T0233882

Lecture Notes in Computer Science 12203

More information about this series at http://www.springer.com/series/7409

Norbert Streitz · Shin'ichi Konomi (Eds.)

Distributed, Ambient and Pervasive Interactions

8th International Conference, DAPI 2020
Held as Part of the 22nd HCI International Conference, HCII 2020
Copenhagen, Denmark, July 19–24, 2020
Proceedings

Editors
Norbert Streitz
Smart Future Initiative
Frankfurt/Main, Germany

Shin'ichi Konomi
Kyushu University
Fukuoka, Japan

ISSN 0302-9743 ISSN 1611-3349 (electronic)
Lecture Notes in Computer Science
ISBN 978-3-030-50343-7 ISBN 978-3-030-50344-4 (eBook)
https://doi.org/10.1007/978-3-030-50344-4

LNCS Sublibrary: SL3 – Information Systems and Applications, incl. Internet/Web, and HCI

This Springer imprint is published by the registered company Springer Nature Switzerland AG
The registered company address is: Gewerbestrasse 11, 6330 Cham, Switzerland

Foreword

The 22nd International Conference on Human-Computer Interaction, HCI International 2020 (HCII 2020), was planned to be held at the AC Bella Sky Hotel and Bella Center, Copenhagen, Denmark, during July 19–24, 2020. Due to the COVID-19 coronavirus pandemic and the resolution of the Danish government not to allow events larger than 500 people to be hosted until September 1, 2020, HCII 2020 had to be held virtually. It incorporated the 21 thematic areas and affiliated conferences listed on the following page.

A total of 6,326 individuals from academia, research institutes, industry, and governmental agencies from 97 countries submitted contributions, and 1,439 papers and 238 posters were included in the conference proceedings. These contributions address the latest research and development efforts and highlight the human aspects of design and use of computing systems. The contributions thoroughly cover the entire field of human-computer interaction, addressing major advances in knowledge and effective use of computers in a variety of application areas. The volumes constituting the full set of the conference proceedings are listed in the following pages.

The HCI International (HCII) conference also offers the option of "late-breaking work" which applies both for papers and posters and the corresponding volume(s) of the proceedings will be published just after the conference. Full papers will be included in the "HCII 2020 - Late Breaking Papers" volume of the proceedings to be published in the Springer LNCS series, while poster extended abstracts will be included as short papers in the "HCII 2020 - Late Breaking Posters" volume to be published in the Springer CCIS series.

I would like to thank the program board chairs and the members of the program boards of all thematic areas and affiliated conferences for their contribution to the highest scientific quality and the overall success of the HCI International 2020 conference.

This conference would not have been possible without the continuous and unwavering support and advice of the founder, Conference General Chair Emeritus and Conference Scientific Advisor Prof. Gavriel Salvendy. For his outstanding efforts, I would like to express my appreciation to the communications chair and editor of HCI International News, Dr. Abbas Moallem.

July 2020 Constantine Stephanidis

HCI International 2020 Thematic Areas and Affiliated Conferences

Thematic areas:

- HCI 2020: Human-Computer Interaction
- HIMI 2020: Human Interface and the Management of Information

Affiliated conferences:

- EPCE: 17th International Conference on Engineering Psychology and Cognitive Ergonomics
- UAHCI: 14th International Conference on Universal Access in Human-Computer Interaction
- VAMR: 12th International Conference on Virtual, Augmented and Mixed Reality
- CCD: 12th International Conference on Cross-Cultural Design
- SCSM: 12th International Conference on Social Computing and Social Media
- AC: 14th International Conference on Augmented Cognition
- DHM: 11th International Conference on Digital Human Modeling and Applications in Health, Safety, Ergonomics and Risk Management
- DUXU: 9th International Conference on Design, User Experience and Usability
- DAPI: 8th International Conference on Distributed, Ambient and Pervasive Interactions
- HCIBGO: 7th International Conference on HCI in Business, Government and Organizations
- LCT: 7th International Conference on Learning and Collaboration Technologies
- ITAP: 6th International Conference on Human Aspects of IT for the Aged Population
- HCI-CPT: Second International Conference on HCI for Cybersecurity, Privacy and Trust
- HCI-Games: Second International Conference on HCI in Games
- MobiTAS: Second International Conference on HCI in Mobility, Transport and Automotive Systems
- AIS: Second International Conference on Adaptive Instructional Systems
- C&C: 8th International Conference on Culture and Computing
- MOBILE: First International Conference on Design, Operation and Evaluation of Mobile Communications
- AI-HCI: First International Conference on Artificial Intelligence in HCI

HCI International 2020 Thematic Areas and Affiliated Conferences

Thematic areas:

- HCI 2020: Human-Computer Interaction
- HIMI 2020: Human Interface and the Management of Information

[illegible]

Conference Proceedings Volumes Full List

1. LNCS 12181, Human-Computer Interaction: Design and User Experience (Part I), edited by Masaaki Kurosu
2. LNCS 12182, Human-Computer Interaction: Multimodal and Natural Interaction (Part II), edited by Masaaki Kurosu
3. LNCS 12183, Human-Computer Interaction: Human Values and Quality of Life (Part III), edited by Masaaki Kurosu
4. LNCS 12184, Human Interface and the Management of Information: Designing Information (Part I), edited by Sakae Yamamoto and Hirohiko Mori
5. LNCS 12185, Human Interface and the Management of Information: Interacting with Information (Part II), edited by Sakae Yamamoto and Hirohiko Mori
6. LNAI 12186, Engineering Psychology and Cognitive Ergonomics: Mental Workload, Human Physiology, and Human Energy (Part I), edited by Don Harris and Wen-Chin Li
7. LNAI 12187, Engineering Psychology and Cognitive Ergonomics: Cognition and Design (Part II), edited by Don Harris and Wen-Chin Li
8. LNCS 12188, Universal Access in Human-Computer Interaction: Design Approaches and Supporting Technologies (Part I), edited by Margherita Antona and Constantine Stephanidis
9. LNCS 12189, Universal Access in Human-Computer Interaction: Applications and Practice (Part II), edited by Margherita Antona and Constantine Stephanidis
10. LNCS 12190, Virtual, Augmented and Mixed Reality: Design and Interaction (Part I), edited by Jessie Y. C. Chen and Gino Fragomeni
11. LNCS 12191, Virtual, Augmented and Mixed Reality: Industrial and Everyday Life Applications (Part II), edited by Jessie Y. C. Chen and Gino Fragomeni
12. LNCS 12192, Cross-Cultural Design: User Experience of Products, Services, and Intelligent Environments (Part I), edited by P. L. Patrick Rau
13. LNCS 12193, Cross-Cultural Design: Applications in Health, Learning, Communication, and Creativity (Part II), edited by P. L. Patrick Rau
14. LNCS 12194, Social Computing and Social Media: Design, Ethics, User Behavior, and Social Network Analysis (Part I), edited by Gabriele Meiselwitz
15. LNCS 12195, Social Computing and Social Media: Participation, User Experience, Consumer Experience, and Applications of Social Computing (Part II), edited by Gabriele Meiselwitz
16. LNAI 12196, Augmented Cognition: Theoretical and Technological Approaches (Part I), edited by Dylan D. Schmorrow and Cali M. Fidopiastis
17. LNAI 12197, Augmented Cognition: Human Cognition and Behaviour (Part II), edited by Dylan D. Schmorrow and Cali M. Fidopiastis

18. LNCS 12198, Digital Human Modeling and Applications in Health, Safety, Ergonomics and Risk Management: Posture, Motion and Health (Part I), edited by Vincent G. Duffy
19. LNCS 12199, Digital Human Modeling and Applications in Health, Safety, Ergonomics and Risk Management: Human Communication, Organization and Work (Part II), edited by Vincent G. Duffy
20. LNCS 12200, Design, User Experience, and Usability: Interaction Design (Part I), edited by Aaron Marcus and Elizabeth Rosenzweig
21. LNCS 12201, Design, User Experience, and Usability: Design for Contemporary Interactive Environments (Part II), edited by Aaron Marcus and Elizabeth Rosenzweig
22. LNCS 12202, Design, User Experience, and Usability: Case Studies in Public and Personal Interactive Systems (Part III), edited by Aaron Marcus and Elizabeth Rosenzweig
23. LNCS 12203, Distributed, Ambient and Pervasive Interactions, edited by Norbert Streitz and Shin'ichi Konomi
24. LNCS 12204, HCI in Business, Government and Organizations, edited by Fiona Fui-Hoon Nah and Keng Siau
25. LNCS 12205, Learning and Collaboration Technologies: Designing, Developing and Deploying Learning Experiences (Part I), edited by Panayiotis Zaphiris and Andri Ioannou
26. LNCS 12206, Learning and Collaboration Technologies: Human and Technology Ecosystems (Part II), edited by Panayiotis Zaphiris and Andri Ioannou
27. LNCS 12207, Human Aspects of IT for the Aged Population: Technologies, Design and User Experience (Part I), edited by Qin Gao and Jia Zhou
28. LNCS 12208, Human Aspects of IT for the Aged Population: Healthy and Active Aging (Part II), edited by Qin Gao and Jia Zhou
29. LNCS 12209, Human Aspects of IT for the Aged Population: Technology and Society (Part III), edited by Qin Gao and Jia Zhou
30. LNCS 12210, HCI for Cybersecurity, Privacy and Trust, edited by Abbas Moallem
31. LNCS 12211, HCI in Games, edited by Xiaowen Fang
32. LNCS 12212, HCI in Mobility, Transport and Automotive Systems: Automated Driving and In-Vehicle Experience Design (Part I), edited by Heidi Krömker
33. LNCS 12213, HCI in Mobility, Transport and Automotive Systems: Driving Behavior, Urban and Smart Mobility (Part II), edited by Heidi Krömker
34. LNCS 12214, Adaptive Instructional Systems, edited by Robert A. Sottilare and Jessica Schwarz
35. LNCS 12215, Culture and Computing, edited by Matthias Rauterberg
36. LNCS 12216, Design, Operation and Evaluation of Mobile Communications, edited by Gavriel Salvendy and June Wei
37. LNCS 12217, Artificial Intelligence in HCI, edited by Helmut Degen and Lauren Reinerman-Jones

http://2020.hci.international/proceedings

8th International Conference on Distributed, Ambient and Pervasive Interactions (DAPI 2020)

Program Board Chairs: **Norbert Streitz, Smart Future Initiative, Germany, and Shin'ichi Konomi, Kyushu University, Japan**

The full list with the Program Board Chairs and the members of the Program Boards of all thematic areas and affiliated conferences is available online at:

http://www.hci.international/board-members-2020.php

HCI International 2021

The 23rd International Conference on Human-Computer Interaction, HCI International 2021 (HCII 2021), will be held jointly with the affiliated conferences in Washington DC, USA, at the Washington Hilton Hotel, July 24–29, 2021. It will cover a broad spectrum of themes related to Human-Computer Interaction (HCI), including theoretical issues, methods, tools, processes, and case studies in HCI design, as well as novel interaction techniques, interfaces, and applications. The proceedings will be published by Springer. More information will be available on the conference website: http://2021.hci.international/.

General Chair
Prof. Constantine Stephanidis
University of Crete and ICS-FORTH
Heraklion, Crete, Greece
Email: general_chair@hcii2021.org

http://2021.hci.international/

HCI International 2021

Contents

Design Approaches, Methods and Tools

Responsive Origami

A Modular Approach to Fabricate Dynamic Surfaces Reactive to Socio-environmental Conditions

Mostafa Alani[1(✉)], Michael C. Kleiss[2], and Arash Soleimani[3]

[1] Aliraqia University, Baghdad, Iraq
mostafa.waleed@aliraqia.edu.iq
[2] Clemson University, Clemson, SC, USA
[3] Kennesaw State University, Marietta, GA, USA

Abstract. This paper presents the design and programming of origami-based, dynamic surfaces. Two functional prototypes were developed: a fixed-site prototype and a modular prototype. The paper discusses the hardware and software design of each prototype. The hardware design part discusses the physical structure of the system. The design of the system software includes developing algorithms to make decisions and providing information to the actuation mechanism to respond by changing the physical state of the system. The design of the modular-based prototype employs a "minimum inventory maximum diversity" strategy to develop programmable units that can be tessellated in a variety of ways to construct culturally inspired, dynamic geometric patterns.

Keywords: Responsive · Interactive · Embedded computation · Origami, reconfigurable · Built environment

1 Introduction

Digital technologies are profoundly changing the way we design and interact with our environment as they are rapidly being embedded in various aspects of our lives. When coupled with reconfigurable forms, digital technologies allow us to experience buildings as living "organs" that respond to occupants' needs as opposed to static entities, ultimately resulting in an improved social and physical experience for the occupants.

Dynamic building components have been incorporated architecture since its early days to accommodate the ever-changing needs of occupants. For instance, a door-and its variations, such as the Shōji in traditional Japanese architecture-is a basic example of a dynamic building component that allows the occupants to have different states for the same space (private and public) [1]. More sophisticated examples incorporate digital technologies to make the reconfiguration process more intelligent through incorporating sensing devices to collect data from the surrounding environment, processing the collected data and making decisions, and initiating the process of a physical shapeshifting [1, 2].

In this paper, we present two functional prototypes for building dynamic surfaces: a fixed-site prototype (Fig. 1) and a modular prototype (Fig. 2). The surfaces reconfigure

N. Streitz and S. Konomi (Eds.): HCII 2020, LNCS 12203, pp. 3–12, 2020.
https://doi.org/10.1007/978-3-030-50344-4_1

aiming at enhancing occupants' social and physical experience of the built environment. The theoretical stance of this study builds on Christopher Alexander's concept of "compressed patterns." In his book, Alexander presented several patterns for designing a humane built environment. He argues that a single space can be formed in a way to house many functions in the same space for economical purposes [3]. The proposed designs aim to manipulate the mode of the room (private and public) and the physical environment allowing more, or less light to pass through. Each prototype is capable of sensing the surrounding environmental conditions, processing the collected data algorithmically, and actuating the system, with the aim of optimizing the social and physical experiences of architectural spaces that we inhabit.

2 Research Through Design Approach

This paper employs Research Through Design (RtD) strategies to cope with the identified issue and develop a suitable response in the form of a physical structure that can be tested. This research method offers an excellent opportunity to take advantage of the iterative nature of the design process to study and refine a solution, which, in the case of this research, significantly helps in developing modular units. The paper takes a "developmental work" approach that involves the "customization of a piece of technology to do something no one had considered before and communicating the results" [4]. As the result of this iterative process, this paper presents an exemplary case of RtD that illustrates a fully functioning prototype that was designed, tested, and improved over various phases to enhance the efficiency of the system.

3 The Physical Metamorphosis

The design of a reconfigurable form requires designers to think about the various states that a form can take under different conditions. This requires "interrogating" the internal structure of the form to understand its morphological transformation [5]. The singular form thus becomes a "keyframe" that, collectively with other keyframes, defines the morphology of a more complex form [6]. In biology, morphological transformation occurs over long periods as a result of environmental forces that make various specious more resistant to ecological threats, as demonstrated by the work of D'Arcy Thompson [7]. This concept has long inspired architects to explore, or more recently, evolve a range of possible solutions for a particular design problem by adding a "temporal dimension" to express the "metamorphosis" of a form. In the case of reconfigurable structures, morphological transformations occur in real time, and thus suitable mechanisms and materials are required to facilitate this process.

After pondering, debating, and experimenting with different aspects of mechanisms and materials to morph the skinning system, our team proposed the use of origami folding techniques to construct the physical metamorphosis to enable the skin to morph from one state to another. Origami provides a convenient mechanism to morph objects while preserving their topological characteristics. Topology is a term related to morphology that refers to the changes occurring within a form that preserve its "internal relational" structure [6]. Figure 1 shows the process of folding a flat sheet of paper into an intricate three-dimensional star geometry. The process is also reversible, which means that the star geometry can devolve back to a flat sheet of paper. This makes it possible to express various states of the geometry without adding or subtracting from the existing material to express the physical metamorphosis. This proved very beneficial for building the dynamic shading device as it allows control of both the permeability of the shade and transformation that preserves the overall look of the system.

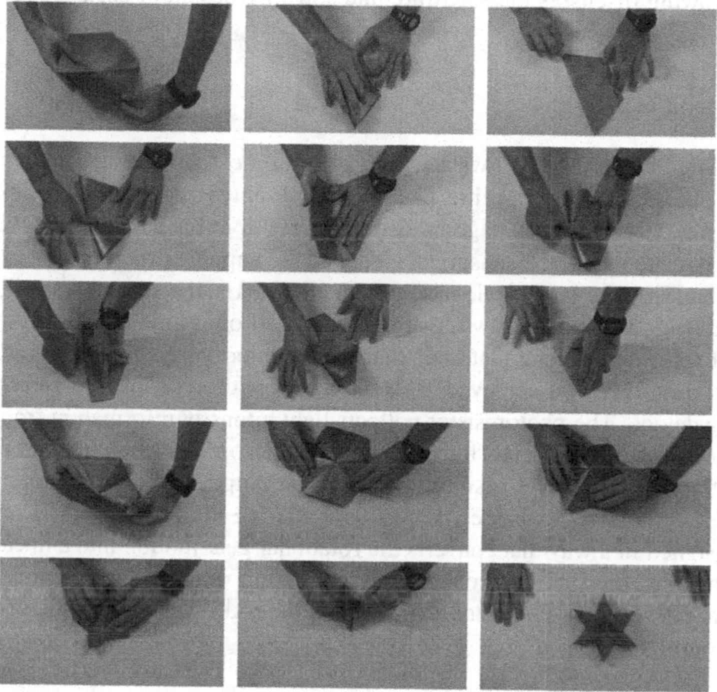

Fig. 1. The process of converting a flat sheet of paper into a star geometry.

In the case of this project, the design of the star geometry is inspired by six-fold Islamic Geometric Patterns. The various lines of the geometric design can be interpreted as hills and valleys. Additional folds added when needed. The same process is applicable for three-fold and four-fold star geometries. These symmetric arrangements enabled a design that completely fills the space while leaving no gaps and being foldable.

4 Responsive Origami Systems

This section presents the two developed prototypes of the responsive origami systems: 1) the fixed-site prototype, and 2) the modular-based prototype. The underlying design structure for both models is based on tessellation, which was utilized to subdivide flat surfaces into smaller parts. Each tessellated surface contains Repeat Units (RUs) and a Repetitive Structure (RS). The RUs are tiles that hold the morphable units, while the RS is the result of the overall organization of the tiles. The RUs consist of the shell, which is the star geometry built using origami techniques; the actuation mechanism, which comprises movable rods, rails, gear, and motor; the sensing device; and the support structure, which holds the RU in place. When attached to the actuation mechanism, the shell's shape changes (shrinking or expanding) in response to data coming from the sensing device through the microprocessor. When stacked together, the tiles collectively form the RS, which covers the required surface area.

The following discusses the hardware and software design of each of the two built prototypes.

4.1 Fixed-Site Prototype

The Fixed-Site Prototype (FSP) was custom built for a certain site, and each piece was designed to be placed in a specific place. The presented prototype was designed to contain 10 RUs stacked in a hexagonal geometric fashion. Each unit includes the shell, the actuation mechanism, the sensing device, and the support structure.

Before building the large-scale model with all 10 RUs, the system was piloted with a single RU (Fig. 2). This pilot was primarily focused on refining the actuation mechanism and exploring building materials that were refined through many iterations until a functional prototype was achieved. This single RU prototype utilized a photoresistor as a sensing device. The photoresistor collects light intensity information from the surrounding environment and sends it to the Arduino microprocessor, which processes the data algorithmically, makes decisions, and sends an output to the servo motor to rotate clockwise or counterclockwise, consequently actuating the central gear. The movable rods are designed in a way that converts the rotational gear motion into a linear motion, thus pushing or pulling the ends of the rods away from or toward the central gear. The foldable star geometry is connected to the end of the rods. Thus, the shape of the tile is altered accordingly.

Fig. 2. Top: the folding process of the morphable shell. Bottom: the metamorphosis process of a single RU in response to light.

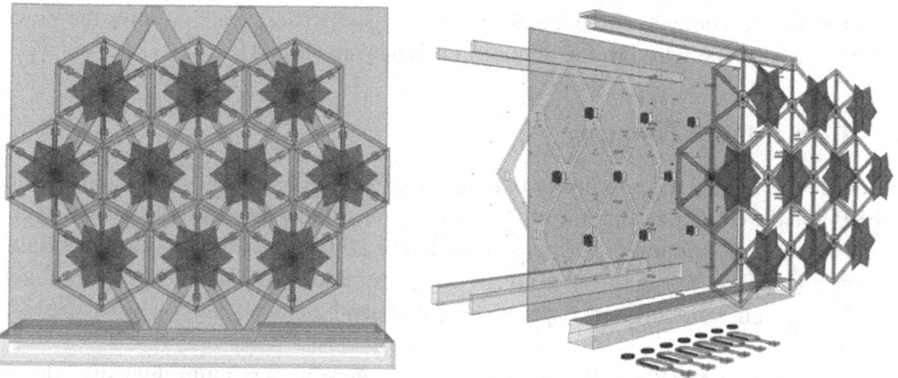

Fig. 3. Left: prototype with 10 hexagonal RUs. Right: exploded view showing the design components, which consist of the diamond shape support structure, plexiglass guiding rails, movable rods, servomotors, and shells.

Fig. 4. Top: the support structure made from CNC'ed MDF used to hold individual RUs. Bottom left: the support structure made from CNC'ed plexiglass. Bottom right: Testing of a single RU in the large prototype.

After arriving at a functional prototype, the refined RU was replicated to build a large-scale geometric pattern that consists of 10 hexagonal cells. The entire system was modeled digitally; the digital manufacturing files were prepared and sent to the machine to be manufactured, and then the parts and servomotors were assembled (Fig. 3). The FSP was built-in sequential stratified fashion. The first layer is a diamond-shaped support structure that holds the servomotors and its associated wiring on one side and the plexiglass rails, central gears, movable rods, and shell layers on the other side. The support structure connects the centers of the star geometries, which allows the power and data cables to be wired to the actuation mechanism (Fig. 4).

4.2 Modular-Based Prototype

Our team investigated the possibility of extending the responsive origami system beyond the FSP and developed modular units that can be tessellated in a variety of ways to create responsive reconfigurable surfaces collectively. Unlike the FSP, the Modular-Based Prototype (MBP) is not built from layers but constructed from smaller programmable units. It is not custom built for a specific site and can be customized on-site to be used as needed.

The developed MBP employs a "minimum inventory, maximum diversity" design strategy [8]. That is, through the use of the same programmable units, the presented modular system allows the construction of three regular tessellation systems: triangle-, square-, and hexagon-based tessellations (Fig. 5). The MBP consists of RUs and an RS. In the case of the MBP system, the RU includes a core and a support structure. The core comprises the shell, actuation mechanism, and sensing device. The core is replaceable, which adds greater flexibility to the system. Unlike the FSP, the guiding rails are not fixed on the support structure and are instead contained within the core. This makes it easier to replace the core when needed, if it malfunctions, or to decorate the unit with different designs without the need to disassemble both the core and the support structure (Fig. 5).

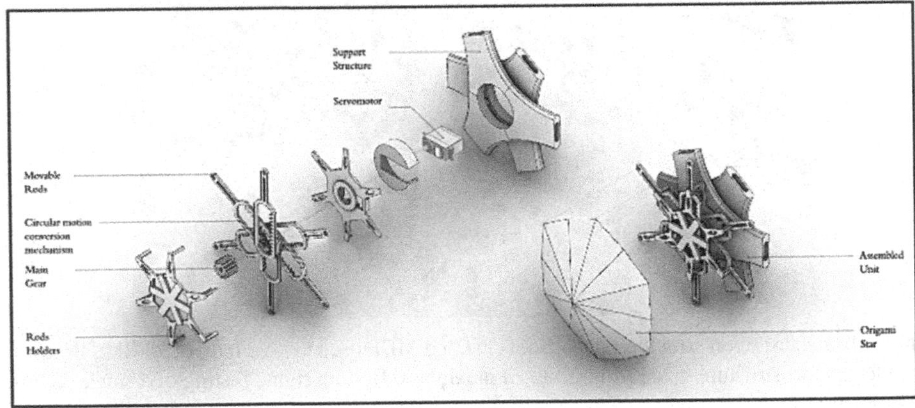

Fig. 5. Left: exploded view of the RU. Right: assembled RU (core and support structure) and shell.

The support structure, on the other hand, consists of two pieces, male and female. This makes it possible for the system to be arranged in different ways, for instance, to switch from a hexagonal tessellation to a rectangular tessellation (Fig. 6). The MBP was modeled digitally and then the manufacturing files were prepared. The entire prototype was built from 3D-printed plastic.

The software for the MBP system was developed using Rhinoceros' Grasshopper and Firefly. Three primary dialogue modes were developed: 1) a preset mode, 2) a responsive mode, and 3) an interactive mode (animation video: https://vimeo.com/377240055). In the preset mode, a human operator is granted full manual control of the system to select the appropriate setting. This mode is particularly useful for testing the system during initial system installation or during maintenance (Fig. 7).

In the responsive mode, a photoresistor is connected to the microprocessor, which senses the light intensity in the surrounding physical environment and sends outputs to the Arduino microprocessor. The data are processed and, if the light intensity is high, the servomotor rotates to unfold the origami shell. If the light intensity is low, the servomotor rotates in the opposite direction to fold up the origami shell star.

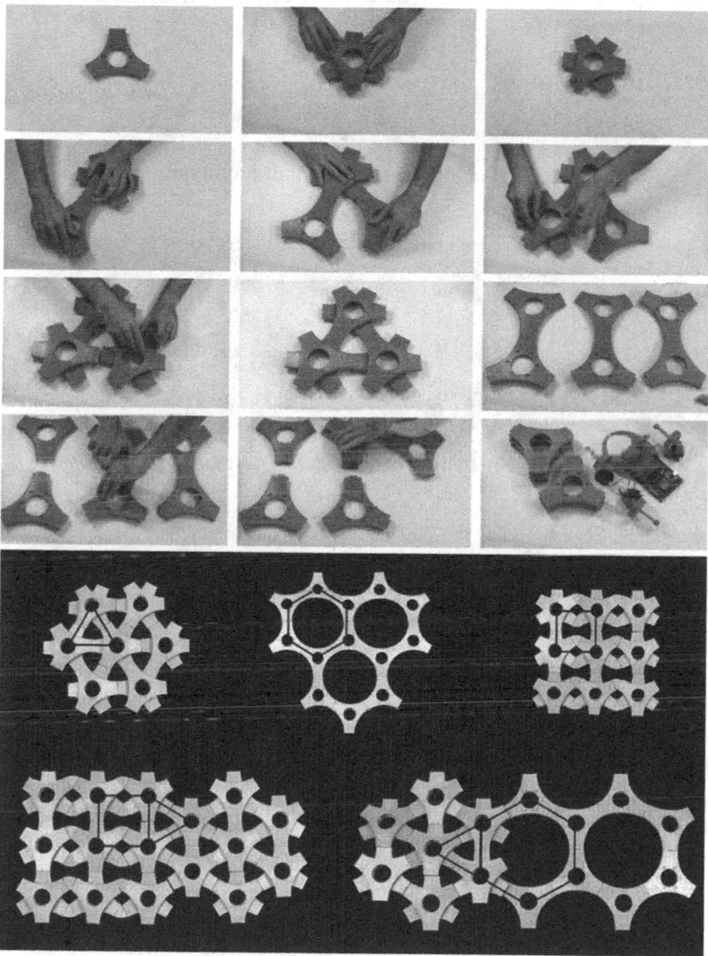

Fig. 6. Top left: the female RU. Top middle: the female and male RU. The rest of the figure shows the process of constructing the support structure of the responsive skin system.

Fig. 7. Testing the modular unit prototype.

Fig. 8. Testing of the interactive mode.

Fig. 9. Left: linear actuator core. Right: the responsive origami core.

In the interactive mode, the MBP system is connected to Microsoft Kinect. Kinect provides "skeletal mapping" data associated with specific parts of the human body to the microprocessors to actuate the system. The data are used to define gestures that allow the user to communicate with the shading device by waving to it. For instance, if the palm hand is higher than the shoulder, this closes the origami star (Figs. 8 and 9).

5 Advantages of the Modular Approach

Compared to the fixed-site prototype, the presented modular-based prototype offers the following advantages:

- Structural Flexibility: The design of the support structure units allows the structure to be assembled in a variety of ways to construct the three regular tessellation systems: triangle-, square-, hexagon-based systems. In addition, it allows the system to be expanded seamlessly or to be disassembled and transported to a different location.
- Customization: The replaceable cores allow the system to be customized with different modules. The replaceable cores allow users to add different hardware to perform additional tasks or to simply decorate the reconfigurable surface with geometric designs.
- Maintenance: Issues with the system can be fixed simply by removing the defective core module or the supporting structure without the need to disassemble the entire system.
- Construction time: The system requires significantly less time to be assembled or disassembled.
- Affordability: With mass customization, the cost of the physical hardware may significantly drop.

6 Conclusion

We present a novel approach to designing modular dynamic shading devices that employ a "minimum inventory, maximum diversity" design strategy. The paper presents the hardware and software designs for two working prototypes: a fixed-site prototype and a modular-based prototype. We compare the modular based prototype to the fixed-site prototype and find that the modular-based prototype offers several advantages over the fixed-site prototype: structural flexibility, customization, maintenance, construction time, and affordability. This makes the modular-based prototype a feasible replacement for use in dynamic shading applications.

7 Future Work

For this project, our future work is twofold:

1. Our next goal is to develop larger units with shells built from fiberglass material and mount the units in an existing building to investigate the effectiveness and usability of the system.
2. We plan to release the digital fabrication files to the public. The proposed modular system can be entirely built from 3D-printed plastic. This makes it possible to communicate the design digitally so that architecture students and design enthusiasts can experiment with it.

References

1. Green, K.E.: Architectural Robotics: Ecosystems of Bits, Bytes, and Biology. MIT Press, Cambridge (2016)
2. Kolarevic, V.B., Parlac, V.: Building Dynamics: Exploring Architecture of Change. Routledge, London (2015)
3. Alexander, C.: A Pattern Language: Towns, Buildings. Construction. Oxford University Press, New York (1977)
4. Frayling, C.: Research in art and design. In: Royal College of Art Research Paper, vol. 1, pp. 1–5 (1993)
5. Lynn, G., Kelly, T.: Animate Form. Princeton Architectural Press, New York (1999)
6. Kolarevic, B.: Architecture in the Digital Age: Design and Manufacturing. Taylor & Francis, New York (2004)
7. Thompson, D.: On Growth and Form. Cambridge University Press, Cambridge (1917)
8. Pearce, P.: Structure in Nature is a Strategy for Design. MIT Press, Cambridge (1990)

A Testbed for Rapid Design and Evaluation of VR Navigation Techniques for Industrial Applications

Jendrik Bulk(✉) and Volker Paelke

Hochschule Bremen University of Applied Science, Flughafenallee 10, 28199 Bremen, Germany
{jendrik.bulk,volker.paelke}@hs-bremen.de

Abstract. VR is making inroads into industrial applications, especially in product design and presentation, training and simulation use cases. A focus of these applications is on the visualization, exploiting 3D immersive graphics as a central feature of VR. While navigation is often required in these applications to select a suitable location for observing the visualization or interacting with the simulation content it is not in the focus of the designers, often leading to the selection of techniques that are convenient during development because they are available in the implementation toolkit. However, these may be less than ideal for the industrial application context. A large variety of VR techniques for navigation have been proposed in the literature and implemented, both for motion control and guidance, but there is currently little established knowledge on their respective benefits and shortcoming, especially in non-gaming applications. To enable designers of industrial VR environments to make informed choices of navigation techniques we present a testbed that enables quick prototyping and comparative evaluation in the specific application context and with the intended target audience, making a user centered selection of navigation techniques viable.

Keywords: Virtual reality · VR · Navigation · Evaluation · Testing

1 Related Work

Navigation is a common term that signifies how a person moves purposefully from one place to another. In virtual environments navigation is a common and ubiquitous activity as it provides the main mechanism for content selection and is often a prerequisite for interaction with objects of interest that are spatially distributed in a virtual environment. Research into navigation techniques for virtual reality applications has a long history. Bowman et al. [1] introduced a useful and widely adopted definition that defines navigation as the combination of wayfinding (the cognitive component of planning the route and making navigation decisions), and travel (the motor component that determines the current direction and speed during the movement phase). Early research like Bowman et al. [2], Jul and Furnas [3] provides a useful conceptual foundation for the design and evaluation of navigation techniques for virtual environments, by identifying central factors of influence and mapping out the design space for techniques to support

N. Streitz and S. Konomi (Eds.): HCII 2020, LNCS 12203, pp. 13–24, 2020.
https://doi.org/10.1007/978-3-030-50344-4_2

both wayfinding and travel activities. Nabiyouni et al. [4] and Boletsis [5] provide an overview of more recent research that aims to classify and evaluate navigation techniques in virtual environments (VE). The selection of suitable navigation techniques for a virtual reality application is highly dependent on the intended users, the application domain and the available hardware. Navigation techniques for games can make use of a wide spectrum of travel techniques ranging from "magic" techniques like teleporting and "magic carpet rides" to more realistic appropriations of normal techniques like walking or skiing (e.g. Paris et al. [6]) and can also design or adjust the virtual space to control the difficulty of navigation, e.g. by creating maze-like structures to purposefully make navigation more challenging or by providing clearly structured environments with landmarks and spatial constraints to simplify navigation. In industrial applications of virtual reality navigation is typically an essential but conceptually secondary activity that should be unobtrusive, intuitive, and easily controlled to support the user in the primary task (e.g. learning about the industrial environment, analyzing information or performing activities by manipulating content) and the spatial structure of the environment is often dictated by the corresponding real world setting. Therefore, many game inspired techniques are not applicable. "Walking" as an analogue of the corresponding real-world activity might seem like the obvious solution, but as the overview by Nilson et al. [7] shows, there are still serious challenges with many of the "natural" walking techniques that have been proposed for virtual environments.

Disorientation and poorly readable user interfaces within a VE have been found to lead to the user breaking off the experience and generally not continuing. The larger the VE, the more complex the requirements for navigation. Therefore, a comprehensible form of navigation and an adaptation to the VE are required [8]. In complex environments users often find it difficult to understand the structure of virtual areas and navigate them successfully [9]. In contrast to entertainment applications VEs for serious use cases are often bound to mimic an existing, potentially complex, spatial layout. The solution to navigation problems in these cases is therefore limited to the provision of suitable navigation aids, e.g. compass displays that show the direction towards the destination or digital maps of the surroundings on which the destination and position of the user are marked (e.g. a minimap) that allow the user to concentrate on the actual task in the application. Sabok et al. [10] have compared two different navigation and different interaction options. They have found that surrounding objects should have the ability to collide with the avatar. The user is prevented from moving through walls, which otherwise quickly leads to disorientation. Top down views and the use of gravity were also found to help test users to orient themselves more quickly.

Santos et al. [11] created a test environment to compare the usability of VR devices. Their results emphasizes that different navigation components may be necessary for different environments. This means that even with good navigation solutions, they cannot be used universally for every scenario. Personal preferences and the experience of the respective user were also found to play a role when evaluating an interface or control. Their research also showed that the "obvious" solution of providing flexibility by offering different options should be balanced so that the user is not burdened by too many options.

The designer of an industrial virtual reality application therefore has to choose navigation techniques based on his specific requirements and validate in user tests that they actually perform as intended. The goal of this research is therefore not to identify an optimal navigation technique, but to provide designers with a toolset that enables them to quickly create and evaluate application specific navigation techniques for their specific project needs.

2 Requirements

As the discussion of the related work shows there are many potential approaches to design navigation solutions for an VR environment and the application specific requirements in the industrial domain are often best addressed by adapting and customizing existing techniques or even developing new approaches. In all cases a user centered approach is required in which techniques can be evaluated easily, rapidly and frequently with users in a scenario that is representative for the specific application context.

To make such a user centered approach viable it needs to be supported by appropriate tools to limit the time and effort required to create the navigation techniques, to create and conduct user tests, to evaluate the test results and to adapt the techniques based on the test results. We established a list of requirements based on experience in previous projects and refined these in discussions with three VR experts. The resulting requirements are:

A. To provide a set of established navigation and locomotion techniques as a baseline for comparison and as a foundation for customized adaptation of these techniques
B. To provide the necessary programming environment to create and modify navigation and locomotion techniques for a wide variety of VR hardware
C. To provide a set of building blocks for navigation tasks that are representative of the application domain
D. To provide tools for composing virtual test environments of varying complexity to rapidly construct environments that are suitable for testing the navigation and locomotion techniques of interest
E. To provide support for conducting user tests in the test environments and provide integrated means of data collection
F. The system and especially the navigation and locomotion techniques should be implemented using widely used technology to ensure that developers don't need to learn new technologies and ideally allow to directly apply the tested navigation and locomotion techniques to the final application.

3 The Testbed Concept

To address these requirements, we have developed a testbed concept that uses a modular approach to both the construction of navigation and locomotion techniques and virtual (test) environments. The design of the concept builds on the modular structures provided in the Unity game engine. This enables developers familiar with Unity to directly use the testbed and also provides a useful starting point for less experienced developers that can refer to the extensive documentation available for the Unity for the general information and then use a template provided to modify and add functionality using connecting points.

To address requirement (A) the testbed provides a set of ready-to-use navigation and locomotion techniques, e.g. common navigation solutions for applications on 2D-displays like Minimaps, as well as 3D solutions for directional disclosures, e.g. a 3D compass. This set of techniques can be used in two ways: First as a baseline reference for user tests against which the performance of other techniques can be compared. Since the creation of such components is a time-consuming task there is often a temptation to just implement rudimentary versions for a test which then can result in suboptimal conditions for the user which can in turn distort the test results [11]. By providing ready-to-use techniques that have already been tested and validated as a baseline, developers can focus of the implementation of new techniques and functionality, while also receiving more meaningful test results. A second use is the use as a basis for the development and adaptation of new techniques. Because the techniques are provided as standard Unity prefabs they can be easily modified and extended, simplifying the development of application specific adaptations. Over time developers can create and expand the library of "proven" baseline techniques by adding their new techniques to the library.

Requirements (B) and (F) are addressed by using the Unity game engine that offers common functionality like collision detection, physics simulation and rendering, so that the developer can concentrate to the more important task like the controls and navigation for the user. Unity is widely used in the development and prototyping of virtual environments, and therefore familiar to many developers and well supported with integration of most VR hardware available today. Using the Unity prefab mechanism, a template for a new navigation technique can be created by pushing one single button. A new navigation technique can thus be constructed in Unity by using either the menu or inside the inspector. The resulting prefab then has to be customized by adding application specific displaying methods. The script created for the prefab already contains commonly required data such as distance and direction data in relation to the destination. If the final application for which the techniques are developed is also implemented in Unity the navigation and locomotion techniques can be directly reused as prefabs in the target application (Fig. 1). If another base technology is used the techniques need to be ported but the implementation concepts of other game engines or VE toolkits are usually similar enough.

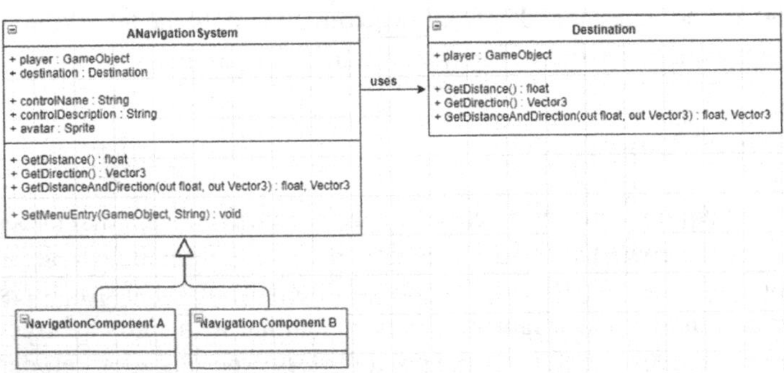

Fig. 1. Implementation of classes for a Navigation Prefab.

Once a new or customized navigation or locomotion technique has been created it needs to be tested. Requirements (C) and (D) address the need of creating virtual environments that are suitable to test different kinds of navigation systems. One possible solution is to test the techniques directly in the virtual environment where they will be used – however, this is usually only an option if a version of this environment already exists. Frequently the environment itself only becomes available later in the development process necessitating the use of a placeholder and even if the environment is already available performance reasons might still make the use of placeholder environments desirable during the development of navigation and locomotion techniques. Without specific support placeholders are often chosen on convenience and availability, leading to either very simplistic environment or ones that do not represent the application domain well (e.g. using a game environment to test techniques for navigating industrial production sites). In our testbed we provide an easy-to-use tile system with different tile stiles reflecting typical, but generic, indoor and outdoor settings from which new environments can be quickly composed, or existing ones adapted quickly, e.g. to support a specific test task. The tiles are again provided as Unity prefabs, allowing to easily adapt and extend the tile collection with new tiles or themes and can therefore use the standard Unity interface to compose new environments.

To support the user tests (requirement (E)) the testbed also includes elements to present test users with descriptions of the test tasks that they should perform within the environment. The different prefabs are also instrumented to automatically provide a standardized protocol of all user interaction during a test and there is an additional mechanism that enables testers to easily add time-stamped event markers to the protocol during a user test (e.g. to mark specific interaction problems) by pressing previously defined buttons.

4 Implementation of the Testbed

The system was created in Unity 2018.3, using the VR API from Unity. In its current form the testbed is independent from device-related SDKs, thus making it possible to use the Unity project with any VR device. Cross-platform builds of the program can also be created with Unity. These two factors make the system flexible.

In the main scene the user can choose between different environments, navigation and control techniques. Every combination is possible, also to combine multiple controls and navigation systems. A laserpointer is used to select the menu entries. The user can see hands of his avatar to get a virtual presence. Figure 2 shows the main menu with its UI.

5 Example: Creating Navigation and Locomotion Techniques

A very simple navigation technique that is commonly used in virtual environments is a 3D virtual compass. The navigation prefab in our testbed already provides a function to calculate the direction and distance from the current position of the user to a specified destination. Such a navigation support technique can therefore be easily created by using this information and mapping it to some appropriate 3D graphics object that then points the user in the right direction. Figure 3 shows how a simple compass was created by simply combining the navigation prefab with some custom geometry for the compass.

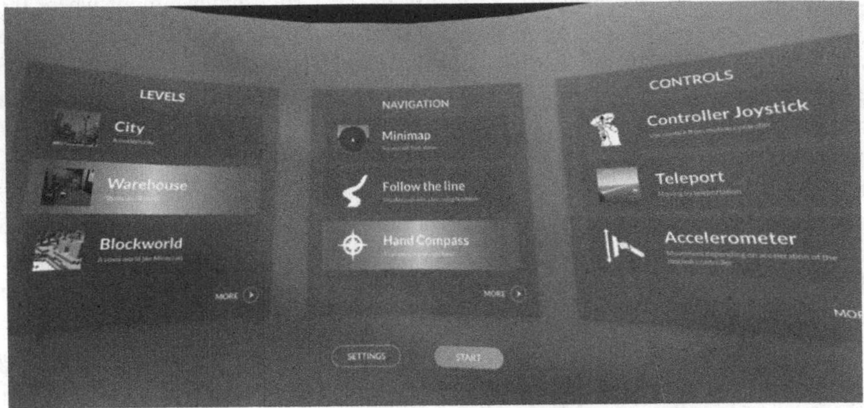

Fig. 2. The main scene of the system. Users can choose between different VEs, navigation and control techniques.

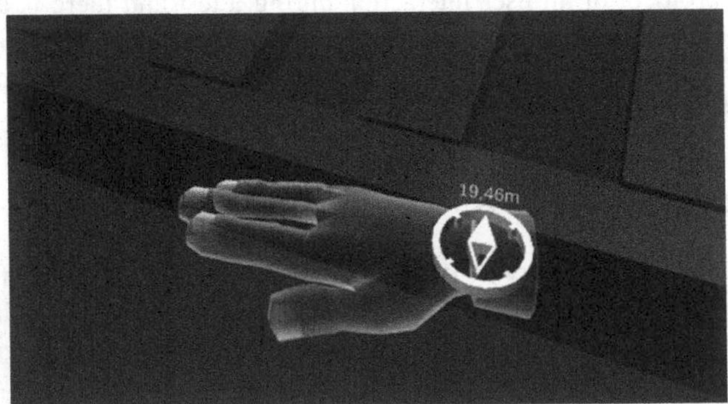

Fig. 3. A model of a compass showing direction and distance to the destination. The compass is installed to the virtual wrist.

More complex navigation techniques support the user by first calculating a route through the virtual environment and then generating appropriate cues to guide and direct the user. As an example, we show how a simple "follow-the-line" technique can be implemented. It is a 3D correspondence to the known 2D presentation in car navigation systems. As a first step the recommended route has to be calculated. In the final application this might be provided by the internal system or be prescribed by some other means. For the user tests we use the Unity Navigation System to generate routes to specified target locations. This system is normally used to move Non-Player-Characters (NPCs) independently. For it to work the developer must mark the walkable areas. Unity visualizes objects that are marked as "Navigation Static" as a blue mesh and saves them in a map data-structure to improve runtime performance (see Fig. 4).

Fig. 4. City environment with blue marked NavMesh.

This enables Unity to rapidly calculate routes to different destinations, which makes it possible to rapidly create a variety of navigation tasks for test, simply by specifying a set of different destinations. In the "follow the line" the calculated route is then simply displayed as a shimmering line between the avatar's location and the destination (Fig. 5). Using the route calculated the returned array with corners is then simply connected to a Line Renderer component to make it visible for the user.

Fig. 5. The "follow-the-line" technique uses Unitys NavMesh and LineRenderer function.

Once a developer has implemented the described navigation concepts they can be easily reused. The corresponding techniques are wrapped in an abstract class so that everybody can work with them without a deeper knowledge of the implementation underlying them.

6 Example: Creating Test Environments

Test environments are created by composing predefined tiles to form an environment that is suitably complex to test the navigation or locomotion technique of interest, without creating unnecessary detail. Depending on the eventual target environment either indoor or outdoor environments might be suitable. Outdoor environments are typically of larger scale and often contain large background objects like landmark buildings or landscape features. Indoor environments are often more limited in size but can be more challenging for navigation, especially if they feature repetitive architectural features. To create test environments that are suitable for serious use cases like industrial training it is essential, that the environment is reflective of the virtual environment in which it is applied later. In our testbed we provide different sets of tiles suitable both for outdoor environments (Fig. 4) and indoor environments (Fig. 6). Developers can easily extend the set with either individual tiles (e.g. to add a specific feature required for a user test) or complete tile sets (e.g. to add a new "theme" with completely different features from those initially provided (e.g. process industry vs. discrete manufacturing). The test environments can be easily combined and modified using standard Unity functionality.

Fig. 6. An indoor VE with training tasks.

As a last step test designers must adjust some variables like jumping and step height, dimensions of the avatars and navigable areas if automatic routing (see above) is required, define the test-tasks and set-up data collection.

7 Evaluation

To evaluate the testbed, we conducted two different tests to (A) validate the functionality and assess in how far the goals of simplification and time saving were achieved (B).

7.1 Comparative User Tests

To validate the functionality, that is to ensure that the testbed is actually suitable to conduct user tests we conducted a test with 13 test users as subjects, using a variety of the navigation techniques in different test environments. The group of 13 test subjects consisted of employees and students of the university. They were between 20 and 40 years old. All participants had previous knowledge in the field of computer science. Only one person had no experience with VR applications.

The test users completed 26 test runs using the testbed system to compare different navigation techniques. In each run the subjects were given the task of reaching a destination in different environments with different control and navigation techniques. Fixed scenarios were used during the tests. All test subjects conduct the tests under the same conditions using the same PC, HMD and controller set and having the same range of motion available (in terms of real space). Data was collected using the automatic logging feature of the testbed and an additional questionnaire on user experience delivered in Google Forms to determine whether the subjects regarded the combination of navigation techniques and environment as suitable. The test scenarios were chosen so that the components clearly differ from one another and the test subjects could clearly perceive this difference. Each subject was given a navigation task. The first task involved comparing a MiniMap in two different environments. The navigation component was first tested in an outdoor environment (a city) and then in an indoor environment (warehouse). These two environments are very different. In the outdoor environment, free movement was possible with the user only being limited by obstacles such as buildings or cars. In this way, an almost direct route to the goal could be taken. In the indoor environment, the user is in a kind of labyrinth. The directions on the MiniMap are not as helpful in an indoor environment in this setting, since this navigation aid only points in the direction of the destination. Due to the labyrinthine structure, it is not possible to find a route according to the cardinal direction. Teleportation was as the locomotion technique in both scenes. This control can be used intuitively by inexperienced subjects and enables rapid progress. Subjects who were not familiar with these forms of navigation and control were instructed and trained in the functions.

The results of the questionnaire confirm the assumption that the MiniMap navigation component is less suitable within the warehouse environment than in the city environment. The next question deals with the deviations made during navigation. The deviations from the specified route are significantly higher than in the city environment. The subjects also rated the MiniMap as more suitable in the city environment than in the warehouse environment, which is shown by the answers to the fourth question. At the end of each test run, the subjects were asked if they considered the software suitable for comparing navigation and locomotion components in VR environments. This was confirmed without exception.

7.2 Expert Review by Experienced VE Developer (B)

To asses in how far the testbed achieves the goal of simplification and time saving (B) we also conducted an expert review with an experienced VE developer. For this purpose, a developer experienced in the development of VR applications was instructed in the system and asked to create her own components. The entire project was made available to the developer, who received personal instruction in the system and documentation of the software.

The software was then used to create a new combination of navigation techniques and a corresponding test environment. In the new system, the user is shown a glowing 3D model of a monster, which must be followed to reach the goal.

The developer stated that the development environment for the navigation components was very clear. The training period in the modular system was about two hours. The development time, including testing of the new component, was approximately one hour. Another hour was spent making optical improvements. The existing navigation components were used as an example in the development of the new system and provided a quick overview of the functions of navigation components. This accelerated the development of the new component. The developer indicated that a quick overview of the modular elements would be helpful to find your way around more quickly. Since a few days passed between the introduction to the system and the actual development, details on how it works can be forgotten. A quick overview would summarize the important key data and clearly illustrate the functionality of the modular system. This overview will be available to future developers.

It was emphasized that the development environment is particularly suitable for inexperienced VR developers. The environment provides a quickly understandable overview of the connection between prefabs, scripts and 3D models. The simplicity of the system motivated the developer to deal with the system beyond the task at hand.

8 Conclusion and Outlook

As part of this work, a testbed environment was created in which it is possible to develop, compare and test navigation and locomotion components.

A review of VR research helped to understand the problems in navigating virtual environments, especially in serious applications. Navigation and locomotion techniques for industrial use cases must find a suitable middle ground between immersive experience and comfortable control that differs significantly from both typical entertainment or training use cases. It is therefore often necessary to adapt techniques and the validate it in an appropriate setting.

The visual structure and complexity of virtual environments has a significant impact on the ability of users to orientate themselves in VR. To be useful test environments should mimic the final application environment both in structure and visual detail. Therefore, an approach for the quick composition of test environments was developed and appropriate assets were developed to create attractive virtual test environments for industrial use cases. The architecture provides for easy extension to additional areas, e.g. additional elements to depict typical environments from process industry.

Building the software architecture and the components based on the concepts of the Unity Editor helped to create a modular system that requires little training, allows developers to get started quickly and often makes the results directly applicable in the target application if this is also created in Unity. Thanks to the modular design of the test environment, it can be expanded quickly and easily. The project already includes three completed VEs, which can be quickly expanded or redesigned using a tile system. The system also offers basic functions for targeting and moving the avatar.

The user tests confirmed that the system can be used for its intended purpose. All subjects confirmed that the application is suitable for comparing locomotion and navigation components. Currently the program is to be made available to future students of the human-computer interaction course at our university in order to train them in the procedures for conducting and evaluating user tests. The automatic report generation offers further evaluation possibilities for tested components. For students who want to implement their own ideas, there is the option to get access to the project files and the documentation. By adapting the Unity interface, future developers will have a clearly designed interface that can be used effectively even with little knowledge of the Unity environment.

The expert review with and experienced developer confirmed that the tested accelerates the creation of components and test environments noticeably and makes it less complicated by providing a lot of common functionality. For the future work we plan to expand both the set of navigation and locomotion techniques provided and the set of themes and tiles for the creation of test environments. We are currently also gathering large scale feedback by using the testbed in student projects. We also aim to apply the testbed in a comparison with the final implementation in an exemplary application to check if the results match and expand the data gathering and analytics functionality to simply the analysis of test results.

References

1. Bowman, D.A., Kruijff, E., LaViola, J.J., Poupyrev, I.: 3D User Interfaces: Theory and Practice. Addison Wesley Longman Publishing Co., Inc., Redwood City (2004)
2. Bowman, D.A., Koller, D., Hodges, L.F.: Travel in immersive virtual environments: an evaluation of viewpoint motion control techniques. In: Proceedings of the 1997 Virtual Reality Annual International Symposium (VRAIS 1997), p. 45. IEEE Computer Society, Washington, DC (1997)
3. Jul, S., Furnas, G.W.: Navigation in electronic worlds: a CHI 97 workshop. SIGCHI Bull. **29**(4), 44–49 (1997) (1997). https://doi.org/10.1145/270950.270979
4. Nabiyouni, M., Saktheeswaran, A., Bowman, D.A., Karanth, A.: Comparing the performance of natural, semi-natural, and non-natural locomotion techniques in virtual reality. In: 2015 IEEE Virtual Reality (VR), pp. 243–244. IEEE (2015)
5. Boletsis, C.: The new era of virtual reality locomotion: a systematic literature review of techniques and a proposed typology. In: Multimodal Technologies and Interaction, vol. 1, p. 24 (2017). https://doi.org/10.3390/mti1040024
6. Paris, R., et al.: How video game locomotion methods affect navigation in virtual environments. In: Neyret, S., Kokkinara, E., Franco, M.G., Hoyet, L., Cunningham, D.W., Świdrak, J. (eds.) ACM Symposium on Applied Perception 2019 (SAP 2019), 7 p. ACM, New York (2019). Article 12. https://doi.org/10.1145/3343036.3343131

7. Nilsson, N.C., Serafin, S., Steinicke, F., Nordahl, R.: Natural walking in virtual reality: a review. Comput. Entertain. **16**(2), 22 (2018). Article 8. https://doi.org/10.1145/3180658
8. Dodiya, J., Alexandrov, V.N.: Navigation assistance for wayfinding in the virtual environments: taxonomy. In: 18th International Conference on Artificial Reality and Telexistence 2008, Yokohama, Japan: ICAT 2008, pp. 339–342 (2008)
9. Herndon, K.P., van Dam, A., Gleicher, M.: The challenges of 3D interaction: a CHI '94 workshop. ACM SIGCHI Bull., pp. 36–43. ACM, New York (1994)
10. Sebok, A., Nystad, E., Helgar, S.: Navigation in desktop virtual environments: an evaluation and recommendations for supporting usability. Virtual Reality **8**, 26–40 (2004)
11. Santos, B.S., Dias, P., Pimentel, A., Silva, S.: Head-mounted display versus desktop for 3D navigation in virtual reality: a user study. Multimed. Tools Appl. **41**, 161–181 (2008)

Accessibility in Pervasive Systems: An Exploratory Study

Diego Addan Gonçalves[1(✉)], Maria Cecilia Calani Baranauskas[1(✉)], and Julio Cesar dos Reis[1,2(✉)]

[1] Institute of Computing, University of Campinas, Campinas, SP, Brazil
diegoaddan@gmail.com, c.baranauskas@gmail.com, juliocesardosreis@gmail.com

[2] Nucleus of Informatics Applied to Education, University of Campinas Institute of Computing, Campinas, SP, Brazil

Abstract. Contemporary computer systems fully integrate people's daily lives in the most diversified contexts. The adequate construction of those systems demands well-defined patterns for including a whole community of users encompassing people with disabilities. Current interaction scenarios with pervasive computing technologies present design challenges for the applicability of standards and guidelines such as those of the W3C Web Content Accessibility Guidelines (WCAG), suited for Web systems. Such scenarios require further studies to deal with the endeavor of supporting designers to project pervasive interactive systems that consider all people, regardless of their condition and ability, allowing different types of interactions to arise. In this article, we conduct an exploratory study to investigate the potential and limitations of current accessibility guidelines for pervasive systems. We explore the last decade of literature studies presenting solutions and challenges for accessibility found for pervasive and ubiquitous computing contexts. The results of this research indicate that it is desirable to define accessibility models for pervasive systems if we consider an accessibility layer that will indicate principles and solutions that should be generic enough to support different categories of impairments and contexts.

Keywords: Pervasive systems · Ubiquitous computing · Accessibility · Guidelines

1 Introduction

Technological advances in computing technology offer new possibilities for interaction as well as opportunities and issues to include people with disabilities in new scenarios of using contemporary digital technology. Enabling all people to access computer systems is a major challenge because there are several types of disabilities by including physical, motor, mental and their combination, and currently 650 million people in the world, live with some type of disability [43].

Accessibility models for computer systems is a key concern in current applications in several domains that range from hardware innovations, such as, robotics [6] to software

N. Streitz and S. Konomi (Eds.): HCII 2020, LNCS 12203, pp. 25–38, 2020.
https://doi.org/10.1007/978-3-030-50344-4_3

projects such as web systems and mobile applications [1, 9]. There are models established to assist in the construction of computer systems intended to include users with physical disabilities; the W3C Web Content Accessibility Guidelines (WCAG) Standard [16] is an example by offering a guide for the construction of web systems that consider people with different conditions (physical, sensorial, intellectual limitations). This contributes to the inclusion of more users and technology propagation. Nevertheless, we understand that there are few defined standards or conventions generic enough to be functional for all types of systems and equipment. This hampers designers in the construction of novel accessible ubiquitous and pervasive technological solutions.

Ubiquitous computing is a new paradigm of computing with omnipresence characteristics, imperceptibility, and naturalness [2]. This kind of computing integrates the concepts of pervasive systems and mobile computing by including the idea of technologies present in people's everyday life interacting invisibly and integrated with daily tasks [6]. According to Rodríguez-Ubeda *et al.* [6], a key feature of ubiquitous computing systems is the ability to adapt their behavior based on user activity and context. In this circumstance, models and guidelines for accessibility purposes can help including all people. The study and proposal of these guidelines should be a priority in the field.

Pervasive computing shares the definition of ubiquitous computing representing technologies that are everywhere, but almost imperceptible to users. These technologies can be used to assist impaired people in daily activities. Kyle Rector [7] highlights the potential for information access that pervasive systems enable for the impaired people's inclusion. These technologies are integrated into everyday life by performing functions subtly enough so that they are not noticeable, such as smart bracelets, physiological readers, trackers.

Existing solutions consider controlled scenarios such as virtual environments in games [5] or the addition of a virtual object that presents adapted information [4]. In general, investigations in literature address a specific deficiency not covering a solution for all. It still lacks a general solution for accessibility considering their different types of interaction, such as IoT systems (Internet of Things), embedded systems, and applications with direct user interaction [17, 18].

The biggest challenge in the context of pervasive computing, however, is to consider different deficiencies in a very diverse computational universe where the devices themselves often do not follow format or construction conventions.In this article, we conduct an exploratory literature review to understand the characteristics and advances of existing work regarding the subject. We investigate the potential and limitations of well known accessibility guidelines in the context of ubiquitous and pervasive computing.

The protocol followed in this study used an exploratory model for reviews and meta-analyses, inspired on [40]. We aim to uncover existing guidelines and analyze to which extent defined accessibility standards are applicable in pervasive computing. To this end, we reviewed literature based on a search in scientific databases in the last 10 years. Our search parameters considered keywords to discover models and techniques for accessibility in pervasive computing. Based on our literature review, we describe and discuss accessibility challenges in ubiquitous computing. Our study provides an analysis of how existing investigations are related to WCAG principles and impairment categories.

Results indicate common characteristics in literature work and the current needs for new considerations and approaches in the pervasive and ubiquitous scenarios considering accessibility. We found which paths recent studies are heading and which models have proven to be functional to include disabled users in pervasive scenarios.

The remaining of this article is organized as follows: Sect. 2 describes the employed research protocol, and o presents classifications of impairments, followed by reference to the WCAG model, used for accessibility in web computing and IoT. Section 3 presents and discusses existing approaches in literature used for the inclusion of disabled people applied to pervasive, enactive and IoT systems. Section 4 presents our analysis by describing open research challenges for the definition of a model for accessibility in ubiquitous computing. Section 5 presents the concluding remarks.

2 Background

In this exploratory work, accessibility solutions in literature are explored considering the research protocol presented in Subsect. 2.1. This section presents the classifications of physical, motor and cognitive disabilities defined by the Web Content Accessibility Guidelines (WCAG) document.

2.1 Protocol

The studies and solutions shown in this work were searched from two scientific bases: IEEE Xplore [42] and The ACM Digital Library [41] considering the 2009 to 2019 period. We considered only full papers written in English language.

The key search terms used in this study were: "accessibility, pervasive systems, IoT, enactive systems, ubiquitous computing, disabilities guidelines". The papers collected in those databases were browsed for:

- The definition of impairments used
- Models and techniques for accessibility in IoT systems;
- Models and techniques for accessibility in pervasive and enactive systems;
- Accessibility layers proposed for use in ubiquitous computing.

In our protocol, we searched for accessibility strategies for pervasive systems considering each disability. For instance, concerning hearing impairment, we describe a system proposed for low hearing people using a smart bracelet to circulate in the external environment, or visors for dautonics.

2.2 Classifications of Impairments

According to Souza & Silva [13], the health condition of a person is relative to sight, hearing, mobility, cognition, self-care and communication. Yuan *et al.* [15] presented the state of the art of accessible development for smart devices where the categories of disabilities were defined as:

- **Visual Impairment:** People who have some degree of visual impairment may be partially or totally blind. Color vision deficiency (CVD) also falls into this category [5].
- **Hearing Impairment:** People with hearing impairment in both ears [4]. These limitations are also classified as deaf or hard of hearing (DHH).
- **Motor Impairment:** People with any limitation of movement, mobility or speech difficulties [19].
- **Cognitive Impairment:** People with psychological limitations may be degenerative as Alzheimer's or limitations as dyslexia and autism [3].

These four categories aid in identifying the completeness of an accessibility model or evaluate a system's ability to attend scenarios where stakeholders have disabilities. Nevertheless, accessibility issues include also [13]:

- not being able to receive feedback;
- not being able to provide input using conventional input devices.

The importance of considering these limitations is vital since not meeting these requirements can exclude a significant portion of people from the use of computational systems.

2.3 WCAG and Guidelines for Accessibility

The WCAG document [16] defines guidelines for Web content accessibility by defining four principles that consider whether the content is perceivable, operable, understandable and robust. Although not anticipated in the WCAG model, these guidelines can be considered for evaluating a pervasive system concerning accessibility. For example, the Authoring Tool Accessibility Guidelines (ATAG), part of WCAG, suggests that editing-views need to be perceivable and operable, which implies the need of alternatives for rendered non-text content, a principle that can be used in ubiquitous systems.

The four principles for accessibility in web systems contained in WCAG are [16]:

- Perceivable: suggests that content should be presented in more than one media.
- Operable: suggests that the system should allow any user to operate inputs without difficulty.
- Understandable: suggests that systems should facilitate languages and outputs to make content easier to understand.
- Robust: suggests that a system should be able to run on assistive platforms.

The challenge in the current study is to find out whether and how the WCAG principles and guidelines fit the ubiquitous and pervasive systems and how current literature on the subject is addressing the accessibility concerns.

3 Accessibility in Ubiquitous Computing

This section presents solutions for accessibility that fit ubiquitous computing. Subsection 3.1 presents solutions found in the literature for accessibility, which address specific deficiencies in computing environments, some of which, pervasive. Subsection 3.2 describes solutions for accessibility to IoT (Internet of Things) systems and the concepts of enactive systems, which should include elements of accessibility in their artifacts.

3.1 Accessibility Solutions of Artefacts Addressing Specific Deficiencies

Some development principles targeting impaired users in mobile computing are presented in Operational Systems (OS) documentation such as Android [28] and BlackBerry, which offer features like Screen reader, sound and vibration alerts; and iOS with features like VoiceOver [27]. These tools offer development features that consider accessibility [13].

K. Rector [7] presents proposals for accessibility in pervasive systems, adapting the format in which information is presented (visually for the deaf, or using sound for the blind, for example) through displays and outputs using sensors. The author suggests that the main point to provide accessibility are adaptations of input and output in a ubiquitous environment.

Challiol et al. [21] and Tanuwidjaja et al. [39] proposed a device to assist colorblind people (cf. Fig. 1). Although this solution is restricted to one type of disability, this could be developed based on an accessibility model for viewers in general. For this purpose, this solution should apply changes to the input information based on the degree of visual impairment, specific chromatic changes, among others.

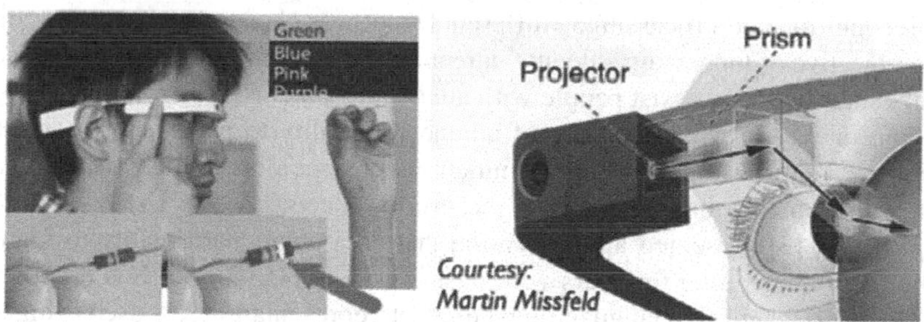

Fig. 1. Pervasive computing assisting users with color blindness [39].

According to Gamecho et al. [10], the solution for accessibility in pervasive systems must be made by matching the inputs and outputs. Gamecho et al. [10] propose an interface layer called Egoki that serves to access pervasive systems and adapt special features to assist users with physical disabilities (cf. Fig. 2). Through a middleware, the Egoki system presents an adapted user interface (UI) with elements that may vary in presentation (sound, purely visual, simplified, etc.) to facilitate or enable understanding by a disabled person.

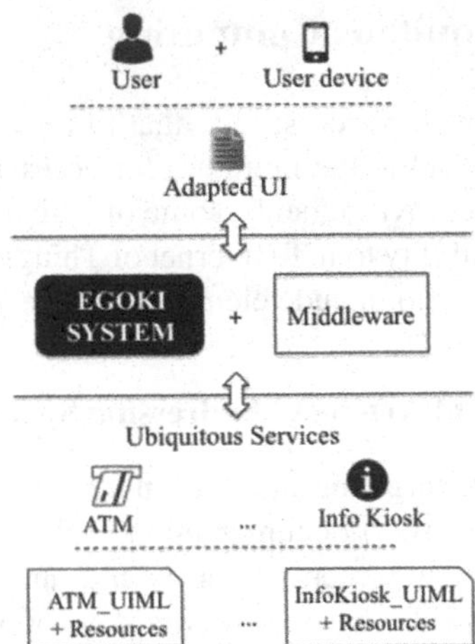

Fig. 2. Egoki Layer for accessibility in pervasive systems [10].

Rector [7] proposed an approach with the use of machine learning to identify notification preferences by Deaf or Hard-of-Hearing (DHH) users. The solution converts the output to lights or flickering screen to alert the user with non-sound elements. The authors present examples of interactive art installation that used Kinect-based proxemic audio interfaces and sound recordings to engage visually impaired as well as sighted patrons (cf. Fig. 3).

Srivastava [37] presented machine learning to identify learning disabilities based on the analysis of student facial expressions. A facial tracking was performed using a thermal camera with four sensors to identify the facial and eye position. By relying on pattern recognition and processing, a different layout was chosen to present the content with the objective of increasing students' attention. This kind of strategy can be used to customize interfaces and assist people with attention problems, for example.

Carro et al. [8] proposed the use of augmented reality to provide accessibility in educational systems, using virtual environments to present more attractive and dynamic content, with elements that interact with real-world objects.

Gupta et al. [3] presented an application that uses augmented reality to highlight texts and facilitate reading for users with dyslexia. A similar approach is proposed by Costa et al. in [4] where sign language and emoticon representations are used to highlight certain content and assist deaf people.

Neto et al. [5] use a speaker to indicate the main elements on the screen in order to assist visually impaired people. This solution can serve for accessibility purposes in ubiquitous devices such as smart wristbands, smartphone applications, and others, informing about elements of locomotion as position of traffic lights or elements of environment as obstacles.

Ubiquitous computing can be used outdoors as a tool to identify people's access. Rodrigo-Ubeda et al. [6] explored physical access data to observe how collective locomotion affects the access for visually impaired users. Pervasive systems of this kind may further utilize access and behavior information in public spaces to determine better access paths or times for impaired persons; or better spaces for visual or sound feedback [9].

Training Technology Probes (TTP) are pieces of technology with augmenting interactivity, used for people with motor difficulties [23]. TTP-based computing is often used to assist people with physical impairments or motor problems due to the ease of the device adjusting to different rhythms or spasms based on user's previous behaviors [24, 25].

Fig. 3. The Oregon Project was an interactive art installation that engages visually impaired using motion recognition by depth channel and sound effects [7].

Specific problems such as color blindness turn difficult for users to understand a color-based message. Khaliq and Dela Torre [29] present solutions for changing game interfaces for users with color blindness (Tritanopia (blue-yellow blindness), Achromatopsia (complete color-blindness), Protanopia (red blindness) and Deuteranopia (green-blindness). Zhou et al. [11] and Flatla et al. [26] present an application that uses a chromatic calculation to set interfaces to understandable patterns by users with Colour Vision Deficiency (CVD).

Automatic Speech Recognition (ASR) can also be used to interpret commands for visually impaired people [12] to assist in the implementation of audio-based access layers enabling voice inputs.

Neuro-Developmental Disorder (NDD) requires specific solutions that are often not limited to the interface. Spitale et al. [30] present an approach called "phygital" as it digitally virtualizes the physical environment of Tangible Objects, in wearables accessories, with environmental intelligence and with the transparent technology of ubiquitous computing (also known as calm technology). The authors concluded that the use of physical elements in conjunction with a digital environment enhances motivation, eventually improving performances; and can help people's learning with NDD.

Buzzi et al. [31] point out a positive relationship between systems that use music for teaching people with Autism, also suggesting the construction of customizable interfaces [36].

For motor problems, an interesting solution may be Smart Clothing [38] because they offer smart devices that enhance user/tool interaction by learning behavior and adapting to different users. This concept is used in prosthetics that can learn behaviors, through pattern recognition and machine learning, or take readings to indicate better actions for disabled users (For example, set rotation speeds by user preference, or indicate incorrect usage through outputs). This type of solution makes it possible to adapt inputs and outputs by integrating systems through an adaptive layer, for example, learning from intelligent systems which output is best suited for which user interactions (visual, sound).

3.2 Accessibility in the Context of Internet of Things and Enactive Systems

The Internet of Things (IoT) represents a system that connects multiple embedded devices exchanging data with each other, with or without involving a human agent in the process. Nguyen et al. [22] point out that a massive amount of personal data is daily collected in IoT devices. According to them, such data can be analyzed to identify preferences regarding inputs and outputs offered by these systems. For example, data collected from a smartwatch can determine physical activity spikes by relating activities or behaviors to the fed data.

Domingo [19] shows an overview of the IoT considering people with disabilities, and proposes a system development architecture consisting of three layers: Perception, Network, and Application layers. Network and application are supported by the technical definitions of the IoT system, such as communication with the database, servers and IP network. The perception layer provides context-aware information concerning the environment for disabled people with alert messages. For example, the messages indicate objects of interest along the way. In this layer, they present solutions for Vision, Hearing and Physical Impairments.

Nitti et al. [1], proposed to use a virtualization layer for Cloud-based IoT architectural solution for people with disabilities. This layer searches and discovery engine that allows the insertion of sound or visual virtual objects. The authors used this model in an IoT system for Accessible Tourism in Smart Cities architecture, implementing all three layers and applying to disabled users, integrating several kinds of users to help guide the environment. The authors used the previous model applied to an IoT for Accessible Tourism in Smart Cities architecture, implementing all three layers and applying to disabled users, integrating several categories of users to help guide the environment design.

Enactive systems are those that present a dynamic coupling between machine and human, allowing a new type of interaction [20]. Since the coupling relationship between a system and a human is a fundamental basis, accessibility criteria have to be considered in the construction of the artifact. According to Hayashi et al. [33], in the enactive system, interactions occur in an "embodied" way, which is guided by the body's involvement and the human agent's spatial presence. Hayashi and Baranauskas [34] propose strategies for the accessibility of visually impaired people in museums using socio-enactive artifacts such as tactile floors and maps.

Rector [7] build an Arduino-based artifact using a soft surface, for children with an autism spectrum disorder. The artifact uses a vibration system to soothe children, showing to be more attractive to people with these disabilities than sound and light responses. Crovari, et al. [32] reinforces this model by developing a Smart Toy artifact for educational interventions with people with Neurodevelopmental Disorder (NDD).

Guidelines for enative systems must consider the perceived sensory input and the engine output and can be defined as a technology interface that is designed for augmented sense-making [35]. Accessibility layers in these systems should consider non-traditional outputs and inputs mostly using sensors and human interaction.

The presented approaches have shown attempts to consider accessibility in pervasive systems such as creating a high-level layer that integrates special access functions into ubiquitous platforms [10, 19, 21]. These layers can be general resources that address the four impairment categories presented in Sect. 3, applying specific strategies to facilitate access to information or services.

In a general analysis of found solutions, even in different technological contexts, they present layers that adapt the inputs or outputs to the special needs of people with specific deficiencies. This is relevant for turning interactions in a way that is understandable for people with the physical limitations. This layer can consider the same principles of WCAG when the adaptations involve software, transforming the presentation of data.

When the adaptation is in hardware, e.g., systems that consider accessibility for people with motor problems, the accessibility layer becomes more specific, making generalizations difficult. The problem in this case is that pervasive systems usually directly involve hardware with very different specifications. In this case, the most generic solution could consider the application of the accessibility layer in the system design, with specific devices being part of a smaller application layer.

4 Accessibility Challenges in Ubiquitous Computing

Based on our literature review results, this section describes open challenges related to the four impairment categories for achieving enhanced accessible pervasive systems. In addition, we present our analysis correlating the WCAG principles with the impairment categories via the existing solutions found.

Visual Impairments. The accessibility layer inserts environment references extracted from trained patterns in the system layer [5–7]. These elements are described using speakers or specific action-sounds. The ubiquitous devices that involve vision, e.g. smart glasses, have no hardware development pattern, but they can implement in their output methods, features that modify the chromatic patterns as well as changes in the focus or position of the displayed elements. The challenge here is the study and design of an accessibility layer to provide elements to call for attention, or color correction for color blindness by eye tracking. For blind people, in addition to speakers, the layer could consider the position of the head and then read obstacles or objects of interest directed where the user is pointing. All of these resources could consider guidelines of a generic logical layer that would be used regardless of the physical architecture of the device.

Hearing Impairments. The solutions require the insertion of visual elements that aid in the understanding of the message, as sign language translations or signals for system sounds [4, 19]. Each country has its own regulations regarding sign languages, but the structures in general are similar as well as the process of computational synthesis. In addition to descriptive visual elements, such as American Signal Language (ASL) sign-writing, there are avatars that can be inserted into devices with a display for transmitting information. Simple visual alerts can be placed on smaller pervasive devices such as lighting alerts. The challenge in these environments is the implementation of an automatic synthesis system that includes the morphological subtleties of sign language. Still, in the case of virtual environments, the computational cost becomes a concern.

Motor and Cognitive Impairments. Screen elements can be highlighted or stabilized, helping to maintain focus or facilitating the understanding of key elements in an interface [27, 28, 30, 36]. There is, however, no document that indicates general principles and solutions for this case. Outlines on objects and elements of interest, or blur on secondary elements can help people with autism on devices with a display or visual representation. In auxiliary pervasive systems, such as bracelets or cybernetic gloves, accessibility features are usually intrinsic to the project. However, the logical accessibility features can share WCAG's accessibility principles by implementing a layer that handles inputs and outputs considering motor or cognitive disabilities. Systems that offer accessibility to cognitive disabilities can apply solutions that adapt inputs and outputs, but the challenge is to propose accessibility solutions for disabilities that affect physical aspects of the user that may require changes in the hardware design of the pervasive device.

Guidelines and Principles, as presented by the referred literature, are addressed as an accessibility layer that is integrated into ubiquitous computing by matching input and output information with the use of this accessibility layer. It is then necessary to build guidelines and principles for accessibility in mobile computing, IoT, and enactive systems that comprise the four classifications of impairments and how to assist people in each/all cases. The challenge in this case is to standardize different context systems for functional guidelines. Enactive systems consider the user's direct relationship and the participation of nonconscious inputs, whereas IoT systems may consider the display feature.

According to [21] services can be adapted to the user's needs or preferences by filtering information and links according to his profile or activity. When considering inputs or outputs in pervasive systems, the focus on standardization of accessibility models can be built on the treatment of information.

Each of the four WCAG principles has recommendations and techniques concerning web applications. Our study reinforces that guidelines for accessibility in pervasive systems can have a parallel with the WCAG (cf. Table 1) model. For the Perceivable and Understandable principles, adaptations of input and output can then be included, being logical adaptations that involve changes of source, color, format of information and aesthetic and functional standards of interface layout.

For accessibility models in pervasive systems applied in the operation principle, the inclusion of peripherals such as audio and light sensors might provide additional or alternative outputs and inputs. Robustness is the most challenging principle in ubiquitous computing environments as there is no hardware construction standard for these

Table 1. Relationship between the works cited and the WCAG principles and impairment categories.

WCAG principle	Visual impairment	Hearing impairment	Cognitive or motor impairment
Perceivable	[1, 5, 10–12, 26, 27]	[1, 10, 27]	[1, 3, 10, 20, 21, 27, 31, 32]
Operable	[6, 9, 14, 18, 29, 39]	[6, 9, 14, 18]	[6, 14, 18, 21, 23, 31, 38]
Understandable	[5, 7, 12, 26, 27, 37],	[7, 27, 37],	[3, 7, 9, 20, 27, 30]
Robust	[4, 6, 11, 13, 15, 19, 22, 24, 34, 36]	[4, 13, 15, 19, 22, 24, 34, 36]	[6, 13, 15, 22, 24, 34, 36]

devices. In this case, performance, interaction format among other parameters can prevent generic guidelines, the most interesting solution being the proposal of a logical layer of accessibility independent of the hardware.

The biggest challenge is to propose a guideline model for accessibility in pervasive scenarios that is generic enough to meet all four principles. The solution can start from the division of the accessibility layer between the WCAG principles. In this case, the biggest challenges are found in operability and robustness because in ubiquitous computing, completely different physical architectures are used. A way to achieve this can be the use of an accessibility layer that is integrated with systems constructed based on different architectures.

5 Conclusion

There is a huge challenge in building new technologies that integrate all people. In this context, it is crucial to define guidelines that help standardize models of access for people with disabilities in the contemporary technology scenarios such as pervasive computing. In this paper, our literature investigation contributed to clarify how accessibility has been considered in ubiquitous computing systems and reflect upon incoming challenges. We found that the lack of a guideline model for accessibility in pervasive systems is a social challenge, which is compounded by the lack of standards in the physical and logical construction of these devices. This work explored solutions proposed in ubiquitous environments, which can be related to the principles of accessibility of the WCAG model. Future work involves the study of solutions that can move towards the development of a specific model for ubiquitous computing that uses an accessibility layer in its design. We plan to investigate its design and evaluation in different contexts to obtain inclusive (i.e. for all) ubiquitous environments.

Acknowledgement. This work was financially supported by the São Paulo Research Foundation (FAPESP) (grants #2015/16528-0, #2015/24300-9 and #2019/12225-3), and CNPq (grant ##306272/2017-2). We thank the University of Campinas (UNICAMP) for making this research possible.

References

1. Nitti, M., et al.: Using IoT for accessible tourism in smart cities, assistive technologies in smart cities, Alejandro Rafael Garcia Ramirez and Marcelo Gitirana Gomes Ferreira, IntechOpen, 5 November 2018. https://doi.org/10.5772/intechopen.77057. https://www.intechopen.com/books/assistive-technologies-in-smart-cities/using-iot-for-accessible-tourism-in-smart-cities
2. Silva, E., et al.: Computação Ubíqua – Definição e Exemplos. Revista de Empreendedorismo, Inovação e Tecnologia, Passo Fundo **2**(1), 23–32 (2015). ISSN 2359-3539. https://doi.org/10.18256/2359-3539/reit-imed.v2n1p23-32
3. Gupta, T., Sisodia, M., Fazulbhoy, S., Raju, M., Agrawal, S.: Improving accessibility for dyslexic impairments using augmented reality. In: 2019 International Conference on Computer Communication and Informatics (ICCCI), Coimbatore, Tamil Nadu, India, pp. 1–4 (2019). https://doi.org/10.1109/iccci.2019.8822152
4. da Costa, S.E., Berkenbrock, C.D.M., de Freitas, L.E.R., Sucupira Ferreira Sell, F.: Development and evaluation of an assistive collaborative resource. In: 2019 IEEE 19th International Conference on Advanced Learning Technologies (ICALT), Maceió, Brazil, pp. 129–130 (2019). https://doi.org/10.1109/icalt.2019.00047
5. Neto, L.V., Fontoura Jr., P.H., Bordini, R.A., Otsuka, J.L.: Design and implementation of an educational game considering issues for visual impaired people inclusion. In: 2019 IEEE 19th International Conference on Advanced Learning Technologies (ICALT), Maceió, Brazil, pp. 298–302 (2019). https://doi.org/10.1109/icalt.2019.00097
6. Rodríguez-Ubeda, D., Rosales, R., Castanon-Puga, M., Flores, D., Palafox, L., Gaxiola-Pacheco, C.: Measuring the accessibility of public places using ubiquitous computing. In: International Conference on Information Society (i-Society 2012), London, pp. 499–500 (2012)
7. Rector, K.: Enhancing accessibility and engagement for those with disabilities. IEEE Pervasive Comput. **17**(1), 9–12 (2018). https://doi.org/10.1109/mprv.2018.011591056
8. Carro, R.M., et al.: eMadrid project: ubiquitous learning, adaptation, adaptability and accessibility. In: 2016 International Symposium on Computers in Education (SIIE), Salamanca, pp. 1–4 (2016). https://doi.org/10.1109/SIIE.2016.7751871
9. Ferrari, L., Berlingerio, M., Calabrese, F., Curtis-Davidson, B.: Measuring public-transport accessibility using pervasive mobility data. IEEE Pervasive Comput. **12**(1), 26–33 (2013). https://doi.org/10.1109/mprv.2012.81
10. Gamecho, B., et al.: Automatic generation of tailored accessible user interfaces for ubiquitous services. IEEE Trans. Hum. Mach. Syst. **45**(5), 612–623 (2015). https://doi.org/10.1109/THMS.2014.2384452
11. Zhou, L., Bensal, V., Zhang, D.: Color adaptation for improving mobile web accessibility. In: 2014 IEEE/ACIS 13th International Conference on Computer and Information Science (ICIS), Taiyuan, pp. 291–296 (2014). https://doi.org/10.1109/icis.2014.6912149
12. Caballero-Morales, S., Trujillo-Romero, F.: Automatic speech recognition of the Mixtec language: an ubiquitous computing application. In: CONIELECOMP 2013, 23rd International Conference on Electronics, Communications and Computing, Cholula, pp. 98–103 (2013). https://doi.org/10.1109/conielecomp.2013.6525767
13. de Sousa e Silva, J., Pereira, A., Gonçalves, R., Gomes, S.: State of the art of accessible development for smart devices: from a disable and not impaired point of view. In: 2014 9th Iberian Conference on Information Systems and Technologies (CISTI), Barcelona, pp. 1–5 (2014). https://doi.org/10.1109/cisti.2014.6876937

14. Using contextual information in Learning Management Systems: managing access control and adaptability/adaptativity/accessibility. In: Proceedings of the 2012 IEEE Global Engineering Education Conference (EDUCON), Marrakech, pp. 1–6 (2014). https://doi.org/10.1109/educon.2012.6201170. http://ieeexplore.ieee.org/stamp/stamp.jsp?tp=&arnumber=6201170&isnumber=6201007
15. Bei Yuan, J., Folmer, E., Harris Jr., F.C.: Game accessibility: a survey. Univers. Access Inf. Soc. 10(1), 81–100 (2011). https://doi.org/10.1007/s10209-010-0189-5
16. W3C. Web content accessibility guidelines 2.0 (2008). http://www.w3.org/tr/wcag20/. Accessed 13 Sept 2019
17. Cavender, A., Trewin, S., Hanson, V.: General writing guidelines for technology and people with disabilities. SIGACCESS Access. Comput. **92**, 17–22 (2008)
18. Dawe, M.: Desperately seeking simplicity: how young adults with cognitive disabilities and their families adopt assistive technologies. In CHI 2006: Proceedings of the SIGCHI Conference on Human Factors in Computing Systems, pp. 1143–1152. ACM, New York (2006)
19. Domingo, M.C.: An overview of the internet of things for people with disabilities. J. Netw. Comput. Appl. **35**(2), 584–596 (2012)
20. Imamura, R.E., Baranauskas, M.C.: Criando uma experiência de leitura colaborativa de histórias fictícias físico-virtuais com realidade aumentada. In: Brazilian Symposium on Computers in Education (Simpósio Brasileiro de Informática na Educação - SBIE), [S.l.], p. 31, out (2018). ISSN 2316-6533
21. Challiol, G., Rossi, L.: Designing pervasive services for physical hypermedia. In: 2006 ACS/IEEE International Conference on Pervasive Services, Lyon, pp. 265–268 (2006). https://doi.org/10.1109/perser.2006.1652238
22. Nguyen, M., Gani, M.O., Raychoudhury, V.: Yours Truly? survey on accessibility of our personal data in the connected world. In: 2019 IEEE International Conference on Pervasive Computing and Communications Workshops (PerCom Workshops), Kyoto, Japan, pp. 292–297 (2019). https://doi.org/10.1109/percomw.2019.8730880
23. Segura, E.M., Vidal, L.T., Bel, L.P., Waern, A.: Using training technology probes in bodystorming for physical training. In: Proceedings of the 6th International Conference on Movement and Computing (MOCO 2019), 8 p. ACM, New York (2019). Article 9. https://doi.org/10.1145/3347122.3347132
24. Boehner, K., Vertesi, J., Sengers, P., Dourish, P.: How HCI interprets the probes. In: Proceedings of the SIGCHI Conference on Human Factors in Computing Systems (CHI 2007), pp. 1077–1086 (2007). https://doi.org/10.1145/1240624.1240789
25. Gaver, B., Dunne, T., Pacenti, E.: Design: cultural probes. Interactions **6**(1), 21–29 (1999). https://doi.org/10.1145/291224.291235
26. Flatla, D.R., Reinecke, K., Gutwin, C., Gajos, K.Z.: SPRWeb: preserving subjective responses to website colour schemes through automatic recolouring. In: Proceedings of the SIGCHI Conference on Human Factors in Computing Systems, Paris, France, pp. 2069–2078. ACM (2013)
27. Apple Developer: iOS human interface guidelines: designing for iOS 7. https://developer.apple.com/library/ios/documentation/userexperience/conceptual/mobilehig/. Accessed 23 Jan 2014
28. Android Developers: Revisions. http://developer.android.com/sdk/index.html. Accessed 22 Jan 2014
29. Khaliq, I., Torre, I.D.: A study on accessibility in games for the visually impaired. In: Proceedings of the 5th EAI International Conference on Smart Objects and Technologies for Social Good (GoodTechs 2019), pp. 142–148. ACM, New York (2019). https://doi.org/10.1145/3342428.3342682

30. Spitale, M., Gelsomini, M., Beccaluva, E., Viola, L., Garzotto, F.: Meeting the needs of people with neuro-developmental disorder through a phygital approach. In: Proceedings of the 13th Biannual Conference of the Italian SIGCHI Chapter: Designing the next interaction (CHItaly 2019), 10 p. ACM, New York (2019). Article 22. https://doi.org/10.1145/3351995.3352055
31. Buzzi, M.C., Paolini, G., Senette, C., Buzzi, M., Paratore, M.T.: Designing an accessible web app to teach piano to students with autism. In: Proceedings of the 13th Biannual Conference of the Italian SIGCHI Chapter: Designing the next interaction (CHItaly 2019), 12 p. ACM, New York (2019). Article 4. https://doi.org/10.1145/3351995.3352037
32. Crovari, P., Gianotti, M., Riccardi, F., Garzotto, F.: Designing a smart toy: guidelines from the experience with smart dolphin "SAM". In: Proceedings of the 13th Biannual Conference of the Italian SIGCHI Chapter: Designing the next interaction (CHItaly 2019), 10 p. ACM, New York (2019). Article 8. https://doi.org/10.1145/3351995.3352041
33. Hayashi, E.C.S., et al.: Socio-enactive systems: the hospital scenario. Technical report - IC-18-03 -Computer Institute - Unicamp, March 2018
34. Hayashi, E.C.S., Cecília, M., Baranauskas, C.: Accessibility and affect in technologies for museums: a path towards socio-enactive systems. In: Proceedings of the XVI Brazilian Symposium on Human Factors in Computing Systems (IHC 2017), 10 p. ACM, New York (2017). Article 7. https://doi.org/10.1145/3160504.3160543
35. Rodríguez, A., López, P.G., Rossi, G.: Sketching for designing enactive interactions. In: Proceedings of the XV International Conference on Human Computer Interaction (Interacción 2014). ACM, New York (2014), 2 p. Article 39. https://doi.org/10.1145/2662253.2662292
36. Abascal, J., et al.: Personalizing the user interface for people with disabilities. In: Proceedings of the 23rd International Workshop on Personalization and Recommendation on the Web and Beyond (ABIS 2019), p. 29. ACM, New York (2019). https://doi.org/10.1145/3345002.3349292
37. Srivastava, N.: Using contactless sensors to estimate learning difficulty in digital learning environments. In: Adjunct Proceedings of the 2019 ACM International Joint Conference on Pervasive and Ubiquitous Computing and Proceedings of the 2019 ACM International Symposium on Wearable Computers (UbiComp/ISWC 2019 Adjunct), pp. 399–403. ACM, New York (2019). https://doi.org/10.1145/3341162.3349312
38. Jansen, K.M.B.: How to shape the future of smart clothing. In: Adjunct Proceedings of the 2019 ACM International Joint Conference on Pervasive and Ubiquitous Computing and Proceedings of the 2019 ACM International Symposium on Wearable Computers (UbiComp/ISWC 2019 Adjunct), pp. 1037–1039. ACM, New York (2019). https://doi.org/10.1145/3341162.3349571
39. Tanuwidjaja, E., et al.: Chroma: a wearable augmented-reality solution for color blindness. In: Proceedings of the 2014 ACM International Joint Conference on Pervasive and Ubiquitous Computing (UbiComp 2014), pp. 799–810. ACM, New York (2014). https://doi.org/10.1145/2632048.2632091
40. Tricco, A.C., et al.: PRISMA extension for scoping reviews (PRISMAScR): checklist and explanation. Ann. Int. Med. 169, 467–473. https://doi.org/10.7326/m18-0850
41. IEEE Xplore. https://ieeexplore.ieee.org. Accessed Oct 2019
42. ACM Digital Library. https://dl.acm.org. Accessed Oct 2019
43. Disabled World Statistics. https://www.disabled-world.com/disability/statistics/. Accessed Jan 2020

Rethinking User Interaction with Smart Environments—A Comparative Study of Four Interaction Modalities

Mohamed Handosa[1], Archi Dasgupta[2], Mark Manuel[2](✉), and Denis Gračanin[2]

[1] Mansoura University, Mansoura, Egypt
handosa@mans.edu.eg
[2] Virginia Tech, Blacksburg, VA 24060, USA
{archidg,mmark95,gracanin}@vt.edu

Abstract. Smart environments, comprised of networked embedded devices, improve the lives of their users by providing them with a variety of assistive services that traditional built environments are incapable of supporting. However, as the number of connected devices in smart environments continue to increase, so does the level of complexity involved in interacting with these environments. Traditional human-computer interaction techniques are not always well-suited for smart environments and this poses some unique usability challenges. To facilitate interactions within such technology-rich smart environments, new models and interaction interfaces need to be developed. In this paper we propose a multi-modal approach to smart environment interaction and explore two novel interaction interfaces: gesture-based interface and mixed-reality-based interface. We also conducted a user study to compare the learnability, efficiency and memorability of these new interfaces to two more commonly used interfaces: voice-based interface and a smartphone GUI-based interface. Our user study experiment involved four light control tasks that subjects were asked to complete using the four interaction interfaces. Study subjects found different interaction techniques to be more suitable for different tasks based on the type, complexity and context of the task. Our analysis of the study results and subject feedback suggest that a multi-modal approach is preferable to a uni-modal approach for interacting with smart environments. We suggest that novel interaction techniques be further explored in order to develop efficient multi-modal approaches along with the widely used techniques.

Keywords: Smart environments · User interaction · Multi-modal interaction · Interaction interfaces · Mixed reality interface · Voice interface · Graphical User Interface · Gestural interface

1 Introduction

A smart environment enables enhanced situated experiences by embedding computational and communication capabilities within everyday objects. The added

N. Streitz and S. Konomi (Eds.): HCII 2020, LNCS 12203, pp. 39–57, 2020.
https://doi.org/10.1007/978-3-030-50344-4_4

capabilities of smart environments open up dramatic new possibilities for interacting and interfacing with these environments. But the burgeoning number of embedded smart devices also pose a challenge to interaction design [20].

Smart environments can gather and apply contextual information in aiding users with autonomous action [25]. However, autonomous action may prove to be inefficient and over-patronizing for users. Users require a simple and convenient user interface (UI) for conducting their day-to-day activities in a smart environment [15,26]. Domestic environment interfaces can be either simple distributed interfaces or can comprise of more complex interfaces [16]. Light switches are an example of simple interfaces while TV and A/V controllers are examples of complex interfaces. These diverse interaction scenarios in smart environments are more intricate and complicated because of the sheer volume of functionalities and interaction opportunities that they provide, thereby, demanding that additional research be conducted in this area [7,15].

Nowadays, Graphical User Interfaces (GUIs), leveraging the ubiquity of smartphones are dominant in supporting user interaction with smart devices [15, 26]. Voice-based UIs have also become popular in recent times. However, smart environments introduce a context where users interact with the physical world in a three dimensional (3D) space where traditional interaction techniques may not perform well. Mapping a 3D physical space to a two dimensional (2D) layout displayed on a smartphone screen can be tricky and may confuse the users. For instance, turning a light switch on/off in a domestic environment using a smartphone GUI (GUI) might be seen as excessive and impractical compared to simply using a physical light switch. Similarly, although voice-based UIs can provide a more natural way of interaction, mapping smart devices to a set of pronounced names may not scale well with the rapidly increasing number of devices in a smart environment. Memorizing voice commands and device names can also introduce a considerable mental workload. Also noteworthy is the fact that current practices of interaction design in smart environments do not leverage the full capabilities of the human body. There is, therefore, a need for more intuitive, seamless, and efficient interaction interfaces for smart environments [15].

To remedy some of these challenges, we propose a multi-modal approach for interaction design and explore the use of two novel modes of interaction: Mixed-Reality (MR) and gesture-based interaction. We considered studying MR as an input modality because a smart environment is likely to have numerous, potentially undetectable smart devices and it can be quite difficult to identify and leverage their smart capabilities to full potential through traditional control interfaces. The enhanced capability of MR devices can assist users in detecting and interfacing with various smart functionalities. We also considered studying gesture-based interaction as it can provide for embodied and instantaneous interaction that leverages the capabilities of the human body. In doing so, gesture-based interaction can allow users to simply point at smart objects to control them, and spares them the burden of having to remember a plethora of complicated device names. Petersen et al. [24] evaluated the potential of using gestures in their user study and determined that 80% of their study subjects preferred to use a gestural interface over more traditional interfaces like GUIs.

To test out the usability of MR and gesture-based interfaces in smart environments we conducted a user study that compared these modalities with two more commonly used interaction modalities(voice-based and GUI-based interaction). Our study evaluated subject task performance in conducting a set of light control tasks using each of the four interaction modalities. We aimed to understand the usability, learnability and memorability of each modality, to identify both their scope and their limitations. Learnability was tested by observing the initial performance of users interacting with the four UIs for the first time. Memorability was tested by evaluating subject task performance between two study sessions. And finally, usability was measured through a combination of qualitative feedback analysis and evaluation of task completion time. By evaluating the usability, learnability and memorability of these four interaction modalities, we sought to understand their strengths and limitations to determine their suitability for interacting with smart environments. We believe that our findings will assist designers in developing efficient, multi-modal interaction approaches for interfacing with smart environments.

2 Related Work

Smart Environments Overview—A smart environment implements ubiquitous computing techniques and provides context-aware automated services [1]. In addition to mechanical and digital devices, everyday physical objects are equipped with computation and communication capabilities in a smart environment [9]. Objects are embedded with sensors and actuators and they form a interconnected communication network creating an Internet of Things (IoT) [1]. As smart environments continue to evolve and become widely accepted, they provide an increasing number of services and diverse interaction scenarios. Here we describe some widely used interaction techniques along with some novel approaches.

Interactions Within Smart Environments—Rashidi and Cook [25] describe an adaptive smart home that identifies user's behaviour patterns and automates the systems according to those patterns. The user can modify and update the automation.

Yamazaki et al. describe a ubiquitous home that uses displays/visual UI and microphones/voice command to interface with the system [31]. Smartphone is an ideal GUI-based interaction interface for smart environments as they have become ubiquitous in recent times. The rapid advancement in smartphone technology, increased computing power and touch and motion sensors have developed it into one of the most promising user interfaces [16].

Intelligent Virtual Agent (IVA) products like Google Home, Apple's HomePod, Amazon's echo are increasingly getting extended to user interaction with smart environments [22]. These devices use voice command as the primary mode of interaction. Swaminathan et al. utilize a speech-recognition system to use voice command for interacting with the objects [27]. Voice-based UI has great potential as it resembles human's natural communication tendencies [11].

Kuhnel et al. evaluate the use of gesture-based interaction in smart home environments. They identify three dimensional gestures using a mobile phone as an interaction device held by the user [30]. They conclude that gesture-based interface is well-suited for smart environments for the most common and basic interactions that elicit similar physical or metaphorical concepts in users. Complicated interactions could be performed by offering additional interfaces such as GUI or allowing the user to define their own set of gestures [16]. Gieselmann et al. suggest that gesture has great potential as an interface for smart environments as it resembles human's natural communication tendencies [11]. Handosa et al. [12] describe a gesture-based approach to control color-adjustable LED lights. The developed lights control system uses a tracking device to capture user gestures. Compared to the use of a glove as described by Mrazovac et al. [21], the tracking device is a hidden interaction proxy that allows for hands-free seamless interaction between users and lights.

Mixed reality is a promising novel interaction modality that can be used to interface with smart, IoT-enabled spaces. IoT enables the creation of enhanced services through a connected network of devices while MR allows for users to interact with these services in ways that are otherwise physically impossible. MR has seen a surge in its popularity in the last decade due to advances in portable mobile devices and computer vision [14,29]. Ladwig and Geiger [18] consider how the advancement of MR technology in the near future will allow us to create the "ultimate device" that will be capable of making the real world indistinguishable from the virtual world. Such a system would provide "realistic and complete embodied experiences" by utilizing multiple human sensory modalities including haptic, sound or even smell and taste [18].

Various studies comparing the different user interfaces show increasing interest among users towards the novel interaction techniques. Kuhnel et al. [16] describe a comparative study between a gesture-based UI, a voice-based UI and a combination of voice, gesture and GUI. Their preliminary results indicate preference towards voice-based UI among half the users and preference towards GUI among the other half [17]. Brumitt et al. describe another comparative study that reports user preference for voice-based interfaces. They also suggested location awareness for voice or GUI to be effective [5].

Gieselmann et al. [11] describe the advantages of providing multi-modal interaction for smart environments. A multi-modal approach provides users with an option to choose a more appropriate interaction technique for each task. It also increases user's overall task performance [2,6,23].

Messaging and Communication Protocols—Sensors form an integral part of a smart environment by acquiring state information of various environmental variables such as energy usage, temperature, occupancy and dust content [1,13]. Certain classes of sensors like motion capture devices and smart speakers can be used to provide additional services and novel interaction techniques to interface with the smart environments [3].

The acquisition of data from numerous sensors spread out across a smart environment can often pose a challenge to the designers of such spaces [28]. Sensor enabled smart spaces often need to interface with large amounts of data and require efficient communication protocols to reduce delays in sending and receiving packets of data. A protocol for data transmission must be reliable and have low power and bandwidth constraints. The Message Queuing Telemetry Transport (MQTT) protocol is one such light-weight protocol that is suitable for use in smart environments. Because of its lightweight properties and small code footprint, MQTT can be used to provide home control and task automation services in smart homes [10,19].

3 Problem Definition

Interaction with smart environments is fundamentally different and more complex compared to the traditional environments. Networked smart objects provide diverse new ways of interfacing with them. The sheer volume of smart functionalities and increased interaction opportunities make the interaction design challenging.

Most of the current interaction techniques have originated in a world of desktop computers and more recently, smartphones. Therefore, they allow for limited interaction that does not leverage the full capabilities of smart environments or the human body. The most common approach for interacting with a smart environment is by using GUIs and web-based portals. However, such an approach does not scale well. As the number of things in a smart environment increases, it becomes harder for a user to maintain a mental model of things and their corresponding apps. This can complicate the user experience rather than simplifying it. Switching between numerous apps to interact with different things introduces an overhead that can degrade user performance and increase cognitive-workload.

Hence, new modalities of human-computer interaction need to be developed to address the enhanced capabilities of smart environments. It is crucial to explore other interaction modalities that can help a smart environment better understand the actions and behavior of its users. A user may provide input through touch/press, speech, gesture, and/or thoughts, while a smart environment may provide output using a graphical, audio, and/or MR user interfaces. Interaction modalities can be device-based (switches, input devices, etc.), where the user monitors and controls the smart environment through a UI. On the other hand, interaction can be done by utilizing the capabilities of the human body (gesture, voice command, etc.), where the smart environment reacts to device-free spontaneous user actions.

Providing a convenient interaction interface while reducing the required mental workload is one of the major challenges in this case. Another big challenge is providing users with a suitable interaction modality based on the task at hand or their personal preferences. Given the drawbacks associated with the current interaction techniques to support interaction with smart environments, it is crucial to adapt these techniques by addressing their drawbacks and explore

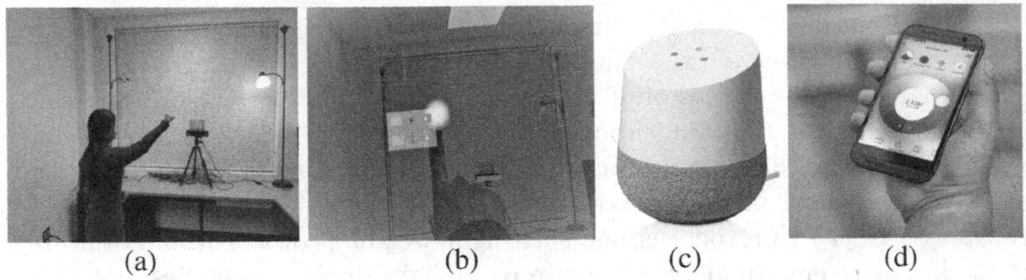

(a) (b) (c) (d)

Fig. 1. From left to right: (a) A user interacting with the smart lights using the gesture-based UI, (b) A user's POV from inside the MR application running on the HoloLens, (c) A Google Home smart speaker, (d) The OSRAM Lightify GUI. (Color figure online)

other alternatives to provide an enhanced interaction experience. In light of this, there is a need for more research into novel interaction interfaces and to conduct experimental studies on different interaction techniques for understanding their strengths and weaknesses. To compare the effectiveness of multiple interaction techniques, they can be evaluated based on metrics such as learnability, memorability and efficiency.

4 Proposed Approach

Smart environments are comprised of many different smart objects, each having their own unique function and interaction mechanism. However, there is no "one-size" interaction interface solution that caters to all smart objects or all smart environments. Users need to be given the ability to control smart objects using interfaces that best suit their needs at a given time. For example, when a user is in the presence of a smart light, controlling it's color and brightness using hand motions might be practical, and might save time. However, if the user is not in the same physical space as the smart object, it might be more sensible to have the user interface with the object by using a application on their smartphone. To address this type of challenges we describe a multi-modal approach that includes two novel interaction techniques: gesture-based and MR-based interaction.

Secondly, to investigate how different user interfaces compare against each other, we designed a simple, multi-modal light control experiment. Among the smart environment activities currently tested, light control is one of the most frequently performed ones making it a prime candidate for a comparative study of interaction modalities. With recent advances in lighting technologies, a lighting control system is no longer as simple as before. We study two novel interaction interfaces: gesture control (Fig. 1a) and MR-based control (Fig. 1b) and compare them to two of the more commonly used smart environment interaction interfaces: voice-based UI (Fig. 1c) and GUI (Fig. 1d).

Multi-modal Approach: We describe a multi-modal testbed that is capable of supporting novel interaction techniques. Our proof of concept light control testbed allows a user to control smart lights using four different UIs.

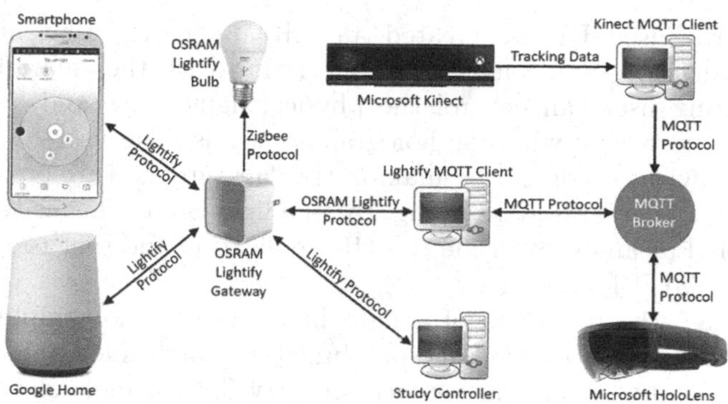

Fig. 2. Light control testbed architecture.

As shown in Fig. 2, our testbed comprises of—a GUI, a voice-based UI facilitated by a Google Home smart speaker, a gesture-based UI that uses the Microsoft Kinect tracking sensor, and a mixed-reality-based UI application that runs on the Microsoft HoloLens. The smart lights (OSRAM Lightify Bulb) can be controlled through a gateway (OSRAM Lightify Gateway). The communication between the gateway and the lights takes place through the Zigbee protocol. The testbed incorporates a vendor-provided GUI (OSRAM Lightify) to test GUI-based interaction. The voice-based UI is also incorporated into the testbed through a vendor-provided configuration mechanism that establishes communication between the gateway and the Google Home smart speaker. An example voice command for controlling lights is—"Set the color of the top right light to soft white".

Besides the vendor-provided GUI and voice-based UI, we developed a gesture-based UI and an MR-based UI. To construct the gesture-based UI, we created a module (Kinect MQTT client) that translates captured hand motions into light control commands and sends them to the gateway via MQTT protocol. Users in the range of the Kinect camera can "take control" of a light by pointing the palm of their hand towards the light and then making a fist. With their closed fist, the user can now move their hand along two dimensions. Moving left-to-right changes the color temperature of the light bulb, while moving up and down changes it's brightness. The extent of a user's hand movement along each dimensional axis is converted into a decimal value between 0 and 1. This value is sent to the Lightify Gateway, as an MQTT message, which changes the corresponding light property (brightness or color) by the specified amount.

The magnitude of the values affect the degree to which the properties of the light are modified. For example, if a user, who is in control of a light, were to lower their fist by a considerable amount with respect to the point where they made the fist gesture, their hand motion would trigger a '0' brightness value which would send a "turn off" signal to the light bulb. To "release control" of a light bulb, the user can raise both of their palms in front of the Kinect sensor.

For the MR-based UI, we created an MR application that allows users to interact with holographic menus for interfacing with the smart lights. The HoloLens-wearing user can control the physical light bulbs and change their properties by interacting with the holographic menus. The user can select the light that they wish to control by making the "air-tap" gesture on a hologram representation (the green square in Fig. 1b) of a light bulb. The air-tap information is registered as an event inside the MR application and sent to the Lightify Gateway as an MQTT message.

"Air-tapping" the hologram of a light bulb causes a holographic menu to appear that allows the user to modify brightness and color values by "air-tapping" the '+' and '−' buttons for each property. The current color and brightness value of the light is represented as a decimal on a slider that takes on values from '0' to '1'. "Air-tapping" the '+' icon increases the brightness of the light by a fixed amount, up to the maximum brightness value, represented by the value '1' on the slider. The color of the light bulb can also be changed by "air-tapping" it's corresponding '+' and '−' buttons.

Both of the above-described user interfaces make use of the MQTT protocol to relay messages to the Lightify Gateway. Being a lightweight and low-latency protocol, MQTT provides a flexible means of establishing communication between these UIs and the Gateway.

5 User Study

As discussed in Sect. 4 of this paper, we designed a multi-modal light control study to compare the usability of four different user interfaces. Our study required subjects to complete sixteen randomized light control tasks. These tasks involved simple procedures like changing the color and the brightness of four smart light bulbs to get them to match the color and brightness of a reference light bulb. The time taken by subjects to complete each task was recorded, along with numerical values representing the color and brightness properties of the light bulbs, as was set by the subjects at the end of each task. At the end of each study, we also collected qualitative feedback from our subjects in order to better understand their interaction experience with each of the four user interfaces.

Our experimental study was set up in a room as shown in Fig. 3. The study equipment included four smart light bulbs that were given memorable names (Top Left, Bottom Left, Top Right, and Bottom Right) to enable study subjects to clearly distinguish between them. The fifth bulb in the middle acted as a reference light during the study. The Kinect motion sensor (tracking device) always faced the study subjects during the study session and was used to capture a set of predefined hand gestures. The "tag device" was used as a marker for the MR headset to register its local coordinate system with the physical surroundings, allowing it to correctly blend the MR holograms with their corresponding physical objects.

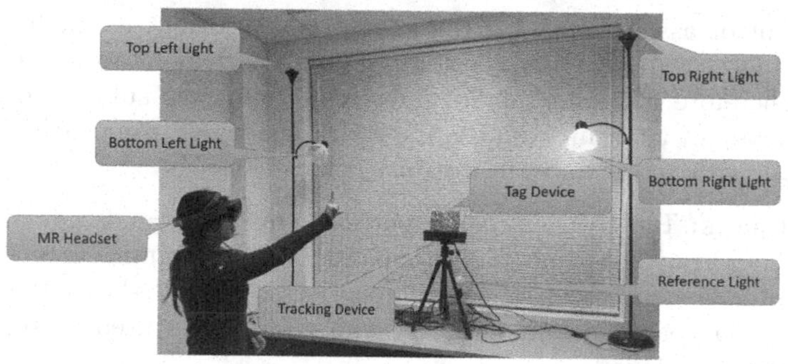

Fig. 3. A user wearing the HoloLens and interacting with the experimental setup.

Study Procedure: The study defines four light control tasks: "turn-on", "turn-off", "set brightness", and "set color temperature". Each subject is required to complete a set of light control assignments. Each assignment asks the subject to control and change the state of a randomly selected light bulb to match the state of the reference bulb using one of the four supported UIs. The study requires the subject to attend two sessions, conducted on two different days to complete three rounds of light control assignments. *Round 1* and *Round 2* take place in *Session 1* while *Round 3* takes place in *Session 2*. Each round consists of sixteen randomly ordered assignments that make the subjects perform each of the four light control tasks using each of the four UIs.

Data Collection: Qualitative data was collected using questionnaires. Each subject completed a background questionnaire at the beginning of *Session 1*. The background questionnaire consisted of a set of demographic questions followed by other questions about the subject's prior experience using any of the devices/interaction modalities used in the experiment. Each subject completed a post-session questionnaire after each of the two sessions. The post-session questionnaire used the System Usability Scale (SUS) [4] to evaluate the usability of each of the four UIs. Having two sets of completed post-session questionnaires allowed us to easily compare the responses of each subject after both sessions and allowed us to identify improvements and/or inconsistencies in subject performance.

Quantitative data was also collected in this experiment. For each light control assignment, the start and finish time of the assignment were recorded in order to measure the total amount of time that it took each subject to complete each of the sixteen assignments.

In *Round 1*, each subject completed their light control assignments for the first time and were relatively unfamiliar with the four UIs. Thus, the amount of time that it took each subject to complete each assignment can act as an indicator of UI learnability. *Round 2*, which took place as part of *Session 2*, was conducted approximately two weeks after *Session 1*. Because of this two-week interim period, the amount of time it took for each subject to perform the light control assignments for the second time can act as an indicator of UI memorability. Finally, *Round 3* took place as part of *Session 2* right after *Round 2*. Therefore, the amount of time that it took each subject to complete the assignments for the third time, while their memory of using each of the four UIs was fresh, can act as an indicator of UI efficiency.

Study Subjects: Ten subjects participated in this study and they all were at least 18 years old at the time of participation. Table 1 summarizes the demographic information of the participating subjects. Table 2 shows the previous experience of the participating subjects with the devices used to support the four interaction modalities.

Table 1. Demographics of the participating subjects.

Age		Gender		Language		Education major	
21–29	30–39	M	F	English	Other	Comp. Science	Other
5	5	8	2	1	9	5	5

Table 2. Experience of the participating subjects.

	Smartphone		Smart speaker		Kinect		HoloLens	
	Yes	No	Yes	No	Yes	No	Yes	No
Used it before	10	0	3	7	4	6	0	10
To control lights	1	0	1	0	0	0	0	0
To control other devices	5	0	3	0	4	0	0	0

6 Results

This section presents the results of analyzing the collected quantitative and qualitative data and discusses the obtained results.

6.1 Quantitative Data Analysis

In *Round 1*, subjects have used the four UIs for the first time. Therefore, the average completion time of a given task using a given UI can provide a good indication of the learnability of that UI. Figure 4 shows the average completion time for each of the sixteen assignments. Results show that the average subject performance varies depending on both the task and the UI in use. The average task completion time using the GUI was less than the other UIs for all light control tasks except for setting color temperature, where the gesture-based UI performed slightly better. This is expected given that the participating subjects have good experience using smartphones and GUIs in general, which made the

GUI feel more familiar compared to the other UIs. Meanwhile, voice-based and MR-based UIs did not perform as good. Forming a voice command can be tricky, especially for tasks requiring relatively long commands. For example, the subject needs to say "Set the brightness of top right light to fifty percent" for changing the brightness. Moreover, voice-based interaction can be inefficient for tasks involving trial and error (e.g. setting light brightness). In such case, it is more feasible to use a UI that allows for fast input and instant feedback. Using the MR-based UI was challenging to the subjects because they were unfamiliar with MR-headsets and MR technology in general.

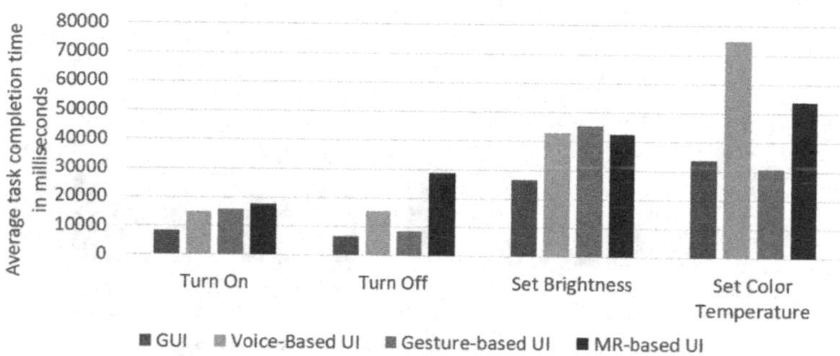

Fig. 4. Average task completion time in round 1 (learnability).

In *Round 2*, subjects have used the four UIs for the second time after days from the first time. Therefore, the average completion time of a given task using a given UI can provide an indication of memorability for that UI. Figure 5 shows the average completion time for each of the 16 assignments. Results show that subjects were able to perform better using the gesture-based UI in three out of four light control tasks while the GUI continued to perform better in the *Turn Off* task. On average, the gesture-based UI has better memorability compared to the other UIs while the voice-based UI has the lowest memorability.

In *Round 3*, subjects have used the four UIs for the third time on the same session right after *Round 2*. Therefore, the average completion time of a given task using a given UI can provide a good indication of efficiency for that UI. Figure 6, shows the average completion time of each of the 16 assignments. Results show that the gesture-based UI has outperformed the other UIs in three out of four tasks while the GUI has performed better in the *Turn On* task. Both voice-based and MR-based UIs did not perform as good. On average, the gesture-based UI is more efficient compared to the other UIs while the voice-based UI is the least efficient.

Although the results mentioned above are preliminary and obtained from a small sample (i.e. 10 subjects), they still show that gesture-based UIs can be promising for supporting user interaction with lights.

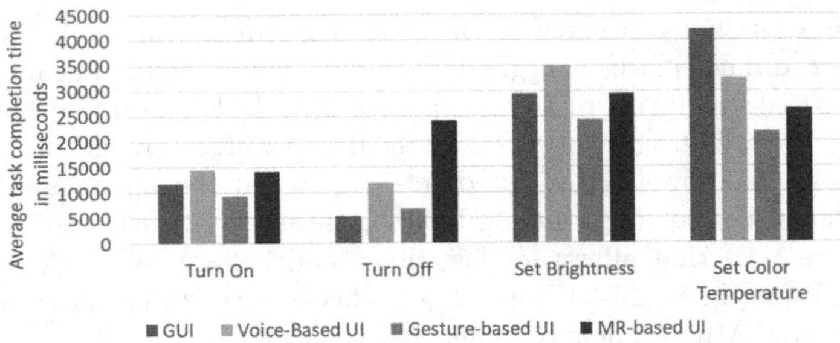

Fig. 5. Average task completion time in round 2 (memorability).

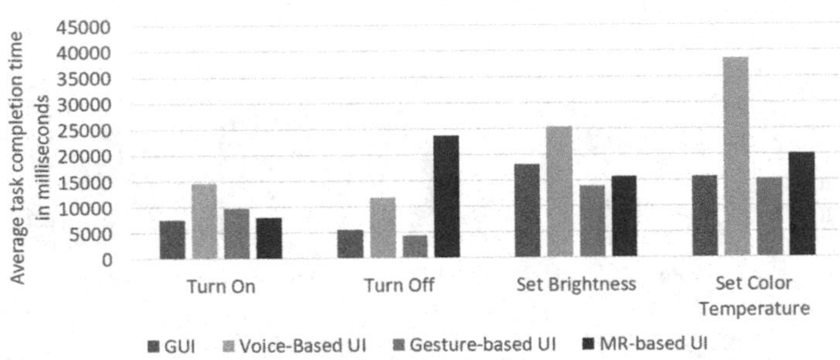

Fig. 6. Average task completion time in round 3 (efficiency).

6.2 Qualitative Data Analysis

Subjects were asked to fill up a post-session questionnaire after each of the two sessions to describe their experiences with each of the four UIs. The post-session questionnaire included the 10 questions of the System Usability Scale (SUS) [4]. Subject responses for each question (Q1 to Q10) were scored on a scale of 0–4. These raw scores were used to calculate a score out of one hundred for each UI. Table 3 shows the average score for each of the four UIs in both sessions. In *Session 1*, the GUI and the voice-based UI have received the highest average score. However, their scores have decreased in *Session 2*. Although the gesture-based UI did not get a high score in *Session 1*, its average score has improved significantly in *Session 2*. This can be interpreted as an indication of gaining acceptance after the subjects got used to it in the second session.

Table 3. The average SUS scores for each of the UIs in both sessions.

	GUI	Voice-based UI	Gesture-based UI	MR-based UI
Session 1	86.25	75.25	64.00	50.00
Session 2	81.75	68.00	74.75	51.25

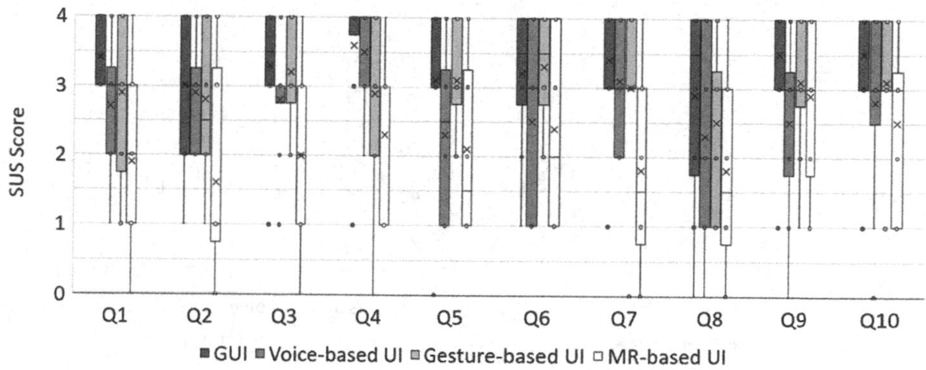

Fig. 7. SUS scores box plot of the UIs for *Session 1*.

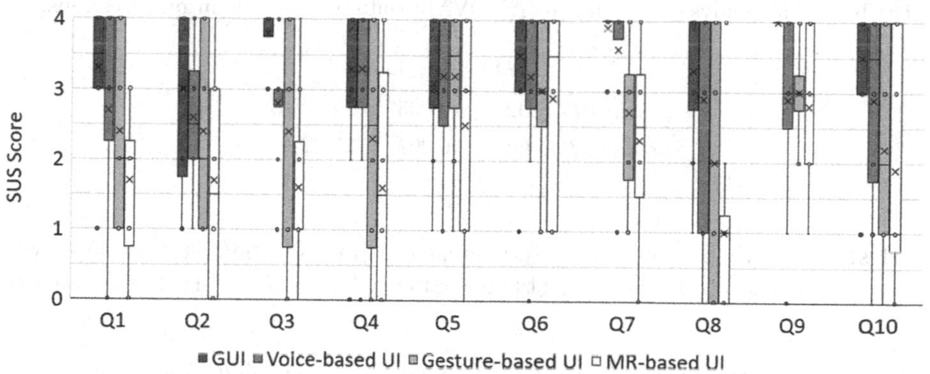

Fig. 8. SUS scores box plot of the UIs for *Session 2*.

The box plots of the raw SUS scores obtained in *Session 1* and *Session 2* are shown in Fig. 7 and Fig. 8. Comparing both box plots (Fig. 9), we can see that the SUS scores for the gesture-based UI have improved in the second session. The outlier in the plot for *Session 2* is a low score (30) given to the GUI by one of the subjects, who commented that the UI design of the app was somewhat complex to understand at first but later the user experience was better. The subject also mentioned that despite being an avid user of GUIs, help was still needed to even understand the navigation design of the vendor-provided app.

The results of the one-way Analysis of Variance (ANOVA) test are shown in Table 4. The p-value in each session is less than 0.05, which leads to rejecting the null hypothesis that all means are equal and confirms that the variability in usability between the four UIs is statistically significant. The R^2 values for *Session 1* and *Session 2* show that the percentage of variation in the response that is explained by the model is 29.51% and 25.82%, respectively.

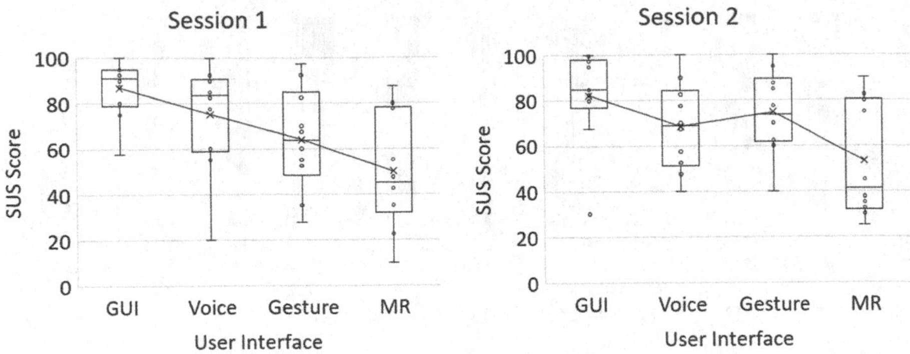

Fig. 9. SUS scores box plot of the UIs for *Session 1 and Session 2.*

Table 4. The analysis of variance (ANOVA) results for the UIs in both sessions.

	F-value	P-value	R^2
Session 1	5.02	0.005	29.51%
Session 2	4.64	0.007	25.82%

Besides the SUS scores collected using the post-session questionnaire, we received comments from the subjects on the four UIs, which we briefly summarize below.

- **GUI**: Subjects found the vendor-provided GUI convenient and easy to use because of familiarity with smartphone apps while some of them complained about the cluttered UI design of the app stating that navigation steps to brightness/color control were unclear. The mapping of the UI to the bulbs were also ill-defined.
- **Voice-based UI**: Some subjects found the voice-based UI to be the most convenient, especially for relatively simple commands (e.g. turn on). However, the lengthy commands for relatively more complex tasks were deemed annoying. Only forty percent of the subjects were fluent English speakers and the non-native English speakers had difficulties while using the voice commands. The smart speaker sometimes had trouble understanding the accent or accepting prolonged pauses between words. Following the specific format of the voice command for long commands and maintaining pauses between words was cxasperating for subjects.
- **Gesture-based UI**: Subjects found the gesture-based UI convenient because it does not require them to hold or wear a device. They also found the gestures to be intuitive. The possibility of fatigue in hands is a significant concern for this UI. The likelihood of false-positives where the system responds to spontaneous gestures and interprets them as device-control commands is another minor concern. This interface also requires the user to be at the same space as the light bulb.

– **MR-based UI**: Some subjects had difficulties providing input to the MR-based UI using the air-tap gesture and reported that they felt fatigue in hand while trying to do the air-tap repeatedly. Wearing a headset to perform a simple task like light control was deemed redundant. However, MR applications would be useful in identifying and controlling smart devices in environments where there are a lot of otherwise hard to detect smart devices (e.g., smart factories).

7 Discussion

In this section, we discuss our overall findings based on the user study and our qualitative and quantitative analyses.

GUIs provide a readily available user interface as smartphones have become a part and parcel of our daily lives. GUI is more useful for relatively complex tasks and for remotely controlling the devices when the user is not in the same physical space. However, complicated UI design can significantly increase the task completion time even for an widely used interaction technique like GUI. One interesting functionality for future researchers to develop would be to point the smartphone towards a smart device resulting in the relevant app page opening up in the GUI. Including a layout plan of the built environment within the GUI and placing device icons in corresponding locations could also be helpful for mapping the UI to the physical device.

Voice-based UI is gaining popularity in recent times specially for smart home scenarios because it resembles natural human communication. Voice allows for intuitive and efficient interaction, especially for simple lighting control tasks (e.g. "turn kitchen lights off"). However, it may not be a wise choice for controlling more complex lighting systems with various parameters (e.g. a room with tens of color-adjustable light sources). Sometimes the verbal commands to interact with a smart object can be too long-winded, causing users to forget these commands. Whereas, a GUI or hand gesture-based interface could prove to be faster and much simpler for that task. In such a scenario users would prefer using other UIs. Voice-based UI also needs to accommodate the issues faced by non-native speakers. For example, making the commands simpler and shorter, allowing for prolonged pauses or filler words.

The gesture-based UI is a hands-free option which does not require the user to carry or have constant access to a controller. Study subjects were intrigued by the intuitiveness of this interface. But along the same lines with the findings of Kuhnel et al. [16], we conclude that gesture is more suitable for straightforward and common interactions that have intuitive gestural perceptions among users. For example, physically inspired gestures like "Up" and "Down" for "On" and "Off". The success of a gesture based system has high dependence on the intuitiveness of the gestures and user familiarity with rotation direction of other interfaces like light/fan regulators or switch on/off direction. Cultural factors (e.g. writing direction) also effect the user's intuition. Gesture-based interaction is more suitable for scenarios where the user and the device are both in the same physical location.

MR-based UI, on the other hand, can be useful in smart environments where there are a lot of smart devices that are relatively inconspicuous. A 3D digital medium like MR provides a greater amount of visual and contextual information using holograms, lending it to be better suited for interfacing with a large number of distributed smart objects, which would be otherwise difficult to control using traditional interfaces. The holographic projection on top of the real environment is useful for complex tasks like maintenance and assembly. Virtual indicators might be useful for indicating proper placement of parts in case of assembly [8]. On the other hand, the use of a head-mounted display for conducting a relatively simple task like light control in smart home scenarios might be redundant. Even though the recent MR devices are fairly light, users prefer even lighter options in case of a wearable device for day-to-day use in a smart home context. Other smart environments like smart factory, smart warehouse, smart industry etc. could be more suitable for MR-based interaction.

The most frequently used interactions need their separate button, gesture or commands which are easy to memorize or placed in a focal point of the GUI. Overall, our findings suggest that different modalities were more suitable for different types of tasks. Therefore, we suggest that a multi-modal interaction system would be more efficient for interfacing with smart environments. Having multiple modalities also improve user task completion performance based on previous studies.

8 Conclusion and Future Work

There is a need for new and improved methods of human-computer interaction when interfacing with smart environments. Smart environments consist of objects that are imbued with computation and communication capabilities. This opens up numerous novel interaction possibilities that leverage recent technological advances, like MR and embodied interaction, to interface with smart environments. We describe a multi-modal approach and explore the use of two novel UIs—an MR-based UI and a gesture-based UI. We conducted a user study with ten subjects to compare the effectiveness of these two UIs to two other more commonly used UIs—GUIs and voice-based UIs. The goal of this study was to explore and evaluate the usability, learnability and memorability of these UIs. We also evaluated subject task performance on four different types of light control tasks in this study.

Our experimental results show that GUI had better learnability rating compared to the other UIs for most of the light control tasks in *Round 1*. In *Round 2* we observed that the gesture-based UI had a better memorability rating compared to the other UIs, while the voice-based UI had the lowest memorability. Lastly, in *Round 3* we observed that the gesture-based UI proved to have better efficiency compared to the other UIs, while the voice-based UI had the lowest efficiency for the light control tasks.

Our analysis suggests that the novelty of the UIs does not affect the overall task completion time. We noted from our subject feedback that different modes of interaction have different strengths and weaknesses based on the type of task that needed to be completed. Hence, a multi-modal approach that combines novel and traditional interaction interfaces provides users with more options to choose from and provides for more flexible and varied interactions with smart environments. Our comparison of the four user interfaces shed light on three different usability aspects of the interfaces: learnability, memorability and efficiency. The qualitative feedback that we obtained from our post-experiment questionnaires also helped us better understand the interface preferences of the study subjects. We believe that our findings will help designers of smart environments in developing more efficient interaction approaches for interfacing with smaart environments.

In the future we plan to further extend this study by investigating other UIs (e.g., web-based portals and wall-mounted touch-screen interfaces) to see how they compare to the ones that we observed in this study. We also plan on increasing the number and type of tasks that the subjects will perform. In subsequent studies we would like to be able to identify and isolate subject UI preferences for a number of different types of smart environment tasks.

References

1. Alam, M.R., Reaz, M.B.I., Ali, M.A.M.: A review of smart homes–past, present, and future. IEEE Trans. Syst. Man Cybern. Part C (Appl. Rev.) **42**(6), 1190–1203 (2012)
2. Ando, H., Kitahara, Y., Hataoka, N.: Evaluation of multimodal interface using spoken language and pointing gesture on interior design system. In: Third International Conference on Spoken Language Processing (1994)
3. Bien, Z.Z., Do, J.H., Kim, J.B., Stefanov, D., Park, K.H.: User-friendly interaction/interface control of intelligent home for movement-disabled people. In: Proceedings of the 10th International Conference on Human-Computer Interaction, pp. 304–308 (2003)
4. Brooke, J., et al.: SUS–a quick and dirty usability scale. In: Usability Evaluation in Industry, vol. 189, no. 194, pp. 4–7 (1996)
5. Brumitt, B., Cadiz, J.J.: "Let there be light": examining interfaces for homes of the future. In: INTERACT, vol. 1, pp. 375–382 (2001)
6. Cohen, P.R., et al.: QuickSet: multimodal interaction for distributed applications. ACM Multimedia, vol. 97, pp. 31–40 (1997)
7. Cook, D., Das, S.K.: Smart Environments: Technology, Protocols, and Applications, vol. 43. Wiley (2004)
8. Coppens, A.: Merging real and virtual worlds: an analysis of the state of the art and practical evaluation of microsoft hololens. arXiv preprint arXiv:1706.08096 (2017)
9. Dasgupta, A., Handosa, M., Manuel, M., Gračanin, D.: A user-centric design framework for smart built environments. In: Streitz, N., Konomi, S. (eds.) HCII 2019. LNCS, vol. 11587, pp. 124–143. Springer, Cham (2019). https://doi.org/10.1007/978-3-030-21935-2_11
10. Froiz-Míguez, I., Fernández-Caramés, T., Fraga-Lamas, P., Castedo, L.: Design, implementation and practical evaluation of an iot home automation system for fog computing applications based on mqtt and zigbee-wifi sensor nodes. Sensors **18**(8), 2660 (2018)

11. Gieselmann, P., Denecke, M.: Towards multimodal interaction with an intelligent room. In: Eighth European Conference on Speech Communication and Technology (2003)
12. Handosa, M., Gračanin, D., Elmongui, H.G., Ciambrone, A.: Painting with light: gesture based light control in architectural settings. In: Proceedings of the 2017 IEEE Symposium on 3D User Interfaces (3DUI 2017), pp. 249–250, 18–19 March 2017
13. Jeon, Y., et al.: Iot-based occupancy detection system in indoor residential environments. Build. Environ. **132**, 181–204 (2018)
14. Jo, D., Kim, G.J.: ARIoT: scalable augmented reality framework for interacting with internet of things appliances everywhere. IEEE Trans. Consum. Electron. **62**(3), 334–340 (2016)
15. Koskela, T., Väänänen-Vainio-Mattila, K.: Evolution towards smart home environments: empirical evaluation of three user interfaces. Pers. Ubiquit. Comput. **8**(3), 234–240 (2004)
16. Kühnel, C., Westermann, T., Hemmert, F., Kratz, S., Müller, A., Möller, S.: I'm home: defining and evaluating a gesture set for smart-home control. Int. J. Hum Comput Stud. **69**(11), 693–704 (2011)
17. Kühnel, C., Westermann, T., Weiss, B., Möller, S.: Evaluating multimodal systems: a comparison of established questionnaires and interaction parameters. In: Proceedings of the 6th Nordic Conference on Human-Computer Interaction: Extending Boundaries, pp. 286–294. ACM (2010)
18. Ladwig, P., Geiger, C.: A literature review on collaboration in mixed reality. In: Auer, M.E., Langmann, R. (eds.) REV 2018. LNNS, vol. 47, pp. 591–600. Springer, Cham (2019). https://doi.org/10.1007/978-3-319-95678-7_65
19. Lee, Y., Hsiao, W., Huang, C., Chou, S.T.: An integrated cloud-based smart home management system with community hierarchy. IEEE Trans. Consum. Electron. **62**(1), 1–9 (2016)
20. Luria, M., Hoffman, G., Zuckerman, O.: Comparing social robot, screen and voice interfaces for smart-home control. In: Proceedings of the 2017 CHI Conference on Human Factors in Computing Systems, pp. 580–628. ACM (2017)
21. Mrazovac, B., Bjelica, M.Z., Simić, D., Tikvić, S., Papp, I.: Gesture based hardware interface for RF lighting control. In: 2011 IEEE 9th International Symposium on Intelligent Systems and Informatics, pp. 309–314. IEEE (2011)
22. Norouzi, N., Bruder, G., Belna, B., Mutter, S., Turgut, D., Welch, G.: A systematic review of the convergence of augmented reality, intelligent virtual agents, and the internet of things. In: Al-Turjman, F. (ed.) Artificial Intelligence in IoT. TCSCI, pp. 1–24. Springer, Cham (2019). https://doi.org/10.1007/978-3-030-04110-6_1
23. Oviatt, S.: Mutual disambiguation of recognition errors in a multimodel architecture. In: Proceedings of the SIGCHI Conference on Human Factors in Computing Systems, pp. 576–583. ACM (1999)
24. Petersen, N., Stricker, D.: Continuous natural user interface: Reducing the gap between real and digital world. In: ISMAR, pp. 23–26 (2009)
25. Rashidi, P., Cook, D.J.: Keeping the resident in the loop: adapting the smart home to the user. IEEE Trans. Syst. Man Cybern. Part A Syst. Hum. **39**(5), 949–959 (2009)
26. Rosendahl, A., Hampe, J.F., Botterweck, G.: Mobile home automation – merging mobile value added services and home automation technologies. In: Proceedings of the International Conference on the Management of Mobile Business (ICMB 2007), pp. 31:1–31:8. IEEE, 9–11 July 2007

27. Swaminathan, R., Nischt, M., Kuhnel, C.: Localization based object recognition for smart home environments. In: 2008 IEEE International Conference on Multimedia and Expo, pp. 921–924. IEEE (2008)
28. Tasooji, R., Dasgupta, A., Gračanin, D., LaGro, M., Matković, K.: A multi-purpose IoT framework for smart built environments. In: Proceedings of the 2018 Winter Simulation Conference, pp. 4240–4241. IEEE Press (2018)
29. Wagner, D., Schmalstieg, D.: History and future of tracking for mobile phone augmented reality. In: 2009 International Symposium on Ubiquitous Virtual Reality, pp. 7–10, July 2009
30. Wobbrock, J.O., Morris, M.R., Wilson, A.D.: User-defined gestures for surface computing. In: Proceedings of the SIGCHI Conference on Human Factors in Computing Systems, pp. 1083–1092. ACM (2009)
31. Yamazaki, T.: Beyond the smart home. In: 2006 International Conference on Hybrid Information Technology, vol. 2, pp. 350–355. IEEE (2006)

Ambient Interaction Design in a Primitive Society

Kei Hoshi[1(✉)] and John A. Waterworth[2]

[1] Auckland University of Technology, 27 St Paul Street, Auckland, New Zealand
kei.hoshi@aut.ac.nz

[2] Umeå University, 901 87 Umeå, Sweden

Abstract. Ambience is about the meaning of silence that cannot be expressed in words, and ambient interaction is about the perception of it. The present paper discusses three critical and fundamental aspects in the way ambient environments can be meaningfully designed in modern information society; 1) how design can merge that which is difficult to externalize together with that which is easy to externalize, and does so in a fulfilling way; 2) what is the most effective method for arriving at a mythological conclusion that could resolve the conflict between the many opposing forces at play?; and 3) what is "emptiness" based on eastern philosophy perspective, and how it can be applied to designing ambient environment? We shed light on how our thinking of design and information-based society should adapt moving forward by using universal thinking and human consciousness in a new, "primitive" coexistence with modern information technology.

Keywords: Ambience · Ambient interaction · Pervasive · Primitive design · Emptiness · Interaction design

1 Introduction

Anthropologists of the 20th century, typified by Levi-Strauss [1], were surprised to find that the "primitive" societies they researched had in fact observed the world around them in excruciating detail. These societies had specific knowledge of the natural objects and events surrounding them, and were able to skillfully take advantage of these in their daily lives.

Logic is an inherent part of the senses, and this logic contains intelligence within it. Since our inception, humans have always been intelligent beings, and our intelligence has manifested itself through the use of ambient interactions. For example, so-called "primitive" societies use their sharpened intellect to record precisely highly minute changes in natural phenomena, such as the sense of belongingness among living creatures (both aquatic and terrestrial), as well as wind, light, the color of the sky, and the size and type of ocean waves, air currents, and water currents.

The use of ambient interaction integrates the intellect with the senses, in which the five senses are used to make logical thinking. Rather than using abstract concepts to understand things, as modern people do, they used concrete things that were readily found

N. Streitz and S. Konomi (Eds.): HCII 2020, LNCS 12203, pp. 58–68, 2020.
https://doi.org/10.1007/978-3-030-50344-4_5

in the natural and human world, fully utilizing their five senses in order to intelligently think about and understand the world. This is the essence of "ambient interaction." Ambient interaction has no words, rather it is a perception of "emptiness." There is really such a thing as "emptiness" that truly primitive people had the capability to perceive. "Emptiness" is perceived to be self-transforming properties, which lead any created object to seem incomplete. As such, people set off to build once more. With a new object comes a new accompanying presence of "emptiness." Emptiness has potential. This is what leads to the formation a rich world of cultures.

In a sophisticated but primitive society, fragments of natural observations and mythological stories are systemized. Large-scale myths began to form, along with the establishment of defined rituals. The world created through "emptiness" is inevitably given mythological properties. This world shares commonalities and properties with self-transforming myths.

The scientific world omits or denies the existence of that which cannot be expressed in words. Consider concepts such as "emptiness." Since these are outside of the realm of science, their existence is not discussed. Herein lies the reason for the incongruity of the design with the scientific approach. The criterion for defining thought as either objective or subjective is whether or not that thought deals with "emptiness." As these concepts are utilized in daily life and in design, such practice is far removed from science. In this way, science has evolved denying the existence of "emptiness."

Design can never be considered a science. The objectivist posits that the non-scientific is subjective, that actions under such a premise merely derive from inertia, and that practitioners of such actions are "primitive." Consider design as inertia stemming from repeated practice. For example, think of a sketch (a drawing) that is being repeatedly drawn to meet the changing needs of the market. This way of thinking posits that design will never propel history; that is to say, design is a part of the "primitive" meaning inferior and savage.

When using objective thought as a yardstick, the thoughts of designers and so-called "primitives" are considered to be underdeveloped, as they do not order things through a logical process of categorization and resort to a wholly illogical "mystical participation" that mixes hierarchies and order without logic. Opinions from an objective standpoint view such people as if they were thoughtless, though such opinions are far removed from reality, and are rife with prejudice. On the contrary, the designer's thought works to destroy the externalized order of the objectivist, and attempts to achieve integration with that which cannot be put into words.

What is the true nature of this misunderstood inertia of design? What changes are needed in our thinking for design to break through this barrier of misunderstanding? Mythological thinking and Eastern philosophy provide specific hints to answering these questions. Both of them share a deeper understanding of human beings as a species on the subconscious level.

2 Mythological Thinking and Eastern Philosophy

Design is a process that merges that which is difficult to externalize together with that which is easy to externalize, and does so in a fulfilling way. In other words, design is able to achieve an enriched world by reintegrating objective and subjective thinking–two divided and separated concepts. The designer may to some extent become a primitive; using methods familiar to some indigenous peoples.

There is one character that perfectly embodies the role of the designer in mythology [2–4]: the "trickster." The trickster transcends time and space, and possesses commonalities seen in numerous myths across the world. He or she disturbs and destroys order, while also creating new order. In mythology, the trickster plays the role of a mediator or arbitrator regarding fundamental conflicts. Myths, or stories based on their models, are commonly enjoyed among all peoples. This is because they are accepted by the common unconscious of human beings and run in line with universal principles that reflect a sense of perception seen in people around the world. They carry universal, stereotypical meaning.

If the essence of the designer is to create things or concepts with a story to which anyone can relate, the designer's ideal way of being is to act or implement the thought of the trickster or the primitive. This follows universal principles that reflect a shared global consciousness. To realize truly universal design, it is necessary to introduce designs that can be shared across the human subconscious, and universally reflect a global shared consciousness.

2.1 Trickster Approach

The "trickster" and the "fool" help to overcome the duality of the mind and body. Restoring the "fool's" sensibility as a critic of science and civilization would serve to balance the relationship between authority, productivity, and theory [5].

There are numerous ways to fragment the world or universe by examining it in a fixed state, ruling over nature, controlling society, and using concepts in their narrowest and so-called strictest sense, though there are very few ways to restore the sensibilities of the "fool", because the terms "fool," "clown," and "buffoon," are generally used in a derogatory way.

To be a fool suggests that one is scatterbrained. To call someone a clown in a political context means that they are unreliable. Positivist rationalism limits itself to visible and quantitative reality. As a ritual framework for communication, the moral view in Western European modern civic society discards all forms of expression except for that which can externally be considered to be "serious." This view only recognizes individual humans as improving statistics, and in other words is of a world dominated by a sense of humanity that denies all variables. In such a world, it is only natural that the "fool," who makes a living by transforming without any awareness of his or her limits, would be made an outcast or a mere entertainment.

The intelligence associated with the "fool" as "trickster" should inform us of the futility of subscribing to a single reality (absolute truth). If the desire to be concerned with only a single reality is a result of seeking coherence, then the process of denying a single reality and freely living in and moving between multiple realities to perpetually reveal hidden features can be considered a type of spiritual technology that develops more dynamic cosmological dimensions. The "trickster" has attracted psychoanalysts like Jung and mythologists like Lévi-Strauss due to this character's hidden potential to revive and invigorate the universe. We cannot underestimate the importance of the role played by the theory of the "trickster" in Lévi-Strauss's work on myths [1, 2]. Lévi-Strauss famously understood that being a "trickster" served as the most effective methods of arriving at a mythological conclusion that could resolve the conflict between the many opposing forces at play.

Intelligence in the 20th century is fundamentally based on expert classification (fragmentation), principles of seriousness (consistency), and a doctrine of strictness (overemphasis). If they are the "center" of intelligence, the intelligence associated with the "fool" as "trickster" is only considered to be unstable, chaotic or confused, which is just about the "periphery" [6].

Areas with a systemized order, known as the "center", include engineering design, systems design, and strategic design and have dominated the design field over the last 20 to 30 years due to their high productivity and their compatibility with our information-based society. While the vitality and polysemy of the "periphery" ideally serves as a driving force to activate the border of the center, design has become a tool to serve system science, engineering, and business. As such, the vitality of genuine design is lost. However, the border between the "center" and the "periphery" is not fixed. The systemized "center" of design constantly attempts to erode and take in the "periphery". The vitality and polysemy of the "periphery" becomes the driving force that propels the border with the "center."

2.2 Center and Periphery

In an interdisciplinary context, design is ambiguous and difficult to define. As such, it is marginalized. The more one tries to define "design," the further one lands from the mark. This is because design (or design culture) is not seen to be built on a fixed state of balance; rather, it is conceptualized as an infringement of regulated, organized boundaries. Historically, the arts and crafts movement and Bauhaus period are obvious examples [7].

In the past, as a result of its influence under functionalism, design was limited to the superficial—to that which could easily be described as the subject of research. It is necessary to adjust our definition of design in terms of its relationship to its own depth. The term "depth" here includes its meaning within psychoanalysis. Rather than strategically limiting design to the superficial, it is necessary to approach design in a way that incorporates into its depth the world captured by all the ability of each individual to make full use of their inhabited space.

The superficial refers to areas that are simple to observe in the field of design research, for these are fields that can be systemized, can be easily articulated through writing, and are easy to organize in the form of text. This may enable us to understand superficial systems of communication that are considered indispensable to design. However, there are clearly areas that cannot be overlooked when dealing with how individuals fundamentally interact with their internal and external environment, though these areas be difficult to articulate through language or discuss systematically. However, it is impossible to grasp the meaning of design on a comprehensive level while turning a blind eye to these areas.

All cultures are fundamentally based around a continual division of the human environment between the "center" and "periphery," the inside and outside, the preferable and not preferable, and the near and far. In other words, in order to strengthen the identity of humans and our culture, we unconsciously create dualities. This becomes clear when observing a child's developmental process. When developing a conscious awareness of the outside world, infants are instinctively able to classify those who are close to them and those who are not. As a provider of intimate contact, the mother is seen as close and familiar by children, though they are fearful of things with which they have no contact, or that are strange or distant.

Even before developing speech, humans tend to divide the world between the inner and outer. In the process of our development and education, we find the things in the world that are preferable to be close—or central—to us, and associate these things with our identity. That which is not preferable is pushed far away onto the "periphery." To put it another way, the "center" and the "periphery" are associated with order and disorder, or the friendly and the hostile. The presence of hostility makes humans aware of that which is inner—or "central"—to them on a fundamental level to elucidate its boundary.

We must consider why the "periphery" is excluded and considered unpleasant despite being impossible to think of the "center" without the "periphery". For example, the political and legal system (the superficial parts of culture) include a basic understanding of the rules involved, and there is a clear purpose and meaning behind the actions that we take. There are "definitions." The act of "defining" has the effect of keeping one thing while excluding another. That which is ambiguous or undefinable is excluded, whereby a system of order is established. Parts that are excluded due to their indefinability are subject to repeated exclusion (however many times they are debated).

Take the moral and amoral person for example. The moral person is easy to define, since that which is "good" is predictable and reliable in any given situation. The amoral person is difficult to define, since their actions are unpredictable and ambiguous. Regardless of the culture, this ambiguity is a target for exclusion.

The scientific world omits or denies the existence of that which cannot be expressed in words. Consider concepts such as "emptiness." Since these are outside of the realm of science, their existence is not discussed. Hereupon lies the reason for the incongruity of the magical with the scientific. As such the criterion for defining thought as either objective or subjective is whether or not that thought deals with emptiness. Did not "primitive" people have the capability to perceive such concepts?

"Emptiness" is perceived to have self-transforming properties, which are chaotic and unstable. Seen from the "center," design is either feared or it is simply used to serve. This is because design provokes instability, transition, and mixtures. In human culture, the target of exclusion tends to be seen as something negative. However, it is an intimate and indispensable element for the depth of human psychology. If we see design (the designer) to take the role of the "trickster" in connecting these two parts and arriving at a synthesis, the work of the designer is to transcend time and look into the "periphery," using it as a fulcrum to assemble new models of totality.

The process of looking into the future past unstable elements may feel uncomfortable, and this process may become the target of exclusion. However, there is a richness to the polysemy of the "periphery," and by using it as a stepping-stone for overcoming boundaries, one discovers the existence of new possibilities.

To date, research into design has eliminated from its focus anything that cannot considered to be the "center" and that is commonly excluded. These excluded areas challenge that which is ordered and fixed. Without these provocative elements, the ingenuity of design cannot be grasped. The more these excluded aspects are perpetually pushed into the margins of consciousness, space, and time, the more they reject the homogeneity that leads to a unified culture. This rejection signifies the dynamic relationship between the "center" and the "periphery."

2.3 Emptiness in Eastern Philosophy

It is speculated that Buddhism was introduced to China around the 1st Century BC, and it is said that the translation of Buddhist scriptures began in earnest in the second half of the 2nd Century AD [8]. At that time, the central issue in the Buddhist world was how to interpret the philosophy of "nothingness" of Taoism (道家), which had attracted the hearts of people instead of Confucianism (儒教), using Buddhist concepts [8]. In the Chinese ideological world at that time, the Prajnaparamita Sutras (般若経) were spreading wide ripples, and efforts were made to understand the idea of "emptiness" preached by the Prajnaparamita Sutra (般若経) with reference to Taoism's idea of "nothingness" [9]. After that, Buddhism was introduced to Japan, and it is said that the idea of "emptiness" was established as "impermanence" or "deficiency."

In the form of Buddhism that developed in Japan, concepts like "impermanence" and "deficiency" were first established. The deficiency philosophy represented by Japanese classical literature (Tsurezuregusa 徒然草) created beauty that included suggestiveness, aftertastes, and blank space as aspects of artistic consciousness [9]. In the case of physical art, it also created "ma" as the spaces between music and performance as well as rhythm and pause in martial arts. These "ma," a characteristic of Japanese culture, have evolved apart from their matrix such as impermanence, and they were developed along with the "ma" of the consciousness in daily life.

If the absolute rule of rationalism is a fulfillment principle that fills "ma," then recognizing "ma," perceiving the meaning of silence that cannot be expressed in words and denying rationalistic sense of fulfillment, can be called deficiency. It can also be called an aesthetic state of mind that does not require eternity from fulfillment. Ambience is about the meaning of silence that cannot be expressed in words, and Ambient Interaction is about the perception of it.

Nietzsche's nihilism [10] is famous as a representative concept of "nothingness" in Western thought. Nihilism is a worldview that refers to a meaningless state that has lost ideals and values. For Nietzsche, "nothingness" was absence, and nihilism was thorough absence. It is the emptiness of where "God" has collapsed, who was the ultimate support of the meaning of living as the highest ground for bringing everything into existence, and it is "eternal meaninglessness." It can be said that it is distinct from the concept of "emptiness" in the East, which has been developed as artistic consciousness and daily life consciousness.

Looking at Japanese architecture, Bruno Taut [11] was deeply impressed and surprised that "emptiness" is valued and plays an important role in architecture. In particular, his attention was drawn to the fact that there was usually nothing placed in a Japanese tearoom, and it was kept "empty." In Western culture, rooms are decorated with ornaments such as curtains, furniture, figurines, paintings, and vases. A tearoom, on the other hand, is empty. From that, he saw the spirit of traditional Japanese beauty, different from the West.

Edward Hall [12] compared the Western sense with "ma" and explains as follows: When Westerners think and talk about space, they keep in mind the distance between things. In the West, we are taught to perceive and react to the arrangement of things and to consider space to be "empty." The meaning of this is apparent when compared to the Japanese. Japanese are trained to perceive the shape and arrangement of space and give meaning to space. This is represented by the word "ma." This space called "ma" is the fundamental architectural break in all spatial experiences of the Japanese people. In Western Europe, people perceive objects but not the space in between them. In Japan, space is perceived, named, and respected as "ma," in essence, intervening space.

The characteristic of the concept of "ma" in the structure of Japanese consciousness is that it is not a blank state or a situation where something that should be there is missing, but it is rather a positive creation. Because "ma" is a creation, it lives in daily life and in the essence of art. For example, Japanese literature such as Waka (和歌) and Haikai (俳諧) has been able to incorporate the excellent art of "ma" because the consciousness of "ma" has been nurtured as the foundation of the Japanese way of thinking itself. As a result, Japanese performing arts were also able to form customs like the Noh (能) dance and tea ceremony (茶道) [13]. From the Japanese perspective there is "ma" in nature. The "wind" is considered as the breath of nature, and the "ma" between those breaths is called "Kazama ("ma" of wind)." In Japan, nature is often expressed by the word "wind (風)," in words such as "landscape (風景)," "topography (風土)," and "scenic beauty (風光)" [14]. It can be inferred that the characteristics of Japan's climate depend on the wind direction in each season, so the Japanese became particularly sensitive to the wind. Because the wind blows through empty space, it matches the Japanese sense of "ma."

The topography of Japan, an island country with many mountains, is densely populated in narrow plains, with cultivated land being managed intensively and with horticultural delicacy. There are almost no monotonous elements in Japan's climate and topography, and there are always many changes. The vibrancy of Japan's nature is something that foreigners who have come to Japan all mention. Japanese have had to live with nature and accept natural disasters such as typhoons, earthquakes, heavy rains, heat waves, and heavy snow. Japan's nature is constantly moving. The Japanese perceive nature as though it smiles and talks to them as human beings do.

The Japanese embodied over a long period of time the diversity and the quickness of changes in nature. There are four seasons in Europe, but severe changes and sudden natural disasters that overwhelm humans are rare. The conditions of being an island nation of the same ethnicity and language and being blessed with nature that is varied and rich in vitality, in which they must survive through farming and fishing, engrained a particular ability of communication into the Japanese. For them, dialogue among humans and dialogue between humans and nature are of the same dimension. Nature speaks to humans, and humans speak to nature. Humans can talk to other humans through and entrusting nature. From Japan's topography, geographical conditions, sharing of the same language, and natural conditions, it can be inferred that the language of silence, the perception of the meaning of emptiness, and the language of speaking without words were inevitably established [15]. Formation of the perception and structure of "ma" also accompanies these backgrounds.

Although everyone in Japan feels, creates, and plays with the aesthetics of "ma," and it is a very familiar thing, it is not always noticeable. Such "ma" has various forms of expression depending on the genre style. What are the common basic conditions of "ma?" "Ma" is a sense of distance when something is being cut temporally and spatially [15]. It varies in size but has this basic condition in common.

The sense of the beauty of "ma" experienced by the Japanese is something unique because they discovered the sense of beauty created by a disconnection in this spatiotemporal "ma," not just the sense of beauty in interlocking and continuous dynamism. The most important condition of "ma" is this disconnection. In other words, it can be said that "ma" is a sense of beauty created by a sense of distance due to a spatiotemporal cut. The sense and concept of "ma" are extremely Japanese. It is often emphasized that the existence of a "ma" is a characteristic of Japanese performing arts and culture in general [11, 12].

Edward Hall, in his book Beyond Culture [12], classifies the types of language communication around the world into high-context and low-context cultures. A low-context culture trusts the power of words, with the conviction that the correct use of words will transmit what is in one's mind. There is absolute trust that "if I use words rationally, the other party can communicate rationally as well." However, for the Japanese, there is an implicit consciousness that we cannot communicate our minds by words alone. The unspoken "implication," which is not expressed by words, is more highly valued subconsciously, and the perception and structure of "ma" are incorporated. High-context cultures include Japan as well as other Asian and Arabic countries, and Japanese is referred to as the most extreme language in this respect. Low-context cultures include Switzerland, Germany, Scandinavia, and the United States, with German being the most extreme example.

2.4 Ambient Interaction Design

In everyday life, we pick up natural sources of ambient information to understand how things are around us. This is not limited to Japanese culture. For example, people can unconsciously interpret the meaning of silence from outside a window. A subtle combination of brightness, wind direction and humidity give us the feeling of coming rain. The perceptual feeling of a peaceful curtain-wave makes people placid, or people foresee a storm when they see the curtain waving in the dim light of the window, with no explicit information or conscious effort.

We tend to think that we always act consciously, but most ordinary everyday activities are subconscious or unconscious and without intervention from our ego. In fact, there are always moments that exist in our ordinary everyday lives where we all behave in the same subconscious way regardless of ethnicity or culture.

J. J. Gibson [16] attempted to demonstrate the act of subconsciously finding value in the environment from the perspective of ecological epistemology. He claimed that humans subconsciously integrate with their environment through series of actions.

George Lakoff [17] described such subconscious thinking and behavior from the perspective of cognitive linguistics. He argued and attempted to demonstrate that the mind is originally embodied and thought is mostly subconscious. People are not like robots that cannot act unless all knowledge is prepared in the brain beforehand, and subconscious actions are the process of dynamic interaction between humans and their environment.

Ambient intelligent computing is a response to this with the – as yet unrealized – ideal of seamless integration of hardware/software, taking account of human experience, the environment, and interaction and learning between them, leading to the idea of using internet-enabled devices with no consciously effort. But conventional design thinking and methods means that this goal cannot be achieved.

Design is thought to inspire and impress people's consciousness, but when things or systems are used in a natural flow or in such an environment or situation, people become unaware of those things and do not consider themselves as "users" of them. Certain things disappear from perception and people subconsciously try to harmonize with things and their environment. When walking on a crowded pedestrian crosswalk, people are unaware of the shoes or socks they are wearing and are not consciously thinking about the ground while walking. On the noisy crosswalk, pedestrians walk across without colliding with each other. "Ma" is subconsciously perceived and each route is created there. "Ma" blends into subconscious acts. Humans are constantly and subconsciously seeking opportunities to maintain balance with things, systems, the environment, and nature. It is also creative. People are creative by nature.

Ambient interaction design is based on providing "ma" and foregoing awareness of things that exist in the flow. The "ma" in design is what is created subconsciously which exists during the process of dynamic interaction between humans and their environment, where we extract information from our accumulated physical experience, classify it, and bring it back into our body.

3 Conclusions

In the present paper, we have argued that while the vitality and polysemy of the "periphery" ideally serves as a driving force to activate the border of the center, design has become a tool to serve system science, engineering, and business. As such, the vitality of genuine design is lost.

Design should serve as a challenger that reinvigorates the "center" through its vitality and ability to provoke. In other words, in order to be perceived as an invigored society in itself, design must be sufficiently provocative in the periphery, and the designer must be able to actively go back and forth through the mechanism of the connection point between the "center" and the "periphery."

Vitality and polysemy decline if the regularity, averageness, and normality of the "center" continues uninterrupted. The vitality of culture is ensured through the conflict between the "center" and concepts divorced from the cultural context such as *infantile play, the heterogenous, the latent/unconscious and emptiness*. Provocativeness is only achieved through being different.

Artificial intelligence (AI) research and its applications are currently flourishing. As a study of the mind and body, Buddhism philosophy speaks to highly relevant topics, including consciousness, mind/body and self/other. Disciplines in science, philosophy, engineering and design need to work together to ensure that human beings will derive a benefit from the rapid growth of technology. When it comes to AI, Buddhism methodology of *subjective* reality plays an especially important role for the creation of better AI.

Science has so far explored only the physical "entity." Paradoxically, technological changes exploiting the progress of science – such as ambient interaction – have made our lives more "primitive", in the sense the word was once applied pejoratively to the cultures of indigent societies.

From now on, the search for "ma" must be included as well. "ma" is not a position to negate or confront science, but rather aims to inherit scientific exploration and encourage new creations. The current limitations of science to entities and their associations should be replaced, and a more liberal universality should be sought. In the process of pursuing the objective facts of entities and their associations, science has called for abandoning the concepts of self and ordinariness while becoming a third party in order to know the essence of an entity or association. The quest for "ma" aims to revive the concepts of self and ordinariness and take a more subjective approach. Taking advantage of self and ordinariness must be much more universal.

Genuine design is entropy that aims to deconstruct order. However, entropy is unable to continue to survive alone. Rather, it fulfills a role as an activator for the mere shell of order that is present within the dynamics of the structure. Design faces the chaos of the "periphery," and confronts its own rebirth as an intermediary between the "center" and the margins.

Society has become more savage and less cultured, despite – or because of – the interactive devices that permeate our lives. In this paper we have tried to shed light on how our thinking of design and information-based society should adapt by using universal thinking and aspects of human consciousness/unconsciousness in a new, "primitive" coexistence with modern information technology.

References

1. Levi-Strauss, C.: The Savage Mind. The University of Chicago Press, Chicago (1966)
2. Levi-Strauss, C.: Myth and Meaning. University of Toronto Press, Toronto (1978)
3. Isao, H., Anne, M., Renata, S.: Play office: toward a new culture in the workplace. GC inc., Tokyo (1991)
4. Masao, Y.: Douke no Minzokugaku. Iwanami Press, Tokyo (2007). (in Japanese)
5. Masao, Y.: Chi no Shukusai. Kawaide Shobo, Tokyo (1988). (in Japanese)
6. Masao, Y.: Bunka to Ryougi-sei. Iwanami, Tokyo (2000). (in Japanese)
7. Frank, W.: The Bauhaus: Masters & Students by Themselves. Overlook Press, New York (1993)
8. Kiyotaka, K.: Nihon no Tetsugaku, vol. 5. Showado, Kyoto (2004). (in Japanese)
9. Kouitsu, Y.: Yuishiki. NHK Press, Tokyo (2002). (in Japanese)
10. Nietzsche, F.: Thus Spoke Zarathustra. Cambridge Text in the History of Philosophy. Cambridge University Press, Cambridge (2006)
11. Taut, B.: Nippon, Japanese edn. Shunjyusha, Tokyo (2008)
12. Hall, E.T.: The Hidden Dimension. Anchor, Doubleday, Garden City (1969)
13. Kunihiko, S.: Ma no Tetsugaku. Liber Press, Tokyo (1986). (in Japanese)

14. Takehiko, K.: Ma no Nihon Bunka. Chobunsha, Tokyo (1992). (in Japanese)
15. Hiroshi, M.: Ma no Kenkyu. Kodansha, Tokyo (1983). (in Japanese)
16. Gibson, J.J.: The Ecological Approach to Visual Perception. Lawrence Erlbaum Associates, Publishers, Hillsdale (1978)
17. Lakoff, G., Johnson, M.: Metaphors We Live By. The University of Chicago Press, Chicago (1980)

Smells as an Interactive Material for Spatial Designing

Jyoti Kapur[1,2](✉)

[1] The Swedish School of Textiles, University of Borås, Borås, Sweden
jyoti.kapur@hb.se, jyoti.kapur@zhdk.ch

[2] Department of Interaction Design, Zurich University of the Arts, Zurich, Switzerland

Abstract. This paper explores design strategies to use smells as a medium of interaction between the body and the space. In a living environment, encounters and experience of smells creates and manifests connections to the space. Along with the other sensory stimuli, smells communicates information about the space. Olfactory interactions can be expressed through its experiential relationship with the body. Design examples as discussed in this paper, express the aesthetics of interaction with smells that are dynamic and temporal. Human perception connects through the patterns and weave the fluid movements across the soft boundaries of smells. Over a range from discrete to ambient presence of smells, this paper discusses tangible and intangible interaction with smells in the design examples. Through active or passive actuation of smells, designing for smell diversity in a living environment would create interactions at many different levels and will add to experiencing spaces in a multisensorial way.

Keywords: Smells · Interaction · Dynamic patterns and textures of smells · Fluid and soft boundaries

1 Introduction

Beyond detection of smells in a space, there is an interaction in the environment through olfaction. Virtual encounters happen in the imagination as the odour memories get triggered with the real and immediate encounter in a space [1]. Through the smells, one is placed in time and space. The encounter in a near environment that involves same space through olfaction is quite similar to a haptic experience and therefore, Rodaway emphasizes that the sense of smell is the most intimate sense, structurally smells create a local geography (reference of a space) and emotionally it makes a strong bond between the person and the environment. A direct bond between the smell and the body is formed due to the chemical basis for the sense, whereas this relationship in the sense of hearing or vision does not take place. According to Rodaway, olfaction is interactive as it is communicating with the environment and since giving out the smells happen in a space, therefore it is spatial or geographical [1].

N. Streitz and S. Konomi (Eds.): HCII 2020, LNCS 12203, pp. 69–84, 2020.
https://doi.org/10.1007/978-3-030-50344-4_6

The emergence of smells in a space and its detection is dependent on the characteristics of the smells, individual´s characteristics and the environment [2]. The intensity of the smells, duration, rate of evaporation, volatility are some of the characteristics for the smells that are influenced by the environmental factors such as flow of air, levels of humidity and change in temperature. Where the familiarity of the smells, associations with the smells, gender and age, social class, bodily state and odour training [2] are individual's characteristics that would direct the odour detection. So where these 3 characteristics of smells, body (individual) and space (environment) overlap- there is the perception of smell for anyone except with someone who has lost the ability to smell. The levels of detection of odours are highly individualistic and varies immensely not just because of differences in the smell receptors in the olfactory but also due to social and cultural differences that strongly influences the associative aspect of smells.

On the characteristics of an olfactory space, Diaconu examines the phenomenological aspect of perception of a space for each sense as written by Merleau-Ponty, well-structured and clear-cut fields or places by Hermann Schmitz and relationship of a body to lived spaces along the axes as written by Husserl, she suggests the olfactory and acoustic spaces are directional and specifically smellscapes are marked with shifting patterns continuously being circulated by the air currents [3]. Rodaway presents two styles of olfaction; a generalised olfaction or a passive encounter with smells in an environment which is rich in details about the quality of the odour but not the location; second style is a specialised olfaction, which focuses on a specific smells for the cause-effect with associations and memories [1]. The odours perceived in a space are episodic in nature and fail to give a continuous information about the environment, however it does revoke memories of events, places or persons as the smells pass by. The interaction with smells in space happens in three ways; the detection of the stimuli, descriptive through the associations (psychological-social-cultural) and at an emotional level. As Rodaway suggests, "olfaction gives a distinctive sensuous experience of space and duration; past, present and potential spaces; and this is both physiologically grounded and culturally defined" [1: pp 71]. The relationship between the smells and the one receiving the smells can be positive or negative. Unfamiliar odours gather negative descriptors and associations as opposed to the familiar odours, which makes it complex to understand the avoidance or pleasure seeking behaviours of the smells [2]. Also, odour sensitivity as discussed by Henshaw beyond the smell performance, could induce behavioural changes [2], however, it is beyond the scope of this research to study the environmental or chemical sensitivities to smells.

Similar to experiential qualities, interaction attributes define the shape of a particular interaction [4], where smell as a material for designing interactions in a space demonstrate the attributes through its experiential quality. Some of the basic responses or the interaction attributes to the smells are; in case of a known or a pleasant smell, has positive descriptors of associations and leads to indulgence in the essence of enjoyment or can be seen as continuity. Also a pleasant smell is often described as open, fresh, wide, light giving an illusion of space being open and welcoming, making one linger in a space; taking time for an immersive experience. Based on the experiments by Weber et al.

natural pleasant smells helped improve emotional states or mood and unpleasant smells diminished the effective positive mood, calmness or alertness [5] demonstrating a positive response of certain pleasant smells on the wellbeing. An unknown smell, is often deciphered as strange or an unpleasant smell and is described with negative connotations and restrictions such as a sense of a hindrance like a wall or closing. It is also associated with probable danger, which takes the olfactory function to its primitive human focus to that of survival, reproduction and orientation [6].

These associations defines the movement in a space in relation to the source of smells, as to embrace or avoid the smells and thereby be able to navigate in the space. The (negative and positive) associations are based on the social-cultural factors, leading to the behavioural change and responses to any future encounters with the (same) smells. Also the perception of smells is attributed to the spatial conditions of air-flow, presence of moisture or relative humidity level and warmer temperatures in a space, creating dynamic presence of smells. The meteorological spatial conditions help create a soft border of a smellscape that one feels it, while going inside and outside of it, but also the borders are created through the connection to the past encounter of the same smell by associating it with a positive or negative experience. Time and duration are equally influential on the intensity of smells that can be present for the nose to detect. However, time does not make smell disappear completely, as certain studies that have investigated communication via chemosignals or bodily sweat reveal that humans can leave contagious emotional residue in physical spaces that linger long after the person has left the space and that anyone who subsequently enters that space, is affected by the residual ambient volatile substances. Guen R. Semin suggests that we communicate with language and movements but unknown until now, we mysteriously communicate through chemosignals [7], giving an opportunity for designing spaces for interactions that are mediated through the embodied experiences [8].

The attributes of smell for an interaction gestalt [9] by reflecting on the "what the thing/system does when we use it" [10], could be summarized smells as a continuum, being open, unfolds, closes, allows movement, directs, is dynamic, creates boundary, is ambient in nature, builds connection, is time based, has depth and intensity, tool for communication, is responsive and helps navigation through the space.

Using textiles as an expression through its materialities, this section explores metaphors [11] as a method to define the aesthetics of interaction with smells in spaces.

Gottfried Semper's theories of architecture have a strong root in the textiles. He defines textiles mainly for two purposes, which is firstly, to string or to bind and secondly to cover or to enclose. According to Semper, 'no material is more ephemeral than woven fabrics' [12]. Smells though being ephemeral, metaphorically and physically enclose or wrap around in a space. Connoting the visual design attributes of colours with "warm" or "cold" emote different habits or morale [11], these associations are metaphors for a kinaesthetic experience of temperature on the skin. Similarly, connected with the emotional aspect of smells, it renders similar feelings.

1.1 Aesthetics of Interaction with Smells

Dynamic nature of smells can be related to the lightweight materials. Smells are volatile without any particular form of moving molecules, constantly changing the intensity and flow of smells with the passing time, flow of air and forms of space. Using the attributes of smells, a designer creates "textile" expression of interaction [10], the term textile used here is as a concept or "thinking". Exploring textiles as an expressive identity of materials [11], for expression of interaction in interior spaces offer sensorial, experiential and temporal point of view. As established above in the interaction attributes, smells as a design material present themselves to be spatially interactive in a direct way. Defining aesthetics of interaction in this case, are the textile expressions of interactions with smell in a space, which are categorised three-fold-

- Expression of connections through patterns and textures

The episodic perceptive quality of smells arranges patterns of memory and connects the past to the present. Also it establishes connection to a space and people. The layers of interaction with a smell over time add to the depth and intensity of the pattern it creates.

Smell is also textural, since the physiology of the olfactory is through the skin, where the smell molecules gets detected and processed as perception.

The textile expressions of interactions are exploring patterns and textures through the embedded smells, as a design element of interaction. The patterns are formed and altered [13] in the way smells get added or revealed in the space through an interaction over a dimension of time or using spatial design variables.

- Expression of fluid movements and soft boundaries

As smell unfolds itself, it moves fluidly in the space. Varied intensities of a smell create soft spatial dividers and boundaries that are similar to textile dividers in the interior spaces that allow fluid movements through and around them. Smell opens up a space for further encounters and welcomes one to "feel-home" or can also close a space and act like a barrier and walls, that compels to change the direction, even though this is a temporal state, it is impactful and unexpected. The fluid nature of smells is continuously forming and re-forming new boundaries and opening up spaces as the smells get carried through the air.

- Dynamic and temporal expressions

Smells are not just dynamic in the sense of their movement rather also that the interaction with smells puts one in different time and space within flash of moments, creating a real-virtual experiential encounter. Smell interactions are temporal. The dynamism of the smells is experienced through the movements in the space. The quality of smells in terms of its intensity changes dynamically, making it responsive of the time based changes.

In the speculative design ideas as discussed further, smells are activated through an active or passive interaction. These expressions change over the dimension of time that exhibits the dynamic and temporal nature of the smells.

2 Design Examples

Selected design examples presented within each category here are developed during classroom workshops with students. These workshops were designed as experimental workshops in the context of artistic research, where the students were asked to develop speculative concepts for spatial interactions using smells as a design material. Workshops were conducted in design schools. The students worked in the groups that were interdisciplinary, where different disciplines were mixed. The master and bachelor students were from the design and health, digital material technology, spatial design, textiles, product design and architectural studies.

The design examples explore the addition of smells or the inherent smells of the materials to create expressions of connections through patterns and textures of smells. These interactions create a dynamic relationship between the artefact, the user and the space.

2.1 Design Example One

Using wood veneer from three different species i.e. birch, ash, and elm, this spatial installation explores the interactivity of the material through the smells. Since each of the selected wood types have distinct inherent smells, the explorations conducted with this material focused on ways of activating the smells. After many explorations, moisture was taken as a design variable to actuate the smells (Figs. 1 and 2).

Fig. 1. Expression of smells through patterns and textures of wood

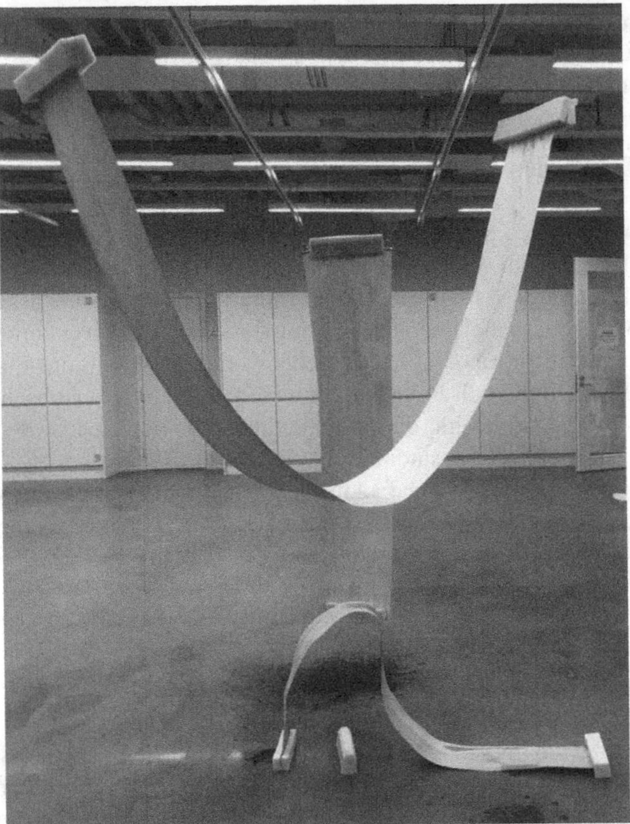

Fig. 2. Explorations with inherent smells of wood

The suspended three different kind of wood veneer had an interactive element made of sponge on the top end to squeeze out water onto the veneer sheet (Fig. 3).

This expression created a random pattern of water droplets on the wood and actuated the smells in this particular wet section of the wood. The physical change in the veneer shrinks and creates a twist in the vertical section.

The three dimensional textures that emerge through the wet wood not only releases the smells but also creates a haptic expression. The pattern and textures created are unique to each interaction, that depends on the amount of water squeezed onto the veneer and also on the room temperature for evaporating or drying the water off the surface over the duration of time. There is a temporality of interaction and that can be repetitive due to the choice of the material.

Fig. 3. Textures of smells created by the shrinking and twisting of the veneer as a result of interaction

2.2 Design Example Two

Adding smells to the structural element of a space, such as bricks, this design example explores ways to activate the smells using spatial design variable of temperature.

Three different sources of smells are used to create bricks and building blocks such as lampshade. Orange peels, freshly grounded coffee and soap detergent are individually mixed with gypsum. When rubbed the smells are activated, however when exposed to the higher temperatures the presence of smells is profound (Figs. 4, 5 and 6).

Fig. 4. Expression of smells through patterns and textures of brick

Fig. 5. Smell diversity (reduced smells) based on activity in living environment

Fig. 6. Smell diversity (amplified smells) based on activity in living environment

Speculating on the presence or absence of smells modulated by the temperature differences, this concept creates a scenario where the room ambience could be designed with smells based on the activity such as waking up in the morning with the touch and smell of a coffee as one switches on the lamp, the heat of the lightbulb makes the smells of coffee fill the room (Fig. 7).

Fig. 7. Smell patterns and textures

Different smellscapes could be designed in a living environment, by placing the bricks with sources of smells in certain specified patterns that adds the smells to the space. This design example brings attention to the haptic interactions with smells [14] which becomes an active interaction with the smells. Dissipation of smells over a period of time and mingling of different smells creates different patterns and textures that are continuously shifting that create temporal expressions.

2.3 Design Example Three

Exploring the change in atmosphere of a space through intervention with the smells, this design example investigates the locker space corridor of the school building which is usually felt as a dull space lacking any social interactions and interest to linger on for more than the required time to operate the lockers (Fig. 8).

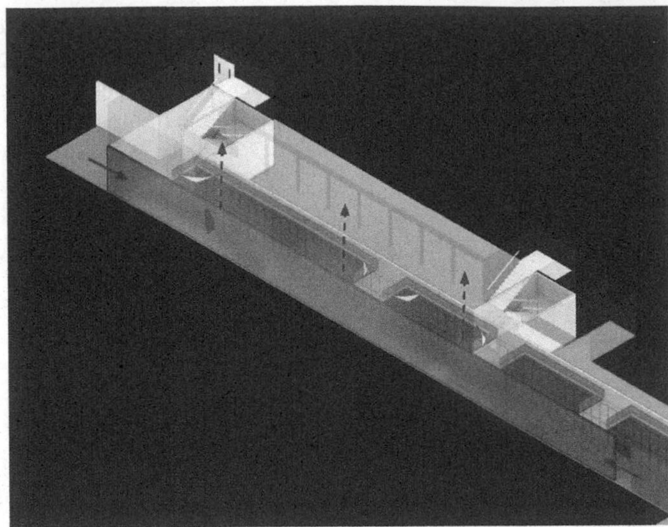

Fig. 8. Soft boundaries created by air and temperature differences

The corridor has two exits at the opposite far ends, which brings in the flow of air and a constant movement of people passing by or the ones who operate the lockers in the corridor. The intervention in this space is to add smells through visually-hidden source and create a smell scape which might induce social interaction. Where passers-by also might either change the speed of walk or linger a bit longer in the corridor due to pleasant atmosphere created by the smells (Fig. 9).

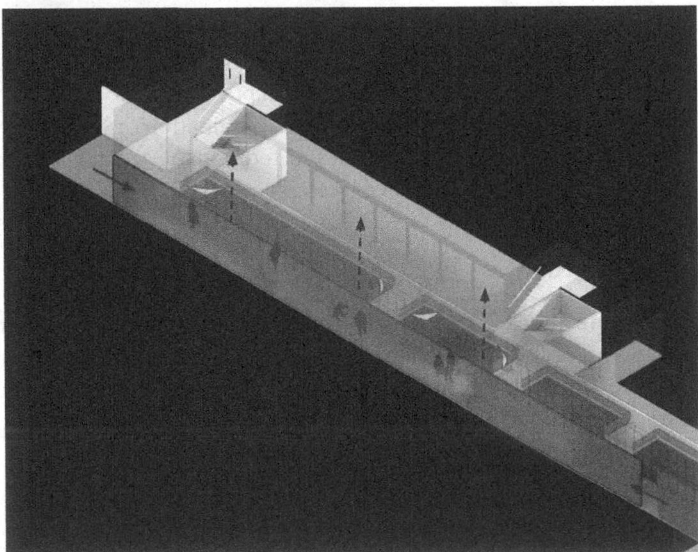

Fig. 9. Intervention by adding smells to induce social interaction

The three smells used at different points in the corridor creates soft boundaries that are dynamic and constantly shifting due to the flow of air and the movement of people in the space. Not only horizontally in that space, rather also vertically up to the second floor level. Due to the stack effect the warm air rises up and so do the smells.

The temporal interactions created in the space changes over the duration of time, based on the individual olfactory capacities and threshold levels of the smells. Also the smells create boundaries, for some these are challenging to cross through based on negative past experience and encounters with the same smell-causing to change the walking path through or around the corridor in the building.

2.4 Design Example Four

In this speculative design concept, smells are embedded in the material surface such as painting smell molecules that are responsive to temperature changes. In this design, the painted smells get activated through the heat of the sunlight. Based on the radiance map through the day as the sunlight falls on the wall, the intensity, the angle of light and warmth, coverage of the surface of the wall is constantly changing.

Mapping the surface of the wall, different smells are planned and placed at certain specific areas of the wall (Fig. 10).

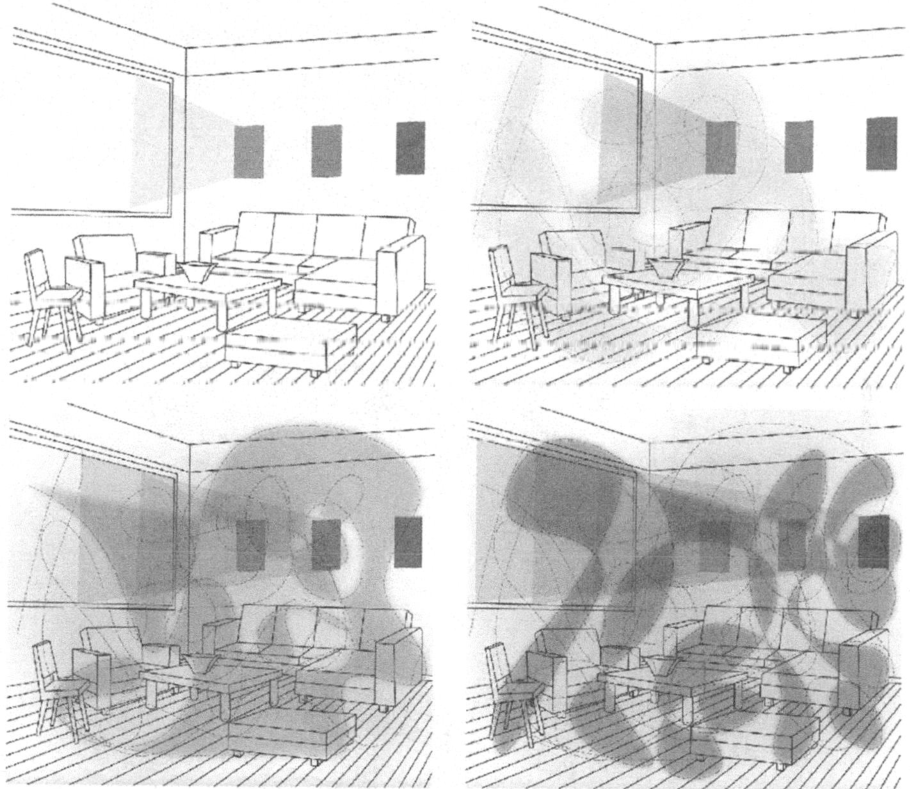

Fig. 10. Dynamic and temporal expression of smells unfolding through the day

The temporal and dynamic nature of smells in this case unfolds itself over a course of time duration before the new smell reveals itself in the space. With a natural rhythm of sun's heat as it changes through the day, smells are activated and allow a certain specific smell to be present in the space for a time duration that then transcends slowly to the next smell and allows for the next smell to unfold. There are different patterns of smells created repetitive each day and there would be a change in these patterns according to the seasons.

Avoiding the clash of smells, this concept creates soft transitions into different smell atmospheres, which could very well be used as an expression of passing time that is analogue, slow although not precise as a clock. Leading to a slow pace of living and perhaps emulating the outside seasons and their smells and creating a similar atmosphere inside.

2.5 Design Example Five

This design example proposes impregnating smells on the ceramic tiles. Which are a part of a dynamic façade system. The example speculates on the existing architectural project by Steven Holl - Storefront for Art and Architecture in New York. This building façade has elements of the wall opening-up and connecting the outside to the inside at different angles, as designed through the width of the façade (Figs. 11 and 12).

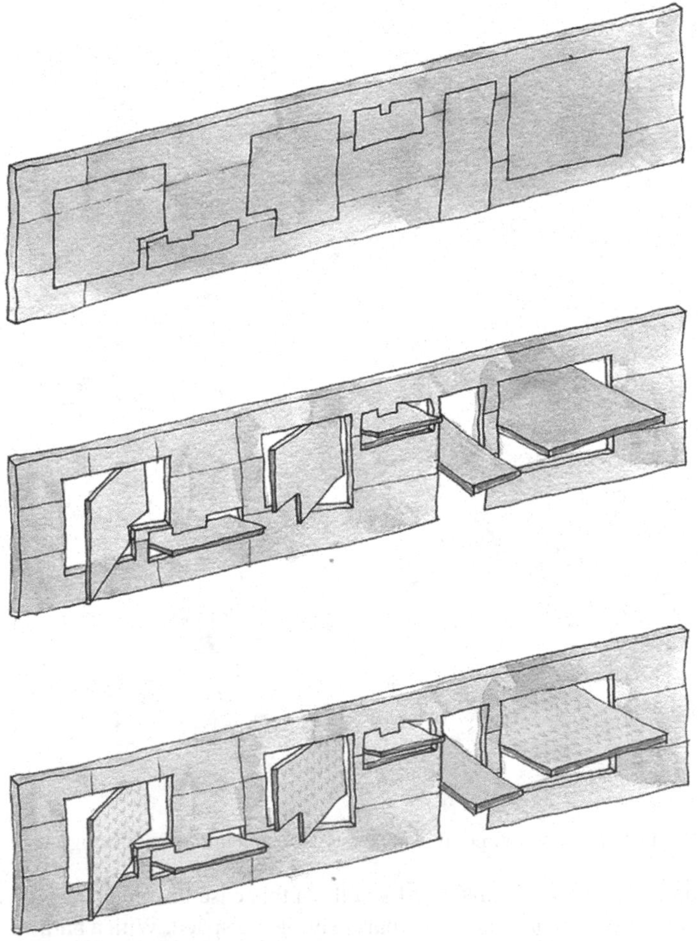

Fig. 11. Adding smells to design dynamic and temporal expressions

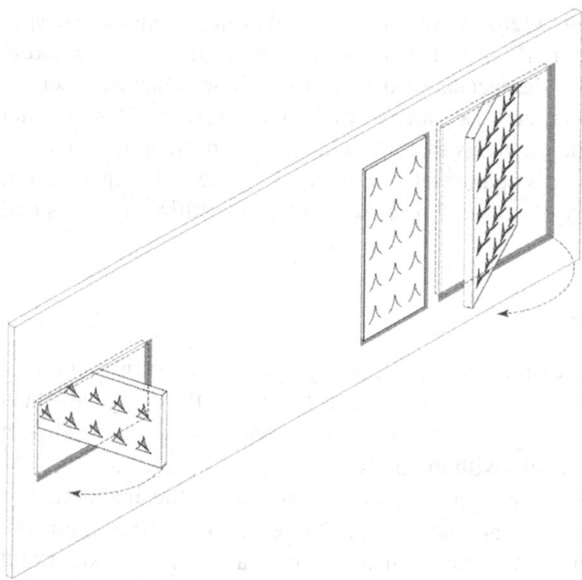

Fig. 12. Thermal temporality to create dynamic expressions of smells

The proposed design concept by the students is to build the façade in hybrid materials. Upon the contact of natural heat of sun on the surface, this hybrid material reacts and opens up at the triangular shaped cut sections. A natural material behaviour of the composite metal sheet on the outer side of the façade element curls up upon being heated. Once the top layer of the surface opens up it exposes the under layer that holds embedded smells in the ceramic layer and releases these in the space (Fig. 13).

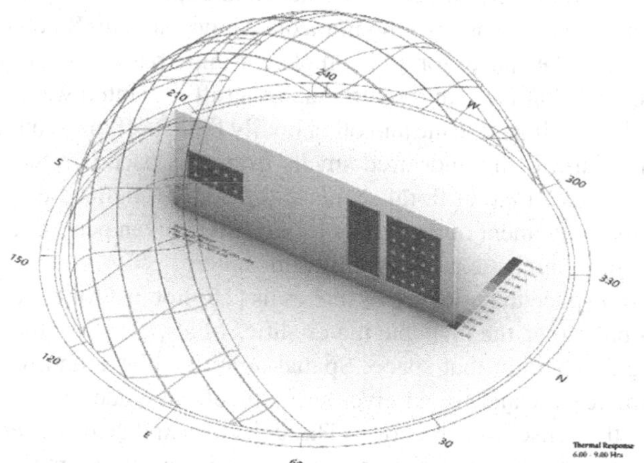

Fig. 13. Site specific radiation analysis

Using the façade elements of the reference project, that can be opened and rotated inside, where the smells from the outside can enter in the space and also through the embedded smells on the façade, would add to the time based experience of these smells.

The temporal interactions with the smell, would create different patterns and textures based on the façade elements that are rotated and on the atmospheric conditions of air flow that drives the dissipation of smells in this space. Also change in temperature and humidity on a daily or seasonal basis would create multiple patterns and expressions of smells.

3 Discussions

The above design examples explore design strategies to use smells as a medium of interaction between the body and the space. Quality of the designed olfactory interactions can be expressed through the connections, movement and temporality in a space and its experiential relationship with the body.

Through the materials inherent or added smells, the interactions are designed to reveal, subside or modulate the smells. The revelation of the smells over a duration of time is dynamic, as slowly the intensity changes and also the extent of the smells in the space. Modes of activating the smells in the presented design examples are either active or passive. Such as actively adding water as an actuator to the wood veneer would create different patterns of smells. Each time the water drops, the volume and the path of its movement is different. Also when the three distinct smells of the veneers are activated, the release of the smells creates patterns and can be perceived variedly.

Passive interactions of the smells, as in the above design examples, actuated due to the spatial variable, such as temperature, creates soft boundaries in the space. These boundaries are dynamic and constantly shifting. Body in relation to the shifting smellscapes either relates to the smells thereby moving through these smellscapes or has a negative association with the smells and movements are negotiated around these smellscapes.

Generally in a living environment, encounters and experience of smells creates and manifests connections to the space or the immediate environment. Smells communicate the information about the space, for an example, an underpass way (subway) communicates an atmosphere that is of an obscure nature, graffiti painted walls, lacking street lighting in the dark, smelling of urine and other bodily fluids, echoing sounds, all making the passers-by insecure. If the undesired smells from this pace is removed or camouflaged by use of desired fragrant floral scents and the street lights are added that glow brighter sensing the movement of the passer by, graffiti is given perhaps a spotlight, this space would then communicate a welcoming atmosphere.

An architectural space that touches or moves us [15] not just for the designers of the building but as inhabitants, the invisible materialities of a space drive the embodied and relational experiences within that space. Spatial qualities like sound, light and smells including the form, texture and colour gives an architectural space an atmosphere, something that touches the senses of perception. Through close and distance senses [16] these spatial qualities effect the human behaviour insofar that can trigger memories or induce moments where one extends the stay and lingers longer in a space than planned. This paper proposes smells as an interactive material to design spaces with. Where smells can be present in an ambient fashion or discretely, connect humans with their environment.

When designing the spatial atmospheres; aesthetical [15, 17] and metrological [18, 19], smells act as an interactive material similar to other sensory stimuli. Although there is no perfect quality of smells that will suit to all. Quite similar to a perfect thermal environment that is difficult to achieve [20], smells render a subjective and associative experience.

Designing for smell diversity in a living environment would create interactions at many different levels. As an explorative approach presented in this paper, expressions of interactions are borrowed from textiles as a leitmotif. These are organised in categories that on one hand render a tangible experience for a touch and visual delight of textures and patterns. On the other hand the dynamism and the temporality of the expressions offer the inhabitants soft boundaries and fluid movements through the space.

Referring to the definitions and etymologies of the term archi-textiles manifests the understanding of the same subject; *tek*, which give ways to the words of textile, technology, text, texture, connection and context. Also, to weave, to connect or to construct means in Latin, *texere*- which is the root of the words technology and textile. Body to space connections are formed due to the embodied experiences of the smells. Textures are experienced through the skin, similar to the thermal comfort and also smells as experienced through the skin of the nose.

Connecting outside to the inside spaces within architecture to create fluidity and continuity is not only a visual design challenge, rather also it is about bringing in the aesthetics of other sensory stimuli. Creating a balance and connectedness to the outside environment, including smells in the spatial design could add these soft boundaries within the space. Designing spaces with the diversity of smells would create patterns of movement and allow the openness or even enclosures of a space in a temporal manner.

The olfactory interactions can be designed through the tangible and intangible materialities of a space. Together with other sensory stimuli, a space is experienced in its multi dimensions. Also multi-sensorial interactions create powerful experiences with the environment.

Acknowledgement to the students. Apoorva Jalindre, Kazi Najeeb Hasan and Hana Nguyenky, Ester, Joon and Leon, Misri Patel, Maryam Aljomairi Alhajri and Shan Chun Wen, Mike Foster and Mike Friese, Mervi Antila, Marina Gavrilenko and Lingfang Shen, *Of*-

- Taubman College of Architecture and Urban Planning, University of Michigan, and
- School of Arts, Design and Architecture, Aalto University.

References

1. Rodaway, P.: Sensous Geographies: Body, Sense and Place. Routledge, London (1994)
2. Henshaw, V.: Urban Smellscapes: Understanding and Designing City Smell Environments. Routledge, New York (2014)
3. Diaconu, M.: Mapping urban smellscapes. In: Diaconu, M., et al. (eds.) Senses and the City, pp. 223–238. LIT Verlag, Vienna (2011)
4. Landin, H.: Anxiety and trust: and other expressions of interaction. In: Department of Computer Science and Engineering. Chalmers University of Technology, Göteborg (2009)
5. Weber, S.T., Heuberger, E.: Smell and be well. In: Diaconu, M., et al. (eds.) Senses and the City, pp. 165–188. LIT Verlag, Vienna (2011)

6. Stepanovic, M., Ferraro, V.: Digitalize limits for increased capability: technology to overcome human mechanisms. In: Ahram, T.Z., Falcão, C. (eds.) AHFE 2018. AISC, vol. 794, pp. 860–870. Springer, Cham (2019). https://doi.org/10.1007/978-3-319-94947-5_84
7. Semin, G.R.: Mysterious communication: the secret language of Chemosignals. In: Brakel, M.V., Duerinck, F., Eikelboom, W. (eds.) Sense of Smell, Breda, The Netherlands, pp. 156–161. Eriskay Connection, Breda (2014)
8. Kapur, J.: Engaging with sense of smell through textile interactions. In: Streitz, N., Konomi, S. (eds.) HCII 2019. LNCS, vol. 11587, pp. 241–257. Springer, Cham (2019). https://doi.org/10.1007/978-3-030-21935-2_19
9. Lim, Y.K., et al.: Interaction gestalt and the design of aesthetic interactions, pp. 239–254 (2007)
10. Hallnäs, L.: Textile interaction design. Nord. Text. J., 104–115 (2008). Special Edition Smart Textiles
11. Ferrara, M., Russo, A.C.: The Italian Design Approach to Materials between tangible and intangible meanings. Cuadernos del Centro de Estudios en Diseño y Comunicación [Ensayos], pp. 67–80 (2018). (Cuaderno 70)
12. Semper, G.: Style in the Technical & Tectonic Arts, or Practical Aesthetics. Getty, Los Angeles (2004)
13. Liotta, S.-J.A., Belfiore, M.: Patterns and Layering: Japanese Spatial Culture, Nature and Architecture. Gestalten, Berlin (2012)
14. Kapur, J.: Smells: olfactive dimension in designing textile architecture. Licentiate dissertation, University of Borås (2017)
15. Zumthor, P.: Atmospheres: Architectural Environments; Surrounding Objects. Birkhäuser, Basel (2006)
16. Exner, U., Spatial design. In: Pressel, D. (ed.) Basics, Spatial Design. Birkhäuser, Basel, Boston (2009)
17. Böhme, G.: The aesthetics of atmospheres. In: Thibaud, J.-P. (ed.) Taylor, and Francis. Routledge, Taylor & Francis Group, London (2017)
18. Rahm, P.: Atmosfere Construite = Constructed Atmoshpere. Postmedia Books, Milan (2014)
19. Roesler, S., Kobi, M.: The Urban Microclimate as Artifact: Towards an Architectural Theory of Thermal Diversity. De Gruyter, Berlin (2018)
20. Heschong, L.: Thermal delight in architecture. MIT Press, Cambridge (1979)

Detecting IoT Applications Opportunities and Requirements Elicitation: A Design Thinking Based Approach

Douglas Lima Dantas[1(✉)], Lucia Vilela Leite Filgueiras[1], Anarosa Alves Franco Brandão[1], Maria Cristina Machado Domingues[2], and Maria Rosilene Ferreira[2]

[1] Escola Politécnica da Universidade de São Paulo, São Paulo, SP 05508-010, Brazil
{douglasdantas,lfilguei,anarosa.brandao}@usp.br

[2] Instituto de Pesquisas Tecnológicas do Estado de São Paulo, São Paulo, SP 05508-901, Brazil
{cmachado,mrosif}@ipt.br

http://www.poli.usp.br

http://www.ipt.br

Abstract. IoT development is complex. To reduce this complexity, IoT platforms provide a set of resources and functionalities to enable application development and support its execution. In this work, we present a human-centered approach for requirements elicitation and mapping them to application resources in IoT platforms, using empathy, definition and ideation methods. A previous study by the authors has identified 11 categories of resources provided by 47 IoT platforms to developers in their application layers. From this set, 6 categories were selected for this work: schedulers and triggers, message and notification triggers, big data and analytics, artificial intelligence and machine learning, dashboards, and services. We invited 18 members of 8 projects for a workshop and divided them in 4 teams, according their project areas, which are: Industry 4.0 (6 participants), Environmental Disasters (4 participants), Environmental Management (3 participants) and Pollution (5 participants). We divided the workshop in 3 phases: warm-up, with user journey mapping, requirements identification using "how might we" questions as a trigger and requirements clustering the questions by the 6 selected categories of resources or an extra category named "others" for those which could not be related to any previous category. Our contribution for the IoT application development is an approach for turning easier requirements elicitation using DT techniques, covering the stages of empathise, definition and ideation, with well-available materials and considering the resources present at application layer of IoT platforms.

Keywords: Design Thinking · Internet of Things · Human centered design · Requirement gathering

N. Streitz and S. Konomi (Eds.): HCII 2020, LNCS 12203, pp. 85–100, 2020.
https://doi.org/10.1007/978-3-030-50344-4_7

1 Introduction

Internet of Things (IoT) technology brings the potential of creating smarter and more connected solutions, making use of intelligent device networks and technological resources such as hardware devices, big data, machine learning, communication protocols, data visualization and others that integrate sensing, actuation, identification, tracking and event processing features [19]. It is expected that in 2020 the Internet has around 100 billion connected devices [20]. IoT technologies have the potential of improving processes in various business domains. However, due the heterogeneity of technologies, IoT application development is complex [16] and requires more interdisciplinary teams when compared with other development fields. For instance, in mobile application development, users' experience is based on established design guidelines [2,3] and on the use of resources powered by the operating system like network access, Bluetooth connection, device sensors, notifications, among other ones [22]. A well-defined set of functionalities and a stable interaction language creates consistency across different mobile applications in different operating systems and domain areas. The same still does not occur with IoT application development, for technologies varies strongly for different projects, mainly when considering IoT applications for different domain areas. In order to reduce this complexity, companies, governments and research institutions work towards the creation of IoT platforms, which are a workbench of integrated technologies providing a set of resources and functionalities to enable application development and to support its execution. IoT platforms are generally available as cloud services, known as Platforms-as-a-Service (PaaS), but are also available for installation in private servers. The mainstream of IoT research is addressing technological aspects such as security and connectivity, or in philosophical questions, such as the representation of physical elements in the digital world, for instance [17]. Nevertheless, for IoT application development, requirements elicitation and their mapping to a given platform is still a challenge. In this work, we present a human-centered approach for requirements elicitation and mapping them to application resources in IoT platforms, using Design Thinking (DT) techniques. We intend to contribute to the process of IoT application development in a platform-agnostic environment, studying how DT can help developers of different domain areas in mapping their requirements to IoT platforms. This paper is structured as follows. Section 2 presents reference IoT architecture models. Section 3 briefly introduces Design Thinking and their phases, detailing the techniques used in our experiment. Section 5 reports our experiment. In Sect. 6, we discuss the experiment findings.

2 IoT Applications Development

According to ITU Telecommunication Standardization Sector [21], IoT is defined as *"a global infrastructure for the information society, enabling advanced services by interconnecting (physical and virtual) things based on existing and evolving interoperable information and communication technologies"*. Figure 1 shows the evolution of the IoT. Over time, the Internet got less people-dependent, networks turned smarter and data gained crucial importance, with devices rising as main data generators. This new paradigm has a potential of application in different vertical markets such as smart cities, industry, smart homes, logistic, health and retail, for example. IoT projects use a diversity of hardware technologies, like sensors, actuators, microcontrollers and communication devices, and software resources, such as data visualization, data processing, machine learning classifiers, etc. This heterogeneity caused a lack of standardization [1]. Over time, government bodies, companies, institutions and others interested organizations have created different architecture reference models in order to standardize the IoT and define guidelines for IoT systems development. Because of these efforts, the ITU-T Architecture Reference Model, IoT Architecture Reference Model (IoT ARM) and ISO/IEC 30141 were defined and are examples of reference models. The application layer, focus of this work, is part of these architectures, as seen in Fig. 2, and it is the place where usually business intelligence is developed. The implementation of an architecture is named IoT platform, that is an integrated solution for a specific or general purpose, reducing complexity, increasing components reuse and bringing development tools for IoT developers. We define as *development resource* as any set of functionalities provided by an IoT platform to an application developer. A resource can be a component, a library, an API or other form of software that can be used in the application development. A previous study by the authors has identified 11 categories of resources provided by 47 IoT platforms to developers in their application layers, listed below:

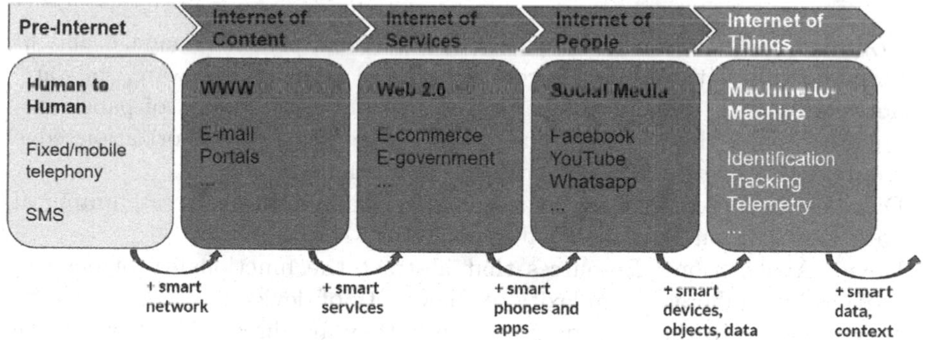

Fig. 1. IoT evolution.

- Artificial Intelligence (AI) and Machine Learning (ML): Resources that allow integrating classifiers and learning algorithms into applications.
- Big Data and Analytics: Resources that deal with the processing and storage of large volumes of data, to give meaning and to extract knowledge from them, generating reports and business strategies.

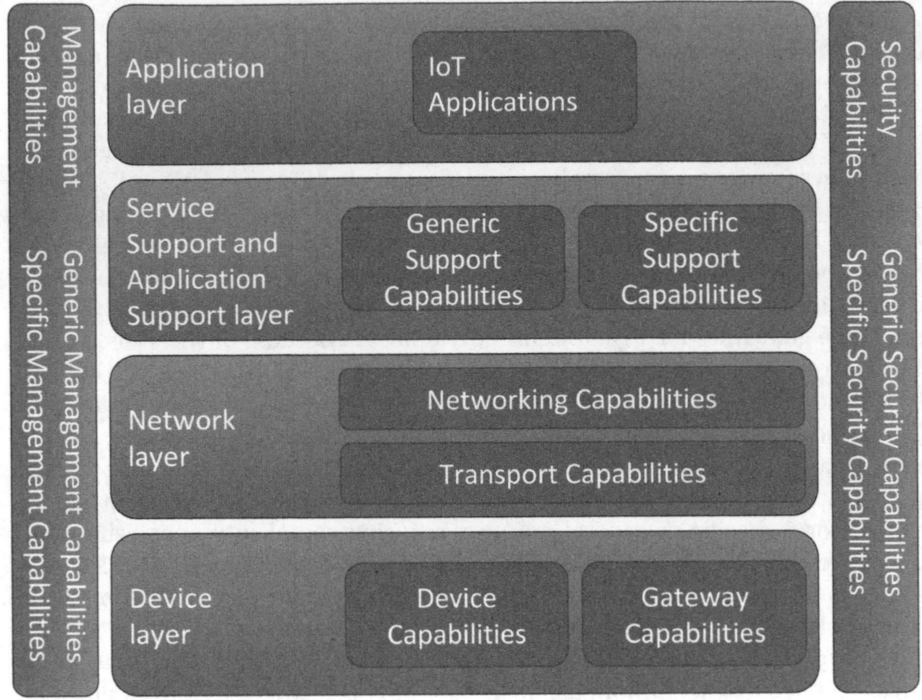

Fig. 2. The ITU-T IoT architecture reference model.

- Control Panels: Resources that help the administrator to manage and to maintain the platform and its resources, these being of hardware, software, network, energy, among others. On IoT platforms, these control panels frequently provide device management, user authentication, authorization, edge computing configuration, and protocol connections.
- Dashboards: Resources of graphical interface capabilities to create graphical data visualization panels, allowing monitoring.
- Device Abstractions: Resources that abstract the functionality of devices, reducing the inherent complexity of the variety of devices.
- Marketplaces: In the context of this work, they are directories at which the developer or end user can find or make available components, applications, data and other products, which permits be commercialized, in catalogue form. These available items can be integrated into applications or used as end applications, depending on the platform.
- Message and Notification Triggers: Resources that aim to send mass messages and notifications to the most varied types of devices. This information can be control messages, event alerts or simply focusing on user interaction.
- Schedulers and triggers: These are resources that trigger actions from a given time, or an expected event.

- Services: Resources of communication interfaces through which functionalities are made available through endpoints, for communication with other applications. The most recurrent form is through HTTP REST and SOAP webservices, in the client-server model, or MQTT, in the publish-subscribe model.
- Software Development Kit (SDK): Resources such as libraries, source codes and templates to facilitate the development of applications, allowing to use platform functionalities within the final applications.
- Wiring Tools: Resources of visual high-level programming tools that consist of links between blocks that represent commands or creation of flowcharts.

3 Design Thinking and Requirements Elicitation

According to Interaction Design Foundation [14], Design Thinking (DT) is "a non-linear, iterative process which seeks to understand users, challenge assumptions, redefine problems and create innovative solutions to prototype and test", and projects in different areas may use its techniques through DT dynamics, where the groups used to be multidisciplinary and their member has skills such as empathy, integrative thinking, optimism, experimentalism and collaboration. The DT process is divided in between three and seven phases, depending the variant. The Fig. 3 shows the five-stage model defined by Hasso-Plattner Institute of Design at Stanford (d.school) [15], which we explain below:

- Empathise: The comprehension of the user's point of view within the context of the project's problem. The success of this phase is crucial, once the definition and ideation processes are dependent of its outcomes. At this stage, we can use methods such as "assuming a beginner's mindset", bodystorming, asking what-how-why, conducting interviews, engaging with extreme users, among others [10].
- Define: The delimitation of the meaningful design challenge on which the team should focus. The Interaction Design Foundation [11] points three desired characteristics of a design challenge: i) human-centered; ii) broad enough for creative freedom; iii) narrow enough to make it manageable. Empathy maps, customer journey, point of view, "how might we" questions are some of the techniques that may we use at this phase.
- Ideate: The effort for idea generation in order to find solutions after one or more design challenges defined. In this phase, the team may find the innovation. There are different ways of conducting it, such as brainstorming sessions, mindmaps and provocation, for instance [12].
- Prototype: The generation of artifacts that can be in different sophistication grades, in order to testing ideas and collect feedback from users. The team may create low-fidelity prototypes, made of simple materials like paper or wood, for example, to validate initial and uncertain ideas and make high-fidelity prototypes, that are closer to the final product, to test the user's behavior with already validated ideas and adjust them [13].

– Test: The presentation of the generated prototypes and users feedback collection. The team may use the outcomes as input for the others stages, like new ideas generation and refining the prototypes, for example [13].

There are several documented techniques to support DT phases. Our requirements elicitation approach used techniques from different DT phases: user journey maps, how might we questions and affinity diagrams.

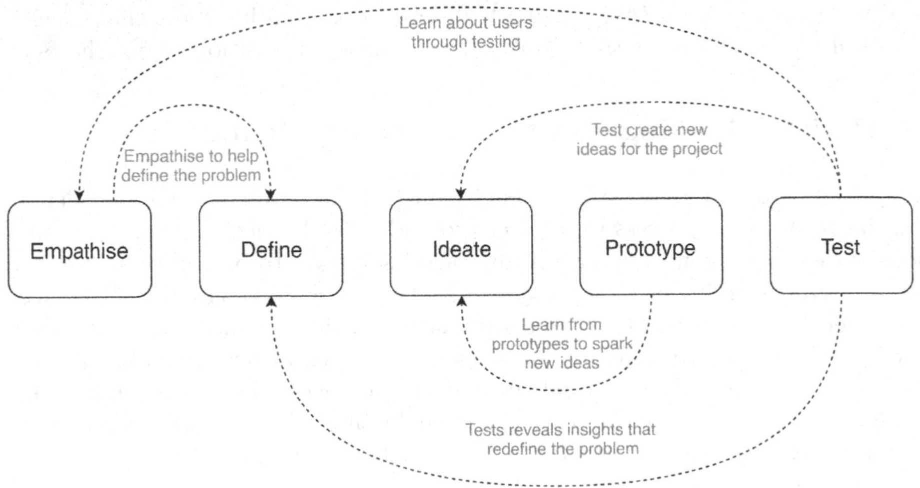

Fig. 3. The 5-stage model purposed by d.school (adapted from [9]).

3.1 User Journey

User journey is a technique to document the steps through which a user approaches a brand, service or product. The journey is composed by a set of touchpoints which represent the moments in which the user interacts with the brand/product/service. For each touchpoint, the map documents user's actions, thoughts and feelings. There is also space for mentioning opportunities for improvements.

The eight basic steps for mapping an user journey are: (1) define a scope of the scenarios to be analyzed; (2) define a user's profile; (3) define scenarios and expectations from the user; (4) create a list of possible actions and interaction points of the user with the product; (5) take into account the user's intentions; (6) draft the interactions step-by-step; (7) consider the user's emotional state for each step of interation; (8) validate and refine the journey [4].

Documenting the user journey is a way of constructing a Point of View (POV), i.e. a description of a problem highlighting its goal, considering the user whom the system if developed for, his needs and others characteristics which may be considered as relevant [11].

Documenting the user journey is one of the ways of to construct a Point of View (POV), i.e. a description of a problem highlighting its goal, considering the user whom the system if developed for, his needs and others characteristics which may be considered as relevant [11].

3.2 How Might We (HMW) Questions

How Might We (HMW) questions is a technique of brainstorming created by Procter & Gamble (P&G) in the 1970's and after adopted by companies such as Google, Facebook and IDEO [8]. Consists in a mean of ideas expression through short questions started with "How Might We", which works as a mind trigger for better ideas flowing considering a given previously defined POV. Design Kit [6] lists a four-step approach for conducing a HMW session that can be summarized as follows: (1) analyze previous statements, POV or other input; (2) rewrite the inputs as how many HMW questions as necessary; (3) verify if the HMW questions allow a variety of solutions, being good triggers for a brainstorm session; (4) verify if the HMW questions are too broad, and delimiter them if necessary.

3.3 Affinity Diagrams

Also known as Space Saturate and Group, is a technique which consists in clustering different types of collected data, resulting of brainstorming, research, interviews and others means, in meaning groups, comparing artifacts and deciding which are similar or different, according with some defined criteria [5].

3.4 IoT-Driven Techniques

Besides these general-purpose techniques, researchers have proposed creativity tools for applying DT to IoT development. The Tiles IoT Inventor Toolkit[1] brings tools such as representations of interfaces, virtual services and physical objects [17]. Besides that, its main characteristic is the working around the non-familiarity with IoT problem using augmentation strategies, i.e. adding computation capabilities to existing everyday objects, mixing existing and new functionalities to them. The toolkit consists in a set of 110 cards divided in six groups and a workshop technique, where the users are inspired for idea generation. Its roadmap contains the prototype creation as a work in progress.

The IoT Design[2] Deck uses different techniques such as User Journey, System Map, Touchpoint Matrix to provide a common language for multidisciplinary teams and is available both in digital or for print versions. While Tiles focuses on the process of the IoT system, this tool is user-centered [7].

The IoT Service Kit[3] also offers a card-based process with items representing things but differs for offering IoT scenario-centered boards with user journeys,

[1] https://www.tilestoolkit.io/.
[2] https://www.iotdesigndeck.com/.
[3] http://www.iotservicekit.com/.

design interaction and 3d-printed tokens, which represents mobile objects such as people and vehicles, for instance.

This work aims to provide empathy, definition and ideation methods for requirements gathering in IoT. It differs from others for using very simple and available tools like sticky notes and papers with user journey diagrams that may be printed or even drew. Besides that, we use "how might we"-started questions as a trigger for ideas generation and representations common resources categories offered by IoT platforms for developers. Table 1 shows a comparison between these techniques and our work considering covered stages of DT.

Table 1. Table captions should be placed above the tables.

Work	Empathise	Define	Ideate	Prototype	Test
IoT design deck	X	X		X	
Tiles			X	In progress	
IoT service kit		X	X	X	
This	X	X	X		

4 Invited Projects

Instituto de Pesquisas Tecnológicas do Estado de São Paulo (IPT)[4], a state research and technology development institute in Brazil, through the São Paulo Research Foundation (FAPESP), started the Institutional Development Plan in the Area of Digital Transformation: Advanced Manufacturing and Smart and Sustainable Cities (PDIP), that aims to implement the research area of Cyber-Physical Systems (CPS), which, according to National Institute of Standards and Technology (NIST) [18], "comprise interacting digital, analog, physical, and human components engineered for function through integrated physics and logic". CPS connected to the Internet are called IoT systems. The PDIP, in turn, is divided in two research axes: 1) Advanced Manufacture; 2) Smart and Sustainable Cities. These axes contains different projects, and we needed, first, to detect IoT applications opportunities, i.e., given the problems, understand how could IoT approach solve them; second, select one of them for implementation and case studies; finally, help their members to meet the requirements of the projects. In order to achieve these goals, we invited the members for a workshop, which were technical personnel of IPT who were in charge of these different projects. The invited projects, with 18 participants, were divided into four areas, and we describe they below:

- Industry 4.0 (6 participants)

[4] http://www.ipt.br/.

    - Analysis of iron ore pellets degradation.
- Environmental Disasters (4 participants)
    - Landslide risk analysis;
    - Flood risk analysis;
    - Forest fragments.
- Environmental Management (3 participants)
    - Tree fall risk analysis and study of forest fragments conservation of.
- Pollution (5 participants)
    - Noise mapping analysis.
    - Air pollution analysis.
    - Management of contaminated areas and environmental waste.

5 Experiment

As Fig. 4 shows, we divided the experiment into three phases: warm-up, requirements identification of each project and clustering the requirements by resources categories.

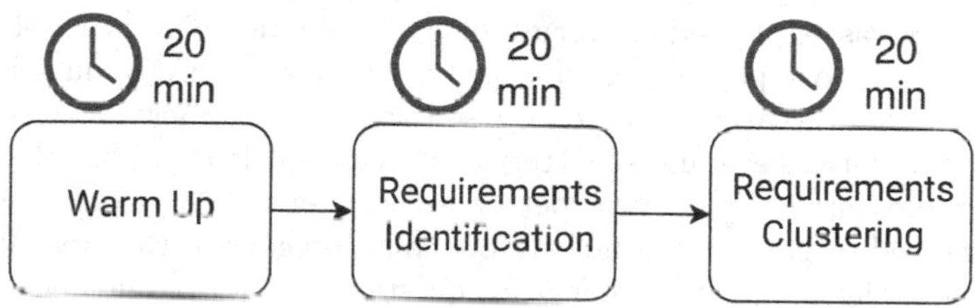

Fig. 4. Representation of the approach.

Firstly, we received the participants and explained to them the workshop goals and how it works. After, in the introducing round, each participant told his or her name, job, expectations about the workshop and described briefly the project which he or she was involved. The warm-up phase had the intention to move the mindset from the technical problems to an user perspective. After, the moderator grouped the participants into four teams according the fields of their projects as follows: 1) yellow: Environment Disasters; 2) lilac: Environmental Management; 3) pink: Industry 4.0; 4) blue: Pollution. So, he showed the user journey concept to them. So, we applied the user journey technique in which each group had to explain which are the touchpoints of their user with their systems and what happens in each stage. Hence, we shared user journeys boards, pencils, rulers and defined a time of twenty-minutes for the teams do this task. Each team chose some user profiles and each member did a board for each one, considering his interactions with the system and the attributes "doing", "thinking", "feeling" and writing, if any, detected opportunities when analyzing the journey. At the end of time, the moderator invited each team to present one of his boards to other teams, to create a mutual understanding of the works. Figure 5 shows an user journey board.

Next step intended to explore the possible usages of IoT environment for applications of each project. So, the moderator explained the HMW questions techniques and the participants received sticky notes in four colors, one for each team, and pens. Hence, we requested for the teams to write HMW questions, considering the user's POVs mapped into the journeys, in a deadline of twenty-minutes. Figure 6 shows two questions created by a team.

The last step intended to explore the resources of IoT platforms, showing the opportunities could be developed using one or more IoT platform built-in solutions. Finally, the moderator presented the resources categories. From the set of eleven resource categories, we select the most commonly used, which are:

- Schedulers and triggers;
- Message and notification triggers;
- Big data and analytics;
- Artificial Intelligence and Machine Learning;
- Dashboards;
- Services

Each resource was explained in terms of what functionality is involved. For each resource category presented, we asked the teams for HMW questions that could be solved by the resource category, so they gave the sticky notes for insert around a label with the name of category in a panel. If any time they detect that a new presented category is better for solving a HWM question, could move the desired sticky notes from any previous category to this one. We made available, too, a label called "Others" for questions that could not be solved by any resource category or don't have technological solution. By this way, all the HMW questions were clustered around the labels, as Fig. 7 shows.

6 Results and Discussion

Figure 8 shows how many HMW questions each team made by resource category, while Fig. 9 shows it by team. The most selected category was "Big Data and Analytics", with 24 occurrences, showing that data and its treatment are very important for these systems and, as we can see also in Fig. 9d, mainly for the ones from Environmental Management, whom the HMW questions presented worries about images processing, data correlations, image and data storage, among others.

"Service" was chosen 21 times, mainly by Environmental Disasters, once its solutions, also from the like the Pollution and Environmental Management teams, need to provide a channel of information for the target audience consume. The Industry 4.0 team, however, did not insert any HMW questions in Service category, probably due to its more operational purpose, without direct need of offering public services.

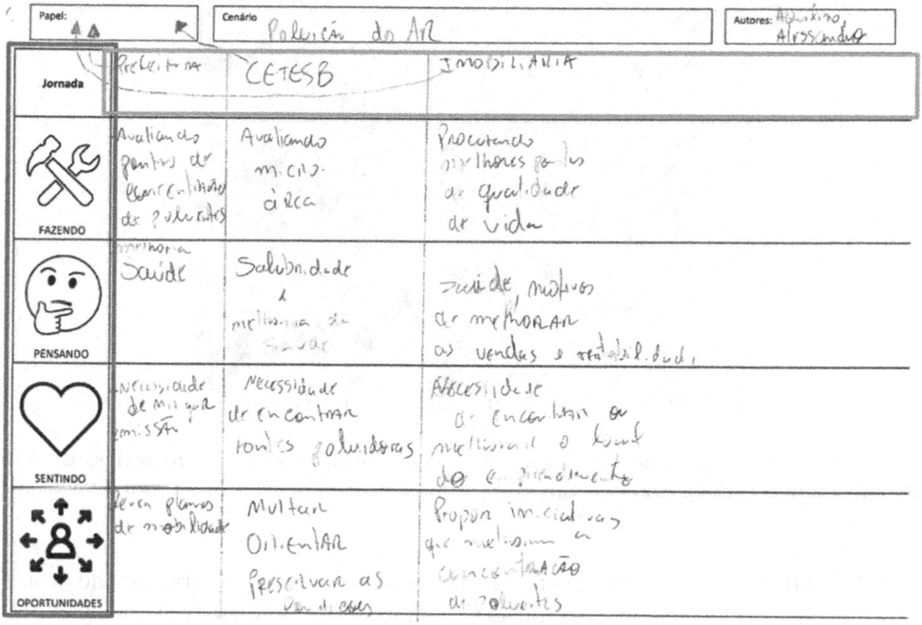

Papel:	Cenário: Poluição do Ar		Autores: Aquino, Alessandra
Jornada	Prefeitura	CETESB	Imobiliária
FAZENDO	Avaliando pontos de concentração de poluentes	Avaliando micro área	Procurando melhores pontos de qualidade de vida
PENSANDO	melhoria Saúde	Salubridade e melhoria da saúde	Saúde, motivos de melhorar as vendas e rentabilidade
SENTINDO	Necessidade de mitigar emissão	Necessidade de encontrar fontes poluidoras	Necessidade de encontrar ou melhorar o local do empreendimento
OPORTUNIDADES	Fazer planos de mobilidade	Multar, Orientar, Preservar as condições	Propor iniciativas que melhorem a concentração de poluentes

Fig. 5. One of the created user journey board. In red, the user's acts and found opportunities and, in green, the points of contact with the system. (Color figure online)

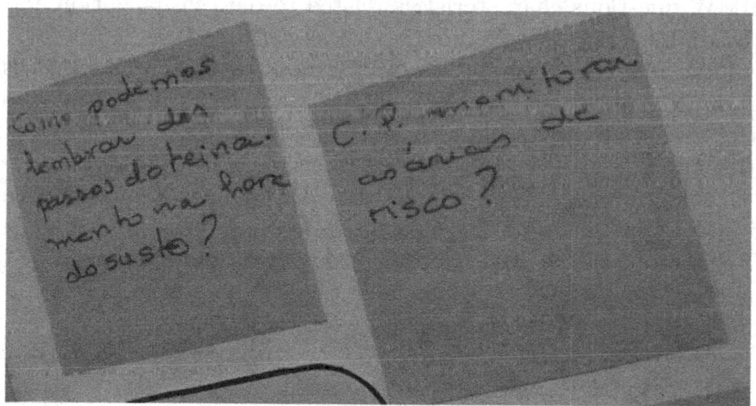

Fig. 6. Two stick notes with HMW questions elaborated by one of the teams.

The teams chose "Messages and Notifications" 12 times. Pollution and Environmental Disasters teams pointed needs focused on alert the population about events of interest and promote their solutions. Industry 4.0 team identified a need of notifying the user of its system.

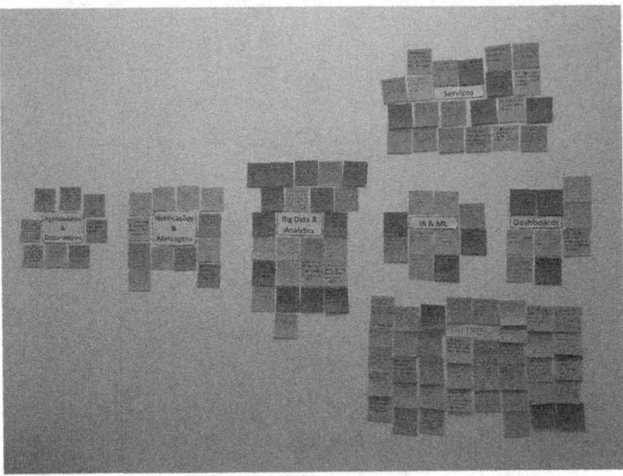

Fig. 7. Panel presenting the HMW questions clustered by resources categories, around the white labels. Sticky notes in the same color were created by the same team.

"IA & ML" category was selected 10 times. All the teams expressed the desire of to use data collected for automatically improve the behaviors of the systems, making them more efficient.

The Environmental Management, Pollution and Industry 4.0 teams chosen the "Dashboard" category 3 times each, totalling 9 occurrences. They presented in their HMW questions characteristics related to data visualization and monitoring. Environmental Disasters didn't selected this one.

"Schedulers and Triggers" was selected 8 times, by Environmental Disasters, Pollution and Industry 4.0. They associate this resource category to automatic reactions for exception events on the systems. Environmental Management didn't selected this one.

The "Other" group, which clusterizes those HMW questions whom the teams doesn't found a category, was the most used, in these percentages: i) Environmental Disasters – 25,71%; ii) Pollution – 34,3%; iii) Industry 4.0 – 55,6%; iv) Environmental Management – 11,5%. These questions reflect the needs whom the resources offered by IoT platforms or even other technologies can not help directly, such as sociopolitical factors, funding, business sustainability, among others.

Some categories such as "Big Data & Analytics", "IA & ML" and "Dashboard" seems to see well-knew by the teams, so we noted the teams did a better correlation of their problems with these categories, like the question "how might we monitor the ore on the way through the milling plant?" which the teams related to "Dashboard" category. However, for the other categories, less familiar for them, the same not occurs, like the "Services", related to webservices creation, a more technical category, which received different questions related to general services, such as "how might we produce more goods at a lower price?", for example.

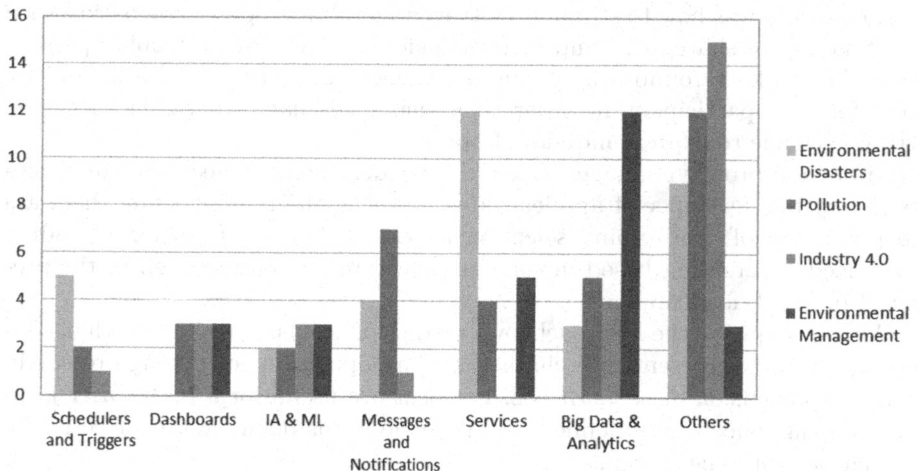

Fig. 8. Chart showing the frequency of HMW questions of the teams by resource category, from less to most selected.

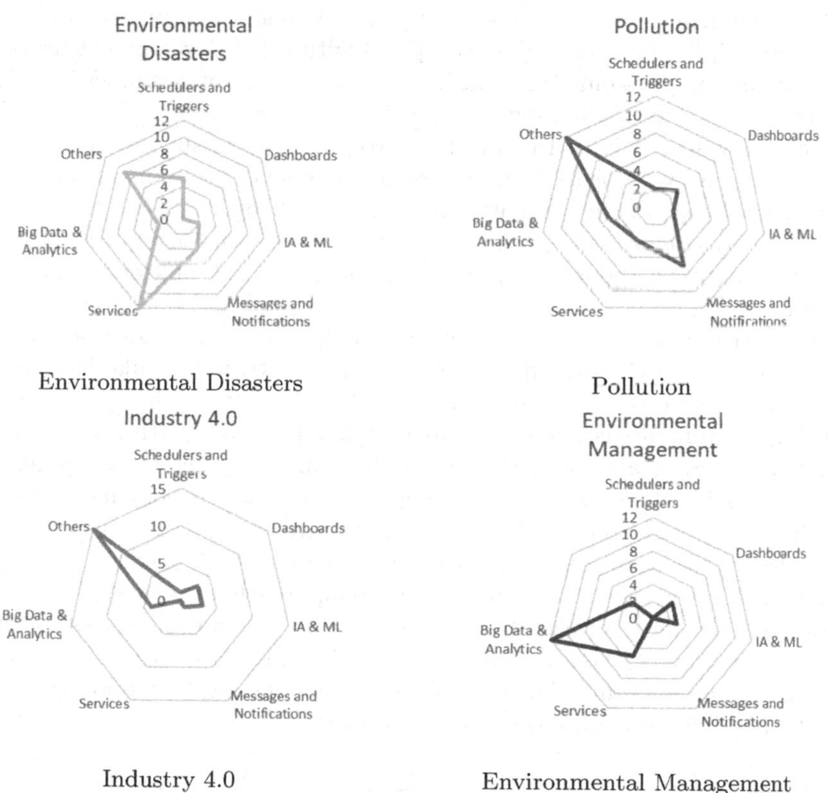

Fig. 9. Radar charts representing the found necessary resources for each team.

A challenge was how to stimulate introvert people's people participation once they tend not to share ideas and be overshadowed by extrovert people's personalities. We worked around it by giving individual user journey boards and sticky notes for each participant in order to permit a discussion between them but letting each one to express individual opinion, yet.

About the prototype stage, once we have identified the necessary resources desired by the developer of application considering the requirements, there are the possibility of prototyping selecting a existing IoT platform for attending those needs or creating based in some architecture reference model, as the presented in Fig. 2, for instance.

We can improve the approach by creating personas, a technique that consists in creating representative characters of a population got through research, for a comprehension of users' needs. Personas are useful for a better user journey mapping, once a well-defined user's profile let us define more correctly the interactions with the system.

7 Conclusions and Future Work

Due to heterogeneity of technologies, IoT development is complex and needs more interdisciplinary teams when compared with other development areas. To work around this problem, IoT platforms provide a set of resources and functionalities to enable application development and support its execution. The common IoT research is addressing technological aspects such as security and connectivity, however, for IoT application development, requirements elicitation and their mapping to a given platform is still a challenge.

In this work, we presented a human-centered approach for requirements elicitation and mapping them to application resources in IoT platforms, using DT techniques.

Our contribution for the IoT application development is an approach for turning easier requirements elicitation using DT, with well-available materials and considering the resources present at application layer of IoT platforms. In other development areas such as mobile, web and desktop, the requirements elicitation processes are more mature, with a huge variety of techniques and less heterogeneity of technologies, in comparison with IoT development. Besides that, the teams could reflect on the needs and problems of their own projects and on the possibilities of solving them through IoT development.

The next steps, we intend to refine the approach developed, look for a method to cover the prototyping stage and review the current classification of resource categories in the application layer of IoT platforms, through the clustered requirements around the "others" label, once those are an opportunity for detecting possible lacks on current IoT platforms.

Acknowledgements. Grant #2018/23052-0, São Paulo Research Foundation (FAPESP). Grant #2017/50343-2, São Paulo Research Foundation (FAPESP).

References

1. Al-Qaseemi, S.A., Almulhim, H.A., Almulhim, M.F., Chaudhry, S.R.: IoT architecture challenges and issues: lack of standardization. In: Proceedings of Future Technologies Conference, FTC 2016, pp. 731–738 (2017). https://doi.org/10.1109/FTC.2016.7821686
2. Apple: Design for Android. https://developer.android.com/design
3. Apple: Human Interface Guidelines. https://developer.apple.com/design/human-interface-guidelines
4. Babich, N.: A Beginner's Guide To User Journey Mapping-UX Planet. https://uxplanet.org/a-beginners-guide-to-user-journey-mapping-bd914f4c517c
5. Dam, R.F., Siang, T.Y.: Affinity diagrams-learn how to cluster and bundle ideas and facts — interaction design foundation (2018). https://www.interaction-design.org/literature/article/affinity-diagrams-learn-how-to-cluster-and-bundle-ideas-and-facts
6. Design Kit: How Might We — Design Kit. https://www.designkit.org/methods/3
7. Dibitonto, M., Tazzi, F., Leszczynska, K., Medaglia, C.M.: The IoT design deck: a tool for the co-design of connected products. In: Ahram, T., Falcao, C. (eds.) Advances in Usability and User Experience. AHFE 2017, Advances in Intelligent Systems and Computing, vol. 607, pp. 217–227. Springer, Cham (2018). https://doi.org/10.1007/978-3-319-60492-3_21
8. Harvard Business Review: The Secret Phrase Top Innovators Use. https://hbr.org/2012/09/the-secret-phrase-top-innovato
9. Interaction Design Foundation: 5 Stages in the Design Thinking Process — Interaction Design Foundation. https://www.interaction-design.org/literature/article/5-stages-in-the-design-thinking-process
10. Interaction Design Foundation: Stage 1 in the Design Thinking Process: Empathise with Your Users. https://www.interaction-design.org/literature/article/stage-1-in-the-design-thinking-process-empathise-with-your-users
11. Interaction Design Foundation: Stage 2 in the Design Thinking Process: Define the Problem and Interpret the Results. https://www.interaction-design.org/literature/article/stage-2-in-the-design-thinking-process-define-the-problem-and-interpret-the-results
12. Interaction Design Foundation: Stage 3 in the Design Thinking Process: Ideate. https://www.interaction-design.org/literature/article/stage-3-in-the-design-thinking-process-ideate
13. Interaction Design Foundation: Stage 4 in the Design Thinking Process: Prototype. https://www.interaction-design.org/literature/article/stage-4-in-the-design-thinking-process-prototype
14. Interaction Design Foundation: What Is Design Thinking and Why Is It So Popular?. https://www.interaction-design.org/literature/article/stage-5-in-the-design-thinking-process-test
15. Kelley, D., Brown, T.: An introduction to design thinking. Institute of Design at Stanford (2018). https://doi.org/10.1027/2151-2604/a000142, https://dschool-old.stanford.edu/sandbox/groups/designresources/wiki/36873/attachments/74b3d/ModeGuideBOOTCAMP2010L.pdf
16. Lepekhin, A., Borremans, A., Ilin, I., Jantunen, S.: A systematic mapping study on Internet of Things challenges. In: Proceedings of the 1st International Workshop on Software Engineering Research & Practices for the Internet of Things, pp. 9–16 (2019). https://doi.org/10.1109/SERP4IoT.2019.00009

17. Mora, S., Gianni, F., Divitini, M.: Tiles: a card-based ideation toolkit for the Internet of Things. In: DIS 2017-Proceedings of the 2017 ACM Conference on Designing Interactive Systems, pp. 587–598 (2017). https://doi.org/10.1145/3064663.3064699
18. National Institute of Standards and Technology: Cyber-Physical Systems. https://www.nist.gov/el/cyber-physical-systems
19. Ngu, A.H., Gutierrez, M., Metsis, V., Nepal, S., Sheng, Q.Z.: IoT middleware: a survey on issues and enabling technologies. IEEE Internet Things J. **4**(1), 1–20 (2017). https://doi.org/10.1109/JIOT.2016.2615180
20. Perera, C., Ranjan, R., Wang, L., Khan, S.U., Zomaya, A.Y.: Big data privacy in the internet of things era. IT Professional **17**(3), 32–39 (2015). https://doi.org/10.1109/MITP.2015.34
21. Sector, I.T.S.: Recommendation itu-t y. 2060: Overview of the internet of things. Series Y: Global information infrastructure, internet protocol aspects and next-generation networks-Frameworks and functional architecture models, pp. 2060–201206 (2012). https://www.itu.int/rec/T-REC-Y
22. Yunisa, F.S.: Push notification system to mobile game player using distributed event-based system approach. In: Proceeding - 2016 2nd International Conference on Science in Information Technology, ICSITech 2016: Information Science for Green Society and Environment, pp. 52–57. Institute of Electrical and Electronics Engineers Inc. (2017). https://doi.org/10.1109/ICSITech.2016.7852607

Aspects of Ambient UX Design Within Design-to-Robotic-Production and -Operation Processes

Milica Pavlovic[1(✉)], Henriette Bier[2], and Margherita Pillan[1]

[1] Interaction and Experience Design Research Lab, Politecnico di Milano, Via Giovanni Durando 38/a, 20158 Milan, Italy
{milica.pavlovic,margherita.pillan}@polimi.it

[2] Robotic Building Lab, Delft University of Technology, Julianalaan 134, 2628 BL Delft, The Netherlands
h.h.bier@tudelft.nl

Abstract. Ambient User Experience design in architecture implies consideration of various intersecting and sometimes overlapping design fields such as interaction and architectural design with the aim to achieve a continuous and cohesive user experience across devices, time, and space. In this paper, Ambient User Experience design is explored in relation to Design-to-Robotic-Production and -Operation processes developed at TU Delft, which link computational design with robotic production and operation. Several case studies involving the integration of sensor-actuators into the built environment are discussed with respect to mapping activities through constraints and enablers and designing with the time as a variable.

Keywords: Ambient User Experience · Design Domains · Interaction design · Architecture design · Design-to-Robotic-Production and -Operation

1 Ambient User Experience

The diffusion of digital technologies imposes an upgrade of design knowledge and skills, and, between others, of drawing capabilities. The design of digitized services that enhance activities within functional physical spaces requires the integration of multiple design competences: service, communication, interaction, product and architectural design. Furthermore, the design of technology-based solutions, requires the collaboration between experts of different disciplines, such as engineers and business managers, and their involvement in co-design processes. In order to manage the complexity of these physical/digital solutions, and to ensure a design result oriented towards the optimal satisfaction of users, new design approaches and mapping techniques focused on experience and on user activities are needed [1, 2].

Ambient User Experience (UX) aims to provide a continuous and cohesive user experience across devices, time, and space. The design of Ambient UX involves various intersecting and sometimes overlapping design fields such as interaction and architectural

N. Streitz and S. Konomi (Eds.): HCII 2020, LNCS 12203, pp. 101–109, 2020.
https://doi.org/10.1007/978-3-030-50344-4_8

design that have subdomains such as design, human–computer interaction, software development, etc.

Ambient UX is a conceptual framework that provides a strategy for structured design processes that target Cyber-Physical Systems (CPSs) [3]. The Ambient UX framework consists of a definition of Design Domains (DDs) (what is to be designed) and User Values (why it is designed) observed within Ambient UX and CPS [4]. Ambient UX design in architecture implies consideration of various intersecting and sometimes overlapping DDs such as interaction and architectural design with the aim to achieve a continuous and cohesive user experience across devices, time, and space. In projects focused on user experience, design activities are not only aimed at defining the physical characteristics of spaces, but also at representing users' physical and cognitive activities in time, and the interactive processes. The overall design integrates the design of interactions with the design of physical environments. In this context, mapping out users' activities through use-case scenarios is considered. From the natural constraints i.e. physical constraints that limit what can be done to the affordances, which convey possible uses, actions, and functions [5], a palette of constraints and enablers is identified. These constraining/enabling points of activities are starting points for designing user experiences.

Fig. 1. Analysing social activities and speculating on new activities within the urban environment.

2 Design Domains

2.1 Mapping Activities Through Constraints and Enablers

Developing design strategies in experience-centred design requires thorough understanding of the users, their goals, motivations and thought-processes, guided by emotional states and contexts. An experience can be observed as an episode, a story within a certain time length, that emerges from the dialogue of a person with the surrounding world through actions [6]. Designing for everyday activities from the perspective of perceived experience through emotions, rather than from the perspective of material output, opens up many possibilities for reflecting on meaningfulness in design scenarios [7]. Such an "an experience" can be seen as a particular meaningful momentary construction [8], with a beginning and an end, that grows from the interaction between people and their environment.

For all the maps, as experience design tools, is common that they are activity-based designs [1, 9]. People are always in an environment that consists of contexts and technologies, in which they are engaged in activities [10]. The activities are enabled within an ecosystem relying on interactions between organisms, and between those organisms and their environment, which together create an ecology that is greater than the sum of its parts [11].

In this context, mapping out users' activities through use-case scenarios is considered. From the natural constraints i.e. physical constraints that limit what can be done to the affordances, which convey possible uses, actions, and functions, a palette of constraints and enablers is identified. These constraining/enabling points of activities are starting points for designing user experiences.

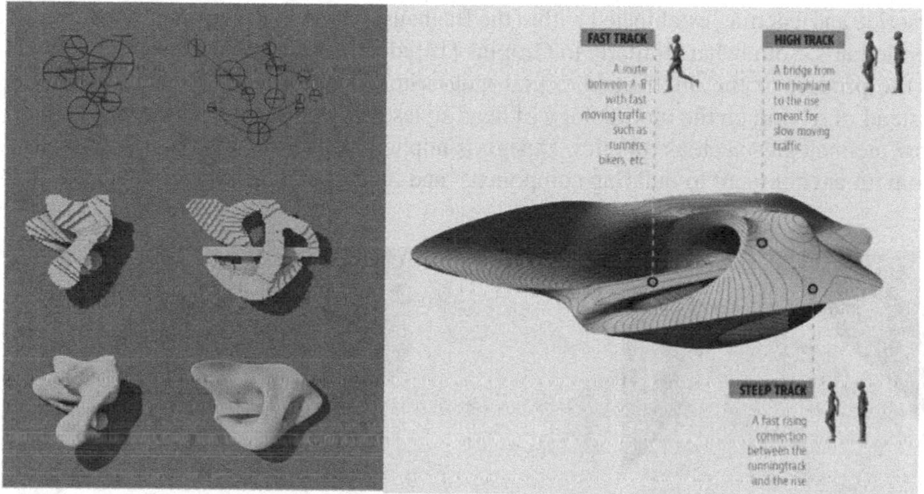

Fig. 2. Mapping out diverse types of activities and routes that the physical shape facilitates.

2.2 Three Architectures with the Time as a Variable

In order to identify Design Domains (DD) for Ambient UX an investigation into cases studies is implemented. The samples of cases were gathered from a course on interactive architecture, that is offered at Robotic Building (RB) (formerly known as Hyperbody), Technical University Delft. Within the design studio course on Design-to-Robotic-Production and =Operation (D2RP&O) for Interactive Urban Furniture [12], Master students were encouraged to represent experiences in architecture by merging physical and digital design aspects and projecting perception and experience of the users. Students developed projects in phases such as analysing the context, defining the concept, developing the project on macro, meso and micro scales, and finally arriving to a tangible prototype of a parametrically defined architectural structure. From analysing and mapping activities, to understanding the needs and developing the concept design, the students defined the physical form while integrating interactive components that support diverse services such as adaptive lighting, sun shading, etc.

In terms of interaction, the emphasis was put on the user-centred approach: When proposing a design concept, students were focusing on the experience of the people that would use the space, and the perceptions of the context of use itself. Mapping activities enabled identification of three networks of interactions with three diverse architectures, where time is a variable: spatial (interaction related to the physical environment), information (interaction related to information flows), and relational (interaction related to human/social relations).

Spatial Architecture by Means of D2RP&O. Spatial architecture, as one of the DDs for Ambient UX, relies on the traditional comprehension of architecture as physically built environment relying on spatial and product/artefact design that finds its roots in the practice and teaching established within the Bauhaus, school of design, architecture, and applied arts. Somewhat similarly to Gropius [13] identifying that the New Architecture is the product of the intellectual, social and technical conditions of its age and time instead of relying on the morphology of dead styles, RB studio explores the potential of new technologies such as robotics. Design is implied as intervention on diverse scales, from an environment to building components and individual artefacts/products.

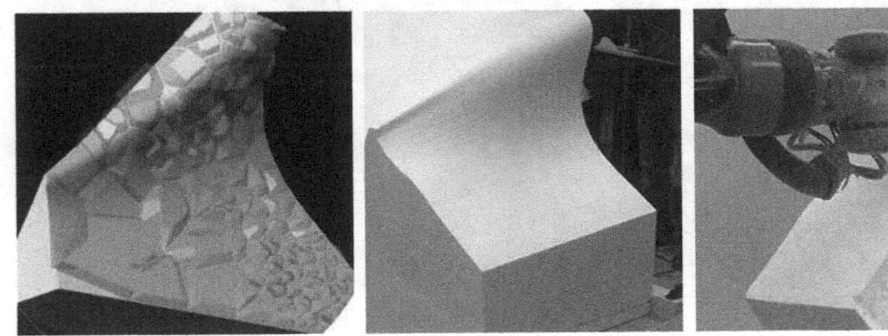

Fig. 3. D2RP process linking parametric 3D model (left) with robotic hot wire cutting (middle) and milling (right).

Architecture as an Ambient UX DD involves design and manufacturing of physically built environments that adapt to human needs. D2RP&O is a particular approach developed at TU Delft [14] that facilitate the integration of advanced computational design with robotic techniques in order to produce performative architectural formations (Fig. 1 and 2). Performances considered are inter al. functional, structural, environmental, and operational.

D2RP&O links design and production with smart operation of the built environment and advances applications in performance optimization, robotic manufacturing, and user-driven operation in architecture. It is relying on human and non-human interaction in the design, production, and operation of buildings. It is fundamentally changing the role of the architect. Architects design increasingly processes not artefacts/buildings, while users operate multiple time-based architectural configurations emerging from the same physical space that reconfigures in accordance to environmental and user specific needs. In this context, D2RP&O empowers architects to regain control over the design implementation into physically built environments and allows end-users to participate as co-creators in the adaptation i.e. customization of their environments over time.

For developing the spatial architecture, students start by mapping the moments and positions of planned and/or predicted activities to take part using simulation tools (Fig. 2). The spatial design is then iteratively defined by taking functional, structural, environmental, materialization, and operational requirements into consideration. While functional requirements refer to use, structural and environmental performances ensure stability and comfort of the structure. Furthermore, materialization requirements involve material properties, production and tools requirements, while operational aspects involve sensor-actuators ensuring responsive and/or interactive behaviours. The D2RP&O approach ensures that the 3D model is linked with robotic production and operation (Fig. 3).

Robotic operation involves sensor-actuators embedded into the built environment and responding to and/or interacting with people. It is relying on information architecture.

Information Architecture. Information architecture, as one of the DDs for Ambient UX, involves management of information [15] and involves patterns and sequences of interaction.

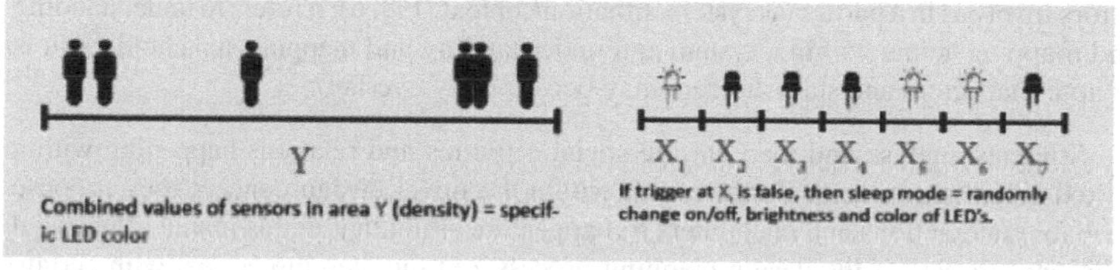

Fig. 4. Design scheme for a dynamically responsive lighting system based on automated inputs was linked real-time to user activities such as seating, walking, running.

In order to develop such patterns, students define the desired interactions enabled by systems of sensors and actuators, such as for example a dynamic change of lighting through intensity and colour, according to the movement of the users within the physical structure and the social moments and settings (Fig. 4 and 5). When shaping inputs and outputs and the information flows, enablers are defined through triggers of pre-designed responses to them, while constraints reflect the fact that only certain triggers and pre-designed responses are selected while all the other possibilities are disabled. Information architecture is visible to the users only when being present within the designated spatial areas and when the triggers for dynamic changes are performed.

The focus of the information architecture in the RB studio 2017 was on light. The dynamically responsive lighting system was linked real-time to user presence and activities such as seating, walking, running (Fig. 4 and 5). Light colour, intensity, turn on-off patterns were correlated to the number of people present as well as the static or dynamic use of space. Embedded sensors identifying presence of people are linked to actuators that respond and/or initiate behaviours such as *stay with me* by turning on or *follow me* by moving ahead a person walking or running.

When defining patterns and sequences of interactions, the challenge is to identify human-nonhuman communication.

Fig. 5. Perspective view of the ambient in which dynamic lighting changes are taking place in relation to people's behaviours.

Relational Architecture. Relational architecture, as one of the DDs for Ambient UX, is intended as anticipation and/or triggering of most probable interactions to happen among actors involved in a particular system/situation/context (Fig. 6); it refers to understanding and mapping actors within a system and understanding and mapping stakeholders (it is to note that actors and stake-holders may occasionally overlap).

Students analyse and map out the social activities and relations happening within an existing environment. Furthermore, within the novel design concept they propose probable interactions and encounters to happen; meaning that in this manner the social relations are part of the design planning process and they are directional with certain enablers and/or constraints within the project.

Variable of Time. Variable of time, as one of the DDs for Ambient UX, is the backbone that puts together all the three architectures described previously; it refers to sequential steps of an activity, and it can reflect diverse time scales and length. When it comes to designing for experiences, story-mapping comes into play [6, 16].

Students analyse and map out time frames of their planed user journeys and activities within the interactive installation (Fig. 4, 5, 6 and 7). Time can be observed as an element that can be enabled or constrained by defining, for e.g., a period in which certain dynamic changes and interactions can happen.

By taking on the approach of designing for experiences, students focus on defining particular journeys, which happen over a certain timespan, i.e. they anticipate possible paths and moments of interaction and encounters, as well as their sequence. Design concepts considering time as a variable is communicated through design tools such as storyboarding, journey mapping, movie plots, etc.

Spatial qualities and functional requirements need to meet story-mapping, hence students identify spatial architecture requirements in relationship to physical and interactive experiences in time. In this context, the overlap and/or intersection between DDs

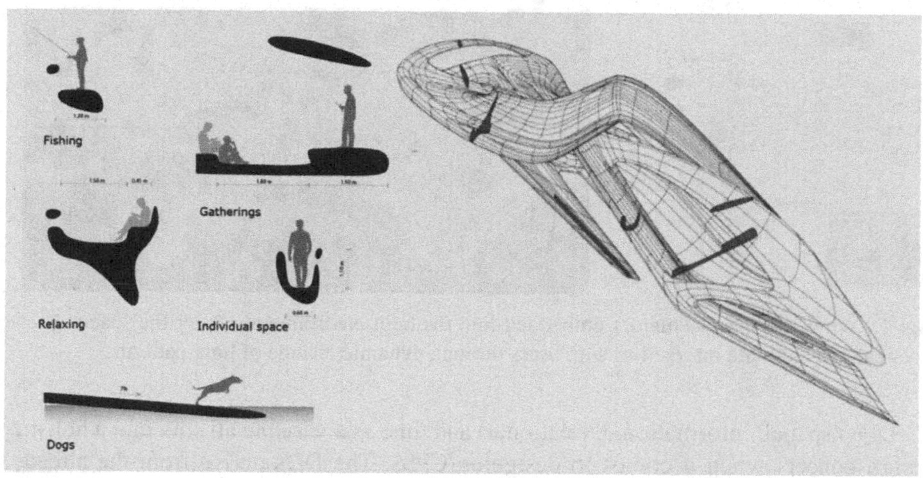

Fig. 6. Planning for probable social activities in relation to spatial qualities and functional requirements.

becomes evident and the interlaced D2RP&O approach becomes a requirement in order to address performances from the very beginning of the process.

When designing for experiences, it is to consider the traversing of the different DDs by identifying DD-specific tools and approaches that are used for modelling, simulating, and prototyping the three architectures. All are contributing to achieving continuous and cohesive Ambient UX across devices, time, and space.

3 Conclusion

This paper presented and discussed Ambient UX design approaches implemented in D2RP&O processes by analysing various case studies implemented at the Robotic Building Lab, TU Delft. All case studies involved the design of physical environments that are incorporating sensor-actuators, hence the DDs for Ambient UX were identified as concerning (1) physical environment and/or artefact (2) information flows and processing, as well as (3) social relations. DDs were discussed with respect to mapping activities through constraints and enablers and designing with time as a variable. The challenges to integrate the design of interactions with the design of physical environments were addressed by establishing feedback loops between D2RP and D2RO. The integration of the two relies on the understanding that the physical environment consists of building components that are cyber-physical in nature (Fig. 7) and their design is informed by structural, functional, environmental, and operational considerations [14, 17].

Architecture as cyber-physical system (CPS) is understood as a network of interacting elements with cyber/physical input and output. Presented studies showcased embedded wireless sensor-actuators that facilitate interaction with users through dynamic change of light patterns (Figs. 4, 5, 6 and 7). By embedding all cyber-physical requirements from the onset of the design process and by traversing the different DDs a continuous and cohesive Ambient UX across devices, time, and space is achieved.

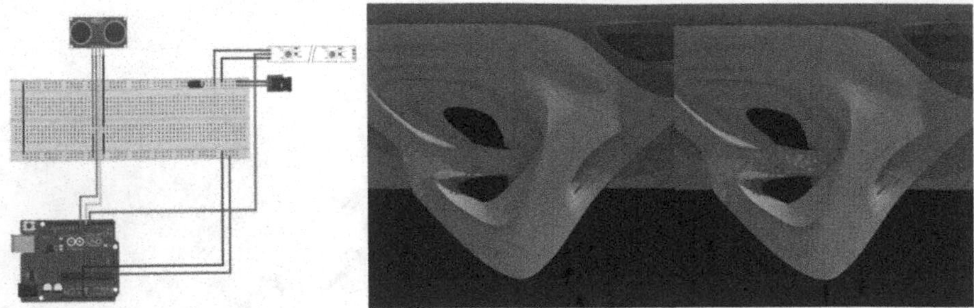

Fig. 7. Wireless sensor-actuators embedded into the built environment render the space cyber-physical and facilitate interaction with users through dynamic change of light patterns.

DDs (spatial, informational, relational) and time as a variable all sink into a holistic design concept when it comes to designing CPSs. The DDs derive from the already established fields, and thus, they are recognizable within design practices; they have different traditions regarding design methods and history of development, as some of them, like spatial architecture, are known and practiced for much longer time period than informational architecture, for example. The element that connects all DDs is the variable of time, which provides a backbone for planning and designing for human activities and interactions. DDs intertwine around the element of time and allow for planning and designing of touchpoints on various levels. Furthermore, as the DDs are known in design practices in terms of the final outcome of the concept and project development, design tools used in the practices are also quite known. The already known tools, being proven as efficient for their peculiar practice, can be used as a starting point for reasoning on a toolkit or a unique tool platform for designing cyber-physical systems.

The next steps in the development of Ambient UX within D2RP&O involves Artificial Intelligence (AI). Even though AI has been developed for several decades now [18], only in recent years it has started to emerge as a significant technology having a large impact in diverse application fields, where the question is not anymore if it will be implemented across industries including architecture and building construction but rather how it should be adopted efficiently [19, 20]. Future research would, thus, target novel design materials, processes and tools in order to establish a blueprint for designers and practitioners in the field. Emerging design approaches need to be discussed as levels of trust, intelligence, automated assistance, and others. The goal will be to provide tangible solutions for how to design interactions that foster trust, when and why to employ non-human-like embodiments of intelligence, how and why might AI resonate empathic responses, and similar.

Acknowledgements. This paper has contributed from the input of IEX researchers and RB tutors, researchers, and students involved in the presented projects.

References

1. Dalton, N.S., Schnädelbach, H., Wiberg, M., Varoudis, T. (eds.): Architecture and Interaction. HIS. Springer, Cham (2016). https://doi.org/10.1007/978-3-319-30028-3

2. Kalbach, J.: Mapping Experiences: A Complete Guide to Creating Value Through Journeys, Blueprints, and Diagrams. O'Reilly Media Inc., Sebastopol (2016)
3. Pavlovic, M., Colombo, S., Lim, Y., Casalegno, F.: Designing for ambient UX: case study of a dynamic lighting system for a work space. In: Proceedings of the 2018 ACM International Conference on Interactive Surfaces and Spaces, pp. 351–356. ACM, New York (2018)
4. Pavlovic, M.: Designing for ambient UX: design framework for managing user experience within cyber-physical systems (Unpublished doctoral dissertation). Politecnico di Milano, Milan, Italy (2020)
5. Norman, D.A.: The Design of Everyday Things: Revised and Expanded Edition. Basic Books, New York (2013)
6. Hassenzahl, M.: Experience Design: Technology for All the Right Reasons. Synthesis Lectures on Human-Centered Informatics, vol. 3, no. 1, pp. 1–95. Morgan & Claypool, San Rafael (2010)
7. Hassenzahl, M., Eckoldt, K., Diefenbach, S., Laschke, M., Len, E., Kim, J.: Designing moments of meaning and pleasure. Experience design and happiness. Int. J. Des. **7**(3), 21–31 (2013)
8. Forlizzi, J., Ford, S.: The building blocks of experience: an early framework for interaction designers. In: Proceedings of the 3rd Conference on Designing Interactive Systems: Processes, Practices, Methods, and Techniques, pp. 419–423. ACM (2000)
9. Carvalho, L., Goodyear, P.: Design, learning networks and service innovation. Des. Stud. (2017). https://doi.org/10.1016/j.destud.2017.09.003
10. Benyon, D.: Spaces of Interaction, Places for Experience. Morgan & Claypool, San Rafael (2014)
11. Levin, M.: Designing Multi-device Experiences: An Ecosystem Approach to User Experiences across Devices. O'Reilly Media, Sebastopol (2014)
12. Bier, H., et al.: Design-to-Robotic-Production and -Operation (D2RP&O) for Interactive Urban Furniture (2017). http://uf.roboticbuilding.eu/. Accessed 29 Jan 2020
13. Gropius, W.: The New Architecture and the Bauhaus, vol. 21. MIT Press, Cambridge (1965)
14. Bier, H., Liu Cheng, A., Mostafavi, S., Anton, A., Bodea, S.: Robotic building as integration of design-to-robotic-production and -operation. In: Bier, H. (ed.) Robotic Building. SSAE, pp. 97–120. Springer, Cham (2018). https://doi.org/10.1007/978-3-319-70866-9_5
15. Rosenfeld, L., Morville, P.: Information Architecture for the World Wide Web. O'Reilly Media Inc., Sebastopol (2002)
16. Lichaw, D.: The User's Journey: Storymapping Products That People Love. Rosenfeld Media, New York (2016)
17. Bier, H.H., Mostafavi, S.: Robotic building as physically built robotic environments and robotically supported building processes. In: Dalton, N.S., Schnädelbach, H., Wiberg, M., Varoudis, T. (eds.) Architecture and Interaction. HIS, pp. 253–271. Springer, Cham (2016). https://doi.org/10.1007/978-3-319-30028-3_12
18. McCorduck, P., Minsky, M., Selfridge, O.G., Simon, H.A.: History of artificial intelligence. In: IJCAI, pp. 951–954 (1977)
19. Brown, S.: What business leaders need to know about artificial intelligence (2019). https://mitsloan.mit.edu/ideas-made-to-matter/what-business-leaders-need-to-know-about-artificial-intelligence. Accessed 29 Jan 2020
20. Ghosh, B., Daugherty, P.R., Wilson, H.J., Burden, A.: Taking a Systems Approach to Adopting AI (2019). https://hbr.org/2019/05/taking-a-systems-approach-to-adopting-a. Accessed 29 Jan 2020

Textile Designer Perspective on Haptic Interface Design: A Sensorial Platform for Conversation Between Discipline

Riikka Townsend[1(✉)], Anne Louise Bang[2], and Jussi Mikkonen[3]

[1] Aalto University, 02150 Espoo, Finland
riikka@townsend.fi
[2] VIA University College, 7400 Horsens, Denmark
anlb@via.dk
[3] University of Southern Denmark, 6000 Odense, Denmark
jumi@sdu.dk

Abstract. Smart textiles have established a foothold in different academic fields, such as in chemistry, engineering, and in human-computer interaction (HCI). Within HCI, smart textiles are present in research in many ways, for example, as context, as means, or as focus. However, interdisciplinary projects tend to leave the implications of and to textile design without notice. How can a project utilise a textile designer's skills to feed back to textile design from an interdisciplinary project? In this paper, we present a case study, where a textile designer's role extends beyond the prototype production, and we analyse the project in light of textile design. Our findings show that textile design can augment data collection and analysis. We conclude with a discussion towards inclusion of textile design in HCI.

Keywords: Smart textile design · Haptic interface · Interdisciplinary · Sensorial

1 Introduction

Textile design typically focuses on the sensorial nuances of material and surface patterns when designing textiles and textile-based products, in order to fulfil both aesthetic, sensorial and functional user requirements in relation to the intended use context. Fabrics that converge electronics and smart materials, namely smart textiles or e-textiles (Poupyrev et al. 2016; Stoppa and Chiolerio 2014), have facilitated fabrics with additional properties that are dynamic, responsive and adaptive, altering their perceivable properties. Consequently, smart textiles have the potential to broaden the experienced sensory spectrum compared to conventional textiles (e.g. Dumitrescu et al. 2018) for everyday living, which can contribute towards e.g. creating applications bridging real-life sensory experiences with digital properties (Abdur Rahman et al. 2010), or creating new forms of haptic-based interpersonal communication (e.g. Samani et al. 2012). However, as a result of textiles transforming into technological material and expanding into fields outside the textile design field, textiles tend to be treated as a technical component such as a surface,

N. Streitz and S. Konomi (Eds.): HCII 2020, LNCS 12203, pp. 110–127, 2020.
https://doi.org/10.1007/978-3-030-50344-4_9

or as a housing or casing in a larger wearable haptic system (Bianchi et al. 2016; Bianchi et al. 2014; Karrer et al. 2011; Parzer et al. 2017). In doing so, the subtle nuances to sensory expression and sensorial characteristics that a textile material can provide becomes lost or even disregarded in favour of new technology. In the overlapping research field of smart textiles, the disciplinary boundaries intertwine (Townsend et al. 2017), and "it is easy for one to jump from qualities of one discipline to another because two things may look similar, but the knowledge of underlying principles or ways of making that may not be as evident on the surface" (Weinthal 2016). Ideally, if the future wearable haptic 'device' is to become 'transparent' and its use as intrinsic to any regular worn garment (Bianchi et al. 2016), our hypothesis is that the understanding of these material sensorial nuances and how to apply this knowledge across disciplinary boundaries is central for all parties. How can a project utilise textile designers' skills to feed back to textile design from an interdisciplinary project? Thus, the design of wearable textile-based systems should include taking textile knowledge into consideration and more importantly, focus on exploiting these sensory nuances.

This paper discusses the influence of textile design and its benefits for HCI through a case study, collaborating in the development and evaluation of Shape Memory Alloy (SMA)-actuated sleeves. We use the sleeves' development and evaluation study to re-examine the design process, and discuss the outcomes through a textile design perspective in reflection with haptic interaction design. We present the overall design process in more detail, to provide insight towards a better utilisation of a textile designers skill-set in future projects. Finally, we include a post-analysis inquiry towards improving the data visualisations to better suit textile designer's utilisation in future projects.

The process presented in this paper is not intended to portray a stereotypical (smart) textile design process, as that does not exist today. Instead, the process underscores the role of the smart textile designer in a state of evolution, and the reciprocal knowledge transfer between two disciplines, textile design and design-engineering. Furthermore, our process highlights how having a textile designer as a core team member in a design team developing smart textiles creates mutual benefits that are relevant to all designers' and researchers' perspectives. This paper calls out to engage and include textile design into future research activities situated in HCI. Rather than using textiles as ready-made material that is merely used as a platform or attaching or encasing haptic technology, we encourage to explore an alternative path, in which technical and design features can co-exist to foster novel research outcomes.

2 Related Work

We first look at the interdisciplinary nature of smart textiles. Our literature search focused on design processes or approaches that use smart textiles either as is, or as material for creating wearables. We also looked at projects that focus or mention haptics, or use smart textiles as sensors. Even though our case-study is not utilising a sensor, we raise these examples to signify the utilisation of smart textiles in the HCI-research.

2.1 Smart Textiles

Smart textiles as a focus of research has grown rapidly in the last decade (Shi et al. 2019). While the approaches towards smart textile research have been described to be relevant to several fields (Castano and Flatau 2016), the multi-and interdisciplinary nature is evident in the majority of the publications. *"Smart textiles are unique in that they require the combined experience from very different disciplines."* (Cherenack and van Pieterson 2012). A call for action towards the interdisciplinary development of smart textiles has been mentioned either directly e.g. *"To address this lack of dialogue, there is a need for mechanisms that bring the different industries closer."* (Baurley 2004), or indirectly *"Besides, with the help of processing units and big data, the textile-based motion sensing systems could even give some analysis and feedbacks about the motions, which benefits the clinical diagnosis and treatment of neurological disorders, such as Parkinson's disease, muscle rigidity and stroke."* (Shi et al. 2019).

There seems to be a division between the textile-design focused smart textile research, such as e.g. (Dumitrescu et al. 2014; Li et al. 2014; Persson 2013) and the HCI-focused research such as e.g. (Parzer et al. 2017; Yoon et al. 2014). Curiously, there have been signs of omissions towards textile design in projects that focus on engineered textile-integration, such as e.g. (Mehmann et al. 2015; Varga and Tröster 2014). This can also be seen in the extensive surveys on smart textiles (Shi et al. 2019; Weng et al. 2016). The review-papers on smart textiles (Castano and Flatau 2016; Cherenack and van Pieterson 2012; Shi et al. 2019; Weng et al. 2016) generally tend to avoid publications that originate from textile-design, unless they are a part of a 'scientific' field, such as e.g. in (Shi et al. 2019), references 176g (Karttunen et al. 2017) and 258a (Mikkonen and Pouta 2015).

2.2 The Role of Textile Design in the Smart Textile Design Process

Recent years have shown an increased capacity building in the design community specifically addressing the field of smart textile design (e.g. (Kettley et al. 2015), (Pailes-Friedman 2016) and (Guler et al. 2016)). As a consequence, also interdisciplinary projects, where the textile designer's role has been more emphasised with respect to HCI have been conducted. These projects focus on making textile design accessible (Devendorf and Di Lauro 2019; Poupyrev et al. 2016; Kim et al. 2019), or describe specific projects that create wearables (Brueckner and Freire 2018; Fransén Waldhör et al. 2017; Heller et al. 2014; Skach et al. 2018), or describe design processes or methods primarily with an artistic textile design lens (Joseph et al. 2017; Nilsson 2015; Persson 2013; Winters 2016). Of these, (Heller et al. 2014) make a distinction between the examples from 'DIY crafting community' and 'scientifically validated' outcomes - only methodically produced numerical values validate the research outcome as science.

Due to the nature of technical HCI-research on interactions or limiting the use to specific situations, smart textiles-as-sensors tend to be presented as an interface with the electronics as a separate platform, isolating the textile as the primary research element: (Gioberto et al. 2014; Hamdan et al. 2016; Leong et al. 2016; Parzer et al. 2018, 2017; Singh et al. 2015; Yoon et al. 2014). Due to this separation, the textile tends to be distanced from the electronics, and as expected, primarily focusing on the capacity of the smart textile as a sensor. This approach implies the smart textile sensor to be a component that could be integrated as part of a system, while the textile design ends at a prototype. Thus, there's no indication of there being any reflection to the actual smart textile process, nor how these are communicated towards textile design.

Regardless of the use, smart textiles within HCI have haptic qualities, as they are being interacted with in some way (Baurley 2004; Bianchi et al. 2016, 2014; Brueckner and Freire 2018; Fransén Waldhör et al. 2017; Greinke et al. 2016; Hildebrandt et al. 2015; Holleis et al. 2008; Joseph et al. 2017; Leong et al. 2016; Schelle et al. 2015; Skach et al. 2018). They can be a natural or an artificial part of a wearable system (Fransén Waldhör et al. 2017; Greinke et al. 2016). However, we point out two papers having the typical test-approach where a separate test-apparatus is constructed to focus on the properties of the textile: this approach is nonsensical for the textile designer. The textile is distanced from the typical textile context by introducing elements that are conventionally not present with textiles, in this case the bulky mechanism for moving the haptic textile (Bianchi et al. 2016, 2014). How can this information be useful for the smart textile design process? If the textile qualities are evaluated in a way that is distant to the textiles as worn items, how can they inform the textile design process on textile qualities?

3 Case Study 'SMA-Sleeve'

This case study involves the development of the actuator knit revolving around three knitted sleeves, with SMA inlaid into the structure. The sleeves were designed with different surface shape-change properties, stimulating the skin with heat and tactile effects. The textile-structural development was employed with textile design methodology, and the overall process was guided by the goal of user-testing towards a garment situated in HCI. The process ended in post-analysis inquiry, making new textile design-relevant analytics.

3.1 The Development of the Actuator Knit

Knit Location on the Body. When designing new textiles, it is customary to create fabric samples, which undergo several iterative cycles of evaluation before producing larger pieces. We started by creating a section of a garment in order to verify a knit structure that would work with a pattern of SMA. To select the body location and the section of a garment for evaluating the actuator knit, we found several studies supporting the placement of the knit onto the forearm. The forearm has been used as an interactive surface (Harrison et al. 2012; Ogata et al. 2013), that not only has good overall detection rates for both static and mobile conditions (Wilson et al. 2011), but thermal perception (Song et al. 2015) can be attenuated when thermal stimulation is accompanied by dynamic tactile stimulation (Green 2009). Similarly, the forearm has also been seen as a preferable location for skin- input (Weigel et al. 2014), and demonstrated as having significant touch acceptance (Abdur Rahman et al. 2010), while having a personal character (Suvilehto et al. 2015). A sleeve, on the other hand, offers an interesting section of a garment, as canvas for fashion (Bloomfield 2014; Heimann 2012; *Shout Out To Statement Sleeves | Lola May Blog*) and for inserting added interactivity and functionality, *i.e.* a metaphorical storage for digital content (Olberding et al. 2013), and for sensing and receiving different types of sensory stimuli (Baurley 2005; Randell et al. 2005).

The Development of the Textile Structure and the Inlaid Shape Memory Alloy. The textile design process grew from the conceptual idea of 'revealing-concealing', to explore the interplay between material, fabric interstices and holes, directing the design towards a lace-like structure.

The development of the knit followed an iterative process from 'sketching' hand-crocheted explorations for an interconnected chain-like structure. The textile's dimensional movement without added actuation (Fig. 1a) was first ascertained through human-material interaction, then explored with inlaid SMA wire, and documented with a video camera. A hand-operated knitting machine, Silver Reed SK 860, was used for establishing a knit structure with similar movement to the sketch, shown in Fig. 1b, before exploration for fabrication using Stoll CMS 340 TC industrial knitting machine (Fig. 1c). During this stage, 15 different knit structures were developed and evaluated, to obtain a single knit pattern - a basis for evaluating the placement and reactions of different SMA inlays. An example of the SMA-induced movement is shown in Fig. 1d.

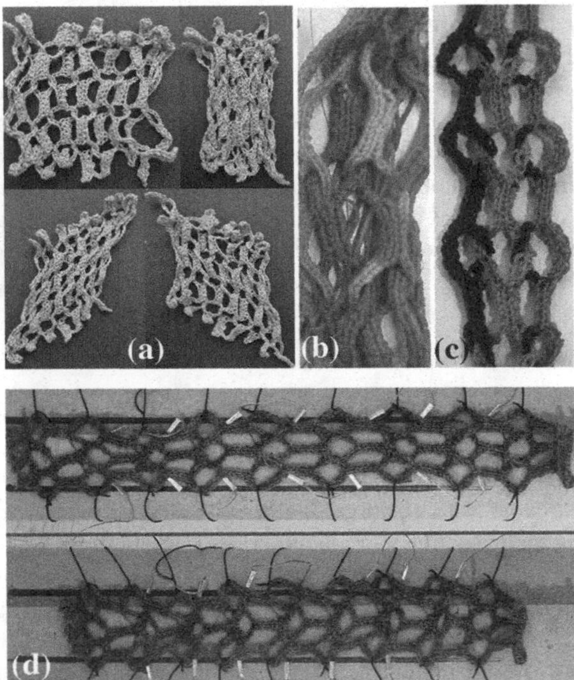

Fig. 1. Stages of the knit's structure development shown through representative samples: (a) dimensional movements of a hand-crocheted sketch without actuation, (b) the sample transformed into knit form with a hand-operated knitting machine, (c) the knit structure developed further with an industrial knitting machine, (d) evaluation of a SMA-knit sample's movement.

The power to the sleeves was controlled with a IRLML2502 n-channel MOSFETs connected to an Arduino Mega and powered by a laboratory power supply. The Arduino was programmed with fixed on-off times and delays in an automated sequence, initiated through a serial interface. The sequence for powering U- and I-sleeves was 7 s on, 10 s off (repeated twice), which enabled complete shape change and adequate time for the SMA to recover from heat.

The Final sleeves (U and I), with actuator placement overlayed in yellow, are shown in Fig. 2. U-sleeve had three separate columns of u-shaped SMA wires embedded across the rows of loops. A total of 34 metallic wire end caps were embedded into the knit structure to connect the conductive yarn to the SMA wire and to secure the SMA wire to the woollen yarn during actuation. This added rigidness to the knit structure, decreasing the sleeve's softness. In I-sleeve, SMA was threaded into a knitted tube forming an s-shaped zigzag connection that held the three individual knit pieces together, making the sleeve partly rigid and partly pliable. The SMA wires were attached to the conductive- and wool yarn with two wire end caps on the top, and two on the bottom end of the sleeve. While the overall feel of the I-sleeve was softer than U-sleeve, there was also a more distinct contrasting feel between hardness and softness across the knit surface. As T-sleeve remained without SMA, the sleeve was the softest and most pliable of all three sleeves.

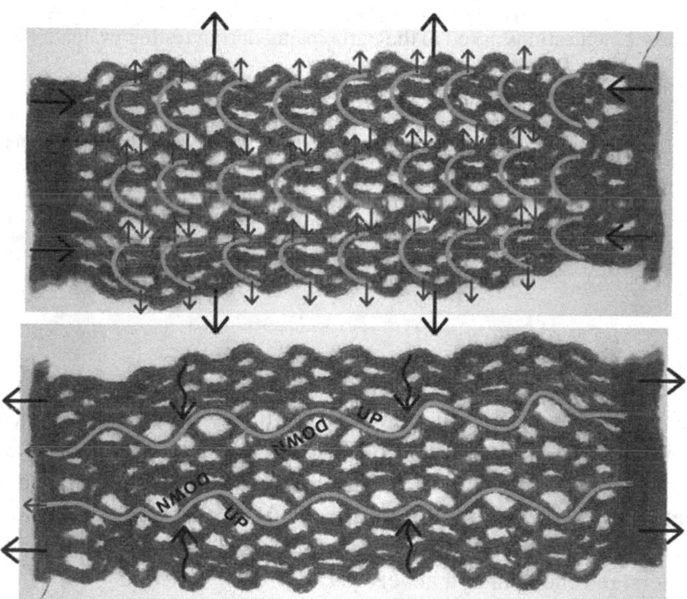

Fig. 2. The placement of SMA wire in U-sleeve (top) and I-sleeve (bottom) are overlayed in yellow, while their respective movements are represented with arrows. The red arrows indicate the movement of the SMA wire, whereas the black arrows depict the sleeve's movement. (Color figure online)

The movement of U-sleeve caused by actuation simultaneously contracts in the vertical axis (along the arm) while expanding in the horizontal axis, whereas I-sleeve expands in the vertical axis while contracting in the horizontal axis. However, due to the longer and larger freedom of movement of the SMA within the I-sleeve, and the alternating shapes of the two SMA wires, the I-sleeve moves in an uneven manner across the surface. The length of SMA wires is directly proportional to the heat produced. Heat generated by U-sleeve is greater than by the I-sleeve, at similar SMA control temperatures. The power required by the U-sleeve is roughly four times greater, 25 W, the I-sleeve actuated with 6 W. The thermal pattern follows the placement of the SMA.

3.2 Evaluation of Sleeves' Sensory Effects and Tactile Appeal for Feedback

Evaluation/Testing Procedure. We invited 3 + 12 participants with design background, for a pre-structured evaluation of the three sleeves. The first three participants were excluded from the results. Their feedback was used to validate the test. The rest were included in the final counterbalanced evaluation. The participants wore each of the three sleeves in succession, and a set of 13 questions were asked for each sleeve on a 5-point Likert scale (1 is strongly disagree and 5 is strongly agree, 3 is neutral). As the focus in this paper is on how the analysis influenced the whole process from a textile design perspective, detailed results are beyond the scope of this case study. Therefore, only questions Q1–Q5 are addressed in this paper, and are seen in Table 1.

Table 1. Questions asked to the participants during testing/evaluation.

Question number	Question
Q1/Q5	The sleeve appealed to my tactile senses (before/after)
Q2	I liked the heat effects in the sleeve
Q3	I liked the tactile effects in the sleeve
Q4	I liked the overall effects in the sleeve

The individual data based on the behavioural observation and the discussions were also analysed using affinity diagramming (Kawakita 1991; Lucero 2015). While this offered some insights, the analysis did not directly add understanding to the numerical data, and in that respect, it was unclear how the feedback could be taken to the next round of development. As a result, this prompted a different way with which to look at the numerical data: by the textile designer developing visually descriptive and relatable patterns to understand the data in a novel way.

3.3 Re-Analysing the Evaluation

Developing Analysis for Textile Design. In an effort to make sense of the data in relation to the textile design part, to draw a connection between the numeral data and the sleeves' materiality and sensoriality, a second set of analysis was developed. Focus was initially placed on the individual sleeve and the distribution of responses collectively

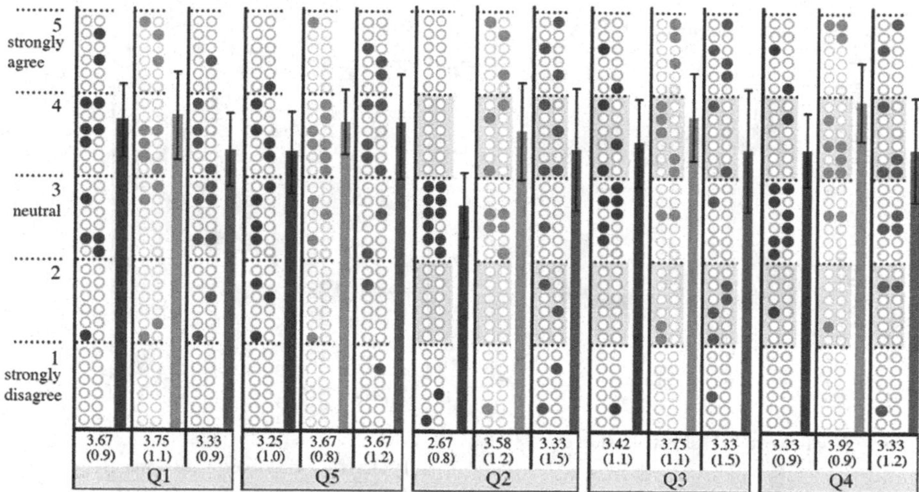

Fig. 3. All participants are represented with an empty circle and placed within the grid of each value (1-5) always in the same order. The participant's numerical response of each question is marked with a coloured circle.

for each question. The first of the textile-designer's visualisations are shown in Fig. 3, illustrated side-by-side with the bar charts.

Although this analysis provided further insight to the overall distribution of responses to each question concerning the individual sleeve, the data was still very static. While it showed clustering of the individual result, it did not show the individual change or combined influence. This prompted the textile designer to draw distribution bars, which show the results as a group, but with individual values. These are shown in Fig. 4a. This distribution can be considered to depict the sensory profile of a sleeve's individual sensory effect, or tactile appeal.

Next, the textile designer developed a "dynamic-droplets", shown in Fig. 4b (bottom) The side-by-side responses of each sleeve are grouped and accordingly colour coded. This portrays the response-relations between the actuation-based sensory effects of each sleeve, while indicating potential differences in the participant answers. The graph in Fig. 4b (top), displays how the perception of the sleeve changed per individual. Thus, the longer the difference between Q1 and Q5, longer the circle-connecting line. Overlapping circles indicate no change in response, *i.e.* represents the same value given to different questions. Additionally, each unchanged value has a pink background colour, further emphasising the pattern-nature of the results.

The Influence of New Analysis to the Results. The new patterns were useful, revealing new perspective to the textile designer. This new way of analysing the data enabled that the sleeves' influences could be seen through the visualisations shown in Fig. 4. All visualisations concerning the response to the dynamic sensory effects are summarised using the results for I-sleeve in Fig. 5., showing the same data through different representations. In the case when the calculated means and standard deviations were identical,

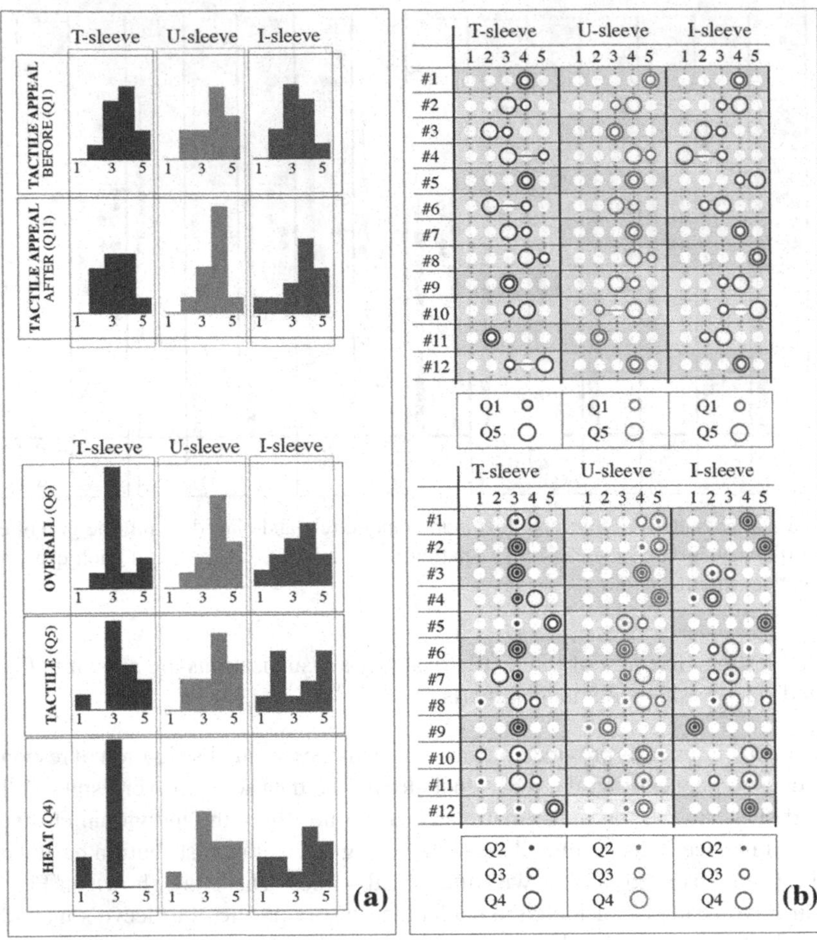

Fig. 4. The responses drawn into distributions bars (a), depicting the sensory profile of a sleeve's individual sensory effect (below) and tactile appeal before and after actuation (top). In the first form of the "dynamic droplets" (b), the representation overlays the responses on liking the respective sensory effects of each individual (bottom). In the second form (top), the smaller circles depict the participants' individual replies to Q1, thus indicating whether the sleeve appealed to the tactile senses of the participant. The larger circles, on the other hand, refer to the tactile appeal of the sleeves after experiencing the textile's dynamic behaviour and sensory effects from the actuation.

the new analysis for textile design revealed more nuances to the data. As an example, with I-sleeve, the statistical values suggested the participants response to heat and tactile effects identically, and with only a subtle difference in liking the overall effects compared to the liking as an individual sensory effect. Figure 5. revealed a clear difference in the liking of each sensory effect. Only 5/12 demonstrated liking all three sensory effects equally. In fact, the responses concerning the tactile effects had the strongest divided opinion.

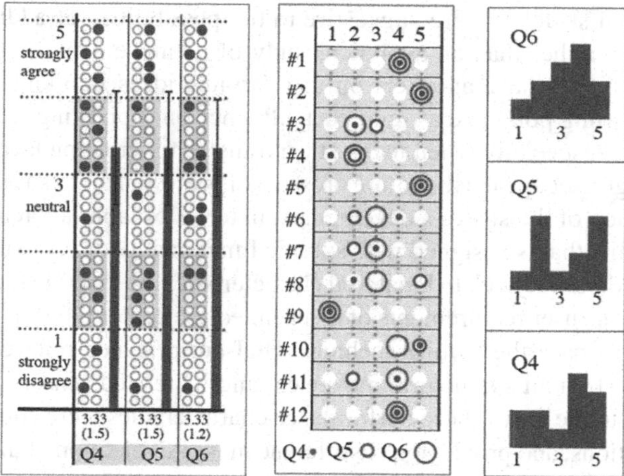

Fig. 5. Three different representations of the same data based on the participants' responses for I-sleeve.

When comparing the sleeves' initial appeal to the tactile senses after the actuation experience, T-sleeve's tactile appeal declined the most, seen both in the dynamic-droplet-representation, as well as in the distribution diagram depicting the sensory profile of a sleeve's individual sensory effect. This could hint that the lack of dynamic behaviour in regards to the two sensory modalities in T-sleeve allowed the focus to be placed more readily/easily on the actual feel of the knit in its conventional state. The visual analysis on tactile appeal of all three sleeves before actuation, revealed U-sleeve having the highest tactile appeal, which was in line with the initial analysis. Unexpectedly, the droplet-form was required for the textile designer to establish and comprehend U-sleeve's appeal. After all, it has 34 wire end caps and more SMA wire, making it the least soft and the most rigid sleeve! Equally surprising was T-sleeve not having the most tactile appeal, as it was the softest and most pliable of sleeves.

4 Discussion: The Sensorial Platform for Conversation Between Disciplines

The discussion revolves around three aspects that emerged from the interdisciplinary actions taking place in the case study. Firstly, we discuss the textile design process for an evaluative HCI process. Secondly, we discuss data visualisation creating a sensorial platform, and thirdly, insights from the visualisation.

4.1 Constructive Textile Design Process Towards an Evaluative HCI Process

The textile designer's role was central in the early development stages of the actuator knit, and even before this, as a creative catalyst. When examining the process of developing the actuator-knit sleeve from a macro-level perspective, the first stages of the design process were similar to a knitted sleeve without actuation. As the initial experiments with SMA embedded material sketches were suggestive to the possibilities of adding movement and shape change, rather than an analytical study of its movements, actuation and its related material did not have an effect on transforming ideas into knit form. Instead, the conceptual starting point had a significant influence on supporting the choice to use a knitted structure, especially when using stitch transfer for creating lace-like patterns. Also, the knit's agile set up, and the future prospect of achievable industrial manufacture, guided the direction of the sleeve's development in terms of fabrication method.

As in any textile that is designed with specific functionality or performance, the textile's utility- and durability-related material characteristics are important considerations that need to meet the user requirements of its intended use context. From a textile design perspective, in this case the textiles technical HCI-performance referred to the functionality of the SMA-knit's structural movement and its related sensory expression, as well as its safety to the user. These performance characteristics were equally important design considerations, and provided a basis for the material selection of the knit, guiding the textile's final surface and structure development process. The decision for the final structure of the design was based on three simultaneous criteria: 1) to enable subtle tactile stimulation; thus, the structure should provide a mildly uneven skin-contact surface, 2) the structure should be open allowing excessive heat dissipation to prevent burns, and 3) allow for both vertical and horizontal movement of the structure. While the choice of using wool yarn supported these three criteria, a counterbalancing influence to the fibres physical properties was, in this case, the knit structure; an open fabric structure exhibits lower thermal insulation as a result of high convective losses, as well as a lower amount of air entrapped in the structure (Kothari 2006). Also, wool's natural crimp contributes to the resilience and elasticity of the fibre (Hatch 1993), an important consideration when designing a textile structure needing to withstand mechanical stress during the knitting process, whereas an open structure also allows for movement in all directions.

However, while the actuator-knit's design process was in the hands of the textile designer, the HCI orientation of the design brief, which emphasised the development of the sleeve's active haptic qualities, caused the main focus to be placed on the actuation and less on the textile itself. Therefore, when the design process entered the stage of fine-tuning the final structural pattern of the industrially knitted sleeve to enable evaluating the movement of all SMA-configurations, some of the taken design decisions regarding material required compromising in areas that are typically at the core of textile design practice. The design decisions had become driven by technical HCI- performance.

Despite the importance of performance considerations, the choice of material and knit structure, especially when designing a worn garment, also requires considering aesthetic and sensorial material characteristics to provide a pleasing sensorial experience as a whole to its user. The neglect of the textile's appearance and feel in the design brief, most notably reflected on the choice of grey wool yarn, was in fact a compromise between performance and sensorial material characteristics. This compromise caused considerable distress to the textile designer. In a response to finding a middle ground between the HCI-orientated design brief and textile-thinking, and 'compensating' for the limited utilisation of specific material sensoriality, the textile designer shifted perspective from the macro-level of the design process to micro-level. This perspective shift to the micro-level of the design process enabled applying 'attention to detail'. In practice, this meant mitigating the effects of the macro-level compromises and making the SMA-inlay functional. As a result, focus was placed on single stitches at the edges of the knits' structural pattern, turning inwards to enable embedding SMA to the knit structure more discreetly.

Because SMA was not knitted into the structure, wire caps were used to ensure electromechanical connectivity, going against the textile aesthetics and sensorial design. As the knit structure was not a ready-made, the textile design-process was balancing between the creative textile design thinking in the micro-level and confronting technical limitations on the macro-level. Overall, the material itself was highly sensorial, and the data resulting from the first round of analysis was not. The post-analysis led us towards the sensorial platform, which we discuss in the next paragraph.

4.2 Data Visualisation Creating a Sensorial Platform

While the post-analysis inquiry increased the understanding of the collected data for the textile designer, from the new analysis also emerged the need to invent ways for making sense of the data, which allows to discuss the process of designing and evaluating the knit actuator-sleeves from both HCI and textile design perspective. Responding to this need led to uncovering the post-analysis inquiry's more profound value: Using the dots and circles to discuss new insight from the post-analysis inquiry creates a foundation through which communication can take place across the disciplinary fields of the case study. This pivotal point transcended data visualisation and transformed the dots and circles into a sensorial platform for conversation between technical HCI & textile design.

One of the challenges that we faced during the initial data analysis, was that the analysis from the Likert scales and the affinity diagram did not include the participants' experiences of materiality and sensoriality of the sleeves. Since textiles are suggested to represent a second skin (Weinthal 2016) and accordingly, can be considered as being inherently personal, the numeral data was insufficient for the further development of the sleeves. Furthermore, the numerical data was especially challenging for the textile designer, who relies directly on the human senses as a tool to design with and through material. The process of re-examining the sleeves' evaluation through visual patterns, provided what we call a sensorial platform and research space for conversation between disciplines. What this meant in practice was that the textile design-led post-analysis inquiry enabled to draw the numerical data closer to the participant's experience of the materiality and sensoriality, Thus, the sensorial platform provided means for fostering interdisciplinary knowledge.

4.3 Visualisation Insights Towards a Set of Guidelines for Textile Design in HCI

In the first form (Fig. 4b bottom), the representation overlays the result-relations between key questions on tactile and thermal feel, as an actuation effect, or an effect created by an external object. It suggests how questions focusing on these aspects are related to each other, and indicating differences in participant answers. As a provocation for further conversation between disciplinary perspectives, the result-relations of all three sleeves implicates to how the liking of 'artificial' sensory effects as an integrated part of the knit possibly differs to the more typical effects, when the sensory stimulation comes from an 'outside' source and is not a permanent part of the knit.

The second form (Fig. 4b top) displays how the overall perception of the sleeve changed per individual: represented by a small circle as before, a large circle as after, and the difference through a connected line. The line, or its absence, was seen to entail the participants' experiences of materiality and sensoriality based on the actuation of the sleeves. We suggest that it allows reflecting on the given responses of the sensory effects of active haptics, in relation to possible changes in tactile appeal; thus, placing material and actuation as equal 'partners' in the future design process.

The larger circles of T-sleeve, in Fig. 4b (top), were discussed as referring to the sleeve's tactile appeal after the knit was touched across its surface with an external object. The feedback from this question was seen connected strongly to material and indicating to the sleeve's *mediated* tactile appeal, having a point of reference to a material experience similar when worn as a regular garment.

From a material perspective, the smaller circles offered valuable insight, functioning as a point of entrance to a conversation to bring the possible tactile differences between the sleeves in their inherent or in their original state to the foreground. The importance of taking into consideration the knit's inherent tactile appeal from the collected feedback is especially relevant in wearable context, since the knit needs to fulfil the sensorial requirements of the user whether activated or not.

Besides the material sensorial characteristics, the small circles also could be seen representing a textile designer's competency to offer aesthetic, sensorial and emotional pleasure through a textile-based product to its users. This competency, (or repertoire) is built on the understanding of the interrelated, complex and hierarchical system of fibre-, yarn-, and fabric construction and finishing process, which is derived from knowledge that is both 'tacit' (e.g. Igoe 2010), 'experiential and implicit' (Bang 2009).

From the outset, a technical HCI perspective made no distinction between the three sleeves in terms of material. The smaller circles of I- and U-sleeve were seen to function as a point of reference to the possible changes shown in the larger circle, which was caused by the effect of the machine-device-system. In fact, it is the embodiment of the smaller circles that the textile designer's skills and knowledge on material sensoriality and sensibility has stronghold; a strength, which is demonstrated in the development process of the actuator knit, described in Chapter 3. From an interdisciplinary perspective, and as a meeting point between technical and designerly skills, the smaller circles, regarding Q1, represent a design space in which negotiations can take place: to negotiate between the sensorial material characteristics of the conventional textile material and the additional material relating to the actuator in relation to its technical functionality.

In this section, we used the visual representation of the data in Fig. 4b to discuss ways in which textile design can act as a value in HCI, and work across disciplines. We learned that this way of analysing the data was meaningful for the entire team since it provided all participating disciplines with a common ground. This we refer to as the 'Sensorial Platform' - and we apply it for further understanding and development of the SMA actuated sleeve. We see this as a starting point for a set of guidelines enabling textile designers and traditional HCI-professionals to benefit from a mutual relationship.

5 Conclusion

This case study was not intended as an argument for or against the design potential of SMA with wearables. Instead, this case study is intended to act as a perspective in a conversation between disciplines that use textiles for various purposes, and to entail a story of the potential sensory-aesthetic and functional diversity that can be exploited when designing a material. Although tangible and sensorial, discussing design decisions and their implications were challenging with the samples at hand. The results could not be found in them. The numerical data, on the other hand, lacked the materials sensorial aspects. The sensorial platform brought these limitations together.

Thus, this paper calls out to engage and include textile design into future research activities situated in HCI. Rather than using textiles as ready-made or a flat material that is merely used as a platform for attaching or encasing haptic technology, we encourage to explore an alternative path, in which technical and design features can co-exist as equal partners. We do this by suggesting an alternative way to analyse the data-set collected by a Likert scale. This approach led to adequate interpretations of the material, and it enabled the researchers (from different disciplines) to apply the professional skill-sets they bring in, in order to get as much knowledge as possible from the experiment.

This case study was not intended to portray a stereotypical (smart) textile design process, as that does not exist today. In this light, the role of the smart textile designer is in a state of evolution. Our case study revolved around three sleeves, and the detailed process needed for creating them. Textile characteristics affecting the feel, is an overall reflection on an interrelated and hierarchical textile system (fibre, yarn, fabric, finishing), also encompassing user related factors. Due to the diverse use of textiles, the design and production of textiles accordingly varies and is subject to adaptability, depending on its intended outcomes. This requires specific knowledge to exploit.

References

Abdur Rahman, M., Alkhaldi, A., Cha, J., El Saddik, A.: Adding haptic feature to youtube. In: Proceedings of the 18th ACM International Conference on Multimedia, pp. 1643–1646 (2010)

Baurley, S.: Interactive and experiential design in smart textile products and applications. Pers. Ubiquitous Comput. **8**(3–4), 274–281 (2004). https://doi.org/10.1007/s00779-004-0288-5

Baurley, S.: Interaction design in smart textiles clothing and applications. Wearable Electron. Photonics, 223–243 (2005)

Bianchi, M., Battaglia, E., Poggiani, M., Ciotti, S., Bicchi, A.: A wearable fabric-based display for haptic multi-cue delivery. In: 2016 IEEE Haptics Symposium (HAPTICS), pp. 277–283 (2016). https://doi.org/10.1109/HAPTICS.2016.7463190

Bianchi, M., et al.: Design and preliminary affective characterization of a novel fabric-based tactile display. In: 2014 IEEE Haptics Symposium (HAPTICS), pp. 591–596 (2014)

Bloomfield, N.: Add-On Fashion Arm Sleeves (United States Patent No. US20140115754A1) (2014)

Brauner, P., van Heek, J., Ziefle, M., Hamdan, N.A., Borchers, J.: Interactive FUrniTURE: evaluation of smart interactive textile interfaces for home environments. In: Proceedings of the 2017 ACM International Conference on Interactive Surfaces and Spaces, pp. 151–160 (2017). https://doi.org/10.1145/3132272.3134128

Brueckner, S., Freire, R.: Embodisuit: a wearable platform for embodied knowledge. In: Proceedings of the Twelfth International Conference on Tangible, Embedded, and Embodied Interaction, pp. 542–548 (2018). https://doi.org/10.1145/3173225.3173305

Castano, L.M., Flatau Alison, B.: Smart textile transducers: design, techniques, and applications. In: Hosseini, M., Makhlouf, A.S.H. (eds.) Industrial Applications for Intelligent Polymers and Coatings, pp. 121–146. Springer, Cham (2016). https://doi.org/10.1007/978-3-319-26893-4_6

Chen, A., Tan, J., Tao, X., Henry, P., Bai, Z.: Challenges in knitted e-textiles. In: Wong, W.K. (ed.) AITA 2018. AISC, vol. 849, pp. 129–135. Springer, Cham (2019). https://doi.org/10.1007/978-3-319-99695-0_16

Chen, W., Dols, S., Oetomo, S.B., Feijs, L.: Monitoring body temperature of newborn infants at neonatal intensive care units using wearable sensors. In: Proceedings of the Fifth International Conference on Body Area Networks, pp. 188–194 (2010)

Cheng, J., Amft, O., Lukowicz, P.: Active capacitive sensing: exploring a new wearable sensing modality for activity recognition. In: Floréen, P., Krüger, A., Spasojevic, M. (eds.) Pervasive 2010. LNCS, vol. 6030, pp. 319–336. Springer, Heidelberg (2010). https://doi.org/10.1007/978-3-642-12654-3_19

Cherenack, K., van Pieterson, L.: Smart textiles: challenges and opportunities. J. Appl. Phys. **112**(9), 091301 (2012). https://doi.org/10.1063/1.4742728

Dagan, E., Segura, E.M., Bertran, F.A., Flores, M., Isbister, K.: Designing 'true colors': a social wearable that affords vulnerability. In: Proceedings of 2019 CHI Conference on Human Factors in Computing Systems, CHI 2019. Scopus (2019)

Devendorf, L., Di Lauro, C.: Adapting double weaving and yarn plying techniques for smart textiles applications. In: Proceedings of the Thirteenth International Conference on Tangible, Embedded, and Embodied Interaction, pp. 77–85 (2019)

Dumitrescu, D., Nilsson, L., Worbin, L., Persson, A.: Smart textiles as raw materials for design. In: Shapeshifting Conference, Auckland, New Zealand (2014)

Foo, E.W., Pettys-Baker, R.M., Sullivan, S., Dunne, L.E.: Garment-integrated wetness sensing for leak detection. In: Proceedings of the 2017 ACM International Symposium on Wearable Computers, pp. 26–33 (2017). https://doi.org/10.1145/3123021.3123056

Fransén Waldhör, E., Vierne, P., Seidler, P., Greinke, B., Bredies, K.: E-textile production of wearable ambient notification devices. In: Proceedings of the 2017 ACM Conference Companion Publication on Designing Interactive Systems, pp. 309–312 (2017)

Gioberto, G., Min, C.-H., Compton, C., Dunne, L.E.: Lower-limb goniometry using stitched sensors: effects of manufacturing and wear variables. In: Proceedings of the 2014 ACM International Symposium on Wearable Computers, pp. 131–132 (2014)

Green, B.G.: Temperature perception on the hand during static versus dynamic contact with a surface. Attention Perception Psychophys. **71**(5), 1185–1196 (2009)

Greinke, B., et al.: Interactive workwear: smart maintenance jacket. In: Proceedings of the 2016 ACM International Joint Conference on Pervasive and Ubiquitous Computing: Adjunct, pp. 470–475 (2016). https://doi.org/10.1145/2968219.2971346

Guler, S.D., Gannon, M., Sicchio, K.: A brief history of wearables. In: Guler, S.D., Gannon, M., Sicchio, K. (eds.) Crafting Wearables: Blending Technology with Fashion, pp. 3–10. Apress (2016). https://doi.org/10.1007/978-1-4842-1808-2_1

Hamdan, N.A., Blum, J.R., Heller, F., Kosuru, R.K., Borchers, J.: Grabbing at an angle: menu selection for fabric interfaces. In: Proceedings of the 2016 ACM International Symposium on Wearable Computers, pp. 1–7 (2016). https://doi.org/10.1145/2971763.2971786

Harrison, C., Ramamurthy, S., Hudson, S.E.: On-body interaction: armed and dangerous. In: Proceedings of the Sixth International Conference on Tangible, Embedded and Embodied Interaction, pp. 69–76 (2012). https://doi.org/10.1145/2148131.2148148

Hatch, K.L.: Textile Science. West Publishing, Eagan (1993)

Heimann, B.: Sleeves for wear with sleeveless or short sleeved garment or bra with sleeves (United States Patent No. US20120324615A1) (2012)

Heller, F., Ivanov, S., Wacharamanotham, C., Borchers, J.: FabriTouch: exploring flexible touch input on textiles. In: Proceedings of the 2014 ACM International Symposium on Wearable Computers, pp. 59–62 (2014). https://doi.org/10.1145/2634317.2634345

Hildebrandt, J., Brauner, P., Ziefle, M.: Smart textiles as intuitive and ubiquitous user interfaces for smart homes. In: Zhou, J., Salvendy, G. (eds.) ITAP 2015. LNCS, vol. 9194, pp. 423–434. Springer, Cham (2015). https://doi.org/10.1007/978-3-319-20913-5_39

Holleis, P., Schmidt, A., Paasovaara, S., Puikkonen, A., Häkkilä, J.: Evaluating capacitive touch input on clothes. In: Proceedings of the 10th International Conference on Human Computer Interaction with Mobile Devices and Services, pp. 81–90 (2008)

Joseph, F., Smitheram, M., Cleveland, D., Stephen, C., Fisher, H.: Digital materiality, embodied practices and fashionable interactions in the design of soft wearable technologies. Int. J. Des. **11**(3), 7–15 (2017)

Karrer, T., Wittenhagen, M., Lichtschlag, L., Heller, F., Borchers, J.: Pinstripe: eyes-free continuous input on interactive clothing. In: Proceedings of the SIGCHI Conference on Human Factors in Computing Systems, pp. 1313–1322 (2011). https://doi.org/10.1145/1978942.1979137

Karttunen, A.J., Sarnes, L., Townsend, R., Mikkonen, J., Karppinen, M.: Flexible thermoelectric ZnO–Organic superlattices on cotton textile substrates by ALD/MLD. Adv. Electron. Mater. **3**(6), 1600459 (2017). https://doi.org/10.1002/aelm.201600459

Kawakita, J.: The Original KJ Method, p. 5. Kawakita Research Institute, Tokyo (1991)

Kettley, S., Bates, M., Kettley, R.: Reflections on the heuristic experiences of a multidisciplinary team trying to bring the PCA to participatory design (with emphasis on the IPR method). In: Adjunct Proceedings of the 2015 ACM International Joint Conference on Pervasive and Ubiquitous Computing and Proceedings of the 2015 ACM International Symposium on Wearable Computers, pp. 1105–1110 (2015). https://doi.org/10.1145/2800835.2807946

Kim, H., Tan, J., Toomey, A.: User experience and interactive textiles: a textile designer's perspective. Int. J. Des. Manag. Prof. Pract. **13**(2), 1–10 (2019)

Kothari, V.K.: Thermo-physiological comfort characteristics and blended yarn woven fabrics. IJFTR **31**(1) (2006). http://nopr.niscair.res.in/handle/123456789/24505

Leong, J., et al.: proCover: sensory augmentation of prosthetic limbs using smart textile covers. In: Proceedings of the 29th Annual Symposium on User Interface Software and Technology, pp. 335–346 (2016). https://doi.org/10.1145/2984511.2984572

Li, L., Au, W.M., Hua, T., Feng, D.: Smart textiles: a design approach for garments using conductive fabrics. Des. J. **17**(1), 137–154 (2014)

Lucero, A.: Using affinity diagrams to evaluate interactive prototypes. In: Abascal, J., Barbosa, S., Fetter, M., Gross, T., Palanque, P., Winckler, M. (eds.) INTERACT 2015. LNCS, vol. 9297, pp. 231–248. Springer, Cham (2015). https://doi.org/10.1007/978-3-319-22668-2_19

Mehmann, A., Varga, M., Gönner, K., Tröster, G.: A ball-grid-array-like electronics-to-textile pocket connector for wearable electronics. In: Proceedings of the 2015 ACM International Symposium on Wearable Computers, pp. 57–60 (2015)

Mikkonen, J., Pouta, E.: Weaving electronic circuit into two-layer fabric. In: Adjunct Proceedings of the 2015 ACM International Joint Conference on Pervasive and Ubiquitous Computing and Proceedings of the 2015 ACM International Symposium on Wearable Computers, pp. 245–248 (2015). https://doi.org/10.1145/2800835.2800936

Nilsson, L.: Textile influence: exploring the relationship between textiles and products in the design process [Doctoral thesis]. University of Borås (2015)

Norooz, L., Froehlich, J.: Exploring early designs for teaching anatomy and physiology to children using wearable e-textiles. In: Proceedings of the 12th International Conference on Interaction Design and Children, pp. 577–580 (2013)

Ogata, M., Sugiura, Y., Makino, Y., Inami, M., Imai, M.: SenSkin: adapting skin as a soft interface. In: Proceedings of the 26th Annual ACM Symposium on User Interface Software and Technology, pp. 539–544 (2013). https://doi.org/10.1145/2501988.2502039

Olberding, S., Yeo, K.P., Nanayakkara, S., Steimle, J.: AugmentedForearm: exploring the design space of a display-enhanced forearm. In: Proceedings of the 4th Augmented Human International Conference, pp. 9–12 (2013). https://doi.org/10.1145/2459236.2459239

Pailes-Friedman, R.: Smart Textiles for Designers: Inventing the Future of Fabrics. Laurence King Publishing, London (2016). https://books.google.fi/books?id=I0XvsgEACAAJ

Pailes-Friedman, R., et al.: Electronic-textile system for the evaluation of wearable technology. In: Proceedings of the 2014 ACM International Symposium on Wearable Computers: Adjunct Program, pp. 201–207 (2014). https://doi.org/10.1145/2641248.2641355

Parzer, P., et al.: RESi: a highly flexible, pressure-sensitive, imperceptible textile interface based on resistive yarns. In: Proceedings of the 31st Annual ACM Symposium on User Interface Software and Technology, pp. 745–756 (2018)

Parzer, P., Sharma, A., Vogl, A., Steimle, J., Olwal, A., Haller, M.: SmartSleeve: real-time sensing of surface and deformation gestures on flexible, interactive textiles, using a hybrid gesture detection pipeline. In: Proceedings of the 30th Annual ACM Symposium on User Interface Software and Technology, pp. 565–577 (2017). https://doi.org/10.1145/3126594.3126652

Persson, A.: Exploring textiles as materials for interaction design. University of Borås (2013)

Persson, N.-K., Martinez, J.G., Zhong, Y., Maziz, A., Jager, E.W.H.: Actuating textiles: next generation of smart textiles. Adv. Mater. Technol. **3**(10), 1700397 (2018). https://doi.org/10.1002/admt.201700397

Poupyrev, I., Gong, N.-W., Fukuhara, S., Karagozler, M. E., Schwesig, C., Robinson, K.E.: Project jacquard: interactive digital textiles at scale. In: Proceedings of the 2016 CHI Conference on Human Factors in Computing Systems, pp. 4216–4227 (2016)

Randell, C., Andersen, I., Moore, H., Baurley, S.: Sensor sleeve: sensing affective gestures. In: Ninth International Symposium on Wearable Computers–Workshop on On-Body Sensing, pp. 117–123 (2005)

Samani, H.A., Parsani, R., Rodriguez, L.T., Saadatian, E., Dissanayake, K.H., Cheok, A.D.: Kissenger: design of a kiss transmission device. In: Proceedings of the Designing Interactive Systems Conference, pp. 48–57 (2012). https://doi.org/10.1145/2317956.2317965

Schelle, K.J., Gomez Naranjo, C., ten Bhömer, M., Tomico, O., Wensveen, S.: Tactile dialogues: personalization of vibrotactile behaviour to trigger interpersonal communication. In: Proceedings of the Ninth International Conference on Tangible, Embedded, and Embodied Interaction, pp. 637–642 (2015). https://doi.org/10.1145/2677199.2687894

Shi, J., et al.: Smart textile-integrated microelectronic systems for wearable applications. Adv. Mater. **32**, 1901958 (2019). https://doi.org/10.1002/adma.201901958

Shout Out To Statement Sleeves | Lola May Blog. (n.d.). Accessed 15 Oct 2018. http://www.lolamay.com/blog/2017/03/22/shout-out-to-statement-sleeves/

Singh, G., Nelson, A., Robucci, R., Patel, C., Banerjee, N.: Inviz: Low-power personalized gesture recognition using wearable textile capacitive sensor arrays. In: 2015 IEEE International Conference on Pervasive Computing and Communications (PerCom), pp. 198–206 (2015)

Skach, S., Xambó, A., Turchet, L., Stolfi, A., Stewart, R., Barthet, M.: Embodied interactions with e-textiles and the internet of sounds for performing arts. In: Proceedings of the Twelfth International Conference on Tangible, Embedded, and Embodied Interaction, pp. 80–87 (2018)

Song, S., Noh, G., Yoo, J., Oakley, I., Cho, J., Bianchi, A.: Hot & tight: exploring thermo and squeeze cues recognition on wrist wearables. In: Proceedings of the 2015 ACM International Symposium on Wearable Computers, pp. 39–42 (2015)

Suvilehto, J.T., Glerean, E., Dunbar, R.I.M., Hari, R., Nummenmaa, L.: Topography of social touching depends on emotional bonds between humans. Proc. Natl. Acad. Sci. **112**(45), 13811–13816 (2015). https://doi.org/10.1073/pnas.1519231112

Townsend, R., Karttunen, A.J., Karppinen, M., Mikkonen, J.: The cross-section of a multidisciplinary project in view of smart textile design practice. J. Text. Des. Res. Pract. **5**(2), 175–207 (2017). https://doi.org/10.1080/20511787.2018.1449076

Vallett, R., et al.: Digital fabrication of textiles: an analysis of electrical networks in 3D knitted functional fabrics. In: George, T., Dutta, A.K., Islam, M.S. (eds.) Proceedings of SPIE 10194, Micro- and Nanotechnology Sensors, Systems, and Applications IX, p. 1019406 (2017)

Varga, M., Tröster, G.: Designing an interface between the textile and electronics using e-textile composites. In: Proceedings of the 2014 ACM International Symposium on Wearable Computers: Adjunct Program, pp. 255–260 (2014). https://doi.org/10.1145/2641248.2666717

Weigel, M., Mehta, V., Steimle, J.: More than touch: understanding how people use skin as an input surface for mobile computing. In: Proceedings of the SIGCHI Conference on Human Factors in Computing Systems, 179–188 (2014). https://doi.org/10.1145/2556288.2557239

Weinthal, L.: Tailoring second and third skins. In: Schneiderman, D., Griffith Winton, A. (eds.) Textile Technology and Design: From Interior Space to Outer Space, 1st ed., pp. 45–55. Bloomsbury Academic, Oxford (2016)

Weng, W., Chen, P., He, S., Sun, X., Peng, H.: Smart electronic textiles. Angewandte Chemie Int. Ed. **55**(21), 6140–6169 (2016). https://doi.org/10.1002/anie.201507333

Wilson, G., Halvey, M., Brewster, S.A., Hughes, S.A.: Some like it hot: thermal feedback for mobile devices. In: Proceedings of the SIGCHI Conference on Human Factors in Computing Systems, pp. 2555–2564 (2011). https://doi.org/10.1145/1978942.1979316

Winters, A.: Building a soft machine: new modes of expressive surfaces. In: Marcus, A. (ed.) DUXU 2016. LNCS, vol. 9748, pp. 401–413. Springer, Cham (2016). https://doi.org/10.1007/978-3-319-40406-6_39

Yoon, S.H., Huo, K., Ramani, K.: Plex: finger-worn textile sensor for mobile interaction during activities. In: Proceedings of the 2014 ACM International Joint Conference on Pervasive and Ubiquitous Computing: Adjunct Publication, pp. 191–194 (2014). https://doi.org/10.1145/2638728.2638746

Designing for Implicit and Positive Interactions - Artificial Intelligence and the Internet of Things in Support of Car Drivers

Mikael Wiberg(✉)

Department of Informatics, Umeå University, Umeå, Sweden
mikael.wiberg@umu.se

Abstract. How can AI (Artificial Intelligence) and IoT (Internet of Things) technologies be combined to support positive interactions in ambient spaces? This was our overarching research question. In addressing this question, we worked in close collaboration with an IT-company and explored one IoT-based design and one AI-based design, and we examined ways of integrating the two designs in an interactive system for the particular use context of a parking lot for cars. In this use context we explored the design of an interactive system that would enable car drivers to easily find an available parking lot, while staying focused on driving rather than being focused on traditional man-machine interaction. With this model in mind we designed two prototype systems based on the idea of "implicit interaction", and we considered how the use of AI (computer vision) and IoT (connected sensors) would enable a reliable solution that would allow the system to "see" available parking lots, and recommend these to the car driver – implicitly and automatically. In this paper we present our work on these two prototypes and our ideas on how to combine AI and IoT in this design. We also report from a preliminary user in order to answer a fundamental question here, i.e. – *"How can we develop interaction models for such ambient spaces that adds to the quality of life for its users and inhabitants?"*. We conclude this paper with our design recommendations for how to design for positive interactions by relying on implicit interaction models and the combination of AI and IoT technologies.

Keywords: AI · Artificial intelligence · Ambient interaction · Ambient spaces · Design models · Implicit interaction · IoT · Internet of Things · Positive interactions

1 Introduction

With the advent of IoT (Internet of Things) and AI (Artificial Intelligence) the basic interaction models for human-computer interaction are fundamentally challenged and in need for development. As we move towards IoT solutions we will not only interact with representations, but also with things (physical objects). Further, and with the adoption of AI technologies we will leave simple turn-taking models for interaction behind in favor of systems that track and adjust its services based on our interactions.

N. Streitz and S. Konomi (Eds.): HCII 2020, LNCS 12203, pp. 128–137, 2020.
https://doi.org/10.1007/978-3-030-50344-4_10

IoT offers tangible interaction models where we can hold, squeeze, lift and move an interactive object. If extending this to ambient spaces it means that we can interact based on our presence, location and movements within such spaces, and through the objects available in one such space. Further, and if combining this with AI technologies, we can imagine ambient spaces that offers not only interactive "things", but spaces that also track our movements and actions in such spaces, and how this collected data might be used to adjusts the space as to offer valuable information based on our actions taken.

This development towards AI and IoT also calls for the development of new interaction design models for the further design of ambient spaces. In this paper I explore this issue by presenting an empirical case where we examined one IoT-based prototype, and one AI-based prototype in an attempt to automatically offer car drivers information about available parking lots (i.e. to implicitly make this information available). Further, we considered what it would mean to combine IoT with AI in this context. As to explore the usefulness of this solution, and what could mean in practice we conducted a preliminary user study where we did follow-up interviews with a pilot group of drivers. In this study we were interested in understanding how one such 'implicit interaction' design model would improve the quality of life for the drivers/users of this interactive system.

The rest of this paper is structured as follows. Before moving towards the practical design and preliminary user study I first present two movements, including the current movements towards IoT and AI. Having described these two trends, I then discuss the combination of IoT (in particular computational and networked objects) and AI (in particular tracking and pattern recognition technologies) from the viewpoint of how the combination of physical and digital materials enable new forms of interaction. I discuss this from the viewpoint of *the materiality of interaction* (Wiberg 2018), and in particular how such configurations might enable new digital services based on an implicit interaction model. I then present the design project, the two prototype installations and the preliminary user study before concluding the paper.

2 A Movement Towards IoT – on Computing and Things

IoT - the Internet of Things - is increasingly described as the next step forward for digitalization in our society. IoT has recently been described as a driver for sustainability - including the development of smart homes and smart cities, for e-health solutions, and for learning. Further, it has been proposed as a solution for more energy efficient transportation solutions, including logistics. IoT is about connected objects, and about the design of systems that enable physical objects to have computational capabilities.

In reviewing the current initiatives taken in this area it is not an understatement to say that the current expectations are high on IoT systems to address a wide range of societal challenges (see e.g. Firner et al. 2011; Pan et al. 2013). Further, we notice initiatives taken on using IoT to address health problems (Savola et al. 2012; Garcia et al. 2017; Chishiro et al. 2017) and as an emergent opportunity for the design of smart physical/digital systems – ranging from e.g. NFC and RFID solutions for mobile payments to finger print based encryption for mobile devices.

Here it should be noted that all of these IoT solutions build on "*material interactions*" as the central interaction model, and that these solution are all dependent on the following three factors: 1) tight integration of computing and networking with physical materials and objects (Want 2015; Romano 2017), 2) alignment to people's needs (Pignotti et al. 2014), and 3) the development of methods and approaches for working across digital and physical materials in interaction design projects (Wiberg 2013; Karana et al. 2016; Garbajosa et al. 2017; Sulistyo 2013).

3 A Movement Towards AI – on the Reading of Patterns

Not only do we have the trend towards IoT, but we also have a parallel trend towards AI – Artificial Intelligence, that also comes with a set of implications for human-computer interaction.

This trend toward AI suggest that in addition to how physical objects around us will have computational capabilities (as envisioned in the IoT paradigm), we will also be able to design interactive systems were the AI system is taking care of some of the interactions (and where other parts of the interactions with the interactive system are still left to the user).

AI enable automated pattern recognition (there is actually a whole scientific ACM conference devoted to this topic, i.e. the AIPR – Artificial Intelligence and Pattern Recognition conference) and with the combination of AI technologies and computer vision it is now possible to write algorithms that can train the computer to "see" and recognize patterns in images and video streams (see e.g. Jaynes 1996), and to design systems that make decisions and take actions based on what the AI system can see.

From an interaction design perspective this is an interesting development where we can now move towards the design of interactive systems that can track physical objects, as well as monitor digital systems, and where we now have the computational power and the algorithms in place for doing advanced pattern recognition. These opportunities do of course come with a call for doing responsible AI design (Dignum 2019) as to make sure that the systems we design are ethically sound, and where individual privacy is carefully considered in the systems design.

4 Combining IoT and AI – Materiality and Material Interactions

But what if we want to combine IoT and AI technologies? Well, if we now move towards a design paradigm where we want to combinate these two strands, we should not focus solely on the technical capabilities that comes with IoT and AI, but foremost focus on the forms of interaction that one such combination could enable. Here I propose "material interactions" and "implicit interaction" as two such interaction models.

"Material interactions" is an emerging approach to interaction design that stretches across physical and digital materials and approaches to the design of interactive systems and networked products (See e.g.: Wiberg 2018; Wiberg et al. 2013a; Wiberg et al. 2012; 2013b).

Over the past few years our field as seen a growing interest in methods and approaches for thinking about interaction design through a material lens (Wiberg 2014). This includes for instance Jenkins (2015) approach to prototyping material interactions for IoT systems, material programming approaches (Vallgårda et al. 2016), ways of designing with material probes (Jung and Stolterman 2011), the work by Berzowska (2012) on approaches to programming materiality, and for instance the work by Karana et al. (2016) on craft-based approaches to the tuning of materials.

With a focus on "material interactions" we can in the use context of car drivers, cars and parking lots imaging that the main focus is on the driver's interaction with the car (i.e. the activity of "driving"). Further, and given a focus on material configurations we can think about the car and the parking lots as physical parts of the interactive system, and how IoT can enable these objects to become integrated parts of this design.

Further, and if we think about the combination of material interactions with Artificial Intelligence, we can think about "implicit interaction" as a fundamental interaction model in that we have an AI system that watches our actions (e.g. where we go with our car), and then combines that with AI-based computer vision (e.g. a system that based on our current location automatically looks for nearby available parking lots). Thus, through the explicit act of driving round, we would also get implicit interaction with the parking lots as a result of the driving. Here the implicit part of the interaction is that as a user I do not need to explicitly do a search via the system for available parking lots based on my current location. Instead, the system does this search automatically based on my actions (in this case driving the car to a particular location).

5 Supporting "Positive Interactions" – Combining AI and IoT

So how do we move from a combination of material interactions and implicit interactions towards something that creates values and positive experiences for the users?

In thinking about how to move from AI and IoT as pure technologies towards interaction design for 'positive interactions' there is a growing trend to focus on how technologies are perceived, and how these technologies work together with other (physical) materials. These efforts concern research on *the materiality of interaction* (Wiberg 2018) and how to work across the physical and the digital in the design of user experiences (See e.g.: Wiberg 2018; Wiberg et al. 2013a; Wiberg et al. 2012, Robles and Wiberg 2010, Wiberg and Robles 2010). As formulated by Wiberg et al. (2013b) this focus on materiality marks an emerging perspective that enable design across physical and digital design, and this approach has its roots in Ishii´s pioneering research on tangible interaction design (see e.g. Ishii and Ulmer 1997 and the most recent Ishii et al. 2012).

Contemporary work in this area includes e.g. Giaccardi and Karana's (2015) approach to understand material experiences, and e.g. Jenkins and Bogost's (2014) approach to prototyping material interactions for the internet of things. Further, these approaches belong to a growing strand of research in interaction design where new design approaches to the materiality of interactive systems are currently being explored – see e.g. Wiberg 2018; Wiberg et al. 2012 including aspects of the form (Jung and Stolterman 2011), and agency (Tholander et al. 2012) of interactive materials and systems, and how these systems are understood and experienced (Pignotti et al. 2014).

As we can see from this review of the existing work in this area it is all about the user experiences, and how that works on top of pure functionality (for an in-depth discussion on the relation between functionality and experience see e.g. Wiberg 2003.

So, a focus for our design project should accordingly be: 1) to address IoT and AI on a technical level, 2) to support 'implicit interaction' on an interaction model level, and 3) to aim for 'positive interactions' on a user experience level.

In the next section we describe how we worked in our practical design project with the design of two prototype systems that were built along these fundamental ideas.

6 Supporting Positive Interactions – A Case Implementation

So, what could it look like in practice if we set out to combine IoT and AI in a practical project? In this Sect. 1 present our current work on one such design project where we set out to support car drivers with a system that can automatically check if there is an available parking lot, and if so notify nearby drivers of this free parking lot.

In the following Sect. 1 present this work and our ongoing collaboration with a local IT-company in Sweden who is currently implementing these solutions.

From a practice perspective there are some commercial solutions already in place for some parking spaces that counts the cars entering the space and displays the number of available parking lots on a display, but more lightweight solutions that builds on data from the cars actually parked in each parking lot are still not available. In relation to this design challenge the IT-company we collaborate with in this project is currently exploring alternative solutions to this design problem trough a trail-and-error design approach that circles around the iterative design and evaluation of simple prototype systems that in a nearby future could combinate IoT technologies (cars and parking lots as physical objects equipped with sensors), and AI technologies (computer vision) that can watch the parking lots and look for available parking lots.

6.1 Design Exploration 1 – Supporting Car Drivers with an IoT System

The first approach we took in relation to this design challenge was to design an IoT-based solution, (see Fig. 1A, 1B and 1C) were ultrasonic sensors for object detection were used to determine if a car is parked in a particular parking lot in the parking garage in the basement of an office building (see Fig. 1A). If there is a car in the parking lot (as in Fig. 1A) the sensor detects that, and the data is transmitted via a LoRa-network (1B), to a server. Then a script sends a signal to an Arduino board to turn a lamp on in a window (Fig. 1C) so that a driver outside the building can see if the parking lot in the basement is occupied or not. Here, a combination of sensors, networks, server tech, and a traditional lamp is used for the system architecture. Accordingly, this solution demonstrates an IoT design across digital materials and physical objects (in this case the position of the car in front of the sensor in the parking lot in the basement), and how this solution offers a new digital service to the user, i.e. to meet a particular user need. However, this first approach has its limitations. It needs sensors installed for every parking lot, and it demand one representation per parking lot (in this case to turn on/off a lamp for each parking lot).

6.2 Design Exploration 2 – Supporting Car Drivers with an AI System

To overcome the design problems we acknowledged with the first prototype installation we explored an alternative solution. For this second solution we experimented with

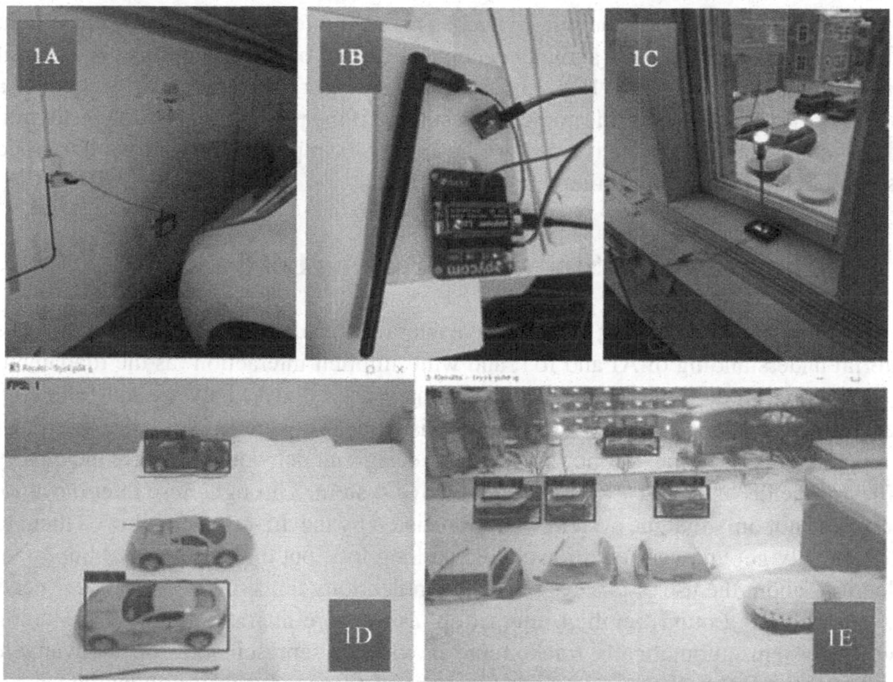

Fig. 1. Two examples of design explorations with IoT technologies (1A, 1B) and with an AI/computer vision-based solution (1D, 1E).

AI and computer vision (see Fig. 1D and 1E). By using a camera and the YOLO v2 framework for object detection we could design a solution where the camera continuously reads the whole parking lot to look for parked cars and available parking lots in this outdoor parking space. To test this design we first conducted a small-scale test with a number of toy cars (Fig. 1D) to test the YOLO framework, before going for a full-scale outdoors implementation (Fig. 1D). This small-scale design allowed for simple tests of the system by moving the toy cars around by hand, whereas the full-scale test allowed for testing the solution in different weather conditions (e.g. during a full snow fall as seen in Fig. 1E) and with actual cars as input to the system.

Similar to the first design exploration this second solution also builds on the tight integration of physical and digital materials, but it is at the same time built on top of a completely different material configuration (in this case a combination of camera tech, AI and computer vision for object detection, and the positions of the cars parked as input to the interactive system). As such this short example illustrates how different material configurations can enable a particular digital service. Further, it illustrates how different material configurations might solve a particular problem, in different ways, but also with different associated pros and cons.

As to increase the precision of the system (in this case to get more accurate notifications from the system that there is in fact an available parking lot in a particular parking space), one can also think about the combination of these two solutions, and to match the input from the sensors with computer vision. This would for instance enable the system to determine if a parking lot is actually occupied by a car, or any other object or material (for instance snow as in Fig. 1E). And, it could also work the other way around. If a sensor is covered with snow, the camera can still see if the parking lot is available or not. This is a third design alternative that we have not yet implemented, but we discussed this combination in our preliminary user study.

7 A Preliminary Pilot Study of the Parking Lot System

As to explore the usefulness of this 'positive interactions' design model built on top of a material understanding of AI and IoT, and with 'implicit interaction' as the fundamental interaction model we conducted a preliminary user study where we did follow-up interviews with a pilot group of drivers. In this study we were in particular interested in understanding how an "implicit interaction" design model would improve the quality of life for the drivers aka users of this interactive system. Through these interviews we discovered not only that the system was appreciated by the drivers, as it allowed them to automatically get an overview of available parking lots, but they also shared important reflections about the use of this system. These reflections concerned: 1) positive aspects of systems build around 'implicit interaction' as the core interaction model, including how the system automatically tracked and provided a representation of the available parking lots, and how the system made recommendations to the driver about the whereabouts of these parking lots, but also 2) critical design aspects, including reflections on how to avoid making the driver feel monitored and tracked by the system. As formulated by one of the participants in our study:

> *-"It is of course a very easy system to use.. you don't really need to do anything except driving to the parking space…but hmm, you know.. it is you know convenient, the system signals that there are free parking lots.. but although it [the system] watches the parking lots, and I don't want it to watch me… you want the service, but you don't want to be watched by the system..".*

It was a recurring topic across the interviews that "implicit interaction" in such ambient spaces where technology is deliberately designed to track objects (cars and parking lots) and users actions, and where the system take action based on this, was appreciated by the users, but also that the system needs to be transparent, and that such systems need to be designed to ensure a feeling of security, control and comfort for the user.

Further, there were concerns raised by the users in this preliminary study about the accuracy of the system, and whether or not it keeps record of not only the available parking lots, but also of who was occupying which parking lot, for how long, and if that was a privacy concern. A design recommendation here is to provide explicit information about how the system deals with these issues (a question that is highly related to designing along the ideas of responsible AI (Dignum 2019).

8 Discussion

Our two prototype installations and the follow up user study led us to some insights and further design reflections. Based on our design studies we think that it could be a fruitful approach to combine IoT and AI technologies as to increase the precision in this system. At the same time, designers that aim for higher precision should also carefully consider if a strive for higher precision also increases the privacy concerns. Clearly there's a fine balance between offering automated solutions based on what the technology can do for us on the one hand, and how that in return might led to other, and more soft issues related to how these systems watches, monitors and track our actions and whereabouts.

In addition to this, and beyond any tradeoff discussions concerning tracking opportunities vs. the monitoring of users we should also address one of the fundamental questions in this project, i.e. –*"How can we develop interaction models for ambient spaces that adds to the quality of life for its users and inhabitants?"*

In relation to this question I think that we were able to get good answers through our design work, and through the preliminary study we conducted. A metaphor for these systems could be a *"servant"*, i.e. someone who looks after your needs (in this particular use context, the need for an available parking lot), and acts in relation to an interpretation of that need (in this case the interpretation is related to entering the parking lot with the car, which the system interpret as an interest in checking if there is an available parking lot that can be used).

Further, increased quality of life might not only be about the big and fundamental questions (such as if we feel that life is meaningful, or if we consider us to be happy), but quality of life can also be related to small things, such as getting appropriate help when needed (e.g. to have a system that works as a servant that checks some information for you, as to make life slightly more comfortable). Still, what "quality of life is", and how it is related to getting help when needed, or being about managing to deal with challenging situations, and feeling good about that, is a question that goes beyond the scope of this paper. However, we did notice that the participants in our study appreciated the system, and they though that it supported them in their everyday lives.

Given these positive statements from the users we suggest that there might be a design space to further explore where the combination of IoT and AI enable the design of interactive systems that rely on 'implicit interaction' as the core interaction model, and that supports 'positive interactions' as to increase the quality of life for its users.

9 Conclusions

In this paper we have considered ways of combining IoT and AI technologies in the design of an interactive system. We have done so with a particular focus on interaction design of a digital service that would enable car drivers to easily find an available parking lot. In collaboration with a local IT-company we designed two prototype implementations of the system with an idea of "implicit interaction" in mind. Based on these two designs we then thought about the combination of AI (computer vision) and IoT (connected sensors) technologies as to enable a more reliable solution that would allow the technology to "see" available parking lots, and to recommend these for drivers.

In this paper we have also reported some initial data on how this new digital service was perceived by its users in order to answer a fundamental question here, i.e. –*"How can we develop interaction models for ambient spaces that adds to the quality of life for its users and inhabitants?"*. Here our initial observations suggest that a focus on design for 'positive interactions', through the use of implicit interaction design models might be a way forward in combining IoT and AI technologies for such purposes.

As an overarching contribution, this paper adds to the current body of research on how to design ambient spaces that takes advantage of new technologies (in this case AI and IoT) while still acknowledging how the fundamental interaction model needs to be carefully adjusted as to support and possible add to the quality of life for its users. In short, we contribute to the existing strands of research by presenting a design model for designing for positive interactions in ambient spaces.

References

Berzowska, J.: Programming materiality. In: Proceedings of the Sixth International Conference on Tangible, Embedded and Embodied Interaction, TEI 2012. ACM (2012)

Chishiro, H., Tsuchiya, Y., Chubachi, Y., Bakar, M., Silva, L.: Global PBL for environmental IoT. In: Proceedings of the 2017 International Conference on E-commerce, E-Business and E-Government, ICEEG 2017. ACM Press (2017)

Dignum, V.: Responsible Artificial Intelligence. Springer, Heidelberg (2019). https://doi.org/10.1007/978-3-030-30371-6

Firner, B., Moore, R., Howard, R., Martin, R., Zhang, Y.: Smart buildings, sensor networks, and the internet of things. In: SenSys 2011. ACM Press (2011)

Garbajosa, J., Magnusson, M., Wang, X.: Generating innovations for the internet of things: agility and speed. In: Proceedings of the XP2017 Scientific Workshops, XP 2017. ACM (2017)

Garcia, C., Fernandes, P., Davet, P., Lopes, J., Yamin, A., Geyer, C.: A proposal based on IoT for social inclusion of people with visual impairment. In: Proceedings of the 23rd Brazillian Symposium on Multimedia and the Web 2017, ACM Press (2017)

Giaccardi, E., Karana, E.: Foundations of material experiences: an approach to HCI. In: Proceedings of CHI 2015, Seoul, Republic of Korea, 18–23 April 2015, pp. 2447–2456. ACM, New York (2015)

Ishii, H., Lakatos, D., Bonanni, L., Labrune, J.B.: Radical atoms: beyond tangible bits, toward transformable materials. ACM Interact. **19**(1), 38–51 (2012)

Ishii, H., Ullmer, B.: Tangible bits: toward seamless integration of interfaces between people, atoms, and bits. In: Proceedings of CHI 1997, pp. 234–241. ACM Press (2017)

Jaynes, C.: Computer vision and artificial intelligence. ACM Crossroads **1**, 1 (1996)

Jenkins, T.: Designing the "Things" of the IoT. In: TEI 2015: Proceedings of the Ninth International Conference on Tangible, Embedded, and Embodied Interaction (2015)

Jung, H., Stolterman, E.: Form and materiality in interaction design: a new approach to HCI. In: Proceedings of CHI 2011, pp. 399–408. ACM, New York (2011)

Karana, E., Giaccardi, E., Stamhuis, N., Goossensen, J.: The tuning of materials: a designer's journey. In: DIS 2016. ACM (2016)

Pan, D., Lam, H.A., Wang, D.: Carrying my environment with me in iot-enhanced smart buildings. In: Proceeding of the 11th Annual International Conference on Mobile Systems, Applications, and Services, MobiSys 2013. ACM Press (2013)

Pignotti, E., Beran, S., Edwards, P.: What does this device do? In: Proceedings of the First International Conference on IoT in Urban Space, URB-IOT 2014. ICST (2014)

Robles, E., Wiberg, M.: Texturing the 'Material Turn' in interaction design. In: Proceedings of TEI 2011, Fifth International Conference on Tangible, Embedded, and Embodied Interaction, pp. 137–144. ACM Press, New York (2010)

Romano, B.: Managing the internet of things. In: Proceedings of the 2017 ACM SIGCSE Technical Symposium on Computer Science Education, SIGCSE 2017. ACM Press (2017)

Savola, R., Abie, H., Sihvonen, M.: Towards metrics-driven adaptive security management in e-health IoT applications. In: BodyNets 2012. ICST (2012)

Sulistyo, S.: Software development methods in the internet of things. In: Mustofa, K., Neuhold, E.J., Tjoa, A.M., Weippl, E., You, I. (eds.) ICT-EurAsia 2013. LNCS, vol. 7804, pp. 50–59. Springer, Heidelberg (2013). https://doi.org/10.1007/978-3-642-36818-9_6

Tholander, J., Normark, M., Rossitto, C.: Understanding agency in interaction design materials. In: CHI 2012. ACM (2012)

Vallgårda, A., Boer, L., Tsaknaki, V., Svanes, D.: Material programming: a new interaction design practice. In: Proceedings of DIS 2016. ACM Press, New York (2016)

Want, R.: The physical web. In: IoT-Sys 2015: Proceedings of the 2015 Workshop on IoT challenges in Mobile and Industrial Systems. ACM Press (2015)

Wiberg, C.: A measure of fun. Extending the scope of web usability. Thesis, Department of Informatics. Umeå University (2003)

Wiberg, M.: Methodology for materiality: interaction design research through a material lens. Pers. Ubiquit. Comput. **18**(3), 625–636 (2014)

Wiberg, M.: The Materiality of Interaction. MIT Press, Cambridge (2018)

Wiberg, M.: Interaction, new materials & computing: beyond the disappearing computer, towards material interactions. Mater. Des. **90**, 1200–1206 (2016)

Wiberg, M., Kaye, J., Thomas, P.: PUC theme issue: material interactions. Pers. Ubiquit. Comput. **18**, 573–576 (2013a). https://doi.org/10.1007/s00779-013-0683-x

Wiberg, M., et al.: Materiality matters – experience materials. ACM Interact. **20**(2), 54–58 (2013b)

Wiberg, M.: Methodology for Materiality: interaction design research through a material lens. Pers. Ubiquit. Comput. **18**, 625–636 (2013). https://doi.org/10.1007/s00779-013-0686-7

Wiberg, M., et al.: Material interactions – from atoms & bits to entangled practices. In: Proceedings of CHI 2012, New York, NY, USA, 2012, pp. 1147–1150 (2012)

Wiberg, M., Robles, E.: Computational compositions: aesthetics, materials, and interaction design. Int. J. Des. **4**(2), 65–76 (2010)

Mood Board Tool - An Innovation Method in Vehicle HMI Design

Qingshu Zeng[1(✉)] and Mingyue Hu[2]

[1] School of Design Art and Media, Nanjing University of Science and Technology, 200, Xiaolingwei Street, Nanjing 210094, Jiangsu, People's Republic of China
qingshuzeng@qq.com

[2] Shanghai International College of Design and Innovation, Tongji University, 1239, Siping Road, Shanghai 200092, People's Republic of China

Abstract. This paper explores conceptual design methods in the vehicle HMI design process. By adopting theory framework construction and case studies, we propose a mood board as the tool to integrate "software" and "hardware" in-vehicle HMI interaction design. The effectiveness and feasibility of this tool are supported by the industrial design undergraduate course, which is the transportation concept design. We were using the proposed mood board tool as an innovative approach assisting electric vehicle HMI design. Students of industrial design and interaction design got involved in the design process. We received positive feedback as to the effectiveness of the method with a satisfactory outcome overall.

Keywords: Mood board · Concept design tools · Vehicle HMI

1 Introduction

A growing integration has taken place between styling design and interaction design on vehicle Human Machine Interfaces (HMI) with the introduction of In-Vehicle Information Systems (IVIS) to the vehicle driving space [1–3]. However, in the current R&D process, car styling design, and interaction design are independent of each other. Both have different design methods and design tools. From the features of vehicle HMI "software" and "hardware," it is necessary to integrate both sides on the level of design methodology for the best results [4–6]. In order to address the problems, this article proposes a concept-oriented design method, the mood board tool for vehicle HMI design. The purpose is to assist car interior designers and interaction designers in the integrated design of the soft and hard interface visual style. Finally, we applied the mood board tool in the transportation design course, which aims to explore new ways of concept design from the perspective of innovation in design integration.

2 Research on Conceptual Innovation Methods and Design Tools

2.1 Car-Styling Concept Design Tools

Conceptual design is a crucial stage in determining the theme of automobile styling and clarifying the design ideas and directions of later stages. For the interior design of the

N. Streitz and S. Konomi (Eds.): HCII 2020, LNCS 12203, pp. 138–149, 2020.
https://doi.org/10.1007/978-3-030-50344-4_11

car interior, the design concept is mainly conveyed by the image information contained in shape [7]. The form is the concrete and perceptible appearance of objective things, while the imagery is a general abstract symbol. Imagery is an essential tool to assist interpersonal cognition and convey imagery and emotion. The tools of styling concept design focus on the organization and transmission of image data [8]. Designers often use visual information boards with emotional atmosphere rendering and visual image stimulation to get design inspiration [9]. The main design tools are image boards, image scale maps, scene boards, brain sketching, etc.

Image boards are collages of collected pictures, illustrations, or brand images that describe specific aesthetic, style, audience, and context aspects of design intent [10]. The image scale map is based on the semantic differential method. On the one hand, it describes the image of the research object by looking for image vocabulary related to the research purpose. On the other hand, it uses the opposite adjective pair to measure the fuzzy image of "image" from different angles. Furthermore, distribute visual material through the way of scale map [11]. The mood board is a tool that associates specific semantics with visual contexts, assists designers in interpreting image information and obtains styling language from it, to model the image. Drawing brainstorming is a derivative of the traditional brainstorming method. The designers draw their concept in sketch form and pass it to other participants to supplement or expand and iterates many times to obtain reconstruction and iteration of modeling image [12].

2.2 Interaction Design Innovation Method

Interaction design is oriented towards user behavior, and interactive design concept innovation tools can: first, analyze and understand the needs of target users; second, translate requirements into specific solutions [13]. The main design methods for user-oriented research include various, such as a persona, role-playing, cognitive mapping, and critical incident technique. Characters are used to analyze the archetypes of target users and describe and outline user behaviors, values, and needs. Role-playing is a relatively low-cost method; that is, the designer plays the role of the user to experience the user's activities and behaviors and considers the problem from the user's perspective [14]. Cognitive diagrams visualize how users understand a specific spatial problem and show the user's experience process and their views on the entire process [15]. The critical event method is to guide the description of the user experience when the user experience is excellent or poor and understand the cause of the event, user behavior, and vision through the critical event method [16].

The design tools and methods for solution transformation mainly include body-storming, affinity diagramming, card sorting, storyboard, etc. Body storm is a dynamic and empirical research method that applies brainstorm to the body. A solution that activates products and services in prototypes that simulate real-life scenarios by combining role-playing and simulation activities [17]. Affinity diagramming is based on user analysis of data analysis, marking user needs, expectations, difficulties, etc. on sticky notes. Designers analyze and cluster similar problems to generate an intuitive understanding of user needs and tasks [18]. Card classification is a user-participative concept design method. By observing the user's classification method, the designer can understand the user's understanding of the connection between different concepts [19]. A storyboard is a visual way to show user roles, purposes, situations, problems, and possible solutions through storyline organization. To sum up, it can be seen that the conceptual innovation method of interaction design is inclined to simulate and analyze the requirements, behaviors, tasks, operations, and the logical relationships behind them from the perspective of the user [20].

2.3 Vehicle HMI Design Concept Tools

Due to the separate design process of soft and hard interfaces, the design tools of vehicle HMI interfaces are mainly tools based on product design, web design, interface design, visual communication design, and human-computer interaction prototypes [21]. For vehicle HMI design itself, the most lacking is the aid of design knowledge. The most significant difference between the conceptual design tools of vehicle HMI interface and the conceptual tools of car styling and interaction design studied above section is the user, that is, software and hardware interface designers [22].

However, with the integration of software and hardware interface design objects, users of design tools will no longer be software or hardware unilateral designers, but teams or groups of software and hardware interface integration design. Therefore, at the conceptual design method level, tools that can simultaneously drive the creation of styling and interaction, designer creativity are needed [23]. For hardware interface designers, the design features, colors, materials, and process quality of the interior parts are driven by the same conceptual theme, expressing the same form image and expressing the same style language. For software interface designers, the visual interface of the system is affected by the interaction paradigm and display medium, and also related to the content, identification, and understanding of visual information display. Therefore, the visual style of software and hardware man-machine interface in the same car may present completely different characteristics. Facing the reorganization of the integration of soft and hard interface design objects and the creative design process, it is of practical significance to explore integrated graphical thinking tools.

By studying the concept of innovation tools of automobile modeling and interaction design, the mood board is considered to be a useful tool for motivating designers to get creative inspiration [24]. It not only has a useful role in visual presentation and theme rendering but also serves as a bridge to communicate the contextual dialogue between designers of soft and hard interfaces. Therefore, the following will focus on the specific problem of the visual style of the soft and hard interface and expand the research on the traditional mood board tools.

3 Mood Board Related Research

The mood board as a design tool has two main functions: one is the inspiration for a designer or design team, and another is communication, supporting both internal and external dialogue with other stakeholders. Images can be used to present designs when textual information is inadequate to get the point across [24]. The essence of the design tool is so-called framing (analog to photographic framing), expressing design intention and design information through framing in order to stimulate a specific visual inspiration, specific styles, and specific design concepts [25]. The mood board provides a medium for designers and practicing designers to respond to perceptions about the design brief.

The mood board is widely used in design teaching. In the industrial design courses, for example, students try to present the design intention of product concepts and design styling by mood board [26]. In graphic design, students express colors, emotions, and decorative styles relying on the boards. While in fashion design, students convey trends and fashion symbols with the aid of the tool [27]. In interior design, students explore space, environment, and atmosphere in different designs through it [28]. Thus, it can be seen that design objects are different though the mood board is widely used in design education. The purpose of introducing mood board into the transportation design courses is to help students from industrial design and interaction design background to establish context-dependent relationships, which allowing hardware and software design driven by the same context materials. Storyboard tools will inspire design ideas and facilitate design communication. The mood board can provide not only a unified graphical representation of the product design theme and interaction paradigm but also perform a unified visual element analysis of the product styling image and the interactive graphical interface image. Therefore, in the teaching of the vehicle HMI, mood board tools will be capable of stimulating students on the collaborative design of "soft" and "hard" interface. Indeed, there are other methods of conceptual design in HCI teaching, for example, storyboard, personas, scenario description swimlanes, etc. [29]. Generally, all of these could help designers to make precise corresponding design tasks and understand design objects to some extent from the perspective of user roles, application environment. Mood board tools, for one thing, have a certain similarity with the above tools on design communication and concept inspiration.

Vehicle HMI combines hardware design, for example, interior design, within the background of industrial design, with the design of information architecture and interactive mode within the background of computer software. This paper proposes mood board tools to integrate "hard" and "soft" interface design. The tools are later introduced in the transportation design course. Preliminary application and verification have been carried out during the design course.

4 Construction and Approach of the Mood Board Tool

4.1 Construction of the Mood Board Tool as a Framework Based on Concepts and Visuals

Donald A. Schön considers that design is action-oriented; designers work by naming the relevant factors in the situation, framing a problem in a certain way, making moves toward a solution, and evaluating those moves [30–34]. The whole design process is considered as a "reflective conversation with the situation" between designers and context materials [35].

In Schön's theory, the so-called naming the relevant factors is the basis of all design activities, and the concept and vision-based mood board is the expression of the design theme (concept) and design elements (vision) by constructing the concept board and visual board out to achieve the "name" of design-related elements.

As shown in Fig. 1, the "concept board" part refers to the visualization and expression consistency in the level of understanding of design concepts by designers from industrial design and interaction design. The "visual board" part indicates the visualization and expression inconsistency in the level of perception on form language by designers from the two aspects mentioned. The former, namely the concept board, is an induction on design concepts and significance, which is ideographic. The latter, comparatively speaking, is an induction on design forms and methods, which is figurative. Both should be considered as expressions of design "framing," as compositing in the viewfinder of a camera. Meanwhile, the concept board and the visual board serve as the bridge in communicating between designers from both sides.

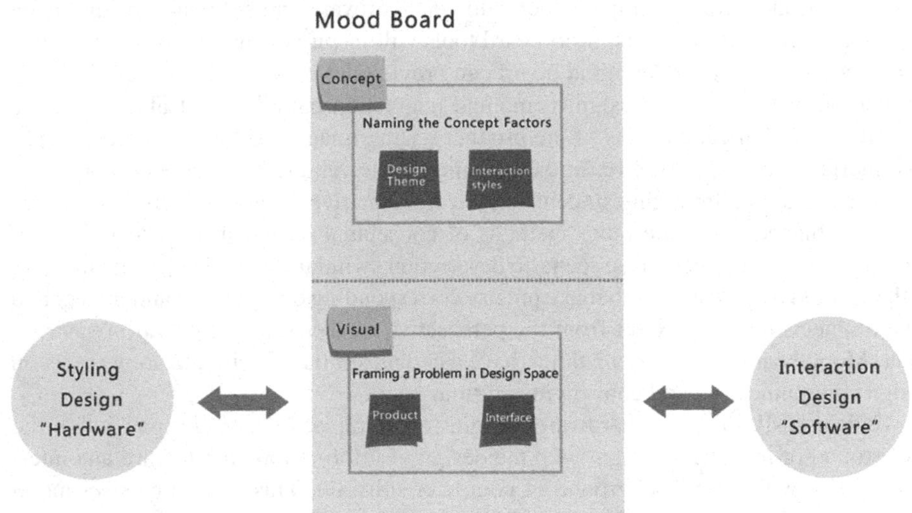

Fig. 1. The framework of the mood board with the concepts and visuals

4.2 Procedure and Approach: The Classification, Association Based on the Mood Board Framework

Based on the framework of the mood board (Fig. 1), Fig. 2 indicates the processing mode of context materials in the mood board, namely the classification, association, and design. The model proposes an operational tool to drive product and interactive design, aiming to integrate hardware and software design in-vehicle HMI R&D.

Step 1: Classification of context materials refers to visualizing the named concepts through pictures based on the design theme, style, intentions, interaction, and interactive technology. Its significance lies in the integration of mutually independent design themes from product design and interaction design into the same conceptual context framework, forming a concept system supporting product and interaction design. Relying on personal intuition and experience, industrial and interaction designers search and accumulate material before classifying through labeling, acquiring, and expressing the design theme and concept of the interface software and hardware, constructing the overall design atmosphere and tone.

Step 2: Association of context materials refers to the refinement and screening of mood materials, forming a systematical design expression.

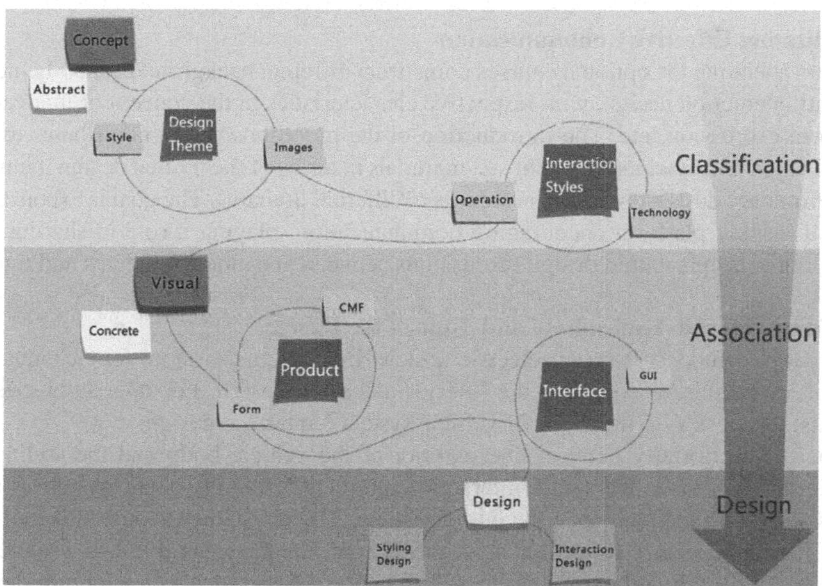

Fig. 2. The classification, association based on the mood board

The students(designers) associates labels based on screening related materials from both perspectives of products and interfaces that reflect visual imagery. The associated labels belong to forms, CMF, and GUI. "Design Framing" is acquired in the visual space through the material clusters. Its significance lies in the integration of mutually dependent visual images from product design and interaction design into the same visual context framework, enabling good communications between industrial and interactive students(designers) in the context of interrelated context, and further, driving the HMI on both software and hardware aspects.

5 Interface Design Practice of Electric Vehicle HMI

In order to verify the above theoretical framework, we used a mood board tool that integrates concepts and vision in the transportation design course to assist students in conceptual design process. In the design practice of this case, the application of the mood board includes two steps: first, the construction of the concept board based on the concept and vision; second, the visual design of the interactive interface based on the scenario board.

This course emphasizes design practices based on theoretical research, the task being to design both car interior styling and interactive interfaces for 2025 electric vehicles.

Participants of industrial design and interaction design use the tool to assist electric vehicle HMI design, obtaining a relatively satisfactory outcome.

5.1 Advantages of Mood Board Tool in Design Education

1 Facilitating Effective Communication
Students attending the optional courses come from different backgrounds, mainly industrial and interaction design, with respective characteristics in the concept of innovation and form expression, etc. The introduction of the mood board tool contributes to the classification and association of chosen materials in terms of the unified design theme in the preliminary design process for students in different domains. The goal is to construct a visual display platform encouraging communication, playing a role in sharing and conveying concepts within design discussions between and among students and tutors.

2 Building Overall Atmosphere and Tone of the Design
In this course, students start with electric vehicle HMI design. Missions for the industrial domain are mainly to complete the interior and parts design. For interaction design students, the work is to finish the in-vehicle system's interface design.

There is uniformity between the exterior of the vehicle body and the styling of the interior. Moreover, the visual interaction interface of the in-vehicle system is also inconsistent with the styling of the entire vehicle. Therefore, the mood board tool can be used as a benchmark for design style throughout. Students can use it as a reference when designing soft and hard interfaces. Teachers can also use it as a guide for design style when guiding students with solutions.

5.2 Mood Board Tool Application in Vehicle HMI Design Course

When the course kicks off, all the participants were divided into four groups, and the students from both domains should be included in each group. In the following passage, one group is selected to demonstrate the application process in the paper.

Step 1. The Construction of the Mood Board Tool
The design theme proposed by this group of students is "at sense of technology and emotional feeling." The interaction method of the in-vehicle system is controlled by APP and gesture. Therefore, when constructing the concept board, students collaged several pictures showing high-tech style and atmosphere around this theme and visualized the concept of interaction. When constructing the visual sign structure, on the one hand, the flexible and emotional styling language is expressed through the characteristic lines and profiles of electronic products and concept cars; on the other hand, the flexible and elegant graphic language is expressed through the interface design of games and web pages. Figure 3 shows the mood board tool conducted by a group of students.

Step 2. Design Based on the Tool's Proposal
The interior hard interface styling elements use keywords such as fashion, futurism, and mobile home, to extend the entertainment activities of people in the future to the car

Fig. 3. The mood board of vehicle HMI and interior design

interior. In terms of the composition of the graphical software interface, the division of the graphical interface not only makes the interface itself visually balanced but also enables it to obtain a high degree of integration in the interior environment. Also, the software interface design uses a large number of rounded corners, streamlines, and circular patterns, adding soft and emotional elements to reflect the feeling of "home," and also echoing the circular design elements in the interior design.

In terms of color, the primary color of the software interface GUI adopts blue, which represents the sense of technology and futuristic, and adds a green gradient to the interface. These designs can make the interface color convey a sense of technology. The lights in the interior design are also embellished with blue light bars, which echo the primary blue color of the software interface. Besides, yellow as the embellishment color of the interface also echoes the fashion sense of metal and wood in the interior design, so that the styling elements of the interior room and the GUI of the software interface can achieve an excellent balance to reflect the future of mobile life technological and stylish family atmosphere. In order to create a sense of fashion and the atmosphere of the "mobile home of the future," the interior hardware interface uses a large number of lights to blur the atmosphere. The software interface design also uses light and shadow and gradients, which not only adds layering and detail to the interface design but also creates an atmosphere for the car interior. Figure 4 shows the interior interface design.

Fig. 4. Interior interface design. (Color figure online)

The hardware interface uses air projection technology to display the virtual screen. As the "remote control" of the concept car interior, the software interface of the App should correspond to the "hardware" interior interface in function and shape. In the entertainment function interface, the user selects the mood mode of the day on the mobile phone. The intelligent entertainment system in the car will recommend corresponding entertainment and relaxation methods such as games, movies, and music. The hardware interface in the interior of the vehicle is an extension and supplement of the software interface of App, and it should be combined with some of the software interfaces of the mobile phone to allow users to see the current operating status more intuitively. Figure 5 shows the App interface design of mobile phone.

5.3 Feedback on the Application of the Mood Board Tool

Some students feedback that the use of the mood board tool enables improvements to the design efficiency within a short time. Due to the time limits of curriculums in design schools, probably the best way to lift the efficiency of the design is to establish an effective communication method. The mood board tool, from the view of visual language, promotes communication in the design process. The remaining students, in their opinion, believe that the tool is capable of spurring creativity, especially in the process of classification and association to mood material. Being exposed to lots of visual information generally provokes innovative design concepts much more accessible.

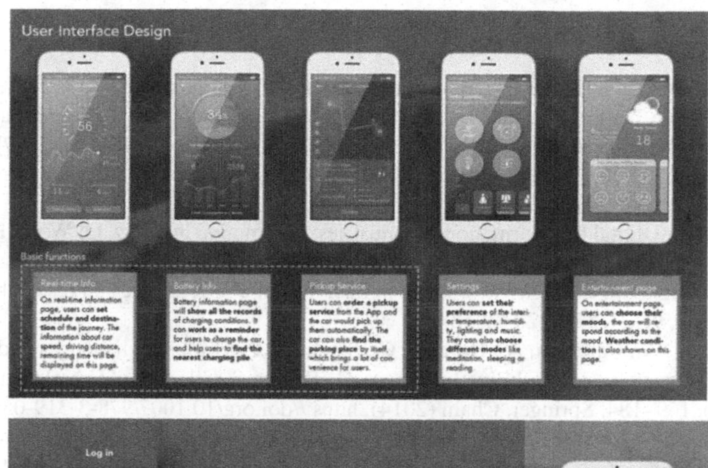

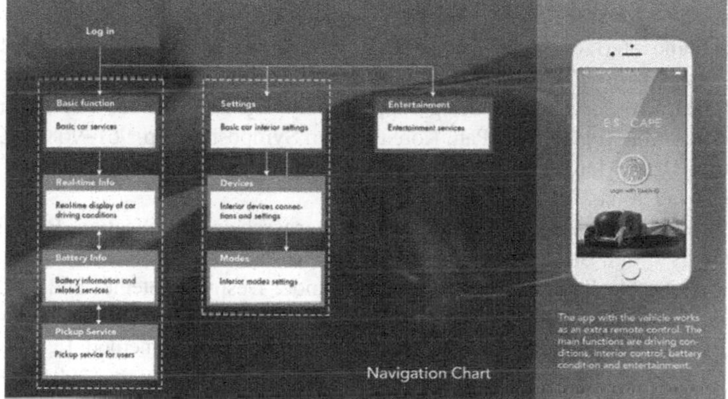

Fig. 5. App interface design of mobile phone

6 Conclusion

Overall, vehicle HMI interaction design has the following characteristics, namely, interdisciplinary, crosscutting. For this reason, it is practically significant to discuss and explore the visual design methods on vehicle HMI for design education. This paper proposed the mood board tool for vehicle HMI interaction design combined with acquiring of positive feedback from the application in the transportation design course. With the trend of artificial intelligence, industrial design and interaction design becoming increasingly integrated. The conceptual tool proposed in the paper that the mood board for vehicle HMI design facilitates effective communication between students(designers) from different domains. Furthermore, the tool promotes the integration of software and hardware interface design.

Acknowledgments. This research was supported by Humanities and Social Sciences Research Funds of the Ministry of Education of the People's Republic of China (19C10288009/19YJC760004), Fundamental Research Funds for the Central Universities (1171090797/30917013111). The authors would like to thank editors and reviewers for their comments.

References

1. Payre, W., Diels, C.: Human-machine interface design development for connected and cooperative vehicle features. In: 8th International Conference on Applied Human Factors and Ergonomics (AHFE 2017), Los Angeles, US, 17–21 July 2017,pp. 145–152 (2017)
2. Schmidt, A., Spiess, W., Kern, D.J.: Driving automotive user interface research. IEEE Pervasive Comput. **9**(1), 85–88 (2010)
3. Weindelt, B.: Digital transformation of industries: automotive industry. In: World Economic Forum in Collaboration with Accenture, vol. 1, no. 4, pp. 125–138 (2016)
4. Hao, T., Jianghong, Z., Wei, W.: Vehicle human machine interface design research. Chin. J. Autom. Eng. **9**(12), 315–320 (2012)
5. Alessandrini, A., Cattivera, A., Holguin, C., Stam, D.: CityMobil2: challenges and opportunities of fully automated mobility. In: Meyer, G., Beiker, S. (eds.) Road Vehicle Automation. LNM, pp. 169–184. Springer, Cham (2014). https://doi.org/10.1007/978-3-319-05990-7_15
6. Zeng, Q., Shi, M.: Story board tools and methods for user-knowledge-based automotive human-machine interface design. In: Rau, P.-L.P. (ed.) CCD 2018. LNCS, vol. 10911, pp. 108–119. Springer, Cham (2018). https://doi.org/10.1007/978-3-319-92141-9_8
7. Lee, S.H., Harada, A.: A kansei design approach by objective and subjective evaluation of kanseiin formation. In: China-JaPan, Korea Design Symposium, pp. 961–968 (1998)
8. Bella Martin, Bruce Hanington. Universal methods of design. Central Compilation Translation Press,Beijin,In,China,2013
9. Zhao, J., Tan, H., Tan, Z.: Car Styling: Theory, Research and Application. Beijing Institute of Technology Press, Beijin (2011)
10. van Boeijen, A., Daalhuizen, J.: Delft Design Guide: Design Strategies and Methods. BIS Publishers, Amsterdam (2014)
11. Sato, K., Sakol, T.C.: Object-mediated user knowledge elicitation method. In: The 5th Asian International Design Research Conference, Seoul Korea, 21–27 October 2001 (2001)
12. Mills, E.: The Art of Visual Notetaking: An Interactive Guide to Visual Communication and Sketchnoting. Walter Foster Publishing, California (2019)
13. Cooper, A., Reimann, R., Cronin, D.: About Face 3: The Essentials of Interaction Design, p. 16. Wiley Publishing Inc., Canada (2007)
14. Pruitt, J., Adlin, T.: The Persona Lifecycle: Keeping People in Mind Throughout Product Design, pp. 45–48. Elsevier & Technology, San Francisco (2006)
15. Sommer, R., Sommer, B.: A Practical Guide to Behavioral Research: Tools and Techniques, pp. 143–145. Oxford University Press, New York (2002)
16. Serenko, A.: The use of interface agents for email notification in critical incidents. Int. J. Hum.-Comput. Stud. **64**(11), 1084–1098 (2006)
17. Spencer, D.: Card Sorting: Designing Usable Categories, pp. 115–118. Rosenfeld Media, New York (2009)
18. Truong, K.N, Hayes, G.R., Abowd, D.: Storyboarding: an empirical determination of best practices and effective guidelines. In: Proceedings of DIS 2006, pp. 210–215 (2006)
19. Kelly, G.: The Psychology of Personal Constructs, vol. 1 and 2. Norton, New York (2015)
20. Sanders, E.B.N., Stappers, P.J.: Co-creation and the new landscapes of design. Co-design **4**(1), 5–18 (2008)
21. Zeng, Q., Duan, Q.: A study on integrated design process of software and hardware interfaces for automotive human-machine interaction. In: Rau, P.-L.P. (ed.) HCII 2019. LNCS, vol. 11576, pp. 105–123. Springer, Cham (2019). https://doi.org/10.1007/978-3-030-22577-3_8
22. Hankey, J.M., Dingus, T.A., Hanowski, R.J.: In-vehicle information systems behavioral model and design support. Virginia Technical Transportation Institute, Blacksburg, VA, pp. 145–150(2001)

23. Bhise, V.D., Hammouded, R.W.: A PC based model for prediction of visibility and legibility for a human factors engineer's tool box. In: Proceedings of the Human Factors and Ergonomics Society 48th Annual Meeting, pp. 110–115 (2004)
24. Liu, Y.C., Bligh, T., Chakrabarti, A.: Towards an ideal approach for concept generation. Des. Stud. **2**(4), 341–355 (2003)
25. Garner, D., McDonagh-Philp, S.: Problem interpretation and resolution via visual stimuli: the use of mood boards in design education. J. Art Des. Educ. **4**(2), 57–64 (2001)
26. McDonagh, D., Bruseberg, A., Haslam, C.: Visual product evaluation: exploring users' emotional relationships with products. Appl. Ergon. **3**(3), 231–235 (2002)
27. Deana, M., Ian, S.: Mood boards as a design catalyst and resource: researching an under-researched area. Des. J. **7**(3), 16–31 (2004)
28. Eckerta, C., Staceyb, M.: Sources of inspiration: a language of design. Des. Stud. **21**(5), 523–538 (2000)
29. Martin, B., Hanington, B.: Universal Methods of Design. Central Compilation Translation Press, Beijing (2003)
30. Schön, D.A.: The Reflective Practitioner How Professionals Think in Action. Education Science Press, Beijing (2007)
31. Valkenburg, A.C.: Shared understanding as a condition for team design. J. Autom. Constr. **7**(2–3), 111–121 (1998)
32. Mazijoglou, M., Scrivener, S.A.: The rich picture of design activity. J. Autom. Constr. **7**(2–3), 157–175 (1998)
33. Schön, D.A.: Problems, frames and perspectives on designing. Des. Stud. **5**(3), 132–136 (1984)
34. Dorst, K.: Describing design—a comparison of paradigms. PhD Thesis, Delft University of Technology (1997)
35. Valkenburg, R., Dorst, K.: The reflective practice of design teams. Des. Stud. **19**(3), 249–271 (1998)

Developing Intelligent Interactions

Teaching by Demonstrating – How Smart Assistive Systems Can Learn from Users

Sebastian Büttner[1,2](✉), Andreas Peda[1], Mario Heinz[1], and Carsten Röcker[1,3]

[1] Ostwestfalen-Lippe University of Applied Sciences and Arts, Lemgo, Germany
{sebastian.buettner,mario.heinz,carsten.roecker}@th-owl.de
[2] Human-Centered Information Systems, Clausthal University of Technology, Clausthal-Zellerfeld, Germany
[3] Fraunhofer IOSB-INA, Lemgo, Germany

Abstract. Projection-based assitive systems that guide users through assembly work are on their way to industrial application. Previous research work investigated how people can be supported with such systems. However, there has been little work on the question on how to generate and author sequential instructions for assitive systems. In this paper, we present a new concept and a prototypical implementation of an assitive system that can be taught by demonstrating an assembly process. By using a combination of RGB and depth cameras, we can generate an assembly instruction of Lego Duplo bricks based on the demonstration of a user. This generated manual can later on be used for assisting other users in the assembly process. By our prototype system, we show the technological feasibility of assistive systems that can learn from users.

Keywords: Assitive system · Authoring · Instruction generation · Computer vision · Teaching by demonstration

1 Introduction

Despite an ever increasing degree of automation, it is predicted that manual industrial assembly work will not disappear in future [12]. In this context, a lot of assistive systems have been presented which provide instructions at the workplace in order to reduce cognitive load of assembly tasks [9,14,21] and first assistive systems have already made it into the market [23,24]. However, the way industrial production is carried out will change: while past production focused on mass production, it is predicted that future industrial production will focus on "mass customization" to allow the production of individual products [16]. In this new scenario, the question is raised how instructions for assistive systems will be provided. When such systems are used in an environment where multiple products or variants are to be produced, the question comes up how the system can be configured to support new products or variants. Writing such instructions is typically a time-consuming and tedious task.

In this paper, we present a concept and a prototype of a smart assistive system that learns by observing users. By integrating RGB and depth cameras

N. Streitz and S. Konomi (Eds.): HCII 2020, LNCS 12203, pp. 153–163, 2020.
https://doi.org/10.1007/978-3-030-50344-4_12

into a workspace, we create a smart environment in the sense of Streitz [26] that is able to store knowledge about assembly processes and to support users in the execution of (new) assembly tasks. Users can teach the system by demonstrating the assembly process of a new product or variant. Later on, the knowledge of the correct assembly process can be used to instruct other people in the process and to check whether the assembly process is being executed in the right way. With our system, we show the technical feasibility of such a smart assistive system based on a Lego Duplo task.

2 Related Work

Over the last decade, there has been a lot of research on different types of assitive systems. According to the definition of Fellmann et al., we understand an assistive system as a "context-aware system consisting of hardware and software that supports a user with the execution of a task and adapts depending on the progress of the task" [12]. Such systems can be realized in various ways. Past systems were implemented by the use of either mobile devices [15] or within augmented reality (AR) environments, realized with head-mounted displays (HMDs) [21,28] or stationary [14,25] or mobile [8] in-situ projections (see overview by Büttner et al. [5]).

While multiple systems have been proposed and their implication on work efficiency [4,17] or on their learning effectiveness [7] has been evaluated, there has been less work on generating or authoring such AR content, even though this is a major requirement if such systems are applied in environments where multiple variants are to be produced.

Authoring can either be done within the AR environment or externally. E.g. Blattgerster et al. [2] present an integrated authoring tool that allows users to author AR instructions within the AR environment. By using Microsoft HoloLens in combination with a smartphone as an additional controller, users can define and manipulate sequences of "action steps" that contain editable AR artefacts.

In the following, we focus on external AR content generation, especially on previous work on activity and object recognition in the context of automated instruction generation out of 3-D models, technical drawings, or videos.

Agrawala et al. [1] presented a system that automatically defines and visualizes assembly sequences based on the 3-D computer-aided design (CAD) model of the complete object. The main focus of their work are design principles for assembly instructions that are intuitively understood. By integrating planning and visualization in one process, they show the feasibility of a system that automatically creates visual instructions for the assembly of everyday products based on CAD data [1]. Mohr et al. [18] use printed technical drawings in combination with CAD models to map 2-D instruction into AR instructions. In contrast to Agrawala et al. [1], they do not generate instruction sequences, but rather mapped 2-D sequence information onto the CAD model of the 3-D object to be able to align content in the 3-D space. Furthermore, they map other types of visualizations into the 3-D space, e.g. explosion diagrams [18].

Since CAD models are not always available, previous work has also focused on instruction generation out of video data (as our approach in this paper). In the context of body movements, Chi et al. [11] presented a system that generates illustrations of body-movements out of video data. By physically demonstrating a movement in front of a depth-camera, body sequences of body postures are recognized and visually prepared, resulting in a movement illustration that can be used for the training of sports or dance steps or as an instruction for gestural interfaces [11]. Mohr et al. [19] use 2-D video tutorials as a basis for AR instructions. They let users extract relevant artefacts from the tutorial video that are automatically mapped into the 3-D space of the AR environment. Even though this is a great tool for authoring AR instructions, it requires already created 2-D video tutorials.

A system that inspired our work was the Active Assembly Guidance presented by Wang et al. [29]. Similar to our work, they integrated a video parser into an assistive system that visually recognizes the assembly sequence of the user and can generate instructions or alert on errors. They can recognize single objects, of which 3-D data need to be known a-priori for the recognition. For the demonstration, they used various toys, such as Lego Duplo bricks, a wooden locomotive and a tricycle [29].

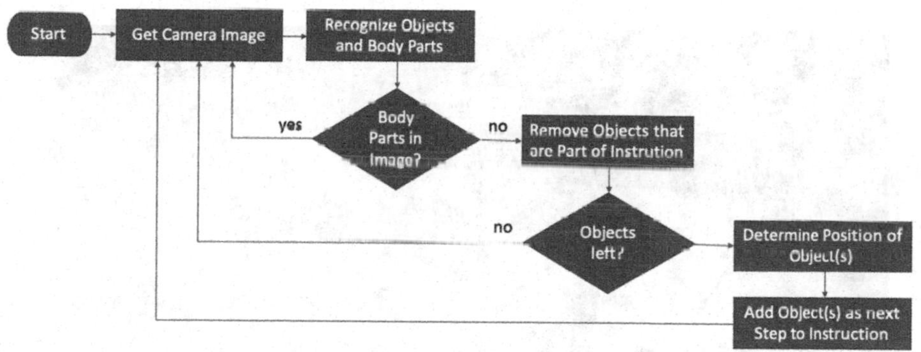

Fig. 1. Flow chart of our conceptual algorithm for the instruction generation.

3 Concept

We envision a stationary or portable system that can be integrated into a commercial assembly station containing a camera system and a computer, similar to our approach presented in [3]. The system makes use of a 3-D camera or an RGB camera to visually recognize single parts in the view of the camera system as well as body parts of the user, such as arms or hands. The positions of all single parts as well as body parts are tracked using computer vision algorithms. Parts that are in a fixed spatial relation are considered as mounted with each other, if there are no body parts in the camera view. Recognized body parts such as arms or hands indicate that the user either moves a new part to the mounting point or that he or she currently mounts a new part. Consequently images containing body parts are excluded from the analysis. If new objects are recognized in an image, their position is determined and they are added as a next assembly step into the instruction. The resulting conceptual flow is shown in Fig. 1. The current flow does not allow parts to be removed. However, this option could be integrated, e.g. for error correction by checking the added parts in every loop or by having an implicit user input in the case that parts are removed.

4 Prototypical Implementation

To show the technical feasibility of such a system, we implemented our concept in a first prototype that is able to create Lego Duplo assembly instructions based on the analysis of the camera images from a camera system. For the implementation, we used an Intel RealSense ZR300 camera system that contains different cameras, such as a structured light depth camera and an RGB camera. The depth camera has a depth range of 55–280 cm and a resolution of 628 × 468 pixels at a frame rate of 30 frames per second. The RGB camera has a resolution of 1920 × 1080

Fig. 2. Prototype System with Intel RealSense ZR300 on tripod.

at 30 frames per second. In addition to these two cameras, the system contains a fish-eye camera and can also be used as an infrared camera, but we do not use these two features for our implementation. The camera system is mounted onto a tripod that is placed above a Duplo base plate (see Fig. 2).

The camera system is connected to a server running Ubuntu 16.04. Our software is implemented in Python 3 using the library [22] and OpenCV [20]. Based on our concept, the software analyses the images in the following three steps: first, coordinates of the base plate are recognized and transformed into a reference coordinate system; second, the objects and body parts are recognized and analysed; and third, the instruction is generated. The following sections describe the three steps in detail.

4.1 Recognition of Mounting Point

We assume a scenario where a portable system (e.g. an a tripod) can be placed next to a workplace. Consequently, the system has to recognize a defined workplace or mounting point. In our case, the mounting point is a green Lego Duplo base plate with a size of 38 cm × 38 cm, which can be placed on any plane surface that differs from the base plate in colour. The base plate is recognized by the

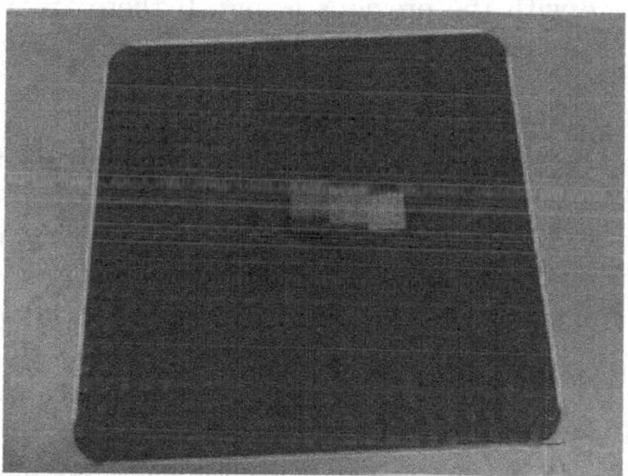

Fig. 3. The base plate is visually recognized in the camera view (purple lines). (Color figure online)

RGB camera based on its colour. We run a colour filter to recognize the parts of the image that are in the broad range of 80°–180° (hue), 25%–100% (saturation) and 25%–100% (value) based on the HSV colour scheme. While the broad range makes sure that the base plate is recognized under different light conditions, it also means that the underground has to differ significantly in colour. Afterwards, we transfer the filtered image into a grey-scale image and run a Canny edge detector [10] to recognize the edges of the base plate. Having the transformed image, we use a contour detection (OpenCV implementation of [27]) and look for the contour with the largest area, which we identify as the base plate. In a next step, we run a line recognition algorithm (Hough transform, see [13]) on the edges of the contour. The recognized four lines are visualized with purple colour in Fig. 3. Finally, we calculate the points of intersection of the four lines and calculate a transformation matrix that transforms the recognized base plate into a square (since we know that the base plate is perspective-distorted in the camera view).

4.2 Recognition of Objects

For the recognition of objects and body parts, we use the depth camera in combination with the RGB camera data. The existence of new Lego Duplo bricks is recognized by using the depth data. Since the bricks are different in colour, we use the RGB camera to verify each single brick and to recognize its colour. Body parts are recognized by the depth camera. The process of object recognition is as follows: first, the depth data is analysed in terms of whether there are new objects or body parts in view ("regions of interest") and the depth data is mapped into the reference coordinate system; second, the location of (potentially) new bricks is determined and their colour is analysed based on the RGB camera data.

Analysis of Depth Image. When analysing a new depth image, we first compare the depth image with the previous image. If there are high variations in multiple regions of the image, we assume that the actual assembly object is (partially) obscured by body parts of the user. Therefore, we reject such images and take the next one from the camera. We repeat this process until we get "stable" images from the depth camera. In a next step, we analyse the depth data in the area of the base plate. We have to take into account that the depth camera does not provide an orthogonal or oblique coordinate system, but provides a distance value for each pixel of the resolution. Consequently, the position of objects in the plane x-y-space of our reference coordinate system can not only be distinguished with the x and y values of the pixels; rather the z-values (height) need to be taken into account as well, since objects close to the camera cover a larger area in the camera view than they do in greater distance. For this purpose, we transfer the visible 3-D surface from the depth data into an auxiliary coordinate system. Again, we compare this data with the previous known 3-D surface and identify regions that are distinct from the previous state. We call these regions "regions of interest."

Recognition of New Bricks. For the actual recognition of single bricks we use the RGB image from the camera, transform it with the transformation matrix of the base plate and analyse the region of interest in terms of two aspects: the layer and the colour of the brick. The advantage of using Lego Duplo building blocks is their clear geometry. Hence, we are able to calculate grids for virtual layers over the space of the base plate. Depending on the height of the camera, we calculate n layer grids and start matching the region of interest with the n layers, starting with the top layer and moving down in the stack to the bottom

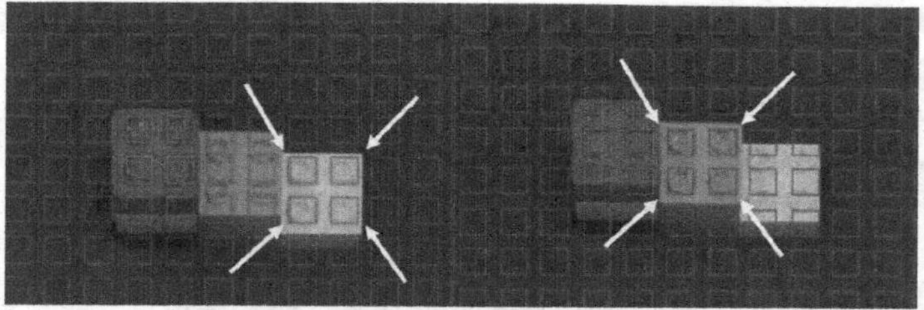

Fig. 4. To determine the position and height, a perspective-corrected grid is placed over the camera image and the bricks are matched according to the grid. Left image: layer 1, right image: layer 2.

layer, as long as a new brick can be matched. For the matching, we recognize the nubs of the bricks in the region of interest based on the RGB image. This recognition is shown in Fig. 4, which includes distinguishing different brick sizes (2×2 vs. 2×4). Finally, the color of the brick is determined based on a histogram build up from the colour data of the part of the image that contains the brick.

4.3 Generation of Instruction and Visualization

If one or multiple new bricks have been recognized, they are added to the instruction. In this step, a plausibility check is included. We assume that no parts are removed during the assembly. Based on this assumption, the plausibility check examines, whether the part can actually be at the specific position given the previous state. This is not the case, if the brick to be added either overlaps with a previous brick or if the brick is not placed directly on top of at least one other brick. If this check is successful, the new bricks are added to the instruction and the next images are analysed. Otherwise, the new recognition is rejected giving the algorithm a further iteration to analyse the scene correctly.

As mentioned previously, our implementation is considered as a proof-of-concept implementation. The created instruction could be used in multiple ways, e.g. to instruct workers by delivering them AR instructions or by checking errors in future repetitions. To show and verify the correctness of our generated model, we implemented a visualization tool. Figure 5 shows an overview of this tool that shows a digital illustration of the current physical state. The image to the upper left shows the live video image of the perspective-corrected base plate. The three images to the right show three different layers of the current state. The generation of the single instruction steps are done in the background based on the occurrence of new parts.

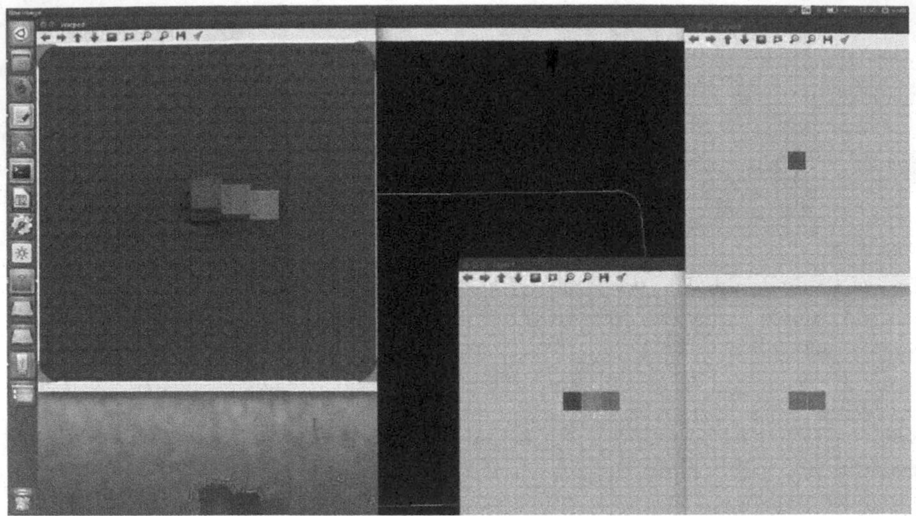

Fig. 5. The software shows the digital illustration of the current physical state.

5 Discussion and Conclusion

With our prototype, we show the technical feasibility of a smart assistive system that automatically generates new instruction manuals by observing users. Our concept supports assembly scenarios with high numbers of products or variations. With the system, the knowledge of experts can be documented digitally through demonstration; new employees can be easily trained with this digital expert knowledge. Furthermore, the system is able to recognize deviations from the correct assembly process. We consider our system as a first step towards the development of smart assistive systems that can be used for the training of new employees.

Of course, our prototype has limitations. The main limitation is the artificial Lego Duplo assembly task used for the implementation. Industrial assembly tasks are much more complex, consisting of much more diverse and smaller parts, which makes the optical recognition more difficult. Furthermore, various joining techniques (such as screwing, pressing, etc.) have to be used in real tasks. A system would not only have to recognize the techniques, but rather check, if the techniques were executed in the right way (e.g. checking the moment of force when screwing). For the latter, we envision digital tools connected to the system to deliver sensor data.

The system that has been described in this paper has been on public display in the SmartFactoryOWL [6] and has been tried out by a lot of users with positive feedback. In our future work, we will systematically test our system within a user study to learn about the implications of the integration of such a system on industrial work.

Acknowledgments. The authors acknowledge the financial support by the Federal Ministry of Education and Research of Germany for the project "Augmented-Reality-Assistenzsysteme für mobile Anwendungsszenarien in der Industrie (FKZ: 03FH005IX6)".

References

1. Agrawala, M., et al.: Designing effective step-by-step assembly instructions. ACM Trans. Graph. **22**(3), 828–837 (2003). https://doi.org/10.1145/882262.882352
2. Blattgerste, J., Renner, P., Pfeiffer, T.: Authorable augmented reality instructions for assistance and training in work environments. In: Proceedings of the 18th International Conference on Mobile and Ubiquitous Multimedia, MUM 2019, pp. 34:1–34:11. ACM, New York (2019). https://doi.org/10.1145/3365610.3365646
3. Büttner, S., Besginow, A., Prilla, M., Röcker, C.: Mobile projection-based augmented reality in work environments-an exploratory approach. In: Mensch und Computer 2018-Workshopband (2018)
4. Büttner, S., Funk, M., Sand, O., Röcker, C.: Using head-mounted displays and in-situ projection for assistive systems: A comparison. In: Proceedings of the 9th ACM International Conference on PErvasive Technologies Related to Assistive Environments, PETRA 2016, pp. 44:1–44:8. ACM, New York (2016). https://doi.org/10.1145/2910674.2910679
5. Büttner, S., et al.: The design space of augmented and virtual reality applications for assistive environments in manufacturing: a visual approach. In: Proceedings of the 10th International Conference on PErvasive Technologies Related to Assistive Environments, PETRA 2017, pp. 433–440. ACM, New York (2017). https://doi.org/10.1145/3056540.3076193
6. Büttner, S., Mucha, H., Robert, S., Hellweg, F., Röcker, C.: HCI in der SmartFactoryOWL - Angewandte Forschung & Entwicklung. In: 4. Workshop zu Smart Factories: Mitarbeiter-zentrierte Informationssysteme für die Zusammenarbeit der Zukunft, Mensch und Computer 2017, Regensburg (2017). [German]
7. Büttner, S., Prilla, M., Röcker, C.: Augmented reality training for industrial assembly work - are projection-based ar assistive systems an appropriate tool for assembly training? In: Proceedings of the 2020 CHI Conference on Human Factors in Computing Systems (forthcoming), CHI 2020. ACM, New York (2020)
8. Büttner, S., Sand, O., Röcker, C.: Extending the design space in industrial manufacturing through mobile projection. In: Proceedings of the 17th International Conference on Human-Computer Interaction with Mobile Devices and Services Adjunct, pp. 1130–1133. ACM (2015)
9. Büttner, S., Sand, O., Röcker, C.: Exploring design opportunities for intelligent worker assistance: a new approach using projetion-based AR and a novel hand-tracking algorithm. In: Braun, A., Wichert, R., Mana, A. (eds.) Ambient Intelligence, Am I 2017. Lecture Notes in Computer Science, vol. 10217, pp. 33–45. Springer, Cham (2017). https://doi.org/10.1007/978-3-319-56997-0_3
10. Canny, J.: A computational approach to edge detection. IEEE Trans. Pattern Anal. Mach. Intell. **6**, 679–698 (1986)
11. Chi, P.Y.P., Vogel, D., Dontcheva, M., Li, W., Hartmann, B.: Authoring illustrations of human movements by iterative physical demonstration. In: Proceedings of the 29th Annual Symposium on User Interface Software and Technology, UIST 2016, pp. 809–820. ACM, New York (2016). https://doi.org/10.1145/2984511.2984559

12. Fellmann, M., Robert, S., Büttner, S., Mucha, H., Rocker, C.: Towards a framework for assistance systems to support work processes in smart factories. In: Holzinger, A., Kieseberg, P., Tjoa, A., Weippl, E. (eds.) Machine Learning and Knowledge Extraction, CD-MAKE 2017. Lecture Notes in Computer Science, vol. 10410, pp. 59–68. Springer, Cham (2017). https://doi.org/10.1007/978-3-319-66808-6_5
13. Fisher, R., Perkins, S., Walker, A., Wolfart, E.: Hough Transform (2003). http://homepages.inf.ed.ac.uk/rbf/HIPR2/hough.htm. Accessed 14 Jan 2020
14. Funk, M., Mayer, S., Schmidt, A.: Using in-situ projection to support cognitively impaired workers at the workplace. In: Proceedings of the 17th International ACM SIGACCESS Conference on Computers, ASSETS 2015, pp. 185–192. ACM, New York (2015). https://doi.org/10.1145/2700648.2809853
15. Hakkarainen, M., Woodward, C., Billinghurst, M.: Augmented assembly using a mobile phone. In: Proceedings of the 7th IEEE/ACM International Symposium on Mixed and Augmented Reality, pp. 167–168. IEEE Computer Society (2008)
16. Hinrichsen, S., Jasperneite, J., Schrader, F., Lücke, B., Fraunhofer, I.I.: Versatile assembly systems-requirements, design principles and examples. Proc. PEM **14**, 37–46 (2014)
17. Korn, O., Schmidt, A., Hörz, T.: The potentials of in-situ-projection for augmented workplaces in production: A study with impaired persons. In: CHI 2013 Extended Abstracts on Human Factors in Computing Systems, CHI EA 2013, pp. 979–984. ACM, New York (2013). https://doi.org/10.1145/2468356.2468531
18. Mohr, P., Kerbl, B., Donoser, M., Schmalstieg, D., Kalkofen, D.: Retargeting technical documentation to augmented reality. In: Proceedings of the 33rd Annual ACM Conference on Human Factors in Computing Systems, CHI 2015, pp. 3337–3346. ACM, New York (2015). https://doi.org/10.1145/2702123.2702490
19. Mohr, P., Mandl, D., Tatzgern, M., Veas, E., Schmalstieg, D., Kalkofen, D.: Retargeting video tutorials showing tools with surface contact to augmented reality. In: Proceedings of the 2017 CHI Conference on Human Factors in Computing Systems, CHI 2017, pp. 6547–6558. ACM, New York (2017)
20. OpenCV: https://opencv.org/ (2020), [Online; accessed 14-January-2020]
21. Paelke, V., Röcker, C., Koch, N., Flatt, H., Büttner, S.: User interfaces for cyber-physical systems. at-Automatisierungstechnik **63**(10), 833–843 (2015)
22. pyrealsense (2020). https://pypi.org/project/pyrealsense/, Accessed 14 Jan 2020
23. rexroth - a Bosch Company: ActiveAssist assistance system - modular, connected, interactive (2019). https://www.boschrexroth.com/en/xc/products/product-groups/assembly-technology/news/activeassist-assistance-system/index, Accessed 11 Dec 2019
24. Röcker, C., Robert, S.: Projektionsbasierte Montageunterstützung mit visueller Fortschrittserkennung [German]. visIT Industrie **4** (2016)
25. Sand, O., Büttner, S., Paelke, V., Röcker, C.: smARt.Assembly - projection-based augmented reality for supporting assembly workers. In: Lackey, S., Shumaker, R. (eds.) Virtual, Augmented and Mixed Reality, VAMR 2016. Lecture Notes in Computer Science, vol. 9740, pp. 643–652. Springer, Cham (2016). https://doi.org/10.1007/978-3-319-39907-2_61
26. Streitz, N.: Beyond 'smart-only' cities: redefining the 'smart-everything' paradigm. J. Ambi. Intell. Hum. Comput. **10**(2), 791–812 (2019). https://doi.org/10.1007/s12652-018-0824-1
27. Suzuki, S., et al.: Topological structural analysis of digitized binary images by border following. Comput. Vis. Graph. Image Process. **30**(1), 32–46 (1985)

28. Tang, A., Owen, C., Biocca, F., Mou, W.: Comparative effectiveness of augmented reality in object assembly. In: Proceedings of the SIGCHI Conference on Human Factors in Computing Systems, pp. 73–80. ACM (2003)
29. Wang, B., et al.: Active assembly guidance with online video parsing. In: 2018 IEEE Conference on Virtual Reality and 3D User Interfaces (VR), pp. 459–466. IEEE (2018)

Towards an Ambient Intelligent Environment for Multimodal Human Computer Interactions

Jeffrey Bennett(✉), Phuong Nguyen, Crisrael Lucero, and Douglas Lange

Naval Information Warfare Center Pacific, San Diego, CA 92152, USA
{jjbennet,nguyen,clucero,dlange}@niwc.navy.mil

Abstract. Recent years have seen an explosion in the academic and commercial applications of digital assistants. These technologies have become increasingly prolific, and their use has resulted in fairly rigid and standardized techniques for achieving a desired result. Whether this includes physical actions, or direct voice queries to the system via predefined wake words and queries, there is a stark boundary between the human and the system. We aim to explore a shift in the paradigm of these current implementations, to that of an Ambient Intelligent (AmI) environment in which users can interface with the system in a more natural, seamless, and multi-modal manner. Applications of this type of technology range from assisted living, to smart conference rooms and meeting spaces. In this paper we introduce an architectural framework for building an ambient intelligent platform using a combination of video and audio sensors to capture and process the data in a given area of interest.

Keywords: Ambient intelligence · Computer vision · Natural language processing · Sensing and reasoning

1 Introduction

The idea of Ambient Intelligent (AmI) environments has been widely explored in works such as [1,2,8,12], and [14]. As these outline, this concept is a logical extension of the trend towards smarter and more interconnected systems that humans interact with on a daily basis. With an increased availability of smart devices and Internet of Things (IoT) networked systems, the manner in which humans can interact with their environments is beginning to shift. The interactions typical of these current day devices falls short of providing a truly AmI environment, but they do provide useful enabling features. Rather than using prescribed wake words and specific query language, an AmI space would support less scripted interactions, and those that can take place beyond strictly defined action and speech interfaces. To work towards realizing such an environment, we have proposed to begin development on a system that can benefit from the explosive advances in two of machine learning's most prolific fields: computer vision

N. Streitz and S. Konomi (Eds.): HCII 2020, LNCS 12203, pp. 164–177, 2020.
https://doi.org/10.1007/978-3-030-50344-4_13

and natural language processing. Initially focusing on the audio and visual input modalities, we have defined a modular architecture capable of achieving baseline functionalities we believe can be further developed to eventually realize a multiple user, interactive AmI space.

1.1 Brief Overview

According to [12], AmI is a vision of systems enabled by technologies that are invisible to the end user, directly embedded in the environment, and capable of autonomous actions. Towards meeting these objectives, an AmI environment should exhibit features that include sensitivity, responsiveness, adaptability, transparency, ubiquitousness, and intelligence [9]. Combined, these features outline a shift in the types of interactions that can take place between people and these technology enabled environments.

In order to realize this new type of environment, [9] outlines specific steps systems must be able to perform, which include: *sensing*, *reasoning*, *acting*, and *interacting* with users. The steps of *sensing* and *reasoning* consist of capturing inputs from the environment and users, and extracting relevant, actionable information from this data. Without these initial steps, the *actions* and *interactions* enabled by the system will not have the required context to be meaningful to its users. Because of this, our initial work has focused heavily on the former steps in the process, in hopes that once in place, they will enable future research on the latter.

1.2 Related Work

Since outlining the abstract vision of AmI environments, the community has seen a great deal of work completed to define, design, and integrate various components, as well as some commercial applications of enabling technologies. A survey of several ubiquitous computing frameworks can be found in [16]. This work also outlines a unique framework and approach for defining and integrating services necessary to build AmI spaces.

Assisted living situations have become a popular application of AmI due to the range of benefits that can be provided to the end users. An example of one of these applications is outlined in [11], which focuses the AmI environment implementation around emergency assistance, autonomy, and comfort.

In the commercial space, smart home devices and digital assistants have become increasingly utilized, and increasingly capable systems. Although they do not encompass all the features of AmI, they provide important components, particularly for the audio input modality. Relevant examples for visual sensory inputs exist as well though, including applications such as the Amazon Go store which utilizes a suite of video cameras to maintain awareness of store occupants and their merchandise. Using "Just Walk Out" technology, the visual inputs are sufficient to create a cashier-less and register-less shopping experience.[1]

[1] https://www.amazon.com/b?ie=UTF8&node=16008589011.

2 Architecture

Developing an architecture around the necessary features of an AmI environment leads to a few critical design considerations, in terms of both the hardware utilized and the software infrastructure. Most importantly, the manner in which a person interacts with the environment should be as seamless and natural as possible. For basic interactions, there should be nothing the user need don upon entering the environment (e.g. a headset or lapel microphone, a GPS or RF tracking device, etc.). Avoiding this requires the passive collection of data from within the space, which for our purposes consists of 3D depth sensors and a ceiling array microphone. Beyond this however, the architecture should remain open to additional sensors and data streams to support follow-on capabilities.

This open architecture approach should also hold for the software employed and the data processing streams that exist. Decoupling discrete functionality as an ideal software practice also helps to enable scalability as the environment is expanded in terms of size, number of users, or volume of data. A final architectural consideration is the need to support adaptability. This can come in the form of capturing directed sensor inputs, or load balancing various processes based on available resources or maintaining critical components. Specific details on how these were achieved for the initial hardware and software implementations follows.

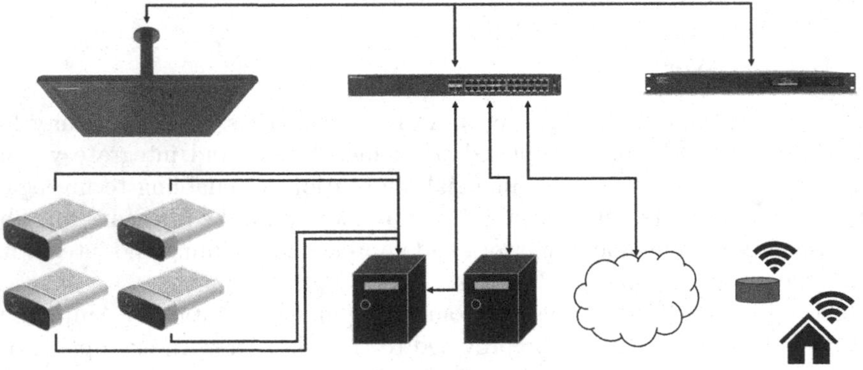

Fig. 1. Physical architecture of the components used to create the AmI environment. The configuration consists of a suite of sensors and compute resources on a local area network, with additional cloud resources and networked smart devices capable of being integrated as well.

2.1 Hardware Architecture

A diagram of an exemplar physical architecture can be seen in Fig. 1. This architecture utilizes a hybrid compute environment to leverage a networked system of local sensors and resources, in addition to cloud compute, storage, and services.

The primary data collection is achieved via local sensors to include a multiple beam, directional microphone, and a collection of synchronized RGB-D video sensors. These meet the requirements for collecting a sufficient amount of data to characterize a given environment, while remaining discrete and unobtrusive to users within that environment. All devices are connected via a local area network (LAN). The microphone is configured to stream raw time series audio to static endpoints on the network, while the depth cameras are directly connected to local general-purpose computers. Data processing can occur on any of the networked resources, including appropriately configured cloud instances. In order to interface with other systems in the environment, each must be connected to an accessible network and provide properly exposed APIs. This is an increasingly common use case as the devices available as part of the IoT continue to proliferate. Ensuring the AmI environment can integrate with these devices, and other available resources effectively, is a must.

2.2 Software Architecture

To support the wide range of functionality required by an AmI environment, a maximally open and modular software architecture is needed. Realizing this with a microservices architecture allows capabilities to be independently developed, and avoids restricting the types of frameworks and tools that can be used. Data flow between the various services comes in the form of a message brokering service designed to support a publisher-subscriber messaging pattern. This allows asynchronous communications between processes, and provides a well defined interface for the structure of data that can be accessed by new services. Another key feature of this design is the ability to scale and distribute processes across available resources as needed. Many of the core services are built using processing intensive deep learning modules, which requires exposing and effectively utilizing compute resources such as GPUs. Each of the core services provide a necessary capability for developing an understanding of the space, and when combined, these services should constitute the minimum viable set of information to enable the desired interactions. The initial set of core services includes a pose estimator, face identifier, fusion mapper, speaker identifier, and transcript generator, all of which are further described in Sects. 3.2 and 3.4.

3 Data and Processing

Capturing appropriate and sufficient data is imperative for building an AmI environment. The various processes employed to transform and analyze the data extracted from the environment provide the necessary information for the system to infer user actions and intents, and respond appropriately. Initial work has focused on the input data modalities of speech and 3D positions, and subsequently outputting audio and visual information as necessary. We believe these modes provide important components of a natural interface, but additional input and output modalities will need to be implemented to increase accessibility and realize the vision of a truly ambient intelligent space.

3.1 Input Video

In order to determine precisely where occupants are in a space, 3D depth sensors are utilized which capture both RGB and depth videos. Also known as RGB-D cameras, these are devices that collect color and depth image frames using both RGB and Time of Flight (ToF) sensors in a time synchronized manner. These sensors are statically mounted on the outer edges of the space, and can be optimally configured to cover a certain area with sufficient overlap to achieve the desired amount of redundancy to handle occlusions.

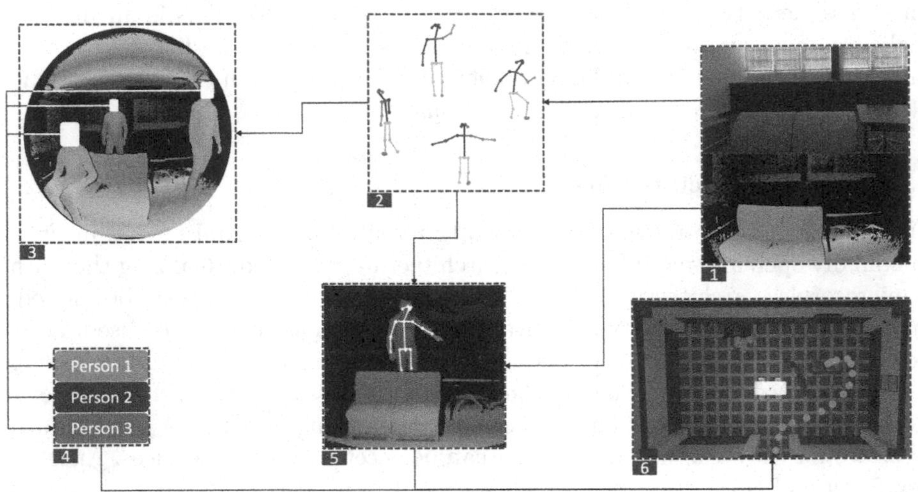

Fig. 2. Video data flow. (1) Input RGB and depth video frames are captured from the sensors. The RGB frames are used to detect and localize people by estimating 25 discrete body points (2). These wireframes are then used to extract the appropriate facial regions if visible (3), and are overlaid on the depth data to determine 3D poses (5). The face images are fed through a face identification module (4), and these ID's are coupled with the 3D pose information by a data fusion module to establish individual tracks in a mapped area.

3.2 Video Processing

Each step in the video processing pipeline is depicted in terms of the data consumed and produced, shown in Fig. 2. Having access to separable RGB-D sensor streams enables an expansive library of computer vision models and algorithms to be applied to the visual aspects of the environment, across application domains.

Pose Estimator. The RGB-D video is streamed directly to one or more local computers on the LAN. Initial processing takes place using the RGB video frames, in order to detect and localize any people present. This module can utilize many different algorithms to implement this capability, but our initial framework leverages OpenPose [5] which provides the ability to predict 25 body keypoints per person identified in the frame. Working with the GPU accelerated implementation, the 2D video frames from all feeds are processed in real-time, and 2D wireframe estimates are generated for each person in each stream.

Face Identifier. The keypoint data is then utilized to extract segments of the frame that correspond to face regions. These subframes are cropped from the RGB data frames and fed into a face identification module. This is again designed to provide flexibility in terms of the implementation utilized, and initial results using the FaceNet architecture [15] have proven successful for identifying individuals that have been pre-trained into the classification layer.

Fusion Mapper. To determine the 3D locations of individuals in the space, the wireframe predictions are overlaid on their corresponding depth frames. From this, 3D pose estimates are generated for every collection of 2D keypoints. If positive face identifications above a given threshold exist for the frame as well, this data is coupled with the 3D pose estimates and fed into a fusion module to generate unique tracks in 3D space. This data is sufficient to represent the locations of specific individuals over time, and with an understanding of the locations of all static objects of interest in the space, the physical content of the environment can be adequately described.

3.3 Input Audio

Our primary method for determining what is happening in the environment is via the collection and processing of human speech. Collecting this type of data requires capturing audio in the appropriate locations within the space. These areas are determined by the video processing techniques described above, and the resulting stream of person locations over time is used by the audio services to dynamically direct the steerable beams of the microphone. Once positioned appropriately, parametric equalization is employed to optimize the levels of this incoming audio.

3.4 Natural Language Processing

The steps for processing the targeted audio into natural language outputs and artifacts is shown in Fig. 3. As the audio data is streamed to a specified endpoint, a transcoding service decodes and resamples the audio to the necessary rates for further processing. This resampled audio is then re-streamed to a hosted speech to text server. The first step in processing each targeted audio stream is to build a buffer of voiced segments using a customized Voice Activity Detection (VAD) module. Using a Gaussian Mixture Model (GMM) to classify audio segments as containing or lacking human speech, the VAD module outputs variable length audio snippets.

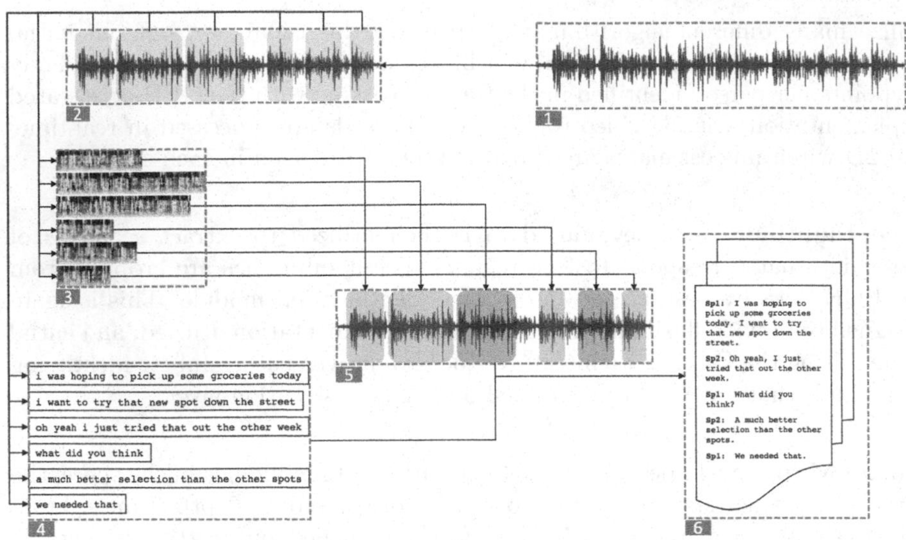

Fig. 3. Audio data flow. (1) Input time series data is captured from the microphone. This is fed through a voice activity detection module to extract the segments identified as human speech (2). These segments are processed to extract spectral features (3), and are fed through a speech to text module to develop rough transcriptions (4). The spectral features are used to identify a source speaker for each segment (5), and are then combined with the rough transcriptions and processed to create a full speaker-aligned transcript (6).

Speaker Identifier. Each audio snippet is consumed by a module to convert the time series audio into the spectral domain. Short time spectrograms are generated for each individual raw audio snippet, and used as inputs into a speaker identification network. As an initial test, this architecture models the one described in [6], but further pre-processing of the snippets and additional architectures will be explored. Estimates of the segment's source speaker that exceed a given threshold for identification are then published to correspond with that snippet.

Audio Transcriber. Simultaneous to the spectral processing and speaker identification, the raw audio segments are fed into a speech to text model. Currently, this model is built using Mozilla's implementation of the DeepSpeech architecture [10], which consists of an acoustic sequence to sequence model to convert time series audio to characters, followed by a beam search decoder scored against a language model to produce context aware text predictions.

Transcript Generator. These text fragments are post-processed to include punctuation and capitalizations, and are correlated to the speaker predictions to generate a final speaker separated transcript. This transcript data is then published to the message broker to feed into additional services designed to extract content of interest, and determine contextual meaning.

3.5 Output Modes

With a general knowledge of who is in the space and where they are (via the video processing steps), and what specific individuals are saying (via the natural language processing), we believe sufficient inputs exist to implement some initial interactive components of the AmI environment. These outputs can span a broad range of capabilities, and will be dependent on the needs of the user and the domain in which the environment is implemented. Our initial efforts have focused on commonly accessible modes that already exist in our target environments, namely visual and audio outputs.

Populating these output modes with appropriate and relevant information will require the implementation of additional modules to represent more complex perceptual tasks. Once developed and determined to better define the goals of the users, these modules can then seed intelligent planning agents to predict the actions and interactions most beneficial to occupants of the space. The vision of an AmI is that the output modes accessible within the environment are then used to effectively support these higher level, contextual interactions.

4 Implementation

Initial prototyping of the system has occurred in a controlled laboratory space. The area covered by the sensors is roughly 18×26 ft, but this does not represent any sensor limitations, as the current configuration is believed to remain functional in a much larger area, and additional sensors can be integrated to further expand the coverage. An example of how the sensors and output devices can be configured within a representative indoor area is depicted in Fig. 4.

Video tracking is achieved through the use of 4 networked Microsoft Azure Kinect depth cameras. These cameras have multiple operating modes that can be tailored to the specific operational environment, but in general the color camera can capture images up to a resolution of 3840×2160 at 30 FPS, while the ToF depth camera can gather data at ranges up to 5.5 m at 30 FPS.[2]

The audio collection equipment consists of a single Shure MXA910 ceiling microphone array, networked to a Q-Sys Core 110f audio processor. The microphone array consists of 8 independently controlled audio beams that can be positioned to specific coordinates and adjusted to narrow (35°), medium (45°) or wide (55°) beam widths. The frequency response is from 180 to 17000 Hz, and audio is natively captured at 48 kHz.[3]

To achieve customized face and speaker identifications, models pre-trained on datasets such as [4] and [6] are fine-tuned on images and audio captured

[2] https://docs.microsoft.com/en-us/azure/kinect-dk/hardware-specification.

[3] https://pubs.shure.com/guide/MXA910/en-US.

prior to the users entering the AmI environment area. This provides a method for initializing new users for development purposes, but a more automated and integrated process is currently under development.

All the models trained to predict human keypoints, speech, face identities, and speaker identities are hosted as servers on the LAN. The necessary input data to these models is pre-processed in their respective services, and connect to the servers as a collection of clients. For the pose estimator and audio transcribers, clients exists for each separate data stream (the RGB camera feeds from each of the Microsoft Azure Kinects, and every audio beam from the Shure microphone array, respectively). The face and speaker identifier services build their data inputs into buffered queues, with additional clients instantiated as necessary.

Fig. 4. Rendering of a simple AmI environment. Audio (green) and video (red) modes are labelled, with inputs and outputs shown using boxes and ovals, respectively. (Color figure online)

5 Early Thoughts

One of the most important considerations for realizing this type of environment has been developing an extensible and scalable architecture that can be modified to meet the needs of different users and use cases. This remains an important aspect of the system, as a large number of additional modules will need to be developed to work towards an increasingly functional AmI space. The baseline components developed to date require relatively robust computational resources, and this requirement will only continue to increase. Along with the need for further capabilities will be the need to support an increased number of occupants in the space. In addition to increasing the amount of data that will need to be processed, steps will also have to be taken to characterize interactions between various groups of individuals, and how to recognize and handle discrete groupings whose interactions with the environment may be reliant, or completely separate, from one other.

Another area that will need to be further explored and addressed relates to individual security and privacy. The use of cameras and computer vision algorithms to analyze images draws a multitude of security and privacy related concerns [8]. As integral parts of AmI, visual data and analysis is critical for sensing and personalization. To reduce concern and earn trust, implementing cybersecurity components via encryption of data at rest, and in transit, are key to protecting the security and privacy of users.

6 Applications

Although the applications of AmI are vast, we have focused our efforts on a specific subset of constrained indoor systems. This offers the appealing benefits of having existing or easily modifiable infrastructures for capturing the necessary sensory inputs, and supplying the appropriate output modes. First, we explore the application of an assisted living area, followed by that of AmI enhanced meeting spaces, and finally discuss how this concept can be applied to command center environments.

6.1 Assisted Living

The healthcare industry offers many potential applications for AmI, among which the services provided via assisted living are very well aligned. With a rapidly growing number of elderly citizens, the demand for assisted living is rapidly increasing [8], making this a highly relevant application domain. AmI provides another care-taking option for elderly citizens by creating a space with features tailored towards mobility related issues. By monitoring and assisting users in this demographic, AmI may provide them the autonomy to live in the comfort of their own homes, in addition to a greater sense of independence. As a result, ambient assisted living options have been shown to have benefits that promote longevity for these individuals [13].

6.2 Meeting Spaces

Conference areas and meeting spaces offer another interesting application of AmI, while requiring a different set of features and posing new challenges. These spaces will typically involve a larger number of participants which can be challenging for a system such as ours, but benefit from the fact that a majority of the time there will only be a small number of actively engaging users and speakers. Benefits of employing AmI capabilities in areas like these include the ability to automatically transcribe meeting notes, provide interactive control of A/V assets in the room based on user roles and locations, and insight generation to assist in decision making and planning processes.

6.3 Command Centers

Similar in infrastructure and layout to conference areas, command centers offer another relevant application of AmI. These environments exist throughout society in the context of transportation systems, energy plants, and crisis/disaster response scenarios. Building AmI into this type of environment has been explored in works such as [1] and [7], while specific technologies have also been tailored to this use case [3]. Realizing an AmI within a command center provides the potential to empower decision makers with the information they require more rapidly and accurately. Enabling these types of interactions between the users and an AmI environment offers the promise of distributing tasks between the two, reducing operator workload and stress, and ultimately resulting in more timely and better informed decisions.

7 Future Work

Although we are in the very early stages of development, the existing system has exposed near and mid term focus areas that will be required to build towards the goal of an AmI enabled interface. Most of the initial work has focused on the *sensing* and *reasoning* steps of AmI systems, and with these in place, follow-on efforts can begin to explore the *acting* and *interacting* phases.

7.1 Improvements to Baseline

Accurately determining what is happening in a given area was the clear initial step. The modules and processes outlined thus far are incremental to achieving this, but further work must be done to improve upon the existing implementations to increase the system's usability and the integration of future capabilities. The sensor and data fusion aspect of the system must be further developed to produce increasingly robust tracks. If the space has well defined ingress/egress points, additional sensors can be mounted here to determine the number of individuals in the room at any given time, which could provide useful bounds to the fusion algorithm.

Another important component will be minimizing any errors that occur in the transcripts from the speech to text module. Depending on the implemented use case, language models will need to be fine tuned to ensure lexicons unique to the domain of interest are properly accounted for. Errors in the transcription portion of the natural language processing pipeline will greatly inhibit the performance of subsequent modules, making efforts to increase the robustness of the speech to text model imperative.

7.2 Capability Enhancements

As the existing capabilities are iteratively improved, new capabilities must be introduced to enhance the interface itself. To incrementally improve upon the existing system, a few key areas have been identified that will be necessary to support further development.

Activity Detection. In addition to the visual modalities currently in the environment, the existing video feeds can be further leveraged to perform activity and gesture recognition. Information on these modalities will allow the system to gain further insight into the user's interaction with the physical environment, and determine intentions to support more intricate context awareness.

Knowledge Framework. To perform any action, the system will require some degree of knowledge representation. This will typically come in the form of a knowledge graph consisting of various types of entities and the relationships between them. In general, some common sense knowledge will be useful across implementations, but domain specific representations will need to be implemented as well.

Natural Language Understanding. Beyond speech to text, higher level natural language processing and understanding techniques will need to be developed and integrated. Named entity recognition will be needed to detect and categorize entities of interest, which can then be linked to the appropriate entities in the knowledge representation. Modules to recognize and classify speaker intent as well as topic modeling techniques, will provide important contextual information. As these are further developed, a process for tracking the state of the ongoing dialogue, including any inputs by the system itself, will be necessary.

Multimodal Outputs. The type of outputs rendered or provided by the system must also be expanded to support increasingly complex interactions. Outside of exposing image or audio based information based on user requests, processes will need to be developed to allow the users to manipulate other aspects of the environment. This will include a combination of integrating existing APIs from other systems in the environment, as well as further developing the audio and visual output modes.

7.3 Human Subjects Studies

User involvement and feedback is an essential component of any research involving human subjects. With the current baseline components in place, a structured study of potential users will need to be designed to better inform future development and capability enhancements, in addition to identifying potential problem areas that must be addressed for the various use cases of the system. These will be necessary for defining and structuring the interactions enabled by the system, and will guide the use of all current and future sensory and perceptual tasks.

8 Conclusion

The developed components provide baseline functionality to infer information about the occupants of an area, and how their actions and intents are related to available assets within the environment. Future work will focus on improving the tracking and identification accuracies of all individuals, as well as decreasing speech to text error rates to enable improved semantic information extraction via natural language understanding models. These will be underpinned by the development of structured knowledge graph representations of information relevant to the domain of interest. Bringing all of these components together will enable rapid feedback and actions based on explicit and implied user requests via a range of outputs, such as displays, speakers, and interfaces to networked resources. With this, an AmI environment begins to emerge with the potential to transform the manner in which humans influence and exploit the data and technologies at their disposal.

References

1. Augusto, J.C.: Ambient intelligence: the confluence of ubiquitous/pervasive computing and artificial intelligence. In: Schuster, A.J. (ed.) Intelligent Computing Everywhere, pp. 213–234. Springer, London (2007). https://doi.org/10.1007/978-1-84628-943-9_11
2. Augusto, J.C., Callaghan, V., Cook, D., Kameas, A., Satoh, I.: Intelligent environments: a manifesto. Hum. Cent. Comput. Inf. Sci. **3**(1), 1–18 (2013). https://doi.org/10.1186/2192-1962-3-12
3. Bagchi, S., Wynter, L.: Method for a natural language question-answering system to complement decision-support in a real-time command center. US Patent 8,601,030, 3 December 2013
4. Cao, Q., Shen, L., Xie, W., Parkhi, O.M., Zisserman, A.: Vggface2: a dataset for recognising faces across pose and age. CoRR abs/1710.08092 (2017). http://arxiv.org/abs/1710.08092
5. Cao, Z., Hidalgo, G., Simon, T., Wei, S.E., Sheikh, Y.: OpenPose: realtime multi-person 2D pose estimation using Part Affinity Fields. arXiv preprint arXiv:1812.08008 (2018)
6. Chung, J.S., Nagrani, A., Zisserman, A.: Voxceleb2: deep speaker recognition. CoRR abs/1806.05622 (2018). http://arxiv.org/abs/1806.05622
7. Coen, M.H., et al.: Design principles for intelligent environments. In: AAAI/IAAI, pp. 547–554 (1998)
8. Cook, D.J., Augusto, J.C., Jakkula, V.R.: Ambient intelligence: technologies, applications, and opportunities. Pervasive Mob. Comput. **5**(4), 277–298 (2009). https://doi.org/10.1016/j.pmcj.2009.04.001. http://www.sciencedirect.com/science/article/pii/S157411920900025X
9. Corno, F., De Russis, L.: Training engineers for the ambient intelligence challenge. IEEE Trans. Educ. **60**(1), 40–49 (2017). https://doi.org/10.1109/TE.2016.2608785
10. Hannun, A.Y., et al.: Deep speech: scaling up end-to-end speech recognition. CoRR abs/1412.5567 (2014). http://arxiv.org/abs/1412.5567
11. Kleinberger, T., Becker, M., Ras, E., Holzinger, A., Müller, P.: Ambient intelligence in assisted living: enable elderly people to handle future interfaces. In: Stephanidis, C. (ed.) UAHCI 2007. LNCS, vol. 4555, pp. 103–112. Springer, Heidelberg (2007). https://doi.org/10.1007/978-3-540-73281-5_11
12. Lindwer, M., et al.: Ambient intelligence visions and achievements: linking abstract ideas to real-world concepts. In: 2003 Design, Automation and Test in Europe Conference and Exhibition, pp. 10–15, March 2003. https://doi.org/10.1109/DATE.2003.1253580

13. Noury, N.: Ambient intelligence might support increased longevity. In: 2014 36th Annual International Conference of the IEEE Engineering in Medicine and Biology Society, pp. 1760–1764, August 2014. https://doi.org/10.1109/EMBC.2014.6943949
14. Ramos, C., Augusto, J.C., Shapiro, D.: Ambient intelligence–the next step for artificial intelligence. IEEE Intell. Syst. **23**(2), 15–18 (2008). https://doi.org/10.1109/MIS.2008.19
15. Schroff, F., Kalenichenko, D., Philbin, J.: FaceNet: a unified embedding for face recognition and clustering. CoRR abs/1503.03832 (2015). http://arxiv.org/abs/1503.03832
16. Yachir, A., Amirat, Y., Chibani, A., Badache, N.: Event-aware framework for dynamic services discovery and selection in the context of ambient intelligence and internet of things. IEEE Trans. Autom. Sci. Eng. **13**(1), 85–102 (2016). https://doi.org/10.1109/TASE.2015.2499792

Making Object Detection Available to Everyone—A Hardware Prototype for Semi-automatic Synthetic Data Generation

Andreas Besginow[1(✉)], Sebastian Büttner[1,3], and Carsten Röcker[1,2]

[1] OWL University of Applied Sciences and Arts, Lemgo, Germany
{andreas.besginow,sebastian.buettner,carsten.roecker}@th-owl.com
[2] Fraunhofer IOSB-INA, Lemgo, Germany
carsten.roecker@iosb-ina.com
[3] Clausthal University of Technology, Clausthal-Zellerfeld, Germany

Abstract. The capabilities of object detection are well known, but many projects don't use them, despite potential benefit. Even though the use of object detection algorithms is facilitated through frameworks and publications, a big issue is the creation of the necessary training data. To tackle this issue, this work shows the design and evaluation of a prototype, which allows users to create synthetic datasets for object detection in images. The prototype is evaluated using YOLOv3 as the underlying detector and shows that the generated datasets are equally good in quality as manually created data. This encourages a wide adoption of object detection algorithms in different areas, since image creation and labeling is often the most time consuming step.

Keywords: Object detection · Synthetic datasets · Machine learning · Deep learning

1 Introduction

Neural network based object detection is used in numerous applications due to speed and accuracy. Examples are medicine [8,18], autonomous driving [4,7] or industrial support [3,5,12]. Regardless of the area of application, neural networks need to be trained using reference images with meta-information, such as the type of object and its position in the image. For the training, large datasets of labeled data can be used, like the COCO dataset [14]. However, most datasets only cover everyday objects, and humans or animals. Therefore, applications that need images of very specific objects can not make use of the available datasets, making it necessary to capture or collect thousands of images of the target object.

To tackle this issue, this work describes the concept, implementation and evaluation of a lightweight and affordable prototype for semi-automatic creation

N. Streitz and S. Konomi (Eds.): HCII 2020, LNCS 12203, pp. 178–192, 2020.
https://doi.org/10.1007/978-3-030-50344-4_14

of image-based training data. With our approach, users without technical knowledge are empowered to create data sets to train machine learning models for their individual purpose. The source code is available on Github.[1]

This work comprises the following sections:

First, other works discussing (semi-)automatic data generation, or which can be extended to, are presented, as well as the applications of object detection in Human-Computer Interaction (HCI). Next, the concept for our system is discussed, separated into hardware and software. Following the concept, the implementation is described, where the programming aspects are discussed in more depth. After this, an evaluation is conducted to decide whether the system is capable of replacing manual training data creation. This work concludes with a discussion of the results and future work.

2 Related Work

This section discusses the implementation of object detection in Human-Computer-Interaction applications as well as different methods to create synthetic data or ease the process of labeling and annotating.

2.1 Object Detection in HCI Applications

Object detection is adopted more and more in the literature. This is used in industrial settings to e.g. recognize which objects are in a specific area, in order to provide further instructions [5]. Object detectors are also used to detect people in images, either to count or track them entering or leaving an area [24]. One very common use for these detectors is to recognize hand gestures to control an environment without direct interaction [17].

2.2 Image Annotation Processes and Implementations

Table 1. The publications assigned to degrees of automation in the annotation process

	Manual	Semi-automatic	Automatic
Image capture		[11] **This work**	
Bounding boxes	[21]	[21]	[11,20] **This work**
Labeling	[20,21]	[11,21,25] **This work**	

[1] https://github.com/ABesginow/SynthTrainDataGenerator.

Broadening the scope of annotating, the following stages can be considered:

1. Taking an image of the target object
2. Marking the position of the object in the image
3. Providing the correct label

These stages can have varying degrees of automation, from manual to automatic (see Table 1).

For all following works, the first step is considered finished. Nevertheless, it is explicitly mentioned since it can be part of the annotation process, as shown in the rest of this work.

The work of Russel et al. [21], focuses on creating a database for object detection in images, where the user is manually labeling images. The user is shown an image in a web editor and can use the editors tools to label objects inside the images. Users can either use simple rectangles to label objects, or choose to draw precise polygons. The labels are also chosen by the user.

In their work, Russel et al. describe how they automated parts of the process.

Labeling of objects has been extended by an electronic dictionary for consistency inside the dataset. And object positions are initially approximated using automatic object detection, leaving verification and refinement to the user. The library had, at the time of publication, a set of 183 classes, with over 30k images annotated. The closest dataset in size provided 101 classes [21]. In terms of degrees of automation, this work went from manual marking of the positions and manual labelling to semi-automating both these processes.

A different work by Russel et al. [20] discusses the automatic recognition of similar looking objects in a large number of images. This approach is based on Scale-Invariant Feature Transformation (SIFT) [16] descriptors which are quantified into visual words [23] using a k-means clustering algorithm. This allows for fully automated object detection in different images, but the objects still have to be labeled by a person [20,22].

Wenyin et al. [25] have developed a tool to decide whether or not a certain image is relevant for a given search query. The implementation displays a number of images with manually or automatically generated tags. Based on the existence of already tagged images, it allows the user to decide whether or not the images belong to the query via a simple yes/no choice. This implementation is similar to the one discussed in this work, since the user is still involved in the process, making it semi-automatic [25]. Since this work doesn't cover marking the objects position, the results would rather be used for different applications than object detection.

A method that uses CAD models to synthesize training images is presented by Hinterstoisser et al. [11]. They created CAD models of a number of objects and placed them in images with a cluttered background and augmented the images e.g. by adding synthetic noise or rotating the object. Given preexisting, or easily created, CAD models this method seems to produce desirable results, but the source code is not available. In addition to generating images, they used a method to freeze layers in a neural network. This helped to learn the objects feature and use pre-trained neural networks to improve the overall performance.

The combination, gave promising results, but the objects were very well distinguishable and the backgrounds used to train were also used for the evaluation, probably making recognition easier.

Crowdsourcing is also used to label datasets. A well known example is the CAPTCHA, developed by Google and used by a large number of websites [1,2].

To the best of the authors knowledge, no system comparable to the one designed and implemented here has been published.

3 Concept

The goal of the system is to capture images of an object, further referred to as OTL (object-to-learn). These images have to show the object from all sides, without the background and ready for further processing. The following section discusses the concept for a system to execute these steps, creating a dataset for training an object detection network.

3.1 Hardware

The hardware necessary for this project consists of a rotating entity to place the OTL on (see Fig. 1). It is placed in front of a well lighted and plain coloured background to increase the background subtraction quality. A motor rotates the plate and a camera captures the scene. It preferably has automatic focus calibration to capture details of the OTL. The final component is a computer for image processing, motor control and training of the neural network.

Fig. 1. Concept sketch of the necessary hardware components

3.2 Software

To create the dataset the following operations are necessary:

1. Create an image of the OTL
2. Subtract the background and cut out the OTL
3. Rotate the OTL
4. Create training images.

These operations can be implemented in various detail, especially the creation of training images allows for a number of possible augmentations. For example a layer of noise on the image causes more variation in the dataset, thus improving the object detection results.

A user specifies what has to be considered background in the image, using an user interface (UI). A rough sketch of the UI is shown in Fig. 2.

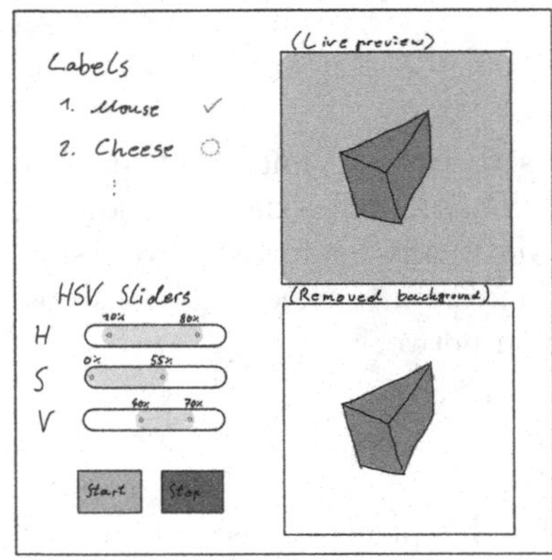

Fig. 2. Sketch of the UI

4 Implementation

This section describes the implementation of the system in hardware and software.

4.1 Hardware

To ensure constant and good lighting conditions, a cube consisting of three light panels, which are adjustable in their brightness, is used. The panel model is V-TAC VT-6137. The cube, including frames, has a side length of 65 cm, with a wooden plate placed in the bottom (see Fig. 4).

A Logitech Brio webcam is used to record images with a maximum resolution of 4096 px × 2160 px. The camera can either be attached to the lighting cube or placed on a tripod (see Fig. 4) to increase flexibility in movement and positioning.

To save and process the images, the single-board computer Raspberry Pi 3 (RPi) is used. Its GPIO pins allow direct control of a step motor connected to the RPi. Furthermore, the RPi keeps the system cheap, small and portable.

The motor is inserted into a custom 3D printed mount, which is secured with double-sided tape. The plate is driven by a 3D printed wheel mounted on the motor tip (cf. Fig. 3). The 3D models are also available on Github.

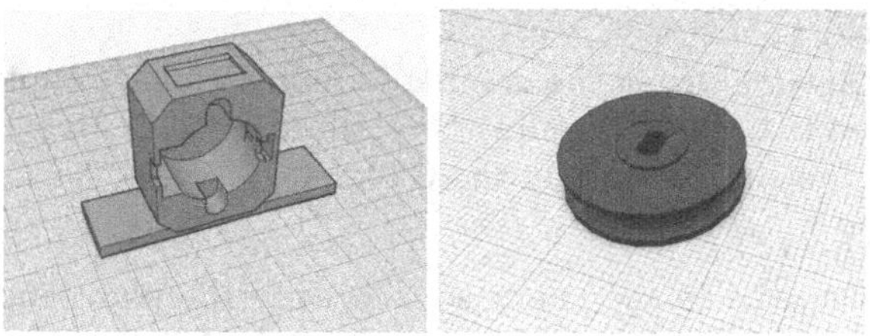

Fig. 3. The 3D models. The left image shows the mount for the motor and the right image shows the wheel placed on the motor tip.

The rotating plate is a plain wooden plate with exchangeable, plain coloured, cardboard covers. A bearing underneath the plate makes it easier for the stepper motor to rotate it, despite the weight of the OTLs.

To train the object recognition network, a desktop PC (further referred to as server) with the following specifications is used: Nvidia 1080 GTX with 8 GB VRAM (GPU), an AMD Ryzen 2700 (CPU) and 16 GB RAM.

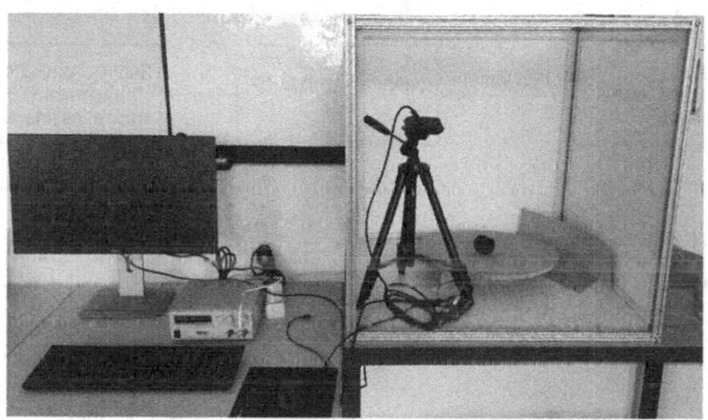

Fig. 4. Hardware setup

4.2 Software

The following sections discuss the code implementation. Figure 5 shows a software process diagram. Since this work is a proof of concept, the Graphical User Interface (GUI) provides just basic functionalities.

Libraries, Tools and Operating Systems

The RPi is running the April 2019 version of the operating system Raspbian and our software, written in Python3. To process images, the OpenCV library for Python is used.

The server is running a Windows 10 operating system and uses the Windows version of YOLOv3[2] [19].

[2] https://github.com/AlexeyAB/darknet.

Image Capture

The images are captured using the standard OpenCV image capture implementation and cut down to only capture the plate and OTL. Here, this results in 600 px × 600 px images, containing the OTL.

Extraction of the OTL

As described above, the image is cut so that only the plate and the OTL are in the window. By leaving out unnecessary areas the following image processing tasks run faster and more stable. A visualization of the process can be seen in Fig. 6.

The image is initially captured using the RGB color scheme, and then translated into the HSV (Hue, Saturation, Value) color scheme. This allows to focus on the hue channel, for further processing. Because the plate is plain colored, the background can be removed easily.

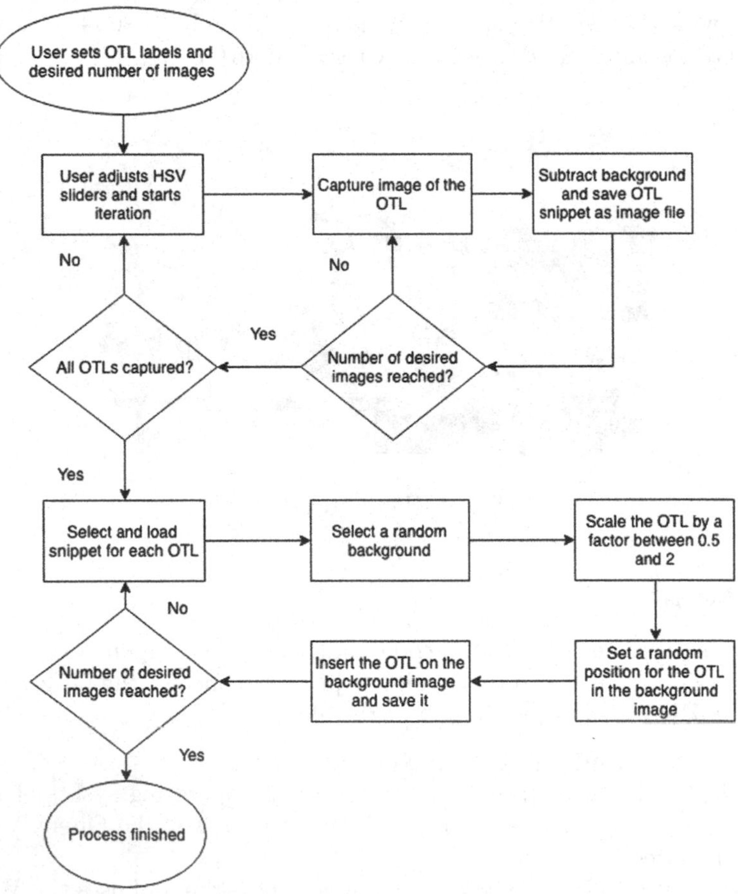

Fig. 5. Software process diagram

The user is provided a basic user interface with sliders for the HSV values and a live preview image. This preview image displays what parts of the image are considered background and are removed (see Fig. 7). When only the OTL can be seen in the preview window the sliders are set correctly. Finally, the extracted OTL is saved.

Augmentations

The number of possible augmentations to increase variety in the dataset and, potentially, improve generalization of the resulting neural network is huge. For test purposes, the minimum of augmentations are implemented, leaving room for improvement in later iterations.

- Randomly selecting backgrounds for the image
- Placing the OTL in a random position inside the image
- Scaling the OTL by a random factor (between 0.5 and 2)

This mitigates several potential errors that the object detector could make, like learning that the object is always in the top left corner, always of the same size, or always has a black background.

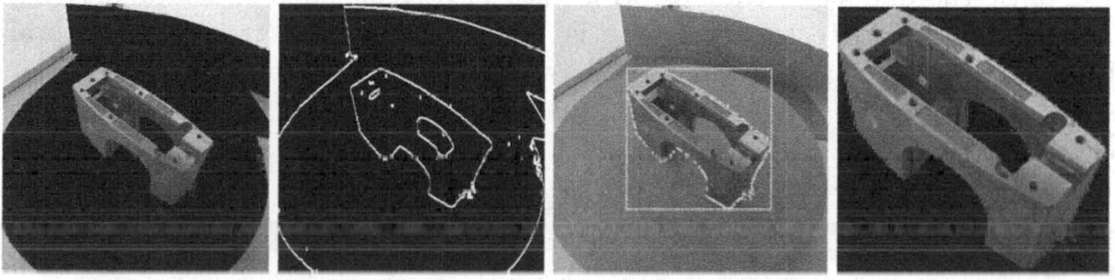

Fig. 6. The first image shows the background subtraction based on the entered HSV values. The second displays the result of the canny edge [6] detection executed on the first image. The third image shows the original image with the selected contour and the corresponding bounding box (the rectangle enclosing the object) drawn in. The final image shows the resulting snippet of the first image, using the bounding box displayed in image three.

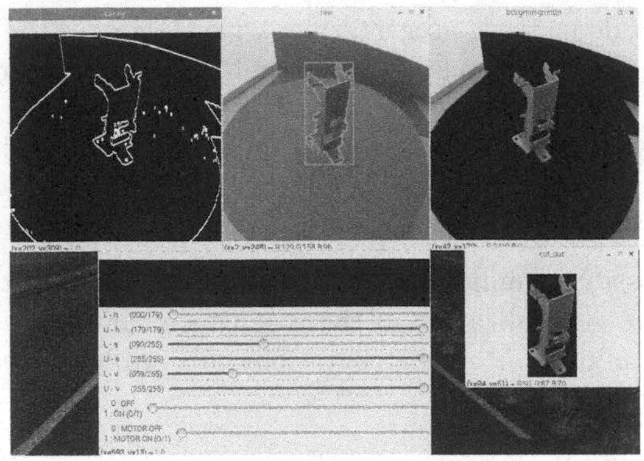

Fig. 7. The GUI displays preview images for all processing steps and HSV sliders, allowing adjustments and updates in the preview images in real time.

5 Evaluation

To evaluate the system, the same object detection algorithm is used in each case, since the quality of the detection then mostly depends on the underlying dataset [13]. The detector used here is YOLOv3 [19]. It is trained on a total of five datasets and later evaluated on two evaluation datasets, which were not used during training. The results on the evaluation datasets show how well the network trained.

5.1 Datasets

The quality of the system is evaluated using the resulting datasets, since this impacts the performance of the final object detector considerably [13]. For this purpose, five datasets are used to train object detectors. They are evaluated by measuring the mAP (mean Average Precision) of the object detectors on a separate dataset. The following section introduces the datasets, an overview is given in Table 2.

Table 2. The different datasets used in direct comparison

	Object	Creation	#Images	Purpose
1	Custom object	Manually	300	Training
2	Custom object	Synthetic	300	Training
3	Custom object	Synthetic	3000	Training
4	Banana	Manually	2200	Training & Testing (2000/200)
5	Banana	Synthetic	2200	Training & Testing (2000/200)
6	Custom object	Manually	56	Evaluation
7	Banana	Manually	57	Evaluation

There are three datasets displaying custom objects, one is created manually and two are created synthetically. The manual dataset consists of 300 images, showing all three objects in each image, from various angles and in different contexts.

The two synthetic datasets consist of 300 and 3000 images. The smaller dataset shows the quality in direct comparison with the manually created dataset. The bigger dataset shows the true potential of semi-automatic data creation, since it takes very little extra effort to create a dataset that big (in total 45 min), whereas the manual dataset took roughly 1 day to make (including the labeling of the objects). The synthetic datasets have been created according to the process described in Fig. 5. Figure 8 shows examples of the synthetic training images. The background images for training are partly self-made, showing e.g. an office environment and partly selected randomly from the internet (e.g. a factory hall, a forest or a cluttered room). A total of 39 background images are used for the datasets.

The remaining two datasets represent everyday objects, bananas, in this case, to run a more exhaustive test of the systems performance. Again, a synthetic dataset is compared against a human-made dataset. For the human-made dataset, the COCO dataset [14] is used. All the images showing bananas were extracted, consisting of approx. 2200 images, of which 2000 are used for training and 200 for testing, during training. The dataset shows bananas in various degrees of ripeness, in tufts or single fruits, cut in slices and arranged in various ways. This variety in presentation is very difficult to create synthetically. We have decided to create three different presentations of the object: as a bundle, as a single banana and cut into slices. Which covers most of the COCO dataset images. The synthetic dataset also consists of 2000 images for training and 200 for testing.

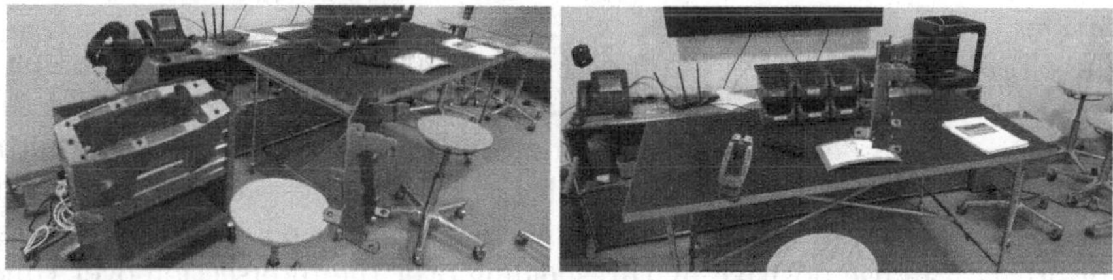

Fig. 8. Synthetic images which were created sermi-automatically using the prototype. The background is photographed beforehand and the three objects have been inserted by the software.

Two evaluation datasets have been created, one for the bananas and one for the custom objects. The banana dataset consists of 57 images (43 taken from the COCO dataset not used for training and 14 images from the internet). The custom objects evaluation dataset consists of 56 images, all created and labeled manually. The labeling includes the position of the objects and the object label, usually referred to as ground truth.

5.2 Training

The object detector trained is YOLOv3 [19]. The training is done from scratch for 13000 iterations and with a learning rate decay at 11000 and 12000 iterations by a factor of 0.1. The number of iterations is set relatively low to keep training time at a reasonable length. Everything else is left to standard configuration.

The networks were initialized randomly for each training, leaving some randomness in the process. This decision was deliberate to allow comparability among the different datasets. The use of the pretrained weights provided for YOLOv3 is common and would improve the final recognition rate of the objects drastically, since the feature layers of the network would have been trained already and only refinement would have been necessary. But since the provided weights were trained on the COCO dataset, this would benefit the banana subset taken for our training, skewing the results. To mitigate this all networks were trained from scratch, which, in combination with the low number of iterations, gives a low mAP value. But since the focus here is on the comparison of the datasets, given the same circumstances, the relative comparison is more important.

All in all this results in five datasets, with five training runs each. Each training takes 13000 iterations and runs approximately 26 h. Therefore the training ran for roughly 27 days on the server described in Sect. 4.1. The training progress is saved every 1000 iterations.

5.3 Analysis and Results

The object detectors, trained on the different datasets, act as proxies for the evaluation.

The object detectors were evaluated every 1000 iterations on the complete dataset, all predictions were noted, including label, predicted position and confidence score. This process is repeated for every run and every dataset, resulting in a total of 325 files containing the predictions for the respective dataset. The predictions are further processed to determine whether or not a prediction was a true positive or a false positive by thresholding over the Intersection over Union (IoU) (or area of overlap a_o), given by this formula [9]:

$$a_o = \frac{area(B_p \cap B_{gt})}{area(B_p \cup B_{gt})}$$

With the prediction bounding box B_p and the ground truth bounding box B_{gt}.

Given $a_o > 0.5$, a prediction is noted as a true positive (TP), else it's a false positive (FP). All objects in an image are considered false negatives (FN) if they have not been found but exist in the ground truth annotations. After sorting the predictions in descending order by their level of confidence, a precision-recall curve is calculated. Precision and recall are calculated as:

$$precision = \frac{TP}{TP + FP} \qquad recall = \frac{TP}{TP + FN}$$

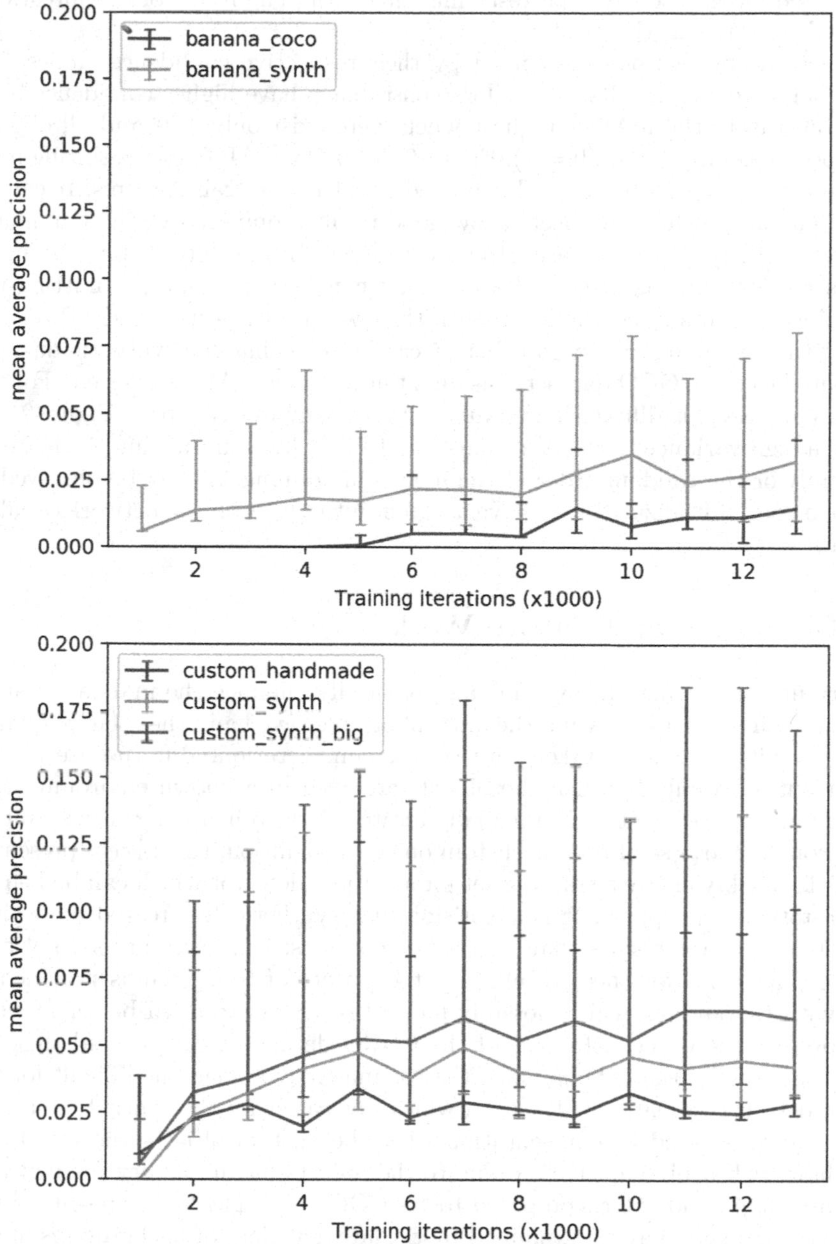

Fig. 9. The mAP values sorted by datasets and plotted over the number of iterations. The continuous line shows the mean of the mAP values over the 5 training runs. The error bars display the min and max values.

The precision is then set to the maximum precision for recall r for any recall $r' \geq r$ and integrated over the resulting curve [10]. The result of the integral is referred to as the mAP.

Since the predictions are sorted by their respective confidence values, the mAP is greater for results where TPs consistently have higher confidence than FPs. Intuitively the mAP is highest when there exist only TPs and all objects have been recognized (recall = 1). Figure 9 shows the mAP curves resulting from the above described process and averaged over the five training runs. It can be seen that the synthetic datasets show good results compared to the handmade datasets. This is true for both object categories. In absolute terms, the mAP values are low, but as discussed above, this can be explained by omitting the pretrained weights in combination with the low number of iterations. But comparing the results against each other, it can be seen that the synthetic dataset, compared to the COCO dataset, has an 2 times higher mAP on average. For the custom objects this difference is similar, at approximately factor 2. Figure 9 also shows a high variance in the error bars, most likely from initializing the network randomly or the random order of the images in training. As can be observed in Fig. 9, a good initialization can have a significant impact on the networks quality (cf. [15]).

6 Discussion and Future Work

The results show that the system can potentially enhance the manual creation of training images. Comparing the amount of time saved and the relative quality of the results, it can be taken into serious consideration. But the use case is important, particularly when the objects are used in a known environment, it is of great importance to add manually created data to increase the recognition rate. For the purpose of tool or custom object recognition, the system presented allows to quickly create a training set for an object detector which can be helpful for prototyping purposes. It is surprising that synthetically created data gives consistently better results than handmade datasets. But there are several possible explanations for these results e.g. the variety of backgrounds provided in the synthetic dataset, which possibly forced the system to learn better features to represent the objects. In case of the COCO dataset it can be said that the wide range of shapes and colors for the bananas maybe made it difficult for the object detector to learn the features, which was easier for the synthetic dataset, since it only showed 3 representations. For the custom objects the results do not show such a big gap, maybe due to the objects having a very distinct and constant shape and color, compared to the COCO set. The better results of the synthetic datasets may be explained by the larger variety of backgrounds in the dataset. This is not given in the handmade dataset since the objects are mostly captured in an office environment Another aspect to take into consideration is the low number of training images in the handmade dataset, which poses the question whether the quality of the object detector would have increased when creating a larger dataset. In any case, the system should be developed further to provide better datasets as there are potential use cases for industries and personal use. Especially since the material cost for the prototype are kept very low with roughly 200€ and can be reduced further by leaving out the lighting panels. The image processing aspects can e.g. be extended by a noise overlay, automatic variations in lighting and color or a synthetic rotation in addition to the physical rotation of the plate. Further, repeated evaluations are necessary to show whether the system can consistently provide such results and if the use of pretrained weights will improve the absolute mAP of the detectors.

Acknowledgements. The authors acknowledge the financial support by the Federal Ministry of Education and Research of Germany for the project "Augmented-Reality-Assistenzsysteme fuür mobile Anwendungsszenarien in der Industrie (FKZ: 03FH005IX6)".

References

1. recaptcha v3 - the new way to stop bots. https://www.google.com/recaptcha/intro/v3.html. Accessed 06 Jan 2020
2. Why captchas have gotten so difficult. https://www.theverge.com/2019/2/1/18205610/google-captcha-ai-robot-human-difficult-artificial-intelligence. Accessed 06 Jan 2020
3. Bian, X., Lim, S.N., Zhou, N.: Multiscale fully convolutional network with application to industrial inspection. In: 2016 IEEE Winter Conference on Applications of Computer Vision (WACV), pp. 1–8 (2016). https://doi.org/10.1109/wacv.2016.7477595
4. Bojarski, M., et al.: End to end learning for self-driving cars. arXiv preprint arXiv:1604.07316 (2016)
5. Büttner, S., Besginow, A., Prilla, M., Röcker, C.: Mobile projection-based augmented reality in work environments-an exploratory approach. In: Mensch und Computer 2018-Workshop Band (2018)
6. Canny, J.: A computational approach to edge detection. In: Readings in Computer Vision, pp. 184–203. Elsevier (1987)
7. Chen, C., Seff, A., Kornhauser, A., Xiao, J.: DeepDriving: learning affordance for direct perception in autonomous driving. In: Proceedings of the IEEE International Conference on Computer Vision, pp. 2722–2730 (2015)
8. Dong, H., Yang, G., Liu, F., Mo, Y., Guo, Y.: Automatic brain tumor detection and segmentation using U-Net based fully convolutional networks. In: Valdés Hernández, M., González-Castro, V. (eds.) MIUA 2017. CCIS, vol. 723, pp. 506–517. Springer, Cham (2017). https://doi.org/10.1007/978-3-319-60964-5_44
9. Everingham, M., Eslami, S.A., Van Gool, L., Williams, C.K., Winn, J., Zisserman, A.: The pascal visual object classes challenge: a retrospective. Int. J. Comput. Vision **111**(1), 98–136 (2015)
10. Everingham, M., Winn, J.: The pascal visual object classes challenge 2010 (voc2010) development kit. http://host.robots.ox.ac.uk/pascal/VOC/voc2010/htmldoc/index.html. Accessed 06 Jan 2020
11. Hinterstoisser, S., Lepetit, V., Wohlhart, P., Konolige, K.: On pre-trained image features and synthetic images for deep learning. In: Proceedings of the European Conference on Computer Vision (ECCV) (2018)

12. Hirano, Y., Garcia, C., Sukthankar, R., Hoogs, A.: Industry and object recognition: applications, applied research and challenges. In: Ponce, J., Hebert, M., Schmid, C., Zisserman, A. (eds.) Toward Category-Level Object Recognition. LNCS, vol. 4170, pp. 49–64. Springer, Heidelberg (2006). https://doi.org/10.1007/11957959_3
13. Junhua Ding, X.L.: An approach for validating quality of datasets for machine learning. In: 2018 IEEE International Conference on Big Data (Big Data), pp. 2795–2803 (2018). https://doi.org/10.1109/bigdata.2018.8622640
14. Lin, T.-Y., et al.: Microsoft COCO: common objects in context. In: Fleet, D., Pajdla, T., Schiele, B., Tuytelaars, T. (eds.) ECCV 2014. LNCS, vol. 8693, pp. 740–755. Springer, Cham (2014). https://doi.org/10.1007/978-3-319-10602-1_48
15. Locatello, F., et al.: Challenging common assumptions in the unsupervised learning of disentangled representations. arXiv preprint arXiv:1811.12359 (2018)
16. Lowe, D.G., et al.: Object recognition from local scale-invariant features. In: ICCV, vol. 99, pp. 1150–1157 (1999)
17. Rautaray, S.S., Agrawal, A.: Vision based hand gesture recognition for human computer interaction: a survey. Artif. Intell. Rev. **43**(1), 1–54 (2012). https://doi.org/10.1007/s10462-012-9356-9
18. Ravì, D., et al.: Deep learning for health informatics. IEEE J. Biomed. Health Inform. **21**(1), 4–21 (2016)
19. Redmon, J., Farhadi, A.: YOLOv3: an incremental improvement. arXiv preprint arXiv:1804.02767 (2018)
20. Russell, B.C., Efros, A.A., Sivic, J., Freeman, W.T., Zisserman, A.: Using multiple segmentations to discover objects and their extent in image collections. In: 2006 IEEE Computer Society Conference on Computer Vision and Pattern Recognition (CVPR 2006), vol. 2, pp. 1–8 (2006). https://doi.org/10.1109/CVPR.2006.326
21. Russell, B.C., Torralba, A., Murphy, K.P., Freeman, W.T.: LabeLMe: a database and web-based tool for image annotation. Int. J. Comput. Vision **77**(1–3), 157–173 (2008)
22. Sivic, J., Russell, B.C., Efros, A.A., Zisserman, A., Freeman, W.T.: Discovering objects and their location in images. In: Tenth IEEE International Conference on Computer Vision (ICCV 2005), vol. 1, pp. 370–377. IEEE (2005)
23. Sivic, J., Zisserman, A.: Video google: a text retrieval approach to object matching in videos. In: Null, p. 1470. IEEE (2003)
24. Subramaniam, A., Chatterjee, M., Mittal, A.: Deep neural networks with inexact matching for person re-identification. In: Advances in Neural Information Processing Systems, pp. 2667–2675 (2016)
25. Wenyin, L., Dumais, S., Sun, Y., Zhang, H., Czerwinski, M.: Semi-automatic image annotation (2000)

On the Integration of Multiple Modeling Methodologies into a Single User Interface

Lawrence Henschen(✉) and Julia Lee

Northwestern University, Evanston, IL 60208, USA
henschen@eecs.northwestern.edu, j-lee@northwestern.edu

Abstract. The development, analysis, and refinement of modern Embedded Systems (ES) and Internet of Things (IoT) applications require the use of complex models. These, in turn, require a variety of modeling techniques that can be used for different aspects of a given ES or IoT project. ES and IoT projects nowadays are well beyond pencil-and-paper development and analysis, so sophisticated tools with well-designed human-computer interfaces are required. Such tools do exist for various modeling techniques individually – for example, tools for Petri Net modeling, tools for UML modeling, etc. Some tools are able to translate a model in one methodology to a second model or to a programming language. However, no tool exists that integrates the major modeling methods used in ES and IoT into a single package that allows designers and engineers to explore through a single interface all the aspects of the project. This makes it difficult for the designers and engineers to see how operations, or even changes, modeled in one methodology impact models in the other methodologies. Designers and engineers can't see the whole picture within a single tool. We argue that such a tool is needed for ES and IoT and propose a set of requirements that such an integrated tool must satisfy in order to be truly useful in the design and analysis of ES and IoT projects.

Keywords: Modeling · Integrated interface · UML · FSM · Petri · BACNet

1 Introduction

The development, analysis, and refinement of modern Embedded Systems (ES) and Internet of Things (IoT) applications require the use of complex models. These, in turn, require a variety of modeling techniques that can be used for different aspects of a given ES or IoT project. ES and IoT projects nowadays are well beyond pencil-and-paper development and analysis, so sophisticated tools with well-designed human-computer interfaces are required. Such tools do exist for various modeling techniques individually – for example, tools for Petri Net modeling, tools for UML modeling, etc. Some tools do include translation to a second modeling methodology or to a programming language. However, no tool exists that integrates the major modeling methods used in ES and IoT into a single package that allows designers and engineers to explore through a single interface all the aspects of the project. This makes it difficult for the designers and engineers to see how operations, or even changes, modeled in one methodology impact

N. Streitz and S. Konomi (Eds.): HCII 2020, LNCS 12203, pp. 193–206, 2020.
https://doi.org/10.1007/978-3-030-50344-4_15

models in the other methodologies. Designers and engineers can't see the whole picture within a single tool. We argue that such a tool is needed for ES and IoT and propose a set of requirements that such an integrated tool must satisfy in order to be truly useful in the design and analysis of ES and IoT projects.

An integrated tool allows designers and other stakeholders, who would be knowledgeable about the application but may not be technically trained, to specify the high-level behavior of the system through a UML-like interface. Designers could then add FSM/SDL models that could implement the behavior. The interface would allow users to tie actors and other information (e.g., timing requirements) from the behavioral model to specific elements in the FSM/SDL model. Similarly, a Petri Net model could be developed, and again specific elements of the behavioral model and the FSM/SDL model tied to places and transitions in the Petri Net model. Finally, as engineers make low-level decisions about specific hardware, the system would allow that information to be added to the system through, for example, a BACNet interface. As before, specific elements of objects defined in the BACNet model could be associated with corresponding items from the other models. With all these models in place and corresponding pieces of each of the models tied together in the system, comprehensive simulations and analyses could be performed. Moreover, all the stakeholders, technical and non-technical, could participate because the integrated model has parts that are easily understandable by each of the stakeholder groups.

We begin with an overview of a sample of existing systems in Sect. 2. We then briefly describe the major modeling systems used in ES and IoT design (and mentioned in the preceding paragraph) in Sect. 3. We present some examples of how an integrated system would present information to users and react to user input in Sect. 4. The major contribution, a list of requirements that an integrated system should satisfy, is then given in Sect. 5.

2 Existing Systems

As mentioned, some systems combine more than one modelling technique. These systems typically implement a single primary modelling methodology with full or nearly full features and provide some translation into a second modelling method.

One class of such systems allows for modeling of a single type with translation between different standards for that type of modeling. Many of these systems also provide generation of code in a variety of programming languages and, in some cases, reverse engineering of existing code in those languages. For example, Enterprise Architect [1, 2] allows high-level modeling of business processes and software in a variety of UML and related standards. It also provides simulation support for sequence and behavioral diagrams of UML and state machines. It supports translation into a variety of programming languages and supports forward and reverse engineering of standard database schemata. It does not provide support for Petri Net modelling or the BACNet-type modelling of the physical level of a system.

There are techniques for limited translation between various modelling methods mentioned in the introduction, although we are not aware of any commercially available systems that implement such translations. For example, [3] describes how to translate colored Petri Nets into FSM format. UML 2.4 supports behavioral state diagrams that are typically derived from the behavioral specification of a UML model. Systems that support simulation of UM 2.4 would provide simultaneous simulation of the UML model and the corresponding FSM model. There is no support for Petri Net modelling or BACNet-level modeling. Unfortunately, translations like these would not likely provide the same level of insight into different portions of a system being designed as would the development of corresponding models from scratch in the different modelling systems. For example, the UML model of a bridge developed by management level designers may simply indicate that under certain conditions the bridge spans go up. An engineer modelling the internal behavior of the motor control system as a finite state machine would have a different and much more detailed view of the span control. Of course, those engineers would be informed by the knowledge from the management designers and the UML model, and vice-verse the engineers would provide information back to the management level designers. But the model produced by the merging of the two models developed semi-independently by corresponding groups of experts will almost surely be better than a UML model in which the FSM portion is derived solely from the UML behavioral specification.

We are not aware of any tool that comes even close to meeting the requirements we have describe in the introduction.

3 Description of Sample Modeling Methodologies

The following represent the major types of modeling systems used in the design and analysis of ES and IoT products. They range from very high-level specification to low-level details of the product implementation. They will illustrate the benefits of an integrated tool and expose requirements that such a tool must satisfy to be useful in the design and analysis of complex products. We use the design of a bridge in an urban environment to illustrate the various modeling techniques.

3.1 Unified Modeling Language (UML)

Early stages of the design of an ES or IoT application typically focus on the external behavior rather than how the product works internally. In other words, the focus is on the interactions of the product with its environment. Universal Modeling Language (UML) [4, 5] is a system that allows non-technical people, such as marketing analysts and government officials, to describe how an application should interact with the people who use it or other products that interact with it. The main diagrams of UML are the use-case diagram and the message sequence chart. UML has many more features, but these two will illustrate the main points of this article – a single human-computer interface system that integrates multiple modelling methods.

The use case diagram lists the various distinct ways in which the product will be used and the users that will participate in those cases. It is important in the early stages of the design to know all the ways in which the product will be used. In the case of a bridge, the use that first comes to mind is to go up to let boats pass under. But the behavior may be different during monthly inspections or maintenance, so these are two additional use cases. Each use case involves its own set of actors, the external entities (people, objects, etc.) that participate in that use case. Figure 1 shows a sample use-case diagram for a bridge project.

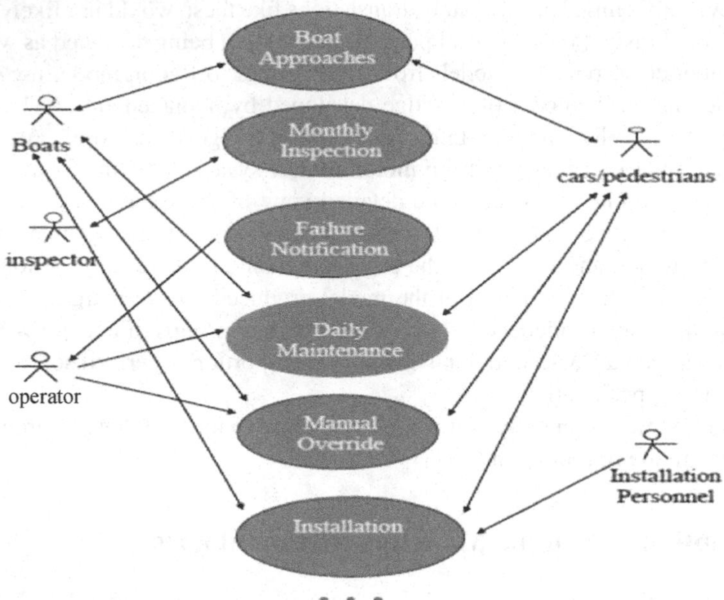

Fig. 1. Sample use cases for a bridge project

The second major diagram in UML is the message sequence chart, a two-dimensional diagram with major modules of the product across the top and progression of time on the vertical axis. Arrows are drawn from one module to another to indicate messages sent from the first module to the second. Arrows further down occur at later times. The message sequence chart shows the totality of messages and their order of occurrence for one scenario. Each scenario (for example, one boat arrives, two boats arrive from opposite directions, etc.) has its own message sequence chart. Figure 2 shows a sample message sequence chart for the bridge project.

UML diagrams allow non-technical people to describe and specify how the product is supposed to behave. These designers would apply their experience and knowledge of the application area to the specification of the product. For example, government officials and river traffic engineers could develop and then analyze message sequence charts to ensure the bridge will operate in accordance with existing laws and protocols. These designers would likely not know about lower-level engineering details, like electrical properties of the motors that raise and lower the bridge spans or specific sensors that could determine how close a boat is to the bridge.

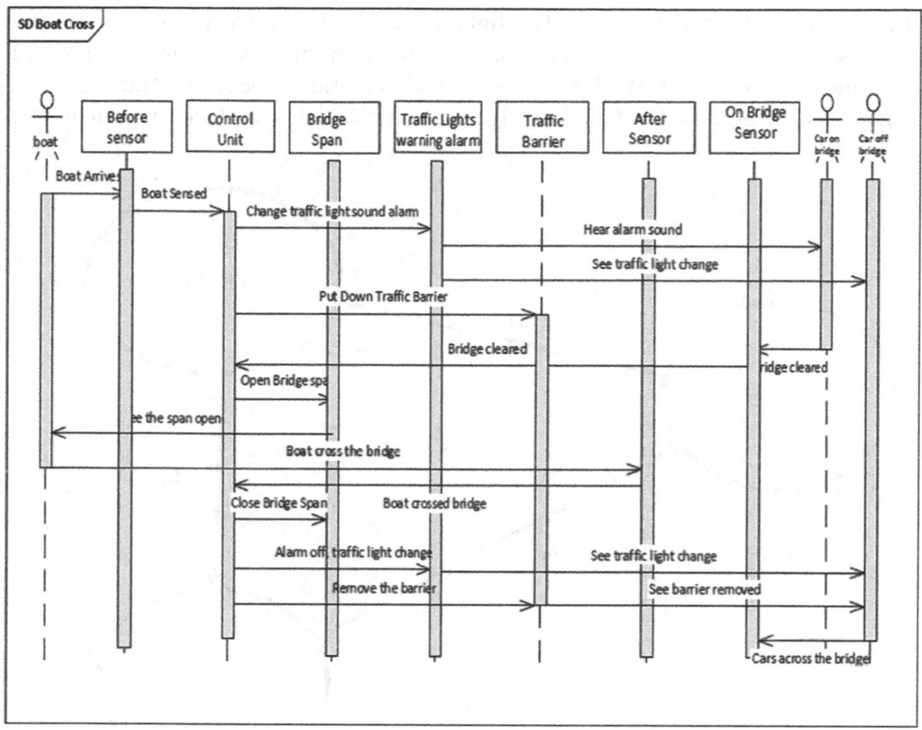

Fig. 2. Sample message sequence chart for the scenario one boat arrives

3.2 Finite State Machine (FSM)

Once the external behavior of the product has been specified designers can focus on the internal behavior, that is, on how the product works internally. One way to model this kind of behavior is the Finite State Machine modeling language [6] and related systems like Specification and Description Language (SDL) [7]. The basic parts of a FSM diagram are states and transitions. A state represents a condition in which the product may exist. Examples of states for the bridge project include (1) that span is down with cars and pedestrians crossing normally and (2) the span is going up in preparation for a boat to pass under. States are drawn as circles. Transitions represent changes from one state to another. A transition has a set of conditions that causes the transition to occur and a set of actions that must occur when the transition is made. An example of a transition for the bridge project is from the normal state (span down, cars/pedestrians using the bridge) to the preparation for span to go up state. The condition that causes this transition to occur is that an approaching boat is sensed. When this transition occurs, many actions must be performed, such as turning the ground traffic warning lights red and other related actions. In a FSM diagram the condition and actions are attached to an arrow leading from the current state to the new state.

Figure 3 shows a portion of a FSM diagram for the traffic lights for the bridge. Conditions c1 and c3 refer to a system variable, ChangeToRed. When a boat is detected the main control module of the bridge sets this variable to 1 to indicate that the street traffic lights should change to red. The light, of course, has to change to yellow for a brief time first, so the action is to turn the green light off, turn the yellow light on, and start a timer. Later, after the boat has passed under the bridge, the main control module would set the variable back to 0, indicating that the traffic light can change back to green.

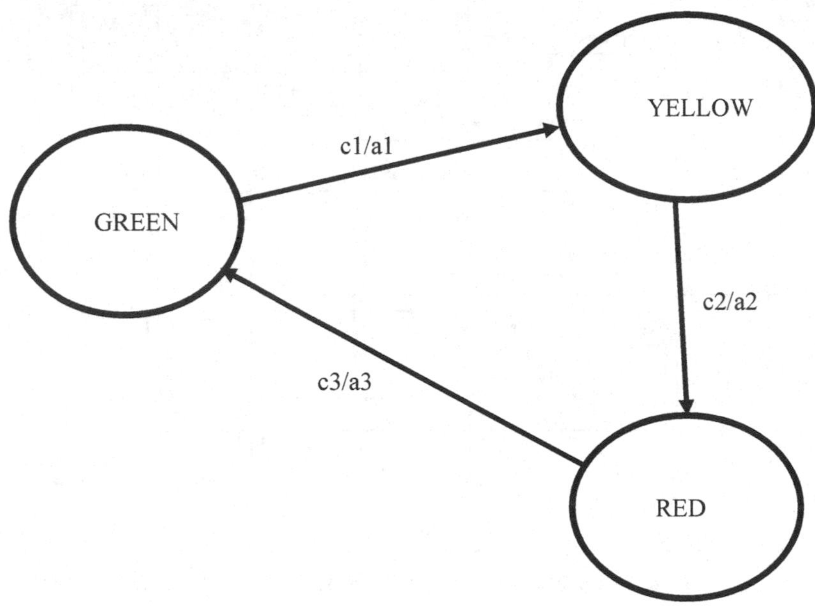

c1	ChangeToRed == 1	a1	Turn off green, turn on yellow, start timer
c2	timer expired	a2	Turn off yellow, turn on red
c3	ChangeToRed == 0	a3	Turn off red, turn on green

Fig. 3. Portion of an FSM for the bridge project

The reader can now appreciate how the various modelling methods relate to each other. For example, states in a FSM diagram may correspond to vertical positions in various message sequence charts, and actions associated with transitions may correspond to messages in those charts. A tool that integrates multiple modelling techniques should provide for relationships between elements of different models to be identified. Further, during simulations of the product changes in one model should be automatically reflected in all the other models. Product designers and analysts should be able to switch from one model to another and see up-to-date diagrams in each of those models.

3.3 Petri Net

The Petri Net representation [8] is useful for modeling distributed systems with modules that must coordinate and share resources. The condition-event format is the original form of Petri Net. Conditions, drawn as circles, represent conditions that can be either true or false. If a dot occurs in the circle it means the condition is true; the absence of a dot means the condition is false. Transitions, drawn as solid rectangles, represent operations that can be performed. An arrow from a place to a transition represents a requirement that the condition at the tail of the arrow (called a precondition) must be true before the transition can occur. There may be several arrows from different places pointing into one transition indicating that the transition requires several conditions to be true. An arrow from a transition to a place represents that a new condition (called a post condition) becomes true after the transition occurs. There may be several arrows leading out of a transition indicating that the transition makes several new conditions true. When a transition "fires", dots in the preconditions are removed (those conditions become false) and dots are placed in the post conditions (making those conditions true).

Figure 4 shows a sample Petri Net for one part of a bridge project. This net models the mutual exclusion of a shared resource – the area where the bridge crosses over the river. We assume a bridge in which the span must go up to allow boats to pass under. Therefore, not both the cars/pedestrians and the boats can be using that area at the same time. Figure 4 shows the situation in which there are cars/pedestrians both on the bridge itself and approaching from the side. Both P4 and P5 have dots. P3 does not have a dot because the common space is not available for other actors (in this case, a boat) to use. P1 is empty, indicating that there are no boats approaching the bridge, and of course P2 is empty because the bridge is currently being used by cars/pedestrians. At some point (see Example 1 in Sect. 4) a boat may appear (a dot appears in P1), requiring the cars/pedestrians to be cleared from the bridge so that they are not using common space. In Fig. 4 this would correspond to the event indicated by the arrows P5 → T3 and T3 → P3. The dot from P5 would be removed, and a dot would appear in P3. At this point transition T1 could occur; that is, the boat could make use of the common space (dot in P2), and the common space would no longer be available for cars/pedestrians (dot removed from P3). Note that for a dot to appear in P2, it must be the case that a boat is approaching and, more importantly for the modelling of the mutual exclusion, the common space is not being used by cars/pedestrians.

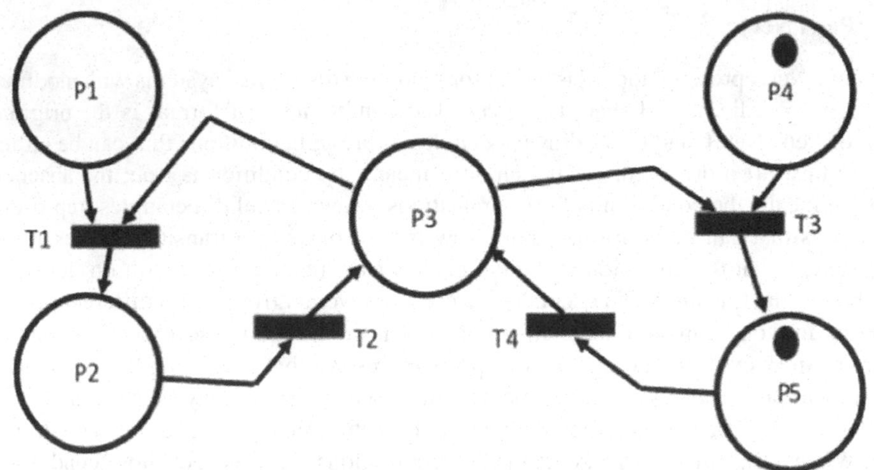

P1	A boat is approaching the bridge.
P2	A boat is currently moving under the bridge.
P3	The common space is not being used by either a boat or cars/pedestrians.
P4	Cars/pedestrians are approaching the bridge.
P5	Cars/pedestrians are currently on the bridge.
T1	The boat is allowed to proceed.
T2	The boat has passed to the other side.
T3	Cars and pedestrians are allowed to use the bridge.
T4	Cars and pedestrians have cleared off the bridge.

Fig. 4. Portion of a Petri Net model for the bridge project

3.4 BACNet

Finally, devices that implement the product being developed must be modelled. These include sensors that provide information about the environment and actuators that cause actions in the environment. Sensors include analog sensors for things like temperature, distance, pressure, etc., digital sensors for things like switches that can be either on or off, and other kinds of input devices. Actuators include analog devices for things like voltage levels, digital outputs for things like relays that can be turned on and off, as well as other kinds of outputs. The BACNet language [9] was designed to model these kinds of devices as well as a host of other devices that might be used in an ES or IoT application. All BACNet objects contain a common set of attributes like device name, device type, etc. Each kind of device then has additional attributes relevant to that kind of device. For example, an analog input device has attributes for current reading, units, minimum/maximum allowed readings, etc. Figures 5 and 6 show partial BACNet models for two devices that might be used in the bridge project. An automated bridge system would need to detect the presence of an approaching boat. Figure 5 shows an input device that senses distance. The system would also need the capability to raise the bridge span through the use of a motor. Figure 6 shows the BACNet model of an output device that represents a relay that turns the motor on and off. Including these implementation objects in the simulation is important because the simulation can help determine whether or not the selected devices perform up to the requirements imposed by the higher-level models.

Name:	boat sensor	Current value:	NONE
ID:	M472sensor	Units:	meters
Type:	analog input	Event detection:	enabled
Description:	distance of incoming boat	Minimum value:	0
		Maximum value:	500

Fig. 5. Partial BACNet specification for the boat-approaching sensor

Name:	span motor up	Current value:	OFF
ID:	K129SRelay	Rating:	200
Type:	digital output	Rating units:	WATTs
Description:	span motor for raising		

Fig. 6. Partial BACNet specification for the span-raising motor

4 Example of Integrated Interface Usage

We suggest that an integrated model can lead to better products that are developed more rapidly than when models are studied independently. Application specialists, such as government and river management officials in the bridge example, would use the UML-like portion of the interface to specify the behavior of the bridge in a variety of use cases and scenarios. Designers and engineers would then develop FSM/SDL and Petri Net models that implement that behavior and also account for the internal operational details of the submodules that make up the product. Engineers could select specific hardware components, such as sensors and motors, and add those to the model through the BACNet interface. Stakeholders from all levels can work together during this model development stage, informing each other of what is required or, conversely, what is feasible or practical.

Similarly, and perhaps more importantly, an integrated system allows all those groups to work together during simulation/testing and analysis. For example, a simulation session might begin by some users specifying that a new boat approaching the bridge has been sensed, i.e., one of the sensors in the BACNet model has detected a boat. The system knows how that sensor relates to inputs and conditions in the FSM/SDL model, places and transitions in the Petri Net model, and actors in the UML model. The change to the sensor reading automatically triggers corresponding changes in the other models. Users can switch back and forth among the models to study the operation of the system in response to that sensor change. Anomalies or unexpected transitions or results in one of the models would be immediately detected by the corresponding participants. The various participants, from government officials to system designers to system implementers, could cooperate to locate and correct errors in one or more of the models and then rerun the simulation to verify that the fixes worked properly. Because errors were found immediately, no matter in which level of modeling they occurred, corrections can be made sooner than if results from, say, a device-based simulation in the BACNet model had to be transferred to the design team (who developed the FSM/DSL and Petri Net models) or even the application specialists (who developed the UML model) to study separately. We believe such close, simultaneous cooperation of representatives from all the levels can also lead to better products as the various groups inform each other and suggest improvements.

We illustrate what we have in mind for the interface with two examples.

Example 1. Simulation from Bottom Up
In the first example we show how the integrated system should work in a simulation based on changes that occur in the devices being used to implement the system. Initially, the boat sensor registers nothing within its range. Then it registers a boat at 490 m. This change in the BACNet model is shown in Fig. 7. Corresponding changes in the other models are shown in Figs. 8, 9 and 10. The changes are highlighted in bold.

Name:	boat sensor	Current value:	**490**
ID:	M472sensor	Units:	meters
Type:	analog input	Event detection:	enabled
Description:	distance of incoming boat	Minimum value:	0
		Maximum value:	500

Fig. 7. The BACNet boat sensor registers an approaching boat.

In the Petri Net model, the presence of an approaching boat is modelled by a dot appearing in P1. Therefore, the change in the sensor value in Fig. 7 should trigger an associated change in the Petri Net, as shown in Fig. 8.

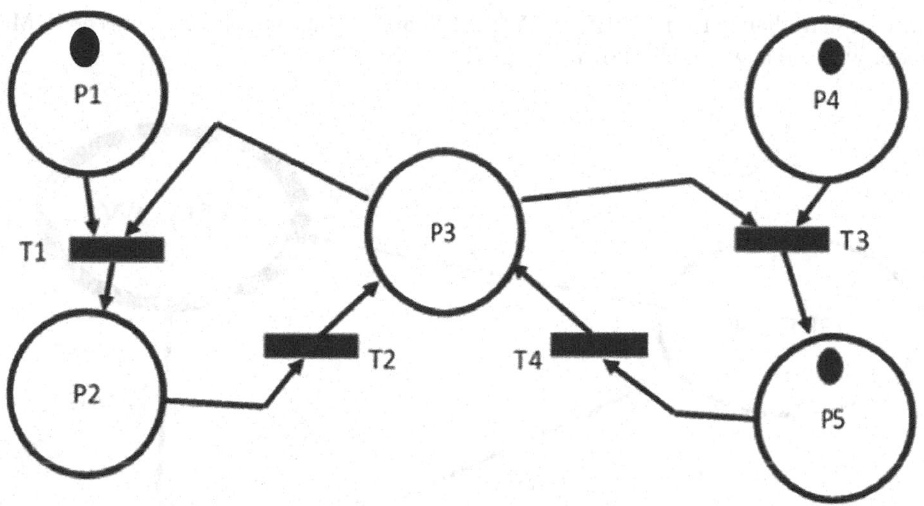

Fig. 8. A dot appears in P1 because of the sensor change in Fig. 7.

In the UML message sequence chart, sensing the arrival of a boat corresponds to a message being sent from the boat to the sensor. This in turn leads to a message being sent to the Main Control module, which then sends a message to the Traffic Lights and Warning Alarm module. The transmission of these three messages is shown in Fig. 9.

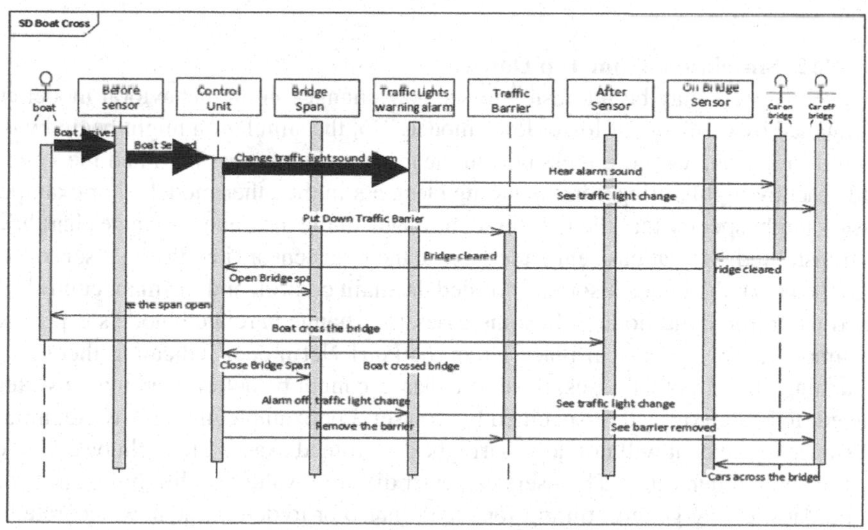

Fig. 9. Messages relating to sensor change in Fig. 7 are highlighted in the message sequence chart.

The message to the Traffic Lights and Warning Alarm module corresponds to setting the variable ChangeToRed in the FSM model to 1. This makes condition c1 true and causes a state change from GREEN to YELLOW and the starting of the timer. The FSM model with the new state is shown in Fig. 10.

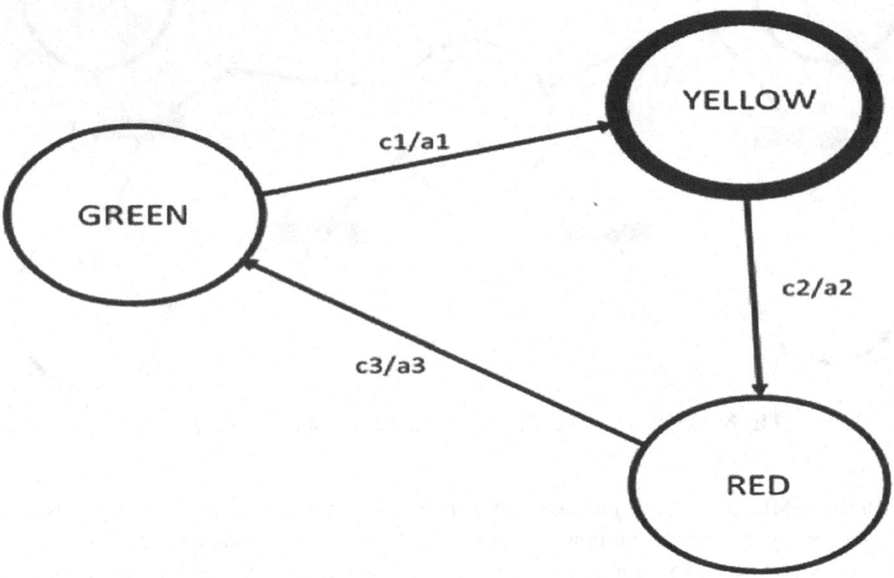

Fig. 10. The traffic light FSM changes state in response to sensor change in Fig. 7.

Example 2. Simulation from Top Down
Conversely, testers may be interested to see how changes in the behavioral model are implemented by elements of lower level models. So, the simulation might begin by the users indicating one or more messages in the message sequence chart, and the system would react by highlighting corresponding elements in the other models. For example, the users might specify that the first three messages in the message sequence chart have been transmitted. A boat has sent a message to the boat sensor (i.e., the boat sensor has sensed the boat), the boat sensor has notified the main control, and the main control has notified the traffic light module. In some cases, the change in related models is precise; for example, a dot appears in place P1 in the Petri Net model indicating there is an approaching boat. In other cases, the exact change cannot be determined by the system and needs to be determined or specified by the user. For example, in the BACNet model the distance to the boat will not necessarily be determined exactly; it might be 500 m or 490 m or some other value. The users can enter different values in different simulation runs, perhaps testing general timing for this scenario or to determine how accurate the boat sensor must be or how often it must be read. The reader can easily imagine how these changes would appear in the interface, so we will not repeat Figs. 7, 8, 9 and 10.

5 Requirements for an Integrated System

The following are what we believe are minimal requirements for a system. As indicated in Sect. 4, such a system should allow users to conduct experiments in which all the models are simulated simultaneously. Any change in one model during the simulation should automatically and instantly be reflected in corresponding changes in the other models. Errors uncovered during a simulation should be correctable in the system itself rather than having to close the system and have the individual teams start up individual applications to make their edits.

An integrated system should have editors for all the modelling techniques that are to be integrated. Users should be able to create new models from scratch in any of the integrated techniques as well as to be able to edit them during simulation runs. Further, users must be able to connect corresponding portions of the various models. Because the models may be developed independently, it is not clear whether the connections can be made automatically or not. Therefore, at a minimum there must be facilities for making these by hand. We anticipated that groups from the various design teams would meet to discuss and determine these connections (Such meetings would also facilitate better understanding between the various design teams from different modeling groups). Alterations to any one model should pop up corresponding edits that may need to be made in the other models. Here are a few examples of alterations possibly requiring changes to other models.

- A change in the order of messages in a message sequence chart may require changes to the FSM model or Petri Net model. For example, designers may have originally indicated that a message should be sent to lower the traffic barriers at the same time as the message to change the traffic light to red is sent. Designers later decide that the traffic barriers should not be lowered until after the light has been red for 5 s so that cars/pedestrians have adequate warning before the gates start to come down. The order of messages in the message sequence chart is changed. This may require a new state in the FSM model – "bridge span cleared". Conditions on the FSM state transitions must be altered correspondingly so that the FSM cannot enter the state "lower traffic barriers" before the state "bridge span cleared" is reached.
- New scenarios may be introduced in the UML model. Similar to the previous bullet point, this may require new states in the FSM model and/or modifications to the conditions and actions on state transitions.
- A different device replaces an existing one in the BACNet model. For example, the engineers want to experiment with a different boat sensor. The new sensor may have a different range, and this may affect timing annotations in the message sequence chart.

The display should provide for layering and zooming into and out of the various models of the system, both during editing and during simulation. Users should be able to click on partially hidden models to bring them to the front. For non-trivial systems the user should be able to zoom out in any model to get the context of the current situation in that model. Conversely, the user should be able to zoom in the see low-level details of the top-layer model. FSM, Petri Net, and BACNet models include hierarchies. For example, one state in an FSM can itself be a complete FSM; for example, the traffic light FSM is one of a set of concurrent FSMs for the whole bridge. Similarly, a BACNet device can include smaller BACNet devices; for example, the BACNet object for the traffic light controller could include several primitive BACNet devices such as switches to turn the individual lights on and off. During editing or simulation a user may want to only see the high-level object or see the internal details.

During simulation the system should alert the user, through pop-ups or other means, of all changes in other models related to any change in the model currently on the top layer. This aspect was illustrated in the examples in Sect. 4.

6 Conclusion

We have proposed the development of a tool that integrates the primary modeling methods used in the design of embedded systems and Internet of Things applications. We have given examples of how such a tool can work to improve design and reduce design time. We have indicated what we believe are the minimum requirements for such an integrated tool.

References

1. Sparx Systems. https://sparxsystems.com/products/ea/. Accessed 18 Jan 2020
2. Wikipedia. https://en.wikipedia.org/wiki/Enterprise_Architect_(software). Accessed 18 Jan 2020
3. Simon, E., Stoffel, K.: State machines and petri nets as a formal representation for systems life cycle management. In: Proceedings of IADIS International Conference Information Systems 2009, pp. 275–272. IADIS Press, Barcelona (2009)
4. DISQUS. https://www.uml-diagrams.org/state-machine-diagrams.html. Accessed 18 Jan 2020
5. Wikipedia. https://en.wikipedia.org/wiki/Unified_Modeling_Language. Accessed 18 Jan 2020
6. Wikipedia. https://en.wikipedia.org/wiki/Finite-state_machine. Accessed 18 Jan 2020
7. Wikipedia. https://en.wikipedia.org/wiki/Specification_and_Description_Language. Accessed 18 Jan 2020
8. Wikipedia. https://en.wikipedia.org/wiki/Petri_net. Accessed 18 Jan 2020
9. Wikipedia. https://en.wikipedia.org/wiki/BACnet. Accessed 18 Jan 2020

VLC-Enabled Human-Aware Building Management System

Yehuda E. Kalay[1,2](✉), Haripriya Sathyanarayanan[1], Davide Schaumann[3], Albert Wang[4], Gang Chen[4], and Ramdas G. Pai[5]

[1] University of California, Berkeley, CA, USA
{kalay,haripriya_snarayanan}@berkeley.edu
[2] Technion, Israel Institute of Technology, Haifa, Israel
[3] Jacobs Technion-Cornell Institute at Cornell Tech, New York, USA
davide.schaumann@cornell.edu
[4] University of California, Riverside, CA, USA
{aw,gachen}@ece.ucr.edu
[5] School of Medicine, University of California, Riverside, CA, USA
ramdas.pai@medsch.ucr.edu

Abstract. "Smart" buildings that can sense and detect people's presence have been in use for the past few decades, mostly using technologies that trigger reactive responses such as turning on/off heating/ventilating, lighting, security, etc. We argue that to be considered truly smart, buildings must become "aware" about the locations and activities of their inhabitants so they can proactively engage with the occupants and inform their decision making with respect to which actions to execute, by whom and where.

To help assess the potential impact of "aware" buildings on their occupants, we are developing a multi-agent simulation-powered building management system that can sense human and building assets, extrapolate patterns of utilization, simulate what-if scenarios and suggest changes to user activities and resource allocation to maximize specific Key Performance Indicators (KPIs). The system is able to evaluate the implications of potential conflict resolution strategies and account for individual and collaborative activities of different types of users in semantically rich environments.

Sensing in our case is based on Visible Light Communication (VLC) technology, embedded in a building's LED lighting system. It can detect the actors, where they are located and what they do. To understand what happens in each space at any given time the information derived from the VLC system is combined with models of users' activity schedules, profiles, and space affordances.

We demonstrate our approach by hypothetically applying it to a Cardiac Catheterization Laboratory (CCL). The CCL is high-intensity hospital unit, second only to the Emergency Department in terms of the urgency of the cases it must handle. An aware building will help both patients and staff to allocate their (always scarce) resources more efficiently, saving time and alleviating stress.

Keywords: Smart environments · Human behavior simulation · Space utilization · Hospital environments · Visible light communication

N. Streitz and S. Konomi (Eds.): HCII 2020, LNCS 12203, pp. 207–222, 2020.
https://doi.org/10.1007/978-3-030-50344-4_16

1 Introduction

Sensing technologies that enable buildings to detect people's presence have been around for the past few decades. Their use was limited mostly to triggering reactive responses to people's presence (heating/ventilating, lighting, security, etc.). We argue that truly "smart" environments can leverage sensed information about the locations and activities of their inhabitants to proactively engage with the occupants and inform their decision-making processes with respect to which activities to execute, by whom and where. We claim that such buildings will be "aware" of their own status, as well as the status of their occupants and the activities that are performed within (and around) them.

To help assess the potential impact of such "aware" buildings on their occupants, we are developing a simulation-powered building management system that can sense the location and activities of human and building assets, simulate what-if future scenarios and suggest user activities and resource allocation that will maximize specific Key Performance Indicators (KPIs). Our system is able to evaluate the implications of potential conflict resolution strategies using a multi-agent simulation system that accounts for individual and collaborative activities of different types of users in semantically rich environments.

Sensing in our case is based on Visible Light Communication (VLC) technology, embedded in a building's LED lighting system (Pan et al. 2019). It can detect who are the actors, where they are located and what they do, as well as how the spaces themselves are used. Information derived from the VLC system is combined with models of actors' activity schedules, profiles, and space affordances, to understand what happens in each space at any given time. This data forms the current state of the building occupancy and utilization, and is used to simulate alternative possible future states for each actor and to resolve possible conflicts that may occur. The simulation and decision-making process are driven by a previously developed narrative-based modeling system that can simulate human behavior in buildings (Schaumann et al. 2017a, b, 2019). It produces alternative future states, revealing the consequences of enacting different resource allocation strategies. A priority function is used to evaluate and compare the alternative futures and choose the one that maximizes some previously agreed-upon utility function. Once the decision is made, the system uses VLC to communicate the information to the relevant actors who enact them.

While the approach being developed is, in principle, agnostic of the sensing and communication technology used, VLC has been chosen because unlike radio frequency it is highly localized and it does not interfere with the building's other sensitive instruments, which is critical in the case of hospitals (our chosen case study). In addition, because it is embedded in the building's LED lighting system, it requires little additional infrastructure compared to other technologies.

We demonstrate our approach by hypothetically applying it to the Cardiac Catheterization Lab (CCL) in a major hospital: an intervention cardiology unit in a hospital with imaging equipment used to diagnose the arteries and chambers of the heart and treat any stenosis or abnormality found. In addition to treating about 20 scheduled patients every day, the CCL also treats 1–2 emergency cases, known as ST-Elevation Myocardial Infarction (STEMI), every day. These acute heart attack cases require immediate attention, and can, therefore, disrupt the scheduled activities of the CCL. A smart building will help allocate resources more efficiently, saving time and alleviating stress in the Cath Lab, the Emergency Department, the in-patient wards, and more.

2 Building Automation

The effects of a given built environment on the people who inhabit it become apparent only after the environment has been built and occupied, making it difficult to assess the impact of technologically rich environments on their inhabitants. Buildings that have embraced truly advanced technological innovations are few, and these mostly focus on improving energy, lighting, and security performances (Jalia et al. 2019). To help understand and assess the potential impact of buildings that can adapt their performance to the dynamic needs of their inhabitants we have identified three levels of building automation (Kalay 2004) feedback regulated adaptability; model-based adaptability; and total environmental adaptability.

Feedback regulated adaptability is based on the concept of automation, where the results of some action are compared against some desired performance measures. Departure from the desired condition triggers another action to bring the results closer to the desired ones. In building automation, the ubiquitous thermostat demonstrates this principle: it instructs the HVAC system to heat (or cool) the air inside a building, until it reaches the desired pre-set temperature. Enabling buildings to sense and respond to such needs is a relatively simple, reactive kind of automation. It has been implemented in areas of control, regulation and supervision of electrical, mechanical and climatic control equipment.

Adding a functional model to networked building systems and appliances allows for a proactive adaptability approach to building automation: it helps to manage the building in expectation of events, rather than in response to them. A functional model of a building is one where the occupants' behavior patterns are programmed in advance, based on learning their typical preferences, so the building can anticipate and position itself to support recurring events, not only to respond to them (Mozer 1988).

We posit that true adaptability will be reached when the building not only responds—reactively or proactively—to its inhabitants' behavior, but it actively engages, even manages them. Such active management depends on much more information than the locations of the inhabitants and prevailing environmental conditions. Broadly, it must include information about *spatial* conditions, *activities*, and the *inhabitants* themselves:

- *Spatial* information includes the configuration of the building (rooms and the connections between them), the intended purpose of each room (e.g., a patient room in hospital, an Emergency Department, a nurse station, etc.), the environmental conditions prevailing in each space (light, temperature, noise, etc.), and current location of each inhabitant within these rooms/corridors.
- *Activities* information includes each inhabitant current, past and future activities: what is s/he doing now, what did s/he do earlier, and what is his/her schedule for the foreseeable future. It also includes information about customary scheduled activity sequences, and what to do in case of unplanned activities (e.g., 'Code Blue' in a hospital).

- *Inhabitants'* (which we call 'actors') information includes the identity of each actor, his/her profile (role in the organization—doctor, nurse, patient, visitor, etc.), abilities, degree of fatigue, and more.

Once the building management system has access to all this information it can form an image of the current state of the whole building and its inhabitants, and predict alternative future states, by means of simulation. It can then evaluate the cost/benefit of alternative future states and recommend choosing the one that seems most profitable in terms of some pre-determined Key Performance Indicators (KPI).

3 The Power of Seeing the Whole Picture

We call the ability to sense the overall state of the building and its occupants, and be able to extrapolate and evaluate future states, "the power of seeing the whole picture."

VLC affords such abilities in buildings, in terms of locating people and equipment in indoor spaces when individuals and equipment are tagged with VLC transponders. Figure 1 shows a hypothetical experiment of locating staff and patients in a medical ward in a hospital. This ability not only allows locating individual staff members, patients and visitors, but also to make assertions about their status: are they busy, free, or in need of medical attention. Likewise, it allows making assertions about the state of occupancy of spaces. When coupled with predefined space profiles, thermal, light, smoke and other detectors, it can inform the building management system about the specific conditions of every space.

The ability to see the whole provides an overview of some situation, not visible from the individual actor's point of view. Furthermore, as evident from Fig. 1, this ability extends from the present to the past: it is possible to trace previous locations of individuals and equipment at prior points in time.

It is our contention that this ability can also be extended into the future, by way of simulation, which will allow the building management system to predict the future locations and activities of the inhabitants. It could, therefore, consider alternative "futures" and help choose the one most desired (according to some predefined criteria). It is this ability which comprises total environmental adaptability.

We are developing a simulation-powered Building Management System (BMS) aimed at Total Environmental Adaptability that leverages the power of "seeing the whole." It will sense the presence and location of humans and building assets, extrapolate patterns of behavior and utilization, simulate what-if scenarios and suggest modifications to user activities and building operations to maximize specific Key Performance Indicators (KPI).

4 Method

The system is composed of four main components: (1) sensing, (2) simulating, (3) evaluating, and (4) acting.

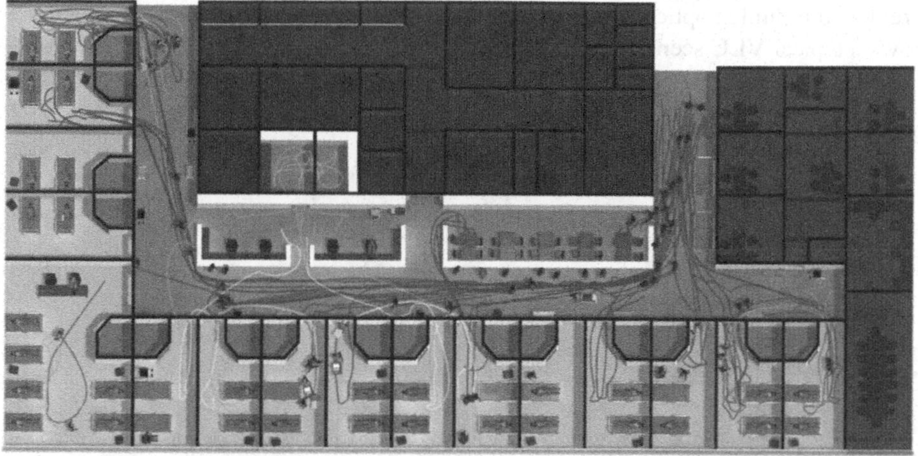

Fig. 1. Locating and tracking people in a hospital ward.

4.1 Sensing

For our case study we have chosen sensing by Visible Light Communication (VLC) system, which is a preferred communication method in hospitals—the domain of our research. Existing RF wireless technologies have many major limitations, including in particular, interference with medical devices that may potentially put patient safety at risk, such as ventilators, pumps, telemetry, defibrillators, brain stimulators, ophthalmic equipment, and many medical implants (Camulli 2014; Berger and Gibson 2013). Another major challenge is that medical-grade wireless must comply with extremely high security and regulatory standards to ensure patient privacy. Such high security cannot be ensured by existing RF wireless networking because RF signals are publicly open and can be intercepted. Any passcode protection may be cracked with enough effort.

Wireless VLC has many advantages over traditional RF technology: it can be embedded in energy-efficient solid-state LEDs (Kim and Schubert 2008). Other than greener lighting, LEDs can be switched ON/OFF at a speed of tens of MHz without flickering visible to the eye, enabling VLC at high data rate by modulating LED light (Conti 2008). The optical spectrum is unlicensed, unrestricted and orders of magnitude wider (300 THz) than the crowded RF spectrum, making wireless streaming of big data possible for large number of users. Visible light allows more emission power for higher data rates and better quality of service (QoS) without risking human health. VLC is unable to penetrate walls, hence ensures high security and privacy. Being interference-free, VLC can co-exist with RF technologies. LED also allows visible light positioning (VLP), due to its beaming nature, which offers indoor locating and navigation in hospitals, parking structures and shopping malls. VLC devices are cheaper than RF components (e.g., expensive 60 GHz mmWave devices). In a sense, VLC wireless is "free" because it is built on existing LED lighting infrastructure, providing VLC wireless streaming at a beyond-Gbps speed.

Ubiquitous VLC wireless systems will consist of modulated LEDs (lamps) for broadcasting and user terminals (smartphones with embedded photodetector as transceivers) to realize full-duplex optical wireless streaming anywhere, anytime for anyone. Figure 2 shows a typical VLC scenario in a hospital.

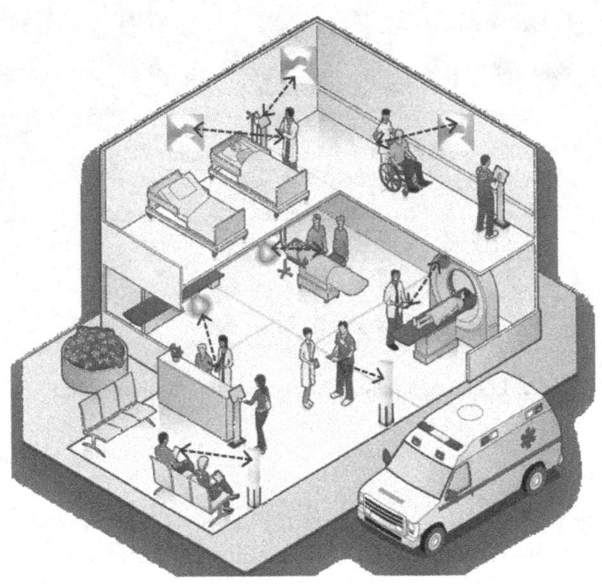

Fig. 2. VLC enables real-time communication positioning in a hospital.

4.2 Simulating

The purpose of the system is to use sensed data, combined with other data, to help make decisions about future actions. Since these decisions involve human activities, which are dynamic and depend on many factors such as spatial, occupational, and personal conditions, the method chosen to help predict future situations is simulation.

Simulation methods have been used to analyze the dynamic relationship between human activities and the surrounding environments in both existing and not-yet-built environments. They include particle-based methods, which describe pedestrians as homogenous particles subject to physical and social forces of attraction and repulsion (Helbing and Molnar 1995). Fluid-based methods describe people flow in fluid-like terms (Henderson 1971; Hoogendoorn and Bovy 2004; Hughes 2003). Cellular automata models provide an inherently spatial representation of occupancy, whereby each cell indicates its occupancy state and transition rules govern the evolution of a cell state (Blue and Adler 1999). Process-driven models consider structured sequences of activities that require a set of resources (e.g., people, equipment) and take a certain (usually stochastic) amount of time (Marmor et al. 2012).

In these models, space is often abstracted in the form of a graph where nodes represent rooms and link represent stochastic traversal times. In hospitals, however, several different processes may take place in the same space, and one process may affect the others. Unplanned social interactions between staff members and patients, for example, have been proven to affect the performing of other medical tasks (Seo et al. 2011). The aforementioned approaches cannot consider interactions among multiple parallel processes occurring in the same space.

We use a Multi-Agent System (MAS) where autonomous agents inhabit virtual environments and sense, plan and act individually or in groups to achieve a specific goal (Yan and Kalay 2004; Helbing et al. 2002; Zheng et al. 2009; Belhaj et al. 2014; Kapadia et al. 2015). While these approaches provide efficient solutions to simulate collision-free movement and social interactions (Thalmann and Musse 2013), they mostly focus on the abstract movement of occupants while ignoring the setting where a behavior is enacted (the specific building type) and the context-dependent activities that people engage in (task-based behaviors in healthcare facilities).

Recent work on narrative-based modeling (Schaumann et al. 2017; Simeone et al. 2013) demonstrated a different approach to simulating day-to-day occupancy scenarios in complex facilities, like hospitals. The approach is centered on the concept of *narratives*, which are rule-based scripts that coordinate the collaborative behaviors of heterogeneous actors (doctors, nurses, patients) who perform a structured sequence of activities (checking a patient, distributing medicine) that unfold in semantically rich spaces.

A key aspect of this approach involves distributing 'intelligence' among the different components of the model. To that effect, the narratives are responsible for the high-level organization of low-level activities into task-based procedures. To relieve the narratives from the need to handle low-level calculation processes, both actors and spaces entities are equipped with autonomous calculation abilities and can dynamically update their status based on contextual social and spatial conditions. That status can be retrieved by the activities and the narratives during their execution so that they can make the most informed decision at any given time.

A narrative manager determines which narrative to trigger at a given time, depending on the current state of the world (the current simulated time or the proximity of actors in a space). In contrast to other approaches that simulate scheduled activities in workplaces, the execution of narratives can adapt to dynamic conditions. For instance, unplanned narratives (such as staff-patient interactions) can cause delays to planned narratives (a patient check).

4.3 Evaluating

Measurable performance indicators are obtained from the simulation results, that can be compared to predefined absolute threshold measures or relatively to one another. They may include patients' length of stay, average waiting times, overall throughput, congestion, staff work schedules and shift loads, staff or space utilization, and other space occupancy indicators.

Performance indicators consists of hard and soft criteria. Hard criteria are quantitative, measurable performances, such as walking distance, length of stay, and throughput of a clinic or ward. Soft criteria are typically qualitative, based on subjective perceptions, such as social, psychological, and organizational policies. In many cases, the same performance results may be valued differently by different stakeholders. To create a building-wide management system, it is therefore necessary to create a shared world-view that incorporates the relative merits of each action from different points of view, and reconciles the differences among them in light of shared, higher-level objectives (Kalay 2004). Since evaluation criteria differ from one other, the evaluation process requires a tradeoff mechanism that balances competing needs: it needs to choose optimization of one performance criterion over others, or strike a balance in the degree to which any performance criterion is achieved, assuring that overall performance is maximized (Kalay 2004).

The process of evaluating the simulation results includes three main phases: (1) identifying the relevant KPI for the simulation; (2) simulation results for the KPIs; (3) comparison of simulation results to benchmark values and normalizing them so they can be compared to one another for evaluation. Evaluating the results and drawing conclusions on the performance of the simulated behavior of the system through the assignment of weights and priorities to arrive at overall scores for a ranking (see Table 2).

The first determines which KPI are needed in relation to time, space, activity, and actors. The second phase is a direct result of the simulations with the metrics for the KPIs. The third phase normalizes the results of the simulation with different numeric measurements to one scale of scores, for example: from 0 (worst) to 5 (best). The normalization is achieved by comparing the simulation (absolute) results to benchmarks based on organizational goals, policies, culture, professional guidelines, norms and regulations, evidence-based design, or expert's opinion.

The evaluation is a study of the implications of the simulation results, based on evidence from research, experience, or precedents. For example, the implications of high level of noise that was predicted in the simulation can be evaluated by their impact on increased patient's stress, pain and depression, decreased patient's privacy and communication with family and staff, decreased staff effectiveness and increased potential of medical errors (Ulrich et al. 2008).

4.4 Acting

Once the comparative evaluations are completed, it is then possible to recommend enacting the most desired—or least disruptive—action. This action is communicated to the relevant stakeholders via the building's two-way communication system, which as mentioned earlier in our case is by means of the VLC system. If the preferred action involves the building's mechanical systems, such as HVAC, lighting, etc., the preferred action may be communicated directly to the assets involved. Like other "recommender" systems, such as GPS-based driving instructions, the actors may accept or ignore the recommended action. Either way, their action will be sensed by the building, and become input for the next round of simulation/evacuation/action.

5 Case Study

We have implemented our system on a hypothetical Cardiac Catheterization Laboratory (CCL). A CCL is a hospital unit equipped with imaging equipment used to visualize the arteries and the chambers of the heart and treat any stenosis or abnormality found. It performs diagnostic, interventional, and electro physiology procedures, serving outpatients, inpatients, and emergency cases.

The CCL while being one of the departments in the hospital, impacts and is impacted by other departments. The challenge is to evaluate those impacts to avoid conflicts and maximize the overall efficacy of the hospital. The simulation process necessarily requires abstraction of a complex system into a simplified model, and experimenting iteratively on it to test the relationship among many variables interacting in complex and often unpredictable ways (Shannon 1998).

The hypothetical case study CCL has five Cath Labs: three Cardiac Catheterization (CC) labs, one Electro Physiology (EP), lab, and one Hybrid Cath Lab. Typically, 20–25 procedures are planned for each workday. In addition, the CCL handles 1–2 unplanned emergency cases every day. The CCL is staffed by 15 medical staff members and operate from 7.30 am to 5 pm every day and may run overtime depending on the procedures and other emergencies. Typically, a diagnostic procedure involves a team of three staff members (a cardiologist and two nurses) and lasts 20–30 min, while an interventional procedure involves a six-member team (cardiologist, anesthesiologist, three nurses and a technician), along with a nurse in the observation area, and lasts 45–90 min. The labs interact with a 15-bed Cardiac Acute Care Unit (CACU) where patients are prepared for the procedure and recover from it (see Fig. 3).

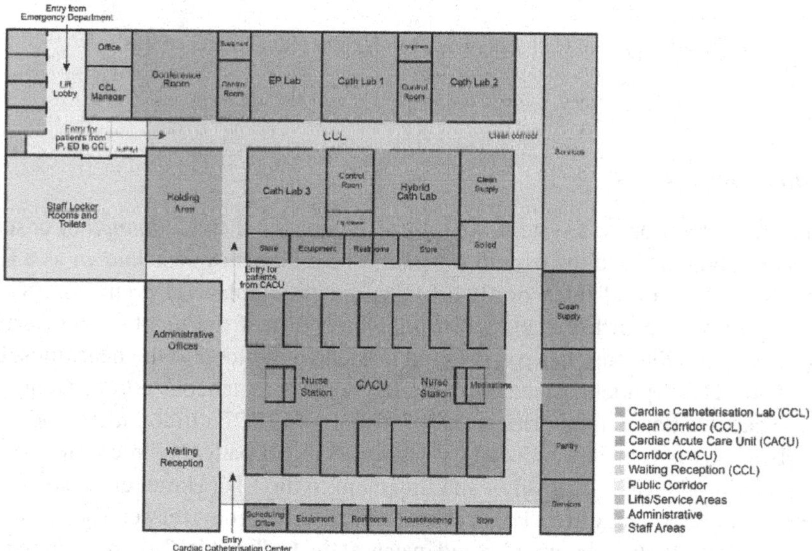

Fig. 3. A typical floorplan of a CCL

5.1 Planned Events

Figure 4 depicts the typical planned activities workflow of the CCL operations. It comprises of four activity blocks that begin after pre-procedure preparation of the patients, either at the CACU for outpatients, the hospital nursing wards for inpatients, or the Emergency Department, depending on the type of patient. These include the 'patient transfer to the procedure room,' 'patient preparation,' 'procedure' and 'transfer back for recovery.' The times depend on the type of patient and type of procedure. There can be additional waiting time dependent on the availability of the cardiologist for the procedure, including other causes for delays such as transfer times and availability of staff for the procedures. The procedure workflow for a patient in the CCL is shown (see Fig. 4) with all the actors and activities involved at various stages in the activity blocks.

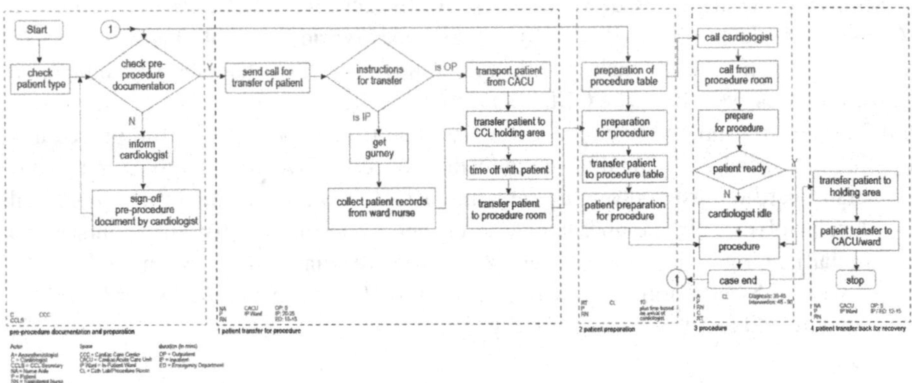

Fig. 4. Typical Cath Lab workflow for the planned procedures.

5.2 Unplanned Events

To demonstrate the proposed system, we look at the impact of an *unplanned* or unscheduled event on the CCL and the overall hospital. The emergency case known as STEMI (ST-Elevation Myocardial Infarction) was taken for the unplanned event. The STEMI is a very serious type of heart attack during which one of the heart's major arteries (one of the arteries that supplies oxygen and nutrient-rich blood to the heart muscle) is blocked. For STEMI patients, access to a facility with percutaneous coronary intervention (PCI) capabilities is time-critical: Door-to-Balloon (D2B) time must be less than 90 min. The D2B is typically reduced by sending STEMI patients directly to the CCL by pre-activating the CCL, instead of sending them to the ED (Martel et al. 2017).

Although the frequency of STEMI cases is typically 1–2 a day, they can be considered as 'unplanned' events that disrupt planned events at the CCL: a STEMI protocol requires an immediate activation of a suitable Cath lab and medical team to prevent delays in care.

Unless the CCL includes a standby un-used CL and medical team to handle such cases (as some hospitals do), this presents a suite of challenges within the CCL, as it may disrupt planned treatments for scheduled patients and medical teams: not all CLs are suitable to treat STEMI patients, and those that are might be occupied with ongoing procedures at different stages of completion. Cardiologists may be occupied or have a scheduling conflict if assigned the STEMI patient. Furthermore, these challenges go beyond the CCL, as changes to the planned schedules can have a negative effect on other outpatients and inpatients: patients that were scheduled to undergo treatment may be bumped, requiring rescheduling (of outpatients) and longer stays (for inpatients). Hence, an action that may seem optimal for the CCL may adversely affect other units of the hospital, and thus be less optimal overall. Such overall implications are often not visible to the CCL staff: resolving them requires "seeing the whole picture," as discussed earlier.

It is the goal of the system described here to critically evaluate all the options facing the CCL in case of a STEMI, and to recommend the overall most suitable plan of action for the hospital as a whole (subject, of course, to the constraints of the STEMI protocol and others).

5.3 Sensing

The overall best course of action is determined by detecting the state of the CCL in term of spaces, actors, and activities, when a STEMI protocol is declared. Table 1 shows the hypothetical state of the five Cath Labs depicted in Fig. 3 in terms of the types of patients and medical teams involved, and the type of ongoing procedures, their expected duration and possibility for interruption of the ongoing procedures by the unplanned STEMI event.

Table 1. Narratives of the planned procedures in the CCL. IP = In-Patient; OP = Out-Patient; CC = Cardiac Catheterization; HCL = Hybrid Cath Lab; EP = Electro Physiology

Space	Type	Procedure	Patient	Duration	Time left
CL1	CC	Intervention	IP1	80 min	40 min
CL2	CC	Intervention	IP2	45 min	45 min
CL3	CC	Diagnosis	OP1	30 min	30 min
CL4	HCL	Diagnosis	OP2	30 min	10 min
CL5	EP	EP	OP3	35 min	30 min

From Table 1 the current state can be determined as follows: the procedure in CL1 is mid-way, the procedures in CL2 and CL3 are yet to commence, the procedure in CL4 is nearing completion, while CL5 is an EP lab, making it unsuitable for the treatment of the STEMI.

5.4 Simulating

The Cath labs need to be evaluated to determine which one of the available labs can be assigned for the STEMI (CL1, CL2, CL3, or CL4), with simulation of the consequences of choosing any one of them and evaluating their relative merits. The Event-Based simulation described earlier is used to determine:

- The procedure in CL1 cannot be interrupted, therefore that lab is not available to treat the STEMI.
- If CL2 is chosen to treat the STEMI, Patient IP2 (an inpatient) who was scheduled to be treated will have to be delayed or rescheduled. The patient will be taken back to the inpatient ward, where (s)he will stay at least another day to be treated (we assume their condition allows such postponement of the treatment). Patient IP2 will not be discharged from the hospital as previously planned and will instead continue to occupy a bed in the cardiac in-patient ward.
- Furthermore, the continued hospitalization of IP2 will prevent admission of an incoming patient from the Emergency Department, who was scheduled to be hospitalized in the cardiac in-patient ward. Instead, she will have to stay in the ED for another 24 h, at a great inconvenience to her and the ED staff.
- If CL3 was chosen to treat the STEMI, Patient OP1 (an outpatient) who was scheduled to be treated will be delayed. He will be taken back to the CACU, delaying treatment of other outpatients scheduled for the day. Since the policy of the CCL is to treat all out-patients that were scheduled for the day rather than sending them home to be treated another day, the CCL clinical staff will have to stay for a longer shift.
- If CL4 is chosen to treat the incoming STEMI, it will take 10 min to complete the ongoing procedure, and another 15 min for the turnaround time (TAT) to make it ready for the incoming STEMI. This will result in an overall 25 min delay in treating the STEMI.

5.5 Evaluating

The results of these simulations are evaluated comparatively to a list of Key Performance Indicators partially drawn from the literature (Brodeschi et al. 2015; Mozer 1988) and discussed with an expert/lead-cardiologist at the hospital's CCL, resulting in sixteen relevant and feasible KPIs that were chosen for this demonstration. The KPIs were grouped into three categories: operational, user related and space related, with eleven operational KPIs, three user-related KPIs, and two space-related KPIs. The KPIs were structured and ranked based on relative importance for the CCL, inpatient and emergency departments, along with executive KPIs for the organization.

For user specific KPIs that address 'patient satisfaction,' proxies such as patient wait times and staff load schedules were used. Inter-departmental relations were accounted for based on the goals or executive KPIs for the hospital to ensure there were no undesired trade-offs where processes within the CCL interact with processes outside the CCL.

Th e simulation results for the KPIs were evaluated based on the method described above to arrive at overall scores for the Cath labs that included the assignment of weights and priorities after normalization.

Figure 5 shows the final evaluation and scores based on category and the Cath lab. While different Cath labs score high in the different categories, if the user-related KPIs are given more weightage by the organization, it is CL3 that is the preferred choice to minimize undesirable consequences such as patient and staff dissatisfaction.

In case of conflicts, the organization's policies and preferences are obtained for the recommended action. Similarly, the scores help understand conflicting needs and consequences of actions on the KPIs.

Table 2. Key performance indicators

	Key Performance Indicators (As defined by Stakeholders)	Simulation Results (Key Performance Indicators)		Benchmark Values	
Operations	Average LOS	Duration of inpatient hospitalization	__days	4.8 days	↓
	Bed turnover rate	Number of discharges / Number of beds	__%	68%	↑
	Cancelled Procedures	Percentage of procedures cancelled/rescheduled	__%	2%	↓
	Average LOS ED	Time between arrival and departure of patient from ED	__hours	9 hours	↓
	First case on-time starts	Percentage of first cases of the day that start on time	__%	100%	↑
	Average procedural time	Procedural time for different procedures	__mins	Diagnosis:30 mins Intervention:50 mins	↓
	Turnaround time (TAT)	Turnaround time between cases (TAT)	__mins	17 mins	↓
	Average time in pre/post procedure holding	Time in pre & post procedure holding area by procedure	__mins	20 mins	↓
	STEMI D2B ≥ 90 minutes	STEMI patients with D2B ≥ 90 minutes	__#	90 mins	↓
	Average LOS post procedure	Duration of time post procedure recovery	__hours	4 hours	↓
	Overall Patient throughput	Time taken by patient from admission to discharge	__hours	6 hours	↓
User	Average Patient Wait Times	Patient wait times	__hours	2 hours	↓
	ED Waiting Time	Wait time in ED	__mins	50 mins	↓
	Staff Load Schedule	Engagement time for treatment and volume of patients	__hours	8 hours	↓
Space	Bed Occupancy	Number of beds occupied/Number of beds	__%	80%	↑
	Room / Asset utilization	Number of rooms utilized/number of rooms	__%	80%	↑

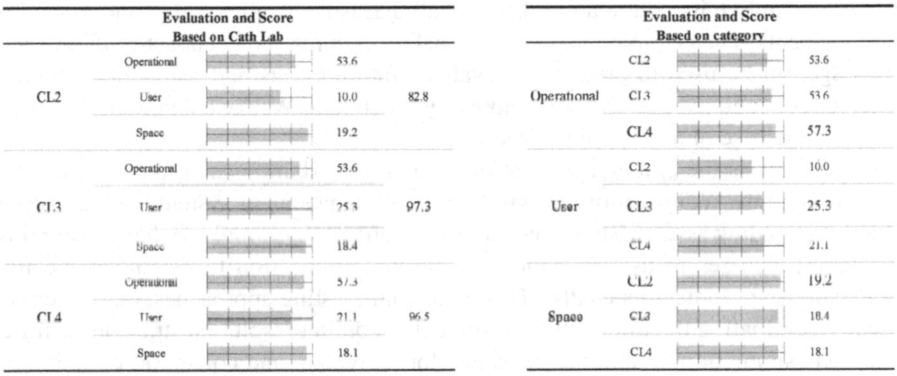

Evaluation and Score Based on Cath Lab			
CL2	Operational	53.6	82.8
	User	10.0	
	Space	19.2	
CL3	Operational	53.6	97.3
	User	25.3	
	Space	18.4	
CL4	Operational	57.3	96.5
	User	21.1	
	Space	18.1	

Evaluation and Score Based on category		
Operational	CL2	53.6
	CL3	53.6
	CL4	57.3
User	CL2	10.0
	CL3	25.3
	CL4	21.1
Space	CL2	19.2
	CL3	18.4
	CL4	18.1

Fig. 5. Scores based on category and Cath Lab for ranking

5.6 Acting

Based on the comparative evaluations, the most desired—or least disruptive—action is communicated to the relevant stakeholders. This is done via the building's two-way communication system, which as mentioned earlier in our case is by means of the VLC.

6 Implementation Details

We use Unity 3D as simulation engine. Unity® 3D is a popular video game engine that features advanced physics and artificial intelligence libraries to model collision avoidance and path-finding.

Spaces have been modeled using Autodesk's AutoCAD® and then imported into Unity 3D using the FBX format. The spaces, actors, activities, narratives and narrative manager have been modeled directly in Unity 3D using Microsoft C#. Activities and narrative have been modeled as co-routines. Narrative co-routines are composed of a structured set of activity coroutines that are nested within the narrative and executed one after the other while yielding at each time step a status to the parent narrative (running or completed). Based on such a status, each narrative updates its own status, which is reported to the narrative manager. To run multiple narratives involving different actors concurrently, we have leveraged Unity 3D's ability to run co-routines in parallel, emulating multi-threading processing.

7 Conclusions

The notion of "smart" buildings has gained popularity with the advent of digital technologies that allow ever-growing sensing and control of building assets and inhabitants. Such systems have mostly been used to improve the energy behavior of buildings and their security by relieving the building's occupants from having to manages such chores. In this paper we argue that true "smartness" will be achieved when the building's omniscience can be harnessed in the service of its inhabitants. Such omniscience implies that the building, unlike its inhabitants, "knows" all that is happening within and around it at any moment. When coupled with operational procedures and occupant profiles, such knowledge can be used to predict and evaluate future events and recommend choosing the most beneficial one for each and every inhabitant. We have demonstrated such abilities in the case of a hospital environment.

To help assess the potential impact of such "aware" buildings on their occupants, we are developing a simulation-powered building management system that can sense human and building assets, extrapolate patterns of utilization, simulate what-if scenarios and suggest changes to user activities and resource allocation to maximize specific Key Performance Indicators (KPIs). Different from existing approaches, our system is capable of evaluating the implications of potential conflict resolution strategies using a multi-agent simulation system that accounts for individual and collaborative activities of different types of users in semantically rich environments.

Sensing in our case is based on Visible Light Communication (VLC) technology, embedded in a building's LED lighting system. It can detect who are the actors, where they located are and what they do. It can also detect how spaces are used. Information derived from the VLC system is combined with models of actors' activity schedules, profiles, and space affordances, to understand what happens in each space at any given time. This data on the current state of the building occupancy and utilization is used to simulate alternative possible future actions for each actor and to resolve possible conflicts that may occur. The simulation and decision-making process is based on a narrative-based modeling system previously developed to simulate human behavior in buildings. It produces alternative future states, revealing the consequences of enacting different resource allocation strategies. A priority function is used to evaluate and compare the alternative futures and choose the one that maximizes some previously agreed-upon utility function. Once the decision is made, the system uses VLC to communicate the information to the relevant actors (i.e., the occupants) who can enact them.

While the approach being developed is agnostic of the sensing and communication technology used, VLC has been chosen because unlike radio frequency it is highly localized, and it does not interfere with the building's other sensitive instruments, which is critical in the case of hospitals (our chosen case study). In addition, because it is embedded in the building's LED lighting system, it requires little additional infrastructure compared to other technologies.

We demonstrate our approach by applying it to a hypothetical Catheterization Lab in a hospital, which treats both scheduled (planned) and emergency (un-planned) patients. Un-planned emergency cases, known as STEMIs, may create scheduling conflicts, as they require immediate attention that can disrupt on-going operations. An aware building can help the CCL staff make decisions that are optimal from the overall hospital point of view, saving time and alleviating stress of both staff and patients.

To build the system we have interviewed medical staff in a major hospital and conducted a literature search for the most pressing issues that need to be handled by a CCL. Models of patient flow, staff work schedules, and space/equipment utilizations were developed. These provide the system with knowledge of past, present and future events at any given time, where each event is comprised of an actor-space-activity triad.

Results indicate that smart environments of the kind described here hold promise to enhance decision-making capabilities of building inhabitants, thus enabling building management strategies that support human needs and efficiency requirements, especially in mission-critical facilities, such as hospitals.

Acknowledgment. The research reported in this paper was made possible through Award #1838702 of Division of Information & Intelligent Systems (IIS), Directorate for Computer & Information Science & Engineering (CISE), U.S. National Science Foundation, and Grant #340753 of the European Research Council (ERC).

References

Belhaj, M., Kebair, F., Ben Said, L.: Agent-based modeling and simulation of the emotional and behavioral dynamics of human civilians during emergency situations. In: Müller, J.P., Weyrich, M., Bazzan, A.L.C. (eds.) MATES 2014. LNCS (LNAI), vol. 8732, pp. 266–281. Springer, Cham (2014). https://doi.org/10.1007/978-3-319-11584-9_18

Berger, H.S., Gibson, H.M.: Managing your hospital RF spectrum. Biomed. Instrum. Technol. **47**, 193–197 (2013). The wireless challenge

Blue, V., Adler, J.: Cellular automata microsimulation of bidirectional pedestrian flows. Transp. Res. Rec. J. Transp. Res. Board **1678**(1999), 135–141 (1999)

Brodeschi, M., Putievsky Pilosof, N., Kalay, Y.E.: The definition of semantic of spaces in virtual built environments oriented to BIM implementation. In: Computer Aided Architectural Design Futures, pp. 331–346 (2015)

Camulli, E.: 5 Wi-Fi performance challenges in hospitals. 7 Signal, March 2014. http://7signal.com

Conti, J.P.: What you see is what you send. Eng. Technol. **3**, 66–68 (2008)

Kalay, Y.E.: Architecture's New Media: Principles, Theories and Methods of Computer-Aided Design. MIT Press, Cambridge (2004)

Mozer, M.C.: The neural network house: an environment that adapts to its inhabitants. In: Coen, M. (ed.) AAAI Spring Symposium on Intelligent Environments, pp. 110–114. AAAI Press, Menlo Park (1988)

Kim, J.K., Schubert, E.F.: Transcending the replacement paradigm of solid-state lighting. Opt. Express **16**(26), 21835–21842 (2008)

Helbing, D., Molnar, P.: Social force model for pedestrian dynamics. Phys. Rev. E **51**(5), 4282 (1995)

Helbing, D., Farkas, I.J., Molnar, P., Vicsek, T.: Simulation of pedestrian crowds in normal and evacuation situations. Pedestr. Evacuation Dyn. **21**(2), 21–58 (2002)

Henderson, L.F.: The statistics of crowd fluids. Nature **229**, 381–383 (1971)

Hoogendoorn, S.P., Bovy, P.H.: Pedestrian route-choice and activity scheduling theory and models. Transp. Res. B Methodol. **38**(2), 169–190 (2004)

Hughes, R.L.: The flow of human crowds. Annu. Rev. Fluid Mech. **35**(1), 169–182 (2003)

Jalia, A., Bakker, R., Ramage, M.: The edge, Amsterdam: showcasing an exemplary IoT building. Technical report, Centre for Digital Built Britain, University of Cambridge, UK (2019)

Kapadia, M., Pelechano, N., Allbeck, J., Badler, N.: Virtual Crowds: Steps Toward Behavioral Realism. Synthesis Lectures on Visual Computing: Computer Graphics, Animation, Computational Photography, and Imaging, vol. 7, no. 4, pp. 1–270 (2015)

Marmor, Y.N., Golany, B., Israelit, S., Mandelbaum, A.: Designing patient flow in emergency departments. IIE Trans. Healthc. Syst. Eng. **2**(4), 233–247 (2012)

Martel, T.J., Nambudiri, V., Kirkman, D., Martel, J., Pappas, L., Jehle, D.: Activation of the cardiac catheterization lab for STEMI patients. Emerg. Med. **49**(6), 259–262 (2017)

Pan, Z., et al.: Visible light communication cyber-physical systems-on- chip for smart cities. J. Commun. **14**(12), 1141–1146 (2019)

Schaumann, D., Pilosof, N.P., Sopher, H., Yahav, J., Kalay, Y.E.: Simulating multi-agent narratives for pre-occupancy evaluation of architectural designs. Autom. Constr. **106**, 102896 (2019)

Schaumann, D., Date, K., Kalay, Y.E.: An event modeling language (EML) to simulate use patterns in built environments. In: Proceedings of the Symposium on Simulation for Architecture and Urban Design, p. 21. Society for Computer Simulation International (2017)

Schaumann, D., Breslav, S., Goldstein, R., Khan, A., Kalay, Y.E.: Simulating use scenarios in hospitals using multi-agent narratives. Build. Perform. Simul. **10**(5–6), 636–652 (2017)

Seo, H.-B., Choi, Y.-S., Zimring, C.: Impact of hospital unit design for patient-centered care on nurses' behavior. Environ. Behav. **43**(4), 443–468 (2011)

Shannon, R.E.: Introduction to the art and science of simulation. In: 1998 Winter Simulation Conference, Proceedings (Cat. No. 98CH36274), vol. 1, pp. 7–14. IEEE (1998)

Simeone, D., Kalay, Y.E., Schaumann, D.: Using game-like narratives to simulate human behavior in built environments. In: Proceedings of the 18th International Conference on Computer-Aided Architectural Design Research in Asia, Singapore, pp. 199–208 (2013)

Thalmann, D., Musse, S.R.: Crowd Simulation. Springer, London (2013). https://doi.org/10.1007/978-1-4471-4450-2

Ulrich, R.S., Zimring, C., Zhu, X., DuBose, J., Seo, H.B., Choi, Y.S., Quan, X., Joseph, A.: A review of the research literature on evidence-based healthcare design. HERD: Health Environ. Res. Des. J. **1**(3), 61–125 (2008)

Yan, W., Kalay, Y.E.: Simulating the behavior of users in built environments. J. Archit. Plann. Res. **21**(4), 371–384 (2004)

Zheng, X., Zhong, T., Liu, M.: Modeling crowd evacuation of a building based on seven methodological approaches. Build. Environ. **44**(3), 437–445 (2009)

IOS Crowd–Sensing Won't Hurt a Bit!: AWARE Framework and Sustainable Study Guideline for iOS Platform

Yuuki Nishiyama[1(✉)], Denzil Ferreira[2], Yusaku Eigen[3], Wataru Sasaki[3], Tadashi Okoshi[3], Jin Nakazawa[3], Anind K. Dey[4], and Kaoru Sezaki[1]

[1] The University of Tokyo, Tokyo, Japan
yuukin@iis.u-tokyo.ac.jp
[2] University of Oulu, Oulu, Finland
[3] Keio University, Tokyo, Japan
[4] University of Washington, Seattle, USA

Abstract. The latest smartphones have advanced sensors that allow us to recognize human and environmental contexts. They operate primarily on Android and iOS, and can be used as sensing platforms for research in various fields owing to their ubiquity in society. Mobile sensing frameworks help to manage these sensors easily. However, Android and iOS are constructed following different policies, requiring developers and researchers to consider framework differences during research planning, application development, and data collection phases to ensure sustainable data collection. In particular, iOS imposes strict regulations on background data collection and application distribution. In this study, we design, implement, and evaluate a mobile sensing framework for iOS, namely *AWARE-iOS*, which is an iOS version of the *AWARE Framework*. Our performance evaluations and case studies measured over a duration of 288 h on four types of devices, show the risks of continuous data collection in the background and explore optimal practical sensor settings for improved data collection. Based on these results, we develop guidelines for sustainable data collection on iOS.

Keywords: Mobile sensing framework · Sustainable sensing · Guideline · iOS · Data collection rate

1 Introduction

Mobile crowd sensing (MCS) is a research method to understand human activities on individual, group, and community levels using data collected by smartphones, which have become ubiquitous worldwide [1]. MCS-based research is being conducted on various scales and terms, including research in fields like computer science, social science, and public health [2–4].

The developments in mobile sensing frameworks [5–7] have accelerated these kinds of MCS research. Such frameworks are capable of dramatically reducing

N. Streitz and S. Konomi (Eds.): HCII 2020, LNCS 12203, pp. 223–243, 2020.
https://doi.org/10.1007/978-3-030-50344-4_17

the developmental and maintenance costs of sensing software. For instance, Ferreira et al. developed the AWARE framework [5], which allows the collection of hardware-based (e.g., accelerometer, GPS, and barometer), software-based (e.g., battery, screen, and network), and human-based (Experience Sampling Method (ESM)) data on the Android platform. In addition, AWARE is designed to manage large-scale human subject studies remotely through a web dashboard.

According to market research [8], Android systems account for 71.94% of the market share, and iOS accounts for 18.89% of the global market share. However, in certain countries (e.g., Japan, the United States of America, the United Kingdom), the market share of iOS is bigger than or comparable to that of Android. For example, in Japan, iOS accounts for 72.45% of the market share, compared to Android's 26.43%. If iOS accounts for more than 50% of the market share in a specific area, then collecting data from both iOS and Android in that region becomes imperative to expand data collection opportunities. Several mobile sensing tools [6,7] have been developed for iOS, but planning and managing a sustainable MCS-based study using iOS remains a challenge.

In this paper, we propose a mobile crowd sensing framework for iOS (namely AWARE-iOS) based on the AWARE Framework [5] which is a mobile sensing framework for Android. AWARE-iOS allows us to collect sensor data sustainably with a few lines of code or through a published client application. Moreover, it provides options for controlling sensors, storage, remote server-connection, and web dashboard to optimize each research purpose. This proposed framework has already been used in various studies [9–11]. Through performance evaluations and case-studies of AWARE-iOS, we demonstrate the potential risks of in-the-wild mobile sensing on iOS and explore a configuration which allows sustainable data collection on iOS. Finally, based on these results, we propose a guideline for realizing sustainable MCS studies using iOS.

The contributions of this study are as follows:

- This study studies the regulations regarding background sensing on iOS, and demonstrates the advantages and disadvantages of iOS in the context of mobile sensing.
- It designs and develops an open-source MCS framework for iOS based on the regulations on iOS.
- It performs basic performance evaluations and in-the-wild studies, demonstrating the risks and modes of their prevention in background sensing on iOS.
- Based on these results, it proposes guidelines for a MCS study using iOS.

2 Mobile Crowd Sensing Studies and Frameworks

MCS-based research in Ubiquitous Computing, Human-Computer Interaction, and/or Public Health collect information regarding human activities using mobile devices to gain an understanding of activities in the daily lives of people. Rachuri et al. [4] developed a mobile sensing platform for social psychology

Table 1. Existing mobile sensing frameworks for iOS

Name	OS	Client	Library	Server	Survey	OSS
AWARE [5]	iOS+Android	✓	✓	✓	✓	Apache 2.0
Sensus [7]	iOS+Android	✓		✓	✓	Apache 2.0
mEMA [21]	iOS+Android	✓		✓	✓	
SensingKit [6]	iOS+Android	✓	✓			LGPL-3.0
StudentLife [3]	iOS+Android	✓				

studies that operated using mobile phones, called EmotionSense. Their developed system can detect individual emotions and verbal and proximal interactions between social group members from the sensors (e.g., microphone, GPS, and accelerometer) on off-the-shelf smartphones. Similarly, StudentLife [3] measured hidden stress and strain in the lives of students based on data gathered by smartphones. In particular, they focused on detecting the day-to-day and week-by-week impacts of workload on stress, sleep, activity, mood, sociability, mental well-being, and academic performances of students. In SmartGPA [12], Wang et al., predicted the academic performance of participants based on the dataset of StudentLife. In addition to passive sensor data gathered by a smartphone, these research projects collect human subject data using a questionnaire on the smartphone. The questionnaire is called ESM and/or Ecological Momentary Assessment (EMA) [13–15]. Participants who have enrolled in a study record temporal thinking and their emotions at the same moment on memos or digital devices. For example, in StudentLife [3] project, they recorded participants' subjective data (e.g., stress-level, social-pressure, and sleep quality.) using EMA during their study.

Various mobile sensing frameworks for Android platform [4,5,16–20] have been proposed and used real studies. For instance, AWARE Framework [5] is an open-source mobile sensing framework, and that allows us to access hardware-, software-, and human-based sensor easily. AWARE is designed to handle a large-scale MCS study remotely through a web dashboard, flexibly extend or import the client and library for satisfying requirements of each study.

Table 1 shows the iOS supported frameworks [3,6,7,21] and functions of each framework. Though stable sensing is an important factor in a mobile sensing framework, these frameworks have not been satisfactorily evaluated the data collection performance in the real condition. SensingKit [6] has evaluated the battery consumption in simple sensor conditions, however, the performance might fluctuate by the sensor and device settings in the real situation. Moreover, Xiong et al. [7] conducted a case study using Sensus, however, the evaluation does not illustrate the stability of data collection during the study. While providing data loss risks and prevention methods assume helps us to plan and manage an MCS study, these risks are not clear and a guideline for sustainable MCS study using iOS platform does not exist.

3 Hindrances of Sustainable Mobile Crowd Sensing

A smartphone possessing multiple sensors is a powerful sensing tool to track the daily lives of people. At the same time, they are frequently used in daily life for multiple purposes such as web-browsing, emailing, gaming, camera, etc.

The Operating System (OS) tries to minimize resource usage for each application that is running as a background process to improve User Experience (UX), because each application on a smartphone uses shared resources like battery, CPU, and storage. On recent versions of OS, an application that does not follow the regulations of the OS is killed or suspended automatically by the OS. In particular, iOS imposes strict regulations on background sensing. This section describes the regulations of iOS regarding MCS-based studies.

3.1 OS Diversity

As a sensing platform, iOS and Android exhibit different characteristics, and they have been tabulated. While Android can access various sensors and distribute an application flexibly, the maintenance costs of the application on it are high because lots of devices are released every year from different manufacturers all over the world, and each Android OS is customized by the corresponding manufacturer.

On the other hand, iOS suffers from various limitations to accessing Application Programming Interfaces (APIs) and distribution methods of an iOS app are limited. However, the maintenance costs are low in its case because iOS devices are released exclusively by Apple. In addition, more than 90% of iOS users use a newer version of OS (iOS 12 or 13[1] on January 10, 2020) while only 38.7% of Android users use Android 8(Oreo) or 9(Pie)[2].

3.2 Resource Limitation

Minimizing resource usage is a common challenge on an off-the-shelf smartphone to improve UX. For example, Low-Power Mode on iOS reduces battery consumption by restricting CPU performance and background activities, especially network connections.

To evaluate storage consumption, we checked the available storage space for 54 undergraduate male students, who possess 16 GB (N = 10), 32 GB (N = 5), or 64 GB (N = 40) storage models, at Keio University, Japan in 2016. As recorded in Fig. 1, 80% of 16 and 32 GB models had less than 1.5 GB free space. The data size of contents increase with time (e.g., Full HD to 4K video), and thus, in this context, available storage is also a significant risk for sustainable data collection.

In addition, an application is barred from using more than 80% of the CPU for more than 60 s while running as a background operation, according to Apple

[1] https://developer.apple.com/support/app-store/.

[2] https://developer.android.com/about/dashboards/index.html.

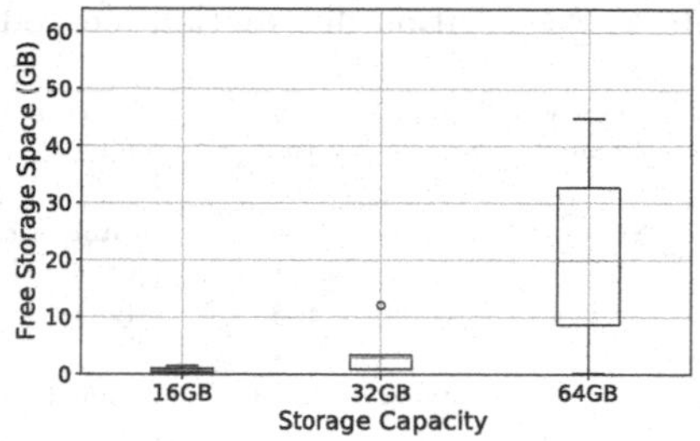

Fig. 1. Free storage space for each specification (16, 32, and 64 GB)

document[3]. If an application oversteps this regulation, the iOS shuts down the application process immediately.

3.3 Restricted Background Sensing on iOS

An iOS app that tracks human activities courteously in the daily lives of people needs to run even if the application is not running as a foreground process. As a lifecycle[4], apps on iOS may have one of the following five statuses: *Not Running*, *Inactive*, *Active*, *Background*, and *Suspended.* If an application is allowed to run in the background, it can continue to run after closing the app. On iOS, if the application serves a function from the following list, it can be run in the background.

- Location updates
- Remote Notifications - Voice over IP (VoIP)
- Audio, AirPlay, and Picture in Picture
- External accessory communication
- Uses Bluetooth LE accessories
- Acts as a Bluetooth LE Accessories
- Background Fetch
- Background Processing

"Location Updates" and "Remote Notifications" functions are commonly used in most applications, and, therefore, such apps easily pass the review by Apple and do not flout iOS regulations. Silent Push Notification (SPN) is a part of remote notification that can be used to send data in JSON format to smartphones from the server-side without any alert and sound to the recipient two or three times per hour[5]. The notification's priority is low, and the system does not guarantee its delivery.

[3] https://developer.apple.com/library/archive/documentation/Performance/Conceptual/EnergyGuide-iOS/WorkLessInTheBackground.html.

[4] https://developer.apple.com/documentation/uikit/app_and_environment/managing_your_app_s_life_cycle.

[5] https://developer.apple.com/documentation/usernotifications/setting_up_a_remote_notification_server/pushing_background_updates_to_your_app.

Table 2. Application distribution methods

Method	Device registration	Deployment platform	Review by Apple	Estimated review time	Account fee	Software update	Private API	Study scale	Build expiration
AppStore	NO	AppStore	YES	1–7 days	99$	Automatic or manual	NO	1–∞	Never
TestFlight (External)	NO	TestFlight or URL	YES	1–7 days	99$	Manual	NO	1–10000	90 days
Apple Developer Enterprise Program	NO	URL	NO	Immediate	299$	Manual	NO	1–100	Never
TestFlight (Internal)	YES	TestFlight	NO	Immediate	99$	Manual	NO	1–100	90 days
DeployGate (AdHoc)	YES	DeployGate	NO	Immediate	99$	Manual	YES	1–100	Never
Xcode	YES	Xcode (PC)	NO	Immediate	99$	Manual	YES	1–100	Never

3.4 Limitation of Application Distribution

Table 2 depicts distribution methods for an application to an iOS user. An application developer and researcher can choose the best way to provide an application for their study from the list.

During the developmental phase, a developed application can be installed on a device that is registered as an Apple Developer Account by Xcode (which is an IDE for Xcode). However, each developer account can register a maximum of only 100 devices. By using AdHoc distribution (like DeployGate), we can deploy the application by URL, but the iOS device is required to be registered to an Apple developer account before building the application. AppStore is a digital distribution platform for iOS applications managed by Apple. iOS devices can download and update applications through the platform. However, releasing an application on AppStore needs to pass a review by Apple. The review is conducted under AppStore review guideline[6], and generally takes a few days.

4 AWARE Framework for iOS

AWARE Framework is an open-source mobile sensing framework for Android which has been developed by Ferreira et al. [5]. The AWARE Framework is composed of an AWARE-Server (hereafter referred to as *AWARE-Server*), which is a common LAMP (Linux + Apache + MySQL + PHP) server, and -Client (hereafter referred to as *AWARE-Android*), which is an Android application.

In this study, we design and implement an AWARE Framework for iOS, namely *AWARE-iOS*, that is compatible with *AWARE-Android* and *-Server*. Figure 2 presents an overview of *AWARE-iOS*. Its architecture is inspired by *AWARE-Android*. *AWARE-iOS* is composed of a Library (see Sect. 4.1) and a User Interface (UI) module (see Sect. 4.2) to improve reusability.

[6] https://developer.apple.com/app-store/review/guidelines/.

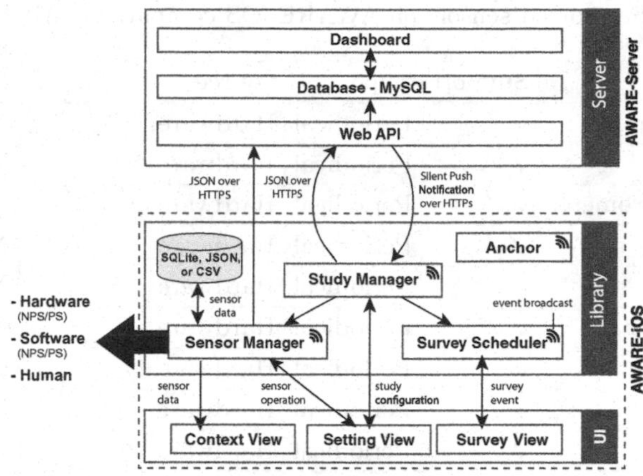

Fig. 2. Overview of AWARE-iOS

Compared to *AWARE-Android* [5], iOS does not allow connections to MQTT for a background process. Thus, instead of MQTT on Android, *AWARE-iOS* uses SPN[7] to transmit data (in JSON format) from the server-side. An SPN can be included as a payload whose maximum size is 4096 bytes[8].

4.1 Core Library

The Library module comprises three sub-modules to manage study, sensors, and survey schedules (see Sect. 4.1). This section describes these sub-modules with sample codes.

Table 3 depicts the supported sensors on AWARE-iOS. The number of supported sensors are less than that of AWARE-Android due to API limitations (e.g., light, proximity, and temperature), but all of the accessible sensors on iOS are supported, to the best of our knowledge [3,6,7]. The source code is written in *Objective-C* and supports iOS 10 or later. *AWARE-iOS* is published under Apache License 2.0 on GitHub[9], similar to *AWARE-Android*.

Library Instruction. The core library is released on CocoaPods[10], which is a library management tool for Xcode project. Just to write `pod 'AWAREFramework'` into Podfile and run `pod install`, a developer and add AWARE-iOS into Xcode project. The developer can use the functions of AWARE-iOS by importing the library into the application by `import AWAREFramework`.

[7] https://github.com/tetujin/aware-push.
[8] https://developer.apple.com/documentation/usernotifications/setting_up_a_remote_notification_server/generating_a_remote_notification.
[9] https://github.com/tetujin/AWAREFramework-iOS.
[10] https://cocoapods.org/.

Table 3. Supported sensors on AWARE-iOS comparing with-Android

Sensors	Support	Type	Source	Permission
Accelerometer	✓✓	Periodical	Hardware	NPS
Gravity	✓✓	Periodical	Hardware	NPS
Linear accelerometer	✓✓	Periodical	Hardware	NPS
Gyroscope	✓✓	Periodical	Hardware	NPS
Rotation	✓✓	Periodical	Hardware	NPS
Magnetometer	✓✓	Periodical	Hardware	NPS
Wi-Fi	✓	Periodical	Hardware	NPS
Location	✓✓	Periodical	Hardware	PS
Barometer	✓✓	Periodical	Hardware	PS
Ambient noise	✓✓	Periodical	Hardware	PS
Bluetooth	✓	Periodical	Hardware	PS
Telephony		Periodical	Hardware	–
Light		Periodical	Hardware	–
Temperature		Periodical	Hardware	–
Processor	✓✓	Periodical	Software	NPS
Timezone	✓✓	Periodical	Software	NPS
Activity recognition	✓✓	Periodical	Software (Auto)	PS
Pedometer	✓✓	Periodical	Software (Auto)	PS
HealthKit*	✓✓	Periodical	Software (Auto)	PS
Weather	✓✓	Periodical	Software (Web API)	NPS
Fitbit	✓✓	Periodical	Software (Web API)	NPS
Proximity	✓	Event	Hardware	NPS
Screen	✓✓	Event	Software	NPS
Battery	✓✓	Event	Software	NPS
Communication	✓	Event	Software	NPS
Installations		Event	Software	—
Applications		Event	Software	—
Keyboard	✓	Event	Software	PS
ESM	✓	Event	Human	NPS

✓✓Supported
✓Partly Supported
*Only iOS

The supported sensors (as depicted in Table 3) can be categorized into the following two types:

- *Non-permission-imposed Sensors (NPS)*: An *NPS* does not require permission for an app to access it. For example, accelerometer, gyroscope, Wi-Fi, and processor are *NPS* on iOS.

- *Permission-imposed Sensor (PS)*: A *PS* requires permission for an app to access it, and might need to describe the reason of requirement during the application review by Apple. On iOS, location, microphone, motion activity, Bluetooth, calendar, contact, and HealthKit are considered to be *PS*.

All applications on *AppStore* or *TestFlight* need to pass the review by Apple. Apple developer guideline demands minimizing the use of *PS* owing to security concerns, and therefore, a developer should focus on minimizing sensor usage. *PS* can be installed separately by using `subpod` function on CococoaPods as shown in Listing 1.1.

```
pod 'AWAREFramework'
pod 'AWAREFramework/Microphone'
pod 'AWAREFramework/MotionActivity'
pod 'AWAREFramework/Bluetooth'
pod 'AWAREFramework/Calendar'
pod 'AWAREFramework/Contact'
pod 'AWAREFramework/HealthKit'
```

Listing 1.1. Podfile

Anchor. To collect data continuously, *AWARE-iOS* maintains a location sensor perpetually activated in the background as an anchor. The iOS location sensor has the following six levels of accuracy: *best*, *best for navigation*, *nearest ten meters*, *hundred meters*, *kilometer*, and *three kilometers*. By default, AWARE-iOS uses a location sensor that is accurate up to *three kilometers*. The battery impact of the low-accuracy location sensor is considered in our basic performance evaluation (see Sect. 5.2).

Sensor Manager. Listing 1.2 depicts a sample code for using the accelerometer sensor in the background. During launch, the app (1) imports AWARE Framework into the project, and (2) requests permission for background sensing from the user. After authorization, `AWARECore` can be activated for background sensing (3). Each sensor can be initialized by (4). `AWARECore`, `AWAREStudy` and `AWARESensorManager` are designed as a singleton class; these classes can be accessed from anywhere in the app. `AWAREStudy` handles study configurations, such as a remote server URL, sensor activation if a study exists, and remote DB sync. In addition, (5) each sensor event can be handled by the `-setSensorEventHandler` method. (6) A sensor instance can be retained on the memory by adding it to `AWARESensorManager`, and can be accessed from any place in the app through the manager. The collected data are saved in SQLite, JSON, or CSV based local storage temporarily.

```
/// (1) import ‘AWAREFramework‘
import AWAREFramework
/// (2) request permission
let core     = AWARECore.shared()
core.requestPermissionForBackgroundSensing{ (status) in
    /// (3) activate AWARECore
    core.activate()
    /// (4) initialize sensor(s)
    let study = AWAREStudy.shared()
    let acc = Accelerometer(awareStudy: study, dbType: AwareDBTypeSQLite)
    /// (5) handle sensor events (option)
    acc.setSensorEventHandler { (sensor, data) in
      // YOUR CODE
    }
    acc.startSensor()
    /// (6) add the sensor(s) into the sensor manager
    AWARESensorManager.shared().add(acc)
}
```

Listing 1.2. A sample code for activating a sensor

Survey Manager. As in the case of *AWARE-Android*, *AWARE-iOS* supports Mobile ESM as a survey function. On *AWARE-iOS*, the following types of survey are supported: *Text, Radio, Checkbox, Likert Scale, Quick Answer, Scale, Date-Time, PAM* [22], *Numeric, Web, Date, Time, Clock, Picture, Audio, and Video* (screenshots can be found here[11]).

Listing 1.3 depicts a sample code for setting a build-in survey with a *Radio* format. The `ESMScheduleManager` manages the entire ESM schedule that is instanced by `ESMScehdule`. An `ESMScehdule` instance possesses parameters for scheduling surveys as notification titles, expiration thresholds, times for notification, and survey items. The survey items support the 16 types of the surveys mentioned above. Moreover, `ESMScheduleManager` can be set up using a JSON file which includes configuration of survey schedule from a connected *AWARE-Server*.

```
let schedule = ESMSchedule()
schedule.notificationTitle    = "Notification Title"
schedule.expirationThreshold = 60
schedule.fireHours            = [9, 15, 21]

let radio = ESMItem(asRadioESMWithTrigger: "trigger", radioItems:
    ["A","B","C"])
radio.setTitle("Title")
radio.setInstructions("Instructions")
schdule.addESM(radio)

ESMScheduleManager.shared().add(schdule)
```

Listing 1.3. Generating an ESM schedule

In addition to the fixed schedule survey, *AWARE-iOS* can implement a context-based survey by using sensors and the `setSensorEventHandler` method.

[11] https://github.com/tetujin/AWAREFramework-iOS/tree/master/Screenshots/esms.

For example, *AWARE-iOS* is able to send a survey to the user when a user finishes a phone call.

Study Manager. *AWARE-iOS* can upload sensor data to a connected remote cloud server if the user has signed up for a study. Studies can be managed on a dashboard on the *AWARE-Server* (accessible at https://api.awareframework.com). The *AWARE-Server* is also an Open Source Project (under Apache 2.0), and thus each researcher can host an AWARE server on the researcher's hosting server, such as Google Cloud Platform, Amazon Web Services, and Microsoft Azure. Listing 1.4 depicts a sample code for signing-up to a study by using a study URL, and for activating sensors with a study configuration on *AWARE-Server*

```
let url = "https://aware.server_url.com/STUDY_ID/PASS"
study.join(withURL: url) { (settings, studyState, error) in
    let manager = AWARESensorManager.shared()
    manager.addSensors(with: study)
    manager.startAllSensors()
}
```

Listing 1.4. Joining a study using a study URL

4.2 User Interface

The AWARE Client iOS is a sample application that serves as the user interface. Users access *AWARE-iOS* APIs through the application. The application is written in *Swift* and has been released on AppStore[12] and GitHub[13] under

Fig. 3. Screenshots of the AWARE Client on iOS

[12] https://apps.apple.com/app/aware-client-v2/id1455986181.
[13] https://github.com/tetujin/aware-client-ios-v2.

Apache License 2.0. As depicted in Fig. 3, the application has three views: settings, ESM, and context cards. A user can modify study settings on the settings view. ESM displays a survey if the survey has been delivered to the app, and context cards show collected sensor data on a card-like view. These functions are changeable through the *AWARE-Server* and on the client.

5 Evaluation and Case Studies

In this section, we evaluate (1) basic performance of SQLite, JSON and CSV-based local storage that is supported on *AWARE-iOS*, and (2) battery consumption of each sensor and configuration. Finally, (3) we conduct case studies to measure data collection rates and coverages in each case study.

5.1 Data Insertion and Fetching Performance

Motion sensors such as accelerometers, gyroscopes, and magnetic-fields are commonly used to detect human and mobile movement. While such sensors are implemented on various devices and are usable for multiple purposes, raw sensor data are collected at high frequencies (1–100 Hz), and this generates a significant amount of data on a smartphone.

Table 4 depicts the table format on the SQLite database on *AWARE-iOS*, which is a sample table format available on AWARE-Android. Accelerometer data are saved with a timestamp, device ID, values (including X, Y, and Z axes), and label. Table 5 depicts the estimated data sizes gathered by the accelerometer at 5 Hz and 50 Hz over an hour, day, week, and month (4 weeks). The total data size exceeds 1 GB in a week at 50 Hz and in a month at 5 Hz and 50 Hz.

Table 4. Table format of accelerometer sensor

Column	Type	Bytes
timestamp	Double	8
device_id	String	32
x	Double	8
y	Double	8
z	Double	8
accuracy	Int32	4
label	String	32

Table 5. Expected data size

Fre	Term	Rows	Estimated size
5 Hz	Hour	18,000	1.72 MB
	Day	432,000	41.20 MB
	Week	3,024,000	288.39 MB
	Month	12,096,000	1.13 GB
50 Hz	Hour	180,000	17.17 MB
	Day	4,230,000	403.40 MB
	Week	30,240,000	2.82 GB
	Month	120,960,000	11.27 GB

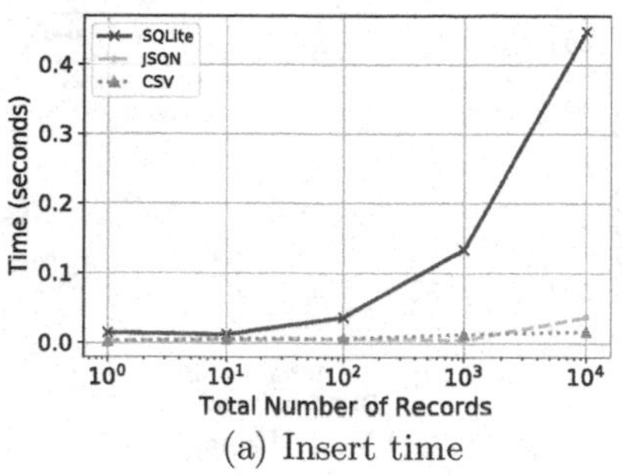

(a) Insert time

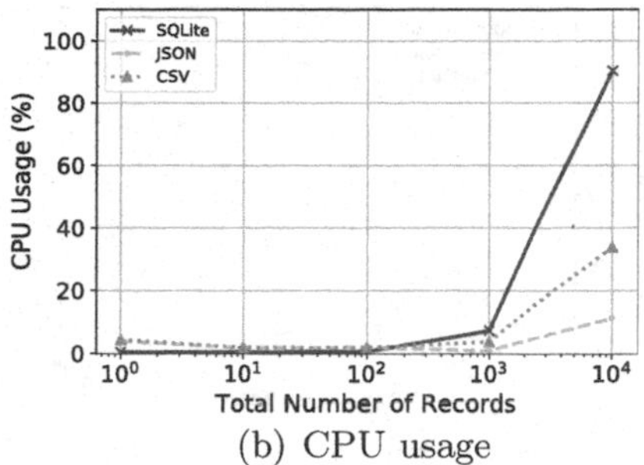

(b) CPU usage

Fig. 4. Resource usage during a data insert operation

Insert Performance. To evaluate insert performance, we measured the time taken and CPU usage during data insertion of different numbers of records (10^0, 10^1, 10^2, 10^3, and 10^4). Generally, accessing a number of files over a period of time influences battery consumption, and thus file access should be minimized. During this evaluation, we explore the best batch size based on CPU usage and execution times for inserting data into each type of local database (SQLite, JSON, and CSV). This evaluation is conducted on the iPhone 7 (iOS 13.2).

As depicted in Fig. 4, data insertion time exceeds 10^3 units. CPU usage (depicted in Fig. 4(b)) also exhibits an almost identical transition with time, except the insertion of 10^3 records per insertion. This result indicates that 10^3 is approximately the correct practical batch size for data insertion.

Fetch Performance. As indicated by the data in Table 5, the amount of stored data continues to increase unless it is cleared. In this evaluation, we measure the time taken and the CPU usage during the process of fetching records from SQLite-, JSON-, and CSV- based storages. As a simulation, we prepared SQLite databases of multiple sizes based on the data presented in Table 5 and measured the performance of each. The fetch request is one of the following three requests:

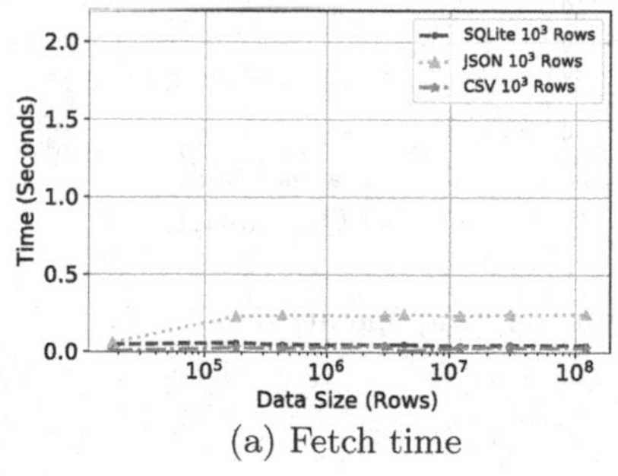

(a) Fetch time

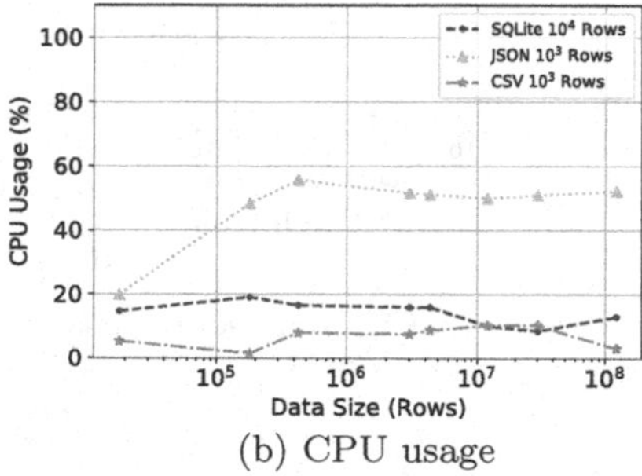

(b) CPU usage

Fig. 5. Resource usage during a data (10^3 rows) fetch operation

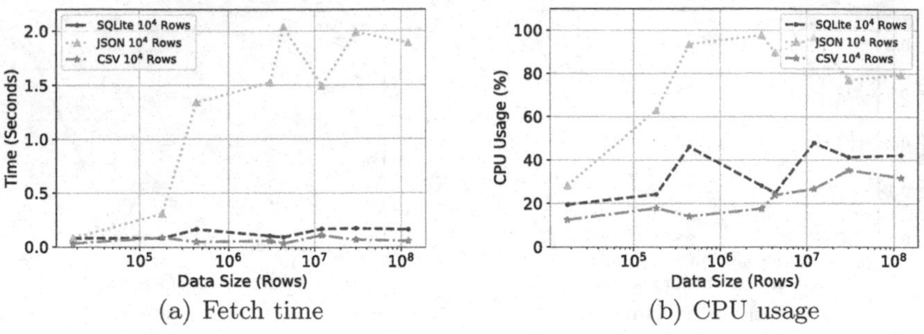

(a) Fetch time (b) CPU usage

Fig. 6. Resource usage during a data (10^4 rows) fetch operation

(1) fetch 10^3 records, (2) fetch 10^4 records, and (3) count number of stored records.

As depicted in Fig. 5(b) and 6(b), CPU usage is observed to increase sharply when the number of stored records exceeds 10^6. CPU usage decreases once the number exceeds 10^7, but, in this case, each fetch takes more than 10 s (as depicted in Fig. 5(a) and 6(a)); 10^6 rows are almost equal with data of 3-days by 5 Hz or 0.5-day by 50 Hz.

As depicted in Fig. 7, operations that read all data in the storage (e.g., counting the number of stored records) significantly affects time consumption and CPU usage. The time taken for the counting process for JSON and SQLite increased to more than 30 s when the size of stored data was greater than or equal to 10^7. However, the CPU usage for SQLite was less than 20% even when the size of stored data was increased. On the other hand, the CPU usage for JSON and CSV increased sharply with increase in the stored data size.

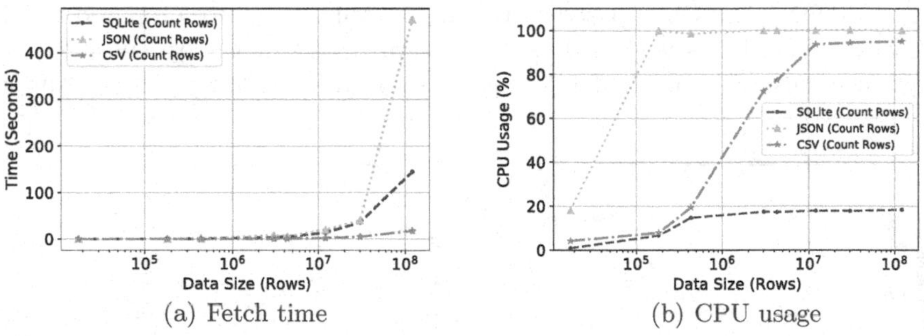

(a) Fetch time (b) CPU usage

Fig. 7. Resource usage during a counting operation

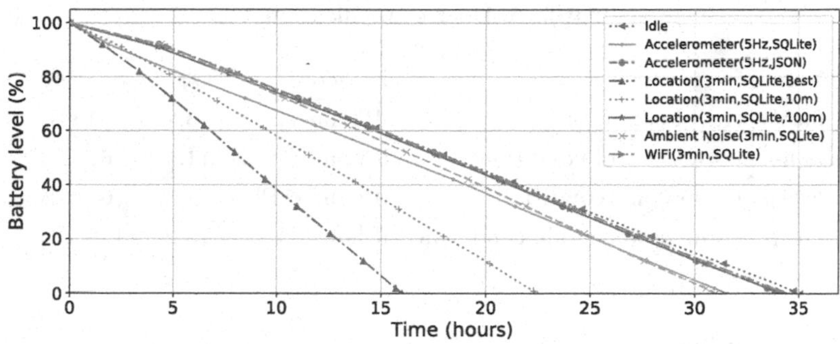

Fig. 8. Battery consumption of *AWARE-iOS*

5.2 Battery Impact

We measured the battery consumption while running *AWARE-iOS* on an iPhone X running iOS 12. All data were erased from the device and the manufacturer's default settings were restored [6]. No other third-party applications were installed or allowed to run in the background. The device was set to flight mode, and wifi, Bluetooth, and cellular connectivities were disabled. Finally, the background app refresh setting was turned off and the low power mode was turned on.

Figure 8 depicts the battery consumption of AWARE-iOS under the aforementioned conditions. In this experiment, we evaluated battery consumption of the library while using the four types of sensors (viz., accelerometer, location, Wi-Fi, and ambient noise from periodical hardware sensor, as recorded in Table 3), which use different storage systems (SQLite or JSON), sampling rates, and accuracies of sensors if required. In the idle condition, a smartphone can be run for a maximum of 35.05 h.

SQLite vs JSON. Battery consumption of the accelerometer that used JSON-based storage was observed to be lesser than that using SQLite-based storage over nearly 5 h. As described in Sect. 5.1, the data insertion time corresponding to the JSON format is lower than that corresponding to SQLite, and the overall CPU usage is lower for the JSON format than for SQLite as well.

Effects of Location Accuracy. We also compared battery consumptions during the use of three levels of accuracy for the location sensors—best for navigation (0 m), 10 m, and 100 m. The battery lives corresponding to the less accurate settings (34.05 and 22.52 h, respectively) were higher than that corresponding to the most accurate setting (16.05 h).

Table 6. Device specification

Name		Device	OS	Storage
ideal	(Ideal condition)	iPhone 11	13.2	64 GB
non-c	(Non-control condition)	iPhone 6 Plus	11.4.1	64 GB
heavy	(Heavy use condition)	iPhone 6 Plus	12.3	64 GB
low-p	(Low-power mode condition)	iPhone 11	13.2	128 GB

5.3 Case Study

As described in Sect. 3.3, iOS imposes several restrictions on apps that run continuous background sensing. In this section, we measure the data collection rates over three days in the following four cases.

BL. A user does not interact with the data collection application during the term as a baseline.
ESM. A user needs to open the application three times a day during the term.
SPN. A user does not interact with the application. Instead, a remote-server sends a silent push notification to the device every 30 min for restart sensors.
ESM + SPN. A user needs to carry out the tasks of ESM and SPN.

In all of these cases, we used AWARE Client iOS (described in detail in Sect. 4.2) with the following sensors: Accelerometer (5 Hz), location (accurate to 3 min and 100 m), weather (accurate to 10 min), pedometer (accurate to 10 min), screen, and battery. The collected data were saved in SQLite and synced with a remote server when the device had access to Wi-Fi and the battery was charged. The results corresponding to the four devices have been recorded in Table 6. The participants carried and used these devices in their daily lives. *ideal* represents the initial setting on the iPhone in which the AWARE Client iOS was installed. *low-p* represents the statistics measured when the phone was in Low-Power Mode during the entire term of investigation. *heavy* represents the case of an iPhone that received memory warnings more than 10 times a day. The memory warning appeared when the user used applications (e.g., YouTube, Instagram, and Camera) that consume significant memory.

Rate of Data Collection Status. Figure 9 depicts the rates of data collection in each of the aforementioned cases. We defined the following three data collection statuses: `Comp`, `Incomp`, and `Loss`. For example, location data are collected every 3 min; thus, ideally, 20 records are collected in 1 h. In this case, records = 20 is categorized as `Comp`, 0 < records < 20 is categorized as `Incomp`, and records = 0 is categorized as `Loss`.

As depicted in Fig. 9(a), corresponding to BL, though *ideal* and *non-c* almost exclusively exhibited the `Comp` status, more than half of the statuses corresponding to *heavy* and *low-p* were observed to be `Loss`. ESM, SPN, and ESM + SPN exhibited nearly 100% `Comp` in all devices except in *heavy* running ESM and SPN; 86.11% of the statuses in *heavy* with SPN condition were `Incomp`. The reason behind this is after receiving a silent push notification once every 30 min, the application was able to run for 30 s after which the device suspended it Thus, As recorded in Fig. 10, data were collected only twice in 1 h on average.

Low power mode restricts network connections when applications are running in the background. Figure 9(b) depicts the number of records each hour corresponding to this mode. As is evident from the figure, if the low power mode is turned on, *low-p* loses weather information (collected by a Web API of OpenWeatherMap (https://openweathermap.org/), even if the application is running in the background.

In all cases, the pedometer sensor (Fig. 9(c)) collected ideal amounts of data. More recent versions of iPhone 5 S and iOS devices run on Apple M-series coprocessors that collect, process, and store sensor data motions even if the iOS device is asleep. This aids the safe collection of data.

Coverage of Data Collection. Each cell in Fig. 10 depicts the total amount of location data collected each hour. *Ideal* and *non-c* phones had collected 100% of the location data under all four conditions. However, *heavy* and *low-c* devices

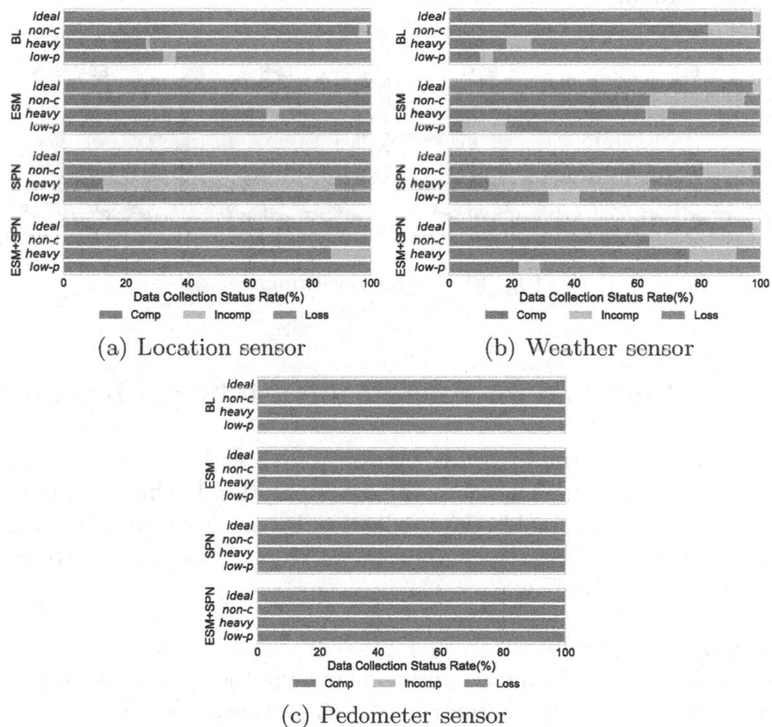

(a) Location sensor (b) Weather sensor

(c) Pedometer sensor

Fig. 9. Data collection status rates

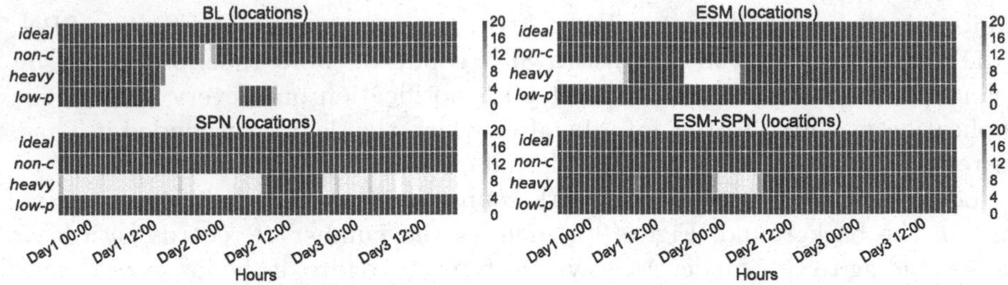

Fig. 10. Coverage of location data collection

had suspended the application after 12:00 h on Day 1 in BL. However, in the cases of ESM and ESM + SPN, data collection was restarted after interaction with the app to take the provided survey.

Memory Warnings. Figure 11 depicts the total number of memory warnings during the study for each case. As is evident from 10, data collection had been suspended on *heavy* devices frequently. On the other hand, *ideal* devices did not suspend the application even once. In this sense, the user of a heavy iOS device runs the risk of reduced data collection rate.

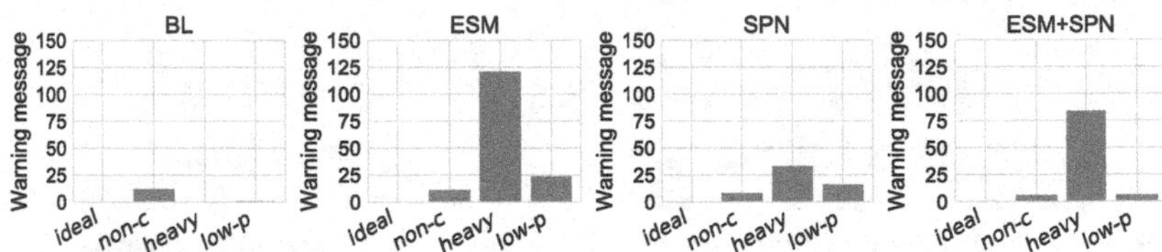

Fig. 11. Memory warnings

6 Design Guideline for Sustainable MCS Studies on iOS

An MCS study involves the following phases: (1) research planning, (2) application development, (3) data collection, and data analytics. In this section, we illustrate a guideline for sustainable data collection by using iOS devices. Based on performance evaluation and case studies, we list recommendations corresponding to each phase for *AWARE-iOS*.

1. Research planning phase
   (a) A researcher should make one or more hypotheses and attempt to collect sensor data as preliminary research to check the difference between Android and iOS using a preset client (Sect. 3.1 and 4.2).

   (b) The number of sensors, durations of sensing intervals, and levels of accuracy on the sensing application should be optimized to reduce battery consumption (Sect. 5.2).
   (c) An application distribution method that agrees with the research plan should be selected for smooth app distribution (Sect. 3.4).
2. Application development phase
   (a) The number of *PS* should be minimized by using `subpod` for smooth app distribution (Sect. 4.1).
   (b) The sensing application should present periodic opportunities to the user to open it, if possible (Sect. 5.3).
   (c) To detecting suspension of the application, a researcher should send Silent Push Notifications to the participants' devices regularly during a study (Sect. 5.3).
   (d) We recommend using a software-based sensor that is collected by motion co-processor automatically if you can replace it from other sensors (Sect. 5.3).
   (e) The table size corresponding to SQLite should be less than 10^6 rows to reduce CPU impact and fetch speed (Sect. 5.1).
   (f) The batch size for data insertion should be less than 10^3 rows to reduce CPU usage (Sect. 5.1).
3. Data collection phase
   (a) Sufficient free storage space should be obtained before beginning the study. In particular, it should be noted that iPhones have models with low storage capacities (e.g., 16 and 32 GB) (Sect. 3.2).
   (b) If possible, low power mode should be turned off during the study (Sect. 5.3).

The performance evaluation in this study was conducted on limited types of iOS devices and OS. Therefore, if a device or OS of a different type is considered, its performance might be drastically different. Moreover, this study was performed over merely three days. The performance of AWARE-iOS needs to be evaluated over much longer durations to draw dependable conclusions regarding it. Moreover, we did not inspect the differences in settings on Anchor (see Sect. 4.1) in this study. Further, location sensors with high accuracy might consume battery at a faster rate, but their superior performance grants them a better data collection rate.

7 Conclusion

MCS is a research method for understanding everyday human activities on the individual, group, and social levels using data collected through smartphones. Even though Android is the most popular OS for smartphones globally, iOS is more popular in certain specific areas or among certain communities. Several MCS frameworks [5–7] for iOS have been proposed. However, planning and managing a sustainable MCS-based study with iOS remains a challenge, in spite of the strict rules that iOS enforces on collecting sensor data in the background.

In this paper, we propose an MCS framework for iOS, namely, *AWARE-iOS*, based on the AWARE framework for Android [5]. *AWARE-iOS* allows us to collect sensor data sustainably based on a few lines of code or by using a published client application, and grants us the opportunity to optimize each research purpose.

Our performance evaluations show that the battery consumption rates of devices depend on sensor settings and storage type. Moreover, case studies illustrate that *ideal-* and *non-control* devices can collect nearly all the data. However, when the device is on low power mode or is being used heavily, it runs the risk of data loss if silent-push notifications or periodical interactions are not employed. Finally, based on these results, we propose a guideline for creating a research plan and managing mobile sensing studies.

Acknowledgment. This work was supported by JSPS KAKENHI Grant Number JP18K11274.

References

1. Center, P.R.: Smartphone ownership is growing rapidly around the world, but not always equally, February 2019
2. Lane, N., Miluzzo, E., Choudhury, T., Campbell, A., et al.: A survey of mobile phone sensing. IEEE Commun. Mag. **48**(9), 140–150 (2010)
3. Wang, R., Chen, F., Chen, Z., Li, T., Campbell, A.T., et al.: StudentLife: assessing mental health, academic performance and behavioral trends of college students using smartphones. In: Proceedings of the 2014 ACM International Joint Conference on Pervasive and Ubiquitous Computing, pp. 3–14 (2014)
4. Rachuri, K.K., Aucinas, A., et al.: EmotionSense: a mobile phones based adaptive platform for experimental social psychology research. In: Proceedings of the 12th ACM International Conference on Ubiquitous Computing - Ubicomp 2010, p. 281 (2010)
5. Ferreira, D., Kostakos, V., Dey, A.K.: AWARE: mobile context instrumentation framework. Front. ICT **2**, 6 (2015)
6. Katevas, K., Haddadi, H., Tokarchuk, L.: SensingKit: evaluating the sensor power consumption in iOS devices. Proceedings - 12th International Conference on Intelligent Environments, IE 2016, pp. 222–225 (2016)
7. Xiong, H., Gerber, M.S., et al.: Sensus: a cross-platform, general-purpose system for mobile crowdsensing in human-subject studies. In: Proceedings of the 2016 ACM International Joint Conference on Pervasive and Ubiquitous Computing, pp. 415–426. ACM Press, New York (2016)
8. Statcounter: Mobile Vendor Market Share. https://gs.statcounter.com/vendor-market-share/mobile/japan
9. Bae, S., Chung, T., Ferreira, D., Dey, A.K., Suffoletto, B.: Mobile phone sensors and supervised machine learning to identify alcohol use events in young adults: implications for just-in-time adaptive interventions. Addict. Behav. **83**, 42–47 (2018)
10. Doryab, A., et al.: Identifying behavioral phenotypes of loneliness and social isolation with passive sensing: statistical analysis, data mining and machine learning of smartphone and fitbit data. JMIR mHealth uHealth **7**(7), e13209 (2019)

11. Kuosmanen, E., Kan, V., Ferreira, D., et al.: Challenges of Parkinson's disease: user experiences with stop. In: Proceedings of the 21st International Conference on Human-Computer Interaction with Mobile Devices and Services, MobileHCI 2019. Association for Computing Machinery, New York (2019)
12. Wang, R., Harari, G., Campbell, A.T., et al.: SmartGPA: how smartphones can assess and predict academic performance of college students. In: Proceedings of the 2015 ACM International Joint Conference on Pervasive and Ubiquitous Computing, UbiComp 2015, pp. 295–306. Association for Computing Machinery, New York (2015)
13. Hormuth, S.E.: The sampling of experiences in situ. J. Pers. **54**(1), 262–293 (1986)
14. Froehlich, J., Chen, M.Y., Consolvo, S., Harrison, B., Landay, J.A.: MyExperience: a system for in situ tracing and capturing of user feedback on mobile phones (2007)
15. Shiffman, S., Stone, A.A., Hufford, M.R.: Ecological momentary assessment. Ann. Rev. Clin. Psychol. **4**, 1–32 (2008)
16. Aharony, N., Pan, W., Ip, C., Khayal, I., Pentland, A.: The social fMRI: measuring, understanding, and designing social mechanisms in the real world. In: Proceedings of the 13th International Conference on Ubiquitous Computing - UbiComp 2011, p. 445. ACM Press, New York (2011)
17. Place, S., Nierenberg, A., Azarbayejani, A., et al.: Behavioral indicators on a mobile sensing platform predict clinically validated psychiatric symptoms of mood and anxiety disorders. J. Med. Internet Res. **19**(3), e75 (2017)
18. Wu, P., Zhu, J., Zhang, J.Y.: MobiSens: a versatile mobile sensing platform for real-world applications. Mob. Netw. Appl. **18**(1), 60–80 (2013)
19. Trossen, D., Pavel, D.: AIRS: a mobile sensing platform for lifestyle management research and applications. In: Borcea, C., Bellavista, P., Giannelli, C., Magedanz, T., Schreiner, F. (eds.) MOBILWARE 2012. LNICST, vol. 65, pp. 1–15. Springer, Heidelberg (2013). https://doi.org/10.1007/978-3-642-36660-4_1
20. Lane, N., Choudhury, T., Campbell, A., et al.: BeWell: a smartphone application to monitor, model and promote wellbeing. In: Proceedings of the 5th International ICST Conference on Pervasive Computing Technologies for Healthcare (2011)
21. ilumivu: mEMA. https://ilumivu.com/
22. Pollak, J.P., Adams, P., Gay, G.: PAM: a photographic affect meter for frequent, in situ measurement of affect. In: CHI (2011)

Driving Innovation with the Application of Industrial AI in the R&D Domain

Fei Xing[1], Guochao (Alex) Peng[1(✉)], Bingqian Zhang[1], Simin Zuo[1], Jiangfeng Tang[2], and Shuyang Li[3]

[1] Sun Yat-sen University, Panyu District, Guangzhou 510000, China
xingf5@mail2.sysu.edu.cn, penggch@mail.sysu.edu.cn
[2] Guangdong Huanuo Qingeng Material Technology Co. Ltd., Guangzhou 510000, China
[3] The University of Sheffield, Sheffield S10 2TN, UK

Abstract. The concept of artificial intelligence (AI) has become increasingly prevalent in the industry, but there is still insufficient understanding about what AI can exactly do for manufacturing companies. This paper focuses on the domain of product research and development (R&D), and aims to depict how AI can assist in industrial R&D activities. Through a comprehensive review of literature, this paper identified three major drawbacks in traditional product R&D approach, namely, low success rate, long research cycle, and difficulty in management. Subsequently, based on the characteristics of AI technology, this paper proposes and discusses a number of scenarios to demonstrate how AI can be applied to support R&D activities. Comparing with traditional product R&D, the advantages of AI-based R&D are proposed and summarized: 1) More objective identification of user requirements to drive enterprise innovation; 2) more precise exploration of market trends; 3) higher efficiency in product design; 4) less risks in R&D process; and 5) improved knowledge sharing ability. This paper will be of interests and value to practitioners and researchers concerned with AI usage in manufacturing contexts.

Keywords: Industrial AI · Enterprise application · AI-based R&D · Advantage

1 Introduction

In the era of Industrial 4.0, utilizing artificial intelligence technologies to enhance business competitiveness has become a key objective for modern companies to achieve. Artificial Intelligence (AI) is a technology to use machines as a substitute of humans in realizing cognition, recognition, analysis, and decision-making, etc. The essence of AI technology is to simulate human's consciousness and thinking processes, so that machine is competent for some complex work that usually requires human intelligence [1, 2]. In recent years, with the development of mobile Internet, big data, Internet of Things (IoT) and breakthroughs in cloud-based large-scale computing capabilities, AI technology has gradually become mature and been applied to all aspects of society. For example, in the medical field, AI is mainly applied to aid diagnosis, medical image interpretation and robotic surgery, etc. [3]. Furthermore, machine vision technology is used to read medical

N. Streitz and S. Konomi (Eds.): HCII 2020, LNCS 12203, pp. 244–255, 2020.
https://doi.org/10.1007/978-3-030-50344-4_18

images, which helps medical staffs to shorten the time of reading images, improve work efficiency and reduce the misdiagnosis rate [4]. In the financial field, AI is primarily used to provide investment consulting services, such as investment decision-making, intelligent customer service, precision marketing, and automatic risk control, etc. The world's most typical intelligent investment advisory platforms are Wealthfront, Betterment, Robo-Advisor, etc. [5, 6]. Moreover, the application of artificial intelligence in the retail field has also been very extensive. It is changing the way people shop, such as cashierless stores, smart supply chains, and unmanned warehouses. These unmanned applications help reduce actual employee participation, reduce operational costs and improve work efficiency [7].

Manufacturing companies are the important cornerstones of social and economic development. The application of AI technology to enterprise management will become the trend of smart manufacturing initiatives, and will cover areas like research and development (R&D), production, marketing, finance, human resource management, etc. [8]. Nowadays, the economic development of a country or region is largely driven by sustained technological innovation. In other words, technological innovation is a major source of economic growth. In light of this discussion, the R&D department is the backbone of any manufacturing enterprise for their survival and development, as well as the key to maintain competitive advantage [9]. In order to maintain its market position and gain consumers' recognition with its products or new technical solutions, a manufacturing firm needs to continuously carry out technological innovation and product innovation. R&D department is the functional department that undertakes the innovation of new products and new technologies of the whole enterprise. Therefore, it is of great significance to apply AI technology in the R&D department to enhance its efficiency, creativity and productivity.

In view of this, this paper aims to investigate potential application of AI technology in the R&D domain through literature analysis. This paper explores the new position and new strategy of product R&D supported by industrial AI technologies. Besides, this paper proposes a new pattern of AI-based R&D by comparing with the steps of traditional product R&D. At the same time, a series of advantages brought by AI-based R&D are summarized, and so providing useful guidance for future practices.

2 Essence and Development of AI

Formed in the 1950s, AI is a comprehensive technology for researching machine intelligence and intelligent machines, involving psychology, cognitive science, thinking science, information science, systems science, biological science, etc. [9]. At present, AI technology has achieved remarkable achievements in knowledge processing, pattern recognition, natural language processing, game playing, automatic theorem proving, automatic programming, expert systems, knowledge bases, intelligent robots, etc., gradually forming diversified development models.

As an important branch of the computer science, AI was proposed by McCarthy at the Dartmouth Conference in 1956 and is now known as one of the world's three cutting-edge technologies [10]. Professor Nelson, at the well-known AI Research Center of Stanford University, defines AI as "a discipline of knowledge – a discipline about how to represent, acquire and use knowledge" [11]. According to Professor Winston of MIT, "AI is to study how to enable computers to do work that required human intelligence" [12]. In addition, there are many other definitions and they all reflect the essence of AI: to study the laws of human's intelligent activities and build an artificial system that acts intelligently.

The 1950s and 1960s were the initial stage of AI development. In this period, the main application of AI focused on the computer programming with heuristic thinking and knowledge of the domain. The most typical program was simulated chess playing program [13]. McCarthy named the Dartmouth Conference as "Artificial Intelligence" in 1956, which started the research on AI. In the same period, the theoretical model of Turing machine proposed by Alan Turing in *Computing Machinery and Intelligence* laid the theoretical foundation for the emergence of modern computers [14]. At the same time, scholars Warren McCulloch and Walter Pitts published *A Logical Calculus of the Ideas Immanent in Nervous Activity*, which proved a certain type of neural network that can be strictly defined, thus creating two research categories of AI: Symbolism and Connectionism [15]. In 1963, people tried to communicate with natural language, which marked another leap in AI: how to enable computers to understand natural language so that they can automatically answer questions and analyze images [16]. In the 1970s and 1980s, AI entered a knowledge-centered development stage, and more scholars recognized the importance of knowledge in analog intelligence. More in-depth explorations were made on knowledge representation, reasoning, machine learning, and the cognitive simulation based on the knowledge of specific problem domain [16].

Therefore, with the rapid development of the IoT and cloud computing technology, it has become more convenient to acquire, transmit, store and analyze data in large amount. Therefore, AI technology is moving towards large-scale distributed AI, multi-expert collaborative systems and parallel reasoning as well as multi-intelligence collaborative systems in large distributed AI development environments and distributed environments. Typical AI research and applications include problem solving, expert system, machine learning, neural networks, and pattern recognition [17]. Specifically, problem solving is to solve the unexpected effect caused by accident or the deviation between unexpected and expected effects in management activities. Expert system (ES) is a computer intelligence program system with expert knowledge and experience for solving specialized problems. Machine learning is to study how to simulate or realize human learning activities with a computer. Learning is a knowledge acquisition process with a specific purpose. It finds expression internally in the continuous establishment and modification of a new knowledge structure and externally in the improvement of performance. A neural network is an operational model consisting of a large number of interconnected nodes (or neurons) to simulate the brain's solution to a particular problem. Pattern recognition is to replace or aid humans in pattern perception with computers, mainly focusing on the recognition of text and two-bit images.

3 Traditional R&D

R&D is the fundamental driving force for the sustainable development and technological innovation of an enterprise. Therefore, it is the fundamental strategy for the survival and development of an enterprise. R&D refers to a series of activities carried out by a company or a research institution to substantially improve technology and products by creatively using technology and new knowledge [18]. Similarly, R&D department is also the specialized venue for a company to develop new services or products or improve existing services or products by carrying out innovative activities. Today, private companies, state-owned companies and large multinational companies all spare no effort in R&D.

The research, development and innovation of new products are undoubtedly the soul of high-tech enterprises. Therefore, the development potential of a high-tech enterprise can be measured by its annual investment in R&D. According to statistics from the UNESCO, worldwide R&D investment reached nearly 1.7 trillion US dollars, a record high, as of June 2018, and all countries have promised to increase their staffing and capital investment in R&D in public (guided by governments, universities, research institutions, etc.) and private (guided by enterprises) organizations by 2030 [19]. Continuous R&D and design is the only way for an enterprise to maintain its core competitiveness. If an enterprise fails to do so, it will be unable to improve its products, and therefore will completely lose the soul of innovation and the market share in future.

The R&D department of a company undertakes the tasks of new product R&D and improvement as well as the enhancement of product functions. Clear work flow of the R&D department and employees will enable the company to develop new products that cater market needs in an efficient, economical and effective manner. From a process perspective, traditional R&D process mainly includes the following steps:

1) Market survey;
2) Project establishment;
3) Preparation of R&D plan, providing scheme design and cost estimation;
4) Carrying out specific R&D tasks;
5) Manufacturing of the first article, which requires cooperation among R&D department, production department, QC department and procurement department;
6) Small-batch production (LRIP);
7) Submit samples to customer for inspection and confirmation before subsequent mass production [20].

With so many steps, therefore traditional R&D has the characteristics of low success rate, long cycle and great difficulty in management, as detailed below:

1) **Low success rate**: The technological innovations in the R&D department of a company mainly include technological development innovation, application basic innovation, production process innovation, market development innovation, etc., all of which are indispensable parts of the development strategy of a company. Industrial R&D is innovative work, which will be affected by many unknown factors. Due to

its low structuredness, the work has high risk level and uncertainty. The century-long enterprise development history of the world tells us that only 16.67% of the technological innovations realized their business value [21].

2) **Long cycle**: This is one of the characteristics of traditional R&D. Generally speaking, a R&D project can take a few months to a year or even longer [22]. In the entire R&D process, no specific R&D results may be achieved in some months or quarters; even if the R&D work is finally successful, it is difficult to averagely allocate the visible results to each month, not to mention failure. Therefore, there is a high probability that the traditional R&D of an enterprise takes a long time but achieves nothing in the end.
3) **Great difficulty in management**: This is another characteristic of traditional R&D. The difficulty in enterprise management is a common problem in business operations; but for R&D department, the great difficulty in management has become a characteristic of traditional R&D. In the process of R&D, the complexity of technology and the integration of work will result in complicated internal relations of the department. Usually, an R&D project requires cooperation between people from different disciplines and various fields. Therefore, it is unable to anticipate collaboration work. In addition, R&D results belong to the whole R&D staff, and it is difficult to measure the contributions of an individual to the final results and define the scope of their respective responsibilities [23].

4 AI-Based R&D

R&D activities of an enterprise rely on the developers' scientific and objective judgments and effective development strategies. AI-based R&D can provide accurate judgment basis for developers, which will enable them more accurately anticipate market demands and improve product development efficiency. Therefore, this section will be elaborated in two aspects: 1) Which steps of R&D activities can be completed using AI technology without human intervention; 2) how AI technology can automatically complete these tasks.

From the perspective of product development and innovation, AI technology is to transform the traditional serial R&D process into a closed-loop intelligent R&D process, which is continuously improved based on market demands with the help of Expert System. AI technology needs to be based on big data. In other words, there will be no AI technology without big data [24]. However, during the traditional R&D, especially in the process of user demands collection, companies often used traditional survey methods, such as questionnaires and interviews. Generally speaking, the information obtained was only a small amount of data, and the samples were selected by sampling method, so there was likely to be a deviation between the survey result and the real market environment [25]. In addition, users only served as the research objects and reference during the collection of R&D requirements, and they did not have the right to decide which concept or product would be adopted. Individual users rarely communicated with each other, so they had low degree of interaction [25]. In this scenario, most users would be unwilling to spend time and energy to assist a company in product development unless they were provided with certain rewards.

However, things will be different in R&D activities with industrial AI. When a product developed by AI technology is manufactured, put on the market and used by users, the intelligent sensors embedded in the product will collect user behavior data at all times during the use of this product, and these data will be continuously sent to the manufacturer's cloud data center, forming big data on user behaviors. In the future, these products developed based on AI technology will have functions such as sensing, monitoring, self-adaptation, interconnection, interaction and coordination, etc. and thus can be called smart products. In the process of interaction between users and smart products, the behavioral big data formed will be intelligently analyzed to form a cycle of user-to-user iterative product development. It is easy to see that AI technology has enabled real-time collection and analysis of market- and user-related data in the early demand analysis. These data are characterized by full coverage, wide range and good effectiveness [26]. Moreover, data about the product itself will also be collected in good time and sent to the user behavior data center. In addition to user behavior and product data, product feedback from netizen users will also be automatically crawled by the system and used as part of market research data. With these text data, text mining and information extraction can be performed through sentiment analysis that is most active in natural language processing (NLP), so that the system can further improve the design based on the users' comments. Therefore, an intelligent R&D process based on reciprocating feedback is formed.

In addition to the early market demand analysis, things will be quite different also in the stage of AI-based product design. In traditional product design, the R&D department needed to conduct a market feasibility and technical feasibility analysis of the project product, prepare an analysis report and submit it to the higher management, so that the management could carry out project approval and review based on risk control and investment budget planning. After that, in a real R&D environment, the product design by the R&D staff would include the specific industrial design, software design and hardware design; debugging and simulation would be performed for the design at different levels to ensure the feasibility of the technical solution. Finally, before mass production, the R&D department and the production department would jointly conduct LIRP and track the small batch production process to confirm the consistency and stability of the product quality, so as to ensure that the product can be put into mass production [26].

However, AI-based R&D can shorten most of these processes to increase the R&D efficiency. In R&D technology feasibility analysis, especially in the verification of the availability of new technologies, new materials and new functions, the AI-based analysis and feedback mechanism can help R&D department create a digital prototype or digital twin of product. A digital twin, as the name suggests, refers to an identical object created in the digital world by digital means for an object in the physical world, so as to achieve in-depth understanding, analysis and optimization of the physical object [27]. The concept of digital twin was first proposed by Professor Grieves at the University of Michigan. He believed that digital twin is "a virtual and digital representation equivalent to the physical product". Later, the concept of digital twin was first introduced to the spacecraft health maintenance by the U.S. Department of Defense, where a fully mapped virtual model was built based on the physical model of a spacecraft, so as to reflect the state of the physical spacecraft with historical data and real-time data collected by sensors in the aircraft

[28]. With the increasing amount of product data (including product performance, user behaviors, market demands, etc.), a digital twin can also be used for the development and test of conceptual products, especially with the vigorous development of deep learning technology that relies on big data. The most typical representative is the concept of "digital twin" proposed by Siemens. It is dedicated to the simulation of finished products in the cyberspace for manufacturing companies, so as to realize the digitalization of the entire process from digital design to manufacturing [29]. When a digital twin is used to support collaborative product design patterns such as overall design, structural design, and process design, different aspects will be examined in these design patterns, such as correct dimension tolerance, functional integrity, interference, material quality, motion analysis, ergonomics analysis, etc. At the same time, during the industrial R&D stage, a digital prototype can also be used to evaluate product processes, including product processing methods, machining accuracy, toolpaths, etc., achieving computer-aided manufacturing (CAM) simulation of prototype and process planning based on 3D digital prototype. By simulation on the digital twin platform, R&D personnel can reduce the number of full-scale tests compared with the traditional R&D process in the past, thereby reducing R&D costs, shortening the R&D cycle. Simulation technology and experimental management can be combined to improve the confidence level of simulation results [29].

Here, R&D in a more complex discrete industry is taken as an example. For automotive engine R&D design companies, the core business is to design an energy-efficient engine. Generally speaking, digital model of drawing, electronic control module design drawings, and engineering design schemes are more common engineering deliverables. However, with the application of AI technology, the classic scenes in the past, such as busy figures in the drawing room, engineering drawings on the desk, will become history in future engine design. 3D model can be automatically converted to drawings. With the increasing amount of data on automobile engines and the continuous upgrading and optimization of computing power and algorithms, AI technology will enable independent software system to develop automobile engines by itself. New products can be continuously optimized based on the ongoing collection and feedback of data from previous generations of engines during driving [30]. At the same time, physical experiments are no longer needed in the functional test. The system will automatically perform the functional test and obtain various parameters. Based on these results, the products developed can be self-optimized with deep learning technology, so that an optimal engine design solution can be obtained during the R&D stage, greatly reducing the time and cost of R&D.

5 Benefits of AI-Based R&D

With the rapid development of AI technology, the deep integration of AI technology and industrial R&D has brought unlimited possibilities and potential advantages to the future R&D models. In general, the advantages brought by AI-based R&D can be divided into the following aspects: **1) More objective identification of user requirements to drive enterprise innovation; 2) more precise exploration of market trends; 3) higher efficiency in product design; 4) less risks in R&D process; and 5) improved knowledge sharing ability**, as follows:

1) **More objective identification of user requirements to drive enterprise innovation**

The main function of R&D department is to develop new products, which is an innovative activity. Product creativity has great significance and plays a vital role in the successful development of new products. In the past, the traditional R&D model was relatively fixed and closed, and creativity mainly relied on the subjective judgment (subjective experience, knowledge, ability) of R&D engineers. That was because the R&D department of companies often used sampling method for user and market demand analysis, and only limited questionnaires were send out for demand survey due to limited time and budget; after questionnaires with low validity were eliminated, the number of valid questionnaires would be even smaller. In addition, in interviews and surveys, investigators lacked in-depth communication with the interviewees due to the short time and thus were unable to obtain effective information. In this case, companies had to rely more on the personal experience of R&D personnel for product R&D. R&D personnel played the role of users, and their judgment result was more subjective [31]. In contrast, under the mode of automatic R&D based on deep learning through AI technology, the samples for demand survey are big data, with more extensive data sources and huge data volume; and more importantly, data acquisition is performed under the users' unconscious state and their intentional concealment is avoided, so the data is more authentic. When the system automatically analyzes the data through AI technology, the conclusions will be more authentic and reliable, achieving more objective identification of user requirements.

2) **More precise exploration of market trends**

The accuracy of product positioning is an important factor in determining the success of a product, and product positioning depends on the decision makers' grasp and judgment of the overall market situation. Traditionally developed products will be mass-produced and then put on the market to face a high uncertainty of market because corporate decision makers cannot ensure that all these products will be favored by consumers. Once these products are not well received by consumers, the manufacturer will face problems such as overcapacity, inventory backlogs, and waste of production resources. This will be considered a R&D failure [32]. Therefore, how to grasp the positioning of products in the market, judge the market trends as accurately as possible, and find out potential user groups have become the problems to be urgently solved by R&D personnel and decision makers of an enterprise. AI technology can be used for accurate positioning of products to clarify the needs of different user groups, thereby increasing the adaptability of products to the market. For example, from a technical perspective, classification mining, cluster analysis, and association rules in AI technology are all used for precise positioning of product users [33]. Cluster analysis is a statistical classification technique in which a set of objects or points with similar characteristics are grouped together in clusters, so that the items in cluster are very similar to one another and very different from the items in other clusters. This technique can be used to classify customer groups and analyze customer backgrounds, so as to predict market trends [33]. Therefore, the needs of users in different groups will be clearer. Then, the AI system can independently develop different types of products with deep learning technology based on user requirements of different groups to achieve product customization.

3) **Higher efficiency in product design**

AI technology has improved the efficiency of product development. The efficiency here is embodied in two aspects. For one thing, from the perspective of the R&D process, AI-based R&D enables more intelligent and efficient acquisition of user requirements information and more extensive and comprehensive data sources. For another, the processes from product scheme design to specific product R&D, material selection, function testing, and finally to the LIRP will be automatically performed by the system, which greatly shortens the development cycle, saves costs and improves product development efficiency. Taking the process-based manufacturing industry as an example, the technical R&D of new materials is of great significance for promoting national prosperity and ensuring national security. However, the development of the material industry has long been dominated by manual trial-and-error R&D model, which has led to a long R&D cycle and high cost of material industry. Studies have shown that it takes at least 20 years from the discovery of a new material to laboratory verification and then to application to demanding products such as aerospace equipment [34]. The traditional empirical trial-and-error method is inefficient and greatly restricted by human energy and experience. In addition, from the successful laboratory application to engineering application, it often takes several years to ensure correct process and operating parameters. With the continuous upgrading of intelligent sensors, more and more R&D process data can be obtained. Based on the data collected in the past experiments, AI technology can be used to simulate materials through simulation modeling tools and software, which can simplify the R&D process. More importantly, all R&D results are driven by data, which ensures the scientificness and authenticity of experiments and improves R&D efficiency.

4) **Less risk in R&D process**

In addition to efficiency improvement, AI technology also lowers the risks of R&D, especially the risks of new products to humans. The most typical application is the R&D in biopharmaceutical industry, which is an important part of the national economy. At present, the R&D of pharmaceuticals are faced with the problems of high cost, long cycle and high risks [35]. There are two problems to be solved in the development of both anticancer drugs and antiviral compounds for agriculture: one is to find the correct chemical structure needed; the other is to determine which chemical reactions can connect the right atoms with the required analysis [35]. For these two problems, if traditional R&D methods are used, the answers often come from random scientific guessing and unexpected discoveries. Not only that, the efficacy of newly developed drugs needs to be proved by clinical application. Therefore, such a research process often has low efficiency, little effect and even certain risks. However, AI technology has gradually become an important means for new drug development. AI technology provides computer-aided research for drug R&D, which can greatly reduce the risks of R&D. At the same time, especially at the stage of clinical trials, AI technology can be used to select target patients that better meet the needs of the trial based on clinical big data, improving the success rate of clinical trials and also reducing the risk of new drugs.

5) **Improved knowledge sharing ability**

In the era of knowledge economy, knowledge management is an inevitable choice for enterprises, and one of its key elements is knowledge sharing. The knowledge sharing ability of R&D personnel directly affects the product development effect [8]. In the previous R&D, the differences in employees' personal knowledge and experience often led to different knowledge levels of individual researchers, which affected the willingness of researchers to share knowledge [36]. In many cases, R&D personnel with rich knowledge and experience will be reluctant or even unwilling to share their knowledge. Today, although with the assistance of AI technology, the system can complete the independent conception and R&D of products, it is also important for R&D personnel to develop the habits and capabilities of lifelong learning and personal knowledge management. AI technology will help the knowledge network based on big data analysis to form a knowledge sharing platform for face-to-face mutual feedback. This platform can also be used as an enterprise's expert system. The AI-based system will independently learn from the accumulated data to enrich the expert database. At the same time, the expert system will classify the acquired explicit knowledge and dig out the tacit knowledge. Employees can continuously learn and share knowledge through this expert system. Therefore, researchers' ability of sharing knowledge is improved.

6 Conclusions

In this paper, AI-based R&D pattern is proposed by combining AI technology with industrial R&D. With the continuous promotion and application of AI technology in the future, R&D pattern will be transformed from the traditional one-way process to enterprise's active connection with user service terminals, thereby achieving benign interaction. The AI-based system automatically performs product development, simulation, and testing based on big data. Users and expert knowledge base will become the subject of technological innovation, and the product development process will also be independently completed by the system.

However, in general, the actual realization of AI-based R&D is a complex and time-consuming process. The realization of the aforementioned elements such as automatic analysis of requirements and the independent completion of R&D process is also a very complicated system project. In addition to establishing and continuously improving their own R&D system and strengthening the expert knowledge base, enterprises also need to realize the data flow automation in the product's entire life cycle, construct intelligent and interconnected products and form a user-centered product ecosystem using AI technology, and develop a closed-loop product R&D service system that can be sustainably optimized by closely linking information (such as user requirements and preferences, and market needs to product R&D) with R&D with AI technology as a driving force.

References

1. McCarthy, J., Hayes, P.J.: Some philosophical problems from the standpoint of artificial intelligence. In: Readings in Artificial Intelligence, pp. 431–450. Morgan Kaufmann (1981)
2. Ramos, C., Augusto, J.C., Shapiro, D.: Ambient intelligence—the next step for artificial intelligence. IEEE Intell. Syst. **23**(2), 15–18 (2008)
3. Jiang, F., et al.: Artificial intelligence in healthcare: past, present and future. Stroke Vasc. Neurol. **2**(4), 230–243 (2017)
4. Bini, S.A.: Artificial intelligence, machine learning, deep learning, and cognitive computing: what do these terms mean and how will they impact health care? J. Arthroplasty **33**(8), 2358–2361 (2018)
5. Gold, N.A., Kursh, S.R.: Counterrevolutionaries in the financial services industry: teaching disruption–a case study of RoboAdvisors and incumbent responses. Bus. Educ. Innov. J. **9**(1), 139–146 (2017)
6. Bahrammirzaee, A.: A comparative survey of artificial intelligence applications in finance: artificial neural networks, expert system and hybrid intelligent systems. Neural Comput. Appl. **19**(8), 1165–1195 (2010)
7. Pantano, E.: Innovation drivers in retail industry. Int. J. Inf. Manage. **34**(3), 344–350 (2014)
8. Kahraman, C., Kaya, I., Çevikcan, E.: Intelligence decision systems in enterprise information management. J. Enterp. Inf. Manage. **24**(4), 360–379 (2011)
9. Li, B.H., Hou, B.C., Yu, W.T., Lu, X.B., Yang, C.W.: Applications of artificial intelligence in intelligent manufacturing: a review. Front. Inf. Technol. Electron. Eng. **18**(1), 86–96 (2017)
10. Moor, J.: The Dartmouth College artificial intelligence conference: the next fifty years. AI Mag. **27**(4), 87–87 (2006)
11. Simmons, A.B., Chappell, S.G.: Artificial intelligence-definition and practice. IEEE J. Oceanic Eng. **13**(2), 14–42 (1988)
12. Beal, J., Winston, P.H.: Guest editors' introduction: the new frontier of human-level artificial intelligence. IEEE Intell. Syst. **24**(4), 21–23 (2009)
13. Vardi, M.Y.: Artificial intelligence: past and future. Commun. ACM **55**(1), 5–5 (2012)
14. Muggleton, S.: Alan Turing and the development of artificial intelligence. AI Commun. **27**(1), 3–10 (2014)
15. Wilson, E.A.: "Would I had him with me always": affects of longing in early artificial intelligence. Isis **100**(4), 839–847 (2009)
16. Cambria, E., White, B.: Jumping NLP curves: a review of natural language processing research. IEEE Comput. Intell. Mag. **9**(2), 48–57 (2014)
17. Duan, Y., Edwards, J.S., Dwivedi, Y.K.: Artificial intelligence for decision making in the era of Big Data–evolution, challenges and research agenda. Int. J. Inf. Manage. **48**, 63–71 (2019)
18. Güngör, A., Alp, G.T.: Cognitive styles affecting the performance of research and development (R&D) employees in the era of Industry 4.0. Industry 4.0 **4**(5), 203–205 (2019)
19. Anthony, S.D., Viguerie, S.P., Schwartz, E.I., Van Landeghem, J.: 2018 Corporate Longevity Forecast: Creative Destruction is Accelerating. Innosight (2018). https://www.innosight.com/insight/creative-destruction
20. Johnson, J.S., Friend, S.B., Lee, H.S.: Big data facilitation, utilization, and monetization: exploring the 3Vs in a new product development process. J. Prod. Innov. Manag. **34**(5), 640–658 (2017)
21. Swink, M., Song, M.: Effects of marketing-manufacturing integration on new product development time and competitive advantage. J. Oper. Manage. **25**(1), 203–217 (2007)
22. Burkart, R.E.: Reducing R&D cycle time. Res.-Technol. Manage. **37**(3), 27–32 (1994)
23. Thamhain, H.J.: Managing innovative R&D teams. R&D Manage. **33**(3), 297–311 (2003)
24. O'Leary, D.E.: Artificial intelligence and big data. IEEE Intell. Syst. **28**(2), 96–99 (2013)

25. Russell, C.A., Stern, B.B., Stern, B.B.: Consumers, characters, and products: a balance model of sitcom product placement effects. J. Advert. **35**(1), 7–21 (2006)
26. Makridakis, S.: The forthcoming Artificial Intelligence (AI) revolution: its impact on society and firms. Futures **90**, 46–60 (2017)
27. Gaggioli, A.: Digital twins: an emerging paradigm in cyberpsychology research? Cyberpsychol. Behav. Soc. Network. **21**(7), 468–469 (2018)
28. Glaessgen, E., Stargel, D.: The digital twin paradigm for future NASA and US Air Force vehicles. In: 53rd AIAA/ASME/ASCE/AHS/ASC Structures, Structural Dynamics and Materials Conference, 20th AIAA/ASME/AHS Adaptive Structures Conference, 14th AIAA, p. 1818, April 2012
29. Vachálek, J., Bartalský, L., Rovný, O., Šišmišová, D., Morháč, M., Lokšík, M.: The digital twin of an industrial production line within the industry 4.0 concept. In: 2017 21st International Conference on Process Control (PC), pp. 258–262. IEEE, June 2017
30. Wang, F.Y.: Artificial intelligence and intelligent transportation: driving into the 3rd axial age with ITS. IEEE Intell. Transp. Syst. Mag. **9**(4), 6–9 (2017)
31. Shin, N., Kraemer, K.L., Dedrick, J.: R&D and firm performance in the semiconductor industry. Ind. Innov. **24**(3), 280–297 (2017)
32. Khanna, R., Guler, I., Nerkar, A.: Fail often, fail big, and fail fast? Learning from small failures and R&D performance in the pharmaceutical industry. Acad. Manag. J. **59**(2), 436–459 (2016)
33. Hsu, F.C., Lin, Y.H., Chen, C.N.: Applying cluster analysis for consumer's affective responses toward product forms. J. Interdisc. Math. **18**(6), 657–666 (2015)
34. Abbe, G., Smith, H.: Technological development trends in Solar-powered Aircraft Systems. Renew. Sustain. Energy Rev. **60**, 770–783 (2016)
35. Sander, T., Freyss, J., von Korff, M., Rufener, C.: DataWarrior: an open-source program for chemistry aware data visualization and analysis. J. Chem. Inf. Model. **55**(2), 460–473 (2015)
36. Inkinen, H.: Review of empirical research on knowledge management practices and firm performance. J. Knowl. Manage. **20**(2), 230–257 (2016)

User Experience in Intelligent Environments

Exploring Users' Eye Movements When Using Projection-Based Assembly Assistive Systems

Mario Heinz[1(✉)], Sebastian Büttner[1,2], and Carsten Röcker[3]

[1] Institute Industrial IT, Ostwestfalen-Lippe University of Applied Sciences and Arts, Campusallee 6, 32657 Lemgo, Germany
{mario.heinz,sebastian.buettner}@th-owl.de
[2] Human-Centered Information Systems, Clausthal University of Technology, Julius-Albert Str. 4, 38678 Clausthal-Zellerfeld, Germany
[3] Fraunhofer IOSB-INA, Campusallee 6, 32657 Lemgo, Germany
carsten.roecker@th-owl.de

Abstract. Projection-based assistive systems have shown to be a promising technology to support workers during manual assembly processes in industrial manufacturing by projecting instructions into the working area. While existing studies have investigated various aspects of these systems, little research has been conducted regarding the way in which the user accesses the provided instructions. In this paper we analyze the eye movements of users during the repeated execution of an assembly task at a projection-based assistive system in order to gain insights into the utilization of the presented instructions. For this purpose, we analyzed eye tracking recordings from a user study with 15 participants to investigate the sequences in which the respective instructions are observed by the users. The results show a significantly lower number of nonlinear gaze sequences as well as a significantly higher number of steps without observing the instructions during the repeated use of the assistive system. In addition, there was a significantly lower task completion time during repeated use of the assistive system.

Keywords: Assistive systems · Eye tracking · Human behavior

1 Introduction

Industrial production is currently undergoing substantial changes. On one hand, there is an ongoing trend towards the automation of manufacturing processes. As a result of these changes, a substantial amount of assembly processes that were previously carried out by hand are now being taken over by automated systems. On the other hand, products are becoming more and more customizable and the production quantities are decreasing accordingly, which is a major challenge for automation [7]. These trends indicate that manual assembly processes will continue to be a part of the production chain in the future. However, it

N. Streitz and S. Konomi (Eds.): HCII 2020, LNCS 12203, pp. 259–272, 2020.
https://doi.org/10.1007/978-3-030-50344-4_19

can be assumed that these assembly processes will become increasingly complex resulting in a higher cognitive load on the workers.

In recent years, various digital assistive systems have been introduced to support workers in executing manual assembly tasks. Alongside systems based on augmented-reality (AR) capable head-mounted displays (HMDs), smartphones and tablet PCs, especially projection-based systems have become very popular [5,13]. These systems use digital projectors to project instructions and additional information directly into the working area. Furthermore, many of these systems also use cameras to implement interactions based on hand positions in oder to provide interactive step-by-step tutorials.

Although numerous studies have been carried out to investigate various aspects in the context of projection-based assembly assistive systems, so far little attention has been paid to the way how users access the provided instructions [5,10]. This raises the following questions: Which elements of the instructions are considered by the users? In which order do users look at the instructions? How does this change with repeated use of the assistive system? In this paper we present the results of a user study tackling these questions. Within the scope of the study, the eye movements of users were recorded during the operation of a projection-based assembly assistive system in order to track the way in which they accessed the provided instructions.

2 Related Work

2.1 Projection-Based Assistive Systems

Various projection-based assistive systems have been introduced to support manual assembly processes in the industrial sector. An early system presented in Bannat et al. used a digital projector to project text-based and image-based instructions into the work environment [1]. In addition, they used a camera combined with a body-worn tracking system to detect the grasping of assembly parts from different boxes. Similar systems have been introduced by Funk et al. [11] and Sand et al. [22] using a depth camera for the tracking of the users' hands. Furthermore, numerous experiments have been carried out to investigate the different aspects of projection-based assistive systems for industrial assembly processes. Büttner et al., for example, compared a projection-based system with an AR assistive system based on a HMD and with a paper-based instruction [2]. They showed that the projection-based system resulted in lower error rates and shorter task completion times compared to paper-based instructions and the HMD system. An evaluation described by Funk et al. comparing projection-based instructions, HMD-based instructions, tablet-based instructions and paper-based instructions showed similar results [11]. In further experiments Funk et al. evaluated different strategies for the creation of instructions for projection-based assistive systems [12] and explored the behavior of expert and novice users at a projection-based system in a long term analysis [8]. Kosch et al. also investigated the use of tactile, auditory, and visual error feedback for projection-based systems [20]. Other studies carried out by Korn et al. have focused on the application of in-situ instructions for people with cognitive impairments [17] as well as the integration of gamification elements [18]. Kosch et al. [19] and Funk et al. [9] further analyzed the challenges and opportunities towards the adaptivity of in-situ instructions. In a recent study, Büttner et al. analyzed the impact of projection-based assistive systems on the learning effectiveness in industrial settings [4].

All in all, previous studies have already analyzed essential aspects in the context of projection-based assembly assistive systems. However, to the best of our knowledge, an investigation of the sequences in which users access the provided instructions has not yet been conducted.

2.2 Eye Tracking

Eye tracking is a method for the recording and analysis of the eye movements of a person. The method is applied in various medical, psychological and linguistic research areas as well as in marketing and human-machine interaction [6]. By analyzing eye movements during the observation of certain views or while performing certain tasks, conclusions can be drawn regarding the underlying cognitive strategies [15]. In the context of manual assembly, Lušic et al. presented a comparative study using eye tracking to investigate the impact of different visualization techniques for screen based instructions [21]. Stoessel et al. further presented an assistive system which uses eye tracking to analyze the cognitive processes of a user during the execution of an assembly task [23]. Huber et al. also used eye tracking in combination with other tracking systems to model human behavior for a hybrid assembly system with a robotic arm [16].

The mentioned publications show that eye tracking has already been used for various investigations in the field of manual assembly. An investigation of eye movements in the context of projection-based assistive systems, however, has not yet been carried out.

3 User Study

To investigate the way how users access to the provided instructions at a projection-based assembly assistive systems, we conducted a user study described in the following sections.

3.1 Design

The study was designed as a longitudinal study with one independent variable: "the number of previous executions" of the assembly task. As dependent variables we measured the task completion time (TCT), the number of steps with linear eye movement sequences and the number of steps without considering the provided text-based and image-based instructions. Furthermore, we collected information about the user experience for the anticipated and the actual use of the assistive system.

3.2 Apparatus

System. For the conduction of the study we used a state-of-the-art projection-based AR assistive system. The system is located in the SmartFactoryOWL, a research and demonstration facility for projects in the scope of industrial digitization and automation in Lemgo, Germany [3]. The system which is based on an assembly workbench consists of a digital projector (CASIO Advanced XJ), a depth camera (Intel Realsense d435), a robotic arm (Universal Robots UR3) and an optical control unit (DATALOGIC). The projector mounted above the user's head is used to project text-, image- and video-based instructions and hints onto the surface of the workbench. The depth camera, which is also located above the user's head, is used to track the hands of the user in order to interact with the system. The interactions involve the detection of an access to one of the component boxes and the activation of virtual buttons. The robot arm of the assistive system supports the user in carrying out various activities such as holding, placing or screwing components. The optical control unit is attached to the right side of the workbench and checks the correctness of the assembly. For this purpose, the component is picked up by the robot arm after the completion of the assembly process and moved in front of the control unit. With this setup the system can be used to provide interactive projection-based step-by-step instructions for manual assembly processes (Fig. 1).

Fig. 1. The assistive system used for the study.

Assembly Task. As an assembly process for our study we used a toy gearbox set. The task involved twelve steps of which four steps are for the picking and four steps are for the assembly of a component. The remaining four steps are for checking the status of the system and controlling the robot arm. An overview of the text-based instructions, interactions and triggered actions for each step is shown in Table 1.

Table 1. Overview of the instructions, interactions and triggered actions for the twelve steps of the assembly task.

Step	Instruction	Interaction	Triggered action
1	Check if the main part is placed correctly on the starting mold	Accept button	Robot moves main part to assembly position
2	Wait until the robot has moved to the assembly position	Accept button	
3	Grasp one part from box 1	Box entrance	
4	Place the part on the main part according to the visualized information	Accept button	
5	Grasp one part from box 2	Box entrance	
6	Place the part on the main part according to the visualized information	Accept button	
7	Grasp one part from box 3	Box entrance	
8	Place the part on the main part according to the visualized information	Accept button	
9	Grasp one part from box 4	Box entrance	
10	Place the part on the main part according to the visualized information	Accept button	Robot moves to optical control unit
11	Wait until the optical control unit has checked the assembly	Optical control	Robot moves the part to resting position
12	The assembly process is complete	Accept button	

To support the picking of a component, the corresponding component box is highlighted by a blue rectangle. In addition, an image of the component, as well as a text-based instruction for the picking, is projected onto the center of the workbench (Fig. 2). To assist the user during the assembly of a component, a video of the assembly, a text-based instruction and a text-based hint are projected onto the center of the workbench (Fig. 2).

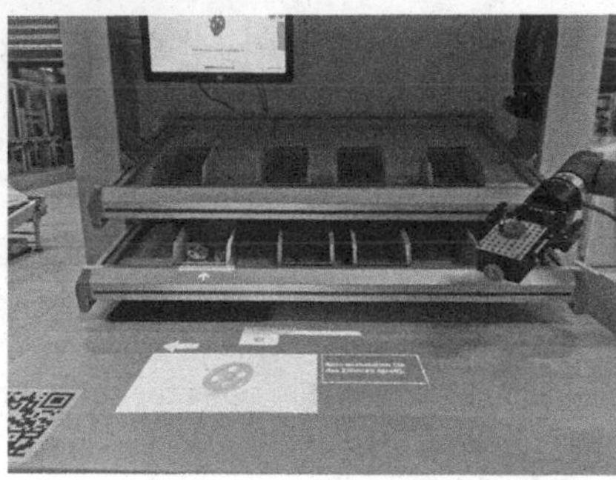

Fig. 2. Example projection for a picking (left) and an assembly step (right).

3.3 Recording Device

For our study we used a mobile eye tracking device (Tobii Glasses 2) to record the eye movements of the participants during the assembly process. In this way we were able to collect information about the way in which the participants accessed the provided instructions. For the attachment, the participants were asked to put on the glasses section of the device and to fasten the retaining strap on the back of their head. The processor unit of the eye tracker was attached to the participants waistband.

3.4 Procedure

Prior to the start of the study, we collected some demographic data (age, gender) of the participants. Subsequently, the participants received a short introduction into the functionality of the assistive system. Then the participants were asked to fill out the User Experience Questionnaire (UEQ). This was intended to collect information about the user experience for the anticipated use of the assistive system. After filling out the questionnaire, the participants were equipped with the eye tracking device and a calibration routine was performed. Afterwards the participants were asked to carry out three repetitions of the assembly process. Thereby, the participants were instructed to follow the instructions of the assistive system and to complete the task at a moderate speed and with as few errors as possible. After each repetition there was a short break during which the assembly object was disassembled and the components were put back into the component boxes. After finishing the third execution of the assembly task, the eye tracking device was removed from the participants and they were asked to fill out the UEQ again. Finally, the participants were thanked for their participation in the study and open questions regarding the study and the assistive system were answered.

3.5 Participants

For the study, we recruited 15 participants, 4 female and 11 male. The participants were aged from 19 and 24 years ($M = 21.5$, $SD = 1.6$). All participants were undergraduate students from our university. None of the participants had previous experience in the field of industrial assembly or was familiar with the components used in the assembly task. The participation in the study was voluntary and the participants did not receive any form of incentive for their attendance. The participants were also informed that they could cancel their participation at any time.

3.6 Data Analysis

A common approach for analyzing eye movements refers to the use of the so-called areas of interest (AOIs), which represent predefined areas in a person's field of view. The sequence of the examination of the different AOIs allows to draw conclusions regarding the access to the information provided in these areas [14]. Thus, for the evaluation of the eye tracking data, we defined multiple AOIs for all relevant areas of the assistive system. Figure 3 shows an overview of the defined AOIs for the assistive system except the AOIs for the starting position and the resting position.

The eye movements of the participants were manually analyzed to collect the sequence of observations of the different AOIs for each step of the assembly process. After the sequences had been recorded, a linear sequence was defined for each step of the assembly process in which users should access the relevant AOIs. The linear sequences are shown in Table 2. Subsequently, the recordings of the individual steps were categorized into linear and non-linear sequences. The recordings that showed the AOIs relevant for the step in the predefined order were classified as linear sequences. Recordings in which at least one of the AOIs relevant for the step was viewed several times, on the other hand, were classified

AOI	AOI Name
1	Display
2	Box 1
3	Box 2
4	Box 3
5	Box 4
6	Progressbar
7	Image/Video
8	Instruction
9	Hint
10	Accept button
11	Main component
12	Robot

Fig. 3. Overview of the areas of interests defined for the study.

Table 2. Overview of the expected linear sequences for the observation of the instructions provided by the assistive system.

Step	Action	Sequence
1	Control	[Image/Instruction/Hint], [Resting place], [Accept Button]
2	Control	[Image/Instruction/Hint], [Robot], [Main component]
3,5,7,9	Picking	[Image/Instruction/Hint], [Box]
4,6,8,10	Assembly	[Image/Instruction/Hint], [Main component], [Accept Button]
11	Control	[Image/Instruction/Hint], [Resting place], [Accept Button]
12	Control	[Image/Instruction/Hint], [Accept Button]

as non-linear sequences. The observation of AOIs not relevant for the step was not considered for the categorization. In addition, we also counted the number of steps for each execution of the assembly task in which the participants skipped the viewing of the text-based and image-based instructions.

3.7 Results

In this section, we present the results of our study. Four participants were excluded from the analysis, because two of them primarily followed the instructions shown on the display instead of using the projection-based instructions and the other two participants were excluded because of technical problems with the eye tracking device.

Task Completion Time. Regarding the TCT, the participants needed an average of 138.73s ($SD = 48.75$) for the first execution, 87.09s ($SD = 22.85$) for the second execution and 87.55s ($SD = 39.91$) for the third execution of the assembly task (Fig. 4). A one-way repeated measures ANOVA was conducted to compare the effect of the number of previous executions on TCT for the first, second and third execution of the assembly task. There was a significant effect on the number of previous executions ($F_{2,9} = 17$, $p = .001$). Pairwise Bonferroni-adjusted post-hoc tests revealed a significant difference ($p = .006$) between the first and the second execution and a significant difference ($p < .001$) between the first and the third execution, but no significant difference between the second and the third execution of the assembly task.

Nonlinear Sequences. In a further step, we analyzed the number of nonlinear sequences of the participants during the three executions of the assembly task. During the first execution, the test subjects showed an average of 5.36 steps ($SD = 2.11$) with a nonlinear sequence. For the second execution there was an average of 2.73 steps ($SD = 1.74$) and for the third execution there was an average of 1.82 steps ($SD = 1.72$) with non-linear sequences. A one-way repeated measures ANOVA was conducted to compare the effect of the number of previous

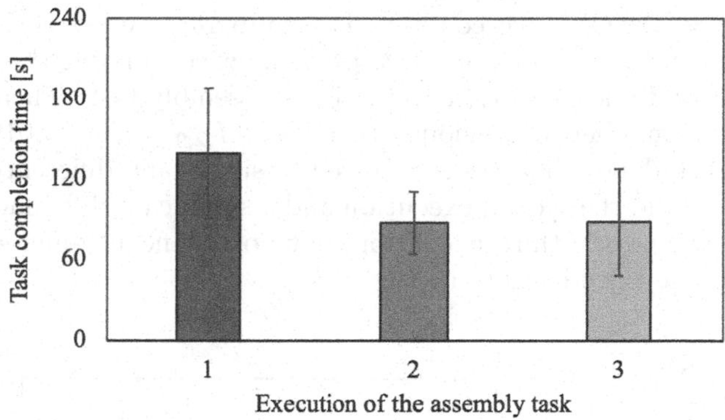

Fig. 4. Result of the study considering the task completion times for the three executions of the assembly task.

executions on the number of non-linear sequences for the first, second and third execution of the assembly task. There was a significant effect on the number of previous executions ($F_{2,9} = 7$, $p = .012$). Pairwise Bonferroni-adjusted post-hoc tests revealed a significant difference ($p = .016$) between the first and the second execution and a significant difference ($p = .007$) between the first and the third execution, but no significant difference between the second and the third execution (Fig. 5).

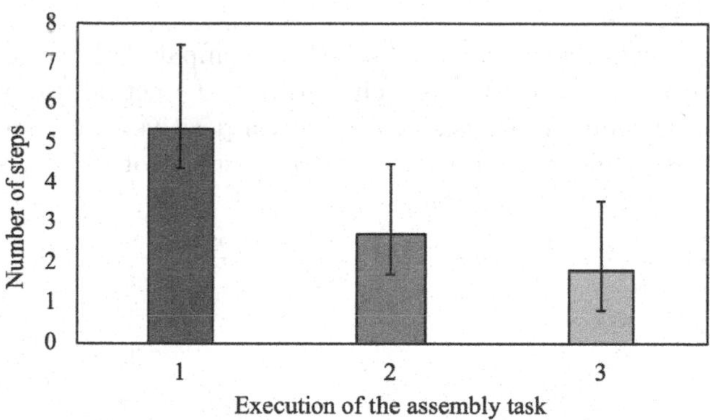

Fig. 5. Result of the study considering the number of non-linear sequences for the three executions of the assembly task.

Information Access. We further analyzed the number of steps in which the participants did skip the text-based and image-based information. The average number of steps without considering the information was 0.18 steps ($SD = 0.40$) for the first execution, 1.82 steps ($SD = 1.83$) for the second execution and 3.18 steps ($SD = 2.68$) for the third execution of the assembly task. A one-way repeated measures ANOVA was conducted to compare the effect of the number of previous executions on the number of steps without considering the information for the first, second and third execution of the assembly task. There was a significant effect on number of previous executions ($F_{2,9} = 6$, $p = .019$). Pairwise Bonferroni-adjusted post-hoc tests revealed a significant difference ($p = .039$) between the first and the second execution and a significant difference ($p = .011$) between the first and the third execution, but no significant difference between the second and the third execution (Fig. 6).

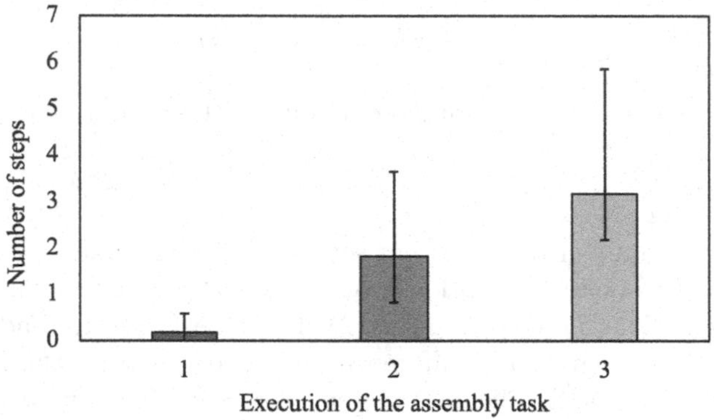

Fig. 6. Result of the study considering the information access for the three executions of the assembly task.

User Experience Questionaire. We further compared the average scores of the six scales of the UEQ for the anticipated and the actual use of the system (Fig. 7). The mean values of the six scales show a positive rating for both points in time of the assessment. T-tests for the comparison of the six scales of the

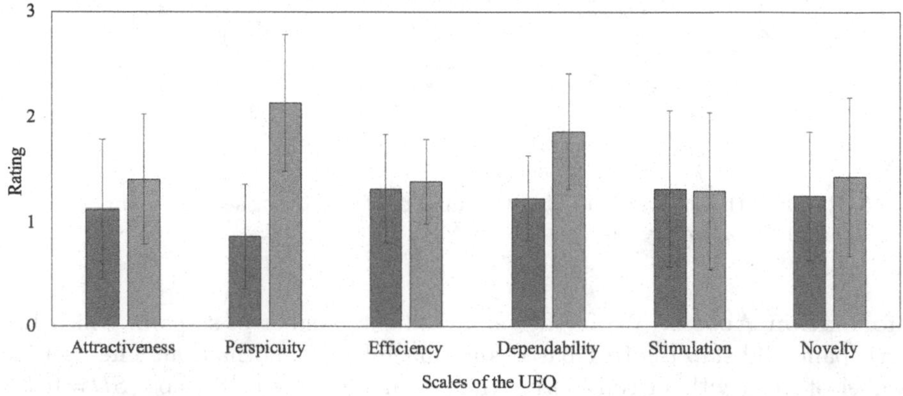

Fig. 7. Results of the UEQ before and after the use of the assistive system.

UEQ for the anticipated and the actual use of the system revealed a significant difference for the perspicuity ($p = 0.0064$), but no significant differences for the other scales.

4 Discussion

Our study shows interesting aspects regarding the repeated execution of an assembly task using a projection-based assistive system. Thus, the repeated executions of the assembly process resulted in a significantly shorter task completion time compared to the first execution. The analysis of the eye movements further revealed a significantly lower number of non-linear viewing sequences when accessing the presented information as well as a significantly increasing number of steps without accessing the displayed text-based and image-based instructions during the repeated execution of an assembly process. These findings indicate the existence of a learning effects regarding the use of the assistive system and the content and structure of the assembly task. In general, the application of eye tracking has shown to be very useful to gain insights into the way how users access the displayed instructions. Considering the analysis of the eye movements during the use of the assistive system, however, it has to be considered that the presented information could also have been accessed and processed by the participants via peripheral vision without any fixation on the corresponding AOI. The evaluation of the user experience questionnaire revealed generally positive results both for the anticipated use before the assembly tasks were carried out as well as for the actual use of the system. The significantly higher rating of perspicuity indicates that the operation of the system is considered less difficult once it has been used.

5 Conclusion

In this paper, we presented the results of an eye tracking study to investigate how users access the instructions provided by a projection-based assistive system during the repeated execution of an assembly process. Our study shows that the repeated use of a projection-based system results in a significantly higher number of steps with a linear viewing pattern and a higher number of steps in which users are skipping the viewing of the text-based and image-based instructions. In addition, there was a significantly shorter task completion time for the repeated execution of the assembly task. All together, these findings suggest the existence of a learning effect regarding the use of the assistive system and the structure of the assembly task. The results obtained provide a general insight into the way how users access the information of the projection-based system and how its changes during the repeated use of the system. It could be argued that the assembly task used for the study is not complex enough and that the number of participants is too small for a more in-depth analysis. Furthermore, the visualization of the instructions can vary considerably between different assistive systems based on the underlying assembly task and the structure of the system. Nevertheless, we argue that the results obtained in our study are primarily linked to the underlying technology and therefore can also be transferred to other projection-based assistive systems. Given the low complexity of the assembly task and the limited number of participants, however, further studies are required to gain a deeper insight into the way how users access the presented information of projection-based assistive systems. Therefore, as future work, we will conduct further studies to investigate the process of information access in more detail.

Acknowledgement. This work was partly funded by the German Federal Ministry of Education and Research (BMBF) under grand number 13FH110PX6.

References

1. Bannat, A., et al.: Towards optimal worker assistance: a framework for adaptive selection and presentation of assembly instructions. In: Proceedings of the 1st International Workshop On Cognition for Technical Systems, Cotesys (2008)
2. Büttner, S., Funk, M., Sand, O., Röcker, C.: Using head-mounted displays and in-situ projection for assistive systems: a comparison. In: Proceedings of the 9th ACM International Conference on Pervasive Technologies Related to Assistive Environments, p. 44. ACM (2016)
3. Büttner, S., Mucha, H., Robert, S., Hellweg, F., Röcker, C.: HCI in der SmartFactoryOWL-Angewandte Forschung & Entwicklung. Mensch und Computer 2017-Workshopband (2017)
4. Büttner, S., Prilla, M., Röcker, C.: Augmented reality training for industrial assembly work - are projection-based AR assistive systems an appropriate tool for assembly training? In: Proceedings of the 2020 CHI Conference on Human Factors in Computing Systems (forthcoming) CHI 2020. ACM, New York (2020)
5. Büttner, S., et al.: The design space of augmented and virtual reality applications for assistive environments in manufacturing: a visual approach. 06 2017. https://doi.org/10.1145/3056540.3076193
6. Duchowski, A.T.: A breadth-first survey of eye-tracking applications. Behav. Res. Methods Instrum. Comput. **34**(4), 455–470 (2002). https://doi.org/10.3758/BF03195475
7. Fellmann, M., Robert, S., Büttner, S., Mucha, H., Röcker, C.: Towards a framework for assistance systems to support work processes in smart factories. In: Holzinger, A., Kieseberg, P., Tjoa, A.M., Weippl, E. (eds.) CD-MAKE 2017. LNCS, vol. 10410, pp. 59–68. Springer, Cham (2017). https://doi.org/10.1007/978-3-319-66808-6_5
8. Funk, M., Bächler, A., Bächler, L., Kosch, T., Heidenreich, T., Schmidt, A.: Working with augmented reality?: a long-term analysis of in-situ instructions at the assembly workplace. In: Proceedings of the 10th International Conference on PErvasive Technologies Related to Assistive Environments, pp. 222–229. ACM (2017)

9. Funk, M., Dingler, T., Cooper, J., Schmidt, A.: Stop helping me-i'm bored!: why assembly assistance needs to be adaptive. In: Adjunct Proceedings of the 2015 ACM International Joint Conference on Pervasive and Ubiquitous Computing and Proceedings of the 2015 ACM International Symposium on Wearable Computers, pp. 1269–1273. ACM (2015)
10. Funk, M., Kosch, T., Kettner, R., Korn, O., Schmidt, A.: motioneap: an overview of 4 years of combining industrial assembly with augmented reality for industry 4.0. In: Proceedings of the 16th international conference on knowledge technologies and datadriven business, p. 4 (2016)
11. Funk, M., Kosch, T., Schmidt, A.: Interactive worker assistance: comparing the effects of in-situ projection, head-mounted displays, tablet, and paper instructions. In: Proceedings of the 2016 ACM International Joint Conference on Pervasive and Ubiquitous Computing, pp. 934–939. ACM (2016)
12. Funk, M., Lischke, L., Mayer, S., Shirazi, A.S., Schmidt, A.: Teach me how! interactive assembly instructions using demonstration and in-situ projection. In: Huber, J., Shilkrot, R., Maes, P., Nanayakkara, S. (eds.) Assistive Augmentation. Cognitive Science and Technology, pp. 49–73. Springer, Singapore (2018). https://doi.org/10.1007/978-981-10-6404-3_4
13. Georgel, P.: Is there a reality in industrial augmented reality?, pp. 201–210, 10 2011. https://doi.org/10.1109/ISMAR.2011.6092387
14. Goldberg, J., Kotval, X.: Computer interface evaluation using eye movements: methods and constructs. Int. J. Ind. Ergon. **24**, 631–645 (1999). https://doi.org/10.1016/S0169-8141(98)00068-7
15. Holmqvist, K., Nyström, M., Andersson, R., Dewhurst, R., Jarodzka, H., Van de Weijer, J.: Eye tracking: a comprehensive guide to methods and measures. OUP Oxford (2011)
16. Huber, M., Knoll, A., Brandt, T., Glasauer, S.: When to assist?-modelling human behaviour for hybrid assembly systems. In: ISR 2010 41st International Symposium on Robotics and ROBOTIK 2010 6th German Conference on Robotics, pp. 1–6. VDE (2010)
17. Korn, O., Funk, M., Abele, S., Hörz, T., Schmidt, A.: Context-aware assistive systems at the workplace: analyzing the effects of projection and gamification. In: Proceedings of the 7th International Conference on Pervasive Technologies Related to Assistive Environments, p. 38. ACM (2014)
18. Korn, O., Schmidt, A., Hörz, T.: Augmented manufacturing: a study with impaired persons on assistive systems using in-situ projection. In: Proceedings of the 6th International Conference on PErvasive Technologies Related to Assistive Environments, p. 21. ACM (2013)
19. Kosch, T., Abdelrahman, Y., Funk, M., Schmidt, A.: One size does not fit all: challenges of providing interactive worker assistance in industrial settings. In: Proceedings of the 2017 ACM International Joint Conference on Pervasive and Ubiquitous Computing and Proceedings of the 2017 ACM International Symposium on Wearable Computers, pp. 1006–1011. ACM (2017)
20. Kosch, T., Kettner, R., Funk, M., Schmidt, A.: Comparing tactile, auditory, and visual assembly error-feedback for workers with cognitive impairments. In: Proceedings of the 18th International ACM SIGACCESS Conference on Computers and Accessibility, pp. 53–60. ACM (2016)
21. Lušić, M., Fischer, C., Braz, K.S., Alam, M., Hornfeck, R., Franke, J.: Static versus dynamic provision of worker information in manual assembly: a comparative study using eye tracking to investigate the impact on productivity and added value based on industrial case examples. Procedia CIRP **57**, 504–509 (2016)

22. Sand, O., Büttner, S., Paelke, V., Röcker, C.: smARt.assembly – projection-based augmented reality for supporting assembly workers. In: Lackey, S., Shumaker, R. (eds.) VAMR 2016. LNCS, vol. 9740, pp. 643–652. Springer, Cham (2016). https://doi.org/10.1007/978-3-319-39907-2_61
23. Stoessel, C., Wiesbeck, M., Stork, S., Zaeh, M.F., Schuboe, A.: Towards optimal worker assistance: investigating cognitive processes in manual assembly. In: Mitsuishi, M., Ueda, K., Kimura, F. (eds.) Manufacturing Systems and Technologies for the New Frontier, pp. 245–250. Springer, London (2008). https://doi.org/10.1007/978-1-84800-267-8_50

Artificial Intelligence and Concerns About the Future: A Case Study in Norway

Kyriaki Kalimeri[1(✉)] and Ingvar Tjostheim[2]

[1] ISI Foundation, Turin, Italy
kkalimeri@acm.org

[2] Norwegian Computing Center, P.O. Box 114, 0314 Blindern, Oslo, Norway
Ingvar.Tjostheim@nr.no

Abstract. Artificial Intelligence (AI) is an integral part of our lives with AI systems to revolutionise our daily practices. At the same time, the rapid pace of AI innovations entails inherent risks that can range from cyber-crime to social discrimination. Here, we administered a large scale survey ($n = 1298$) assessing peoples' concerns and expectations regarding AI's influence on society in the future decade. The AI concerns employed in this study, originate from the "One hundred year study on Artificial Intelligence" project. Taking Norway as a case study, we discuss the participants' prioritisation of concerns for their socio-demographic characteristics. Our findings show a divide in the society; with younger generations to expect a positive impact of AI on our lives in the future decade. More sceptical groups are afraid of structural changes in the economy and job losses, while supporters see opportunities that will improve our life quality. These findings can inform both academics and policymakers that should work closely to ensure fairness, explainability and maintain a trusting relationship between AI and society.

Keywords: Artificial Intelligence · Fairness · Explainable AI · Ethics · Morals · AI for social good

1 Introduction

Algorithmic systems are increasingly more present in our lives, shaping our daily practices in a wide range of high impact domains such as healthcare [25], justice [21], education [1,22]. AI applications tackle some of the world's most challenging social problems, having a significant positive impact on many different sectors of the global economy and society [6]. Success stories include applications regarding AI for good [35], such as prediction of diseases outbreak [12], or poverty mapping employing satellite imagery [33].

The accelerating pace in which AI blends into our lives raises numerous concerns. The major ones are ethical due to AI becoming ubiquitous [31]; for

N. Streitz and S. Konomi (Eds.): HCII 2020, LNCS 12203, pp. 273–284, 2020.
https://doi.org/10.1007/978-3-030-50344-4_20

instance, AI applications inform decision-making in sensitive domains like justice [21], where incorrect judgments come with tremendous implications. As a consequence, an increasingly active research community is established around the topic of fairness in algorithms and ethics [4,17] aiming, among other issues, to carefully assess biases in the algorithms [23].

This study takes inspiration from the "One hundred year study on Artificial Intelligence" (AI100) project [34] which focuses on salient domains of AI and their impact on the future of humanity. A team of international experts including technology pioneers, innovators, developers, business and policy leaders, researchers and activists expressed their concerns, that summon up around the following topics: (i) human agency, (ii) data abuse, (iii) job loss, (iv) dependence lock-in, (v) propaganda, and (vi) mayhem. We contribute to the above discussion assessing the concerns from the perspective of the consumers of AI, people. Taking Norway as a case study, we surveyed a large, nearly representative, sample of the population as to their opinions and concerns regarding the role of AI the future.

From our analysis we notice a clear division in the Norwegian society. Common concerns across socio-demographic groups are the vagueness of decision-making processes relying on AI systems and possible future exclusion of human supervision and control. On the contrary Norwegian citizens seem less concerned with topics related to cyber-security or eventual spread of propaganda [8,16]. Sentiment analysis revealed that the more sceptical segment of the population expresses emotions of fear and mistrust towards future AI applications [36]. Overall, younger generations are more optimistic about the role AI will have in the forthcoming decade.

Our findings support the demand for transparency, fairness, and explainability of the future AI systems necessary to ensure a smooth integration of the technology in the society [29]. Creating systems that people understand will help avoid misconceptions and establish a trusting relationship between AI and public perception.

2 Experimental Design and Data Description

Taking Norway as a case study, we carried out an online survey, including 1,289 participants (51% Females). After signing informed consent, the participants were asked to provide their basic demographic information, including gender, age, education, income, and region of residence. The recruited cohort is a nearly representative sample of the Norwegian population, in terms of age, gender and geographic distribution. Figure 1 depicts the expected population size according to the official census data versus the geographic distribution of our sample[1]. Table 1 provides an analytical breakdown of the demographic attributes of our cohort.

[1] The census data originate from the national statistical institute of Norway and can be download from the following link: https://www.ssb.no/en/statbank/table/07459/.

Participants were then asked to fill in a series of questions regarding the use of social media, the use of smart agents and internet of things (IoT) as well as their privacy concerns and practices. The survey developed around the six concerns raised by the experts of the AI100 project [15].

The core of the survey was phrased according to the following scheme:

General AI Attitude. *In newspapers and media, news stories about machine learning and artificial intelligence are increasing. What do you think about this new technology?* The responses ranged from "Very sceptical" to "Very positive" in a 5-point Likert scale.

AI in 2030. *By 2030, do you think it is most likely that advancing AI and related technology systems will enhance human capacities and empower them? That is, most of the time, will most people be better off than they are today? Or, people will not understand how decisions are made, and the outcomes of AI-based decisions.* Then, participants were invited to write their opinions on the matter in an open form.

AI1 - Human Agency. *Decision-making on key aspects of digital life is automatically ceded to code-driven, "black box" tools. People will not understand how decisions are made, and the outcomes of AI-based decision.*

AI2 - Corporate Data Abuse. *Most AI tools are and will be in the hands of companies striving for profits. Values and ethics are often not baked into the digital systems making people's decisions for them.*

AI3 - Government Data Abuse. *Most AI tools are and will be in the hands of governments striving for power. Values and ethics are often not baked into the digital systems making people's decisions for them.*

AI4 - Dependence Lock-in. *Many see AI as augmenting human capacities, but some predict the opposite – that people's deepening dependence on machine-driven networks will erode their abilities to think for themselves, take action independent of automated systems and interact effectively with others.*

AI5 - Fake News. *Artificial intelligence will be used for propaganda and fake news. One of the consequences would be a more unstable world.*

AI6 - Mayhem. *Some predict further erosion of traditional sociopolitical structures. Individuals will experience a loss of control over their lives.*
In all above items, participants were asked to provide their responses in a 5-point Likert scale ranging from "Strongly disagree" to "Strongly agree".

3 Results and Discussion

3.1 Is the Society Positive or Sceptic Towards AI?

Figure 2 depicts the level of scepticism, expressed by the participants, regarding the tenacious presence of AI in our lives and society. With lower values to represent more sceptic individuals and higher ones to depict more positive

Table 1. Demographic Information breakdown of our dataset and the respective information from the official Norwegian census. The sample sizes refer to a total number of participants $n = 1,289$.

Attribute	Demographic variables	Dataset	Census
Gender	Males	48%	51.5%
	Females	51%	49.5%
Age	Baby Boomers (1945–1964)	22%	24.7%
	Generation X (1965–1980)	31%	29.5%
	Millenials (1981–1996)	32%	31.6%
	Generation Z (1997–2010)	14%	14.2%
	Average age (years)	41.5	40.5
Income	Kr. 0–99.000	6.3%	11.3%
	Kr. 100–199.000	5.5%	8.2%
	Kr. 200–299.000	11.9%	14.6%
	Kr. 300–399.000	14.0%	15.7%
	Kr. 400–499.000	15.4%	15.3%
	Kr. 500.–799.999	18.9%	22.3%
	Kr. 800.–999.999	4.9%	7.0%
	Kr. over 1.000.000	4.2%	5.7%
	No answer	19%	–
Education	Primary school level	13%	13.6%
	Secondary school/real school level	42%	42.9%
	University/college, lower grade	29%	25.8%
	University/college, higher degree	15%	11%

in a 5-point Likert scale, we notice that in average people's opinion fluctuate around average scores showing an evident indecisiveness. We also see a slightly more sceptical position of the older generations concerning the younger ones. Interestingly, education and income follow the same pattern.

We also trained a regression model to predict the general attitude of the Norwegian society with respect to whether people will be better off than today in 2030 (see Sect. 2). We predict the overall level of concern per topic inferring from the primary demographic attributes available, gender, education, income, and generation group, we find a few small but statistically significant differences. Table 2 (AI_D) reports the metrics of the model. Overall, Millennials are the most open to having more AI systems in the future, followed by the people that have completed higher education studies. Then, Generation X and Generation Z are supporting in the openness towards AI.

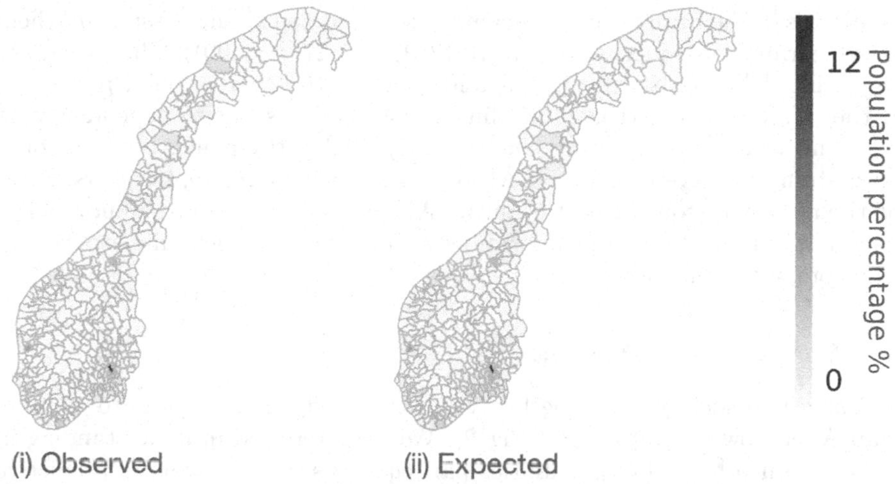

Fig. 1. Geographic distribution of the population in our dataset (i) versus the expected population percentages according to the official census of Norway (ii) per municipality. Both observed and expected values are expressed in percentages.

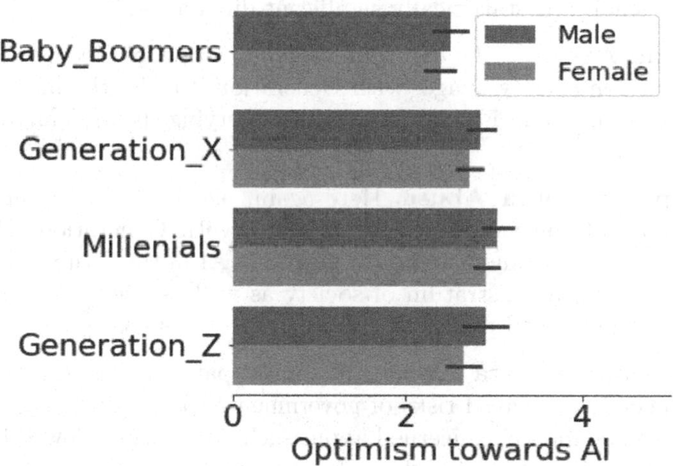

Fig. 2. Scepticism towards AI in the future according to generational group and gender. The higher the score, the more positive the attitude people have towards AI in the future. Societies are going to benefit from AI technologies. Participants are grouped according to their birth date in Baby Boomers (1945–1964), Generation X (1965–1980), Millenials (1981–1996), and Generation Z (1997–2010) respectively.

3.2 What Are People Most Concerned About?

To individualise Norwegians' primary concern regarding the role of AI in the future decade, we ran a linear regression on the six factors (AI1-AI6) proposed in Sect. 2. From the analysis it emerges that those who are eager for more AI applications in the future are significantly less concerned about possible mayhem and cybercrime consequences (AI6, $F(6,1289) = -.27$, $p < .00$)). They see fewer dangers in AI being used for propaganda, (AI5, $F(6,1289) = -.09$, $p < .00$)), and they also see fewer risks of eroding human abilities due to dependency on AI systems (AI4, $F(6,1289) = -.08$, $p < .02$)). All participants, both the ones with a strong positive opinion on AI as well as their more sceptic peers, agree that the most worrisome aspect of future AI technologies is transparency (AI1). "Black-box" applications that inform decision-making in crucial life aspects are at the core of the public concern.

3.3 What Concerns Whom?

The Norwegian society seems perfectly dichotomised when it comes to embracing an AI-empowered future (see Fig. 2). We are interested in understanding in depth the concerns and opportunities participants see. We trained a predictive regression model on each topic, namely: (i) human agency, (ii) data abuse, (iii) job loss, (iv) dependence lock-in, (v) propaganda, and (vi) mayhem (see Sect. 2). We predict the overall level of concern per topic inferring from the primary demographic attributes available, gender, education, income, and generation group, we find a few small but statistically significant differences.

AI1 - Human Agency. The determinant factor of people seeing dangers in a "black-box" driven society is age, with Generation Z to be the most concerned about this. Automated decision making is also worrying the Millennials, followed by Generation X.

AI2 - Corporate Data Abuse. Here again, age is the determinant factor explaining most of the variability in the data, with Generation Z to be the most sceptical regarding increased data misuse in AI in the future. Contrary, we have the higher educated stratum of society as well as the men to maintain a favourable, less concerned profile.

AI3 - Government Data Abuse. A similar pattern can be noted regarding with respect to perceived risks of governmental data abuse. Again we have Generation Z to be mostly concerned about such a scenario followed by the Millennial's, while participants of higher education and male are contradicting this trend.

AI4 - Dependence Lock-In. Moving to the risk of humans losing their critical ability and crafting skills due to over-dependency on AI systems we have again Generation Z and the Millennials to express the more concerns. Interestingly, participants with lower income are also concerned about job loss due to AI.

AI5 - Fake News. Regarding the scenario of a future raise of propaganda raising due to AI, the demographic profile of the population segment that is mostly concerned includes Generation Z and the Millennials, followed by Generation X.

AI6 - Mayhem. A similar emerges regarding the risk of sociopolitical destabilisation and increase of cyber-crime the demographic profile of the population segment that is mostly concerned is as before, Generation Z and the Millennials, followed by Generation X.

Table 2. Logistic regression models predicting attitudes towards AI using demographics (D) including age as generational groups, Gender, Income, Education, the six concern factors (AI1), (AI2), (AI3), (AI4), (AI5), (AI6). We also present the model that predicts AI attitude in general from demographics (AI_D). Only features significant at $p < 0.01$ level shown alongside their coefficient estimate. Confidence levels: $p < 0.001$***, $p < 0.01$**, $p < 0.05$*.

	AI_D	AI1	AI2	AI3	AI4	AI5	AI6
n	1298	1298	1298	1298	1298	1298	1298
R^2_{MF}	.040	.047	.031	.020	.019	.022	.046
(Intercept)	2.08***	3.53***	3.32***	3.30***	3.71***	3.78***	4.00***
GenX	.37***	−.23**				−.24**	−.33***
Millennials	.53***	−.40***	−.26**	−.18*	−.24**	−.39***	−.58***
GenZ	.27**	−.72***	−.39***	−.25*	−.47***	−.41**	−.66***
Income					−.04*		
Education	.08*		.09**	.09**			
Gender(M)			.13*	.15*			

3.4 Content Analysis - People's Reflections of AI in 2030

As a final part of this study, we asked the participants to explicitly state in an open form, their concerns or the opportunities they see about a future AI-empowered society. Such direct communication with the cohort allows us to capture elements that are missing or understated in our predefined survey, giving the possibility to people to express themselves fully.

We analysed the user-generated text employing natural language processing methods. Overall, we have 324 optimistic and 520 sceptic comments. Initially, we translated into the English language the text[2]. Then, the text was lemmatised with the removal of common English stopwords as well as the words "artificial intelligence" which appeared in almost all posts. We build two probabilistic language models, one for the positive comments and one for the concerns. The most common terms, along with their probability scores, are reported in Fig. 3.

On the sceptic side, emerging concepts include "abuse", "control", and "job loss". On the favouring side, people are optimistic about new emerging opportunities that are going to improve the quality of life.

Lastly, we compute the emotional connotation of the words used to describe the role of AI in the future society (Fig. 3). We employed the DepecheMood++

[2] Link to the library used for the automatic text translation https://pypi.org/project/translate/.

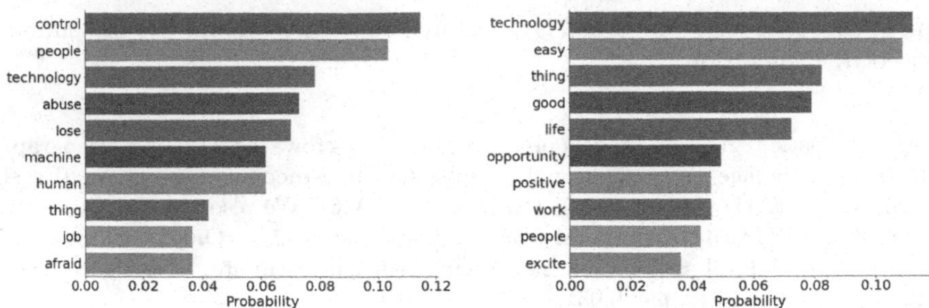

Fig. 3. Content analysis on the open question: "In newspapers and media, news stories about machine learning and artificial intelligence are increasing. What do you think about this new technology?". The most frequent words used by participants to express their concerns (on the left) and optimistic views (on the right) respectively.

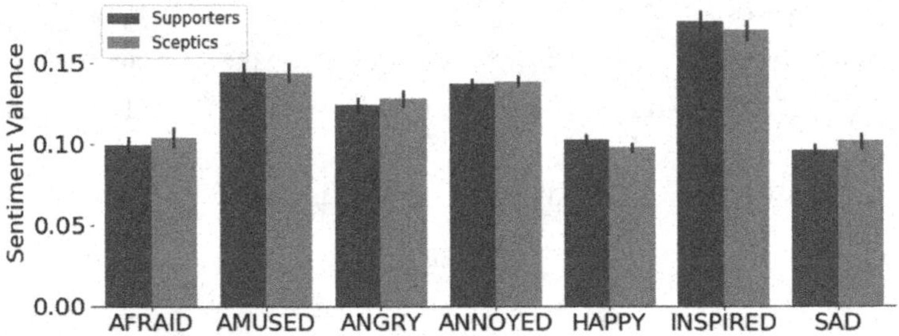

Fig. 4. Sentiment Analysis on the open question: "In newspapers and media, news stories about machine learning and artificial intelligence are increasing. What do you think about this new technology?"

lexicon [3], which provides fine-grained emotion analysis for seven basic emotions, fear, amusement, anger, annoyance, happiness, inspiration, and sadness. As for the narrative analysis, we lemmatised the message of every comment and calculated the average emotion per sentence according to the lexicon. In this way, we avoid introducing biases due to the varying lengths of the messages.

We also assess the moral narratives of the messages employing the MoralStrength lexicon [2] (Fig. 4). MoralStrength operationalizes moral values in the text according to the Moral Foundations Theory (MFT) [14]. Expressing morality in terms of innate intuitions, MFT defines five moral foundations: care/harm, fairness/cheating, loyalty/betrayal, authority/subversion, and purity/degradation. We automatically assess the average moral valence of the messages; similar to the sentiment analysis, on the lemmatised text we estimate the average moral valence per sentence according to the lexicon. We notice that both AI supporters and sceptics express themselves using very similar narratives for all moral dimensions but one, authority. The sceptic community is dominated by concerns highly related to authoritarian aspects for instance control,

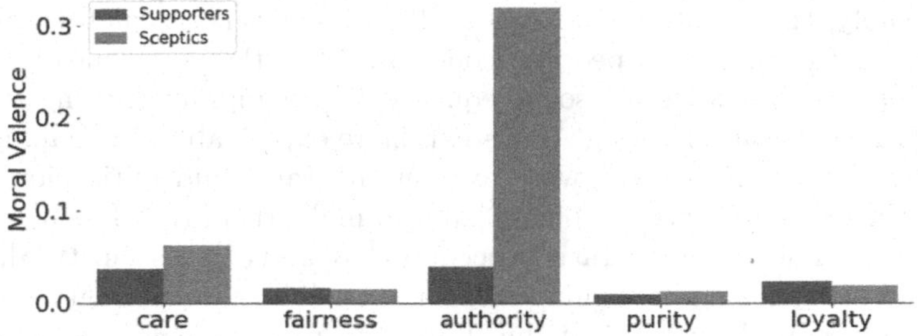

Fig. 5. Moral Valence Analysis on the open question: "In newspapers and media, news stories about machine learning and artificial intelligence are increasing. What do you think about this new technology?"

obligations, and respect, related to the ownership of the data or the automatic decision-making processes made by AI applications (Fig. 5).

Despite the preliminary character of this study, the encouraging message is that all differences are small, and people are not expressing themselves in a drastically positive or negative way. We observe that for the sceptics express themselves in a slightly more afraid, angry, annoyed, and sad way. Interestingly, the more optimistic portion of the population expresses themselves with an "inspiring" ton while they are more "happy" and carefree in their communication.

4 Conclusions

Artificial intelligence (AI) applications are revolutionising our everyday lives in a wide range of domains like: agriculture [27], disaster prevention and response [10], education and productivity [9,11,18], health care and well-being [20,24,30,32], and ubiquitous personalisation [19]. Substantial increase in the future uses of AI will reinforce human efficiency, bringing economic and social benefits shared across society. With technology moving at a rapid pace, risks from potentially malicious AI applications are not to be neglected; instead, they should be fully understood. Misunderstandings about AI could fuel opposition to innovation and technology while creating socio-political conflicts.

Surveying a large, nearly demographic representative sample of the Norwegian population ($n = 1298$), we assess peoples' opinions and attitudes towards the role and increasing presence of AI in our lives. Our analysis shows that the Norwegian society is divided on the topic, with the more sceptic group to express worries about decision-making informed by "black-box" algorithm but also pronounced anxiety for potential job losses [13]. The predominant sentiments in their communication are fear, anger, and displeasure. On the contrary the part of society that embrace AI is excited and believes that the new technological advances and believe that the emerging technologies will improve the quality of life and transform society for the better in the coming decade.

Fortunately, the debate is not intense. If policymakers, regulators, and academics respond promptly to peoples' concerns, AI in the years ahead will augment its impact while fostering social equality [26]. A rapidly growing academic community focuses on rendering AI systems more explainable [5], enabling users to understand how AI systems work avoiding mistakes and mitigation of misuse risks. Unveiling algorithmic biases [23] will make them look less like "black-boxes" which will foster democratic procedures [16] and cyber-security [8]. Establishing good practices and assigning moral responsibility is essential to seize the opportunities created by AI [7]. Ethical analyses must be extended to account for the invisible influence exercised by AI on human behaviour. The design of the new algorithms should be created in a way that keeps humans in the loop [28]. Such efforts are crucial for building a trusting relationship with people. Regulators and stakeholders should not merely aim to improve AI systems' accuracy and performance, instead, aim for regulating the behaviour of AI systems identifying and pursuing the best strategies for AI to support prosperity while respecting human dignity.

Acknowledgements. KK acknowledges support from the "Lagrange Project" of the ISI Foundation funded by the Fondazione CRT. This work was partly supported by the Research Council of Norway under the grant 270969.

References

1. Aoun, J.E.: Robot-Proof: Higher Education in the Age of Artificial Intelligence. MIT Press, Cambridge (2017)
2. Araque, O., Gatti, L., Kalimeri, K.: MoralStrength: exploiting a moral lexicon and embedding similarity for moral foundations prediction. Knowl.-Based Syst. **191**, 105184 (2019)
3. Araque, O., Gatti, L., Staiano, J., Guerini, M.: Depechemood++: a bilingual emotion lexicon built through simple yet powerful techniques. IEEE Trans. Affect. Comput. 14 Aug 2019
4. Baleis, J., Keller, B., Starke, C., Marcinkowski, F.: Cognitive and emotional responses to fairness in AI-A systematic review (2019)
5. Bhatt, U., et al.: Explainable machine learning in deployment. In: Proceedings of the 2020 Conference on Fairness, Accountability, and Transparency, pp. 648–657 (2020)
6. Castro, D., New, J.: The promise of artificial intelligence. Center for Data Innovation, pp. 1–48 (2016)
7. Conitzer, V., Sinnott-Armstrong, W., Borg, J.S., Deng, Y., Kramer, M.: Moral decision making frameworks for artificial intelligence. In: Thirty-First AAAI Conference on Artificial Intelligence (2017)
8. Darraj, E., Sample, C., Justice, C.: Artificial intelligence cybersecurity framework: preparing for the here and now with AI. In: ECCWS 2019 18th European Conference on Cyber Warfare and Security, p. 132. Academic Conferences and Publishing Limited (2019)
9. Do, T.M.T., Kalimeri, K., Lepri, B., Pianesi, F., Gatica-Perez, D.: Inferring social activities with mobile sensor networks. In: Proceedings of the 15th ACM on International Conference on Multimodal Interaction, pp. 405–412 (2013)

10. Fan, C., Zhang, C., Yahja, A., Mostafavi, A.: Disaster city digital twin: a vision for integrating artificial and human intelligence for disaster management. Int. J.f Inf. Manage. 102049 (2019)
11. Finnerty, A.N., Kalimeri, K., Pianesi, F.: Towards happier organisations: understanding the relationship between communication and productivity. In: Aiello, L.M., McFarland, D. (eds.) Social Informatics, pp. 462–477. Springer, Cham (2014). https://doi.org/10.1007/978-3-319-13734-6_33
12. Fisman, D.N., Hauck, T.S., Tuite, A.R., Greer, A.L.: An idea for short term outbreak projection: nearcasting using the basic reproduction number. PLoS ONE **8**(12), 1–8 (2014). https://doi.org/10.1371/journal.pone.0083622
13. Frey, C.B., Osborne, M.A.: The future of employment: how susceptible are jobs to computerisation? Technol. Forecast. Soc. Change **114**, 254–280 (2017)
14. Graham, J., Haidt, J., Nosek, B.A.: Liberals and conservatives rely on different sets of moral foundations. J. Pers. Soc. Psychol. **96**(5), 1029 (2009)
15. Grosz, B.J., Stone, P.: A century-long commitment to assessing arDtificial intelligence and its impact on society. Commun. ACM **61**(12), 68–73 (2018)
16. Helbing, D., et al.: Will democracy survive big data and artificial intelligence? In: Helbing, D. (ed.) Towards Digital Enlightenment, pp. 73–98. Springer, Cham (2019). https://doi.org/10.1007/978-3-319-90869-4_7
17. Hutchinson, B., Mitchell, M.: 50 years of test (un)fairness: lessons for machine learning. In: Proceedings of the Conference on Fairness, Accountability, and Transparency, pp. 49–58 (2019)
18. Kalimeri, K., Lepri, B., Pianesi, F.: Causal-modelling of personality traits: extraversion and locus of control. In: Proceedings of the 2nd International Workshop on Social Signal Processing, pp. 41–46 (2010)
19. Kalimeri, K., Lepri, B., Pianesi, F.: Going beyond traits: multimodal classification of personality states in the wild. In: Proceedings of the 15th ACM on International Conference on Multimodal Interaction, pp. 27–34 (2013)
20. Kalimeri, K., Matic, A., Cappelletti, A.: RFID: recognizing failures in dressing activity. In: 2010 4th International Conference on Pervasive Computing Technologies for Healthcare, pp. 1–4. IEEE (2010)
21. Kugler, L.: AI judges and juries. Commun. ACM **61**(12), 19–21 (2018)
22. Luckin, R., Holmes, W., Griffiths, M., Forcier, L.B.: Intelligence Unleashed: An Argument for AI in Education. Pearson, London (2016)
23. Mehrabi, N., Morstatter, F., Saxena, N., Lerman, K., Galstyan, A.: A survey on bias and fairness in machine learning. arXiv preprint arXiv:1908.09635 (2019)
24. Mejova, Y., Kalimeri, K.: Effect of values and technology use on exercise: implications for personalized behavior change interventions. In: Proceedings of the 27th ACM Conference on User Modeling, Adaptation and Personalization, pp. 36–45 (2019)
25. Miotto, R., Wang, F., Wang, S., Jiang, X., Dudley, J.T.: Deep learning for healthcare: review, opportunities and challenges. Briefings Bioinform. **19**(6), 1236–1246 (2018)
26. Mouzannar, H., Ohannessian, M.I., Srebro, N.: From fair decision making to social equality. In: Proceedings of the Conference on Fairness, Accountability, and Transparency, pp. 359–368 (2019)
27. Patrício, D.I., Rieder, R.: Computer vision and artificial intelligence in precision agriculture for grain crops: a systematic review. Comput. Electron. Agric. **153**, 69–81 (2018)

28. Rahwan, I.: Society-in-the-loop: programming the algorithmic social contract. Ethics Inf. Technol. **20**(1), 5–14 (2017). https://doi.org/10.1007/s10676-017-9430-8
29. Renda, A.: Artificial intelligence: ethics, governance and policy challenges. CEPS Task Force Report (2019)
30. Saitis, C., Kalimeri, K.: Identifying urban mobility challenges for the visually impaired with mobile monitoring of multimodal biosignals. In: Antona, M., Stephanidis, C. (eds.) Universal Access in Human-Computer Interaction. Users and Context Diversity, pp. 616–627. Springer, Cham (2016). https://doi.org/10.1007/978-3-319-40238-3_59
31. Shahriari, K., Shahriari, M.: IEEE standard review–ethically aligned design: a vision for prioritizing human wellbeing with artificial intelligence and autonomous systems. In: 2017 IEEE Canada International Humanitarian Technology Conference (IHTC), pp. 197–201. IEEE (2017)
32. Spagnol, S., et al.: Model-based obstacle sonification for the navigation of visually impaired persons. In: Proceedings of the 19th International Conference Digital Audio Effects (DAFx 2016), Brno, Czech Republic, pp. 5–9 (2016)
33. Steele, J.E., et al.: Mapping poverty using mobile phone and satellite data. J. R. Soc. Interface **14**(127), 20160690 (2017)
34. Stone, P., et al.: Artificial intelligence and life in 2030. One hundred year study on artificial intelligence: Report of the 2015–2016 study panel. Stanford University, Stanford, CA (2016). http://ai100.stanford.edu/2016-report. Accessed 6 Sept 2016
35. Taddeo, M., Floridi, L.: How AI can be a force for good. Science **361**(6404), 751–752 (2018)
36. Toreini, E., Aitken, M., Coopamootoo, K., Elliott, K., Zelaya, C.G., van Moorsel, A.: The relationship between trust in AI and trustworthy machine learning technologies. In: Proceedings of the 2020 Conference on Fairness, Accountability, and Transparency, pp. 272–283 (2020)

Extended User Interface: NFC-Enabled Product Packaging for Enhanced User Experience

Justina Lydekaityte(✉)

Aarhus University, Birk Centerpark 15, 7400 Herning, Denmark
justina@btech.au.dk

Abstract. User-centered physical-digital systems let designers create interactive interfaces filled with special moments and experiences, giving brand owners the chance to have profound communication with their consumers. In fact, product's packaging has recently begun to investigate as one of such interfaces to form a strong link between manufacturers and their end-users. Microprocessors, sensors, actuators and wireless data-exchange supporting chips can be embedded, into packaging design creating an extended user interface – a touchpoint for a visual, tactile and digital encounter with consumers. Near Field Communication (NFC) is one of the rapidly increasing technologies that researchers begin to investigate as a potential tool for enhanced consumer-brand communication. However, although NFC is available in the market since late 2010, the technology is still not widely applied to the packaging industry. As a result, the main purpose of this research is to investigate the current state-of-the-art and potentials of NFC system. The results of this study provide a systematic review of NFC characteristics, including technological capabilities, consumer- and brand-oriented benefits, and technology- and user-centered potential barriers for NFC to become widely accepted. The findings of this study are expected to contribute to a better understanding of the effectiveness of NFC-enabled packaging, allowing brands to dynamically adapt to emerging consumer needs by improving their products and services.

Keywords: Near field communication · Smart packaging · Technological capabilities

1 Introduction

In the recent years, the accelerating adoption of enabling technologies, such as Internet of Things (IoT), cloud computing, augmented reality, smart sensors, touch-sensitive surfaces and gestural interfaces, has induced the emergence of interconnected systems, where smart, sensory and interactive objects communicate among themselves, as well as with their users [1, 2]. At the same time, the cost of the tools needed to connect products to the internet has dropped down to enable the continued growth of the Internet of Everything [1]. As a result, the increasing use of the internet and the development of interconnected digital-physical systems have merged engineering and design due to a common objective to enhance user experience [3]. Consequently, according to [4], the

N. Streitz and S. Konomi (Eds.): HCII 2020, LNCS 12203, pp. 285–304, 2020.
https://doi.org/10.1007/978-3-030-50344-4_21

concept of Human-Computer Interaction (HCI) has gone beyond the traditional mechanical computer systems and begun to penetrate into everyday objects and environments people are in touch with in their daily life.

User-centered physical-digital systems let designers create interactive interfaces filled with special moments and experiences, giving brand owners the chance to have profound communication with their consumers [5]. In fact, product's packaging has recently begun to investigate as one of such interfaces to form a strong link between manufacturers and their end-users [6–8]. Microprocessors, sensors, actuators and wireless data-exchange supporting chips can be embedded, laminated or directly printed onto packaging design creating an extended user interface – a touchpoint for a visual, tactile and digital encounter with consumers.

Although the traditional passive packaging already served as an effective communication medium [8], advances in conductive ink and nanomaterials, printed electronics techniques and ICT allowed packaging to enter digital innovation and become connected. In this work, such packaging is referred to as Smart Interactive Packaging. The latter provides an interactive dimension between the consumer and the brand with the help of informing and measuring sensors, light-emitting displays, standardized communication protocols and other electronic elements that increase the design freedom for new packaging applications.

Near Field Communication is one of the rapidly increasing technologies that researchers begin to investigate as a potential tool for enhanced consumer-brand communication. In general, NFC is a standard for a wireless data transmission that provides secure, short-range, and paired communication capability between devices triggered by a simple touch [9]. However, despite the fact that NFC is available in the market since late 2010, the technology has not yet reached its way to enhanced consumer engagement through the product's packaging. Even though the technology has been already commercialized, it is still not widely applied to the packaging industry. As a result, the main purpose of this research is to investigate the current state-of-the-art and potentials of NFC system, including the overview of the main characteristics, technological capabilities, benefits, and potential barriers for NFC to become widely accepted.

2 Methodology

This research methodology employs multi-method research approach to combine the current theoretical knowledge about NFC technology from the scientific literature with real-world empirical cases to expand the understanding of both theory and observed phenomena [10]. As a result, the study is based on a systematic literature review focused on scientific publications related to the topic of Near Field Communication and its application, particularly for smart packaging. Moreover, this research employed a set of empirical examples from the industrial cases of diverse NFC technology providers collected by desk research (including product datasheets, technical reports, press releases, whitepapers), direct observations and semi-structured interviews with companies' representatives during the attended industrial events. Practical industrial data was needed to verify current NFC specifications, to broaden the scope of collected knowledge, and increase data triangulation.

Literature review used the keyword-based search approach in the largest databases of peer-reviewed literature, namely Scopus and Web of Science. A wide range of keyword variations was used to come up with the best combination yielding publication results concerning and related to the selected research scope.

During the keyword search, a few insights were gained that allowed to limit the search process. For instance, the abbreviation of NFC also refers to fluorescent nanofibrillated cellulose/carbon dot (NFC/CD) that is also present in the packaging research, and therefore in order to prevent confusion and irrelevant research outcomes, the abbreviation was changed to the specific phrase of "near field communication".

Another observed insight was that packaging could also be referred to electronic packaging, where research is carried out in regards to sophisticated electronics systems. Therefore it was decided to limit the search specifically to product packaging.

Also, some publications related to materials science and fabrication of the NFC, as [11–14], were included only to support the theoretical background of the research in terms of NFC components.

Moreover, a handful list of research [7, 13, 15–17] investigates NFC as a way to communicate sensor information in regards to food spoilage, track and trace, monitoring of the package surrounding environment.

However, this study aims to take a more novel approach and investigate NFC potentials substantially related to enhanced consumer, retailer and brand experiences, such as engagement and entertainment, confirmation of authenticity, prevention of counterfeiting and grey market division. It has been an increasing interest from the industry for anti-counterfeiting and entertaining capabilities provided by NFC technology [18–24], therefore the search was narrowed down to these specific experiences. Also, several studies [25–27] have been selected to include that identified factors facilitating or impeding the adoption of NFC technology and consumer acceptance of NFC system.

The final determined limitation was not to take into consideration the mobile payment possibilities with NFC since a significant number of researches towards NFC and user experience is done in terms of contactless payment.

The outcomes from systematic literature review based on keyword search and empirical data collection yielded results presented in this paper as (1) an overview of the main components of NFC system, (2) a list of technologies capabilities provided by NFC attached to product packaging, (3) a list of contributed/created consumer and brand experiences, (4) an overview of potential barriers for NFC to become widely accepted.

3 Theory

3.1 From Passive to Connected: Smart Interactive Packaging

Nowadays, the consumer market brings into play many different digital interfaces to create the link between consumers, products and brands in order to deliver unexpected and unique user experiences [5]. Recently, product packaging also became one of such digital interfaces. The emerging infrastructure of digital-physical systems consisting of everyday items and advanced wireless communication devices, such as wireless networks, light-emitting devices, smart sensors and tags, opens a new digital dimension for human-packaging interaction (Fig. 1).

In general, the packaging is defined as a combination of product, package, and distribution, which is intended to provide protection, convenience, containment, and communication throughout the entire supply chain until goods reach the end-user [8, 28]. However, recent advances in enabling technologies improved the communication function profoundly and allowed the packaging to become connected. As a result, such packaging improves the traditional one-way information flow and triggers continuous interaction between the consumer and the brand [29]. Therefore we define smart interactive packaging as packaging that provides an interactive dimension between the consumer and the brand with the help of various enhanced communication devices, where the user initiates the interaction willingly to get some response.

In fact, there are several different environments/touchpoints, where users-packaging interaction takes place: manufacture, distribution system, retail or in-store, and at-home. This study investigates human-packaging interaction enabled by NFC technology in retail and at-home settings – the environments that are likely to benefit the most from of NFC systems. The following section will provide more detailed information about the main characteristics of NFC technology.

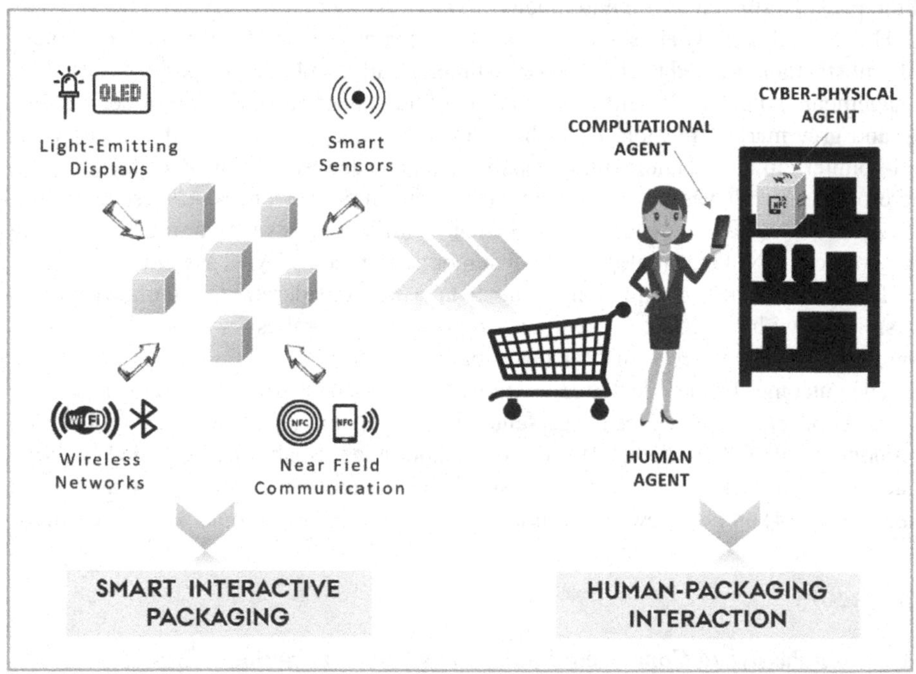

Fig. 1. Smart Interactive Packaging as interactive system that includes actions from the human agent, computational agent (mobile device), and cyber-physical agent (packaging).

3.2 Near Field Communication

In recent years, different types of short-range communication technologies have been integrated into smartphones, including Bluetooth, infrared transceivers, RFID, and NFC [25]. The former is currently perceived as one of the most promising technologies for mobile devices in the coming years [25]. Although NFC has existed for more than a decade, it has just recently come into the surface with the remarkable growth of the Internet of Things [16].

In general, NFC is a standard for a wireless data transmission that provides secure, short-range, and paired communication capability between devices triggered by a simple touch [9]. NFC technology is based on the ISO/IEC14443 protocol. It operates at 13.56 MHz frequency with a maximum transmission speed of 424 kbit/s within an operation radius of 4 cm (up to a maximum of 10 cm) to create a peer-to-peer network for sending and receiving information between the initiator and target [11, 30]. In the NFC system, the initiator or the reader is always an element that actively functions, e.g. mobile device, whereas the target or receiver is usually a passive element, such as NFC tag [31]. In order to initiate the data exchange, the target (NFC tag) is placed in the magnetic field created by the reader (mobile phone), the tag antenna harvest energy received from the mobile device to wake the tag up, and data is then sent to the reader using a standardized format created by NFC Forum called NFC Data Exchange Forman (NDEF) [16]. NDEF permits to storage and transport various types of information, like Uniform Resource Locators (URLs), Record Type Definition (RTD), or Multipurpose Internet Mail Extensions (MIME) messages [31].

Currently, NFC applications are widespread in transport cards, door access, contactless payment, and other mediums where simple data as an identification number or text is exchanged securely and promptly between devices without pairing [16]. NFC technology is becoming more commonly used for various purposes for product packaging as well. First of all, food and beverage packaging industries utilize NFC tags to read, store and transmit data from oxygen, relative humidity, temperature and other sensors to monitor the conditions of the packaged products to ensure their quality [7]. Also, packaging can be equipped with an NFC chip to provide brands with an additional level of protection by enabling traceability and authenticity of the product, especially to fight against counterfeiting [6]. Finally, digitalizing products via NFC technology allows personalized and customized mobile promotions and reward-based interactions to increase product perception and brand loyalty [6].

Below, in Table 1, there is a list of NFC technology providers that manufacturer, create and build various elements or services related to NFC technology. Some of the given providers present fully-integral NFC systems, where all physical and digital components are developed in-house. On the other hand, other providers specialize in specific NFC system elements. For instance, NXP's expertise lies in NFC chips, whereas Avery Dennison specializes in printed NFC antennas and inlays. Providers are also establishing collaborations to create joint technological solutions.

Table 1. The summary of NFC providers (retrieved from products' datasheets [32–39])

Provider	Key NFC technologies	Main capabilities
Thinfilm	OpenSense™ and SpeedTap™ NFC tags, opening sensors	Refill fraud, anti-counterfeiting, identification, track and trace, authentication, tampering, real-time monitoring
NXP	NTAG 213, NTAG® 424 DNA & DNA TagTamper, sensors (touch, magnetic, capacitive, motion, pressure)	Cryptography, secret keys, authentication, tampering, real-time monitoring, refill fraud, anti-counterfeiting, cloud-based services
Toppan	CorkTag™, Cachet-Tag™ with antenna circuit, InTact, OD Tag	Detection of removal and piercing of the cork, prevention of fraudulent re-labelling, cork protection, authentication and opening detection
Avery Dennison	AD-740/750 NFC Wet/Dry Inlays, T Sensor Plus™ NFC tag	Temperature data logging, originality signature, automatic serialization NDEF messages, password protection, fraud prevention, unique 7-byte serial number
PragmatIC	ConnectIC®, FlexIC®	Flexible integrated circuits, item-level monitoring, grey market, authentication, gamification, promotional offers
Identiv	NXP ICODE® SLIX, NXP ICODE® SLIX HC, ST SRI	Consumer interaction, brand protection, product integrity, status awareness, anti-counterfeiting, authentication, physical security
Stora Enso	Bobbin NTAG213	Authentication, password protection, targeted marketing, consumer engagement and experience
WISeKey	WISeCryt™ based digital authentification, NanoSeal®	Anti-counterfeiting, authentication, brand loyalty, consumer insights, access control, tamper/opening detection, traceability, maskable identifier

4 Results

Technological capabilities of NFC system have been divided into three main groups: data and information services, security services, and other services (Table 2).

4.1 Data and Information Services

Data Storage. As discussed in the theory section, the NFC tag mainly consists of a chip and antenna. The majority of technological capabilities provided by NFC technology rely on its chip. NFC tags specifically designed for smart packaging application usually comprise Read/Write memory size of between 144 and 888 bytes and they are wirelessly powered by a smartphone [11, 33]. NFC tags can store NDEF (NFC data exchange format) data in the form of URL, telephone number, geolocation, SMS, plain text, network connection and similar that makes them fully compatible with every NFC-enabled smartphone and the entire ISO/IEC 14443 infrastructure [33]. As a result, the very primary NFC functionality is to store encoded/written data in heterogeneous formats. Usually, the product-specific or customer-specific data is already encoded in the chip before the tags are shipped to the manufacturer [32].

The most common type of stored data is the URL that redirects the user to particular content, in most cases, hosted by the brand owner's CMS [32]. Consequently, NFC provides novel opportunities for brands and retailers to communicate engaging and dynamic content, such as more explicit product information, proof of legitimate distribution, region and year of production, recipes and etc [34, 40], in different means of media. For instance, NFC tag attached to a wine bottle can contain information about the product's origin, traceability, or even all processes followed up for its fermentation [18].

Data Collection. Some of the data not only can be encoded/written in advance but also it can be collected during the entire life-cycle of packaging. The combination of sensing devices and NFC connectivity allows the autonomous data collection. The collected data is uploaded securely into the cloud via NFC by a simple tap with a smartphone [33]. There are various smart sensors that can be incorporated in the overall NFC integrated circuit to monitor conditions such as relative humidity, shocks, vibrations, oxygen levels, temperature and similar, and, in turn, to collect the quantitative data of the current status of the packaged product and its surrounding environment [7, 33]. For instance, reference [15] fabricated a flexible system of NFC and sensing devices that collected data regarding ammonia (NH3) and oxygen levels in the meat packaging. Similarly, reference [17] demonstrated an NFC-enabled sensing system that was able to detect and collect the data about the level of water-soluble gases in the packaging atmosphere.

Data Logging. Another method of data collection is manual or autonomous data entry by human agents. Even though this activity might happen in every process of the supply chain, NFC technology due to its short-range reading capability is mostly related to data entry or logging that happen in the retail and at-home environments. Therefore, marketing campaigns in-store are increasingly interested in NFC capabilities for instantaneous feedback, streamlined data collection and entry that allow capturing real-time consumer interaction with products [40].

Data Transmission. Once data is stored, automatically collected or manually entered, it can be transmitted, read or exchanged between devices upon the initial request from the human agent, commonly, to receive access to the respective additional information

[7, 30]. Data from sensors not only can be collected but also be read by NFC reader to retrieve the information in a visual form on the smartphone's screen [13, 41]. According to [7] more recently, NFC has been adopted as main technologies attached to the packaging for the reading of the sensors and the transmission of data by a remote NFC reader.

Furthermore, data transmission is becoming more favorable in the retail setting, where shoppers can check and obtain diverse data about the products, for instance, the availability or stock information directly at the point of sale with their NFC-enabled smartphones [19]. When the NFC tag is positioned in the RF field, the transmission of the data is around 106 kbit/s [33]. In terms of peer-to-peer communication, NFC Simple NDEF Exchange Protocol (SNEP) permits an application on an NFC-enabled device to exchange (NDEF) messages with another NFC Forum device while operating in NFC Forum peer-to-peer mode [42]. This protocol utilizes particular connection-oriented transport modes to ensure a reliable data exchange that, for instance, is essential for voucher transmission [42].

In practice, all the sub-functions of data services capability are connected and operate in succession. For instance, Bon-Ton, a regional, departmental store company, launched an initiative to inform shoppers about the current stock status of particular sizes of [40]. First, the data about the inventory was stored and continuously updated in the NFC chip and the database. Once the consumers tap on the NFC-enabled packaging, the data transmission is initiated and the specific information, if a specific size shoe is in stock or not, is provided. NFC-enabled packaging provides shoppers with access to information through their mobile devices [43].

4.2 Security Services

Identification. Currently, the majority of NFC applications contain simple data such as an identification number or text that are exchanged immediately and safely between two devices [16]. Similarly to barcodes that contain the International Article Number (EAN), RFID tags are designed to store the Electronic Product Code (EPC) – a standard for automated item-level product identification [19]. In the last decade, there were many attempts to develop a solution of NFC that uses HF frequencies to be compatible with EPC [19, 44]. At the moment, NFC chips store a unique identifier that provides the capability to be uniquely identified in through the Internet or managed in a supply chain [18, 20, 45]. As a result, NDEF on the NFC tag can store unique (serialized) identifiers in Unique Resource Identifier (URI) format [19], or Unique Identifier (UID) format [33]. For example, in the manufacturing line, Industrial Line Manager (ILM) consisting of a computer and NFC reader can detect any thresholds and deviations from accepted standards by reading product/packaging information written in its tag's UID [34].

Validation and Redirection. In regards to validation and redirection, UID is closely related to database and cloud services, where identities of items are protected and controlled, giving each product a persistent, addressable web-based presence [32]. For example, NXP provided NFC solutions use could services that are accessible using standard RESTful APIs to permit straightforward and prompt integration into brand owners database/business intelligent system and software [32]. In other words, validation and redirection processes link products to manufacturers' digital platforms. As a result, NFC tags obtain a specific code that allows brands to identify and launch a unique experience for each individual package in-store [37].

Authentification. NFC-enabled intelligent packaging applications encompass a wide variety of other technological capabilities related to product's security and authenticity [31, 46]. Contrary to a prime understanding of authenticity as an action for authenticating who is accessing the information, smart packaging applications are more about the user aiming to know that the system, in this case, a product, is a product it claims to be. Consequently, some research has already been carried out to analyze the potential of NFC technology as means of the authenticity of the product [22, 45, 47, 48, 55]. According to [48], NFC tags grant a simple, small-sized and secure way to verify the genuineness of the product. NFC technology permits any object to securely authenticate itself and communicate this information online through NFC readers [39]. Currently, smart packaging contains NFC tags that are not only capable of detecting counterfeits, grey-market products, and tampering, but also implement secure marketing campaigns by assuring that only requests originated from authentic tags are forwarded to brand's web systems [32, 45]:

- Anti-counterfeiting. Counterfeit products are one of the main threats to commerce accounting up to 5–7% of all world trade goods and global economic value of over $ 865 bn [45, 48]. The development of consumer-centered NFC tags allows shoppers to determine the legitimacy of a product at the point of purchase, and, in turn, enhances direct-to-consumer digital strategies [45]. EPC standard can be used as an anti-counterfeiting measure by tracking the physical location of a tag and uploading the results in the database [45]. Consequently, product diversion can be detected by a simple scan and reported directly to the manufacturer contributing to grey market prevention [34].
- Tampering. Product tampering is another threatening factor to modern commerce. Diverse tamper-related incidents might happen in the entire supply chain that can be handled and controlled by adherence of NFC tags, including prevention of fraudulent re-labelling, opening detection/unopened product proof, refill fraud, detection of removal and piercing of the bottle cork, and other fraudulent events [33, 34]. For instance, once the wine bottle protective cork foil is removed, a brittle antenna circuit is damaged, and the tag is unreadable that might indicate a refill fraud.

Encryption. Another, more sophisticated, anti-counterfeiting approach is based on cryptography [42, 45]. In this method, each tag contains a secret encrypted value that is unreadable by anyone who does not possess a decryption key [45]. In general, this approach utilizes an encrypted challenge-response protocol and may be based on symmetric key or asymmetric key cryptography (or Public Key Cryptography (PKC)) [45]. In-store environment, where shoppers use their smartphones to read NFC tags, PKC is preferable for authentication purposes [22].

There are to main categories of counterfeiting prevention based on cryptography: off-line and on-line [45]. The former encompasses no shared secret between the NFC reader and the tag attached to a product, i.e. if the tag's contents are verified, and the tag is authenticated, the packaged product is presumed to be genuine [45]. The latter contains secret information shared between the reader and a tag, i.e. in order to determine the authenticity of a product, the reader requires access to a server containing a database of secrets [45].

NXP developed cryptography solutions in NTAG™ 424 DNA and NTAG 424 DNA TagTamper support relevant cryptographic operations and offer trust provisioning services, including creation, provisioning and managing of (1) customer dedicated keys in hardware secure modules that have access to master secrets, (2) secure key exchange and management, (3) SUN (Secure Unique NFC) message and encrypted SUN message verification, (4) tamper message verification (5) mutual authentication [32]. Such advanced security solutions: encrypt all critical data in transit and storage, protect access to target URL or tag memory, protect the master secret against malicious attacks or breaches, permit logging of data requests and changes, detect valid/invalid authentication request, provide patent ending dynamic cryptographic digital signature [32]. To summarize, based on NXP developed products, NFC uses symmetric cryptography with secret keys for encryption and decryption to protect the information, therefore whenever a key exchange is needed, it is done with encryption applying a secure communication channel [32].

4.3 Other Capabilities

Coupons and Vouchers. NFC technology proposes several diverse opportunities for brands and retailers to interact and engage with consumers with promotional efforts, especially couponing [24, 30, 40]. Reference [42] states that "the system is responsible for diffusion, distribution, sourcing, validation, redemption and managing of vouchers, loyalty cards and all kind of mobile coupons using NFC". The potential scheme of the NFC-coupon system might be as presented by [42]: at the point of sale, the shopper uses his/her smartphone to touch the NFC-equipped product to redeem a voucher, then the information is read from the smartphone and sent to the server for the voucher validation, once the validity is confirmed, the voucher is sent to the shopper.

NFC technology also employs location-based promotional offers, when users receive coupons on their mobile phones depending on their physical location and can redeem them at the offered retail outlet [40]. Furthermore, the NFC-based promotions can also be personalized. Depending on the shopper's previous visits to the stores, time-stamped promotion coupon can be forwarded and displayed on shopper's mobile phone to facilitate purchase decisions, when a shopper enters the store [20].

Loyalty, Bonus and Memberships. With the use of NFC technology, brands and marketers can carry out better customer loyalty programs in several techniques [40]. First of all, if loyalty, bonus and membership cards are stored on the mobile phone, NFC provides a possibility to automatically accumulate points, receive discounts, coupons, priority reservations, special offers, event invitations, product samples or other incentives [30, 34, 35]. Also, NFC allows instantaneous consumer feedback and streamlined data collection and entry [40] that benefits brands with in-depth real-time insight about their products and enables instant response to a consumer to contribute and enhance consumer loyalty.

Location-Based Services. NFC technology can be used for a wide range of context-aware services, including:

- Previously described location-based couponing, advertising, in-store marketing, and mobile marketing [21, 30, 49]. Once a registered shopper carrying an NFC-enabled smartphone with an app for personalized promotion system comes to a close range of a passive NFC tag attached to any items in the store, the is activated, and its unique ID and its location information is collected to grant a shopper with special promotions [20].
- Transparent tracking in the supply chain [32, 34, 35]. NFC enables traceability solutions relation to serialization, aggregation and data handling to provide real-time supply chain visibility in order to protect brands against grey market distribution, i.e. NFC scan allows to detect item's location at the specific time.

Social Networks. Reference [43] argues that the purchase of a product is motivated by the attempted acquisition of a certain status that is granted by a social reference group. In other words, the buying decision is highly dependent on suggestions and opinions from other consumers, such as friends, relatives, partners, etc., i.e. people tend to seek information before choosing [43]. Consequently, the opinions of others might reduce or increase the perceived credibility of the product [43]. If there is no physical presence of other consumers, the opinions and recommendations can also be derived from social networks. The NFC-enabled system is able to make links with social media to provide first-hand experience and recommendations from others [30, 34, 50].

Energy Harvesting. In general, a passive NFC tag is able to obtain energy from the radio frequency generated from the active NFC reader (smartphone) due to the electromagnetic field induced by the active device [7, 20]. Recently, NFC-based energy harvesting has been attracting more research attention in regards to its promising potential [16]. It might not only be used for data transmission, but also for powering up embedded sensor modules that measure diverse environmental parameters such as pH, soil moisture, temperature, gas concentration, humidity, and similar [16]. Reference [16] has fabricated battery-free smart sensor capable of less than 1 mW of power consumption, thus the energy from active NFC reader is enough to power up the sensor and read its data. NFC-based energy harvesting reduces the system cost by removing the need for a specialized NFC reader [16].

Network Access. The capability to provide network access is twofold. First, NFC technology redirects the user to the web through the encoded links (URLs). Second, users tapping on an NFC tag can also be logged onto a Wi-Fi or connected to a Bluetooth [30].

Device Pairing. By a simple tap, for instance, on a Bluetooth speaker, NFC technology makes the pairing process effortless, and the two devices are securely paired automatically with no need to search for a connection or type a code [30, 33].

Table 2. The summary of investigated NFC technological capabilities

Technological capabilities	Short descriptions
Data storage	To store encoded/written data in heterogeneous formats
Links to URL	To redirect the user to a particular content hosted by the brand owner's CMS
Data collection	To collect data autonomously using sensing devices that monitor different conditions
Data logging	To allow manual or autonomous data collection by human agents (e.g. feedback)
Data transmission	To transmit, read or exchange data between devices upon the initiative request from the human agent
Identification	To store a unique identifier that provides the capability to be uniquely identified in through the Internet
Validation and redirection	To protect and control product identities giving each item a persistent, addressable web-based presence
Authentication	To provide a simple and secure way to verify the genuineness of the product
Encryption	To secure data with secret keys and provide trust provisioning services/cryptography
Coupons and vouchers	To diffuse, distribute, source, validate, redeem and manage coupons and vouchers based on location or personalization
Loyalty, bonus, membership	To implement better customer loyalty programs by automatically accumulating points, providing discounts, offers and other incentives
Location-based services	To grant a user with diverse incentives based on location, and to enable traceability solutions to provide real-time supply chain visibility
Social networks	To provide a link with social media to provide first-hand experience and recommendations from others
Energy harvesting	To enable data transmission and power up embedded sensors and read their data
Network access	To log onto Wi-Fi or get connected to a Bluetooth by a tap
Device pairing	To securely and automatically pair two devices without searching for a connection or typing a code

5 Discussion

In this section, two different matters are addressed: consumer- and brand/retailer-oriented benefits from NFC, and potential user- and technology-centered barriers for NFC to become widely accepted.

5.1 Consumer-Oriented Benefits

Consumer Engagement. By attaching NFC tags to traditional customer engagement mediums, such as signage, posters and packaging, brands can create unique interactions and experiences for their customers [37, 40]. NFC-enabled packaging is able to transform products into a direct engagement channel to connect with shoppers directly at any time [34]. Reference [43] concurs and states that context-awareness technologies and ubiquitous networks provide users with access anywhere and anytime to information through their smartphone with no need of special assistance in the retail environment. As a result, the retail settings are shifting to new forms of store/space filled with increasing use of advanced technologies, such as NFC [43]. These technological innovations impart unique, interactive and entertaining tools to search, compare, and purchase products [43]. Consequently, the progressively increasing use of technologies during shopping may have an impact on consumers' shopping practices and behavior [42, 43].

Fast-moving technology-based shopping experience induced by NFC capabilities allows facilitating such elements as convenience, trust, loyalty or even intent to purchase the product. Previously presented cased of the NFC-enabled packaging for shoes not only converts the package to engaging media but also provides a straightforward and convenient way for customers to get the information about the right size availability [40]. Furthermore, NFC capability to verify authenticity, integrity, safety and quality of the packaged items builds consumer trust in both products and manufacturer/service provider [34, 49]. Finally, context-based NFC technology is also used as a mean to motivate customers to come to stores. Depending on interpreted customer interests in the displayed items, the personal promotion strategies are formulated in order to increase the intent to purchase [20].

Customization. Naturally, the employment of NFC technology allows gathering a vast amount of customer-related information about their preferences, behaviors, and responses [30, 50]. For instance, based on the purchase history from customer's previous visits to the stores, personalized promotion strategies are built and sent to customer's smartphone in forms of coupons or vouchers [20]. As a result, customization and geo-localization have beneficial effects in regards to increased market visibility for brands and products [30], as well as a deeper and more personal relationship with consumers [33].

5.2 Brand/Retailer-Oriented Benefits

There is a handful list of benefits NFC-enabled packaging brings to brand owners, including sales process optimization and increase, brand protection, enhanced brand-consumer relationship, consumer satisfaction and loyalty, and new marketing positions. Reference [19] presented the Mobile Sales Assistant (MSA) system allowing users to instantly check the availability and stock information of products might increase customer satisfaction with a fast and simple experience that, in turn, might can a positive outcome for product sales. Consequently, increased NFC-enabled engagement with consumers can be directly related to driving sales. Likewise, the combination of digital product authentication and enhanced consumer engagement help brands improve their reputation and maintain valuable relationships with consumers.

On the other hand, NFC-based packaging also creates new forms of in-store marketing campaigns. An example of such campaign given by [20] describes a promotion scheme to increase the number of shoppers visiting the stores, where each checking with an NFC tag provide a bonus mark to the consumer. The accumulated points can be transformed into discount and purchase benefits [20].

Real-Time Analytics. Web-based or cloud-based data management and analytic platform is an integral part of the NFC system. In general, such a platform is responsible for collecting data from consumers using NFC tags and performing advanced analytic techniques to gain meaningful and actionable insights for business development [23, 34]. This platform is capable of providing:

- Real-time analysis of scan/tap activity to measure the effectiveness of the integrated NFC technology [32, 34].
- Real-time analysis of regionally-focused data (geolocation), product status awareness, notification of use-by-date and other [34].
- Real-time analysis of products' performance [32].
- Real-time detection of irregularities related to authenticity, tampering or counterfeiting that can be dealt with momentarily [32].
- Recognized changes in consumers' shopping behavior due to the impact of NFC technology [23, 43].
- Captured real-time consumers interaction with the NFC-enabled product and their experiences based on feedback [34, 35].
- Captured individual consumer engagement to provide personalized and customized promotions [35].

Overall, described capabilities contribute to product and brand data management system, customer content management system, distribution management system, marketing analysis and other with the main purpose of increasing revenue from consumers' repeated purchases due to successful analytics [23, 34]. All the findings from collected data analysis are seamlessly linked to the brand's business intelligent system in order to help gather knowledge to make better decisions and take corrective actions [32].

5.3 Technology-Centered Barriers

Despite all the advanced and beneficial capabilities and benefits of NFC, the technology is still not widely accepted by the end-users or brand owners [26]. It might be related to any technological obstacles, consumer acceptance of the technology, or the economic benefit to implementing the technology into the business model, therefore this section shortly describes the possible and potential barriers for NFC to become widely accepted.

In relation to HCI theory, the design of NFC-enabled packaging, as a digital interactive system, has to follow the main principles of the interaction design in order to create a functional and effective connection between the consumer and the brand. However, the success of creating this bond highly depends on whether the created digital-physical object can impart a pleasing interface with the user addressing both technology- and human-related factors. Reference [27] concurs and states that the intention to adopt NFC technology is affected mostly by product-related factors, personal-related factors and attractiveness of alternatives. Likewise, reference [26] also distinguishes factors regarding NFC adoption into user-oriented and system-oriented.

Two studies [26, 27] employed the Technology Acceptance Model (TAM) to provide a profound understanding and identify factors facilitating or impeding the adoption of NFC technology. Study [26] identified four system-centric variables beneficial for such adoption, including user mobility, reachability, compatibility, and user convenience. Any issue related to these factors might have a negative impact on the user's decision to use an NFC system [26]. Likewise, study [27] identified six product-related factors: perceived usefulness, perceived ease of use, compatibility, perceived risk, perceived cost, and trialability. However, named factors by [27] are highly related user's belief and perception rather than engineering- and technology-related concerns. Overall, based on both studies, product- or system-related elements seem to have a stronger effect on the intention to adopt NFC systems [26, 27].

In addition, based on the literature review, other more practical/technological obstacles have also been identified, including:

- The stability of the regulated voltage by the NFC chip. According to the authors, there are two external parameters that have an impact on stability: the powering time and the position of the mobile device when it is brought close to the NFC antenna. The chip requires a particular level of the induced electromagnetic field to provide the regulated power supply, therefore not every position of the smartphone can activate the tag. Only a small displacement is permitted to avoid the deactivation [7].
- Transmission speed. Due to low transmission speed (up to 424 Kbps), NFC technology is not capable of large files transfer, therefore it intercommunicates with other wireless networks as Wi-Fi and Bluetooth that permits greater in size transfers [31].
- Battery saving mode. Consumers are used to switching off various settings of mobile apps connecting the mobile device with a service provider to save battery power [40]. It might cause inconvenience during data transmission, as several intermediate steps will be necessary to enable the process, i.e. set up the right settings permitting internet connection.
- Privacy settings. Very commonly due to privacy concerns customers also switch of the permission to always track their geographical location on mobile devices [40]. In this case, personalized promotion strategies might not function as accurate as expected.
- A limited number of devices that support NFC technology [51].
- Awareness of NFC technology. Finally, NFC is still not widely known by consumers, therefore public prominence has to take place before the exponential growth in usage of this communication protocol [30].

5.4 User-Centered Barriers

Since interaction design is about creating the overall essence and structure of products and systems to ensure that they support user's needs, desires, goals, perspectives and address their problems to provide enhanced user experience in their everyday lives, it is essential that interaction would be intuitive, enjoyable and effortless [52–54]. However, NFC technology has not yet reached its way to enhanced consumer engagement through the product's packaging. Even though the technology has been already commercialized (Seritag, Toppan, Identiv), it is still not widely applied to the packaging industry. The investigated literature addresses several user-related factors regarding the efficient adoption of NFC technology.

Three different studies related to Technology Acceptance Model and NFC that include consumer-related factors very investigated [25–27]. A study by [26] indicated the main two user-oriented factors, i.e. personal innovativeness and NFC knowledge, and two additional belief factors, i.e. perceived ease of use and perceived usefulness. Similarly, reference [25] included a few more concerns: personal innovativeness, convenience, perceived ease of use, perceived usefulness, perceived security, and perceived compatibility. Research by [27] tested two individual constructs, namely innovativeness in new technologies and absorptive capacity, and two additional constructs, namely trust and attractiveness of alternatives. User-oriented factors that are common amongst three studies:

Personal innovativeness. It refers to user's willingness to try out or embrace new information technology [25–27]. Therefore the difference in consumers' personal innovativeness should be taken into account in order to facilitate the usage of NFC technology. Also, one should consider that there are two different groups of people: early adopters and late adopters, i.e. users with a higher degree of personal innovation find NFC system more approachable [26].

- Perceived ease of use. It relates to the degree to which a user believes that the NFC system would require no substantial effort, i.e. NFC system has to be easy to use and easy to learn [25, 26].
- Perceived usefulness. The acceptance of NFC system highly relies on its provided unique advantage in comparison to existing solutions, like barcodes, QR codes, or Electronic Article Surveillance (EAS) tags [25, 26]. If users perceive alternatives as more attractive, it will have a negative effect on the intention to adopt NFC [25].
- Security and trust. According to the survey results by [25], users are more willing to use the NFC technology, if the perceived security is high. Users seem to be more interested in the security and trust of the NFC operations than on its ease of use [25, 27]. Moreover, it might also raise some privacy concerns, thus NFC system, for instance, has to offer valuable incentives in exchange for data [30].
- Knowledge and absorptive capacity. Users already having some knowledge about NFC would find the technology easier and more encouraging to adopt [26]. Moreover, understanding, acquisition and application of knowledge play a major role in user's absorptive capacity [27].

6 Conclusion

Equipped with NFC and other supporting computational devices capabilities physical items become uniquely identifiable, traceable, and, most importantly, interactive so they are able to increase the value from the point of manufacture to the end-user hands. NFC ability to connect products to the network by a single tap brings the technology to light to be spotted by innovation-seeing brand owners and retailers. The engaging and interactive medium provided by the Internet can be handed over to consumers' palms through NFC and mobile devices. Technology-enriched stories about products, instant verification of product's genuineness, just-on-time received offers can significantly improve consumers' experiences and positively influence their perception of products. Likewise, since brand identity and reputation are built through consumers' interaction with their products, NFC enables brands to dynamically adapt to emerging consumer needs by improving their products and services, and deliver personalized value-added solutions.

This study brought a comprehensive understanding of prominent technological capabilities provided by NFC technology applied to the product packaging. The incorporation of NFC into overall packaging design allows the package to become an interactive digital interface with infinite possibilities depending on brands and retailers creativity. Based on the results, NFC technology can contribute and create better experiences for consumers, brands, and retailers. Furthermore, in order to build an intuitive, enjoyable and effortless system, packaging designers have to take into consideration technology- and user-centered factors that might form barriers for successful adoption of NFC technology.

To conclude, the study aimed to build a bridge and establish a close relationship between the industry and academia and merge both sources of knowledge to contribute to a better and more practical understanding of the current state-of-the-art of the NFC and overall human-packaging interaction.

References

1. Horan, B.: Branded interactions: trends and strategies for digital-physical products. Appl. Des. **64**(1), 16–19 (2016)
2. Tolino, U., Mariani, I.: Do you think what I think? Strategic ways to design product-human conversation. Strateg. Des. Res. J. **11**(3), 254–262 (2018)
3. Lowgren, J.: The Encyclopedia of Human-Computer Interaction. https://www.interaction-design.org/literature/book/the-encyclopedia-of-human-computer-interaction-2nd-ed/interaction-design-brief-intro. Accessed 11 Oct 2019
4. Carli Lorenzini, G., Olsson, A.: Towards patient-centered packaging design: an industry perspective on processes, functions, and constraints. Packag. Technol. Sci. **32**(2), 59–73 (2019)
5. Bezerra, P.F., Arruda, A., Araujo, K.: Experience Design as a tool to promote interaction among users in the beverage market: proposal for a new emotional approach in usability. Procedia Manuf. **3**, 6028–6035 (2015)
6. Forcinio, H.: Smarter Packaging Comes to the Pharma Market: active and intelligent packaging technologies benefit brand owners, caregivers, and patients. Pharm. Technol. Eur. **31**(1), 12+ (2019)
7. Escobedo, P., et al.: Flexible passive near field communication tag for multigas sensing. Anal. Chem. **89**(3), 1697–1703 (2017)
8. Schaefer, D., Cheung, W.M.: Smart packaging: opportunities and challenges. Procedia CIRP **72**, 1022–1027 (2018)
9. Coskun, V., Ozdenizci, B., Ok, K.: The survey on near field communication. Sensors **15**(6), 13348–13405 (2015)

10. Dubois, A., Gadde, L.E.: Systematic combining: an abductive approach to case research. J. Bus. Res. **55**(7), 553–560 (2002)
11. Zhu, L., et al.: Silver nanowire mesh-based fuse type write-once-read-many memory. IEEE Electron Device Lett. **39**(3), 347–350 (2018)
12. Jung, M., Kim, J., Koo, H., Lee, W., Subramanian, V., Cho, G.: Roll-to-roll gravure with nanomaterials for printing smart packaging. J. Nanosci. Nanotechnol. **14**(2), 1303–1317 (2014)
13. Zhang, X., Shan, X., Wei, J.: Hybrid flexible smart temperature tag with NFC technology for smart packaging. In: 2017 IEEE 19th Electronics Packaging Technology Conference (EPTC), pp. 1–5. IEEE, December 2017
14. Yang, Y., Zhang, H., Li, J.: Effects of sintering temperature on microstructure and magnetic properties of NiCuZn ferrites for NFC application. In: 2018 19th International Conference on Electronic Packaging Technology (ICEPT), pp. 928–932. IEEE, August 2018
15. Li, S., et al.: Achieving humidity-insensitive ammonia sensor based on Poly (3, 4-ethylene dioxythiophene): poly (styrenesulfonate). Org. Electron. **62**, 234–240 (2018)
16. Nguyen, T.B., Tran, V.T., Chung, W.Y.: Pressure measurement-based method for battery-free food monitoring powered by NFC energy harvesting. Sci. Rep. **9**(1), 1–10 (2019)
17. Barandun, G., et al.: Cellulose fibers enable near-zero-cost electrical sensing of water-soluble gases. ACS Sens. **4**(6), 1662–1669 (2019)
18. Jara, A.J., Skarmeta, A.F., Parra, M.C.: Enabling participative marketing through the Internet of Things. In: 2013 27th International Conference on Advanced Information Networking and Applications Workshops, pp. 1301–1306. IEEE, March 2013
19. Karpischek, S., Michahelles, F., Resatsch, F., Fleisch, E.: Mobile sales assistant-an NFC-based product information system for retailers. In: 2009 First International Workshop on Near Field Communication, pp. 20–23. IEEE, February 2009
20. Lam, K.Y., Ng, J.K.Y., Wang, J., Ho Chuen Kam, C., Wai-Hung Tsang, N.: A pervasive promotion model for personalized promotion systems on using WLAN localization and NFC techniques. Mob. Inf. Syst. **2015**, 1–13 (2015)
21. Rohm, A.J., Gao, T.T., Sultan, F., Pagani, M.: Brand in the hand: a cross-market investigation of consumer acceptance of mobile marketing. Bus. Horiz. **55**(5), 485–493 (2012)
22. Urien, P., Piramuthu, S.: Framework and authentication protocols for smartphone, NFC, and RFID in retail transactions. In: 2013 IEEE Eighth International Conference on Intelligent Sensors, Sensor Networks and Information Processing, pp. 77–82. IEEE, April 2013
23. Wang, Q., Mohammed, S., Fiaidhi, J.: Near field communication tag-based system in retail marketing. Int. J. Future Gener. Commun. Network. **10**(7), 67–76 (2017)
24. Yildirim, K., Dalkiliç, G., Duru, N.: Formally analyzed m-coupon protocol with confirmation code (MCWCC). Turk. J. Electr. Eng. Comput. Sci. **27**(1), 484–498 (2019)
25. Bandinelli, R., Fani, V., Rinaldi, R.: Customer acceptance of NFC technology: an exploratory study in the wine industry. Int. J. RF Technol. **8**(1–2), 1–16 (2017)
26. Pal, D., Vanijja, V., Papasratorn, B.: An empirical analysis towards the adoption of NFC mobile payment system by the end user. Procedia Comput. Sci. **69**, 13–25 (2015)
27. Pham, T.T.T., Ho, J.C.: The effects of product-related, personal-related factors and attractiveness of alternatives on consumer adoption of NFC-based mobile payments. Technol. Soc. **43**, 159–172 (2015)
28. Mumani, A., Stone, R.: State of the art of user packaging interaction (UPI). Packag. Technol. Sci. **31**(6), 401–419 (2018)
29. Lydekaityte, J.: Smart interactive packaging as a cyber-physical agent in the interaction design theory: a novel user interface. In: Lamas, D., Loizides, F., Nacke, L., Petrie, H., Winckler, M., Zaphiris, P. (eds.) INTERACT 2019. LNCS, vol. 11746, pp. 687–695. Springer, Cham (2019). https://doi.org/10.1007/978-3-030-29381-9_41

30. Basili, A., Liguori, W., Palumbo, F.: NFC smart tourist card: combining mobile and contactless technologies towards a smart tourist experience. In: 2014 IEEE 23rd International WETICE Conference, pp. 249–254. IEEE, June 2014
31. Cerruela García, G., Luque Ruiz, I., Gómez-Nieto, M.Á.: State of the art, trends and future of bluetooth low energy, near field communication and visible light communication in the development of smart cities. Sensors **16**(11), 1968 (2016)
32. NXP Whitepaper. https://www.nxp.com/docs/en/brochure/NXP-NFC-E2ESOLUTION.pdf. Accessed 01 Mar 2020
33. NXP Ntag213 Datasheet. https://www.nxp.com/docs/en/data-sheet/NTAG213_215_216.pdf. Accessed 01 Mar 2020
34. Toppan Whitepaer. https://www.toppan.com/event/aipia2019.html. Accessed 1 Mar 2020
35. Avery Dennison Whitepaper. https://label.averydennison.com/content/dam/averydennison/lpm-responsive/na/doc/case-studies/product/intelligent-labels/industry-solutions/cs-eu-mineral-fusion-directLink-12172015-en.pdf. Accessed 01 Mar 2020
36. PragmatIC Website. https://www.pragmatic.tech. Accessed 01 Mar 2020
37. Identiv Report. https://www.identiv.com/community/2019/11/06/identiv-collaborates-with-nxp-to-power-new-kraft-heinz-intelligent-instant-redeemable-coupon-for-more-meaningful-frictionless-customer-connections/. Accessed 01 Mar 2020
38. Stora Enso Bobbin NFC Datasheet. https://www.storaenso.com/-/media/documents/download-center/documents/product-brochures/intelligent-packaging/bobbin-nfc-label.pdf. Accessed 01 Mar 2020
39. WISeKey Website. https://www.wisekey.com/nfctrusted/. Accessed 01 Mar 2020
40. Abhishek, Hemchand, S.: Adoption of sensor based communication for mobile marketing in India. J. Indian Bus. Res. **8**(1), 65–76 (2016)
41. Zhu, R., Desroches, M., Yoon, B., Swager, T.M.: Wireless oxygen sensors enabled by Fe (II)-polymer wrapped carbon nanotubes. ACS Sens. **2**(7), 1044–1050 (2017)
42. Borrego-Jaraba, F., Garrido, P.C., García, G.C., Ruiz, I.L., Gómez-Nieto, M.Á.: A ubiquitous NFC solution for the development of tailored marketing strategies based on discount vouchers and loyalty cards. Sensors **13**(5), 6334–6354 (2013)
43. Pantano, E., Gandini, A.: Exploring the forms of sociality mediated by innovative technologies in retail settings. Comput. Hum. Behav. **77**, 367–373 (2017)
44. EM Microeletronic. https://www.eejournal.com/industry_news/20150414-01/. Accessed 01 Mar 2020
45. Saeed, M.Q., Bilal, Z., Walter, C.D.: An NFC based consumer-level counterfeit detection framework. In: 2013 Eleventh Annual Conference on Privacy, Security and Trust, pp. 135–142. IEEE, July 2013
46. Simske, S.J.: Smart packaging for security and logistics. In: NIP & Digital Fabrication Conference, vol. 2011, no. 2, pp. 801–804. Society for Imaging Science and Technology, January 2011
47. Przyswa, E.: Protecting Your Wine. Stop counterfeiters from selling cheap imitations of your premium brand. Wines and Vines, pp. 38–47 (2014)
48. Schilling, J., et al.: Secured miniaturized system-in-package contactless and passive authentication devices featuring NFC. In: 2016 Euromicro Conference on Digital System Design (DSD), pp. 439–445. IEEE, August 2016
49. Violino, S., et al.: Are the innovative electronic labels for extra virgin olive oil sustainable, traceable, and accepted by consumers? Foods **8**(11), 529 (2019)
50. Kneißl, F., Rottger, R., Sandner, U., Leimeister, J.M., Krcmar, H.: All-i-touch as combination of NFC and lifestyle. In: 2009 First International Workshop on Near Field Communication, pp. 51–55. IEEE, February 2009
51. Đurđević, S., Novaković, D., Kašiković, N., Zeljković, Ž., Milić, N., Vasić, J.: NFC technology and augmented reality in smart packaging. Int. Circular Graph. Educ. Res. **11**, 52–65 (2018)

52. Stolterman, E., Wiberg, M.: Concept-driven interaction design research. Hum. Comput. Interact. **25**(2), 95–118 (2010)
53. Coiera, E.: Interaction design theory. Int. J. Med. Informatics **69**(2–3), 205–222 (2003)
54. Wray, T.B., Kahler, C.W., Simpanen, E.M., Operario, D.: User-centered, interaction design research approaches to inform the development of health risk behavior intervention technologies. Internet Interv. **15**, 1–9 (2019)
55. Yiu, N.C.: An NFC-enabled anti-counterfeiting system for wine industry. arXiv preprint arXiv:1601.06372 (2016)

Ambient UX Research: User Experience Investigation Through Multimodal Quadrangulation

Marco Mandolfo[1(✉)], Milica Pavlovic[2], Margherita Pillan[2], and Lucio Lamberti[1]

[1] Department of Management, Economics and Industrial Engineering, Politecnico di Milano, Via Lambruschini 4/B, 20156 Milan, Italy
{marco.mandolfo,lucio.lamberti}@polimi.it

[2] Department of Design, Politecnico di Milano, Via Durando 38, 20158 Milan, Italy
{milica.pavlovic,margherita.pillan}@polimi.it

Abstract. Cyber-physical systems refer to environments that are sensitive and responsive to people, where users' activities in a physical environment are enhanced by digitized services, thus calling for an Ambient UX design approach. Designing for experiences in such complex systems implies facing UX investigation in a holistic manner. The present work encompasses an initial overview of the methods employed to investigate systematically different facets of UX by actively involving users and based on experiments involving biometrics monitoring and other solutions to collect data. Investigation approaches are conceived as belonging to four layers of analysis, namely (i) physiological, (ii) behavioural, (iii) self-reported, and (iv) expert evaluation. The major contribution of the current research lies in the methodological integration firstly adopting a theoretical stance for UX investigation through multimodal quadrangulation, and secondly in a discussion on the applications of the approach as performed in a multidisciplinary research laboratory.

Keywords: Ambient UX · UX investigation · Research methods · User testing · Biometrics · Behavioural analysis

1 Introduction

Cyber-Physical Systems (CPS) [1] refer to environments that are sensitive and responsive to people; they integrate a variety of devices operating in concert to support human activities in an unobtrusive way, using intelligence that is hidden in the network connecting them. Designing a CPS implies planning for user interactions that are contextual and open-ended, triggered by the unrestricted activity of the users within the environment; therefore, CPS design is influenced by user-centric methods where the user is placed at the centre of the design activity and asked to give feedback through evaluations and tests to improve the design, or even co-create the design with a design team [2]. Pavlovic [2] observes an enlargement of current user experience (UX) design practices towards the

N. Streitz and S. Konomi (Eds.): HCII 2020, LNCS 12203, pp. 305–321, 2020.
https://doi.org/10.1007/978-3-030-50344-4_22

design of CPSes and proposes Ambient UX as a novel suitable approach for the emerging applications. Ambient UX approach, thus, targets the design of physical environments in which activities are enhanced by digitized services.

Within the research field, UX has been studied by various authors that have been proposing approaches towards reasoning on UX beyond mere usability. Norman [3] talks about "emotional design" in terms of visceral, behavioural, and reflective experiences, while Hassenzahl [4] underlines that products have hedonic attributes, besides the pragmatic ones (e.g., an ability to evoke feelings of pleasure). Desmet [5] provides a conceptual model for emotional responses that results from the perception of consumer products. In this context, MacDonald and Atwood [6] suggest that the exploration of UX evaluation methods, implying both pragmatic and hedonic dimensions, is a valuable research direction for real-world interaction design projects, as it is recognized that usability is not enough.

Pragmatic and hedonic dimensions of UX can be observed as correspondent to "what" and "why", where the main aim is to understand the "why" behind the "what" [7]. This is to say that investigating experiences is a complex quest and requires merging of diverse inquiry methods as well as diverse professional fields that conduct investigations. Such professional fields that tackle research on UX span from Human-Computer Interaction to Design of Services, Interfaces and Spaces, as well as Marketing and Communication. All of these fields investigate diverse dimensions of experience; bringing together diverse methods of inquiry could help to comprehend UX in a more holistic manner and facing its complexity accordingly. In UX Design an in-depth investigation of complexity of the human experience, with respect to the interaction with spaces and contexts, is a key issue, suitable to provide insights and suggestions in all phases of the design process, from the conception of innovative solutions to the progressive improvement of existing systems and services [8]. Evidence-based investigation of users' experience provides inspiration in the design of new solutions [9, 10]; it supports the reduction of the mismatch between the value proposition as it is conceived by designers with respect to users [8] provides information about the users' efforts in their interaction with the adaptive ambient and their satisfaction [11]; it provides awareness about the diverse human attitudes, and supports interoperability, consistency and coherence of connected systems [12].

This paper aims to respond to the need of facing UX investigation in a holistic manner, by proposing a methodology for investigating the experience of users of CPSes based on quadrangulation of methods borrowed from diverse fields of practices that shown to be efficient for comprehending hedonic dimensions of experiences, i.e. users' affective responses. The major contribution of the current research lies in the methodological integration, firstly adopting a theoretical stance and secondly providing a discussion of the approach as applied at the PHEEL (PHysiology, Emotion, and Experience, Lab) research laboratory (which authors are part of), based on case-studies developed in collaborations with industries.

The present work proposes quadrangulation of diverse levels of analysis for investigating systematically different facets of UX. The here presented approach is based on the assumption that the crossing of information, provided by monitoring of physiological parameters with the record of the behaviours of users and their subjective perception of the interactive process with environments and contexts, can provide meaningful insights about the "how" of the experience and subsequently hints on the "why". The paper presents the methods and an overview of some meaningful application. Each presented method is compared in terms of methodological specificities including time accuracy, instrumentation invasiveness, the possibility to assess top-down or bottom-up user responses, and the role of the researcher. From such an appraisal, a comprehensive framework is drafted highlighting applicability best practices, critical success factors and limitations associated with each method.

The discussion is centred on the importance of the experimental model in terms of scientific reliability, validity and transparency associated with the four layers of user experience analysis as provided by the experimental studies.

2 Framework of Reference

The present work encompasses an initial overview of the methods employed to investigate systematically different facets of UX. The overview summarises the scientific background of the experimental activities performed by the PHEEL Lab, a research laboratory created in collaboration by the Departments of Design, Management Engineering and Bioengineering within Politecnico di Milano, and focused on multi-purposes analysis of user experience. Investigation approaches are conceived as belonging to four layers of analysis, namely (i) physiological, (ii) behavioural, (iii) self-reported, and (iv) expert evaluation. After an illustration of the four layers' perspective and tools, a methodological comparison is presented to discuss quadrangulation modalities.

2.1 Physiological Level of Analysis

Physiological analyses are intended to gauge user reactions based on responses related to either the individual's central or peripheral nervous system activity. In its broadest sense, this level of investigation encompasses both a focus on the cognitive as well as the affective user responses [13]. The theoretical foundation of this level is rooted in the established mind-body relationship, which posits that for every person "every change in the physiological state is accompanied by an appropriate change in the mental-emotional state, conscious or unconscious, and conversely, every change in the mental-emotional state, conscious or unconscious, is accompanied by an appropriate change in the physiological state" [14]. According to this principle, which stems from early research on physiological responses specificity [15], by means of the measurement of the physiological state of a person, information about her psychological state can be assessed.

This line of thought is not novel. Indeed, evidence both in communication and behavioural research is found in previous literature. For instance, Kroeber-Riel [16] investigated individual's psychobiological activations to test the efficacy of advertising or Weinberg and Gottwald [17] conceptualised the assessment of perceived arousal during impulse buying processes through electrodermal activations. However, thanks to the technological and scientific developments, the last decade has seen a rising interest in the adoption of tools for assessing users' reactions, beyond the clinical setting. The fields of consumer neuroscience and cognitive psychology provide exemplary evidence [18, 19]. The former specifically aims at understanding instinctive conscious and unconscious human behaviours in response to marketing stimuli to ultimately provide information about the underlying consumer's cognitive and affective mechanisms and improve behavioural predictions [20, 21].

The added value of the physiological layer of analysis lays in the possibility of gauging user's unconscious information about their preferences, overcoming fundamental limitations related to traditional research methods, such as surveys or interviews. Indeed, such methods of investigation based on self-reporting may be impaired by biases related to self-deception, social desirability or acquiescence [20, 22]. By doing so, these analysis techniques are expected to support the early product or service design providing accurate and quantifiable insights into the user experience itself [23].

Concretely, the physiological level of analysis includes the analysis of physical responses such as (i) cortical and sub-cortical activations, as a direct quantitative measure of the central nervous system activity; (ii) cardiac and respiratory responses, as an expression of sympathetic and parasympathetic bodily activations; (iii) electrodermal activity, as an manifestation of sympathetic activations; (iv) muscular responses, related the muscle action potential produced by motor units; (v) peripheral temperature, as changes in skin temperature of the human body; (vi) pupil dilation, as the variation in the size of the eye pupil; and (vii) other biometric methods related to the measurement of nervous system-related activity (e.g. salivary or lacrimal glands responses).

In non-clinical settings, such analysis is employed for the investigation of a vast amount of cognitive and affective processes as, for instance, user experienced engagement during the use of a mobile app [24] or decision-making dynamics [25]. Overall, previous literature has shown that through the analysis of physiological activations it is possible to assess individual's exogenous and endogenous attention [26], affect [27], memory-related processes [28], and approach-withdrawal tendencies [29], arousal and stress [30].

2.2 Behavioural Level of Analysis

Behavioural responses encompass information related to instinctive nonverbal responses of the user. Contrastingly to physiological responses that gauge internal bodily reactions related to the nervous system activity, the behavioural level aims at assessing user involuntary expressions and behavioural exteriorisation. The study of nonverbal behaviours has been the centre of interest of various disciplines ranging from social psychology to anthropology [31], and from psychopathology [32] to sociology and marketing [33].

A specific fil rouge that bonds such distant fields is found in the analysis of the person's affective states. Indeed, significant evidence shows how expressions of affect can be conveyed through nonverbal cues [34] or that deception may be linked to specific nonverbal correlates [35]. Following such a line of thought, behavioural analyses result to be an alternative way to overcome biases related to self-reports in-field interviews. The observation of nonverbal behaviours enables descriptions of user behaviours both in social and individual settings, thus providing further sources of information about the individual's intentions.

As conceived by the present research, the behavioural level of analysis is focused on user responses such as (i) facial expressions, as the combinations of movements of facial landmarks such as eyes, eyebrows, lips, mouth, nose, and cheeks; (ii) gaze behaviour, as the analysis of the typologies of eye contact, ocular movements, gaze direction, and blink rates; (iii) paralinguistic cues, including the investigation of vocal pitch, loudness or amplitude, pitch pattern variations or pauses; (iv) proxemics, namely the postural patterns and structuring of space adopted from the user; (v) kinesics, as the body movements including head and limbs moves; and (vi) interaction behaviours, as the actions performed by the user during an interaction including touch and haptic behaviours.

Previous literature has broadly investigated nonverbal behaviours and various codings have been proposed [36]. Facial expression analysis may be performed through different methods (i.e. experts coding based on the Facial Action Coding System, by means of surface electromyography or through real-time software analyses). Despite the assessment methodology, facial expression analysis is commonly adopted to investigate user reactions in terms of arousal and valence, generally related to universal emotions [37].

Eye movement and gaze direction are classified according to voluntarily or involuntarily moves such as eye direction, focus change, or objects following [38]. Gaze analysis is commonly employed to track visual saliency during space exploration or during an interaction with a digital interface [39]. In addition, blink rates, as the measure of the frequency of eye blinks has often related to stress-related indexes [40].

Verbal communication features are an additional parameter considered. Specifically, paralinguistic cues as vocal pitch, intensity, frequency, glottal characteristics, and speech rate are among the common parameters analysed [36, 40]. These extracted features have been related to affective states such as frustration, annoyance, tiredness, or amusement classifiable based on valence and arousal [41] or potential stress levels [42].

Proxemics and kinesics represent a broad cluster of non-verbal cues where the physical behaviour is exercised to express or convey information. Such behaviour embraces body poses, posture, hand movements as well as body motion. Common metrics include distance, body orientation, touch, limb static positions or movements to provide inference on user engagement, disengagement or distress [36].

Lastly, interaction behaviours embrace the relational aspects occurring between the user, the object of investigation and the environment. Interaction behaviours may occur by means of devoted input peripherals (e.g. keyboard, mouse, touchscreen in case of a digital interface), or by means of specific event recording. Interactive patterns provide information about the user's understanding of an artefact as well as affective responses related to the interaction.

2.3 Self-reported Level of Analysis

Self-reported analyses are a family of research approaches based on personal statements stemming either from a conversation between the user and the researcher or as written user's opinions. This level of analysis represents a widely adopted methodology in social sciences to investigate user's understanding, opinions, attitudes or feelings [43]. Self-reports are commonly supported by a constructivist stance, positing that individual's understanding is not objective. Therefore, these research approaches are intended to investigate user's rationalisation of phenomena [44, 45].

Differently from the physiological and behavioural levels of analysis, the self-reported process grants an opportunity to explore the meanings that individuals give the object of interaction. Indeed, this layer aims at studying the content of thoughts and to support the respondent to articulate perceptions and understandings otherwise not observable. Such process proves specifically valuable in case of longitudinal research, where self-reports are collected over a period of time [43].

In its essence, the self-reported layer encompasses: (i) interviews, intended as a conversation between the user and an interviewer on a specific topic; (ii) surveys and questionnaires, as a collection of written questions; (iii) think aloud, referred to the analysis of the user's verbalisations during a task; and (iv) focus groups, as inquiries taking place in a group setting. Interviews consist of a process where the interviewer works directly with the respondent and seeks to understand the central themes of the user experience. Such a practice may be carried out in either a structured, semi-structured, or unstructured way [46].

Surveys and questionnaires encompass a set of structured queries provided in written form. Such methods of investigation include both open and closed questions which participants are required to answer in an individual manner. Personal answers do commonly guarantee the responder's anonymity especially in case of sensitive and personal topics of research. Overall, surveys and questionnaires result suitable for probability sampling and represent a tool associated with easier study replicability [45].

Think aloud investigations represent a process where the individual is asked to verbalise her thought while being involved in a task [47]. It consists of a source of information on the user's cognitive processes, which are gathered during a specific interaction, object of the study. However, unlike other methods for verbal data gathering, the participant is neither interrupted, nor suggestive prompts are provided. Instead, the subject is encouraged to express her understanding and interpretation of the task at hand.

Lastly, focus groups consist of group interviews with a heterogeneous set of respondents. Participants are asked for their perceptions, opinions, or attitudes towards the object of investigation in a way that they are open to discuss with peers under the guidance of a moderator [48]. The added value related to focus groups stems from the group interaction to novel idea generation, as respondents build on peers' comments. Specifically, the technique proves valuable to extract insights about complex issues and topics.

2.4 Expert Evaluation

The three levels of analysis described in the previous paragraphs refer to methods and techniques that can provide information on the experience of people interacting with CPSes, in experiments where users are directly involved and monitored while performing free activities or goal-oriented actions.

The fourth level of the quadrangulation scheme is the one we refer to as *expert evaluation*, and it provides the framework for the creation of suitable experiments and data processing, aimed at generating design hints and opportunities for the CPS. Expert here is a design professional that manages with his/her sensibility, developed over time and through experience working on projects, to model a CPS with respect to the possible user paths enabled by the environment and technologies, and conceptual description of the activities enabled/constrained by the characteristics of the system.

The final aim of our investigation is the production of knowledge that supports the design and re-design of CPSes with respect to the fulfilment of user needs and expectations, with an emphasis on the freedom of action and resilience. The description of a CPS in terms of tasks and paths of users [8], flows of activities and processes, and the envisioning of structural dimensions of the physical and digital architectures [2] is a preliminary activity in the investigation of experience, and the benchmark for the interpretation of data provided by experiments. For this reason, expert evaluation is crucial for tailoring an evaluation process related to experiences. Such professional figure is knowledgeable about the whole design process flow as well as the aspects of a product-service system that can be redesigned for supporting desirable experiences. This level of analysis provides insights within an overall context of usage, potential expectations from the usage, as well as the adequacy of the design concept for undertaking foreseen activities. The insights provided by the experiments with users can confirm and enrich the interpretation and expectations of the experts, or they can offer different and unforeseen perspectives on possible experiences related to the interaction with a CPS emerging from the quadrangulation process.

Roots of this method that we employ within the work of our research group can be found among UX research methods referred to as heuristic evaluation. Author Nielsen [49, 50] defines heuristic evaluation as a "usability engineering method for finding the usability problems in a user interface design so that they can be attended to as part of an iterative design process". In this context, such evaluation implies having a number of usability evaluators within the research team that can analyse the interface according to recognized usability principles, which are referred to as *heuristics*.

Usability principles, i.e. heuristics, according to Nielsen [50] are: (1) visibility of system status, (2) match between system and the real world, (3) user control and freedom, (4) consistency and standards, (5) error prevention, (6) recognition rather than recall, (7) flexibility and efficiency of use, (8) aesthetic and minimalist design, (9) helping users recognize, diagnose, and recover from errors, (10) help and documentation. It is to note, however, that evaluators can develop further category-specific heuristics according to peculiarities of a design product that is being analysed. One of such examples is performing a competitive analysis among existing products within a specific category, and further extracting principles that would support the definition of usability problematics [51].

Heuristic evaluation principles refer to usability aspects of an interface, while in our research group we expand the expert evaluation on a broader level considering experiences beyond mere usability problematics. This is due to the nature of projects that the group deals with, where projects of interaction design go beyond graphical user interfaces and shape complex cyber-physical service systems. Role of a design professional as an evaluator is to identify all the problematic and/or potentially dominant aspects of design that can influence user experience. Such evaluation brings to a further definition of a study protocol for investigating UX according to very specific design aspects and features, even those not among the recognized heuristics.

In this context, expert evaluation refers to conducting an analysis of a design product from the side of design professionals, in order to identify a further study protocol. This activity ensures having a tailored UX research methodology according to the very specific design in question, which comprises of some of the previously described physiological, behavioural, and self-reported methods. After defining a protocol and conducting studies, a design professional performs another activity by translating the research insights into potential design recommendations.

The scope of identifying a necessity for an activity such as expert evaluation, within the process of investigation of user's experience, is to underline the importance of including a design professional within the research methodology. Such a professional is capable of detecting problematics and features with design potential in order to further improve/re-design a product-service system by bridging the research and design process.

The four described layers of analysis (physiological, behavioural, self-reported, expert evaluation) are parts of a quadrangulation strategy for investigating users' experiences. Table 1 in Sect. 3.1 on quadrangulation strategies summarises the structure of each layer and the related information provided.

3 Methodological Considerations

Each presented perspective and measurement tool demonstrate specificities in terms of skills and knowledge, methodological procedure and context of use requirements. However, the present discussion intentionally leaves aside punctual considerations related to each tool for the sake of framework generalization. Accordingly, we develop a broad discussion that encompasses applicability features of each layer of analysis. Our argumentation begins with the comparison of the four layers in terms of temporal accuracy, instrumentation invasiveness (i.e. the necessity to potentially insert disturbing elements in the analysed experience), possibility to assess instinctive (i.e. top-down or bottom-up) user responses, and the role of the researcher. Next, we draft possible quadrangulation strategies combining each layer's features.

3.1 Methodological Perspective Appraisal

Each layer provides a different lens of analysis (Table 1); each one is characterised by a specific level of impact on users (as an instance, eye-tracking and the monitoring of physiological parameters require the user to wear instruments that in some circumstances can affect the experience; video recording and direct observation of contexts are subjected to different constraints of privacy depending on the location of the experiments), and some require calibration and settings that should be carefully handled to interfere with the normal development of events. In terms of temporal accuracy, more precisely the possibility to assess real-time information, the physiological layer grants continuous data gathering. Temporal information may range from milliseconds (in case of cortical responses gathered through EEG) to minutes (in relation to peripheral temperature analyses). Such information may be collected prior, during and after the experience, in the event of long-term physiological recordings. Despite the temporal accuracy, the physiological recording is commonly bounded to the physical application of measuring instrumentation to the body of the subject, which may restrain movements either completely (in the case of sub-cortical inferences) or partially (in the event of electrodermal activity measurements). On this line of thought, physiological measurement tools imply a high degree of invasiveness. Furthermore, the physiological layer of analysis allows the possibility to measure instinctive user responses, related to physiological involuntary responses. Such a possibility is provided in the face of a fairly actively involved researcher that must monitor physiological responses during each experimental session. In general terms, we argue that the physiological layer is characterised by a robust temporal accuracy, a high degree of invasiveness, a significant possibility of gathering user's instinctive responses and a fairly active role of the researcher.

By the same token, the behavioural level of analysis shows good temporal accuracy. Gaze behaviour or facial expressions are commonly accounted in the range of seconds, as well as proxemics and kinesics that are frequently assessed in time windows of a few seconds. Information is commonly gathered during the experience through less invasive technology which, for the large majority, is not in contact with the user's body (such as ambient cameras, infrared cameras, or audio-recording devices). Like the physiological layer, behavioural analyses grant the possibility to assess user's instinctive and involuntary responses in the face of a fairly active researcher that should often actively code user responses during the investigation. Based on such reasons, we posit that the behavioural level shows an average level of temporal accuracy, low invasiveness, a significant possibility of collecting instinctive responses and a fairly active role of the researcher.

During experiments, the accuracy of timing for physiological and behavioural analysis is crucial for the aim of producing information about the correlation between the events, the activities, the stimuli enacting actions, and the reactions that take place in the context.

Conversely, the self-reported layer of analysis shows distinct features. Despite specific methodologies that allow collecting self-reported responses of the user during the experience (e.g. think aloud), self-reported measures commonly are assessed either prior or after the experience. Self-reported analyses investigate the experience rationalisation of the user, providing a time-lag between the user action and the data collection. As concerns the experience invasiveness, self-reports do not constitute any concern, since they do not insert any element of potential disturb. Furthermore, this layer of analysis does not provide, by its nature, insights on the instinctive user responses rather it shed light on the user's cognitive understanding. Self-reported investigations do require, however, a committed role of the researcher who has often to actively conduct interviews or moderate focus groups discussions.

Expert evaluation as an activity is not defined by a certain timeframe, but within the overall study methodology is meant to save time by identifying specific design features that the study should focus on. This level of analysis engages in two phases of the study, in the very initial phase when the study protocol is being defined, and in the final phase when it comes to interpreting research results. This level of analysis differs from the other three as it does not involve direct feedback from the users, rather it relies on the expertise of the design professional. Therefore, the design professional in this case takes on a user's perspective, performing diverse tasks with a design product, while simultaneously being knowledgeable about the design process and certain heuristics that comply with good

Table 1. Confrontation of four layers of analysis for investigating user experience.

Layer of analysis	Response	Instrumentation	Information provided
Physiological	Cortical activations	Electroencephalography, magnetoencephalography, steady-state topography	Attention-related processes, memory-related processes, approach-withdrawal tendencies
	Sub-cortical activations	Functional magnetic resonance imaging, positron emission tomography, functional near-infrared spectroscopy	Exogenous and endogenous attention, affect, memory-related processes, approach-withdrawal tendencies
	Cardiac and respiratory responses	Electrocardiography, respiration bands or respiratory tubes	Stress, arousal
	Electrodermal activity	Surface skin electrodes	Stress, arousal
	Muscular responses	Electromyography	Stress
	Peripheral temperature	Skin thermometers	Stress, arousal
	Pupil dilation	Eye tracking infrared based technology	Stress, arousal, engagement
Behavioural	Facial expressions	Video-recording	Valence, arousal
	Gaze behaviour	Eye tracking infrared based technology	Attention-related processes
	Paralinguistic cues	Audio-recording	Valence, arousal
	Proxemics	Video-recording	Engagement-related processes, stress
	Kinesics	Video-recording	Engagement-related processes, stress
	Interaction behaviours	Video-recording	Attention-related processes, user understanding

(*continued*)

Table 1. *(continued)*

Layer of analysis	Response	Instrumentation	Information provided
Self-reported	Individual response	Interview, think aloud, survey	Cognitive evaluation (understanding, opinions, attitudes or feelings)
	Group response	Focus group	Cognitive evaluation (understanding, opinions, attitudes or feelings)
Expert evaluation	Design professional's estimation	Design brief, description of main features of the artefacts under analysis, functional inspection	Definition of design and functional features to be tested

design. Information provided from this activity is a definition of design features to be tested, through one or more methods deriving from the other three levels of analysis previously described.

3.2 Quadrangulation Strategy

At the PHEEL Lab, each experiment follows a typical process including a sequence of activities that we summarize in four main steps: (i) framing; (ii) preparation; (iii) test; (iv) data post-processing.

Our research is usually commissioned by an institution or company that manages a service, product or system, and that intends to analyse the user experience in order to seize the opportunities for improvement or, more simply, to understand the real attitudes of people towards their design. We also collaborate with companies that are developing innovative and experimental solutions, and therefore we support the development process by carrying out tests on prototypes.

The framing phase includes a preliminary inspection of the artefacts that will provide the context of analysis, and a collaboration with the stakeholder to identify goals and priorities of the investigations. Second phase, the preparation, includes the expert evaluation of the artefacts performed by designers and giving as output a conceptual description of the context including topology, structure, design characteristics; the expert evaluation also provides a description of the main tasks of users of the CPS in the timeline, and of the expected procedures of interactions with it. Based on these descriptions, we prepare an experimental protocol including tasks and activities we will focus on during the tests with users. Finally, we define a strategy for recruiting people to be involved in the experiments as representatives of the final users of a CPS. The third phase is dedicated to the tests with users, that we perform keeping under control potential external interferences on the normal development of activities. The last phase is dedicated to the data post-processing with an approach that is schematically reported in Fig. 1.

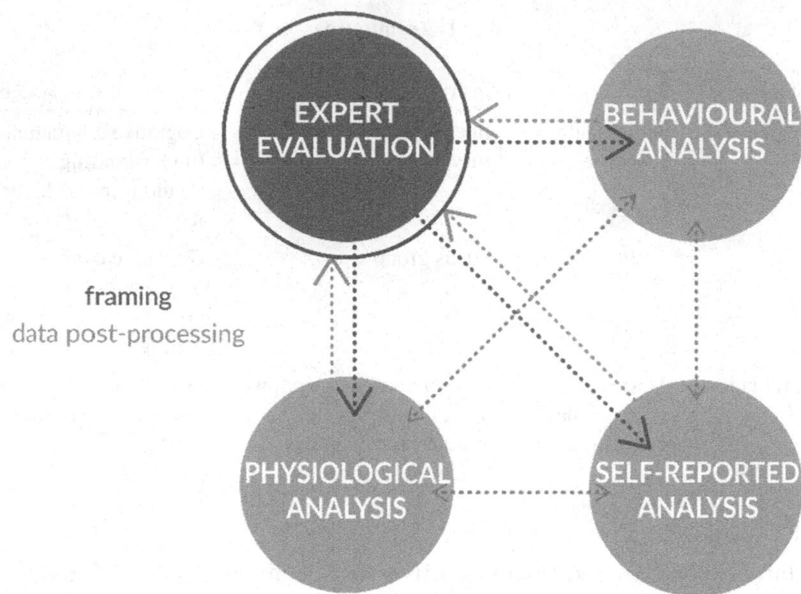

Fig. 1. Quadrangulation of layers of analysis for investigating user experience according to the activities within an experiment flow.

3.3 Case Studies of Investigating User Experience

The methodology has been applied in experiments performed by the PHEEL Lab in a variety of application fields, from entertainment to retail, from gaming to driving experience. Most projects are funded by industries requiring investigation to support the design of very innovative solutions and the upgrading of the existing ones; due to the industrial sponsorship, most experiments are subjected to non-disclosure agreements, but we can provide here an overview of some experiments we performed in some fields we consider as meaningful for the purposes of the present work. We recall here: (i) experiments in large retail environments, (ii) analysis of the driving experience, (iii) investigation of playing.

In regard to retail as a domain of human experience, we consider physical stores as interesting for the experimental use of digital solutions employed to support information and decision processes. Retail spaces are complex environments where the senses are overstimulated, the attention of users is disputed by intentional activities and external inductions to action, and where task-positive and task-negative perception processes alternate frantically. Large stores provide several different concurring layers of information, related to the spatial organization and including the references to conventional or innovative semantic category-management of goods. In stores, users perform tasks under the compulsion of personal tasks and in free exploration of the space, sometimes also guided by information searched on personal devices. The application of the assessment methodology based on our four different analysis provides insights on cognitive and emotional experiences with respect to the spatial organization, the single objects and products, the social interactions and the evaluation of the journey. With this aim, we commonly track the user's cortical activations, cardiac, respiratory, and ocular activity as well as user's verbalisations. We report in Fig. 2 an archetypal setting.

Fig. 2. Illustrative research setting in the shopping context

We are presently performing an investigation of the driving experience in real-world environments and in simulation rooms. The entire automotive sector is currently undergoing a phase of major changes due to the transition from combustion engines to electric ones, to the increasingly massive role played by sensors and digital technologies, and to the development of technologies for autonomous vehicle driving. The evolution of engines and control systems requires an extensive investigation of the new modalities of engagement of drivers, that involve all senses and the development of automatism. The application of our approach for the analysis of the experience of drivers supports the understanding of the impacts related to the sensorial stimuli provided by the new cars (including sound and haptic effects), related to the physical characteristics of the vehicles, as well as with respect to personal attitudes and expertise of pilots. In such a setting, we specifically monitor users' cardiac and respiratory activity to infer states of arousal, as an expression of the physiological layer of analysis. Furthermore, we track users' gaze activity in conjunction with driving interaction patterns, as indexes of behavioural expressions. Self-reporting takes place prior and after the experience to compare expectations with actual users' rationalisations. Expert evaluation represents a fundamental layer in several process phases. First, these include the framing and preparation phases to outline user interaction possibilities in relation to context topology and expected users' mental mappings. Second, expert evaluations steer the conception of the experimental protocol in the definition of tasks and procedures requested to the user. Lastly, during the data post-processing, expert evaluation has the role of bridging research outcomes with the future (re)design process. A typical research setting is shown in Fig. 3.

In collaboration with one of the Italian state's concessionary agencies, we conducted research on gambling with digital games by applying our methodology of investigation in the laboratory and in game arcades. In the controlled experimental setting we explored player's physiological and behavioural reactions to slot machines gambling outcomes

Fig. 3. Illustrative research setting in the driving context

and in-game features. The physiological layer of analysis encompassed most of the responses listed (i.e. cortical, cardiac, respiratory, dermal, and pupillary responses) due to the seated posture of the subjects. The behavioural layer embraced the gaze, proxemics, and interactive behaviours, whereas the self-reported layer included surveys prior to and after the experience. Expert evaluation played a central role in the understanding of the interaction dynamics with the gaming platform in the problem setting stage as well as in the generation of conclusive insights. The experiment allowed to produce metrics and models of the different ways of engagement in relation to the intrinsic characteristics of the games, highlighting the potential to leverage on such physiological responses to prevent possible unhealthy gambling behaviours. In particular, users' behaviours underscored the possible exploration of in-game pop-up message usage to nudge online responsible gambling behaviours [52]. Secondly, we explored social dynamics in the ecological setting, namely arcades and slot halls. In such settings, we relied on unobtrusive behavioural expressions gauged from facial expressions, proxemics, paralinguistic cues, and kinesics gathered from ambient cameras. Our findings showed that the presence of other players might influence the individual gambling conduct, constituting an element of prevention in the onset of negative valence behavioural responses [53].

4 Conclusion

The development of physical/digital environments is based on the integration of traditional and innovative technologies aimed at improving lifestyles, wellbeing and providing sustainable cities. The introduction of digital technologies in these environments has impacts on human activities and induces new ways of actions/interactions that can only be partially predicted in the design phases. The development of suitable approaches for the analysis of the user experience plays a fundamental role in the development of CPSes, providing the means for an awareness of the impacts of the design choices. The development of neuroscience and the availability of instruments for monitoring physiological responses enable new approaches for such analysis, offering the means to understand the impacts of the design choices with respect to the variety of human characteristics and attitudes. By developing more comprehensive approaches to the investigation of user experiences in CPSes, the authors intend to provide a contribution to the development of design methods capable to support awareness and responsibility within the design processes.

Acknowledgements. This paper has benefitted from the input of PHEEL Lab researchers involved in the presented projects.

References

1. Bier, H., Liu Cheng, A., Mostafavi, S., Anton, A., Bodea, S.: Robotic building as integration of design-to-robotic-production and -operation. In: Bier, H. (ed.) Robotic Building. SSAE, pp. 97–120. Springer, Cham (2018). https://doi.org/10.1007/978-3-319-70866-9_5
2. Pavlovic, M.: Designing for ambient UX: design framework for managing user experience within cyber-physical systems. Unpublished doctoral dissertation (2020)
3. Norman, D.: Emotional Design: Why We Love (or Hate) Everyday Things. Basic Books, New York (2004)
4. Hassenzahl, M.: The thing and I: understanding the relationship between user and product. In: Blythe, M.A., Overbeeke, K., Monk, A.F., Wright, P.C. (eds.) Funology. HCIS, vol. 3, pp. 31–42. Springer, Dordrecht (2003). https://doi.org/10.1007/1-4020-2967-5_4
5. Desmet, P.: A Multilayered Model of Product Emotions Resilient@work: development of an application for a more positive outlook on life View project. Artic. Des. J. **6**, 4–13 (2003)
6. MacDonald, C.M., Atwood, M.E.: Changing perspectives on evaluation in HCI: past, present, and future. In: Conference on Human Factors in Computing Systems – Proceedings, pp. 1969–1978. Association for Computing Machinery (2013)
7. Kim, J.H., Gunn, D.V., Schuh, E., Phillips, B.C., Pagulayan, R.J., Wixon, D.: Tracking real-time user experience (TRUE): a comprehensive instrumentation solution for complex systems. In: Conference on Human Factors in Computing Systems – Proceedings, pp. 443–451 (2008)
8. Kalbach, J.: Mapping Experiences: A Complete Guide to Creating Value Through Journeys, Blueprints, and Diagrams. O'Reilly, Sebastopol (2016)
9. Buxton, B.: Sketching User Experiences – Getting Right Design, and Getting the Design Right. Morgan Kaufman, San Francisco (2007)
10. Stickdorn, M., Hormess, M., Lawrence, A., Schneider, J.: This is Service Design Doing: Applying Service Design Thinking in the Real World. O'Reilly (2018)
11. Tullis, T., Albert, W.: Measuring the User Experience: Collecting, Analyzing, and Presenting Usability Metrics. Morgan Kaufman, San Francisco (2013)
12. Rowland, C., Goodman, E., Charlier, M., Light, A., Lui, A.: Designing Connected Products: UX for the Consumer Internet of Things. O'Reilly (2015)
13. Kreibig, S.D.: Autonomic nervous system activity in emotion: a review. Biol. Psychol. **84**(3), 394–421 (2010)
14. Green, E.E., Green, A.M., Walters, E.D.: Voluntary control of internal states: psychological and physiological. J. Transpers. Psychol. **2**, 1 (1970)
15. James, W.: Discussion: the physical basis of emotion. Psychol. Rev. **1**(5), 516 (1894)

16. Kroeber-Riel, W.: Psychobiology and consumer research: a problem of construct validity: rejoinder. J. Consum. Res. **7**, 96 (1980)
17. Weinberg, P., Gottwald, W.: Impulsive consumer buying as a result of emotions. J. Bus. Res. **10**(1), 43–57 (1982)
18. Plassmann, H., Ramsøy, T.Z., Milosavljevic, M.: Branding the brain: a critical review and outlook. J. Consum. Psychol. **22**, 18–36 (2012)
19. Mather, M., Cacioppo, J.T., Kanwisher, N.: How fMRI can inform cognitive theories. Perspect. Psychol. Sci. **8**, 108–113 (2013)
20. Plassmann, H., Venkatraman, V., Huettel, S., Yoon, C.: Consumer neuroscience: applications, challenges, and possible solutions. J. Mark. Res. **52**, 427–435 (2015)
21. Lim, M.: Demystifying neuromarketing. J. Bus. Res. **91**, 205–220 (2018)
22. Dimoka, A., Pavlou, P.A., Davis, F.D.: NeuroIS: the potential of cognitive neuroscience for information systems research. Inf. Syst. Res. **22**, 687–702 (2011)
23. Ariely, D., Berns, G.S.: Neuromarketing: the hope and hype of neuroimaging in business. Nat. Rev. Neurosci. **11**, 284 (2010)
24. Chai, J., et al.: Application of frontal EEG asymmetry to user experience research. In: Harris, D. (ed.) EPCE 2014. LNCS (LNAI), vol. 8532, pp. 234–243. Springer, Cham (2014). https://doi.org/10.1007/978-3-319-07515-0_24
25. Stevens, R.H., Galloway, T., Berka, C.: EEG-related changes in cognitive workload, engagement and distraction as students acquire problem solving skills. In: Conati, C., McCoy, K., Paliouras, G. (eds.) UM 2007. LNCS (LNAI), vol. 4511, pp. 187–196. Springer, Heidelberg (2007). https://doi.org/10.1007/978-3-540-73078-1_22
26. Foxe, J.J., Snyder, A.C.: The role of alpha-band brain oscillations as a sensory suppression mechanism during selective attention. Front. Psychol. **2**, 154 (2011)
27. Sabatinelli, D., Bradley, M.M., Fitzsimmons, J.R., Lang, P.J.: Parallel amygdala and inferotemporal activation reflect emotional intensity and fear relevance. Neuroimage **24**, 1265–1270 (2005)
28. Zola-Morgan, S., Squire, L.R.: Neuroanatomy of memory. Annu. Rev. Neurosci. **16**, 547–563 (1993)
29. Sutton, S.K., Davidson, R.J.: Prefrontal brain asymmetry: a biological substrate of the behavioral approach and inhibition systems. Psychol. Sci. **8**, 204–210 (1997)
30. Venkatraman, V., et al.: Predicting advertising success beyond traditional measures: new insights from neurophysiological methods and market response modeling. J. Mark. Res. **52**, 436–452 (2015)
31. Depaulo, B.M., Lindsay, J.J., Malone, B.E., Muhlenbruck, L., Charlton, K., Cooper, H.: Cues to deception. Psychol. Bull. **129**, 74–118 (2003)
32. Keltner, D., Kring, A.M.: Emotion, social function, and psychopathology. Rev. Gen. Psychol. **2**, 320–342 (1998)
33. Sundaram, D., Webster, C.: The role of nonverbal communication in service encounters. J Serv Mark. **14**(5), 378–391 (2000)
34. Ekman, P., Friesen, W.: The repertoire of nonverbal behavior: categories, origins, usage, and coding. Semiotica **1**, 49–98 (1969)
35. Mehrabian, A.: Nonverbal betrayal of feeling. J. Exp. Res. Personal. **5**, 64–73 (1971)
36. Mehrabian, A.: Some referents and measures of nonverbal behavior. Behav. Res. Methods Instrum. **1**, 203–207 (1968). https://doi.org/10.3758/BF03208096
37. Ekman, P.: An argument for basic emotions. Cogn. Emot. **6**, 169–200 (1992)
38. Van Der Stigchel, S., Meeter, M., Theeuwes, J.: Eye movement trajectories and what they tell us. Neurosci. Biobehav. Rev. **30**, 666–679 (2006)
39. Djamasbi, S.: Eye tracking and web experience. AIS Trans. Hum. Comput. Interact. **6**(2), 37–54 (2014)

40. Sharma, N., Gedeon, T.: Objective measures, sensors and computational techniques for stress recognition and classification: a survey. Comput. Methods Programs Biomed. **108**, 1287–1301 (2012)
41. Ang, J., Dhillon, R., Krupski, A., Shriberg, E., Stolcke, A.: Prosody-based automatic detection of annoyance and frustration in human-computer dialog. In: Interspeech (2002)
42. Hopkins, C.S., Ratley, R.J., Benincasa, D.S., Grieco, J.J.: Evaluation of voice stress analysis technology. In: System Sciences, HICSS 2005 (2005)
43. Arksey, H., Knight, P.: Interviewing for Social Scientists: An Introductory Resource with Examples. SAGE Publications, Thousand Oaks (1999)
44. Lune, H., Berg, B.L.: Qualitative Research Methods for the Social Sciences. Pearson Higher Education, Boston (2016)
45. Nardi, P.: Doing Survey Research: A Guide to Quantitative Methods. Routledge, Abingdon (2018)
46. Fontana, A., Frey, J.: The Art of Science. The Handbook of Qualitative Research. Thousand Oaks (1994)
47. Van-Someren, M., Barnard, Y., Sandberg, J.: The Think Aloud Method: A Practical Approach to Modelling Cognitive Processes. Academic Press, London (1994)
48. Morgan, D.: Focus Groups as Qualitative Research. Sage Publications, Thousand Oaks (1997)
49. Nielsen, J., Molich, R.: Heuristic evaluation of user interfaces. In: Conference on Human Factors in Computing Systems – Proceedings, pp. 249–256. Association for Computing Machinery (1990)
50. Nielsen, J.: Heuristic evaluation. In: Usability Inspection Methods (1994)
51. Dykstra, D.: A comparison of heuristic evaluation and usability testing: the efficacy of a domain-specific heuristic checklist. Ph.D. dissertation, Department of Industrial Engineering, Texas A&M University, College Station, TX (1993)
52. Mandolfo, M., Bettiga, D., Lolatto, R., Reali, P.: Would you bet on your physiological response? An analysis of the physiological and behavioral characteristics of online electronic gaming machines players. In: NeuroPsychoEconomics Conference, p. 28 (2019)
53. Mandolfo, M., Bettiga, D.: Better off alone? An analysis of behavioral characteristics of electronic gaming machine players. In: Riunione Scientifica Annuale AiIG (2018)

Dynamic Consent: Physical Switches and Feedback to Adjust Consent to IoT Data Collection

Henrich C. Pöhls[1(✉)] and Noëlle Rakotondravony[2]

[1] Institute of IT-Security and Security Law, University of Passau, Passau, Germany
hp@sec.uni-passau.de
[2] Worcester Polytechnic Institute, Worcester, MA, USA
ntrakotondravony@wpi.edu

Abstract. From smart homes to highly energy-optimized office building and smart city, the adoption of living in smart spaces requires that the inhabitants feel comfortable with the level of data being collected about them in order to provide smartness. However, you usually provide this consent on—or best before—your very first interaction. Thus, firstly your consent might vary over the time of usage. Secondly, it is not always obvious if data is currently collected or not. This paper addresses two missing elements in the interaction with a smart environment: First, the general concept of dynamicity of consent to data collection. Second, provision of a physical interaction to gather and change consent and a physical feedback on the current data collection status. By the feedback being physical we mean being visual, haptic or accoustic, in order to allow natural perception by the users in the physical space. For both components we provide examples which show how one could make both the current status as well as the consent physical and discuss the user perception. We argue that having a physical interaction to start potentially privacy-invasive data collections is a useful enrichment for legal consent, and physically visible status is helpful to make a decision.

Keywords: Privacy · Security · Consent · Smart living · Internet-of-Things

1 Introduction and Motivation

We need privacy in the smart spaces that are enabled by the technological advances of the Internet-of-Things (IoT). Privacy can be seen as a legal right, like the European Union's General Data Protection Regulation (GDPR) [1], or even as a human right [2]. Regardless how you see it, it might get demanded by your users as their fundamental criteria for adopting smart spaces, and thus the invasiveness of smart objects must be limited and users' control on data collection must be enabled.

Henrich C. Pöhls—Supported by EU H2020 grant n°780315 (SEMIoTICS).

N. Streitz and S. Konomi (Eds.): HCII 2020, LNCS 12203, pp. 322–335, 2020.
https://doi.org/10.1007/978-3-030-50344-4_23

Data protection laws, like the mentioned GDPR in the EU, require—among other things—to "minimise the amount of collected data" [3] and that the data subject, which is the individual person whose personal data is handled, needs to give their informed consent a-priori to the data gathering process and must be able to intervene. There are different technical mechanisms to achieve the recommendation that "Device manufacturers should limit as much as possible the amount of data leaving devices" [3]. For instance, reasearch findings from the EU-funded project RERUM (2016)[1] sparked works that allow for more configurable privacy and data minimisation of private information such as location) [4–6]. And clearly, the need for privacy(-by-design) is acknowledged not only within the EU [7], but also elsewhere, e.g. Canada [8].

Following the EU's GDPR the data subject has the right to intervene or update/revoke their consent. M. Weiser's vision of ubiquitous computing [9] partly become reality, with smart things that monitor us directly or indirectly in our physical surrounding: in our smart homes [10], in the smart city with smart street lamps[2], and smart buildings[3].

Allhoff et al. [11] also outlined that even if the monitored inhabitant of a such a smart space, i.e. the legal data subject, would have been informed of the personal information being collected and would have given consent, there will still be occasions were they would not want to leave the usual traces in the smart space, e.g. during private celebrations. However, after having initially consented to the collection there would still be occasions were one would like to object and avoid to leave the usual traces in the smart space, e.g. if you hide easter eggs, secretly prepare birthday cakes, have surprise parties or play Papa Noël.[4]

Furthermore, as we are at the level of physical interaction with smart spaces, we propose that the human-computer interaction interface for those dynamic adaption of consent should also be a physical one. We would like to extend the statement that "Truly smart gadgets should have built-in intelligence"[5] [12], such that the users of those smart gadgets shall be enabled to easily adjust the data collection dynamically to provide them "[...] the ability to perceive and control who is observing or disturbing a user in her private territory [...]" [13]. In this work we introduce first the general requirement for dynamicity in consent and then discuss physical-interaction based human-computer-interaction (HCI) concepts—physical both in the signalling of the inhabitants' wish of consent and in the signalling of the smart devices' or smart spaces' current collection activity. In the following, we first discuss our first contribution of the notion of dynamicity in Sect. 2 and then discuss existing related works that allow physical interaction with the privacy settings within the SmartHome use-case Sect. 3, before we conclude in Sect. 4.

---

1 `ict-rerum.eu` (accessed 30 Nov 2019).

2 https://www.tvilight.com (accessed 30 Nov 2019).

3 https://www.greenerbuildings.eu (accessed 30 Nov. 2019).

4 These examples emerged from several open discussions with users of IoT enabled spaces we conducted in preparation of this work.

5 Proclaimed by Tony Fadell, the inventor of Nest thermostats.

2 New Concepts: Dynamicity of Consent and Physical Interaction Patterns

In this work we introduce two new concepts: dynamicity of consent and physical interaction patterns. The terminology are briefly distinguished and defined in this section.

2.1 Definition: Dynamicity of Consent for Data Collection in the Physical Space

We would define the general concept of changing consent for data collection in a physical surrounding, in contrast to the virtual world, e.g. when browsing the WWW, in a dynamic manner as follows:

> *Dynamicity of consent allows the user who is subject to data collection in the physical space the user interacts with to adapt their consent to a defined set of rules for data collection.*

In EU GDPR [1] terms the user is known as the 'data subject' and thus dynamic consent enables data subjects to change their informed consent dynamically from (partial or full) opt-in to (partial or full) opt-out or vice-versa. In the following we will use the term context, there are two contexts in our environment: the context of the physical world, with buttons and sensors and actuators; and the virtual context, requiring the use of additional devices for the interaction, like smart phones, tablets, computers, touch screens. In this respect the notion of a context switch would mean that the user is required to change between the contexts to fulfil a task, e.g. a switch from physical to virtual interfaces would be to take out the smartphone, open an app to dim the light. From the perspective of the user the following requirements shall be fulfilled:

- *change of consent requires no context switch*
- *checking current status requires no context switch*
- *the currently signalled status is correctly representing the data collection*

The final point requires that the system is designed and deployed such that a certain data collection would not be carried out if the visual suggests to the user that it is not taking place, i.e. no malicious application can circumvent the indication of the current status [14].

2.2 Definition: Physical Switch

> *A physical switch allows the user, who is subject to data collection in the physical space that the user interacts with, to change their consent to a different defined set of rules for data collection by a physical interaction.*

In this context it is important to note, that our current work sees voice commands not as a physical interaction. This has several advantages, firstly an attacker could not carry out the change and maliciously re-enable previously disabled data collections from a distance, e.g. not like the laser attack on voice-enabled which allows to inject commands over long-distances of line of sight [15] or by maliciously playing non-hearable commands [16,17]. Secondly, it allows to use the physical gesture or interaction as a stronger signal signalling informed consent.

2.3 Definition: Physical Kill Switch

A physical kill switch allows the user, who is subject to data collection in the physical space that the user interacts with, to physically either completely disable the data collection or reduce it to a defined lower level by a physical interaction.

This is slightly different to the physical switch, that would not require the data collection opt-out to be physically enforced or at least physically diminished. An obvious example for a kill switch is to take the battery out of a device or put a covering lid over a camera.

2.4 Kill Switch Compared Normal Switch

Both, the physical kill switch as well as the physical switch, can be used to opt-in or opt-out of data collection. For a discussion of opt-in or opt-out and problems the reader shall turn to other works, e.g. [8,18,19]. We note no effect with respect to the general opt-in vs. opt-out discussion whether or not the switch is physical or virtual. Thus, both switches suffer from the generic problem of how they should be initially configured.

The subtle difference is that the physical *kill* switch is defined to physically diminish or remove the device's ability to collect the data in question. This means that when a *normal* switch is turned to the 'off' position the device could still technically gather the data and signal the back-end to not safe or process the data further, i.e. it can still physically collect the data. The beauty of having a user physically interact with the device allows to use the physical switch to also physically disable (or diminish) the device's ability, i.e. the power supply is physically disconnected, or the sensor physically blocked.

Note that the information of the current consent, i.e. if the user allows data being currently collected or not, is not part of the information that the physical switch is trying to disable.

Finally, whether or not this physical blockage is easy to understand or note for the average user is not part of the differentiation. If it is easy to note for the user, the physical kill switch often also doubles as a physical indicator, which we define next.

2.5 Definition: Physical Status Indicator

A physical status indicator allows the user to physically perceive the current state of the data collection it is subject to while acting within this space.

Note, this makes two important underlying assumption: Firstly, the user understands what level of data collection means what level of privacy-invasiveness, which requires that the user needs to be previously informed about the consent. Secondly, the status indicated must not be circumvented maliciously [14].

3 Use-Case and Examples

Taking the terminology previously sated, we are briefly describing and discussing different physical kill switches and physical status indicators of data collections; we do not strictly limit ourselves to those in IoT or smart home scenarios when it comes to widely used existing ones.

3.1 Physical Kill Switches

Many physical kill switches found in existing products offer a physical gesture and result in two or more visually different positions of the switch, thus they immediately can serve as physical status indicators as described in Subsection 3.3. Examples of kill switches are physical switches which require physical interaction to opt-out or opt-in into data collection, but instead of programmatic switching the status of data collection they physically diminish the ability to collect certain data. However, as a physical switch usually has different states, e. g., on- and off-state, they can also serve as physical indicators for the state they control. Different in their physical feedback to switches are push buttons, as they do not have a state; so even though they are physical they offer no indication of their position by themselves; but they require a physical interaction with the human user.

In general, the same discussion on opt-in being better than opt-out for privacy is the same in the physical world as in virtual worlds and has been discussed there, e. g., for cookies and tracking in websites.

As an example take the Amazon Echo depicted in Fig. 1. The device has "[...] a microphone off button that electronically disconnects the microphones"[6]. The device features a physical push button, for which the device manufacturer claims it controls the power supplied to the audio collection circuit and thus physically disables the all device's microphones. It also turns an LED-illuminated ring to the color red. The state survives reboots, but the transparency, i.e., the understandability, of the physical disablement of the data collection is not as obvious as a physical lid that covers a camera (Fig. 4, 5), or a physically disconnected sensor (Fig. 3). To make sure that it is not maliciously tampered with might require skilled third-parties to confirm the physical kill by testing a device sample (e.g. someone who dissects such hardware to see if it truly disables the power[7]).

---

[6] https://www.amazon.com/Alexa-Privacy-Hub (accessed Nov. 2019).
[7] Compare the attacks to bypass the indicator of a webcam [14].

Fig. 1. Amazon's button to turn off the microphone and the red-illuminated ring as an indicator [www.amazon.com/Alexa-Privacy-Hub] (Color figure online)

3.2 Physical Status Indicators

Regardless of the way data collection is controlled, there is the possibility to offer feedback in the physical world about the current status of the data collection. Probably the most common example of such an indicator is a visual indication by turning on a light emitting diode (LED). This can be found on many devices, e.g. on voice-controlled products the "[...] button turns red [when] the microphone is off. The device won't respond to the wake word or the action button until you turn the microphone on again."[8]. Additionally, other visual feedback can be provided, e.g. as depicted in Fig. 1 the red-illuminated ring also signals that microphones and thus voice data collection is turned off. On the contrary, when data is being collected "[...] a blue light indicator will appear or an audio tone will sound [...]"[9].

Another example of a physical status indicator is the LED next to many webcams, that shall light-up while the device is capturing images. This is a visual that is well understood by human users and allows to identify when live images are captured, however it usually does not flash when still images are taken.

A note on the security requirements on status indicators: Special care needs to be taken to make sure the status indicator would stay in-sync with the data acquisition, e.g. Apple build their hardware such that usually software would not be able to turn on the live-imaging without turning on the light, i.e. the visual indicator is paired in hardware. "Since the LED is controlled by the same output that controls STANDBY [meaning the camera is not capturing], there is no danger that firmware on the EZ-USB could deassert STANDBY and turn the LED off [...]" [14]. We say 'usually' because researchers were able to modify the hardware's programming (firmware) to enable the capturing while still signalling that the camera is in "STANDBY" and thus "[...] control the LED without affecting the operation of the image sensor." [14]. However, it is out of scope to discuss the security of the status indicator operation in this paper.

[8] https://www.amazon.com/Alexa-Privacy-Hub (accessed Nov. 2019).

[9] https://www.amazon.com/Alexa-Privacy-Hub (accessed Nov. 2019).

Noteworthy, for the physical status indicators—the same for software ones—it is a requirement that the indicator is always truly reflecting the current state of the data collection.

Fig. 2. External disconnect-able microphone serves as both (a) physical kill switch and (b) indicator; taken from the Candle IoT project [www.candlesmarthome.com]

Fig. 3. Big red handle serves as both (a) physical switch and (b) indicator for the Candle IoT project's carbon sensor [www.candlesmarthome.com] (Color figure online)

3.3 Mixes of Switch and Status Indicators

As mentioned earlier, a lot of examples offer physical kill switches serve a double role and also function as physical status indicators. For example, the switch in Fig. 3 also serves as an indicator. Following the designer's statement the "big red toggle will automatically move to the correct position to indicate it's no longer sending data. This allows you to always figure out if the device is currently transmitting data, even when looking at it from across the room."[10]. Other switches might provide more subtle status indicators, e.g. the camera being covered and some orange-red-coloured plastic appears as depicted in Fig. 4 and 5. Another way of switching on or off data collection is to disconnect the sensors relevant for data collection physically, as depicted in Fig. 2. Except for the first one, depicted in Fig. 3, the physical kill switches also physically hinder the data collection, i.e. covering or disconnecting the sensor. We thus introduced a distinction of the physical kill switch from the physical switch as discussed in Sect. 2.

A completely different form of physical interaction was for example executed during a security and privacy related conference (S&P conference in May 2019): They distributed black stickers that participants had to stick on their badges if they did not want to be filmed. This is again an opt-out, and signals privacy non-consent in the physical world. Technically, it would be possible to create recognisable visuals that people put on visible areas on their body for cameras

[10] https://www.candlesmarthome.com/jesse-howard-innovations (accessed Dec. 2019).

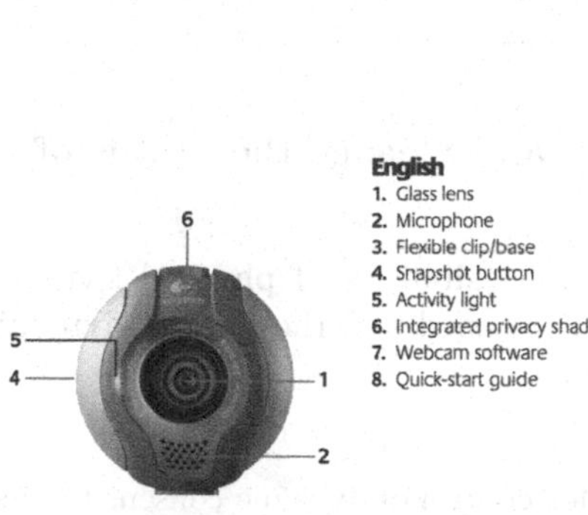

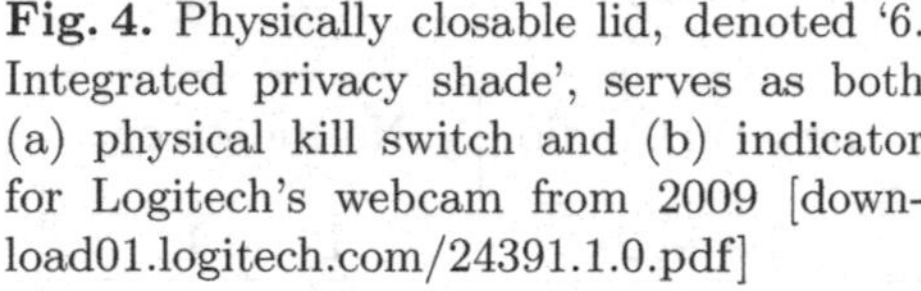

Fig. 4. Physically closable lid, denoted '6. Integrated privacy shade', serves as both (a) physical kill switch and (b) indicator for Logitech's webcam from 2009 [download01.logitech.com/24391.1.0.pdf]

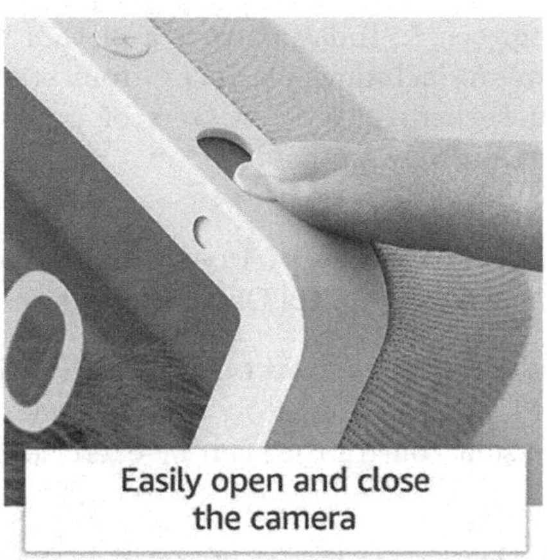

Fig. 5. Physically closable lid acts as both (a) physical kill switch and (b) indicator for the camera build in the Amazon Echo Show 5 [www.amazon.com/Alexa-Privacy-Hub]

to pick-up and recognise to then consequently blur their faces locally before forwarding their images. As a side note, of course this shall not be confused and lead to the discussion if criminals would abuse those stickers to blur their images on security cameras. This is not acceptable, but areas that require constant video monitoring for security should also be limited. To conclude this side discussion, this work's scope is on the ability of legally opting out of data collection dynamically due to changes in the privacy-invasiveness tolerate-able by users due to changes in their situations.

Another example is the updates Amazon made to their devices of the models including a camera, named Echo Show: Compared to earlier models they added a "[...] built-in shutter [that] also lets you easily cover the camera." as depicted on their website and reproduced as Fig. 5. Noteworthy to say, Amazon is not the first to produce this hardware kill switch for their camera-including products, many notebook vendors, amongst them market leaders Lenovo[11], HP[12]; also some early external USB webcams already had the physical lid on them, e.g. the 1.3 MP Webcam C500 V-U0006 from 2009 featuring an "integrated privacy shade" (see Fig. 4). Note that this switch was not continued throughout all models of

[11] See for example Lenovo's Blog Post from 2010 on the ThinkCentre M90z http://blog.lenovo.com/en/blog/watch-that-webcam (accessed Jan. 2020).

[12] See for example the top-listed feature of "a physical shutter to protect from malicious surveillance." https://www8.hp.com/uk/en/solutions/computer-security.html (accessed Jan. 2020).

Logitech[13]. Today there is a plethora of webcam covers as physical add-ons for camera-including products, from sticky tape, as used quite famously by Mark Zuckerberg [20], to stickers of pro-privacy NGOs[14], to 3D-printed covers for certain webcam models[15].

3.4 Overview of Possibilities to Signal and Change the Status of Consent to Data Collection

Table 1 gives an overview how the discussed possibilities of physical switches and physical indicators for feedback can be combined and the level of dynamic consent control that can be exercised by them.

Table 1. Combination of switch and indicator for control of dynamic consent (higher level means better control; above level 2 is recommended)

Switch \ Indicator	Visual	Haptical/Audio	No Indicator
Physical Switch	Level 3	Level 2	Level 1
Physical Kill Switch	Level 5	Level 4	Level 1
No Switch	Level 1	Level 1	Level 0

We have categorized the control that can be exercised into four ascending levels, starting from level 0 that allows no easy physical control of the data collection activities. We suggest any smart environment to achieve at least level 2 for an interactive physical consent management, thus we have marked those as grey in Table 1. The following descriptions, especially the examples, of the levels are written explicitly in non-technical language to allow them to be used to ask participants in a more formal user study. In all levels we assume that the user did give informed consent to data collection before the first interaction, i.e. during initial setup.

Level 0: In the physical environment the user does not know if data is currently being collected and he can not change the current data collection. The user can only go to a website or interact with an app on its mobile to see the current status and change the current data collection.
Example 0: User does not know if the smart home currently collects any data and can not change that without opening an app on the smartphone.

[13] For example there are third-party vendors selling physical covers, like for the Logitech C920 Webcam https://www.youtube.com/watch?v=2uNMcJXt0fo (accessed Jan. 2020).

[14] https://supporters.eff.org/shop/eff-sticker-pack (accessed Dec. 2019).

[15] https://www.thingiverse.com/thing:2003903 (accessed Dec. 2019).

Level 1: In the physical environment the user either does not know if data is currently being collected or the user can not change the current data collection from within the physical environment. The user still has to go to a website or interact with an app on its mobile to either see the current status of the data collection or change the current data collection.
Example 1a (no indicator, but switch): User can flip a physical switch, but then has to go to an app on the smartphone to see if its really changed the data collection.
Example 1b (no switch, but indicator): User can see a physical indicator, e.g. a red blinking LED, but then has to go to the app on the smartphone to turn off the data collection.

Level 2: In the physical environment the user is able to change the current data collection and on change is provided with a haptical or acoustical feedback. The user either has to interact with the switch again to receive feedback of the current data collection or go to a website or interact with an app on its mobile to see the current status of data collection.
Example 2a (vibration after toggling switch): User can flip a physical switch, which then vibrates twice if data collection is turned off or once if its turned on.
Example 2b: (spoken announcement after pressing a physical button): User can press a physical button, which then results in an audible announcement like 'collection off' if data collection is turned off or 'collection on' if collection is turned from off to on.

Level 3: In the physical environment the user is able to change the current data collection by a physical interaction and on change the user is visually provided with the current status. Thus the user does neither need to physically interact with the switch again to receive feedback of the current data collection, nor does need to switch to a website or an app.
Example 3 (LED changes color after pressing a physical button): User can press a physical button, which then results in an LED to glow in green color if data collection is turned off or glow in red color if collection is turned on.

Level 4: In the physical environment the user is able to change the current data collection and on change is provided with a haptical or acoustical feedback. The user either has to interact with the switch again to receive feedback of the current data collection or go to a website or interact with an app on its mobile to see the current status of the data collection. Additionally, the user's action physically intervenes with the sensor's ability for collecting the data[16].
Example 4: (spoken announcement after pressing a physical button): User can press a physical button, which then results in an speaker giving a spoken announcement like 'collection off' if data collection is physically disabled and thus turned off or 'collection on' if collection is turned on.

Level 5: In the physical environment the user is able to physically interrupt the current data collection by a physical interaction and the user can review the

[16] We note here, that of course the fact that data is not being collected is information that can still be collected.

current status easily by visual inspection. Thus the user does neither need to physically interact with the kill switch again to receive feedback of the current data collection, nor does need to switch to a website or an app. Additionally, the user's action physically intervenes with the sensor's ability for collecting the data[17].

Example 5 (visual indicator plus a physical kill switch): User can remove the sensor's cable, which physically disconnects the power to the sensor, which results in the sensor to stop glowing white and stop working which means that the collection is turned off; plugging it in will result in it starting to glow white and to collect data again.[18]

Table 2 shows which level the previously discussed real-life examples from Sect. 3 achieve. This table and the collected examples are by no means complete, finding real-life examples for the other levels is left for further research.

Table 2. Levels of physical control over dynamic consent reached real-world examples

Switch \ Indicator	Visual	Haptical/Audio	No Indicator
Physical Switch	**Level 3:** Big-handed switch (Fig. 3)	Level 2: -	Level 1: –
Physical Kill Switch	**Level 5:** disconnect-able microphone (Fig. 2); lid over webcam (Fig. 4,5); red LED on powerless, thus muted microphones (Fig. 1)	Level 4: –	Level 1: –
No Switch	**Level 1:** LED next to laptop webcam	Level 1: –	Level 0: –

3.5 Initial User Pre-study

We did conduct a very initial pre-study by open discussions with selected user groups. This was conducted to initially understand if users would value the concept of dynamic consent. We fully disclose all the details in this subsection. We did interview two groups: The first group consisting of five computer science students that are technically savvy and privacy-aware and a group consisting of eight normal users that were explained the ideas of living in a smart home

[17] We note here, that of course the fact that data is not being collected is information that can still be collected.

[18] We are aware that a non-glowing sensor would not enable the user to distinguish from a malicious or faulty sensor that is plugged-in and collecting data but not glowing; however we wanted to convey to users an example that physically disconnects the data gathering device.

environment. Both were presented the concept of dynamic consent and the idea of having physical switches to control the data collection of devices, e.g. presence monitoring and behavioural monitoring, using some of the real-world examples as given in this paper. Note, that the second group was not chosen totally distinct, it included older people and people exposed to new technology as users only, i.e. parents and friends of the computer science students from the first group.

As expected the first group explained that one might want to technically control the devices' ability to communicate with external servers, e.g. "flash open source firmware", "run your own MQTT-server locally", and "give suspicious devices no Internet by using a firewall rule" where among the answers. None of the participants found the concept of physical interaction bad in principle, some stated that they might not need it as they "already put tape over the laptop's webcam", or raised concerns that they might be "too lazy to get up to turn certain device functions physically off and thus leave it always on".

The second group—the group of normal users—seemed mostly reluctant to put technical 'gadgets' into their homes themselves and made statements, like "I do not want my home to always spy on me", which indicated to us that they have to be considered as privacy-aware as well. After being explained the concept of dynamic consent and physical interactions to control the consent, the members of the second group liked the idea, mainly making statements indicated that this allows them being "in control of all that technical stuff". During the discussion members of the second group also came up with more concrete usage scenarios: "having a switch near the front door which turns all monitoring on only when I want it".

As mentioned, due to the setup and the open discussions we had with them, the results can not be considered a user study, but we wanted to share the initial feedback we gathered. More structured interviews with focus groups especially including not-yet privacy-aware users would be beneficial for further research.

4 Conclusion

Clear and informed consent from the legal data subject is essential for smart spaces in order to comply to legal requirements and for human users in order to wisely adopt privacy-invasive technologies [21]. While in general, most users provide their consent to data collection mechanisms during initial device configuration, only few are aware of available interaction mechanisms with their smart surroundings for adjusting already accepted data collection terms.

We describe the concept of physically giving consent and also signalling the current state of data collection through visual, haptical, or audio feedback. This enables to interact easily and enables dynamically adaptable consent to data collection; a concept which we introduced in this paper as well. The concept describes how to leverage state-of-the-art devices' physical interfaces to dynamically empower users to dynamically adapt their consent to change from an already defined level of consent to data collection to another one. This means the user can make a physical interaction with the user's physical surroundings to control the data collection the smart devices in the user's physical surroundings are gathering.

This way the user regains some control over the privacy invasion by smart things, as Könings et al. put it "The goal of territorial privacy is to control all physical or virtual entities which are present in the user's virtual extended territory in order to mitigate undesired observations and disturbances, and to exclude undesired entities from the private territory." [22]. Especially, the physical interaction with consent controls requires no change of context, i.e. the user does not have to use an app on the smart phone—switch to the virtual context—to dynamically change the consent to a physical spaces's data collection.

Further research is needed to show which other physical switches and feedback mechanisms are possible and what combinations thereof, and how users conceive more precise implementations of the concept.

Acknowledgment. H. C. Pöhls was partially funded by the European Union's H2020 grant n°780315 (SEMIoTICS). This paper reflects only the authors' views.

References

1. European Parliament and the Council of the European Union: Regulation (EU) 2016/679 of the European Parliament and of the Council of 27 April 2016 on the protection of natural persons with regard to the processing of personal data and on the free movement of such data, and repealing Directive 95/46/EC (General Data Protection Regulation). Off. J. **OJ L**, 1–88, May 2016. 119 of 4.5.2016
2. OECD: The OECD Privacy Framework (2013). http://oecd.org/sti/ieconomy/oecd_privacy_framework.pdf. Accessed Jan 2020
3. EU Article 29 Data Protection Working Party (WP 223): Opinion 8/2014 on the Recent Developments on the Internet of Things, pp. 1–24, September 2014
4. Pöhls, H.C., et al.: RERUM: building a reliable IoT upon privacy- and security-enabled smart objects. In: Wireless Communications and Networking Conference Workshop on IoT Communications and Technologies (WCNC 2014), April 2014, pp. 122–127. IEEE (2014)
5. Tragos, E.Z., et al.: Enabling reliable and secure IoT-based smart city applications. In: Proceedings of the International Conference on Pervasive Computing and Communication Workshops (PERCOM 2014), March 2014, pp. 111–116. IEEE (2014)
6. Staudemeyer, R.C., Pöhls, H.C., Watson, B.W.: Security and privacy for the Internet of Things communication in the SmartCity. In: Angelakis, V., Tragos, E., Pöhls, H.C., Kapovits, A., Bassi, A. (eds.) Designing, Developing, and Facilitating Smart Cities, pp. 109–137. Springer, Cham (2017). https://doi.org/10.1007/978-3-319-44924-1_7
7. Danezis, G., et al.: Privacy and data protection by design - from policy to engineering. Tech. rep. European Union Agency for Network and Information Security, December 2014
8. Cavoukian, A.: Privacy by design: the 7 foundational principles. Revised Version. http://www.privacybydesign.ca/content/uploads/2009/08/7foundationalprinciples.pdf. Accessed Nov 2019
9. Weiser, M.: Some computer science issues in ubiquitous computing. Commun. ACM **36**(7), 75–84 (1993)

10. Frizell, S.: This Startup is Trying to Create - and Control - the Internet of Your Home. Time Mag. **184**(1) (2014). https://time.com/magazine/us/2926387/july-7th-2014-vol-184-no-1-u-s/
11. Allhoff, F., Henschke, A.: The Internet of Things: foundational ethical issues. Internet of Things **1**, 55–66 (2018)
12. Vella, M.: Nest CEO Tony Fadell on the future of the smart home. Time Mag. **184**(1) (2014). https://time.com/magazine/us/2926387/july-7th-2014-vol-184-no-1-u-s/
13. Könings, B., Schaub, F.: Territorial privacy in ubiquitous computing. In: 8th International Conference on Wireless On-Demand Network Systems and Services, pp. 104–108. IEEE (2011)
14. Brocker, M., Checkoway, S.: iSeeYou: disabling the MacBook webcam indicator LED. In: 23rd USENIX Security Symposium (USENIX Security 14), pp. 337–352 (2014)
15. Sugawara, T., Cyr, B., Rampazzi, S., Genkin, D., Fu, K.: Light commands: laser-based audio injection on voice-controllable systems (2019). https://lightcommands.com/. Accessed 13 Dec 2019
16. Zhang, G., Yan, C., Ji, X., Zhang, T., Zhang, T., Xu, W.: Dolphinattack: inaudible voice commands. In: Proceedings of the 2017 ACM SIGSAC Conference on Computer and Communications Security, pp. 103–117. ACM (2017)
17. Roy, N., Shen, S., Hassanieh, H., Choudhury, R.R.: Inaudible voice commands: the long-range attack and defense. In: 15th USENIX Symposium on Networked Systems Design and Implementation (NSDI 18), pp. 547–560 (2018)
18. Karegar, F., Gerber, N., Volkamer, M., Fischer-Hübner, S.: Helping john to make informed decisions on using social login. In: Proceedings of the 33rd Annual ACM Symposium on Applied Computing, SAC 2018, New York, NY, USA, pp. 1165–1174. Association for Computing Machinery (2018). https://doi.org/10.1145/3167132.3167259
19. Johnson, E.J., Bellman, S., Lohse, G.L.: Defaults, framing and privacy: why opting in-opting out. Mark. Lett. **13**, 5–15 (2002)
20. The Guardian - Alex Hern: Mark Zuckerberg tapes over his webcam. Should you?, June 2016. https://www.theguardian.com/technology/2016/jun/22/mark-zuckerberg-tape-webcam-microphone-facebook. Accessed Dec 2019
21. Rosner, G., Kenneally, E.: Clearly opaque: privacy risks of the Internet of Things. In: Rosner, G., Erin, K. (eds.) Clearly Opaque: Privacy Risks of the Internet of Things, 1 May 2018. IoT Privacy Forum (2018)
22. Könings, B., Schaub, F., Weber, M.: Privacy and trust in ambient intelligent environments. In: Ultes, S., Nothdurft, F., Heinroth, T., Minker, W. (eds.) Next Generation Intelligent Environments, pp. 133–164. Springer, Cham (2016). https://doi.org/10.1007/978-3-319-23452-6_4

Towards a UX Assessment Method for AI-Enabled Domestic Devices

Davide Spallazzo(✉), Martina Sciannamé, and Mauro Ceconello

Department of Design, Politecnico di Milano, 20158 Milan, Italy
davide.spallazzo@polimi.com

Abstract. Artificial Intelligence is increasingly integrating into everyday life and is becoming an increasingly pervasive reality. Domestic AI-enhanced devices are aggressively conquering new markets, nevertheless such products seem to respond to the taste for novelty rather than having a significant utility for the user, remaining confined to the dimension of the gadget or toy. Interestingly, although AI has been indicated as a new material for designers, the design discipline has not yet fully tackled this issue. Moving from these premises, the MeEt-AI research program aims at developing a new UX assessment method specifically addressed to AI-enhanced domestic devices and environments. Accordingly, we frame the project within the vast and variegated field of UX assessment methods, focusing on three main aspects of UX assessment – methodology, UX dimensions and analyzed objects – by looking at what current methods propose from the standpoint of AI-enhanced domestic products and environments. What emerges are general considerations that are at the basis of the positioning of the MeEt-AI research program.

Keywords: User experience · Assessment method · Artificial Intelligence · Domestic environment

1 Introduction

1.1 AI in the Domestic Environment

Today, computation is spreading throughout the physical space and across multiple devices to build environments that help people in their ordinary activities [1]. Undoubtedly, the integration of Artificial Intelligence (AI) into everyday life is becoming an increasingly pervasive reality, even if AI, for sure, is not new and brings us back to the theorization of the universal machine by Turing. Nevertheless, only the contemporary technological development has made it possible to create pervasive systems capable of simulating human behavior, finding significant application in various sectors (e.g. medicine, security, transport, education).

Given that conversational AI-based agents such as Amazon Alexa, are spread in more than 100 million houses [2], we may state that the domestic environment is increasingly populated by products that, based on learning algorithms, are able to adapt autonomously

N. Streitz and S. Konomi (Eds.): HCII 2020, LNCS 12203, pp. 336–347, 2020.
https://doi.org/10.1007/978-3-030-50344-4_24

to the context and the needs of users, entertaining a dialogue, recognizing them and tracking/anticipating their behavior.

Just looking at first party hardware, namely products that integrate AI agents developed by the same producers, in the third quarter of 2019, 28.6 millions smart speakers were sold across the world [3], with Amazon leading the market with 10.4 million shipments and about 32% market share, followed at great distance by Alibaba (3.9 million), Baidu (3.7 million), Google (3.5 million) and Xiaomi (3.4 million). To these million products we may add all those that embed AI agents from third party, being them speaker or other home appliances.

Even if not relevant in terms of market share, we may also mention an overabundance of personal and domestic robots (e.g. Asus Zenbo) provided with conversational agents and powered by AI, which accompany users across the house helping in more or less complex tasks.

Accordingly, we consider relevant to look at those products we see as representative of the first wave of materialization of AI in the domestic landscape, namely virtual assistants, trying to understand and frame the User Experience (UX) they entail. Indeed, given the great success of these devices on the market, it becomes mandatory for the design discipline to reflect on their real potential on the one side and the meaning of use on the other.

As a matter of fact, such products seem to respond to the taste for novelty rather than having a significant utility for the user, remaining confined to the dimension of the gadget or toy [4]. Moreover, they are not particularly significant in terms of quality of interaction, generating sometimes frustration and a basic use unable to unlock their potential [5]. A condition made evident by initiatives developed by the research centers of Amazon, Google, Microsoft such as glossaries, booklets or guidelines to support the design, also towards a human-centered approach (Google PAIR).

Surprisingly, so far, the world of design, and the academic one in particular, has not yet fully tackled this issue, although AI has been indicated as a new material for designers [6, 7] and some studies have analyzed machine learning as a design subject [8], the use of virtual assistants in everyday life [5] and their aesthetic-functional dimensions in the domestic realm [9]. If studies focused on conversational interfaces [10], reviewing the questionnaires available to date for the evaluation of user experience [11] we identified a gap in literature regarding UX assessment methods specifically designed to cope with the complex nature of AI-enhanced domestic devices and environments in a holistic manner.

Relying on these premises, we frame here preliminary reflections that are guiding the start of the MeEt-AI – Metadesign Evaluation Method for AI – research program, aimed at defining a new method specifically aimed to assess the user experience of domestic devices and environments powered by AI.

Describing the research program is not the aim of the paper, but it is worthy briefly outlining the MeEt-AI project in order to better frame the present contribution. Funded by the Department of Design of Politecnico di Milano as basic research, the 12 months project delves into the topic of UX in the era of AI, with the aim of understanding what does it mean – from a UX standpoint – to introduce other intelligences in the domestic environment. To meet this challenge, the project moves from the end, namely from

UX assessment, trying to understand which are the UX dimensions currently analysed, the employed tools and the studied systems. These elements will be at the basis of (i) assessment sessions of existing domestic AI-enhanced systems and subsequent (ii) co-design workshops involving researchers, designer, early adopters, companies active in the field. The aim is understanding the dimensions and tools that better describe these complex and novel ecosystems and introducing new ones. Accordingly, a new assessment method will be formulated and validated through (i) confrontation with international experts and (ii) multiple assessment sessions with a relevant sample of users. The reflections here discussed lay in the very beginning of the project and configure this contribution as a position paper.

1.2 UX Evaluation: A Variegated Picture

Since the emergence of the term User Experience (UX) around the turn of the millennium, researchers looked for novel ways of understanding and evaluating the quality-in-use of interactive systems [12]. Leading this transition, initially started in the HCI field, was the feeling that contemporary evaluation methods were too tied to the usability and efficiency of systems, overlooking more general but no less important aspects such as quality, pleasantness and meaning.

Accordingly, over the years several researches advanced diverse methods to understand, conceptualize and support the design for meaningful experiences with interactive systems [13], thus animating a debate resulting from different epistemological standpoints. At the same time, the scope of the analyses gradually moved from the mere instrumental and task-oriented evaluation of usability to include, pleasure [14], positive emotions [15] and aesthetics [16] just to name a few.

The academic world, alone or in collaboration with companies, as well as consulting agencies, actively embraced this new perspective resulting in a plethora of publications more or less directly dealing with the UX evaluation for interactive systems, being them industrial products, digital interfaces or services. Eventually, the proposed solutions spanned from specific tests [17], to the implementation of evaluative tools [18–23] to more comprehensive and broad methodologies [24–27].

The large amount of material produced, soon led researchers to take stock of the situation, trying to classify and analyze all the tools and methods proposed. In 2010 Vermeeren et al. [28] collected 96 relevant and original UX evaluation methods, coming from academia and industry, and categorized them according to different parameters. The analyzed methods mostly applied to digital interfaces (e.g. websites and mobile apps) and to fully functional systems or to working prototypes, thus intervening at an advanced stage of development. These methods collected equally – and sometimes both – qualitative and quantitative data, gathered mostly from one user at a time.

One year later, Bargas-Avila and Hornbæk conducted a similar wide-ranging critical analysis focusing on empirical methods for the evaluation of the UX, with an in-depth enquiry of 51 publications out of the 1254 resulting from researches on digital libraries [12]. Their study portrayed a prevalence of digital interfaces as analyzed systems and a tendency to assess the overall UX as well as less traditional dimensions of UX such as affect, emotion, enjoyment, aesthetics, appeal and hedonic qualities. They also evidently showed that researchers mostly used self-developed questionnaires and that traditional enquiry methods such as questionnaires, interviews, diaries were the most commonly employed to collect qualitative data.

In 2017, Rivero and Conte [29] conducted a systematic analysis of UX evaluation methods for digital interfaces, identifying 227 relevant papers out of 2101 retrieved. Their results do not substantially differ from those of the previously mentioned researches: the enquiry methods are mostly traditional (e.g. questionnaires, observation) and employed with samples of final users in a controlled environment, during or after the experience of use. In contrast to the previously described analyses, this survey highlights a prevalence of quantitative data as main outcome of the UX evaluation.

Analogously, Pettersson and colleagues conducted a systematic analysis on 100 academic papers, written between 2010 and 2016, describing empirical studies on UX evaluation with a specific attention to reliability, by specifically addressing the triangulation of methods in UX assessment [30, 31]. This up-to-date analysis of the state-of-the-art highlights results comparable to the studies above discussed. In particular the overall UX and the pragmatic qualities (usability) are the most addressed UX dimensions, digital interfaces are the most commonly evaluated products and self-developed questionnaires are frequently employed as enquiry method. The authors further point out a current tendency to employ – and triangulate data from – diverse methods of inquiry in order to better understand and frame the results.

Interestingly, in their paper presented at CHI 2018 [31] the authors highlight four open questions for next UX research that perfectly match those guiding the MeEt-AI research program. In particular they point out: the need of further guidelines and practical examples for effective combinations of different methods, a lack of a significant number of studies focusing on the early stages of the project and on users' expectations, the need to address complex systems based upon diverse touch points/devices and finally the necessity to cope with ever evolving technologies and non-human intelligences.

2 Framing the Approach: Preliminary Reflections

2.1 AI-enhanced Domestic Devices

The current panorama of AI powered devices portrays a great dominance of first party smart speakers as show by the data reported at the beginning of the article. They appear to be the first massive embodiment of AI in the domestic landscape, and as such, functions highly influence the general [9]: as a consequence, looking at the simple physical appearance, these devices are nothing more than discreet ornaments. Nevertheless, the simple appearance betrays a complexity determined by numerous features that make such products difficult to analyze from a UX point of view.

The main evident characteristic is that they are not just "simple products", but actually ecosystems consisting of several interfaces and touch points. As a matter of fact, most of them integrate multiple interfaces – namely physical, digital, conversational – sometimes overlapping. Being an ecosystem means also communicating with – and even control – other devices: a condition particularly evident for domestic devices, that commonly act – or are supposed to act – as control hub for home entertainment and for an ever-growing number of connected objects in complex dynamic environments such as our homes.

A second element of complexity can be found in their technological core, based on learning algorithms (machine learning) and neural networks (deep learning). This means that the same device could provide different outputs at the same input over time, a condition that can affect UX evaluation if conducted in traditional ways.

To increase the complexity of these devices, at least from an UX evaluation standpoint, there's the fact that their real potential is rarely exploited by the majority of users which mainly uses routine actions such as reading news, weather forecasting and controlling simple home appliances [5, 32]. A condition that may open on the one side a discussion on discoverability as that proposed by White [32], and on the other a deeper reflection on the meaning smart speaker may have in our daily life.

The elements above listed, that in our opinion make AI-powered smart speakers complex or even wicked artifacts, are at the basis the MeEt-AI research project, which aims to address these issues working on both the methodologies and the dimensions of UX to be explored.

Concurring with Bargas-Avila and Hornbæk [12], we argue that three areas of interest for the project are the methodologies to be applied, the dimensions of the user experience as well as the kind of products to be analyzed. Accordingly, in the next sections we reflect on both methodological and content-related issues, advancing preliminary reflections that will guide the start of the MeEt-AI project.

2.2 Considerations on the Methodological Approach

The complex nature of AI-powered home devices briefly described above entails a coherently deep reflection on the methodology to be adopted in order to evaluate the UX they may foster.

A first question to be addressed regards the specific nature of these devices, often characterized by different interfaces. Let's consider, for the sake of clarity, the case of Amazon Echo. It is a smart speaker with four physical buttons on the top: two of them raise and lower the volume, one activates Alexa – Amazon's AI-powered assistant – and the last turns the microphone off. A LED ring gives feedbacks employing 7 different colors – blue, orange, purple, white, red, yellow and green – in diverse configurations. Alexa can even be turned on and prompted through voice interface by simply saying "Alexa". Additionally, a companion mobile app allows users to set up the device and perform several actions including broadcasting music or turning on/off connected devices just to name a couple.

In order to assess the experience of use of Amazon Echo, we could certainly consider separately tasks involving one specific interface. Methods such as SUS [33], Kansei [34] AttrakDiff [35] can be employed to evaluate the usability/pragmatic or hedonic qualities of the product in its hardware side. Likewise, we could refer to the renowned Nielsen and Molich's heuristics [36] to assess the UI of the companion app, and eventually rely on specific methods to evaluate the UX of conversational interfaces [23, 37]. The open question is how to assess user experience in a comprehensive, holistic manner.

Analogously, we may encounter the same complexity considering the entire domestic ecosystem controllable through this smart speaker. So far, hundreds of devices can be connected to/controlled by Amazon Echo – e.g. light bulbs, doorbells, cameras, thermostats – creating an integrated system that finds in the smart speaker its hub. It is evident that the user experience enabled by an ecosystem of this kind can be different over time, and entails several touchpoints, be them physical, digital or based on voice interfaces. A complexity made evident since the emergence of the IoT paradigm, and the introduction of the first connected devices characterized by several touch points [31]. Again, how to evaluate the user experience in its totality is matter of discussion.

In our opinion, the possible ways to cope with this level of complexity are essentially two: (i) developing a bespoke method, eventually integrating existing methods or (ii) proposing a generic one, able to catch the essence of the overall experience. The second path seems the most popular, looking at the results emerging from the critical analysis of the existing UX evaluation methods. In Bargas-Avila and Hornbæk's study, 41% of the methods assess the generic UX [12] and the percentage rises to 56% in the more recent analysis by Pettersson and colleagues [31]. On the contrary, following the first path, thus assessing specific aspects related to different interfaces and multiple touchpoints requires a method vast and modular enough to be adapted to each specific case to be analyzed.

These choices necessarily involve a reflection on the temporal stage of the analysis: if the assessment of generic UX seems to best fit with evaluation sessions that happen before – thus focusing on expectations – and after use of the systems to be assessed, a more articulated analysis may need assessment during use, in order to gain reliable information not based on memory.

Analogously, defining a methodology means also taking a position in the long-lasting debate between the quantitative and qualitative approaches, that move from different epistemological standpoints, one considering UX as something quantifiable and the other considering simplistic the idea of measuring the experience [12, 31]. In their 2000 study, Vermeeren and colleagues found a fair distribution between methods employing quantitative only data, qualitative data only and both [28]. These percentages are different in the results discussed by Bargas-Avila and Hornbæk which found a predominance of pure qualitative methods (50%) in respect to quantitative ones (33%) and to those employing both (17%) [12]. In the more recent study by Rivero and Conte the percentages are completely reversed with about the 58% methods collecting quantitative data, 14% methods exclusively qualitative and finally 28% methods collecting both types of data [29]. Very dissimilar results may be motivated by different ways the researchers employed to filter the available articles used to conduct the study and, consequently, these results do not portray a reliable evolving picture. Nevertheless, in the divergences of the above listed studies we may recognize the need for triangulation of different methods postulated by [28] and studied by Pettersson and her colleagues [31], who underline a growing tendency to use more than one method to increase the reliability of the results.

We feel that a promising path to be followed in order to better understand the complex nature of the UX triggered by AI-enhanced domestic devices is meaningfully cross-referencing the data obtained by applying several methods. As a consequence, for now, our position in the debate on the value of qualitative and qualitative data to describe an experience places exactly in the middle, envisioning a multi-method approach, able to exploit both kinds of data. It is not surprising, then, that one of the first studies conducted specifically on Amazon Echo [5] adopted a multi-method strategy based on logs and qualitative interviews.

Another topic of discussion is the assessed period of the experience. As shown in the studies used as reference across the article, different methods take into account different time spans of experience ranging from specific snapshots/episodic activities, to episodes/specific tasks to long term usage [28]. Given the aim of the research project, namely to develop a method able to asses a multifaceted experience in a holistic way, the strategies we could envision are essentially two: (i) to assess diverse single episodes – that may refer to different interfaces or touch points – or (ii) to consider the entire experience – during or after the experience.

Furthermore, one of the main characteristics of AI-enhanced devices is that of being based on learning algorithms (machine learning) or neural networks (deep learning), that means that the same system may give different outputs to the same inputs over time. As a consequence, evaluating the experience across single episodes or even an entire day may result in data that is not completely reliable, whereas a longitudinal study may render a better picture of the user experience.

All the reflections made since now take the usage as reference, but it is evident that some issues that may emerge during an UX assessment can be better addressed in an early stage of development. As underlined by two studies regarding specifically Amazon's products [5, 32], it is evident how their real potential is rarely exploited, often due to poor discoverability and lack of proactivity. In particular, understanding the real usefulness and meaning of interacting with an alter intelligence embedded in an object is something to be anticipated in the concept phase. Our impression is that an evaluation method addressing just the usage, even if properly designed, may only highlight few issues that can be coped with the iterations that commonly characterize the design process. Returning to the studies on Amazon's devices, it is clear that proactivity can partially solve problems connected to discoverability [32]. But it is equally true that a use of such device only for weather forecasts betrays some leaks in the reflection about the meaning of such a product in the home environment. As a consequence, we envision a method able to be applied even in the early stages of a product development.

2.3 Reflections on UX Dimensions

The above-mentioned reflection on the meaning of interacting with AI-enhanced domestic devices opens up the discussion regarding the UX dimensions. They are at the core of any assessment method and, more than other features, they change over time reflecting an ever-evolving way of understanding and framing UX.

Relying again on comprehensive analyses of UX methods [12, 31] we may state that generic UX is by far the most investigated dimension, even if its definition is actually unclear. As reported in [12], generic UX is mostly assessed with qualitative methods and seems to refer to an overall perception of the experience. Analogously, generic UX is defined as a general construct in [31], something that can be assessed in a holistic way. As already discussed in the previous section, looking at the overall experience could allow to manage complexity in multi interfaces and multi touchpoints systems, but at the same time it may be limiting, and incapable of providing relevant feedbacks in the design process.

Pragmatic qualities – namely usability – are the second more assessed qualities in the study by [31] and surprisingly they were not even present as UX dimension 7 years before in [12]. A condition that seems to describe an intentional initial detachment from usability issues – to mark the new approach – and a subsequent new inclusion. In a previous study on domestic AI-enhanced devices [9], we highlighted how some of the most sold ones are not completely tackling usability questions, lacking deep reflection on the basics of interaction design, such as input, output and feedback modalities. For example, one of the results of the analysis is that the AI-enhanced devices under examination offer almost no inherent feedback, as physical actions are required in a very limited manner; therefore, only functional feedbacks and augmented feedbacks seems to characterize the current domestic assistants [9]. Preliminary reflections of this kind suggest that pragmatic issues cannot be taken for granted and should be assessed, especially in early stages.

Nevertheless, there is no doubt that dimensions such as pleasantness of use, emotion/affect, enjoyment, play a prominent role in the UX, especially in a domestic context. Not surprisingly, these dimensions are the most assessed ones after the general UX [12, 31] and groups such as the Delft Institute of Positive Design run by Desmet and Pohlmeyer specifically focus on these dimensions. As a matter of fact, reflecting on how the integration of AI capabilities into domestic products and environments could work towards (positive) emotions is, for sure, a matter of design as shown by Google's installation *A Space for Being* at Fuorisalone 2019, where three multi-sensorial domestic environments have been used to affect visitors' emotional state, (partially) tracked through wristbands.

The reflection on the emotional response to objects/environments entails a consideration on the aesthetics/hedonic qualities of products. Our preliminary study on the embodiment of AI capabilities in the domestic environment [9] highlights two main formal trends, one related to speaker-like devices and the other to robot-like sci-fi ones, formal solutions driven by their preeminent and different functional purpose: on the one hand smart speaker whose main evident characteristic is the conversational interface and on the other devices aimed at triggering social contact. What comes up is a still immature reflection on the embodiment of AI in the domestic landscape and the consequent need to address the aesthetic dimension in the assessment method, especially in the early prototyping phases.

The UX dimensions discussed till now are more or less addressed by the methods developed in the last twenty years as shown in [12, 31]. Nevertheless, our preliminary impression is that current assessment methods are not completely able to address the meaning of interacting with other intelligences embedded in domestic devices and environments. Understanding sense and meaning as describable – and even assessable – constructs in the UX is at the same time one of the main efforts of the MeEt-AI research program and a challenging aim. The meaningfulness of a UX, in fact, entails a reflection on the physical context, very often not considered in current paradigms, as well as on the social one. Furthermore, it implicates a strict correlation with users' background and motivations as well as with their ethical positions. Accordingly, the research program will explore these issues as potential UX dimensions, understanding when and how they could be addresses during the design process.

2.4 Addressing the Analysis

The third element of discussion regards the objects of analysis: what kind of objects/systems the novel method will assess?

The answer to the question is anything but simple. As highlighted across the article, the first wave of materialization of AI in the domestic environment has the shape of speakers or sci-fi robots that can be controlled through several interfaces and that are able to connect with hundreds of other devices thanks to an ever-growing number of protocols. Taking the current situation as a reference, the objects of analysis could be several, ranging from the physical device (e.g. the smart speaker) and its companion app, to the conversational interface and even to associated/controlled devices.

Nevertheless, thinking of AI as only embedded in this kind of devices may be simplistic and, in the next future, we could assist to the integration of AI capabilities in a wide range of domestic products or even the disappearance of physical touchpoints in favor of computational capabilities widespread across the house acting without user intervention to provide a seamless experience.

These considerations make evident the need of flexibility for the evaluation method to be designed, that, in our opinion, should be capable of addressing a wide range of interfaces and touchpoints both considering them in their specificity and as part of a more complex ecosystem.

3 Final Remarks

The paper retraces the theoretical reflections that are guiding the start of the MeEt-AI research program, trying to frame it within the vast and variegated field of UX assessment methods.

In particular the effort made is that of discussing three main aspects of UX assessment – namely methodology, UX dimensions and analyzed objects [12] – by looking at what current methods propose from the standpoint of AI-enhanced domestic products and environments. What emerges are general considerations that are at the basis of the positioning of the MeEt-AI research program, useful in a very preliminary phase to better define the project's aims and approach.

Even if still very blurry, the portrait of the new UX assessment method we have outlined along the pages has some general characteristics listed below.

Following the considerations made in the previous pages, the new method should be able to address complexity by zooming in and out, so as to allow both an overall and detailed view. Furthermore, it must be carefully designed to be applied at different stages of the design process, with a particular focus on the early phases, that we consider particularly relevant and crucial.

We envision a multi-method approach able to cross-reference different data that can be gathered through both quantitative and qualitative analysis, and, eventually, across a long-lasting experience. In addition, the method should allow a multi-dimensional analysis able to capture both the overall UX and specific dimensions, including meaning.

Finally, the method should be valid for a great variety of interfaces and touch points, since the analyzed systems very often entail a complex ecosystem and we are not still aware of the future directions of AI in the domestic realm.

References

1. Kaptelinin, V., Nardi, B.A.: Acting with Technology: Activity Theory and Interaction Design. The MIT Press, Cambridge (2009)
2. Bohn, D.: Exclusive: Amazon says 100 million Alexa devices have been sold (2019). https://www.theverge.com/2019/1/4/18168565/amazon-alexa-devices-how-many-sold-number-100-million-dave-limp
3. Canalys Newsroom- Canalys: Amazon smart speaker shipments crossed 10 million mark in Q3 2019. https://www.canalys.com/newsroom/worldwide-smartspeaker-Q3-2019. Accessed 30 Jan 2020
4. Levinson, P.: Toy, mirror, and art: the metamorphosis of technological culture. ETC Rev. Gen. Semant. **34**, 151–167 (1977)
5. Sciuto, A., Saini, A., Forlizzi, J., Hong, J.I.: "Hey Alexa, What's Up?": a mixed-methods studies of in-home conversational agent usage. In: Proceedings of the 2018 Designing Interactive Systems Conference, New York, NY, USA, pp. 857–868. ACM (2018). https://doi.org/10.1145/3196709.3196772
6. Antonelli, P.: AI is design's latest material (2018). https://design.google/library/ai-designs-latest-material/
7. Holmquist, L.E.: Intelligence on tap: artificial intelligence as a new design material. Interactions, **24**, 28–33 (2017). https://doi.org/10.1145/3085571
8. Dove, G., Halskov, K., Forlizzi, J., Zimmerman, J.: UX design innovation: challenges for working with machine learning as a design material. In: Proceedings of the 2017 CHI Conference on Human Factors in Computing Systems, New York, NY, USA, pp. 278–288. ACM (2017). https://doi.org/10.1145/3025453.3025739
9. Spallazzo, D., Sciannamè, M., Ceconello, M.: The domestic shape of AI: A reflection on virtual assistants. In: DeSForM 2019 Beyond Intelligence (2019)
10. Vitali, I., Arquilla, V.: Conversational smart products: a research opportunity, first investigation and definition. In: DeSForM 2019. Beyond Intelligence (2019)
11. Kocaballi, A.B., Laranjo, L., Coiera, E.: Measuring user experience in conversational interfaces: a comparison of six questionnaires, 4 July 2018. https://doi.org/10.14236/ewic/HCI2018.21
12. Bargas-Avila, J.A., Hornbæk, K.: Old wine in new bottles or novel challenges: a critical analysis of empirical studies of user experience. In: Proceedings of the SIGCHI Conference on Human Factors in Computing Systems, New York, NY, USA, pp. 2689–2698. ACM (2011). https://doi.org/10.1145/1978942.1979336
13. Hassenzahl, M., Tractinsky, N.: User experience - a research agenda. Behav. Inf. Technol. **25**, 91–97 (2006). https://doi.org/10.1080/01449290500330331
14. Jordan, P.W.: Designing Pleasurable Products: An Introduction to the New Human Factors. CRC Press, Cleveland (2000). https://doi.org/10.1201/9780203305683
15. Norman, D.A.: Emotional Design: Why We Love (or Hate) Everyday Things. Basic Books, New York City (2004)
16. Tractinsky, N., Katz, A.S., Ikar, D.: What is beautiful is usable. Interact. Comput. **13**, 127–145 (2000). https://doi.org/10.1016/S0953-5438(00)00031-X
17. Schmettow, M., Noordzij, M.L., Mundt, M.: An implicit test of UX: individuals differ in what they associate with computers. In: CHI 2013 Extended Abstracts on Human Factors in Computing Systems, Paris, France, pp. 2039–2048. Association for Computing Machinery (2013). https://doi.org/10.1145/2468356.2468722

18. Lugmayr, A., Bender, S.: Free UX testing tool: the LudoVico UX machine for physiological sensor data recording, analysis, and visualization for user experience design experiments. In: Proceedings of the SEACHI 2016 on Smart Cities for Better Living with HCI and UX, San Jose, CA, USA, pp. 36–41. Association for Computing Machinery (2016). https://doi.org/10.1145/2898365.2899801
19. Minge, M., Thüring, M., Wagner, I., Kuhr, C.V.: The meCUE questionnaire: a modular tool for measuring user experience. In: Soares, M., Falcão, C., Ahram, T.Z. (eds.) Advances in Ergonomics Modeling, Usability & Special Populations, pp. 115–128. Springer, Cham (2017). https://doi.org/10.1007/978-3-319-41685-4_11
20. Sivaji, A., Nielsen, S.F., Clemmensen, T.: A textual feedback tool for empowering participants in usability and UX evaluations. Int. J. Hum. Comput. Interact. **33**, 357–370 (2017). https://doi.org/10.1080/10447318.2016.1243928
21. Almeida, R.L.A., Darin, T.G.R., Andrade, R.M.C., de Araújo, I.L.: Towards developing a practical tool to assist UX evaluation in the IoT scenario. In: Anais Estendidos do Simpósio Brasileiro de Sistemas Multimídia e Web (WebMedia), pp. 91–95 (2018). https://doi.org/10.5753/webmedia.2018.4575
22. Zhou, Z., Gong, Q., Qi, Z., Sun, L.: ML-process canvas: a design tool to support the UX design of machine learning-empowered products. In: Extended Abstracts of the 2019 CHI Conference on Human Factors in Computing Systems, Glasgow, Scotland UK, pp. 1–6. Association for Computing Machinery (2019). https://doi.org/10.1145/3290607.3312859
23. Maguire, Martin: Development of a heuristic evaluation tool for voice user interfaces. In: Marcus, Aaron, Wang, Wentao (eds.) HCII 2019. LNCS, vol. 11586, pp. 212–225. Springer, Cham (2019). https://doi.org/10.1007/978-3-030-23535-2_16
24. Obrist, M., Roto, V., Väänänen-Vainio-Mattila, K.: User experience evaluation: do you know which method to use? In: CHI 2009 Extended Abstracts on Human Factors in Computing Systems, Boston, MA, USA, pp. 2763–2766. Association for Computing Machinery (2009). https://doi.org/10.1145/1520340.1520401
25. Kujala, S., Roto, V., Väänänen-Vainio-Mattila, K., Karapanos, E., Sinnelä, A.: UX curve: a method for evaluating long-term user experience. Interact. Comput. **23**, 473–483 (2011). https://doi.org/10.1016/j.intcom.2011.06.005
26. Jiménez, C., Rusu, C., Roncagliolo, S., Inostroza, R., Rusu, V.: Evaluating a methodology to establish usability heuristics. In: 2012 31st International Conference of the Chilean Computer Science Society, pp. 51–59 (2012). https://doi.org/10.1109/SCCC.2012.14
27. Otey, D.Q.: A methodology to develop usability/user experience heuristics. In: Proceedings of the XVIII International Conference on Human Computer Interaction Interacción 2017, Cancun, Mexico, pp. 1–2. ACM Press (2017). https://doi.org/10.1145/3123818.3133832
28. Vermeeren, A.P.O.S., Law, E.L.-C., Roto, V., Obrist, M., Hoonhout, J., Väänänen-Vainio-Mattila, K.: User experience evaluation methods: current state and development needs. In: Proceedings of the 6th Nordic Conference on Human-Computer Interaction: Extending Boundaries, Reykjavik, Iceland, pp. 521–530. Association for Computing Machinery (2010). https://doi.org/10.1145/1868914.1868973
29. Rivero, L., Conte, T.: A systematic mapping study on research contributions on UX evaluation technologies. In: Proceedings of the XVI Brazilian Symposium on Human Factors in Computing Systems, Joinville, Brazil, pp. 1–10. Association for Computing Machinery (2017). https://doi.org/10.1145/3160504.3160512
30. Pettersson, I., Frison, A.-K., Lachner, F., Riener, A., Nolhage, J.: Triangulation in UX studies: learning from experience. In: Proceedings of the 2017 ACM Conference Companion Publication on Designing Interactive Systems, Edinburgh, United Kingdom, pp. 341–344. Association for Computing Machinery (2017). https://doi.org/10.1145/3064857.3064858

31. Pettersson, I., Lachner, F., Frison, A.-K., Riener, A., Butz, A.: A bermuda triangle? A review of method application and triangulation in user experience evaluation. In: Proceedings of the 2018 CHI Conference on Human Factors in Computing Systems, Montreal, QC, Canada, pp. 1–16. Association for Computing Machinery (2018). https://doi.org/10.1145/3173574.3174035
32. White, R.W.: Skill discovery in virtual assistants. Commun. ACM **61**, 106–113 (2018). https://doi.org/10.1145/3185336
33. Brooke, J.: SUS: a quick and dirty usability scale. Usability Eval. Ind. **189**, 4–7 (1995)
34. Schütte, S., Ayas, E., Schütte, R., Eklund, J., Ayas Alikalfa, E.: Developing software tools for kansei engineering processes: Kansei Engineering software (KESo) and a design support system based on genetic algorithm. In: 9th International Quality Management for Organizational Development (QMOD) Conference, 9–11 August, Liverpool, England (2006)
35. Hassenzahl, M.: The effect of perceived hedonic quality on product appealingness. Int. J. Hum. Comput. Interact. **13**, 481–499 (2001). https://doi.org/10.1207/S15327590IJHC1304_07
36. Nielsen, J., Molich, R.: Heuristic evaluation of user interfaces. In: Proceedings of the SIGCHI Conference on Human Factors in Computing Systems, Seattle, Washington, USA, pp. 249–256. Association for Computing Machinery (1990). https://doi.org/10.1145/97243.97281
37. Pyae, A., Joelsson, T.N.: Investigating the usability and user experiences of voice user interface: a case of Google home smart speaker. In: Proceedings of the 20th International Conference on Human-Computer Interaction with Mobile Devices and Services Adjunct, Barcelona, Spain, pp. 127–131. Association for Computing Machinery (2018). https://doi.org/10.1145/3236112.3236130

Inverting the Panopticon to Safeguard Privacy in Ambient Environments: An Exploratory Study

Ingvar Tjostheim[1] and John A. Waterworth[2](✉)

[1] Norwegian Computing Center, P.O. Box 114, Blindern, 0314 Oslo, Norway
Ingvar.Tjostheim@nr.no
[2] Umeå University, Main Campus, 901 87 Umeå, Sweden
jwworth@informatik.umu.se

Abstract. Jeremy Bentham is known for designing an institutional building, a prison named a panopticon and some alternatives to this concept. One of the alternatives are the inverted or constitutional panopticon in which the purpose is to let the governed, the citizens' see and monitor the governors. Hence, the concept of inverted panopticon can be used to describe an analyze privacy protecting devices. In this paper we report on a national study on citizens' opinion and attitudes to devices that can protect the user from being seen and listened to, with 1289 participants. At this stage of the work, we have not done statistical analysis of factors that might reveal differences between citizens, but as an exploratory study, we provide an overview of how the two privacy protecting devices were received by Norwegian citizens, based on survey responses. Our aim is to build a foundation for future studies that will investigate the inverted panopticon concept in a society in which personal data has become a currency.

Keywords: Privacy · Personal data · Privacy protection · Privacy enhancing technologies

1 Introduction

In today's digital economy we pay for technological services with our data (Elvy 2017). Our data is used to build profiles, for advertising and marketing. In the loT context, the collection of data does not end after the consumer purchases a device online or in a store, but instead increases once the consumer begins to use the device, as well as accessible websites and mobile applications (Elvy 2018). In a review article on AmI (ambient intelligence), Augusto et al. (2010) asks: "*how can you defend your privacy if wearing networked devices makes you trackable everywhere you go?*" This question is becoming more and more relevant to everyday life. According to Streitz et al. (2019) the big challenges for ambient intelligence concern two trade-offs: "*Keeping the human in the loop and in control ... (and) Ensuring privacy by being in control of making decisions over the use of personal data vs. intrusion of often unwanted, unsupervised*

N. Streitz and S. Konomi (Eds.): HCII 2020, LNCS 12203, pp. 348–361, 2020.
https://doi.org/10.1007/978-3-030-50344-4_25

and importunate data collection methods as a prerequisite of providing smartness, for example, in terms of smart services."

In this paper we are primarily concerned with privacy and not with how data can be used to offer customized services. The current study builds on findings from two national consent studies (Tjostheim and Waterworth 2020) in which we tested willingness to share personal data and attitudes towards the use of data to build personal profiles and assess susceptibility to phishing. Our analysis indicated that a willingness to share data makes users vulnerable to phishing. This is only one aspect that illustrates that the citizen is the weaker party in the data and services economy. In these two national studies, in response to the statement: "*it should be made harder to collect data and build digital profiles*", 75% and 69%, respectively, indicated full or partial agreement. The studies revealed particularly strong negative attitudes towards the sharing of data with third parties and the analysis of data "*to learn as much as possible about their users,*" with 89% negative and 86%, respectively, responding negatively.

There is an asymmetry of knowledge or power if we are monitored without being aware of the monitoring. Some authors use the metaphor a one-way mirror to explain how it works (Cyphers and Gebhart 2019). Even more well-known is panopticism, a term that first was used for the architectural design of a prison by Jeremy Bentham. Usually, we think of a panopticon as embodying an oppressive, top-down system of observation and control, with Big Brother watching us, as in Orwell's 1984. But Bentham distinguished between four different types of panopticon. In this paper, we focus on his constitutional panopticon, as described in Constitutional Code (Bentham 1830). We use this also referred to as the inverse panopticon, or reversed panopticon; (Galič e al. 2017) as a theoretical concept within an explorative study of users of apps and smart environments.

For most readers the word panopticon has a negative connotation. But with an inverse panopticon, there is envisaged to be a bottom-up surveillance through which governing functionaries are monitored through panoptic methods (Brunon-Ernst 2013) rather than the other way around. Mann (2004) calls this sousveillance or watching from below through procedures of using technology to mirror and confront bureaucratic organizations (Mann et al. 2003).

In the Constitutional Code the focus is on the governing functionaries of public officials, ministers in a government. In this architectural arrangement the prime minister is in the center, in an oval shaped building but without the central inspection tower. The key to good behavior, good government, according to Bentham is transparency and publicity – the many should watch the few rather than the other way round.

The literature on the inverse panopticon is sparse, but research on privacy and the sharing on personal data gives us an indication on what we might expect. Given the widespread concern about how data is used and shared with third parties (Barth and de Jong 2017; Preibusch 2013), we expected that the inverse panopticon concept will be perceived as a meaningful and useful concept, but we have not identified any studies with large samples on this subject. Against this backdrop, our research addresses citizens' perspectives on surveillance and the inverse panopticon within ambient environments. The most well-known devices are perhaps smart speakers, but in a modern house smart-home technologies to control light, temperature and door-locks are also common.

In the present study we focus on attitudes towards devices that the citizen could use to protect privacy, which can be termed inverse panopticon applications.

2 Method

We carried out the study in cooperation with a market research companies PollStat AS, to achieve our aim of national studies on an issue affecting a broad section of the population. The market research company uses quota sampling to provide a sample that is nationally representative in terms of age, gender, education and geographical region. In our survey, we targeted citizens 16–69 years old.

From the national panel of online users, we recruited 1289 participants. In Norway, nearly all citizens own a smartphone and therefore a high percentage are categorized as online users. There are citizens that are hard to recruit in surveys, these are primarily citizens with very low socio-demographic characteristics, but for this study they are not a targeted group. In a longer perspective it is likely that IoT devices will be even more common among all groups of citizens.

The national bureau of statistics in Norway, Statistics Norway, has the demographic profile of Norwegians in the population register. In the first table we compare the profile of our respondents with a similar survey but not from the national bureau of statistics. The market research company cannot recruit directly from the population registry, but it is a goal to recruit a sample with a similar profile. Table 1 shows that our sample is similar to the sample of the ICT-survey named the use of ICT in Norwegian households by Statistics Norway, 2019.

Table 1. Educational profile of the participants in the survey.

	No answer	Primary education	Secondary education	University & college
Statistics Norway, targeted profile based on the population registry 2019 (N = 1865)	9%	19%	37%	35%
Statistics Norway, ICT-survey 2019 (N = 1011)	4%	18%	35%	42%
PollStat-survey 2020 (N = 1389)	–	14%	42%	45%

After asking the respondents about IoT-devices, we introduced two devices. The first was an application for smart speakers is an ultrasonic jammer that prevents smart speakers from recording human speech (Chen et al. 2019). A similar device was also featured in a later New York Times article (New York Times 2020). The second device was similar to the SpecEye application (Li et al. 2019), a screen exposure detection system that can be used to identify the presence of digital cameras. Another solution is AudioSentry, an application that hides reflections off the user from the sensing signal by covering them with the reflections from an obfuscation signal (Gao et al. 2019).

We presented the illustrated devices to respondents after the questions about digital profiles and privacy (see Fig. 1). Studies show that respondents can be influenced by the question order. According to Strack (1992), when respondents perceive survey questions as belonging to the same conversational context, the responses tend to adhere to Grice's (1975) principle of conversation, that is the content of previous conversation. "*When respondents answer questions that pertain to the ongoing conversation, they make their responses as relevant to the conversation as possible.*" (DeMoranville and Bienstock 2003: 2018)

We did not assume that the respondents had knowledge about devices such as the bracelet or a device that can detect cameras. Our assumption was that online users have limited knowledge about the idea of an inverse panopticon. The text above the four pictures was: "*PCs, tables, smartphones and smart speakers have cameras and microphones. They can be on or off. In some occasions you decide when they are on or off. In other occasions, the recording takes place without the possibility for you to check that this is happening. This is an example of a bracelet that is sending ultrasound to jam the microphones – as a consequence the audio-recording is damaged.*"

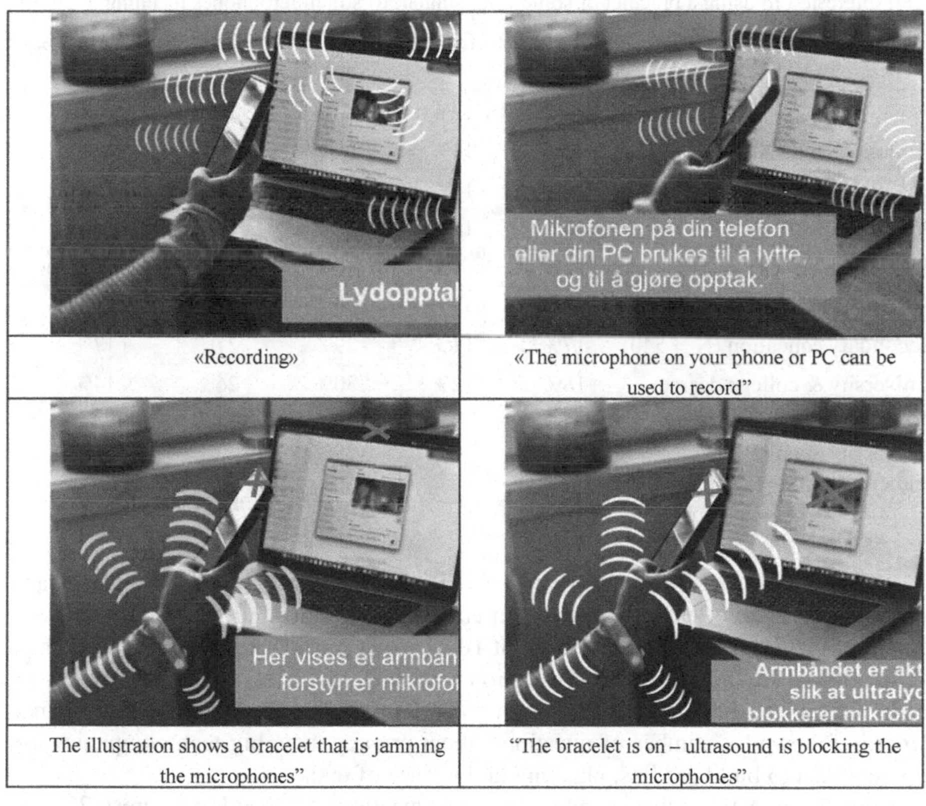

«Recording»

«The microphone on your phone or PC can be used to record"

The illustration shows a bracelet that is jamming the microphones"

"The bracelet is on – ultrasound is blocking the microphones"

Fig. 1. The Bracelet (the Norwegian text is translated under the pictures)

We decided to illustrate a bracelet similar to the one by the Chen et al. (2019). It is a prototype, but as an illustration it served our purpose. Since the survey started in January 2020, we could not use photos from the New York Times article (which was published February 14, 2020).

3 Results

3.1 Concerning Privacy Protecting Devices

After showing the illustrations we asked the respondents to choose an alternative from low interest to high interest. Table 2 shows that across gender, age and education 30% had low interest, 30% no opinion, and 40% were interested in a device jamming microphones. These numbers are for all that answered the survey regardless of use of IoT-devices.

Table 2. Demographics and attitudes to a device jamming microphones

I am interested in using a bracelet or something similar, to stop microphones listening					
	Very low	Quite low	Neither & nor	Quite high	Very high
Male (N = 625)	17%	12%	30%	28%	14%
Female (N = 664)	19%	11%	28%	27%	15%
16–29 years old (N = 400)	15%	14%	29%	29%	14%
30–49 years old (N = 479)	17%	11%	28%	29%	15%
50–69 years old (N = 410)	22%	9%	30%	24%	15%
Primary education (N = 175)	18%	13%	30%	25%	14%
Secondary education (N = 540)	17%	11%	29%	27%	17%
University & college degree, lower level (N = 380)	18%	12%	30%	26%	14%
University & college degree, higher level (N = 194)	21%	10%	25%	33%	11%

Many devices such as smartphones and PCs have cameras. Inside buildings and outdoors, there are often surveillance cameras. After the illustration about the bracelet for jamming microphones, we asked about a device that can detect cameras in the vicinity of the person. We did not use an illustration for his device, only text.

In the survey, the illustration about the bracelet and the question about surveillance cameras followed a number of questions about privacy, how big tech companies use personal data to build profiles, phishing and misuse of data.

Table 3 shows that across gender, age and education 25% had low interest, 25% no opinion, and 50% were interested in a device for detecting cameras in the vicinity of the person. Figures 2, 3 and 4 present these findings graphically.

Table 3. Demographics and attitudes to a device for detecting cameras

	Very low	Quite low	Neither & nor	Quite high	Very high
Male (N = 625)	12%	9%	25%	35%	19%
Female (N = 664)	16%	11%	24%	29%	21%
16–29 years old (N = 400)	10%	11%	23%	34%	22%
30–49 years old (N = 479)	13%	10%	24%	32%	21%
50–69 years old (N = 410)	19%	8%	26%	29%	18%
Primary education (N = 175)	14%	11%	27%	27%	21%
Secondary education (N = 540)	14%	8%	22%	32%	23%
University & college degree, lower level (N = 380)	12%	12%	26%	33%	17%
University & college degree, higher level (N = 194)	16%	10%	24%	32%	20%

The survey-data do not reveal demographic differences– 40% had an interest in using a jamming device. The patterns in Figs. 2, 3 and 4 are similar.

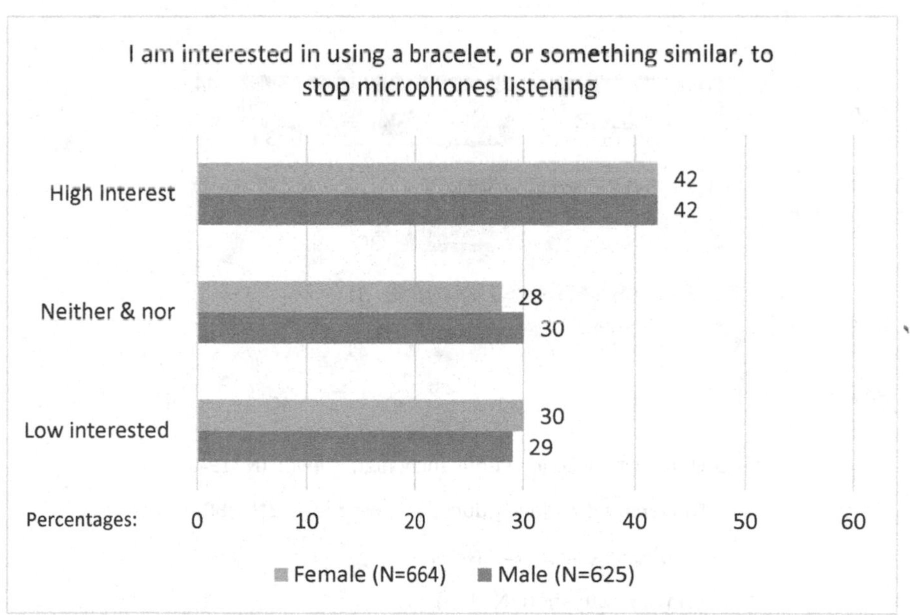

Fig. 2. Interest in the bracelet for different genders

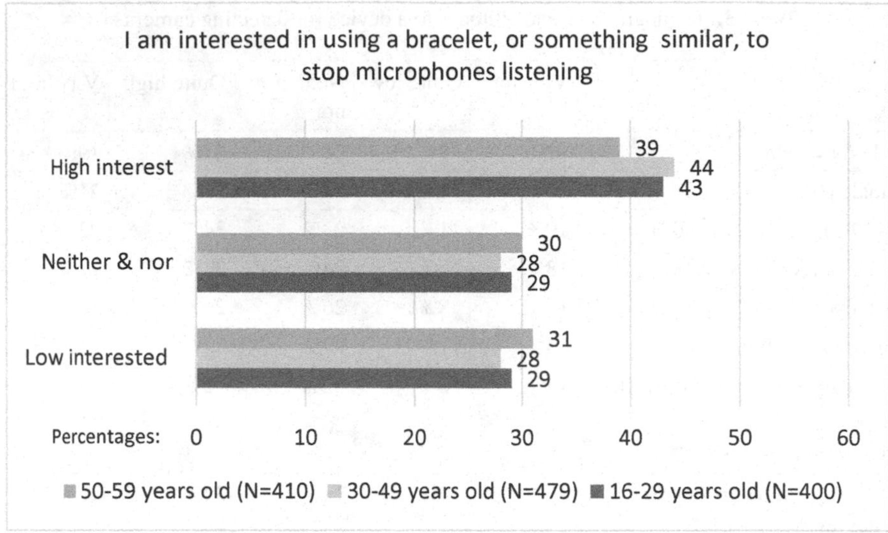

Fig. 3. Interest in the bracelet for different age groups

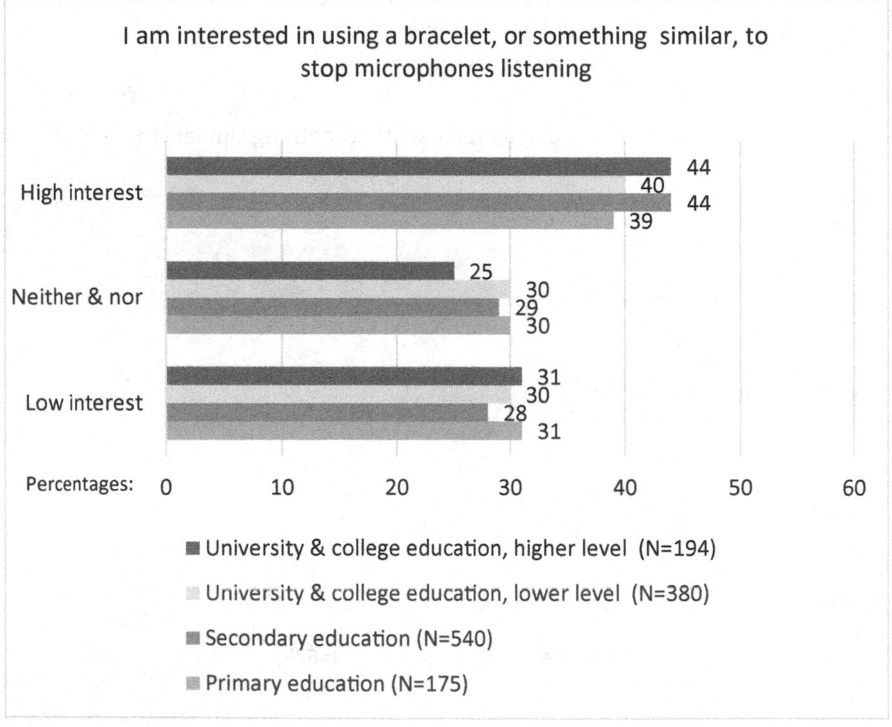

Fig. 4. Interest in the bracelet with different educational levels

Figures 5, 6 and 7 present the results for a device that can detect cameras. Figure 5 shows that approx. 50% of both male and female answered that were interested in using the device about twice as many that answered low interest. For all three age-groups, slightly more than 50% answer high interest (Fig. 6). Also, for all four educational groups, approximately 50% answered high interest twice as many as those who answered low interested (Fig. 7).

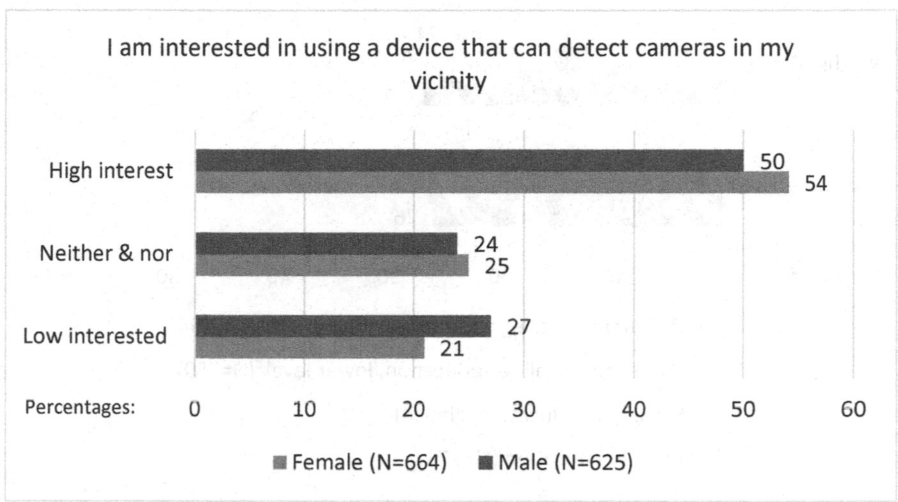

Fig. 5. Interest in a device for detecting cameras for different genders

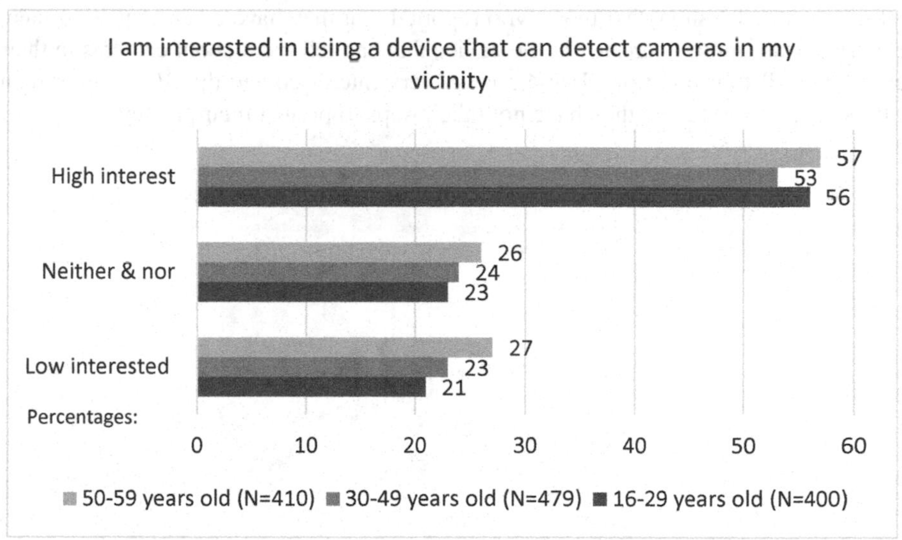

Fig. 6. Interest in a device for detecting cameras for different ages

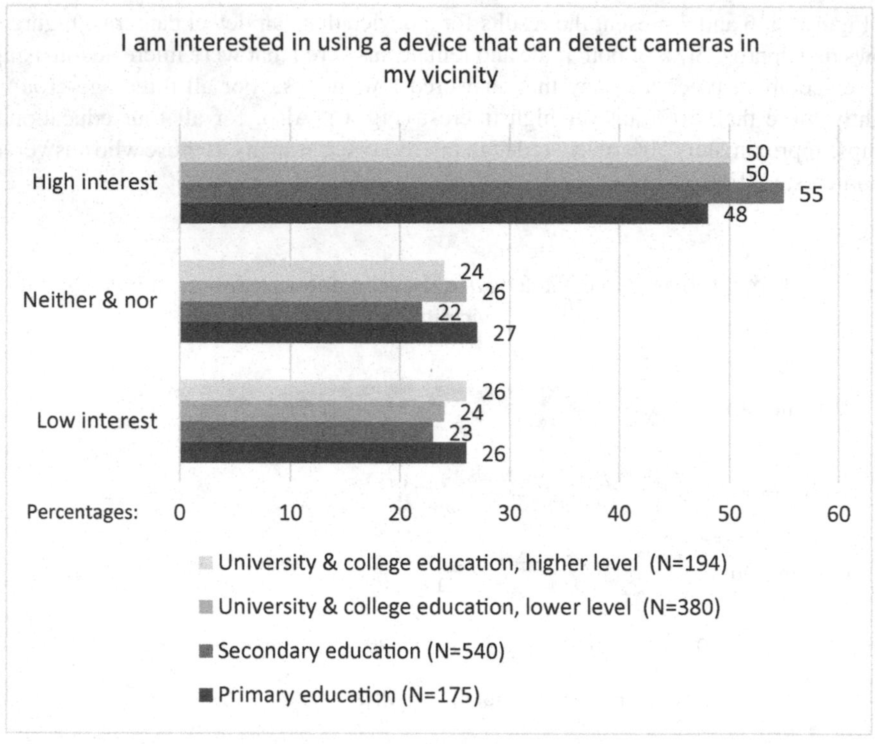

Fig. 7. Interest in a device for detecting cameras for different educational levels

Figures 8 and 9 show that those who reported that they have taken steps to protect their privacy are more interested in the device that can tell them about cameras in their vicinity. For all four questions 1-in-4 answer very interested and this 10% higher than for those that reported that they have not taken steps to protect their privacy.

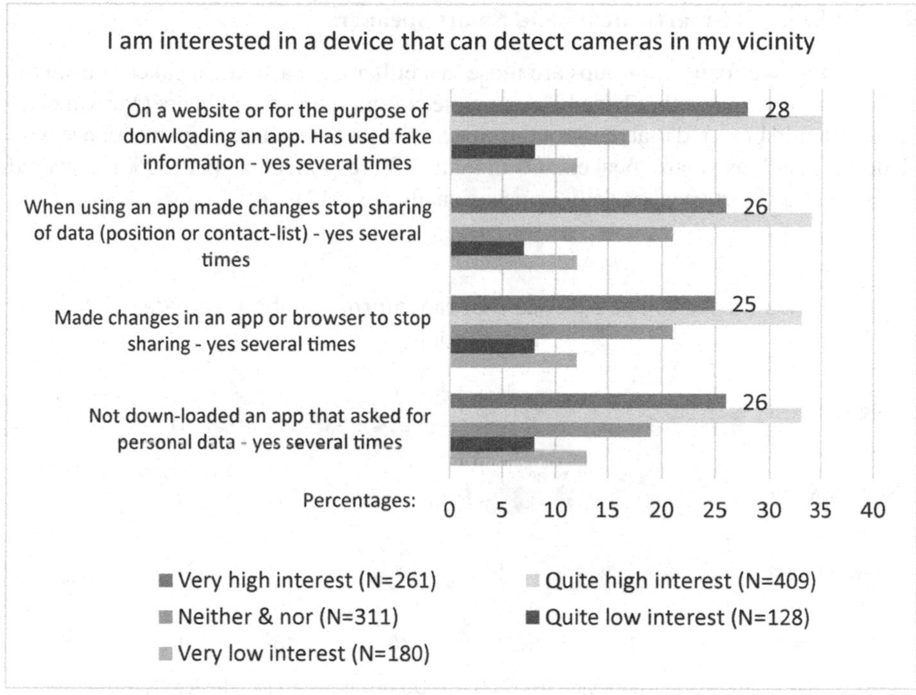

Fig. 8. The citizens who have taken steps to protect privacy

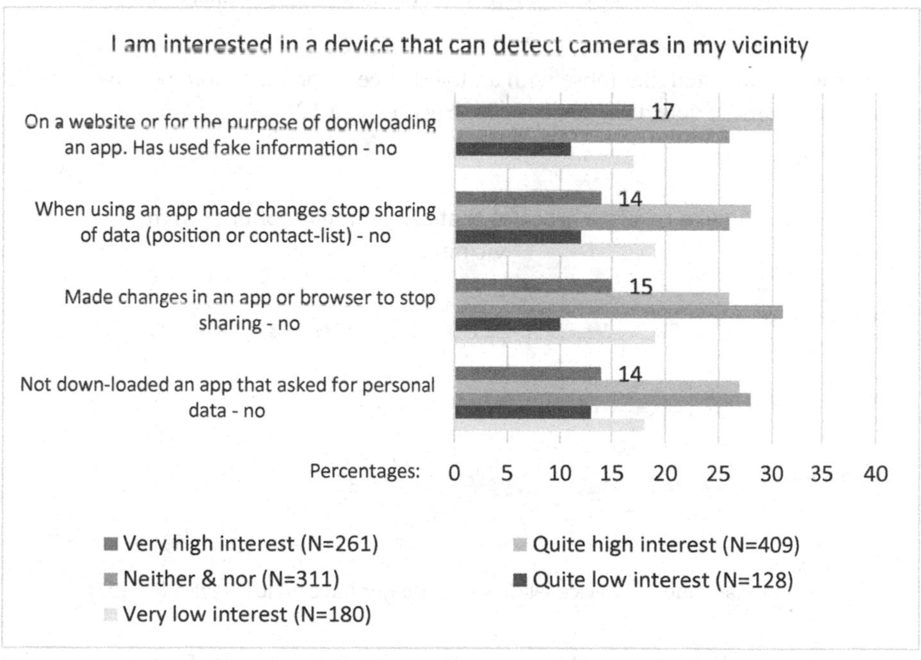

Fig. 9. The citizens who have not taken steps to protect privacy

3.2 The Users of Smartwatches and Smart Speakers

In this section we focus on groups are those that either have a smart speaker or a smartwatch, two IoT devices that have become quite common the recent years (Malkin et al. 2019). It should be noted that many of the citizens do not own or have any experience with IoT-devices such as smart speakers. Of in total 1289 respondents, 451 (32%) answered that they use a smart speaker daily or occasionally (Fig. 12).

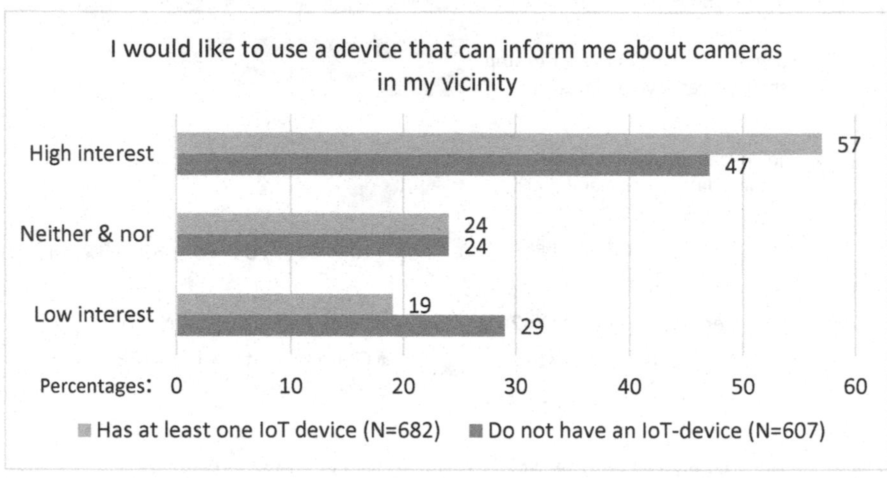

Fig. 10. Responses to a camera detecting device for those with or without an IoT device

The survey indicated that those with an IoT device responded more positively to the jamming and camera detection devices (see Figs. 11 and 12).

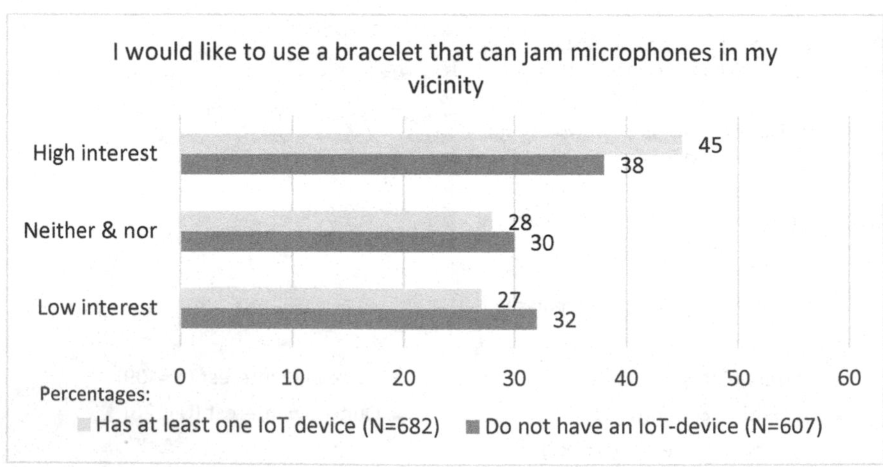

Fig. 11. Responses to a bracelet for those with or without an IoT device

There might be a difference between owning device, but not using it often and using the IoT device on a daily basis. We asked those with a smartwatch connected to the Internet and those with a smart speaker about daily use (see Fig. 12). In a survey, it is easier to answer a specific question than a more general one and to interpret the answers.

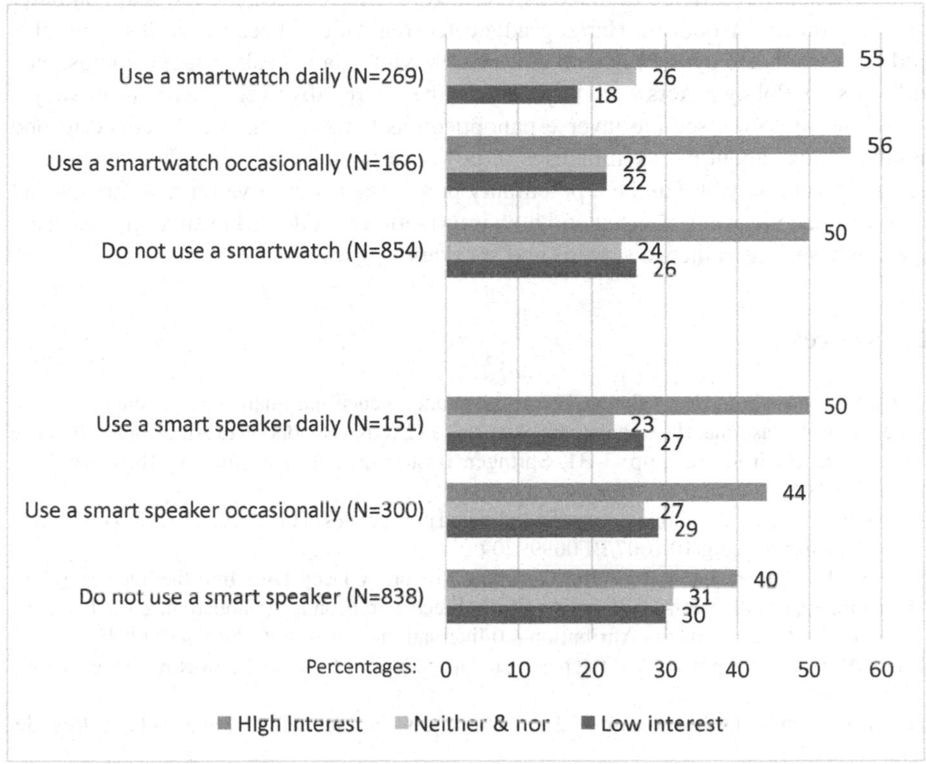

Fig. 12. Responses of citizens with/without an IoT smartwatch and a smart speaker

4 Discussion and Conclusions

How do we support users' decision-making regarding the collection and distribution of their data within ambient environments? For a possible approach to this difficult issue, we go back almost two centuries to the concept of the (constitutional) panopticon, as envisaged by moral philosopher Jeremy Bentham.

We presented two devices that are not consumer products today and we assume that the devices were new to the citizens. It is therefore not a surprise that many, approximately 30%, did not have an opinion. We illustrated the bracelet device with pictures. Then we asked about the opinion about this device and a similar device. Before that we had asked a number of questions about privacy. With reference to Starck (1992), we assume that many of the respondents already think about privacy when answering the question about the two devices. We do not think that the answers, their stated preferences, can necessarily be used as a good indication of revealed preferences (Ben-Akiva et al. 1994), their likely behavior. However, in an exploratory study such as this, the illustrations with questions serve our purpose. We have identified an interested in privacy protecting devices – approximately 40% answered that they were interested in using the devices.

In a newspaper article February 14 (New York Times 2020), the law and computer science professor Woodrow Hartzog advocated regulations because, in his view, this kind of surveillance by the big tech companies, with smart speakers and cameras, etc., will not stop. Policymakers need to pass laws that more effectively guard our privacy.

While we do not see the inverse panopticon as the single answer to concerns and dissatisfactions about the asymmetries of power in favor of the big tech companies in the digital economy, it may be a potentially promising perspective for new studies and design work concerning if, what and how information is collected in smart homes from equipment such as cameras, screens and speakers.

References

Augusto, J., Nakashima, H., Aghajan, H.: Ambient intelligence and smart environments: a state of the art. In: Nakashima, H., Aghajan, H., Augusto, J.C. (eds.) Handbook of Ambient Intelligence and Smart Environments, pp. 3–31. Springer, Boston (2010). https://doi.org/10.1007/978-0-387-93808-0_1

Ben-Akiva, M., et al.: Combining revealed and stated preferences data. Market. Lett. **5**(4), 335–349 (1994). https://doi.org/10.1007/BF00999209

Cyphers, B., Gebhart, G.: Behind the One-Way Mirror: A Deep Dive Into the Technology of Corporate Surveillance. A Publication of the Electronic Frontier Foundation, 2019 Released Under a Creative Commons Attribution 4.0 International License (CC BY 4.0) (2019)

Elvy, S.A.: Paying for privacy and the personal data economy. Columbia Law Rev. **117**(6), 1369–1459 (2017)

Elvy, S.A.: Commodifying consumer data in the era of the Internet of Things. B.C. L. Rev. **59**, 423, 446 (2018)

Barth, S., de Jong, M.: The privacy paradox – investigating discrepancies between expressed privacy concerns and actual online behavior – a systematic literature review. Telematics Inform. **34**(7), 1038–1058 (2017)

Bentham, J.: Constitutional code, vol. 1. Rosen, F. (ed.) Clarendon Press, Oxford, 1983 (1830)

Brunon-Ernst, A.: Beyond Foucault: New Perspectives on Bentham's Panopticon. Ashgate, London (2013)

Chen, Y., et al.: Understanding the Effectiveness of Ultrasonic Microphone Jammer, vol. 1, no. 1, April 2019 (2019). 17 pages

DeMoranville, C.W., Bienstock, C.C.: Question order effects in measuring service quality. Int. J. Res. Mark. **20**(3), 217–231 (2003)

Galič, M., Timan, T., Koops, B.-J.: Bentham, Deleuze and beyond: an overview of surveillance theories from the panopticon to participation. Philos. Technol. **30**(1), 9–37 (2017). https://doi.org/10.1007/s13347-016-0219-1

Gao, C., Fawaz, K., Sur, S., Banerjee, S.: Privacy Protection for Audio Sensing Against Multi-Microphone Adversaries (2019). https://doi.org/10.2478/popets-2019-0024

Grice, H.P.: Logic and conversation. In: Cole, P., Morgan, J.L. (eds.) Syntax and Semantics 3: Speech Acts, pp. 41–58. Academic Press, New York (1975)

Li, Z., Rathore, A.S., Chen, B., Song, C., Yang, Z., Xu, W.: SpecEye: towards pervasive and privacy-preserving screen exposure detection in daily life. In: The 17th Annual International Conference on Mobile Systems, Applications, and Services (MobiSys 2019), 17–21 June 2019 (2019)

Malkin, N., Deatrick, J., Tong, A., Wijesekera, P., Egelman, S., Wagner, D.: Privacy Attitudes of Smart Speaker Users (2019). https://doi.org/10.2478/popets-2019-0068

Mann, S., Nolan, J., Wellman, B.: Sousveillance: inventing and using wearable computing devices for data collection in surveillance environments. Surveill. Soc. **1**(3), 331–355 (2003)

Mann, S.: 'Sousveillance': inverse surveillance in multimedia imaging. In: 12th Annual ACM International Conference on Multimedia. ACM, New York (2004)

New York Times (2020). https://www.nytimes.com/2020/02/14/technology/alexa-jamming-bracelet-privacy-armor.html. Accessed 24 Feb 2020

Preibusch, S.: The value of privacy in web search. In: Proceedings of the Twelfth Workshop on the Economics of Information Security (WEIS) (2013)

Strack, F.: "Order effects" in survey research: activation and information functions of preceding questions. In: Schwarz, N., Sudman, S. (eds.) Context Effects in Social and Psychological Research, pp. 23–34. Springer, New York (1992). https://doi.org/10.1007/978-1-4612-2848-6_3

Streitz, N., Charitos, D., Kaptein, M., Böhlen, M.: Grand challenges for ambient intelligence and implications for design contexts and smart societies. J. Ambient Intell. Smart Environ. **11**(1), 87–107 (2019). Tenth Anniversary Issue

Tjostheim, I., Waterworth, J.A.: Predicting personal susceptibility to phishing. In: Rocha, Á., Ferrás, C., Montenegro Marin, C.E., Medina García, V.H. (eds.) ICITS 2020. AISC, vol. 1137, pp. 564–575. Springer, Cham (2020). https://doi.org/10.1007/978-3-030-40690-5_54

LNCS Homepage. http://www.springer.com/lncs. Accessed 21 Nov 2016

Designing Unconscious and Enactive Interaction for Interactive Movie Experience

Laura Varisco[1(✉)] and Giulio Interlandi[2]

[1] Department of Design, Politecnico di Milano, Milan, Italy
laura.varisco@polimi.it

[2] School of Design, Politecnico di Milano, Milan, Italy

Abstract. In a world full of sensors that gather personal data and digital solutions that use these data to provide feedback and personalized experiences, biofeedback is increasingly involved in the definition of new paradigms for tailoring interactions. Companies are collecting and using personal data to propose personalized services. Content providers are pushing users to produce data in order to create personalized storytelling experiences. In this context, the tech market is offering new low-cost solutions able to gather biodata. The paper reports the results of evidence-based explorations aimed at formalizing knowledge regarding the use of passive and unconscious interaction to control the fruition of storytelling artifacts. We investigate a new interaction paradigm that promise to seamlessly enable unconscious and enactive interactions for movie experiences. We propose the use of emotion recognition and eye-tracking as exploratory technologies that promise to be a potential contribution to richer access to the spectators' emotional involvement. We reflect on disruptive power of non-invasive technologies, given by the possibility to be used for home-cinema experiences. Investigating on emotional states of users in their decision we leverage on the emotive-cognitive data as a matter of creation and enabling of tailored movie experiences. Our research intends to explore the possibility of extracting knowledge from recognition of facial expressions that will contribute to foster its use in real-time passive interaction using emotion recognition as a trigger of enactivity that is not limited to interactive storytelling but opens new scenarios in the design of proactive systems for screens, spaces and environments. Furthermore, we provide suggestions as guidelines for the design of enactive experiences that leverage on emotion recognition and eye-tracking.

Keywords: Real-time interaction · Enactive interaction · Eye-controlled interfaces · Emotion recognition · Evidence-based design research

1 Introduction

We are living in a world that is pervasively filled with sensors and devices that are able to take advantage of data about people to create information that is capable to enable new interactions. Ubiquitous computing and pervasive sensing allow the gathering, collection of such data that, once elaborated, can be used to extract knowledge.

N. Streitz and S. Konomi (Eds.): HCII 2020, LNCS 12203, pp. 362–375, 2020.
https://doi.org/10.1007/978-3-030-50344-4_26

Furthermore, the services enabled by the interaction with devices provide not only useful feedback, but also personalized and even tailored experiences [4–7]. While companies are collecting and using personal data to propose personalized services for commercial purposes, also content providers are pushing users to produce data in order to create personalized storytelling experiences [8]. In this context, the tech market is offering new low-cost solutions able to gather biodata. One meaningful example of such solution is eye-tracking technology. Eye trackers are currently used for immersive gameplay through hands-free interaction as well as for healthcare purposes for disability [1], representing a step forward in the interaction with visual content for displays and smart-TVs.

Considering eye-trackers as an easily implementable technological add-on due to their decreasing price together with increasing performances, our research focuses on new possible paradigms for tailoring experiences that leverage on this technology as well as looking for a step further and exploring and reasoning on the introduction of emotion recognition through built-in cameras. We aim to take advantage of the ability to collect biodata and biological evidence such as eye-gaze, saccades and fixations, and merge it with emotion analysis so to personalize the providing of content for storytelling experience. These promising devices are in fact the enablers not only of hands-free, but also for passive and unconscious interactions that can represent the new interaction paradigm for future fruition of entertaining content.

The paper reports the results of an evidence-based exploration aimed at formalizing knowledge regarding the use of passive and unconscious interaction to control the fruition of storytelling artifacts. Through the use of both active and passive (gaze-based) interaction together with the collection of emotional states during the fruition, the reported experiment intends to explore and understand the possibilities offered by the merging of the two technological solutions as providers of meaning carried by the knowledge that can be extracted from the data they collect. The possible application of such new interaction paradigm for visual content, spaces from the framed screen to an entire indoor space, opening new scenarios of interaction design and adaptive environment design allowing the creation of enactive spaces and architectures.

2 Enactive Interaction for Storytelling

Interaction and storytelling have always been developed in parallel. From ancient paintings found in caves, to nowadays complex artifacts there's a long history strictly related to the human capability of crafting tools and technologies and create languages, knowledge, and meanings. Starting with gamebooks or CYOA (Choose Your Own Adventure) books, the interaction with storytelling experiences in modern times follows non-linear paths that allow people to make choices so to define how the storyline develops.

The form of interactive storytelling and the advancement of technology opened the ground to new kinds of interactive artifacts, Hypertext fiction, Interactive fiction, Interactive narration, Interactive narrative, and Adventure games. One of the trends of today is the Streaming of Interactive movie experiences on platforms like Netflix [9] in which the interaction takes place choosing the path to follow between different options through the TV remote control. This new kind of movie experiences can be cinematographic (Black Mirror's Bandersnatch [10]), graphic adventures (Minecraft Story Mode [11]) documentaries (You vs. Wild [12]) and animated films (Puss in book [13]).

In order to study how a traditional fiction film can take a step forward to a new kind of form of interaction in terms of emotion-driven enactive cinema, we based our approach on Tikka's research [2] that revisited and extrapolated knowledge through research-based practical experiments, actualizing Eisenstein's idea of cinema as a psychological laboratory for the general study of the emotional dimensions of the human mind [2] with today's scientific knowledge, theories, and technologies.

For the experiment that is the object of the paper, we considered the cinematographic experience *Black Mirror's Bandersnatch* [10] as a suitable expedient to embed the enactivity and unconsciousness of the interaction in the cinema experience.

The core idea is that "What emerges in the mind, in the form of an idea, corresponds to some structure of the body, in a particular state and set of circumstances" [14]. The unconscious response in space and time precedes the conscious evaluation and any change reinforces the organism's awareness. The emotional survival kit humans have (neurochemical and hormonal), works enabling immediate responses to the changes in the surrounding environment or to the behavior of other entities, guiding the organism towards wellbeing [2]. Paul Ekman's research on facial expression suggests the similarity of emotions across cultural borders of humanity [3–15]. According to the Paul Eckman group, the Facial Action Coding System (FACS) is a comprehensive, anatomically based system for describing all visually discernible facial movements. The FACS (Facial Action Coding System) can provide a tool to make sense of the emotional responses of the spectator to the cinematic content. "The understanding of the psychophysiological dynamics of embodied simulation could enable discovering those aspects of the human perception-action system that are automated" [2]. The human mind is survival-driven, and sensory-based categorization forms part of this survival process. Cinema as an artistic audiovisual product can be a creative laboratory for modeling the world, in which the relationship between the author's embodied relation with the world (first-order modeling), enables cognitive mapping of the world for the observer (second-order modeling) who is determined to model a first-order mind in the act of modeling the world [2].

As good reference example of enactivity embedded in the cinema experience, we consider Tikka's *Obsession* [16], an installation that performs a continuous montage of cinematic indexed and classifieds elements, according to the algorithm fed with data coming from the observer. This enactive cinema installation was "designed so as to play with the anticipation and expectations of the spectator, that is, with those uncontrollable fears and desires that the author assumes the unfolding of the story to elicit in the spectator's experience" [2] using biological signals. "Obsession's bio-sensitive interface is designed to detect the emotional affect that the cinematic installation has on the spectator and to channel it back to control the installation's narrative dynamics." [16]. This interface consists of an infrared sensor for the fingertip that calculates the heart rate (HR), and a device under the spectator's hand, measured the electrodermal activity. "Enactive cinema involves creating, controlling, and maintaining complex emotion-driven interaction between an enactive mind and dynamical cinema montage." [2]. For this reason, the cinema montage is driven by the spectator's unconscious emotional experience.

"The data captured from the sensors was interpreted in terms of three emotion theoretical dimensions: valence, arousal, and dominance" [2]. One effective emotion-tracking method taken into account for obsession was the electromyography (EMG) of facial muscle activity, however, it was not included in the installation experience because this measurement requires sensors to be applied on the skin resulting in an invasive instrument that could affect the experience.

3 Evidence-Based Exploration of Interactive Storytelling

As anticipated, starting from Tikka's approach, we conducted an exploratory evidence-based test using modern already implementable gaze interaction (eye-tracking) and including the promising emotion recognition so to understand further development of passive and unconscious interaction of storytelling content's personalization that merges the two technologies. The purpose of the experiment is to understand how modern, less invasive and more affordable technologies can be used nowadays as enablers to support an enactive interaction with storytelling experiences.

While EMG was considered as too invasive also in Tikka's experiments, we consider Facial Action Coding System as a suitable solution that allows to code the activation of 44 muscles at the same time [17] avoiding the intrusiveness of the electrodes. Furthermore, being eye-movement tracking a potential contribute to even richer access to the spectators' emotional involvement [16], in the experiment we included an eye-tracking device as a controller for the interactive experience so to compare conscious and unconscious decision making. Today is easy to find low price eye-tracking device, and facial muscle activity has become non-invasive thanks to webcams that use computer vision algorithms.

3.1 Prototyping the Experience

During previous research, the authors developed a first prototype of a storytelling experience using passive and unconscious interaction that triggers the personalization of the experience through the user's gaze. This first prototype is a sequence of selected scene from the interactive storytelling Bandersnatch created by Netflix [9, 10]. The original content (the one published by Netflix) allow the users to select how to continue the storyline by making active choices when asked. The choice has to be made through the remote in the time of 15 s. The revised prototype we developed during the Professional Workshop held at Politecnico di Milano within the Master Course in Digital and Interaction Design, hide the consciousness of the choice. In fact, the trigger of the selection is made only through the gaze fixation and the users don't receive any feedback about that. The main purpose of the first exercise during the workshop was to speculate and raise awareness in the spectators about both the possibilities and the issues, in terms of privacy, of modern technologies' trend of increase automation in providing contents. While this first prototype's interaction seemed promising, we soon realized that using only the gaze's fixation for the interaction was not meaningful enough in terms of significance of the choices. In fact, some of the choices are triggered during scenes that have a high visual component (e.g. the choices between two cereal boxes), while other choices mostly rely on emotional triggers (e.g. the choice to take a drug or not). While a generic eye-tracking device allows obtaining basically two kinds of data, saccades, and fixations, for the first prototype, we created an algorithm that compares two different dynamics areas of the screen (eye-areas) in order to determine which of the two has been watched for more time. The feedback received by users of the first prototype confirmed that gaze's fixation could be a contribution in terms of data for the detection of a decision-making process. However, we realized also that, due to the emotional component of the choices, the eye gaze cannot be considered as symptomatic of a decision or of a willing. Even choices that has to be made in scenes where the visual characteristics are predominant (e.g. choosing between two packs of cereals that are shown), the emotional component cannot be excluded from the analysis. This is particularly true during scene with high emotional predominance with less visual clues for the choice (e.g. taking or not taking a drug) [18]. For this reason, we decided to move forward our research and explore how to improve the unconscious interaction with the introduction of emotion recognition.

We created a second prototype specifically to perform an experiment aiming at extracting knowledge on how to include emotion recognition in the unconscious interaction and create enactivity. The second prototype consisted of a sequence of scenes during which the users has to make four choices in total. Considering both high visual and high emotional components, two of the selections were made consciously by clicking on the choice with the mouse, the other two were triggered passively by using the detection of the eye gaze on a dynamic invisible area (eye-area). Figure 1 shows the matrix of the choices the viewer makes while experiencing the second prototype that consider both the visual or emotional prominent characteristic of the scene and the type of choice (unconscious or conscious).

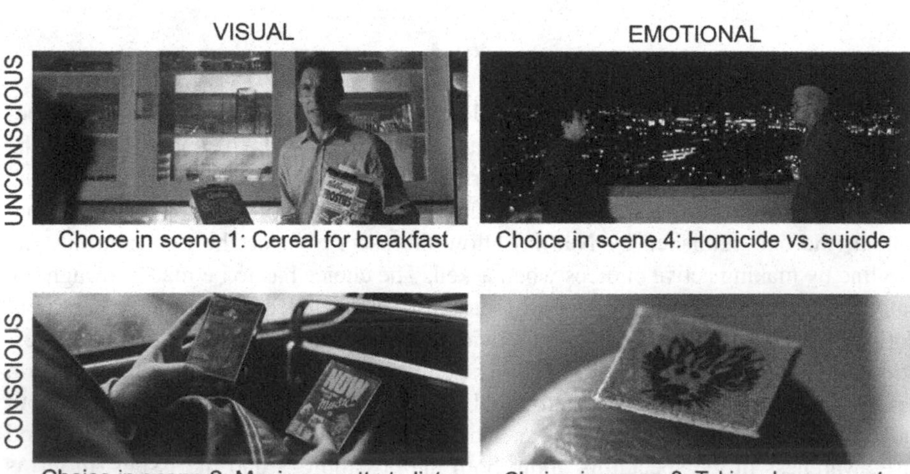

Fig. 1. The scenes' choices matrix of the second prototype.

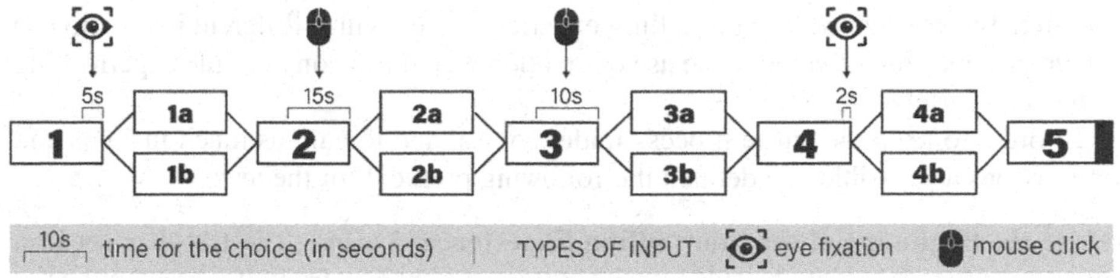

Fig. 2. Flow of the scenes in the narrative sequence of the prototype.

During the test, the face of the subject was monitored through a webcam connected to a face reading software. We included both conscious and unconscious selection so to compare the two results of emotion recognition.

The narrative of the prototype follows the scheme described in Fig. 2 and the 4 choices' interaction are performed as following:

Scene 1 - Cereal for Breakfast. The scene contains the unconscious visual choice. Two invisible eye-areas have been created above two packs of cereals (Sugar Puff & Kellogg's Frosties) that one of the characters is showing to the protagonist. For the selections made using the eye-tracker as a triggering device, the prototype counts the duration of eye gazes on each of the areas and a script select the most fixated one through the comparison of the two values.

Scene 2 - Music Cassette to Listen. During the conscious visual choice, the protagonist extracts two music cassettes from a bag, at the same time two buttons appear allowing the subject to choose one with the mouse within 15 s (if no choices are made, the first option is chosen automatically).

Scene 3 - Taking Drugs or Not. The conscious and emotional choice is contained in a scene in which a drug (LSD) is offered to the protagonist. The subject has the possibility to choose whether to take it or not by clicking on one of two buttons (same as for scene 2) within 10 s.

Scene 4 - Homicide vs Suicide. This scene contains the last choice of the experience, the unconscious emotional one. Here the subject face an unconscious choice with a high emotional impact. He decides (without knowing) which one of two characters will jump from a balcony going for a sure death. The choice is determined by the ocular fixations as for scene 1, but this time the moment in which the two eye-areas are shown is shorter (about 2 s) so to avoid a broader exploration of the scene with the eye-gaze.

3.2 The Evidence-Based Test

We conducted the experiment on 20 subjects so to capture their emotional involvement during the fruition. We group the subjects into two main categories: the first group was composed by 10 people who didn't see Bandersnatch (G1); the second one was composed by 10 people who have seen Bandersnatch before (G2). We decided to consider people who already experienced the storytelling experience even with a different interaction so to have evidence on the value of the use of emotion recognition on multiple experiencing for the same artefact.

In order to keep the entire process under control and to gain as much insights and comparisons as possible, we defined the following protocol for the test:

Before the Beginning of the Storytelling Experience (5 min). The test was set in a laboratory office in which the subject was sitting on a chair in front of a desk on the top of which there was the laptop running the prototype with a mouse device, a webcam and a fixed eye-tracker connected to it. This step consisted in welcoming the subject, reading a brief introduction to the experiment, signing the consent and calibrating the eye-tracker device. For the introductory text, we kept relevant information of the scope and aim of the test, as well as the role of the eye-tracker and the camera for the end of the test so to avoid spoiling the use of emotion recognition and the passive triggering of choices. This helped us to have as less biased data as possible.

The Experience with the Prototype (10 min). This phase consisted of the main experience of using the prototype. During the experience, the subject is contributing to the development of the story during the four trigger moments as described previously. At the beginning of the experience we start running the emotion-analysis software that collected the data about facial expressions. The emotion-analysis was set so to keep data only about the triggering times (in which the subject has to make a choice) including the part of the scene that introduce the choice.

After the Experience (5 to 10 min). At the end of the experience with the prototype, we conducted a semi-structured interview for each of the subjects so to collect insights about self-report of the experience and compare them with data collected during the test. We investigated on previous experiences of storytelling experiences in general, about conscious feelings emerged during the experience, and the choices they would have done in scene 1 and 4 if they had the possibility to choose consciously. Right after the interview, we declared the real purpose of the test and informed the subject about the unconscious choices on scene 1 and 4.

4 Results Obtained

The experiment results, as we explained above, are divided in the two groups of subjects, both groups consist of ten subjects and we followed the same protocol for all of them. The data we analyzed are the ones gathered from Noldus FaceReader and from the prototype developed using the video game engine Unity [19], and from the audio-recorded interviews. Concerning the data obtained from the emotion-analysis, we used Noldus FaceReader [20], a validated automated facial coding (AFC) software, for the recognition of specific properties in facial images and classification of people's emotions into discrete categories of basic emotions [21]. AFC algorithms use a set of fixed rules to code facial expressions on the 20 webcam recordings (one for each subject). The software estimates human affective states making interpretations through theoretical methods supported by literature [21]. For each of the subjects' choice we extrapolated a graph that visualize the data related to emotional values analyzed by the software of 6 emotions (happy, sad, angry, surprised, scared, disgusted - Fig. 3), valence and arousal (Fig. 4). In the graphs, we represent, on the x-axis, the timespan of the choice as inclusive of the part of the scene that introduced the selection, while the y-axis represents the emotional value as defined by the software. Consistently with the data gathered, we considered as significative the values that reached the minimum threshold of 0,1 for any emotional value, and of 0,5 for the arousal. For the valence, we considered as relevant the values smaller than −0,1 and bigger than 0,1 to determine if it is negative or positive [22]. Both of the figures report these thresholds as colored areas so to highlight whether the value is considered as a relevant emotional engagement. The valence value reveals whether the emotional state of the subject is positive or negative. The only positive expression that the software recognize is 'Happy', while negative expressions are 'sad', 'angry', 'scared' and 'disgusted'. 'Surprised' could be considered either positive or negative. Arousal indicates whether the subject is active or not active.

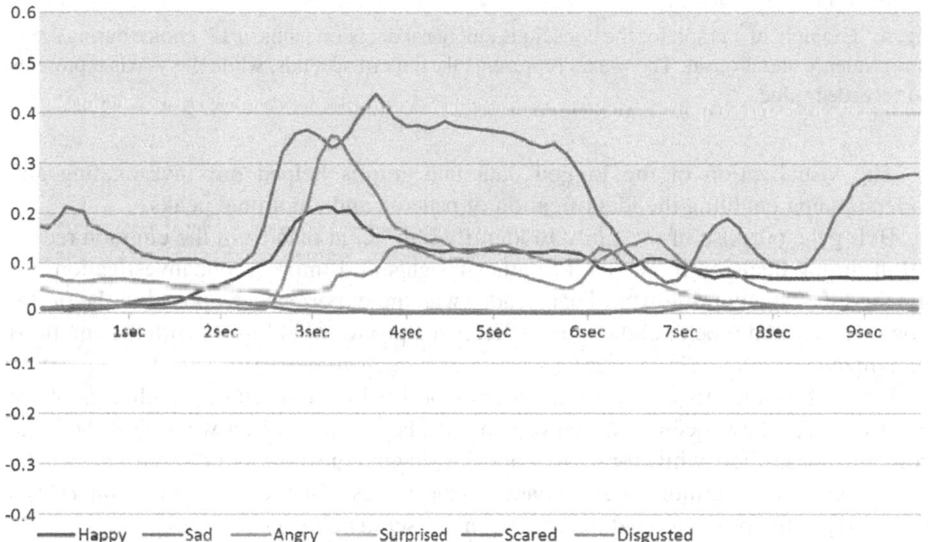

Fig. 3. Example of a graph for the conscious emotional decision (subject 13, choice during scene 3) for the 6 emotions. The x-axis represents the time in seconds, while the y-axis represents the recorded value.

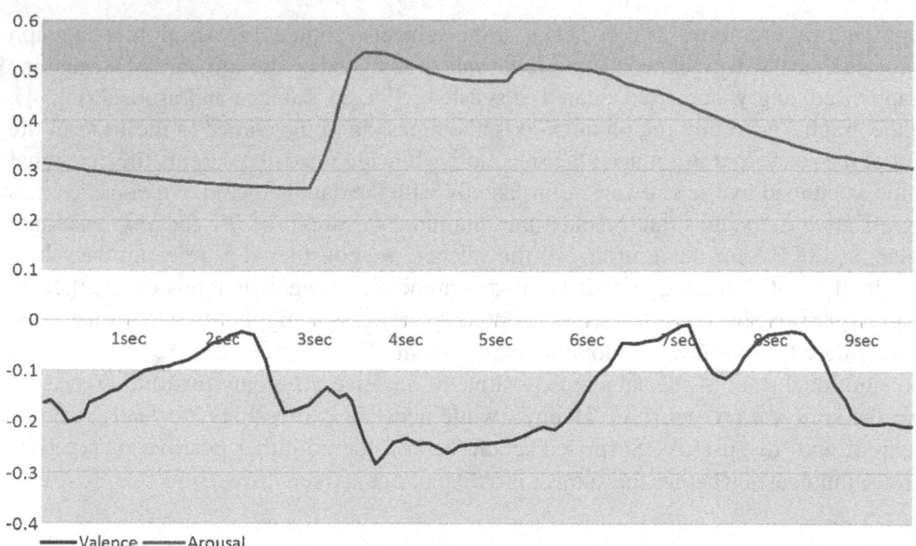

Fig. 4. Example of a graph for the conscious emotional decision (subject 13, choice during scene 3) for valence and arousal. The x-axis represents the time in seconds, while the y-axis represents the recorded value.

The visualization of the logged data into graphs helped our investigating and understanding enabling the identification of patterns and emotional peaks.

Being the purpose of the study to identify significant data from the emotion recognition during decision moments, to gather insights and improve our investigation, we matched the data coming from FaceReader with the experience proposed in the prototype relating each type of choice (as in the matrix proposed in Fig. 1) with the emotions recognized.

For each of the subjects we related emotional values to each of the choices of the experience that have been recorded in a log file. For scene 1 and 4 we logged the input from the mouse click, while for scene 2 and 3 we logged the most fixated area between the two proposed. Furthermore, we compared the outcomes with the results of the interviews to identify both consistent and misleading unconscious choices.

4.1 Data Outcomes

In order to be able to compare the data between emotion recognition and choices made during the experience, we summarized the emotional values as number of overcoming of the thresholds for each of the emotions and for valence and arousal (if any) and assigned a 'TRUE' value for each of the emotions that overcame the threshold at least once during the timespan of the choice (an example is shown in Table 1). Then, knowing which of the options the subject chooses, we related the two data aggregating the subjects of each group. Figure 5 and Fig. 6 show the number of subjects (y-axes) that overcome the thresholds for each of the 6 emotions, valence and arousal (x-axis). Additionally, they report the data in relation to the choice made (a or b).

Table 1. Number of overcoming of the thresholds (subject 13, choice during scene 3).

Happy	Sad	Angry	Surprised	Scared	Disgusted	Valence	Arousal
60	123	30	0	0	55	91	25
True	True	True	False	False	True	True	True

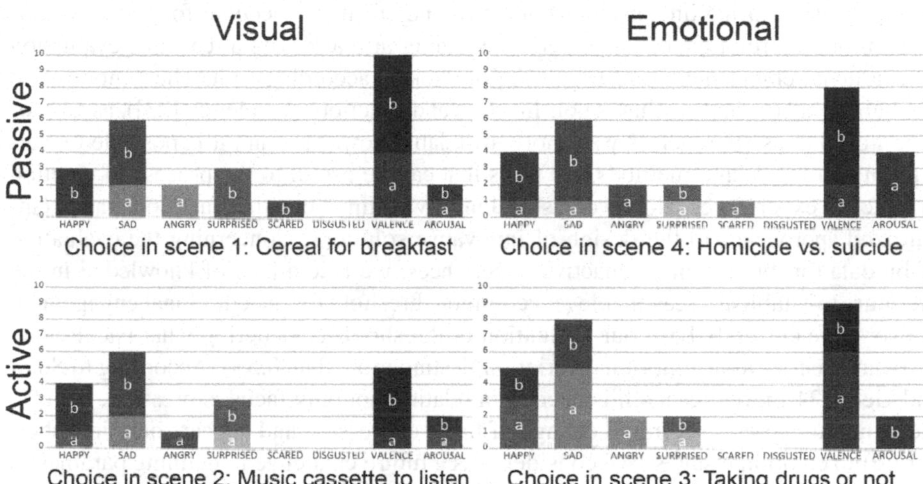

Fig. 5. Aggregation of values of G1 for all the 4 choices made considering the overcome of the threshold (number of subjects) and the option chosen.

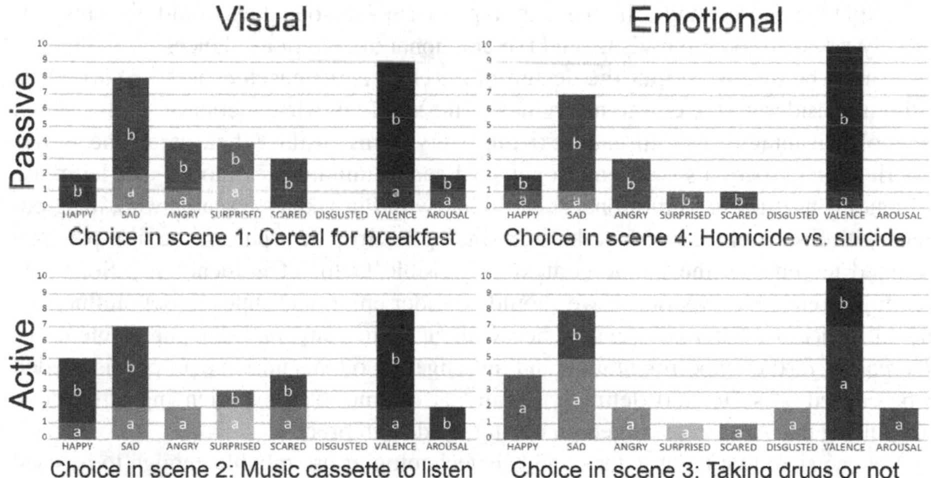

Fig. 6. Aggregation of values of G2 for all the 4 choices made considering the overcome of the threshold (number of subjects) and the option chosen.

5 Discussion and Conclusions

The aggregation of the values shows that for both the groups of subjects (the ones that are seeing Bandersnatch for the first time, and the ones that have already experienced the interactive storytelling through the Netflix platform), is possible to identify significant emotional engagement during the choices. It also shows that there's no significant difference in the engagements between the unconscious and the conscious choice, so the value of engagement during unconscious choice can be taken into account for further development of the prototype of the experience aiming at integrating a real-time evaluation of emotional engagement and triggering of choices according to it. The "unobtrusive measurement" (a solution that is non-invasive and functions seamlessly [23]), as an evolution of Tikka's approach is way more affordable nowadays and it is possible to start thinking on the design methods and tools that can be useful to the process of creation of enactive experiences. However, as designers we aim at creating functional and standardized approaches to the design of innovative solutions. Concerning the evaluation of biodata for the design of enactive experiences, we face a lack of knowledge in the literature to establish a reasonable and common threshold for the emotional engagement in users. We currently base our evaluation of thresholds considering what FaceReader software identify as an emotional variation (lasting more than 0.5 s). According to Sumi and Ueda [24], more research is needed in relating not only facial expression, but also facial micro-expressions (rapid change of facial expression and appears only in a short period) to emotional states. We consider it as a future challenge in defining parameters related to emotion recognition for the creation of enactive experiences. Furthermore, the comparison between the prototype's data and the declared opinions coming from the interviews supported our assumption that the exclusive use of the eye-gaze as a source of data is not representative of the choice of the user. In fact, many of the interviewees stated that the choice made 'by the prototype' wasn't the one they would have made if actively asked for both the visual and the emotional unconscious choices.

It must be discussed that the design of enactive experiences cannot be carried on without considering the emotional values of the whole movie experience. In this study, we took advantage of an already existing storytelling artifact that, as all the movie experiences, embeds its own emotional load and communicates moods and leitmotiv influencing the viewer's emotional state. In line with Pia Tikka's research who, in agreement with Eisenstein, considers the surrounding environment part of the film product, we need to consider the whole context as possible factor of influence [2]. So, while creating an enactive experience we should consider emotional states as both influenced and influencer of the whole experience without taking any variation for granted. For this reason, further experimentation and investigation on this iterative process is needed to be carried on so to start defining a grammar of emotional experiencing of enactive storytelling that can be leveraged on during the design process.

We can state that today's face analysis technologies are reliable enough to be used as a tool for designing enactive experiences considering it as both a tool for emotional analysis of the elements of the artifacts, and a tool for enabling the enactivity of the experience.

5.1 Suggestions and Guidelines

By comparing the data provided from the technologies we chose (saccade, fixation, single emotion value, valence, and arousal), with those used in the Obsession installation by Pia Tikka (HR, EDA), we started creating guidelines and suggestions to consider while creating enactive interactions. These elements have been identified thanks to the results of the described study that demonstrated the possibility to find significant emotional engagement from face analysis and combine those values with the use of an eye-tracking device to target the focus of the visual area. They can be considered a starting point for further experimentation on real-time gaze and emotional analysis to enable enactivity. These experimentations could contribute to knowledge not only in the field of interaction and experience design, but also in the field of cinema authorship.

Direction of Change. Aligned with Tikka's [16] principle, consider the increase or decrease in the values to affect the emotional mood through the management of the narrative flow including or excluding scenes and other ontologically organized content. Positivity or negativity of the valence and the value related to arousal can be particularly useful to detect the direction of change, especially for scenes with a predominance of emotional characteristics.

Areas of Focus. The eye-tracking can provide a further focus on the user's gaze when the emotion analysis is performed. In scenes with a high visual component, the eye-tracking data can be crossed with the facial ones to understand the user's emotions with respect to a single eye-area. This means that from the author's or designer's point of view it is possible to know the valence and arousal, as well as the single emotion involved respectively to a visual element of the montage. Therefore, there is the possibility to compare different visual elements both in terms of duration of the fixation and in terms of comparison of emotional analysis. Hence psychology and bio-marketing studies can be useful in the design of emotional triggers and could provide an analysis of the like or dislike of the visual elements.

Unexpected Interactive Elements. In order to open new scenarios, it is possible to work on placing visual "Easter-eggs" within the enactive experience. Thanks to eye-tracking technology, it is possible to know if a single visual element has been looked at by the user and for how long.

5.2 Applicability of the New Paradigm

Considering the enactive interaction with storytelling artifact as a new paradigm for an unconscious and/or passive control of interfaces, we can speculate on possible further applications of such interaction within different solutions belonging not only to the field of cinema and movie experiences. It is easy to imagine how an unconscious and passive interaction that leverage on emotional statuses of the users, could be a contribution in several fields. The most promising ones are interactive spaces and digital environments such as ambient intelligence. We foresee future technological advancement that will allow a multi-user interaction for both eye-gaze and enactive control of contents and information creating a personalized space that consider all the inhabitant and users of an environment.

5.3 Ethical Concerns

On the point of view of ethics, it is necessary to discuss the possible consequences of the future spreading of enactive experiences in everyday entertainment (such as embedding the necessary devices in smart TVs). Considering current technological trends that move fast to the hyper-personalization of services and systems so to create tailored experiences (e.g. recommender systems, personalized suggestions, adaptive solutions), we see enactivity a possible way to influence both the artifact and the viewer. We strongly believe in a need of future in depth investigation of such interactive paradigm seen as an agency for possible individual and social consequences of the use of bio-information (emotional state) in everyday life in terms of privacy, and individual and social issues [27]. In order to foster the solutions' resilience [28], we can address the possible individual and societal impacts of the use of this new paradigm according to criticalities emerged from previous research on the possible consequences of the use of personal information [25, 26]. First, on the topic of data privacy, we have to consider that the awareness of the user of the tracking of emotions and the subsequent use of such information is key to foster the social acceptability giving to the individual the power to decide if and when to be tracked as well as the control on data access management. Secondly, the users should have the right to access to the knowledge extracted from the analysis of their data so to increase their knowledge about both themselves and how the system decided for them. However, the amount and depth of this knowledge that the users get back has to be carefully balanced to avoid dangerous misperception of the self, due to self-mirroring into data and to avoid information overload that could increase psychological impacts leading to changes in the attitude and disposition of the individuals due to the raising of concerns on problems derived from self-analysis through data. Third, the knowledge extracted from the data analysis by the system can make social labeling and misuse of data even easier than before, leading to the increase of effectiveness of targeted subliminal messages as well as nudging and influencing for improper purposes. However, it has to be noticed that, especially for neuroscience and cognitive science researchers that work on human emotions, the information gathered from the systems that embed enactivity, can represent an interesting source of value in terms of massive amount of data for research purposes and a voluntary donation of the data from the user should be taken into consideration as a possible option so to allow them to contribute to the public good.

References

1. Calvo, A., et al.: Eye tracking impact on quality-of-life of ALS patients. In: Miesenberger, K., Klaus, J., Zagler, W., Karshmer, A. (eds.) ICCHP 2008. LNCS, vol. 5105, pp. 70–77. Springer, Heidelberg (2008). https://doi.org/10.1007/978-3-540-70540-6_9
2. Tikka, P., Korkeakoulu, T.: Enactive cinema: simulatorium Eisensteinense. University of Art and Design Helsinki, Helsinki (2008)
3. Ekman, P., et al.: What the Face Reveals: Basic and Applied Studies of Spontaneous Expression Using the Facial Action Coding System (FACS). Oxford University Press, Oxford (1997)
4. Mitchell, W.J.: Me++: The Cyborg Self and the Networked City. MIT, Cambridge (2010)

5. Young, N.: The Virtual Self: How Our Digital Lives are Altering the World Around Us. McClelland & Stewart, Plattsburgh (2013)
6. Neff, G., Nafus, D.: Self-Tracking. The MIT Press, Cambridge (2016)
7. Lupton, D.: The digitally engaged patient: self-monitoring and self-care in the digital health era. Soc. Theory Health **11**(3), 256–270 (2013). https://doi.org/10.1057/sth.2013.10
8. Quesenbery, W., Brooks, K.: Storytelling for User Experience: Crafting Stories for Better Design, p. 569 (2010)
9. Netflix. https://www.netflix.com/
10. Slade, D.: Black Mirror: Bandersnatch. Netflix (2018)
11. McManus, S.: Minecraft: Story Mode. Telltale Games, Mojang (2015)
12. Buchta, R., Grylls, B.: You vs. Wild. Netflix (2019)
13. Burdine, R., Castucciano, J.: Puss in Book: Trapped in an Epic Tale. Netflix (2017)
14. Damasio, A.R.: Looking for Spinoza: Joy, Sorrow, and the Feeling Brain, First Harvest edn. Harcourt, Orlando, Toronto, London (2003)
15. Ekman, P.: Facial expressions of emotion: new findings, new questions. Psychol. Sci. **3**(1), 34–38 (1992). https://doi.org/10.1111/j.1467-9280.1992.tb00253.x
16. Tikka, P., Vuori, R., Kaipainen, M.: Narrative logic of enactive cinema: Obsession. Digit. Creat. **17**(4), 205–212 (2006). https://doi.org/10.1080/14626260601074078
17. Maison, D., Pawłowska, B.: Using the FaceReader method to detect emotional reaction to controversial advertising referring to sexuality and homosexuality. In: Nermend, K., Łatuszyńska, M. (eds.) Neuroeconomic and Behavioral Aspects of Decision Making. SPBE, pp. 309–327. Springer, Cham (2017). https://doi.org/10.1007/978-3-319-62938-4_20
18. Kahneman, D.: Thinking, Fast and Slow, 1st pbk. edn. Farrar, Straus and Giroux, New York (2013)
19. Unity. Unity Technologies. https://unity.com/
20. FaceReader. Noldus. https://doi.org/www.noldus.com/facereader
21. Lewinski, P., den Uyl, T.M., Butler, C.: Automated facial coding: validation of basic emotions and FACS AUs in FaceReader. J. Neurosci. Psychol. Econ. **7**(4), 227–236 (2014). https://doi.org/10.1037/npe0000028
22. Jansen, J.: Automated Identification and Measurement of Suppressed Emotions using Emotion Recognition Software, p. 16 (2015)
23. Mandolfo, M.: You trust me, and I feel it. Influence of foreign live biofeedback on interpersonal trust-related behaviour. Politecnico di Milano (2017)
24. Sumi, K., Ueda, T.: Micro-expression recognition for detecting human emotional changes. In: Kurosu, M. (ed.) HCI 2016. LNCS, vol. 9733, pp. 60–70. Springer, Cham (2016). https://doi.org/10.1007/978-3-319-39513-5_6
25. Schneier, B.: Data and Goliath: The Hidden Battles to Collect Your Data and Control Your World, Norton Paperback. W.W. Norton & Company, New York, London (2016)
26. Polaine, A., Lovlie, L., Reason, B.: Service Design: From Insight to Implementation. Rosenfeld Media, Brooklyn (2013)
27. Pillan, M., Varisco, L., Bertolo, M.: Facing digital dystopias: a discussion about responsibility in the design of smart products. In: Alonso, M.B., Ozcan, E. (eds.) Proceedings of the Conference on Design and Semantics of Form and Movement - Sense and Sensitivity, DeSForM 2017, pp. 121–131. InTech (2017)
28. Varisco, L.: Personal Interaction Design: introducing the discussion on the consequences of the use of personal information in the design process. Ph.D. dissertation, Politecnico di Milano, Milan, Italy (2019)

Smart Cities and Landscapes

Development of One-Stop Smart City Application by Interdisciplinary Data Linkage

Kenro Aihara[1,2,3](✉) and Atsuhiro Takasu[1,2]

[1] National Institute of Informatics, Tokyo, Japan
{kenro.aihara,takasu}@nii.ac.jp
[2] The Graduate University for Advanced Studies, Tokyo, Japan
[3] Joint Support-Center for Data Science Research, Research Organization of Information and Systems, Tokyo, Japan

Abstract. The development of open data by local governments and data platforms for each field is progressing. These are broad ranged data on each area, such as traffic, disaster prevention, restaurants and services, and are expected to be useful information sources for citizens and tourists. On the other hand, these data are usually deployed in a network reachable place, but when they have to be handled individually according to its own format, and in some cases, conversion both in format and in semantics are required, which is a barrier to use.

By the way, in existing information services for tourists, especially smartphones application services for tourists, the content provided are selective and limited in some specific fields and target areas covered. That is, there is a problem on coverage in content. In addition, there are many cases where has a problem with the cost of maintaining and updating content, and the content may often be obsolete.

Given the existence of data platforms developed for each field, the paper presents the data linkage challenges that enable them to be integrated and used. And also the paper shows a one-stop smart city application that has been developed using that function. This application provides information for tourists during normal times, and it can handle the situation in town, such as congestion, in real time in order to grasp the flow and local stagnation that occur in bursts at the time of events or accidents.

Keywords: Location-based service · Smart city · Behavior log · Integration of heterogeneous contents · Data linkage · Crowdsourcing

1 Introduction

The development of open data by local governments and data platforms for each field is progressing. These are broad ranged data on each area, such as traffic, disaster prevention, restaurants and services, and are expected to be

N. Streitz and S. Konomi (Eds.): HCII 2020, LNCS 12203, pp. 379–390, 2020.
https://doi.org/10.1007/978-3-030-50344-4_27

useful information sources for citizens and tourists. On the other hand, these data are usually deployed in a network reachable place, but when they have to be handled individually according to its own format, and in some cases, conversion both in format and in semantics are required, which is a barrier to use.

By the way, in existing information services for tourists, especially smartphones application services for tourists, the content provided are selective and limited in some specific fields and target areas covered. That is, there is a problem on coverage in content. In addition, there are many cases where has a problem with the cost of maintaining and updating content, and the content may often be obsolete.

Given the existence of data platforms developed for each field, the paper presents the data linkage challenges that enable them to be integrated and used. And also the paper shows a one-stop smart city application that has been developed using that function. This application provides information for tourists during normal times, and it can handle the situation in town, such as congestion, in real time in order to grasp the flow and local stagnation that occur in bursts at the time of events or accidents. The application enables crowdsourcing to collect information on situations in town from users.

2 Background

2.1 Location-Based Information Services

A lot of network services with location data are proposed, and some of them, such as foursquare[1], are getting popular. Usually location information is given as geographical coordinates, that is, latitude and longitude, a location identifier such as ID for facilities in geographical information services (GIS), or a postal address. Google has launched Google Places[2], which gathers place information from active participating networkers and delivers such information through Google's web site and API (application programmable interface). Google may try to grasp facts and information on activities in the real world where it has not enough information yet even though it seems to have become the omniscient giant in the cyber world. Google already captures some real world phenomena in its own materials. For example, it gathers landscape images with its own fleet of specially adapted cars for the Google Street View service[3]. However, the cost of capturing and digitizing facts and activities in the real world is generally very expensive if you try to obtain more than capturing photo images with geographical information. Although Google Places may be one of the reasonable solutions to gathering information in the real world, it's not guaranteed that it can grow into an effective and reliable source reflecting the real world.

Existing social information services, such as Facebook and Twitter, are expanding to attach location data to users' content.

---

[1] http://foursquare.com/.
[2] http://www.google.com/places/.
[3] http://www.google.com/streetview/.

2.2 Open Data

Open Definition describes open data as "Open means anyone can freely access, use, modify, and share for any purpose (subject, at most, to requirements that preserve provenance and openness)." [10] Although the idea of open data has been around for a long time, the term "open data" has been used to refer specifically to the activities of open-data government initiatives, such as data.gov, data.go.uk, and data.go.jp, in recent years. To promote government transparency, accountability, and public participation, governments make information publicly available as machine-readable open data.

Linked Open Data (LOD) is Linked Data which is released under an open license, which does not impede its reuse for free [5]. Linked Data is structured data which is interlinked with other data to share information to enable to be processed semantically by computers. Tim Barners-Lee advocated the five star rating scheme of LOD as follows:

1. Available on the web (whatever format) but with an open licence, to be Open Data
2. Available as machine-readable structured data (e.g. excel instead of image scan of a table)
3. as (2) plus non-proprietary format (e.g. CSV instead of excel)
4. All the above plus, Use open standards from W3C (RDF and SPARQL) to identify things, so that people can point at your stuff
5. All the above, plus: Link your data to other people's data to provide context

Usually, when considering the use of open data by machine processing, it is considered that three or more stars are required.

2.3 Crowdsourcing for Civil Problems

The term "crowdsourcing" was described by Jeff Howe in 2006 [7] and defined that crowdsourcing is the act of taking a task traditionally performed by a designated agent and outsourcing it by making an open call to an undefined but large group of people [8]. This can take the form of peer-production, but is also often undertaken by sole individuals [6].

The concept of smart cities can be viewed as a recognition of the growing importance of digital technologies for a competitive position and a sustainable future [11]. Although the smart city-agenda, which grants ICTs with the task to achieve strategic urban development goals such as improving the life quality of its citizens and creating sustainable growth, has gained a lot of momentum in recent years.

Tools such as smartphones offer the opportunity to facilitate co-creation between citizens and authority. Such tools have the potential to organize and stimulate communication between citizens and authority, and allow citizens to participate in the public domain [4,12]. One example is FixMyStreet[4] that

[4] https://www.fixmystreet.com/.

enables citizens to report broken streetlights and potholes [9]. It is important that these approaches will not succeed automatically and social standards like trust, openness, and consideration of mutual interests have to be guaranteed to make citizen engaging in the public domain challenging.

Waze[5] is another crowdsourcing service to collect data of traffic. Even though Waze provides users to traffic information collected from users and route navigation function, it seems not enough to motivate users to get involved in, because recommended routes are not as adequate as car navigation appliances, especially in Japan where such appliances are well-developed.

The authors have researched and proposed some crowdsourcing applications. One is an online driving recorder service to collect both sensor data and videos, recorded from the view of the driver; by using this application, users benefit from a free record of their driving, and the authors obtain large amounts of low-cost sensor data. Then, the authors estimate road surface conditions by analysing such collected sensor data [1,3]. Another application can collect and share the location information of mobile phones cheaply in a public place like a bus [2].

3 Zap Sapporo: An LBS for Explorers in Town

3.1 Service Description

The service can be accessed via smartphone application. The authors have developed a locatiton-based service application called “Zap Sapporo”. This application was made available to the public in February 2020.

The service is designed for strollers who visit Sapporo area. Sapporo is the fifth largest city in Japan, with a population of about 1.91 million. The city receives an average of about 6 meters snowfall annually, with an average maximum snow depth of about 1 m in February. The city spends more than 15 billion yen every winter on road management activities such as snowplowing and snow removal. Sapporo appears to be one of the most “challenged” cities in the world because its citizens demand good facilities and services even though the climate is severe. Sapporo has almost twice as much snowfall as Quebec City, while its population is nearly four times larger, and is increasing.

When visitors arrive in the service area and access the service, they can get information about scheduled events and integrated contents.

Zap Sapporo is more than just LBS, it is an application that enables crowdsourcing, especially sharing real-time city conditions.

Major functions of the service are as follows.

3.2 User Experience

The application screen is composed of the following tabs, and the user switches the desired item by selecting the tab.

[5] https://www.waze.com/.

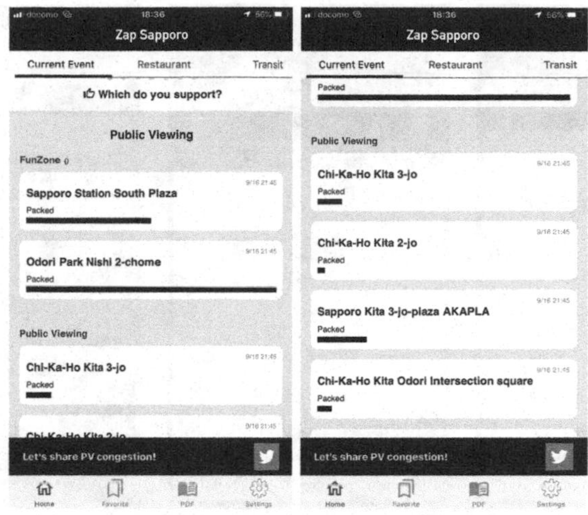

Fig. 1. Snapshot images of current events in the Zap Sapporo application

- Current Event
- Restaurant
- Transit
- Bear
- Hospital
- Other

The application can select English, Chinese (Traditional and Simplified), and Korean in addition to Japanese, and content according to the set language is provided.

Current Event. The current event is displayed on the application home page. This page contains information about the event and useful links to external sites, such as the official website.

Along with receiving the event information, the user can transmit the event information. Such user-generated information can be shared in the page. Figure 1 shows an example of current event tab. This example contains public viewing information about an international sporting event held in Sapporo in the fall of 2019. In the city center, several public screens have been deployed to show the match live. The page includes such venue list of public viewing screens with the last congestion status posted by users. In this example, all venues are fully packed, but the length of the bar is different because the length indicates its capacity.

Users can post the congestion status of the venue where they are staying, tapping the blue button in the lower right corner. After tapping the button, the venue selector appears (Fig. 2(a)). Then, users are requested to select a category of congestion degree (Fig. 2(b)). Given categories are as follows:

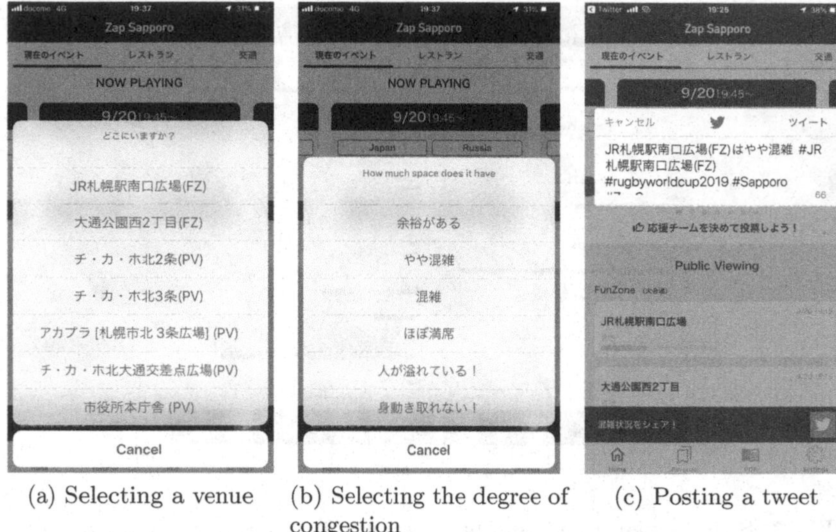

(a) Selecting a venue (b) Selecting the degree of congestion (c) Posting a tweet

Fig. 2. Snapshot images of posting a tweet on current congestion status in the Zap Sapporo application

- vacant
- has room
- crowded
- full
- so many people
- cannot move

Users can choose one of them subjectively. Finally, they add comments and then complete posting the tweet (Fig. 2(c)).

Posted tweets including congestion status are processed automatically and the information in the application is updated as shown in Fig. 1. Figure 3 shows the scene of another event in Sapporo in the winter of 2020.

Restaurant. The second tab is for restaurants and bars. The list of restaurants can be sorted by distance from the user's location. Users can also filter the list by specified tags that correspond to categories. Figure 4 shows the list of restaurants sorted by the distance order.

The restaurant information provided here uses information integrated from several information sources such as Sapporo City, Sapporo Tourism Association, and the Sapporo Chamber of Commerce and Industry. The integrated content used here is described in Sect. 4.

Fig. 3. A scene of an event in Sapporo in the winter of 2020

Transit. Information such as real-time traffic information and transfer guides may be important for visitors in the city. Transit tab shows the transit information. Current traffic information are displayed on the top. This traffic information is provided at Data Smart City Sapporo (DSCS), the open data platform of Sapporo City. The information is updated every 10 min.

Six major transports, subway, street car, Japan Railway (JR), bus, taxi, and rental bicycle, are displayed in the center of the page (Fig. 5(a)). The subway sub page displays a route map and timetables that are also provided at DSCS (Fig. 5(b)).

Others. The Zap Sapporo application has three more tabs: Bear, Hospital, and Other. Bear includes information on the appearance of wild bears collected at the city hall. The spot where the bear was sighted is plotted on the map. The Hospital tab displays a list of hospitals in the Sapporo area collected by the Hokkaido government.

The "Other" tab provides miscellaneous information, especially for foreign visitors (Fig. 6). Public Wi-Fi spots, restrooms in public parks, and foreign diplomatic locations are provided (Fig. 6(a)). For example, a list of consulates of oversea countries located in Sapporo is provided. Almost all of the information on the list has been taken from the Ministry of Foreign Affairs of Japan website.

3.3 Sensing Functions

User Data. The Zap Sapporo service collects the following user attributes:

- nationality
- country of residence
- purpose of visiting Japan

Fig. 4. Snapshot images of restaurant list in the Zap Sapporo application

Onboard Location and Motion Sensors. The Zap Sapporo application retrieves position and movement data from onboard sensors even in background mode. The collected data is pooled in a local data store and sent to a log server.

Collected data are as follows:

- Location (latitude, longitude, altitude, horizontal/vertical accuracies)
- Heading (magnetic, true, accuracy)
- Move (course, speed)

The collected data will be used for city dynamic analysis.

4 Integration of Distributed Contents

4.1 Issus of Integration

In the conventional LBS application that provides information for visitos, such as tourists, contents are individually prepared and maintained. However, individual content development has the following problems:

- Aggregating a lot of content and maintaining it is costly.
- Data provided by individual content providers only covers some stores, and coverage is low.
- Content provided by individual content providers is heterogeneous and not easy to integrate.

Generally, various types of data are managed and provided in an autonomous distributed manner. From the viewpoint of data linkage, the same data has different formats, structures, and expressions, and is an obstacle to cross-use. At present, data that should be connected is not connected. There are the following issues regarding data linkage:

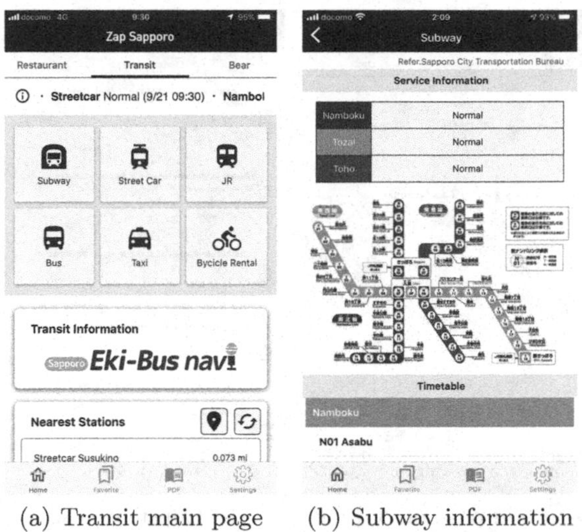

(a) Transit main page (b) Subway information

Fig. 5. Snapshot images of transit information in the Zap Sapporo application

- a large variety of data, a large amounts of data
- distributed management of data
- data written in different ways
  - the same data in different formats
  - the same data in different structures
  - the same data in different expressions

Here, the authors focus particularly on the third issue. The difference between formats may correspond to 2-star class of five star rating scheme of LOD shown in Sect. 2.2, while the difference between structures is regarded as 3-star class. In order to actually use different data by computational integration, a match at the expression level, that is, a 4-star class is required. In particular, when trying to use data in different fields, the use of words is generally quite different, and there are many technical issues in realizing these integration.

This paper will try to integrate content from various information sources, targeting the disambiguation at the level of attribute labels, and make them available through Zap Sapporo.

4.2 Integration of Restaurant Contents of Sapporo

Restaurant contents used in Zap Sapporo are realized by integrating contents from multiple information sources. One of fundamental sources is Sapporo City. It delivers List of Food Business Permits in DSCS. This list can be considered as a kind of a complete list of restaurants in the city, as it is necessary to obtain this permission to legally operate a restaurant in the city. Unfortunately, the list consists of few attributes, such as name of the operator and postal address.

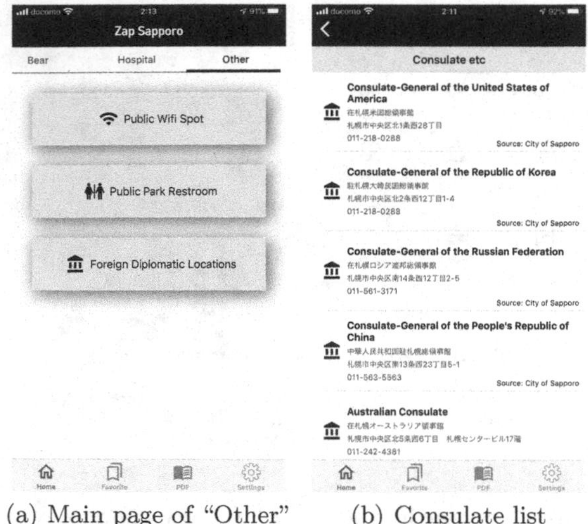

(a) Main page of "Other" (b) Consulate list

Fig. 6. Snapshot images of miscellaneous information in the Zap Sapporo application

Table 1. Data collections

Collection	# of records	Main attributes
List of Food Business Permits	34,351	name, address
Sapporo Gourmet Coupon	212	name, address, description
Yokoso Sapporo	33	name, succinct address, phone, description
Tourist friendly restaurant	30	name, address, phone
Sweets	64	name, address, phone
Night map	47	name, succinct address, phone

Another source is Sapporo Tourism Association, a non-profit organization that promotes tourism in Sapporo. It operates "Yokoso Sapporo (welcome to Sapporo)", an official website of Sapporo tourism, and also produces leaflets and guidebooks for visitors. In addition, it provides a smartphone application called "Sapporo Gourmet Coupon".

The Sapporo Chamber of Commerce and Industry also has some lists of restaurants to promote local business. One is a restaurant list in English, another is a list of confectionaries in greater Sapporo area.

Table 1 shows data to be integrated.

Sapporo Gourment Coupon and Yokoso Sapporo contains not many attribures but rich description of restaurants. Tourist friendly restaurant has usuful attributes for foreign visitors, such as available languages and cashless payment. Night map is unique because they contain many restaurants that are different from other collections, but there are challenges in integrating items such as simplified names and addresses.

At this stage, this paper has manually integrated these collections. As a result, it was found that there was a lot of problems with the accuracy of name matching on characters, and that the address was not perfect because it contained spelling errors and mistakes. Intuitively, phone numbers seem to be the most consistent and dependable, that is, useful for matching.

For example, "Ramen SORA", a ramen restaurant, is appeared in three collections: List of Food Business Permits, Sapporo Gourmet Coupon, and night map. For name, two variations are shown: "らーめん　空" and "ラーメン　空". Both "らーめん" and "ラーメン" are phonetic characters, so these two can be easily integrated automatically. Each expression of postal address is different: "北海道札幌市中央区南３条西５丁目２０－2", "札幌市中央区南 3 条西 5 丁目　20-2", and "南３条西５丁目 20". The third expression is succinct and rough. Matching may be probabilistic. Phone number is contained in Sapporo Gourmet Coupon and night map. The two numbers are exactly the same.

Another example is an okonomiyaki restaurant. Its name in the List of Food Business Permit is "焼き好み　風月", while the name in tourist friendly restaurants is "～お好み焼き・焼きそば～　風月＜パセオ店＞" which is decorated to attract attention. Postal address in tourist friendly restaurants is rough and in English, "060-0806 West exit PASEO 1F, Kita 6, Nishi 4, Kita-ku, Sapporo".

Based on the above analysis, a heuristic-based matching program has enabled some integration of collections. In the future, the authors aim at automatic and high-accuracy integration by natural language processing technologies and machine learning approaches.

5 Conclusions

This paper shows a one-stop smart city application that has been developed using that function. This application provides information for tourists during normal times, and it can handle the situation in town, such as congestion, in real time in order to grasp the flow and local stagnation that occur in bursts at the time of events or accidents.

Given the existence of data platforms developed for each field, we present the data linkage challenges that enable them to be integrated and used.

The authors continues to develop and provide both our application and data linkage platform. To evaluate the effectiveness of the proposed systems, experiments are being planned.

Acknowledgments. The authors would like to thank City of Sapporo, Hokkaido Government, Sapporo Tourist Association, and the Sapporo Chamber of Commerce and Industry for their cooperation with this research.

This work was supported by Cabinet Office, Government of Japan, Cross-ministerial Strategic Innovation Promotion Program (SIP), "Big-data and AI-enabled Cyberspace Technologies" (funding agency: the New Energy and Industrial Technology Development Organization, NEDO).

References

1. Aihara, K., Bin, P., Imura, H., Takasu, A., Tanaka, Y.: On feasibility of crowd-sourced mobile sensing for smarter city life. In: Streitz, N., Markopoulos, P. (eds.) DAPI 2016. LNCS, vol. 9749, pp. 395–404. Springer, Cham (2016). https://doi.org/10.1007/978-3-319-39862-4_36
2. Aihara, K., Bin, P., Imura, H., Takasu, A., Tanaka, Y.: Collecting bus locations by users: a crowdsourcing model to estimate operation status of bus transit service. In: Streitz, N., Konomi, S. (eds.) DAPI 2018. LNCS, vol. 10921, pp. 171–180. Springer, Cham (2018). https://doi.org/10.1007/978-3-319-91125-0_14
3. Aihara, K., Imura, H., Piao, B., Takasu, A., Tanaka, Y.: Mobile crowdsensing to collect road conditions and events. In: Yasuura, H., Kyung, C.-M., Liu, Y., Lin, Y.-L. (eds.) Smart Sensors at the IoT Frontier, pp. 271–297. Springer, Cham (2017). https://doi.org/10.1007/978-3-319-55345-0_11
4. Amichai-Hamburger, Y.: Potential and promise of online volunteering. Comput. Hum. Behav. **24**(2), 544–562 (2008)
5. Berners-Lee, T.: Linked data, July 2006. https://www.w3.org/DesignIssues/LinkedData.html
6. Howe, J.: Crowdsourcing: A definition Crowdsourcing. Tracking the Rise of the Amateur (2006)
7. Howe, J.: The rise of crowdsourcing. Wired Mag. **14**(6), 1–4 (2006)
8. Howe, J.: Crowdsourcing: How the Power of the Crowd is Driving the Future of Business. Random House (2008)
9. King, S.F., Brown, P.: Fix my street or else: Using the internet to voice local public service concerns. In: Proceedings of the 1st International Conference on Theory and Practice of Electronic Governance, pp. 72–80 (2007). https://doi.org/10.1145/1328057.1328076
10. Open Definition. http://opendefinition.org/
11. Schuurman, D., Baccarne, B., De Marez, L., Mechant, P.: Smart ideas for smart cities: investigating crowdsourcing for generating and selecting ideas for ict innovation in a city context. J. Theor. Appl. Electron. Commer. Res. **7**(3), 49–62 (2012)
12. Stembert, N., Mulder, I.J.: Love your city! an interactive platform empowering citizens to turn the public domain into a participatory domain. In: International Conference Using ICT, Social Media and Mobile Technologies to Foster Self-Organisation in Urban and Neighbourhood Governance (2013). http://resolver.tudelft.nl/uuid:23c4488b-09e1-4b90-85e3-143e4a144215

Evaluation of the Tourists' Satisfaction of Smart Tourist Attractions Using Importance-Performance Analysis

— Taking Jiuzhaigou as an Example

Chufan Jin(✉), Dian Zhu, Xi Chen, and Jingran He

Shanghai Jiao Tong University, Shanghai 200240, People's Republic of China
470193648@qq.com

Abstract. Taking Jiuzhaigou Scenic Area as an example, on the basis of combing the literature and combining the characteristics of the intelligent scenic area, a smart landscape composed of 14 indicators.

District service quality evaluation system, through the questionnaire survey method to obtain tourist evaluation data on these indicators. Based on the IPA analysis method, SPSS 21.0 was used to analyze the importance-satisfaction difference analysis of the sample data. Evaluation indicators are classified into advantage area, maintenance area, improvement area and opportunity area, and put forward suggestions to improve wireless network coverage, strengthen the construction of a personalized service intelligence system, and strengthen the connection between virtual networks and physical landscapes.

Keywords: Smart Tourist Attractions · IPA · Tourists' satisfaction

1 Background

With the development of artificial intelligence, big data, 5G and some other technologies, the Smart Tourist Attractions (STAs) have been widely developed in China. In the past six months, lots of STAs have successively build some latest functions such as AI navigation assistants, height screening system, online dynamic queuing, future population heat prediction and so on.

Recently, the ranking of Chinese top 100 of STAs has become a hot topic, and the degree of smart development of the STAs will also have a huge impact on the domestic tourism and service industries. Due to the popularization of technology, the development of STAs has shifted from technology-centric to demand-centric. Satisfaction of tourists has become the key to the quality of STAs.

According to the research of literature, as early as the end of the 20th century, western countries applied information technology to the practice of tourism. Western countries related research mainly explores the intelligent service system of tourist attractions and the practical application of intelligent information technology in the tourist attractions. For example, Owaied et al. proposed the framework model of smart travel guide system in

N. Streitz and S. Konomi (Eds.): HCII 2020, LNCS 12203, pp. 391–399, 2020.
https://doi.org/10.1007/978-3-030-50344-4_28

2011; Joan Borràs et al. surveyed the existing intelligent travel recommendation system in 2014 and summarized the corresponding construction guidelines and recommendations.

According to the CNKI search, it is known that the development of domestic STAs is good, and the number of related literatures in STAs is increasing. The research content of related literature is mainly focused on the concept of STAs, the construction of STAs, research based on the perspective of tourists, the development status and countermeasures of STAs, and the management and services of STAs. Regarding the discussion of the concept of STAs, Shao Zhenfeng and others believe that "STAs" are innovative scenic spot management systems that can most thoroughly perceive the three major aspects of the environment, society, and economy, wider interconnection and more scientific visual management. Ji Guobin and others proposed that the smart scenic area is based on the integration of modern communication and information technology, with the purpose of improving the quality of tourists' experience, and combining innovative service and management concepts to achieve intelligent management of scenic areas, intelligent service of scenic areas, and intelligent marketing of scenic areas Into. This concept points out the purpose of the construction of a STA, the means to rely on, and the ultimate goal to be achieved. With regard to the construction of STAs, scholars use field surveys, field surveys and other research methods to take representative STAs as research objects, and research smart facilities, equipment and platforms from various aspects in order to provide advice for the construction of domestic STAs. In recent years, STAs have also paid more and more attention to tourists' experience and perception evaluation. With reference to reasonable suggestions made by tourists, the scenic spots have been improved and optimized. Wang Xia and others believe that tourists are the most important experiencers of smart projects in scenic spots and the core objects of STA services. Zhang Chuncao and others based on the IPA analysis method and the perspective of tourists perception to construct the Qingming Shanghe Garden STA and concluded that the STA should be optimized and upgraded in terms of basic information and intelligent information system construction, scenic spot publicity means, and resource allocation optimization.

Through the review of the literature, it is found that the research results of STAs based on the perspective of tourists have gradually increased, but the research on tourist satisfaction is still at a shallow level. The essence of a STA is to serve tourists, improve the quality of tourism services, and meet the individual needs of tourists, thereby increasing tourists' satisfaction with the scenic spot. Based on previous research, this article selects the indicator system related to STA services, obtains data through questionnaire survey, uses SPSS21.0 for IPA analysis, and uses a four-quadrant grid chart to separate the indicators in the evaluation index system. It is classified into advantage area, improvement area, opportunity area, and maintenance area, and corresponding countermeasures are proposed for different areas. This article studies the service quality of STAs based on the IPA analysis method from the perspective of tourists' perception evaluation. It can not only enrich the research content of smart tourism, but also provide theoretical guidance for the construction and development of STAs to a certain extent.

2 Objective

Based on previous studies, this article selects an index system related to STAs services, and obtains data through questionnaire survey for Jiuzhaigou STAs, using SPSS21.0 for

IPA analysis. Jiuzhaigou Scenic Area was rebuilt due to the earthquake two years ago. This year 9 The park was reopened as STAs in January, but the analysis of its visitor satisfaction has remained in 2012, targeting its traditional infrastructure. Selecting it as the research object, the research results can be compared with the results of traditional scenic spots. From the perspective of tourist perception evaluation, the service quality of STAs based on IPA analysis can not only enrich the research content of smart tourism, but also provide theoretical guidance for the construction and development of STAs to a certain extent.

3 Method

3.1 Importance-Performance Analysis

IPA analysis (Importance-Performance Analysis, IPA) was proposed by John A. Matila and John C. James (John A. Martilla and John C. James) to analyze marketing sales, Pointed out that "importance-performance analysis is a useful technique for evaluating marketing plan elements." Since the 1990s, it has been widely used in government management, service industry, marketing and other fields, mainly focusing on product macro policy formulation, regional competitiveness assessment, and service quality assessment. At present, the research methods of academic satisfaction for tourists include American Consumer Satisfaction (ACSI), Service Quality Method (SERVQUAL), Fuzzy Comprehensive Evaluation Method (IPA), etc. Passengers' needs, looking for market positioning and improving service standards. Among them, the IPA analysis method has been widely used due to its advantages of intuitiveness, image, easy interpretation and favorable decision-making.

3.2 Data Sources

This article takes tourists in the Jiuzhaigou Scenic Area as the research object, and obtains data through field survey methods to reflect tourists' evaluation of the quality of Jiuzhaigou, so as to find out the existing problems in the area of smart services. 2 October 2009 on the 7th and 7th and 11th November, the author distributed questionnaires in the Jiuzhaigou Scenic Area. The target of the survey was tourists. A total of 250 questionnaires were distributed and 225 valid questionnaires were returned. The questionnaire recovery rate was 90%.

3.3 Questionnaire Design

The questionnaire consists of two parts. The first part is the characteristics analysis of tourists. Including items such as source area, age, gender, education, etc. The second part is the evaluation of STAs service quality. Combined with the uniqueness of STAs travel services, a total of 14 smart service quality evaluation indicators have been designed: intelligent forecasting system, wireless network coverage, self-service ticket checking system, online learning of scenic road conditions, mobile client electronic voice explanation service, mobile phone The client conducts electronic tour of the interior of the scenic spot, online purchase of scenic souvenirs, official WeChat and other platforms such as online parks, intelligent access control systems, intelligent passenger flow control systems, intelligent vehicle control, smart hotels and smart restaurants, travel information services, and consulting and complaint services. Questionnaire responses were in the form of Likert 5 scales.

Using the reliability analysis function of the Scale module in SPSS21.0 to examine the statements, the cloned Baha factor of the tourist satisfaction measurement scale consisting of 14 statements is 0. 861, and the cloned Baha coefficient of the importance measurement scale is 0.775, the cloned Baha coefficients of the two scales were above 0.7, the internal consistency of the questionnaire data was good, and the reliability was high.

4 Results and Analysis

4.1 Descriptive Analysis of Traveler Characteristics

The characteristics of tourists are shown in Table 1.

Table 1. Tourist characteristics

Questions	Options	Percentage %
Gender	Male	49.3
	Female	50.7
Age	Under 18 years of age	16.2
	18–29 years	38.1
	30–45 years	28.3
	Over 45 years old	17.4
Education	Junior high school and below	11.2
	High school, secondary school	23.7
	College	15.5
	Undergraduate	43.3
	Graduated students and above	6.3
Source	Province	64.6
	Outside the province	35.4
Number of visits to the scenic area	1 time	60
	2–3 times	26.4
	4 times and above	13.6
Ways to know the scenic area	Travel app	24.2
	Scenic site	18.6
	WeChat public account	15.7
	Introduction by others	34.7
	Travel agency	16.7
	TV, newspaper	41.4

Among the interviewed tourists, the sex ratio is relatively balanced. The age of tourists is mainly concentrated in the ages of 18–29, followed by 30–45, indicating that the tourists in Jiuzhaigou Scenic Area are mainly young and middle-aged. Age is related to tourism needs, and young groups travel Motivation is stronger. In terms of the educational level of tourists, more than half of the tourists are well-educated and belong to intellectuals. Generally speaking, tourism is largely a spiritual consumption. The higher the education, the more spiritual Level of satisfaction, the stronger the demand for travel. The source of tourists is mainly in Sichuan Province, which indicates that Jiuzhaigou Scenic Spot has occupied a certain market share in Sichuan Province, and 34.3% of tourists come from other provinces and cities, indicating that the scenic spot is in The country already has a certain popularity and influence. Regarding the number of tourists visiting the scenic area, most of the tourists in Jiuzhaigou are visiting the scenic area for the first time. 38.9% of tourists visit the scenic area more than once. To improve the rate of tourists' revisit and cultivate loyalty High-level tourists also need to continuously improve the service quality of the scenic spots. Regarding the channels for tourists to understand the scenic spots, most tourists pass through friends The introduction and TV, newspapers and other understanding of the scenic spot indicate that the word of mouth effect of tourists is very important, and the satisfaction of tourists directly affects the evaluation of Jiuzhaigou by tourists. Tourists understand the Jiuzhaigou scenic spot through traditional media such as television and newspapers, which indicates that the Jiuzhaigou scenic spot needs to use traditional media Carry out publicity so that more people understand the scenic spot. In addition, there are still a small number of tourists who understand the scenic spot through the scenic spot's official website and WeChat public account, indicating that the scenic spot needs to continuously strengthen its own platform construction and guide tourists to pay attention to the official website of the scenic spot and the public No., to understand the culture and development trend of the scenic spot. In addition, the scenic spot needs to strengthen cooperation with third-party platforms such as travel apps and travel agencies to continuously improve its popularity and brand effects.

4.2 Calculation of the IPA Index

The calculation formula is: $IPAI = (I - P)/I \times 100$. In the formula, IPAI is the IPA index, I is the score of importance, and P is the score of performance. The smaller the IPA index, the smaller the gap between performance and importance, which means that the satisfaction of tourists is higher. According to the size of the IPAI, the satisfaction can be divided into five levels: $\leq$1.00, 1.01–5.00, 5.01–10.00, 10.01–15.00 $\geq$ 15.01, respectively: very satisfied, satisfied, average, dissatisfied and very not dissatisfied (Table 2).

Table 2. Importance-performance score

Evaluation item	I	P	I – P	IPA	Satisfaction
Smart forecasting system	3.56	3.58	−0.02	−0.56	Very satisfied
Wireless network coverage	3.98	3.36	0.62	15.58	Very dissatisfied
Self-service ticket buying and checking system	3.92	3.69	0.23	5.87	General
Online access to scenic road conditions	3.67	3.59	0.08	2.18	Satisfied
App voice guide service	3.89	3.81	0.08	2.06	Satisfied
App electronic guide	4.01	3.62	0.39	9.73	General
Purchasing souvenir online	3.54	3.35	0.19	5.37	General
Visiting online attractions	3.65	3.61	0.04	1.10	Satisfied
Smart access control system	3.61	3.74	−0.13	−3.60	Very satisfied
Visitor flow intelligent control system	4.14	3.16	0.98	23.67	Very dissatisfied
Vehicle intelligent control	3.75	3.37	0.38	10.13	Dissatisfied
Smart hotel and smart catering	3.78	3.63	0.15	3.97	Satisfied
Tourism information service	3.49	3.48	0.01	0.29	Very satisfied
Consulting complaints service	3.46	3.26	0.20	5.78	General

Note: Very satisfied = 5, satisfied = 4, generally = 3, dissatisfied = 2, very dissatisfied = 1; very important = 5, important = 4, generally = 3, not important = 2, very not important = 1

The IPA index results: the importance score distribution of each evaluation item is 3.46–4.14; the satisfaction score distribution is 3.16–3.81.

Satisfaction	Evaluation item
Very satisfied	Smart forecasting system, smart access control system, tourism information service
Satisfied	Online access to scenic road conditions, app voice guide service. visiting online attractions, smart hotel and smart catering
General	Self-service ticket buying and checking system, app electronic guide, purchasing souvenir online, consulting complaints service
Dissatisfied	Vehicle intelligent control
Very dissatisfied	Wireless network coverage, visitor flow intelligent control system

4.3 Quadrant Analysis

Taking the importance of the observed items and the mean value of satisfaction as the intersection, taking the importance (I) as the vertical axis and the satisfaction (P) as the horizontal axis, constructing a two-dimensional four-quadrant coordinate map, forming four quadrants. They are: Advantage Zone, Improvement Zone, Opportunity Zone, and Maintenance Zone.

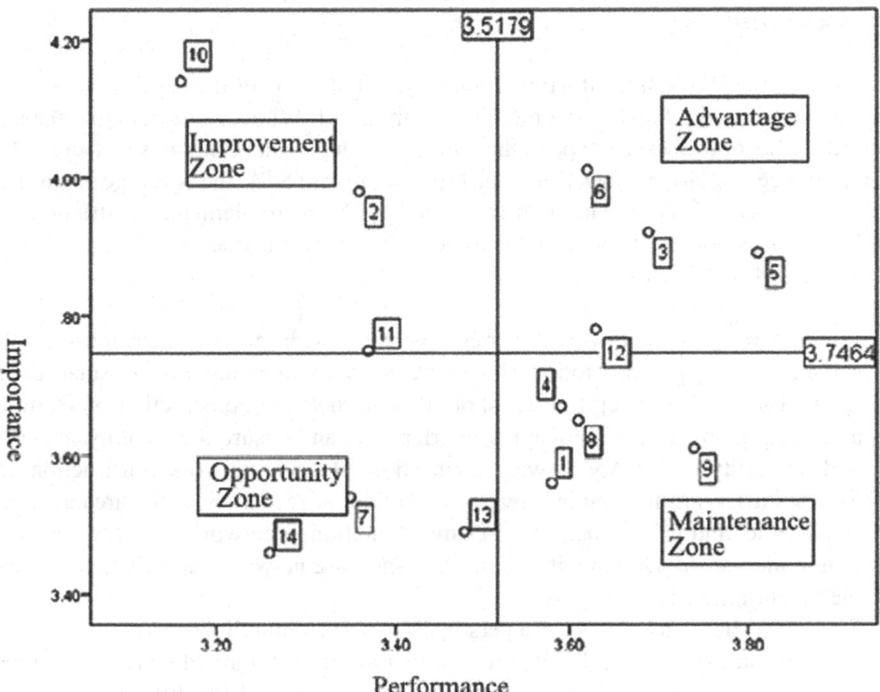

Quadrant Analysis Results
The first quadrant (Advantage Zone): the area with high importance and satisfaction is the advantage part of the Jiuzhaigou STA. It includes the self-service ticket checking system, app voice guide service, app electronic guide, smart hotels and smart restaurants. They are the advantages of Jiuzhaigou Scenic Area in terms of smart services and should be highlighted in the tourism marketing activities of tourist destinations, making it the core factor for Longmen Grottoes to attract tourists.

The second quadrant (Improvement Zone): high importance and low satisfaction area. It includes: coverage of wireless network, intelligent adjustment of visitor flow and intelligent regulation of vehicles. Aiming at these three smart service evaluation indicators, the scenic spot should prescribe the right medicine, focus on improving, and make it show a good development trend.

The third quadrant (Opportunity Zone) low scores on importance and satisfaction, and does not occupy priority status, including: online purchase of scenic souvenir, tourism information services and consulting and complaint services. The three indicators in this quadrant can be used as sub-improved objects. With the change of tourists' attitudes, the indicators in this area may be transformed into the competitive advantage of the scenic spot.

The fourth quadrant (Maintenance Zone): the importance is not very high, but the satisfaction is high. It includes: online access to the scenic road route, visiting online attractions, intelligent access control system, intelligent forecasting system. This shows that Jiuzhaigou Scenic Area has developed well in these three aspects. To continue to maintain it, you can also continue to innovate.

5 Discussion

According to the IPA results, the importance and satisfaction of the explanation service and e-guide service related to the mobile app are good. While, the electronic maps of other platforms or the service type of the online garden type have higher satisfaction, but the importance is relatively low. But as the infrastructure of STA, the coverage of wireless networks is unsatisfactory. Although Jiuzhaigou STA has implemented restrictions on people flow, it is not satisfactory in the survey of tourists' satisfaction.

Strategies for STAs:

(1) Strengthen wireless network coverage to create conditions for smart tours. At the same time, it is planned to introduce a 5G network to create a better smart experience for tourists. Scenic areas should strengthen the construction of facilities and equipment, try to avoid signal interference, and ensure the stability, security, and reliability of WLAN network connections. During network construction, try to avoid affecting the original features and human resources of the area as much as possible, and fully consider the Demand, including network coverage, capacity requirements, etc. Domain, it also needs to increase network capacity to fully meet the potential needs of tourists.

(2) Strengthen the construction of a personalized service intelligence system. According to the statistics of big data on tourists, tourists can be more refined and classified, and more personalized recommendations can be realized for different tourists in tourism information services, online souvenir purchase and other services.

(3) Strengthen the connection between virtual networks and physical landscapes. Use AR, VR technology to enhance the viewing experience.
Using mobile apps to design interactive games with physical landscapes in the AR environment can help visitors better see and understand the attractions. This way is more attractive to young people and children. The AR environment can bring more unachievable in a limited environment. Landscapes, for example, allow tourists to use mobile phones at a certain time to enjoy different scenery of the four seasons.

(4) Improve the passenger flow management system to divert time and space to travellers.

Excessive pedestrian flow in the scenic area not only affects the quality of tourists' viewing, but also affects the satisfaction of tourists. Therefore, it is necessary to divert tourists during peak periods, mainly in terms of time and space. The diversion in time mainly guides tourists in different periods Enter the scenic area or tourists visit the main attractions of the scenic area at different times. First, tourists can be diverted through the ticket reservation platform. When the tourist volume of the scenic area approaches the maximum capacity, the booking and purchase of tickets should be suspended. The flow of visitors is determined by the time when tourists buy tickets. The tourists can enter the area in batches at intervals of 20 min. In addition, the area should break the traditional publicity method and comprehensively use the platform's WeChat public account and official website to announce The number of tourists recently received by the scenic spot and the capacity of the scenic spot to guide tourists stagger the peak period of the scenic spot.

The spatial diversion is mainly aimed at controlling the flow of people at the popular attractions in the scenic spot. When the number of tourists is large, it will not only affect the viewing effect, but also endanger the safety of the tourists. At that time, the scenic spot can send someone to take charge of the tourists at the scenic spot to queue in batches to limit the viewing time of the tourists. In addition, the tour guide should pay attention to the diversion between the group tourists and individual tourists when leading the team.

References

1. Jin, Z., Liao, B.: Reform and innovation of smart scenic spots in China. Beijing Second Foreign Lang. Acad. **37**(1), 73–83 (2015)
2. Hao, G., Zhang, S., Liu, Y.: Research on the application mode of the concept of Zhihui scenic area in the tourism scenic area. World Digital Commun. (10), 123 (2018)
3. Ji, S., Wang, J., Gao, L., et al.: Research on infrastructure construction of Zhihuijing District: taking Qiannan District of Hebei Province as an example. Inf. Manag. China **20**(20), 127–128 (2017)
4. Qi, X.: Construction strategy of smart tourism scenic area in Xining wild zoo under the background of "internet". Anhui Agric. Sci. **44**(3), 219–220 (2016)
5. Shi, Y., Liang, Y., Xu, L.: Construction of personalized service system for tourists in smart scenic spots based on tourism e-commerce platform. J. Taiyuan Univ. (Nat. Sci. Ed.) **34**(4), 51–54 (2016)
6. Wang, Q., Peng, J., Sun, G.: Evaluation of tourist satisfaction in traditional scenic areas based on IPA method: taking Langya mountain scenic area as an example. Reg. Res. Dev. **36**(4), 110–115 (2017)
7. Xu, F., Huang, L.: Study on the willingness to use smart tourism system in scenic spots: based on integrated TAM and TTF models. Travel Tour. Sci. J. **33**(8), 108–117 (2018)
8. Song, Z., Li, C.: Research on the development status and countermeasures of smart scenic spots in Liaoning Province: from the perspective of tourist satisfaction. Special Econ. Zone **10**, 109–113 (2017)
9. Rina, U.: Based on management of tourism scenic spots from the perspective of smart tourism transformation and upgrade. Time Financ. (2), 336 (2018)
10. Shao, Z., Zhang, X., Ma, J., et al.: Management of Jiuzhaigou Zhihui District based on the Internet of Things. Geogr. Inf. World (5), 12–16 (2010)
11. Ji, G., Chen, L., Po, Y.: Development status and countermeasures of Zhihuijing District, Dalian City. China Econ. Trade Herald (5), 56–59 (2016)
12. Pan, C.: The construction and strategy of the management system of "Zhihui District" in the internet age: taking Jinci scenic area as an example. J. Taiyuan Univ. (Nat. Sci. Ed.) **35**(4), 62–67 (2017)
13. Fan, Y.: Planning of infrastructure construction in the wisdom scenery area under the "internet +" background: take Xingtai's Qiannan District as an example. Hous. Real Estate (18), 8 (2017)
14. Tang, L.: Study on the countermeasures and models for the construction of Zhihuijing District: a case study on the scenic spot of Gulangyu in Xiamen, Xiamen. J. Cent. South For. Univ. Sci. Technol. (Soc. Sci. Ed.) **10**(6), 81–88 (2016)
15. Dong, Z., Yang, Y.: Research on the perception and development strategy of the Zhihui scenic area based on the tourist's experience and perspective: taking Nanjing Sun Yat-sen Mausoleum smart scenic area as an example. Bus. Econ. (12), 51–53 (2018)
16. Wang, X., Zhen, F., Wu, X.: Evaluation system and empirical analysis of smart scenic spots based on tourist perspective: taking the Qinhuai scenery belt of confucius temple in Nanjing as an example. Prog. Geogr. **34**(4), 448–456 (2015)

Digitally Enhancing Society Through Structuralism: Virtualizing Collective Human Eyesight and Hearing Capabilities as a Case Study

Risa Kimura(✉) and Tatsuo Nakajima

Waseda University, Tokyo, Japan
{r.kimura,tatsuo}@dcl.cs.waseda.ac.jp

Abstract. Information technologies have dramatically changed our real world. There are two major concepts have played a role to change the real world. Through the computation concept, our various tasks can be automated. Also, the informatization concept makes us possible to quantify our daily activities. These concepts offer infinite possibilities for our future. However, another concept named the digital enhancement through virtualization concept has not been well discussed previously for changing the real world, but the concept has strong power to refine our real world. In this paper, we use the concept to virtualize collective human eyesight capabilities. We have developed a prototype implementation of the distributed platform to virtualize collective human eyesight and hearing capabilities and extracted some insights from the current platform. The paper concludes by exploring several future challenges to enhancing our current approach.

Keywords: Digital enhancement · Sharing economy · Collective human eyesight and hearing · Eye gaze gesture · Virtual reality · Smart city and society · Structuralism

1 Introduction

Information technologies have dramatically changed our real world [26, 29]. There are two major concepts have played a role to change the real world. Through the first concept named the computation concept, our various tasks can be automated. For example, automatic car driving is one of typical current trends using the concept. The second concept named the informatization concept makes us possible to quantify our daily activities. For example, the quantified-self approach monitors our physical activities correctly for increasing our health. These concepts offer infinite possibilities for our future. However, another concept named the digital enhancements through virtualization concept has not been well discussed previously for changing the real world, but the concept has strong power to refine our real world.

The sharing economy concept [10] is promising to digitally enhancing the real world through virtualization. In this paper, we use the concept to virtualize collective human

N. Streitz and S. Konomi (Eds.): HCII 2020, LNCS 12203, pp. 400–414, 2020.
https://doi.org/10.1007/978-3-030-50344-4_29

eyesight and hearing capabilities. Investigating the feasibility of sharing other types of physical resources, particularly human bodies, as sharable resources to enhance body ownership [18] and agency [31] is an interesting direction in which to expand the current scope of the sharing economy. The relationship between humans and computers has been dramatically changed.

In this study, we present a case study to digitally enhancing the real world. The case study is a distributed platform to virtualize collective human eyesight and hearing capabilities in a lightweight way, as shown in Fig. 1; the platform makes it possible to develop novel services to hijack anyone's eyes and ears as one's own. The platform adopts a gesture based on a user's gaze to choose which eye view he/she wants to see and to navigate the selected person's gaze orientation.

Fig. 1. Sharing parts of the bodies of everyone in the world

2 Background: Digitally Enhancing Society Through Structuralism

Digitally enhancing the real world through structuralism is a promising approach to systematically develop novel digital services by refining the meanings of the real world. Structuralism discusses that an abstract structure in our natural and social world is essential to generally define various phenomena explained in mathematics, physics, biology, psychology, social science, anthropology and so on [19, 28]. We believe that the structure becomes a key mechanism to virtualize the real world. Each structure virtualizing our society regulates human everyday behavior and also offers new opportunities to our future. For example, the real world can be reframed through several structures investigated by information concepts for engaging people from increasing the meaningfulness of the real world [25, 35].

In [30], *virtual form* is proposed as abstraction to digitally enhancing our real world. Virtual form presents dynamically generated visual expressions containing information that ascribes some additional values to the artifacts. Using virtual forms is a very promising way to enhance our real world, and to make our daily life and business richer and more enjoyable. Virtual forms can be used as a tool to enhance our real world for achieving *alternate reality experience* [13]. Alternate reality experiences are typically achieved by modifying our eyesight or replacing our five senses to others, and they make our world interactive by implicitly influencing human attitudes and behaviors.

The *dimension world model* is a model for analyzing the real world and to guide to design alternate reality experience. In Fig. 2, the dimension world model is presented. Dimension classifies our real world into the seven abstract components to model the world to take into account its meanings. The seven components are Living Things, Objects, Landscape, Information, Institution, Occurrences and Narrative, and a way to redefine our real world. By examining each component in the real world, we can systematically consider the refinement of the real world based on the model and framework. In [13], the authors explained how the seven components are introduced and use them to improve existing services. For achieving alternate reality experience, designers consider how virtual forms can be introduced according to respective dimensions in the real world.

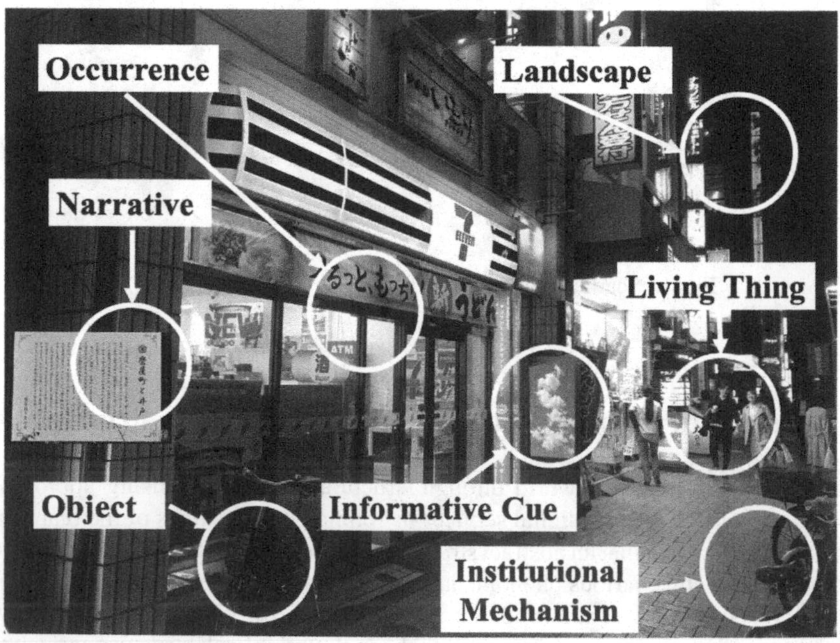

Fig. 2. Dimension world model

For designing virtual forms, we have developed design concepts called values and rhetorics. In Fig. 3, values and rhetorics are proposed for assisting to design and analysis for developing alternative reality experiences by digitally enhancing the real world through virtuality. The value is used for designing the playful aspect and the rhetoric is used for designing the gameful aspect in alternative reality experiences. As shown in Fig. 4, the rhetorics are extracted from various literatures [31]. In the paper, rhetorics are collected into *gameful digital rhetoric*, where five rhetorics: curious, social, economic, collective and narrative rhetoric are defined. In games, various virtual objects are embedded in the game worlds to influence players' behavior. Digital games consist of various digital rhetorical elements. Gameful digital rhetoric are as expressions that inform, persuade and inspire human behavior through digitally mediated virtual objects incorporated into the real world using digital technologies. In Fig. 5, the values are extracted from various disciplines [30], where six values: empathetic, persuasive, informative, economic, aesthetic and ideological values are introduced. Each value represents the specific quality that may attract users. As shown in [30], values are useful to analyze existing virtualized services and how to improve the service by considering which value was currently degraded and which value will be able to be increased.

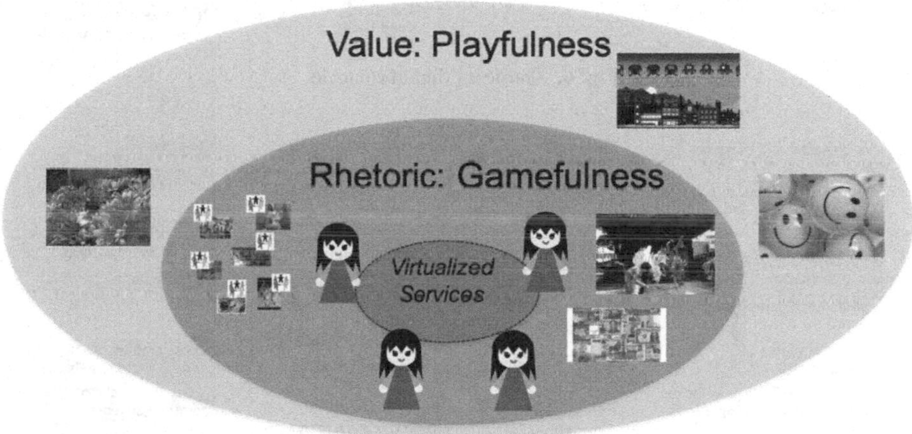

Fig. 3. Value and rhetoric

Figure 6 show three approaches to consider the digital enhancement of the real world for incorporating virtual forms in the real world. The first approach is "*replacing*". The approach is to replace a component in the real world to a fictional component. For choosing a replaced component, values and rhetorics can be used to design fictional components. [12] and [24] are typical examples to use "replacing" to incorporate virtuality in the real world. The second approach is "*adding*". The approach is to add fictional component in the real world. This is the most typical use case to use virtualization in previous approaches. For example, adding virtual agents is a well-known example. [16] and [25] are typical approach to use "adding" to incorporate virtuality in the real world. The last approach is "*reframing*". A typical way to use the approach is to add a new

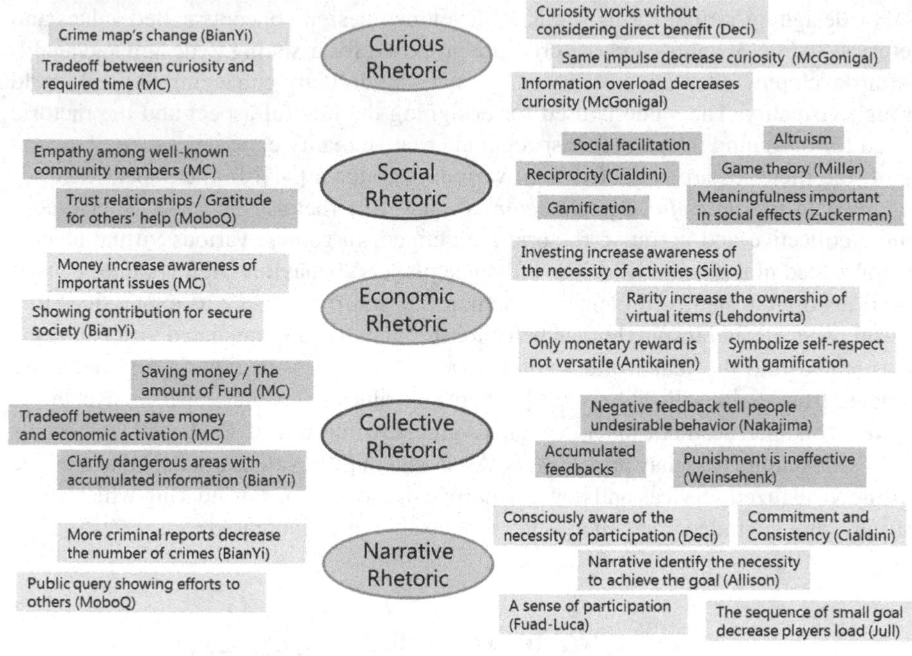

Fig. 4. Gameful digital rhetoric

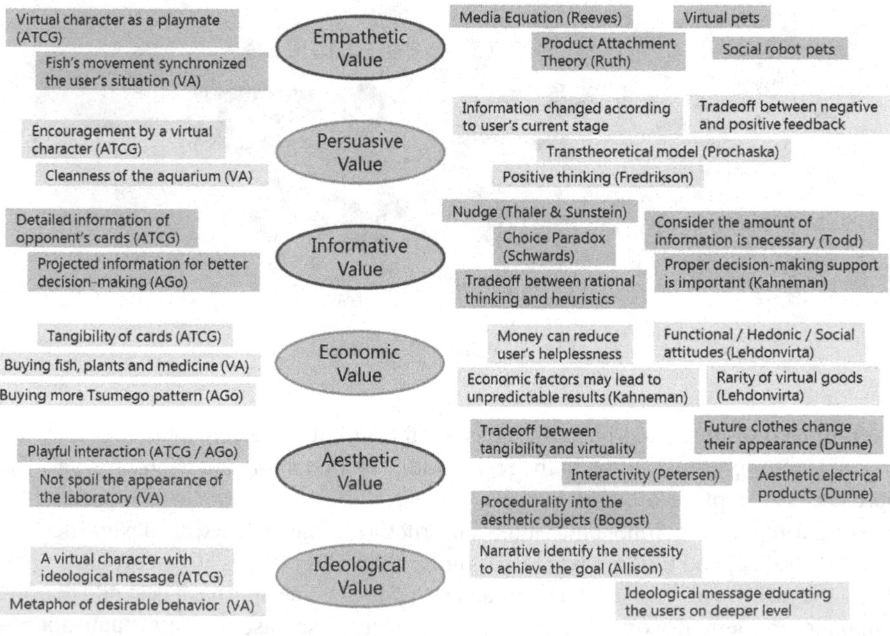

Fig. 5. Value-based analysis framework

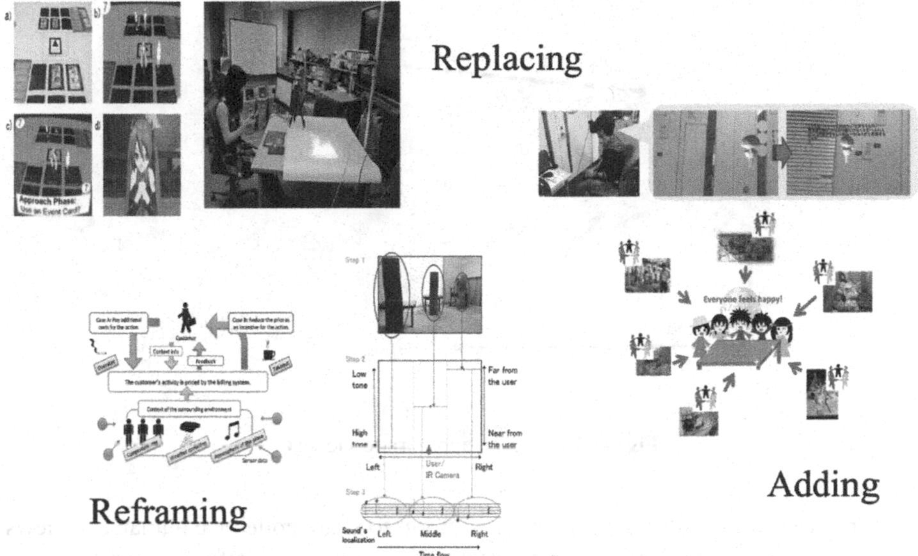

Fig. 6. Three approaches for digitally enhancing the real world

regulation for governing commons in the real world through an abstract structure (or a set of rules). Using "reframing" is a new way to incorporate virtuality in the real world, and in this paper, we like to show an example to use "reframing" to incorporate virtuality in the real world.

3 Basic Design for Virtualizing Collective Human Eyesight and Hearing Capabilities

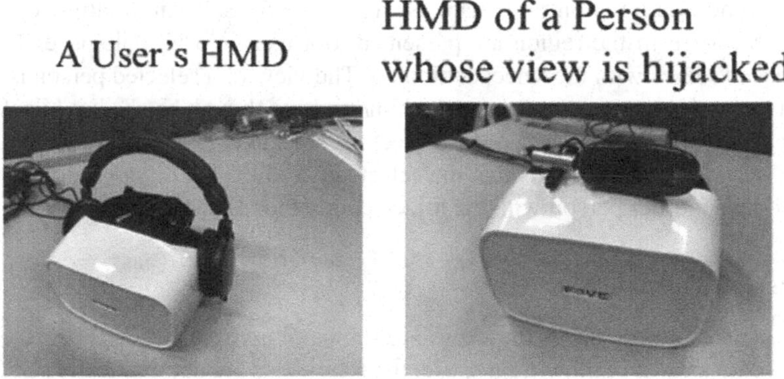

Fig. 7. Head-mounted display used in the proposed platform

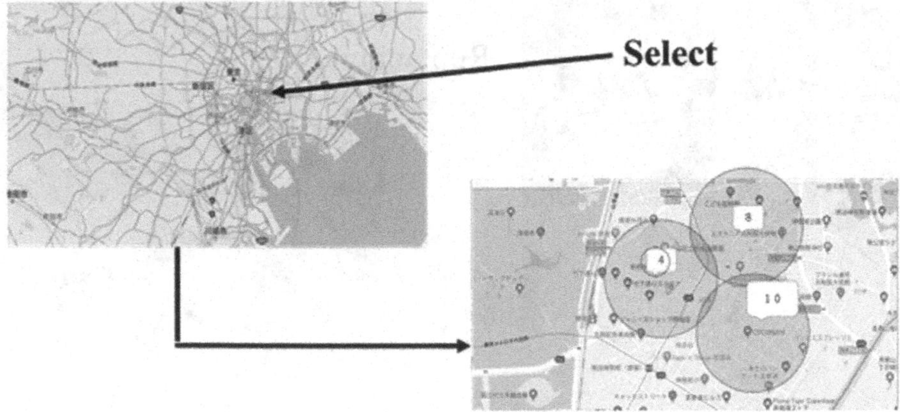

Fig. 8. Finding an appropriate view (1)

In this section, we introduce a digital platform to share collective human eye views and hearings for virtualizing the real world. The proposed platform consists of the following four functionalities: We assume that each person is equipped with a wearable device containing a camera and microphone, typically wearable glasses. The current version of the platform uses a head-mounted display (HMD) and puts a camera and microphone in front of the HMD, as shown in Fig. 7. The HMD projects the view captured by a camera. However, the future platform will use a lightweight smart glass to improve the ease of daily use.

The proposed platform also uses the eye gaze based gesture to change the direction of a selected person's head orientation by presenting a small moving/blinking visual object for turning the selected person's head orientation towards the object that a user wants to see based on techniques described in [1, 8]. More details can be found in [17].

3.1 Finding an Appropriate Eye View

First, a user chooses a region on a map, as shown in Fig. 8. Then, multiple eye views of persons who are in the region are presented to a user in a virtual space. The user chooses one of views with the select command. The view of a selected person is shown instead of the user's own eye view to make him/her to as though he/she has hijacked the selected person's eye. The user can then direct the selected view with his/her eye gaze, as shown below. If the user finds that the selected person is not an appropriate person, he/she chooses another person with the hijack command, as shown in Fig. 9.

3.2 Watching Multiple Eye Views

When showing multiple views, the views are shown in a virtual space (Fig. 10). When many views are shown in the virtual space, the four views are automatically selected. If one of views does not interest a user, the remove command is used to indicate the view is not necessary. Then, another view is shown instead of the removed view. Additionally, the change command can replace all views at the same time.

Fig. 9. Finding an appropriate view (2)

Fig. 10. Watching multiple eye views

3.3 Eye Gaze Based Gesture

One of the characteristics of our approach is to use gaze-based gestures for all controls in the platform. We defined the following five basic commands based on the design shown in [11, 33]. The first command named select command is employed by the user to select a target person by moving his/her eyesight from top to bottom. The second command named deselect command is used to return to the previous view by the user moving his/her eyesight from bottom to top. The third command named hijack command is employed by the user to choose another person whose eye view the user wants to hijack by watching a selected person and moving his/her eyesight from top to bottom around the person. The fourth command named change command is used to change the current view to the view of the randomly selected another person near the user by the user moving his/her eyesight from top to bottom in the current view. The fifth command named replace command is used for removing a view that the user wants to replace by the user moving his/her eyesight from bottom to top on the view.

4 A Preliminary User Study

In this user study, we wanted to extract some insights on the feasibility of our approach based on research through design [9]. We knew that the proposed approach might not be familiar for most of the participants. Since we predicted that they might not understand how to use the platform just by experimenting with the prototype, we have developed a fictive use case scenario based on the design fiction method. By playing a role in the scenario that was based on user enactments [27], they could understand the potential merits of the design and investigate the possibilities and pitfalls of the approach.

The experiment was conducted for an entire day at our university; we hired 16 participants (age m = 24.8, sd = 8.4, 15 males), and each participant was first introduced to the basic idea of the proposed approach and then asked to play the role of Risa in the following scenario by using the prototype system. Finally, we conducted an interview with him/her to extract some insights into the current approach.

4.1 Scenario

Risa, who is a college student, has strong interests in the landscape of urban cities such as Odaiba in Tokyo, where there is much fantastic scenery. In order to investigate the landscape of Odaiba, she first tries to find some people who are the place. Their eye views are presented in a VR space, and she chooses one of them. Then, she wants to explore other scenery so she starts to find another person who is slowly walking to the direction of a bridge that she wants to see, and uses the hijack command to change her current eye view to the newly selected person's eye view. She uses the gaze-based navigation function to orient the selected person's head to look at the bridge

4.2 Extracted Insights

We classified the labels extracted from the interviews into three categories in accordance with affinity diagram [23] and grounded theory [5].

Gaze-based Gesture Control. Most participants said the gaze-based gesture was natural and easy to use, and it was easy to remember how to use the respective gesture commands. On the other hand, one participant said, "*For performing gestures, moving my eyesight should be minimal.*" Another participant noted that "*When using the platform for a long time, I felt my eyes get tired.*"

Effect of Hijacking Others' View. All participants answered that hijacking other persons' eye views is enjoyable and useful because they can easily investigate the selected location from multiple angles, but one participant noted that "*Hijacking an eye view is dangerous in terms of privacy because I can easily know whose view is now hijacked. Selecting a person's view randomly may be more preferable.*" Another participant also mentioned: "*I may be confused on whether I'm now watching my view or others' views. Therefore, the platform should clearly indicate whether the current view is not my view. This is like the metacommunication proposed by Bateson* [2]." On the other hand, one participant said, "*Hijacking multiple persons' views consecutively offers serendipitous thinking to expand my creativity.*"

Additionally, "*Eye views of foreign people who visit in Tokyo may offer me serendipitous ideas on well-known places for me as shown in the video.*" (The video that the participant showed is [36]).

Privacy Issues. One important concern of this approach is how participants felt about privacy issues. Their comments noted that the issue would not be serious if the anonymity of a person who offers his/her eye view is preserved. However, one participant asserted: "*I think that it is necessary to consider the privacy of the person within their own field of vision; I don't want to show the information presented on my mobile phone.*" Another participant said, "*I would not like my vision being controlled while reading books, talking to people, or relaxing at home.*"

5 Related Work

5.1 Telepresence Robots

There are several approaches to using robots, not human eyesight, to capture remote views in the real world. Robots that are remotely deployed in sightseeing locations can travel around the locations in place of a user [4]. The user can then visit any location without physically going there [34]. Additionally, it has become common to use moving robots when a person cannot attend a conference. These robots perform various activities on behalf of the user's physical body. The approach is especially effective when working in dangerous locations.

5.2 Jack-In Head

Jack-In is a concept for augmenting human capability and human existence [14, 15]. The concept enables immersive connection between humans and other artifacts or between humans. The technique of hijacking another person's eyesight that is used in our approach is similar to the Jack-In concept.

5.3 KinecDrone

A KinecDrone enhances our somatic sensation of flying in the sky [12]. A video captured by drone is transmitted to a user's smart glasses. While a user behaves like he/she is flying in the sky, he/she can watch the scene captured by flying drone while still in a room. Thus, the user feels like he/she is truly flying in the sky.

5.4 Crowdsourcing

Crowdsourcing divides a task into various microtasks and asks crowds to complete them. Typical crowdsourcing uses monetary rewards to motivate crowds. Amazon Mechanical Turk is currently the best-known commercial crowdsourcing service [7]. As shown in [22], humans can be used to monitor real-world information as a sensor based on collective human power.

5.5 Metagames

A metagame concept [3] may be becoming a key to redefining the meaning of the real world because the concept has developed various approaches to enhancing the original meaning of existing games to incorporate more real-world social activities [3].

6 Challenges and Opportunities

When using others' eye views, one important issue is to preserve their privacy as pointed in the previous section. Our prototype system allows us to choose a view anonymously, but we still need to consider the following two issues. The first issue is the possibility of identifying a person from surrounding situations found in views. For example, if the person looks at his/her belongings, someone may become aware of who he/she is. The second issue is that the view may be used to know someone's current situation. For example, if a view contains a person who meets another person secretly, that fact may be suddenly disclosed to others.

The proposed approach requires diving into a VR space for accessing multiple views. For using the approach in our daily lives, a more lightweight method for accessing a VR space is desirable. One approach is to present multiple views in real space by using augmented reality technologies. However, the views should be carefully shown in the real world because these views may increase a user's cognitive load and disturb his/her current tasks. Additionally, mirror worlds offer new possibilities for representing a variety of real-world information in a virtual space [24]. Remixed reality offers technologies that can synchronize the virtual and real worlds [20]. Additionally, layered representation, such as [32], provides a new way to present multiple people's views simultaneously, as shown in Fig. 11. In the next step, we aim to investigate these new approaches to information representation.

In our study, we consider only sharing human eyesight and hearing capabilities. However, it is not easy to share other human capabilities, such as a sense of taste and smell, because these senses are not easy to detect and actuate. The use of robots' arms and feet has become popular for supporting a person's activity in remote places. However, it is not easy to use others' arms and feet without explicitly requesting to use them. However, it may be interesting to investigate the possibility of sharing these capabilities.

In [17], the authors show that showing multiple eye views offer a new possibility for stimulating reflective thinking. Li, Dey and Forlizzi present a five-stage model of personal informatics systems and identify the barriers in each stage. Reflection is one of the stages in the model, and the problems caused by the barriers occur exploring,

Fig. 11. Layered representation

and understanding information [21]. Our system helps people to retrieve and explore a variety of information in the world where our current aim is to offer technologies to support the R0-R2 level defined in [6] but where it is not ensured whether the quality of the information is sufficient for reflective thinking. One issue is that the system relies on users understanding information because it does not offer deep information, so a misunderstanding or shallow understanding of the information may become a barrier to reflective thinking.

7 Conclusion

In this paper, we presented a case study to digitally enhancing the real world though virtualization. In the case study, the virtualization concept is adopted to virtualize collective human eyesight and hearing capabilities. A distributed platform to implement the virtualization to develop services that use collective human eyesight and hearing capabilities. The platform offers a user the ability to navigate through multiple people's views with his/her eye gaze. We showed a prototype implementation of the distributed platform to virtualize collective human eyesight and hearing capabilities and extracted some insights from the current platform. The paper concludes by exploring several future challenges to enhancing our current approach.

References

1. Åkerström, A.: Comparison between gaze and moving objects in videos for smooth pursuit eye movement evaluation. Department of Electrical and Information Technology, Lund University (2015)
2. Bateson, G.: A Theory of Play and Fantasy. In: Bateson, G. (eds.) Steps to a Ecology of Mind, pp. 177–193. Ballantine Books (1972)
3. Boluk, S., Lemieux, P.: Metagaming: Playing, Competing, Spectating, Cheating. Making, and Breaking Videogames, University of Minnesota Press, Trading (2017)
4. Cain, W., Bell, J., Cheng, C.: Implementing robotic telepresence in a synchronous hybrid course. In: Proceedings of the IEEE 16th International Conference on Advanced Learning Technologies, pp. 171–175 (2016). https://doi.org/10.1109/ICALT.2016.79
5. Corbin, J.: Basics of Qualitative Research: Techniques and Procedures for developing Grounded Theory. Sage, Thousand Oaks (2008)
6. Fleck, R., Fitzpatrick, G.: Reflecting on reflection: framing a design landscape. In: Proceedings of the 22nd Conference of the Computer-Human Interaction Special Interest Group of Australia on Computer-Human Interaction (OZCHI 2010), pp. 216–223 (2010). http://dx.doi.org/10.1145/1952222.1952269
7. Kittur, A., Chi, E.H., Suh, B.: Crowdsourcing user studies with Mechanical Turk. In: Proceedings of the SIGCHI Conference on Human Factors in Computing Systems (CHI 2008), pp. 453–456 (2008). https://doi.org/10.1145/1357054.1357127
8. Ghosh, S., et al.: NotifiVR: exploring interruptions and notifications in virtual reality. IEEE Trans. Vis. Comput. Graph. **24**(4), 1447–1456 (2018). https://doi.org/10.1109/TVCG.2018.2793698
9. Giaccardi, E., Stappers, P.J.: Research through Design. Chapter 43: The Encyclopedia of Human-Computer Interaction, 2nd edn. Interaction Design Foundation (2017)
10. Hamari, J., Sjöklint, M., Ukkonen, A.: The sharing economy: why people participate in collaborative consumption. J. Assoc. Inf. Sci. Technol. **67**(9), 2047–2059 (2015). https://doi.org/10.1002/asi.23552
11. Heikkilä, H., Räihä, K.-J.: Speed and accuracy of gaze gestures. J. Eye Mov. Res. **3**(2) (2010). http://dx.doi.org/10.16910/jemr.3.2.1. ISSN 1995-8692
12. Ikeuchi, K., Otsuka, T., Yoshii, A., Sakamoto, M., Nakajima, T.: KinecDrone: enhancing somatic sensation to fly in the sky with Kinect and AR.Drone. In: Proceedings of the 5th Augmented Human International Conference (AH'14). Article 53, p. 2 (2014). http://dx.doi.org/10.1145/2582051.2582104
13. Ishizawa, F., Sakamoto, M., Nakajima, T.: Extracting intermediate-level design knowledge for speculating digital-physical hybrid alternate reality experiences. Multimed. Tools Appl. **77**(16), 21329–21370 (2018). https://doi.org/10.1007/s11042-017-5595-8
14. Kasahara, K., Rekimoto, J.: JackIn: integrating first-person view with out-of-body vision generation for human-human augmentation. In: Proceedings of the 5th Augmented Human International Conference (AH 2014). Article 46, p. 8 (2014). http://dx.doi.org/10.1145/2582051.2582097
15. Kasahara, S., Ando, M., Suganuma, K., Rekimoto, J.: Parallel eyes: exploring human capability and behaviors with paralleled first person view sharing. In: ACM SIGGRAPH 2016 VR Village (SIGGRAPH 2016). Article 16, p. 2 (2016). https://doi.org/10.1145/2929490.2929495
16. Kinoshita, Y., Nakajima, T.: Making ambient music interactive based on ubiquitous computing technologies. In: Proceedings of the 9th International Symposium on Ambient Intelligence. pp. 199–207 (2018)

17. Kimura, R., Nakajima, T.: Sharing collective human's eyesights towards reflective thinking. In: Proceedings of the 17th International Conference on Mobile and Ubiquitous Multimedia, pp. 341–349 (2018). https://doi.org/10.1145/3282894.3289724
18. Kilteni, C., Maselli, A., Kording, K.P., Slater, M.: Over my fake body: body ownership illusions for studying the multisensory basis of own-body perception. Front. Hum. Neurosci. **9**, March 2015, Article. 141. https://doi.org/10.3389/fnhum.2015.00141
19. Levi-strauss, C., Structural Anthropology, Basic Books (2000)
20. Lindlbauer, D., Wilson, A.D.: Remixed reality: manipulating space and time in augmented reality. In: Proceedings of the 2018 CHI Conference on Human Factors in Computing Systems (CHI 2018). Paper 129, p. 13 (2018). https://doi.org/10.1145/3173574.3173703
21. Li, I., Dey, A., Forlizzi, J.: A stage-based model of personal informatics systems. In: Proceedings of the SIGCHI Conference on Human Factors in Computing Systems (CHI 2010), pp. 557–566 (2010). https://doi.org/10.1145/1753326.1753409
22. Liu, Y., Alexandrova, T., Nakajima, T.: Using stranger as sensors: temporal and geo-sensitive question answering via social media. In: Proceedings of the 22nd International Conference on World Wide Web (WWW 2013), pp. 803–814 (2013). https://doi.org/10.1145/2488388.2488458
23. Lucero, A.: Using affinity diagrams to evaluate interactive prototypes. In: Abascal, J., Barbosa, S., Fetter, M., Gross, T., Palanque, P., Winckler, M. (eds.) INTERACT 2015. LNCS, vol. 9297, pp. 231–248. Springer, Cham (2015). https://doi.org/10.1007/978-3-319-22668-2_19
24. Maeda, K.: Mirrorworlds. http://blog.leapmotion.com/mirrorworlds/. Accessed 28 Dec 2019
25. Nakajima, T., Lehdonvirta, V.: Designing motivation using persuasive ambient mirrors. Pers. Ubiquit. Comput. **17**(1), 107–126 (2013). http://dx.doi.org/10.1007/s00779-011-0469-y
26. Niksirat, K.S., et al.: Approaching engagement towards human-engaged computing. In: Extended Abstracts of the 2018 CHI Conference on Human Factors in Computing Systems (CHI EA 2018). Paper SIG14, p. 4 (2018). https://doi.org/10.1145/3170427.3185364
27. Odom, W., Zimmerman, J., Davidoff, S., Forlizzi, J., Dey, A.K., Lee, M.K.: A fieldwork of the future with user enactments. In: Proceedings of the Designing Interactive Systems Conference (DIS 2012). pp. 338–347 (2012). https://doi.org/10.1145/2317956.2318008
28. Piaget, J., Structuralism. Psychology Press, New York (2015)
29. Ren, X.: Rethinking the relationship between humans and computers. Comput. **49**(8), 104–108 (2016). https://doi.org/10.1109/MC.2016.253
30. Sakamoto, M., Nakajima, T., Alexandrova, T.: Enhancing values through virtuality for intelligent artifacts that influence human attitude and behavior. Multimed. Tools Appl. **74**(24), 11537–11568 (2015). https://doi.org/10.1007/s11042-014-2250-5
31. Sakamoto, M., Nakajima, T., Akioka, S.: Gamifying collective human behavior with gameful digital rhetoric. Multimed. Tools Appl. **76**(10), 12539–12581 (2017). https://doi.org/10.1007/s11042-016-3665-y
32. Saraiji, M.H.D.Y., Sugimoto, S., Fernando, C.L., Minamizawa, K., Tachi, S.: Layered telepresence: simultaneous multi presence experience using eye gaze based perceptual awareness blending. In: ACM SIGGRAPH 2016 Emerging Technologies (SIGGRAPH 2016). Article 14, p. 2 (2016). https://doi.org/10.1145/2929464.2929467
33. Singh, H., Singh, J.: Real-time eye blink and wink detection for object selection in HCI systems. J. Multimod. User Interf. **12**(1), 55–65 (2018). https://doi.org/10.1007/s12193-018-0261-7
34. Tsui, K.M., Desai, M., Yanco, H.A., Uhlik, C.: Exploring use cases for telepresence robots. In: Proceedings of the 6th International Conference on Human-robot Interaction (HRI 2011), pp. 11–18 (2011). https://doi.org/10.1145/1957656.1957664

35. Yamabe, T., Nakajima, T.: Playful training with augmented reality games: case studies towards reality-oriented system design. Multimed. Tools Appl. **62**(1), 259–286 (2013). https://doi.org/10.1007/s11042-011-0979-7
36. Tokyo cute, strange, weird travel tips! Suspiria horror bar, Pokemon cafe, Line Friends, Gundam. https://www.youtube.com/watch?time_continue=30&v=VuTPA3uk0h0. Accessed 28 Dec 2019

Investigating Users Attitudes and Perceptions Towards the Usage of Smart City Apps

Sirong Lin, Xinting Liang, Bingqian Zhang, Fei Xing, and Guochao (Alex) Peng(✉)

Sun Yat-Sen University, Panyu District, Guangzhou 510000, China
penggch@mail.sysu.edu.cn

Abstract. The important role of citizens towards smart city success has been increasingly recognized by police makers, practitioners and academics. In light of this, smart apps are probably the most appealing smart city element to citizens, who are using these on a daily basis. Nevertheless, little was known about citizens attitudes and perceptions regarding the usage of smart city apps. In this paper, we reported the results derived from a questionnaire survey with 577 citizens in Guangzhou, China. The study investigated their use experience of smart city apps, in order to identify potential shortcomings of these apps and provide reference for their future optimization. The results show that Chinese citizens have high intention to use smart city apps, but they also have concerns about app service responsiveness, information accuracy, system reliability, perceived cost, and perceived risk.

Keywords: Smart city · Smart city app · User perspective

1 Introduction

With the advancement of urbanization and increasing urban population, the daily lives of urban residents and the public management of local infrastructure and services are becoming more and more complicate [1]. In response to the emerging "urban problems", the concept of "smart city" was proposed by IBM in 2008. A smart city utilizes the information to effectively integrate infrastructure, increases the participation of citizens in urban governance, and thus improves the efficiency of urban operations and residents' quality of life [1, 2]. The construction of smart cities has achieved initial results. With the help of smart technology, residents can carry out urban activities such as consultation appointments, parking inquiries, and real-time traffic inquiries without leaving home. China has proposed the development prospects of "smart society" construction [3].

The progress from a smart city to a smart society will completely change people's mode of production and lifestyle [4], which will inevitably require the full use of various urban data and ensuring the full coverage of city residents by smart services. This goal cannot be realized without the support of various smart city apps. Only through smart city apps can residents be connected with various smart infrastructures [5, 6] to enjoy the convenience of life brought by the smart environment. Governments of countries in the world have invested a lot of money in building smart city infrastructures. At

N. Streitz and S. Konomi (Eds.): HCII 2020, LNCS 12203, pp. 415–430, 2020.
https://doi.org/10.1007/978-3-030-50344-4_30

present, there are many apps supporting smart services, but the actual utilization is not optimistic. In China, researchers have found that residents' awareness and utilization of mobile medical apps are at a low level [7]. Government apps also have the problems such as uneven quality, poor functions, blind development, few users, and low user stickiness [8, 9]. There are also similar problems in foreign countries. The London government has invested a lot of money in building a smart parking system, but the supporting app is rarely used by residents [10]. The widespread application of smart technologies in cities will indeed facilitate residents' participation in urban governance, but inadequate use of these technologies by residents will be a waste of resources [11–13]. At present, smart city has a good momentum of technical development, but there is still a lack of humanities. Smart city is implemented by people, not technology [14], and technology is valuable only when it is embedded in the social environment [15]. Research on the use of smart services by residents is also an important subject in smart city construction.

At present, there have been related studies focusing on user behaviors under smart services. Researchers have used empirical research to build user adoption models of specific smart services in the context of smart cities, and explore factors that affect users' adoption of and intention to use services. These studies have provided a good theoretical basis for understanding users' adoption behavior in the smart city context. These models mainly clarify the relationships and influence paths of various factors. Although they can also provide a reference for the development and improvement of smart services, smart services can be improved and optimized in a more targeted manner by learning about the current user experience of smart services to find the gap between user needs and actual services. As such, this study differentiates itself from most previous studies by learning about the residents' use experience of and comments on smart city apps from multiple dimensions through questionnaires, and finding out the problems in the apps to provide references for its optimization. The next section outlines the literature on smart services and users, followed by discussion on research methodology. Then, the results of the study are discussed. The last section is the summary and outlook.

2 Related Work Between Smart City Services & Users

Smart city is a rich concept that involves all aspects of the city, so the services provided in a smart city are diverse [16]. The existing smart services and applications cover smart transportation, smart healthcare, and smart education, smart energy, smart public security, smart building management, smart waste disposal, etc. [10]. Most researchers believe that the construction of smart cities requires advanced information and communication technologies in order to provide more effective public information and services and thus a smarter city life for residents [10]. Accordingly, city managers overemphasize the fundamental role of smart technology in the construction of smart cities, and put more effort into building infrastructure to provide smart services regardless of time and location [17].

Although smart services have brought many innovative means to urban governance, substantial improvement of quality of life cannot be brought by sensors only [11–13]. The implementation of technology works only when it is accepted by end users. In this regard, ICT (Information and Communication Technology) companies focus on not only sensor-based systems, but also the value of these systems for the communities they serve, as well as communication with residents [18]. Similarly, researchers have begun to pay attention to users' acceptance of information and communication technologies in the context of smart cities. Yeh [19] found that if a smart service is innovative and have high quality without unauthorized disclosure of privacy, residents will be willing to accept and use such a service. Research by Tony et al. [20] showed that residents' perceived usefulness and perceived ease of use of City113 app will affect their attitude towards it, and thus affect their intention to use the app. Daniel et al. [21] studied smart cards and found that the ease of use has a high positive effect on perceived privacy, perceived usefulness, and perceived security, and convenience plays a decisive role in continuance of users. In addition, research shows that users of smart city services value safety, security as well as information quality and service quality [22]. These studies mainly clarify the relationships and influence paths of various factors, providing a good theoretical basis for understanding user adoption behavior in the context of smart cities.

Smart phones are considered an ideal carrier for developing smart applications and services [23]. Smart apps will be an important medium for experiencing smart services. However, previous research shows that smart apps fails to achieve the desired result even if its development has cost a lot of money and energy of the government [7–10]. The low utilization has made smart apps useless. How to improve the acceptance of smart apps by residents is an important issue for the promotion of smart services. As mentioned above, most of the current related studies are based on user behavior theory, focus on the identification of the factors that influence the users' intention to use and clarify the mechanism of their interaction. However, smart services can be improved and optimized in a more targeted manner to increase the utilization rate by learning about the current user experience of smart services to find the gap between user needs and actual services. Different from previous research, this research surveys the residents through questionnaires to learn about their use experience of and comments on smart city apps from multiple dimensions and find out the problems in the apps.

3 Methodology

3.1 Questionnaire Design

As mobile applications, smart city apps are also information systems. Most of the user-perspective studies on information systems use Technology Acceptance Model (TAM) [24], Unified Theory of Acceptance and Use of Technology model (UTAUT) [25], and the Delone and McLean Model of Information Systems Success (D&M model) [26] or other theoretical models coupled with external variables to study multiple factors affecting user adoption of information system. The data collected by this research aims to reflect the experience and comments of residents in using smart city apps. A large number of studies [27–29] have proven that factors such as perceived ease of use, perceived cost, perceived risk, system quality, information quality, and service quality can affect users' intention to use information systems and their satisfaction. Relevant research on user adoption behavior has also proved that the above factors play an important role in user adoption behavior. Therefore, learning about users' comments on these dimensions is of great significance for the targeted optimization and improvement of the systems. In addition, most of the above studies quantify these factors by examining the user experience during the use of the system, which shows that the above factors can be used to measure the user experience of the information systems.

In summary, by reference to the previous research and based on the characteristics of smart city apps, some factors were selected and refined to obtain user perception indicators of smart city apps in this research (Table 1).

Table 1. User perception indicators of smart city app

Indicator	Definition	Subdivision indicator	Source
Perceived ease of use (PEU)	The ease of use of smart city apps perceived by residents	1 Ease of use 2 Flexibility	Davis [24]
Perceived cost (PC)	Time, energy and economic cost perceived by residents for using smart city apps	1 Perceived financial cost 2 Perceived effort	Luarn & Lin [27], Hu & Kettinge [28]
Perceived risk (PR)	Risk perceived by residents in the use of smart city apps	1 Privacy risk 2 Performance risk	Featherman & Pavlou [29], Jacoby & Kaplan [30]
System quality (SYSQ)	Residents' evaluation of the system reliability of smart city apps	System reliability	Petter et al. [31], Zhou [32]
Information quality (IQ)	The accuracy and timeliness of information transmitted by smart city apps perceived by residents	1 Information accuracy 2 Information timeliness	
Service quality (SERQ)	The service quality of smart city apps perceived by residents	1 Service responsiveness 2 Service effectiveness	
Behavioral intentions to use (BI)	Residents intention to use smart city apps	Attitude toward using	Moon & Kim [33]

Questions in the questionnaire described the experience of using the apps from various dimensions in the form of statement (Table 2). Each indicator is measured using a Likert 5-level scale, and respondents answered the questions based on their real feelings in using smart city apps.

3.2 Selection of Sample

In this study, Guangzhou is selected as the representative of China's "smart cities" for a case study. In 2012, Panyu District and Luogang District of Guangzhou became the

Table 2. Design of questionnaire on user perception of smart city apps of Guangzhou

Indicator		No.	Content	Options
Basic question		Q1–Q5	Area of residence, gender, age, education level, income	N/A
Core problem	PEU1	Q6	The mobile smart city apps are easy to operate	1. Strongly disagree 2. Disagree 3. Neutral 4. Agree 5. Strongly agree
	PEU2	Q7	Smart city apps are easy to use most of the time and place	
	PC1	Q8	I think the economic cost of using smart city apps is high	
	PC2	Q9	I think the use of smart city apps costs a lot of time and energy	
	PR1	Q10	I worry about privacy leakage when using smart city apps	
	PR2	Q11	I think there is great risk in using smart city apps	
	SYSQ	Q12	Smart city apps generally have no problems such as crash, white screen or inability to open	
	IQ1	Q13	Smart city apps always send me accurate information	
	IQ2	Q14	I think smart city apps send timely information	
	SERQ1	Q15	The offline service of smart city apps can be well connected with the corresponding online service	
	SERQ2	Q16	The services provided by smart city apps make my life more convenient	
	BI	Q17	I have a positive and supportive attitude towards the use of smart city apps	

first pilot areas of China's smart cities. After several years of development, Guangzhou has a more mature strategic deployment in the construction of smart cities, developing a relatively complete social activity system. There are increasingly sound technical support systems to provide strong support for the construction of smart cities [34], and smart city services such as smart transportation, smart ports, and e-government have made great progress [35]. Guangzhou has won multiple awards at Smart China Annual Conference, won the fourth place in the "Top 20 Cities in Smart City Construction" in 2017 [36], and won the Smart City Leadership Award in 2018 [37]. It can be seen that Guangzhou has made good achievements in smart city construction. To some extent, Guangzhou represents the current level of smart city construction in China. It is appropriate to select this city as a survey sample.

3.3 Questionnaire Distribution

The targeted sampling frame is the users of smart city apps in Guangzhou, China. The sample data is collected by means of online questionnaire filling and paper questionnaire distribution. In order to ensure that the collected sample data is comprehensive and can fully reflect the use of smart city apps by residents in Guangzhou, on the one hand, researchers spread the questionnaires by forwarding online; on the other hand, considering that the scope of online spread will be restricted by the breadth of the social circle, the research team distributed questionnaires offline in 11 districts of Guangzhou. Finally, the data collected online and offline were integrated and cleaned, and quantitative analysis was performed.

4 Data Analysis and Results

4.1 Sample Demographics

A total of 577 valid questionnaires were collected in this study. The sample data covered 11 districts of Guangzhou. According to the data released by the Guangzhou Statistics Bureau, the urbanization rate of Guangzhou by the end of 2018 was 86.38% [38]. It can be seen that the collected sample data is basically consistent with the distribution of urban and rural population in Guangzhou. The proportions of different genders are roughly equal. In terms of age structure, respondents aged 19 to 44 accounted for the largest proportion, and this age group is also the most frequent users of mobile applications. In terms of education level, undergraduates and above account for nearly 80% of the respondents, indicating that the users of smart city apps of Guangzhou are mainly people with higher education level. In terms of income, the respondents mainly have a monthly income of less than 5,000 yuan and 5,000 to 20,000 yuan; and those with a monthly income of more than 20,000 yuan are only a small proportion (Table 3).

4.2 Overall Situation of Users' Perception on Smart City Apps

According to the collected valid questionnaires, the arithmetic mean value[1] of the results of each question were calculated to obtain the residents' evaluation scores on smart city apps as a whole and each indicator (Table 4). The higher the score given by users, the higher the evaluation of smart city apps, and the better the user experience will be.

[1] During data analysis, for the questions with positive meanings (Q6–Q7, Q12–Q17), the options "strongly disagree", "disagree", "neutral", "agree" and "strongly agree" are assigned scores of 1, 2, 3, 4 and 5 respectively; for questions with negative meanings (Q8–Q11), the scores are assigned reversely, that is, 5 for "strongly disagree" and 1 for "strongly agree" and so on.

Table 3. Sample demographics

Measure	Item	Percentage
Region	Urban	73.3%
	Rural	26.7%
Gender	Male	46.4%
	Female	53.6%
Age	≤18	10.9%
	19–44	78.3%
	≥45	10.7%
Education level	Senior high school or lower	21.7%
	Undergraduate	59.1%
	Graduate and above	19.2%
Monthly income	≤5000 yuan	48.0%
	5,000–20,000 yuan	47.5%
	≥20,000 yuan	4.5%

Table 4. Results of user perception measurement of smart city apps of Guangzhou

Indicator	Score (out of 5)	Question	Score (out of 5)	Order
BI	4.02	Q17 (Attitude toward using)	4.02	2
SERQ	3.89	Q16 (service effectiveness)	4.08	1
		Q15 (service responsiveness)	3.69	6
PEU	3.87	Q7 (Flexibility)	3.91	3
		Q6 (Ease of use)	3.82	5
IQ	3.77	Q14 (Information timeliness)	3.87	4
		Q13 (Information accuracy)	3.68	7
SYSQ	3.44	Q12 (System reliability)	3.44	8
PC	2.76	Q9 (Perceived effort)	2.83	9
		Q8 (Perceived financial cost)	2.82	10
PR	2.44	Q11 (Perceived financial cost)	2.65	11
		Q10 (Privacy risk)	2.23	12
Overall score 3.41				

The overall score of smart city apps given by residents was 3.41, still far from the full score, indicating that smart city apps currently cannot bring the best user experience to residents, and there is a great room for improvement. Among the subdivision indicators, "service effectiveness" in SERQ got the highest score, and the "privacy risk" in PR got the lowest score.

(1) BI
The score for BI was 4.02 (reflected by "attitude towards using"), which was the highest among the seven indicators. 79.4% of the residents had a positive and supportive attitude towards the use of smart city apps. Less than 1% of the residents held the opposite opinion, and the remaining 19.8% had a neutral attitude. From this point of view, smart city apps are highly accepted among residents, indicating that the development of smart city apps meets the needs of residents. At the same time, less than 30% of the residents with a positive attitude gave a score of 5, which shows that smart city apps need to be improved in many aspects although it is recognized by most residents.

(2) SERQ
The overall score given by residents on the SERQ of smart city apps was 3.89, which was relatively high. From the perspective of subdivision indicators, the service effectiveness got the highest score among all subdivision indicators. 81.8% of the residents agreed with the statement "the services provided by smart city apps make my life more convenient", indicating that smart city apps play a better role in the daily life of residents and bring convenience to them. However, in terms of service responsiveness of smart city apps, the score was 3.69. In addition to assisting residents with information inquiry and acquisition, smart city apps can also assist citizens in handling various affairs. When residents' requests can be quickly responded, it will improve the users' perception of effectiveness [22]. Therefore, ensuring effective response is an important dimension for improving the user experience. If a resident registers online to see a doctor, but he is told that there is no registration record at the hospital. The bad experience brought by this disconnection of online and offline information will greatly curb the enthusiasm of residents for using smart city apps. According to the survey results, there is still room for improvement in the service response of smart city apps.

(3) PEU
The overall score given by residents on the PEU of smart city apps was 3.87, which indicates that smart city apps perform better in this regard. In terms of each subdivision indicator, the ease of use got a score of 3.82, and the flexibility got a score of 3.91. An app can attract users and solve their needs only if it is easy to use, otherwise users may abandon it the first time he opens it due to tedious operations. According to the survey results, there is no big problem in the operation design of smart city apps, but there is still room for improvement. The residents gave a generally high score to flexibility. Smart city apps rely on smart phones, so they have good mobility and can be used anytime and anywhere. However, in some special scenarios, they may bring hidden safety hazards. For example, navigation apps are likely to bring unsafe driving behaviors [39]. In addition, most smart city apps need access to the Internet to obtain the latest real-time information, and the completeness of communication facilities will also affect their use.

(4) IQ
Smart city apps integrate city data to provide residents with basis for various information decision-making and convenient city services. Information is one of the core elements of smart city apps. According to the statistical results, residents gave a relatively low score of 3.77 on IQ, which is a key indicator of smart city apps. Among the subdivision indicators, the information timeliness scored higher, indicating that smart city apps can basically deliver real-time information to users in a timely and fast manner. Information accuracy scored lower. Ensuring information accuracy is an important foundation for smart city apps. Only based on accurate information can users make correct decisions. Without accuracy, no matter how timely the information is provided, it will not help users make decisions, and may even bring reverse results. At present, the information quality of smart city apps still have potential for improvement.

(5) SYSQ
The smart city apps' system reliability got a score of 3.44. Less than 50% of residents think that smart city apps generally do not have problems such as crash, white screen or failure to open. This reflects that the system cannot ensure its proper operation during the use of smart city apps. Although there are many smart city apps on the market, the statistics of mobile app store[2] show that most apps have fewer downloads and low software ratings except for some familiar applications, and many comments suggest that apps have problems such as "inability to open normally", "inability to log in", "connection failure", "crash", etc. It indicates that some smart city apps have the poor system stability, which will directly affect the user experience. Therefore, more attention should be paid to system stability in the smart city app development process.

(6) PC
There is a great gap between the score of PC and those of the aforementioned indicators. The perceived cost of smart city apps includes the effort and money spent on using the apps. Both subdivision indicators scored lower than the median score of 3, which shows that most residents believe that using the smart city apps will bring them higher costs. The use of smart city apps will inevitably consume a certain amount of time and energy, and sometimes users need to learn the corresponding knowledge in order to master the use method. Certain apps may also charge fees during the use, thus bringing burdens to residents and complicating matters that could have been done easily [40]. Seen from the survey results, residents currently have a poor evaluation of smart city apps in terms of the perceived cost.

(7) PR
PR also received a low score, ranking last among the eight indicators, and the "privacy risk" scored the lowest among all questions, indicating that residents are paying great attention to personal privacy when using smart city apps. Smart city apps are data-driven and will inevitably need to collect a large amount of user data. Most of people's information and behavior data will be recorded, and some smart city apps also require users to provide their real names and bind their bank cards. Therefore, the privacy and security of information can easily cause residents'

[2] The data source is Android App Store.

concerns [41, 42], and solving security issues is vital to smart services [43]. The data shows that current residents' evaluation of smart city apps is low in terms of both privacy protection and security performance.

4.3 Users' Perception on Smart City Apps Under Different Demographics

Previous studies have shown that user groups with different socio-demographic characteristics may have different intentions to use technology products [44], and age, gender, or education level may all have an effect on this [45]. In addition to grasping residents' perception of the smart city apps as a whole, the study also horizontally compares the respondents with different socio-demographic characteristics in order to obtain different user groups' perception of the smart city apps. According to the results, the male and the female groups show no obvious differences in the choice of the answers to the questions, but differences are shown between the groups in the dimensions of area of residence (Table 5), education level (Table 6), age (Table 7), and monthly income (Table 8).

(1) Difference between urban and rural residents

Table 5. Statistics of answers given by urban and rural residents (partial)

Question	Group	Strongly disagree	Disagree	Neutral	Agree	Strongly agree
Mobile smart city apps are easy to operate.	Urban residents	0.2%	3.1%	25.5%	53.0%	18.2%
	Rural residents	0.6%	3.2%	34.4%	48.7%	13.0%
The services provided by smart city apps make my life more convenient.	Urban residents	0.0%	1.4%	14.4%	54.6%	29.6%
	Rural residents	0.6%	1.9%	22.1%	52.6%	22.7%
Smart city apps always send me accurate information.	Urban residents	0.0%	4.3%	33.8%	47.5%	14.4%
	Rural residents	1.3%	5.2%	41.6%	40.9%	11.0%
I think the use of smart city apps costs a lot of time and energy.	Urban residents	1.9%	23.9%	35.2%	29.8%	9.2%
	Rural residents	4.5%	19.5%	48.1%	20.8%	7.1%
I worry about privacy leakage when using smart city apps.	Urban residents	0.9%	4.7%	30.7%	39.5%	24.1%
	Rural residents	1.3%	3.2%	41.6%	36.4%	17.5%

In terms of ease of use, the proportion of urban residents with a positive attitude was 71.2%, while that of rural residents was 61.7%, nearly ten percentage points lower compared with urban residents. At the same time, the rural residents who encountered problems such as crash and white screen on the apps accounted for 39%, 11.4% more than urban residents. This shows that in the operation and use of the smart city apps, rural residents perceive higher difficulty than urban residents, which may be because rural residents have lower education level than urban residents and accept new things slowly.

In terms of service quality and information accuracy, rural residents' evaluation of smart city apps is also lower than that of urban residents. Rural residents' perception of the service effectiveness of smart city apps is not as obvious as that of urban residents. The reason may be that the difficulties encountered in using apps have weakened their perception of the convenience to a certain extent. Urban residents who agreed with the statement "smart city apps always send me accurate information" accounted for 61.9%, while the proportion of rural residents was 51.9%, indicating regional difference in the quality of information provided by smart city apps. The reason may be that the infrastructures supporting smart city services in rural areas are inferior to those in urban areas.

Urban residents appear to be more sensitive than rural residents in terms of perceived effort and privacy leakage. 39% of urban residents think that it costs a lot of time and energy to use smart city apps, and this value has dropped to 27.9% in rural areas. Regarding privacy, 63.6% of urban residents are worried about privacy leakage when using smart city apps, while only 53.90% of rural residents are concerned about privacy leakage. Compared with rural residents, urban residents pay more attention to their time and energy costs and privacy security when using smart city apps, raising higher requirements for the use costs and security performance of apps.

(2) Difference among different education levels

Table 6. Statistics of answers given by respondents with different education levels (partial)

Question	Group	Strongly disagree	Disagree	Neutral	Agree	Strongly agree
The services provided by smart city apps make my life more convenient.	Graduate	0.0%	2.7%	11.7%	57.7%	27.9%
	Undergraduate	0.0%	0.6%	16.1%	54.8%	28.4%
	High school	0.8%	3.2%	21.6%	48.8%	25.6%
I have a positive and supportive attitude towards the use of smart city apps.	Graduate	0.0%	0.9%	18.0%	55.9%	25.2%
	Undergraduate	0.0%	0.3%	16.4%	59.2%	24.0%
	High school	0.8%	1.6%	30.4%	47.2%	20.0%
I worry about privacy leakage when using smart city apps.	Graduate	0.9%	4.5%	21.6%	41.4%	31.5%
	Undergraduate	0.9%	3.5%	33.1%	39.6%	22.9%
	High school	1.6%	6.4%	45.6%	33.6%	12.8%

Residents with undergraduate or high education level did not show outstanding group characteristics, and residents with a high school or lower education level showed differences in certain dimensions.

The group with a high school or lower education level had lower evaluations of smart city apps in terms of "service effectiveness" and "behavioral intention to use" than the other two groups. In terms of perceived effectiveness brought by smart city apps, 74.4% of the group with a high school or lower education level believed that the services provided by smart city apps make city life more convenient, while the proportions of graduate group and undergraduate group with the same opinion both exceeded 80%. In addition, more than 80% of graduate and undergraduate groups have a positive attitude towards the use of smart city apps, and this value dropped to less than 70% of the group with high school or lower education level. It can be found that, along with the low evaluation of service quality perception, the intention to use smart city apps among people with high school or lower education level also dropped. Compared with the groups with other education levels, the group with high school or lower education level includes respondents under the age of 18, who have insufficient knowledge of urban life, use smart city apps less frequently and thus have limited perception.

In terms of privacy, the respondents with a high school or lower education level do not pay as much attention as the other two groups. 72.90% of the respondents with graduate education level are worried about privacy leakage when using smart city apps, 62.50% of the respondents with undergraduate education level also hold the same opinion, and only 46.40% of respondents with high school and below education level are concerned about privacy leakage. With the improvement of educational level, people are more aware of information security, and will pay more attention to their privacy protection and the privacy protection function of apps.

(3) Differences among different age groups

Table 7. Statistics of answers given by respondents of different age groups (partial)

Question	Group	Strongly disagree	Disagree	Neutral	Agree	Strongly agree
The services provided by smart city apps make my life more convenient.	≤18 years old	0.0%	1.6%	28.6%	47.6%	22.2%
	19-44 years old	0.2%	3.1%	27.0%	52.4%	17.3%
	≥45 years old	1.6%	4.8%	33.9%	51.6%	8.1%
I worry about privacy leakage when using smart city apps.	≤18 years old	1.6%	9.5%	42.9%	27.0%	19.0%
	19-44 years old	0.9%	3.8%	32.7%	39.4%	23.2%
	≥45 years old	1.6%	3.2%	30.6%	45.2%	19.4%
I have a positive and supportive attitude towards the use of smart city apps.	≤18 years old	0.0%	0.0%	30.2%	46.0%	23.8%
	19-44 years old	0.0%	0.9%	18.8%	56.2%	24.1%
	≥45 years old	1.6%	0.0%	16.1%	64.5%	17.7%

Among the three age groups, the 19–44 age group did not show significant differences from the other two groups.

Regarding the ease of use of smart city apps, nearly 70% of people under the age of 44 have a positive attitude, while only 59.7% of those aged 45 and above have the same attitude. This shows that compared with other age groups, the middle-aged and elderly group have some difficulties in using smart city apps, and further optimization is needed to meet the requirements of this group.

The consciousness of privacy protection among people aged 18 or below is relatively weak. Only 46.0% of this group are worried about privacy leakage when using smart city apps, while more than 60% of the other two age groups are worried about privacy leakage. In addition, the group under 18 years of age hold a less positive attitude towards the use of smart city apps than the other two groups, which may be related to the fact that this group has not started an independent life and has less exposure to smart city apps.

(4) Difference among groups with different income levels

Table 8. Statistics of answers given by respondents with different income levels (partial)

Question	Group	Strongly disagree	Disagree	Neutral	Agree	Strongly agree
The services provided by smart city apps make my life more convenient.	≤5,000 yuan	0.4%	1.4%	19.5%	55.2%	23.5%
	5,001–20,000 yuan	0.0%	1.5%	14.2%	54.0%	30.3%
	≥20,000 yuan	0.0%	3.8%	7.7%	42.3%	46.2%
I have a positive and supportive attitude towards the use of smart city apps.	<5,000 yuan	0.4%	0.4%	24.9%	54.2%	20.2%
	5,001–20,000 yuan	0.0%	0.7%	15.0%	59.5%	24.8%
	≥20,000 yuan	0.0%	3.8%	15.4%	38.5%	42.3%

The high-income group with monthly income of more than 20,000 yuan gave higher evaluation in some indicators than the other two groups. In terms of the service effectiveness of smart city apps, the respondents with monthly income of more than 20,000 yuan who choose "strongly agree" accounted for the highest proportion among the three groups. At the same time, the proportion of people who hold positive attitudes on this topic in this group is also higher than that of the other two groups. In addition, in terms of intention to use, the proportion of people who gave a score of 5 is also much higher than that of the other two groups.

5 Discussion and Conclusion

The purpose of this study is to investigate residents' perception and attitudes towards the use of smart city apps, so as to find out issues that should be focused on in the optimization of smart city apps. In addition to the planning and design of government agencies and technological innovation, the construction of smart cities is inseparable from the support and adoption by urban residents. Therefore, it is of great significance to study residents' views of smart city services. This can provide guidance for targeted optimization of smart city apps. In this study, a Chinese city with good achievements in smart city construction has been selected a sample, and the survey results come from representative respondents among local residents. The study mainly draws the following conclusions:

(1) The overall evaluation of smart city apps by citizens is not very high. Although the data reflects residents' high intention to use smart city apps, some indicators got a low evaluation and there is still room for improvement.
(2) Among the multiple evaluation indicators, smart city apps got relatively high evaluation in terms of service effectiveness, perceived ease of use, and information timeliness and can basically meet the residents' requirements for use.
(3) Smart city apps got low evaluation in terms of service responsiveness, information accuracy, system reliability, perceived cost, and perceived risk, showing a great gap from residents' expectations. Smart city apps should be improved in these aspects.
(4) High-income residents and highly educated residents showed a higher intention to use smart city apps.
(5) In terms of ease of use, urban residents and high-income group have shown higher recognition, while the elderly group still has obstacles in the operation of smart apps.
(6) In terms of service quality and information accuracy, urban residents gave higher evaluation than rural residents.
(7) Urban residents, highly educated residents and adult group pay more attention to perceived risk and perceived cost.

6 Limitations and Direction for Future Studies

The indicators in this study were mainly extracted from previous empirical studies, so there are certain limitations in the construction of the indicator system. In addition, from the results of data analysis, it can be seen that the evaluations of smart city apps by different demographic groups shows differences. Since the data were collected from questionnaires and the questions in the questionnaires were closed, it was unable to find the reasons behind the difference. Further exploration can be made in this aspect in the future. In terms of research object, this study took all different types of smart city apps as a whole for the research. However, different types of smart services have different focuses, so whether this will lead to the differences in people's evaluations remains to be studied in the future.

References

1. Aldama-Nalda, A., et al.: Smart cities and service integration initiatives in North American cities: a status report. In: Proceedings of the 13th Annual International Conference on Digital Government Research, pp. 289–290. ACM, June 2012
2. Neirotti, P., De Marco, A., Cagliano, A.C., Mangano, G., Scorrano, F.: Current trends in smart city initiatives: some stylised facts. Cities **38**, 25–36 (2014)

3. www.qstheory.cn. Report of Xi Jinping at the 19th National Congress of the Communist Party of China (Full Text) [EB/OL], 09 04 2019. http://www.qstheory.cn/llqikan/2017-12/03/c_1122049424.htm
4. www.besticity.com. Interpretation of the "smart society" in the report of the 19th National Congress of the Communist Party: What exactly is the "smart society" mentioned by Xi Jinping? [EB/OL], 09 04 2019. http://www.besticity.com/newsExpress/174629.html
5. Liang, T., Peng, G.C., Xing, F.: Application status and problem analysis of China's smart city app. Libr. Inf. Serv. **63**(8), 65–73 (2019)
6. Cifaldi, G., Serban, I.: Smart cities-smart societies. In: Karwowski, W., Ahram, T. (eds.) IHSI 2018. AISC, vol. 722, pp. 700–707. Springer, Cham (2018). https://doi.org/10.1007/978-3-319-73888-8_108
7. Zhou, S.S., Ma, L.Y., Xing, L., Hu, X.P.: Lanzhou Citizens' Awareness and Demand for Mobile Medical Apps. Chin. J. Publ. Heal. **11**, 126–128 (2017)
8. Chen, Z.Q.: Analysis of typical problems of china mobile government app. E-Government **3**, 12–17 (2015)
9. Xue, W.Q., Xie, M.R.: Development status and strategic thinking of government app from the perspective of service-oriented government. E-Government **3**, 38–42 (2015)
10. Peng, G.C.A., Nunes, M.B., Zheng, L.: Impacts of low citizen awareness and usage in smart city services: the case of London's smart parking system. Inf. Syst. e-Business Manag. **15**(4), 845–876 (2016). https://doi.org/10.1007/s10257-016-0333-8
11. Nam, T., Pardo, T.A.: Conceptualizing smart city with dimensions of technology, people, and institutions. In: Proceedings of the 12th Annual International Digital Government Research Conference: Digital Government Innovation in Challenging Times, pp. 282–291. ACM, June 2011
12. Thomas, V., Wang, D., Mullagh, L., Dunn, N.: Where's wally? in search of citizen perspectives on the smart city. Sustainability **8**(3), 207 (2016)
13. Townsend, A.M.: Smart cities: Big Data, Civic Hackers, and the Quest for a New Utopia. WW Norton & Company, New York (2013)
14. Oliveira, Á., Campolargo, M.: From smart cities to human smart cities. In: 2015 48th Hawaii International Conference on System Sciences, pp. 2336–2344. IEEE, January 2015
15. Murphie, A., Potts, J.: Culture and technology. J. Documentation **3**(3), 285–288 (2003)
16. Oktaria, D., Kurniawan, N.B.: Smart city services: a systematic literature review. In: 2017 International Conference on Information Technology Systems and Innovation (ICITSI), pp. 206–213). IEEE, October 2017
17. Lee, J., Lee, H.: Developing and validating a citizen-centric typology for smart city services. Gov. Inf. Q. **31**, S93–S105 (2014)
18. Chong, M., Habib, A., Evangelopoulos, N., Park, H.W.: Dynamic capabilities of a smart city: An innovative approach to discovering urban problems and solutions. Gov. Inf. Q. **35**(4), 682–692 (2018)
19. Yeh, H.: The effects of successful ICT-based smart city services: from citizens' perspectives. Gov. Inf. Q. **34**(3), 556–565 (2017)
20. Susanto, T.D., Diani, M.M., Hafidz, I.: User acceptance of e-government citizen report system (a case study of city113 app). Procedia Comput. Sci. **124**, 560–568 (2017)
21. Belanche-Gracia, D., Casaló-Ariño, L.V., Pérez-Rueda, A.: Determinants of multi-service smartcard success for smart cities development: a study based on citizens' privacy and security perceptions. Gov. Inf. Q. **32**(2), 154–163 (2015)
22. Schumann, L., Stock, W.G.: The information service evaluation (ISE) model. Webology **11**(1), 1–20 (2014)
23. Balakrishna, C.: Enabling technologies for smart city services and applications. In: 2012 Sixth International Conference on Next Generation Mobile Applications, Services and Technologies, pp. 223–227. IEEE, September 2012

24. Davis, F.D.: Perceived usefulness, perceived ease of use, and user acceptance of information technology. MIS Q. 319–340 (1989)
25. Venkatesh, V., Morris, M.G., Davis, G.B., et al.: User Acceptance of Information Technology: Toward a Unified View. MIS Q. **27**(3), 425–478 (2003)
26. Delone, W.H., McLean, E.R.: The DeLone and McLean model of information systems success: a ten-year update. J. Manag. Inf. Syst. **19**(4), 9–30 (2003)
27. Luarn, P., Lin, H.H.: Toward an understanding of the behavioral intention to use mobile banking. Comput. Hum. Behav. **21**(6), 873–891 (2005)
28. Hu, T., Kettinger, W.J.: Why people continue to use social networking services: developing a comprehensive model. In: Proceedings ICIS 2008, p. 89 (2008)
29. Featherman, M., Pavlou, P.: Predicting e-services adoption:a perceived risk facets perspective. Int. J. Hum Comput Stud. **59**(4), 451–474 (2003)
30. Jacoby, J., & Kaplan, L. B. (1972). The components of perceived risk. ACR Special Volumes
31. Petter, S., DeLone, W., McLean, E.R.: Information systems success: The quest for the independent variables. J. Manag. Inf. Syst. **29**(4), 7–62 (2013)
32. Zhou, T.: An empirical examination of continuance intention of mobile payment services. Decis. Support Syst. **54**(2), 1085–1091 (2013)
33. Moon, J.W., Kim, Y.G.: Extending the TAM for a World-Wide-Web context. Inf. Manag. **38**(4), 217–230 (2001)
34. Zhang, Z.G., Zhang, X.J.: Status, problems and countermeasures of Guangzhou smart city construction. Sci. Technol. Manag. Res. **35**(16), 87–93 (2015)
35. Huanan, Z., Shijun, L., Hong, J.: Guangzhou smart city construction and big data research. In: 2015 International Conference on Behavioral, Economic and Socio-cultural Computing (BESC), pp. 143–149. IEEE (2015)
36. http://www.echinagov.com. Internet + Smart China Annual Conference 2017 [EB/OL], 09 04 2019. http://www.echinagov.com/zt/90/
37. http://www.echinagov.com. Fruitful Achievements of Smart China Annual Conference 2018 [EB/OL], 09 04 2019. http://www.echinagov.com/news/243207.htm
38. Guangzhou Statistics Bureau. Guangzhou's population size and distribution in 2018 [EB/OL], 09 04 2019. http://tjj.gz.gov.cn/gzstats/tjgb_qtgb/201902/da07f05ce86a41fd97415efec5637085.shtml
39. Siuhi, S., Mwakalonge, J.: Opportunities and challenges of smart mobile applications in transportation. J. Traffic Transp. Eng. (Engl. Ed.) **3**(6), 582–592 (2016)
40. AlAwadhi, S., Morris, A.: The use of the UTAUT model in the adoption of E-government services in Kuwait. In: Proceedings of the 41st Annual Hawaii International Conference on System Sciences (HICSS 2008), pp. 219. IEEE, January 2008
41. Welch, E.W., Hinnant, C.C., Moon, M.J.: Linking citizen satisfaction with e-government and trust in government. J. Public Adm. Res. Theory **15**(3), 371–391 (2005)
42. Scuotto, V., Ferraris, A., Bresciani, S.: Internet of Things: Applications and challenges in smart cities: a case study of IBM smart city projects. Bus. Process Manag. J. **22**(2), 357–367 (2016)
43. Dunkerley, K., Tejay, G.: Theorizing information security success: Towards secure e-Government. Int. J. Electron. Gov. Res. (IJEGR) **6**(3), 31–41 (2010)
44. Arts, J.W., Frambach, R.T., Bijmolt, T.H.: Generalizations on consumer innovation adoption: A meta-analysis on drivers of intention and behavior. Int. J. Res. Mark. **28**(2), 134–144 (2011)
45. Sun, H., Zhang, P.: The role of moderating factors in user technology acceptance. Int. J. Hum Comput Stud. **64**(2), 53–78 (2006)

Adaptability and Attuning in Smart Cities: Exploring the HCI Grand Challenge of Learning and Creativity

H. Patricia McKenna(✉)

AmbientEase, Victoria, BC V8V 4Y9, Canada
mckennaph@gmail.com

Abstract. This work addresses the grand challenge for human-computer interaction of learning and creativity, in the context of smart cities. Through a review of the research literature for learning in relation to attuning and then for creativity in relation to adaptability, a theoretical perspective and conceptual framework is developed for learning and creativity in smart cities. Using an exploratory case study approach combined with an explanatory correlational design, relationships for learning and creativity in urban environments are explored using survey data and in-depth interviews. Additionally, emotion/affect is explored in relation to learning and creativity in terms of the experience of comfort in urban environments. This work is significant in that it provides a hybrid approach to understanding the grand challenge of learning and creativity through the use of both quantitative and qualitative data and analysis. This paper contributes to the research literature for smart cities, learning cities, and creativity in smart environments; develops and operationalizes a conceptual framework for learning and creativity in smart cities; and points to the importance and potential for learning and creativity relationships in smart, urban environments.

Keywords: Adaptability · Attuning · Comfort · Correlation · Creativity · Emotion/Affect · Learning

1 Introduction

In response to one of several grand challenges for human-computer interaction (HCI) identified by Stephanidis et al. [1], the purpose of this work is to focus on the 7th challenge, that of *learning and creativity,* in an "intelligent era" in the context of urban life, smart cities, and learning cities. Where Vertesi [2] pointed to the creativity and adaptability of people in working with seamful, multiple, and heterogeneous infrastructures when interacting in and with daily life (e.g., physical, etc.), McKenna [3] calls for a re-thinking of learning in smart cities by introducing an exploration of potentials for "emergent behavior in relation to awareness, autonomy, creativity, and innovation." Gil-Garcia, Zhang, and Puron-Cid [4] provide a conceptualization of smartness in government along 14 dimensions, two of which are creativity and innovation.

N. Streitz and S. Konomi (Eds.): HCII 2020, LNCS 12203, pp. 431–442, 2020.
https://doi.org/10.1007/978-3-030-50344-4_31

Theoretically, this work focuses on the construct of urbanizing in more aware environments, as in, adapting spaces and elements for urban uses, where *adaptability* is employed in this paper as a proxy for *creativity* in relation to the construct of *learning*, where attuning to urban spaces is used as a proxy. As such, this work looks for a correlation between adaptability and attuning in relation to sensibilities in smart cities as a way of exploring the grand challenge for HCI of learning and creativity identified by Stephanidis et al. [1]. Additionally, creativity and learning are also explored in relation to emotion/affect through assessments of the experience of comfort in the city. This background and context gives rise to the research question under exploration – *Are creativity and learning related in the context of contemporary and future smart urban environments and regions?*

2 Theoretical Perspective

Stephanidis et al. [1] describe creativity and learning as "two strongly associated concepts that have shaped the notion of creative learning." This, together with the background and context provided for this work will be probed in this section through a review of the research literature for creativity in terms of adaptability and for learning in terms of attuning to urban environments in smart cities.

2.1 Creativity and Adaptability

Amabile [5] evolved a definition of creativity as "the production of a novel and appropriate response, product, or solution to an open-ended task." Amabile [5] adds that an open-ended task is one that is heuristic as distinct from "having a single, obvious solution" as in "purely algorithmic." Creativity for Amabile [5] contains two assumptions, that of a "continuum from low, ordinary levels of creativity found in everyday life" extending "to the highest levels found in historically significant inventions, performances, scientific discoveries, and works of art." The second assumption is that of "degrees of creativity" where "the level of creativity that a person produces at any given point in time is a function of the creativity components operating, at that time, within and around that person." Tursić [6] observes that Lévy [7] "stresses the role of serendipity as a particularly creative force of urban public spaces." Amabile [8] pointed to the need for "studies of creative behavior" that are "in situ, as it is happening" as "everyday creativity" interpreted by McKenna [9] in the context of smart cities as "ambient creativity" in "everyday spaces, in real time." McKenna [10] articulates the concept of ambient creativity as "a more dynamic, adaptive, and evolving understanding of creativity, enabled by more aware people interacting with more aware technologies and with each other." Gil-Garcia, Zhang, and Puron-Cid [4] identify creativity as one of 14 dimensions of smartness in government. McCullough [11] identifies the notion of "architecture's grid edge" described as "a distinct new category of creative work and experience" in a forthcoming work (McCullough, 2020) [12] whereby an inquiry is proposed into "what it means to turn architecture on, but also off" and to "have well made places" affording "occasional off-grid independence, unconditional natural operations, social practices of at least some intermittency, and a more versatile local resilience." Indeed, for McCullough [11], resilience gives way to "smarter" as in "more everyday flexibility, even new pursuits of comfort" while "more humane approaches to local energy microgrids suggest a simple change of attitudes in **design for living**."

It is worth noting that part of the definition of artificial intelligence (AI) pertains to "flexible adaptation" where according to Haenlein and Kaplan [13], AI is "commonly defined as a system's ability to interpret external data correctly, to learn from such data, and to use those learnings to achieve specific goals and tasks through flexible adaptation." Also of note is the need for accommodating the creative, serendipitous, and unpredictable nature of people [9], in keeping humans in the loop [14]. Stephanidis et al. [1] claim that, "beyond the learning context, human creativity is expected to have a central role in the forthcoming intelligent era." As such, Stephanidis et al. [1] maintain that, "tools will need to reconsider how creation in real world environments can be fostered when the digital will be blended with the physical." Additionally, Stephanidis et al. [1] indicate that "the role of big data and AI towards empowering human creativity needs to be further explored, taking into account the potential risks for creativity entailed by over-automation." Using the notion of "little C" creativity as defined by Ferrari, Cachia, and Punie [15] as "a behavioral and mental attitude or the ability to find new and effective solutions to everyday problems" Stephanidis et al. [1] highlight that while "this type of creativity depends on education and training", importantly, "it can also be fun, involves play and discovery, and requires hard work, good field knowledge, and development of thinking skills" [15].

2.2 Learning and Attuning

Rickert [16] refers to rhetoric as "something world-transforming for individuals and groups immersed in vibrant, ecologically attuned environments." Rickert [16] noted that, "we are entering an age of ambience" where "boundaries between subject and object, human and nonhuman, and information and matter dissolve" so as to "transform our knowledge about self and world." As such, according to Rickert [16], "an ambient age calls us to rethink much of our rhetorical theory and practice" and "to understand rhetoric as ambient." For Rickert [16], "ambience refers to the active role that the material and informational environment takes in human development, dwelling, and culture" while having an awareness of the ambient. It is this awareness and attuning that assists in formulating new understandings of urban life as ambient and multidimensional, as in, urbanities [10] while McKenna et al. [17] advanced learning as ambient and emergent. Indeed, a key aim of the work by Coletta, Evans, Heaphy, and Kitchin [18] "is to explore the various critiques of smart city rhetoric and deployments and to suggest social, political, and practical interventions that would enable better designed and more equitable and just smart city initiatives."

In seeking spaces for people and their voices in the making of responsive cities, McKenna [19] explored attuning to urban spaces in relation to sharing and to trust in smart cities. In the context of *creating smart cities*, Coletta et al. [18] note that, "the public and private sectors seem more attuned to co-production as they are accustomed to collaborating with partners." Bolivar [20] claims that, "scholars studying the smart city domain stress the importance of attuning technological innovation to the capabilities and requirements of people that use and drive it." Citing Cichia et al. [21], Stephanidis et al. [1] describe the notion of creative learning as "any learning that is learner-centered and involves understanding and new awareness" and "allows the learner to go beyond knowledge acquisition, and focus on thinking skills." Additionally, in learning environments, "technology should be customizable and adaptable" [1]. Drawing on the work of Loveless [22], Stephanidis et al. [1] highlight that "digital technologies can be used in the context of creative learning to develop ideas, to facilitate connections with other people, projects, information and resources, to collaborate and co-create, as well as to present and promote one's work." Stephanidis et al. [1] point to the combining of creative learning, creative classrooms [23] and "support for creativity in education" as "totally aligned with the notion of ubiquitous learning."

2.3 Summary and Conceptual Framework

A summary of the literature review is presented in Table 1, organized by year (from 2007 to 2020) and author for learning and creativity.

Table 1. Literature review summary for learning and creativity in smart cities.

Author	Year	Creativity	Learning
Loveless	2007	Learning	Creative, adaptable tech
Ferrari et al.	2009	Small c	
Lévy	2011	Serendipity	
Bocconi et al.	2012	Creative classroom	Formal/informal/personalized
Amabile, T. M.	2013	Definition	
McKenna et al.	2013		Ambient & emergent
Rickert, T.	2013		Attuning
Gil-Garcia et al.	2016	Dimension of smartness	
McCullough, M.	2017	Work/experience	
Tursić	2017	Urban public spaces	
McKenna, H. P.	2018	Ambient	
Bolivar	2019		Technology/people attuning
Coletta et al.	2019		Public/private co-production
Haenlein & Kaplan	2019	Flexible adaptation	AI and data
McKenna, H. P.	2019	People	
Stephanidis et al.	2019	Learning/classrooms/education	Ubiquitous
McCullough, M.	2020	Downtime/flexibility	

Loveless [22] points to the importance of new technologies for creativity and learning while Ferrari et al. [15] distinguish between big C and small c creativity, focusing on the importance of the latter for everyone in addressing issues in everyday life. Bocconi et al. [23] advance the notion of creative classrooms as an ecosystem in support of both formal and informal learning as well as personalized learning [1]. Amabile [5] provides an expansive definition of creativity incorporating the importance of the environment and context. McKenna et al. [17] advance the notion of ambient and emergent learning in technology-pervasive environments while Rickert [16] articulates the notion of ambient rhetoric in a world transformed by technologies where traditional boundaries dissolve, influencing attuning and awareness. McCullough [11] speaks of creative work and experience in relation to architecture and the potential of microgrids. Bolivar [20] emphasizes the importance of taking the capabilities and requirements of people into consideration so as to attune technological innovations accordingly. Coletta et al. [18] speak of attunement in relation to public and private collaborations for smart city interventions and initiatives while Haenlein & Kaplan [13] address artificial intelligence (AI) in relation to data learning potentials and flexible adaptations. McKenna [19] focuses on the importance of finding spaces for people in smart environments and Stephanidis et al. [1] advance creative learning, classrooms, and creativity in education as aligned with ubiquitous learning. McCullough [11, 12] encourages the notion of design for living, involving more creative and flexible ideas for comfort and resilience.

This literature review enables the development of a conceptual framework for adaptability in support of creativity and for attuning in support of learning in smart cities as depicted in Fig. 1, as operationalized for use in this paper. Creativity and learning, in the context of a people – technologies – cities dynamic, enabled through interactions with aware applications and aware people influence learning, extending to emotion/affect (e.g., the experience of comfort), shedding light on patterns, partnerships, and relationships, extending to affective, social and other dimensions, with implications for learning, smart, and future cities.

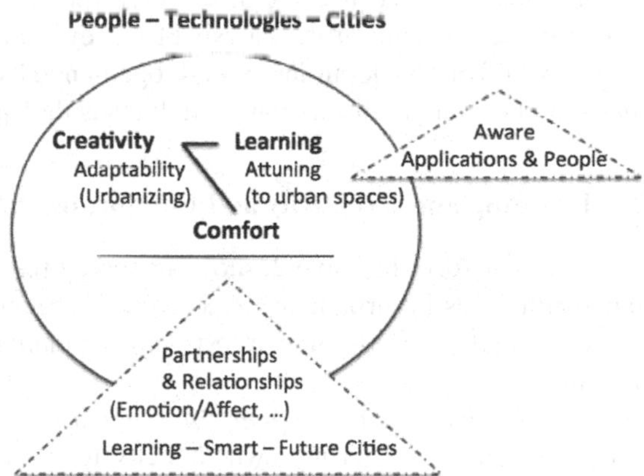

Fig. 1. Conceptual framework for learning and creativity in smart cities.

The research question for this work is reformulated as a proposition under exploration in this work as:

P1: *Creativity and learning are related in the context of contemporary, smart urban environments and regions through adaptability and attuning, with relationships for each extending to emotion/affect, such as comfort.*

3 Methodology

Methodologically, a hybrid approach is used in this paper incorporating an explanatory correlational design [24] and an exploratory case study [25]. Yin [25] points to the "complementarity of case study and statistical research" indicating that "case studies have been needed to examine the underlying processes that might explain a correlation." This study employs multiple methods of data collection including in-depth interviews and a survey involving a cross-section of people in small to medium to large sized cities in Canada, Europe, Israel, and the United States. Content analysis is used as an analytic technique for qualitative data and descriptive statistics for quantitative data, in the form of correlational analysis using the Spearman Correlation Coefficient for ordinal data.

A website was used to describe the study and invite participation. During online sign up for the study, demographic data were gathered including age range, gender, city, and people could self-identify in one or more categories (e.g., student, educator, city official, business, community member, visitor, etc.). The sampling technique used in this work is heterogeneity sampling, a form of purposive sampling, enabling the inclusion of a broad spectrum of perspectives.

In parallel with this study data were also systematically collected from a wide range of sectors in several Canadian cities through group and individual discussions. Overall data were collected in this work for n = 76, consisting of 59% males and 41% females for people ranging in age from their 20 s to 70 s.

4 Results and Discussion

Results are presented in terms of the correlating of survey responses for learning and creativity using proxies for each. Quantitative analysis of survey data is enriched with an analysis of qualitative data from in-depth interviews, open-ended survey questions, and group and individual discussion. A discussion of findings is then presented.

4.1 Correlations for Learning and Creativity and Comfort in Smart Cities

Results are presented in tabular form in Table 2, showing survey responses pertaining to creativity (using adaptability, as in, urbanizing as a proxy), learning (using attuning to urban spaces as a proxy), and extending to comfort with correlations calculated for creativity and then learning.

When asked to assess *urbanizing as in adapting for urban uses* (on a 7 point scale with 1 = not at all and 7 = absolutely) in terms of whether city-focused social media and other aware technologies give rise to many possibilities, 75% of participants responded toward the upper end of scale at 5 and 25% responded at 7. When asked to assess *attuning to urban spaces* (on a 7 point scale with 1 = not at all and 7 = absolutely) in terms of whether city-focused social media and other aware technologies give rise to many possibilities, 25% of participants responded also toward the upper end of the scale at 6 and 75% at 7.

The Real Statistics [26] software Resource Pack add-in for Microsoft Excel is used to conduct correlations, consisting as it does of a range of supplemental statistical functions

Table 2. Correlations for learning and creativity in smart cities, extending to comfort.

Constructs	Survey responses	Correlations
Creativity (Adaptability/Urbanizing)	75% (5); 25% (7)	.33
Learning (Attuning to urban spaces)	25% (6); 75% (7)	
Creativity (Adaptability/Urbanizing)	75% (5); 25% (7)	−.57
Comfort	50% (3); 50% (7)	
Learning (Attuning to urban spaces)	25% (6); 75% (7)	.57
Comfort	50% (3); 50% (7)	

and data analysis tools, including a correlation feature for determining the nature of the relationship between constructs. As shown in Table 2, based on ordinal data, a Spearman Correlation coefficient of .33 emerges in this work between *creativity* and *learning*.

Using an adapted version of Anderson's [27] body insight scale (BIS) for the exploration of the experience of comfort in urban environments, survey participants were asked to assess body awareness in their city, as follows – "Would you agree that you feel comfortable in your city most of the time?" Using a scale of 1 to 7 on a continuum of disagree to agree, 50% of participants responded at position 3 on the scale and 50% responded at the upper end of the continuum with agree at position 7. While other scales exist such as that by Teixiera, Dublon, and Savvides [28], the focus is on human sensing through the use of computing technologies enabling the detection of presence, count, location, and so on. By contrast, Anderson's BIS [27] is intended for use by people in human sensing. Responses for *comfort* were correlated with *creativity* using *adaptability/urbanizing* as a proxy and then with *learning* using *attuning to urban spaces* as a proxy. A Spearman correlation coefficient of −.57 emerges in this work between *creativity* and *comfort* revealing a negative direction while a positive correlation of .57 emerges between *learning* and *comfort*.

4.2 What People Said About Learning and Creativity in Smart Cities

From a qualitative data perspective, based on in-depth interviews, open-ended survey question responses, and group and individual discussions, findings are presented for learning, creativity, and feelings of comfort in urban environments and regions.

Creativity. City information technology (IT) staff noted that the emergence of urban data enable "data analysis that you've not thought of" with "serendipitous or accidental" or "unintended" potentials that were not "even in our mindset." The need for funding in support of data analysis initiatives was identified by city IT staff who commented that "we haven't had any kind of funding to do these things" while highlighting the importance of education. For example, city IT staff stated "we're starting to look at the tools to help us mine the data that we already have an interest in" and "beyond that, we're very much immature in that overall data sense." A community leader/member referred to a "conversations" series with the mayor of the city, particularly that pertaining to "creativity in public spaces" with the potential for focusing on "the interactive art idea."

Learning. A community leader/member stated that, "the biggest benefit" social media and other aware technologies "can offer is to assist in citizen/visitor education and awareness" adding "unfortunately, most cities are not utilizing them in this manner." Regarding the notion of smart cities, another community leader/member stressed the need for "educating people on why it's important" and "what opportunities exist." City IT staff pointed to "that hurdle of just really starting to educate" about "what could be done" and "educating ourselves" while a community leader/member identified the need for "finding fun and meaningful ways to engage the public and visualize this data, and 'simplify' it for the larger public." An educator spoke of continuous learning, as in "what you are doing everyday" noting that, "you are all learning, all the time." An educator/business person commented on the need for "schools to open their 'walls'" in order to develop "place based projects" in the community. While all respondents agreed on the need to "Make engagement smarter" as in, "break down the silos and collaborate more" it is worth noting that a community leader spoke of the "major governance silo problems" and the need to move from "that silo/sectoral approach" toward "clusters, things that would bring industries and sectors together." The educator/business person also identified the option of "smart city projects" that could be "conducted by high-tech companies" involving "collaboration with students and other community centers."

Comfort. An educator suggested use of the concept "wise city" encompassing "friendly, comfortable" which "reflects human values and needs." A community leader/member commented on the importance of smart cities as a "catalyst for the changes that are needed in cities" adding, "primary efforts should be focused around people and their needs, with everything else playing a supporting role." The element of comfort in urban spaces also emerged in terms of the placement of urban elements such as benches where a community leader/member observed that, "I feel like a lot of them aren't actually designed for people to stay there" as in, "they're not comfortable" in that "you want to be able to see your environment and you want to feel protected in some way too." Indeed, where smart cities are often associated with "IoT, Big Data, and other tech systems" the educator/business person suggested that the "'Wise Way' is to find the way to include both together" encompassing both the wise city and the smart city.

4.3 Discussion

In terms of whether the relationship between *creativity* and *learning* as strongly associated concepts [1] holds in the context of evolving and emerging environments in smart cities, this work found a correlation of .33 between proxies for the concepts. It is important to note that Creswell [24] advises that, "when correlations range from .20 to .35 there is only a slight relationship" adding that "this size of a coefficient may be valuable to explore the interconnection of variables but of little value in prediction studies." As such, findings from this work suggest the presence of a relationship between creativity and learning in the smart cities context, although slight, with the potential to increase as more support in the way of funding and education occurs for smart city projects and initiatives. Also of note is the need for the removal of hurdles to education, the removal of walls around schools in order to extend learning beyond the notion of the school, and the removal of silos that would enable cross-sector collaboration, all of which are suggestive of the potential for adaptability associated with learning in smart environments. Attuning to "people and their needs" emerged as a "primary focus" of smart cities in this work, and this is important, serving as it does as a proxy for learning.

It is worth noting that the connection between creativity and serendipity [6, 7] emerged in this work in relation to urban data potentials while the notion by Amabile of "everyday creativity" that is "in situ" emerged in the context of smart cities in the form of ideas for "conversations" about "creativity in public spaces." In the case of correlations for *learning* with *comfort* and then for *creativity* with *comfort* where a correlation of .57 and −.57 was found, respectively, Creswell [24] advises that, for the .35 to .65 range, "when correlations are above .35, they are useful for limited prediction" and the inter-correlation of variables. The direction of the correlation is negative or inverse for *creativity* and *comfort* while the direction of the relationships for *learning* and *comfort* is positive, as is that for *creativity* and *learning* in urban environments. Regarding the negative direction of the correlation between *creativity* and *comfort,* this is in keeping with the work of de Vries [29] who advances the need for improvisation in "educating the inventors of our future to address creativity as a condition for innovation" and "step out of their comfort zone and focus on the things that are happening in the here-and-now." For de Vries [29] "the essence of improvisation touches the heart of creativity" so as to respond in the moment in real world environments while "accepting mistakes and learning to look for novel associations." Perhaps among the key challenges and opportunities emerging from this work for smart cities will be how to improve the correlation for *learning* and *creativity* going forward.

5 Limitations and Future Directions

Limitations. A key limitation of this paper is the small sample size focusing on small to medium to large-sized cities in only a few countries, which is mitigated by the potential to extend this work to many more cities in additional countries and to mega-cities. Another limitation of this paper is the use of proxies thought to be suitable for assessing the relationship between learning and creativity.

Future Directions. Going forward, future studies could explore learning and creativity more directly, without the use of proxies for learning and creativity in smart urban environments and regions. Potential applications of the *conceptual framework for learning and creativity in smart cities* (Fig. 1) along with the potential impact are presented below.

Potential Applications. The *conceptual framework for learning and creativity in smart cities* (Fig. 1) opens spaces for learning collaborations in smart cities; introduces the learning and creativity dynamic to smart environments with improvisatory activities as a possible approach; and combines the emotion/affect dimension, in the form of comfort, with learning and creativity in smart spaces and regions. More specifically, potential applications emerging in this work point to urban data analysis initiatives; interactive art in public spaces projects; and education and awareness opportunities.

Potential Impact. The impact of the *conceptual framework for learning and creativity in smart cities* (Fig. 1) has the potential to influence urban theory and approaches to learning and creativity, along with considerations for emotion/affect in the context of smart environments and regions. This framework also has the potential to open the way for "studies of creative behavior" as articulated by Amabile [8] "in situ, as it is happening" in the context of smart city projects and initiatives, while attuning to, and incorporating, "people and their needs" as part of the smart cities dynamic of people-technologies-cities. A learning and creativity framework for smart cities also supports the importance of keeping people in the loop [14] in purposeful and meaningful ways that are possibly even creative and fun while drawing attention to the complexities and opportunities associated with comfort in relation to learning and to creativity.

6 Conclusion

This work provides an exploration of learning and creativity in the context of smart cities and regions through a review of the research literature followed by an analysis of what people said and their assessments of proxies for these constructs. While a relationship between creativity and learning was found with a positive correlation of .33 through the use of proxies (e.g., adaptability and attuning, respectively) in smart cities in this work, it is worth noting some of the contextual factors, possibly influencing "creativity components" [5], identified by participants pertaining to financial, educational, and other "hurdles." As such, a stronger correlation may occur with the direct use of learning and creativity in future studies and with the evolving of smart city supports. The positive direction of the relationship between *learning* and *comfort* in smart cities shows a correlation of .57 while the negatively correlated relationship between *creativity* and *comfort* at −.57 highlights challenges and opportunities associated possibly with comfort zones for creativity [29] in smart urban environments.

This work is significant in that it develops and operationalizes a *conceptual framework for learning and creativity in smart cities,* incorporating the notion of comfort while opening spaces for research and practice going forward. Future directions are discussed in terms of potential applications for the *conceptual framework for learning and creativity in smart cities* along with implications. A key take away from this work is the relationship between *learning* and emotion/affect, in the form of *comfort*, on the one hand and *comfort* and *creativity* on the other, as a way of considering "people and their needs" in smart environments and regions. This work will be of interest to an interdisciplinary audience, from creativity and learning researchers, practitioners, and educators to city officials and community members, and anyone concerned with learning, creativity, and comfort in smart environments.

References

1. Stephanidis, C., et al.: Seven HCI grand challenges. Int. J. Hum. Comput. Interact. **35**(14), 1229–1269 (2019). https://doi.org/10.1080/10447318.2019.1619259

2. Vertesi, J.: Seamful spaces: heterogeneous infrastructures in interactions. Sci. Technol. Human Values **39**(2), 264–284 (2014). https://doi.org/10.1177/0162243913516012
3. McKenna, H.P.: Rethinking learning in the smart city: innovating through involvement, inclusivity, and interactivities with emerging technologies. In: Gil-Garcia, J.R., Pardo, T.A., Nam, T. (eds.) Smarter as the New Urban Agenda. PAIT, vol. 11, pp. 87–107. Springer, Cham (2016). https://doi.org/10.1007/978-3-319-17620-8_5
4. Gil-Garcia, J.R., Zhang, J., Puron-Cid, G.: Conceptualizing smartness in government: an integrative and multi-dimensional view. Gov. Inf. Q. **33**(3), 524–534 (2016). https://doi.org/10.1016/j.giq.2016.03.002
5. Amabile, T.M.: Componential theory of creativity. In: Kessler, E.H. (ed.) Encyclopedia of Management Theory, Sage (2013)
6. Tursić, M.: Aesthetic space: the visible and the invisible in urban agency (Thèse No. 6445). EPFL, Lausanne (2017)
7. Lévy, J.: La sérendipité comme interaction environnementale. La Sérendipité: Le Hasard Heureux, pp. 279–285 (2011)
8. Amabile, T.M.: In pursuit of everyday creativity. Working Paper 18-002. J. Creative Behav. (2017). https://doi.org/10.1002/jocb.200
9. McKenna, H.P.: Creativity and ambient urbanizing at the intersection of the internet of things and people in smart cities. In: Antona, M., Stephanidis, C. (eds.) UAHCI 2018. LNCS, vol. 10908, pp. 295–307. Springer, Cham (2018). https://doi.org/10.1007/978-3-319-92052-8_23
10. McKenna, H.P.: Evolving urban understandings: cultures, economies, and everything as ambient. In: Ambient Urbanities as the Intersection Between the IoT and the IoP. IGI Global, Hershey (2019)
11. McCullough, M.: Downtime on the microgrid: Abstract (2017). http://www-personal.umich.edu/~mmmc/BOOKS/AboutDowntimeOnTheMicrogrid.pdf. Accessed 18 Sept 2019
12. McCullough, M.: Downtime on the Microgrid: Architecture, Electricity, and Smart City Islands. MIT Press, Cambridge (2020)
13. Haenlein, M., Kaplan, A.: A brief history of artificial intelligence: on the past, present, and future of artificial intelligence. Calif. Manag. Rev. **6**(4), 5–14 (2019). https://doi.org/10.1177/000812561986425
14. Streitz, N.: Beyond 'smart-only' cities: redefining the 'smart-everything' paradigm. J. Ambient Intell. Humaniz. Comput. **10**(2), 791–812 (2018). https://doi.org/10.1007/s12652-018-0824-1
15. Ferrari, A., Cachia, R., Punie, Y.: ICT as a driver for creative learning and innovative teaching. In: Villalba, E. (ed.) Measuring Creativity: Proceedings of the Conference, Can Creativity be Measured? pp. 345–367. Publications Office of the European Union (2009)
16. Rickert, T.: Ambient Rhetoric: Attunements of Rhetorical Being. University of Pittsburgh Press, Pittsburgh (2013). https://doi.org/10.2307/j.ctt5hjqwx
17. McKenna, H.P., Arnone, M.P., Kaarst-Brown, M.L., McKnight, L.W., Chauncey, S.A.: Ambient and emergent learning with wireless grid technologies. In: Proceedings of the 5th International Conference on Education and New Learning Technologies (EduLearn13), International Association of Technology, Education, & Development (IATED), pp. 4046–14053 (2013)
18. Coletta, C., Evans, L., Heaphy, L. (eds.): Creating Smart Cities (Regions and Cities). Routledge, London (2019)
19. McKenna, H.P.: Exploring the quantified experience: finding spaces for people and their voices in smarter, more responsive cities. In: Arai, K., Bhatia, R., Kapoor, S. (eds.) FTC 2018. AISC, vol. 880, pp. 269–282. Springer, Cham (2019). https://doi.org/10.1007/978-3-030-02686-8_22
20. Bolívar, M.P.R., Muñoz, L.A. (eds.): E-Participation in Smart Cities: Technologies and Models of Governance for Citizen Engagement. Springer, Cham (2019). https://doi.org/10.1007/978-3-319-89474-4

21. Cichia, R., Ferrari, A., Ala-Mutka, K., Punie, Y.: Creative learning and innovative teaching: final report on the study on creativity and innovation in education in the EU member states. Publications Office of the European Union (2010). https://doi.org/10.2791/52913
22. Loveless, A.: Literature review in creativity, new technologies and learning. A NESTA Futurelab research report – report 4 (2007). https://doi.org/10.1094/pdis-91-4-0467b. https://telearn.archives-ouvertes.fr/hal-00190439
23. Bocconi, S., Kampylis, P.G., Punie, Y.: Innovating learning: key elements for developing creative classrooms in Europe. IRC-Policy and Scientific Reports, Luxembourg (2012). http://publications.jrc.ec.europa.eu/repository/handle/JRC72278
24. Creswell, J.W.: Educational Research: Planning, Conducting, and Evaluating Quantitative and Qualitative Research, 6th edn. Pearson, Boston (2018)
25. Yin, R.K.: Case Study Research and Applications: Design and Methods. Sage, Thousand Oaks (2018)
26. Zaiontz, C.: Real statistics using excel (2019). www.real-statistics.com
27. Anderson, R.: Body intelligence scale: defining and measuring the intelligence of the body. Humanist. Psychol. **34**, 357–367 (2016)
28. Teixiera, T., Dublon, G., Savvides, A.: A survey of human-sensing: methods for detecting presence, count, location, track, and identity. ENALAB Technical report 09-2010, 1(1), (2010)
29. de Vries, E.: Improvisation as a tool to develop creativity mini-workshop divergent thinking. In: 2014 IEEE Frontiers in Education Conference (FIE) Proceedings, Madrid, pp. 1–3 (2014). https://doi.org/10.1109/FIE.2014.7044132

Participatory Governance in Smart Cities: Future Scenarios and Opportunities

Nicole Shadowen(✉), Thomas Lodato, and Daria Loi

Mozilla Corporation, Mountain View, CA 94041, USA
{nshadowen,tlodato,dloi}@mozilla.com

Abstract. In smart cities, citizens' lives and data will be increasingly intertwined with the systems used by local, state, and federal governments. Given such a context, this paper focuses on the role that automated decision(-making) systems (ADS) play—and could play—within smart cities and unpacks the challenges of stakeholder participation in determining this role. To address future scenarios and propose a provisional framework for participating in and with ADS-laden cities and government, we begin with the case of New York City's Automated Decision Systems Task Force as a concrete example of the challenges of regulating, governing, and participating with ADS. As a single example, we explore the particularities surrounding the Task Force, including the mobility of its policy, the difficulty of defining the issue, and finally the proposed framework for overseeing ADS in New York City. We introduce two practices of participating in city-making: participatory governance and participatory design. As we explain, these practices emphasize the role of stakeholders—e.g. citizens, bureaucrats, private industry actors, and community groups—in crafting the policy and technology that they use or are impacted by. We then propose a provisional framework for ADS transparency and accountability based on these participative practices. We recommend enabling citizens to directly help regulate and design automated decision-making systems with the caveats that doing so can be messy, contextual, and frictional. In sum, this paper advocates that all communities should be empowered to understand and impact the systems determine their destiny.

Keywords: Smart cities · Automated decision-making systems · Participatory governance

1 Introduction

The global urban landscape is populated by an increasing number of information and communication technologies (ICTs), internet-connected devices and sensors (often called "Internet of Things" or IoT), and other digital and computerized systems. Motivating this technology adoption are predictions that 68% of the global population will reside in urban areas by 2050 [1] depleting resources and straining governments. Many claim that these smart city technologies, systems, and services can play a key role in optimizing resources, enabling informed decision-making, and serving citizens with greater efficiency, ease, and equity [2–4]. These smart technologies promise that cities will not

N. Streitz and S. Konomi (Eds.): HCII 2020, LNCS 12203, pp. 443–463, 2020.
https://doi.org/10.1007/978-3-030-50344-4_32

need to cut back as they could "use technology to do more with less" [5]. With investment, procurement, and deployment from private and public actors, the market for smart cities is estimated to grow from $308.0 billion (USD) in 2018 to $717.2 billion (USD) by 2023, at a Compound Annual Growth Rate (CAGR) of 18.4% during the forecast period" [6].

The term smart city has been applied to a variety of different approaches, technologies and values within cities. Broadly speaking, the term refers to approaches to urban government, development, and management that depend on digital, computational, and networked technologies to collect, process, and act on various data sources [7–10]. Although varied and debated, smart cities share many characteristics. Below are four paraphrased from Albino et al. [11]:

1) Technology is used for governmental efficiency, and social and cultural development;
2) Business-led urban development emphasizes creativity [cf. 12, 13];
3) Initiatives for social inclusion and social capital;
4) Natural resources and their management play a critical role.

The emphasis on technology in smart city design has led many to question who smart cities are actually for. Wiig [14] argues the term smart cities comes from corporate narratives that, while not excluding citizens, do not figure them in. Others argue that citizens are highly constrained by the modes of participation as data collectors or transactions [15–18]. Still others have argued that smart city programs marginalize and disenfranchise groups by emphasizing particular discursive practices around technology [19–22]. There is a unique opportunity and need for increased citizen participation and influence in the use of smart city technology. In this paper, we focus on the potential for participation in one such technology: automated decision systems (ADS).

The use of ADS and other automated processes in smart cities mark a shift toward "algorithmic bureaucracy" where "some organizational practices previously based on office procedures [...can] be carried out by algorithms" [23]. Many of these systems can both inform and enact decision-making. Delivering simplicity, efficiency, and reliability by mitigating human repetition and intervention, algorithms also promise to reduce human biases, thereby producing more equitable outcomes (even though evidence shows equity is not the outcome [24]). Providing the value of consistency, equity, and ease, the use of ADS could precipitate a reduced role for people in governmental operations.

On the other hand, the wider discourse of smart cities frequently emphasizes the importance of citizen participation in decision-making through new mechanisms of feedback, data collection, and civic engagement. From data collection as citizenship [15, 16] to new sites of public discourse [25], smart cities could facilitate a democratization of bureaucracy—opening up the inner working of cities to the people who reside there. Even with an emphasis on participation, many critiques have emerged about the terms, characteristics, and legitimacy of claims and activities of participation in smart cities [19–22, 26, 27].

As a paradox, the smart city competes against itself for what it represents. One future of (smart) cities is inherently technocratic, where procurement and participation require expertise in algorithms, training data, databases, and computational systems. Another future is inherently democratic, where citizens of many kinds and interests can contribute to the joint project of city-making. The question, then, is how do these futures co-exist rather than compete?

In this paper, we attempt to provide a foundation for a larger body of work that will explore aspects of how people are impacted by the increasing use of intelligent agents in the spaces they inhabit. Specifically, in this work we focus on the use of intelligent agents, like ADS, in smart city design. Our contributions, to this end, are as follows:

1) We review definitions and examples of automated decision systems in smart city contexts.
2) We provide a detailed case study of the New York City Automated Decision System Task Force, to highlight specific successes and challenges of stakeholder participation in smart city decision making.
3) We include a review of existing participatory practices, like participatory governance and design, that provide methods that may be adapted to stakeholder involvement in smart city ADS implementation.
4) We identify framework scaffolding for disambiguating factors to consider when enabling participation in smart city design and apply these factors to a scenario in context.

Using these contributions, we explore what successful participation looks like, from past examples and other domains, in an effort to build on work that enables stronger collaboration and participation between governments and their citizens in shaping the way that intelligent technologies affect them.

2 Background

2.1 Automated Decision Systems

A key subset of the technologies that make up a smart city include ADS. The term has been used to account for a diversity of technical solutions, but typically it is used in a government context to describe a program used to supplement or replace human decision making by finding patterns in data. According to the AI Now Institute, an NYU social justice research institute focused on the impact of artificial intelligence on society, an ADS "refers to data-driven technologies used to automate human-centered procedures, practices, or policies for the purposes of predicting, identifying, surveilling, detecting, and targeting individuals or communities. They are often used to assist or supplant human decision making" [28]. These systems utilize diverse approaches (e.g. deep learning, neural networks, etc.) to achieve a variety of goals (e.g. machine learning, natural language processing, etc.) and ultimately make suggestions, predictions, or decisions from relevant datasets. ADS exhibit varying degrees of sophistication, automation, and processing. Often, ADS leverage public and private data, using machine learning (ML) and artificial intelligence (AI) or more manual means, (e.g. query able database) of analysis and discovery.

ADS is often used synonymously with AI or machine learning. However, as the New York City ADS Task Force discovered, the term is so broad that it could be applied to almost every automated process, from excel spreadsheet macros to artificial intelligence.

The following diagram shows a simple framework for understanding automated decision systems in the context of artificial intelligence and machine learning (Fig. 1).

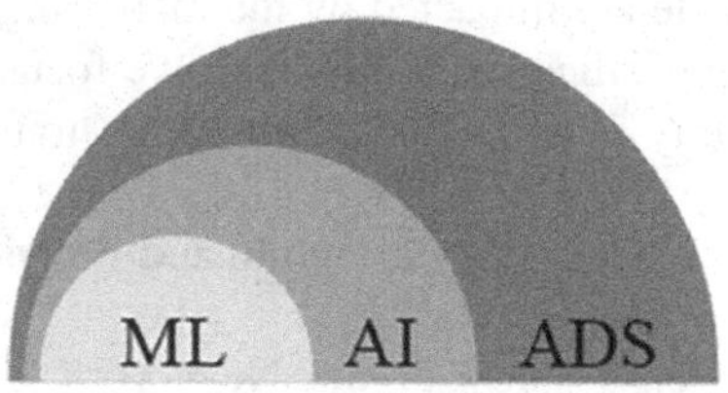

Fig. 1. Framework for understanding Automated Decision Systems (ADS), Artificial Intelligence (AI), and Machine Learning (ML) in context.

ADS are part of a broader trend to automate (parts of) decision-making in various domains, including bureaucratic and public sector procedures. Widely used in the financial and insurance industries, ADS originated as formalizations of "actuarial processes that made [workers] think more like computers than people, but human discretion" was still involved [24]. Prior to the late 1970s and early 1980s, Eubanks explains [24], the risk associated with loan assessment was assessed by humans. Over time—and quite pervasively now—decisions like whether to grant a loan or whether a transaction is fraudulent are made through the combination of data, algorithms, and behavioral models that are "inscrutable, invisible pieces of code [...that] are so deeply woven into the fabric of social life, that most of the time, we don't even notice we are being watched and analyzed." [24] The technology is being developed and deployed at a rapid pace, but oversight is comparatively slow. As a result, watch-dog groups, technology experts, and citizens worry that without transparency and careful planning these technologies will generate the basis for deeply unequal societies [29, 30], where vulnerable groups will be negatively impacted by these systems due to cycles of surveillance and prediction based on historical data [24].

These systems, in and out of the public sector, determine the lived reality of people, and often rely on public sources of data to produce decision outcomes. As Eubanks explains, "[m]ost people are targeted for digital scrutiny as members of social groups, not as individuals." [24] As a result, "oppressed and exploited populations bear a much higher burden of monitoring and tracking than advantaged groups" because of their transit in the world across borders, through public services, through rental properties in particular neighborhoods, and similar circumstances. [24] In short, ADS reproduce existing conditions rather than renovating them.

2.2 Examples of ADS in Smart Cities Around the World

ADS in use today already have a significant impact on human lives, such as predictive policing, facial recognition, or school assignment algorithms [31]. In the United States, as in other countries, law enforcement and government agencies have more access to citizen data than ever before, often through public-private partnerships. These partnerships are sometimes formed after a period of time in which consumers interact with a service without understanding that their data may be provided to third party or public sector entities. For example, in November 2019, a judge in Florida approved a warrant allowing a detective to access the DNA database of GEDmatch, a consumer DNA site with nearly one million users [32]. Other sensitive information is being passed from products like Google's Sensorvault to law enforcement from anyone with Google Maps installed on their android or iPhone device [33]. The database stores users' location data from almost a decade ago from anyone who opted in (unknowingly or not) to the service [33], and can now be accessed as evidence in investigations.

In other cases, governments may elect to build their own ADS with help from other governments or private companies. In 2018, the Zimbabwean government announced a partnership with Chinese-owned, CloudWalk, as a part of the Chinese government's "Belt and Road Initiative", to build a facial recognition software and database to monitor citizens' behavior in the nation's capital, Harrare [34]. The choice to leverage existing tools or build in-house can depend on factors such as resourcing and bandwidth. The consequences of these decisions may be increasingly opaque, depending on the number and type of stakeholders involved.

3 The Case of New York City's Automated Decision Systems Task Force

Aiming to gain intelligence and increase efficiency, the local government of New York City, USA, has integrated algorithms into citizens' everyday experience, including healthcare, education, housing, and criminal justice. While some of these applications have been successful, such as the high school admissions algorithm that helped overhaul a faulty school acceptance program in the city [35], others are not so innocuous. In 2016, a lawsuit was filed against the NYPD for their use of predictive policing software [36] as stop and frisk numbers reported by the NYCLU indicated that outsized percentages of African American and Latinx communities were targeted [37]. Without sufficient transparency, it is impossible for the public to know why they are being targeted and how they (and their data) are protected in the process. Luckily, just as the use of automated decision-making systems is growing, so is awareness of their risks.

In 2018, NYC passed one of the first laws of its kind in the US, with a mandate to form a task force that would examine how automated decision-making systems are used in the city and how they affect citizens [38]. Many in the technology and policy communities celebrated the approach as a step in the right direction to establishing and maintaining oversight of these systems from committed stakeholders. However, nearing the end of their allotted tenure in 2019, members of the task force voiced concerns that the city was not giving them access to what they needed to conduct tactical evaluation of the systems. In return, city officials cited intellectual property as one of the reasons for not providing specific details about agency ADS implementations [39]. The NYC ADS Task Force final report was published by Mayor Bill de Blasio in November 2019, but remaining discrepancies about the Task Force's success highlight the challenges in true oversight of government agency ADS implementations.

3.1 Origin of the Task Force

The NYC Task Force originated from a growing awareness of the need to constrain government ADS use due to citizen harms, as well as an uncertainty of what realistic policy should entail. In March of 2012, the Committee on Technology by the New York City Council initiated an effort towards transparency, enacting the Open Data Law, which required the "Accessibility to Public Data Sets" by citizens of New York City. The law also provided definitions, public data sets availability, web portal administration, open data legal policy, internet data set policy and technical standards, as well as an agency compliance plan to uphold it [40]. Since its enactment, datasets have been made open by many agencies in the New York City government, thus increasing involvement from citizen activists, researchers, engineers, and data scientists. For example, civic action projects such as, JailVizNYC by Navena Chaitoo [41] from the Vera Institute of Justice, uses data from NYC agencies to visualize statistics about those jailed in NYC, and better understand the local criminal justice system.

The NYC Council Technology Commission has continued to listen to the concerns of its citizens as well as subject matter experts on issues like open data and algorithms. In October 2017, James Vacca, Chair of the Technology Committee, held a hearing to discuss proposed legislation on algorithmic transparency. Based on the belief that "we have a right to know what goes into decisions made by city government and how they arrived at the conclusion they arrived at," [42] the proposed legislation read as follows:

> *Each agency that uses, for the purposes of targeting services to persons, imposing penalties upon persons or policing, an algorithm or any other method of automated processing system of data shall:*

1) *Publish on Such Agency's Website, the Source Code of Such System; and*
2) *Permit a user to (i) submit data into such system for self-testing and (ii) receive the results of having such data processed by such system* [43].

The hearing was, notably, one of the most attended in the committee's history, and included testimony from both government officials and private citizens [42]. Although all witnesses agreed that algorithmic transparency is a worthy cause, representatives from the NYC Mayor's Office of Data Analytics (MODA) objected to the legislation on the basis that (1) open sourcing agency algorithms would be an added cybersecurity risk, (2) the scope of 'algorithms in use' is too broad, (3) public testing of all algorithms used on context-dependent agency systems would not be possible, and (4) open sourcing could result in unintended consequences, such as gaming the system.

Due to these technical and practical concerns (whether based on substantive experience or not), and an acknowledgement of the complexity of the ask, the NYC Committee of Technology adopted Local Law 49 based on an amended version of Introduction No. 1969. The first of its kind in the country, Local Law 49 obliged the Mayor to convene a task force of experts to arrive at further legislation to make automated decision making systems affecting NYC more transparent [44].

3.2 Task Force in Action

Given the progressive and complex nature of potential legislation around algorithmic accountability, many private and public industry experts were involved in the discussion from its early stages. Just over a week after the law was passed, expert stakeholders, including AI Now, a social justice research institute at NYU, sent a letter to Mayor de Blasio recommending potential members of the task force [45]. It wasn't until May of 2018 that the much-awaited Automated Decision Systems Task Force members were announced on Mayor de Blasio's website. The Task Force co-chairs were Emily W. Newman, Director of the Mayor's Office of Operations, and Brittny Saunders, Deputy Commissioner for Strategic Initiatives at the NYC Commission on Human Rights. Task Force members included both city agency commissioners, as well as experts from a variety of fields including data science and technology [38].

The mandate of the Task Force was to release a report at the end of 2019 containing recommendations on the following: (1) a set of criteria to determine which ADS to prioritize and assess across agencies; (2) a process to explain the decisions of these prioritized ADS; (3) a process to identify bias or discrimination occurring from an ADS; (4) a process to address bias or discrimination once identified; (5) explain ADS so that the public can assess; and (6) the feasibility of a process to archive ADS and data once out of use [44].

As the Task Force was set to begin their work, they received recommendations from experts in the field, including a letter sent by over twenty organizations and individuals in August of 2018 with a set of detailed recommendations as well as definitions to advise the Task Force and offer help [46]. Task Force members, as well as industry experts, hoped the group would be able to participate in operational decisions regarding NYC implemented ADS, define ADS more specifically across city agencies, and provide a list of ADS in use by the city. Despite these goals and the momentum around their work, almost a year later in an April 2019 oversight hearing on the Task Force's progress, two appointed members of the Task Force testified regarding their belief that "the work of the Task Force so far has failed" [47]. In Stoyanovich and Barocas' testimony [47], they cited a failure by city officials to provide the insight into agency ADS required for the Task Force to issue meaningful recommendations. The Task Force members concerns reflected a broader uncertainty that the law would be enough to compel real accountability of city agencies towards algorithmic transparency [39].

In response to Task Force members' concerns, after the April 2019 hearing, the Task Force was subsequently presented with four specific examples of ADS in operation from city agencies, including the Department of Transportation, the Police Department, the Department of Education, and the Fire Department. Almost a year after its formation in late April 2019, the group held their first public forum to enable public engagement and collect citizen recommendations across NYC's five boroughs [48].

In November of 2019, the first Task Force released its final report on recommendations based on NYC Local Law 49. The group's recommendations included outlines for (1) an ADS management capacity across the city government, (2) public engagement with ADS acquisition and implementation, and (3) operations management of city agency ADS (NYC Automated Decision System Task Force Report, 2019). Shortly thereafter, based on Task Force recommendations, Mayor de Blasio announced an executive order creating an Algorithms Management and Policy Officer position [49]. Government officials celebrated the Task Force's report and executive order as successful progress towards the mandate of LL49, while many industry task members reported disappointment and concern that their recommendations could not be more specific or transparent [50].

3.3 Challenges

The Task Force efforts demonstrate an awareness, across private and public interests, that algorithmic transparency is a worthy focus of resources to enable government accountability and uphold fairness and equity across a city's inhabitants. However, the trajectory of the group's work revealed the challenge of reaching consensus amongst a group of multi-disciplinary stakeholders on a complex and broadly defined set of emerging technologies. Despite city officials claiming the task force's success, many members and involved advocates and researchers voiced frustration about the lack of specificity in the group's recommendations and the delayed inclusion of public participation in the process. To them, it seemed that the task force's recommendations were rendered less substantive due to a lack of access to real examples of city agency ADS and the data they used.

When the algorithmic accountability bill [43] was first introduced to the NYC Council, it included the requirement of city agencies to release the source code of their ADS. After city employees testified on the subject about issues like cyber security risk and resourcing, the committee amended the bill to include the formation of a task force, omitting the requirement for open source code. The NYC ADS report highlights some of the challenges the Task Force experienced over the course of their tenure. These included the challenge of identifying a shared definition of the term automated decision system, ambiguity around the level of specificity of recommendations, and the authority granted to the task force to demand higher access. Notably, the report reflects the challenges listed early in the process by city employees, including privacy and data security amongst city agencies (resulting in caution or hesitation when sharing real examples) and the logistics of coordinating public forums for participation.

3.4 Related Contexts

New York City's attempts to enact algorithmic accountability represents a growing recognition that automated decisions meant to supplement or replace human decision making could pose a significant risk to numerous aspects of private and public life, if not bounded in scope by legislative forces. Policymakers' efforts in New York City seem to have precipitated a number of similar initiatives across the United States. In April 2019, the U.S. House and Senate introduced the Algorithmic Accountability Act, which would require the Federal Trade Commission (FTC) to determine protocol for assessing automated decision system impact [51, 52]. Just after the formation of the New York City Task Force, Vermont announced a state-wide Artificial Intelligence Task Force, who released their report in January of 2020 [53]. Additionally, Washington state legislators in the state House and Senate proposed companion bills on AI accountability that would outline guidelines for automated decision system procurement as well as implementation in government agency activities [54–56].

Initiatives to regulate automated decision systems are not limited to the United States. In January 2020, the Norwegian Minister of Digitalization, Nikolai Astrup, released a report covering Norway's national strategy on AI. The report lists a number of regulatory strategies the country is considering related to artificial intelligence systems, including "regulatory sandboxes", which give corporations the chance to test technologies within pre-determined regulatory constraints and geographic regions [57, 58].

Open data projects, initiatives, and markets are a related area which stakeholders and researchers may look to as a reference. For example, Copenhagen's City Data Exchange (CDE) project uses an open data platform for private and public data sharing and exchange. The CDE team predicts that collaboratives like the City Data Exchange will become more common as central places for collective data sharing, and will require data brokers to facilitate data exchange [59, 60].

4 Approaches to Participation

The NYC case shows that having oversight on how ADS are built, acquired, implemented, and maintained within a smart city infrastructure is a complex endeavor facing numerous challenges. Nonetheless, local, state, and federal governments considering such optimizations, especially systems that directly affect citizens through the allocation of resources or access to services, must engage a complex array of stakeholders to ensure that outcomes consider their wide-reaching impact. Rather than mere oversight, participation, then, is an imperative for government agencies leveraging these technologies. As we will show in this section, collaborative and participatory means of creating policy and technology offer means to create safe, fair, and equitable systems for those affected by these systems.

As much as participation is a tenet of democracy, what is meant by participation is multi-faceted. Often when (democratic) participation is mentioned, the term implies voting, community meetings, and/or campaigning, that is, officially sanctioned means for influencing decisions with aggregated preferences, group representation and delegation of decision-making. These methods foster participation along existing channels of power. Yet in democracy and otherwise, participation can also mean dissensus and contest that challenges entrenched power, such as various types of conflictual, aggressive, and even violent political actions [61–64]. These too are forms of participation insofar as they sway decision and impact policy and often demand official response. Participation can also entail emerging means of expression and creation, such as the civic technology and open data movement, as well as the always on participation of ambient urbanities [65]. Acknowledging that many more unmentioned forms of participation exist, the point here is that who, what, and why such forms of participation exist or come into existence is because of the agendas, channels, and outcomes deemed necessary by participants. In short, participation is far from one dimensional.

In this section we highlight approaches to participation that involve citizens and stakeholders directly in the processes of making cities and governments through decisions about the policies and technologies that comprise cities. Participation is a process of creating, negotiating, and enacting particular present and future agendas through avenues of representation, skill, and power. The approaches of participatory governance [66] and participatory design [67] were selected because of their focus on opening up how decisions are made about the worlds that we live in, and enact what McKenna advocates for as "meaningful access, involvement, and collaboration" through the "interrelatedness" of the various domains that comprise technologized landscapes [65]. A key characteristic of these approaches is that participation can be a prefigurative activity, constructive of the world participants want to see, thereby constantly encouraging reinvention, revision, and openness.

4.1 Participatory Governance: Citizen Policymakers

Although participatory governance [66] is a relatively new practice in the context of smart city systems, principles of collaborative and participatory governing are not new. As early as 1766, Sweden for instance passed legislation guaranteeing Swedish citizens access to government processes and public data [68] and Nordic countries have a long history of participatory governance with citizens directly involved in shaping the spaces they inhabit and services they use daily [69]. Key to participatory governance is that citizens have the ability to impact public policy at the point of its making. Rather than being consulted before at a public meeting or after at the voting booth, participatory governance means involving people at the level of crafting and enacting policy and initiatives.

A commonly cited framework for participation is Sherry Arnstein's "ladder" of participation [70]. Written in response to failures to engage citizens effectively during the US-based Model Cities Program [71, 72], Arnstein defines citizen participation as "a categorical term for citizen power" [70]. Using the metaphor of the rungs of a ladder, Arnstein's framework places citizen control over projects and initiatives as the goal of citizen participation in government. For Arnstein, citizens create, oversee, and manage government programs to ensure their outcomes. In this framework, citizens themselves, not government employees, are the *deciding* force in projects by comprising the steering committee, task force, or administration of initiatives.

Critical of Arnstein's ladder, Tritter and McCallum [73] argue that a hierarchical notion of participation based on power misses key aspects about the implementation and execution of policy. To them, Arnstein's notion of citizen control is an effective rallying cry and polemic position but does not realistically address the long timescales of programs, initiatives, and policy development. Instead, they advocate for a more "mosaic" approach to participation. Tritter and McCallum write "[b]uilding a successful user involvement system requires connecting with diverse individuals and groups at local, organizational, and national levels" [73]. As opposed to positioning experts and officials at odds with citizens, the authors envision various stakeholders as "co-producers", and so co-participants in the process of policymaking and governance. They conclude that such a model of participation where "user involvement [is] a small part of a larger system helps bridge the divide between micro level changes and system-wide reforms" [73]. What Tritter and McCallum seem to envision are collaborative forums—task forces, working sessions, and episodic meetings—through which an array of individuals collectively impact decisions and directions. Citizens, as much as other stakeholders, all have a seat at the table to represent various interests defined upfront.

Similarly critical of Arnstein's ladder, Collins and Ison [74] argue that citizen participation as equated to power fails to account for context, "in situations when the nature of the issue is highly contested or undefined" [74]. In other words, participation is always participation in *something*. As such, most instances of citizen participation depend on issues that have interdependent, complex, uncertain, and contested conditions. In these cases, what individuals are participating in and for is not agreed upon, making the problem different for different parties, or "wicked" [75]. Although groups may be convening or debating related points, stakeholders in such circumstances are actively defining the problem itself as much as the policy around it.

Rather than assuming "a fixed form of knowledge applied to a problem", Collins and Ison propose that participation includes aspects of social learning—"knowing [that] occurs within the act of constructing the issue"—as a contributing process for citizen participation in policymaking [74]. For them, social learning assumes that participation is not acting upon an issue, but actively constructing its boundaries, understanding, and course of action. In these ways, the groups and sites of debate and feedback, such as a forum, are important sites of negotiation not just of direction, but of the issue itself. In many ways, the Task Force was critiqued for precisely this—their discussion about the definition of an ADS is a discussion of who gets to determine such a definition. In practice, participatory governance can take many forms and is complex and messy.

One long standing example of participatory governance in action is legislation implemented by the nation of Sweden. In Sweden, the values of liberty and justice are predicated on individual and collective participation in legislative processes. A leader in information transparency, Sweden issued "The Act on the Freedom of Publishing and the Right of Access to Official Documents" in 1766. This act institutionalized a cultural belief that knowledge of governmental activities is a contributing factor to social equality insofar as the collective oversight holds officials to their promises. The Swedish government's laws and initiatives, especially in recent years, provide an example in using technology to facilitate this historical tradition of open government and participation. Technologies like open-source software and online platforms, promise "the citizen's right to monitor the activity of public sector in various spheres of national economy and advancing the development of civil society institutions" [66]. Even still, a gap exists between intent and outcome. Reviewing open source software, as the policy intends, is only possible with a degree of comfort and expertise with such technologies, and so limits who can be involved and on what terms.

It is clear that the ability to participate does not equate to the ability to impact. In a study of participation through government portals, Bernades et al. [76] note "administrations tend to reproduce in its government portals the same pre-existing governance structure, making decisions in a vertical way (top-down), with reduced transparency and openness to popular participation." Where individuals can shape policy through a portal, doing so requires considerations of how the system is actually designed.

Participatory governance is a conceptualization of citizen participation in the decisions of policymaking and programs. Due to the many forms and goals citizens may have in participating, participatory governance is far from simple, and requires evaluation and ongoing support. Rather than problems, the challenges of participatory governance are important outcomes. By opening up government processes to the messiness of participation, participatory governance provides a means for different voices, modalities, and avenues for affecting change from those the governments serve.

4.2 Participatory Design: Users as Designers

Participatory Design (PD) provides another—and increasingly overlapping—touchpoint for understanding participation in city-making projects. Rising out of a similar period as Arnstein's ladder (1960s-70s), PD [77, 78] was initially "a response to the transformation of workplaces driven by the introduction of computers" [79] wherein management did not consult the workers—the users of such workplace computers—in the process of development and implementation. Early work in PD discovered that "[w]hen those who would use these new computer-based systems were not actively involved and influential in their development and use, they were unable to create visions of future working conditions and practices that would improve or even match their current ones" [79]. In other words, as computers were introduced in workplaces, the systems poorly addressed the work processes, practices, and skills of workers. As a result, these computers ultimately undermined the intended purpose of increasing efficiency and productivity. In response, designers sought to involve workers early in the design process to shape technologies they used. Kensing & Greenbaum [80] provide a thorough historical account of PD's early practices.

From these early experiments, PD has grown as an approach and practice in design rather than a formal set of design methods or techniques. The driving perspective is that PD aims "to enable those who will use technology to have a voice in its design, without needing to speak the language of professional technology design" [79]. In order to achieve this, practitioners leverage "interactions with prototypes, mock-ups and other tools that can represent developing systems and future practices" [79]) as well as, facilitate common design activities such as ideation, conceptualization, and refinement. These interactions and activities are all done with a diverse array of participants who use systems in various ways (e.g. as workers, as managers, and as customers/recipients). Central to this practice is the assertion that users of systems are experts in their own right—experts about their work, lives, needs, and aspirations. As such, designers seek to understand the life worlds of users through what they create and conceptualize. A key aspect of PD is the role of users and stakeholders in the design and use of the technologies they use.

Characteristic of PD is a commitment to rework power relations in the process of constructing new technology [80]. Participation is more than a functional or pragmatic consideration for practitioners (e.g. making *better systems*): it is also an ethical and political position (e.g. *better making of* systems). By engaging and enacting the (re)distribution of power and control, PD activities apply to a diverse array of contexts outside of the workplace. This is true of projects and activities with community groups and government institutions [81–88]. In these settings, scholars have revised the political practice of PD from work that engages in developing and sustaining workplace democracy to a practice of experimenting with various types of democratic configurations [89].

As a design approach, PD has largely developed through practice, and examples of this practice vary greatly. Early formative work from Nygaard and Bergo was a partnership with a union in Sweden. Union workers "met every other week [...] to discuss problems with computer systems and management—and how to deal with such problems [...and then] produced reports that were primarily written by the workers" [80]. Using a traditional output of design (a requirements and recommendations document) to allow workers to advocate to management about the changes they wanted to affect through the creation of a practical set of recommendations. In other cases, PD practice is more focused on the creation of groups (what practitioners refer to as design Things) and infrastructures to help groups and systems persist over time. For example, DiSalvo et al. [90] document community-based PD done in the city of Braddock (PA, USA). With limited resources, the Neighborhood Networks project used participatory methods for residents to envision new futures for their neighborhood through prototyping, sketching, and modeling technologies. In doing so, the design activities created an avenue for a community that felt largely invisible and marginalized in local politics and programming to become *visible* contributors to their city.

The key lesson to learn from PD related to participation in smart city design, is the importance of enabling participation and projects that can sustain and the role of designers in supporting diverse stakeholders. Referred to as *infrastructuring* [91], a critical activity for participation is the development of resources to sustain participation over time. Sustaining in this context means, not that the same people will be involved, but that projects and programs are able to persist as participants ebb and flow. As an activity, infrastructuring requires designers to consider the means and modes through which individuals can participate both at the point of developing a new system or program ("design before use") and for future interventions ("design after design") [92]. Additionally, PD demonstrates that the design of technology requires mutual learning by all users as well as an engagement with and redistribution of power through substantive performances of different politics.

5 Participating in ADS Smart City Implementation

5.1 Framework

In this paper, we imagine and discuss future scenarios where frameworks for transparency and accountability, based on participatory governance and design, enable citizens to directly help regulate their smart cities' automated decision-making systems. The NYC Automated Decision System Task Force report produced broad recommendations for what the city should do when implementing agency ADS, but the group was unable to provide specific feedback to make changes to the ADS in use today or intended for the future. Drawing from the lessons of participatory governance and design, we know that a sustainable infrastructure for multi-stakeholder participation in context is the best way to empower citizens to have an impact on smart city decision making. We pull from the traditions of participatory governance and participatory design, as well as recent approaches to smart city and automated decision systems analysis to provide a sense of the key factors to consider: context driven accountability and transparency.

The first step in framing participation over time, is identifying the types of people who are accountable to parts of the system. According to a number of smart city infrastructure reviews, including Van der Hoogen et al., four key stakeholder types can be described generally as follows:

- **Enabler** – Enablers create a vision, allocate resources, provide strategic leadership, and promote networking;
- **Provider** – Providers engage academicians and professionals as innovators, provide innovative research and design (R&D) methods, augment knowledge and manage knowledge distribution systematically;
- **Utiliser** – Utilisers create suitable products and services, set small-scale objectives derived from the vision, learn new practices to produce accessible knowledge and innovate; and
- **User** – Users participate in experiments, empower citizens through co-creation and produce place-based experience [2]

Transparency, for the sake of participation, must be defined as the ability of stakeholders to understand, audit, and/or impact a system. Based on work done by Sinders[1] in outlining methods to make machine learning algorithms (and the data they use) transparent, these steps help disambiguate methods from outcomes. Here, what's most important is a stakeholder's ability to influence the decisions being made in context:

1. **Ability to understand** - stakeholder is able to understand description of a system
2. **Ability to audit** - stakeholder is understand the way the system works, the context around it, and the intention of the system. Stakeholder can provide feedback
3. **Ability to impact** - stakeholder can change system based on understanding and ability to audit [93].

Last, we articulate some of the basic phases of automated decision system implementation based on the New York City case study and related initiatives. These phases help delineate between distinctly implicated stakeholders. However, they are not comprehensive and should be considered rough guidelines for the types of decisions to be made. Notably, iteration is required between and within each of these phases to reflect participant input and refine outcomes. The process phases are:

1. **Plan** - process by which implicated stakeholders collaborate and make decisions to prepare for implementation of an automated decision system
2. **Procure and/or build** - how an automated decision system comes to be in an agency's possession. May acquire and adapt the system from another agency, private industry, or open source or decide to develop independently.
3. **Regulate** - necessary limitations imposed on system at time of procurement, implementation, or execution.
4. **Archive** - process by which abandoned or broken systems are recorded, stored, maintained, or destroyed.

[1] Caroline Sinders was a recent Mozilla Fellow for the Mozilla Foundation focused on the problems of bias in AI to create more equitable and ethical technology systems. More on her work can be found on her website here: https://carolinesinders.com/.

Using these three components together, one can begin to shape a framework based on a given context or case. By completing the following sentence, one could better understand the levels of transparency required for particular stakeholders in given process phases, depending on the scenario.

A **[stakeholder]** needs to have **[level of transparency]** to participate in decisions about how to **[process phase]** the system.

5.2 Frameworks in Practice

Based on an understanding of participatory traditions like policymaking and design described above, we know that these frameworks are useful in theory, but they may be limited in practice. We enumerate a few reasons for this limitation here, although there may be others. First, stakeholder identities may be highly amorphous and fluid. A Provider may be a User as well as an Enabler. Identities may change over time. Stakeholders may have different capacities to participate on varying levels. And, who gets to decide the stakeholder identities of the others?

Similarly, levels of transparency, and potential participation, are iterative and fluid in practice. They are often limited by "wicked" problems that constrain the potential for stakeholders to participate equally. Participation may be more practically approached through existing participatory governance methods.

We note these limitations in attempting to find a unified and analytical approach to understanding the key requirements in participatory decision making for ADS implementation, but there may be others we have not considered. Given these limitations, reassessment of the components over time and how they work together to achieve ideal outcomes is highly recommended.

5.3 Contextualizing with Scenario

In order to understand how categories of transparency, accountability, and process could help to organize the strategy of ADS implementation in smart cities, we briefly touch on a scenario of the future. This exercise is for illustration purposes only and is in no way meant to suggest that these components are the only designations to consider when drafting a plan for a given ADS.

In a city of the future, geo-spatial public health data has revealed that citizens inhabiting particular locations in the city are more likely to contract a particular illness than others. Using pattern recognition and other predictive analysis tools, experts are able to connect illnesses to environmental conditions in different areas. Newly able to link illnesses with regional criteria, Health Department employees use the analysis reports to make more informed decisions about where to locate additional clinics, and eventually, access to unique services. As the dataset becomes increasingly large and granular, the Health Department needs more employees to make sense of the reports to make decisions. Eventually, the department reaches the limit of its budget and cannot hire any more employees. After hearing about an initiative run by the city's Office of Data Analytics to develop automated decision systems, an entrepreneurial employee crafts a system that takes in reports generated from these tools and provides recommendations on where to place healthcare services for the city's citizens. The system "works so well" that the rest of the department wants to adopt it.

In this scenario, we can see how an automated decision system may be deployed without employees knowing it is one. From the start, there are questions that should be answered before the department adopts a system for official city government decisions. Some questions to consider in the context of our framework:

Stakeholders

- Who are the users of this system?
- Which government employees will have access to the system and the data?
- Who decides whether or not the system can be implemented?
- What does this mean for the citizens of this city?
- Will some be more at risk by being further from health services if they are an "anomaly" according to the system?
- Who else will be involved along the way?

Transparency levels

- What level of transparency will the related stakeholders need?
- Who provides these levels of transparency?

Process phase

- Which stakeholders need to be involved in the planning, building (or refining in this case), regulating, and possible archiving of the project?
- How are structures for participation implemented and maintained?

6 Conclusion: Recommendation and Next Steps

Using a specific case study in New York, as well as participatory approaches across domains, we hope to provide work that supports participation in smart city infrastructure decision making. More work is required to understand gaps in what we know and identify additional use cases. Particularly, we see a need for comparative empirical work related to governmental use of ADS that documents the debates, decisions, and implementations of systems, policies, and programs. Future work should make sure to consider the full life cycle of automated decision systems, using participatory design infrastructuring, to consider pre-conditions and "design after design." One area that is most opaque in our study and elsewhere [94] are vendor interactions and procurement procedures. Because ADS are often not homegrown, upfront agreements (legal or otherwise) are critical points for understanding what these systems do, who they affect, and their underlying motivations. On the other side, empirical interventionist work that uses PD approaches is vital to shaping ADS through participation. This type of work would take considerable resources and commitment on the part of many parties, including cities and vendors, but it is work that we feel is vital to social justice and equitable outcomes in the public domain.

Researchers and legislators alike have voiced concerns about the long-term impacts of ADS on citizen participation. As James Vacca, Chairperson of the NYC Council Committee on Technology, put it:

> *We have a right to know what goes into the decisions made by city government and how they arrived at the conclusion they arrived at. It's called transparency... the ability to evaluate government decision making and the ability to hold government accountable are key features of our democracy* [42].

As the New York City Task Force use case demonstrated, attempts to define and guide the use of automated decision systems in smart city infrastructure will be a challenge for even the most expert and senior authorities on the topic. Core to these challenges is the way in which stakeholders interact and share information with each other. Given this, our recommendation is that ADS in smart cities be made open to implicated stakeholders, especially those impacted by them, and acquired and implemented iteratively.

We recommend that these systems be made open, because transparency is not possible without being able to see in. One of the most often cited reasons for not opening code is due to cybersecurity concerns. There are significant projects and organizations (including the one we work for) that have sustained years of successful use while growing vibrant open source communities to maintain them. Open source does not necessarily mean less secure. As our case study of New York City's ADS Task Force shows us, it is difficult – if not impossible – to assess automated decision systems and their impact without knowing the details of the system and the data it uses. For citizens to be and feel protected, they must know that their governments are aware and in control of the systems that are meant to better serve them. Although smart city infrastructure is often adopted for speed and efficiency, it is critical that government officials consider not just the short-term gains of automated decision systems, but the long-term ramifications to citizen well-being and protected freedoms. Along with smart cities, we should be growing smart citizens, capable of interacting with and participating with the systems that determine key decision points in their lives.

We also recommend acquiring or building automated decision systems iteratively. Participatory Design, User Centered Design and design thinking all deploy multi-iteration loops to keep overhead low and align with user, consumer, or citizen expectations early. In many of the examples we have explored, those initiatives that have been most successful are those that started small and built on the projects that worked while deprioritizing or ending those that do not. Ultimately, it will take a combined multi-stakeholder participatory approach to ensure the successful implementation of smart city ADS for citizens. By using a combination of frameworks to structure an open and iterative approach, governments will be better equipped to use resources efficiently and maintain democratic processes for the citizens they serve.

References

1. United Nations, Department of Economic and Social Affairs, Population Division: World Urbanization Prospects: The 2018 Revision (ST/ESA/SER.A/420). United Nation, New York (2019)
2. Van der Hoogen, A., Scholtz, B., Calitz, A.: A smart city stakeholder classification model. In: 2019 Conference on Information Communications Technology and Society (ICTAS), pp. 1–6 (2019)

3. Alawadhi, S., et al.: Building understanding of smart city initiatives. In: Scholl, Hans J., Janssen, M., Wimmer, Maria A., Moe, C.E., Flak, L.S. (eds.) EGOV 2012. LNCS, vol. 7443, pp. 40–53. Springer, Heidelberg (2012). https://doi.org/10.1007/978-3-642-33489-4_4
4. Washburn, D., Sindhu, U., Balaouras, S., Dines, R.A., Haye, N., Nelson, L.E.: Helping CIOs Understand "Smart City" Initiatives: Defining The Smart City, Its Drivers. And the Role of the CIO, Forrester (2010)
5. Townsend, A.M.: Smart Cities: Big Data, Civic Hackers, and the Quest for a New Utopia. WW Norton & Company (2013)
6. IoT in Smart Cities Market by Solution (Remote Monitoring, Network Management, Analytics, RTLS, Security), Service, Application (Smart Transportation, Buildings, Utilities, Healthcare and Public Safety), and Region - Global Forecast to 2023. MarketsandMarkets Research (2019)
7. Anthopoulos, L.G., Janssen, M., Weerakkody, V.: Comparing smart cities with different modeling approaches. In: Proceedings of the 24th International Conference on World Wide Web, pp. 525–528. International World Wide Web Conferences Steering Committee, Republic and Canton of Geneva, Switzerland (2015)
8. Batty, M., et al.: Smart cities of the future. Eur. Phys. J. Spec. Top. **214**, 481–518 (2012)
9. Chourabi, H., et al.: Understanding smart cities: an integrative framework. In: 2012 45th Hawaii International Conference on System Science (HICSS), pp. 2289–2297 (2012)
10. Concilio, G., Rizzo, F. (eds.) Human Smart Cities. Springer, New York
11. Albino, V., Berardi, U., Dangelico, R.M.: Smart cities: definitions, dimensions, performance, and initiatives. J. Urban Technol. **22**, 3–21 (2015). https://doi.org/10.1080/10630732.2014.942092
12. Florida, R.: The Rise of the Creative Class. Revisited. Basic Books, New York (2012)
13. Florida, R.: Cities and the Creative Class. Routledge, New York (2005)
14. Wiig, A.: IBM's smart city as techno-utopian policy mobility. City **19**, 258–273 (2015). https://doi.org/10.1080/13604813.2015.1016275
15. Gabrys, J.: Programming environments: environmentality and citizen sensing in the smart city. Environ. Plann. D Soc. Space **32**, 30–48 (2014)
16. Gabrys, J., Pritchard, H., Barratt, B.: Just good enough data: figuring data citizenships through air pollution sensing and data stories. Big Data Soc. **3**, 2053951716679677 (2016)
17. Rossi, U.: The variegated economics and the potential politics of the smart city. Territory, Politics, Governance, pp. 1–17 (2015). https://doi.org/10.1080/21622671.2015.1036913
18. Vanolo, A.: Smartmentality: The Smart City as Disciplinary Strategy. Urban Studies. **51**, 883–898 (2014). https://doi.org/10.1177/0042098013494427
19. Shelton, T., Zook, M., Wiig, A.: The 'actually existing smart city'. Cambridge J. Reg. Econ. Soc. **8**, 13–25 (2015)
20. Cardullo, P., Kitchin, R.: Smart urbanism and smart citizenship: the neoliberal logic of 'citizen-focused'smart cities in Europe. Environ. Plann C Politics Space **37**, 813–830 (2019)
21. Greenfield, A.: Against the Smart City. Do Projects (2013)
22. Shelton, T., Lodato, T.: Actually existing smart citizens: expertise and (non)participation in the making of the smart city. City **23**, 35–52 (2019)
23. Vogl, T., Seidelin, C., Ganesh, B., Bright, J.: Algorithmic bureaucracy. In: Proceedings of the 20th Annual International Conference on Digital Government Research, pp. 148–153. ACM, New York (2019)
24. Eubanks, V.: Automating Inequality: How High-Tech Tools Profile, Police, and Punish the Poor. St. Martin's Press, New York (2017)
25. Array of Things. https://arrayofthings.github.io/index.html
26. Capra, C.F.: The smart city and its citizens: governance and citizen participation in amsterdam smart city. IJEPR **5**, 20–38 (2016). https://doi.org/10.4018/IJEPR.2016010102

27. Taylor, L., Richter, C., Jameson, S., de Pulgar, C.: Customers, Users or Citizens? Inclusion, Spatial Data and Governance in the Smart City. Social Science Research Network, Rochester, NY (2016)
28. Confronting Black Boxes: A Shadow Report of the New York City Automated Decision System Task Force. AI Now Institute, New York (2019)
29. Loi, D.: Ten guidelines for intelligent systems futures. In: Arai, K., Bhatia, R., Kapoor, S. (eds.) FTC 2018. AISC, vol. 880, pp. 788–805. Springer, Cham (2019). https://doi.org/10.1007/978-3-030-02686-8_59
30. Harari, Y.N.: Are we about to witness the most unequal societies in history? (2017). https://www.theguardian.com/inequality/2017/may/24/are-we-about-to-witness-the-most-unequal-societies-in-history-yuval-noah-harari
31. Automated Decision Systems: Examples of Government Use Cases (2019). https://ainowinstitute.org/nycadschart.pdf
32. Hill, K., Murphy, H.: Your DNA Profile is Private? A Florida Judge Just Said Otherwise (2019). https://www.nytimes.com/2019/11/05/business/dna-database-search-warrant.html
33. Lynch, J.: Google's Sensorvault Can Tell Police Where You've Been. https://www.eff.org/deeplinks/2019/04/googles-sensorvault-can-tell-police-where-youve-been
34. Goitom, H.: Regulation of Artificial Intelligence: Sub-Saharan Africa. https://www.loc.gov/law/help/artificial-intelligence/africa.php#_ftn18
35. Roth, A.E.: Who Gets What - and Why: The New Economics of Matchmaking and MarketDesign - from Birth to Death and Along the Way. HarperCollins Publishers Limited (2015)
36. Levinson-Waldman, R.: Re: Freedom of Information Law Request (2016). https://www.brennancenter.org/sites/default/files/NYPD%20Palantir%20FOIL%20061416.pdf
37. Stop-and-Frisk Data. https://www.nyclu.org/en/stop-and-frisk-data
38. Mayor de Blasio Announces First-In-Nation Task Force To Examine Automated Decision Systems. http://www1.nyc.gov/office-of-the-mayor/news/251-18/mayor-de-blasio-first-in-nation-task-force examine-automated-decision-systems-used-by
39. Lecher, C.: New York City's algorithm task force is fracturing. https://www.theverge.com/2019/4/15/18309437/new-york-city-accountability-task-force-law-algorithm-transparency-automation
40. Open Data Law. https://www1.nyc.gov/site/doitt/initiatives/open-data-law.page
41. Chaitoo, N.: JailVizNYC. http://nycod-wpengine.com/
42. Vacca, J.: Transcript of the Minutes of the Committee on Technology, New York City (2017)
43. Vacca, J.: Introduction No. 1696 (2017)
44. Vacca, R., Johnson, S., Gentile, C., Williams, K.: Menchaca: Local Law No. 49: In relation to automated decision systems used by agencies (2018)
45. Cahn, A.F., et al.: Re: NYC Automated Decision Systems Task Force (2018)
46. Ferguson, A.G., et al.: Re: New York City's Automated Decision Systems Task Force (2018)
47. Stoyanovich, J., Barocas, S.: Testimony of Julia Stoyanovich and Solon Barocas before New York City CouncilCommittee on Technology, regarding Update on Local Law 49 of 2018 in Relationto Automated Decision Systems (ADS) Used by Agencies, New York City (2019)
48. New York City Automated Decision Systems Task Force Report. Automated Decision Systems (ADS) Task For, New York City (2019)
49. de Blasio, B.: Establishing an Algorithms Management and Policy Officer (2019)
50. Cahn, A.F.: NYC's task force to regulate AI was a spectacular failure. https://www.fastcompany.com/90436012/the-first-effort-to-regulate-ai-was-a-spectacular-failure
51. Budds, D.: New York City's AI task force stalls. https://ny.curbed.com/2019/4/16/18335495/new-york-city-automated-decision-system-task-force-ai
52. Clarke, Y.D.: Algorithmic Accountability Act of 2019

53. Breslend, B.: Artificial Intelligence Task Force Final Report. Artificial Intelligence Task Force, Vermont (2020)
54. Pangburn, D.J.: Washington could be the first state to rein in automated decision-making. https://www.fastcompany.com/90302465/washington-introduces-landmark-algorithmic-accountability-laws
55. Hasegawa, N., McCoy, K.: Washington (State) Senate Bill 5527
56. Hudgins, Z., Shea, M., Morris, J., Kloba, S., Valdez, J.: Washington (State) HB1655
57. Javaid, A.: Norway's first National Strategy for Artificial Intelligence launched - NORA - Norwegian Artificial Intelligence Research Consortium. https://www.nora.ai/news-and-events/news/norway%E2%80%99s-first-national-strategy-for-artificial-in.html
58. Ministry of Local Government and Modernisation: The National Strategy for Artificial Intelligence. https://www.regjeringen.no/en/dokumenter/nasjonal-strategi-for-kunstig-intelligens/id2685594/
59. Wray, S.: Copenhagen shares takeaways from its City Data Exchange. https://www.smartcitiesworld.net/news/news/copenhagen-shares-takeaways-from-its-city-data-exchange-2961
60. Municipality of Copenhagen and Capital Region of Denmark: City Data Exchange: Lessons learned from a Public/Private Data Collaboration. Municipality of Copenhagen and Capital Region of Denmark, Copenhagen (2018)
61. Habermas, J.: Three normative models of democracy. Constellations **1**, 1–10 (1994). https://doi.org/10.1111/j.1467-8675.1994.tb00001.x
62. Mouffe, C.: The democratic paradox. verso (2000)
63. Marres, N.: The issues deserve more credit: pragmatist contributions to the study of public involvement in controversy. Soc. Stud. Sci. **37**, 759–780 (2007). https://doi.org/10.1177/0306312706077367
64. Frantz, F.: Wretched of the Earth. Penguin Books (1995)
65. McKenna, H.P.: Ambient Urbanities as the Intersection Between the IoT and the IoP in Smart Cities. IGI Global (2019)
66. Kassen, M.: A promising phenomenon of open data: a case study of the Chicago open data project. Gov. Inf. Q. **30**, 508–513 (2013)
67. Simonsen, J., Robertson, T.: Routledge International Handbook of Participatory Design. Routledge, New York (2012)
68. Fischer, F.: Participatory governance: from theory to practice. In: Levi-Faur, D. (ed.) The Oxford Handbook of Governance, pp. 457–471. Oxford Univeristy Press (2012)
69. Stefanescu, A., Mocanu, M., Eugeniu, T.: Participatory governance in the public healthcare systems of the scandinavian and baltic countries. Ann. Fac. Econ. **1**, 625–630 (2011)
70. Arnstein, S.R.: A ladder of citizen participation. J. Am. Inst. Plann. **35**, 216–224 (1969)
71. Warren, R.L.: Model cities first round: politics, planning, and participation. J. Am. Inst. Plann. **35**, 245–252 (1969). https://doi.org/10.1080/01944366908977228
72. Weissman, S.R.: The limits of citizen participation: lessons from San Francisco's model cities program. W. Polit. Q. **31**, 32–47 (1978). https://doi.org/10.1177/106591297803100105
73. Tritter, J.Q., McCallum, A.: The snakes and ladders of user involvement: moving beyond Arnstein. Health Policy **76**, 156–168 (2006)
74. Collins, K., Ison, R.: Dare we jump off Arnstein's ladder? Social learning as a new policy paradigm (2006)
75. Rittel, H.W.J., Webber, M.M.: Dilemmas in a general theory of planning. Policy Sci. **4**, 155–169 (1973)
76. Bernardes, M.B., de Andrade, F.P., Novais, P., Lopes, N.V.: Participatory governance of smart cities: a study upon Portuguese and Brazilian government portals. In: Proceedings of the 11th International Conference on Theory and Practice of Electronic Governance, pp. 526–536. ACM, New York (2018)

77. Sanoff, H.: Participatory Design: Theory & Techniques. H. Sanoff (1990)
78. Schuler, D., Namioka, A.: Participatory Design: Principles and Practices. CRC Press, Boca Raton (1993)
79. Robertson, T., Simonsen, J.: Participatory Design: an introduction. In: Simonsen, J., Robertson, T. (eds.) Routledge International Handbook of Participatory Design. Routledge, New York (2012)
80. Kensing, F., Greenbaum, J.: Heritage: having a say. In: Simonsen, J., Robertson, T. (eds.) Routledge International Handbook of Participatory Design. Routledge, New York (2012)
81. Light, A., Akama, Y.: The human touch: participatory practice and the role of facilitation in designing with communities. In: Proceedings of the 12th Participatory Design Conference: Research Papers - Volume 1, pp. 61–70. Association for Computing Machinery, Roskilde (2012)
82. Light, A., Simpson, G., Weaver, L., Healey, P.G.T.: Geezers, turbines, fantasy personas: making the everyday into the future. In: Proceedings of the Seventh ACM Conference on Creativity and Cognition, pp. 39–48. ACM, New York (2009)
83. Heitlinger, S., Bryan-Kinns, N., Comber, R.: Connected seeds and sensors: co-designing internet of things for sustainable smart cities with urban food-growing communities. In: Proceedings of the 15th Participatory Design Conference: Short Papers, Situated Actions, Workshops and Tutorial - Volume 2, pp. 1–5. Association for Computing Machinery, Hasselt and Genk (2018)
84. Brown, A.V., Choi, J.H.: Refugee and the post-trauma journeys in the fuzzy front end of co-creative practices. In: Proceedings of the 15th Participatory Design Conference: Full Papers - Volume 1, pp. 1–11. Association for Computing Machinery, Hasselt and Genk, Belgium (2018)
85. Huybrechts, L., Benesch, H., Geib, J.: Institutioning: Participatory Design, Co-Design and the public realm. CoDesign **13**, 148–159 (2017). https://doi.org/10.1080/15710882.2017.1355006
86. DiSalvo, C., Lodato, T., Fries, L., Schechter, B., Barnwell, T.: The collective articulation of issues as design practice. CoDesign **7**, 185–197 (2011). https://doi.org/10.1080/15710882.2011.630475
87. Lukens, J., DiSalvo, C.: Speculative design and technological fluency. Int. J. Learn. Media **3**, 23–40 (2011). https://doi.org/10.1162/IJLM_a_00080
88. Ehn, P., Nilsson, E.M., Topgaard, R. (eds.) Making Futures: Marginal Notes on Innovation, Design, and Democracy. MIT Press, Cambridge (2014)
89. Binder, T., Brandt, E., Ehn, P., Halse, J.: Democratic design experiments: between parliament and laboratory. CoDesign **11**, 152–165 (2015). https://doi.org/10.1080/15710882.2015.1081248
90. DiSalvo, C., Nourbakhsh, I., Holstius, D., Akin, A., Louw, M.: The neighborhood networks project: a case study of critical engagement and creative expression through participatory design. In: Proceedings of the Tenth Anniversary Conference on Participatory Design 2008, pp. 41–50. Indiana University, Indianapolis (2008)
91. Le Dantec, C., DiSalvo, C.: Infrastructuring and the formation of publics in participatory design. Soc. Stud. Sci. (2013). https://doi.org/10.1177/0306312712471581
92. Bjögvinsson, E., Ehn, P., Hillgren, P.: Design things and design thinking: contemporary participatory design challenges. Des. Issues **28**, 101–116 (2012)
93. Sinders, C.: Designing for transparency in machine learning. https://interaction19.ixda.org/program/talk-designing-for-transparency-in-machine-learning-caroline-sinders/
94. Lodato, T., DiSalvo, C.: Institutional constraints: the forms and limits of participatory design in the public realm. In: Proceedings of the 15th Participatory Design Conference: Full Papers - Volume 1, pp. 1–12. Association for Computing Machinery, Hasselt and Genk (2018)

Civic Crowdsensing Through Location-Aware Virtual Monsters

Takuro Yonezawa[1(✉)], Mina Sakamura[2], Nobuo Kawaguchi[1], and Jin Nakazawa[2]

[1] Nagoya University, Aichi, Nagoya, Japan
{takuro,kawaguti}@nagoya-u.jp
[2] Keio University, Kanagawa, Fujisawa, Japan
{mina,jin}@ht.sfc.keio.ac.jp

Abstract. We present a new model for encouraging people to get involved with monitoring and taking part in the life of cities. Cities could be smarter if IoT and people could serve as engaged and pro-active data resources (i.e., crowd sensing). This study tackles two challenges: methods by which the privacy of people who act as sensors/actuators can be guaranteed and methods to create a unified programming model for crowd sensors alongside other IoT functions. To achieve these goals, we introduce a new concept called Lokemon (Location Monster). Each sensing space is characterized as a personified target. Lokemon asks users to imagine themselves to be monsters associated with target spots when achieving sensing tasks. Lokemon is also expressed as a PubSub node so that the data from Lokemon can be easily accessed in the same way as data from IoT is assessed. The article explains the concept of Lokemon and its programming model. We report our evaluation of the effectiveness of Lokemon in a campus experiment that was performed for four weeks.

Keywords: Crowdsensing · Urban computing

1 Introduction

Computing is now widely applied in the management of urban activities and resources. The internet of things (IoT) will be ubiquitously embedded in equipment and infrastructure throughout cities. Real-time sensor data from IoT underpins the monitoring of a variety of city contexts for tasks such as day-to-day activities, which include city management, disaster management, enhancing the quality of life and encouraging economic growth. Another important resource in the cities is people. By using smartphones and wearable devices, people can act as sensors (e.g., reporting city happenings by capturing photos or counting the number of people in a line) and even actuators (e.g., picking up garbage or erasing graffiti). Since both IoT and people each have advantages, utilizing them in a complementary and transparent manner is the next paradigm for a programmable world.

N. Streitz and S. Konomi (Eds.): HCII 2020, LNCS 12203, pp. 464–476, 2020.
https://doi.org/10.1007/978-3-030-50344-4_33

We tackle following two challenges: 1) how can we persuade people to act as active sensors/actuators by reducing concerns that they will thereby sacrifice their privacy and 2) what might be suitable as a programming model/platform that would combine data from both IoT and crowd sensing. First, as several papers have already shown, crowd sensing requires incentives to motivate people to participate in sensing tasks. Also, people who report sensor data at a certain location are sometimes faced with a problem of loss of privacy - in location-aware reporting the position of the user can be identified when the report is made. It is, therefore, necessary to reduce privacy concerns to involve more people in crowd sensing. Secondly, though many platforms have been proposed and developed for IoT and crowd sensing, they are mainly designed for supporting either IoT or crowd sensing. To access data transparently and write programs effectively, any sensing method should be managed and applied in a unified way.

To solve these issues and provide a unified method for computing with both IoT and people, we introduce Lokemon, a new crowd sensing concept and platform that will embody the concept. Lokemon is short for location monster, an example of which is to be virtually placed at each point of interest (PoI) in cities. Lokemon asks users to imagine themselves to be the monsters as they perform sensing tasks. Any users currently located near the PoI identify with the Lokemon and complete tasks or answer questions from other remote users. To reduce the loss of privacy, people's actions are assigned to the Lokemon rather than being labeled with the user name or even an anonymous name. Moreover, Lokemon provides a new experience whereby the user can collect data while mimicking as a Lokemon. It is implemented by using a universal sensor network system based on the PubSub protocol [9], so that Lokemon provides an open API, which is same to that for IoT. This article presents details of the Lokemon and reports our first campus-wide experiment to evaluate its potential. In summary, the article establishes the following three developments:

- Introducing a new concept called Lokemon that achieves crowd sensing by mimicking monsters that are installed virtually at PoIs
- Providing a system architecture that integrates IoT and crowd sensing and adapting it for Lokemon
- Presenting an initial evaluation of Lokemon in a four-week experiment on campus

2 Lokemon

This section begins by describing the problems involved in crowd sensing and then introduces the concept of Lokemon as a solution.

2.1 Problems of Crowdsensing

Recent progress with mobile devices such as smartphones allows people to refine and integrate their perceptive faculties as a part of sensing framework. This sensing framework, so-called crowd sensing (or participatory sensing) [1], distributes various sensing tasks (such as reporting the weather, waiting time in a queue and traffic conditions) to potential participants. By people sending a text, photo, sound data and so on, we can get subjective and qualitative data that it has been hard for physical sensors to collect hitherto, such as the mood of a place. It would make wide and high density sensing possible. However, there are some problems with existing crowd sensing systems, as follows:

1. Privacy
   Users who are participating in sensing send information to each PoI. As a result, the system knows where they are at particular times.
2. Motivation
   It is important to give an incentive because getting involved in crowd sensing is a burden on users. Without adequate incentive mechanisms, most users may not want to participate.
3. Quality of information
   It is possible to allow users to contribute information anonymously to protect their privacy. However, such information may lead to difficulties such as deterioration of quality (false information), ravage and allegations of libel and slander.

Recent researches have described many existing efforts to solve these problems [2–4]. For example, Groat et al. [2] proposed a way of protecting privacy by reconstructing reports from users using a 'Negative Survey' technique. In terms of incentive for participation, Sasank et al. [4] explored what kind of monetary rewards work effectively in crowd sensing. However, several limitations remain. For example, the privacy protection method works only for multiple-choice questions. Using external factors such as monetary rewards is insufficient for enhancing motivation compared to internal factors. Previous research has been tackled the problems by using "username" or "anonymous user" as the alias for the information sender. We, on the other hand, explore the possibility of solving these problems by providing an alternative: namely, mimicking location-aware virtual monsters.

2.2 Concept of Lokemon

We developed the concept of Lokemon to solve the three aforementioned issues simultaneously. The basic idea of the Lokemon is very simple: users can achieve crowd sensing as monsters, which are virtually located at each PoI. Figure 1 shows a comparison between the typical crowd sensing model and the Lokemon model. In the typical crowd sensing model, users usually use their user names (real names or pseudonyms) to send sensing data. In Lokemon model, by contrast, users send sensor data in the name of a nearby Lokemon virtually located at each sensing. We explain the detail of the Lokemon in the following scenario.

Scenario: Today is the first day of Bob's trip to Kyoto. Because of a bad case of jet lag, he wakes up at his hotel at noon and goes outside to have lunch with his

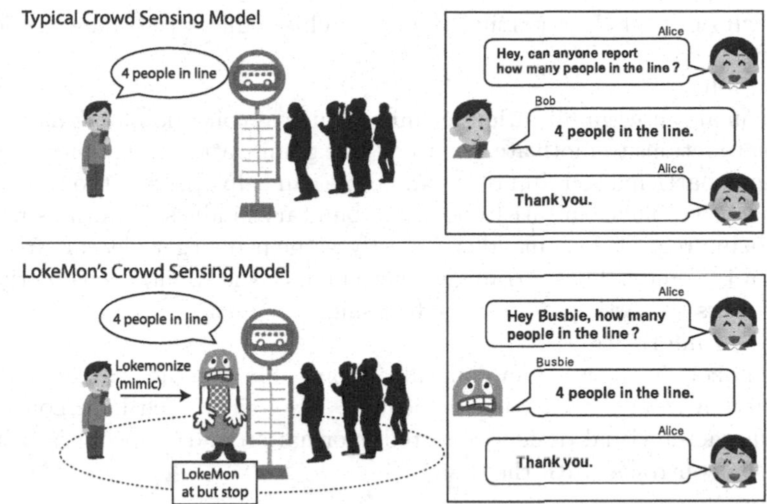

Fig. 1. Comparison of current participatory sensing model and Lokemon's sensing model. In typical crowd sensing model, a user sends sensor data by using his/her user name. In Lokemon model, a user sends sensor data by using monster name which is virtually located at a sensing spot.

smartphone in which the Lokemon application is installed. He is a great lover of ramen noodles, so he heads to a famous ramen restaurant by bus. While he waits for a bus at a bus stop, he gets notification that a new Lokemon is located at the bus stop. He opens the Lokemon application and adds the new Lokemon named Busbie to his Lokemon collection. At the same time, he finds that a user named Alice is asking Busbie how many people there are in the line. Being at the bus stop, he is able to give the information and he reports the number of people in the line identifying himself as Busbie. After a 15 min bus ride, he finally arrives at the ramen restaurant. But the restaurant is full of people; more than 20 people are waiting outside. He gives up to eat ramen noodle, however, he collects a new Lokemon called ramen-man in the restaurant. The next day, he considers giving the ramen restaurant another try. He opens the Lokemon application and asks ramen-man about current congestion at the ramen restaurant. Ramen-man reports that there are only a few people in the restaurant, and he decides to go there to eat.

As shown in the scenario, Lokemon enables users to perform the following actions: 1) collect a Lokemon by visiting a place where it virtually lives, 2) use a Lokemon as an alias to report information near to its site, and 3) ask a question remotely of a collected Lokemon. The scenario suggests solving the three aforementioned issues as follows:

1. Privacy
   Since the users can send data in the name of Lokemon, other users cannot

know who is actually reporting the data. This reduces the chance of loss of privacy.

2. Motivation
   Lokemon also uses gamification techniques such as collection, ranking or cooperation functions to motivate the users. The gamification techniques motivate the users' participation. In Lokemon, people can help others without revealing their identity. This can satisfy people's voluntary kindness for others without them being regarded as 'meddlers'. Lastly, some people get pleasure from acting as a Lokemon. These strategies may enhance the spontaneous motivation of the users to participate in crowd sensing.
3. Quality of information
   Using Lokemon, people can concentrate on achieving the task of reporting information from that particular location. Also, since each Lokemon has an each character visual design, reported information and/or people's behavior might be controlled with the design.

2.3 Sociological Theory Behind Lokemon

Lokemon's potential for solving the issues can also be explained by introducing several sociological theories. First, dramaturgy theory [5] suggests that the design of Lokemon might enhance information quality. Dramaturgy, originally developed by Erving Goffman, argues that human interactions are always influenced by time, place, and audience. It suggests that a person's identity is not a stable and independent psychological entity, but rather gets remade as the person interacts with others. In other words, people always have to aware of whether they are playing an expected role, or change their behaviors to manage the impression they make on others. Since Lokemon forces users to act as the Lokemon rather than themselves, they can focus on playing a more stable role/character as the Lokemon, rather than varying their behavior to make a particular impression on others. Thus, Lokemon provides a stable front stage and guide of performance for the users. In addition, the concept of positive/negative face or face-threatening acts in politeness theory [6] also suggests that Lokemon provides safe opportunities to help others while avoiding excessive mutual interference. In the real world or when using a user name that identifies each user, it is difficult for users to balance positive face and negative face. By mediating their communications through a virtual monster that is characterized by a common identity for the PoI, users can meld into a common identity shared by other people. This could help to enhance users' motivation to participate in crowd sensing.

3 Programming Model

We propose a programming model for computing people (leveraging people as a part of sensing/actuating in program) through Lokemon. Instead of requesting users directly to undertake various tasks such as sensing or acting, our

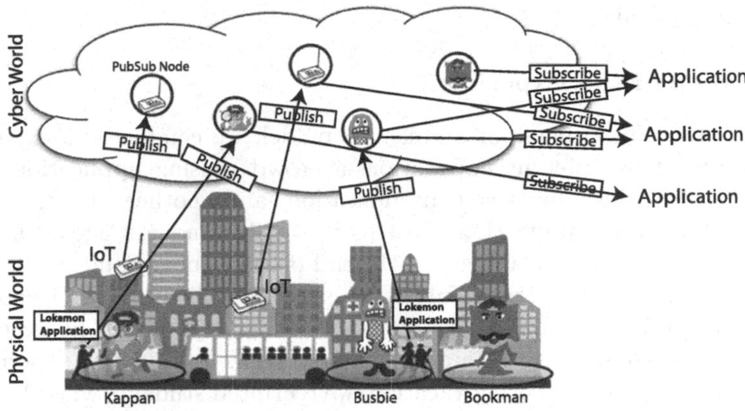

Fig. 2. IoT sensors are placed to physical world. Lokemons are placed virtually to each locations. Applications can access them via PubSub nodes, which are associated to each IoT and Lokemon, by subscribing or publishing the nodes.

model places requests to users indirectly by doing it through Lokemon. Moreover, our model enables developers to access data both from IoT and people (Lokemon) via unified APIs. We adapted the Publish-Subscribe model to access sensors/actuators including IoT and Lokemon. Each IoT/Lokemon is managed as a PubSub node, and applications can leverages data of the node by subscribing the node or publishing data to the node. This allows developers to make applications easily because both IoT and Lokemon can be treated in the same way as real-time data streams. Figure 2 represents how data from IoT and Lokemon are flowed in the same manner. In the figure, two IoT sensors are deployed in the physical world. They periodically publish sensor data to the PubSub node corresponding to the each IoT sensor. In addition, three Lokemons named Kappan, Busbie, and Bookman are deployed virtually at several locations, and people who are located closely to each Lokemon publish sensor data as Lokemon by using the Lokemon application. Third party applications can retrieve data from both IoT and Lokemon in a unified way by subscribing to PubSub nodes corresponding to each IoT and Lokemon. Thus, information from Lokemon can be regarded as open sensor data streams just like public IoT sensors. One of advantages of the programming model is to provide simplicity; developers do not have to specify exact users to interact with. Developers can make use of sensor data from people who are in PoI by accessing virtual sensors as Lokemon. For the PubSub-based platform, we extended the sensor-over-xmpp protocol [7,8] to manage not only IoT sensors/actuators but also crowd sensing nodes with Lokemon. In addition, we also made use of our XMPP server implementation, SOXFire [9], which is designed for distributed and federated infrastructure for data sharing among various users/organizations in a way that is scalable, extensible, and easy to use and secure.

4 Experiment

4.1 Purpose of the Experiment

To evaluate the effectiveness of a Lokemon model, we conducted a experiment that compared two different applications-a crowd sensing application with a Lokemon mode (called the Lokemon application) and another lacking Lokemon (called the Lokerepo application). We recruited 34 students aged 19–30. We offered them a reward of 3,800 yen at the end of experiment, and divided them into two groups (17 each) randomly. One group installed only Lokemon, and the other group installed only Lokerepo on their smartphones. The experiment took place between January 24th and February 28th. Because the experimental period coincided with the spring vacation, we recruited students who planned to visit the campus for more than seven days during the period. At the beginning of the experiment, we taught each group how to use Lokemon or Lokerepo as appropriate. We did not force the users to use Lokemon/Lokerepo. We required only that the users always have Bluetooth turned on, allowing notification from the application. The experiment allowed us to compare the difference between of the number of reports and communications among participants using Lokemon and those equipped with Lokerepo. Finally, we conducted a questionnaire survey to help us understand the participants' impression of the applications.

4.2 Prototype Applications and Experiment Setting

We implemented two iOS applications - Lokemon and Lokerepo. In both applications, the users' basic task is defined as to reporting current information from each location. For each PoI, we prepared a virtual noticeboard at the locations where participants could report current information. Messages in noticeboard can be also accessed remotely so that remote users can ask questions to possible users who are/will be at the locations. In other words, prototype applications were designed to work as a location-oriented Q&A service. In Lokemon, participants can report sensing information by mimicking monsters, which are virtually placed in each PoI (though those asking remotely were supposed to use their username). In Lokerepo, on the other hand, participants have to use their registered username (real name or a pseudonym) every time they used the application.

We defined nine locations in our campus as PoI - Theta building, the bus stop, the Subway restaurant, building Iota, Kappa building, the Yukichi statue, the Gulliver pond, the co-op store and Omega building. Figure 3 shows the nine locations and the Lokemons designed by the authors and placed in each PoI. We also installed iBeacon nodes in each PoI to specify the users' location. We set iBeacon's signal strength as "far" mode, which can be detected within a distance of about 10 m. When the users enter each PoI (i.e., the iBeacon signal area), a notification is sent to the user's smartphone to make them aware of the existence of the PoI. Users with the Lokemon application can then pretend to be the Lokemon associated to the PoI to report information. GPS can also useful for specifying the users' location, for implementing Lokemon, but in this experiment we used iBeacon to specify location more precisely. Figure 4 shows screenshots of implemented applications. We designed and implemented iOS applications of Lokemon and Lokerepo to provide very similar usage for the users. The only difference was that the Lokemon application expresses each PoI as its Lokemon, enabling the users to pretend to be a Lokemon. Other functions such as receiving notifications when users are within PoIs, when any reports/questions are posted, the interface design for map and posting messages take the same form in the two applications (see Fig. 4).

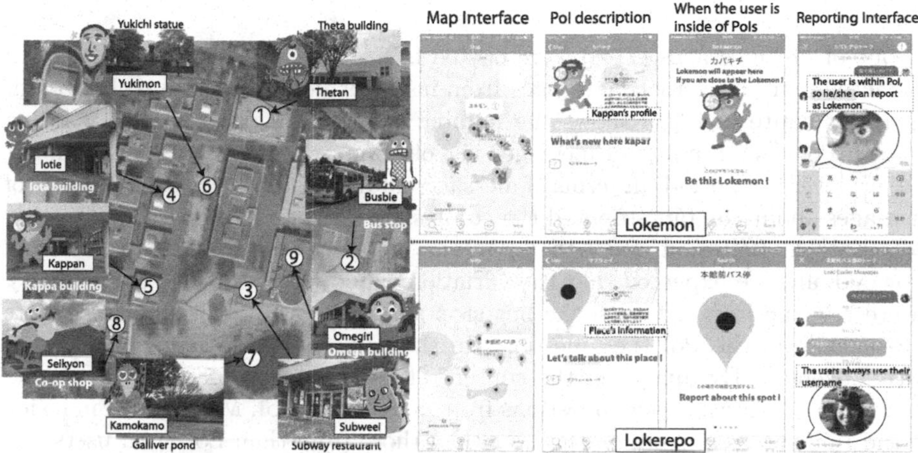

Fig. 3. Locations of the nine PoIs in the campus, and the identities associated with the Lokemon at each PoI (left). Screenshots of Lokemon and Lokerepo (right).

4.3 Experimental Result

This section describes experiment result and discusses the particular effect of Lokemon. In both applications, participants asked/replied questions about current information near each PoIs such as the current length of waiting line at bus stop, or whether the shop was open or closed. All communication in both Lokemon and Lokerepo was done in Japanese. We translated the original messages into English as far as possible in the explanation below while retaining original nuances of messages.

Difference of Collected Information. In all, we received 153 messages in Lokemon, and 114 messages in Lokerepo. Thus, Lokemon collected 134% number of messages compared to Lokerepo. In addition, in the case of Lokemon application, 72 out of 153 messages (47%) were posted as Lokemon (i.e., posted within PoI area). On the contrary, in the case of Lokerepo application, only

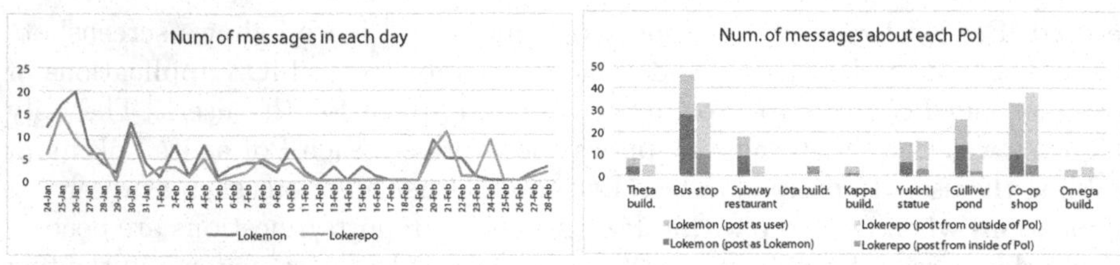

Fig. 4. Comparison of the number of messages in Lokemon and Lokerepo in each day (left) and in each PoI (right).

24 out of 114 messages (21%) were posted from inside of PoIs. Thus, Lokemon attracted more than twice messages from inside of PoIs compared to Lokerepo.

Right figure in Fig. 4 shows the number of messages each day and relating to each PoI. The number of messages in Lokemon and Lokerepo show a similar pattern over the period. In terms of messages about each PoI, the total number of messages about the bus stop and the co-op shop are larger compared with other PoIs both in Lokemon and Lokerepo. The bus stop and co-op shop are often crowded, and we expected that the variation would be reflected in participants' interest in the PoIs. At both the bus stop and co-op shop, Lokemon gets more messages from the PoI (i.e., messages in the name of the Lokemon) compared with Lokerepo. By analyzing the content of the Lokerepo messages, we found that most of messages were questions from outside the PoI. Messages from inside of the PoI were relatively much fewer than those from than Lokemon users.

Next, in both Lokemon and Lokerepo, buildings Theta, Iota, Kappa, and Omega collected only a few messages. Those buildings are usually used for lectures; however, the experimental period was during spring vacation and no lectures took place in those buildings. That why those buildings did not get messages. In the Subway restaurant and Gulliver pond, Lokemon again collected more messages than Lokerepo. The differences were mainly due to the number of messages from inside the PoIs - about half the messages from the Subway restaurant and the Gulliver pond in Lokemon were posted using the Lokemon alias. Even when there were no questions from other users, participants voluntarily pretended to be a Lokemon to post messages about the PoI's current situation or their feeling about the mood as the Lokemon such as "No one here. I am very lonely. (posted by user A as Kamokamo)," or "Today's special lunch is Tuna sandwich! (posted by user B as Subweei)." In Lokerepo, we could not see this kind of messages.

Through these observations, we confirmed that Lokemon provided more than twice the opportunities to collect information from people who are in PoIs. This result implies that the Lokemon model could motivate people better than the traditional username model. Moreover, some users voluntary play a role as Lokemon to establish or assume the identity of the Lokemon's identity when they report current information about the PoIs.

Differences of Communication Between Users. We also observed that there are significant differences between the types of communication that take place between the Lokemon and Lokerepo users.

1. Many-to-one communication (Lokemon) vs. many- to-many communication (Lokerepo)
   In Lokemon, participants usually asked questions that address the Lokemon such as "Hey Subweei, what is your recommendation today? (posted by user C)" or "The wind seems to be strong today, are you OK Busbie? (posted by user B)." On the contrary, in Lokerepo, participants often addressed questions to "someone" who could help them such as "Does anyone know whether the Subway is opened now? (posted by user D)." In other words, the users in Lokerepo were often concerned about possible communication with unknown people. Lokemon provides a more simple communication option from many users to one Lokemon. Also, many people actually played a role as the Lokemon when they responded.
2. Casual communication (Lokemon) vs. Polite communication (Lokerepo)
   Another interesting observation in Lokemon was that people tended to communicate more casually compared with Lokerepo. When people address questions to a Lokemon, they say things like "Hey Busbie," "Are you cold?" or "Thanks!." Replies from Lokemon were also expressed in a casual or monster-like way such as "No one here!," "We are closed!," with attaching onomatopoeia at the end of messages to express the Lokemon's character, such as "(messages) kapa!," "(messages) BusBus!" or "(sentences) yo!." This onomatopoeia style was developed by the users themselves. On the contrary, in Lokerepo, people tended to ask/answer questions in a more polite way such as "Could someone tell me whether the shop is open or not?," "Thank you very much." or "Opening time in spring vacation is from 11:00 to 15:00. (in a polite way in Japanese)." We consider that Lokemon has the potential to enhance a friendly mood that contributes to the increase in the number of messages.

Questionnaire Survey. After finishing the experiment, we asked the participants to complete a questionnaire. Table 1 represents statements and averages of results obtained from the questionnaire. The respective ratings of agreement are: 1 = strongly disagree, 2 = partly disagree, 3 = neither agree nor disagree, 4 = partly agree, and 5 = strongly agree. In terms of pleasant, easiness, and motivation, Lokemon users gave better feedbacks than Lokerepo users. In addition, Lokemon users seemed to feel that the risk of loss of privacy is reduced by using Lokemon as a mediator of crowd sensing. These results show that we were right to predict that users of Lokemon would use this modality more. On the other hand, users of Lokemon seemed to consider that the reliability of messages is decreased slightly compared with Lokerepo. We take this to be a result of its anonymity feature. In future we need to evaluate Lokemon's reliability, by looking at the effect of feedback.

Table 1. Result of questionnaire.

Question	Lokemon	Lokerepo
It was pleasant to post message	3.6	3.2
Using Lokemon name (for Lokemon users) or Using username (for Lokerepo users) made it easy to post messages	3.8	2.5
The application enhanced my motivation to participate	3.3	2.5
The application decreased the reliability of messages	2.8	1.9
The application decreased the risk of loss of privacy	3.8	2.5

5 Related Work

To motivate people to participate in crowdsensing, a lot of work have been conducted on incentive study. For example, the effect of monetary incentives has been investigated in [10,11]. For non-monetary incentives, researchers mainly focus on psychological factors. For example, the study of gamification has been conducted in [12,13]. The work of [14,15] studied to use compliance-without-pressure technology to improve the receptiveness of participants. Our proposal is a new comprehensive approach of non-monetary incentives which uses techniques from sociology, psychology and anthropomorphism which have not been utilized in crowdsensing by now.

Lots of work have studied the use of avatars in virtual space communication and demonstrated that avatars does place an effect on people's behavior in both real and virtual worlds. For example, Yoon et al. [16] investigated whether certain types of avatars and avatar behaviors could promote pro- or anti-social actions of humans in daily behavior. Rosenberg et al. [17] illustrated the potential of using experiences in virtual reality technology to increase pro-social behavior in the physical world. To our best of knowledge, this work is the first attempt to promoting people's participation in crowdsensing via avatars. Moreover, in Lokemon, each monster can be mimicked by a group of people while in the aforementioned study each avatar can only be manipulated by one person.

Anthropomorphic design has also been widely applied to mascot characters, robotics, and entertainment games. Jetter et al. [18] explored how the physical design of urban sensors can change citizens' attitudes and perceptions toward being sensed. They found that anthropomorphic design resulted in greater engagement and trust while neutral or less visible designs created rejection and anxiety. Osawa et al. [19] proposed a direct anthropomorphic method that agentizes an artifact by attaching anthropomorphic parts to it. The study indicated that the examinees noticed the target artifact and memorized functions using direct anthropomorphism method more than doing so using an independent humanoid-agent. Compared with these study, our design applies an anthropomorphism of the property of location rather than physical objects, which has not been studied before.

6 Conclusion

We have presented a new crowd sensing model called Lokemon that mediates sensing subjects as location-aware virtual monsters. We addressed issues such as loss of privacy, providing motivation and controlling data quality in crowd sensing and showed that they are strongly related to aspects of the way of the sensing subject is structured such as whether the user identifies themselves using individual username or an alias. To address the issue, we introduced the concept of Lokemon that enables users to mimic location-aware monsters when they participate in crowd sensing. In addition, we also presented a programming model where a Lokemon can work as a virtual sensor node. Our programming model enables developers to create an application in a unified way that can handle data from both IoT sensors and people via Lokemon sensors. Through a small-scale four-week comparison experiment, we confirmed that the Lokemon concept was positively accepted by the users: Lokemon increased the number reporting from PoIs, and fostered casual communication among users while reducing their concerns about loss of privacy. In future, we will conduct a large-scale experiment to evaluate Lokemon's effectiveness. In addition, we will focus more on how the design of the Lokemon monster will affect the quality of information that people supply. Finally, we will make our Publish-Subscribe APIs public so that the Lokemon's crowd sensing data can be easily accessed. This should play an important role in realizing a programmable world that combines information from both IoT and people.

Acknowledgment. This research is supported by JSPS KAKENHI Grant Number 19K11945 and MIC SCOPE project.

References

1. Estrin, D., et al.: Participatory sensing: applications and architecture [Internet Predictions]. IEEE Internet Comput. **14**(1), 12–42 (2010)
2. Groat, M.M., Edwards, B., Horey, J., He, W., Forrest, S.: Enhancing privacy in participatory sensing applications with multidimensional data. In: 2012 IEEE International Conference on Pervasive Computing and Communications, Lugano, pp. 144–152 (2012)
3. Crowley, D.N., Breslin, J.G., Corcoran, P., Young, K.: Gamification of citizen sensing through mobile social reporting. In: 2012 IEEE International Games Innovation Conference, Rochester, NY, pp. 1–5 (2012)
4. Reddy, S., Estrin, D., Hansen, M., Srivastava, M.: Examining micro-payments for participatory sensing data collections. In: Proceedings of the 12th ACM International Conference on Ubiquitous Computing (UbiComp 2010), pp. 33–36. ACM, New York (2010)
5. Goffman, E.: The Presentation of Self in Everyday Life. Anchor Books (1959)

6. Brown, P., Levinson, S.C.: Politeness: Some Universals in Language Usage, vol. 4. Cambridge University Press, Cambridge (1987)
7. Rowe, A., et al.: Sensor Andrew: large-scale campus-wide sensing and actuation. IBM J. Res. Dev. **55**, 6:1–6:14 (2011)
8. Sensor-over-XMPP: https://xmpp.org/extensions/inbox/sensors.html
9. Takuro, Y., Ito, T., Nakazawa, J., Tokuda, H.: SOXFire: a universal sensor network system for sharing social big sensor data in smart cities. In: Proceedings of the 2nd International Workshop on Smart (SmartCities 2016) (2016). Article no. 2, 6 pages
10. Danezis, G., Lewis, S., Anderson, R.J.: How much is location privacy worth? In: WEIS, vol. 5 (2005)
11. Lee, J.-S., Hoh, B.: Dynamic pricing incentive for participatory sensing. Pervasive Mob. Comput. **6**(6), 693–708 (2010)
12. Crowley, D.N., Breslin, J.G., Corcoran, P., Young, K.: Gamification of citizen sensing through mobile social reporting. In: 2012 IEEE International Games Innovation Conference (IGIC), pp. 1–5. IEEE (2012)
13. Deterding, S., Dixon, D., Khaled, R., Nacke, L.: From game design elements to gamefulness: defining gamification. In: Proceedings of the 15th International Academic MindTrek Conference: Envisioning Future Media Environments, pp. 9–15. ACM (2011)
14. Brady, E., Morris, M.R., Bigham, J.P.: Gauging receptiveness to social microvolunteering. In: Proceedings of the 33rd Annual ACM Conference on Human Factors in Computing Systems, pp. 1055–1064. ACM (2015)
15. Masli, M., Terveen, L.: Evaluating compliance-without-pressure techniques for increasing participation in online communities. In: Proceedings of the SIGCHI Conference on Human Factors in Computing Systems, pp. 2915–2924. ACM (2012)
16. Yoon, G., Vargas, P.T.: Know thy avatar: the unintended effect of virtual-self representation on behavior. Psychol. Sci. **25**(4), 1043–1045 (2014). 1153
17. Rosenberg, R.S., Baughman, S.L., Bailenson, J.N.: Virtual superheroes: using superpowers in virtual reality to 1138 encourage prosocial behavior. PloS One **8**(1), e55003 (2013)
18. Jetter, H.-C., Gallacher, S., Kalnikaite, V., Rogers, Y.: Suspicious boxes and friendly aliens: exploring the physical design of urban sensing technology. In: Proceedings of the First International Conference on IoT in Urban Space, pp. 68–73. ICST (Institute for Computer Sciences, Social-Informatics and Telecommunications Engineering) (2014)
19. Ohmura, R., Osawa, H., Imai, M.: Evaluation of function explaining from artifacts using a direct anthropomorphization method. J. Hum. Interface Soc. **10**(3), 305–314 (2008). http://ci.nii.ac.jp/naid/10024261805/

Factors Influencing the Acceptance and Usage of Smart City Services: A Systematic Review and Meta-analysis

Bingqian Zhang, Guochao (Alex) Peng(✉), Xinting Liang, Qi Gao, and Fei Xing

Sun Yat-sen University, Panyu District, Guangzhou 510000, China
Zhangbq5@mail2.sysu.edu.cn, penggch@mail.sysu.edu.cn

Abstract. Smart city services and applications have gradually come into the life of citizens. Citizens' use of smart city services is necessary for the sustainable development of such services. However, the existing literature has a large difference in research conclusions on the relationship between smart city service user behaviors and their influencing factors. In this paper, the meta-analysis method was used to review 54 independent samples in 52 studies, the related effects of 33 influencing factors were analyzed. The meta-analysis results show that 31 influencing factors have significant effects on the adoption, use, and continuance behaviors of smart service users. In addition, sample groups have a moderating effect on the relationship between user behaviors and variables such as social influence. This paper has clarified the effects of influencing factors and one moderator, which has a certain reference value for improving the use intention and participation of users of smart services and applications.

Keywords: Smart city · Mata-analysis · User behaviors

1 Introduction

Victor Mayer Schoenberg, author of Big Data Age, points out that the information storm caused by big data is transforming our life, jobs, and thinking. The great value generated by big data is being recognized by people. It provides a new way of looking at the world through technological innovation and development, as well as the comprehensive perception, collection, analysis, and sharing of data. Therefore, scientist Andreas Weigend said, "data is the new oil".

Big data is the general term for a very large system. The development and wide application of ICT has brought convenient services to people's travel and life, and also promoted the progress of cities. In recent years, with the development of Internet of Things, cloud computing and mobile Internet, modern digital and network-based cities are moving towards automated and smart cities [1]. Smart city is a strategic issue that many countries in the world have focused on in recent years, and it is regarded as an important means to solve urban development problems, improve people's livelihood, and enhance competitiveness of a city.

N. Streitz and S. Konomi (Eds.): HCII 2020, LNCS 12203, pp. 477–490, 2020.
https://doi.org/10.1007/978-3-030-50344-4_34

Smart social applications and services have incorporated massive data based on emerging technologies, transmit processed and integrated information of city. They are important carriers to connect smart society and citizens and can help achieve rational allocation and intelligent response of urban resources [2], with the characteristics of real-timeliness, mobility, integration, etc., covering government affairs, transportation, home services, energy, medical and other fields. By providing citizens with a variety of real-time mobile online services such as urban transportation, health care, and government affairs guidance, smart services can assist urban governance and improve citizens' quality of life. Therefore, they have great practical significance in addressing urban problems and a series of social and livelihood issues, enhancing competitiveness of a city, etc [3].

In addition to urban construction and governance, various smart services and applications in the fields of transportation, medical care, energy, public security, construction planning and education (such as Smart Community Comprehensive Information O2O Service Platform, "Cloud Health" Service Platform, Smart Parking Systems, etc.) also require the active participation of citizens and users [4]. The research by Chourabi et al. indicated that related technical factors (e.g. service stability, system security and data integration), organization and users are key factors for the success of smart city services [5]. Peng et al. pointed out in the case study of the British smart parking system that the government should decide on the selection, implementation and deployment of smart city services based on the actual needs of potential users, namely local residents [3]. Many user-related factors (e.g. user information literacy, user awareness, public acceptance, user participation, etc.) will affect the final results and effects of smart city service implementation.

From different theoretical perspectives, scholars have done a lot of research on the adoption, use behavior and intention of the users of smart services and applications such as wearable medical devices, smart home services, and smart government, etc. to explore the factors influencing user behaviors. However, previous studies differ widely in their conclusions. In addition, previous research didn't fully explore into the following problems:

- What are the attributions of user behaviors in smart services and applications in different fields?
- Is there any difference in influence strength?
- Will different research conclusions be caused by different subject groups?

Therefore, it is necessary to systematically review and integrate existing literature in order to draw a comprehensive and universal research conclusion.

Based on the above research gaps, this study focuses on the use intention and behavior of smart services and applications, and adopts the meta-analysis method to quantitatively analyze the factors that influence the behaviors of smart service users, comprehensively evaluates the strength of the relationship between the use of smart services and various influencing factors, and explores the moderating effects of the types of smart services and applications and the sample population characteristics, with a view to promoting the implementation and improvement of smart city applications and services from the micro perspective of use, providing support for decision making in smart city construction and development.

2 Literature Review

The research on smart services and applications is mainly focused on the following three aspects:

- Mobile APP development, focusing on smart city mobile services and application design [6, 7];
- Exploring the barriers and obstacles in smart city APP promotion based on social background and local policies [8, 9];
- Analyzing the users' adoption behavior and related influencing factors based on existing theoretical models in the field of information systems [9, 11].

Focusing on the user behaviors of smart services and smart devices, scholars have explored the factors that affect user intention and behavior from the aspects of adoption, use, and continuance.

In terms of adoption intention and behavior, literature suggests that user perception factors are major factors affecting users' intention to use smart services. Users are likely to adopt a smart service or smart device only when they perceive such a need [12]. In addition, some scholars have analyzed factors such as demographic characteristics and environment. Taking the fields of smart medical care as example, in addition to user perception factors such as perceived usefulness, perceived ease of use and privacy concerns, users' technical acceptance intention is also moderated by demographic factors such as age, gender, and educational level [13]. Besides, external factors such as social influence and cost, and platform system factors such as service quality and system quality also have significant effects on user adoption behavior and intention [14].

The research on use behavior and intention of smart service and application users has been conducted from multiple theoretical perspectives. For example, Klobas et al. used Reasoned Action Theory to conduct research on users' intention to use smart home devices from the aspects of perceived security risk and perceived controllability [15]. In addition, from the perspective of Innovation Diffusion Theory, some studies have discussed the influence of relative advantage, observability, complexity, compatibility, trialability and other innovative attributes of smart services on the use intention and behavior of users [16]. Some other research built a theoretical framework using information resources, management services, platform technology, and equipment effectiveness and other system factors and service factors as core variables by reference to the Delone and McLean Model of Information Systems Success (D&M Theory), and the research fields covered smart communities, smart medicine, smart transportation, etc. [17]. The theoretical foundations involved in the research on use intention and behavior also include the Value-based Adoption Model [18], Social Cognition Theory [14], transaction cost theory [19], and motivation theory [20], etc.

The continuance behavior has been a focus of researches in the field of information systems. In terms of smart services and applications, however, there are not much research literature on users' continuance intention and behavior, and they mostly focus on smart government services, smart tourism, and smart life services and applications. Among them, most of the literature analyzes the factors that influence users' continuance intention and behavior from the aspects of intrinsic motivation (including user perception dimensions such as satisfaction, privacy concerns, and expectations confirmation) [21] and extrinsic motivation (including system and environmental factors such as service quality, cost of use, and social support) based on the continuance theory [22].

By sorting out the existing literature on user behavior of smart services and applications, it can be seen that empirical researches have been conducted on the motivation of smart applications and services. However, there has been no paper that comprehensively evaluates the factors that affect the user behaviors of smart services and thus no comprehensive and universal conclusion. At the same time, due to different sample sources, sample sizes, methods and models, and research perspectives, existing studies on user behavior in the context of smart cities have significant differences in the aspects of research field, research conclusion, test subjects, and theoretical basis. The differences include:

- Different natures of influencing factors. Taking the research on the users' intention to adopt smart meters as an example, based on TAM theory, Zamrudi et al. pointed out that perceived ease of use can significantly increase users' intention to adopt smart meters [23]. However, Wunderlich et al. believed that users have no in-depth interactive use of smart meters, so perceived ease of use is not important for users' intention to adopt smart meters; and internal and external incentives are the key factors affecting their intention to adopt [24].
- Different strengths of influencing factors. For example, research by Yuen et al. showed that reliability has almost no influence on the user behavior of smart express cabinets ($r = 0.08$) [19]. Park et al. found that there was a weak correlation between system reliability and users' intention to use smart home devices ($r = 0.289$) [20]. However, Sepasgozar et al., based on social cognition theory, pointed out that technical reliability can significantly affect the use of smart city service technology ($r = 0.660$) [14].
- Different research subjects. Most of the studies are targeted at users of their respective smart service and application, but some are targeted at special populations such as the elderly. Whether the difference in demographic characteristics affects the influencing strength of various factors needs to be explored to test its moderating effects.

This study uses a Meta-Analysis method to quantitatively analyze the factors influencing user behaviors of smart city services, quantify and merge the research results of existing literature, to solving the problem of different research conclusions in existing literature and providing a more objective conclusion for the research on user behaviors in the context of smart city.

3 Methodology

Meta-analysis is an empirical research method for statistical analysis of a large number of independent research results. It can draw a more universal conclusion from multiple similar research results under the same topic. It is a secondary comprehensive analysis and evaluation of existing research literature and has a more convincing conclusion than a single research. Trahan [25] and Salang [26] discussed Meta-Analysis in the field of information systems early; Ankem then introduced in details about how to use Meta-Analysis in the field of information management, and discovered that there had been extremely limited applications of meta-analysis in the field of library and information [27]. The application of meta-analysis mainly includes two aspects. 1) Meta-analysis can be used to obtain the weighted average effect value of different study results to check the strength of the relationship between two variables; 2) Meta-analysis can be used to explore the moderating effects of factors such as research scenarios and research objects on the relationships between variables [28].

Meta-analysis provides an effective method for unifying academic differences. The specific steps of the Meta-Analysis include:

- Extensively search for empirical research results of specific research subject;
- Select research results and based on a predetermined set of transparent literature selection criteria to form a database;
- Perform comprehensive analysis using specific statistical analysis techniques and calculate the accurate effect value [29].

According to the characteristics of meta-analysis, this paper conducts research in accordance with the process of literature search and screening, literature coding, analysis of influence factors, analysis of moderating effects, and interpretation of results.

3.1 Collection and Selection of Publications

The publications collection in this paper was carried out jointly by two researchers, and the search results were compared and supplemented. Search platforms used included English databases such as Web of Science (SCIE, SSCI, ISTP, ISSHP), EBSCO, Taylor & Francis Online and ProQuest Dissertations & Theses (PQDT) Full Text, PsycInfo, SAGE Journals Online, Springer, and Elsevie Science. The keywords "smart city", "smart service", "IoT", "wearable technologies", "smart library", "smart home", "smart devices", "AI" were matched with "user", "user behavior", "usage", "Behavior", "adopt", "adoption", "accept", "continuance", etc. for search in the databases for English literature.

The publications retrieved were sorted according to the following criteria:

- The papers must be empirical research on the users behaviors or intention to use smart applications or smart services, excluding qualitative research papers such as review research, theoretical research and case research.
- The papers clearly report the sample size, the coefficient r of correlation between user behavior, intention and related influencing factors, or t, p, or F value that can be used to calculate such correlation coefficient.

In addition, we checked references in review papers and empirical research papers to avoid missing relevant references. In the end, 52 publications suitable for meta-analysis were obtained, two of which contained two independent samples each, so there were a total of 54 independent samples; the total number of subjects reached 17,407.

3.2 Coding and Analysis Process

This study adopted coding procedure recommended by Lipsey and Wilson [30]. In order to reduce the occurrence of coding errors, two researchers first compiled a coding manual and coding instructions, which were discussed with other two researchers and modified before used as the reference basis for coding. The main information of the coding manual includes two parts. One is the basic information of the literature, including author publication date, publication platform, topic, subjects, research object, research field, theoretical basis and other research characteristics. The other is the effect value, including sample size, influencing factors and their effect value r or regression coefficient t, etc.

Each independent sample is used as a coding unit. If a paper contains multiple independent samples, they will be coded separately. At the same time, moderators were tested, so the samples were grouped according to the moderators during the coding process. After each paper was coded, a certain number of papers were randomly selected and coded by another researcher to ensure the accuracy of the coding. For those inconsistent contents, a consensus was reached through backtracking and discussion. The coding results of some papers are shown in Table 1.

Independent variables with frequency of 3 or more were selected based on behavior theme for Meta-Analysis. Among them, the adoption, use, and continuance intentions had 7, 3, and 23 influencing factors respectively suitable for meta-analysis.

Referring to the meta-analysis method and steps proposed by Lipsey and Wilson, this review uses the correlation coefficient r as the effect value. Some papers do not report r, but reported P, t. These coefficients must be converted into correlation coefficient r. The entire Meta-Analysis calculation process was performed by the software CMA 2.0 (Comprehensive Meta-Analysis 2.0). For effect value test, the software first weighted the r value according to the sample size, and then converted it into related indicators such as Fischer Z; finally, they were calculated to obtain the final correlation coefficient, confidence interval and variance, etc., and whether to use a fixed effect model or a random effect model was determined based on the result of the heterogeneity. The fixed effect model assumes that all samples originate from the same population, so it applies to homogeneous meta-analysis results; the random effect model assumes that each sample comes from a different population, and there are differences between different studies, so it applies to heterogeneous meta-analysis results.

4 Findings

4.1 Correlation Effect Analysis

Table 2 shows the meta-analysis results on relationship between adoption, use and continuance behaviors and intention of smart service and application users and some of their influencing factors.

In this study, the analysis of publication bias was performed using the fail-safe number method. Rosenthal et al. pointed out that there is no publication bias when the value of the fail-safe number N is greater than 5 * the number of studies K + 1031. Publication bias refers to that in academic research, empirical studies with conclusions showing

Table 1. Publications coding table (part)

No.	Author (Year)	Behavior theme	Sample size	Subjects	Research object	Field	Theoretical basis	Influencing factors (effect value)
1	Pal D. et al. 2018	Intention to use	239	Elderly	Healthcare Home System	Smart medicine	UTAUT	Perceived Trust (0.653), Facilitating Conditions (0.474), Social Influence (0.586), Technology Anxiety (−0.620), Perceived Cost (−0.730), Effort Expectancy (0.692), Performance Expectancy (0.677), Expert Advices (0.416)
2	Yang H., Lee H., Zo H. 2013	Intention to use	216	Citizens	Smart home services	Smart home	TPB Theory	Automation (0.589), Mobility (0.625), Inter-operability (0.611), Privacy Risk (−0.323), Physical Risk (−0.168), Trust in service provider (0.555), Attitude (0.691), Subjective Norm (0.693), Perceived Behavioral Control (0.556)
3	Baudier P., Ammi C., Rouchon M. D. 2018	Intention to use	316	Students	Smart home device	Smart home	UTAUT TAM2	Safety Security (0.465), Health (0.505), Convenience Comfort (0.591), Sustainability (0.446), Performance Expectancy (0.663), Effort Expectancy (0.426), Social Influence (0.421), Hedonic Motivation (0.513), Price Value (0.469), Habit (0.725), Personal Innovativeness (0.493)
4	Nascimento B., Oliveira T., Tam C. 2018	Continuance intention	574	Common citizens	Smart watch	Smart life	Continuance Theory	Habit (0.64), Perceived Usefulness (0.59), Confirmation (0.42), Perceived Usability (0.44), Perceived Enjoyment (0.44), Satisfaction (0.62)
5	Li H. et al. 2016	Adoption behavior	333	Common users	Wearable medical device	Smart medicine	Privacy Calculus	Information Sensitivity (−0.221), Personal Innovativeness (0.211), Legislative Protection (0.145), Perceived Prestige (0.209), Perceived Informativeness (0.253), Functional Congruence (0.252), Perception Privacy Risk (−0.251), Perceived Benefits (0.315)

Table 2. Meta-analysis results on the of relationship between smart service and application user behaviors, intention and some influencing factors

Behavior	Influencing factor	Model	*K*	Sample size	Point estimate	*Z* value (2-tail)	95% interval	*Q* value	*df* (*Q*)	I^2	Fail-safe number *N*
Adoption	Trust	Fixed	6	1759	0.274	11.751	0.230–0.317	53.538	5	90.661	202
		Random			0.286	3.588	0.133–0.425				
	Social influence	Fixed	5	1908	0.469	22.154	0.433–0.504	122.98	4	96.747	746
		Random			0.626	4.924	0.415~0.733				
	Perceived privacy risks	Fixed	6	2694	−0.288	−15.332	−0.322~−0.253	79.818	3	93.736	392
		Random			−0.379	−4.592	−0.515~−0.225				
Continuance	Expectation confirmation	Fixed	3	1139	0.511	18.965	0.467–0.553	21.159	2	90.548	284
		Random			0.531	5.875	0.375–0.658				
	Satisfaction	Fixed	3	1139	0.655	26.336	0.620–0.687	8.883	2	77.486	528
		Random			0.660	12.129	0.581–0.726				
Use	Service quality	Fixed	4	1372	0.371	14.356	0.324–0.416	165.144	2	98.183	223
		Random			0.395	2.05	0.018–0.673				
	Convenience	Fixed	6	1814	0.472	21.751	0.436–0.508	171.121	5	97.078	735
		Random			0.476	3.740	0.241–0.658				
	Perceived usefulness	Fixed	13	4740	0.58	43.375	0.560–0.598	299.364	12	95.992	6375
		Random			0.569	8.731	0.463–0.659				

a significant correlation are more likely to be published than those with conclusions showing no significant correlation. Therefore, the results are more representative if the Meta-Analysis has no publication bias. According to the Meta-Analysis results, there is publication bias in the adoption behavior and intention influencing factor age (N = 16), and the use behavior and intention influencing factors technicality (N = 0), affordability (N = 6), and privacy concerns (N = 35), and other influencing factors passed the publication bias test.

The heterogeneity test is mainly to determine the model of Meta-Analysis. In the Meta-Analysis results, the Q value, df (Q), and its significance test value p are used to indicate the heterogeneity between the effect sizes. Taking the effect value of use influencing factor perceived usefulness as an example, the Meta-Analysis results show that the Q value is 299.365 (df = 12, p = 0.000), and it is significant, indicating that heterogeneity among the effect values. Excluding the 4 independent variables with publication bias, for the remaining 29 independent variables, the Q values obtained in the heterogeneity test are much greater than df (Q), and all p values are less than 0.001, indicating high heterogeneity in the effect values. Therefore, a random effect model is selected for effect value analysis.

According to the point estimated effect value in the random effect model, there is no significant correlation between age and adoption behavior and intention (r = −0.076, p = 0.366); among the influencing factors of use behavior and intention, affordability (r = 0.166, p = 0.661), privacy concerns (r = −0.162, p = 0.382), and technicality

Table 3. Correlation between behaviors and intention of smart city service and application users and their influencing factors

Behavior theme	Correlation	Influencing factors
Adoption behavior and intention	Strong r > 0.5	Social influence, Perceived usefulness, Perceived ease of use
	Average 0.3 < r < 0.5	Trust, Personal innovation, Perceived privacy risk (negative correlation)
Use behavior and intention	Strong r > 0.5	Self-efficacy, Performance expectancy, Trust, Compatibility, Habits, Perceived value, Practicality, Enjoyment, Perceived ease of use
	Average 0.3 < r < 0.5	Hedonism, Reliability, Economic value, Service quality, System quality, Effort expectancy, Social influence, Convenience, Perceived usefulness, Perceived risk (negative correlation), Personal innovation
	Weak 0.1 < r < 0.3	Perceived cost
Continuance behavior and intention	Strong r > 0.5	Perceived usefulness, Satisfaction, Expectation confirmation

(r = −0.105, p = 0.774) have no significant effects on the use behavior and willingness of smart city service users. Other influencing factors all have different degrees of correlation with user behavior and intention. According to Cohen's criteria for dividing the strong and weak effect values [32], the correlations between different behavior themes and their influencing factors were divided according to the strength, as shown in Table 3.

4.2 Moderating Effect Analysis

This paper examines the moderating effect of the subjects on the relationship between user behaviors and intention and their influencing factors. Specifically, if the groups pass the heterogeneity test, it means that the research on different groups has different characteristics, indicating significant moderating effect. In view of the limited number of studies, user behavior themes were not grouped for moderating effect test; instead, the subjects and smart areas were grouped, and the influencing factors were selected from each group in which the number of studies (k) is greater than or equal to 2 for meta-analysis. Based on the above conditions, the factors social influence, convenience and performance expectancy were selected for the moderating effect analysis. Due to their limited number of empirical studies, other influencing factors were not included in this analysis to ensure the reliability of Meta-Analysis result. Table 4 shows the analysis results of the moderating effects of subjects on the relationship between the user behavior, intention and some influencing factors under the random effect model.

Table 4. Results of analysis on the moderating effect of subjects

Moderator	Heterogeneity			Group	*K*	Sample size	Effect size and 95% interval		Test of null (2-tail)	
	Q value	*Df (Q)*	*P* value				Point estimate	95% interval	*Z* value	*P* value
Social influence	6.176	2	0.046	Elderly	2	537	0.594	0.536–0.646	15.751	0.000
				Students	4	1077	0.410	0.222–0.569	6.422	0.000
				Common users	11	3980	0.487	0.354–0.601	4.063	0.000
Performance expectancy	6.853	2	0.037	Elderly	2	569	0.636	0.577–0.688	15.708	0.000
				Students	4	1077	0.51	0.304–0.669	4.449	0.000
				Common users	5	972	0.515	0.426–0.594	9.738	0.000
Convenience	46.890	2	0.000	Elderly	2	569	0.522	0.433–0.600	9.882	0.000
				Students	2	398	0.084	0.354–0.693	4.953	0.000
				Common users	5	1713	0.546	−0.015–0.181	1.671	0.095

According to the heterogeneity test results, the subject group has a significant moderating effect on the relationship between convenience and user behaviors (Q = 46.890, p = 0.000). The convenience can positively affect the elderly and common users' use of and intention to use smart city services, and the effect values of two groups have no significant difference. However, for the student group, there is no significant relationship between this independent variable and user behaviors (r = 0.084, p = 0.095).

The subject group has a certain impact on the relationship between social influence (Q = 6.167, p = 0.046), performance expectancy (Q = 6.853, p = 0.037) and the smart city service user behaviors, with less significant moderating effect than convenience.

Specifically, the social influence has a more significant effect on the smart service use behavior and intention of the elderly group, showing a strong correlation (r = 0.594), followed by the common user group (r = 0.487) and the student group (r = 0.410). For performance expectancy, it shows different strengths of impact on different groups of subjects. Similar to social influence, performance expectancy shows the most significant effect on the behaviors and intention of smart service users in the elderly group (r = 0.636), and has almost similar effects on common users (r = 0.510) and student groups (r = 0.515).

5 Discussion and Conclusion

5.1 Adoption

This study has identified the influencing factors in the adoption, use, and continuance stages of smart service users through coding analysis of existing literature, and obtained the effect values of the influencing factors on user behaviors and intention, classified the influencing factors according to their correlation significance. In this paper, based on the correlation strength evaluation criteria proposed by Cohen, we found that perceived usefulness (0.696), social influence (0.626), and perceived ease of use (0.568) are the three most important factors influencing the adoption behavior and intention of smart service users, the following are personal innovation (0.444), personal privacy risk (−0.379), and trust (0.3). It indicates that the users' emotional perception factors play an important role in the adoption of smart city services.

However, age has no significant influence on the adoption behavior and intention of smart city service users. This meta-analysis result is contrary to traditional cognition. In previous research assumptions, the elderly group was mostly considered to have low intention to adopt new technologies due to limited information literacy. However, with people's deepening understanding of smart city technology in modern society, as well as the more unified and user-friendly functions of smart services and mobile APP's UI design, demographic factors such as age and gender longer play an important role in the adoption of smart services and smart technologies.

5.2 Use

Different from the adoption behavior, platform factors such as compatibility, practicality, service quality, and system quality can also significantly affect the use behavior and intention. This is related to the behavior stages of users. After a user has used the smart service for a period of time, his focus will shift from the initial psychological cognition to system and platform services. Therefore, compatibility, practicality, reliability and other platform functional characteristics will play an important role in the stage of use.

Some personal characteristics, such as self-efficacy, habits, and personal innovation also have a certain effect on use behavior. Users' self-efficacy and innovation awareness are the keys to determining whether users can effectively explore the system and use it in depth. In addition, the pleasure motivations of users such as pleasure and enjoyment have a significant influence on use behavior. Many smart devices (such as smart home devices) are designed to create convenience and pleasant experiences for users' life, promoting users to further use the devices.

In addition, the influence of trust in the stage of use is much greater than that in adoption. The reason is that users' adoption of smart services mostly comes from the innovation awareness and impact of the surrounding environment, and users do not have a high level of trust in smart service operators. With the deepening of the understanding of the smart services, the level of trust is getting higher and higher, and the degree of influence on the use behavior is also increasing.

5.3 Continuance

Most research on the continuance of smart city services in the existing literature is based on the theory of information system continuance. Therefore, there are fewer influencing factors, and only perceived usefulness, expectation confirmation and satisfaction are suitable for meta-analysis. All the three factors have significant positive correlations with users' continuance behavior and intention, with satisfaction having the most significant influence.

In addition, unlike perceived privacy risk that can negatively affect users' adoption, privacy concerns have significant relationship with use and continuance. There are two possible reasons for this: 1) During the stages of use and continuance, users' level of concern on the collection and use of their personal information by service operators is not as high as in the stage of adoption; 2) users feel the security of personal privacy information during the use and will not reduce personal intention of use or continuance due to high concern on personal privacy.

5.4 Discussion on the Meta-analysis Result of Moderating Effect

The paper finds that the subject group can also affect the relationship between some factors and the behaviors of smart service users to a certain extent. Social impact, performance expectancy and convenience show a higher impact on the elderly group compared with common users and students, which also confirms the research conclusion of Workman et al. However, subjects of different ages differ greatly in their use experience, habits, and personal cognition. For example, the elderly group is apt to make decisions on whether to use smart services based on the suggestions of others, so the correlation between social influence and user behavior and intention is stronger when the subject is elderly group. Similarly, the student group has relatively rich experience and high information literacy, so factors such as the convenience of service acquisition do not play a decisive role in the use of smart services.

6 Research Conclusion and Limitations

6.1 Research Conclusions

By integrating the research conclusions with large differences, a more comprehensive and universal research conclusion is obtained. In this paper, the research conclusions with different influence natures, influence strengths and effect directions in the existing literature were integrated and quantitatively analyzed with the meta-analysis method; common effect values were used to clarify the relationship between service users' behaviors and intention and the influencing factors, providing a more unified conclusion for the subsequent research in this field. This has certain reference value for smart city service operators in terms of user retention, system development, and advertising, enabling smart city services to be closer to the life of citizens and pay more attention to user experience and requirements, and to some extent also helping with the implementation of smart city services. In addition, smart service operators also need to consider the user groups of their services, and design product service and functions according to the characteristics of the user groups, thus providing targeting smart services and reflecting the human-oriented concept of smart city development from the user level.

6.2 Limitations

In terms of research method, the meta-analysis method requires that k must be greater than 2, so some influencing factors with low frequency of occurrence were not extracted for analysis. In the future, systematic review and meta-ethnography can be combined to conduct a more comprehensive analysis of the factors affecting the behaviors of smart city service users by both qualitative and quantitative analysis. In addition, the paper only examines the moderating effect of the subject group as a moderator on the relationship between some influencing factors and user behaviors. In the future, the moderating effect of moderators such as smart service areas and cultural environments can be tested to explore more moderators, which is also a direction of further research.

References

1. Hollands, R.G.: Will the real smart city please stand up? City **12**(3), 303–320 (2008)
2. Lombardi, P., Giordano, S., Farouh, H., et al.: Modeling the smart city performance. Innov. Eur. J. Soc. Sci. Res. **25**(2), 137–149 (2012)
3. Peng, G.C.A., Nunes, M.B., Zheng, L.: Impacts of low citizen awareness and usage in smart city services: the case of London's smart parking system. IseB **15**(4), 845–876 (2017)
4. Kanter, R.M., Litow, S.S.: Informed and interconnected: a manifesto for smarter cities. Harvard Business School General Management Unit Working Paper, 09-141 (2009)
5. Chourabi H., et al: Understanding smart cities: an integrative framework. In: Proceedings of the 45th Hawaii International Conference on System Sciences, Maui, HI, USA (2012)
6. Su, K., Li, J., Fu, H.: Smart city and the applications. In: International Conference on Electronics. IEEE (2011)
7. Mitton, N., Papavassiliou, S., Puliafito, A., et al.: Combining cloud and sensors in a smart city environment. EURASIP J. Wirel. Commun. Netw. **2012**(1), 247 (2012)
8. McGrath, Kathy: Identity verification and societal challenges: explaining the gap between service provision and development outcomes. MIS Q. **40**(2), 486–500 (2016)
9. Ma, R., Lam, P.T.I., Leung, C.K.: Potential pitfalls of smart city development: a study on parking mobile applications (apps) in Hong Kong. Telemat. Inf. **35**(6), 1580–1592 (2018)
10. Papa, A., Mital, M., Pisano, P., et al.: E-health and wellbeing monitoring using smart healthcare devices: an empirical investigation. Technol. Forecast. Soc. Change, 1–10 (2018)

11. Hsiaoping, Y.: The effects of successful ICT-based smart city services: from citizens' perspectives. Gov. Inf. Q. **34**(5), 556–565 (2017)
12. Workman, M.: New media and the changing face of information technology use: the importance of task pursuit, social influence, and experience. Comput. Hum. Behav. **31**(1), 111–117 (2014)
13. Marakhimov, A., Joo, J.: Consumer adaptation and infusion of wearable devices for healthcare. Comput. Hum. Behav. **76**, 135–148 (2017)
14. Sepasgozar, S.M.E., Hawkenb, S., Sargolzaeic, S., Foroozanfa, M.: Implementing citizen centric technology in developing smart cities: a model for predicting the acceptance of urban technologies. Technol. Forecast. Soc. Change **142**, 105–116 (2019)
15. Klobas, J.E., McGill, T., Wang, X.: How perceived security risk affects intention to use smart home devices: a reasoned action explanation. Comput. Soc. **87**, 1–13 (2019)
16. Hubert, M., Blut, M., Brock, C., et al.: The influence of acceptance and adoption drivers on smart home usage. Eur. J. Mark. **53**(6), 1073–1098 (2019)
17. Fu, H.: Factors influencing user usage intention on intelligent logistics information platform. J. Intell. Fuzzy Syst. **18**, 1–10 (2018)
18. Kim, Y., Park, Y., Choi, J.: A study on the adoption of IoT smart home service: using value-based adoption model. Total Qual. Manag. Bus. Excell. **28**(10), 1149–1165 (2017)
19. Yuen, K.F., Wang, X., Ma, F., et al.: The determinants of customers' intention to use smart lockers for last-mile deliveries. J. Retail. Consum. Serv. **49**, 316–326 (2019)
20. Park, E., Kim, S., Kim, Y.S., et al.: Smart home services as the next mainstream of the ICT industry: determinants of the adoption of smart home services. Univ. Access Inf. Soc. **17**, 175–190 (2018)
21. Belanche-Gracia, D., Casaló-Ariño, L.V., Pérez-Rueda, A.: Determinants of multi-service smartcard success for smart cities development: a study based on citizens' privacy and security perceptions. Gov. Inf. Q. **32**(2), 154–163 (2015)
22. Liu, D., Tong, C., Liu, Y.: Examining the adoption and continuous usage of context-aware services: an empirical study on the use of an intelligent tourist guide. Inf. Dev. **32**(3), 608–621 (2016)
23. Zamrudi, Z., Karim, S., Farida, M., Maharani, D., Kuraesin A.D.: Smart meter adoption: the role of consumer experience in using smart device. In: 1st International Conference on Advance and Scientific Innovation (ICASI), pp. 1–6 (2019)
24. Wunderlich, P., Veit, D.J., Sarker, S.: Adoption of sustainable technologies: a mixed-methods study of German households. MIS Q. **43**(2), 673–691 (2019)
25. Trahan, E.: Applying meta-analysis to library and information science research. Libr. Q. **63**(1), 73–91 (1993)
26. Salang, M.M.C.: A meta-analysis of studies on user information needs and their relationship to information retrieval. J. Philipp. Librariansh. **18**(1–2), 36–56 (1996)
27. Ankem, K.: Approaches to meta-analysis: a guide for LIS researchers. Libr. Inf. Sci. Res. **27**(2), 164–176 (2005)
28. Miller, D., Toulouse, J.: Chief executive personality and corporate strategy and structure in small firms. Manag. Sci. **32**(11), 1389–1409 (1986)
29. Borenstein, M., Hedges, L.V., Higgins, J.P.T., Rothstein, H.R.: Introduction to Meta-Analysis. Wiley, Chichester (2009)
30. Lipsey, M.W., Wilson, D.B.: Practical Meta-Analysis, pp. 105–142. SAGE Publications Inc, Thousand Oaks (2008)
31. Rosenthal, R.: Meta-analytic procedures for social science research. Educ. Res. **15**(8), 18–20 (1986)
32. Cohen, J.: Statistical Power Analysis for the Behavioral Sciences, pp. 77–80. Academic Press, New York (1977)

Well-Being, Learning and Culture in Intelligent Environments

Computer Vision on Wheelchairs: Detecting Sleeping Behavior of People with Intellectual Disabilities

Lang Bai and Jun Hu(✉)

Eindhoven University of Technology, Eindhoven, The Netherlands
j.hu@tue.nl

Abstract. There have been few products or research efforts on designing for people with intellectual disabilities. The caretaking companies have no enough caretakers to keep an eye on the clients with intellectual disabilities, who are suffering from circadian rhythm disorder. We report on the design of a system to detect the sleeping behavior of people with intellectual disabilities in the daytime. The system utilizes an inexpensive 2D camera with computer vision techniques to track whether a user is falling asleep. The system wakes up the clients gradually in several steps when a long-time sleeping is detected. Our study explores taking eye aspect ratio, head orientation as inputs, and a support vector machine to managing complex situations in real life.

Keywords: Circadian cycle · Eye aspect ratio · SVM · Intellectual disabilities

1 Introduction

There have been few products or research efforts on designing for people with intellectual disabilities. The caretaking companies have no enough caretakers to keep an eye on the clients with intellectual disabilities, who are suffering from circadian rhythm disorder. CARE[1] is one of these companies running for providing care of hundreds of disabled people in serval resident locations in the Netherlands. In the summer of 2015, CARE collected the 24-h heart rate data of three groups of clients. These clients are taken care of differently by the level of cognitive disability. By analyzing the activities in day and night, the clients with Serious Intellectual Disabilities (SID) or Moderate Intellectual Disabilities (MID) are with difficulty in understanding the routine activities. The SID and MID clients have no idea on what to do according to a regular timetable. It mainly shows from their above-normal heart rate at night and low heart rate at daytime. Therefore, clients are considered to have circadian rhythm disorders. Since the clients are seriously intellectually limited, even pressing a button will build up a barrier. It's difficult to use a system with complicated interaction to educate them to be aware of the appropriate routine. The primary step in this problem, it's to detect their sleeping behavior in the

[1] The real company name is not used here for the concern of the privacy of the clients mentioned in this paper.

N. Streitz and S. Konomi (Eds.): HCII 2020, LNCS 12203, pp. 493–504, 2020.
https://doi.org/10.1007/978-3-030-50344-4_35

daytime and awake them. Due to the limited number and full-loaded work of caretakers, it's impossible to provide one-on-one or one-on-two supervise. Thus, an autonomous device of detecting and waking would be in demand.

There are many methods in drowsiness detection; however, in our problem setting, there are constraints in choosing a method. Additional hardware should be with cost control of CARE, hence sophisticated biosensing methods [1, 2] and smart environments [3, 4] are our of consideration because of such a requirement. From the observation, clients are sitting in the wheelchairs all day. They are mostly quiet, with no movement in large amplitude. The quickest and easiest way to detect motion is to compute the difference between the initial frame and the subsequent frame of a camera image. However, due to the complexity of the real-life situation, namely, some people might pass or stand behind the clients. To recognize the face, especially the eye, could boost the detection part in this scenario. It is also a challenge on how to wake up the sleeping clients properly. According to Roenneberg [5], an alarm clock is hazardous to health. An alternative way is to set multiple wake-up stages, with gradually increasing intensity level.

2 Related Work

2.1 Facial Landmark

Facial landmark is a computer-based function for automatically dealing with detecting distinctive features in human faces. According to recent surveys, facial landmark detection has long been impeded by the problems of occlusion and pose variation [6]. What is noticeable is that most of these works assume a densely connected model that can support the need for matching algorithms. For example, based on a mixture of trees with a shared pool of parts, every facial landmark can be used to capture topological changes due to viewpoint [7]. Another team presents an interactive model that allows for improving the appearance fitting step by introducing a Viterbi optimization process that can operate along the facial contours [8]. Other notable recent works explore how they use appropriate priors exploiting the structure of image data to help with efficient feature selection [9].

2.2 Head Pose Estimation

Estimating the head pose of a person is a common human ability that presents a challenge for the computer system. With the recent increasing technologies, a few notable works have shown the usefulness in solving this problem. Some use a unique cue [10], which uses random regression forests for giving their capability to handle large training datasets. Another method can be combined with 2D image data, and a regularized maximum likelihood deformable model fitting (DMF) algorithm is developed, with special emphasis on handling the noisy input depth data [11].

2.3 External Influences

Many factors can influence the robustness of the algorithm. The light environment can be one of them. The light field is considered as the set of features on which to base recognition. These features can be the pixel intensities used in appearance-based face and object recognition [12]. Shelters that cover the face can also influence the detection a lot. People from certain religious groups and occupations occlude faces where only their particular regions are visible for biometric identification [13].

3 Design

We present a design that can detect the sleeping and tenderly wake up the clients. It consists of eye recognition and multi-stage waking up. Our study was conducted in an activity room environment of CARE. It used a co-design approach involving people with intellectual disabilities, their caregivers, and students from Eindhoven University of Technology. We adopted this approach to get meaningful insights regarding sleeping behavior detection, their reaction to the alarm.

3.1 Observation and Interviews

To understand the context and the problem, we conducted semi-structured interviews and observations in two care centers of CARE. To get insights about the everyday life of people with intellectual disabilities, we directly observed the clients' behavior and also interviewed the caretakers.

We focused only on the SID and MID clients because there were already on-going projects aiming at changing other clients' behavior due to their better ability in basic interaction, while SID and MID clients are in a more urgent need of help. We observed 12 clients (5 females and 7 males). Their age ranged from 19 to 62. we conducted interviews with two professional managers and two caretakers from care centers. All of them visited and participated in the group-based sessions or the training sessions regularly.

After the observations and interviews, the system tailored to their behavior and environments was designed and implemented, followed by a user test conducted in the care center on three clients. We want to see the performance of the system and find out the complexity of the environments that we haven't concerned about. In the meanwhile, video data were recorded with permission for further analysis.

Data Collection. We conducted semi-structured interviews with 12 SID and MSL clients and 4 of their caretakers. Interview questions concentrated on their illness condition, daily routines, and the interaction between caretakers and clients, and the difficulties that the caretakers had. The participants were encouraged to elaborate freely upon these topics. All the interviews were conducted face-t-face by the researchers, each of which lasted 30 to 60 min. The conversations were recorded and transcribed. The researchers directly observed the participants' interactions and took notes while observing.

To increase the reliability of data, we took the two methods: (1) talking about similar topics to all the caretakers, (2) test our design concepts and prototypes with the manager of caretakers, who was considered to be an expert in the field, especially on the aspects he thought to be important.

To observe the sleeping behavior, it would be time-consuming to record the video of clients and analyze the video recordings. The privacy concern also prevented us from doing so. Instead, we try to mimic the behavior of the clients such as the sitting posture and blinking frequency based on our observations, to provide the parameters and training data for our algorithm. The parameters were then fine-tuned after the test on three clients.

Qualitative Data Analysis. There were two stages of data analysis. The first stage was to analyze the qualitative data from the observation and the interviews. The second stage was to analyze the data for system parameters. The qualitative data analysis provided the guideline for the algorithm design. Thematic analysis was applied. After generating the initial codes, researchers searched for the themes and reviewed them. The themes with refined specifics and clear definitions were: user privacy, the cost of the system, mobility of the system, the benefits and drawbacks of using the system, humanization of the system, the learning curve of caretakers, and workload of caretakers.

Figure 1 shows the daily routines of the SID and MID clients. The circadian rhythm disorder happened to many clients due to sleeping behavior when they were sitting in their wheelchairs in the activity room. To prevent sleeping behavior in the daytime could lead to more sleep at night.

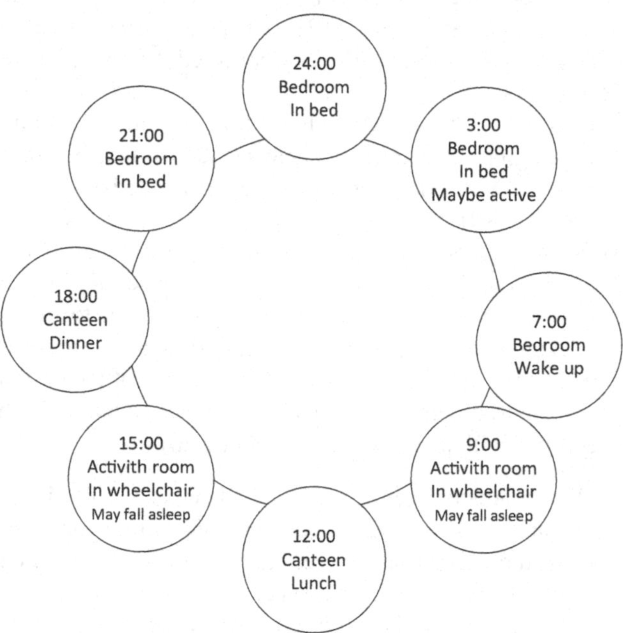

Fig. 1. Daily routines of SID and MID clients

3.2 Overall System Design

The system consists of detection, alarming, and communication components (see Fig. 2). A camera, a diffused light source, and a small speaker are mounted on the wheelchair. The system collects the Eye aspect ratio (EAR) and 3D head orientation data, and stores it on the cloud. No image is recorded or stored. The caretakers can access the cloud to review the status of clients over a given period. They can also get the notification from the system. The components are integrated into a system with a cute pet shape.

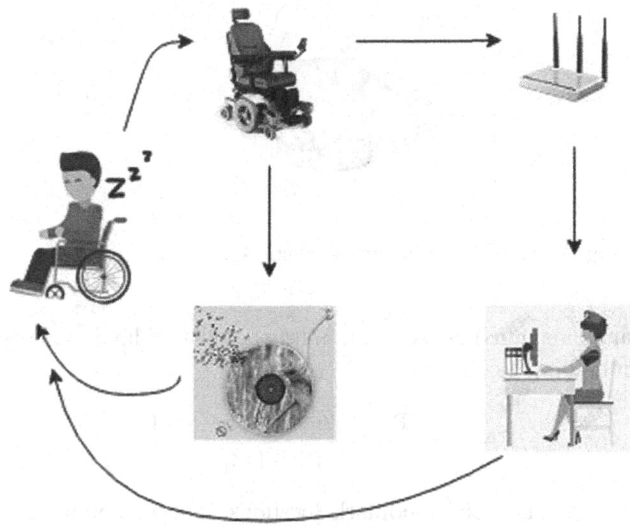

Fig. 2. System structure.

4 Algorithms

4.1 Eye Aspect Ratio Detection

Based on the result of the qualitative data analysis, we took the activity room of CARE as the environment of the use case. Most of the time, the clients were sitting in wheelchairs and listening to soft music. With 12 clients in a room, sound-based methods were sensitive to the sound of music; hence they were not appropriate to be applied in this scenario. With computer vision, the challenge was how to detect the sleeping behavior from the camera facing the client in the wheelchair. Concerned with the speed and computation cost, the initial choice was to compute the absolute difference between the previous frame and the current frame. We had observed that these clients most of the time kept quiet, with only small movements, which brought two constraints when using the absolute difference of the frames: (1) people walked behind the client from time to time, and the background might change because clients could have possibly moved position. Predicting the background by computing the mean of previous frames could hardly work due to the change of background. (2) body recognition can ignore the effect of background changing. However, clients' body movements were very small, even when they were awake. Instead of using body movement as the metrics for sleeping behavior, eye recognition is not only robust but also intuitive.

The eye aspect ratio [14] is an efficient tool to determine whether the eye is closed or not. The eye aspect ratio involves a simple calculation based on the ratio distance between facial landmarks of eyes. In this method, each eye is represented by 6 points, starting at the left corner of the eye and going clockwise around the remainder of the eye region (P1 to P6 in Fig. 3).

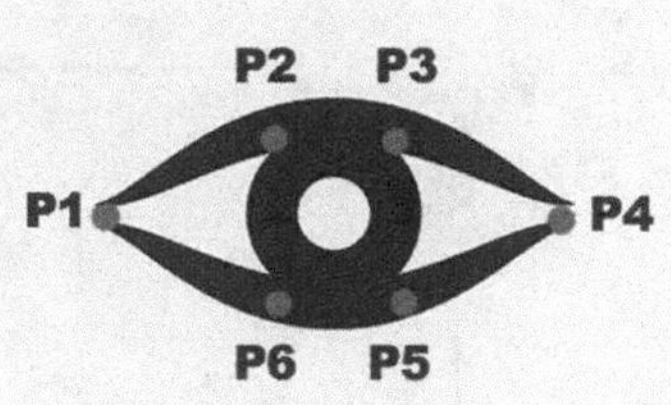

Fig. 3. The 6 facial landmark points associated with the eye

The EAR can be regarded as the relation between the width and the height of these points. The calculation is as follows:

$$\mathrm{EAR} = \frac{||P2 - P6|| + ||P3 - P5||}{2||P1 - P4||},$$

where p1, …, p6 are 2D facial landmark locations. The numerator of this equation computes the distance between the vertical eye landmarks (height), and the denominator computes the distance between horizontal eye landmarks (width).

We use the sleeping and awake video from ourselves as the training data set. Each video has around 10 s, 30fps, with a resolution of 640 × 480 pixels. We have three types of eye behaviors to examine - closing, opening, and blinking. The landmark recognition is implemented through OpenCV and the *dlib* library in Python. Figure 4 shows examples of the EAR distribution histograms.

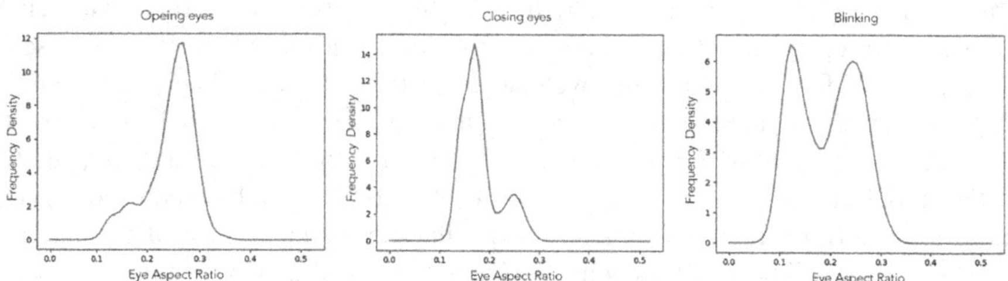

Fig. 4. Examples of EAR distribution histograms of eyes opening, closing, and blinking.

An interesting threshold value from the examples in Fig. 4 can be observed, which is supposed to be between 0.18–0.22.

However, the result of the first-round test showed a drawback of such thresholding. In the real-life application, the clients are in a much more complicated situation than the training video, for example, with or without glasses, in different light conditions, and with different head poses direction, etc. For a more robust detection, the following approaches were applied: (1) using videos with different light conditions for training,

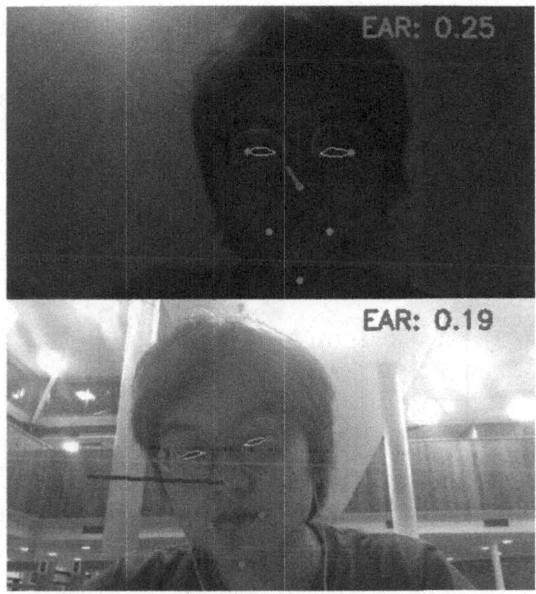

Fig. 5. Training data in different light conditions, with head orientation estimation.

(2) using videos with and without glasses for training, and (3) estimating 3D head pose direction. Figure 5 shows examples of new training data.

After the field testing, the new dataset was annotated with EAR, roll angle, yaw angle, pitch angle, and whether sleeping or being awake. This dataset contains light settings in both bright and dark conditions, subjects with and without glasses, different head orientations in up, down, left, and right directions, with a maximum of 45° in each direction.

4.2 Head Orientation Estimation

The implementation of head orientation estimation follows the solution of the Perspective-n-Point problem in OpenCV. The aim is to find the position and orientation of an object from a 2D image, given the camera intrinsic parameters such as the focal length and the optical center), and the 3D model of n points and the corresponding 2D features in the image.

For each PnP problem, there are three coordinate systems: the world coordinates (U, V, W), the camera coordinates (X, Y, Z), and the 2D image coordinates (x, y). The 3D points in the world coordinates can be transformed into 3D points in camera coordinates through rotation R (a 3×3 matrix) and translation t (a 3×1 vector). The 3D points in camera coordinates can be projected on 2D image coordinates through the known camera intrinsic parameters.

The location (X, Y, Z) of the point P in the camera coordinate system can be yielded from the following equation:

$$\begin{bmatrix} X \\ Y \\ Z \end{bmatrix} = [\boldsymbol{R} \mid \boldsymbol{t}] \begin{bmatrix} U \\ V \\ W \\ 1 \end{bmatrix},$$

which can be also written as:

$$\begin{bmatrix} X \\ Y \\ Z \end{bmatrix} = \begin{bmatrix} r_{00} & r_{01} & r_{02} & t_x \\ r_{10} & r_{11} & r_{12} & t_y \\ r_{20} & r_{21} & r_{22} & t_z \end{bmatrix} \begin{bmatrix} U \\ V \\ W \\ 1 \end{bmatrix},$$

For the point P in the camera coordinates (X, Y, Z), the 2D image coordinates (x, y) can be calculated from the equation involving camera matrix (M), where

$$M = \begin{bmatrix} f_x & 0 & c_x \\ 0 & f_y & c_y \\ 0 & 0 & 1 \end{bmatrix},$$

and (f_x, f_y) is the focal lengths and (c_x, c_y) is the optical center. In most cases, the lens distortion is assumed as not existing. And the equation is given by

$$\begin{bmatrix} x \\ y \\ 1 \end{bmatrix} = s \begin{bmatrix} f_x & 0 & c_x \\ 0 & f_y & c_y \\ 0 & 0 & 1 \end{bmatrix} \begin{bmatrix} X \\ Y \\ Z \end{bmatrix}.$$

The position in 2D image coordinates can be predicted from a given 3D point in the world (a facial landmark), if the right pose (***R*** and) is given.

For the equations above, Direct Linear Transform [15] (DLT) is used for getting the pose ***R*** and ***t***. However, the DLT algorithm does not minimize the reprojection error. Reprojection error represents the sum of squared distances between the projected 3D face points and the 2D image points. Since the 2D points of face and body can be detected using *dlib*, an intuitive way to converge the error curve is to adjust ***R*** and ***t*** to align the projected 3D points with detected 2D image points. Levenberg-Marquardt optimization is widely used to minimize reprojection error. In our implementation, CV_ITERATIVE in OpenCV's function *solvePnP* was chosen, which is based on Levenberg-Marquardt optimization.

4.3 Influence of Head Orientation, Glasses, and Light Condition

The support vector machine (SVM) classifier has four inputs: EAR, and the angles of roll, yaw, and pitch. The Radial Basis Function (RBF) kernel SVM approach performs best among all the SVM methods we have tried, with an accuracy of 0.84 on a total of 7390 frames. After a close look into the details of the data, we found the facial landmark detection algorithm worked terribly when the head orientation was downward. We reach the accuracy of 0.94 on the remaining 5485 frames, after excluding the head downward orientation data. The ROC curve of SVM with RBF kernel is shown in Fig. 6. Since there is no strict rule of mounting a camera on the wheelchair, a lower position is recommended to avoid head downward orientation as much as possible.

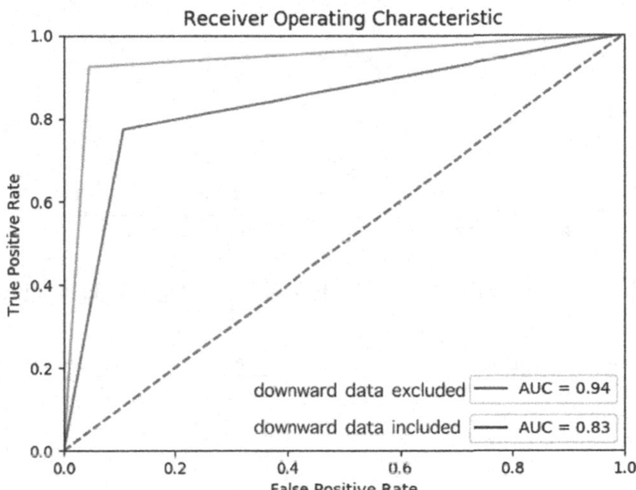

Fig. 6. ROC curve of SVM with RBF kernel on including and excluding head downward orientation data.

Using a between-group experiment design, we divide data into dim condition group and bright condition group according to the light conditions. In the dim condition, the accuracy is 0.81 on 2959 frames, and in contrast, our approaches accuracy rises to 0.90 on data in the bright condition (shown in Fig. 7). A good light condition dramatically increases detection accuracy.

A pair of glass is widely considered to lead to a decrease in detection accuracy. However, our experiment on the data shows the opposite situation. When subjects are wearing the glasses (3650 frames), the accuracy is 0.88, while it drops to 0.82 when subjects are not wearing the glasses (3740 frames), as Fig. 8 shows. However, a detailed inspection of the data provides us the insights that the exceptional conditions happen when the subjects turn head downward while wearing glasses. After excluding the downward data, the accuracy in the without-glasses group reaches the highest number, 0.96; while the with-glasses group also climbs to 0.94. In this case, the difference between the glass conditions can be ignored.

In summary, the experiments provide us the insights into the position of mounting the camera - a relatively low position is better than a high position. Besides, if under the cost control, a low-power and diffused light source would be recommended. Glasses are not a barrier to using our system.

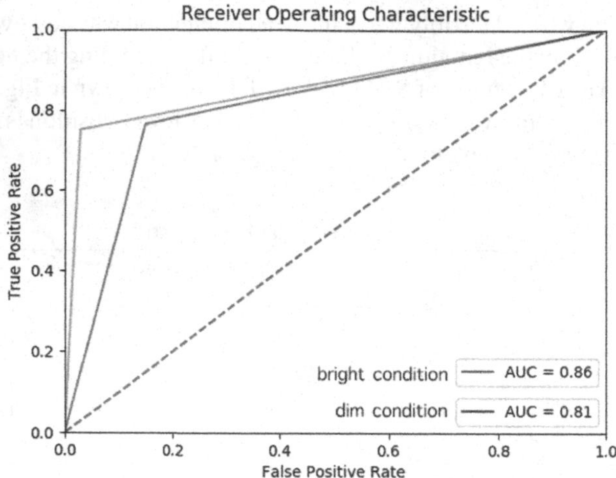

Fig. 7. ROC curve of SVM with RBF kernel on different light conditions.

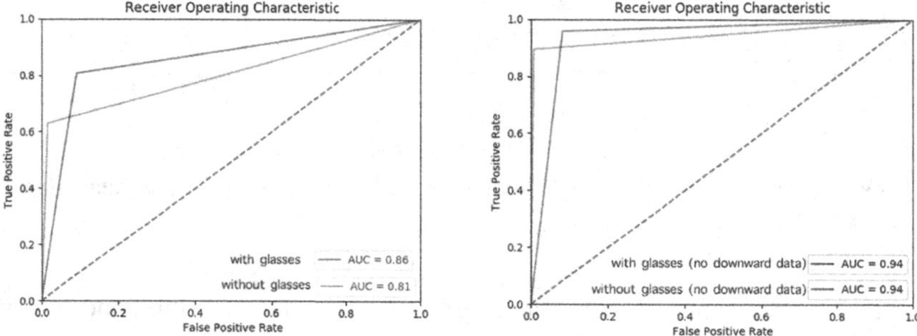

Fig. 8. ROC curve of SVM with RBF kernel on different glasses conditions.

4.4 Multi-step Alarm

A sleeping behavior within a certain time does not only involves closing eyes. For example, people might close their eyes for the first three-quarters of the time while blinking their eyes in the last quarter. To make our approach flexible, we set a window of 200 ms, which moves at the step of 100 ms. Each window has a flag and the highest EAR. For the EAR values in every window, we use the Gaussian Kernel Density Estimation to smooth the histograms. The average of the highest three EAR is regarded as the highest EAR of this window. Since each flag (predicted label) is assigned to one EAR value, the flag of the window is aligned with the flag of the three highest EAR values (the flag that appears at least two times). For every 10 s, a stop-alarm flag is on when the half of the last-2.5-s window flags are labeled as eyes-open. Otherwise, if half of the window flags are eyes-closed, the level-1 alarm is on, which is designed to use the sound of birds singing and colorful blinking lights. The volume of the alarm increases gradually if the client is still asleep. The alarm soundtrack turns into the sound of waves at level 2. When the volume increases to a certain value, the system turns off the alarm and texts to the caretaker. There is a limit on the volume since multiple clients sitting in the same room to avoid bothering or disturbing the others.

5 Conclusion

In this paper, we have analyzed the approach of helping clients with intellectual disabilities with a system that can detect whether they fall asleep in their wheelchairs and that tries to wake them up with a three-level alarm. We found the trait of closing and opening eyes from the EAR values. The field test showed the drawback of the thresholding method. The SVM approached was then introduced on the data we collected from the different conditions of lighting, head orientations, and wearing glasses. We discussed the influence of different conditions. The results suggested that the position of mounting the camera should be mounted relatively low, and a low-power and diffused light source is also recommended. Ideally, our detection approach can reach an accuracy of 0.96. However, our approach should be fine-tuned with more subjects, since different facial features would also affect the detection accuracy. With this effort, we hope to inspire more designs for people with intellectual disabilities.

References

1. Yu, B., Feijs, L., Funk, M., Hu, J.: Designing auditory display of heart rate variability in biofeedback context. Georgia Institute of Technology (2015)
2. Yu, B., Funk, M., Hu, J., Wang, Q., Feijs, L.: Biofeedback for everyday stress management: a systematic review. Frontiers ICT **5**, 23 (2018)
3. Van der Vlist, B., Niezen, G., Hu, J., Feijs, L.: Design semantics of connections in a smart home environment (2011)
4. Hu, J., Feijs, L.: An agent-based architecture for distributed interfaces and timed media in a storytelling application. In: Proceedings of the Second International Joint Conference on Autonomous Agents and Multiagent Systems, pp. 1012–1013 (2003)
5. Roenneberg, T., Allebrandt, K.V., Merrow, M., Vetter, C.: Social jetlag and obesity. Current Biol. **22**(10), 939–943 (2012)
6. Zhang, Z., Luo, P., Loy, C.C., Tang, X.: Facial landmark detection by deep multi-task learning. In: Fleet, D., Pajdla, T., Schiele, B., Tuytelaars, T. (eds.) ECCV 2014. LNCS, vol. 8694, pp. 94–108. Springer, Cham (2014). https://doi.org/10.1007/978-3-319-10599-4_7
7. Zhu, X., Ramanan, D.: Face detection, pose estimation, and landmark localization in the wild. In: 2012 IEEE Conference on Computer Vision and Pattern Recognition, pp. 2879–2886. IEEE (2012)
8. Le, V., Brandt, J., Lin, Z., Bourdev, L., Huang, Thomas S.: Interactive facial feature localization. In: Fitzgibbon, A., Lazebnik, S., Perona, P., Sato, Y., Schmid, C. (eds.) ECCV 2012. LNCS, vol. 7574, pp. 679–692. Springer, Heidelberg (2012). https://doi.org/10.1007/978-3-642-33712-3_49
9. Kazemi, V., Sullivan, J.: One millisecond face alignment with an ensemble of regression trees. In: Proceedings of the IEEE Conference on Computer Vision and Pattern Recognition, pp. 1867–1874 (2014)
10. Fanelli, G., Gall, J., Van Gool, L.: Real time head pose estimation with random regression forests. In: CVPR 2011, pp. 617–624. IEEE (2011)

11. Cai, Q., Gallup, D., Zhang, C., Zhang, Z.: 3D Deformable Face Tracking With A Commodity Depth Camera. In: Daniilidis, K., Maragos, P., Paragios, N. (eds.) ECCV 2010. LNCS, vol. 6313, pp. 229–242. Springer, Heidelberg (2010). https://doi.org/10.1007/978-3-642-15558-1_17
12. Gross, R., Matthews, I., Baker, S.: Appearance-based face recognition and light-fields. IEEE Trans. Pattern Anal. Mach. Intell. **26**(4), 449–465 (2004)
13. Juefei-Xu, F., Savvides, M.: Subspace-based discrete transform encoded local binary patterns representations for robust periocular matching on NIST's face recognition grand challenge. IEEE Trans. Image Process. **23**(8), 3490–3505 (2014)
14. Soukupová, T., Cech, J.: Eye blink detection using facial landmarks. In: 21st Computer Vision Winter Workshop, Rimske Toplice, Slovenia (2016)
15. Sutherland, I.E.: Three-dimensional data input by tablet. Proc. IEEE **62**(4), 453–461 (1974)

Motivating Physical Exercise in the Elderly with Mixed Reality Experiences

Mark Chignell(✉), Henrique Matulis, and Brian Nejati

University of Toronto, Toronto M5S3G8, ON, Canada
chignell@mie.utoronto.ca

Abstract. The rapid aging of developed societies is creating an increasing number of cases of dementia and other aging-related diseases. Physical exercise has been shown to be beneficial for retaining cognitive, as well as physical function. In this paper we describe a system that we have developed for motivating older people to exercise. We begin by demonstrating how activity declines with age using an analysis of survey data (from 2003–2015) reported by the U.S. Bureau of Labor and Statistics on American Time Use Usage. We use multiple discriminant analysis to characterize which activities tend to become more, or less frequent as people age. We then review previous exergame approaches for motivating physical activity. After this we discuss a pedaling system that is designed to motivate and facilitate physical activity in the elderly using a combination of competition, social interaction, and engaging video content. We conclude with a discussion of how to adapt exergaming innovations to the context of use.

Keywords: Exercise · Time usage · VR · Mixed reality · Aging

1 Introduction

The demographic distribution is being transformed in developed societies, with fewer younger people and an increasing proportion of older people. In some countries, such as Italy and Japan, this transformation is highly advanced, but even in developing countries this transformation is generally happening, with notable exceptions in sub-Saharan Africa.

The rapid aging of societies has strong implications for the availability of labor, and overall productivity, but it also has implications for the cost and viability of the healthcare system, with the prevalence of health conditions increasing as people age (see Fig. 1 for illustrative data from New Zealand).

Can we reduce the devastating increase in age-related diseases that is accompanying the demographic transformation? In the long term, innovations such as genetic engineering, new drug therapies, etc., may reduce the disease burden in aging. However, in the short term, promoting physical exercise and better managing cognitive decline may be the most promising ways to delay the diseases, and associated loss of function, that are typically associated with aging.

According to the U.S. Centers for Disease Control and Prevention (CDC 2019): "Regular physical activity is vital for healthy aging. It can help delay, prevent, or manage

N. Streitz and S. Konomi (Eds.): HCII 2020, LNCS 12203, pp. 505–519, 2020.
https://doi.org/10.1007/978-3-030-50344-4_36

many costly chronic diseases faced by adults 50 years or older. Physical activity can also reduce the risk of premature death. Despite these benefits, 31 million adults age 50 or older are inactive." The CDC goes on to say: "Getting any amount of physical activity still offers some health benefits. Some is better than none. Helping inactive people become more active is an important step towards better health."

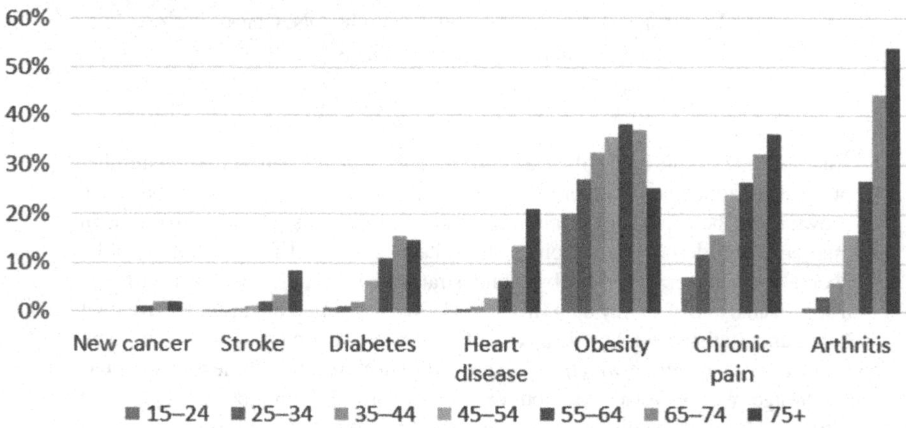

Fig. 1. Prevalence of health conditions by age. Data from the New Zealand Ministry of Health.

In this paper we start by examining activity time use data from the U.S. Bureau of Labour and Statistics to track how activities change as people age. After demonstrating a general decline in physical activity as people age we discuss the use of exergames to motivate more physical exercise in the elderly. We then describe the development of an innovative pedaling system that motivates elderly people to exercise more through a combination of social interaction, competition, and engaging video content.

2 Background

According to the US Department of Health and Human Services (HHS 2008) in its Physical Activity Guidelines for Americans: "For substantial health benefits, adults should do at least 150 min (2 h and 30 min) a week of moderate-intensity activity" with longer amounts of activity, as well as aerobic activity, being preferred. The HHS goes on to say that adults over the age of 65 should follow the general adult guidelines where possible, adjusting as necessary for fitness levels and safety issues associated with chronic disease.

Schneider and Pichora-Fuller (2000) analyzed the causes of perceptual and cognitive decline over aging. The authors concluded that age-related cognitive deterioration is more extensive than the loss of visual and auditory sensitivity, suggesting that cognitive impairment may in general be a greater problem than perceptual impairment in aging.

Another issue concerns depression and dementia which are both common in older people. Bennet and Thomas (2014) reviewed 34 studies that explored cause, consequence and coincidence of dementia and depression and found convincing evidence that early life depression is associated with an increased risk of dementia and that late-life depression is associated with dementia.

The problem of inactivity is particularly challenging in dementia, where people who are institutionalized may spend most of the day either sitting around or lying down (MacRae et al. 1996). This state of affairs continues even though physical exercise has been shown to protect against cognitive decline in aging generally, as well as in Alzheimer's disease (Norton et al. 2014). Consistent with low rates of exercise in older people, people living with dementia tend to be short of exercise, and the problem is particularly severe for people living in long-term care (Salguero et al. 2011).

In summary, older people typically do not get enough physical activity, and they often suffer from problems like cognitive impairment and depression that may be treatable, or preventable, through greater levels of activity.

3 Aging and Activity

In order to characterize how activity changes with age, analyses were carried out using American Time Use Survey (ATUS, 2003–2015) downloaded from the Kaggle website (https://www.kaggle.com/bls/american-time-use-survey). The goal of the ATUS is to measure how people spend their time, as assessed using a large set of coded activities. In the annual ATUS survey, each respondent was interviewed only one time about how they spent their time on the previous day, where they were, and whom they were with. Figure 2 shows the demographic distribution of the survey. Note that data for people aged from 80 to 84 (N > 5000), and aged 85 and above (N > 2500) were assigned a single age code (hence the two large spikes on the right side of the graph).

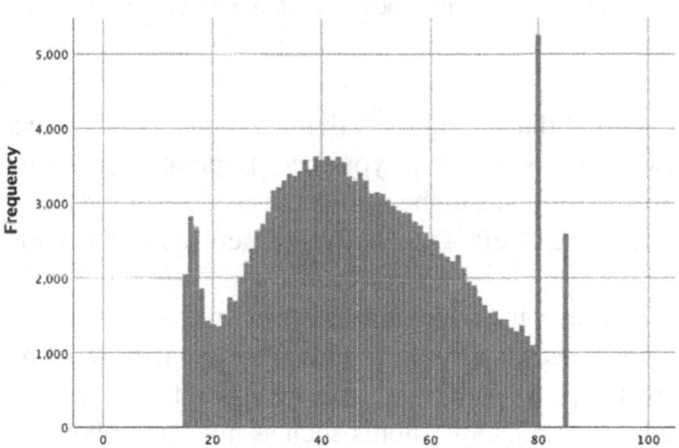

Fig. 2. Demographic distribution of the ATUS survey.

In order to characterize changes in activity as people age, two discriminant analyses were carried out. The first analysis contrasted people 65 and older vs. people between the ages of 40 and 64. Measures used to predict membership in the two age groups were based on activity codes that were assigned, on average, more than a minute a day. Stepwise discriminant analysis was carried out and 49 activity codes were included in the resulting discriminant function which significantly differentiated between the groups (Wilk's Lambda - .791, p < .001). Table 1 shows the activities that had the largest discriminating function coefficients.

Table 1. ATUS activities that maximally distinguish between seniors and non-seniors. (Standardized discriminant function coefficients in decreasing order of absolute value, "hh" stands for "household")

Reading for personal interest	0.424
Television and movies	0.394
Work main job	0.376
Relaxing, thinking	0.262
Eating and drinking	0.221
Gap/can't remember	0.188
hh and personal mail and messages	0.162
Washing, dressing and grooming oneself	0.14
Playing games	0.139
Physical care for household children	0.138
Sewing and repairing	0.128
Travel related to caring for hh children	0.125
Talking with/listening to hh children	0.094
Health related self care	0.093
Shopping except groceries, food and gas	0.086

It can be seen in Table 1 that sedentary activities, such as reading, watching television, and eating, increase in the senior (vs. younger) population (as shown by the larger discriminant function coefficients in the right hand column of the table). Unsurprisingly, time spent at work decreases after normal retirement age, and gaps in memory also increase.

Other activities and measures that increase with age include relaxing and thinking, and gaps of time when people couldn't remember what they were doing. Thus the ATUS data indicates that people are more sedentary, and less active, both physically and cognitively, over the age of 65. Other items such as not remembering what people were doing hint at possible increases in subjective impairment in the seniors, but that topic is outside the scope of this paper.

We then carried out a second discriminant analysis, contrasting people aged between 70 and 79 with those people aged 80 or over. Stepwise discriminant analysis was again carried out and 33 activity codes were included in the resulting discriminant function, which significantly differentiated between the groups (Wilk's Lambda - .942, p < .001).

Table 2 shows the activation codes that had the largest discriminating function coefficients when comparing those 80 or over with people in their seventies. It can be seen

Table 2. ATUS activities that maximally distinguish between people aged 70–79 and those aged 80 and over.

Relaxing, thinking	0.542
Sleeping	0.539
Television and movies	0.483
Reading for personal interest	0.467
Eating and drinking	0.321
Washing, dressing and grooming oneself	0.314
HH and personal mail and messages	0.24
Playing games	0.202
Sleeplessness	0.197
Work main job	−0.196
Gap/Can't remember	0.191
Listening to the radio	0.177
Socializing, communicating with others	0.161
Health related self care	0.154
Shopping except groceries, food and gas	−0.131
Sewing, repairing and maintaining textiles	0.119
Vehicle repair and maintenance	−0.116
Financial management	0.112
Computer use for leisure	−0.112
Playing with non HH children	−0.111
Kitchen and food cleanup	0.105
Travel related to socializing and communicating	−0.1
Care for animals and pets	−0.096

that there is considerable overlap in the most discriminating activities for the two age contrasts (comparing Table 1 and Table 2). However, sleeplessness seems to be a more important issue for people over the age of 80.

Communicating and socializing with others is also noted more by people 80 and older, perhaps because there are few opportunities for communication and socialization in formal work environments or when carrying out activities such as shopping outside the house. Other hints about changing lifestyle in the 80s include less playing with household children (likely because grandchildren are reaching adulthood) and less time on vehicle repair (as people drive less). However, the tendency for people to use computers for leisure less over the age of 80 may be a generational change rather than a consequence of aging per se.

The following bar charts (with error bars showing 95% confidence intervals) show the time associated with some of the activity codes for different age groups.

As can be seen in Fig. 3, time spent "thinking and relaxing" is a major correlate of age, increasing from around 10 min a day in the 40s to close to an hour a day in the 80s.

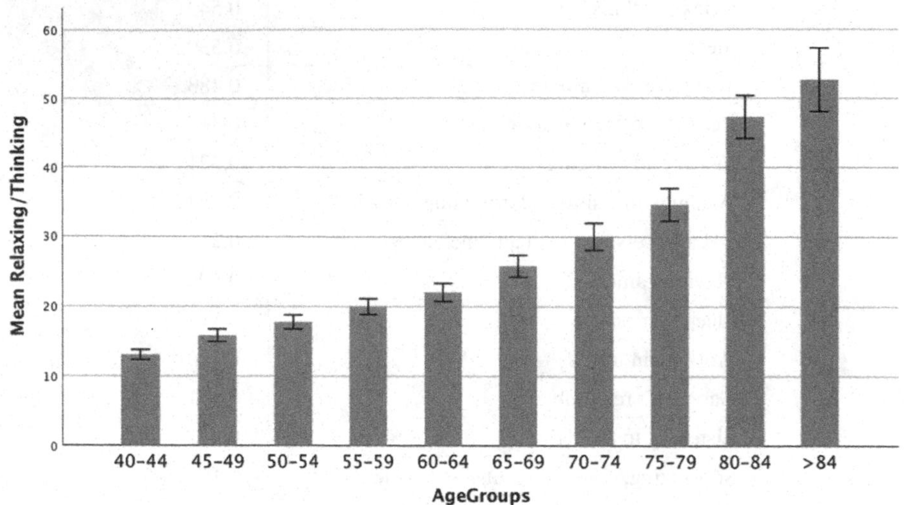

Fig. 3. Time spent "relaxing or thinking" per day for different age groups (minutes).

As shown in Fig. 4, time watching television appears to increase steadily before asymptoting around age 75.

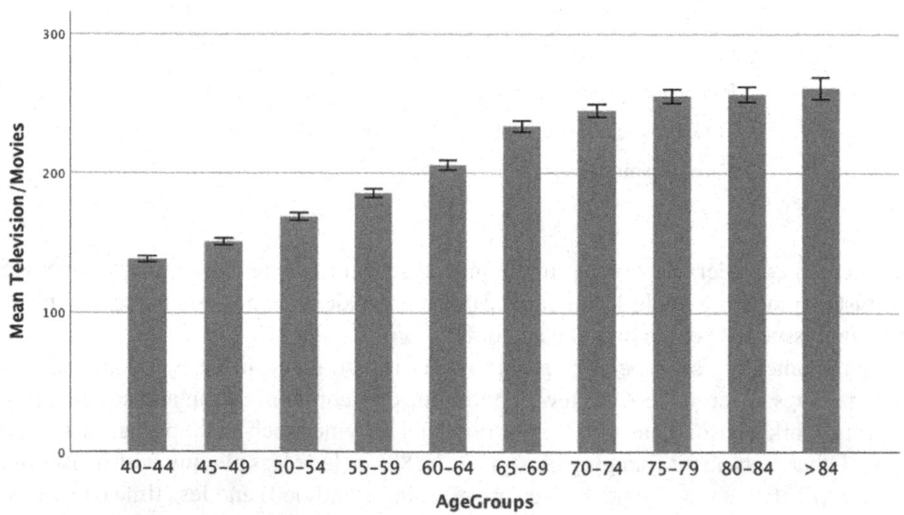

Fig. 4. Time spent watching television and movies for different age groups (minutes).

Time reported sleeping is relatively stable at a little over 8 h prior to retirement age after which it rises steadily to around 9 h a day (Fig. 5).

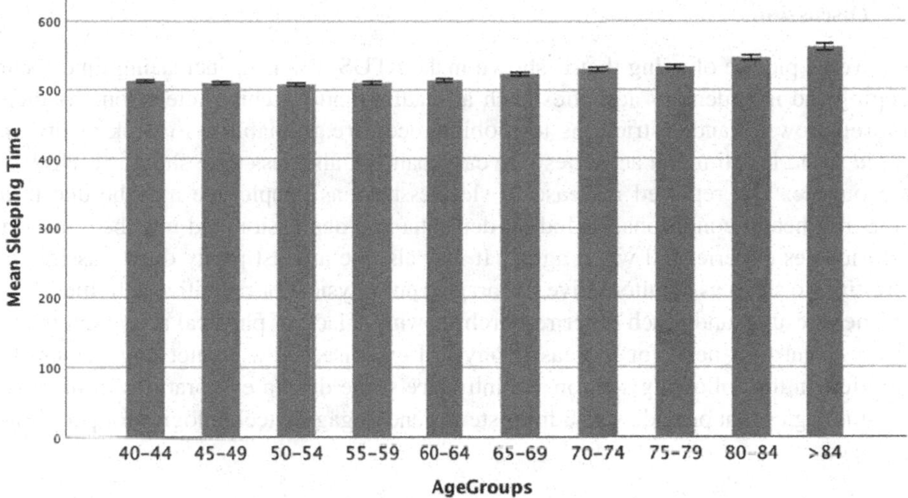

Fig. 5. Time spent sleeping for different age groups (minutes).

Figure 5 shows that self-reported sleeping tends to increase after retirement age while Fig. 6 shows that the general increase in sleeplessness tends to accelerate after retirement age, rising to around 5 min a night on average in the early 70s and then increasing to around 10 min a night after the age of 85. This tendency to sleep more, sometimes unsuccessfully, may reflect a reduced ability and/or motivation to organize and carry out activities, which shows up first in increased television viewing and subsequently in a tendency to allocate more time to sleep.

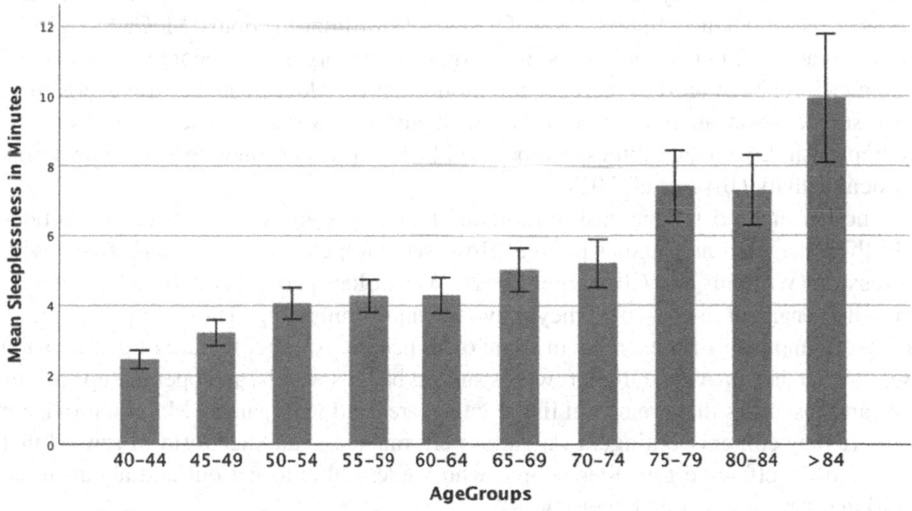

Fig. 6. Reported sleeplessness as a function of age.

3.1 Discussion

The overall picture of aging that is shown in the ATUS data is of increasing time spent sleeping and in sedentary activities such as reading and watching television. As their children grow up and restrictions to mobility occur (e.g., inability to walk or drive), people spend less time on activities like car repair but also less time shopping and less time outside. The reported increase in sleeplessness as people age may be due to a number of health conditions, including dementia and depression and may be a marker of difficulties experienced when aging. It may also be at least partly due to assigning more time to sleep as an alternative to carrying out physical or cognitive activities.

These results, and much other research showing a lack of physical activation in the elderly, point to a need for increased physical exercise and a greater engagement in activities. In the following section we introduce some design explorations in the area of technologies that provide self-administering and engaging technologies for people as they age.

4 Motivating Physical Exercise

There are many reasons why physical exercising may decline with age, including the effects of physical ailments, but one primary reason appears to be lower motivation to exercise. Making exercise more fun and game-like with the assistance of technology has become an important strategy for motivating increased amounts of physical exercise in the population in general. This approach has been referred to as exergaming, a combination of exercise and videogames (Yim and Graham 2007).

Exergames use active body motions as part of game play and hence encourage physical activity in a fun and engaging way (Chan et al. 2019). Well-known early commercial games that promoted physical exercise include: Wii Fit, Just Dance, Zumba fitness, My fitness coach, and Kinect Sports, each of which sold millions of copies (McCallum 2012). There has also been growing interest in exergames that target older people. A number of strategies have been used to increase the motivation for older people to use exergames. For instance, social interaction is paired with physical exercise in the social exergaming approach. Social exergames can be used both to prevent loneliness and encourage physical activity (Brox et al. 2011).

Another method for increasing motivation in videogames is competition, particularly those targeted at younger people. However, competition is often associated with aggression (Williams and Clippinger 2002). While older people tend to be less aggressive when engaged in activities, they may still enjoy competing. Thus competition may be a useful motivator for exercise in some older people. Another feature of games is the rewards that they provide. Often, rewards such as badges, levels, and opening up various tools and resources that are useful in the game, are used with games. Making provision of interesting content contingent on game performance is another form of reward that may be more effective for older people who are less able to get out and about in the world and have interesting experiences.

4.1 Pedaling Games

Pedal exercise has been a focus of a number of exergames. For instance, PaperDude (Fig. 7) was a Virtual Reality cycling based exergame system inspired by the arcade game Paperboy (Bolton et al. 2014).

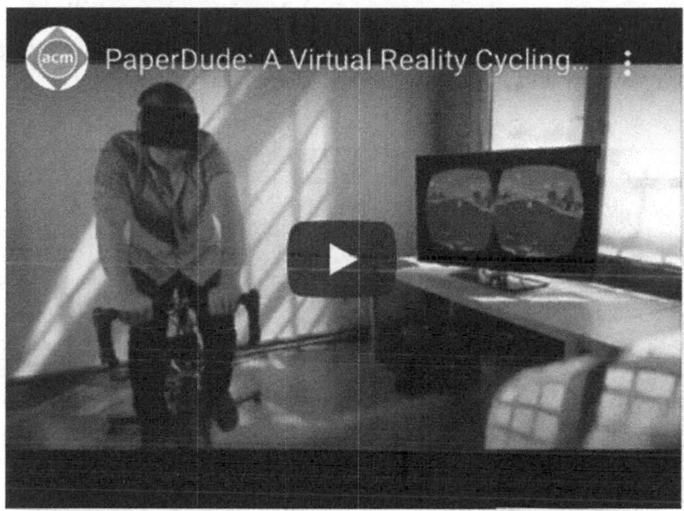

Fig. 7. A participant playing PaperDude.

Pedaltanks (Hagen et al. 2016) was another pedaling game where pedaling was incorporated into a game with tanks, adding competition with another human player (Fig. 8). Unlike PaperDude, Pedaltanks did not use a VR (virtual reality) headset.

Fig. 8. Participants playing Pedaltanks.

Campbell and Fraser (2019) developed VeRitas, a physiologically controlled exergame in which the player's exertion influenced their avatar's performance. Anderson-Hanley et al. (2018) described the interactive Physical and Cognitive Exercise System (iPACES) which combined pedaling with cognitive exercise and which is targeted at older users (Fig. 9).

A commercial system that uses pedaling exercise aimed at older users is Motiview by Motitech. This system combines an exercise bike with video and allows users to take cycle trips through familiar surroundings and childhood memories. Thus the goal in this case is not only exercise but also reminiscence.

Fig. 9. The iPaces gaming system where elliptical pedaling is combined with an game intended to provide cognitive exercise.

5 Physical Centivizer

As part of research funded by the AGEWELL National Centre of Excellence (NCE) we are developing serious games for cognitive assessment (e.g., Tong et al. 2016) as well as products intended to increase the amount of physical and cognitive activity in the elderly (Tong et al. 2017). The motivation behind this product development is to create enjoyable experiences, providing external motivation for carrying out physical and cognitive activities. Ideally, a system for increasing activity should become part of an older person's daily routine. The system should also offer a variety of options so each user can find her own way to interact with the system. Devices should be adjustable, and where necessary, different versions of a device should be developed so as to accommodate a wide range of elderly users.

Figure 10 shows an example of motivating exercise by having a face that smiles as long as the person is pedaling. While this is an example of a motivating feature that can be added when pedaling, it is unlikely to provide sustained motivation,

Figure 11 shows a second pedaling scenario where an element of social interaction (and possible competition) is added by having a second person pedal around the same course. In this case the participants are pedaling around a rocky seaside path and the split screen allows each person to have their own view of where they are on the course. The button box shown in front of the screen can be used to select different courses to travel on while pedaling. Note that the system is highly portable, consisting of the button box and pedalers. In the example shown in Fig. 11 the system has been set up for a special session with seniors in a public library.

In the situation shown in Fig. 11 the two people who are pedaling can have a conversation that is facilitated by the shared experience not only of pedaling but also of traversing the same course. When two participants pedaling side by side choose to make it so, there can also be a competitive challenge that motivates faster pedaling. The faster a person pedals, the faster the video plays for that person. The person who pedals the fastest overall gets to the end of the course first and "wins".

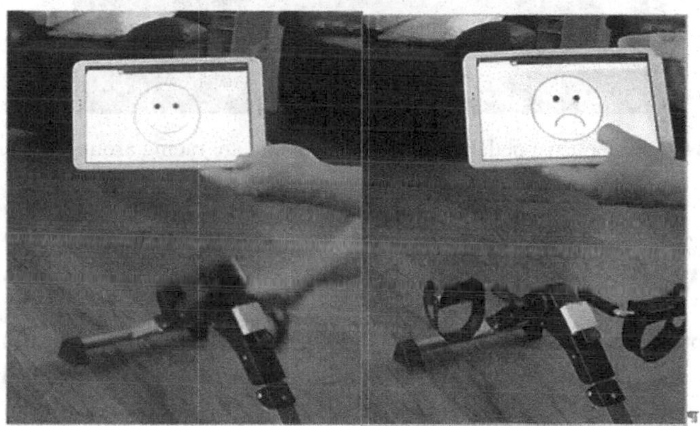

Fig. 10. Pedal exercise to make a face smile.

While pedaling is a physical activity, other activities involve moving through a virtual environment and are experiential in nature. One of the most important experiences in the lives of many people over the age of 65 is driving. People who were driving all their lives may find it difficult not to drive any more and people who can no longer travel like they used to may regret not being able to experience new places and cultures. In order to bring back the experience of driving and travel we developed the Experiential Centivizer. Early prototypes of the Experiential started with a set of 360 degree world travel videos that the user could select and then use a joystick to rotate the viewpoint in the 360 degree video. In our testing we found that 3D manipulation of the viewpoint with the joystick was too complex for many older people. Thus we decided to use a steering wheel in order to allow a more simple interaction (panning around the video without changing the vertical dimension) and to bring back the familiar, driving-related experience of turning a wheel.

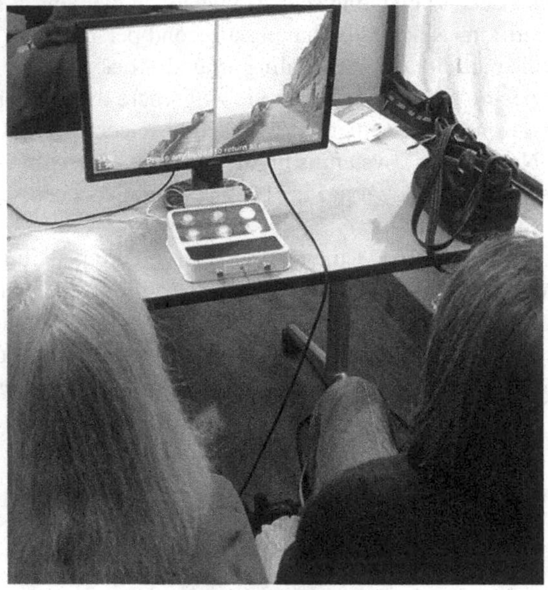

Fig. 11. Competitive pedaling where two people are racing around a course.

6 Adapting Innovation to the Context of Use

How can the products and approaches discussed in the previous two sections be implemented in environments and contexts where the target users (people over the age of 65 in need of more exercise) can use them naturally and enjoyably? As with the diffusion of new products in general, the challenge is to identify the right user, in the right place, at the right time, where a particular product may have a number of feasible combinations of user type, location/environment/context, and time. In our experiential marketing of pedal exercise prototypes we have identified the following potential sweet spots for VR and AR (augmented) exercise, although we expect that there are many more yet to be examined (Table 3).

In our work with community dwelling seniors we have provided pop-up events at a local library, billed as introducing new technology for seniors. The events have generally been fully subscribed (around 15 attendees per session). While self-selected, the attendees are probably representative of a fairly large subtype of seniors that is active, educated, and motivated to remain physically and cognitive intact. These attendees are very open to new experiences such as VR, but also appreciate the opportunity to engage socially with like-minded seniors. Responses to a session which included a VR option were also informative with roughly half of participants being greatly taken by the VR experience and the other half wanting nothing to do with it, either because it was strange

Table 3. Synergistic combination of user/place/time for seniors' pedal exercise.

User type	Place	Time
Community-dwelling seniors	Library	Afternoon presentations/demos
Patient undergoing rehabilitation	Rehab Hospital	Therapy sessions
Patient waiting for discharge	Reactivation Centre	Free use/therapy sessions
Resident	Long Term Care	Group programs

and unfamiliar or because they were worried that it would make them feel nauseous. In all cases though, people enjoyed pedaling and the content that they viewed while pedaling distracted them from the effort of pedaling. Around half of the seniors enjoyed competitive pedaling where they were explicitly racing against the other participant, but clearly it needs to be a choice, since other participants didn't want to do pedaling exercise competitively.

Our experience in institutional settings is that staff, including nurses, physiotherapists recreational therapists and administrators, act as gatekeepers for the use of new technologies for motivating and providing exercise. In settings where equipment is continuously available in the ambient environment, there are challenges in maintaining it. One lesson that we learned early on was to plug everything in to the mains rather than using batteries because staff tend not to recharge batteries on a regular basis and users assume that equipment is broken (and stop using it) when it is out of battery power. Getting people to use equipment for the first time, and to build up habits of use is very important. An equipment installation can succeed or fail depending on the buy-in from staff and how enthusiastically they promote and facilitate the use of the equipment.

Our experience has been that innovative exercise equipment for the elderly works best when it is integrated into existing exercise and activity programs. Thus our latest product (4VRYoung, pronounced "Forever young") has been co-designed with managers of adult day programs at a long term care centre. This has resulted in exercise programs being built around our equipment in this setting. Co-design worked in this case because there was a need for leg exercise in the context of VR and we created a new version of our product that was configured according to the specifications provided to us by the day program managers.

What has our experience in many different settings over the past few years taught us about device design for older users? In particular, when should VR, AR and mixed reality be used in contexts such as exercising, and simulated driving? Large screens can be engaging and they have the advantage of having the "real environment" at the edges of the screen. Curved displays, and particularly concave displays (Chignell et al. 2019), can be highly immersive and engaging. For full immersiveness however, VR goggles provide the most compelling experience, although they may be contra-indicated for seniors with difficulties maintaining time and place orientation. In the future we expect that AR exercising applications should be particularly effective. In this case computer graphics and text can overlay images in a 360 degree video or computer graphics generated virtual world. Overlaid graphics can be used to signify reward (e.g., fireworks when an exercise goal is reached) or they can be used to increase interest in content or further distract from the physical effort as the person becomes more tired.

Individual differences tend to increase as people age and acquire different types of disability. Inclusive and adaptive interfaces can be used to accommodate various disabilities, and there is always a tension between having a single product with an inclusive interface and having different products that are customized for different types of user. In our approach we have a product with a common core of functionality and content, and provide different types of input and output to accommodate users with different abilities and with special needs. These accommodations have include the use of a button box as input for people who do not have fine motor skills, providing hand pedals for people in wheelchairs, and using a range of display devices (flat screen, curved displays, VR goggles) to accommodate different types of user. We have also found that VR displays have special characteristics deriving from both their immersiveness and their tight coupling between input and output. Thus features such as virtual clouds, animals, and birds can enrich scenes and increase engagement when VR displays are used.

7 Conclusions

In this paper we reviewed a small portion of the growing evidence that activation is an important part of improving health, and reducing decline, in aging. We then carried out an analysis of the ATUS data to document how sedentary activities increasingly predominate as people age and to show the rise in sleeplessness as an example of a marker that indicates possible problems such as depression and dementia. After considering the problems of declining activation we then reviewed earlier research on exergames that facilitate exercise through pedaling. We introduced a novel approach to activating people with technology that combines the extrinsic motivators of engaging video content (which can only be viewed while pedaling), social interaction, and competition.

The research reported in this paper shows how devices can be created to motivate people to be active, with a focus on pedaling as form of physical exercise. These devices have been created in response to the urgent need for new activation technologies for people to use as they are aging. These technologies should be inclusive, usable, and enjoyable to use. Fortunately, there is a wide and welcoming design space with a range of inexpensive technologies that can be brought to bear on the problem as the example of exergames for physical interface shown in this paper demonstrate.

References

Anderson-Hanley, C., et al.: The interactive Physical and Cognitive exercise system (iPACes™): effects of a 3-month in-home pilot clinical trial for mild cognitive impairment and caregivers. Clin. Interv. Aging **13**, 1565 (2018)

Bennett, S., Thomas, A.J.: Depression and dementia: cause, consequence or coincidence? Maturitas **79**(2), 184–190 (2014)

Bolton, J., Lambert, M., Lirette, D., Unsworth, B.: PaperDude: a virtual reality cycling exergame. In: CHI 2014 Extended Abstracts on Human Factors in Computing Systems, pp. 475–478. ACM, April 2014

Brox, E., Luque, L.F., Evertsen, G.J., Hernández, J.E.G.: Exergames for elderly: social exergames to persuade seniors to increase physical activity. In: 2011 5th International Conference on Pervasive Computing Technologies for Healthcare (PervasiveHealth) and Workshops, pp. 546–549. IEEE, May 2011

Campbell, J., Fraser, M.: Switching it up: designing adaptive interfaces for virtual reality exergames. In: Proceedings of the 31st European Conference on Cognitive Ergonomics, pp. 177–184. ACM, September 2019

CDC: Adults need more physical activity (2019). https://www.cdc.gov/physicalactivity/inactivity-among-adults-50plus/index.html. Accessed 18 March 2019

Chan, G., Arya, A., Orji, R., Zhao, Z.: Motivational strategies and approaches for single and multi-player exergames: a social perspective. PeerJ Comput. Sci. **5**, e230 (2019)

Chignell, M., et al.: Immersiveness and perceptibility of convex and concave displays. In: Proceedings of the Human Factors and Ergonomics Society Annual Meeting, vol. 63, no. 1, pp. 396–400. Sage Publications, Los Angeles, November 2019

Hagen, K., Chorianopoulos, K., Wang, A.I., Jaccheri, L., Weie, S.: Gameplay as exercise. In: Proceedings of the 2016 CHI Conference Extended Abstracts on Human Factors in Computing Systems, pp. 1872–1878. ACM, May 2016

HHS: U.S. Department of Health and Human Services. 2008 Physical Activity Guidelines for Americans. U.S. Department of Health and Human Services, Washington, DC (2008). http://www.health.gov/paguidelines

MacRae, P.G., Schnelle, J.F., Simmons, S.F., Ouslander, J.G.: Physical activity levels of ambulatory nursing home residents. J. Aging Phys. Act. **4**(3), 264–278 (1996)

McCallum, S.: Gamification and serious games for personalized health. In: pHealth, pp. 85–96, January 2012

Norton, S., Matthews, F.E., Barnes, D.E., Yaffe, K., Brayne, C.: Potential for primary prevention of Alzheimer's disease: an analysis of population-based data. Lancet Neurol. **13**(8), 788–794 (2014)

Salguero, A., Martínez-García, R., Molinero, O., Márquez, S.: Physical activity, quality of life and symptoms of depression in community-dwelling and institutionalized older adults. Arch. Gerontol. Geriatr. **53**(2), 152–157 (2011)

Schneider, B.A., Pichora-Fuller, M.K.: Implications of perceptual deterioration for cognitive aging research. In: Craik, F.I.M., Salthouse, T.A. (eds.) The Handbook of Aging and Cognition, pp. 155–219. Lawrence Erlbaum Associates Publishers, Mahwah (2000)

Tong, T., Chignell, M., Tierney, M.C., Lee, J.: A serious game for clinical assessment of cognitive status: validation study. JMIR Serious Games, **4**(1) (2016)

Tong, T., Wilkinson, A., Nejatimoharrami, F., He, T., Matilus, H., Chignell, M.: A system for rewarding physical and cognitive activity in people with dementia. In: Proceedings of the International Symposium on Human Factors and Ergonomics in Health Care, vol. 6, no. 1, pp. 44–49. Sage Publications, New Delhi, June 2017

Williams, R.B., Clippinger, C.A.: Aggression, competition and computer games: computer and human opponents. Comput. Hum. Behav. **18**(5), 495–506 (2002)

Yim, J., Graham, T.N.: Using games to increase exercise motivation. In: Proceedings of the 2007 Conference on Future Play, pp. 166–173, November 2007

Tele Echo Tube for Historic House Tojo-Tei in Matsudo International Science Art Festival 2018

Hill Hiroki Kobayashi(✉) and Daisuké Shimotoku

Division of Joint Usage and Research, Center for Spatial Information Science, University of Tokyo, Chiba 277-8568, Japan
{kobayashi,shimotoku}@csis.u-tokyo.ac.jp

Abstract. Sustainable interface design has been receiving a great deal of attention in efforts towards a sustainable society. The Tojo-Tei Historic House exhibition at Matsudo International Science and Art Festival 2018 focused on a new type of interface with the aim of raising mythological awareness in the midst of a modern city. A tele echo tube (TET) is a speaking tube interface that interacts acoustically with a deep mountain echo via a slightly vibrating lampshade-like interface. TET allows users to interact with a mountain echo in real time, through an augmented echo-sounding experience with vibration, over a satellite data network. Since 2009, we have continuously improved the architecture of this system to increase the interaction performance and improve the experience. In order to evaluate the interaction performance, an experimental system was constructed to study general rather than laboratory use. In this paper, we discuss the basis requirements for the system for the Tojo-Tei Historic House exhibition at the Matsudo International Science Art Festival 2018.

Keywords: HCBI (Human-Computer-Biosphere Interaction) · Nature interface · Sustainability · Sustainable design

1 Introduction

A comparable type of complex presence existed in Japanese culture (Fig. 1). For cultural and mythological reasons, interactions between nature and human societies in ancient times were more balanced than those that characterize modern society. Before human beings became capable of dramatically altering natural landscapes, humanity and nature were physically separated but spiritually and emotionally connected. Although Japanese farmers interacted with nature within their local environments, the mountainous wilderness areas of Japan were considered to be the domain of gods and mythological creatures. Consequently, wild animals and their habitats in the mountains were left undisturbed for the most part, and Japanese culture was characterized by respectful and benevolent interaction with nature. Recent technological and information advancements, including satellite imaging, have been unable to confirm the presence of mythological

N. Streitz and S. Konomi (Eds.): HCII 2020, LNCS 12203, pp. 520–532, 2020.
https://doi.org/10.1007/978-3-030-50344-4_37

creatures in undeveloped natural locations, and very few humans now believe in the existence of the creatures that control the weather or other farming conditions. However, since we no longer embrace the presence of such cultural and imaginable metaphors in our daily lives, especially in city life, there has been little outcry at the severe materialism brought about by the globalization process. The tele echo tube (TET) aims to increase mythological awareness in the midst of a modern city, transcending our cultural and imaginable boundaries (Fig. 2). It is a speaking tube installation that acoustically interacts with a deep mountain echo via a networked remote-controlled speaker and microphone. This allows users to interact with the echo in the forest around Mount Fuji in real time, through an augmented echo-sounding experience. In this way, TET can help us to design an interactive system that leverages the boundary between the real and virtual worlds by engaging in culturally cognition to perform a nonhuman-centric interaction with a culturally imaginable creature.

Fig. 1. "Yamabiko", the echo in Japanese mythology. Left: "Yamabiko" in a collection of pictures known as "Hyakkai-Zukan" [6]. Right: The "Illustrated Night Parade of A Hundred Demons" [3].

2 Background

TET is based on the concept of human-computer-biosphere interaction (HCBI) (Fig. 3), which is an extension of human-computer interaction (HCI) and human-computer-pet interaction (HCPI). Computer-supported cooperative work (CSCW) is based on computer-interaction paradigms to support specific activities. For example, we can exchange ideas, thoughts, theories, and messages by encoding them into transferable words, communicating them through computer systems, and then decoding them. However, in our daily lives, we implicitly exchange and share a great deal of additional nonverbal information that

Fig. 2. Urban users in the Tojo-Tei Historic House interacting with Mr. Yamabiko in the forest around Mt.Fuji, via a TET interface, at Matsudo International Science and Art Festival 2018

maintains our social relationships, such as messages acknowledging the presence and moods of others. The concept of HCBI proposes that these elements can be extended to philosophical interactions with countable objects, such as pets and plants in space, and their "surrounding world," which is an uncountable, complex, nonlinguistic "something" that exists beyond our imagination.

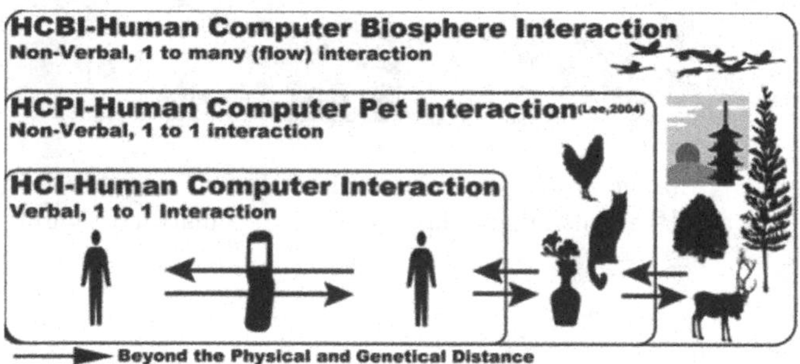

Fig. 3. The concept of human-computer-biosphere interaction (HCBI), an extension of HCI (human-computer interaction) and HCPI (human-computer-pet interaction) [2]

3 Tele Echo Tube System

TET consists of local and remote speaking tube systems with a one-way echo canceler that uses a full duplex audio I/O system. The remote and local systems perform a remote interaction and create a pseudo echo experience. The system is designed to emulate the imagined response of Yamabiko, or "Echo," a mythological tree spirit (Fig. 1), who is believed to answer when one calls out. A remote system consisting of weather-resistant microphones and speakers was also placed in the forest around Mount Fuji, Japan. To interact with "Echo," users speak into the local speaking tube, as illustrated in Fig. 2. Users typically enthusiastically shout something like "yoo-hoo." The loop back call at the remote host occurs because the sound from the speaker is captured and transferred back to the user by the remote host with a spontaneous network delay. When users hear the loop back call, that is, "their voices within the soundscape" from the forest, accompanied by a slight vibration in their hands provided by the interface, they recognize that their vocalization did actually travel through the forest environment.

4 Tele Echo Tube Exhibition at Matsudo International Science and Art Festival 2018

In a future city in which nature, science, and culture coexist seamlessly, expressways and tunnels can also evolve into a creative space that connects nature with cutting-edge technology. Matsudo City in Japan is developing a variety of initiatives with the aim of creating a city brand based on culture and a town in which creators and artists can play active roles. As part of this effort, the "Matsudo International Science and Art Festival 2018" [4] was held on November 16 (Sat) and 17 (Sun), 2018, with the theme of "Citizens of the Future". Visitors could enjoy special exhibitions, talks, and workshops at Tojogaoka Historical Park [5]. The main venue, Tojo-Tei House, was built in 1884 by Akitake Tokugawa, the last lord of the Mito clan, and was surrounded by state-of-the-art gardens when it was constructed. Akitake himself was educated abroad, and was a global pioneer in terms of incorporating new cultures and technologies. In this historic place of innovation, Matsudo city held an exhibition that considered the world of the future, which extended to the rich nature surrounding the historical park, the earth that gives us life, and the universe that humanity will step out into in the future. In future cities, advanced technologies such as IoT and artificial intelligence (AI) can be connected with nature in new ways, to enable societies to better coexist with their environments.

The exhibition at Tojo-Tei Historic House is an interactive installation based on research and technology from the University of Tokyo, which connects the voices of visitors with the sounds of nature and its wildlife. TET aims to increase mythological awareness in the midst of a modern city, beyond our cultural and imaginable boundaries. TET connects the Tojo-Tei visitors with the forests surrounding Mt. Fuji, and can not only receive sounds from nature but also send the voices of the visitors to the forest to enable interaction with wildlife and the mountain echo. It is a speaking tube installation that acoustically interacts with a deep mountain echo via a networked remote-controlled speaker and microphone. It allows users to interact with the echo in a forest around Mount Fuji in

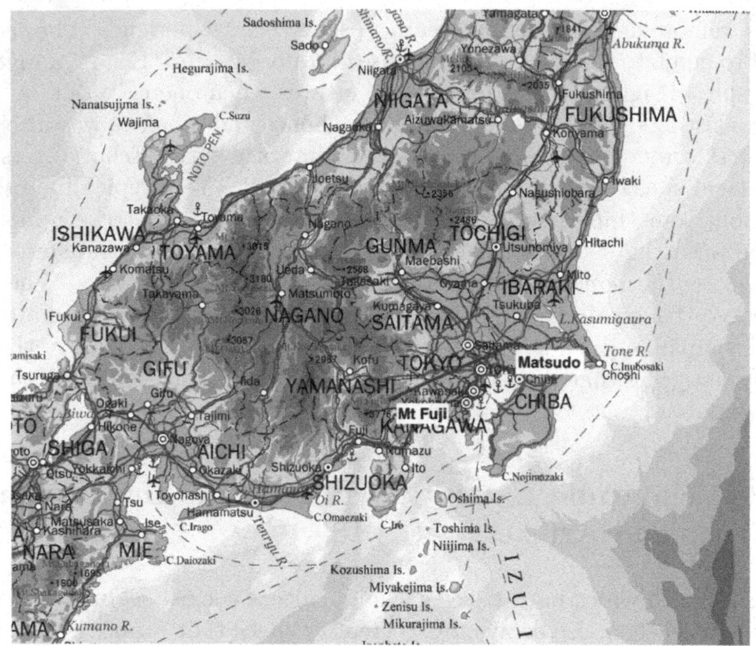

Fig. 4. Map of experiment. [1]

real time through an augmented echo-sounding experience. In this way, TET can help us design an interactive system that leverages the boundary of the real and virtual worlds by engaging cultural cognition to perform a nonhuman-centric interaction with a culturally imaginable creature.

4.1 Design of the System

TET (Mt. Fuji version) consists of remote, communication, local, and interaction systems. The subsystem consists of the following four components: the remote system, the communication system, the local system and the interaction system (Figs. 5 and 6).

4.2 Remote System

The remote and local systems perform a remote interaction to create an echo-sounding experience with "Yamabiko" ("Echo", represented as a mountain nymph in Greek mythology), as shown in Fig. 1, through a live sound pipe via the mobile-networked Internet. Networked microphones and speakers were placed in the forest around Mt. Fuji at Fuji Iyashinomori Woodland Study Center [8] in the University of Tokyo Forests (Fig. 4) to create the echo-sounding experience, for 24 h per day over 365 days. The environmental sound and video in the forest were recorded and monitored by a landscape monitoring system. In addition,

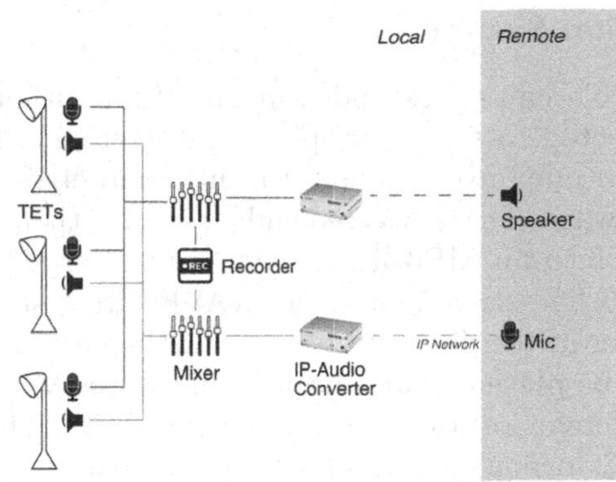

Fig. 5. Schematic of the system.

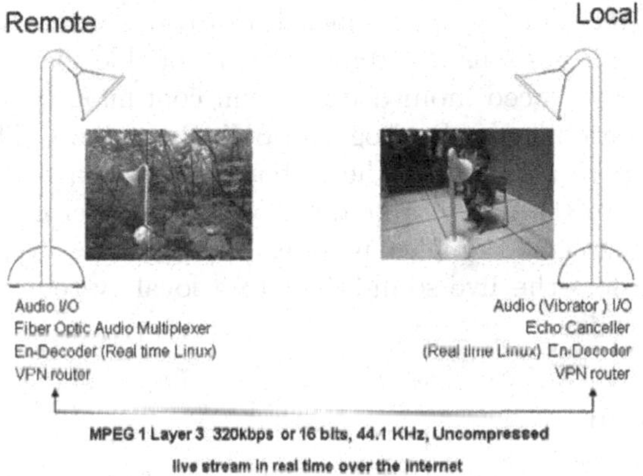

Fig. 6. TET (Mt.Fuji version): system diagram of remote and local installation.

real-time sound and video archives were broadcast via an Internet website called the "Cyber Forest Project" [7]. The real-time streaming system was improved several times to achieve long-term stability under unmanned operating conditions. The remote system, shown on the right in Fig. 5 and on the left in Fig. 6, was placed in the forest. The weatherproof microphone consisted of a nondirectional microphone wrapped in a sheet of thick waterproof sponge and a hard plastic mesh. The joints of the microphone and an audio cable connector were shielded by waterproof putty and tape to protect them from moisture. The microphone was tied to the trunk of a tree. An A/D device converted the analog audio signal from the microphone (speaker) to a digital audio signal, and transferred the signal to an audio processing system with extremely low noise.

4.3 Communication System

The digital signal cable can be extended up to 10 km without any digital distortion, and is connected to the audio processing system. This audio signal is digitally processed to enhance its quality using remotely controlled real-time audio processing software. The processed audio signal is then sent to the recording system, encoded into an MP3 live stream, and recorded as WAVE format sound files. The MP3 live stream (and the WAVE direct stream over UDP) is sent to a stream server in the date archive system, directly via the Internet. The MP3 live stream can be played simultaneously on various MP3-based audio software packages at different locations all around the world. The storage/analysis system stores WAVE format sound files that are sent from an audio encoding/recording system to its storage system, and is capable of storing audio files recorded continuously over several decades. The data communication system provides a satellite-based internal computer network as part of the audio digitizing/streaming/recording system, and also provides Internet access to/from the system. Thus, all systems are remotely controllable via the Internet. Furthermore, a remotely placed monitoring system continuously keeps track of all the system information using SysLog and SNMP software. This management capability allows us to monitor all the system information from the input level on the microphone to the data traffic delay on the Internet connection over the satellite from the data communication system in Fig. 6. The system continuously captures and transfers the live soundscape to a local system over the Internet within several seconds.

4.4 Local System

The local speaking tube system consists of networked microphones, speakers with vibrator, and an echo canceler as described in Fig. 6. An embedded CPU system receives live soundscape data from the remote mountain via the satellite network, immediately performs echo cancelling on the sound signal, and sends it back to the remote site, as shown in Fig. 6. TET (Mt. Fuji version) runs on a full-duplex audio pipe over the Internet and uses an echo-canceling process to prevent audio feedback in the loop.

4.5 Interaction System

The songs of small birds, the trickling of a stream, and the sounds of insects moving in the mountain forest represent the arrival of spring in the mountain area (Fig. 8). These interactions create an echo-sounding experience with "Yamabiko" (Fig. 1) through a live sound pipe via the satellite-networked Internet. To interact with "Yamabiko," users can call out in a loud voice from the local speaking tube (Fig. 2) to the speakers on the mountain at the remote site, as described in Fig. 4. The loopback call at the remote host occurs because the playback sound from the speaker is captured and transferred to the user by the remote host with a spontaneous network delay (Fig. 8). When the users hear the loopback

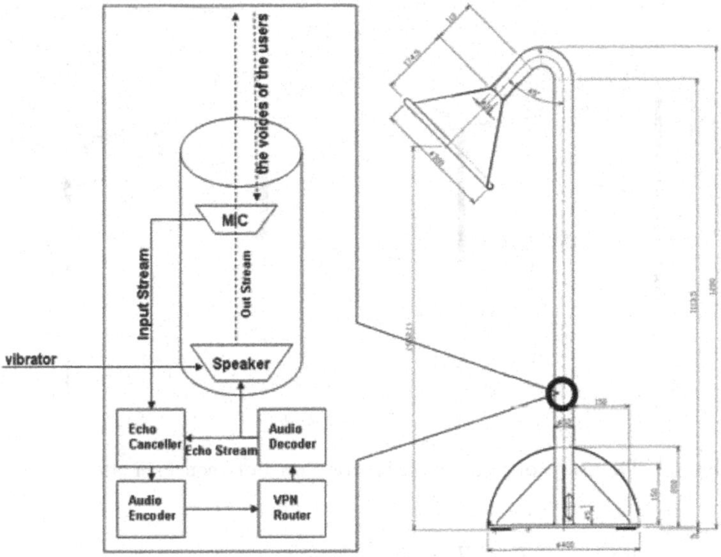

Tele Echo Tube : Tube Diagram

vibrator
the voices of the users
MIC
Input Stream
Out Stream
Speaker
Echo Canceller
Echo Stream
Audio Decoder
Audio Encoder
VPN Router

Fig. 7. Tube diagram of TET.

call (that is, "their voices within the soundscape" from the mountain) with the slight vibration in their hands through the interface, they recognize that their voices actually traveled to the mountain environment. This echo-sounding loop with the spontaneous network delay, which transfers live sounds bidirectionally from the remote and local sites, creates an echo-sounding effect, and in doing so gives the user the opportunity to interact remotely with the "fickle echo" (Fig. 1) of the deep mountain. These acoustic interactions support nonlinguistic believability in the form of a mythological metaphor of the mountain echo.

4.6 Interaction Measurement Design

First, we introduce some of the notations used in our interaction measurement. When measuring the performance conditions of the "echo-sounding experience," or in this case, conditions related to transmission, network congestion, effects from temporary blackouts and the required buffer size in memory stack vary significantly. In situations where multiple units are deployed via the Internet and operated for extended periods from a remote area, the stability of the system must be carefully controlled. However, since the careful regulation of numerous units is unfeasible, the development of a robust method that used commercial products for a long period of continuous operation was considered essential. In this study, the system performance was investigated by measuring the cumulative value of the network delay to remotely create the presence of "a fickle echo" on the deep mountain. The cumulative value of the network delay in the user's input was calculated using Eq. (1) below:

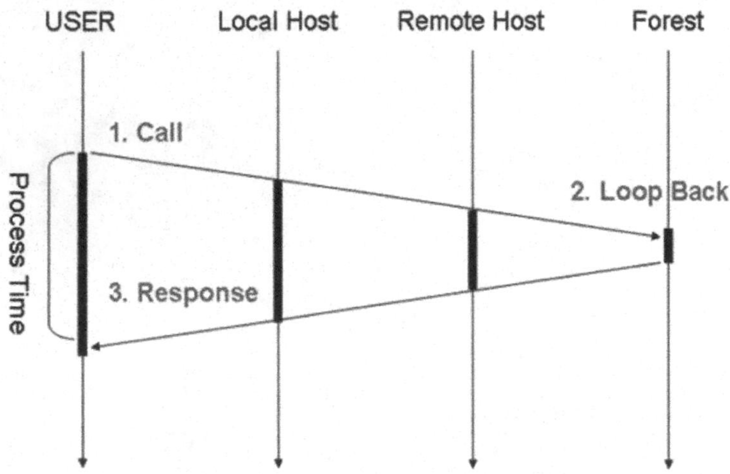

Fig. 8. Diagram of nonverbal interaction between user and echo.

$$T = T_c + T_l + T_r. \tag{1}$$

In the TET system, we have three stages, i.e. call, loopback, and response, as shown in Fig. 8. T represents the time of processing for a single echo-sounding experience. T_c is the time taken for the user's calls travel from the local to the remote site (i.e. the outbound travel time), and T_l means the time during which the user's call makes a loopback at the remote site in the forest. T_r denotes the travel time of a single call from the forest to the local site (i.e. the inbound travel time). True means the time taken to respond from the remote to the local site.

However, unlike a VoIP application, the MP3 live stream system is designed to transmit live stream data over a robust network with a large memory buffer. In addition, special tuning of the TCP/IP stack to avoid network clipping is essential. We also used a commercial off-the-shelf product that can reduce the operating cost to demonstrate the validity and usefulness of the time system. We note that the microphone-speaker distance in the forest that affects T_l is about 1 m, and T_l is therefore less than 10 ms, which is negligible compared to T_c and T_r. Hence, this system can be used to evaluate the network travel delay $\Delta t = T_c + T_r$.

4.7 System Configuration

The system conditions cause the network travel delay Δt to fluctuate. Subjects were located in an isolated space, and stood or sat facing the installation, as shown in Fig. 9. A speaker and microphone were placed inside the tube, as shown in Figs. 6 and 7, located 30 cm from the bottom. A single computer provided recording, communication and processing with CUI-based operation. The setup comprised a Barix Instreamer, Exstreamer 100, audio mixer (Behringer Xenyx 802 Mixer) and audio mic/speaker with echo cancellation (Yamaha PJP-25UR).

Our real-time sound streaming system was previously developed from Iriomote island [2] and the Cyber Forest project site. The whole system was designed to operate for several years. An absolute delay throughout the system of 0 ms was obtained by using an analog bypass with the audio interface. One of the authors (D.S.) listened to and watched all of the recorded digital files, and calculated the processing times for all users. To measure the interaction, we used Adobe Audition sound processing software to measure the amount of time that elapsed between the call and the response.

4.8 Trials

The experiment was conducted on November 16 (Sat) and 17 (Sun), 2018, in Matsudo City, Chiba, Japan. The system was installed in the Tojo-Tei House [5], which was built for and used by the ex-Japanese samurai governor Tokugawa and is protected as an important historical property by the Agency for Cultural Affairs of the Japanese Government (2006). While the building was strictly under protection, no additional construction for this event was allowed. Thus LTE wireless internet in means to protect the building served by the local telecommunications company NTT was employed and no dedicated network was available. The processing time T_p varied with time and location, and each subject performed a trial only once. The calling process, which involved singing out "yoo-hoo!", was randomly initiated by the subject in each trial (Fig. 9).

The experiment was conducted on 16 (Sat) and 17 (Sun), 2018 at Matsudo City, Chiba, Japan. The system was installed on the Tojo-Tei (the historical residence house)[5], which was built and used for the ex-Japanese samurai governor the Tokugawa was and thus protected as an important historical property assigned by the Agency for Cultural Affairs of Japanese Government (2006). While the building strictly under protection, no special construction was allowed; i.e. LTE wireless internet served by the local tele-communicator NTT was employed and no dedicated network was available. The processing time Tp. was varied over time and locations. Each subject performed each trial once only. Calling by singing out "YO-HOOOOO!" in each trial was randomly initiated by the subject (Fig. 9). The subjects were ordered to wait for the reaction from the echo until the arrival of the response. Overall, one session took about less than one minute to complete. Subjected actions in the movie were analyzed visually and manually to measure.

4.9 Analysis

When the sound captured at the local side (i.e. the sound transmitted from the local side to the forest, as shown by the red line in Fig. 5) and the sound captured at the remote side (i.e. the sound transmitted from the forest to the local side, as shown by the blue line in Fig. 5) had been recorded on different channels, the sum of the travel time was measured by comparing the spectrogram (Fig. 10). To enable a better comparison, the audio was normalized and the background noise suppressed using software.

Fig. 9. Setting of the experiment.

As described in [2], the first 50 participants were sampled and Δt was measured. Figure 11 shows the estimated network travel time observed using echo sounding. The figure yields the changes in Δt over time: the delay for the first sample was $\Delta t = 9.809$ s, while that for the last sample was $\Delta t = 8.240$ s. Figure 11 shows that the delay gradually decreased over time.

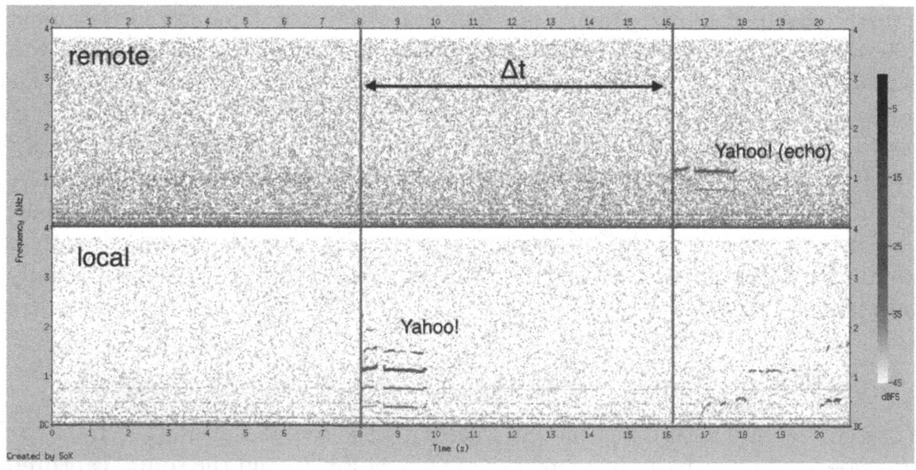

Fig. 10. Example of call and response

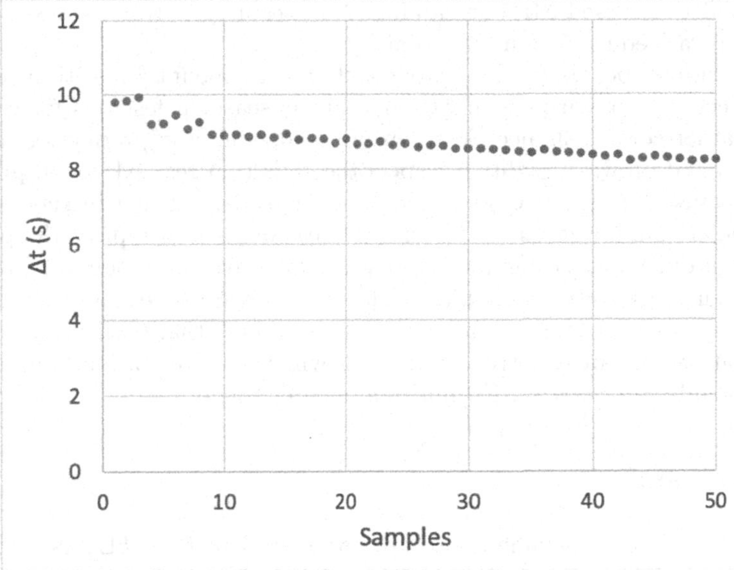

Fig. 11. Estimated network delay

5 Discussions

In general, a reduction in computational power was caused by heat and memory leaks. Heat was generated by the recording system itself, as the recording system was running in an environment with extremely high moisture and temperature, in a subtropical forest. Memory leakage, i.e. the loss of memory blocks necessary for a computational process, occurred in the recording system as it ran for 24 h over 365 days. Hence, to solve these problems, two identical systems were created, and these were run separately in alternate shifts of 12 h each. Using this shift system, the CPU temperature of the two identical systems was reduced and the memory leak problem was solved. A previous study confirmed that the delay increased due to the effects of this heat [2], and on average, the time required for interaction increased from the first to the 50th by about 7 s. However, in this study, the measurements showed the opposite result, and the response time became shorter as the number of users increased. This indicates that the measures to compensate for the heat and network delay were more appropriate in comparison with the previous experiment.

There was a major technical difference between the previous study, in which 40 s was required for the calling time, and the current study, in which only 10 s was required. Previously, MP3 streaming was used for both two-way audio communication from the local to the remote stations. This has the advantage that stable communication can be performed without requiring a large band, but has the disadvantage of causing large delays. Hence, only the outbound route was transmitted in the uncompressed direct WAVE format this time, and only the inbound route used MP3 streaming. As a result, the time required for the interaction was reduced from 40 s to about 8 s.

Before human beings became capable of leveling mountains with heavy construction equipment, farmers prayed to gods at seasonal festivals for the tools or the weather conditions needed to ensure successful crop production, and the general population was taught to respect the gods that resided in and protected the mountains (Fig. 1). The sounds of singing birds, buzzing insects, swaying leaves, and trickling water in a mountain forest implicitly imprint the presence of nature in our cultural memory, and when we leave the mountains, recalling them takes us back to the same place. The crucial factor here is not the means of conveyance (words or language), but the "something" that manifests; an atmosphere that we cannot exactly identify but which endures beyond our cultural and imaginable boundaries with information technology.

6 Conclusions

On the basis of our experiment, we are now confident that TET is a practical means of realizing mythological awareness in the midst of a modern city beyond our cultural and imaginable boundaries. In order to make this type of exhibition more lively and interesting, technical improvements to create a more believable interaction are required.

Acknowledgment. This study was supported by JSPS KAKENHI Grants (18H04089 and 19K22839), the Telecommunications Advancement Foundation, and the Tateisi Science and Technology Foundation.

References

1. Geospatial Information Authority of Japan: Geospatial information authority of Japan. https://www.gsi.go.jp/
2. Kobayashi, H., Hirose, M., Fujiwara, A., Nakamura, K., Sezaki, K., Saito, K.: Tele echo tube: beyond cultural and imaginable boundaries. In: Proceedings of the 21st ACM International Conference on Multimedia (MM 2013), pp. 173–182. ACM, New York (2013). https://doi.org/10.1145/2502081.2502125
3. Kyōgoku, N., Tada, K.: Yōkai zukan. Kokusho Kankōkai, Tōkyō, shohan. edn. (2000)
4. Matsudo International Science Art Festival, Matsudo City, Chiba Pref, Japan (2018). https://science-art-matsudo.net/
5. Tojo Museum of History, Matsudo City, Chiba Pref, Japan (2020). https://www.city.matsudo.chiba.jp/tojo/
6. Suushi, S.: Hyakkai-Zukan: The Illustrated Volume of a Hundred Demons. Sawaki Suushi, Tōkyō, shohan. edn. (1737)
7. University of Tokyo: Cyberforest (2020). http://www.cyberforest.jp/
8. University of Tokyo Forests: Fuji Iyashinomori Woodland Study Center (2020). http://www.uf.a.u-tokyo.ac.jp/fuji/

Smart Learning in the Community: Supporting Citizen Digital Skills and Literacies

Pen Lister[(✉)]

University of Malta, Msida MSD 2080, Malta
pen.lister@penworks.net

Abstract. This paper discusses how smart learning in urban environments can mediate citizen digital skills and competences learning initiatives supported by standards such as the European Commission citizen Digital Competences Framework [8], thus helping a broad range of urban populations to gain essential knowledge and skills for navigating the digitised services of the societal urban systems around them. Smart learning, based on cultural, civic or community interests and placed within a context of ad-hoc urban learning experiences set in authentic learning hyper-local environments might support and develop citizen digital literacies and competences through a wide variety of informal learning activities. This kind of technologically mediated learning acts as an implicit conduit to channel the development of a number of skills and literacies involved in the use of digital apps and devices, and the manipulation of knowledge content both digitally created as well as consumed. Additionally, development of 'soft' skills such as community participation, confidence building and language literacy are increased in digitally connected spheres, enabling citizens to act with more self assured agency within these territories. The paper refers to the author's own doctoral research findings developed from a phenomenographic investigation into smart learning journeys to suggest a 'pedagogy of experience complexity' for smart learning as support for these kinds of learning activities.

Keywords: Smart learning · Smart pedagogy · Digital skills · Phenomenography · Smart cities

1 Introduction

As society moves towards realisation of a comprehensive digitisation, consideration must be given to the conditions of rapidly transforming technically mediated provision of urban society support systems, and the necessary digital literacies of citizens who are the intended users of those systems. In this context, this paper reflects on findings and further implications of doctoral research based at the University of Malta [35], in relation to conceptualisations for pragmatic application of a pedagogical approach to ad-hoc informal smart learning, to support digital skills, literacy and competences development for the digital citizenry of urban populations.

Focus is on emerging ideas of applying a smart learning pedagogical relevance structure [39, pp. 143, 202] formed as a 'Pedagogy of Experience Complexity' for

N. Streitz and S. Konomi (Eds.): HCII 2020, LNCS 12203, pp. 533–547, 2020.
https://doi.org/10.1007/978-3-030-50344-4_38

smart learning [35], derived from a phenomenographic investigation into smart learning conceptualised as smart learning journeys, with suggestions for ways to move forward in the support of developing the digital literacies of urban citizens.

Though there is now an almost ubiquitous digitisation of many of society's essential services, citizens remain unable to fully or even partially engage with these systems. Urban populations specifically may be at most risk of being 'left behind' [5, 26], and reasons for this are manifold, including language, culture, new migrant communities or others such as age and gender [37]. The challenges of engaging citizens in digitally mediated learning activities to support their digital skills development might therefore manifest in a variety of guises: limited digital device experience and knowledge; limited time available to participate; language literacy for reading or writing in an additional language; limited experience in aspects of information literacy to enable sourcing and selection of relevant useful information; limited confidence to participate digitally; or a mixture of several of these or other issues. Provision of community wide digitally mediated learning activities might therefore need to acknowledge the wide range of citizens they may be catering for, and be planned according to an inclusive, accessible and flexible design and development [54].

2 Defining Terms and Literature

Key terms are defined here within the context of relevant literature, and clarified into two groups: generic terms and more specific terms. It is acknowledged that many of these terms can mean more than one thing to different disciplines and discourses, so here context and meaning are described for this paper, referring to relevant literature to provide useful background.

2.1 Inclusivity, Digital Skills, Literacies and Informal Learning

Generic terms used in this paper that may benefit from brief summary definition with examples from the literature would be inclusivity, digital skills, soft skills and literacies, and informal learning activities. Inclusivity here can be defined as pertaining to citizen involvement both in terms of the conceptualization and development of a smart city for all citizens and communities [3], and for how digital experiences, with any subsequent implicit or explicit technically mediated learning, are structured and created in those communities. Inclusivity is an important part of interpreting digital literacy, and in conjunction with closely related literacies of media and information, can be defined as being able to navigate and understand role, agency and potentials of these domains and territories, for example as outlined by Thompson [51]. Digital skills are best defined here by the digital competence framework for citizens, also known as DigComp 2.1 [8], which is the most recently devised and widely adopted comprehensive set of factors involved in such a set of skills. Of particular note here is that Bloom's revised taxonomy [1] forms a part of the DigComp 2.1 framework, giving an indication of proficiency level in relation to cognitive domain.

Discourse around soft skills has circulated for some years and often forms part of '21st century skills', e.g. [2], [10] in [53, 51] and [52]. Soft skills can be thought of here as life skills [2] that are transferrable [54]. These are variously described as communication, problem solving, teamwork, collaboration, critical thinking and so on, and part of the three literacies of information, media and digital. Informal learning is understood here in its most general form of non-assessed learning, as opposed to non-formal [59] or formal learning [46]. To illustrate context for this paper, Carroll et al. [9] describe "a sustainable process of informal learning about information technology - helping community organizations learn how to discover, understand, and respond to their own information technology needs" [9, p. 5]. Informal learning can be thought of as learning that happens implicitly as well as explicitly. For example, gamified community activities that are ostensibly for fun can have learning impact as a more covert agenda, e.g. [18, 19, 21], supporting practice with mobile apps, creating digital identities or encouragement to contribute to community discussion and feedback on a particular issue via digital communication channels [9, 48].

2.2 Smart Cities, Learning, Environments and Urban Hyper-localisation

Terms such as smart city, smart learning and smart learning environments, hyper-local environments [25], urbanised learning and smart learning pedagogies form the specialised scope of this paper. Beginning with the term 'smart city', Ojo et al. [44] offer a comprehensive literature analysis of concepts for a smart city, highlighting a city is smart when investments in human and social capital, traditional transport and modern (ICT) communication infrastructure fuel sustainable economic growth as being representative of much smart city design and approach. This is further supported by de Lange & de Waal [14] who state "... the notion of 'smart cities' often invoked in policy and design discourses [...] is mainly understood as a series of infrastructures that must be managed as efficiently as possible." They go on to state that "(q)uestions about the role of digital media technologies in shaping the social fabric and built form of urban life are all the more urgent in the context of challenges posed by rapid urbanization" (ibid, p. 90). This supports a smart city as primarily concerned with building smart citizen spaces [3], placing emphasis on the people, e.g. [42], not (only) the technological implementations of such city spaces, e.g. [23].

Smart learning and environments are variously discussed in literature within two contrasting positions. The first is the idealised aim of a learning experience provided by sophisticated technological infrastructures and an assumption of personalisation driven by data interactions, for example [32] or [20], or, where focus is more emphasised on human and pedagogical aspects, such as [42] or [17]. Some of the literature outlines complex technological-pedagogical systems, for example [43] or [4]. In this paper the meaning of the term smart learning is summed up best by Liu et al., as "learning to do, learning to learn and learning to self-realisation" [34, p. 209]. Dron makes clear that much learning in a smart learning environment is "a complex conversational process that can and usually does lead to much that is of value beyond what is planned" [17, p. 3].

In considering smart city localised places, here it is helpful to use the term *hyper-local*, more commonly applied to news content as hyper-local media (in weblogs, for example). Hyper-local places and place-making articulate the very localised nature of often limited lifespan digital community experiences situated in very specific small local areas. Carroll et al. [9] state "(w)eb 2.0 infrastructures can be hyper-local. Mechanisms for geocoding allow information and interaction to be located in space [...] within a geographically local area..." and "...the rapidly expanding ecology of Internet devices, notably smartphones and rich information infrastructures for geo-location..." means that "... members of a community may now upload, share, comment, and collaborate on information when and where it is of interest". The author's own doctoral research conceptualises and develops 'smart learning journey' activities located around St Pauls in the City of London, UK, and then Republic Street in the centre of Valletta, Malta. A smart learning journey is defined here as a smart learning activity in geo-spatially relevant locations: forming a journey of several close by locations that are related to the topic of learning. These would be examples of hyper-local (smart) learning locations, very specific to a small area.

Sacré & De Visscher [47] shed light on ways to think of urbanised learning, stating "urban education is concerned with all forms of learning in the urban context", that "civic learning (is) an essential component of the city", and "(a) cultural understanding of civic learning..." is the "citizens' assemblage of the social, the material and the symbolic, as a kind of wayfinding in society". This is how urbanised learning is conceptualized in this paper, as urban space situated learning activities. Within these types of learning activities, as situated 'smart' urban spaces, we then consider the potential of smart learning pedagogies. Lorenzo & Gallon [36] have useful input, stating that "...digital transformation ... generates a need for rethinking educative roles in the digital age", and "Smart Education Models will have to include social dimensions and collaborative approaches..." [36, pp. 52, 53]. They stress student centred 'individual awareness': "(i)t is difficult to understand the personal mechanisms that incentivize engagement and motivation [...]. Smart learning spaces can be a useful element in this personalized approach" (ibid, p. 54). Dron emphasizes the purpose of smart learning environments to learn and teach effectively, and how intrinsic and extrinsic motivations play a crucial role in any learning participation [17, p. 11]. Reasons for motivation are considered in this paper as part of a pedagogical 'structure of relevance' [39] for smart learning.

3 Global Urbanization

The world's population is rapidly becoming ubiquitously urbanised. Consider the following quotes, first from 2007, The United Nations Fund for Population Activities:

> *"In 2008 the world reaches an invisible but momentous milestone for the first time in history and half its human population, three 3.3 billion people, will be living in urban areas. By 2030, this is expected to swell to almost 5,000,000,000. Many of the new urbanites will be poor. The future, the future of cities in developing countries, the future of humanity itself, all depend very much on decisions made now in preparation for this growth.", [56].*

Then, the 2018 revision from the World Urbanisation Prospects:

> *"Globally, more people live in urban areas and in rural areas, with 55% of the worlds population residing in urban areas in 2018. In 1950, 30% of the worlds*

population was urban and by 2050, 68% of the worlds population is projected to be urban […] to ensure that the benefits of urbanisation are shared and that no one is left behind, policies to manage urban growth need to ensure access to infrastructure and social services for all, focusing on the needs of the urban poor and other vulnerable groups for housing, education, health care, decent work and a safe environment." [58].

These key quotes provide a clear message, that without adequate consideration and support for the most vulnerable in society, many members of urbanised populations risk being 'left behind' in the post digitised urban landscape. Much other relevant discourse is available on this problem, for example [5, 26].

4 The Issue of Digitalization

Brennen & Kreiss [6] refer to digitalization "as the way many domains of social life are restructured around digital communication and media infrastructures", and digitization refers to "the technical process of converting streams of analog information into digital bits of 1s and 0s", also stating that they are "interrelated, concepts". Here it is suggested that a digitized society is both meanings.

Digitalization of societal systems to support citizen urban life has become pervasive [57], creating for many an unfamiliar and difficult terrain to negotiate for access to civic infrastructures [37]. Many citizen user groups might be ill prepared for this changeover when important civic services move from face-to-face access to only digitised provision. The challenge then, is to find ways to support all citizens in society to enable them to access the services they need, are entitled to and enjoy the benefits of adequate digital skills and literacies [21]. In urban contexts these issues become more urgent, as populations require digital skills and awareness to participate in almost every aspect of life: jobs, housing, health, education and so on [18].

4.1 Digital Citizen Skills and Competences

Studies show that those most vulnerable and 'at risk' of being left behind in a digitized society are lower income groups, lower educational achievers and women [37]. We need to design digital solutions to support development of digital skills and competences with consideration for these citizens groups, for issues of context as well as individual competence levels. Vasloo [54], provides practical guidance for digital skills design awareness using the DigComp 2.1 framework [8] and this approach can be acknowledged as pragmatic guidance in the scope of planning and development of 'in the wild' smart learning activities.

Industry reports stress the urgency for initiatives to develop digital skills and competences relevant or even vital to urban citizen life. For example, the Mckinsey Global Institute, in [7], indicate significant changes in almost every aspect of labour, emphasising the growth of the technically skilled workforce: "France expects a shortage of 80,000 workers in IT and electronics jobs by 2020 … there could be a shortfall of some 250,000 data scientists in the short term in the United States … 23% of the UK population, or

12.6 million people, lacked basic digital skills, at a time when about 90% of new jobs require them". Need for digital skills extends beyond work, for example "(a) study of a South African SMS platform for reporting water and sanitation grievances found that although elderly, disabled, and infirm individuals in a township faced significant barriers in accessing water and sanitation services, they also lacked the technical capacities to communicate their issues via mobile devices, thus preventing their participation", [26]. But in devising initiatives to support development of citizen digital skills, measurable aims and outcomes should ideally be in place to ensure effective skills improvement. Utilizing existing digital skills frameworks, perhaps along with a flexible pedagogical guide, might provide measurable outcomes.

4.2 Digital Skills and Literacy Frameworks

Three related current digital competence frameworks are briefly outlined here. Though frameworks often have similarities, the DigComp 2.1 [8] is useful as incorporates a cognitive domain using Bloom's revised taxonomy [1]. This permits a direct relationship with the author's proposed pedagogy of experience complexity [35]. Included for historical reference is Dede [13], who examines several frameworks in relation to the P21 initiative for 21st century skills for the period 2003–2010.

The Digital Competence Framework for Citizens (DigComp 2.1) 2018. The DigComp 2.1 contains five competences and eight proficiency levels for different purposes and skill levels, with examples of how to apply them. Along with practical ideas is a cognitive domain scale that matches skills and competences to Bloom's revised taxonomy [1], to help provide a learning measurement and pedagogical approach. It is therefore more possible to devise pedagogically based learning experiences that might support specific activities and develop particular aspects of digital skills.

A Global Framework of Reference on Digital Literacy Skills for Indicator (SDG) 4.4.2. [55] Developed by the Unesco Global Alliance to Monitor Learning, their website [41] explains: "(t)o offer a more comprehensive view of the digital skills of youth and adults, [...] the first step has been to develop a global framework of digital literacy skills based on a technical review of more than 40 digital literacy frameworks used by countries around the world." Essentially closely related to the competences of the DigComp framework this adds 'career competences' composed of soft, transversal skills as a sixth category [33].

The National Standards for Essential Digital Skills. Produced by the UK Department for Education (2019), again has generally similar categories of competences, adding 'transacting', the use of online services and buying securely online, as a separate category. The idea of the framework is to contribute to awarding qualifications in digital skills, beginning in April 2020 [16].

Worth further consideration, Dede [13] uses the 2006 'Partnership for 21st Century Skills Framework' (P21) as a benchmark to evaluate six other frameworks of the period. The P21 has six categories incorporating much of what is included in the more recent frameworks listed here. A clear development timeline seems evident from reading Dede's work.

5 Research Context

A pedagogical relevance structure for smart learning is being developed by the author, derived from doctoral research at the University of Malta into smart learning journeys. This will form the foundation of a 'pedagogy of experience complexity' based in participatory connectivist-inspired pedagogical approaches. Here discussion is focused on implications relating to this pedagogical guide. The research is outlined in brief in the following paragraphs. To reiterate, smart learning in this research was conceptualized as a smart learning journey, that is, a smart learning activity in geo-spatially relevant locations: forming a journey of several close by locations that are related to the topic of learning and mediated by technology.

5.1 Methodology and Research Design

The experience of learners participating in smart learning journeys was the focus of interest in the research, and phenomenography was selected as the most suitable methodology. Two relevant fields of inquiry demonstrate the benefit of phenomenography as a methodological approach: technology enhanced learning (e.g. [12, 31, 50]), and user experience (e.g. [30, 60]). These fields have increasingly looked to phenomenography to understand more about what users or learners do and why they do it. Phenomenography analyses learner experience, looking for experience variation at a collective rather than individual level, though context is retained. Phenomenography draws on Gurwitsch's [24] ideas about theme, thematic field and margin to analyse experience using a 'structure of awareness' analytical framework [11]. Known as a second order perspective [38], phenomenography is non-dualist in nature, making an epistemological assumption that there is only one world as experienced by the learner, "where there is an internal relation between the inner world and the outer world" [28]. Here we are not concerned with ontological discussions of reality, or of the essence of a phenomenon [39, p. 117], but rather only the reality concerning phenomena of interest to the research as experienced by the individuals being researched.

The sample was purposive and convenience [50, p. 4], recruiting 24 undergraduate and postgraduate participants on a voluntary basis, including cohorts from several education-related degrees based at University of Malta, and an additional cohort from London Metropolitan University studying English Literature and Creative Writing.

5.2 Smart Learning in This Study

Within a connectivist inspired [35] scope, HP Reveal[1], Edmodo[2] and Google MyMaps[3] were used to mediate learning interactions and a route of locations that together formed the smart learning journey. Employing digital augmented reality technology to augment specific features of locations, context-aware learning content, participative learning tasks and opportunity for location-based interactions were effectively provided to the learner

[1] HP Reveal (formerly Aurasma) https://www.hpreveal.com/.

[2] Edmodo https://www.edmodo.com/.

[3] Google MyMaps https://www.google.co.uk/maps/d/u/0/.

at that time and place. Learning content was hyperlinked from knowledge sources such as Wikipedia[4], Wikimedia Commons[5] or specialist websites, with some content created by tutors and hosted on independent webpages[6].

Two smart learning journeys were developed, 'Literary London', approximately 2.5 km, around St Paul's Cathedral and the City of London, UK, and 'Malta Democracy', approximately 600 m, along Republic Street, Valletta, Malta. Both locations are rich in cultural history and heritage, providing multiple authentic sites for learning experiences and offering learners a creative and critical participation within an autonomous learning activity. This attempts to support Dron, who "consider(s) smartness as an emergent consequence of dynamic interactions between the environment's constituent parts, including those of its human inhabitants and the artefacts and structures they wittingly or unwittingly create." [17, p. 3].

5.3 Discovering a Pedagogy of Experience Complexity for Smart Learning

Four categories of learner experience variation, defined as a phenomenographic outcome space [39, p. 136] for experiencing a smart learning journey were discovered from analysis of participant interviews. This resulted in a table of experience complexity for a smart learning journey, comprising the four categories, with four levels of complexity for each category [35]. Categories were 'Tasks and Obligations, Discussing (and collaborating), Being There and Knowledge and Place as Value. These categories potentially indicate that learners might be considered within a pedagogical relevance structure [39, pp. 143, 202] to support different aspects of experience complexity, in addition to any desired specific topic learning outcomes. Experience complexity understanding means that aspects of experience can be supported in multiple ways. A 'pedagogy of experience complexity' for smart learning [35] that the author is developing may provide a pragmatic way of understanding how for example the DigComp 2.1 might be applied to citizen smart learning journey activities for activity design and digital skills development approach. This pragmatic pedagogical guide draws on concepts from connectivist style participatory pedagogies [49, p. 10], as "communication skills, participation, networking, sharing – overlap with what are viewed as essential 21st-century learning and employability skills", [40]. Levels of surface to deep learning reflected in use of Blooms revised taxonomy [1] and articulated by work in for example [27] assist in outlining a pedagogical relevance structure applied to the four categories and levels of complexity of each. Table 1 shows category experience variation and complexity that forms the basis for the 'pedagogy of experience complexity' reasoning.

6 Compiling the Citizen Learning City

Thinking about the potential for these kinds of urban situated learning activities described as smart learning journeys, we can consider possibilities for engaging citizens in cultural

[4] Wikipedia https://www.wikipedia.org/.

[5] Wikimedia Commons https://commons.wikimedia.org/.

[6] Smart Learning research website http://smartlearning.netfarms.eu/.

Table 1. Illustration of experience complexity for a smart learning journey pedagogical relevance structure.

	Category A **Tasks, Obligations**	Category B **Discussing**	Category C **Being There**	Category D **Knowledge & place as value**
Level 4	Research tasks and topic beforehand, take time doing and reflecting on tasks	Share tasks, content, do additional learning, discuss related experience and knowledge	Live it, being in the picture, live the atmosphere, take more time, seeing the whole and related parts	Knowing, seeing knowledge and place as valuable, personal experience, deeper engagement, 'possibilities'
Level 3	Tasks indirectly related to coursework or assessment	Discuss tasks and topic in relation to time and place	Experience place relating to other people, aspects, memories, connections between places and knowledge	Engage further with knowledge in topics, create upload content for tasks and at locations
Level 2	Do the tasks of interest, directly related to coursework or assessment	Discuss the tasks, help each other with tasks and tech	Locations are of some interest, potential for learning, creativity or inspiration	Click a few content links, save links 'for later', make screenshots of augmentations or tasks
Level 1	Do the tasks, go home	Discuss who does the tasks, how technology works	Go to locations, do tasks, go home	No engagement with content or knowledge, don't create or upload content
Notes on pedagogical structure of relevance	About tasks and assessment. Relevance of activity to coursework or purposes, assessment, further usefulness	About discussion and collaboration. Considerations concern how to expand participation to include the 'dialogic space'	About being in the place, support by showing learner how to engage in the place, with specific indicators and clues or prompts	About value of knowledge in the place, specified by location, time and relevance to other categories. Applying, creating knowledge bound by place with value

or community real world activities, and in so doing, develop their digital skills to support engagement with key civic services. Five relevant initiatives are provided here as examples. Community organisation, research based projects as well as personal activity concepts are highlighted. Projects discussed serve to illustrate how citizen digital skills and literacies could be supported and developed through engagement and participation, potentially enhanced by a pedagogical approach. Purposes of projects vary from creative, artistic and narrative driven to cause and issue related. What each project has in common is that it is situated within an urban environment and makes use of simple to use yet sophisticated technology to build community engagement. The common subtext is that digital skills are developed, and digital, media and information literacies are expanded and explored for those who participate in these activities.

6.1 Participatory Creative Activities and Mapping the City

Mapping the city has a long tradition, for example "urban geographer Kevin Lynch uses the term 'wayfinding' to describe the process of navigating through the 'vast sprawl of our cities'…" [29]. Mapping has been absorbed into smart city cultural communication perhaps partially through use of wayfinding and alert apps such as ThunderMaps (now SaferMe)[7] or Waze[8]. Mapping content to geo-tagged locations has steadily become part of urbanised digital interaction, for example apps such as DB Pedia Places[9] or Geoflow[10] display local content geo-tagged to a GPS smartphone location. Projects outlined here either use specific bespoke smartphone apps, sometimes in conjunction with websites, or free smartphone apps.

Community Maps in Hackney Wick[11]. Community mapping in the Hackney Wick area of East London, UK, records places of interest or concern and is created by residents for residents. A map is developed showing hyper-local points of interest, features or issues and information is attached to each map pin.

Map Local[12]. Map Local was a Birmingham based research project for urban planning, with input from 50 selected residents in specific areas of Birmingham. The project sought to 'unlock the creativity of communities by gathering materials to inform neighbourhood planning'. A bespoke app, 'MapLocal' allowed people to create audio and image content on smartphones that was uploaded to a map on the MapLocal website.

Wood Street Walls[13]. Wood Street Walls is an artist's collective based in East London, UK, and orientates towards encouraging local involvement of the community in arts activities as well as providing affordable studio space for local artists. Wood Street Walls use What3Words[14] and 3WordPhoto[15] as an innovative way to discover local

[7] ThunderMaps, now known as SaferMe, https://play.google.com/store/apps/details?id=com.thundermaps.saferme&hl=en_GB.

[8] Waze https://www.waze.com/en-GB/.

[9] DBPedia Places https://wiki.dbpedia.org/project-categories/user-applications.

[10] Geoflow app https://apps.apple.com/us/app/geoflow-learn-something/id1235949045.

[11] Community mapping in Hackney Wick, London, UK https://communitymaps.org.uk/project/hackney-wick?center=51.5443:-0.0340:15.

[12] Map Local project available at https://chrisspeed.net/?p=1303.

[13] Wood Street Walls Community Art project uses What3Words https://www.youtube.com/watch?v=O-lhbhfibDI.

[14] What3Words https://what3words.com/.

[15] 3WordPhoto app and other what3words photography integration https://what3words.com/products/?category=Photography.

street-art created by these artists and others in the community. The apps are used to document the work available and help to brighten up the community and engage citizens in aspects of urban space ownership.

Tokyo Paper Hunt[16]. The Tokyo paper hunt case study available on the What3Words website outlines a knowledge hunt activity using What3Words, for finding a series of bookshops amongst the complex Tokyo address structure. This kind of concept could be repurposed for many kinds of activities, using maps to find things and then perhaps record further input as a result of finding the locations.

Smart Learning Feedback Maps[17]. Smart Learning Feedback Maps are an outcome of the author's research, being a concept investigated as a solution to participant feedback for the smart learning journeys developed for the research. Feedback could be generated by participants while at locations on a smart learning journey, and pinned to map coordinates from where they submitted the feedback, adding text and images. This would give future participants an idea of what to expect and over time develop a rich source of community generated informal knowledge about smart learning journey activities in the area.

In addition to these examples, the Planetizen[18] website contains numerous other examples of social, civic and more high profile arts projects and apps, and is shared here for information to encourage the reader to investigate these ideas further.

7 Implications and Significance of This Paper

The scope for this kind of smart learning activity offers opportunity for learning that can be both overt (for example arts, environment, or cultural appreciation), and covert (digital skills and competences). That is, in addition to entertainment, civic support or community engagement, digital skills and competences, together with their associated soft skills, can be developed as implicit learning.

Framing smart learning as conceptualised in autonomous smart learning journeys, and utilising both a digital skills framework such as the DigComp 2.1 (or partials of it) and a pedagogy of experience complexity (or aspects of it) may provide engaging practical mechanisms to support citizen digital skills and competences in flexible alternative ways to the more common 'computer training sessions' approach. Digital skills are often not perceived as being limited by a user themselves, e.g. [45], therefore citizens may not be inclined to attend such training courses. Perhaps gamifiying [22] or similar approaches to digital skills development introduces a more attractive option, placing digital skills

---

[16] Tokyo Paper Hunt with What3Words https://what3words.com/news/general/3-word-address-paper-hunt-around-tokyo/.

[17] Smart learning feedback maps webpage demonstration http://smartlearning.netfarms.eu/scl-learner-feedback-map/.

[18] Planetizen examples of relevant apps and projects: https://www.planetizen.com/news/2019/05/104255-neighborhood-based-apps-and-socialized-fear-crime; https://www.planetizen.com/news/2019/08/105653-augmented-reality-and-public-art-new-era-begins-today; *Can Technology Help Involve More Low-Income Residents in the Planning Process* https://www.planetizen.com/node/60880.

development in a covert learning strategy. Learning happens without learners even being aware of it.

8 Conclusions

The research sought to develop a pragmatic fluid pedagogy for smart learning by using smart learning journeys as a simple model of activity, and in so doing highlighted the creative, social and participatory nature of these activities, perhaps demonstrating the potential for ad hoc 'in the wild' urban community engagement that might benefit from these kinds of activities. Further to that realisation was a significant implicit aspect of these kinds of activities, the learner experience of digital tools and functionalities. The process of uncovering how to use apps and platforms was an aspect of learning that itself offered value, indicating that within informal citizen digital skills and competences development contexts this value might be a significant aim and reason for any journey being developed.

Jordon [29] emphasises the importance of participation in the urban environment. His quote from the UK Department of Business, Innovation and Skills sums it up: "… a Smart City should enable every citizen to engage with all the services on offer, public as well as private, in a way best suited to his or her needs. It brings together hard infrastructure, social capital including local skills and community institutions, and (digital) technologies", [15]. If we want all citizens to engage in urban life, we need to find better, easier ways for them to develop their digital skills and competences. Perhaps informal smart learning journeys supported by a framework of digital competences and a flexible pedagogical approach can be part of that effort.

References

1. Anderson, L.W., Krathwohl, D.R. (eds.): A Taxonomy for Learning, Teaching, and Assessing: A Revision of Bloom's Taxonomy of Educational Objectives. Addison Wesley Longman, New York (2001)
2. Anderson, R.: Implications of the information and knowledge society for education. In: Voogt, J., Knezek, G. (eds.) International Handbook of Information Technology in Primary and Secondary Education, vol. 20, pp. 5–22. Springer, Boston (2008). https://doi.org/10.1007/978-0-387-73315-9_1
3. Aurigi, A.: No need to fix: strategic inclusivity in developing and managing the smart city. In: Caldwell, G.A., Smith, C.H., Clift, E.M. (eds.) Digital Futures and the City of Today - New Technologies and Physical Spaces. Intellect, Bristol (2016)
4. Badie, F.: Knowledge building conceptualisation within smart constructivist learning systems. In: Uskov, V.L., Bakken, J.P., Howlett, R.J., Jain, L.C. (eds.) SEEL 2017. SIST, vol. 70, pp. 385–419. Springer, Cham (2018). https://doi.org/10.1007/978-3-319-59454-5_13
5. Bailey, D., Perks, M., Winter, C.: Supporting the digitally left behind. Opinion, Ingenia Issue 76, September 2018
6. Brennen, J.S., Kreiss, D.: Digitalization. In: Jensen, K.B., Rothenbuhler, E.W., Pooley, J.D., Craig, R.T. (eds.) The International Encyclopedia of Communication Theory and Philosophy, pp. 556–566. Wiley-Blackwell, Chichester (2016)
7. Bughin, J., Hazan, E., Lund, S., Dählström, P., Wiesinger, A., Subramaniam, A.: Skill Shift: Automation and the Future of the Workforce. McKinsey, Toronto (2018)

8. Carretero, S., Vuorikari, R., Punie, Y.: Digital Competence Framework for Citizens (DigComp 2.1). European Commission. Publications Office of the European Union, Luxembourg (2017)
9. Carroll, J.M., Hoffman, B., Han, K., Rosson, M.B.: Reviving community networks: hyper-locality and suprathresholding in Web 2.0 designs. Pers. Ubiquit. Comput. **19**, 477–491 (2015). https://doi.org/10.1007/s00779-014-0831-y
10. Cobo, C.: Mechanisms to identify and study the demand for innovation skills in world-renowned organizations. On the Horizon **21**(2), 96–106 (2013). https://doi.org/10.1108/10748121311322996
11. Cope, C.: Educationally critical aspects of the concept of an information system. Inf. Sci. **5**(2), 67–78 (2002)
12. Cutajar, M.: The student experience of learning using networked technologies: an emergent progression of expanding awareness. Technol. Pedagogy Educ. (2017). https://doi.org/10.1080/1475939x.2017.1327451
13. Dede, C.: Comparing frameworks for "21st century skills". In: James Bellanca, J., Brandt, R. (eds.) 21st Century Skills: Rethinking How Students Learn. Solution Tree, Bloomington (2010)
14. De Lange, M., De Waal, M.: Owning the city: new media and citizen engagement in urban design. In: Urban Design: Community-Based Planning, pp. 89–110 (2013)
15. Department for Business Innovation and Skills: Smart cities: background paper (2013). https://www.gov.uk/government/publications/smart-cities-background-paper
16. Department for Education, Gov UK.: Guidance, National standards for essential digital skills (2019). https://www.gov.uk/government/publications/national-standards-for-essential-digital-skills
17. Dron, J.: Smart learning environments, and not so smart learning environments: a systems view. Smart Learn. Environ. **5**, 25 (2018). https://doi.org/10.1186/s40561-018-0075-9
18. EAEA: Manifesto for Adult Learning in the 21st Century: The Power and Joy of Learning (2019)
19. Fang, J.: Colorful robots teach children computer programming: how do you make coding something that kids want to do? Meet Bo and Yana: covert teaching machines. ZdNET (2013). https://www.zdnet.com/article/colorful-robots-teach-children-computer-programming/
20. Freigang, S., Schlenker, L., Köhler, T.: A conceptual framework for designing smart learning environments. Smart Learn. Environ. **5**, 27 (2018). https://doi.org/10.1186/s40561-018-0076-8
21. Goggin, G.: Afterword: why digital inclusion now? In: Ragnedda, M., Mutsvairo, B. (eds.) Digital Inclusion: An International Comparative Analysis. Lexington Books, Lanham (2018)
22. Goh, D.H., Ang, R.P., Tan, H.C.: Strategies for designing effective psychotherapeutic gaming interventions for children and adolescents. Comput. Hum. Behav. **24**(2008), 2217–2235 (2008)
23. Goodspeed, R.: Smart cities: moving beyond urban cybernetics to tackle wicked problems. Cambridge J. Reg. Econ. Soc. (2014). https://doi.org/10.1093/cjres/rsu013
24. Gurwitsch, A.: The Field of Consciousness. Du-quense University Press, Pittsburgh (1964)
25. Han, K.: Understanding the application of mobile technology in local community contexts. Doctoral dissertation (2015)
26. Hernandez, K., Roberts, T.: Leaving no one behind in a digital world. K4D Emerging Issues Report. Institute of Development Studies, Brighton, UK (2018)
27. Hounsell, D.: Contrasting conceptions of essay-writing. In: Marton, F., Hounsell, D., Entwistle, N. (eds.) The Experience of Learning: Implications for Teaching and Studying in Higher Education, 3rd edn., pp. 106–125. University of Edinburgh, Centre for Teaching, Learning and Assessment, Edinburgh (2005). (Internet)

28. Ireland, J., Tambyah, M.M., Neofa, Z., Harding, T.: The tale of four researchers: trials and triumphs from the phenomenographic research specialization. In: AARE 2008 International Education Conference, Changing Climates, Education for Sustainable Futures, 30th November–4th December 2008, Queensland University of Technology, Brisbane, QUT Digital Repository (2009)
29. Jordan, S.: Writing the smart city: "relational space" and the concept of "belonging". Pract.: J. Creative Writ. Res. **1** (2015)
30. Kaapu, T., Tiainen, T.: Consumers' views on privacy in e-commerce. Scand. J. Inf. Syst. **21**(1), 3–22 (2009)
31. Koole, M.: A social constructionist approach to phenomenographic analysis of identity positioning in networked learning. In: Hodgson, V., Jones, C., de Laat, M., McConnell, D., Ryberg, T., Sloep, P. (eds.) 2012 Proceedings of the 8th International Conference on Networked Learning (2012)
32. Koper, R.: Conditions for effective smart learning environments. Smart Learn. Environ. **1**, 5 (2014). https://doi.org/10.1186/s40561-014-0005-4
33. Law, N., Woo, D., de la Torre, J., Wong, G.: A Global Framework of Reference on Digital Literacy Skills for Indicator 4.4.2. UNESCO Institute for Statistics (2018). https://unesdoc.unesco.org/ark:/48223/pf0000265403
34. Liu, D., Huang, R., Wosinski, M.: Future trends of smart learning: Chinese perspective. In: Liu, D., Huang, R., Wosinski, M. (eds.) Smart Learning in Smart Cities. LNET, pp. 185–215. Springer, Singapore (2017). https://doi.org/10.1007/978-981-10-4343-7_8
35. Lister, P. J.: Understanding experience complexity in a smart learning journey. J. Appl. Res. High. Educ (2020). (Manuscript submitted for publication)
36. Lorenzo, N., Gallon, R.: Smart pedagogy for smart learning. In: Daniela, L. (ed.) Didactics of Smart Pedagogy, pp. 41–69. Springer, Cham (2019). https://doi.org/10.1007/978-3-030-01551-0_3
37. Martínez-Cantos, J.L.: Digital skills gaps: A pending subject for gender digital inclusion in the European Union. Eur. J. Commun. **32**, 419–438 (2017)
38. Marton, F.: Phenomenography - describing conceptions of the world around us. Instr. Sci. **10**(1981), 177–200 (1981)
39. Marton, F., Booth, S.: Learning and Awareness. Lawrence Erlbaum Associates, Mahwah (1997)
40. McLaughlin, C., Lee, M.: Personalised and self regulated learning in the Web 2.0 era: international exemplars of innovative pedagogy using social software. Australas. J. Educ. Technol. **26**(1), 28–43 (2010)
41. Montoya, S.: Meet the SDG 4 Data: Indicator 4.4.1 on Skills for a Digital World. UNESCO website (2018). http://uis.unesco.org/en/blog/meet-sdg-4-data-indicator-4-4-1-skills-digital-world
42. Mullagh, L., Blair, L., Dunn, N.: Beyond the 'smart' city: reflecting human values in the urban environment. In: The Third International Conference on Smart Systems, Devices and Technologies (SMART 2014). Thinkmind (2014)
43. Nikolov, R., Shoikova, E., Krumova, M., Kovatcheva, E., Dimitrov, V., Shikalanov, A.: Learning in a smart city environment. J. Commun. Comput. **13**(2016), 338–350 (2016)
44. Ojo, A., Dzhusupova, Z., Curry, E.: Exploring the nature of the smart cities research landscape. In: Gil-Garcia, J.R., Pardo, T.A., Nam, T. (eds.) Smarter as the New Urban Agenda. PAIT, vol. 11, pp. 23–47. Springer, Cham (2016). https://doi.org/10.1007/978-3-319-17620-8_2
45. Porat, E., Blau, I., Barak, A.: Measuring digital literacies: junior high-school students' perceived competencies versus actual performance. Comput. Educ. (2018). https://doi.org/10.1016/j.compedu.2018.06.030

46. Pyyry, N.: Geographies of hanging out: playing, dwelling and thinking with the city. In: Sacré, H., De Visscher, S. (eds.) Learning the City. SE, pp. 19–33. Springer, Cham (2017). https://doi.org/10.1007/978-3-319-46230-1_2
47. Sacré, H., De Visscher, S.: A cultural perspective on the city. In: Sacré, H., De Visscher, S. (eds.) Learning the City. SE, pp. 1–17. Springer, Cham (2017). https://doi.org/10.1007/978-3-319-46230-1_1
48. Salim, F., Haque, U.: Urban computing in the wild: a survey on large scale participation and citizen engagement with ubiquitous computing, cyber physical systems, and Internet of Things. Int. J. Hum.-Comput. Stud. **81**, 31–48 (2015)
49. Siemens, G.: New structures and spaces of learning: the systemic impact of connective knowledge, connectivism, and networked learning. Paper presented at the Encontro Sobre Web 2.0, Braga, Portugal (2008)
50. Souleles, N., Savva, S., Watters, H., Annesley, A., Bull, B.: A phenomenographic investigation on the use of iPads among undergraduate art and design students. Br. J. Educ. Technol. (2014). https://doi.org/10.1111/bjet.12132
51. Thompson, K.M.: Multiple layers of digital inclusion. Online Curr. **30**(1), 38–40 (2016)
52. Quieng, M.C., Lim, P.P., Lucas, M.R.D.: 21st century-based soft skills: spotlight on non-cognitive skills in a cognitive-Laden dentistry program. Eur. J. Contemp. Educ. **11**(1), 72–81 (2015). https://doi.org/10.13187/ejced.2015.11.72
53. van Laar, E., van Deursen, A., van Dijk, J., de Haan, J.: The relation between 21st-century skills and digital skills: a systematic literature review. Comput. Hum. Behav. **72**, 577–588 (2017). https://doi.org/10.1016/j.chb.2017.03.010
54. Vosloo, S.: Guidelines: Designing Inclusive Digital Solutions and Developing Digital Skills. United Nations Educational, Scientific and Cultural Organization (2018)
55. UNESCO: Sustainable Development Goal Four targets (2016). https://en.unesco.org/education2030-sdg4/targets
56. United Nations Population Fund: State of world population 2007. Unleashing the Potential of Urban Growth (2007). https://www.unfpa.org/sites/default/files/pub-pdf/695_filename_sowp2007_eng.pdf
57. Wildemeersch, D., Jütte, W.: digital the new normal-multiple challenges for the education and learning of adults. Eur. J. Res. Educ. Learn. Adults **8**(1), 7–20 (2017). https://doi.org/10.3384/rela.2000-7426.relae13
58. World Urbanization Prospects: The 2018 Revision (2018). https://population.un.org/wup/Publications/
59. Yarosh, M., Beneitone, P.: Introduction. In: Yarosh, M., Serbati, A., Seery, A. (eds.) Developing Generic Competences Outside the University Classroom. Editorial Universidad de Granada, Granada (2016)
60. Zoltowski, C.B., Oakes, W.C., Cardella, M.E.: Students' ways of experiencing human-centered design. J. Eng. Educ. **101**(1), 28–59 (2012)

Learning Analytics Data Flow and Visualizing for Ubiquitous Learning Logs in LMS and Learning Analytics Dashboard

Songran Liu[1(✉)], Kousuke Mouri[2], and Hiroaki Ogata[3]

[1] BiiiiiT, Inc., Tokyo, Japan
liu.songran@biiiiit.com
[2] Tokyo University of Agriculture and Technology, Fuchu, Japan
mourikousuke@gmail.com
[3] Kyoto University, Kyoto, Japan
hiroaki.ogata@gmail.com

Abstract. In this paper, we describe about a kind of data flow design that between ubiquitous learning log system called SCROLL and learning analytics and visualizing system called Learning Analytics Dashboard (LAD). SCROLL is a ubiquitous learning system what is logging students' learning behaviors data in database, and SCROLL can provide students suitable learning method and location to learn efficiently. Lots of paper show that it is appreciate to share the learning data in SCROLL to the other learning analytics system like LTI, Bookroll, Moodle and so on. Learning Analytics Dashboard (LAD) is also a learning data analytics and visualizing system. So share students' learning data from SCROLL to LAD to show and help students to know their students' learning situation is the proposal of this paper.

Keywords: SCROLL · Learning Analytics Dashboard · Ubiquitous learning · xAPI

1 Introduction

1.1 Ubiquitous Learning

Ubiquitous learning can be defined as an everyday learning environment that is supported by mobile and embedded computers and wireless networks in our everyday life [1]. It is aimed to provide learners with content and interaction anytime and anywhere [2]. The learning process includes the real-life experience augmented with virtual information and is adapted to the learner and learner's environment. The content objects, activities, and the interaction with the system and with other humans (including instructors and peers) are customized according to learner's current goals of learning, interests and preferences, cognitive characteristics, history and current state of competency in the subject matter in hand, the characteristics and demands of the location, the technology being used as the medium and facilitator for learning, and the context of the situation in which the learning is taking place. Figure 1 shows the position of ubiquitous learning.

N. Streitz and S. Konomi (Eds.): HCII 2020, LNCS 12203, pp. 548–557, 2020.
https://doi.org/10.1007/978-3-030-50344-4_39

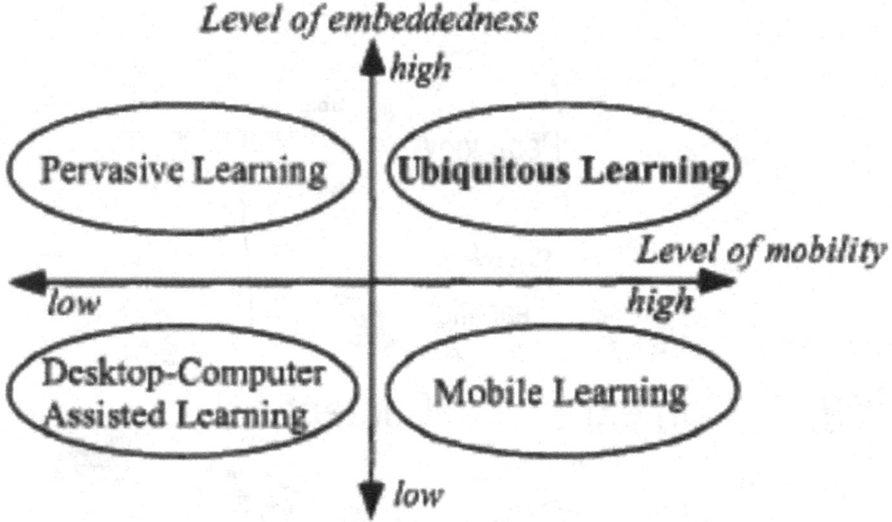

Fig. 1. The position of ubiquitous learning.

In past ten years, with the development of mobile networking, like 4G or 5G, Ubiquitous learning is easier and more comfortable for students. Students can watch much more kind of learning content with various media format, like audio, video even AR and VR in their mobile phone.

What kind of learning content and behavior are more suitable for students is always a point of issue.

1.2 Seamless Learning

Seamless learning is a learning notion that emphasises the bridging of different learning efforts across a variety of learning settings (such as formal and informal learning, individual and social learning, and learning in physical and digital realms), ideally by leveraging mobile technology in 1:1 (one-device-or-more-per-student) to assist individual students in carrying out cross-space learning on a 24 × 7 basis. Building on the outcomes of the existing NIE seamless learning research team in the past 6 years, this research area is intended to further investigate and theorise the nature of seamless learning as well as derive design principles for nurturing the disposition (or a culture) of lifelong seamless learning among the young students beyond school-based episodic seamless learning interventions [3].

Classroom learning is important for student to share their learning behavior data to teachers. Most time, students learning out classroom. If teachers can know what the students have learned or how they have learned out classroom, teachers can give more advice to students. Figure 2 shows mobile seamless learning and its pedagogy [4].

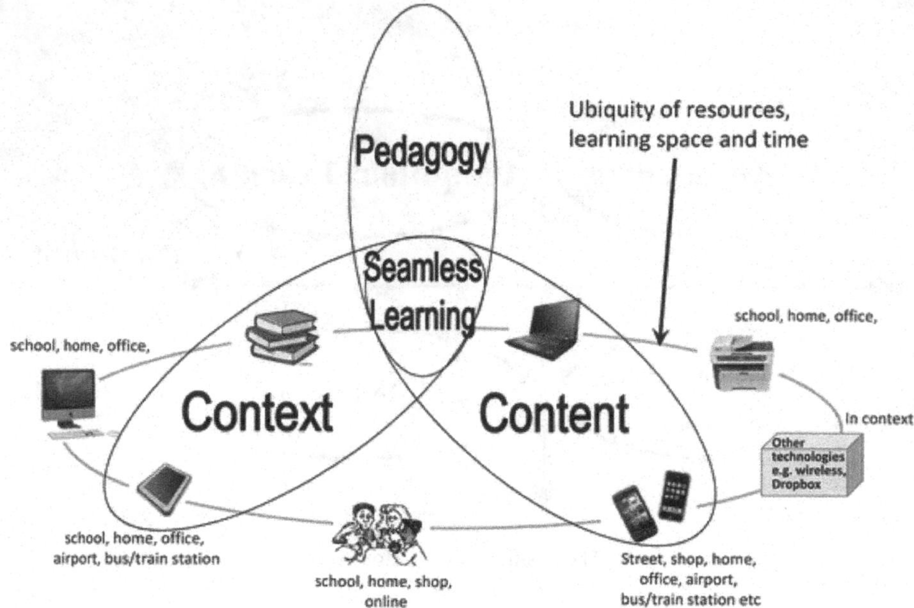

Fig. 2. Mobile seamless learning and its pedagogy

1.3 Approach

To share students' learning data between teachers and students seamlessly, this paper describe a kind of data flow between SCROLL, the ubiquitous learning system, and Learning Analytics Dashboard, the real-time analyzing and visualizing learning data system, to make a seamless learning environment using SCROLL.

2 Related Works

2.1 Scroll

With the evolution of the mobile device, People prefer to record learning contents using mobile devices instead of taking memos on paper. Most of the language learners have their own learning note. In this paper, learning log is defined as a recorded form of knowledge or learning experiences acquired in our daily lives. SCROLL has been developed for supporting international students in Japan to learn Japanese language from what they have learned in formal and informal setting. It adopt an approach of sharing user created contents among users and is constructed based on a LORE (Log-Organize-Recall-Evaluate) model which is shown in Fig. 1. And the SCROLL system UI is shown in Fig. 3 [5].

SCROLL has been developed for ten years, recently it is renewable developed with more useful UI and it can be easily integrated with LTI and other LMS. Therefore this paper's data flow design chooses SCROLL as base project.

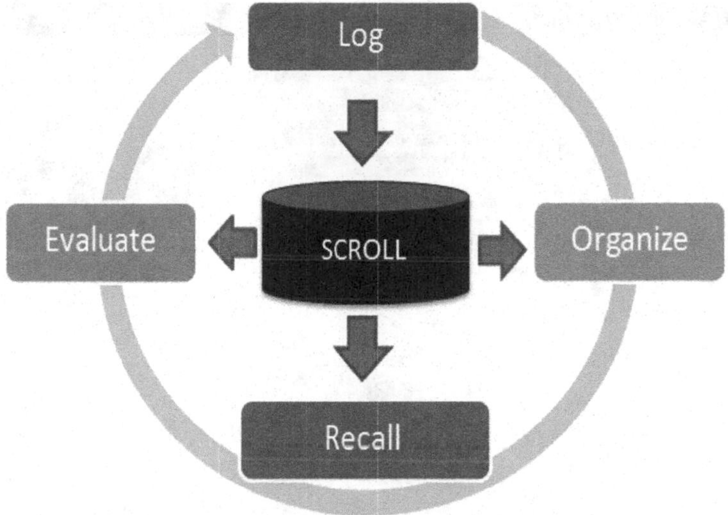

Fig. 3. LORE model in SCROLL.

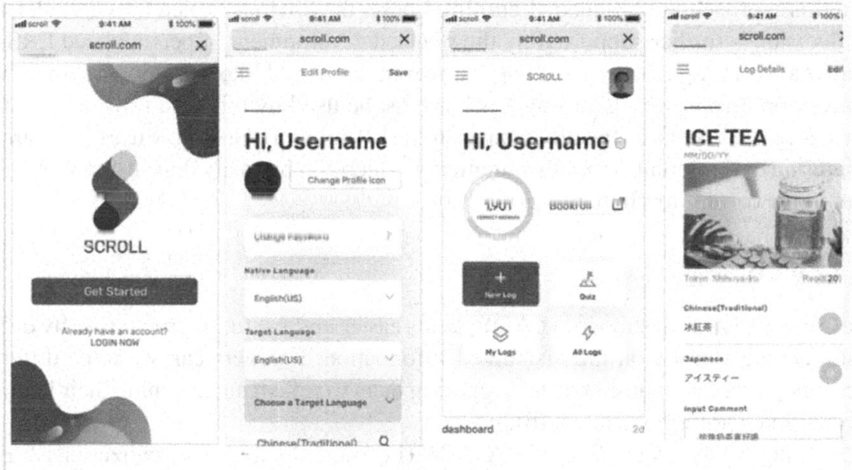

Fig. 4. SCROLL system UI.

2.2 Learning Locker

A LRS is required to share students' data from SCROLL to other learning system. Although more are likely to become available as the xAPI is more broadly adopted, two solutions currently exist that are independent of a LMS: Learning Locker, which is an open source LRS championed by HT2, and distributed under a GPL3.0 li-cense.; and SCORM Engine/Cloud & Watershed LRS which are commercial solutions developed by Rustici software [6].

Figure 5 shows the UI of Learning Locker.

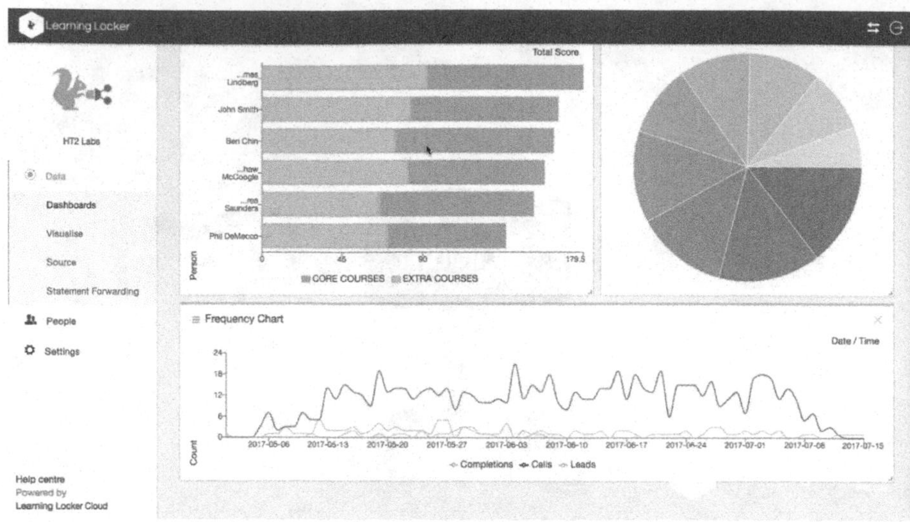

Fig. 5. Learning Locker system UI

In this approach, we has made Learning Locker the obvious choice for a default LRS. This decision is further supported by the planned development of personalized LRSs in the current Learning Locker roadmap. However, we would like to emphasize that there is no a priori reason why Learning Locker must be used by this data flow design. Any other LRS could be used. Indeed, changing the LRS that the data flow uses is as simple as changing the endpoint for xAPI statements, which can be easily done using web based forms in the current implementation.

2.3 LaViEW

A learning analytics dashboard (LAD) assists easier and useful interpretation by different stakeholders based on the visualized information. Learners can view the different indicators presented in dashboards, triggering them to reflect and examine their learning behavior and learning outcomes [6].

Learning Analytics Dashboard LAViEW (Learning Analytics Visualizations & Evidence Widgets) can be added as an external tool in LMS and accessed by both teachers and students. LAViEW automatically handles the role from the LTI and displays different panels of graphs based on customized views. When the user login to the system, they need to select the content and the period of time they want to analyze from Context Selector panel (see Fig. 4 as reference). According to the user's selection the data in every panel is updated. We created an Overview panel which gives aggregated statistics about selected course. In this section both teachers and students can see average statistics of the class on the bottom and selected student's record on the top [7]. The architecture of LaViEW is shown as Fig. 6.

Currently none of the LADs capture this preference of the teachers to relate problems and indicators and assist them to plan interventions directly from the dashboard. This paper presents LAViEW (Learning Analytics Visualizations & Evidence Widgets),

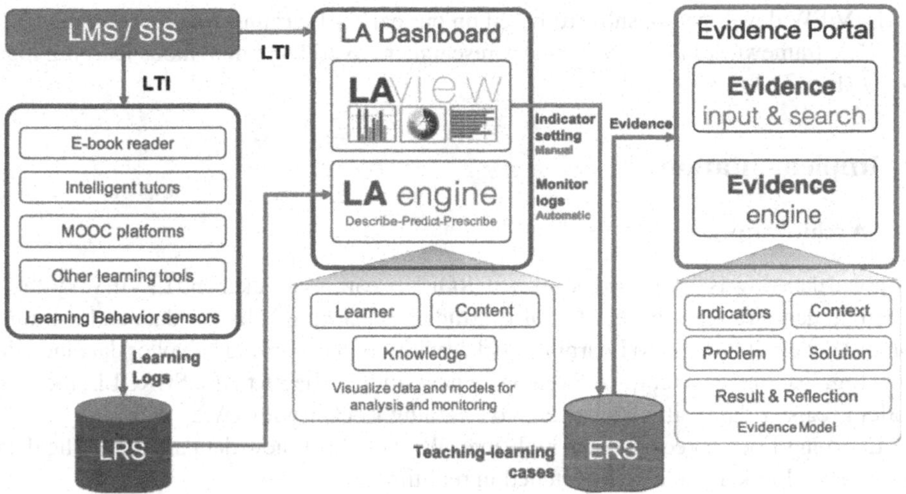

Fig. 6. The architecture of LaViEW

a LAD that supports the users to analyze learning logs and gather evidence of learning. Figure 4 gives sample visualizations in the current version of the LAViEW dashboard. Readers can access the system at live.let.media.kyotou.ac.jp/analysis to explore the features with anonymized dataset [8].

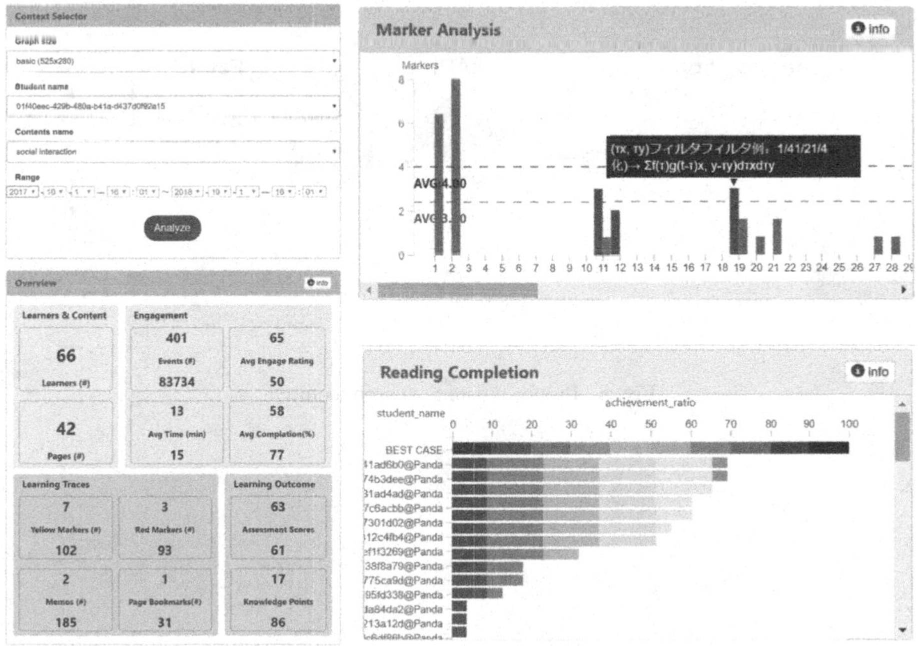

Fig. 7. Analytics modules in LaViEW.

LaViEW developed dashboard based on our earlier Learning Analytics Framework [7]. This framework helps teachers and researchers to collect anonymous learning logs easily (Fig. 7).

3 Implementation

3.1 Architecture

Proposal data flow is developed base on SCROLL, Learning Locker and LaViEW system. When student are learning in SCROLL. Students' learning behavior data and learning content data will be send to Learning Locker with xAPI. Learning behavior data include view log, like log, answer quiz. Even when new students begin to use SCROLL, the new student register data will also be send to Learning Locker with xAPI.

Learning Locker receive data real-time. We can check new data anytime. The data in Learning Locker can also be fetched in real-time.

In LaViEW, we develop a data tracking module to fetch data every 15 min to collect data. Then sink the data to database to use. Once data has sinked, analytics module will update UI to show newest data as graph in system.

All system architecture is shown as Fig. 8.

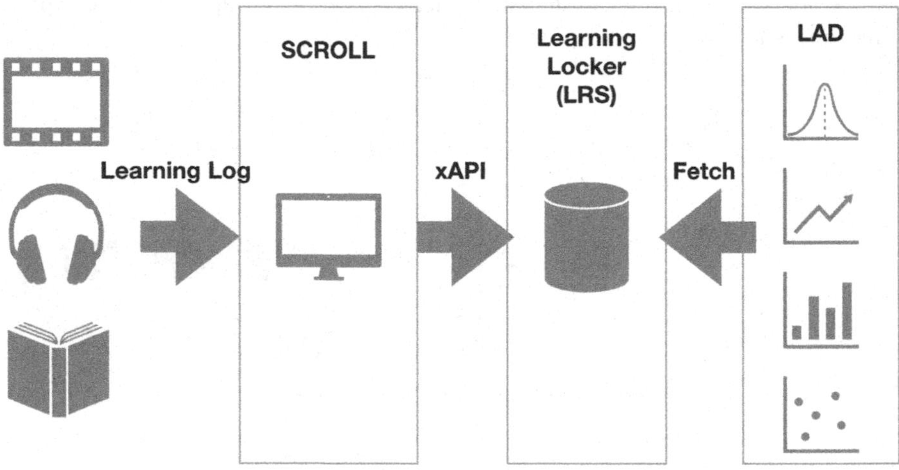

Fig. 8. Proposal data flow architecture.

Figure 9 shows sample behavior type in SCROLL which will be send to Learning Locker.

A	B
Major Actions	**Description**
Play Audio	A user wants to listen the pronunciation of the word
ALL	A user wants to browse logs in SCROLL server
GROUP	A user wants to see his/her's peers activities
SEARCH	A User is looking for a particular word/log
Too easy	A user remembers the word/The word wasnot difficult to recall
Easy	A user finds the word easy to remember
General	The user finds the word neither easy nor difficult
Difficult	The user finds the word difficult in answering the quiz
Too difficult	The user finds the word very difficult to answering the quiz
More quiz	The user is ready for next quiz
Yes	The user acknowledge that he/she remembers the word
No	The user acknowledge that he/she doesnot remembers the word
GROUP	A user wants to see the Group features of the SCROLL
ADD	A user wants to form/create a new group in SCROLL
Sign out	

Fig. 9. Sample action type in SCROLL.

Learning Locker receive data and show as JSON format. We can check data in anytime. Like this, when student with account id a8139d78b3f147dcaf4ca2942675c16d view log with log id d36ff13daf9e4742a0493bc0b616a015 in SCROLL, data will be send. In Learning Locker page, it shown like Fig. 10. The learning content data also are shown in Learning Locker.

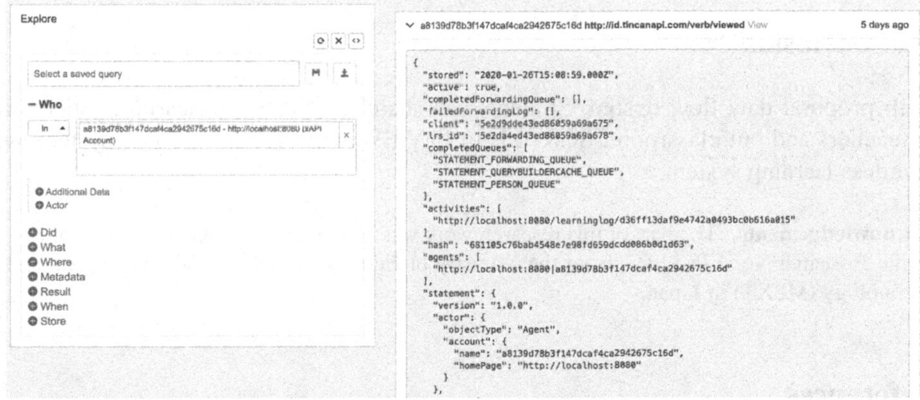

Fig. 10. Behavior data in Learning Locker.

In LaViEW, analytics module will show learning situation for teacher or students theirselves. Shown as Fig. 11.

フィードバックパネル　すべて選択　メールを送る　説明

10 件を表示　検索

学生名	時間（分）	達成	操作	日	長期操作	赤マーカ...	黄マーカ...	メモ	ブッ...
Yoshitake Daichi	54	100	281	6	57	0	4	6	2
劉 松然	0	0	0	0	0	0	0	0	0
Wille Luiza	0	0	0	0	0	0	0	0	0
ScrollTeststudent1LN ...	0	0	0	0	0	0	0	0	0
ScrollTeststudent2LN...	12	17	22	3	9	0	0	1	0
ScrollTestteacher2LN...	0	0	0	0	0	0	0	0	0
ScrollTestteacherLN ...	0	0	0	0	0	0	0	0	0

7 件中 1 件から 7件 を表示中　前 1 次

リアルタイムグラフ　On Off 説明

Fig. 11. Learning situation in LaViEW.

4 Conclusion

With proposal data flow design. Students can share their data and learning situation to teachers and out classroom. SCROLL in LaViEW will become learning system as seamless learning system.

Acknowledgements. The part of this research work was supported by the Grant in-Aid for Scientific Research No. 17K12947 from the Ministry of Education, Culture, Sports, Science and Technology (MEXT) in Japan.

References

1. Ogata, H., Matsuka, Y., El-Bishouty, M.M., Yano, Y.: LORAMS: linking physical objects and videos for capturing and sharing learning experiences towards ubiquitous learning. Int. J. Mob. Learn. Organ. **3**(4), 337–350 (2009)

2. Hwang, G.-J., Tsai, C.-C., Yang, S.J.H.: Criteria, strategies and research issues of context-aware ubiquitous learning. Educ. Technol. Soc. **11**(2), 81–91 (2008)
3. Wong, L.-H., Looi, C.-K.: Vocabulary learning by mobile-assisted authentic content creation and social meaning making: Two case studies. J. Comput. Assist. Learn. **26**(5), 421–433 (2010)
4. Nicholas, H., Ng, W.: Mobile seamless learning and its pedagogy. In: Wong, L.-H., Milrad, M., Specht, M. (eds.) Seamless Learning in the Age of Mobile Connectivity, pp. 261–280. Springer, Singapore (2015). https://doi.org/10.1007/978-981-287-113-8_13
5. Ogata, H., Yin, C., Okubo, F., Shimada, A., Kojima, K., Yamada, M.: E-book-based learning analytics in university education. In: International Conference on Computer in Education (ICCE 2015), pp. 401–406 (2015)
6. Kitto, K., Cross, S., Waters, Z., Lupton, M.: Learning analytics beyond the LMS: the connected learning analytics toolkit. In: Proceedings of the Fifth International Conference on Learning Analytics and Knowledge, pp. 11–15 (2015)
7. Durall, E., Gros, B.: Learning analytics as a metacognitive tool. In: Proceedings of the 6th International Conference on Computer Supported Education - Volume 1, Portugal, pp. 380–384 (2014)
8. Majumdar, R., Akçapınar, A., Akçapınar, G., Flanagan, B., Ogata, H.: LAViEW: learning analytics dashboard towards evidence-based education (LAK 2019) (2019)

Applying Deep Learning in Creative Re-creation of Changsha Kiln Cultural Relics

Wen Lu(✉)

School of Fine Arts, Hunan Normal University, 36, Lushan Street, Changsha 410081, Hunan, China
luwen@hunnu.edu.cn

Abstract. Changsha Kiln, world-renowned for its rich under-glazed porcelain, is a famous export porcelain kiln in the Tang Dynasty, began to thrive during the middle and late periods of the Tang Dynasty (618–907 AD), but then declined during the Five Dynasty periods (907–960 AD). Since the beginning of the new century, with the country's increasing emphasis on the protection and innovation of cultural heritage, Changsha Kiln has gradually moved towards revival. However, the lack of ceramic products design talents, difficult to blend traditional and modern styles, and lack of support for creative design are obstacles to revival. To this end, this paper proposes an open creative design platform for cultural relics re-creation in Changsha kiln. Three basic components built based on deep learning technology in this platform: cultural relics knowledge base, cultural relic image feature database, and search engine based on semantics and images. With this platform, provide cultural relics element retrieval and creative design services for the general public, cultural creative designer and SMEs, which can promote the integrated development of culture and technology, and promote the cultural industry to become a pillar industry of the national economy.

Keywords: Changsha Kiln · Cultural relic elements · Deep learning · Creative design

1 Introduction

The ceramic industry is a special industry with dual attributes of industry and art, practical and aesthetic functions, and shoulders the dual tasks of promoting the Chinese culture and revitalizing the national industry. Changsha Tongguan Kiln, a private-run commercial kiln, began to thrive during the middle and late periods of the Tang Dynasty (618–907 AD), but then declined during the Five Dynasty periods (907–960 AD). The site of the kiln was discovered in the 1950s at WaZhaping in Tongguan town. It was later named "Changsha Kiln", or "Tongguan Kiln" or "WaZhaping Kiln" in the academia, but during the Tang dynasty, it was called "Shizhu Kiln". Since the beginning of the new century, China has increasingly paid attention to the protection and utilization of cultural heritage. In 2006, the Changsha Tongguan Kiln Site was identified as one of the 100 major national heritage protection projects. In 2010, the Changsha Tongguan Kiln Site was included

N. Streitz and S. Konomi (Eds.): HCII 2020, LNCS 12203, pp. 558–568, 2020.
https://doi.org/10.1007/978-3-030-50344-4_40

in the list of the first batch of National Archaeological Site Parks and officially started construction [1, 2].

For a long time, China's deconstruction, reconstruction, and innovation of folk culture and art have been achieved through a complete cultural heritage and institutional system. At the beginning of the 21st century, the concept of "intangible cultural heritage" was introduced in China government, and a variety of folk cultural arts were incorporated into the entire society management system to promote innovation. Changsha Tongguan Kiln ceramic technology is no exception [3]. In 2009, it was included in the Hunan Intangible Cultural Heritage List, and in 2011 it became the third batch of national intangible heritage protection projects. As "Chinese elements" become more and more popular in modern design, the local folk ceramic art in Tongguan Kiln has also returned to the market. Today, more than a hundred home-made ceramic workshops, ceramic art studios, and ceramics dealers are scattered throughout the ancient town. Their products include four main varieties: collectibles, daily necessities, art ceramics, and tourist souvenirs. In March and October 2018, the author and his team surveyed Tongguan town and found that the main problems faced by local ceramic producers are: 1. overlapping product types and serious homogeneity; 2. long development cycles and high costs; 3. low product market competitiveness, and it can not meet the user's personalized needs for ceramic products on time. The reason is mainly due to the poor communication channels between producers and end consumers. To solve these problems, this paper proposes an open Changsha Kiln cultural relics creative design platform. This platform uses deep learning technology to realize the redesign of cultural relic elements and provide developers with support for elements search and creative production [4].

2 Platform Design

2.1 Platform Functional Architecture Design

The Changsha Kiln cultural relics creative design platform includes basic service layer, application support layer, and operation interaction layer, as shown in Fig. 1.

Basic Service Layer. Includes web crawler module, cultural relics knowledge management module, ceramic product databases, and data cleaning module. The web crawler module is mainly used to collect, aggregate, and extract the cultural and historical information, research literature, and graphic image data of Changsha Kiln cultural relics and other handicraft products on the Internet, and import them into the ceramic product database. The cultural relics knowledge management module is mainly used for the extraction of Changsha Kiln cultural relic elements' text and image features to build the Changsha Kiln cultural relics knowledge base and cultural relics image feature database. The ceramic product database is mainly used for unified management of all ceramic product data while providing professionals with the ability to fill in or upload related data and images of ceramic products. The data cleaning module mainly completes a series of data pre-processing tasks, such as data cleaning, conversion, deduplication, denoising, and standardization of the collected ceramic product data.

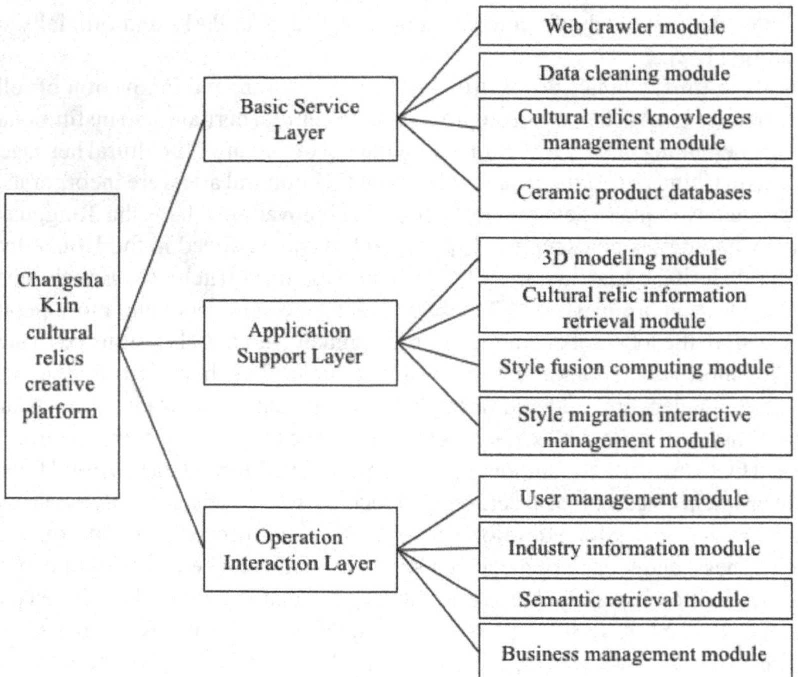

Fig. 1. Platform functional framework

Application Support Layer. Includes a cultural relic information retrieval module [5] based on semantics, a cultural relic elements style fusion computing module, a style migration interactive management module, and the 3D modeling module [6, 7]. The cultural relics information retrieval module is mainly used to provide semantic-based element data retrieval, including ceramic product data, cultural relics knowledge data and cultural relics image feature data. The style transfer interactive management module realizes the fusion of content images and style images to generate new creative materials. The style fusion calculation module obtains a neural network model, which contains a large number of cultural relic image features, through the training of convolutional neural networks in a large number of ceramic relics and ceramic product images. The 3D modeling module realizes the 3D display of creative products.

Operation Interaction Layer. Mainly aimed at designers, the public and enterprises and other end-users, which provides interactive re-engineering design functions [8] of cultural relic elements in Changsha Kiln: including user management module, industry information module, business management module, and semantic retrieval module. The user management module is used to manage user information and permissions. The industry information module is used to manage the news and announcements issued by the platform. The business management module is used to monitor and manage the business requests that occur on the platform. The semantic retrieval module is used for the retrieval and browsing of cultural relic materials based on the semantic retrieval of cultural relics.

2.2 Platform Interaction Design

This research uses related technical means such as multimedia and deep learning and adopts a parallel design working mode. Users can store, model, design, and improve activities of cultural relics in real-time, intuitive, and visual in immersive or non-immersive environments. Through the design service and orientation service for the reconstruction of cultural relic elements, the one-time success rate of product design is improved.

The user enters a search sentence on the search page, calls the cultural relics semantic retrieval module of the application support layer to obtain related cultural relics samples (as shown in Fig. 2); then the cultural relics related features, including the shape, the pattern and the glaze are obtained by querying the cultural relics image feature database.

Then use the ceramic product sample search the relevant features of modern artifacts from the cultural feature image feature database; after choosing types, patterns and glazes to be fused (as shown in Fig. 3), the platform calls the style fusion calculation module to define artifact fusion rules (as shown in Fig. 4).

Finally, through the style transfer interactive management module, a two-dimensional image of the fused artifact is generated, and then the 3D modeling module is called to output the final design rendering (as shown in Fig. 5).

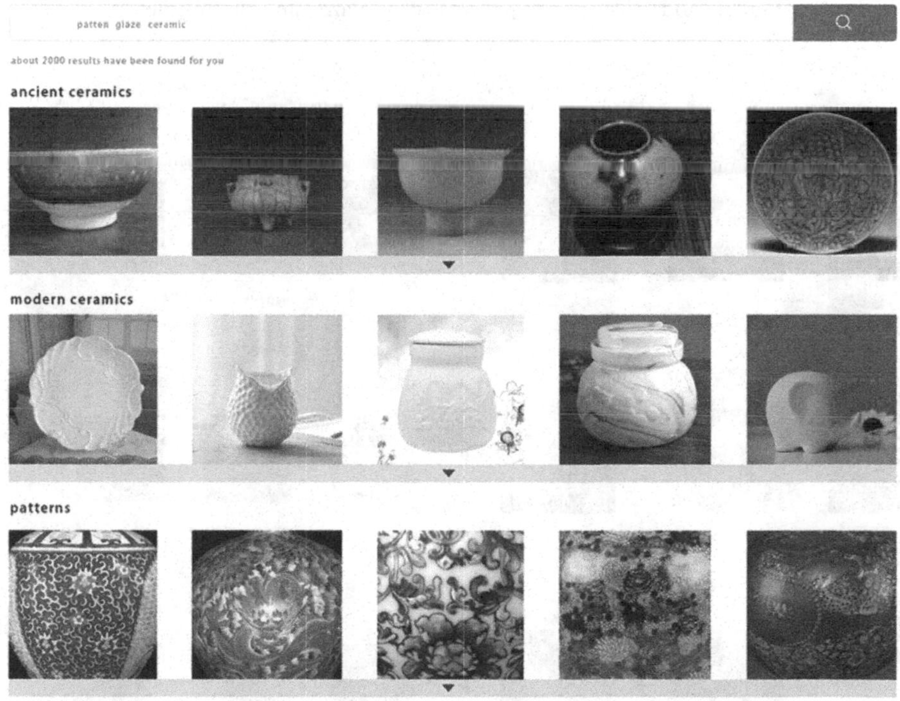

Fig. 2. Retrieve cultural relic elements in search page

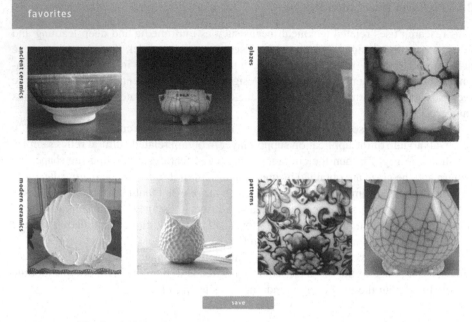

Fig. 3. Add the shape, the pattern and the glaze into your favorites

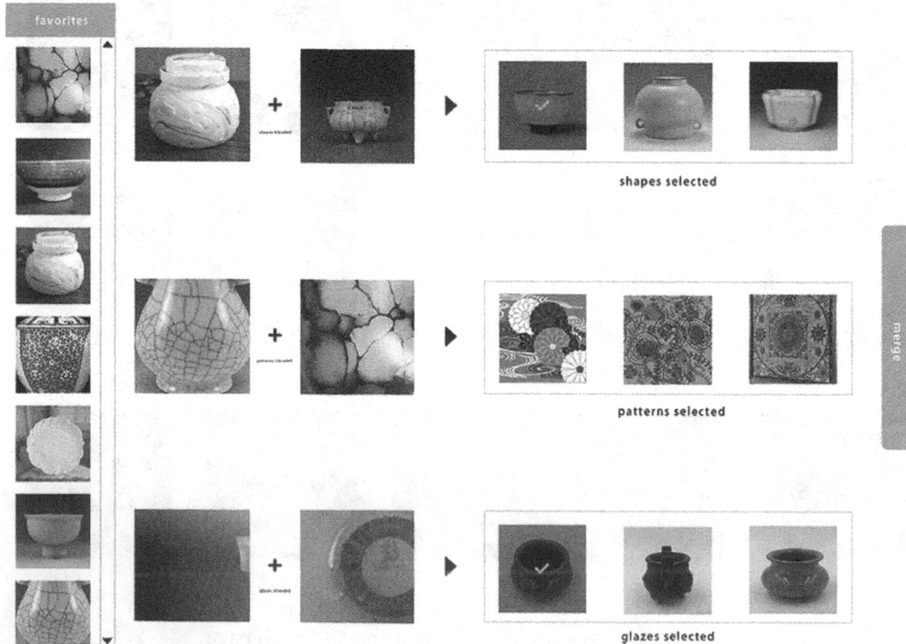

Fig. 4. Style fusion calculation

Fig. 5. Generate a 2D image of the fused artifact and then call the 3D modeling module

3 Technology Overview

The innovative design of this research aims to start with the construction of Changsha Kiln's cultural relic knowledge ontology library and material synthesis system with deep learning technology and build a cultural relics creative design platform to open up all links of the entire ceramic creative design service industry chain.

In recent years, the rise of artificial intelligence can be said to benefit from the success of deep learning. The three main factors driving deep neural network breakthroughs are massive training data, powerful computing architecture, and related advances in the academic field. Therefore, the performance of deep learning in image classification, style transfer, and natural language processing not only surpasses traditional methods but also exceeds the human level. All of this creates huge potential for new businesses that use deep learning to solve practical problems.

Convolutional Neural Network. After 2015, given the outstanding performance of deep learning algorithms such as convolutional neural networks in image feature extraction, and the fit of VGG-19 networks to image style extraction and content extraction tasks, convolutional neural networks have become the mainstream framework in this field. Convolutional Neural Network (CNN) provides an end-to-end learning model, and parameters in the model can be trained by traditional gradient descent methods. The trained convolutional neural network can learn the features in the image and complete the extraction and classification of image features. As an important research branch in the field of neural networks, the characteristics of convolutional neural networks are that the features of each layer are excited by the local area of the previous layer through a convolution kernel that shares weights. This feature makes convolutional neural networks more suitable for image feature learning and expression than other neural network methods. Therefore, by training the convolutional neural network in a large number of ceramic relics and ceramic product images, a neural network model containing a large number of cultural relic image features can be obtained.

Image Style Transfer Based on Deep Learning. In recent years, as deep networks have made breakthrough results in computer vision-related fields, some researchers have begun to focus on artistic creation, and style transfer is one of the more successful attempts. Style transfer is a fusion of classical art forms and artificial intelligence technology, which has greatly influenced both the art and technology fields. Not only that, but the products with the core of style transfer technology attracting a large number of users in a short period time also proved its broad application scenarios. The image style migration process extracts features from a specified style image, without destroying the structure of the content image, and the extracted features are used to make a style transform for the content image. The resulting output image is the perfect blend of content and style images. Image style transfer technology mainly solves three problems: first, how to extract image pattern features without interfering with content features; second, how to extract image content features without interfering with image pattern features; third, how to fuse the two features to generate a target image.

Natural Language Processing Based on Deep Learning. At present, deep learning has been successfully applied in natural language processing and has made significant progress. Natural Language Processing has five main tasks: classification, matching, translation, structural prediction, and sequential decision-making processes. Except for the last task, deep learning methods have surpassed or significantly surpassed traditional methods. End-to-end training and representation learning are key features of deep learning, which makes deep learning a powerful tool for natural language processing. Because of the model (deep neural network) has powerful representation capabilities, and the information in the data can be efficiently encoded in the model, deep learning can often be trained end-to-end in applications. Data in different forms (such as text and images) can be used to train and it represented as real-valued vectors in deep learning. This makes it possible to process information across modalities. For example, in image retrieval, you can match a query (text) to an image and find the most relevant image, because all of this information is represented as a vector.

4 Platform Practice

4.1 Construction of Changsha Kiln Cultural Relic Knowledge Database

The Changsha Kiln Cultural Relics Knowledge Database [5] is based on combing the cultural relics knowledge system [9], constructing a cultural relics knowledge base by extracting cultural relics elements' text features and image feature extraction, and providing data retrieval services based on semantic Changsha kiln cultural relics information retrieval.

Cultural Feature Text Extraction, including text preprocessing and feature extraction. Text preprocessing mainly includes document segmentation, text segmentation, and text stop words. Feature extraction is based on the BiLSTM-CRF [10] model, the first step of the model is to process the corpus and use word2vec [11–13] to embed the words of the corpus. Every word is 50 dimensions; the second step is to input the word embedding feature to BiLSTM, then, add a linear layer to the hidden layer of the output, and finally add a CRF layer (Conditional Random Field is an undirected graph model, has achieved good results in word segmentation, part-of-speech tagging, named entity recognition and other sequence tagging tasks, in recent years); the model shows better flexibility than traditional machine learning methods, and is particularly suitable for scenarios with large corpora, using GPU (Graphics Processing Unit mainly performs floating-point operations and parallel operations. The floating-point operations and parallel operations can be hundreds of times faster than the CPU) can greatly improve the training speed [14]. The extracted text features are stored in the Changsha Kiln Cultural Relics Knowledge Base [15]. As shown in Fig. 6.

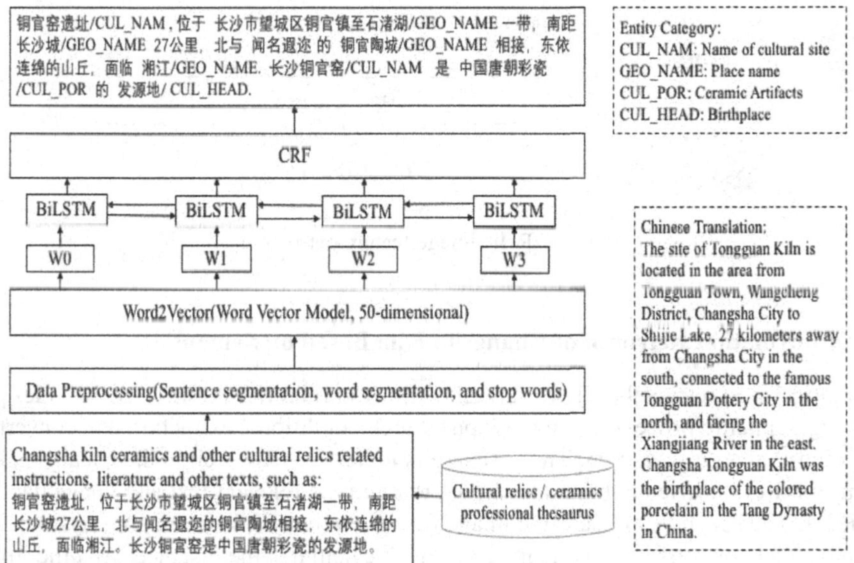

Fig. 6. Relic text information extraction

Cultural Relic Image Feature Extraction, based on deep learning technology to extract cultural relics' features (including color features, pattern features, shape features, spatial relationship features, and so on), and store them in the Changsha Kiln Cultural Relics Knowledge Image Feature Database to establish related indexes; this module includes image preprocessing and feature extraction. Image preprocessing mainly includes image damage inspection, image format conversion, image format scaling, and image noise processing. Feature extraction is performed by a fast region-based convolutional network method (Faster R-CNN [16]) for image feature extraction. The faster

R-CNN algorithm consists of two major modules, one is the candidate frame extraction module of the candidate area network, and the other is the Fast R-CNN monitoring module. Extracted features stored as a tensor in the Changsha Kiln Cultural Relics Knowledge Image Feature Database and indexed. As shown in Fig. 7.

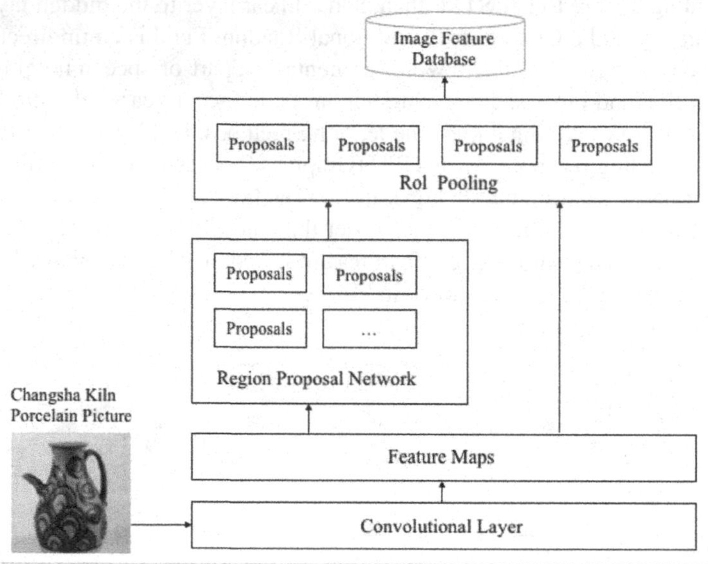

Fig. 7. Relic image feature extraction

4.2 Information Retrieval of Changsha Kiln Based on Semantics

Semantic-based retrieval [17] of Changsha kiln cultural relics information includes performing semantic processing on the input search conditions, extracting and converting them into a search paradigm. The first step is to perform a search in the Changsha kiln cultural relics knowledge base, and the system returns relevant text and image data for retrieval. The second step reads the image resource returned from the previous step into memory and converts it into a feature tensor. It calculates the distance from the image feature tensor in the Changsha Kiln Cultural Relic Design Element Database and selects the image with the shortest distance of the feature tensor [18, 19]. Finally, the text data returned in one step is combined with the similar image data returned in the second step and output to the user.

4.3 Style Fusion of Cultural Relic Elements in Changsha Kiln

Changsha Kiln cultural relics creative platform through the convolutional neural network training on a large number of ceramic cultural relic images to obtain a neural network model containing a large number of cultural relic image features; style fusion based on the style image and content image input by the user, and finally blend the text and similar image to generate target image to the user with a good fusion of content and style. This study defines the following fusion rules for style transfer [20, 21] (as shown in Fig. 8):

Fusion rule 1: ancient and modern shapes are blended to generate a set of alternative new shapes;

Fusion rule 2: ancient patterns and modern glazes are blended to generate a set of alternative patterns;

Fusion rule 3: ancient glazes and modern glazes are blended to generate a set of alternative glaze colors;

Fusion rule 4: combine the new shapes, the new patterns, and the new glazes output by rules 1, 2, and 3 to generate selectable products.

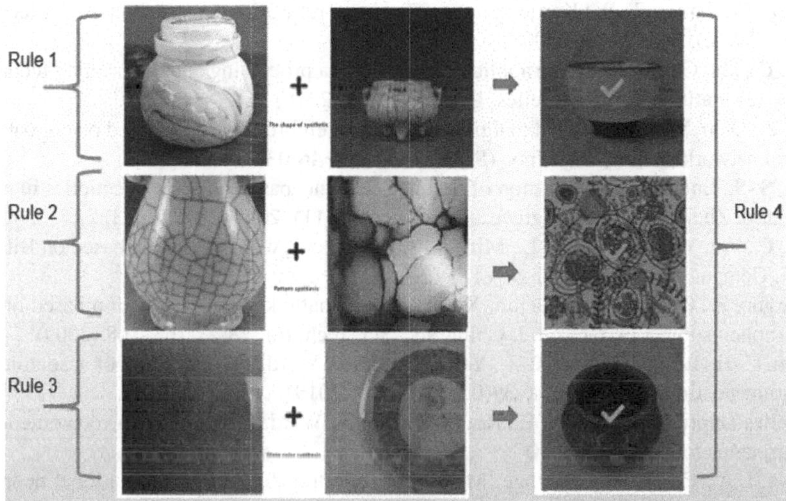

Fig. 8. Style fusion rules

5 Conclusion

Under the impact of the market economy and modern industry, the production of ceramics in Changsha Kiln's is shrinking, and the inheritance mode is fragile. From the perspective of intangible productive protection, Changsha Kiln's cultural relics creative platform can promote inheritance and development through industrialization. Therefore, this study attempts to promote the organic combination of traditional cultural relics elements and modern creative design through the construction of a creative platform for recreating cultural relic elements in Changsha kiln and to stimulate the sustainable development of regional cultural resources, provide cultural relics product creative design services for public, promote the integrated development of culture and technology, and promote the cultural industry to become a pillar industry of the national economy.

Acknowledgment. This work was supported partially by the Project from the Science & Technology Department, Hunan, China (No. 2016SK2017), and a grant from the Education Department of Hunan Province (No. 19A309).

References

1. Xiao, X.: A survey of the Tongguan kilns in Changsha in Tang Dynasty. J. Archaeol. **1**, 67–96 (1980)
2. Li, S.: Strolling the bronze official: research and design practice of modern ceramics based on Changsha Kiln. Hunan University (2016)
3. Zhang, Z., Guo, Y.: Study on the colored glaze and porcelain of Changsha Tongguan kiln. J. Jingdezhen Ceram. Inst. **01**, 2+15–21+81 (1985)
4. Chen, X.: Changsha Kiln porcelain poem: a masterpiece of Chinese packaging history. Packag. World **06**, 62 (2001)
5. Zhang, Q.-J.: Research on Bronze Orientation Retrieval Based on Semantic Web, Xi'an University of Technology (2010)
6. Qiu, Z.-W., Zhang, T.-W.: Key techniques on cultural relic 3D reconstruction. Acta Electronica Sinica **36**(12), 2423–2427 (2008)
7. Zhu, C., Ma, C., Shen, J.: The application of 3D data processing and 3D printing technology in the restoration of cultural relics. Digit. World **8** (2018)
8. Rui, Z., Qian, W., Xu, D., et al.: Digital synthesis of embroidery style based on convolutional neural network. J. Zhejiang Univ. (Science Edition) **46**(03), 13–21 (2019)
9. Zhu, S.-S., Luo, S.-J.: Re-creation of heritage elements based on design semiotics in product design. J. Zhejiang Univ. (Engineering Science) **47**(11), 2065–2072 (2013)
10. Wei, C., Wu, Y.-Z., Chen, W.-L., Min, Z.: Automatic keyword extraction based on BiLSTM-CRF. Comput. Sci. **45**(S1), 91–96+113 (2018)
11. Qingguo, Z., Chengzhi, Z., Dejun, X., et al.: Automatic keyword extraction based on KNN for implicit subject extraction. J. China Soc. Sci. Tech. Inf. **28**(2), 163–168 (2009)
12. Chen, C.-H., Li, X.-T., Zou, X.-Z., Ye, Z.-F.: A New Word2Vec algorithm of academic paper recommendation. Libr. Tribune **39**(05), 110–117 (2019)
13. Caselles-Dupré, H., Lesaint, F., Royo-Letelier, J.: Word2vec applied to recommendation: hyperparameters matter (2018)
14. Gatys, L.A., Ecker, A.S., Bethge, M.: Image style transfer using convolutional neural networks. In: 2016 IEEE Conference on Computer Vision and Pattern Recognition (CVPR). IEEE (2016)
15. Zhu, K.-Q.: Study of the construction on cultural relics foundational database. Sci. Conserv. Archaeol. **3** (2011)
16. Hao, L.: A new facial detection model based on the Faster R-CNN. In: Advanced electronic materials in 2018, p. 6. Nanyang Technological University, Hong Kong Global Scientific Research Association (2018)
17. Hsu, G.S.J., Shie, H.C., Hsieh, C.H., Chan, J.S.: Fast landmark localization with 3D component reconstruction and CNN for cross-pose recognition. IEEE Trans. Circ. Syst. Video Technol. **28**, 3194–3207 (2017)
18. Wang, Y., Yang, C., Liu, S., Wang, R., Meng, X.: Grid-enabled Chinese natural language-based information retrieval system in digital museum. In: International Conference on Pervasive Computing & Applications. IEEE (2007)
19. Liddy, E.D., Paik, W., Mckenna, M.E., Li, M.: Natural language information retrieval system and method (1999)
20. Liu, L., Xi, Z.-X., Ji, R.-R., Ma, W.-G.: Advanced deep learning techniques for image style transfer: a survey. Sign. Process. Image Commun. **78**, 465–470 (2019)
21. Brunetti, A., Buongiorno, D., Trotta, G.F., Bevilacqua, V.: Computer vision and deep learning techniques for pedestrian detection and tracking: a survey. Neurocomputing **300**, 17–33 (2018). S092523121830290X

Visualizing Studying Activities for a Learning Dashboard Supporting Meta-cognition for Students

Min Lu[1(✉)], Li Chen[1], Yoshiko Goda[2], Atsushi Shimada[1], and Masanori Yamada[1]

[1] Kyushu University, 744, Motooka, Nishi-ku, Fukuoka 819-0395, Japan
lu@artsci.kyushu-u.ac.jp

[2] Kumamoto University, 2-39-1, Kurokami, Chuo-ku, Kumamoto 8600862, Japan

Abstract. The existing researches and developments of dashboard visualizing results from learning analytics mainly serve the instructors instead of learners in a direct manner. Effective visualizations extracted from learning log data can help the students to reflect and compare studying activities and access their metacognition to improve their self-regulated learning. For such purposes, we designed a reading path graph for visualizing the studying activities on slide pages used as teaching materials in classes intuitively, as one of the key functions of the learning dashboard. By providing the comparisons between the user's own situation and the class overview, the visualization is expected to motivate the further actions of using other tools of the learning dashboard and reflecting studies. This paper introduces our exploration of the data process flows of extracting necessary data from a large number of operational logs for the visualization, and the techniques and strategies applied for rendering the graphics effectively. We implemented the data processing module with Python3 and the web-based visualization module of the reading path graph with JavaScript based on D3.js considering the extensibilities. The issues engaged in the development of prototypes are discussed, which will lead to the improvement of future prototypes and better designs of user experiments for formative evaluations as the next step of this research.

Keywords: Visualization · Learning analytics · Self-regulated learning · Learning dashboard

1 Introduction

Researches and developments of dashboards with visualized results of Learning Analytics (LA) based on large-scale educational log data accumulated in e-learning environments have become popular. Generally speaking, the major part of the current LA dashboard developments aims at feeding back the analytic results to the instructors rather than the learners directly. To help the learners to be aware of their deficiencies in learning progress, and regulates their learning strategies by themselves, monitoring their own learning processes and behaviors is an essential process [1]. Thus, making the information of past studying activities, such as what the learner has been doing and what

N. Streitz and S. Konomi (Eds.): HCII 2020, LNCS 12203, pp. 569–580, 2020.
https://doi.org/10.1007/978-3-030-50344-4_41

the others have in the same class, salient for the learner can be helpful to reflect one's study and learn from each other [2]. Our prior research has designed a learning analytics dashboard supporting metacognition to improve self-regulated learning in online environments through the collection, analysis, and visualization of learning log data [3]. A very early prototype of the proposed dashboard has been introduced in [4]. This paper focuses on the details of our latest effects on visualizing studying activities extracted from the operational logs of digital teaching materials to support self-monitoring as part of the in-progress development of the learning dashboard.

Because the learners are expected to focus on the learning processes rather than the outcome only in self-monitoring [5], the learning dashboard is designed to provide the students with summarized and visualized studying activities organized with the teaching materials (i.e., slide pages) used in the classes. The visualization includes an overview summarizing the activities on all the slide pages in a class and a view of the detailed activities on a single page. Both views provide side-by-side comparisons between the overall situations of all the students in the class and one's own activities, as it accords with the point of self-evaluation [6]. This paper will mainly introduce a realization of visualizing the above-mentioned overview and detailed view from the operational event logs of a digital teaching material delivery system named "BookRoll" [7] operated by Kyushu University in Japan. The expected impact of the visualizations is to stimulate the student's curiosity about the differences between their own study activities and the others by providing intuitive contrasts, in order to motivate her/his further actions of using other tools to find more details and reflecting their studies.

2 UI Designs for Visualizing Study Activities

We currently focus on the page-viewing activities within the slide of a class, which include the slide reading path and page viewing duration, as well as the learner-generated content, which includes highlight markers and memo annotations created on the slide pages by students. As the accumulated operation event logs on the e-book system from different courses and students are stored in the same database table, the event records need to be filtered according to the classes, slides, and students' IDs. To get the reading paths, we extract the sequences of page-navigation-related events, with the high-frequency page changes filtered. From such sequences, we can calculate the time spent on each page by each student and the "from-to" links between the pages. The overall states of all the students in a class before/during/after the class time can be summarized from all the students' results indicating the start time and end time of the class.

2.1 Graph for Reading Path Overview

We designed a graph to visualize the slide reading path and durations with the nodes standing for the pages arranged on a circle and the links standing for the "from-to" relations between the nodes for the reading path. As illustrated in Fig. 1, the color intensity of a node with a page number indicates the reading duration on the page; the thickness of a link shows the number counting the same page transit; and the colors of the link shows the directions (light gray for going to the next page, dark gray for going

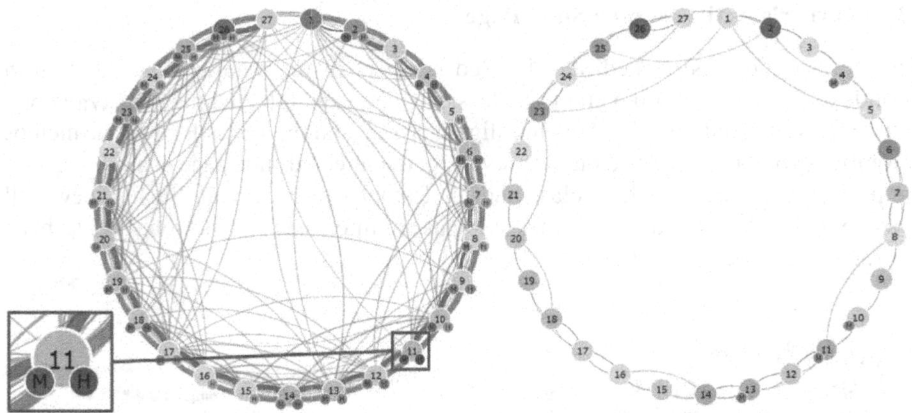

Fig. 1. Reading path graphs on a 27-page slide of a 70-student class (left) and one of the students in the class (right) during class time

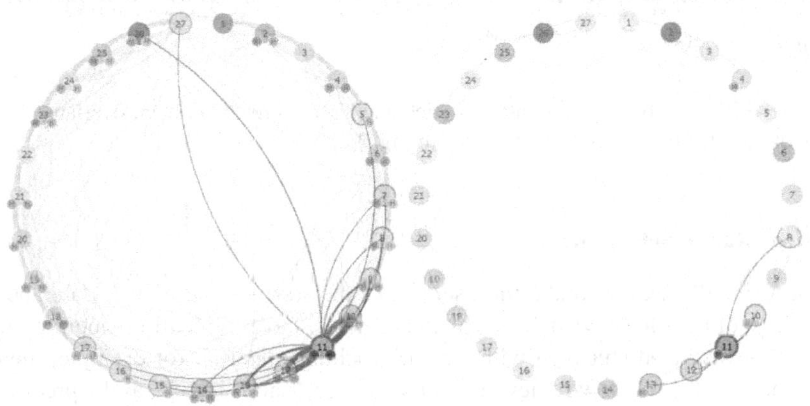

Fig. 2. Reading path graphs highlighting a selected page and the links related to the page after clicking the node of Page No. 11 in Fig. 1

to the previous page, mint for jumping forward and orange for jumping backward). The accessories, which are smaller circles attached to a page node, appear if there is learner-generated content on the page, including highlight markers (circle with the letter H) and memo annotations (circle with the letter M), with their color intensities present the total numbers created on the same page. A pair of such graphs for the teaching material will be presented to the learner for them to compare her/his studying activities with the overall situation of the whole class. For the graph of the class overview, the color intensity of a node stands for the average reading time spent on the page over all the students. When a page node in the graph is clicked, the node and the "from-to" links related to the page will be highlighted with all the other nodes and links in much higher transparency. As illustrated in Fig. 2, two different colors are used to distinguish the links from the selected node with those coming to the node.

2.2 Learner's Activities on a Slide Page

When a page node is clicked, the detailed numbers of the reading time duration in seconds (class average for the graph of class overview) and total learning behaviors will be listed. As shown in Fig. 3, all the highlight markers and the symbols of all the memos annotations will be overlapped on the preview of the selected slide page in a side-by-side comparison between the whole class and the learner's own content. Such a view will help the user to find out the part other students are interested in but probably has been ignored by the user at a glance.

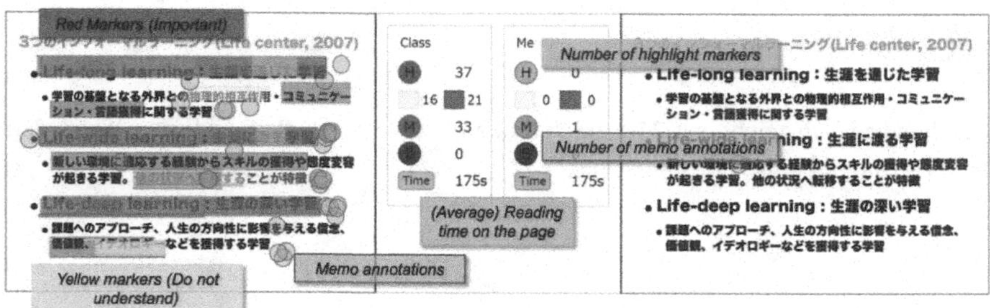

Fig. 3. Detailed view of the studying activities and learner-created content overlapped on the preview of the slide page (No. 11 as selected in Fig. 2)

2.3 Time Range Selection

It is not a friendly way to make the users input the starting and ending date and time as the range of data to be visualized, as the user will have to recall the memory of the specific time spent on studying with certain teaching material, for example, the class time or the time for preview/review. It is also not necessary to do so, as the precise time specified to minutes or seconds is not meaningful. Also, class days and class time are usually the most concerned time ranges. Therefore, we designed a two-step operation to select a time range with predefined easy-to-understand options. The first step is the date selection. The users can either select from a list of all the class days or select other days from the calendar. The second step is the time slot selection. If the users have chosen a class day in the first step, then they can choose from the options of *Before*, *During,* or *After* the class. Otherwise, they may choose *Morning*, *Afternoon*, *Evening,* or *Night*.

3 Data Processing

3.1 Data Sources

The raw data used to visualize the study activities is mainly from the database of BookRoll. More specifically, we mainly use the event stream from the log data table to generate the reading paths and other page-navigation-related information, and records

Table 1. Example of the operation types and their counts from the event logs generated by a class of 70 students on a 27-page slide, with the types related to page navigation highlighted

Operation type code	Meaning	Count
ADD BOOKMARK	Added a bookmark to the page	6
ADD MARKER	Added a highlight marker to the page	268
ADD MEMO	Added a memo annotation to the page	205
ADD_HW_MEMO	Added a hand-written memo to the page	13
BOOKMARK_JUMP	**Jumped to a page using a bookmark**	**1**
CHANGE MEMO	Edited the text of a memo annotation	42
CLEAR_HW_MEMO	Cleared a hand-written memo	1
CLICK_RECOMMENDATION	Clicked the link of recommendation	10
CLOSE	**Closed the teaching material**	**243**
DELETE BOOKMARK	Deleted a bookmark	1
DELETE MARKER	Deleted a highlight marker	26
DELETE_MEMO	Deleted a memo annotation	2
GETIT	Clicked the "Get It" button	41
LINK_CLICK	Clicked an URL link on a page	16
NEXT	**Clicked the "Next Page" button**	**9670**
NOTGETIT	Clicked the "Not Get It" button	16
OPEN	**Opened the teaching material**	**332**
PAGE_JUMP	**Jumped to a page (using the slide bar)**	**87**
PREV	**Clicked the "Previous Page" button**	**4299**
SEARCH	Searched certain text	1
SEARCH_JUMP	**Jumped to a page from the search results**	**1**
UNDO_HW_MEMO	Undo when inputting a hand-written memo	12
Total		15293

from the content tables (e.g., tables of highlight markers and memo annotations) to visualize the learner-generated content. We also access the database of the LMS to get the class dates and times of a certain course.

The event stream consists of a series of data records, with each of them describes an operational log event. The fields of each record mainly include the user's (student's) id, the teaching material's id, the page number in the teaching material, the type code of the operation, and additional descriptions according to the event types, with the date and time when the event is logged. Table 1 shows all of the operation types and their counts from the event logs generated by a single class of 70 students on a single slide of 27 pages. The highlighted operation types are those related to page view and navigations. Actually, there are operation types that never appeared in this data example, such as *MEMO_JUMP*.

From other content tables, we got the number of highlight markers created by the same class on the same slide is 242, while the number of memo annotations is 203. The data include the activities during and out of class time.

3.2 Raw Data Preprocess

As all the event logs generated by all the students on teaching materials of different courses applying BookRoll are accumulated in the same table, we have to at first query the data rows according to the id of the teaching material, screen out the interested records according to the type codes (e.g., only page navigation-related events for reading path generation), and then group them by student ids.

3.3 Reading Path Generation

With the preprocess data that are grouped event log records according to the student ids, we can generate reading paths for visualization by the following steps.

Page Navigation Event Log Filtering
The events of each student are sorted by time from early to late, and then the events having too short time interval (intuitively, less than 0.5 s) since their previous ones or have the same page number as their previous ones are filtered out to make the data more meaningful. This means, for example, if a user clicked the "Next Page" button frequently in a short time, such behavior is considered as a "jump" from the page just before the series of frequent operations to the page after them. Such data filtering processes can help us to obtain the students' behaviors closer to their real purposes through the surface of the log data.

Page Navigation Sequence Constructing
The sorted and filtered event log records of a single student are divided into several segments according to the pairs of *OPEN* and *CLOSE* events. From each segment, we can construct a page navigation sequence, which contains a *start time* from the *OPEN*, an *end time* from the *CLOSE* event, ordered items each having the *page number* from the corresponded event log record and *time duration stayed at the page* in seconds calculated from the timestamp of the event and its next one's.

Creating Data for Nodes and Links in Reading Paths
By going through each page navigation sequence, we can sum the total time duration stayed at each page for the nodes in the reading path graph and collect all the links between different pages from each pair of two neighbored items in the sequence. The number of links with the same source page and target page is then counted. After that, additional data, such as the numbers of highlight markers and memo annotations, are appended to the nodes (i.e., pages). The set of the nodes and links of a reading path are then stored with the start time and end time.

3.4 Class Overview Generation

With all the reading paths of all the students in a class generated for teaching material, the data for visualizing the class overview graph can be collected and generated. As discussed in Sect. 2.3, a time range is selected by the user to request the visualization. Thus, all the reading paths whose time ranges intersect with the requested range can be searched out. In the next step, by going through all of these reading paths all over the class, data of all the nodes and links are merged according to the same page numbers to generate the nodes and links of the class overview. The sum of time durations stayed on a certain page is replaced by its average over the number of students in the class.

4 Visualization Techniques

The visualization of the data generated above can be realized in different approaches. In our prototype implementation, which will be introduced in Sect. 5, we developed a web-based visualization module using JavaScript on the basis of D3.js [8] (Data-Driven Documents, a widely used JavaScript library for dynamic and interactive data visualizations in web browsers). This section will discuss several technical issues in our experience of visualizing the reading path graphs.

4.1 Reading Path Graph Automatic Generation

The reading path graph has to adapt different learning materials that have different numbers of pages. Thus, it should be able to calculate the size and position of each node according to the number of pages and the size of its container in a web page, and then render the nodes and links between them automatically. We applied a technique combining the APIs for drawing donut charts and force directed graphs in the quick implementation of our reading path graph.

For the first step, an invisible donut chart is generated, in which the slices are equally divided, and the number of them is the same as the number of pages. The purpose of this donut chart is just to get the center coordinates of the arcs, which can be utilized as the center of the nodes without additional codes for calculation. The radius of each node can be calculated as, for example, 1/4 of the arc's length, and then the positions and sizes of the accessories of each node can also be derived with a simple calculation. In the next step, a force-directed graph is automatically generated by binding the data of nodes and links. By disabling the animation of the force-directed graph and fixing the final coordinates of each node at the corresponded arc's center derived in the first step, our reading path graph can be generated with only a few lines of source codes.

4.2 Visual Variable Settings

We need to set up the visual variables, such as colors of the nodes and links, the line width of the links, of reading path graph generated in Sect. 4.1 to provide effective visualization. Although it is possible to define such variables manually with the APIs provided by D3.js, we try to provide several integrated programming interfaces to determine these variables with easy-to-understand settings according to the characteristics of the data. As one of the main purposes is to provide a comparison between the student's own learning activities and the overall class situation, the two graphs must be in the same settings of visual variables to make sure the comparison is meaningful. Our strategy here is to set up the class overview graph at first and then use the generated settings to render the student's graph.

Node Color Scales

As introduced in Sect. 2, the intensity of the color that fills a node indicates the time duration stayed on the page. By setting up the colors of the minimum and maximum values of the time duration of all the nodes, we can generate a linear color scale with the API of D3.js and apply it to each node in the graph. When applying the color scale generated using the data of the class overview to the student's view, it is possible that some values are out of the color scale's range, as the nodes in the class overview apply the average values. In this case, we simply use the minimum's color for the values smaller than it and the maximum's color for the values larger than it. The accessories of the nodes visualizing the numbers of highlight markers and memo annotations also use the same strategy to set up the color scales.

Link Width Scales

We use different stroke widths of the links to indicate the numbers of the same moves between the pages. As the numbers of actions moving to the next page or the previous page is overwhelmingly larger than the others (i.e., "jumps" between the pages not neighbored), if we generate a linear scale from the minimum and maximum numbers over all of the links for the range of the stroke width, most of the "jump" links will have the smallest stroke width. However, the jumps are usually more concerned as they usually provide more information than the commonly appeared "next" and "previous". Therefore, we ignore the "next" and "previous" links and generate a linear scale with the minimum and maximum numbers over all of the "jump" links, in order to make the link width more meaningful. Similar to the node color scales, we use the minimum's width for the links have smaller numbers, and the maximum's width for the links has larger numbers. Thus, usually, all the "next" and "previous" links in the class overview graph have the largest width.

Link Colors

If we set up the same color for all the links, the reading path graphs will look messy, especially when the number of pages is large. This will make the visualization less effective, as the user cannot draw useful information, such as important links and pages of jumped from/to, from the messy graph. As clarified above in link width settings, "jump" links are considered more important than "next" and "previous", thus we can set up different colors and transparencies on them as follows to distinguish the concerned ones.

- **"Next"** links are considered the least important, as it is the most common and necessary action when browsing the teaching material. Thus, we can apply the least distinct color (e.g., light gray) and the highest transparency.

- "**Previous**" links can be more important than "next" links, as there must some reasons for the students to refer to the page just viewed. Thus, we can apply a more distinct color (e.g., dark gray) and lower transparency than the "next" links.
- "**Jump**" links are much fewer and more informative, so we can apply distinct colors on them with the least transparency. As jumping **forward** and **backward** can have different meanings, we can apply different colors to distinguish the difference of directions.

Highlights for the Selected Page

When a node (i.e., page) in the reading path graph is selected, all the other nodes and the links not related to the selected node will be displayed in with high transparency to distinguish the selected node and the links from/to it. In addition, we can modify the colors stoking the links to distinguish the links from the selected node from those moved to the node. Take Fig. 2 as an example, and we use cerulean for the links from the selected node, as well as the outline of the selected node. For the links towards the selected node, magenta is used as a contrast, also for the outlines of the nodes at the other end of the links.

5 Prototype Development

The initial prototype implementing the proposed visualization is developed with some small dumps of event logs on a very limited number of teaching materials from the database. In this stage, we mainly experimented with the data processing flows and visualization techniques with this prototype to make sure they are correct and effective to generate our expected graphs. A data processing module developed with Python3 and a web-based visualization module developed with JavaScript on the basis of D3.js was developed. In the next stage, these two modules are wrapped into our learning dashboard prototype as plugins of the LMS operated by Kyushu University for educational technology researches. The students, who are the users of the LMS, will be able to access the learning dashboard from the course page of the LMS and browse the reading path graphs of their own and the whole class for each BookRoll slide with details. In this under-going stage, we mainly work on the issues in optimizing the data processing workflows to deal with the real-time request of data period for visualization and the detailed information of the users and courses passed by the web sessions. After completing the current stage, we will prepare the prototype for the experiments of formative evaluations.

5.1 Data Processing Module

The main task of this module is to extract necessary data from the database according to the requests of visualization and process the raw data to generate the data that can be used by the visualization module to render the graphs. The data sources to be processed by this module mainly include the follows:

- Information passed by the web sessions: such as the identities of the users, courses, and teaching materials, the requested range.

- Information from the LMS: mainly the time periods of the classes of each course and the list of students registered to the courses.
- Raw data from the database of BookRoll: operational event logs, and learner-generated content, as clarified in Sect. 3.1.

Considering the balance of processing load and storage cost, we strategically use offline processing for preprocesses and the data expected to be used frequently, while using online processing for the less frequently used or incidentally requested data. The offline processes can be conducted regularly at, for example, the late-night every day. Typically, offline processes include:

- Preprocesses: as introduced in Sect. 3.2, screen out and group up the data needed from the operational event log data table in the database of BookRoll.
- Page navigation sequence construction: as introduced in Sect. 3.3, form the time-ordered sequences of page numbers and time durations for each student over each teaching material.
- Reading path generation for the class time: as the time periods of classes are known and reviewing of these time periods are expected to be frequently used, the data for visualization can be prepared in advance. Therefore, the nodes and links for the student's view, as well as the class overview during the class time, can be generated and stored following the steps introduced in Sects. 3.3 and 3.4. When the user requests to view the graphs of the class time, the stored results will be directly used instead of processing in real-time.

On the other hand, the online processes mainly deal with generating reading paths for the requests other than the class time. In this case, the data of the nodes and links will be created after the user has chosen a range of time to view the graphs.

5.2 Web-Based Visualization Module

To deploy the visualization module in the web framework of the learning dashboard prototype, the web container of it is also developed with Flask, which a micro web framework is written in Python3. The visualization functions are developed with JavaScript based on D3.js and wrapped up in an independent module as a.js file. This module provides programming interfaces for binding data to generate the reading path graphs and leaner-generated content overviews and to set up visual variables, including sizes and colors. The module will output the graphs in SVG (Scalable Vector Graphics) format that to be displayed in the web container. The module also handles and delivers some of the interactive events. For example, all the mouse-click events on the graphics of nodes, links, accessories, and symbols of learner-generated content will be raised to the upper layers (e.g., the web container of the graph). This also brings expansibility to this module that is can potentially work with other functions of the learning dashboard as well as other plugins of the LMS.

6 Discussions and Future Work

When implementing the proposed visualization of studying activities for the learning dashboard, preliminary evaluations by interviews with several graduate students and teachers in our university obtained positive opinions as well as useful comments and suggestions. Besides, we also engaged in many issues that are worth discussing for further improvements and future studies.

The first issue is how many visual variables should be used for providing useful information to the users. In other words, should we use as many visual variables as possible to provide as much information as possible to achieve effective visualization? The answer is often negative. Although we managed to distinguish more important links in the reading path graph by introducing more colors, however, when we tried to add more variables, for example, using the color intensity of a node's outline to indicate its in/out degrees, the graph became difficult to understand. Accordingly, here comes the question of what are the proper visual variables for what kinds of information should be applied in the graphs to achieve effective visualization for the students. In our opinion, the reading path graph should distinct the important messages about the differences in learning activities or styles and make them easy to find to arouse the student's curiosity. In our future user experiments, we will try different combinations of visual variables and find out the effective designs by checking how fast the users can distinguish the important messages and their preferences.

The second issue is that when the teaching material has too many pages (e.g., more than 50), the reading path graph will become a message as there are too many links, while the nodes will be too small to see or operate. Enlarging the graph may solve the problem of too small nodes, but the user will lose the side-by-side comparison view of the two graphs, which will make the visualization less effective. One possible solution is to group the pages by the internal structures of the teaching material, such as sections in a slide, which are displayed as collective nodes, in order to reduce the number of nodes on the graph. When the user clicks the collective nodes, they will be unfolded to show more details. Such a solution will visualize the relations between sections instead of pages. We will develop the functions to support the collective nodes in our future prototypes and test their effectiveness in formative evaluations.

The third issue is the possible loss of some important information on a reading path when visualized with our proposed design. As our reading path graph mainly focuses on the importance of the pages by displaying the reading time of a page and the degrees of its relations with other pages, the order and timing of how the pages have been read are not reflected directly. For example, when a page was read more than once in a reading path, only the total reading time spent on it can be displayed, and we cannot tell if the student spent more time when reading the page for the first time or the later times. In our opinion, the information of reading orders and timing should be presented using other forms of visualizations with a time axis. We argue that such visualizations based on the time axis is not good at giving an overview of the relations between pages, and different forms of visualizations cannot replace the others without loss of functions. We may develop different views of the reading path in our future prototypes for different functions and combine them together in the learning dashboard. We can also test and compare their effectiveness with user experiments.

There can be more issues to be discovered in our future development of the visualizations of study activities for the learning dashboard, and the discussions on them will lead to more refined details of our proposed graphs and better designs of user experiments for formative evaluation. In the future, we are going to explore visualizations of other types of data and forms to enhance the functions of the learning dashboard to support self-regulated learning, including self-monitoring, knowledge monitoring, planning, and regulation, for the students.

Acknowledgments. This research is supported by a JST AIP Grant No. JPMJCR19U1, Japan.

References

1. Hofer, B.K., Yu, S.L., Pintrich, P.R.: Teaching college students to be self-regulated learners. In: Schunk, D.H., Zimmerman, B.J. (eds.) Self-regulated Learning: From Teaching to Self-reflective Practice, pp. 57–85. Guilford, New York (1998)
2. Yen, M.H., Chen, S., Wang, C.Y., Chen, H.L., Hsu, Y.S., Liu, T.C.: A framework for self-regulated digital learning (SRDL). J. Comput. Assist. Learn. **34**(5), 580–589 (2018)
3. Chen, L., Lu, M., Goda, Y., Yamada, M.: Design of learning analytics dashboard supporting metacognition. In: Proceedings of 16th International Conference Cognition and Exploratory Learning in Digital Age (CELDA 2019), pp. 175–182 (2019)
4. Lu, M., Chen, L., Goda, Y., Shimada, A., Yamada, M.: Development of a learning dashboard prototype supporting meta-cognition for students. In: Companion Proceedings of the 10th International Conference on Learning Analytics & Knowledge (LAK20), pp. 104–106, FrankFurt (online), Germany, 23–27 March (2020)
5. Zimmerman, B.J.: Developing self-fulfilling cycles of academic regulation: an analysis of exemplary instructional models. In: Schunk, D.H., Zimmerman, B.J. (eds.) Self-regulated Learning: From Teaching to Self-reflective Practice, pp. 1–19. Guilford, New York (1998)
6. Belfiore, P.J., Hornyak, R.S.: Operant theory and application to self-monitoring in adolescents. In: Schunk, D.H., Zimmerman, B.J. (eds.) Self-regulated Learning: From Teaching to Self-reflective Practice, pp. 184–202. Guilford, New York (1998)
7. Ogata, H., et al.: E-Book-based learning analytics in university education. In: International Conference on Computer in Education (ICCE 2015), pp. 401–406 (2015)
8. Data-Driven Documents. https://d3js.org/. Accessed 31 Jan 2020

Visualization and Analysis for Supporting Teachers Using Clickstream Data and Eye Movement Data

Tsubasa Minematsu(✉), Atsushi Shimada, and Rin-ichiro Taniguchi

Kyushu University, Fukuoka, Japan
minematsu@ait.kyushu-u.ac.jp

Abstract. Recently, various educational data such as clickstream data and eye movement data have been collected from students using e-learning systems. Learning analytics-based approaches also have been proposed such as student performance prediction and a monitoring system of student learning behaviors for supporting teachers. In this paper, we introduce our recent work as instances of the use of clickstream data and eye movement data. In our work, the clickstream data is used for representing student learning behaviors, and the eye movement data is used for estimating page areas where the student found difficulty. Besides, we discuss advantages and disadvantages depending on the types of educational data. To discuss them, we investigate a combination of highlights added on pages by students and eye movement data in page difficulty estimation. In the investigation, we evaluate the similarity between positions of highlights and page areas where the student found difficulty generated from eye movements. It is shown that areas in the difficult pages correspond to the highlights in this evaluation. Finally, we discuss how to combine the highlights and eye movement data.

Keywords: Learning analytics · Eye movement · Machine learning · Neural network

1 Introduction

Improving learning support for students is a vital task for teachers to reduce at-risk students and to enhance students' performances. To provide better supports for students, teachers need to understand how the students learn and their characteristics. For example, it is useful to find contents students feel difficult in their lectures because teachers can provide more detailed explanations of the contents more carefully thanks to the finding. However, to investigate such useful information manually is time-consuming for teachers by themselves. To understand students' learning behavior automatically, recent works in learning analytics analyze their learning behaviors based on educational data using machine learning techniques and data mining techniques, and provide various results and findings for supporting students and teachers [1,5].

N. Streitz and S. Konomi (Eds.): HCII 2020, LNCS 12203, pp. 581–592, 2020.
https://doi.org/10.1007/978-3-030-50344-4_42

Various types of educational data are collected from digital learning systems such as Massive Open Online Courses (MOOCs) and M2B systems in Kyushu University [14]. The collected data is responses written in e-portfolio systems, eye movement of students reading a digital textbook, and clickstream data and event logs such as students' access logs and page browsing logs. The number of students that can be measured at the same time and the degree of detail of the measured learning behavior differs depending on the data type. For example, clickstream data can be collected from more than 100 students simultaneously, and it is difficult to capture reading behaviors on e-book pages. Therefore, the functions of systems for supporting teachers also differ depending on the collected educational data.

In this paper, we introduce our recent works [9–11] using clickstream data and eye movement data to discuss learning analytics-based approaches for helping teachers support students when using different types of educational data. The first topic is a visualization of the relationship between quiz scores and reading behaviors using clickstream data to understand the characteristics of a large number of students, and the second topic is page difficulty estimation using eye movement data to help teachers find contents students feel difficult.

2 Related Work

In learning analytics, it is essential to understand student learning behaviors and feedback results of the analysis to teachers and students. To measure student learning behaviors, recent online digital learning management systems is available because they can store interaction by students reading digital textbooks. Besides, teaching materials, quiz scores, and responses written by students are also collected in such systems.

One of the major educational data is clickstream data representing the interaction between e-learning systems and students. There are several studies using clickstream data for predicting student achievement and grades [2], and monitoring student learning behaviors [3,16]. These studies using interaction such as page transition can help teachers detect and support at-risk students. Besides, interactions such as adding highlights and memos are used for a concept map tool [18] and a knowledge map tool [15]. Teachers can use such tools to confirm if the students comprehend. Our method [10] also visualizes student characteristics based on clickstream data. As shown in the previous studies, a large amount of clickstream data can be collected from numerous students. However, it is difficult to measure the more detailed learning activity of students such as reading paths in pages of digital textbooks.

On the other hand, an eye tracker is used for the measurement of eye movement of students reading teaching materials. Reading paths measured from students learning contents by eye trackers is attractive to analyze student performances and difficulty of teaching materials. Nakamura et al. predicted subjective impressions of difficulty of English word tests by using eye movements [13]. The analysis of eye movement data can be useful for understanding learning behaviors within pages. Findings are shown related to effective attention guidance techniques in [4] and relationships between students' reading paths and performance in [7,17]. Therefore, we can use eye movements for analyzing student learning behaviors deeply. The eye trackers can measure eye movement, however, it is hard to measure eye movements from many students because of the difficulty regarding preparing many eye trackers and expertise to use eye trackers.

3 Visualization of Quiz Scores and Reading Behaviors Based on Clickstream Data

We introduce a visualization method to overview student's quiz scores and reading behaviors [10]. Teachers can use quiz scores as a criterion to understand student's achievement and select strategies of learning supports for students. However, such learning supports based only on the quiz scores can not consider students' learning behaviors during lecture time. Even if some students obtain the same score, appropriate learning supports for them are not always the same support. In this study, we provide reading behaviors during lecture time as another criterion, and teachers can have an opportunity to consider how to individually support. Our visualization method defines an action score to represent reading behaviors, and show a distribution between quiz scores and action scores. We apply our visualization method to Kyushu University clickstream data provided by the LAK19 data challenge [5].

3.1 Method

We compute action scores of each student from clickstream data which contain pages read by students, their timestamps, and operations done by students. An action score is defined based on pages read by many students in a class and the number of operations except operations of page access.

In this study, we observed many students read the same page at the same time. Figure 1 shows a heatmap of students reading a textbook. In the heatmap, red color means that many students read a page. We assume that teachers' instruction can affect students' page transitions. Under the assumption, we focus on the majority page transitions, and we compute differences between a student's page transition and the major page transition. When a student follows the major page transition, the action score increases. We can evaluate rare reading patterns such as the yellow reading pattern in Fig. 1.

Besides, the used clickstream data provides several operations such as "ADD MARKER" and "ADD BOOKMARK". Teachers did not force students to do such operations. Therefore, analysis of the operations can be helpful to understand students' learning behaviors. To consider such operations as learning behaviors, we count the number of operations done by each student, and the count is quantized to four-level scores between 0 and 1. When the number of operations increases, the action score also increases. After computing action scores, we plot quiz scores and action scores of students to visualize them.

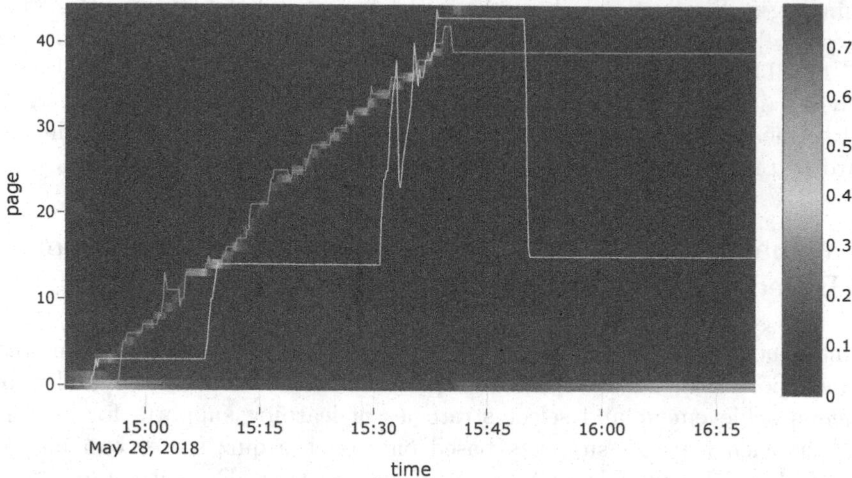

Fig. 1. Reading behaviors in a course. The green and yellow lines represent instances of the reading behavior of the two students. (Color figure online)

3.2 Results

We show a result of the Kyushu University data by our visualization method in Fig. 2. This figure illustrates a quiz score and an action score for each student. To select strategies for learning supports, teachers can use this figure. For example, we can focus on some points in the bottom-right of Fig. 2. The students have higher action scores and lower quiz scores. In this study, such students indicate that their activity did not contribute to higher quiz scores because the action scores are computed from their students' behaviors such as page transition and interactions between students and e-learning systems.

Our visualization method can provide some suggestions for teachers when supporting students in the bottom-right and bottom-left of Fig. 2. We can consider that these two types of students have different learning behaviors during lectures. In the bottom-right, we can estimate that the students follow teachers' instruction or proactively perform operations. Therefore, teachers can provide supplementary teaching materials to help the student learn more detailed content. For students in the bottom-left, teachers can provide a summary of lectures to encourage reviewing previous lectures.

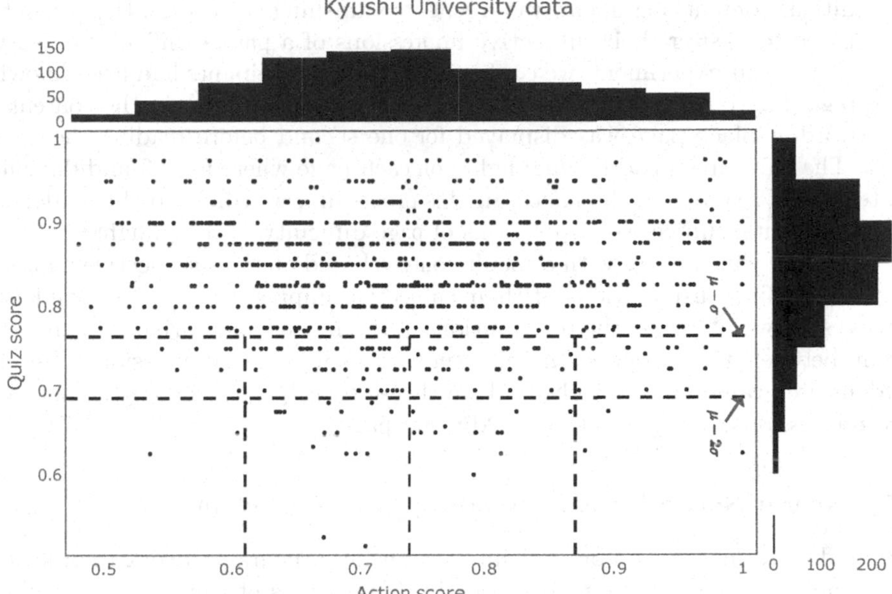

Fig. 2. Distribution of quiz scores and action scores. μ and σ are a mean and a standard deviation of quiz scores.

4 Region-Wise Page Difficulty Using Eye Movement Data

We investigate the relationship between subjective impressions of a page's difficulty and eye movements of students while studying by themselves [9]. Eye movement data can have information on more detailed reading behaviors than clickstream data. The purpose of this study is to estimate where on pages students found difficulty using their eye movement data. In this study, we use a neural network to model eye movements in pages with difficult content. This work can contribute to helping teachers revise teaching materials.

4.1 Data Collection

To analyze eye movements of students reading pages of teaching materials, our eye movement data were collected from 15 Kyushu University students reading a digital textbook. In this study, a Tobii eye tracker we used (Tobii pro spectrum 150 Hz) was attached to a monitor in a dark room, and its sampling rate was set to 150 Hz. The participants started to learn teaching materials after a calibration of the eye tracker. The contents of teaching materials were a statistical test and correlation, and it was included figures, tables, text, formulations, and images.

In addition, content alignment was free. After finishing each page, the students were asked to answer their subjective impressions of a page's difficulty on each page. Before our experiment, we confirmed that all participants had little knowledge regarding information science and statistical mathematics in the contents. Afterward, a black page was displayed for one second before reading the next page. The participants added highlights on each page where they found difficult content after reading all the pages. In this procedure, we collected the students' eye movements, subjective impressions of page difficulty, and highlights.

To decide which pages with difficult content based on their subjective impression, we confirm distributions of their subjective impressions for each student. As a result, we observed the distributions of the means and variances were different between the students. In this study, the subjective impressions of each student are evaluated relatively, and we choose some pages with higher subjective impressions in each student as "difficult pages".

4.2 Neural Network-Based Reading Pattern Modeling

We model eye movements on difficult pages using a neural network in order to find reading patterns related to subjective impressions of the page's difficulty. Recently, neural networks become to extract effective features automatically in several tasks such as image classification [6]. Eye movement data consist of sequences of gaze points and contain both spatial and temporal information. It is difficult to design manual features for modeling such eye movements. Therefore, we choose a neural network as our model.

Our neural network estimates whether eye movement data belong to a difficult page, and the output is a probability of page difficulty. To input eye movement data to our neural network, we use a reading pattern code [12] as the input. The reading pattern code represents T density maps of gaze points. We divide a sequence of gaze points into T time slots, and each heatmap is computed at each time slot. Therefore, a reading pattern also contains both spatial and temporal information. Our neural network accepts a reading pattern code and provides the probability of page difficulty. Training our neural network is performed based on difficult pages. Afterward, our neural network models relationships between eye movements and difficult pages.

We analyze which parts of eye movements our neural network focuses on to interpret the relationships our model learns. In other words, we investigate eye movements when the eye movements are classified as ones of difficult pages by our neural network. In this study, layer-wise relevance propagation (LRP) [8] is used for computing relevance maps, which represent the contribution to the classification result at each element of the input. An element with a high score in a relevance map means related to difficult pages. Therefore, we focus on the relevance maps to visualize page areas where students found difficulty.

4.3 Evaluation

Qualitative Evaluation. Figure 3 illustrates relevance maps of pages with more than five students who found difficulty on those pages. We compare the relevance maps with two types of maps; gaze maps and highlight maps. The gaze maps and highlight maps are heatmaps of the number of gaze points and highlights added by students. A figure in blue has a smaller value than a figure in red.

We roughly observe that the relevance maps are similar to the highlight maps. Especially, both these maps focus on equations. The gaze maps are distributed on each page, and the relevance maps focus on specific regions in the gaze maps. Therefore, we believe that our neural network learns relationships between the eye movements and subjective impressions of the pages with difficult content.

Table 1. Questionnaire about the quality of the relevance maps. n is the number of pages.

Question	Evaluation					
	Agree A (1)	Agree A a little (2)	Neither agree nor disagree (3)	Agree B a little (4)	Agree B (5)	Weighted average ($n = 33$)
Q1	11	6	8	6	2	2.45
Q2	1	4	22	3	3	3.09

Q1: Which of the systems present similar results to what you find difficult for the students?
Q2: Which system do you want to refer to when modifying teaching materials?

Evaluation for Modification of Teaching Materials. We investigate whether relevance maps help teachers revise teaching materials. For the investigation, we administered a questionnaire to the creator of the teaching materials. First, the relevance maps and the gaze maps are shown to the creator of the teaching materials. We tell the creator that these maps are generated from two different systems. In Table 1, system A is a generator of gaze maps, and system B is a generator of relevance maps. After viewing the maps, the creator answers two questions for each page.

According to Table 1, the relevance maps do not help the creator modify teaching materials. However, we expect that teachers modify contents in difficult pages. Therefore, we focus on difficult pages in the two questions. Table 2 shows some weighted averages when easier pages were removed based on thresholds. We ignore pages if the number of students finding difficulty in a page is less than threshold values. In Q2, almost all weighted averages increase. Therefore, the relevance maps can help the creator modify difficult pages.

5 Discussion

The number of students to be analyzed and the level of detail of the analyzed results differ depending on the type of educational data. Clickstream-based

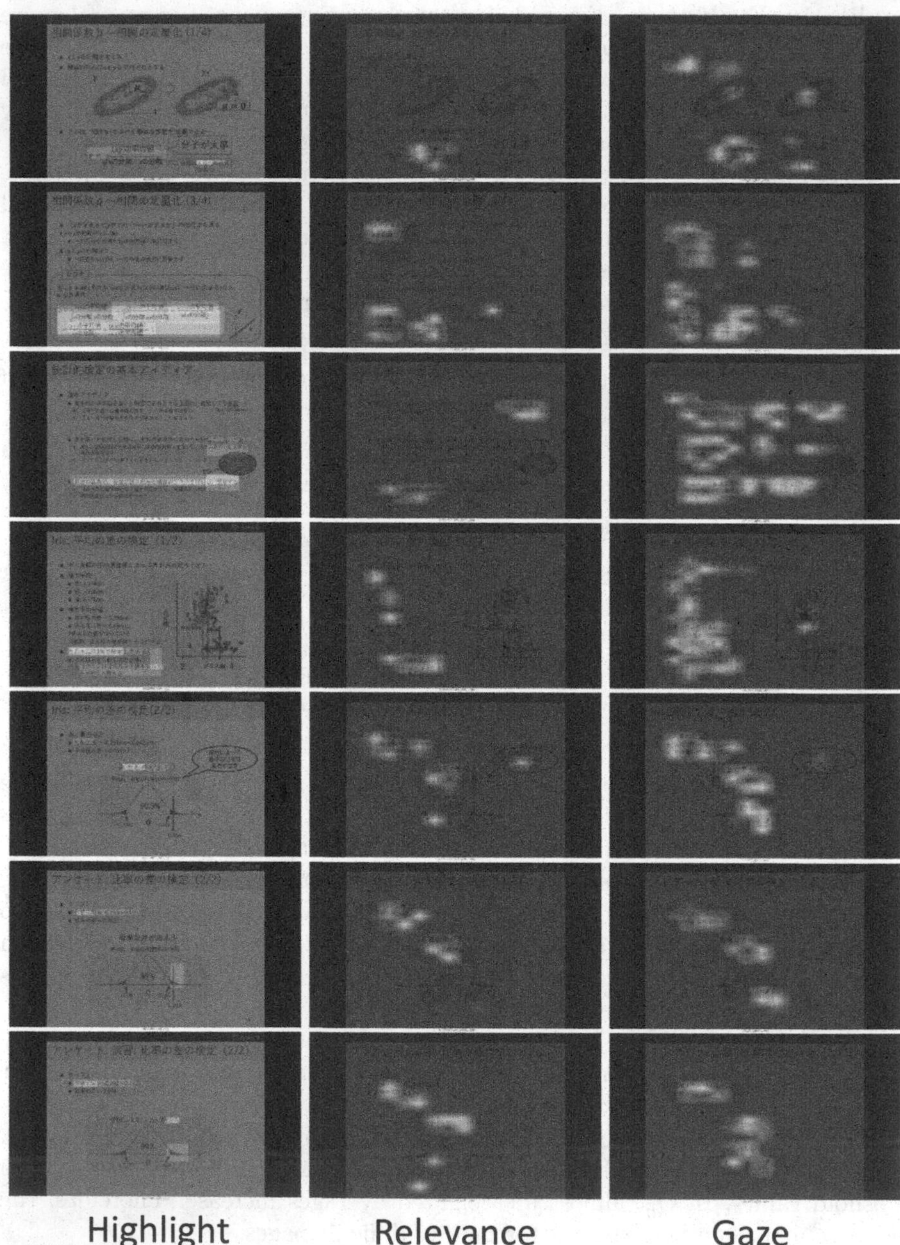

Fig. 3. Highlight maps, relevance maps, and gaze maps in pages with more than five students who found difficulty. (Color figure online)

approaches apply to many students and provide analytics at the page and course level. Eye movement-based approaches, on the other hand, can provide detailed analysis at the word level, however, it is difficult to apply the approach to more than 100 students. This argument applies to other educational data such as electroencephalogram (EEG). We discuss a combination of different educational data to perform a detailed analysis of many students. To discuss it, we focus on highlights and eye movement data [11].

Table 2. Results of the questionnaire when focusing on difficult pages. n is the number of pages used for calculating the weighted average.

Question	Threshold							
	≥ 0 (n = 33)	≥ 1 (n = 23)	≥ 2 (n = 17)	≥ 3 (n = 15)	≥ 4 (n = 11)	≥ 5 (n = 7)	≥ 6 (n = 4)	≥ 7 (n = 3)
Q1	2.45	2.26	2.35	2.47	2.55	2.57	2.00	2.00
Q2	3.09	3.13	3.18	3.27	3.36	3.57	3.25	3.33

Table 3. Averaged precision, recall, and F-measure values comparing the three maps.

	Highlight vs. relevance			Highlight vs. gaze		
	Precsion	Recall	Fmeasure	Precsion	Recall	Fmeasure
Top 3 difficult pages	0.483	0.497	0.394	0.292	0.749	0.334
The other pages	0.108	0.316	0.129	0.098	0.604	0.15

To investigate the similarity between a large amount of clickstream data and a small amount of eye movement data, we collect highlights from approximately 1,200 students using the same e-book system. The students have the opportunity to add or delete highlights on the digital textbook when they found difficulty. Highlight maps are generated from these highlights. For this discussion, we compare the relevance maps with the highlight maps and gaze maps. The three maps are binalized in the comparison. Figure 4 illustrated the binalized highlight, relevance, and gaze maps for the three most difficult pages.

To evaluate the similarities between the different types of the data, Table 3 shows the precision, recall, and F-measure values that were calculated by comparing the highlight maps with the two maps that were generated from eye movement data. According to Table 3, the relevance maps achieved higher precision than the gaze maps in the top three most difficult pages. This indicates that the relevance maps have more similar information about the highlight maps in difficult pages.

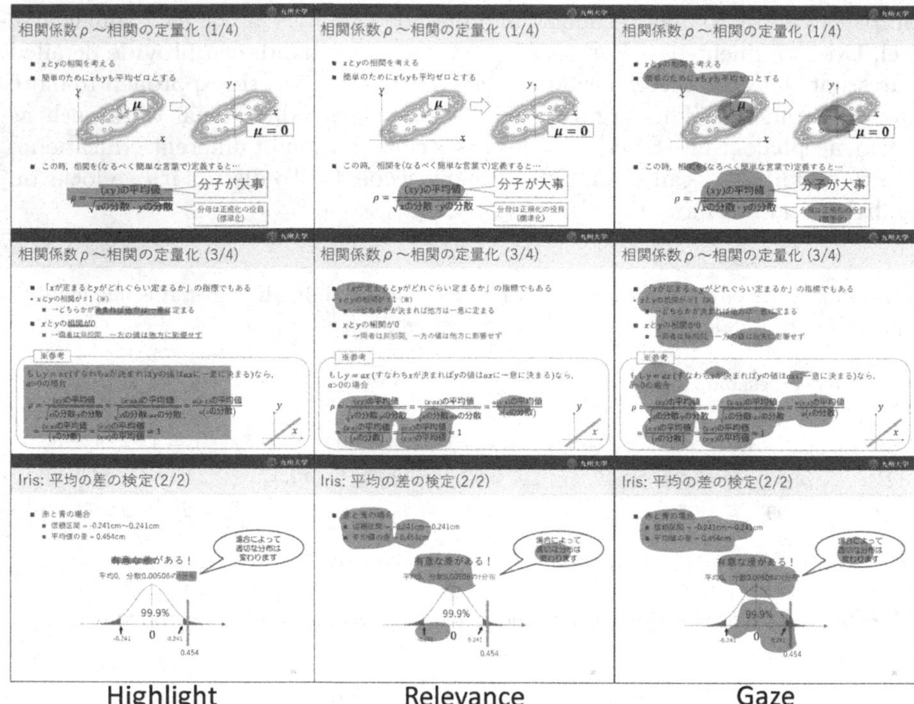

Fig. 4. Binary maps in highlight maps, relevance maps, and gaze maps for the three most difficult pages.

We observed that the highlight maps are similar to, but not completely the same as the relevance maps. Therefore, we expect to combine highlights and eye movements complementarily for estimating page difficulty. For instance, when a page area is detected in both a highlight and a relevance map, this suggests that the area has higher confidence than areas that were detected in either a highlight map or a relevance map. In this study, we do not discuss reading paths on each page and the other combinations of different resources such as texts of memos. For example, locations and the number of highlights may be related to the reading paths. We need to find how to choose related features.

6 Conclusion

We introduced our methods for supporting teachers. In our study, clickstream data and eye movement data were used to analyze relationships between students' learning behaviors and their quiz scores and to estimate region-wise page difficulty. Our works help teachers select strategies for learning supports and revise teaching materials.

Depending on the type of educational data, the advantages and disadvantages are different in the number of students and data collection. To solve the disadvantages, we evaluated the similarity between eye movement data and highlights in clickstream data and discussed the combination of different resources. In future work, we investigate the different combinations of the other resources such as memos written by students. In addition, we need to develop methods for finding effective combinations and features.

Acknowledgments. This work was supported by JSPS KAKENHI Grant Number JP19K20421.

References

1. Blikstein, P., Worsley, M.: Multimodal learning analytics and education data mining: using computational technologies to measure complex learning tasks. J. Learn. Anal. **3**(2), 220–238 (2016)
2. Brinton, C.G., Chiang, M.: MOOC performance prediction via clickstream data and social learning networks. In: 2015 IEEE Conference on Computer Communications (INFOCOM), pp. 2299–2307. IEEE (2015)
3. Davis, D., Chen, G., Hauff, C., Houben, G.J.: Gauging MOOC learners' adherence to the designed learning path. International Educational Data Mining Society (2016)
4. De Koning, B.B., Tabbers, H.K., Rikers, R.M., Paas, F.: Attention guidance in learning from a complex animation: seeing is understanding? Learn. Instr. **20**(2), 111–122 (2010)
5. Flanagan, B., Shimada, A., Yang, S., Chen, B.L., Shih, Y.C., Ogata, H.: Predicting performance based on the analysis of reading behavior: a data challenge. In: Companion Proceedings 9th International Conference on Learning Analytics & Knowledge (LAK 2019), March 2019
6. He, K., Zhang, X., Ren, S., Sun, J.: Deep residual learning for image recognition. In: Proceedings of the IEEE Conference on Computer Vision and Pattern Recognition, pp. 770–778 (2016)
7. Jian, Y.C., Ko, H.W.: Influences of text difficulty and reading ability on learning illustrated science texts for children: an eye movement study. Comput. Educ. **113**, 263–279 (2017)
8. Lapuschkin, S., Binder, A., Montavon, G., Müller, K.R., Samek, W.: The LRP toolbox for artificial neural networks. J. Mach. Learn. Res. **17**(1), 3938–3942 (2016)
9. Minematsu, T.: Region-wise page difficulty analysis using eye movements. In: International Conference Cognition and Exploratory Learning in Digital Age, pp. 109–116, November 2019
10. Minematsu, T., Shimada, A., Taniguchi, R.I.: Analytics of the relationship between quiz scores and reading behaviors in face-to-face courses. In: Companion Proceedings 9th International Conference on Learning Analytics & Knowledge (LAK 2019) (2019)
11. Minematsu, T., Shimada, A., Taniguchi, R.: Analytics of multimodal learning logs for page difficulty estimation. In: 10th International Conference on Learning Analytics & Knowledge, Frankfurt, Germany (2020)

12. Minematsu, T., Tamura, K., Shimada, A., Konomi, S., Taniguchi, R.: Analytics of reading patterns based on eye movements in an e-learning system. In: Graziano, K. (ed.) Proceedings of Society for Information Technology & Teacher Education International Conference 2019, Las Vegas, NV, United States, pp. 1054–1059, March 2019
13. Nakamura, K., Kakusho, K., Murakami, M., Minoh, M.: Estimating learners' subjective impressions of the difficulty of course materials in e-learning environments. In: APRU 9th Distance Learning and the Internet Conference, pp. 199–206 (2008)
14. Ogata, H., et al.: E-book-based learning analytics in university education. In: International conference on computer in education (ICCE 2015), pp. 401–406 (2015)
15. Onoue, A., Shimada, A., Minematsu, T., Taniguchi, R.I.: Clustering of learners based on knowledge maps. In: Proceedings of the 16th International Conference on Cognition and Exploratory Learning in the Digital Age, CELDA 2019, pp. 363–370, November 2019
16. Park, J., Denaro, K., Rodriguez, F., Smyth, P., Warschauer, M.: Detecting changes in student behavior from clickstream data. In: Proceedings of the Seventh International Learning Analytics & Knowledge Conference, pp. 21–30 (2017)
17. The, B., Mavrikis, M.: A study on eye fixation patterns of students in higher education using an online learning system. In: Proceedings of the Sixth International Conference on Learning Analytics & Knowledge, pp. 408–416 (2016)
18. Yamada, M., Shimada, A., Terai, M., Taniguchi, Y., Konomi, S.: Br-map: concept map system using e-book logs. In: Sampson, D., Sampson, D., Isaias, P., Ifenthaler, D., Ifenthaler, D., Rodrigues, L. (eds.) Proceedings of the 15th International Conference on Cognition and Exploratory Learning in the Digital Age, CELDA 2018, pp. 248–254, January 2018

Returning to Nature: VR Mediated States of Enhanced Wellness

Henry J. Moller[1,2,3,4(✉)], John A. Waterworth[5], and Mark Chignell[3]

[1] Department of Psychiatry, Faculty of Medicine, University of Toronto, 1 King's College Circle, Toronto, ON M5S 1A8, Canada
[2] PRAXIS Holistic Health, 101-785 Carlaw Avenue, Toronto, ON M4K 3L1, Canada
drmoller@praxisholistic.ca
[3] Department of Mechanical and Industrial Engineering, Faculty of Applied Sciences, University of Toronto, 5 King's College Road, Toronto, ON M5S 3G8, Canada
[4] Music and Health Research Collaboratory, University of Toronto, 80 Queens Park, Toronto, ON M5S 2C5, Canada
[5] Department of Informatics, Umeå University, Umeå 901 87, Sweden

Abstract. A visit to a place of natural beauty is known to have restorative potential. Immersing oneself in nature - relaxing, contemplating, meditating, walking and so on – can help improve one's mental and physical wellbeing. Suitably designed VR can encourage beneficial meditative states as well as healthy physical activities. We see fully immersive forms of VR as a form of "synthetic consciousness" that is a modern addition to the three clearly established classic states of consciousness: wakefulness, dreamless, and rapid-eye-movement (REM) sleep. Certain therapeutic and self-care mental health therapies such as mindfulness based stress reduction (MBSR) meditation can assist individuals to achieve relative peace of mind. We describe the development of aesthetically appealing VR programs that were designed to induce mental states of equanimity, hopefulness and child-like wonder, referring back to historical aspects of art and design. We also report work where VR was used to embed actions required for exercise within a meaningful experience with the exercise itself, and the associated effort, becomes secondary in the mind of the participant to the flow, and narrative logic, of the interaction being performed. To increase the "stickiness" or attractiveness of our VR approach to exercise we also introduce the idea of rewards for exercise carried out correctly. User groups of "healthy normal" adults, mental health patients with clinically significant anxiety, and frail elderly at risk of institutionalization have provided helpful and generally positive feedback.

Keywords: Virtual reality · Health design · Disability · Rehabilitation · Meditation · Nature therapy · Behavioural activation

1 Introduction

The industrial revolution of the late 18th and early 19th centuries had a transformational effect throughout Europe and North America. These societies transitioned from agrarian

N. Streitz and S. Konomi (Eds.): HCII 2020, LNCS 12203, pp. 593–609, 2020.
https://doi.org/10.1007/978-3-030-50344-4_43

to urban, with resulting enhanced capacities for economic growth through mass production, as well as greater geographic and social mobility for workers. While societies became richer overall, cities became overcrowded and there was widespread poverty as described by Dickens and others. The breakdown of traditional social bonds between the individual and family/community system was associated with a near-epidemic rise of mental unwellness and suicides (Durkheim 1893; 1897; Mulder 2008).

These dramatic industrial and societal revolutions were accompanied and followed by new approaches to art and design, including the Romantic and Bauhaus movements, with the former emphasizing aesthetic values and the latter practical utility (i.e. form and function). Both served to counter the human toll of an increasingly mechanized and urbanized world. In the case of Romanticism this involved nostalgically peering back at the intertwined relationship of human beings and nature, with an emphasis on emotionally evocative landscapes; by contrast, the Bauhaus movement embodied a starker minimalism that considered the relationships of human beings and machines. We propose that the flourishing of these new approaches to art and design played a therapeutic role in countering the delirious and often dehumanizing effects of industrialization and urbanization through enhanced aesthetic sensibility and functional utility of design, supplemented by restorative trips to the countryside for those who could afford it. The current late post-modern era is undergoing a technological revolution that is potentially just as disruptive as the earlier era of mass industrialization, While the earlier invitation/compulsion was from countryside to city, the current invitation is from everyday physical reality to virtual reality (VR).

VR offers entertainment as a readily available and inexpensive form of escape from a variety of dilemmas and anxieties but what are the social, ethical and utilitarian values promulgated by this new medium? Rather than merely moralizing on this matter, scientific (and, neuroscientific) principles should be used to evaluate the impact of VR on human behaviour and mental wellbeing. Through the science of neurophysiology, we now have a clearer understanding of brain and behaviour states, such as discrete states of consciousness mediating sleep and wakefulness (Aserinsky and Kleitman 1953). Progress is also being made in clarifying how shifts in cognition and emotion correlate with changes in electroencephalographic (EEG) patterns that mediate states of mind such as, for example, calmness versus agitation.

Fully immersive forms of VR can be understood as a form of "synthetic consciousness" that is a modern addition to the three clearly established classic states of consciousness: wakefulness, dreamless sleep, and rapid-eye-movement (REM) dream mentation. This could be viewed either as an augmentation or encroachment upon natural human neurobiological functionality. We also note that certain therapeutic and self-care mental health therapies such as mindfulness-based stress reduction (MBSR) meditation can assist individuals to achieve relative peace of mind even at the most distressing of times. Meditation can be laborious to learn and given the current predominant hyper-culture of immediacy and instantaneity, is not readily sought out either by entertainment-seeking escapists, nor those experiencing actual psychological illness or distress.

Thus, we have involved ourselves in the development of aesthetically appealing VR programs that include elements of hedonic reward reminiscent of Romantic art designed to induce mental states of equanimity, hopefulness and even child-like wonderment.

These VR meditation programs, delivered either via head-mounted display (HMD) or external display typically involve majestic nature vistas that have been recorded in numerous bucolic sites in Europe and North America over the past several years. In order to further induce relaxation effects, immersive audio accompaniments have been designed to entrain slowing/calming of brain states. User groups of "healthy normal" adults as well as mental health patients with clinically significant anxiety and frail elderly at risk of institutionalization have provided helpful and generally positive feedback to date.

With respect to a Bauhaus-like focus on craft and function, the second arm of this endeavour has involved the development of interactive devices intended to induce "behavioural activation" and enhancement of functional capability, a proven psychological therapy for some of the most difficult to reach patients affected by mental unwellness. As a supplement for those who experience simulator sickness in immersive VR, a virtual world can be presented on a curved screen, so that the person has a form of mixed reality where the physical world is available at the edges of the virtual world. Within this virtual world we have created a driving simulator that provides a set of immersive tasks (shopping, reminiscing, touring scenic places) predicated on the act of driving and navigating through the virtual world. We have also created virtual worlds where the goal is to motivate physical exercise so that the person needs to pedal with arms or legs (or both) in order to keep moving through the virtual world. These devices for behavioural activation and exercise are currently being tested and trialled in hospitals, libraries and long-term care homes and appear to be a promising way to motivated increased levels of exercise and activity in older people.

While VR can potentially become a dangerous departure from everyday reality, we will show in this paper how it is possible to create therapeutic versions of VR to best serve the wellness needs of individual and society-at-large in years to come.

2 Background

2.1 Virtual Reality, Leisure and Wellbeing

VR is emerging as a widespread societal phenomenon in industrialized nations In Marshall McLuhan's prophetic "The medium is the massage" (McLuhan and Fiore 1967, its original title due to a type-setting error and later popularized to "the medium is the message"), he opined:

> *All media work us over completely. They are so pervasive in their personal, political, economic, aesthetic, psychological, moral, ethical, and social consequences, they leave no part of us untouched, unaffected, unaltered.* (p. 26)

Our position is that VR, like other media, can work us over, but due to its immersive nature and its property as a novel from of consciousness, it can also be designed and utilized in beneficial ways that promote wellness. This paper is a reflection regarding the value-added upon individuals and society of a more pervasive presence of immersive media of various forms. More specifically, we seek to clarify the role of VR in the domains of health, wellbeing, productivity and leisure. In particular, the interconnected role of leisure and wellbeing is of interest. Leisure can be broadly defined as freely chosen activities (to be distinguished from obligatory, professional activities), and ***"perceived freedom in leisure"*** may be defined as a cognitive motivational construct of control over leisure experiences, the satisfaction of **leisure** needs and the participation in leisure behaviour and global life satisfaction (Ellis and Witt 1994). Further, this may be experienced either as **"freedom from"** (e.g. an unpleasant experience or environment) or **"freedom to"** (e.g. to engage with a meaningful or rewarding experience/environment), with the latter being conventionally understood as a higher order of leisure experience than the former (Harper 1986) in terms of Maslow's classic hierarchy of needs (Maslow 1943). Free choice as a point of departure technically may involve an infinite number of possibilities, however, leisure affordances are often narrowed for those with limitations in health, ability, mobility and economic means, amongst others. We have previously established that having leisure opportunities to engage with the physical splendour of nature in its various manifestations has demonstrable benefits for overall health and wellbeing outcomes both as a preventative and definitive health-care strategy (Moller et al. 2016; Moller et al. 2018). Yet, in many of today's modern, developed societies, access to leisure and wellbeing can be difficult to arrive at due to constraints in health, income, location and time (Moller et al. 2020).

2.2 Aesthetics, Form and Function: Historical Perspectives

In this paper, we will discuss aesthetic and functional elements of VR through the lens of two distinct movements in the history of art and design: the pre- and early Victorian Romantic movement and the Weimar Republic's Bauhaus movement, while looking to link these movements to aspirational and practical aspects of current VR therapeutics.

Romanticism (also known as the *Romantic era*) was an artistic, literary, musical and intellectual movement that originated in central and northern Europe toward the end of the 18th century, and in most regions peaked from about 1800 to 1850. In part, an artistic push-back against the evolving march of modernity to transform society into an ever more mechanical/industrial one, the Romantic Movement can be viewed as existing either as a complement to or cautionary opposition against changing societal standards, mores and values during this era. In contrast to the Rationalism and Classicism of the Enlightenment, Romanticism revived themes of heroism, mysticism, medievalism and elements of art and narrative perceived as authentic virtuous human qualities within nature in order to address population growth, early urban sprawl, and industrialism. The general emphasis often returned wistfully to the primacy of the central role of the human in the context of the natural world, and a nostalgic reminiscence of the Graeco-Roman classical period. Artists typifying the aesthetics of this era included luminaries such as Caspar Friedrich, William Blake, William Turner and Ferdinand Delacroix; it was a time of intense creativity for the arts in union with the natural world, and this included Romantic writers, poets and playwrights. Within the visual arts, the Romantic movement's backward-looking historical perspective would eventually be eclipsed late in the 19th century by **Impressionism**, a more contemporaneous take on the natural world, and the perceptual after-image a snapshot or prolonged experience might have on an observant individual.

A doctor's sage advice to members of the beleaguered bourgeoisie during this time might well have been to leave behind the stifling inner-city miasmas and interpersonal dog-eat-dog stresses of the rapidly expanding Metropolis of the industrial revolution for the refreshing airs of the seaside or mountains. While empirically sound health advice in terms of a classic Hippocratic preventative medicine model, it soon became apparent that such scenic getaways were not to be a reality for the majority, as widening economic disparities created a scarcity of access to places of nature, wellbeing and leisure; thus, attendance of a bucolic countryside sanatorium became financially and practically unrealistic for the majority of less than privileged urban dwellers. To this day, while general tourism and leisure has attained a far more widespread favour amongst the masses, the specific employment of the splendour of nature for the purpose of health and wellness is today more limited to those with adequate resources, be they in terms of finances, ability/mobility or simply even free time. Indeed, engagement in leisure past-times that can be defined as **medical tourism** either for definitive or preventative care has been trending in recent years, although largely limited to the affluent. The rise of medical tourism has been criticized in terms of its emphasis on the privatization of health care, its growing dependence on technology, the uneven access to health resources that is provided, and the accelerated globalization of both health care and tourism (Connell 2006; Crooks et al. 2010).

Aspects of tourism could naturally be viewed as a form of mental health therapy by virtue of imbuing the human need for perceived freedom (i.e. leisure in its classic definition), wellbeing and mobility outside the mundanities of day-to-day existence. In the early decades of the industrial revolution, the epidemic emergence of mental illness, with the most devastating outcome being suicide, was explained through the emergence of "anomie" (i.e. meaningless, anonymized existence) of city life in the rapidly developing urban centres at the turn of the 20th century. If there was a contagion to this epidemic, one could ascribe it to the socioeconomic pressures that uprooted established social and community structures (largely from rural/agrarian to urban/industrial) and redefined the meta-narrative of individual and societal roles within a very short span of history. Unfortunately, not long after this, World War I broke out, with its resulting devastati an apparent manifestation of the perils of full-scale industrialization at the expense of peace-time human values.

This breakdown of reason as an outcome of the industrial age of the machine was the societal outcome that the art and aesthetic of the Romantic era sought unsuccessfully to prevent. It is noteworthy that the Romanticism-inspired practice of the restorative return to nature as a regenerative health tourism practice persisted beyond World War I, though now more limited to the bleaker leisure affordances of this era. Romantic artists and writers, as well as the moneyed class continued to seek out opportunities to "get away from it all by journeying to environments with established reputation for conferring wellbeing on the ailing: e.g., green rolling meadows or an Alpine mountain environment, as eminent central European writers of the maturing industrial age such as Thomas Mann or Hermann Hesse might have approved of as remedies in times of physical and/or emotional weakness and lassitude (Mann 1924; Hesse 1925).

Overall, however, the post-World War 1 period was one of survivalism for the majority. Practicality, pragmatism and austerity replaced notions of splendour, wonderment and mysticism. Out of this environment emerged the design-oriented "form and function" imperative of the (Staatliche) **Bauhaus Movement**, a central German art and design school movement operational from shortly after World War I until 1933. Bauhaus combined crafts and the fine arts and emphasized functionality/utility as a valuable element of art within society. If Romanticism was a push-back against an all-too-rapid industrial age, then the Bauhaus Movement can be viewed as a counterweight to a mechanical/industrial society that imperils rather than assists human endeavours (Gaddis 2004).

Figure 1 illustrates aspects of the aesthetic framework underlying our endeavor into VR-naturescape meditation. German Romantic artist Caspar David Friedrich's mid- and late-career masterpieces "Wanderer Above the Sea of Fog" (1818) and "The Stages of Life" (1835) demonstrate his stylistic approach of placing the viewer into an immersive first-person perspective, seemingly inviting him or her to enter the scene as active participant rather than merely a passive observer. By employing this technique, an appeal for an engagement of meditative oneness with the nature scene is created. Thus, Victorian art presages Nature VR.

Fig. 1. **a** Caspar Friedrich "Wanderer über dem Nebelmeer" (1818) Kunsthalle Hamburg (Google Cultural Institute, Licensed under Public Domain via Wikimedia Commons). **b, c** Caspar Friedrich "Die Lebensstufen" (1835) Museum der bildenden Künste, Leipzig

2.3 Modernizing Old Romantic and Industrial Notions

In a modern-day context, a Bauhaus-informed utility has been described as **user-centred design**, with aesthetic becoming a secondary function, as opposed to the primary function of serving the needs of the user (Norman 1988). This is of interest to anyone involved in the care and rehabilitation of individuals with illness and/or disability, whether chiefly physical or mental. Growing further out of this movement to maximize ease-of-use and intended action outcome has come the conceptual framework **of inclusive design** (Abascal and Azevedo 2007); here, the focus is on optimized user acceptance in a lead user population that may have compromised perceptual/sensory capacity or a disability in integrative capacity of a "normal", fully intact and holistically experienced reality. It is thought that healthy normal users will also gravitate to those designs offering greatest ease-of-use and lowest encumbrance, i.e. those designed to serve those with handicaps, disabilities and varied accessibility issues.

Given the fact that those with compromised physical and especially mental function typically enjoy a diminished level of functionality in various instrumental and even basic activities of daily living, often paired with cognitive impairment, therapeutic approaches need to be mapped out sequentially and realistically. Rather than assuming the immediate ability to engage in Bauhaus-style form and function in a rehabilitative context, it must be understood that many affected individuals are easily tired, and vulnerable to loss of self-confidence in their abilities, as well as disturbances in focus and concentration. To this end, an approach of "working with what's there" is less aggressive and potentially threatening to a consumer of health-care therapeutics who may begin their health journey from a place of quite significant disability or impairment.

In our therapeutic approach, we induce a meditative worldview of tried and true aesthetic appeal. Naturally, it is not intended to replace actual time spent in nature, but rather to use a simulation that primes the neural circuits that would otherwise be activated in the *bona fide* great outdoors. Our choice of AV content is very much informed by the parallel contributions of the art and design communities to the past modern age's industrial revolution. Being faithfully entrenched in the nuances and complexities of the present historical epoch, we seek to place effective VR therapeutics into the context of our current postmodern age's embrace of technology and entertainment while remaining very much mindful of the central role of health psychology and perceptual phenomenology.

2.4 Reinstating Leisure as Mindful Meditation in the Modern Context

Meditation, including mindfulness-based stress reduction (MBSR) is now a mainstream therapy in mental health care, with good evidence to support its effectiveness in treatment of anxiety and mood disorders. No longer viewed as a fringe, new-age therapy, meditation is included in treatment guidelines for numerous serious mental illnesses, including mood and anxiety disorders in conventional medicine. (e.g. anxiety disorders guidelines for American family physicians; Locke et al. 2015).

In its typical manifestation, meditation requires active engagement and participation and is a learning process, far removed from the kind of healthful leisure experience one might get at a European spa or Japanese onsen hot-spring. Many users in the clinical arena are unable to readily practice meditation on their own because they find it hard to rehearse mental imagery or meditative affirmations, particularly if suffering from psychiatric illness or trauma that impacts neurocognitive capacity. (Moller and Bal 2013) These patients may lack imaginal capacity for visualization exercises: "…some patients refuse to engage in the treatment, and others, though they express willingness, are unable to engage their emotions or senses" (Difede and Hoffman 2002). A further roadblock that might impede the effectiveness of meditation-based relaxation therapies is the consistency and quality of the user's experience.

Meditation involves the ability to autonomously control one's mental function more optimally, while also learning to feel less overwhelmed by thoughts, emotions and/or mental phenomena that previously may have been negative, distressing, or overwhelming through a practice of acceptance and self-care. On a technical level, meditation may also involve the conjuring up of mental imagery or helpful self-talk through creative visualizations and/or meaningful mantras. These are difficult higher-level operations of consciousness; they are not readily learned or intuited by individuals experiencing acute or chronic distress, whether it be physical (e.g. pain), emotional (e.g. fear) or psychosomatic.

Meditation also requires intensive and repetitive practice by patients, who may have difficulty performing their practice autonomously. This has led to a clinical demand for developing standardized meditation techniques that can readily be provided to patients in a safe, effective and reproducible manner. For the past few years the first author has been researching and developing forms of VR-based mindful meditation at PRAXIS/Holistic Health (Moller and Bal 2013; Moller et al. 2016, 2018) that mimic the leisure experience of travel to spas and scenic spots in earlier times. The resulting TEMM (technology-enhanced multimodal meditation) program was designed to provide the benefits of meditation while making fewer demands on the patient in terms of self-discipline and cognitive effort.

TEMM is motivated by an inclusive design approach where it functions as a universal entry point to pleasant and hedonically rewarding meditative experience regardless of the physical and cognitive functions of the user. Up to this point TEMM has been targeted for use in a psychiatric practice, but it should also be useful for consumers in other settings (e.g. use in school settings to teach meditation to children with ADHD or anxiety, a stressed-out employee needing a rest-break in a corporate setting, a weary busy traveler stuck on a long flight or commuter train) as well as for people in long term care, including those with dementia.

TEMM utilizes immersive programs that entrain mental states of calmness, relaxation and wellbeing. These programs have been expanded in the "Windows to the World" project funded by the Canadian federal government's Social Sciences and Humanities Research Council (SHHRC) to focus on the capture, display and therapeutic use of immersive VR naturescapes, using majestic, authentically inspiring settings such as mountains, seashores, forests and fields paired with musical programs designed to effect brainwave entrainment congruent with meditative calmness, e.g., analogous to enjoying a relaxing sunset or sunrise while on a vacation. TEMM offers: a replicable, protocol-based, technology-delivered meditation session (with all its inherent benefits) monitored by a human attendant. It is a timely intervention as use of mobile devices with 3D AV capacities will become widespread within the next decade, with the likelihood that VR will be used increasingly extensively for medical, educational and recreational/entertainment purposes.

3 Making Meditative Content

In this section we discuss some of the techniques that we have used to create content that engenders states of mindful meditation[1].

3.1 Design of Video Content

For the development of TEMM content we created original immersive 3D video using a set of 7 GoPro HERO4 BLACK cameras. Video was shot in a variety of places of scenic

[1] We gratefully acknowledge the excellent technical input of Mr. Lee Saynor (PRAXIS Holistic Health) in the construction and ongoing development of the described VR-meditation naturescapes.

beauty. Post-production operations included synching, stitching, horizon correction, and colour/brightness normalization in the Kolor software suite.

The video was augmented with four interchangeable visual effects layers. These layers reside in the virtual space between the end user's eyes and the skybox—the polygonal sphere onto which the nature panoramas are projected (Gauthier 2005). We experimented with adding a number of different visual effects aimed at increasing the viewer's sense of wonder, and emphasizing the presentation of spectacle as opposed to the representation of narrative (Ryu 2007).

Videos were shot in Flat colour mode (similar to a photographer "shooting RAW" on a DSLR camera for editing flexibility) and expected colour intensity was restored in the stitching process, further colour adjustment could be activated during playback, inspired by the enduring popularity of photo filters. Older users could compensate for macular degeneration (Haegerstrom-Portnoy et al. 2014) by exaggerating colour saturation and possibly aligning the product closer to the end user's recollection of nature. Colour can also have intense personal associations, including correlation with personality type, as studied in the use of Instagram filters (Ferwerda and Tkalcic 2018). Thus colour adjustment is a relatively expedient way of adding a breadth of personalization to visual digital experiences, which users generally respond to positively, in our experience.

Another graphical effect that we have used is billowing mist, which simulates water vapour with particle clouds, to create atmosphere. This can either restore realism to an overcast panorama where the camera autofocused on objects (losing weather detail and motion in the process) or for enhancement through occlusion. A thick fog refracts colour and can be used for stylistic effect (Willis 1987; Narasimhan 2003).

The video environments are naturally tranquil unless more active scenes are filmed (e.g. through weather, camera motion, actors both human and animal). Activity can also be added through objects in the virtual space. We have found that radial, open, upward motion is preferred and is emotionally associated with happiness. This has both evolutionary and physiological roots in nature. One might contemplate, for example, a wide variety of curvilinear natural elements seemingly defying gravity: plants spiralling out, reaching for the rising sun, human and animal standing and being active.

In contrast downward motion tends to be associated with danger, evoking fear and anger. Examples include angular forms like predator teeth, chasms, jagged rock, death and decay, and dark water. Curvilinear elements also appear to be compatible with the physical structure of the eye (Lima 2017).

Lighting, and variations in lighting can also be used to meditative effect (see Fig. 2). Prolonged fixation on a bright moving object fatigues parts of the brain and induces trance, a state unique from sleep (Braid 1843). Following W. Gray Walter's experiments with strobe lights and EEG monitoring equipment in the 1930s and 40s, modern lighting and circuit technology enabled popular "mind machines"—oscillating LED glasses—through the 60s and 70s (Budzynski 1991). Affordable HMD's are only the latest medium for experiments in entrainment of brainwaves. Flickering of light is another way to modify conscious experience. Strobe lights can also make time appear slowed (low Hz) or simulate colours (high Hz) known as the Fechner effect: illusory arcs of pale colour among moving objects (Bagley 1902).

Fig. 2. Adding graphical effects to video for presentation to test subjects for evaluation

There is a large design space of graphical effects that can potentially enhance the experience of natural scenes present in VR. Figure 1 shows incremental levels of graphical effects being added to an originally unadulterated 3D- naturescape video. Users are asked to give quantitative and qualitative feedback upon random presentation of each meditative scenario via Oculus Go HMD.

3.2 Design of Audio Content

While VR therapeutics to date have largely focused on visual elements to produce compelling simulations, we note a relative dearth of research on the role of audio in enhancing the healing process. In our approach to TEMM, audio content is composed based on principles of correlating tempo of a variety of instrumental classical music pieces presented in a continuous mix with electroencephalographic (EEG) frequencies associated with states of inspiration, calmness and tranquillity. This is based on understanding of brainwave frequencies associated with alpha-EEG, or approximately 8–12 Hz or beats per second, representing calm awareness, and theta-EEG (4–8 Hz) (Markland 1990; Kabuto et al. 1993) and has been used to digitally weave together a series of audio suites based upon neuroscientific principles of meditative calmness and relaxation.

As with recurring EEG patterns, there are simple repetitive music phrases which can be employed to neutrally entrain positive states of being with transformative value. Our compositional method for meditative audio involves repetitive harmonic progression with layered melodic fragments intended to emotionally evoke/trigger brainwave states. with the final delivery symbiotically merged into a union with the nature visuals

(Moller et al. 2020). While the bulk of research, by necessity, continues to focus on the visual aesthetics, it is clear the contribution of the hedonics, aesthetics, resonance and immersiveness of audio ought not to be underestimated to create a more evocative, unified holistic VR experience conferring the intended perception of enhanced leisure and wellbeing.

3.3 User Feedback

In our testing thus far, the most memorable and resonant elements as reported by participants were the presence of dynamic natural "creature features" such as, e.g. flocks of peaceful grazing sheep or a graceful circling birds. This was true whether these creatures were embedded in the "real video" (e.g. sheep walking through a stone circle) or added post-hoc via CGI effects, making this the most successfully "integrated" visual effect. Participants also positively recollected the sun, clouds, mountains, the "spaciousness" of the valley, and the presence of any "unnatural" man-made features in a scene, such as the boulders that make up a stone circle surrounding a green meadow in a scenario captured in England's Lake District.

Quite a bit of early user feedback in iterative testing also focused on the immersive audio content. The choice of classical music was more evocative than expected, described by participants at times as "sad", "tense", "too loud", and "ornate" but at times positively "magical". Some participants noticed an uncanny mismatch between bird sounds and the scenery, for instance, hearing a woodpecker in a Swiss valley. The most technical participant criticized the "shifting sound channels" of the 3D-spatialization, suggesting it might best be used more judiciously. It was also noted that relatively minor shifts in audio content (e.g. using non-identical classical music segments in evaluating similar nature vistas) could shift aesthetic preference rankings that were intended to primarily evaluate alterations in visual content. To this end, we note that audio content ought to be minded as a likely contributing as well as confounding factor to be controlled for in content creation and evaluation.

The rising mist and oscillating lights visual effects were broadly deemed "distracting" and "unnatural"; "blocking" the scenery, not enhancing it. Changing the colour of mist from pink to white did not improve reception. Oscillating lights are being moved from the more foveal eye-space to the more peripheral environment in continued user testing, according to iterative design principles.

4 VR for Exercise

In addition to enjoying its beauty and relaxing qualities, when we are in nature we are also active: we walk, cycle and run as well as relaxing, sleeping and meditating. We will now review the compelling arguments for focusing on exercise as a central part of well-being.

Physical exercise is known to improve longevity and cognitive status, but older people get insufficient exercise. The problem is particularly acute in long term care. Lack of exercise leads to muscle wasting and poor metabolism, and increased likelihood of frailty, falls, and cognitive impairment. Tavares et al. (2014) found that even elders with depression can benefit from better quality of life when exercising. Rejeski and Mihalko (2001) reviewed more than 60 studies that reported improvement in quality of life when the amount of physical exercise increased. The current state of physical exercise and the elderly has been summarized by the 2018 Physical Activity Guidelines Advisory Committee Scientific Report, pages F9-1 to F9-2 (US Department of Health and Human Services, 2018) as follows. "*Ample evidence now exists that regular physical activity is key to preventing and managing major chronic diseases common to older people. Physical activity is also important for preserving physical function and physical function in aging, however, the proportion of older adults meeting recommended physical activity guidelines remains low (27%).*"

The problem of inactivity is particularly challenging in dementia, where people who are institutionalized may spend most of the day either sitting around or lying down (MacRae et al. 1996). This is in spite of the fact that physical exercise has been shown to provide a protective effect against cognitive decline in aging generally, as well as in Alzheimer's disease (Norton et al. 2014). As well as older people generally, people living with dementia are short of exercise, and the problem is particularly severe for people living in long-term care (Salguero et al. 2011).

It is not surprising that physical inactivity may lead to cognitive decline since the efficiency of brain metabolism and therefore the health of the brain networks and pathways that underlie cognition depend on body metabolism generally, and good blood flow (i.e., vascular efficiency) in the brain in particular. Current evidence suggests that increased or maintained cortical thickness might be one mechanism by which aerobic exercise preserves cognitive function in older adults (Lisanne et al. 2018). Vascular problems in the brain are associated with impaired executive functions, functional decline, and increased dementia risk (Roman et al. 2002; Vermeer et al. 2007). Aerobic exercise is a promising approach to delay the progression of vascular problems in the brain due to its direct effect on these cardiometabolic risk factors (Drexel et al. 2008).

Older people typically do not get enough physical activity, and as a result they suffer from preventable cognitive impairment, loss of physical function and energy, and depression, all of which may be treatable through greater levels of activation. Any intervention that can increase physical activation of the elderly, and those in nursing homes in particular, should have a beneficial impact on a range of outcomes including physical functioning, cognitive functioning, levels of depression, and quality of life. However, while many of the benefits of exercise for the elderly have been known for decades, most older people continue to get far less exercise than they need. Why is this?

A recent review of the problem attributed lack of exercise in the elderly to "failures of motivation and self-regulatory mechanisms" (Lachman et al. 2018). Simply put, older people generally know that physical exercise is good for them, but they are not motivated to exercise and they are unable to force or persuade themselves to do exercise. To deal with this problem Lachman et al. recommend "a personalized approach to motivation and behaviour change, which includes social support, goal setting, and positive affect coupled with cognitive restructuring of negative and self-defeating attitudes and misconceptions."

VR has been used to motivate exercise in the elderly. In appropriately designed VR applications, exercise occurs naturally as part of an immersive experience that includes a physical activity (e.g., rowing). However, VR solutions tend to focus on the upper body perhaps due to the fact that people are functionally blind to the external surroundings when using immersive VR, and moving around while using VR is dangerous. Thus there is a need for VR applications that can motivate people to exercise their legs. We have developed a solution ("Forever young" or 4VRYoung) that solves the problem of insufficiently motivated leg exercise by using leg pedalling in an immersive VR setting where people are motivated to pedal in order to move through engaging 360-degree travel videos. Pedalling works particularly well in this case because the legs move but not the body so that there is no safety concern with the person bumping into, or tripping over, objects.

Another feature of VR exercise solutions is that they allow exercise to be personalized and adaptive to the user. In the absence of technology, providing exercise to older adults is labour intensive and often expensive in terms of acquiring standard exercise equipment. Group exercise is often used as a cost-effective way for one person to supervise exercise carried out by a number of people. However, group exercise tends to be driven by the physical capability of the frailest member of the group. When a number of people are in wheelchairs this means that arm exercises are prioritized over leg exercises. In contrast, the VR approach uses pedals to exercise the legs as well as arms and the application can adapt the task to user capability. People can work individually, with little supervision, and at their own pace.

Figures 3 and 4 show a staff member at a Hospital Reactivation Centre learning how to use a pedal exercise game. This game can be played with immersive VR goggles or with a large screen display depending on the preferences of the user. In Fig. 3 the participant is choosing from a set of available courses to pedal on. There are five choices (buttons) on the screen with the sixth button being pressed if the person wants to see more choices.

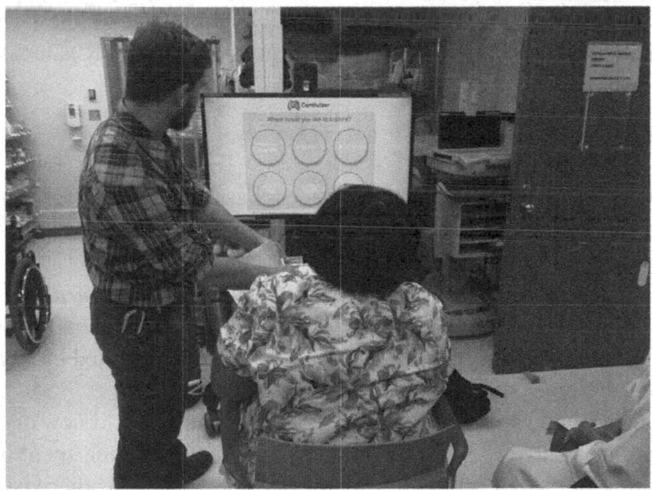

Fig. 3. Selecting a course in the pedal exercising game

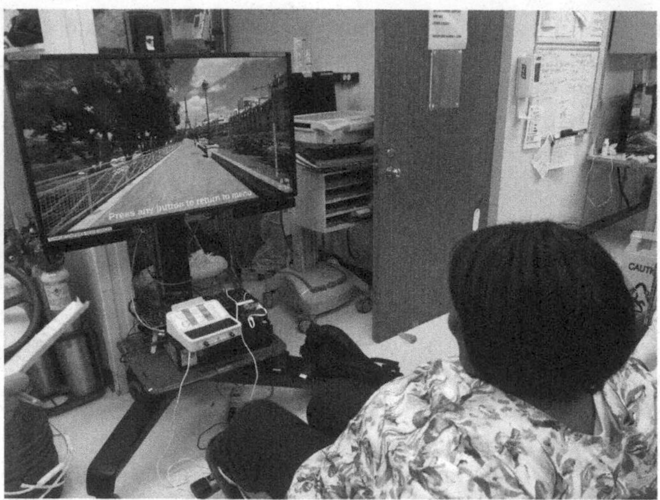

Fig. 4. Pedalling through a course.

Figure 4 shows the person pedalling through the course. Shown below the screen is the button box that is used to select courses. If the player gets tired of the course s/he is on she can hit any button on the button box to return to the menu screen and select a new course. In another version of the task (not shown here) the participant is moving through 360-degree travel videos. These may be shown with VR googles in which case the person can look around the video with head movements to change the viewpoint. Alternatively, the video can be shown on a large screen in which case participants use a steering wheel to pan around the video. Since a fairly large proportion of older people may be unwilling to wear goggles, or may suffer from simulator sickness when they use them, we typically use screens as alternatives to goggles in our VR games.

5 Discussion

The first thread of our research on VR for wellness has focused on leisure and aesthetics, a second thread is more functional in nature, inspired by the Bauhaus approach of form following function and of art being subservient to craft. As Gropius (1919) commented in his manifesto: "*The mere drawing and painting world of the pattern designer and the applied artist must become a world that builds again*". In our Bauhaus informed view, the immersive aesthetic of multimedia VR needs to be supplemented by a craft-oriented view, where perception is situated within meaningful interactions.

In our first therapeutic approach, we induced a meditative worldview of tried and true aesthetic appeal. Naturally, it is not intended to replace actual time spent in nature, but rather to use a simulation that primes the neural circuits that would otherwise be activated in the *bona fide* great outdoors. Our choice of AV content is very much informed by the parallel contributions of the art and design communities to the past modern age's industrial revolution. Being faithfully entrenched in the nuances and complexities of the present historical epoch, we seek to place effective VR therapeutics into the context of our current postmodern age's embrace of technology and entertainment while remaining very much mindful of the central role of health psychology and perceptual phenomenology.

In later work, the goal of interaction was exercise, and the purpose of using VR was to embed the actions required for exercise within a meaningful experience where the exercise itself, and the associated effort, becomes secondary in the mind of the participant to the flow, and narrative logic, of the task like interaction being performed. To increase the "stickiness" or attractiveness of our VR approach to exercise we also introduce the idea of reward, so that the exercise that is carried out is rewarded in some way.

6 Conclusion

A visit to a place of natural beauty is known to have restorative potential. Immersing oneself in nature - relaxing, contemplating, meditating, walking and so on – can help improve one's mental and physical wellbeing. Suitably designed VR can encourage beneficial meditative states as well as healthy physical activities. Those involved in the technological endeavour of ameliorating the human condition may well be advised to remain mindful of the history of aesthetics and ethics, while observant of current trends in this field of applied health science. While VR can potentially become a dangerous departure from everyday reality, it is possible to create therapeutic versions of VR that will serve the wellness needs of individual and society-at-large in years to come.

References

Abascal, J., Azevedo, L.: Fundamentals of inclusive HCI design. In: Stephanidis, C. (ed.) UAHCI 2007. LNCS, vol. 4554, pp. 3–9. Springer, Heidelberg (2007) https://doi.org/10.1007/978-3-540-73279-2_1

Aserinsky, E., Kleitman, N.: Regularly occurring periods of eye motility, and concomitant phenomena, during sleep. Science **118**, 273–274 (1953)

Bagley, F.W.: An investigation of Fechner's colors. Am. J. Psychol. **14**(4), 488–525 (1902)

Braid, J.: Neurypnology; or The rationale of nervous sleep, considered in relation with animal magnetism. London, UK (1843)

Budzynski, T.: The Clinical Guide to Sound and Light. Synetics Systems, Seattle (1991)

Connell, J.: Medical tourism: sea, sun, sand and…surgery? Tourism Manag. **27**(6), 1093–1100 (2006)

Crooks, V.A., Kingsbury, P., Snyder, J., Johnson, R.: What is known about the patient's experience of medical tourism? A scoping review. BMC Health Serv. Res. **10**, 266 (2010)

Difede, J., Hoffman, H.G.: Virtual reality exposure therapy for world trade center post-traumatic stress disorder: a case report. Cyberpsychol. Behav. **5**(6), 529–535 (2002)

Drexel, H., et al.: Metabolic and anti-inflammatory benefits of eccentric endurance exercise—a pilot study. Eur. J. Clin. Invest. **38**(4), 218–226 (2008)

Durkheim, E.: The Division of Labour in Society. Trans. W. D. Halls, intro. Lewis A. Coser. Free Press, New York, 362 pp (1997, first published 1893)

Durkheim, E.: Suicide: a Study in Sociology. Trans. J. A. Spaulding, G. Simpson. Free Press, New York (1997, first published 1897), 405 pp (1997)

Ellis, G.D., Witt, P.A.: Perceived freedom in leisure and satisfaction: exploring the factor structure of the perceived freedom components of the leisure diagnostic battery. Leisure Sci. **16**(4), 259–270 (1994)

Ferwerda, B., Tkalcic, M.: Predicting users' personality from Instagram pictures: using visual and/or content features? In: Proceedings of UMAP 2018, Singapore, Singapore, 8–11 July 2018 (2018)

Gaddis, J.L.: The Landscape of History. The Landscape of History: How Historians Map the Past, pp. 1–2. Oxford University Press (2004)

Gauthier, J.M.: Building Interactive Worlds in 3D: Pre-visualization for Games, Film, and the Web, pp. 90–91. Focal Press, Oxford (2005)

Gropius, W.: Bauhaus Manifesto and Program (1919). http://mariabuszek.com/mariabuszek/kcai/ConstrBau/Readings/GropBau19.pdf. Accessed 30 Jan 2020

Haegerstrom-Portnoy, G., Schneck, M.E., Lott, L.A., Hewlett, S.E., Brabyn, J.A.: Longitudinal increase in anisometropia in older adults. Optom. Vis. Sci. **91**(1), 60–67 (2014)

Harper, W.: Freedom in the experience of leisure. Leisure Sci. **18**(2), 115–130 (1986)

Hesse, H.: Kurgast: Aufzeichnungen von einer Baderner Kur, 160 pp. S. Fischer Verlag, Berlin (1925)

Kabuto, M., Kageyama, T., Nitta, H.: EEG power spectrum changes during to listening to pleasant music and their relation to relaxation effects. Nippon Eiseigaku Zasshi **48**(4), 807–818 (1993)

Lachman, M.E., Lipsitz, L., Lubben, J., Castaneda-Sceppa, C., Jette, A.M.: When adults don't exercise: behavioral strategies to increase physical activity in sedentary middle-aged and older adults. Innov. Aging **2**(1), igy007 (2018)

Lisanne, F., Hsu, C.L., Best, J.R., Barha, C.K., Liu-Ambrose, T.: Increased aerobic fitness is associated with cortical thickness in older adults with mild vascular cognitive impairment. J. Cogn. Enhanc. **2**(2), 157–169 (2018)

Locke, A.B., Kirst, N., Schultz, C.G.: Diagnosis and management of generalized anxiety disorder and panic disorder in adults. Am. Fam. Physician **91**(9), 617–624 (2015)

MacRae, P.G., Schnelle, J.F., Simmons, S.F., Ouslander, J.G.: Physical activity levels of ambulatory nursing home residents. J. Aging Phys. Activity **4**(3), 264–278 (1996)

Mann, T.: Der Zauberberg (2 vol.'s, pp. 578 & 629). S. Fischer Verlag, Berlin (1924)

Markland, O.N.: Alpha rythms. J. Clin. Neurophysiol. **7**, 163–189 (1990)

Maslow, A.H.: A theory of human emotion. Psychol. Rev. **50**(4), 370–396 (1943)

McLuhan, M., Fiore, Q.: The Medium is the Massage: An Inventory of Effects, 157 pp. Penguin Books, Random House, New York (1967)

Moller, H.J., Sudan, K., Saynor, L.: Multisensory meditation environments promote wellbeing. Univ. J. Public Health **4**(2), 70–74 (2016)

Moller, H., Saynor, L., Chignell, M.: Towards transformative VR meditation: synthesizing nirvana, naturally. In: Proceedings, 12th ICDVRAT with ITAG, Nottingham, England, 4–6 September 2018 (2018)

Moller, H.J., Barbera, J.: Media presence, dreaming and consciousness. In: Riva, G., Anguera, M.T., Wiederhold, B.K., Mantovani, F. (eds.) From Communication to Presence: The Integration of Cognition. Emotions and Culture Towards the Ultimate Communicative Experience. IOS Press, Amsterdam (2006)

Moller, H.J., Bal, H.: Technology-enhanced multimodal meditation: clinical results from an observational case series. In: Burdea, G., Weiss, T. (eds.) Proceedings of 10th International Conference on Virtual Rehabilitation, Philadelphia, PA, USA, August 2013 (2013)

Moller, H.J., Saynor, L., Butler, G.: Immersed in sound, with vision. In: Proceedings, 6th International Conference of Music and Medicine, Boston, MA, USA, 28–30 May 2020 (2020)

Mulder, R.T.: An epidemic of depression or the medicalization of distress? Perspect. Biol. Med. **51**(2), 238–250 (2008)

Narasimhan, S.G.: Models and algorithms for vision through the atmosphere. Ph.D. thesis, Columbia University, 223 pp (2003)

Norman, D.: The Design of Everyday Things, 240 pp. Basic Books, New York (1988). ISBN 978-0-465-06710-7

Norton, S., Matthews, F.E., Barnes, D.E., Yaffe, K., Brayne, C.: Potential for primary prevention of Alzheimer's disease: an analysis of population-based data. Lancet Neurol. **13**(8), 788–794 (2014)

Rejeski, W.J., Mihalko, S.L.: Physical activity and quality of life in older adults. J. Gerontol. Ser. A: Biol. Sci. Med. Sci. **56**(Suppl. 2), 23–35 (2001). https://doi.org/10.1093/gerona/56.suppl_2.23

Roman, G.C., Erkinjuntti, T., Wallin, A., Pantoni, L., Chui, H.C.: Subcortical ischaemic vascular dementia. Lancet Neurol. **1**(7), 426–436 (2002)

Ryu, J.H.: Reality & effect: a cultural history of visual effects. Dissertation, Georgia State University, pp. 11–16 (2007)

Salguero, A., Martínez-García, R., Molinero, O., Márquez, S.: Physical activity, quality of life and symptoms of depression in community-dwelling and institutionalized older adults. Arch. Gerontol. Geriatr. **53**(2), 152–157 (2011)

Tavares, B.B., Moraes, H., Deslandes, A.C., Laks, J.: Impact of physical exercise on quality of life of older adults with depression or Alzheimers disease: a systematic review. Trends Psychiatry Psychother. **36**(3), 134–139 (2014). https://doi.org/10.1590/2237-6089-2013-0064

Vermeer, S.E., Longstreth Jr., W.T., Koudstaal, P.J.: Silent brain infarcts: a systematic review. Lancet Neurol. **6**(7), 611–619 (2007)

Willis, P.J.: Visual simulation of atmospheric haze. Comput. Graph. Forum **6**(1), 35–41 (1987)

Going Beyond Computer-Assisted Vocabulary Learning: Research Synthesis and Frameworks

Mohammad Nehal Hasnine[1](✉), Masatoshi Ishikawa[2], Kousuke Mouri[1], and Keiichi Kaneko[1]

[1] Tokyo University of Agriculture and Technology, Tokyo 184-8588, Japan
nehalhasnine@gmail.com

[2] Tokyo Seitoku University, Tokyo 114-0033, Japan

Abstract. This paper introduces three computer-assisted applications designed for learning foreign vocabulary in an informal setting. The first one, images recommendation application, generates appropriate image recommendations for representing a word. It tackles the challenge for a foreign language learner to determine appropriate images from a standard web search engine such as Google, Yahoo, Flicker, etc. The second application, learning context representation application, generates learning contexts automatically from lifelogging images. It addresses problems associated with describing a learning context in the forms of hand-written descriptions, keeping notes, or taking memos. The third application we discuss here, namely location-based associated word recommendation application, generates recommendations of associated words in a particular learning location by analyzing word learning histories. It seeks to answer a critical question: what I should learn next? This is a critical challenge for the users of ubiquitous learning tools. In order to recommend potential vocabularies which a learner could be learning in a particular location, this study recommends associated words and topic-specific vocabularies. These applications are for AIVAS (Appropriate Image-based Vocabulary Learning System), a platform for computer-assisted vocabulary learning. We report here several evaluations, including human assessment and data-driven assessments, that have been carried out to reveal the importance of these systems.

Keywords: Artificial intelligence in language learning · Images recommendation · Informal learning · Learning context representation · Location-based associated word · Vocabulary learning technologies

1 Introduction

Research on foreign vocabulary learning has received considerable attention in recent years for many reasons. The first reason is that vocabulary learning is an inseparable part of foreign language development. Second reason is, foreign language learning is a must in many countries hence students are required to take courses such as English as the Second Language (ESL), French as the Foreign Language (FFL), Spanish as the Additional Language (SAL) or English for the Speakers of Other Languages (ESOL) in school. The third reason is that vocabulary expansion helps in expanding knowledge of

N. Streitz and S. Konomi (Eds.): HCII 2020, LNCS 12203, pp. 610–623, 2020.
https://doi.org/10.1007/978-3-030-50344-4_44

new information. To describe the importance of vocabulary in language learning, Wilkins stated that-without grammar, very little could be conveyed, but without vocabulary, nothing can be conveyed [1]. Lam addressed vocabulary as a vital element of language capability and delivers much of the foundation for how well novice learners communicate [2]. As a result, various systems have been developed to support web-based, mobile, and ubiquitous learning contexts. One of the aims of these systems is to assist learners in experiencing a systematic vocabulary learning process using ubiquitous technologies and multimedia-supported learning materials [3].

To support computer-assisted vocabulary learning, we develop a framework called AIVAS (Appropriate Image-based Vocabulary Learning System). In this framework, learners can create their learning materials. To support this framework, we developed three computer-assisted applications, namely an image recommendation system, a learning context representation system, and a system for location-based associate vocabulary recommendation. In this paper, we introduce them to the readers. We also report here several evaluations, including human assessment and data-driven assessments, that have been carried out to reveal the importance of these systems. Besides, we discuss the scope of employing learning techniques such as spaced-repetition, memory palaces, and mnemonics elaboration, etc. in computer-assisted vocabulary learning systems.

This paper is structured as follows. To begin with (in Sect. 2), we discuss other frameworks that can be referred for vocabulary learning in informal settings. After that, in Sect. 3, we introduce the AIVAS framework. Section 4 is about our contribution to image recommendation. Section 5 is about the learning context of representation. Next, in Sect. 6, we discuss the location-based associated word learning study. Finally, in Sect. 7, we conclude the paper by summarizing the outcomes.

2 Existing Platforms for Vocabulary Learning

Computer-assisted vocabulary learning is a much-explored research domain, and therefore, many frameworks are developed to assist in foreign vocabulary development. In 2005, PhotoStudy was developed to assists English as foreign language learners in improving their vocabulary by studying words associated with images that have been uploaded to a shared database [4]. In 2007, PSI [5] and MultiPod [6] systems were developed that allow creating a 5-second-long learning material consisting of the spelling, the meaning, and a short video clip together with the pronunciation data to acquire an English word is generated that aids English as second language learners. In 2010, a Mobile-assisted Content Creation system was proposed to facilitate elementary school students in the creation of vocabulary (English preposition and Chinese idioms) learning contents based on photos captured in real-life contexts [7]. In 2011, SCROLL, a ubiquitous language learning system that allows learners to capture and record their lifelong learning experiences as vocabulary learning logs [8], was introduced to the research community. In 2012, UEVL was introduced to aid learners in experiencing a systematic vocabulary learning process by displaying hints and providing a piece of guided information [3]. In 2013, Mobile Assisted Language Learning System, an online activities program was proposed that intends to assist elementary level Russian language learners enrolled at Macquarie University, Australia [9]. In 2015, Word Learning-CET6, an android application to assist English as Foreign Language learners in intentional vocabulary learning, was introduced. In 2016, U-Arabic, a context-aware ubiquitous learning system for Arabic language learning for non-native Arabic speakers [10], was introduced.

Our development AIVAS (Appropriate Image-based Vocabulary Learning System) was introduced in 2017. AIVAS is a web-based language learning system that, in the context of informal language learning, allows on-demand creation of vocabulary learning materials [11]. In this paper, we discuss the development of AIVAS. In addition, we discuss our research outcomes on three aspects, namely image recommendation, learning context generation, and location-based associated word recommendation.

3 AIVAS: The Platform for Vocabulary Learning

The initiative to develop AIVAS (Appropriate Image-based Vocabulary Learning System) was started in 2014. In the prototype of the system [12], we developed a web-based system for on-demand creation of learning materials for words that one intends to learn. Here, the system made it possible for the learners to create five-second-long learning material for a word that includes its spelling, meaning, pronunciation, and a corresponding image. From 2014 to 2017, the system has been much-researched and modified in terms of vocabulary memorization, retention, image recommendation, noun's imageability, and multimedia annotations. At present, AIVAS runs in web browsers. The user interface of the system is shown in Fig. 1. The main features of the system are:

On-demand learning materials creation: the system allows the users to create their learning materials on demand. Each of the learning materials is a five-second-long in length include its spelling, meaning, pronunciation, and a corresponding image. The on-demand architecture allows a learner to create his/her learning material without relying on instructors, and learn at their best times. The entire process of creating learning material happens automatically, so the learner does not need to gather learning resources such as image, text data, translation data, or pronunciation data by himself/herself [13].
Multiple foreign languages are supported: learners can acquire vocabulary in many languages using just one system.
Reuse the created materials: the system allows learners to generate their learning materials, save it in the system database, and reuse it [13].
Appropriate image recommendation for nouns: the system can decide the most appropriate image for a concrete noun, and recommend images based on image features for abstract nouns.
Rate learning materials: the system allows a learner to rate previously created learning material, and also to refer to the ratings given by other learners.

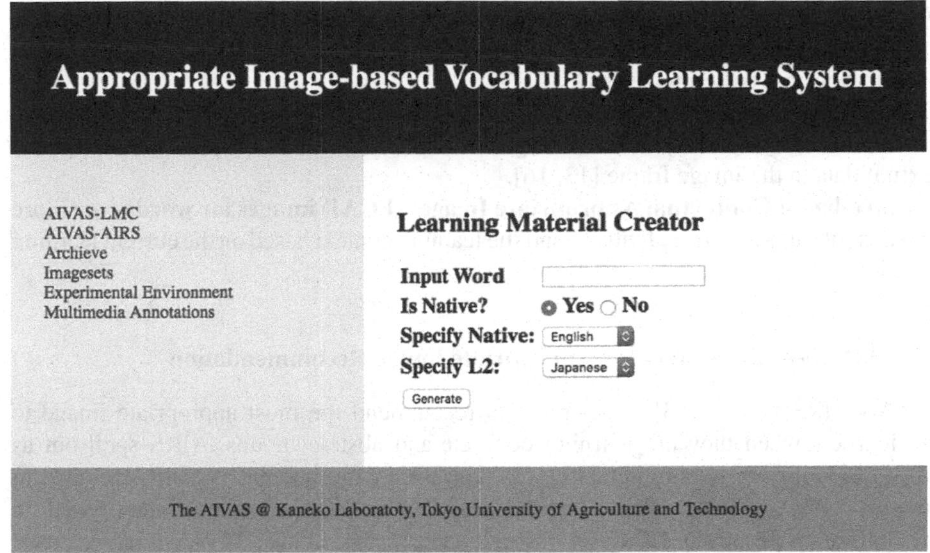

Fig. 1. The user interface of the system.

4 Research and Development on Image Recommendation

There are many advantages of using images for memorizing words. For instance, images are processed sixty-thousand times faster in the brain than text [14]; images affect learners on the cognitive level and stimulate their imagination and triggers our feelings by engaging with the visuals [15]. Nowadays, search engines are powerful. A search query in Google or Yahoo image search engine will result in thousands of images to represent a word, but it is not very easy for a human instructor or a technology-assisted agent to determine which images can be used for vocabulary learning purposes. As a result, it is crucial to research on image recommendation for vocabulary learning from pedagogical and educational perspectives. In our study, the objective is to develop a system that will assist learners in determining the most appropriate image to represent a word.

4.1 Theoretical Background

Concrete and abstract nouns are different in creating imageability in our brains. Concrete nouns are easy to create imageability. In contrast, abstract nouns are much tricky to form a clear image in our minds. Therefore, the definitions of appropriate images for abstract and concrete nouns are introduced. We assumed that the images that meet the definitions could be recommended to the learners for word learning. The definitions are:

For a basic concrete noun - an appropriate image for representing a concrete noun is the one having the actual object(s) located in the middle-ground, with the highest proportion of the actual object(s) in the image frame [11, 13].

For basic abstract nouns that represent social contexts between humans - a still image that contains only textual data (texts/characters) in the image frame can be suggested [13, 16].

For abstract nouns that are related to feeling and emotion - still images that are visually too abstract are may be inappropriate learning resources; hence, the system will have to filter out these images [13, 16].
For abstract nouns that represent human's social and religious beliefs - still image that contains multiple objects including the existence of human, object, animation, and textual data in the image frame [13, 16].
Feature-based Contextual Appropriate Images (FCAI) images for words - are those that describe unique image features and the learning context based on the current learning location [17].

4.2 AIVAS-AIRS System for Appropriate Image Recommendation

AIVAS-AIRS system [13] is designed to recommend the most appropriate image to the learners when they are learning concrete and abstract nouns. AIRS spell out as Appropriate Image Recommendation System is an experimental system developed to support AIVAS users. In this system, appropriate images are recommended based on the definitions proposed earlier for abstract and concrete nouns. AIVAS-AIRS is based on AIVAS-IRA (AIVAS-Image Ranking Algorithms) [11, 13, 16]. AIVAS-IRA has four phases, namely the initial phase, the intermediate phase, the re-ranking phase, and the re-determining centroid(s) phase. The initial phase and the re-calculate initial phases of the AIVAS-IRA are non-repetitive. On the other hand, the intermediate and the re-ranking phases of the algorithm are iterative.

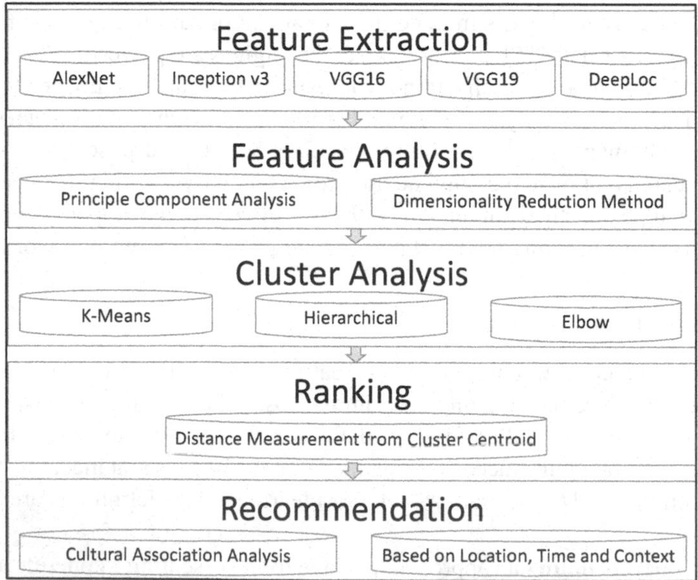

Fig. 2. The method of image feature analysis for image ranking

4.3 A Distributed Semantics Model for Feature-Based Contextual Appropriate Images (FCAI) Recommendation

This Distributed Semantics Model (DSM) [18, 19], is designed for Feature-based Contextual Appropriate Images (FCAI) Recommendation [17] in the context of ubiquitous learning. In this model, we first quantify and measure the semantic similarities between various educational data. After that, the model analyzes the relationship between a word and its visual image features. In doing this, the model also considers learning context, geographical location, demographic information, time of learning, etc. After that, the model analyses the learner's cultural-association and learning context of a word and its image representation. Finally, using AIVAS-IRA (introduced in Sect. 4.2), the DSM determines the most appropriate FCAI image that can be used to represent a word under a particular learning location. In Fig. 3, the overview of the DSM is shown.

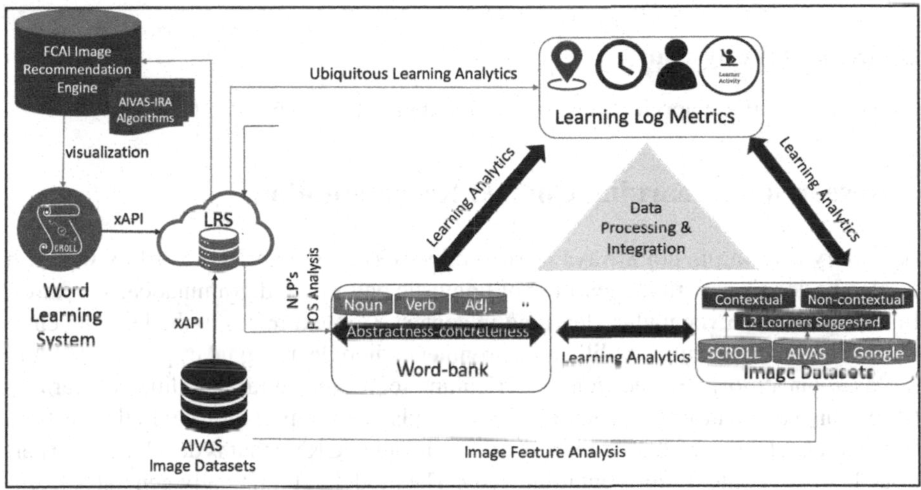

Fig. 3. The distributional semantics model for feature-based contextual appropriate images

4.4 Image Datasets

In order to implement the frameworks introduced in Sect. 4.2, we prepared four image datasets. These datasets contain sample images that can be used as vocabulary learning resources. We briefly introduce these datasets.

AIVAS-CNCRT59 dataset is a collection of 59 sample appropriate images for representing 59-English words. These images are accumulated by the authors from the Google image search engine. In selecting these images, two measures were our key considerations—first, images in which the actual object(s) highlighted in the center position. Second, the higher proportion of the actual object(s) in the image.

AIVAS-ABST-LS68 dataset contains 68 sample appropriate images representing 14-English abstract nouns. Unlike the AIVAS-CNCRT59 dataset in which images were chosen by the authors, images in the AIVAS-ABST-LS68 dataset were chosen by the learners of foreign languages. We carried a survey for accumulating images in this dataset.

AIVAS-ABST-LS795 dataset is our third image dataset. This dataset contains 795 sample appropriate images for representing 83 frequently used English abstract nouns. The learners of foreign languages choose the images in this dataset. In collecting the images, a survey was conducted.

AIVAS-ABST8300 dataset is a collection of 8300 sample appropriate images. Eight thousand three hundred images represent 83 frequently-used abstract nouns in the English language. The authors accumulated these images. In preparing this dataset, 100 images for representing each of those 83 abstract nouns are downloaded from the Google image search engine using the Fatkun batch downloader.

SCROLL dataset [20] is a collection of learning logs collected using a ubiquitous learning system. Till today, the dataset has 30000 learning logs. There are approximately 10000 images in this dataset. The images are lifelong learning images.

4.5 Demo of the Systems

Some demos of these applications can be found in [11–13, 16–19, 21].

5 Research on Learning Context Representation

Vocabulary learning is not always learned directly (i.e., memorized word by word); it can also be acquired with the learning of linguistic patterns and grammatical structures. This often refers to vocabulary learning in context. Context refers to the learning environment and socio-cultural-political environment where learning takes place, including the classroom atmosphere, academic curriculum, social and cultural tradition of learning [22]. In language learning, the learning context plays an important role. In this section, we introduce a learning context representation model (LCRM) that is developed as a part of our learning context representation study. The model automatically generates learning contexts from the pictures that users used to create a learning material. In order to produce learning contexts, we analyzed the visual contents of images. We refer to these contexts as the special learning contexts for vocabulary learning. The assumption was that those special learning contexts would help learners in enhancing their vocabulary [23].

5.1 Overview of the Framework

Our framework is based on the integration of three modular systems. First, a Context Representation Model (LCRM). Second, a Learning Context Analytics (LCA). Third, a Picture-assisted Quiz System (PQS). The framework (shown in Fig. 4) can be used independently or as a function of the AIVAS system.

Learning Context Representation Model (LCRM) First takes a picture as an input. After that, it analyzed the scene of the picture. Next, it detects the objects of the picture and generates vocabulary using an LSTM (Long Short-Term Memory) model. Finally, it generates sentences using automatic image captioning technology.

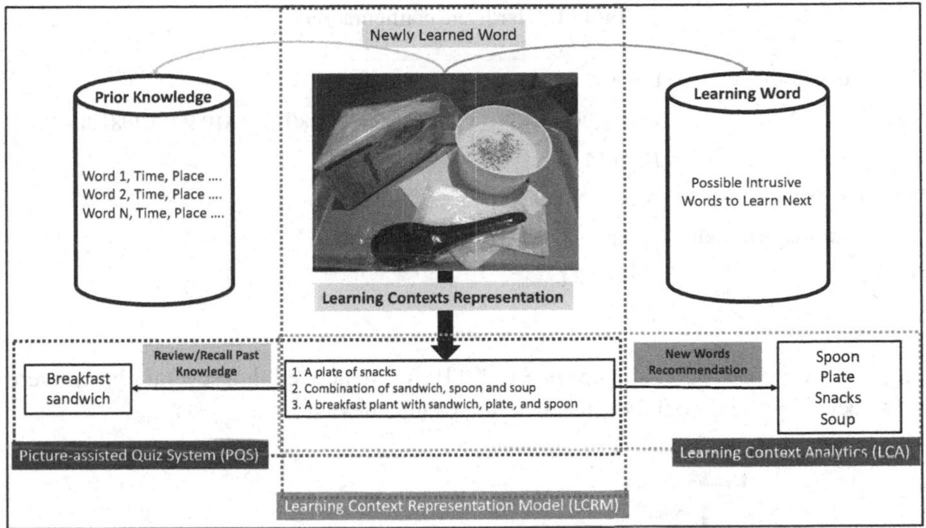

Fig. 4. The framework of learning context representation research

Learning Context Analytics (LCA) is used to analyze the sentences generated by the LCRM. In general, we use POS (Parts-of-Speech) analysis in the LCA.

Picture-assisted Quiz System (PQS) is used to generate quizzes to assess one's vocabulary skills. The PQS is used as the reflection tool.

5.2 Development of the Learning Context Representation Model (LCRM)

Learning context representation is a complex task, although artificial intelligence is gaining much popularity to build various learning systems. In order to develop LCRM, we leveraged automatic image captioning, which has connected computer vision and artificial intelligence. We used a neural network-based model called Show-and-Tell for analyzing the scenes from the natural images and generating reasonable contexts in plain English. The LCRM model encodes an image into a compact representation. Then it uses a recurrent neural network to generate the threes corresponding sentences. The model presents each of the sentences with its corresponding accuracy. Our model uses Microsoft's COCO dataset. Table 1 shows the hardware details and the training time require to train the model.

5.3 Output of the Model

In Fig. 5, we demonstrate an example output of the model. Here, we used a lifelong learning image from a context-aware learning system. The picture was used by a learner to memorize the word *computer*. The learner described the learning context as: *this is a computer running Oculus Rift for language research.* Our LCRM represented the learning contexts as: (1) a laptop computer sitting on top of a desk ($p = 0.008150$), (2) a laptop computer sitting on top of a wooden desk ($p = 0.007242$), and (3) a laptop

Table 1. Hardware configuration

Characteristics	Details
GPU	ZOTAC GAMING GeForce RTX 2080 Ti AMP ZT-T20810D-10P
Time	10 to 14 days
Libraries/Packages	Bazel, Python, Numpy, punkt
Natural language toolkit	NLTK
Dataset	MSCOCO

computer sitting on top of a table (p = 0.001166). We noticed that several objects were not detected by the model. For instance, the Oculus device.

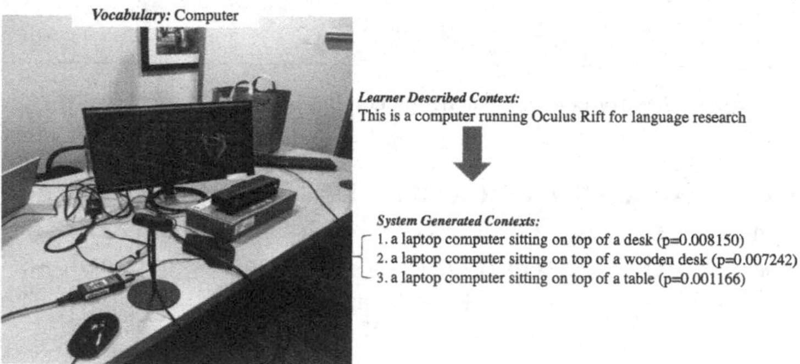

Fig. 5. An output of the LCRM model

5.4 Scope of Intrusive Word Learning Using this Technology

With this technology, learners of foreign language can learn their intended vocabulary as well as multiple intrusive vocabularies using one learning material. Figure 6 displays a screenshot of the learning environment developed for intrusive vocabulary learning.

6 Research on Location-Based Associated Vocabulary Recommendation

A common criticism of traditional word learning tools are - the scope of learning new words covering diverse topics is limited. Besides, existing tools do not support learning associated words synonymously related words while associated words are important to memorize. Associated words are often addressed as the related words by the linguists. In vocabulary development, associated words to another set of words are useful because they often contain lots of collocations that are important for enhancing sentence construction skills, particularly crucial for academic writing, speaking ability, passing proficiency tests such as IELTS, TOEFL, etc. To overcome this limitation, Google,

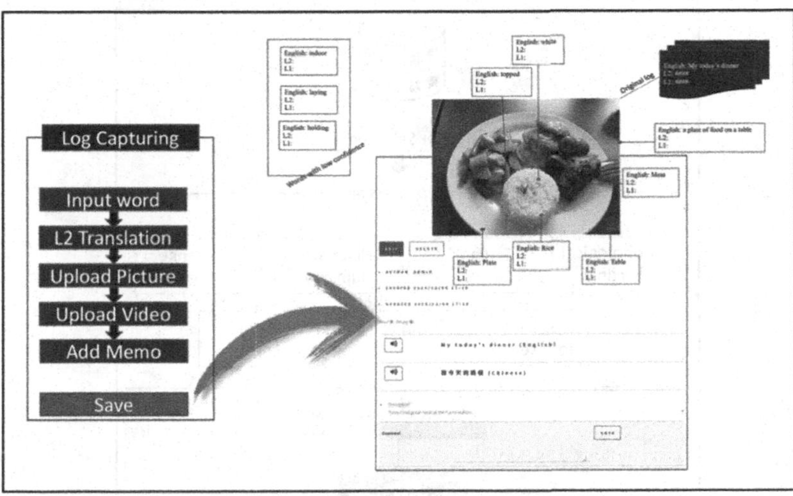

Fig. 6. Intrusive vocabulary learning using the framework

in 2018, developed Google coach where related and associated words are suggested. Inspired by Google, we aimed to develop an intelligent word recommendation agent in the context of ubiquitous learning that can suggest associated words. The following sections describe our approach and contribution to support location-based associated word recommendation literature.

6.1 Design of the Model

In order to recommend associated and related words, our approach is to understand word cooccurrence information in learners' ubiquitous learning behavior. Word cooccurrence information clues about learners such as learning behavior (i.e., eastern - vs.- western learners), learner-to-context interaction, and stage of learning (novice, intermediate, or advanced), etc. can be discovered from word cooccurrence information. A paradigm is proposed to discover word cooccurrence information and associated word recommendation. Figure 7 shows the design of the model.

6.2 An Exploratory Analysis to Test the Model

To test the accuracy of the model, we carried out an exploratory data analysis. For the analysis, we used the SCROLL dataset [20] as it contains ubiquitous learning logs collected from learners of foreign languages. We selected 20-users' data from the dataset. The common grounds for the participants are- first, they registered English as their default language, and second, they created the highest number of logs while their study location was the Tokushima region. We used Geolocational clustering for location similarity to determine the location. Figure 8 shows the geolocational clustering for location similarity using k-means.

After that, we preprocessed their logs by eliminating stop words, irrelevant characters, missing values, and missing numbers. We used manual operation for preprocessing.

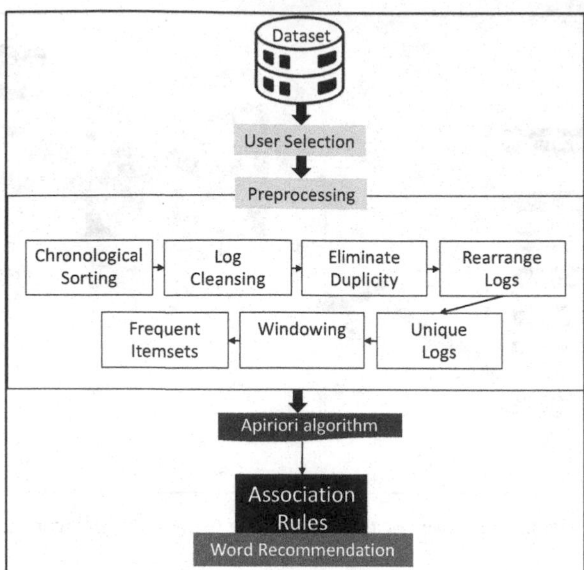

Fig. 7. The model of the location-based associated word recommendation tool [24]

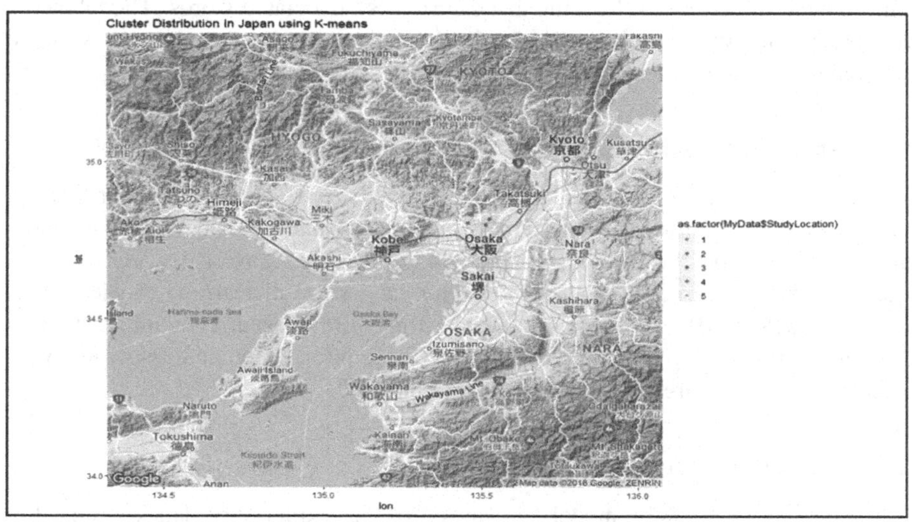

Fig. 8. Geolocational clustering for location similarity using k-means

In addition, we used Mecab and TreeTagger for data preprocessing. At last, we employed Apriori and FP-growth algorithms [25] on the preprocessed text data.

The result indicates that - IF a learner studies the word collapse THEN he/she may study the word plead (Minimum Confidence = 13%, Support = 0%, Confidence = 0.01). However, the confidence level is low. It is because students' learning location and time varied a lot [24].

6.3 Output of the System

Based on the training data, we yield this that- the possibility of recommending intrusive vocabulary is higher than associate words. For instance, if a learner learns *apple, orange, kiwi,* and *powder* at a supermarket, we expected the associated words such as *buy* and *eat*. However, our model recommends random and intrusive words such as *cloths, street, milk, cloud,* and *streaming*. Our analysis also suggested that- in informal learning context, English as the Foreign Language learners' word learning interests diverse although the learning location remains to be the same [24]. We show an output of the system in Fig. 9.

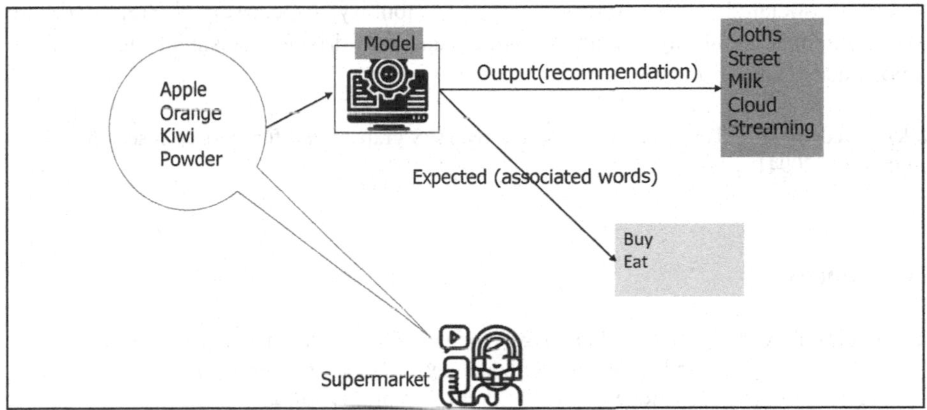

Fig. 9. An output of the model

7 Summary

In this paper, we introduced computer-assisted applications designed for learning foreign vocabulary. At first (in Sect. 3), we introduced a web-based vocabulary learning system named AIVAS (Appropriate Image-based Vocabulary Learning System). Using this system, foreign language learners can create their learning materials without the help of human instructors. Next (in Sect. 4), an image recommendation system is presented. The system generates appropriate image for representing abstract and concrete nouns. This system tackles the challenge for a foreign language learner to determine appropriate images from a standard web search engine. We address this challenge using the image ranking algorithms. Our algorithms are based on feature extraction on image datasets. Therefore, the algorithms extract and analyze various hand-crafted and deep image features in determining the most appropriate image. Moreover, the image recommendation system is capable of categorizing images based on feature similarity. After that (in Sect. 5), a learning context representation application is presented. This system generates learning contexts automatically from lifelogging images. It addresses problems associated with describing a learning context in the forms of hand-written descriptions, keeping notes, or taking memos. To overcome it, this system produces three possible learning contexts using lifelog images. The assumption behind using a lifelogging image is that visuals stay in memory for a longer time. This technology leverages the power of automatic image captioning, and the field of artificial intelligence that connects computer vision, image processing, and natural language processing. The final application (in Sect. 6) is a location-based associated word recommendation tool. It generates recommendations of associated words in a particular learning location by analyzing word learning histories. It seeks to answer a critical question: what I should learn next? This is a critical challenge for the users of ubiquitous learning tools. In order to recommend potential vocabularies which a learner could be learning in a particular location, this study recommends associated words and topic-specific vocabularies. Association rule mining and topic modeling methods are used to analyze learning histories before recommending associated words and topic-specify vocabulary, respectively. We reported here several findings, including human assessment and data-driven assessments, to reveal the importance of our applications.

Acknowledgement. This work is supported by JSPS grant-in-aid for start-up research activity number 19K20941.

References

1. Wilkins, D.A.: Linguistics in Language Teaching. E. Arnold, London (1973, 1972)
2. Richards, J.C., Renandya, W.A.: Methodology in Language Teaching: An Anthology of Current Practice. Cambridge University Press, Cambridge (2002)
3. Huang, Y.-M., Huang, Y.-M., Huang, S.-H., Lin, Y.-T.: A ubiquitous English vocabulary learning system: evidence of active/passive attitudes vs. usefulness/ease-of-use. Comput. Educ. **58**(1), 273–282 (2012)
4. Joseph, S., Binsted, K., Suthers, D.: PhotoStudy: vocabulary learning and collaboration on fixed & mobile devices. In: IEEE International Workshop on Wireless and Mobile Technologies in Education (WMTE 2005), p. 5 (2005)
5. Hasegawa, K., Amemiya, S., Ishikawa, M., Kaneko, K., Miyakoda, H., Tsukahara, W.: PSI: a system for creating english vocabulary materials based on short movies. J. Inf. Syst. Educ. **6**(1), 26–33 (2007)
6. Hasegawa, K., Amemiya, S., Kaneko, K., Miyakoda, H., Tsukahara, W.: MultiPod: a multilinguistic word learning system based on iPods. In: Proceedings of the Second International Conference on Task-Based Language Teaching (2007)
7. Wong, L.-H., Looi, C.-K.: Vocabulary learning by mobile-assisted authentic content creation and social meaning-making: two case studies. J. Comput. Assist. Learn. **26**(5), 421–433 (2010)
8. Ogata, H., Li, M., Hou, B., Uosaki, N., El-Bishouty, M.M., Yano, Y.: SCROLL: supporting to share and reuse ubiquitous learning log in the context of language learning. Res. Pract. Technol. Enhanced Learn. **6**(2), 69–82 (2011)
9. Kalyuga, M., Mantai, L., Marrone, M.: Efficient vocabulary learning through online activities. Procedia-Soc. Behav. Sci. **83**, 35–38 (2013)
10. Alobaydi, E.K., Mustaffa, N., Alkhayat, R.Y., Arshad, M.R.H.M.: U-Arabic: design perspective of context-aware ubiquitous Arabic vocabularies learning system. In: 6th IEEE International Conference on Control System, Computing and Engineering (ICCSCE), pp. 1–6 (2016)

11. Hasnine, M.N., Ishikawa, M., Hirai, Y., Miyakoda, H., Kaneko, K.: An algorithm to evaluate appropriateness of still images for learning concrete nouns of a new foreign language. IEICE Trans. Inf. Syst. **100**(9), 2156–2164 (2017)
12. Hasnine, M.N., Hirai, Y., Ishikawa, M., Miyakoda, H., Kaneko, K.: A vocabulary learning system by on-demand creation of multilinguistic materials based on appropriate images. In: Proceedings of the 2014 e-Case & e-Tech, pp. 343–356 (2014)
13. Hasnine, M.N.: Recommendation of appropriate images for vocabulary learning. Ph.D. thesis, Tokyo University of Agriculture and Technology, Japan (2018)
14. Alliance, V.T.: Professional development for primary, secondary & university educators/administrators. Retrieved from Professional Development for Primary, Secondary & University Educators/Administrators (2014)
15. Gutierrez, K.: Studies confirm the power of visuals in elearning. Shift Disruptive ELearning (2014)
16. Hasnine, M.N., Hirai, Y., Ishikawa, M., Miyakoda, H., Kaneko, K., Pemberton, L.: An image recommender system that suggests appropriate images in creation of self-learning items for abstract nouns. Int. J. Manag. Appl. Sci. **2**(5), 38–44 (2016)
17. Hasnine, M.N., Mouri, K., Flanagan, B., Akcapinar, G., Uosaki, N., Ogata, H.: Image recommendation for informal vocabulary learning in a context-aware learning environment. In: Proceedings of the 26th International Conference on Computer in Education, pp. 669–674 (2018)
18. Hasnine, M.N.: A distributional semantics model for image recommendation using learning analytics. In: Early Career Workshop Proceedings of the 26th International Conference on Computer in Education, pp. 10–12 (2018)
19. Hasnine, M.N., Flanagan, B., Ishikawa, M., Ogata, H., Mouri, K., Kaneko, K.: A platform for image recommendation in foreign word learning. In: Companion Proceedings of the 9th International Conference on Learning Analytics and Knowledge (LAK 2019), pp. 187–188 (2019)
20. Ogata, H., Uosaki, N., Mouri, K., Hasnine, M.N., Abou-Khalil, V., Flanagan, B.: SCROLL dataset in the context of ubiquitous language learning. In: Workshop Proceedings of the 26th International Conference on Computer in Education, pp. 418–423 (2018)
21. Hasnine, M.N., Hirai, Y., Ishikawa, M., Miyakoda, H., Kaneko, K.: Learning effects investigation of an on-demand vocabulary learning materials creation system based on appropriate images. In: Proceedings of the 4th ICT International Student Project Conference (2015)
22. Gu, P.Y.: Vocabulary learning in a second language: person, task, context and strategies. TESL-EJ **7**(2), 1–25 (2003)
23. Hasnine, M.N., Flanagan, B., Akcapinar, G., Ogata, H., Mouri, K., Uosaki, N.: Vocabulary learning support system based on automatic image captioning technology. In: Streitz, N., Konomi, S. (eds.) HCII 2019. LNCS, vol. 11587, pp. 346–358. Springer, Cham (2019). https://doi.org/10.1007/978-3-030-21935-2_26
24. Hasnine, M.N., et al.: Design of a location-based word recommendation system based on association rule mining analysis. In: Proceedings of the 8th International Conference on Learning Technologies and Learning Environments, pp. 250–253 (2019)
25. Agrawal, R., Imieliński, T., Swami, A.: Mining association rules between sets of items in large databases. In: Proceedings of the 1993 ACM SIGMOD International Conference on Management of Data, pp. 207–216 (1993)

Circuit Game

A Craft-Based Electronic Building Practice

Farzaneh Oghazian(✉) and Felecia Davis

The Pennsylvania State University, State College, USA
{Fxo45,Fud12}@psu.edu

Abstract. In this research, through a project named Circuit Game, a conceptual framework has been developed by which new processes of integrating craft and technology for educating electrical concepts are explored. The framework incorporates Do It Yourself (DIY) methods through making and assembly procedures. The intention is to engage architecture students in the process of crafting a new technological artifact while understanding difficult concepts related to electronics. Buechley & Hill define HCI as the development of new interfaces for interaction between people and technology (Buechley and Hill 2010). The authors seek to discover how a composite textile interface can invite people into thinking about electronics, materials, and design processes and eventually engage them in the process of designing circuits through crafting. Base materials, DIY making, and DIY assembly processes are three interwoven components of the circuit game. The role of these elements in the learning process are investigated through the development of a circuit game.

Keywords: Game · Circuit · Composite textiles · Craft-based game · Interaction

N. Streitz and S. Konomi (Eds.): HCII 2020, LNCS 12203, pp. 624–635, 2020.
https://doi.org/10.1007/978-3-030-50344-4_45

1 Background Research

In the last decades, HCI has been researched from different perspectives. This part explores literature studies mostly related to the gaming, integration of electronics and craft, as well as educating through materiality.

1.1 Educating Through Materiality

Base materials that are the interest of this research include crafts, Arduino boards, and computers that enable the craft to play as the interface for interaction with a human. Based on a discussion by Wiberg et al. (2013) a material perspective offers very different implications of HCI practice and a new way of seeing. In addition, a good material understanding helps to expand the boundaries of HCI. Therefore, materiality is one of the main elements of HCI and its role should be explored through the experience. This section investigates how the material has been defined in HCI research practices

Based on Davis (2017), Papert, Eisenberg, Buechley, Elumeze, and MacFerrin are some researchers that represent computers as material. Papert introduces computers as "an object to think with" (Papert 1980), play and experiment with Davis (2017). His approach requires human participation and interaction with computers to enhance the learning process. Eisenberg goes further and looks at computing as an act of bringing things to life by making them do things (Davis 2017).

Redstrom and Maze identify computational materials and assert that temporal form is the main difference between these materials and the conventional materials. In their research, they focus on the shift from form to experience. The temporal form that they refer to will be apparent when they are used by people to create new expressions (Mazé and Redström 2005). In this regard, Davis declares that to make, invent, combine, select and recycle a material indicate where a person is in relationship with the material and determine the degree of completeness, openness, and lifespan of that material (Davis 2017).

Using forgotten histories as the material and practice of innovation for reconfiguring the present as well as creating and visualizing our relationship to the design in the future is proposed by Rosner (2018).

1.2 Integration of Craft and Technology-Educating Through DIY Making Process

Buechley et al. (2008) introduce three approaches toward technology and these are technology as automation, entertainment and expanding human expression. While the first two aim to ease the learning and improve the productivity and human condition, the latter focuses on whether the human can do things or express things that are beyond their capacities. One way that people can challenge themselves for their potentials is engaging in Do It Yourself activities. In general, DIY comprises modification through creative activities to make new things and it can be an important alternative for design practices (Buechley et al. 2009) which requires the active participation of people in making and assembly processes.

Craft has been incorporated in research practices as a material for educating people in electronic concepts. for example, the implementation of printed circuit boards (PCB) in crafts using techniques like sewing, carving, and painting is the focus of research by Buechley and Perner-Wilson (2012). Integrating craft materials like sequins and buttons as part of the circuit device engages the users and makers of the device due to the familiarity with the materials (Buechley and Eisenberg 2007).

Regarding the integration of textile and electronics, in their book "Textile messages", the authors point out that e-textiles use the materials and practices that were traditionally the domain of women as pathways into engineering for the women and under-represented groups through a playfully combining of electronics with textile, crafts, clothing, and jewelry (Buechley et al. 2013). This act of piecing together "help establish design as a site to invite more intimate and longstanding relationship with technological things" (Rosner 2018). Overall, the makers are designers of the devices, who will learn something new through playful making processes and integrating familiar craft-based materials and electronics.

1.3 Game Practices-Educating Through DIY Assembly Process

The other approach is educating through assembly and game strategies. Based on Björk (2008), there are three interwoven area in gamed-based design:

- Codes or the systems that embed the process in themselves (game)
- People who are doing the game practices (gamers)
- The type of interaction that people have with the game (gaming)

Each of the elements of the game differently affects the educating process. Papert suggests that games like LOGO, as a tool for education, should be easily accessible to get into it but should not be a toy. The game language should also be accessible but challenging enough to help users make progress in learning new things (Papert 1980). Researchers and hobby designers are exploring the methods of embedding technology into toys for the educational purposes (Buechley and Hill 2010; Salgado et al. 2017). Buechley and Perner-Wilson point out that education researchers like Eisenberg and Kafai investigate the role of combining art and technology in hand-on projects to enrich the quality of learning. In their study, the methods by which technology can be augmented through developing hybrid crafts integrated with electronics is presented (Buechley and Perner-Wilson 2012). Kafai and Vasudevan (2015) recognizes games as models of richer and collaborative learning environments and board game design as a computational thinking activity. In their approach, combinatorial interactive games will be developed by combining physical and digital or low-high interfaces through the integration of craft boards (crafting) and digital screens (coding).

Rosner (2018) refers to Critical fabulations as ways of storytelling that evoke how things that we design come into being and what they do in the world. This approach is related to what (Mazé and Redström 2005) argue about temporal forms. These forms will emerge according to the ways that people use an open-ended design to explore more and understand better. In fact, based on different assembly strategies, there can be different ways of storytelling and developing temporal forms. Allowing users to manipulate the configuration of the pieces enables them to tell their own stories or tell the same story in a preferred way.

Related to the type of interaction that people might have (Giles and van der Linden 2014) incorporated non-visual effects in quilt electronics as an output to the interactions, where senses go beyond the appearance of the device and give the semantic meaning to the material such as recalling childhood memories by touching the material.

2 Understanding the Critical Parts of the Circuit Game

If we consider the circuit game in the center, Material, DIY making process, and DIY assembly process are the main components of this game (Fig. 1). These game elements are distinct but have overlapped at some points and can assist the learning process in different ways. The remainder of the paper discusses these elements came together in Circuit Game to satisfy the objective of this research.

The overall structure of the game is inspired by interwoven sculptural structures designed by Erwin Hauer to weave all three components of the game.

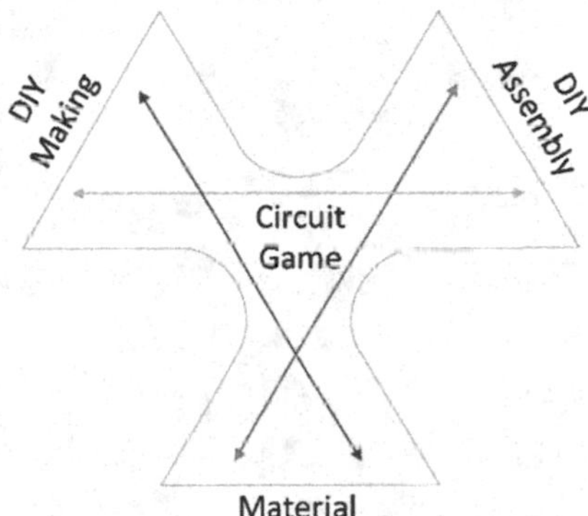

Fig. 1. Three main elements of the Circuit Game and their relationship (Material, DIY making, DIY assembly).

2.1 Base Materials in Circuit Game

This research was part of a practice related to the "Responsive Architectural Fiber Composites" course that required students to work with composite textiles. Therefore, composite textiles made of woven glass fiber, carbon fiber, felt and cotton knitted textiles with distinct patterns are selected to develop the game pieces (Fig. 2, Fig. 3). Flexible and shapeless textiles have been impregnated with resin to procure the fixed complex shapes. The textile-based composite material with the LED lights integrated into the pieces perform as an interface for the circuit game. The LEDs respond to the stimuli, which is the accurate assembly of pieces, by blinking. For the sake of simplicity, the response is limited to the blinking LEDs, however, other types of responses such as playing a piece of music, change of color, vibration will make the game more interactive and interesting to play with.

Any circuit has four parts: the energy source that provides the voltage, conductor which is the wiring system of the circuit, switch for controlling and the load that is the amount of energy source used by device to complete its task[1]. Additionally, to design any electronic integrated craft the main parts are inputs (sensor), connector (wires) and outputs (actuators) (Buechley and Perner-Wilson 2012).

In general, to make the whole structure there are two approaches: seamless and aggregation method. Since it is a game-based project, therefore, it is required to have separate pieces to explore different combination strategies. In addition, the interwoven geometry of the structure does not allow it to make one continuous piece. Therefore, the aggregation method is chosen and the pieces are made accordingly.

Fig. 2. Pieces made of different types of fabrics. Black pieces are Carbon Fiber, semi-transparent pieces are Glass Fiber and the samples in the bottom are Felt.

2.2 Circuit Game and DIY Making Process

The next step is making the pieces of the circuit game using the composite textile materials as the base and to bring the pieces to life as Eisenberg calls it Davis (2017), other materials are integrated into the pieces and these are conductive materials, LEDs, Arduino boards, and craft joinery materials. Making the main part of the electronic circuit from the craft materials, a research study revealed that most students participated enthusiastically in the projects of making functional electronic-based artifacts. In addition, the result of their study shows that different crafts can engage people with a

[1] https://www.hunker.com/12003706/the-four-and-more-basic-parts-of-an-electrical-circuit.

Fig. 3. Knitted samples with different patterns are knitted and the shape is fixated through impregnation with resin. The knitted patters are modified by adding holes in their structure to add conductive fibers.

distinct background in race, ethnicity, and socioeconomics differently (Buechley and Perner-Wilson 2012).

Conductive fibers have close characteristics to the textiles and can substitute the wires as well as connect the game pieces. Additionally, to be reliable as a connector the material should have low resistance (Buechley and Perner-Wilson 2012). Conductive fibers used here are in three different colors which means having different levels of resistance, however, the resistance of all the colors is suitable enough to flow the current. The integration of conductive fibers and the composite textiles is in the way that fibers are not connected directly in one piece to avoid the short circuits. Different joinery details are developed based on the joint location using knotting technique, sewing, metal snap buttons, and earring post pins (Fig. 4).

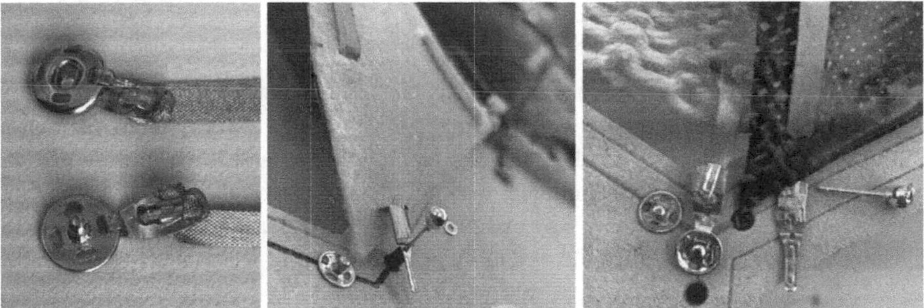

Fig. 4. Details of the joints for connecting pieces. Left: snap buttons for connecting conductive fibers to others and conductive fibers to the middle part of the board. Middle: connecting conductive fibers to the terminal points of the board using ear studs and earring post pins. Right: two types of connections on the board

LEDs are embedded inside the composite pieces and attached to the conductive fibers in a way that red fibers are always positive and dark gray fibers are negative (Fig. 5). The light gray fibers can be positive or negative based on their position and adjacency with dark gray and red fibers respectively (Fig. 6).

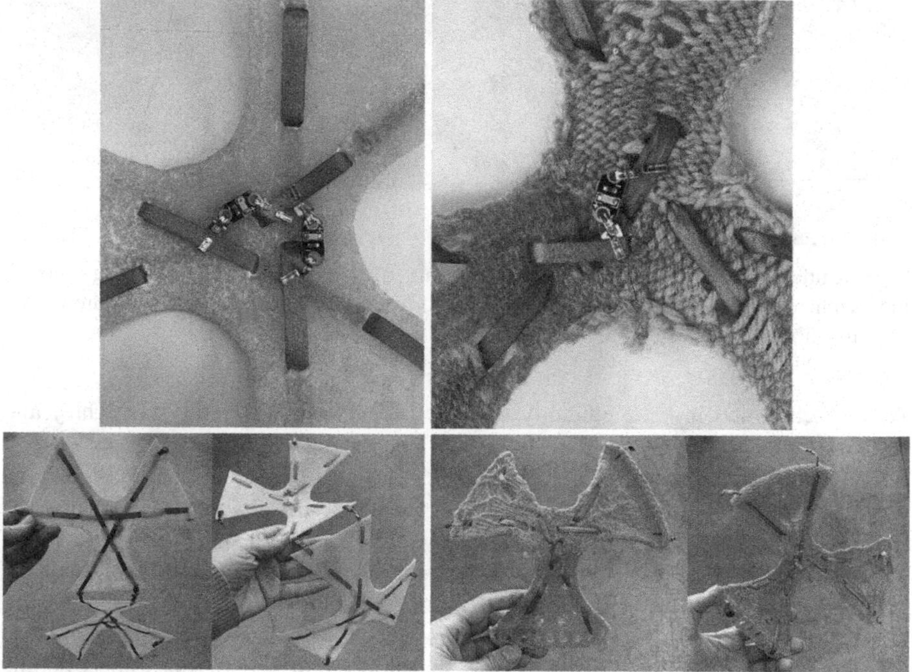

Fig. 5. LEDs attached to the conductive fibers

2.3 Circuit Game and DIY Assembly Process

The third step is to assemble the pieces and play the game to complete the circuit. At this step, the application of the game will be tested. Participants will receive the instruction on how to play the game to explore the design alternatives and learn more about the circuits. Through assembly techniques, multiple design alternatives will emerge and each assembly can be a different way of storytelling as Rosner asserts (Rosner 2018).

There are two strategies for the assembly of the pieces:

1. First is having pieces attached to a board: In this approach, the wires are embedded into the solid board and connected to the Arduino board. Here, the Arduino board and the terminal points are the fixed components. Users attach the pieces together and to the terminal points to get the response. In this approach, because of using the Arduino board it is possible to add other types of responses like plying music, change of color, and kinetic response.

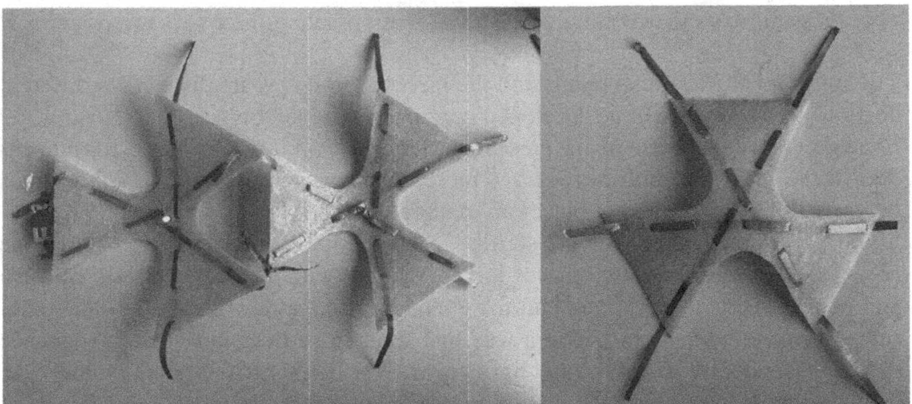

Fig. 6. The structure of conductive fibers is in a way that fibers have no connection with each other, therefore, avoiding the short circuits (Color figure online)

2. The second approach is to have pieces freely attached to other pieces: In this system, there is no need for the baseboard and the game can have any overall form at the end. Some pieces have batteries embedded in them and based on the connection that the player makes between the pieces they will receive the response. Here, the possibility of a connection between the pieces is limited compared to the first approach because the connection of pieces to receive the response is limited to the location of the batteries.

This practice followed the first approach and as it is shown in Fig. 7, a board with the hexagonal openings is selected as a base for embedding wiring and terminal points.

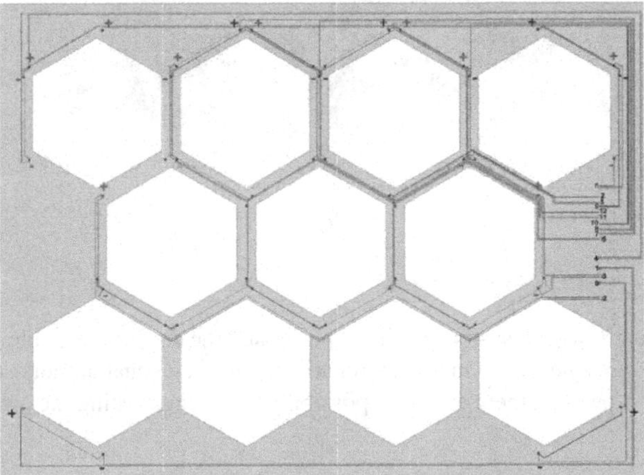

Fig. 7. Baseboard with the hexagonal openings. Terminal points are marked on the board and wiring plan is showed that connect terminal points to the Arduino board

For the game to work according to the goals of this practice, there are some principles:

- The joints for the terminal points and the pieces themselves are distinct, so different design alternatives might be developed considering the joint types.
- Even accurate attachment of one piece to the terminal points will turn the LED embedded in the piece on, however, to get more lights on, the appropriate connections between this piece and other pieces are required.
- Some rules can be defined before starting the game, for example, in this practice one rule was to have at least two pieces joined together with the same color in concave and convex sequence. Although all the conductive fibers flow the current, the other rule was try to connect pieces in a way that conductive fibers attached in sequence have the same color as red (+) and light gray (−) or light gray (+) and dark gray (−).
- Negative and positive terminal points are marked on the board and these are the fixed points.
- Players should attach more pieces with the same color in series as they complete the circuit board.

There are multiple possibilities for completing the circuit game. Figure 8 shows the base case that authors started the game design with, however, other design alternatives will emerge as different users approach differently to the game (Fig. 9). The main point is having users to discover the circuit logic and learn it through playing the game.

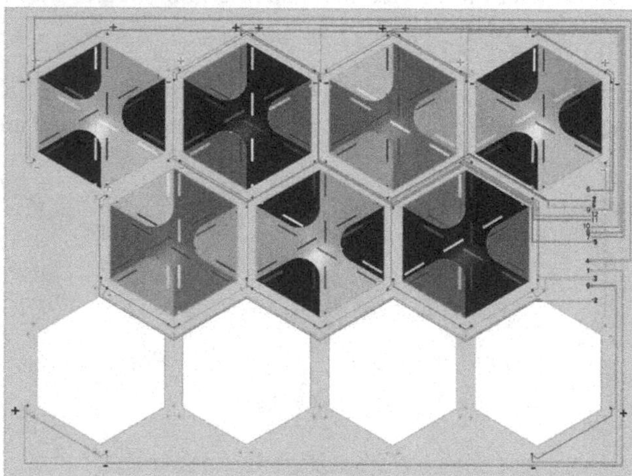

Fig. 8. The baseboard, wiring system, terminal points and the composite textile pieces connected accordingly. These are one of the many aggregation alternatives that authors started to develop the game based on, however, there are other possibilities for aggregating the pieces.

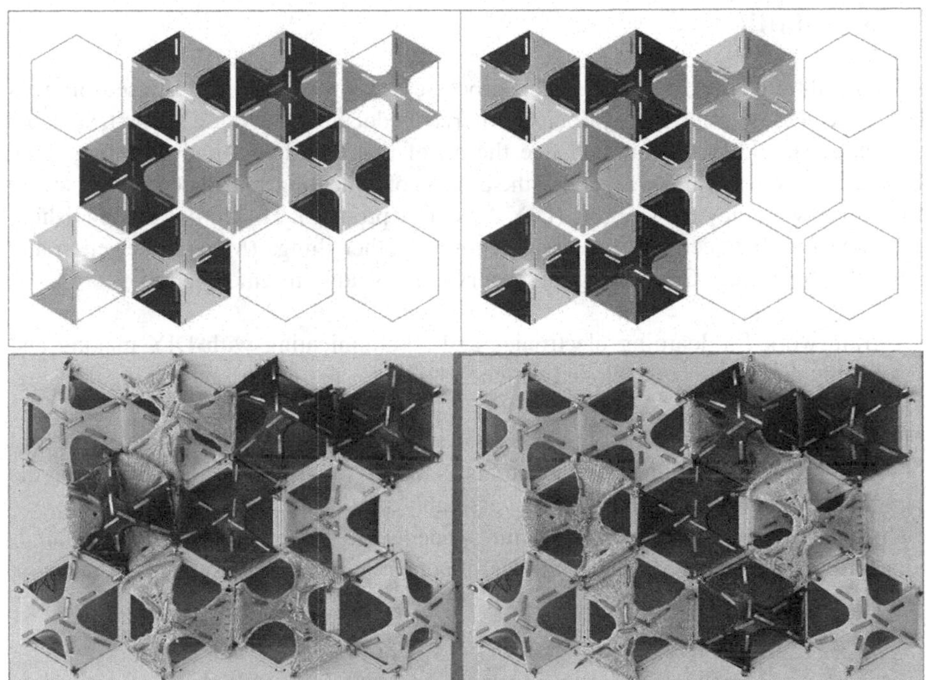

Fig. 9. Other design alternatives

3 News and Future Research Recommendations

Besides developing craft integrated electronics strategies using common toolkits like Arduino and Lilypad, other researchers emphasize on the personal fabrication of electronics instead of using available toolkits bringing novice practitioners closer to commercial electronic products (Mellis et al. 2016). Therefore, the next step would be exploring the potentials of customizing the whole fabricated circuit game from scratch.

In addition, in this practice, two types of joints are designed connecting the pieces together and pieces to the board. It would have given more flexibility to the game if there was only one type of joint with the possibility of converting it to other types using a converter connector. In this way, the players could change the connection joint based on the assembly strategy they choose and explore more assembly alternatives.

It was found that carbon fiber textiles will keep their semi-conductivity even though, they are completely impregnated with resin. In this practice, these pieces were used as fillers. However, based on the type of piece that the player selects to start the game with, different levels of complexity could be defined in advance.

The concept of the game introduced here can be a self-assembled, changeable responsive interior wall or the screen for light filtration. Multiple possibilities of connecting the pieces bring more variability to the design and help to develop more temporal forms.

4 Contribution

Educating through making and assembly processes is central to this study. Based on Cross (1982), Peters suggested three principal criteria of education and these are first, valuable knowledge should be transmitted like the art of making, doing, and inventing (DIY Making Process). Second is related to the process of educating and students being aware of what and why they are learning (DIY Assembly process). The third is distinguishing the connection between what students learn and other things (Material selection and material application). Connecting this theory to the study presented here:

- A framework for learning electronics and communicating with DIY making and assembly processes is developed which is relied on the culture of making, sensing, and electronics.
- During the process of assembly, we learned about the circuit logic, the role of material behavior and their conductivity potentials as well as material selection by playing the game and exploring through different assembly strategies.
- Through this game children, architecture students and other groups who are not familiar with the electronic concepts will learn more about circuits through a combination of common craft materials and electronics.

References

Björk, S.: Games, gamers, and gaming understanding game research. Paper Presented at the MindTrek 2008: Proceedings of the 12th International Conference on Entertainment and Media in the Ubiquitous Era (2008)

Buechley, L., Eisenberg, M.: Fabric PCBs, electronic sequins, and socket buttons: techniques for e-textile craft. Pers. Ubiquit. Comput. **13**(2), 133–150 (2007). https://doi.org/10.1007/s00779-007-0181-0

Buechley, L., Eisenberg, M., Catchen, J., Crockett, A.: The LilyPad arduino: using computational textiles to investigate engagement, aesthetics, and diversity in computer science education. Paper Presented at the CHI Florence, Italy (2008)

Buechley, L., Hill, B.M.: LilyPad in the wild: how hardware's long tail is supporting new engineering and design communities. Paper Presented at the ACM, Aarhus Denmark (2010)

Buechley, L., Peppler, K.A., Eisenberg, M., Kafai, Y.B.: Textile messages: dispatches from the world of e-textiles and education: Peter Lang (2013)

Buechley, L., Perner-Wilson, H.: Crafting technology. ACM Trans. Comput. Hum. Interact. **19**(3), 1–21 (2012). https://doi.org/10.1145/2362364.2362369

Buechley, L., Rosner, D., Paulos, E., Williams, A.: DIY for CHI: methods, communities, and values of reuse and customization. Paper Presented at the CHI, Boston, MA, USA (2009)

Cross, N.: Designerly ways of knowing. Des. Stud. **3**(4), 221–227 (1982)

Davis, F.A.: Softbuilt: computational textiles and augmenting space through emotion. (Doctor of philosophy in the field of architecture: design and computation). Massachusetts Institute of Technology (2017)

Giles, E., van der Linden, J.: Using eTextile objects for touch based interaction for visual impairment. Paper Presented at the Proceedings of the 2014 ACM International Symposium on Wearable Computers Adjunct Program - ISWC 2014 Adjunct (2014)

Kafai, Y., Vasudevan, V.: Hi-Lo tech games: crafting, coding and collaboration of augmented board games by high school youth. Paper presented at the Proceedings of the 14th International Conference on Interaction Design and Children - IDC 2015 (2015)

Mazé, R., Redström, J.: Form and the computational object. Digit. Creat. **16**(1), 7–18 (2005)

Mellis, D.A., Buechley, L., Resnick, M., Hartmann, B.: Engaging amateurs in the design, fabrication, and assembly of electronic devices. Paper presented at the Proceedings of the 2016 ACM Conference on Designing Interactive Systems - DIS 2016 (2016)

Papert, S.: Mindstorms: Children, Computers, and Powerful Ideas. Basic Books Inc., Publishers, New York (1980)

Rosner, D.K.: Critical Fabulations: Reworking the Methods and Margins of Design. The MIT Press, Cambridge (2018)

Salgado, J., Soares, F., Leão, C.P., Matos, D., Carvalho, V.: Educational games for children with special needs: preliminary design. Paper Presented at the 4th Experiment@ International Conference (exp.at 2017). University of Algarve, Faro, Portugal (2017)

Wiberg, M., et al.: Materiality matters-experience materials. Paper Presented at the ACM (2013)

Designing an Interactive Platform for Intangible Cultural Heritage Knowledge of Taoyuan Woodcarving Craft

Mingxiang Shi[1(✉)] and Qingshu Zeng[2]

[1] School of Fine-Arts, Hunan Normal University, 36, Lushan Street, Changsha 410081, Hunan, People's Republic of China
64149555@qq.com

[2] School of Design Art and Media, Nanjing University of Science and Technology, 200, Xiaolingwei Street, Nanjing 210094, Jiangsu, People's Republic of China

Abstract. This paper conducts literature research from the fields of art research, digital protection, and productive protection. We build an intangible cultural heritage knowledge platform, which aims at the protection of Taoyuan woodcarving craft. Furthermore, it conducts interactive design research and practice of the system. The purpose of this study is to establish a knowledge platform, to speed up the industrial process of Taoyuan woodcarving craft by sharing the database, and to improve the innovative design and development system of Taoyuan woodcarving. By extracting basic knowledge, modeling knowledge, functional knowledge, process knowledge, and aesthetic knowledge, a case specification and data model are established to create a rapid design channel. The goal is to shorten the practice cycle of design innovation to help the economic and design value conversion of Taoyuan woodcarving craft intangible cultural heritage.

Keywords: Taoyuan woodcarving craft · Intangible cultural heritage · Knowledge platform · Interactive system

1 Introduction

Taoyuan woodcarving craft (TWC)-a precious gem among intangible cultural heritages in Hunan Province-is essential to the region's folk culture because it bears a precious cultural memory, as well as the sentiments, life, and faith of this region's people. However, under the pressure of the market economy and the modern industry, this art has been gradually declining for two reasons. First, the wood carving culture that accompanies the traditional agricultural lifestyle can neither keep up with the changing times nor integrate into modern life; second, methods by which artisans pass on these skills are very fragile. It mostly relies on one-on-one teaching from masters to apprentices or among family members, with high risks of interruption or variation [1, 2]. Moreover, it is passed down through family lines as a marketable skill.

The purpose of this paper is to establish intangible cultural heritage (ICH) for Taoyuan woodcarving, to speed up the industrial process of woodcarving by sharing

N. Streitz and S. Konomi (Eds.): HCII 2020, LNCS 12203, pp. 636–647, 2020.
https://doi.org/10.1007/978-3-030-50344-4_46

the database, and to improve the innovative design and development system of Taoyuan woodcarving. By extracting basic knowledge, modeling knowledge, functional knowledge, process knowledge, and aesthetic knowledge, a case specification and data model are established to create a rapid design channel. The purpose is to shorten the practice cycle of design innovation to help the economic and design value conversion of Taoyuan woodcarving intangible cultural heritage.

2 Related Work

2.1 Study of Woodcarving Art

The research in the art field mainly focuses on the artistic style and cultural connotation of woodcarving. By studying the shapes, patterns, themes, and techniques of woodcarving, it analyzes its artistic and aesthetic values. Guo Le studied the components of Taoyuan woodcarving, analyzed its structure and patterns, and proposed a design method for woodcarving cultural and creative products [3]. Chen et al. studied the animal patterns in Taoyuan woodcarvings and summarized the pattern combination and aesthetic characteristics to assist the innovative design of modern furniture [4]. Wen et al. studied the artistic characteristics and carving techniques of Taoyuan woodcarving, explored the cultural origin of woodcarving art, and proposed methods of application in interior design [5]. Kang analyzed the composition of Taoyuan's woodcarving works and studied the artistic methods of blank space to propose the aesthetic rules of woodcarving furniture design [6]. Zhou studied the creative theme of Taoyuan wood carving auspicious patterns from the perspective of regional culture to explore the artistic value of wood carving art [7]. Some scholars believe that the integration of wood carving art and artistic, creative design can enhance the cultural connotation of products and public acceptance [8]. Lin divides the fusion of carving art knowledge in the product innovation design process into the fusion of inner knowledge (including story, emotion and cultural characteristics), the fusion of middle knowledge (including function, operation, availability, and safety), and the integration of outer knowledge. The fusion includes three levels of color, texture, form, decoration, surface decoration, line quality, and detail) [9]. Chai et al. used a continuous fuzzy Kano model to analyze the application of the above three levels of knowledge in creative cultural design [10]. The results show that the inner "intangible" knowledge and the middle "behavioral" knowledge are more important than the outer "tangible" knowledge can increase public satisfaction with wood carving art products. Based on the definition and classification of woodcarving cultural and creative products, Liu Wenjia et al. put forward the design principles of woodcarving cultural and creative products, supplemented the design system of intangible cultural heritage, and promoted the innovation of woodcarving art products [11].

2.2 Digital Protection Research

The development of information technology has opened the era of digital protection of ICH. How to use digital technology to protect ICH is a crucial study. It is not only necessary to protect intangible cultural heritage, but also to reinterpret ICH through new methods and means and give them new meanings. Comprehensive domestic and foreign-related research, the main types of protection are as follows.

1. **Digital archive.** With the development of information technology, high-precision digital archives are becoming increasingly abundant. Using technologies such as 3D scanning, digital photography, and image processing, it is possible to achieve high-precision acquisition and storage of information such as the graphic structure and texture of the ICH. Provide accurate digital materials for ICH's information sharing, protection, dissemination, development, and utilization [12]. The Dong Brocade Digital Museum, developed by the School of Design & Art of Hunan University, has displayed a variety of digital pictures of brocades online, providing design inspiration for designers. The materials on the platform are classified in detail, and designers can always find the patterns they want easily and quickly [13].
2. **Digital resource library.** Oz University in Japan has digitized the living cultural heritage "Lion Dance" in the Oz area. Hitachi has successfully used digital technology to reproduce the "Genji Monogatari Map" and become Japan's "Digital Culture Ambassador. Meyer established a network-based cultural heritage management system, and Dong and others established the Digital Science and Technology Museum System China Digital Science and Technology Museum to diversify the display of intangible cultural heritage. Luo Shijian has proposed an ICH design integrated system for artistic, creative design. Lou's research solves the problems of low relevance, insufficient knowledge reasoning, and low utilization of artifacts in the cultural creative design field, which carries out cultural creative design activities for designers Assisted [14].
3. **Build ICH digital museum with virtual reality technology.** The digital museum can play the role of disseminating non-heritage knowledge, and the content is most popular and exciting to attract public attention. At present, domestic scholars are exploring design methods for integrating VR technology into the protection of intangible cultural heritage. "Development and Construction of Intangible Cultural Heritage Museum Based on Virtual Reality Technology" (Cultural Research Project of Jiangsu Province) "Research on the Application of Virtual Reality Technology in the Protection of Intangible Cultural Heritage in Hebei Province", "The Application of Virtual Reality Technology in the Protection of Folk Crafts" Applied research (protection of Yunnan's characteristic folk crafts), "exploration and research on the protection of Mongolian saddle making process by virtual reality technology", "application concept of virtual reality in Inner Mongolia Museum" and other topics on the reproduction of intangible cultural heritage by virtual reality technology Applying forms and methods for theoretical research [15]. The "Shuo Shuo" Dong ICH design museum constructed by Hunan University has demonstrated the craftsmanship of the Dong people's handicrafts through multi-dimensional integration of pictures, videos, and virtual reality technology. Users can gain Dong culture and art knowledge through this platform, and also design and customize gifts through online museums. "Shuo Shuo" Digital Museum applied virtual reality technology to protect the intangible cultural heritage of the Dai people and explored it from the practical and application level.

2.3 Productive Protection Related Research

The productive protection of intangible cultural heritage refers to the maintenance of the authenticity, integrity, and inheritance of intangible cultural heritage in the practice of productive nature, with the premise of useful inheritance of intangible cultural heritage skills as a prerequisite [17]: circulation, sales, and other means to protect intangible cultural heritage and its resources into cultural products. In productive protection, production means a combination of craftsmanship and technology. In the process of "combination", "maintain the authenticity, integrity, and inheritance of intangible cultural heritage, and premise the effective inheritance of intangible cultural heritage skills", that is, respect the core value of intangible heritage. The degree of object and technology participation varies. Zhang Xinyu proposed that the methods of technical participation, including two aspects, which is the first technical assistance in the production and research and development of wood carving techniques, providing new materials and new ideas; the second technology promotes the integration of wood carving crafts into daily life products and drives market consumption [18].

In summary, the above methods are subject to certain restrictions and constraints. The display area limits the woodcarving art collection; digital protection methods solve some of the above problems, but it is still challenging to enhance the on-site situational sense of artworks, the craftsmanship, and experience. Also, the application of intangible cultural heritage in other fields is often rough and rough, and it does not convey the beauty of traditional crafts. Therefore, the following article will analyze the integration and application of TWC art in artistic and creative design for the above problems, and structure the classified management of non-heritage knowledge according to the application requirements of creative design to realize the organization and expression of design knowledge. An interactive system of non-heritage knowledge of TWC was established, and an example verified the feasibility of the system.

3 Establishing an ICH Knowledge Platform for the TWC

3.1 ICH Knowledge Source of TWC

ICH knowledge is the sum of design information and experience that has reference significance to the design process and can provide designers with creative, artistic, and cultural elements [19]. The TWC related ICH knowledge is structured and classified according to the requirements of the design application. The ICH knowledge of TWC for knowledge-oriented design innovation comes from multiple knowledge sources, mainly from TWC artists, product designers, and system interaction designers, as shown in Fig. 1. They not only provide knowledge reserves but also provide such knowledge with vibrant, dynamic, implicit, heuristic, and other characteristics, which is a high degree of unification of cultural and technical elements [20].

TWC artists provides basic knowledge of wood carving, including utensil types, process methods, and design knowledge that product designers pay attention to, including modeling, color, material, structure, and function. The system interaction designer is devoted to the design and research of the data lesson and interaction interface of the ICH digital platform of TWC.

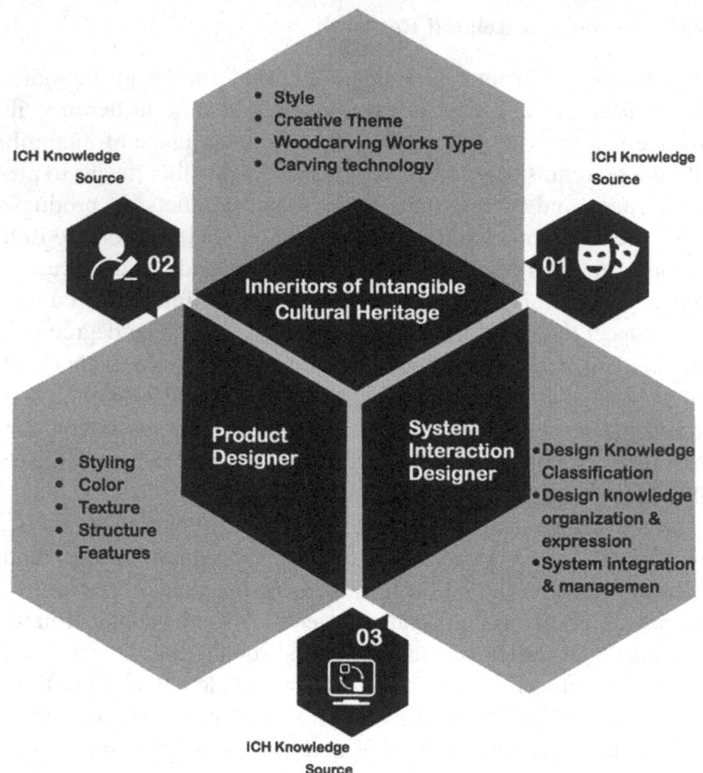

Fig. 1. The source of ICH knowledge of TWC

3.2 ICH Knowledge Source of TWC

ICH knowledge for design innovation can be divided into the following types:

Basic knowledge, which describes the essential attributes of TWC. Including name, type, size, creator.

Styling knowledge, which describes the sculptural elements of TWC. Including TWC's component form, decoration, composition, and color.

Technical knowledge, which describes the technical information related to TWC. Including TWC's structure, material, and carving technology.

Functional knowledge, which describes technical information related to practical functions, aesthetic functions, symbolic functions, and also saves materials, processes.

Cultural knowledge, which describes the specific cultural meaning contained in the subject matter of the work, and presents the value characteristics of the work. Including folk allusions, auspicious allegations, or enlightened meanings.

Establish an ICH knowledge classification framework model based on classification, as shown in Fig. 2.

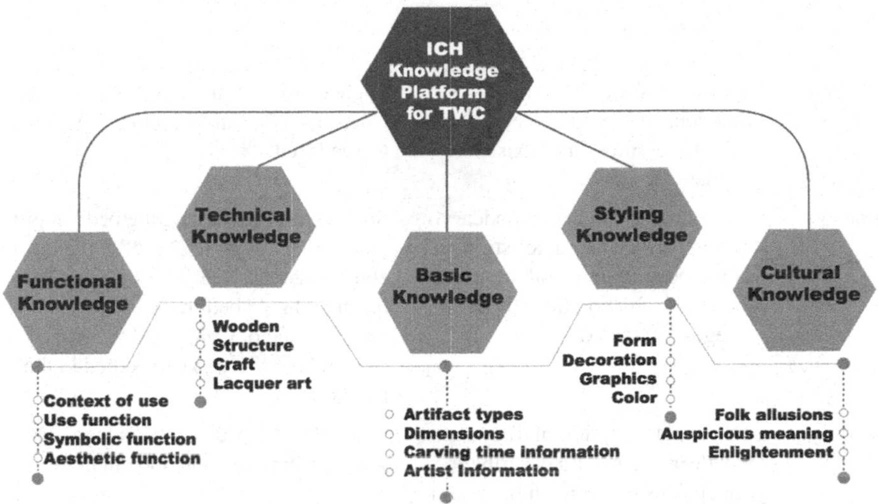

Fig. 2. The ICH knowledge classification framework model

3.3 ICH Knowledge Source of TWC

In order to ensure the typicality and reliability of the data of the ICH knowledge platform, we have convened art researchers, Taoyuan woodcarving artists, and woodcarving collectors to hold seminars. We adopted the opinions and suggestions of experts and determined 3166 pieces of woodcarving legends from the catalogs of the Taoyuan County Museum and Changde Museum of Intangible Culture. The sources of wood carving mainly include the following categories:

- **Architectural woodcarvings,** carved boards are sourced from the door waist plate (大门腰板), heart plate (心板), skirt board (裙板), window grille (窗花), corbel (牛腿), door dang (门当) etc.
- **Furniture wood carving,** carving board source washbasin (洗脸架), clothes rack (衣架), chair back (椅背), carved bed (雕花床), incense case (香案), altar (祭台), bookshelf (书架) etc.
- **Sacrifice wood carvings,** including Tunkou (吞口), fairy statues (神仙雕像), ancestral statues (祖宗雕像) etc.

Based on previous research, sort out the ICH knowledge interpretation specification table (as shown in Table 1). Knowledge interpretation of the selected TWC cases to form a case base. Keywords are extracted from each type of interpretation knowledge, and a Taoyuan woodcarving domain knowledge table for design innovation is formed for ontology knowledge modeling.

Table 1. The ICH knowledge interpretation specification table.

Basic information		
Category	Types of TWC, divided by functions of building decoration, daily necessities, and household appliances	Such as: Eight Immortals Table, Taishi Chair, Double Cabinet, Dressing Table, Carved Bed
Name	The name of Taoyuan woodcarving should include characteristics such as period and time, craftsmanship, the motif of decoration, furniture category, and so on	Such as the "Xiaoxiangjing bed" in gilt gold (鎏金 "潇湘景拔步床"), the luoshi zhuanjing bed (螺蛳转井), the carved lacquered gold bed in the early years of the Republic of China, and the "Sui he san dai" (隋和三代) carved bed in the late Qing
Size	The size description of Taoyuan woodcarving should describe the dimensions of the main body and components such as length, width, height, step depth, and perimeter	Example: The bed is 220 cm long, 230 cm wide, 45 cm deep and 300 cm high
Carved plate	Describe the number of carved plates, carved characters, flowers, and birds, etc. for a single work	Such as more than 150 carved boards, 106 characters, more than 100 patterns of flowers and birds
Styling knowledge		
Style	Describe the overall style of TWC	For example: exquisite, elegant, vivid characters
Color	Describe the decorative colors of TWC	Such as: Zhu lacquered gold (朱漆髹金), Gold (鎏金)
Decoration	It describes the motifs, decorative patterns, and decorative patterns of Taoyuan woodcarvings	Such as people, flowers and birds, scenery, auspicious animals
Process knowledge		
Craft	It describes the carving method of TWC	Such as round sculpture, relief sculpture, open sculpture, hollow sculpture
Material	It describes the wood and material selection of TWC	Such as poplar, camphor
Structure	It illustrates the structural parts of TWC	Such as Quan kou ya zi (券口牙子), Jiao ya (角牙), Yatiao (牙条),roll top (卷篷顶), hanging (挂落), door covers (门罩), vertical strips (垂条), pillows (遮枕)

(*continued*)

Table 1. (*continued*)

Basic information		
Functional knowledge		
Usage scenarios	Describe the usage scenarios of Taoyuan woodcarving, and information about users' lifestyle, including application areas such as building decoration, furniture furnishings, and daily necessities	Such as door waist board (大门腰板), heart board (心板), skirt board (裙板), corbel, beam (牛腿), door dang (横梁), building carving (门当), Jinping (锦屏)
Instructions	It describes the furnishings of TWC, the functions, and uses of daily necessities	For example, the "Luoshi rao jing" (螺蛳转井) bed occupies an area of an nearly 20 square meters and has four entrances-the first entrance is a shoe changing place, the second entrance is a locker room, the third entrance is a toilet, and the fourth entrance is a sleeping area. On rainy days, the owner can also live on the bed, as if the snail coiled around the wellhead.
Aesthetic function	Aesthetic Analysis and Explanation of TWC	Such as: lifelike shapes, solemn atmosphere, smooth lines
Cultural knowledge		
Drama story	It describes stories and characters in Chinese classical literature.	Celebrating Guo Ziyi's birthday (郭子仪拜寿), Xiao He chased Han Xin on a moonlit night (萧何月下追韩信), Guan Gong fought with Huang Zhong (关公战黄忠)
Folk life scene	Describe the life scenes of ancient Chinese folk, wood carvings as a daily necessity to express the atmosphere of the countryside and the beauty of simplicity	Such as spinning thread (纺线), lotus picking (采莲), weaving (织布), farming (农耕), sacrifice (祭祀), fishing (渔猎), hunting (婚嫁), marriage (招亲), throwing hydrangea (抛绣球), learning (苦读), Guanyin child delivery (观音送子), unicorn tossing jade books (麒麟吐玉书), Queen star fighting (魁星点斗)
Auspicious meaning	Describe auspicious meaning to express good wishes	Such as Xi shang mei shao (喜上眉梢)\Zhi ri gao sheng (指日高升)\Wu fu peng shou (五福捧寿)\San yan kai tai (三阳开泰)\Lian sheng gui zi (连生贵子)
Landscape	Carving board depicting the scenery	Such as Eight scenic spots in Xiaoxiang (潇湘八景): Pingsha Luo yan (平沙落雁), Xiaoxiang Ye yu (潇湘夜雨), Yan si Night Bell (烟寺晚钟), Shanshi Qing lan (山市晴岚), Jiang Tian mu Snow (江天暮雪), Yuanpu Guifan (远浦归帆), Dongting Qiuyue (洞庭秋月), Fishing Village Evening Photo (渔村夕照)

4 Establishing an ICH knowledge Platform for the TWC

4.1 System Architecture

Based on the above research, an interactive system of the TWC intangible knowledge platform for design and innovation is constructed, which could manage and display the Taoyuan woodcarving intangible knowledge effectively. The system is designed to provide knowledge services to architecture, furniture, product designers, and handmade art researchers to assist design creativity. The system architecture is divided into four levels:

1. **Storage layer** Stores wood carving multimedia data resources for creative design and provides relational data sets and non-relational data sets for web-service for other system calls.
2. **Description layer** The description of TWC case data, including modules such as knowledge management and knowledge retrieval.
3. **Organization layer** Including two modules of retrieval mechanism and authority management, copy the business logic of system retrieval.
4. **Application layer** It mainly displays information and an operable window for users.

4.2 Functional Architecture

The ICH knowledge platform of TWC needs to implement functions such as resource sharing, information retrieval, product display, design application, and knowledge dissemination. Divided into TWC primary information database, sample case material library, product library, research dynamic tracking library. The case material library is the core part of the knowledge platform. According to the interpretation table of TWC knowledge, the sample case material library is divided into the necessary knowledge, modeling knowledge, functional knowledge, technical knowledge, and cultural knowledge of TWC (Fig. 3).

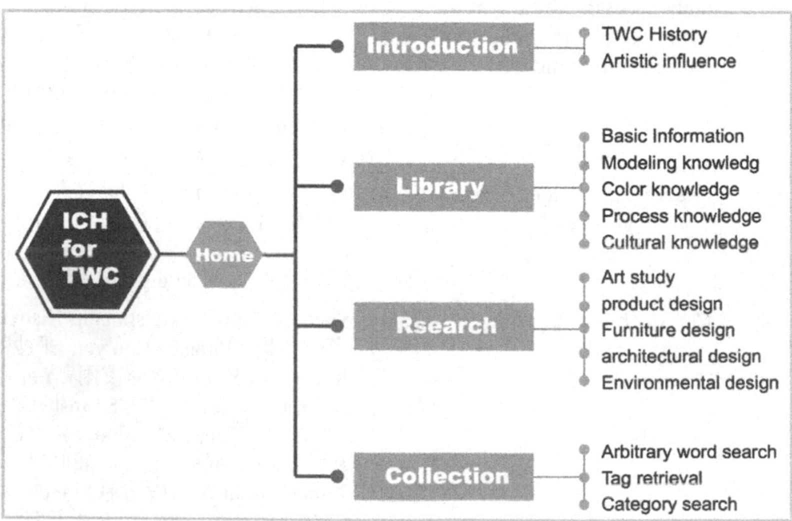

Fig. 3. The functional architecture

4.3 Interface Visual Design

The interface design takes into account the user's habits and style expression, adheres to the easy-to-understand, refined design principles, the overall interface shows national characteristics, and at the same time can well display the main content body of the website.

The database system itself has the complexity of data, and it should be as concise and transparent as possible in visual style. With content as the main body of the design, return to function. Emphasize clear functional division, unified and coordinated visual elements, and smooth browsing.

- **Visual strategy:** local characteristics and efficiency;
- **Design style:** concise and refined;
- **Style elements:** pixels, classic wood carving patterns.

The system interface uses the classic color matching and classic totem of TWC to reflect the national characteristics. Adopt the principle of content first to ensure sufficient display space of materials on the website. Reduce the appearance of decorative elements, adhere to the consistent use of elements, and adhere to the concise and straightforward practical style.

The home page has three parts: text introduction (basic information, modeling knowledge, color knowledge, craft knowledge, functional knowledge, cultural knowledge), a wood carving gallery, and a catalog axis.

According to the user's left-to-right page browsing habits, the text is on the left side of the page, and the auxiliary text is used to separate the information between each page to make the information clear. The right side of the page serves as a guide, including the gallery and the tracking axis. The gallery contains pictures and descriptions of the wood carvings; the directory axis tracks the browsing of this article to remind visitors of the current reading progress. Part of the interface design is shown in Figs. 4, 5 and 6.

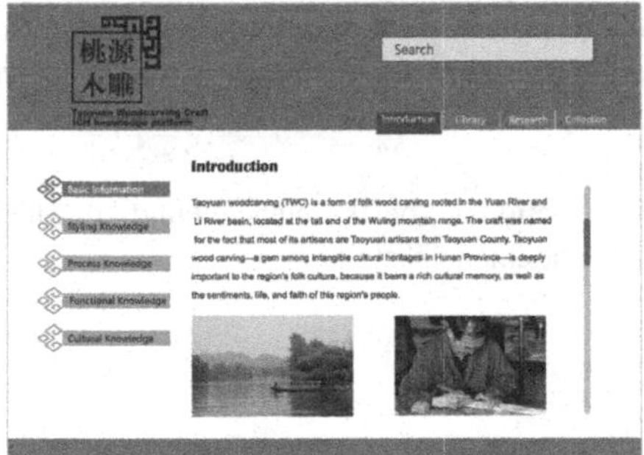

Fig. 4. Introducing interface design.

Fig. 5. Collection interface design

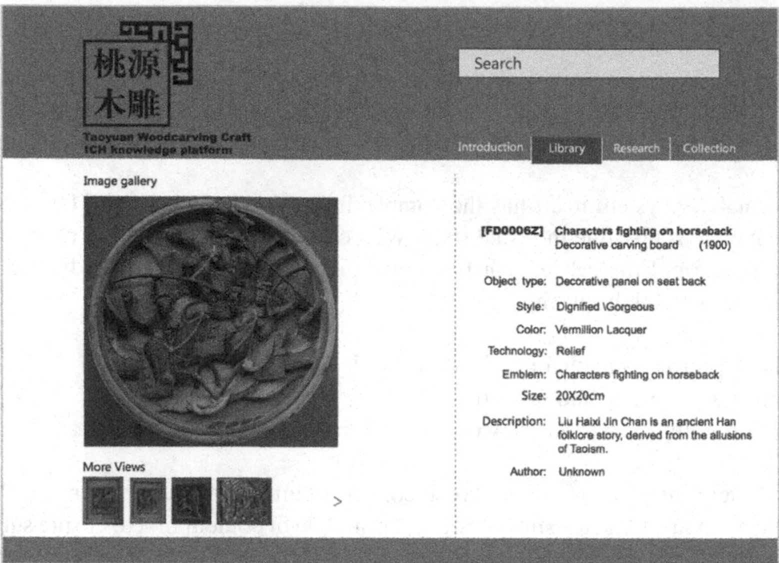

Fig. 6. Case library interface design

5 Conclusion

Aiming at the protection and inheritance of TWC intangible cultural heritage, the ICH knowledge platform of TWC is constructed to accelerate the industrial process of TWC by sharing the database and promote the innovative design and development of TWC. This platform can meet the needs of people in different design fields to acquire the knowledge of TWC design and promote the dissemination and application of TWC in the fields of products, furniture, architecture, and interaction design.

Future research work is as follows: on the one hand, improve the case data of the knowledge platform and improve the efficiency of database construction. On the other hand, improve the system function based on the designer's test and feedback so that the designer can use the resources of the knowledge platform for design innovation more efficiently.

Acknowledgement. This research is supported by National Social Science Fund of China program (17BG149). We also gratefully acknowledge the financial support.

References

1. Zhao, X.: The artistic achievements of taoyuan wood carving. J. Art China. **3**(7), 82–90 (2014)
2. Shi, M., Ren, S.: A study on productive preservation and design innovation of Taoyuan wood carving. In: Rau, P.-L.P. (ed.) HCII 2019. LNCS, vol. 11576, pp. 203–214. Springer, Cham (2019). https://doi.org/10.1007/978-3-030-22577-3_14
3. Le, G., Fen, W.: Research on cultural and creative products of Taoyuan woodcarving "Niu tui". Art Technol. **11**(24), 71–75 (2018)

4. Chen, Z., Peng, K.: A brief analysis of the animal patterna of Taoyuan woodcarving. Furnit. Inter. Design **3**(6), 35–39 (2018)
5. Wen, R., He, T.: Taoyuan woodcarving cultural details. Art Educ. Res. **4**(8), 40–48 (2018)
6. Kang, P., Chen, Z., Tang, L.: Discussion on composition features of white space in Taoyuan woodcarving decorative patterns. Furnit. Inter. Design **4**(8), 66–72 (2018)
7. Zhou, M.: On the influence of witchcraft culture on Taoyuan woodcarving. Fine Arts Times **5**(10), 49–54 (2019)
8. Qi, Y.: Changde characteristics of the city's cultural construction of folk-art resources. J. Wuling **6**(37), 65–69 (2012)
9. Lin, R.: Transforming Taiwan aboriginal cultural features into modern product design: a case study of a cross-cultural product design model. Int. J. Design **1**(2), 47–55 (2007)
10. Chai, C., Bao, D., Sun, L.: The relative effects of different dimensions of traditional cultural elements on customer product satisfaction. Int. J. Ind. Ergon. Elem. Custom. Prod. Satis. **48**(10), 77–88 (2015)
11. Liu, W., Wu, Z.: Cultural creative product made of hongmu and its principle of development design. Packag. Eng. **37**(14), 169–173 (2016)
12. Wang, X.: On the practical significance of Huxiang wood carving. J. Hunan Univ. Sci. Technol. Soc. Sci. Edn. **5**(17), 166–175 (2014)
13. Hu, Y., Jiang, Y.: A study based on Guangxi Hunan and Guizhou Province's Dong nationality paper cutting participatory interaction design. Art Design **10**(20), 112–118 (2014)
14. Luo, S., Dong, Y.: Integration and management method of cultural artifacts knowledge for cultural creative design. Comput. Integr. Manuf. Syst. **4**(24), 964–977 (2018)
15. He, S.: Analysis of intangible heritage digital protection under new media diversification. Cult. J. **5**(10), 86–92 (2018)
16. Ji, T., Guo, M.: Social transformation and design participation in rural cultural construction. Zhuangshi **4**(300), 39–43 (2018)
17. Qiu, C.: Productive protection: 'self-hematopoiesis' of intangible cultural heritage. J. China Cult. Daily **2**(21), 15–18 (2012)
18. Zheng, X.: Traditional and modern technology. Zhuangshi **5**(301), 55–59 (2018)
19. Zhang, D., Ji, T.: Collaborative design "trigger" revival of traditional community. J. Zhuangshi **12**(284), 26–28 (2016)
20. Li, J., Ying, J.: Taoyuan folk wood carving art. J. Cent. South Univ. (Soc. Sci. Edn.) **4**(2), 84–90 (2003)

Learning Support for Career Related Terms with SCROLL and InCircle

Noriko Uosaki[1(✉)], Kousuke Mouri[2], Takahiro Yonekawa[3], Chengjiu Yin[4], Akihiko Ieshima[1], and Hiroaki Ogata[5]

[1] Osaka University, Osaka 565-0871, Japan
n.uosaki@gmail.com
[2] Tokyo University of Agriculture and Technology, Tokyo 184-8588, Japan
[3] Brain Signal, Inc., Tokyo 105-6027, Japan
[4] Kobe University, Kobe 657-8501, Japan
[5] Kyoto University, Kyoto 606-8501, Japan

Abstract. In this paper, we describe the support system for job-hunting students to learn job-hunting related terms by using an eBook and a chat system. Job-hunting process is very unique and complicated in Japan. Job-hunting students face difficulties in many phases. Many job-hunting related terms are not used in daily conversation and very new to them. Therefore, it is necessary to support them to learn them. The objectives of this study are (1) to clarify whether there is a positive correlation between active involvement of eBook learning and test performance and (2) to clarify whether the use of our chat system was effective in learning job-hunting related terms. The result of the evaluation showed that as for (1), there was no statistically significant correlation between the two factors. However when focusing on the international students, the correlation coefficient increased. It was aligned with the fact that this system was originally designed to support international students. As for (2), when the comparison was made between with and without InCircle delivery, there was no statistically significant difference between them in terms of Pre- and Post-test improvement. However the students gave the high score when they were asked its helpfulness. The score implies that the students were satisfied with its helpfulness.

Keywords: Career support · Career related term · Chat system · Collaborative learning · eBook · Job-hunting

1 Introduction

The typical job-hunting process in Japan is very different from most other countries in the world. It is long and complex. The earliest the job-hunting process can start as early as the summer of two years before they graduate. They start with internship screenings, writing CVs (curriculum vitae) and entry sheets, taking exams, written or web-based, such as general knowledge tests, aptitude tests, and personality tests, participating group discussion observed by recruiters, and multiple rounds of group interviews and individual interviews until they finally achieve official job offers.

N. Streitz and S. Konomi (Eds.): HCII 2020, LNCS 12203, pp. 648–662, 2020.
https://doi.org/10.1007/978-3-030-50344-4_47

There are many terms used in job-hunting processes, which are rarely used in daily conversation. The objective in this study is to propose an effective learning system for job-hunting related terms in order to facilitate their job hunting in Japan. The system supports individual learning and collaborative learning with eBook and a chat system. The results of our previous study [1] showed a superiority of eBook-based learning to the Blogger-based learning when compared in terms of pre- and post-test improvement though there was no statistically significant difference. The effectiveness of chat system, however, was not detected in [1]. There are two objectives in this study: (1) to clarify whether there is a positive correlation between eBook learning involvement and test performance and (2) to clarify whether the use of our chat system was effective in learning job-hunting related terms. The rest of this paper is constructed as follows. Section 2 describes related researches to clearly identifying the difference between related works and our research. Section 2 describes the design of eBook called SCROLLeBook and a chat system called InCircle. Section 3 describes the evaluation and Sect. 4, discussion and our conclusions.

2 Related Researches

2.1 Technology Enhanced Career Support/Career Support Using Information Technology

There are some researches on ICT implementation on career support. In particular quite a few researchers have been working on utilization of ePortfolios for career education [2–5]. [2] proposed the use of ePortfolio in career education. [3] pointed out that there was a gap between the students' skill sets expected by companies and their actual abilities, and contended the necessity of ePortfolio utilization for their career development. [3] also pointed out that there are three issues yet to be solved for its effective use. 1) the information accumulated in ePortfolios has not been systematically organized nor utilized. 2) Data accumulated through career education (formal learning) is not enough. Some information is missing such as relationship between the two data and information accumulated through informal learning. 3) Related to 1), it is difficult for students to reflect and determine their suitable career based upon the data accumulated in ePortfolios. [4] proposed 'Portfolio Cycle', cyclic model for effective use of Portfolios, It consists of 5 cyclic factors: 1) goal setting 2) collecting data, accumulation of their achievments, 3) reflection, 4) evaluating setting, 5) self-assessment and peer reviewing. [5] implemented ePortofolio, Mahara for career assistance and insisted that motivation is pivotal for the effective use of Portfolios. Other ICT implementations are such as implementation of portal sites for students' career support [6], e-Learning contents in career development for university students [7], and e-mentoring for career development [8]. But no such learning system as eBook and chat-system blended learning system has been developed except our previous studies [1, 9].

2.2 SCROLL eBook

SCROLL (System for Capturing and Reusing Of Learning Log) was designed and developed by [10]. It aims to assist learners to record, organize and remind what they have learned in both informal and formal settings using a web browser and a mobile device and to share them with other learners beyond the limits of time and space. The system supports various learning fields including task-based language learning, vocabulary learning, science communicator, career support for international students living in Japan. The system is enriched with eBook reader, automatic quiz generator, analytics to share-and-reuse learning logs, learning activity tracker, and recommendation functionalities. This is an on-going project still in progress with new functions being added to the system one after the other. SCROLL eBook is one of the functions of SCROLL developed by using EPUB format [11].

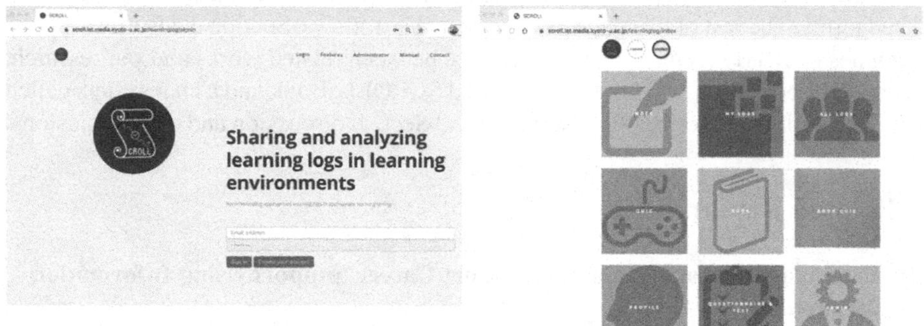

Fig. 1. Login interface of SCROLL (left) and SCROLL top page (right).

Figure 1 (Left) shows the web version of SCROLL login interface. Figure 1 (right) shows the SCROLL top page on the web. Book icon is the link to eBook system. Figure 2 shows SCROLL eBook contents. Teachers create e-book contents using PowerPoint or Keynote before classes. The contents created with PowerPoint/Keynote are converted to EPUB format and uploaded to the system. Learners can access the eBook contents by using smartphones and PCs. Figure 2 shows the digital textbook list.

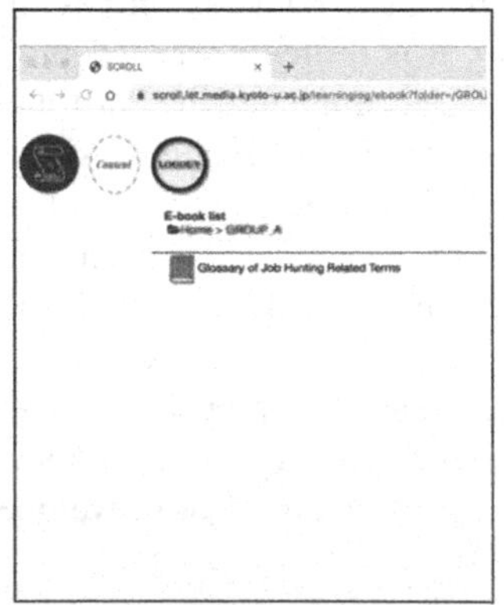

Fig. 2. SCROLL eBook contents.

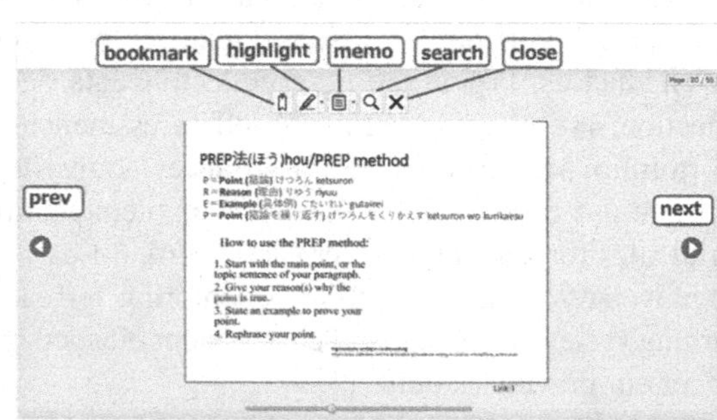

Fig. 3. SCROLL eBook viewer interface.

Figure 3 shows the eBook viewer interface and its functions. When a learner clicks the highlight button, he/she can highlight the word. he/she can find the page number corresponding to the target word in the e-book by clicking the search button. When a learner clicks the memo button, he/she can write memos about what they learned or questions about their target words.

2.3 InCircle

InCircle is a product developed by AOS Mobile Inc., Tokyo, Japan with the third-author joining this project as a chief software architect. It is a client-server application. The server side runs on Linux OS and Windows Server. The client side is working on iOS, Android, and PC Web browser. Messages are transmitted and received through the network (Fig. 4).

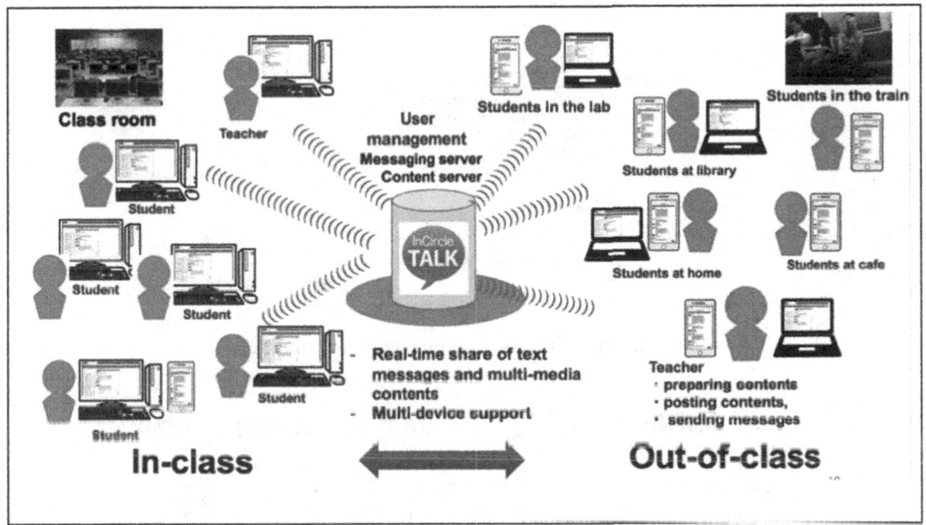

Fig. 4. InCircle system configuration.

Users can create groups. Group members are able to send and receive messages and multimedia files in their talk room with an easy operation. Messages are synchronized in real-time to facilitate smooth communication. Figure 5 shows a talk room interface when the instructor posted an interrogative sentence: "Do you have the system of 年功序列 (promotion by seniority)?" since interrogative sentences trigger active interaction among learners which leads to mutual cross-cultural understanding. InCircle was introduced in our learning scenario because it is reported that collaborative learning among students is effective especially in language learning [12]. The implementation of InCircle which allows us to realize synchronized communication anytime anywhere with easy handling is believed to contribute to the facilitation of collaborative learning.

2.4 SCROLLeBook & InCircle Combined Learning

In this study, the learning scenario was designed to combine self-learning with group learning. Figure 6 shows SCROLLeBook & InCircle combined learning. Students learn

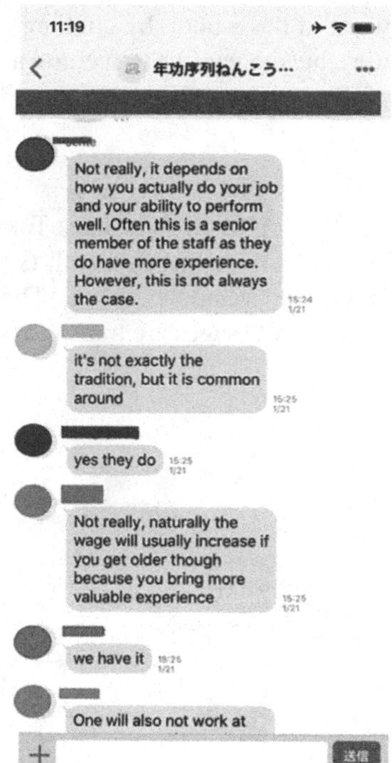

Fig. 5. InCircle talk room interface on mobile.

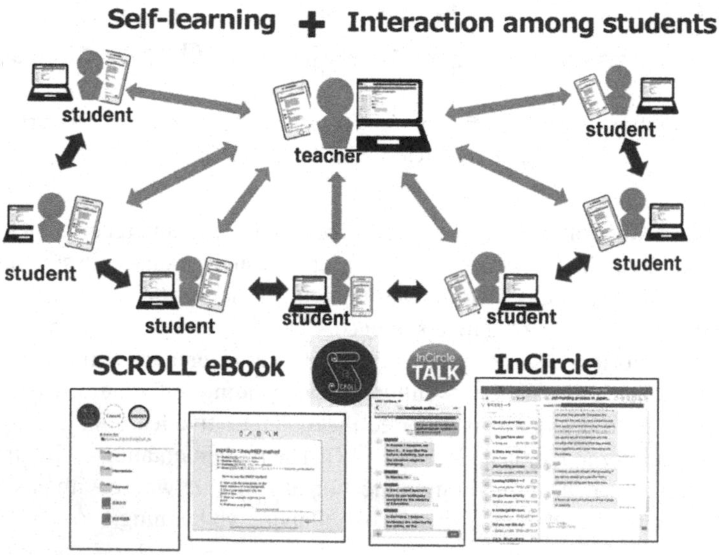

Fig. 6. SCROLL eBook & InCircle combined learning

career-related things with SCROLLeBook alone and interact with other class-mates and the teacher at the same time. In order to encourage students to collaborate during the task, the teacher posted a topic which would be helpful to learn career-related things via InCircle. Students were encouraged to interact via InCirle by telling them the number of InCircle posts will affect their grades.

3 Evaluation

3.1 The Target Classes

Seventeen students (7 Japanese, 3 Chinese, 2 British, 1 Finnish, 1 Brazilian, 1 Australian, 1 German, 1 Brunei), who were taking the classes called "Career Design and Business Communication" (Class A) and "Second Language Learning with Online Resources" (Class B), participated in the evaluation experiment. The target classes were held once a week in 2019 spring semester. Each student had PCs in classes. The objectives of Class A were (1) To develop one's self-concept during preparation for job hunting, and (2) to develop the skills of problem finding and solving, and cross-cultural communication in a diversity of workplace environments. The evaluation was conducted during April 25th to May 16th as an out-of-class activity. The objectives of Class B were to (1) to improve the skills of their target language, Japanese and (2) to enhance cross-cultural understanding as well as to learn Japanese affairs. The evaluation was conducted during June 18th to July 16th as an out-of-class activity.

3.2 Procedures

Figure 7 shows the learning scenario.

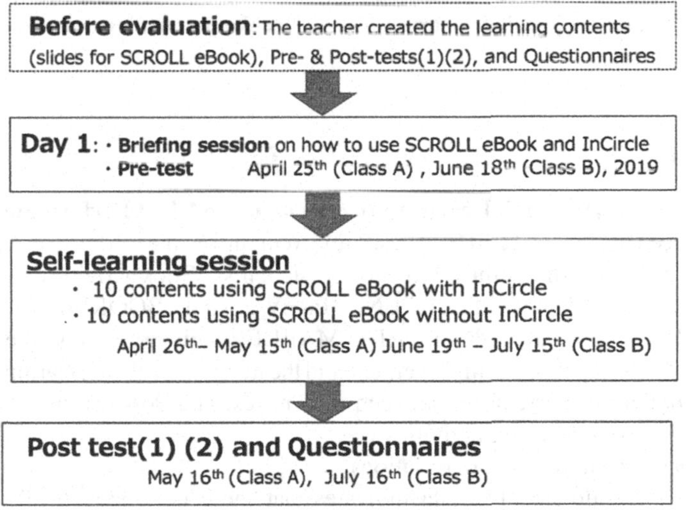

Fig. 7. Evaluation Procedures

The teacher created 20 contents for SCROLL eBook of career related terms such as "年功序列 (nenkoujoretsu)" (promotion by seniority), "終身雇用(shushinkoyou)" (permanent employment). The objective of the contents was to learn useful terms in terms of job-hunting. At the beginning of the session (Day 1), the participants received a briefing session to learn how to use SCROLL eBook and InCircle and took the pre-test to examine whether they know the meanings of 20 target terms. They were assigned to learn the target terms on a self-learning basis using SCROLL eBook (Fig. 8). Then the teacher delivered 10 learning contents via InCircle. In order to examine the effectiveness of InCircle, the comparison was made between with and without InCircle delivery. In order to give an equal opportunity of education, there was no control group created. Therefore the whole class experienced both with and without InCircle delivery. During the evaluation session, students were free to use InCircle both on PC and on Mobile to communicate with other classmates and the teacher. After the evaluation, Post-tests (1) & (2) were taken by the participants and the questionnaire was conducted.

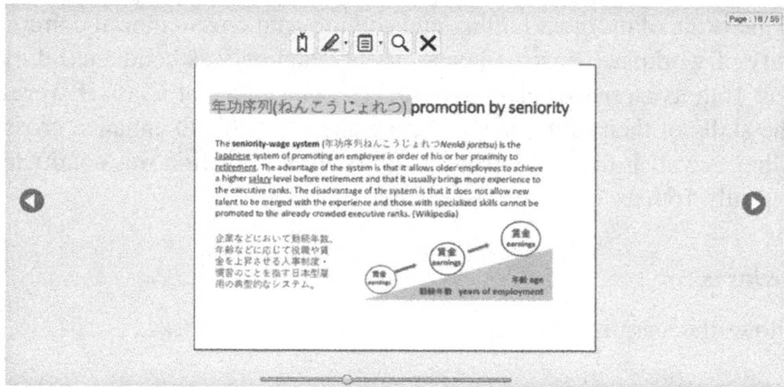

Fig. 8. SCROLL eBook learning content "年功序列(nenkoujoretsu)" (promotion by seniority)

3.3 Results

Correlation Between eBook Learning Involvement and Test Performance. The correlation between the Pre-test and Post-test improvement and the eBook learning activities was examined. Table 1 shows the number of the students' eBook activities. E-Book activities include 'CLOSE', 'NEXT', 'OPEN', 'PREV', 'ADD BOOKMARK' 'DELETE BOOKMARK', 'PAGE_JUMP' and 'ADD MARKER'. Figure 9 shows the correlation between pre-test and post-test improvement and the number of eBook learning activities.

The coefficient of correlation between the Pre-test and Post-test improvement and the number of eBook learning activities was:

$/r/ = 0.332$ (weak positive correlation)

However the following formula indicates that there is no statistically significant correlation:

$r^2 = 0.1103 < 0.21 \{4/(n + 2)\}$

Table 1. eBook learning activities.

	'CLOSE'	'NEXT'	'OPEN'	'PREV'	'ADD BOOKMARK'	'DELETE BOOKMARK'	'PAGE_JUMP'	'ADD MARKER'	Total
student #1	6	155	8	12			6	3	190
student #2	10	132	11	5	1	1	3		163
student #3	2	112	2	6					122
student #4	2	97	6	12			2		119
student #5	1	56	2	21			1		81
student #6	2	75	2						79
student #7	1	60	3	8				2	74
student #8		64	3		1	1	1		70
student #9	2	61	2	2					67
student #10	2	58	2	2					64
student #11	1	51	1	2					55
student #12	2	29	7	11	2	2	1		54
student #13		10	1	8					19
student #14	1	10	1						12
student #15									0
student #16									0
student #17									0

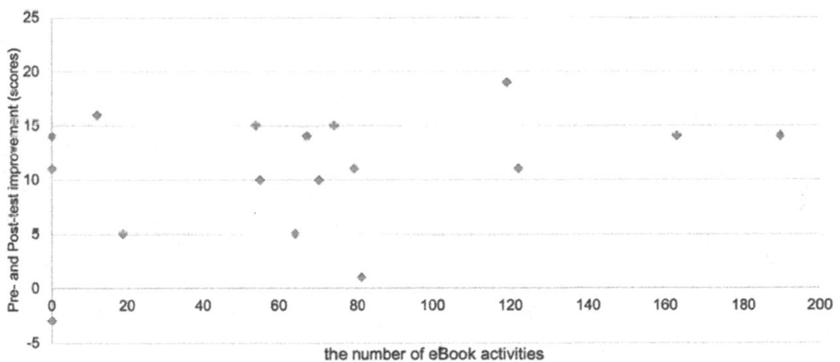

Fig. 9. Correlation between Pre-test and Post-test improvement and the number of eBook learning activities.

Our learning system was originally developed for international students. Therefore we analyzed the correlation between the Pre-test and Post-test improvement and the number of eBook learning activities focusing on the international students. Table 2 shows the number of the students' eBook activities. Figure 10 shows the correlation between Pre-test and Post-test improvement and the number of eBook learning activities of international students.

The coefficient of correlation between the Pre-test and Post-test improvement and the number of eBook learning activities of international students was:

$/r/ = 0.512$ (weak positive correlation)

Table 2. eBook learning activities focusing international students.

	'CLOSE'	'NEXT'	'OPEN'	'PREV'	'ADD BOOKMARK'	'DELETE BOOKMARK'	'PAGE_JUMP'	'ADD MARKER'	Total
int'l student #1	6	155	8	12			6	3	190
int'l student #2	2	97	6	12			2		119
int'l student #3	1	60	3	8				2	74
int'l student #4	0	64	3	0	1	1	1		70
int'l student #5	2	61	2	2					67
int'l student #6	2	58	2	2					64
int'l student #7	2	29	7	11	2	2	1	0	54
int'l student #8	0	10	1	8					19
int'l student #9	1	10	1	0					12
int'l student #10		0		0					0

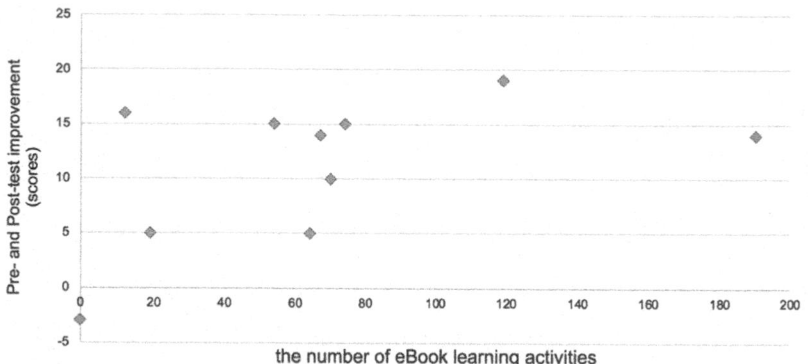

Fig. 10. Correlation between Pre-test and Post-test improvement and the number of eBook learning activities of international students.

The correlation focusing on the international students is stronger than that of the whole participants.

However the following formula indicates that there is no statistically significant correlation:

$r^2 = 0.2621 < 0.33 \{4/(n + 2)\}$

Effectiveness of InCircle Delivery of Learning Contents. Table 3 shows the result of the Pre- and Post-test (1) and (2). Pre- and Post-test (1) were identical to ask them the meaning of 10 Japanese career-related terms to be taught via eBook with InCircle delivery. Pre- and Post-test (2) were also identical to ask them the meaning of 10 career-related terms to be taught via eBook without InCircle delivery. The full mark was 10 points for Pre- and Post-test (1) and Pre- and Post-test (2). The mean scores of the Pre-test (1) and (2) were 2.82 and 2.94 with the standard deviation(SD) of 1.81 and 1.85. After the learning session, the result of Post-test (1) was 8.35 with the standard deviation of 2.47, while that of Post-test (2) was 8.12 with the standard deviation of 3.02. T value, 0.448 and effect size (d), 0.12 shows that there is no statistically significant difference between them. However, as Fig. 11 shows, there was a slight difference in the mean score increase between the two methods. With-InCircle-delivery method shows more improvement than without- InCircle-delivery method.

Table 3. The result of Pre- and Post-tests.

	Pre-test (1) (full mark 10)	Post-test (1) after eBook and InCircle learning (full mark 10)	t-value of Pre-&Post-test improvement of with/without InCircle delivery	Effect Size (d)
Mean	2.82	8.35	0.448 ($p < 0.05$)	0.12 (Small)
SD	1.81	2.47		
	Pre-test (2) (full mark 10)	Post-test (2) after eBook learning (full mark 10)		
Mean	2.94	8.12		
SD	1.85	3.02		

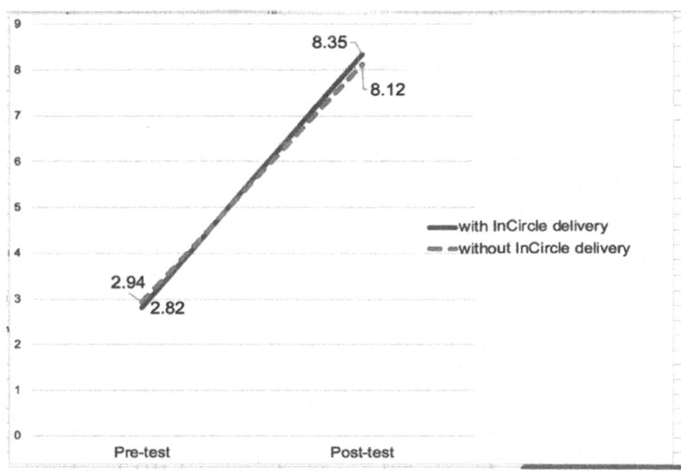

Fig. 11. Comparison between eBook learning with InCircle without InCircle in terms of the means of Pre- and Post-tests.

As mentioned above, our system was originally developed for international students. Therefore we analyzed it focusing on the international students. Table 4 shows the result of the Pre- and Post-test (1) and (2) of the international students. The mean scores of the Pre-test (1) and (2) were 2.20 and 2.30 with the standard deviation (SD) of 1.81 and 2.11. The result of Post-test (1) was 7.80 with the standard deviation of 2.90, while that of Post-test (2) was 7.70 with the standard deviation of 3.47. T value, 0.784 and effect size (d), 0.05 show that there is no statistically significant difference between them. Figure 12 shows the comparison between eBook learning with InCircle without InCircle in terms of the means of Pre- and Post-tests of international students. After all, no particular difference was found between all the participants and foreign students.

Table 4. The result of Pre- and Post-tests of international students.

	Pre-test (1) (full mark 10)	Post-test (1) after eBook and InCircle learning (full mark 10)	t-value of Pre-&Post-test improvement of with/without InCircle delivery	Effect Size (d)
Mean	2.20	7.80	0.784 (p = 0.39)	0.05 (Small)
SD	1.81	2.90		
	Pre-test (2) (full mark 10)	Post-test (2) after eBook learning (full mark 10)		
Mean	2.30	7.70		
SD	2.11	3.47		

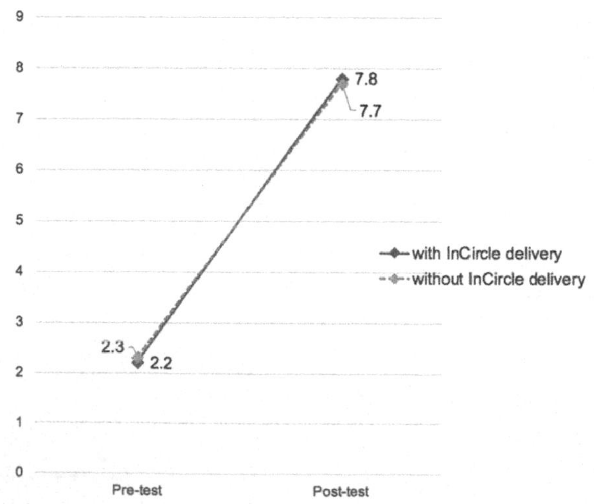

Fig. 12. Comparison between eBook learning with InCircle without InCircle in terms of the means of Pre- and Post-tests of international students.

Table 5 shows the number of InCircle post of the students and the teacher during the evaluation. Totally there were 72 posts by the students and 140 by the teacher. The students were not so active in InCircle compared with the teacher's active posting. They tended to react when the teacher posted interrogative messages. [13] reported that there was an active interaction among students when they used InCircle such that one student's post lead to another students' reaction. Such a phenomenon rarely happened in this evaluation except once when a student asked the teacher about an entry sheet writing task, another student reacted to her message.

Table 5. The number of InCircle post during the evaluation.

	The number of InCircle post
Students	72
Teacher	140

4 Discussion and Conclusion

4.1 Discussion

At the end of the evaluation, they were asked to answer the five-point-scale-questionnaire as shown in Table 6. Q1and Q6 were created to examine the fun factor of SCROLLeBook and InCircle. Q2and Q5 were created based on the technology acceptance model proposed by [14]. Q3 and Q7 were created to examine the user acceptance of its interface. The highest score, 4.69 was given when they were asked about the user-friendliness of InCircle (Q.5). Its functions and interface are almost the same as other chat tools such as LINE, Messengers, and WhatsApp. They felt it was easy to handle. The second highest score, 4.19 was given when they were asked about its helpfulness of InCircle (Q.4). The mean score of 4.19 can be safely said that they regarded it as helpful for learning job-hunting related terms. The lowest score, 3.81 was given when they were asked about

Table 6. The results of the 5-point-scale questionnaire.

	Questions	Mean	SD
Q.1	Was it fun to learn career related terms with SCROLL eBook contents	3.94	1.26
Q.2	Was it easy for you to handle SCROLL eBook?	4.13	0.79
Q.3	Please rate its interface of SCROLLeBook	3.81	1.00
Q.4	You also learned career related terms via InCircle. Was it helpful?	4.19	1.02
Q.5	Was it easy for you to handle InCircle?	4.69	0.50
Q.6	Was it fun to learn career related terms via InCircle ?	4.00	1.21
Q.7	Please rate its interface of InCircle	4.13	0.83

rating of the interface of SCROLLeBook (Q.3). As Fig. 8 shows, its interface is just like other eBook system developed based on ePub system, it seems that they regarded it as nothing new. Besides, as Table 6 shows, there were some students who had a difficulty in zooming-in and -out the eBook screen. This user-unfriendliness might be one of the reason why they graded low.

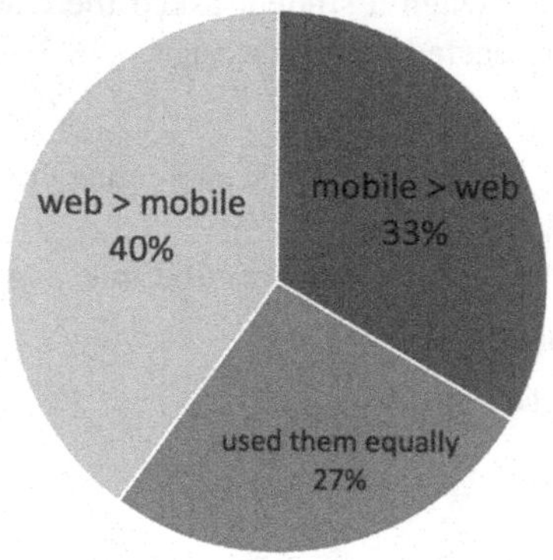

Fig. 13. Which media did you use more often web or mobile?

Table 7. The students' impressions of the eBook and InCircle combined learning.

	Comments
#1	It's okay I guess. The design is pretty basic but easy enough for anyone to use
#2	It was fun
#3	It was lots of interesting information, I learned a lot of new things about Japanese society and careers
#4	I think it is helpful because students can share learning materials together
#5	It was helpful for me to learn lots of information which is necessary for job-hunting
#6	It worked quite well in my opinion. It was simple and easy to use, so I didn't have any complaints
#7	Okay, but not really special
#8	I'm not fond of scroll. The eBook was no different from a PowerPoint
#9	I think it doesn't work with all web browsers, it would be nice to know which browsers don't work
#10	Difficult to handle to utilize this site effectively
#11	I could not find zoom-in function, So I could not see the slides well
#12	I could not make the eBook full screen, so It was difficult to see the contents
#13	I have a problem opening the eBook at first

Figure 13 shows the result of the question: Which did you use more often web-based InCircle or InCircle on mobile? Forty % of the students used InCircle on the web more often than on mobile, 33% of the students used mobile more often than the web, and 27% used equally. Compared with our previous study [9] where the majority used mobile more often than the web, the result was opposite. The fact that InCircle on the web was introduced in class earlier than InCircle on mobile might have affected the result.

Table 7 shows the participants' free comments on the eBook and InCircle combined learning. Comments #1, 2, 3, 4, 5, and 6 are positive ones, they seemed to enjoy learning using the system. As for Comment #9, the teacher repeated to tell them to use Chrome. but it turned out that it was not enough. As the comment #9, 10, 11,12 pointed out, there are some students who had some difficulty to enlarge the slide. Users needed to use one of the Chrome functions located in the right upper corner of the browser to enlarge the screen. It also turned out that some users did not grasp this function thoroughly. It should be considered in our next evaluation.

4.2 Conclusions

In this study, we described facilitating the learning of job-hunting related terms by using SROLLeBook and InCircle. The objectives of our research were: (1) to clarify whether there is a positive correlation between active involvement of eBook learning and test performance and (2) to clarify whether the use of our chat system was effective in learning job-hunting related terms. As for (1), there was no statistically significant correlation between the two factors. However when focusing on the international students, the correlation coefficient increased from 0.332 to 0.512. It was aligned with the fact that this system was originally designed to support international students. From the students' free comments, it was found out that some students had some difficulties in adjusting slide sizes. Adjusting the screen size is one the functions provided by Chrome, but this information was not thoroughly conveyed to the participants. It is necessary to instruct them how to adjust the size repeatedly. It will be considered in our next evaluation. As for (2), when the comparison was made between with and without InCircle delivery, there was no statistically significant difference between them in terms of Pre- and Post-test improvement. However the students gave the high score of 4.19 when they were asked its helpfulness. The score implies that the students were satisfied with its helpfulness. Therefore our hypotheses (InCircle content delivery system contributes to facilitating their learning job-hunting related terms) was proved correct in terms of the users' impressions. However compared with the teacher's active posting on InCircle (140 times), the students were not so active (72 times in all). It is among our future works to find out some solutions to encourage more involvement in our chat system since it is reported, as mentioned, that a collaborative learning method is effective especially in language learning.

Acknowledgements. Part of this research work was supported by the Grant-in-Aid for Scientific Research No.18K02820, No.17K12947, No.16H06304 and 16H03078 from the Ministry of Education, Culture, Sports, Science and Technology (MEXT) in Japan.

References

1. Uosaki, N., et al.: Seamless collaborative learning method to learn business Japanese with eBook and chat system. In: Streitz, N., Konomi, S. (eds.) HCII 2019. LNCS, vol. 11587, pp. 442–458. Springer, Cham (2019). https://doi.org/10.1007/978-3-030-21935-2_34
2. Arame, M., Naganuma, S., Kobayashi, M., Komatsu, M., Tamaki, K.: Consideration about how to use the e Portfolio in career education, IPSJ Trans. Comput. Educ. (Kenkyu Houkoku:Computer to Kyouiku) 2013-CE, **120**(3), 1–8 (2013). (in Japanese)
3. Maeda, Y.: An Improvement study of career portfolio to support the career development of university students. Fukuyama Univ. Dept. Bull. Paper **3**, 65–73 (2017). (in Japanese)
4. Ogawa, K.: Utilization of ePortofolios for Career Support -Toward Sustainable Systems - (in Japanese)
5. Murayama, M.: Utilization of Career Portfolio for Career Assistance - Implementation of Open Sourse ePortfolio called Mahara, Nagaoka University Lifelong Learning Center Yearly Report, vol. 4, pp. 55–59 (2010). (in Japanese)
6. Calitz, A., Evert, C., Cullen, M.: Promoting ICT careers using a South African ICT career portal. African J. Inf. Syst. **7**(2), 1 (2015)
7. Teshima H., Kawasaki C., Komatsu Y.: Integrated program of the academic skills and the career development for university freshers: a report, Bull. Osaka Jogakuin College, **5**, 119–144, (2008). On the Course "Skills for Self Establishing" at Osaka Jogakuin College (Japanese)
8. Headlam-Wells, J., Gosland, J., Craig, J.: "There's magic in the web": e-mentoring for women's career development. Career Dev. Int. **10**(6/7), 444–459 (2005)
9. Uosaki, N., Mouri, K., Yonekawa, T., Yin C., Ogata, H.: Supporting job-hunting students to learn job-hunting related terms with SCROLL eBook and InCircle. In: Conference Proceedings Volume 1 of the 27th International Conference on Computers in Education, ICCE2019, pp. 478–483 (2019)
10. Ogata, H., Hou, B., Li, M., Uosaki, N., Mouri, K., Liu, S.: Ubiquitous learning project us-ing life-logging technology in Japan. Educ. Technol. Soc. J. **17**(2), 85–100 (2014)
11. Kiyota, M., Mouri, K., Uosaki, N., Ogata, H.: AETEL: supporting seamless learning and learning log recording with e-book system. In: Proceedings of the 24th International Conference on Computers in Education, ICCE 2016, pp. 380–385 (2016)
12. Oxford, R.L.: Cooperative learning, collaborative learning, and interaction: three communicative strands in the language classroom. Mod. Lang. J. **81**(1), 443–456 (1997). https://doi.org/10.1111/j.1540-4781.1997.tb05510.x
13. Uosaki, N., Yonekawa, T., Yin, C.: Enhancing Learners' Cross-Cultural Understanding in Language and Culture Class Using InCircle. In: Yoshino, T., Yuizono, T., Zurita, G., Vassileva, J. (eds.) CollabTech 2017. LNCS, vol. 10397, pp. 145–152. Springer, Cham (2017). https://doi.org/10.1007/978-3-319-63088-5_13
14. Davis, F.D.: Perceived usefulness, perceived ease of use, and user acceptance of information technology. MIS Q. **13**(3), 319–339 (1989)

Non-invasive Sleep Assistance System Design Based on IoT

Dong Wang, Shiyao Qin, and Zhenyu Gu(✉)

School of Design, Shanghai Jiao Tong University, Shanghai, China
wangdong_sjtu@163.com, zygu@sjtu.edu.cn

Abstract. With the accelerated pace of life in modern society, various sleep problems have become increasingly prominent and spread to younger groups. Meanwhile, people are beginning to accept the use of IoT products to improve their sleep quality. This paper designs a non-invasive sleep assistance system based on IoT that integrates a non-invasive device of collecting sleep data, a sleep-assisted light linkage and a mobile application. Before the design, we conduct questionnaires and in-depth interviews to understand user characteristics and related demands, construct personas, and conduct competitive product analysis to determine the specific product form. The sleep data collection device is a circular mat based on the Arduino platform and the EMFi sensor, and the light linkage is a sleep-assisted device coordinated with the circular mat. The mobile application can display some information vividly, such as the user's physiological data, sleep quality, sleep suggestions, and so on. We complete the functional prototype of the data collection device and the light linkage, and the high-fidelity prototype of the mobile application. In addition, we collect feedbacks and discuss the improvement direction of the sleep assistance system in the future.

Keywords: Smart home · Sleep assistance · Non-invasive · IoT · EMFi

1 Introduction

1.1 Research Background

According to a survey report by the Chinese Sleep Research Association in 2018, nearly 80% of Chinese people between the ages of 10 and 45 fell asleep poorly, and 13% of them suffered from physical and mental discomfort due to insufficient sleep. At the same time, sleep problems are getting younger, and young people are becoming the main population of insomnia [1].

Sleep is an important physiological process of the human body. It plays an important role in replenishing body energy, enhancing immunity, promoting bone development, and slowing down human aging. It is extremely significant to protect people's physical and mental health. The human sleep phase is divided into non-rapid eye movement (NREM) and rapid eye movement (REM). During the non-rapid eye movement phase, the deep sleep phase occurs periodically. The length of the deep sleep phase largely determines the human body's sleep quality. Sleep problems such as insomnia, irregular

N. Streitz and S. Konomi (Eds.): HCII 2020, LNCS 12203, pp. 663–676, 2020.
https://doi.org/10.1007/978-3-030-50344-4_48

sleep and daytime drowsiness can damage human health over time. Experts on sleep health have stated that irregular schedules are harmful to health, and can easily induce physical and mental diseases such as cardiovascular disease, metabolic diseases, cancer, and depression, and may be life-threatening in severe cases [2].

Traditional healthcare mainly relies on manual or large-scale medical equipment, which costs consumers a lot of time and money, therefore many people are unwilling to get healthcare service. Nowadays, smart home products have entered millions of households with their advantages of portability, intelligence, and affordability, enabling people to enjoy the comfort and convenience of life given by technology. Combining the Internet of Things (IoT) technology with healthcare products, and designing smart healthcare products to replace traditional healthcare methods are the current hotspots and industry trends.

Therefore, an intelligent sleep care product combined with the IoT technology can well fill the market demand and meet people's expectations for sleep health. The product monitors the sleep quality of the human body in a reasonable and effective way, presents visual analysis results to the user, and gives effective suggestions based on the analysis results, to help users improve sleep quality and achieve the efficacy of sleep care.

1.2 Related Work

The historical achievements on sleep monitoring methods include Polysomnography (PSG), Portable Monitoring (PM), Actigraphy, Micro-movement Sensitive Mattress Sleep Monitoring System (MSMSMS), and Electro Mechanical Film (EMFi) sensors (see Fig. 1).

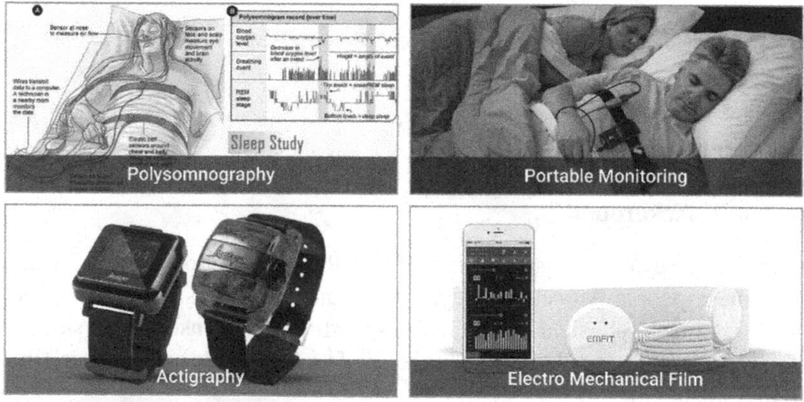

Fig. 1. Sleep monitoring methods

(1) Polysomnography (PSG) is a standard test for the diagnosis of sleep-related breathing disorders and narcolepsy, positive airway pressure titration, and assessment of abnormal sleep. Monitoring parameters include electroencephalogram, electrooculogram, mandibular electromyography, oral and nasal airflow and respiratory movement, electrocardiogram, blood oxygen, snoring, limb movement, body position,

etc., which has the advantages of accuracy, reliability, intuitiveness and detailedness. At present, it's the standard physiological diagnosis method in hospital for patients with sleep disorders [3]. However, polysomnography requires the installation of detection electrodes of various instruments on the subject, which is tedious and complicated. At the same time, the cost is high, the learning cost is high, the portability is insufficient, and it is inconvenient to use outside the hospital.

(2) Portable Monitoring (PM) is also called Home Sleep Testing (HST). Compared with polysomnography, the equipment is more compact, and it monitors at least 3 parameters: airflow, breathing effort, and Pulse oxygen saturation, but it is still necessary to wear sensors on more than 3 parts of the subject, and patients have a high failure rate when using alone [4].

(3) Actigraphy is a wearable device that records physical activity over a period of time, such as a smart bracelet, etc., using the static and movement data collected by the acceleration sensor to estimate the amount of body movement, awake time and other parameters. The actigraphy is convenient to wear and use, and can be used to evaluate some sleep disorders, such as circadian disorder, insomnia, sleep apnea, excessive sleep, sleep movement disorders, etc. [5], which is suitable for assisting polysomnography. Its accuracy and professional is not as good as polysomnography.

(4) Micro-movement Sensitive Mattress Sleep Monitoring System (MSMSMS), developed by Academician Yu Mengsun, uses pressure sensors to record any small changes in a person's bed, including even heartbeat signals [6]. The sleep monitoring process of this system tends to be natural, without the need for medical staff to pre-process, electrodes, and wiring. It only requires the subject to lie on a special mattress to be monitored, and the monitoring results are more reliable. In this system, the heart rate is calculated from the pulse wave signal recorded by the finger-tip photoelectric volume pulse wave detection recorder, which requires the subject to wear the detector at all times during night sleep, which brings certain inconvenience to the subject.

(5) Electro Mechanical Film (EMFi) sensor, first invented by Finnish company VTT in 1980, has a long strip shape, light weight and thin shape, and can be isolated from external interference [7]. The sensitivity of EMFi sensors is an order of magnitude better than that of ordinary piezoelectric materials. Due to the high resistance and the hole-like structure of organic materials, the charge can last for a long time, which is convenient for the timely collection of electrical signals [8]. The Finnish company Emfit uses self-developed EMFi sensors for sleep monitoring and has designed an Emfit QS health monitor that can monitor multiple sleep data such as heart rate, breathing, and turning over during sleep. The sleep monitor is currently the most convenient mat-type sleep monitoring product. Users do not need to wear any equipment and can lay on a smart mat based on an EMFi sensor to get non-invasive sleep quality monitoring. It gets rid of the problem that the original smart products need to be replaced frequently, and there is no need to learn how to use it, which significantly improves the convenience of monitoring.

In view of the many excellent characteristics of the EMFi sensor, this paper will use the EMFi sensor to design and develop intelligent sleep assistance system. The electrical signals collected by the EMFi sensor will be used to analyze and calculate physiological signals including respiratory frequency, heart rate, and body movement by the sleep analysis algorithm. The user's sleep quality can be visualized on the mobile phone, and the system can help the user to harvest a healthy and comfortable sleep experience and develop good sleep habits through sound and light, relatives and friends supervision, and sleep reward program, etc.

2 Investigation and Analysis

2.1 Questionnaire

According to a survey report by the Chinese Sleep Research Association in 2018, nearly 80% of Chinese people between the ages of 10 and 45 fell asleep poorly, and 13% of them suffered from physical and mental discomfort due to insufficient sleep. At the same time, sleep problems are getting younger, and young people are becoming the main population of insomnia. This paper conducts a questionnaire on sleep quality and sleep-related products. The results are shown in Fig. 2.

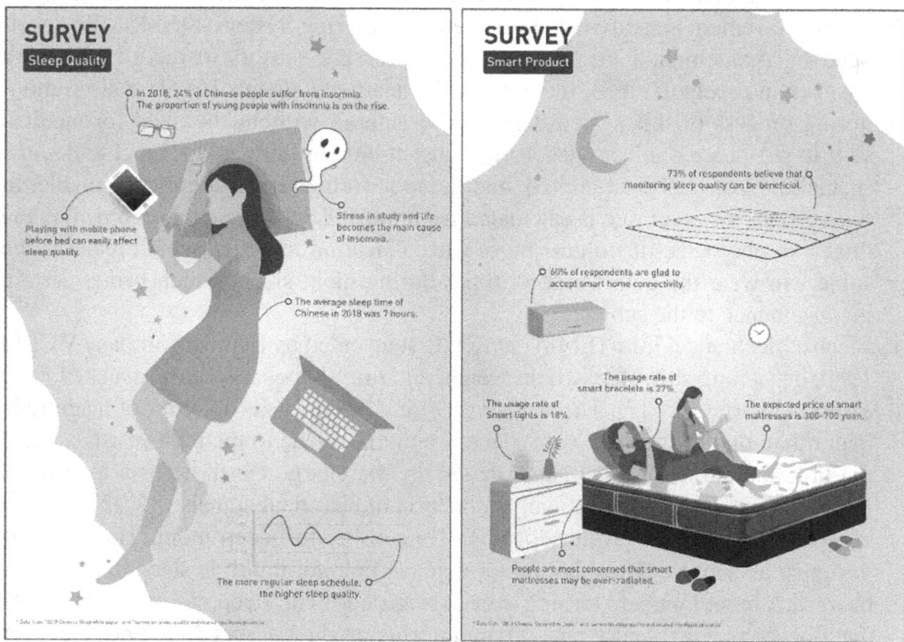

Fig. 2. Information visualization of survey results

Of the respondents in this survey, 54% slept less than 7 h a day, and 49% rated their sleep quality as average or poor. Among the main reasons that affect people's sleep quality, using electronic devices before bedtime ranks first, accounting for 64%, and study/work stress accounts for 61%, followed by insufficient exercise, strong light/noise, and so on. Among related sleep products, the use rate of smart bracelets was the highest, accounting for 27%, followed by smart sleep aid lamps, accounting for 18%. When asked opinions on a smart product that can monitor and improve sleep quality, 89% of the respondents said they would like to try to accept it, and 30% of them are looking forward to the arrival of this product very much. For the beneficial functions of smart sleep products, 73% of respondents chose monitoring sleep quality, 59% chose adjusting indoor temperature during sleep, 58% chose turning off music and indoor lights after falling asleep, and 52% chose playing music or the radio to adjust the mood. Regarding the concerns about smart sleep products, 77% of the respondents are worried that there may be radiation, and long-term use will be harmful to health, and 47% of them are worried about inconvenience. Finally, regarding the price expectations of smart products, 46% of the respondents chose 200–500 yuan, and 27% chose 500–1000 yuan.

The above questionnaire analysis results show the respondents' overall sleep status, the opinions and acceptance of sleep-related smart products, the expectations of the functions, deficiencies and prices of sleep-related smart products, and the related product forms still need to be further explored.

2.2 User Interview

User interview is a face-to-face exchange between the designer and the interviewee. It can provide insight into special phenomena, specific situations, specific problems, common habits, special situations, and consumer preferences. It helps designers to understand consumers' perceptions, opinions, consumption motivations and behaviors of products or services [9]. In order to better understand the sleep status of young people, this paper conducted user interviews to conduct in depth questions and investigations on the questions in the questionnaire.

The experiences and feelings of one of the interviewees are highly representative. She is an undergraduate student, and she usually suffers from insomnia, mostly because the exam is approaching and the deadline for submitting homework is imminent. She needs to stay up late to study and work. In daily life, the mobile phone is not left for a long time, it is easy to play the mobile phone and watch videos for too long. At night, the spirit is in a state of excitement. When she realized that she should sleep, she did not have a strong sleepiness. In most cases, she usually goes to bed at 11 or 12 in the evening, depending on the situation in the morning. She wakes up at about 7 o'clock in the morning or when there is something. She can sleep late at about 10 o'clock.

She has not used any sleep-related smart devices, and has accepted the products of wristbands, but also admitted that she does not have the habit of wearing a watch. It feels a bit uncomfortable to wear things while sleeping, which may affect the quality of sleep. For products such as bedside lamps, it is considered useful to have different light responses in different situations, such as eye protection lights when reading at night, and sleep assistance lights at night. For the new products of a smart mat, she expects practicality and convenience. At the same time, she wants to ensure that there is no electronic radiation that may harm physical health.

For the post-90s generation who started on the health road, she expressed understanding and support. Because of insomnia and stresses of study and work, acne appeared on her face, she said "the body began to automatically fight against bad habits and required to be taken good care of". When asked about self-regulation, she thought it was important to develop a regular sleep routine, but she did know it was easy to know and hard to implement.

She said, "Insomnia is a fierce self-resistance. There is a flood of thoughts at night, a variety of beautiful visions of life in the mind, conflicts with various realistic dilemmas and inadequate abilities, huge pressure and confusion sweeping through the body. It is impossible to sleep peacefully". At the same time, she also firmly believes that it is necessary to work hard to cope with sleep problems, reasonably plan future careers, and maintain a relaxed attitude, and everything will gradually get better.

2.3 Competitive Products Analysis

This paper collects 8 typical sleep-related competitive products and evaluates them in four aspects. The evaluation of each competitive product is shown in Table 1.

Table 1. The evaluation of competitive products

Product Name	Picture	Practicability	Appearance	Portability	CP ratio	Total
Mi Band 2		●●●○○	●●●○○	●●●○○	●●●●○	13
Mijia bedside lamp		●●●●○	●●●●○	●●●●○	●●●●○	16
Nox aroma lamp		●●●●○	●●●○○	●●○○○	●●●○○	12
RestOn sleep device		●●●●●	●●●●●	●●●●○	●●○○○	16
Dot fastener		●●○○○	●●●○○	●●●●●	●●●●●	15
Monna		●●○○○	●●●○○	●●●○○	●●○○○	10
Somnox		●●○○○	●●●○○	●●○○○	●○○○○	8
Circa		●●●○○	●●●●●	●●●○○	●●○○○	13

Based on the above product evaluation table, the two products with the highest scores stand out-Mijia bedside lamp and RestOn smart sleep device, which have the functions of assisting sleep light and monitoring sleep data. Therefore, these two functions can be used as the focus of subsequent design work.

The Mijia bedside lamp has a unique and effective function, which can help to fall asleep, wake up, and adjust the light mode. The price is average and it is fashionable. It does not collect enough sleep data.

The RestOn smart sleep assistance device has a large monitoring area, and the measured data is more accurate and reliable. It does not need to be worn, is easy and comfortable, has dedicated functions, and is expensive.

Combined with the competition product analysis, we can infer the two functions that the user needs most-sleep monitoring and light sleep assistance, while ensuring good practicability.

3 Sleep Data Collection and Analysis

3.1 Sleep Data Collection

The intelligent sleep assistance product designed in this paper uses the Arduino platform to carry out the design of intelligent hardware. The EMFi sensor is used to collect sleep information.

The EMFi sensor is thin and light, and is sensitive to changes in its surface force. It can convert pressure changes into output electrical signals, but the output electrical signals are very weak [10]. The voltage fluctuation range of human body movement is 0–20 mV, while the voltage fluctuation range corresponding to breathing is only in the range of 0–0.3 mV. The change of electrical signals cannot be obtained directly through the Arduino analog input, and it is easy to be interfered by the power frequency of 50 Hz mains. Therefore, more sophisticated data collection and processing circuits need to be designed. By consulting the literature, the overall circuit layout of "EMFi sensor → charge amplifier → filter → AD converter → Arduino development board" was determined [11]. The overall circuit is shown in Fig. 3.

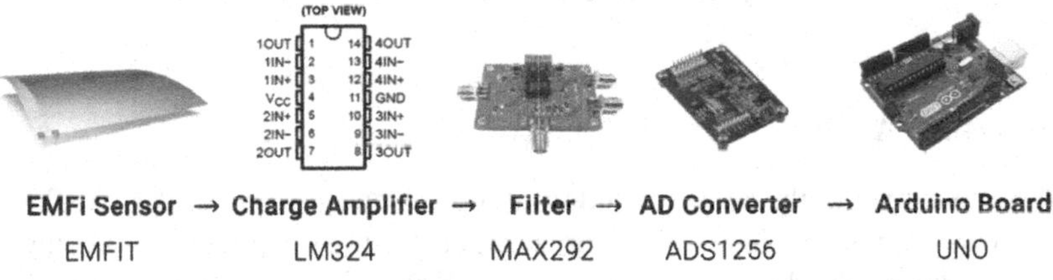

Fig. 3. Circuit layout

After some circuit study, we decided to use LM324 quad operational amplifier to design the amplifier circuit, MAX292 eighth-order low-pass filter to design the low-pass filter circuit, and 24-bit AD converter ADS1256 to design the high-precision AD acquisition circuit. After reading and researching the relevant data manual, complete the design of the overall circuit, and cooperate with the EMFi sensor for debugging. We selected the appropriate DC power supply, clock signal, resistance, and capacitance, to complete the design of Arduino program and high-precision data acquisition. The actual effect of the detection circuit is good. it can capture human body movements in time, roughly observe the signal fluctuation caused by breathing, and observe the signal fluctuation caused by heartbeat while holding the breath.

In order to obtain the values of breathing frequency and heart rate from the data analysis of electrical signals, it was decided to use MATLAB for data analysis. The electrical signals in the time domain were subjected to fast Fourier transform (FFT) to obtain the frequency domain distribution map of the electrical signals. (see Eq. 1)

$$\hat{f}(\xi) = \int_{-\infty}^{\infty} f(x)e^{-2\pi ix\xi}dx \tag{1}$$

The crest distribution can accurately obtain the values of respiratory frequency and heart rate. The analysis of each electrical signal and frequency is shown in Fig. 4.

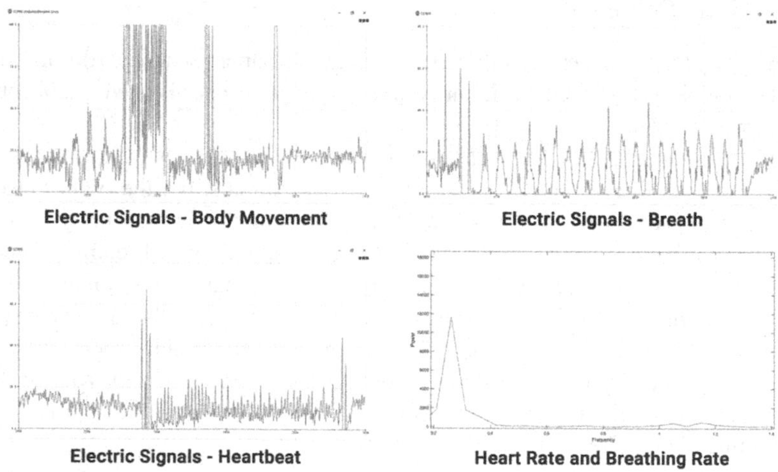

Fig. 4. Electrical signals and frequency

3.2 Sleep Data Analysis

According to research, the basis for judging good sleep quality includes 10–20 min of falling asleep, deep sleep, less waking up at night, getting up quickly, and being awake during work during the day and so on. The length of deep sleep largely determines our sleep quality. The deeper people sleep during the night, the higher the sleep quality is.

The determination of the degree of sleep can be processed based on the data collected by the mat, including heart rate, breathing rate, and body movement. To simplify the user's understanding, we divide the sleep phase into the awake phase, light sleep phase and deep sleep phase. Among them, the user does not fall asleep during the awake phase, and the user may be in a light sleep phase or a deep sleep phase after falling asleep. The condition for the judgment is that when the body movement frequency exceeds 3 times per minute, we think that the user is still awake; when the body movement frequency is less than 3 times per minute, we think that the user starts to fall asleep, and continue to judge whether the user is in the light sleep stage or in the deep sleep phase. When the user's heart rate falls to 80% before falling asleep, we determine that the user has entered the deep sleep phase, otherwise the user is in the light sleep phase [12]. The sleep phase flow chart is shown in Fig. 5.

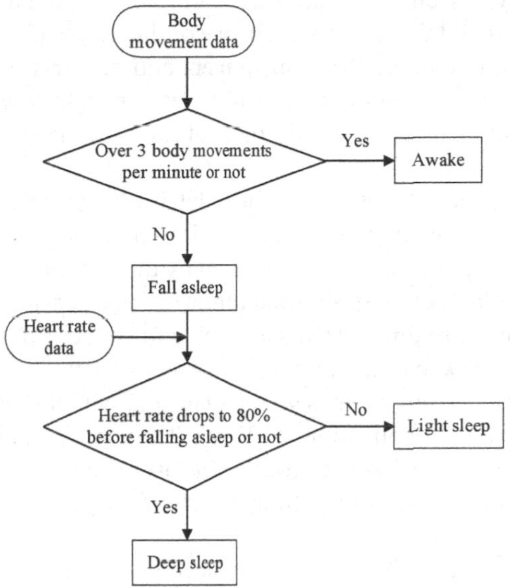

Fig. 5. The sleep phase flow chart

In addition, the mat can also determine whether the user is lying down and ready to sleep. This can be determined based on the heart rate value. When the user is sitting on the bed for reading or playing with a mobile phone, his heartbeat is difficult to be captured or in a huge fluctuation range because the human heart is far from the mat. When the user is lying in bed and ready to sleep, the back of the human body is close to the mat, and the sensor can accurately capture a stable heartbeat value, so as to make a judgment that the user has been lying down.

4 Intelligent Sleep Assistance System

4.1 Product Form and Interaction Process

After completing the collection and analysis of sleep data, this paper began to establish the brand image of smart sleep assistance products-LotusLeaf sleep assistance equipment, and product form-smart mat combined with smart bedside lamps. The inspiration of LotusLeaf's brand is derived from the ancient Chinese poetry, "Little lotus leaf only showed sharp pointed corners, and a dragonfly stood on its head", which depicts a pleasant and peaceful pastoral scene. The natural beauty can bring great relaxation and stress relief.

The specific usage scenarios and interaction processes are as follows:

When the user goes to bed, he can choose to turn on or off the bedside lamp. If it is turned on, he releases soft sleep aids. At the same time, he can choose to play white noise, music or audio programs on the mobile application. The mat will record the sleep data of the user's body movement, breathing, heart rate from the moment the user goes to bed. It can be determined that the user is in one of the awake phase, light sleep phase, and deep sleep phase based on the body movement and heart rate.

After the user switches from the awake phase to the light sleep phase or the deep sleep phase, the bedside lamp will slowly turn off, and the sleep assistance audio will slowly disappear.

When the user wakes up at night to go to the toilet, the bedside lamp will automatically turn on, and it will automatically turn off after going to bed.

According to the sleep plan and alarm time set by the user on the mobile application, combined with the user's sleep stage obtained from the mat sensing analysis, in the light sleep moment near the alarm time, the alarm clock will sound and the bedside lamp will shine as the sun rises, awaken users, and welcome a new day.

After the user wakes up, all devices stop monitoring, and the related sleep data will be transmitted to the mobile application via Wi-Fi. The mobile application will analyze and obtain the sleep quality assessment results. The user can view the sleep scores, sleep data, sleep map, sleep analysis information at night, and get suggestions on adjusting personal habits.

During the long-term use, the user can set sleep goals (such as the length of sleep, the time to fall asleep, the time to get up, etc.) according to his own situation and official recommendations. The virtual image lotus leaf will grow with the quality of the user's sleep. When establishing good sleep habits, the lotus will bloom, and users can get reward medals and physical prizes. At the same time, they can add relatives and friends' accounts to supervise themselves, and develop good sleep habits. They can also link their elders' mobile phones with theirs to regularly know the elders' sleep quality.

4.2 Product Design

After thinking about some complicated or simple design concepts, we decided to stick to the original intention of the product design, to design a non-invasive, comfortable and easy-to-use smart product. The most user-related experience is the feeling of the user sleeping on the mat: the thinner and lighter, the more comfortable. Therefore, based on the thinness of the EMFi sensor, we decided to design the product as a thin and light mat covering the EMFi sensor. The wire was connected to the cylinder that wrapped the circuit of the development board. The wire was powered on, and the desk lamp interface was reserved on the cylinder. Choose whether to use a matching table lamp, and the table lamp base and development board circuit are combined in a cylinder, the overall design is simpler. In order to ensure the maximum monitoring perimeter under the smallest area, and combined with the natural shape of the lotus leaf, the final shape of the mat is changed to a circular shape, which is convenient for monitoring user data.

The product design of the LotusLeaf sleep assistance device includes a lotus leaf mat and a bedside lamp, which are simple and elegant in shape. The mat is made of skin-friendly linen material, and a thin EMFi sensor is embedded inside, which can ensure that the user does not feel its presence when sleeping; bedside lamp is made of flame-retardant PC material, withstands high strength, and feels soft and comfortable. It integrates all communication modules, speakers, data processing modules and control units, and embeds LED strips with chips in round tubes to switch multi-color. The appearance of the product is shown in Fig. 6.

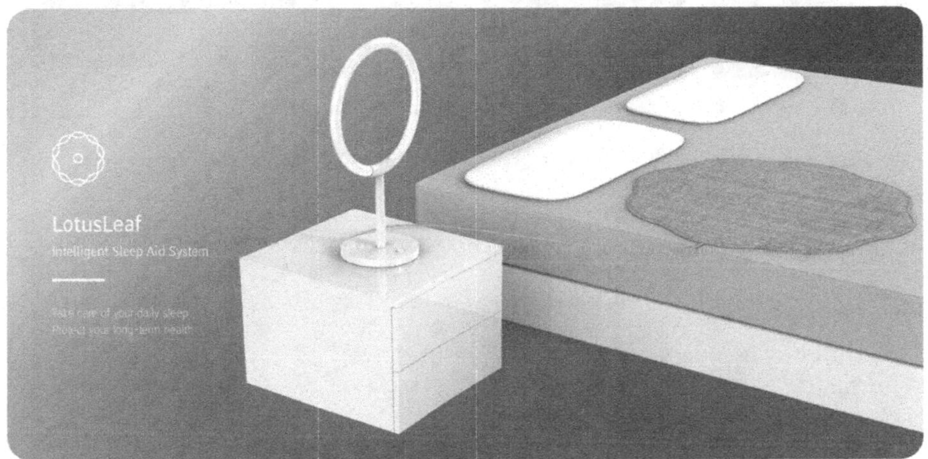

Fig. 6. The LotusLeaf product rendering

4.3 Mobile App Design

LotusLeaf App is a tool to assist the smart mat. It displays and processes data from the smart mat. It aims to let users understand their sleep status and establish good sleep habits. With the main intention and visual element of the lotus leaf, we will be able to analyze and visualize the data collected by the sleep assistance device.

Comprehensive data such as heart rate, breathing frequency, body movement frequency, sitting position in bed, and time can be used to obtain the analysis results of total sleep time, deep sleep time, bed time, falling asleep time, number of waking at night, and sleep pattern. These analysis results finally calculate the user's total sleep score and rating at night. When the rating is poor, the homepage animation will show the dry lotus with bitterness and sentimentality, so as to remind users to pay attention to improving sleep quality; when the rating is medium, the homepage animation will show the lotus leaves exposed in early summer a cute corner, with a tender green hope, indicates that the user's sleep quality has improved; when the rating is good, the homepage animation will show a flourishing scene like the lotus leaves shining in the sky, and a beautiful lotus flower embellishes it, which means to the user full affirmation and praise of sleep quality. These animations will have a certain visual impact on the user and give the user intuitive and easy-to-understand visual feedback. At the same time, the user can jump to the analysis of sleep details by clicking the animation. The user can make self-adjustment according to his specific sleep problems and official suggestions, gradually improve his sleep quality, develop good sleeping habits, and achieve the ultimate goal of maintaining good health. The application UI design is shown in Fig. 7.

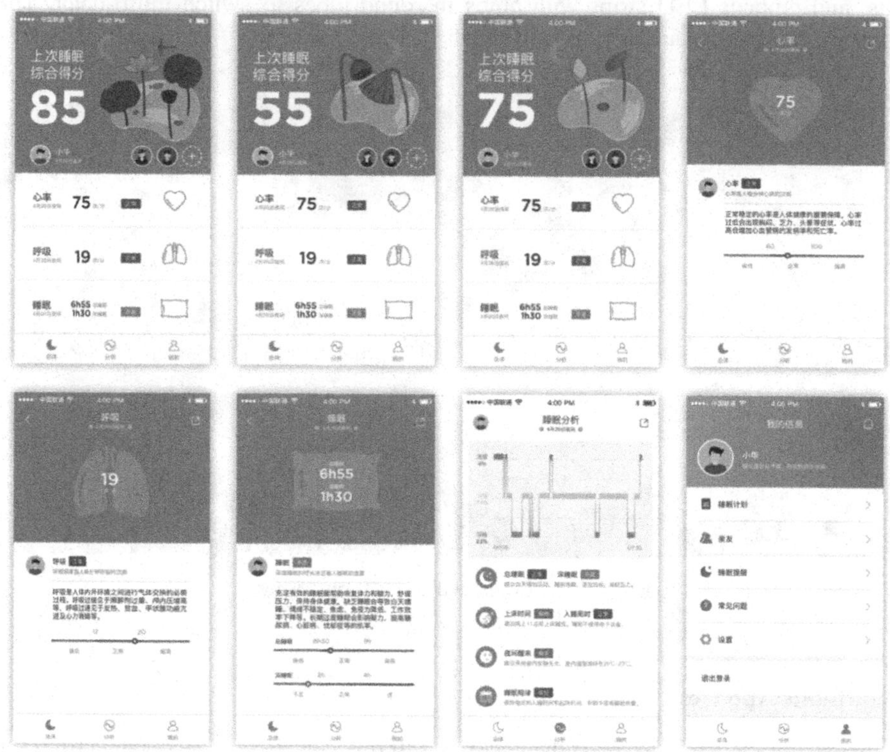

Fig. 7. The UI of LotusLeaf mobile application

The main color of the application is blue with high lightness. High lightness conveys a light and lively sensory experience, and blue symbolizes peaceful sleep. The application is divided into three major sections: General, Analysis, and Me.

The General page, which is also the home page, will display comprehensive sleep scores and information such as breathing, heartbeat, and sleep duration, accompanied by "normal", "low", and "high". The user can click to enter the heart rate page, breathing page, and sleep page. Each page has its own data curve and shows sleep-related knowledge.

The Analysis page displays the results of various analysis of sleep data all night. Above is the fluctuation image of the awakening stage, light sleep stage and deep sleep stage with time, and the image visually shows the sleep situation all night. The four columns below show the length of sleep (total sleep and deep sleep), the state of falling asleep (time to go to bed and time to fall asleep), the judgment of waking at night and sleep patterns, which are divided into "normal", "insufficient", "late", "good". Advice and guidance are given on sleeping conditions in the four columns.

The Me page is a collection of user information and settings, including sleep plans, relatives and friends, sleep reminders, FAQs, settings, etc. Users can refer to the application guidance to set a sleep plan, and obtain rewards after completing the corresponding goals. The user can also check the sleeping status of relatives and friends, supervise and communicate with each other, and develop good sleeping habits.

The LotusLeaf application selects the Android system for software development work, uses the ESP8266 Wi-Fi communication module to communicate with Arduino, and uses the Gizwits IoT platform as a background data transmission hub.

5 Conclusion

This paper takes sleep problems and sleep assistance demands as the starting point, and researches and designs a smart product that can collect sleep data, visualize sleep quality, and assist users to develop good sleep habits. It meets the needs of young people for smart sleep assistance products. Through objective and rational design method, this paper carries out scheme design, the appearance model, the intelligent hardware and the mobile application.

In terms of product form and function, it has carried out in-depth exploration and self-innovation, meeting the functions of sleep monitoring and light assisting sleep, and it can more intelligently detect the user's sleep at night and give sleep assistance by the light change. The shape of the LotusLeaf mat is beneficial for full contact with the human body and sleep data collection, which is non-invasive. The design of the base can reduce the thickness of the mat, which is convenient for the product to be carried apart. In terms of intelligent hardware, combined with the Arduino platform, EMFi sensor, and ESP8266 module, it realizes the functions of sleep data collection and intelligent interconnection. In terms of the application, the growth and wilt of lotus leaves are used to visualize the user's sleep quality. The combination of sleep information generates a night sleep map. Sleep quality analysis can help users understand their sleep status and improve their sleep quality.

Sleep healthcare is a social issue that attracts much attention. The design and development of smart home devices based on the IoT and new sensing devices is also a major industry hotspot. This paper's smart sleep assistance system is a design case based on this background. There are also some deficiencies that the entire system is not fully developed for real use. With regard to the design of emotional care, this paper stays at the level of sleep suggestion feedback and sleep quality visualization. It does not dig deep into the emotional needs behind sleep problems. In the future study, we will use cutting-edge technologies to learn the user's sleep characteristics, analyze the user's emotional needs, achieve more effective physical and mental care, and design a more intimate smart sleep assistance system.

References

1. Zou, Y.: Do You Sleep Well? Report: 56% of Chinese netizens suffer from sleeping troubles. https://news.cgtn.com/news/33496a4d79454464776c6d636a4e6e62684a4856/share_p.html. Accessed 21 Mar 2018

2. Zhao, Z.: Sleep Medicine. People's Medical Publishing House, Beijing (2016)
3. Kushida, C.A., et al.: Practice parameters for the indications for polysomnography and related procedures: an update for 2005. Sleep **28**(4), 499–523 (2005)
4. Collop, N.A.: Portable monitoring for the diagnosis of obstructive sleep apnea. Curr. Opin. Pulm. Med. **14**(6), 525–529 (2008)
5. Morgenthaler, T., et al.: Practice parameters for the use of actigraphy in the assessment of sleep and sleep disorders: an update for 2007. Sleep **30**(4), 519–529 (2007)
6. Zhang, H., et al.: Judgment rules for detection of sleep breathing events by Micro-movement Sensitive Mattress Sleep Monitoring System. Chin. J. Aerosp. Med. **1** (2010)
7. Paajanen, M., Lekkala, J., Kirjavainen, K.: ElectroMechanical Film (EMFi)—a new multipurpose electret material. Sens. Actuators Phys. **84**(1-2), 95–102 (2000)
8. Zhang, T.: Piezoelectric Film Material and Device Fabrication Technology. Northwestern Polytechnical University Press, Xi'an (2012)
9. Van Boeijen, A., et al.: Delft Design Guide: Design Strategies and Methods (2014)
10. Rajala, S., Lekkala, J.: PVDF and EMFi sensor materials—a comparative study. Procedia Eng. **5**, 862–865 (2010)
11. Junnila, S., Akhbardeh, A., Värri, A.: An electromechanical film sensor based wireless ballistocardiographic chair: Implementation and performance. J. Signal Process. Syst. **57**(3), 305–320 (2009)
12. Li, S.: Design and implementation of non-contact sleep monitoring system. MS thesis. Harbin Institute of Technology (2016)

PuzMap: Designing a Multi-sensory Puzzle Map for Children to Learn Geography

Junwu Wang[1(✉)], Lijuan Liu[2], Muling Huang[3], Weilin Jiang[3], Cheng Yao[2], and Fangtian Ying[1]

[1] School of Industrial Design, Hubei University of Technology, Wuhan, China
354227128@qq.com, yingft@gmail.com

[2] College of Computer Science and Technology, Zhejiang University, Hangzhou, China
{liulijuan,yaoch}@zju.edu.cn

[3] College of Software Technology, Zhejiang University, Hangzhou, China
{583185319,21951221}@zju.edu.cn

Abstract. Geography is a broad subject, and maps are essential tools for learning geography. It is necessary to educate children about geography and maps at an early age. Digital educational tools play an increasingly important role in children's education. However, few studies focus on digital map design for children conforming to their cognitive abilities. Inspired by that, we propose PuzMap, a novel puzzle map, which facilitated with various sensory channels, visual, auditory, tactual, and olfactory. It can create specific experiences when it is manipulated. PuzMap delivers knowledge of geographical distribution to children. It also introduces the concept of ocean current and its movement principle through the multi-sensory approach, which is rarely mentioned before. When finishing the puzzle map, children can scan the pattern on each distribution module to enjoy the AR patterns about this area. In this paper, we detail the system design of PuzMap and present the design principles of children map. We also conducted studies to explore our system's usability. The results showed that PuzMap could help children learn geography knowledge, and it is engaged for children to play.

Keywords: Children map · Jigsaw puzzles · Geography · Multi-sensory design · Interaction design

1 Introduction

To know a country or a region, one must first know its geographical location. The geographical position of a country or region is generally analyzed from four aspects: hemispheric position, land and sea position, longitude and latitude position, and relative position with neighboring countries or adjacent areas. By learning geography, children can learn about nature and the history and culture of different countries in the world.

N. Streitz and S. Konomi (Eds.): HCII 2020, LNCS 12203, pp. 677–688, 2020.
https://doi.org/10.1007/978-3-030-50344-4_49

According to mathematical laws, maps reflect the natural and human phenomena of the earth on a plane or sphere at a particular scale. Children as young as already have a certain level of cognitive ability with maps, which increases with age. Exposing children to maps in early childhood has an enlightening effect on their map recognition ability, spatial cognition ability, and logic ability.

The design of children's maps should accord with children's psychological and cognitive ability, and the map should be interesting and informative. The multisensory approach is a common way to improve interactions. It enriches the product experience, avoids unwanted conflicting messages, and results in products that are also comprehensible for users with chipmaker impairments [1]. In this paper, we designed a children's map that combines multiple sensory interactions. Desert, forest, ocean and ice land are textured differently, allowing for visual and tactile interaction. Ocean areas have salty odors, and the flow of water will simulate the movement of ocean currents, which can help children learn knowledge more intuitively.

Jigsaw puzzles are a popular game. They have been shown to be good at stimulating cognitive development, as well as helping children learn and develop skills such as problem-solving, shape recognition, and hand-eye coordination [2]. In this article, we use the puzzle approach, let children participate in the game to complete the map puzzle. Once the splicing is complete, scan the corresponding area icon to see the AR image, which shows the typical resident animals in the area. PuzMap offers children the opportunity to learn in many ways. Our contribution is to provide an interactive puzzle map. The multi-sensory approach is applied to children's map design. Present the strategy of children map design.

2 Related Work

2.1 Children's Tangible Design

Many researchers believe that tangible objects are very suitable for children's learning, and have also discussed that tangible products are more interesting than digital products [3, 4]. In design activities, designers must consider children's development skills and abilities and ensure that tangible products are suitable for the expected age [5]. Kian Teck, Lee made an attempt to use the combination of tangible objects and mobile technology to enhance the participation and mobility of stem children's education. He proposed bloxels, which consists of color blocks and bloxels builder game board. We can see the effectiveness in engaging and activating their learning through reversible learning [6]. Programming concepts are often difficult to understand, and Yunfeng Qi and Lan Zhang et al. present a new tangible programming tool – TanProStory [7]. The device uses three modules: program block and animation Game and sensor input module. Children can create initialization characters and program characters through the arrangement and combination of modules, so as to achieve the learning function.

2.2 Multi-sensory Design

Multi perception design has always been an important part of HCI. Guide the design of five senses: vision, hearing, smell, touch, and taste to provide users with interesting and rich experience [1]. In the process of interaction between users and products, all senses are open and can receive information to obtain sensory impressions [8]. Daniel Harley and Alexander Verni et al. [9] applied multi perception design to virtual reality. The system included 2 scenes at the beach and red hat to increase the sensory experience outside the VR scene, to get a more real perception. Uttara Ghodke and Lena Yusim et al. presented a learning aid for blind and low vision users. Three audio-tactile spheres enable blind and low vision users to perceive geospatial information [10]. Our PuzMap system combines olfactory, sound, touch, and vision, focusing on the multi-sensory approach to foster children's geography knowledge.

2.3 Jigsaw Puzzles

In recent years, the design of puzzles in the field of human-computer interaction is more inclined to the combination of hybrid products. Jigsaw puzzle is a fun way for children to learn and play. Sarah Hayes and Michelle O'Keeffe present PuzzleBeo. The device was an interactive installation comprised of a computer-mediated jigsaw puzzle and multimodal display [11]. Yang Ting Shen and Ali Mazalek put forward PuzzleTale, which combines the tangible puzzle with the storytelling system. Assembling tangible puzzles can influence digital characters and create a flexible story scenario [12].

Based on previous research and inspiration, tangible jigsaw puzzles are more suitable for children's learning. We propose a multi-sensory interactive puzzle map to provide rich interactive experiences through vision, touch, and olfactory.

3 Learning with PuzMap

Geography is like a link that connects people, countries, and history, allows students the chance to explore and understand where they come from, where they live, and all of the places surrounding them [13]. We designed the PuzMap system based on the Pacific World Map [14]. PuzMap can convey the following knowledge to children:

Location and significant geographical features of the world's continents and oceans. By stitching together maps, children can learn about the seven continents and four oceans, including their locations and major geographic features.

Typical animals in each region and their living environment. Studies found that a child is spontaneously attracted to other organisms from birth [15]. The AR function of the PuzMap system introduces children to the typical animals of the various continents and oceans.

Ocean current. Coriolis force caused by the Earth's rotation [16], capable of affecting the direction of the flow of water in the southern and northern hemispheres. The ocean current flows clockwise in the northern hemisphere and counterclockwise in the southern hemisphere. On the ocean modules, we set up water flow-related interactions where children can understand the concept of ocean currents and the differences in the current movement of the north and south hemispheres.

4 System Description

PuzMap system consists of two parts (Fig. 1). The hardware part includes the map puzzle modules (Fig. 2), and the software part presents the AR contents. Puzzle modules differ in texture, color, and material to provide a variety of interactive effects.

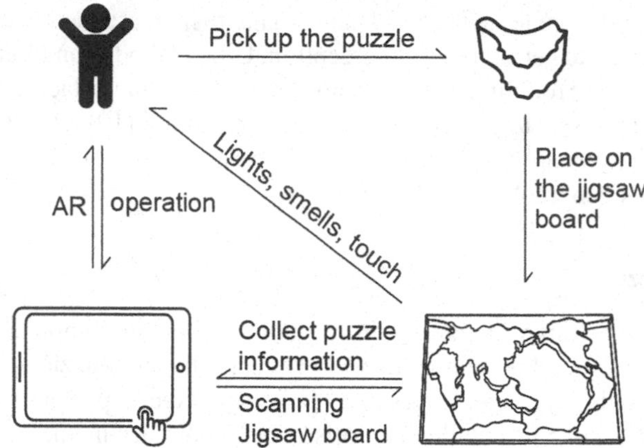

Fig. 1. Interaction framework of PuzMap.

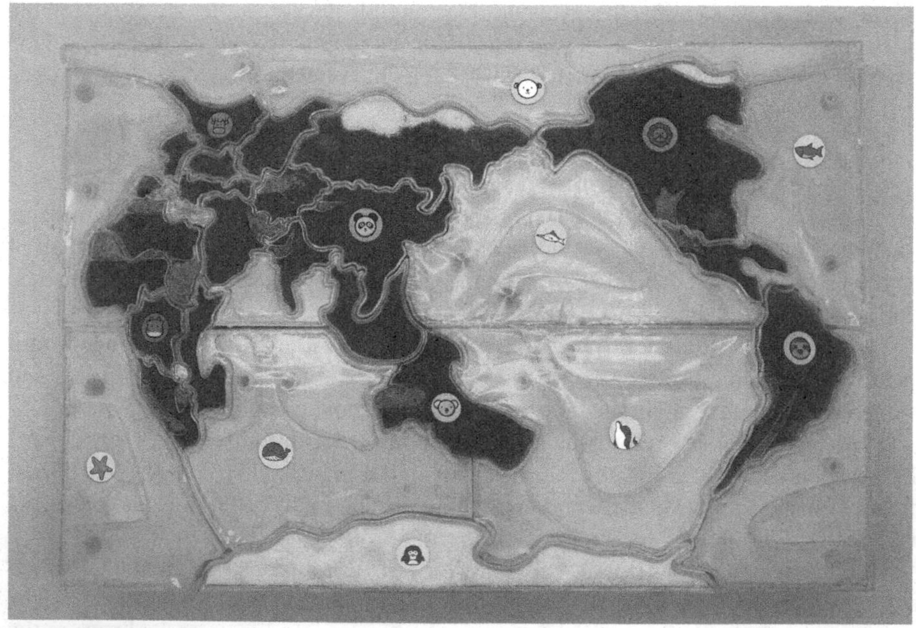

Fig. 2. PuzMap.

4.1 PuzMap Modules

According to the layout of the world map, we made 30 pieces of map modules (Table 1) by 3D printer. The module consists of two layers. The bottom layer consists magnets and electronic components, such as pumps and LEDs. The upper layer is used to place materials to provide different textures. The system consists of four elements from natural - grass, sand, water, and snowflake powder, to simulate vegetation, desert, ocean, and ice land on earth (Fig. 3). In this way, children can learn regional distribution and geographical features.

Table 1. Distribution of 30 modules.

Asia (6)	Europe (5)	Africa (5)	Americas (3)	Other continents (2)	Ocean (9)
East Asia	East Europe	East Africa	South America	Oceania	Pacific Ocean (2)
South Asia	South Europe	South Africa	North America	Antarctica	Indian Ocean (2)
Central Asia	Central Europe	Central Africa	Central America		Atlantic Ocean (4)
West Asia	West Europe	West Africa			Arctic Ocean
North Asia	North Europe	North Africa			
Southeast Asia					

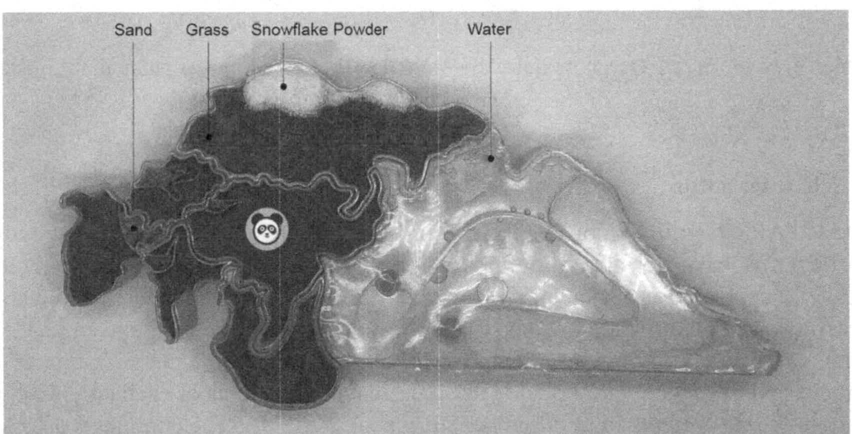

Fig. 3. Four materials used in PuzMap.

Moreover, they get an intuitive sense of how many areas of the earth's oceans are, how many areas of the earth's lands are desert, and how many areas are covered by ice. These areas are not suitable to provide living needs; the green space for human survival is not much. This system can help children build environmental and ecological awareness from an early age.

The map modules are placed on the base plate. The bottom plate is made of acrylic material and is divided into four layers. The bottom layer is for batteries and gas generator; The third layer puts the LED lights and the frame of the area boundary; The second layer contains magnets; The top layer is a 0.5 mm photosensitive resin plate, marked with the names of the continents. When the power is turned on, the LEDs work, and the colored light is projected onto the top panel, giving a clear view of the continents and oceans.

We have built nine ocean modules, which are divided into two parts of the northern and southern hemispheres according to the equator. Each ocean module is divided into upper and lower layers; the upper layer has a tank and two water ports, which are connected to the water pump in the lower layer with a soft pipe. When the ocean module is properly placed on the base, the water in the tank begins to flow. The ocean current in the northern hemisphere flows clockwise (Fig. 4), and the southern hemisphere flows counterclockwise. The upper layer of the ocean module is silicone, and the hand touch can feel the flow of water. The ocean module also includes a shock pad as a seawater odor generator. When completing a puzzle of an ocean area, ocean odors are released.

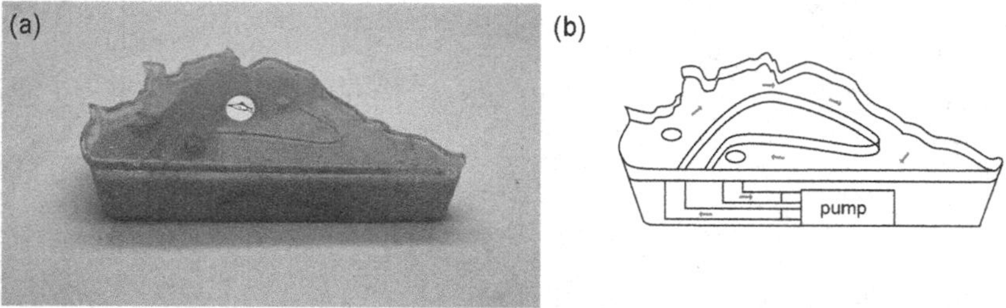

Fig. 4. (a) North Pacific Ocean module; (b) Water flow direction of water pump in the module.

4.2 AR Interaction

We added AR recognition icons on the specific modules and matched the corresponding AR effect. We have developed an application (Fig. 5), when completing the module puzzle of a continent or ocean, an AR scan icon will be used to animate the animals of the corresponding continent or ocean. The animation mainly introduces the typical local animals and their living environment. We have made the animal classification of the continent and the ocean, and selected the representative animals of each continent, the common marine animals in children's picture books (Fig. 6). The continents are: Asia for pandas, Africa for giraffes, Europe for bonasus, South America for pumas, South America for sloths, Oceania for koalas and Antarctica for penguins. The oceans are: whales, starfishes, dolphins, sharks, tunas, polar bears.

Fig. 5. Application for PuzMap AR. (a) Application main interface; (b) Scan the Asia module to get the panda scene; (c) Learn more about panda.

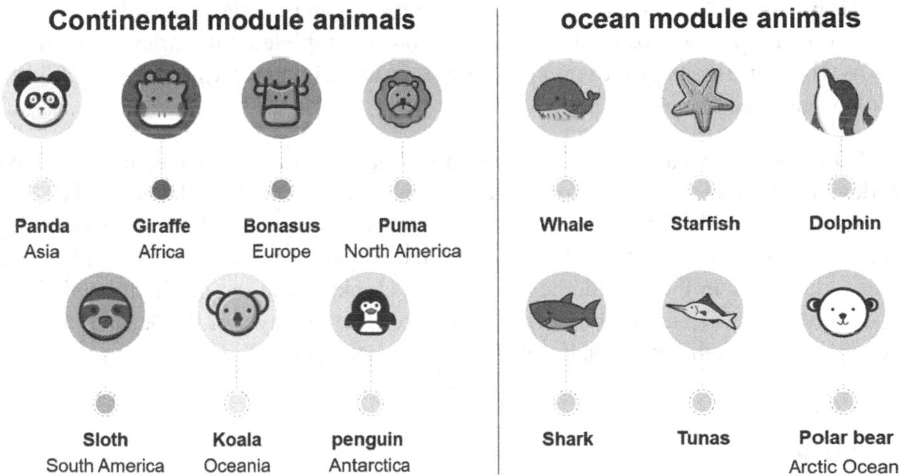

Fig. 6. Animal distribution in AR module.

4.3 Multi-sensory Interaction

Vision. When the child places the map module on the base, the module glows (Fig. 7). When splicing correctly, the base and module will display the same color of light. We set up 7 colors of light for different areas. Red, yellow, purple, green, pink, white, and blue correspond to Africa, Asia, Europe, America, Oceania, Antarctica, and the ocean. This way gives visual and shape cues, making it easy for children to assemble maps.

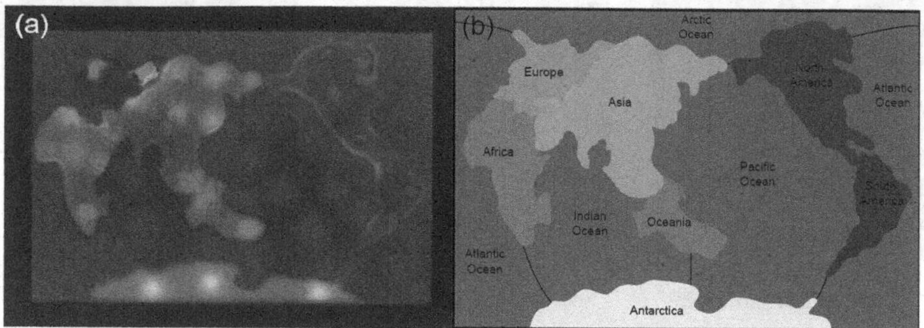

Fig. 7. (a) PuzMap base; (b) Base color and pattern distribution.

Olfaction. We added an ultrasonic atomizer to the ocean module to provide odor interaction. When a jigsaw puzzle of an ocean region is completed, the ultrasonic atomizer goes to work, turning the water into the water mist and giving off a salty smell. Children can also sense the ocean by smell.

Touch Feeling. We made four kinds of modules, grass, sand, blue water, and snowflake powder, to simulate the vegetation, desert, ocean, and ice field on the earth. The four materials can provide different tactile sensations and increase the child's understanding of the regional characteristics. We designed the ocean currents. When the splicing is correct, the water in the module begins to flow, clockwise in the northern hemisphere and counterclockwise in the southern hemisphere. The top layer of the ocean module is silicone, and when the user touches it, he can sense the flow of water.

5 Studies

To understand the usability of the PuzMap system, we recruited 16 children ages 5 to 10 (M = 7.44, SD = 1.62) for user test. The whole experiment was recorded and transcribed with the consent of the children's parents.

We introduced the PuzMap system to participants for 10 min, and then they were given 5 min to play PuzMap to familiarize themselves with the system. For the next 30 min, participants explored and played PuzMap freely. After that, we conducted semi-structured interviews with participants and their parents to understand the usability of the system and users' satisfaction with the system (Fig. 8).

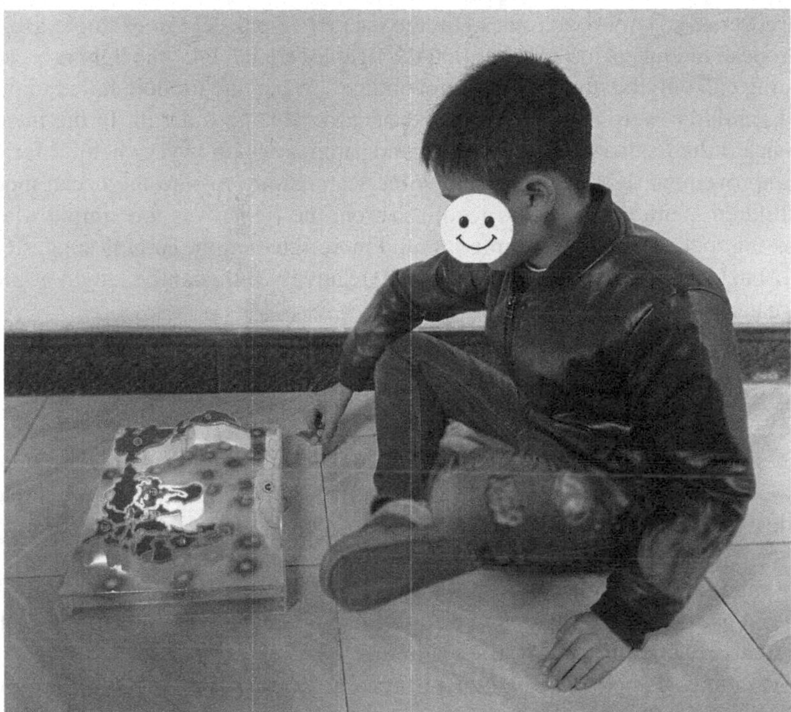

Fig. 8. Children playing puzzles in the experiment.

6 Results

During the test, we observed participants' reactions, such as body movements, facial expressions, and conversations with parents during play, and then sorted out the interview records. We found that children could judge the position of the module by observing the shape of the map module and touching the texture of the module during the stitching process. When children spliced successfully, the lights of the module came on, and the children would clap their hands in celebration. We also found that children were pleasantly surprised when they touched the movement of water in the ocean modules. The results showed that PuzMap could convey geography knowledge to children and stimulate their interest in learning geography.

Thirteen of the 16 people said PuzMap was interesting. From the dialogue between children and parents, we also find that PuzMap can trigger children's thinking and motivate them to explore new knowledge. For example, P3 says, "there is water flowing in the tank, the water is flowing in a different direction. Why is that?" P8 said, "dad, the modules are different colors. Yellow, green, and white. Why do they have these colors?" P7 scanned the icon with the APP after finishing the Asian module and said, "mom, the panda is moving on this screen. Let's see what other animals are! "There are also children who need their parents' help to complete the puzzle together. When the AR module was identified, the children would share their joy with parents and friends, inviting them to watch the AR scenes together.

There were also some bad reviews in the interactive puzzle. For example, P10 says: "the European module is too small to find the right location". P4: "the light is broken, so the splicing can only be done through the outline". When the module failed to provide feedback, children were disappointed, and the task became difficult. In the interview, we also heard the feedback from children and parents, which is very helpful for future design improvement. For example, add some sea creature toys to the ocean modules. Other children mentioned that the feedback from the lights was too simple when the map was misspelled, and they wanted to add more interaction. Parents suggested that although PuzMap is a creative jigsaw puzzle, relatively little can be taught at present, and more can be improved in the future.

7 Design Principles of Children's Map

Children's maps can be divided into wall charts, desktop maps, atlas, jigsaw puzzle, globe, and so on. Based on PuzMap's design and study feedback, we propose principles for the design of children's maps:

- The symbol and color design in the map should be equal to the level of children's cognition and understanding. Map design should be simple graphics, clear outlines, more realistic symbols, less abstract symbols.
- Properly apply colors to help distinguish between different areas. Children more easily understand the colors that follow the nature of things.
- Maps can show information of interest to children, such as animals.
- Image, text, sound, video, and animation can be used as the supplement of the map, and the multimedia display can be combined with AR technology to inspire children to explore geographical knowledge.

8 Discussion and Future Work

PuzMap is a multi-sensory interactive map for children to learn about geographical area distribution. It can help children learn geography knowledge. However, the current system still has some limitations. First, the equipment is unstable, and sometimes it does not work, affecting the completion of the puzzle and users' experience. Besides, the system now provides less geographical knowledge.

In the future, we will continue to study the multi-sensory interaction map. We will improve the interaction ways and add new interactions in the system, which involves more sensory feedback. For example, adding RFID in the module can identify whether the module is splicing correctly. Add more geographical knowledge to the design through interactive means, such as temperature changes, monsoon signals, seasonal changes, etc. For the AR function, more identifiable modules and scene information will be added in the future to make the AR experience better.

9 Conclusion

In this paper, we propose PuzMap, a map design based on multi-sensory interaction. The system has interactive design in visual, tactile, and olfactory elements, and combines AR technology to enable children to learn geography knowledge from multiple dimensions. The system also motivates children to explore and become interested in geography. According to the design process and experiment of PuzMap, we also present the design principle of children's map. PuzMap can motivate children to learn geography in exciting interactive ways.

Acknowledgements. The authors thanks all the reviewers for providing valuable insights and suggestions that have helped in substantially improving this paper, as well as all volunteers for general support. This research was supported by the National Natural Science Foundation of China (No 51675476).

References

1. Schifferstein, H.N.J.: Multi-sensory design. In: Proceedings of the Second Conference on Creativity and Innovation in Design, DESIRE 2011, Eindhoven, the Netherlands, pp. 361–362 (2011)
2. Chen, F.: Multimodal behaviour and interaction as indicators of cognitive load. ACM Trans. Interact. Intell. Syst. **2**(4), 1–36 (2013)
3. Zaman, B.: Editorial: the evolving field of tangible interaction for children: the challenge of empirical validation. Pers. Ubiquitous Comput. **16**(4), 367–378 (2012)
4. Xie, L.: Are tangibles more fun? Comparing children's enjoyment and engagement using physical, graphical and tangible user interfaces. In: Proceedings of the 2nd International Conference on Tangible and Embedded Interaction, TEI 2008, Boon, Germany, pp. 191–198 (2008)
5. Bekker, T.: Developmentally situated design (DSD): making theoretical knowledge accessible to designers of children's technology. In: Proceedings of the SIGCHI Conference on Human Factors in Computing Systems, CHI 2011, Vancouver, BC, Canada, pp. 2531–2540 (2011)
6. Lee, K.T.: Demo: use of tangible learning in STEM education. In: SA'16 SIGGRAPH ASIA 2016 Mobile Graphics and Interactive Applications, SA 2016, Macao, pp. 1–2 (2016)
7. Qi, Y.: TanProStory: a tangible programming system for children's storytelling. In: Proceedings of the 33rd Annual ACM Conference Extended Abstracts on Human Factors in Computing Systems, CHI EA 2015, Seoul, Korea, pp. 1001–1006 (2015)
8. Schifferstein, H.N.J.: Tools facilitating multi-sensory product design. Int. J. All Asp. Des. **11**(2), 137–158 (2008)
9. Harley, D.: Sensory VR: smelling, touching, and eating virtual reality. In: Proceedings of the Twelfth International Conference on Tangible, Embedded, and Embodied Interaction, TEI 2018, Stockholm, Sweden, pp. 386–397 (2018)
10. Ghodke, U.: The cross-sensory globe: participatory design of a 3D audio-tactile globe prototype for blind and low-vision users to learn geography. In: Proceedings of the 2019 on Designing Interactive Systems Conference, DIS 2019, San Diego, CA, USA, pp. 399–412 (2019)
11. Hayes, S.: Piecing together the past: constructing stories with Jigsaw puzzles in museums. In: Proceedings of the 2017 ACM Conference Companion Publication on Designing Interactive Systems, DIS 2017, Edinburgh, HK, pp. 79–83 (2017)

12. Shen, Y.T.: PuzzleTale: a tangible puzzle game for interactive storytelling. Comput. Entertain. **8**(2), 1–15 (2010). Article no. 11
13. Gandy, S.K.: Developmentally appropriate geography. Soc. Stud. Young Learn. **20**(2), 30–32 (2007)
14. World Maps Online. https://www.worldmapsonline.com/detailed-world-physical-pacific-centered-wall-map.htm. Accessed 11 Oct 2019
15. Anderson, D., de Cosson, A., Mclntosh, L.: Research Informing the Practice of Museum Educators, 1st edn. Sense Publishers, Rotterdam (2015)
16. Wikipedia Coriolis force. https://en.wikipedia.org/wiki/Coriolis_force. Accessed 14 Oct 2019

Internet of Toys for Measuring Development of Ball Handling Skills in Support of Childcare Workers

Keiko Yamamoto[1(✉)], Koshiro Matsumoto[1], Tomonori Usui[1], Ichi Kanaya[2], and Yoshihiro Tsujino[1]

[1] Kyoto Institute of Technology, Kyoto, Japan
kei@kit.ac.jp
[2] University of Nagasaki, Nagasaki, Japan

Abstract. During childhood, play is important for promoting the mental and physical development of children. For this reason, those involved with childcare (guardians and childcare workers) need to create an environment suitable for child development and provide children with support and guidance. However, because there are unique elements to the development of each individual child, childcare workers caring for large numbers of children, and guardians in remote areas, may struggle to oversee the daily development of the children in their care. In this paper, we propose toys with built-in sensors are used to acquire motion data during play activities, and a system intended to aid in estimating the child development stage by creating a data visualization for childcare workers. To establish the proposed system, a ball-type device was created using a built-in acceleration sensor as a prototype of a toy with a built-in sensor. Using this prototype, we conducted an experiment to verify whether it is possible to discern five types of ball activities when focusing on changes in ball-throwing movements related to child development. As the results based on two types of learning algorithms (SVM and RF) indicate, in each case the activity could be identified with approximately 70% accuracy.

Keywords: Childcare · IoT · Machine learning

1 Introduction

1.1 Background

Children engage in various forms of activities, such as tag, playing house, drawing, and dodgeball. For children, such play is simply a form of daily entertainment. However, regarding the effects of play on child development, the "Childcare Guidelines for Nursery Schools" [1] put out by the Ministry of Health, Labor, and Welfare, which is the government body in charge of nursery schools, has stated that "in the case of infant care, based on the nature of development at this age, through the enrichment of life and play, we can cultivate a foundation for children's physical, social, and mental development," and "children while immersed in play developing their own activities steadily

N. Streitz and S. Konomi (Eds.): HCII 2020, LNCS 12203, pp. 689–698, 2020.
https://doi.org/10.1007/978-3-030-50344-4_50

develop various skills, such as thinking, planning, and using their imaginations, along with learning other aspects of life, such as cooperating with friends and relating to their environment". In the early childhood exercise guidelines [2] put out by the Ministry of Education, Culture, Sports, Science, and Technology, which has jurisdiction over kindergartens, it is stated that "in early childhood, engaging in sufficient physical activity, particularly play, in addition to helping children learn various physical movements, contributes to health later in life by improving cardiopulmonary function and bone formation, etc., and establishes the foundation for a rich life by cultivating a positive and proactive attitude". Based on these comments regarding the importance of athletic play, play for young children is crucial to promoting their physical development and forming relationships with others, showing that childcare and play are inseparable.

The type of children's play generally changes with age. Referencing international studies on the topic, Kosaka [3] states that play at each stage of development from infancy (0 to 1 year old) to early childhood (1 to 6 years old), childhood (6 to 12 years old), and puberty and adolescence (12 to 20 years old) moves from play with few aspects to play with numerous aspects, and from playing alone to play involving others. Given these effects of play on childhood development, an environment that allows for play and activities to change along with the development of the child in an active and healthy way is required.

Still, because children are mentally and physically undeveloped, it is difficult for them to prepare such an environment on their own. Therefore, to allow each child to have effective and safe experiences for their development, childcare workers (e.g., nursery school teachers and guardians) need to be able to oversee the play and activities of the children under their care and have the ability to provide appropriate help and guidance at the proper time.

1.2 Problem

In recent years, the number of dual-income households in Japan has increased significantly, and in many homes, couples do not have sufficient time to observe the daily play and activities of their children, as described in Sect. 1.1. In addition, few parents have the expertise to know what type of guidance they should give and when to give it. For these reasons, children, particularly during infancy, are generally taken to nursery schools and kindergartens, where teachers are asked to help the children as they develop.

Because childcare workers have the necessary expertise regarding infant development, if the stage of a child's development can be understood through observation, the appropriate help and guidance can be provided. However, the work of a childcare worker goes beyond playing with children, including tending to the surroundings, researching new teaching materials, maintaining a log of events, and creating class newsletters. In addition, they are also often responsible for multiple infants. For this reason, they are unable to set aside sufficient time to observe the daily play and activities of each infant under their care, making it difficult to determine each infant's particular developmental stages. In addition, one of the causes of such a large amount of work is due to a severe shortage of childcare workers. Because current childcare workers may end up carrying the burden of any personnel shortages at school, this can make it even more difficult for them to observe the play of each infant in their care and to provide assistance and guidance suitable to each child's individual developmental needs.

2 Related Studies

In an attempt to address the problems discussed in Sect. 1.2, several studies have been conducted on the observation of infant activities and supporting the estimation and evaluation of childhood development.

To clarify the developmental changes in the solo play of children, Shinno et al. [4] used a camera in a longitudinal study on 3 and 4 year-olds, and through an analysis, it was shown that the characteristics of play differ for these two ages. Moreover, Suzuki et al. [5] facilitated child health supervision and childcare in nursery schools using a proposed monitoring system that allows for the sharing of information among childcare workers, guardians, and nutritionists by applying sensor bands wrapped around the upper arms of the children. However, the cameras and wearable devices used to observe the activities of the children in these studies may have interfered with the normal activities of the children owing to restrictions regarding where they could be placed and the children's dislike of wearing the devices. In this study, because the activities of the children were observed by incorporating sensors into their toys, which are not worn, such issues did not arise.

Similar to the present study, prior studies have evaluated the development of children through play using toys with built-in sensors. Kamide et al. [6] used building blocks with built-in acceleration sensors, and play with the modified building blocks was quantified for children aged 2 to 6; it was shown that the children's ages could be estimated based on the data as an index reflective of their cognitive development. In addition, Mironcika et al. [7] developed a block with a built-in acceleration sensor that can be used to detect developmental delays in motor skills early without the need for professional help. However, both studies evaluated only one type of play or ability. In the present study, by incorporating various sensors into an assortment of items such as balls, stuffed animals, and writing tools, we aim to estimate the developmental stage of a child from multiple perspectives, rather than using data obtained from only a single form of play.

Furthermore, in recent years, studies using machine learning to evaluate motion have been conducted. In Wang et al. [8], the researchers looked at the learning of effective spiking in volleyball, and estimated the skill levels of different spikes using machine learning. In the present study, following in the footsteps of Wang et al.'s approach, we used machine learning to automatically estimate the child's stage of development.

With the introduction of sensors and Internet of Things (IoT) technology, Kimura et al. [9] conducted research aimed at building a system that can test the user's physical fitness while allowing the user to continue working out unimpeded. Still, because this approach was intended for use in physical fitness tests and not everyday recreation, the system may operate differently in relation to natural daily activities, and because the measurement frequency in relation to the speed of childhood development is low, the response to the data might potentially be delayed.

3 Proposed System

3.1 Function

To help childcare workers assess the stages of childhood development, we propose a system that supports the estimation of the developmental stages in children by presenting data on what toys they play with and how they play with them as measured in an unrestricted and real-time manner using toys incorporating sensors and wireless communication devices.

Figure 1 shows an overview of the proposed system, which is divided into the following three parts:

- Measurement: A toy with a built-in sensor is used to conduct the measurements. In this part of the system, movement data from the children's play (acceleration, angular velocity, pressure, etc.) are continually being sensed, and when a specific condition is detected, that particular portion of the sensor data and the ID of the child are sent to the processing unit through a wireless transmission.
- Deep Learning: In this processing part of the system, a learning model is constructed for each toy using various movement data acquired during play, and the play and usage of the sensor data received from the measurements are estimated. The child's ID, the date, and the time are all recorded in the database.
- Visualization: This presentation part of the system takes the recommended play and usage data related to development collected during the deep learning stage, and creates a visualization of the time sequence for each child for application by the user (e.g., a childcare worker).

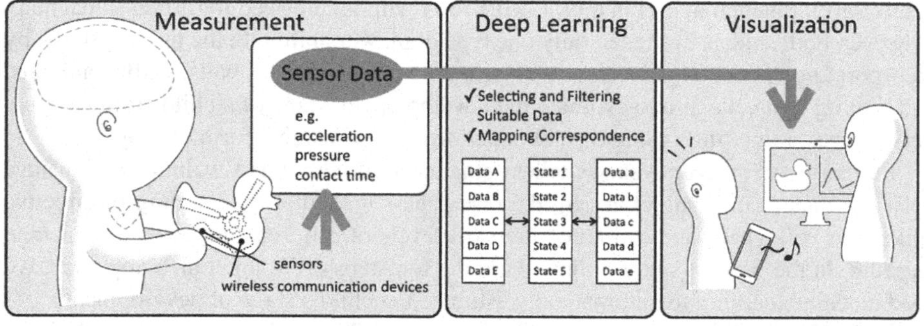

Fig. 1. Overview of proposed system

3.2 Implementation

Among the toy categories mentioned by Senda [10], referencing domestic and foreign studies on the topic, many can be found in nursery schools, and as a representative toy commonly played with by children, for the development of our prototype, we used a playground ball with an acceleration sensor attached.

In a polyurethane resin ball (16 cm in diameter), a triple-axis MMA8452Q accelerometer was installed along with an Arduino MKR1000 and its battery as a wireless communication device capable of transmitting over Wi-Fi. The appearance and internal configuration of this ball-type device are shown in Fig. 2.

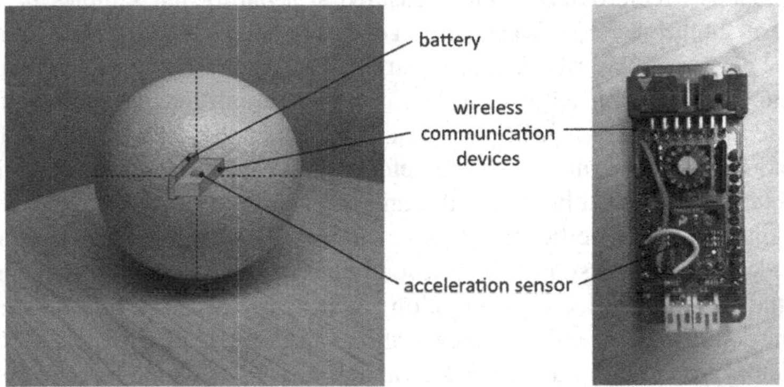

Fig. 2. Ball-type device prototype

4 Experiment: Verifying the Discriminability of Ball Activities

4.1 Different Ball Activities to Recognize

To test the feasibility of the proposed system, we used the ball-type device described in Sect. 3 to see whether a specific action related to the developmental stages of play could be recognized. Looking at other studies on this topic conducted in both Japan and abroad, we considered basic movements such as "throwing" and "kicking," and based on Shoji's assessment method for evaluating the motor functions of children with learning disabilities [11], we came up with the following specific actions.

1. Throwing the ball underhand with both hands
2. Throwing the ball over one's head with both hands
3. Throwing one-handed (no stepping into the throw or wind-up)
4. Stepping and throwing with the same arm and leg to throw (no wind-up)
5. Winding up with the arm behind, and stepping and throwing with the opposite arm and foot.

These five ball activities are designated as tasks 1–5, respectively.

4.2 Procedure

The experiment was conducted in a room with sufficient space to allow the tasks above to be conducted. There were ten collaborators (seven male, three female, ages 20 to 24), all of whom are right-handed.

After describing the experiment to the participants, they each conducted tasks 1–5 ten times each. After confirming whether the participant was in the starting position (with the ball-type device held with both hands in front of the chest), the experiment leader signaled the participant to perform the task. While the task was being performed, the ball-type device communicated the data wirelessly to a PC over Wi-Fi, and the values of the triple-axis accelerometer were measured at a rate of ten samples per second. When the ball hit the ground, the acquisition of acceleration data was ended. In addition, because the degree of maturity, including strength and motor nerves, of the experiment and the intended research targets (children) completely differ, the participants were instructed to throw the device with their non-dominant hand, while keeping in mind the strength of a child. Furthermore, the characteristics of each task were communicated to the participants beforehand both verbally and in writing, and they were asked to form a mental image of the specific actions of each task by watching a video of a toddler playing dodgeball. They also practiced several times before the data were recorded.

After the data were collected, the motion was extracted based on the collected acceleration sensor values. Because the acceleration values are approximately 0 [G] along any axis in the air, the point at which the value is near 0 [G] immediately after a large increase in acceleration from motion occurs immediately following the throw; thus, we look back a set amount of time from that point to extract the motion portion of the data. After this part of the process, the feature values of all acceleration data are calculated. These feature values, described in Sect. 4.3, are used to check the accuracy of the verification through machine learning. In this experiment, we used scikit-learn, which is an open-source machine learning library using Python. Two types of learning algorithms were used: a support vector machine (SVM) and random forest (RF). A leave-one-out cross-validation was used for verification, and the optimal parameters for the SVM were found using a grid search.

4.3 Results

Using the procedure described in Sect. 4.3, 500 data points were collected (10 people × 5 tasks × 10 repetitions). Figure 3 shows examples of the acceleration data collected for each task. There were ten types of feature values used for learning based on the characteristics of the acceleration data for each of these tasks (i.e., the magnitude of the acceleration, which is the square root of the sum-of-squares of the output data from the triple-axis accelerometer), namely, the (1) average, (2) dispersion, (3) standard deviation, (4) kurtosis, (5) skewness, (6) root-mean-square, (7) minimum value, (8) maximum value up to the point of the minimum value, (9) angle of the direction of gravity of the ball just prior to accelerating as it is thrown, and (10) slowness of the acceleration from (9) to the point where the acceleration peaks.

After verifying the collected data, ten data points were excluded, the time series of which was interrupted owing to communication problems, leaving a total of 490 acceleration data points, which had their motion portion extracted using software programmed in C. To extract the motion, (a) the threshold value for approximating 0 [G] to determine the point immediately after the throw was set to 0.6, (b) the minimum value for the difference between (a) and the peak was 2.0, and the duration for the motion portion used to calculate the (3) feature values was 1.0 (ten samples of acceleration data); based

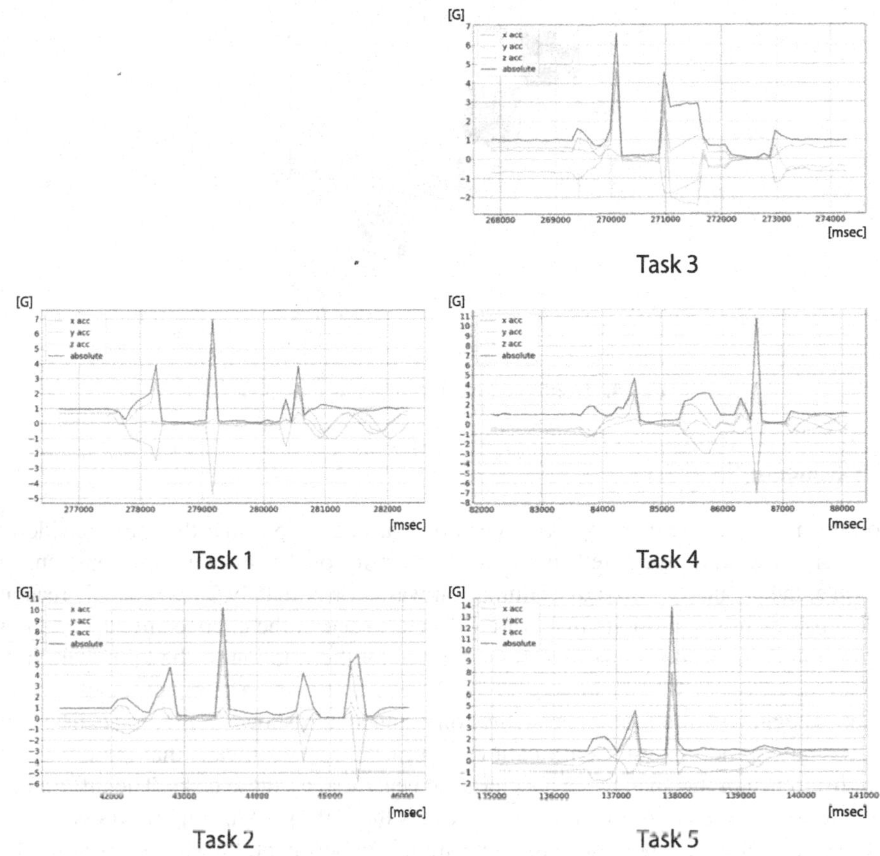

Fig. 3. Examples of acceleration data

on the calculated results, 470 points of acceleration data for the throwing motions were obtained.

For these 470 data, the identification rate from the results of conducting the leave-one-out cross-validation was 71% for SVM ($C = 1{,}000$, $\gamma = 0.1$) and 72% for RF (estimates = 100). In addition, Fig. 4 shows the confusion matrix used by the learning model applying SVM to verify which ball activity was being conducted. The labels in Fig. 4 match the tasks listed in Sect. 4.1, where the vertical axis shows the accurately guessed labels, and the horizontal axis indicates the predicted labels. This confusion matrix is for the case of 80% training data and 20% test data. In the confusion matrix, task 1 was not misidentified, and for the other tasks, a minor misidentification occurred. In particular, tasks 3–5 showed approximately the same degree of misidentification.

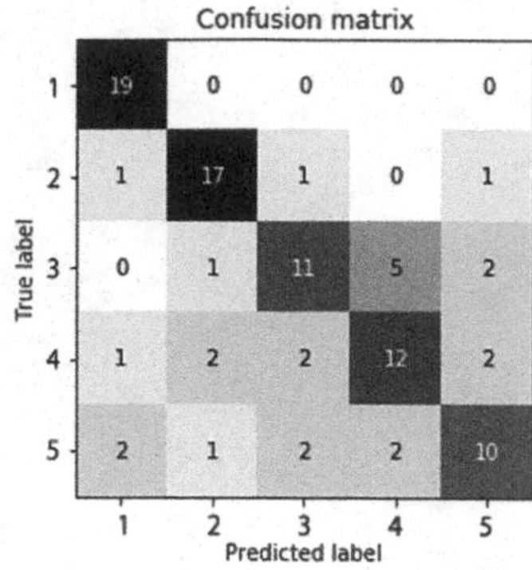

Fig. 4. Confusion matrix for SVM classifier

4.4 Discussion

Through this experiment, using two types of learning algorithms that are considered to be highly accurate, we determined the verifiability of the throwing motions, and in each case, the accuracy of the discrimination was approximately 70%. For this reason, the differences in the motions that were difficult to see in the changes in acceleration, and the influence of the centrifugal force caused by the rotation of the ball, were both considered.

Let us begin with the former. From the confusion matrix shown in Fig. 4, it can be seen that there are numerous misidentifications in tasks 3–5. This means that there was not much difference in the changes in acceleration generated by these tasks. The differences in the motions for tasks 3–5 is in the use, or lack thereof, of a wind-up (pulling back of the arm) and stepping when throwing. During this experiment, the starting position for performing each task was holding the ball with both hands in front of the chest, and Tasks 3 and 4 were throwing motions not using a wind-up, although to conduct a one-handed throw, the ball must be raised to the shoulder level. The motion from the initial state to the raising of the ball to the shoulder level is not significantly different from task 5, and shares the same starting position; however, the thrower employs a wind-up in this case. Therefore, it is thought that the difference in movement characteristics of tasks 3–5 would be difficult to tell based on changes in acceleration.

To resolve this issue, it is thought that new feature values can be added. This time, feature values (7) through (10) were based on the characteristics of the acceleration changes in each task, but there may be other useful feature values as well. Moreover, in addition to the acceleration sensor, by including angular velocity sensors and magnetic sensors, the angle of rotation and direction of the ball could be measured accurately, which would provide sufficient potential for differentiating tasks 3–5.

Next, let us consider the latter issue. Looking directly at the acceleration data, after the ball is thrown, despite the ball being in the air, it was found that the acceleration value was not approximately 0 [G]. As the root cause of this, because the built-in sensor itself was not located at the center of gravity of the entire ball-type device, centrifugal force is likely acting on it when the ball is rotating. Therefore, a threshold was set to automatically remove the motion. However, by setting this threshold, tasks 3, 4, and 5, in which data could not be extracted automatically, showed numerous misidentifications in a total of approximately 20 data points. Because the amount of data is an extremely important parameter in machine learning, it is thought that this was a factor that considerably affected the identification rate. In addition, by setting the threshold itself, it is possible that a portion of data that did not indicate a part of the motion was extracted. Therefore, designing the overall device to house the sensor at its center of gravity will be necessary for minimizing the generation of centrifugal force.

5 Conclusion

Because play is important to the mental and physical development during early childhood, it is necessary to provide suitable help and guidance for play throughout the childhood development stages. However, children develop differently, and it is difficult for childcare workers to track the developmental stages of children on a daily basis. Therefore, in this study, we proposed a support system for estimating the progress of these developmental stages that acquires and visualizes motion data from children's play using toys with built-in sensors. To make this proposed system a reality, a ball-type device with a built-in acceleration sensor was created as a prototype, and using it, we conducted an experiment focusing on throwing motions associated with child development, selecting five such motions to verify whether they could be accurately identified. Based on the results of two types of learning algorithms (SVM and RF) used to identify motions, it was found that both algorithms identified the motions with an accuracy of approximately 70%.

To improve the accuracy, it will be necessary to redesign the ball-type device such that the sensor is positioned at its center of gravity. In addition, sensors for determining the angular velocity and other factors allowing the accuracy to be reverified should potentially be added. Furthermore, future issues that need to be addressed include implementing prototypes of non-ball toys (such as stuffed animals and writing utensils), designing a GUI for visualization, and determining whether such devices are useful in supporting childcare workers in estimating the stages of development of the children under their care.

Acknowledgement. This work was supported by JSPS KAKENHI Grant Number JP18K11396.

References

1. Ministry of Health, Labor, and Welfare: Childcare Guidelines for Nursery Schools. https://www.mhlw.go.jp/_le/06-Seisakujouhou-11900000-Koyoukintoujidoukateikyoku/0000202211.pdf. Accessed 31 Jan 2020. (in Japanese)
2. Ministry of Education, Culture, Sports, Science and Technology, "Early Childhood Exercise Guidelines". https://www.mext.go.jp/amenu/sports/undousisin/1319771.html. Accessed 31 Jan 2020. (in Japanese)
3. Kosaka, K.: What is play? https://blog.goo.ne.jp/kodomogenki/e/4964c4f5b892be54d4b1e6420eb5f769. Accessed 31 Jan 2020. (in Japanese)

4. Shinno, T., et al.: A study of play in preschool children's play. —a study of solitary play in preschool children—. Technical Report from the Bulletin of Faculty of Education, Nagasaki University Educational Science (1993). (in Japanese)
5. Suzuki, S., Kurashima, S., Hikosaka, S., Abe, N.: Watching over system for children in a kindergarten based on a human-monitoring technology. IEEJ Trans. Electron. Inf. Syst. **137**(1), 46–53 (2017). (in Japanese)
6. Kamide, H., Takashima, K., Ishikawa, M., Adachi, T., Kitamura, Y.: Quantitative evaluation of children's developmental stage in building block play. Trans. Hum. Interface Soc. **20**(1), 107–114 (2018). (in Japanese)
7. Mironcika, S, et al.: Smart toys design opportunities for measuring children's fine motor skills development. In: Proceedings of the Twelfth International Conference on Tangible, Embedded, and Embodied Interaction, pp. 349–356 (2018)
8. Wang, Y., et al.: Volleyball skill assessment using a single wearable micro inertial measurement unit at wrist. IEEE Access **6**, 13758–13765 (2018)
9. Kimura, N., Satoh, A.: System for evaluating ball throws using a motion sensor. In: Multimedia, Distributed, Cooperative, and Mobile Symposium 2018 Collected Papers, pp. 567–572 (2018). (in Japanese)
10. Senda, T.: Playground equipment and play involving children in childcare environments, Technical Report, Aichi University of Education, Early Childhood Research (2007). (in Japanese)
11. Shoji, H.: Normative study to validate developmental sequences of fundamental movement skills to assess children with intellectual disabilities. Technical report, Center of Developmental Education and Research Publication (2012). (in Japanese)

Author Index

Printed in the United States
By Bookmasters